Glencoe Science
Indiana Science
Grade 7

Lake County

Tom Campbell/Index Stock

 Glencoe

New York, New York   Columbus, Ohio   Chicago, Illinois   Peoria, Illinois   Woodland Hills, California

ISBN: 0-07-861781-2 *(Indiana Student Edition)*

Indiana

Contents

Indiana Teacher Advisory Board IN3

The Glencoe Formula IN4

Indiana's Academic Standards Overview IN6

Indiana's Academic Standards Expanded and Correlated to *Glencoe Indiana Science, Grade 7* IN8

Monty Sloan

Lafayette wolf preserve

Teacher, Student, and Parent One-Stop Internet Resources

JUST FOR INDIANA

Log on to in7.msscience.com

ONLINE STUDY TOOLS
- Section Self-Check Quizzes
- Interactive Tutor
- Chapter Review Tests
- Indiana Standards Review
- Vocabulary PuzzleMaker

ONLINE RESEARCH
- WebQuest Projects
- Prescreened Web Links
- Career Links
- Internet Labs

Exclusively from Glencoe!

INTERACTIVE ONLINE STUDENT EDITION
- Complete Interactive Student Edition available at mhln.com

FOR TEACHERS
- Teacher Bulletin Board
- Teaching Today—Professional Development

SAFETY SYMBOLS

SAFETY SYMBOLS	HAZARD	EXAMPLES	PRECAUTION	REMEDY
DISPOSAL	Special disposal procedures need to be followed.	certain chemicals, living organisms	Do not dispose of these materials in the sink or trash can.	Dispose of wastes as directed by your teacher.
BIOLOGICAL	Organisms or other biological materials that might be harmful to humans	bacteria, fungi, blood, unpreserved tissues, plant materials	Avoid skin contact with these materials. Wear mask or gloves.	Notify your teacher if you suspect contact with material. Wash hands thoroughly.
EXTREME TEMPERATURE	Objects that can burn skin by being too cold or too hot	boiling liquids, hot plates, dry ice, liquid nitrogen	Use proper protection when handling.	Go to your teacher for first aid.
SHARP OBJECT	Use of tools or glassware that can easily puncture or slice skin	razor blades, pins, scalpels, pointed tools, dissecting probes, broken glass	Practice common-sense behavior and follow guidelines for use of the tool.	Go to your teacher for first aid.
FUME	Possible danger to respiratory tract from fumes	ammonia, acetone, nail polish remover, heated sulfur, moth balls	Make sure there is good ventilation. Never smell fumes directly. Wear a mask.	Leave foul area and notify your teacher immediately.
ELECTRICAL	Possible danger from electrical shock or burn	improper grounding, liquid spills, short circuits, exposed wires	Double-check setup with teacher. Check condition of wires and apparatus.	Do not attempt to fix electrical problems. Notify your teacher immediately.
IRRITANT	Substances that can irritate the skin or mucous membranes of the respiratory tract	pollen, moth balls, steel wool, fiberglass, potassium permanganate	Wear dust mask and gloves. Practice extra care when handling these materials.	Go to your teacher for first aid.
CHEMICAL	Chemicals can react with and destroy tissue and other materials	bleaches such as hydrogen peroxide; acids such as sulfuric acid, hydrochloric acid; bases such as ammonia, sodium hydroxide	Wear goggles, gloves, and an apron.	Immediately flush the affected area with water and notify your teacher.
TOXIC	Substance may be poisonous if touched, inhaled, or swallowed.	mercury, many metal compounds, iodine, poinsettia plant parts	Follow your teacher's instructions.	Always wash hands thoroughly after use. Go to your teacher for first aid.
FLAMMABLE	Flammable chemicals may be ignited by open flame, spark, or exposed heat.	alcohol, kerosene, potassium permanganate	Avoid open flames and heat when using flammable chemicals.	Notify your teacher immediately. Use fire safety equipment if applicable.
OPEN FLAME	Open flame in use, may cause fire.	hair, clothing, paper, synthetic materials	Tie back hair and loose clothing. Follow teacher's instruction on lighting and extinguishing flames.	Notify your teacher immediately. Use fire safety equipment if applicable.

 Eye Safety Proper eye protection should be worn at all times by anyone performing or observing science activities.

 Clothing Protection This symbol appears when substances could stain or burn clothing.

 Animal Safety This symbol appears when safety of animals and students must be ensured.

 Handwashing After the lab, wash hands with soap and water before removing goggles.

Indiana Teacher Advisory Board

The Indiana Teacher Advisory Board gave the editorial staff and design team feedback on the content and design of the Student Edition. They provided valuable input in the development of the 2005 edition of *Glencoe Indiana Science.*

Chuck Beeson
Math/Science Division Leader
Penn High School
Mishawaka, Indiana

Brian R. Conner
Science Teacher
New Haven Middle School
New Haven, Indiana

David Kyle Dahlquist
Science Teacher
Grissom Middle School
Mishawaka, Indiana

Jody Duncan
Applied Physics and Chemistry
   Teacher
Bloomington High School South
Bloomington, Indiana

Margaret A. Flack
Science Department Chair
Science Teacher
Jasper Middle School
Jasper, Indiana

Erika Hummel
8th Grade Science Teacher
Stonybrook Middle School, M.S.D.
Warren Township
Indianapolis, Indiana

Nancy Moore
Science Teacher/Dept. Chair
Franklin Township Co. Schools
Franklin Township Middle School
Indianapolis, Indiana

Rick Schuley
Science Department Chair
Seymour High School
Seymour, Indiana

Pam Schumm
Biology and Genetics Teacher
Wawasee High School
Syracuse, Indiana

Susie Seal
Science Teacher
Westfield Middle School
Westfield, Indiana

Phyllis Speicher
Science Department
   Chairman/Teacher
Taft Middle School
Crown Point, Indiana

Joyce Striclyn
7th Grade Science Teacher
Honey Creek Middle School
Terre Haute, Indiana

Jan Carroll Weir
Science Department Chair
Lawrence Central High School
Indianapolis, Indiana

Daniel Wunderlich
Chemistry Teacher
Terre Haute South Vigo High
   School
Terre Haute, Indiana

Indiana

The Glencoe Formula
for successfully mastering Indiana's Academic Standards for Science, Grade 7.

Learning + Practicing = *Success!*

Learning

Academic Standards
- Each chapter opener lists the Academic Standards you'll learn in that chapter.

Standards
- Each section opener lists the portion of the Standard you'll learn in that section.

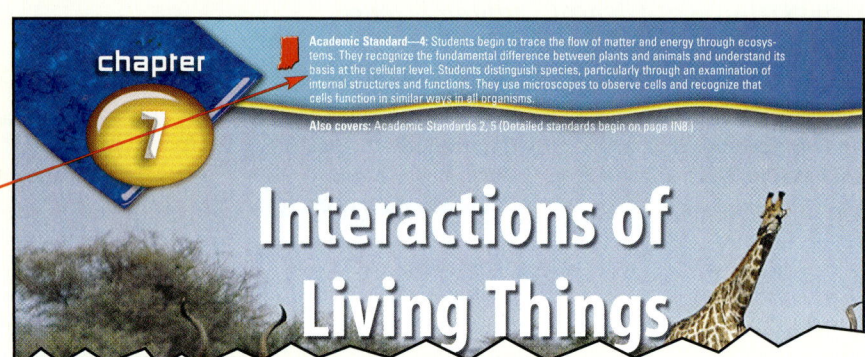

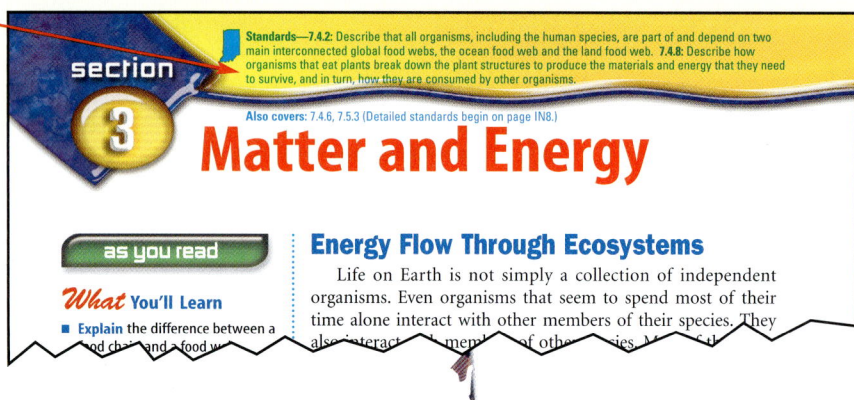

Indiana State Capitol Building

Bob Rowan: Progressive Image/CORBIS

Practicing

Indiana Academic Standard Check

7.4.2: Describe that all organisms . . . are part of and depend on two main interconnected global food webs, the ocean food web and the land food web.

✔ Where might humans fit in an ocean food web?

Standard Check
- focuses on and assesses the Standard covered on that page

Indiana Standards Review
Two pages created specifically for Indiana covering Indiana's Academic Standards for Science.

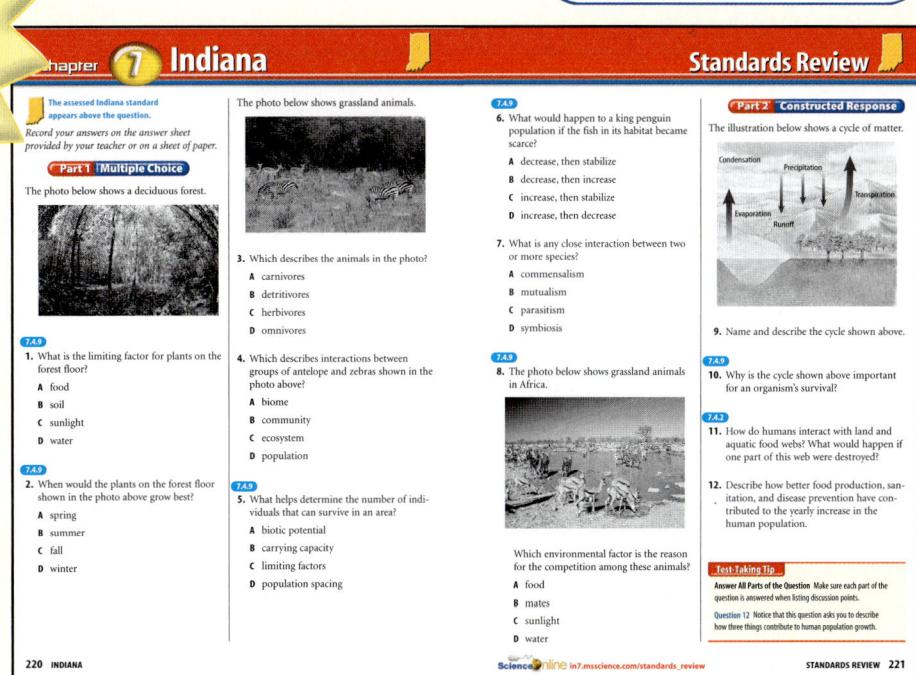

Test-Taking Tips

✔ Go to bed early the night before the test. You will think more clearly after a good night's rest.

✔ Read each problem carefully, underline key words, and think about ways to solve the problem before answering the question.

✔ Relax. It's natural to be nervous when taking a test. Just do your best.

✔ Try to answer each question in order. If you are unsure of an answer, mark your best guess and then mark the question in your test booklet. This will be a reminder to come back to the question at the end of the test.

✔ Think positively. Some problems may seem hard to you, but you may be able to figure out what to do if you read each question carefully.

✔ If no figure is provided, draw one. If one is furnished, mark it up to help you solve the problem.

✔ When you have finished each problem, reread it to make sure your answer is complete and reasonable.

✔ Make sure that the number of the question on the answer sheet matches the number of the question on which you are working in your test booklet.

GLENCOE INDIANA SCIENCE, GRADE 7   IN5

Indiana

Indiana's Academic Standards Overview

Beginning with Grade 6, Indiana's Academic Standards for science contain seven Standards, with the addition of Historical Perspectives. Each Standard is described below. On the pages that follow, age-appropriate concepts are listed underneath each Standard. These ideas build a foundation for understanding the intent of each Standard.

Standard 1 THE NATURE OF SCIENCE AND TECHNOLOGY

It is the union of science and technology that forms the scientific endeavor and that makes it so successful. Although each of these human enterprises has a character and history of its own, each is dependent on and reinforces the other. This first Standard draws portraits of science and technology that emphasize their roles in the scientific endeavor and reveal some of the similarities and connections between them. In order for students to truly understand the nature of science and technology, they must model the process of scientific investigation through inquiries, fieldwork, lab work, etc. Through these experiences, students will practice designing investigations and experiments, making observations, and formulating theories based on evidence.

Standard 2 SCIENTIFIC THINKING

There are certain thinking skills associated with science, mathematics, and technology that young people need to develop during their school years. These are mostly, but not exclusively, mathematical and logical skills that are essential tools for both formal and informal learning and for a lifetime of participation in society as a whole. Good communication is also essential in order to both receive and disseminate information and to understand others' ideas as well as have one's own ideas understood. Writing, in the form of journals, essays, lab reports, procedural summaries, etc., should be an integral component of students' experiences in science.

Standard 3 THE PHYSICAL SETTING

One of the grand success stories of science is the unification of the physical universe. It turns out that all natural objects, events, and processes are connected to each other. This Standard contains recommendations for basic knowledge about the overall structure of the universe and the physical principles on which it seems to run, with emphasis on Earth and the solar system. This Standard focuses on two principle subjects: the structure of the universe and the major processes that have shaped planet Earth, and the concepts with which science describes the physical world in general—organized under the headings of *Matter and Energy* and *Forces of Nature*. In Grade 7, students continue to learn about the relationships between physical objects, events, and processes in the universe.

IN6 GLENCOE INDIANA SCIENCE, GRADE 7

Standard 4 THE LIVING ENVIRONMENT

People have long been curious about living things—how many different species there are, what they are like, how they relate to each other, and how they behave. Living organisms are made of the same components as all other matter, involve the same kinds of transformations of energy, and move using the same basic kinds of forces. Thus, all of the physical principles discussed in Standard 3—The Physical Setting, apply to life as well as to stars, raindrops, and television sets. This Standard offers recommendations on basic knowledge about how living things function and how they interact with one another and their environment. In Grade 7, students trace the flow of matter and energy through ecosystems.

Standard 5 THE MATHEMATICAL WORLD

Mathematics is essentially a process of thinking that involves building and applying abstract, logically connected networks of ideas. These ideas often arise from the need to solve problems in science, technology, and everyday life—problems ranging from how to model certain aspects of a complex scientific problem to how to balance a checkbook.

Standard 6 HISTORICAL PERSPECTIVES

Examples of historical events provide a context for understanding how the scientific enterprise operates. By studying these events, one understands that new ideas are limited by the context in which they are conceived, are often rejected by the scientific establishment, sometimes spring from unexpected findings, and grow or transform slowly through the contributions of many different investigators. The historical events listed in Grade 7 are certainly not the only events that could be used to illustrate this Standard, but they provide an array of examples. Through these examples, students will gain insight into germ theory.

Standard 7 COMMON THEMES

Some important themes pervade science, mathematics, and technology and appear over and over again, whether we are looking at ancient civilization, the human body, or a comet. These ideas transcend disciplinary boundaries and prove fruitful in explanation, in theory, in observation, and in design. A focus on *Constancy and Change* within this Standard provides students opportunities to engage in long-term and on-going laboratory and fieldwork, and thus understand the role of change over time in studying The Physical Setting and The Living Environment.

Indiana

Indiana's Academic Standards Expanded and Correlated to *Glencoe Indiana Science, Grade 7*

This correlation "expands," or breaks down, each standard into its components. The chapter and section that address each component are listed. Some standards do not require expanding.

Academic Standards	Chapter-Section
Standard 1 — THE NATURE OF SCIENCE AND TECHNOLOGY	
Students further their scientific understanding of the natural world through investigations, experiences, and readings. They design solutions to practical problems by using a variety of scientific methodologies.	
7.1.1 Recognize and explain that when similar investigations give different results, the scientific challenge is to judge whether the differences are trivial or significant, which often takes further studies to decide.	1-1, 19-1, Science Skill Handbook
7.1.2 Explain that what people expect to observe often affects what they actually do observe and provide an example of a solution to this problem.	
expanded standard — what people expect to observe affects what is observed	1-3, Science Skill Handbook
expanded standard — provide a solution to the problem of bias.	Science Skill Handbook
7.1.3 Explain why it is important in science to keep honest, clear, and accurate records.	1-1, 1-4, Science Skill Handbook
7.1.4 Describe that different explanations can be given for the same evidence, and it is not always possible to tell which one is correct without further inquiry.	
expanded standard — different explanations can be given for the same evidence	1-1, 1-3, 19-1, 21-3, Science Skill Handbook
expanded standard — it is not always possible to tell which explanation is correct	1-1, 1-3, 19-1, 21-3, Science Skill Handbook
7.1.5 Identify some important contributions to the advancement of science, mathematics, and technology that have been made by different kinds of people, in different cultures, at different times.	1-3, 2-2, 2-3, 4-3, 6-4, 9-1, 9-2, 9-3, 12-1, 12-2, 14-3, 15-2, 16-1, 16-3, 16-4, 17-3, 18-1, 21-2, 22-3
7.1.6 Provide examples of people who overcame bias and/or limited opportunities in education and employment to excel in the fields of science.	2-3, 5-4, 17-3
7.1.7 Explain how engineers, architects, and others who engage in design and technology use scientific knowledge to solve practical problems.	2-2, 2-3, 7-1, Unit 6 Project
7.1.8 Explain that technologies often have drawbacks as well as benefits. Consider a technology, such as the use of pesticides, which help some organisms but may hurt others, either deliberately or inadvertently.	1-1, 4-3, 8-1, 8-2, 13-3, 15-2, Unit 3 Project
7.1.9 Explain how societies influence what types of technology are developed and used in fields such as agriculture, manufacturing, sanitation, medicine, warfare, transportation, information processing, and communication.	5-4, 6-1

Academic Standards		Chapter-Section
7.1.10	Identify ways that technology has strongly influenced the course of history and continues to do so.	
expanded standard	technology has influenced the course of history	4-3, 13-2
	technology continues to influence the course of history	4-3
7.1.11	Illustrate how numbers can be represented using sequences of only two symbols, such as 1 and 0 or on and off, and how that affects the storage of information in our society.	
expanded standard	illustrate how numbers can be represented using sequences	15-2
	illustrate how numbers represented using sequences affects the storage of information	15-2

Standard 2 SCIENTIFIC THINKING

Students use instruments and tools to measure, calculate, and organize data. They frame arguments in quantitative terms when possible. They question claims and understand that findings may be interpreted in more than one acceptable way.

7.2.1	Find what percentage one number is of another and figure any percentage of any number.	Applied and reinforced in the Math Skill Handbook and Applying Math Features
7.2.2	Use formulas to calculate the circumferences and areas of rectangles, triangles, and circles, and the volumes of rectangular solids.	Applied and reinforced in the Math Skill Handbook and Applying Math Features
7.2.3	Decide what degree of precision is adequate, based on the degree of precision of the original data, and round off the result of calculator operations to significant figures that reasonably reflect those of the inputs.	Applied and reinforced in the Math Skill Handbook and Applying Math Features
7.2.4	Express numbers like 100, 1,000, and 1,000,000 as powers of 10.	Applied and reinforced in the Math Skill Handbook and Applying Math Features
7.2.5	Estimate probabilities of outcomes in familiar situations, on the basis of history or the number of possible outcomes.	Applied and reinforced in the Math Skill Handbook and Applying Math Features
7.2.6	Read analog and digital meters on instruments used to make direct measurements of length, volume, weight, elapsed time, rates, or temperatures, and choose appropriate units.	11-1, 12-3, 13-3, 21-3
7.2.7	Incorporate circle charts, bar and line graphs, diagrams, scatterplots, and symbols into writing, such as lab or research reports, to serve as evidence for claims and/or conclusions.	
expanded standard	incorporate circle charts into writing	1-4
	incorporate bar and line graphs into writing	1-4, 8-2, 11-1, 11-2, 13-2, 13-3, 21-3
	incorporate diagrams into writing	1-4, 4-1, 4-3, 5-4, 7-1, 11-3, 15-2, 19-2
	incorporate scatterplots into writing	1-4, Unit 2 Project
	incorporate symbols into writing	1-4, 4-3, 5-4
7.2.8	Question claims based on vague attributes, such as "Leading doctors say…," or on statements made by celebrities or others outside the area of their particular expertise.	1-1

GLENCOE INDIANA SCIENCE, GRADE 7   IN9

Academic Standards	Chapter-Section
Standard 3 — THE PHYSICAL SETTING	
Students collect and organize data to identify relationships between physical objects, events, and processes. They use logical reasoning to question their own ideas as new information challenges their conceptions of the natural world.	
7.3.1 Recognize and describe that the sun is a medium-sized star located near the edge of a disk-shaped galaxy of stars and that the universe contains many billions of galaxies and each galaxy contains many billions of stars.	16-4
7.3.2 Recognize and describe that the sun is many thousands of times closer to Earth than any other star, allowing light from the sun to reach Earth in a few minutes. Note that this may be compared to time spans of longer than a year for all other stars.	14-3, 16-2
7.3.3 Describe how climates sometimes have changed abruptly in the past as a result of changes in Earth's crust, such as volcanic eruptions or impacts of huge rocks from space.	21-3
7.3.4 Explain how heat flow and movement of material within Earth causes earthquakes and volcanic eruptions and creates mountains and ocean basins.	
expanded standard — heat flow and movement of material within Earth causes earthquakes and volcanic eruptions	19-1, 19-2, 20-3
expanded standard — heat flow and movement of material within Earth creates mountains and ocean basins	19-1, 19-2
7.3.5 Recognize and explain that heat energy carried by ocean currents has a strong influence on climate around the world.	21-1, 21-3
7.3.6 Describe how gas and dust from large volcanoes can change the atmosphere.	21-3
7.3.7 Give examples of some changes in Earth's surface that are abrupt, such as earthquakes and volcanic eruptions, and some changes that happen very slowly, such as uplift and wearing down of mountains and the action of glaciers.	
expanded standard — some changes in Earth's surface are abrupt	19-1, 19-2, 20-1, 20-2, 20-3
expanded standard — some changes in Earth's surface happen slowly	19-1, 19-2
7.3.8 Describe how sediments of sand and smaller particles, sometimes containing the remains of organisms, are gradually buried and are cemented together by dissolved minerals to form solid rock again.	18-4, 22-1
7.3.9 Explain that sedimentary rock, when buried deep enough, may be reformed by pressure and heat, perhaps melting and recrystallizing into different kinds of rock. Describe that these reformed rock layers may be forced up again to become land surface and even mountains, and subsequently erode.	
expanded standard — sedimentary rock may be reformed by pressure and heat	18-3, 18-4
expanded standard — reformed rock layers may be forced up again and subsequently erode	18-4
7.3.10 Explain how the thousands of layers of sedimentary rock can confirm the long history of the changing surface of Earth and the changing life forms whose remains are found in successive layers, although the youngest layers are not always found on top, because of folding, breaking, and uplift of layers.	
expanded standard — thousands of layers of sedimentary rock can confirm the long history of the changing surface of Earth and the changing life forms	22-1, 22-2
expanded standard — the youngest layers are not always found on top	22-2
7.3.11 Explain that the sun loses energy by emitting light. Note that only a tiny fraction of that light reaches Earth. Understand that the sun's energy arrives as light with a wide range of wavelengths, consisting of visible light, infrared, and ultraviolet radiation.	14-3, 16-2, 16-3
7.3.12 Investigate how the temperature and acidity of a solution influences reaction rates, such as those resulting in food spoilage.	10-2, 10-3
7.3.13 Explain that many substances dissolve in water. Understand that the presence of these substances often affects the rates of reactions that are occurring in the water as compared to the same reactions occurring in the water in the absence of the substance.	3-1, 3-2, 10-1, 10-2
7.3.14 Explain that energy in the form of heat is almost always one of the products of an energy transformation, such as in the examples of exploding stars, biological growth, the operation of machines, and the motion of people.	3-3, 13-1, 13-2

Academic Standards		Chapter-Section
7.3.15	Describe how electrical energy can be produced from a variety of energy sources and can be transformed into almost any other form of energy, such as light or heat.	
expanded standard	electrical energy can be produced from a variety of energy sources	13-2, 13-3
	electrical energy can be transformed into almost any other form of energy	13-2, 13-3
7.3.16	Recognize and explain that different ways of obtaining, transforming, and distributing energy have different environmental consequences.	
expanded standard	different ways of obtaining energy have different environmental consequences	8-1, 8-2, 8-3, 13-3
	different ways of transforming energy have different environmental consequences	8-1, 8-2, 8-3, 13-3
	different way of distributing energy have different environmental consequences	13-3
7.3.17	Investigate that an unbalanced force, acting on an object, changes its speed or path of motion or both, and know that if the force always acts toward the same center as the object moves, the object's path may curve into an orbit around the center.	
expanded standard	an unbalanced force, acting on an object, changes its speed or path or both	12-1, 12-2, 12-3
	if the force always acts toward the same center as the object moves, the object's path may curve	12-2
7.3.18	Describe that light waves, sound waves, and other waves move at different speeds in different materials.	
expanded standard	light waves move at different speeds in different materials	14-1, 14-3
	sound waves move at different speeds in different materials	14-1, 14-2
	other waves move at different speeds in different materials	14-1, 19-1, 20-1, 20-3
7.3.19	Explain that human eyes respond to a narrow range of wavelengths of the electromagnetic spectrum.	14-3
7.3.20	Describe that something can be "seen" when light waves emitted or reflected by it enter the eye just as something can be "heard" when sound waves from it enter the ear.	
expanded standard	something can be "seen" when light waves emitted or reflected enter the eye	14-3
	something can be "heard" when sound waves enter the ear	14-2

Standard 4 THE LIVING ENVIRONMENT

Students begin to trace the flow of matter and energy through ecosystems. They recognize the fundamental difference between plants and animals and understand its basis at the cellular level. Students distinguish species, particularly through an examination of internal structures and functions. They use microscopes to observe cells and recognize that cells function in similar ways in all organisms.

7.4.1	Explain that similarities among organisms are found in external and internal anatomical features, including specific characteristics at the cellular level, such as the number of chromosomes. Understand that these similarities are used to classify organisms since they may be used to infer the degree of relatedness among organisms.	
expanded standard	similarities among organisms are found in external anatomical features	1-2, 1-4, 4-2
	similarities among organisms are found in internal anatomical features	1-2, 4-2
	similarities are used to classify organisms	1-4, 4-2
7.4.2	Describe that all organisms, including the human species, are part of and depend on two main interconnected global food webs, the ocean food web and the land food web.	5-2, 7-3
7.4.3	Explain how, in sexual reproduction, a single specialized cell from a female merges with a specialized cell from a male and this fertilized egg carries genetic information from each parent and multiplies to form the complete organism.	
expanded standard	a single specialized female cell merges with a single specialized male cell	4-2
	a fertilized egg carries genetic information	4-2
	a fertilized egg multiplies to complete the organism	4-2

	Academic Standards	Chapter-Section
7.4.4	Explain that cells continually divide to make more cells for growth and repair and that various organs and tissues function to serve the needs of cells for food, air, and waste removal.	
expanded standard	cells continually divide for growth and repair	1-2, 2-2, 2-3, 4-1, 4-3, 6-1
	various organs and tissues function to serve the needs of cells for food	2-1, 3-3, 5-1, 5-2, 6-1, 6-2, 6-4
	various organs and tissues function to serve the needs of cells for air	2-1, 3-3, 5-3, 6-1, 6-2, 6-4
	various organs and tissues function to serve the needs of cell for waste removal	2-1, 3-3, 5-4, 6-1, 6-2, 6-4
7.4.5	Explain that the basic functions of organisms, such as extracting energy from food and getting rid of wastes, are carried out within the cell and understand that the way which cells function is similar in all organisms.	
expanded standard	basic functions of organisms are carried out within the cell	1-2, 1-4, 2-1, 2-2, 2-3, 3-2, 3-3
	cells function in similar ways in all organisms	1-2, 1-4, 2-1, 2-2, 2-3, 3-2, 3-3
7.4.6	Explain how food provides the fuel and the building material for all organisms.	
expanded standard	food provides the fuel for all organisms	1-2, 5-1, 5-2, 7-3
	food provides the building materials for all organisms	1-2, 5-2, 5-4, 7-3
7.4.7	Describe how plants use the energy from light to make sugars from carbon dioxide and water to produce food that can be used immediately or stored for later use.	2-1, 2-3, 3-3
7.4.8	Describe how organisms that eat plants break down the plant structures to produce the materials and energy that they need to survive, and in turn, how they are consumed by other organisms.	
expanded standard	organisms break down plant structures to produce materials and energy needed to survive	1-2, 3-3, 5-1, 5-2, 7-2, 7-3
	organisms are consumed by other organisms	1-2, 3-3, 5-2, 7-2, 7-3
7.4.9	Understand and explain that as any population of organisms grows, it is held in check by one or more environmental factors. These factors could result in depletion of food or nesting sites and/or increase loss to increased numbers of predators or parasites. Give examples of some consequences of this.	
expanded standard	a population of organisms is held in check by depletion of food or nesting sites and give examples	1-2, 7-1, 7-2
	a population of organisms is held in check by an increased number of predators or parasites and give examples	7-1, 7-2
7.4.10	Describe how technologies having to do with food production, sanitation, and disease prevention have dramatically changed how people live and work and have resulted in changes in factors that affect the growth of human population.	
expanded standard	food production and sanitation technologies have dramatically changed how people live and work	6-3, 6-4
	disease prevention technologies have dramatically changed how people live and work	6-3
7.4.11	Explain that the amount of food energy (calories) a person requires varies with body weight, age, sex, activity level, and natural body efficiency. Understand that regular exercise is important to maintain a healthy heart/lung system, good muscle tone, and strong bone structure.	
expanded standard	the amount of calories required by a person varies with body weight, age, sex, activity level, and natural body efficiency	5-2
	regular exercise is important to maintain a healthy heart/lung system, good muscle tone, and strong bone structure	6-2
7.4.12	Explain that viruses, bacteria, fungi, and parasites may infect the human body and interfere with normal body functions. Recognize that a person can catch a cold many times because there are many varieties of cold viruses that cause similar symptoms.	
expanded standard	viruses may infect the human body and interfere with normal body functions	2-3, 5-3, 6-4
	bacteria may infect the human body and interfere with normal body functions	2-3, 5-3, 6-4
	fungi may infect the human body and interfere with normal body functions	5-3, 6-4
	parasites may infect the human body and interfere with normal body functions	5-3, 6-4
	many varieties of cold viruses cause similar symptoms	2-3, 6-4

Academic Standards		Chapter-Section
7.4.13	Explain that white blood cells engulf invaders or produce antibodies that attack invaders or mark the invaders for killing by other white blood cells. Know that the antibodies produced will remain and can fight off subsequent invaders of the same kind.	
expanded standard	white blood cells engulf invaders or produce antibodies that attack invaders or mark invaders for killing by other white blood cells	6-1, 6-3
	antibodies produced will remain and fight off subsequent invaders	6-1, 6-3
7.4.14	Explain that the environment may contain dangerous levels of substances that are harmful to human beings. Understand, therefore, that the good health of individuals requires monitoring the soil, air, and water as well as taking steps to keep them safe.	
expanded standard	the environment may contain dangerous levels of harmful substances	6-4, 8-2, 8-3
	good health requires monitoring the soil as well as steps to keep them safe	8-2, 8-3
	good health requires monitoring the air as well as steps to keep them safe	8-2, 8-3
	good health require monitoring the water as well as steps to keep them safe	8-2, 8-3

Standard 5 THE MATHEMATICAL WORLD

Students apply mathematics in scientific contexts. They use mathematical ideas, such as relations between operations, symbols, statistical relationships, and the use of logical reasoning, in the representation and synthesis of data.

7.5.1	Demonstrate how a number line can be extended on the other side of zero to represent negative numbers and give examples of instances where this is useful.	21-1
7.5.2	Illustrate how lines can be parallel, perpendicular, or oblique.	14-1
7.5.3	Demonstrate how the scale chosen for a graph or drawing determines its interpretation.	1-4, 4-2, 6-4, 7-2, 7-3, Math Skill Handbook
7.5.4	Describe that the larger the sample, the more accurately it represents the whole. Understand, however, that any sample can be poorly chosen and this will make it unrepresentative of the whole.	Unit 2 Project, Science Skill Handbook

Standard 6 HISTORICAL PERSPECTIVE

Students gain understanding of how the scientific enterprise operates through examples of historical events. Through the study of these events, they understand that new ideas are limited by the context in which they are conceived, are often rejected by the scientific establishment, sometimes spring from unexpected findings, and grow or transform slowly through the contributions of many different investigators.

7.6.1	Understand and explain that throughout history, people have created explanations for disease. Note that some held that disease had spiritual causes, but that the most persistent biological theory over the centuries was that illness resulted from an imbalance in the body fluids. Realize that the introduction of germ theory by Louis Pasteur and others in the nineteenth century led to the modern understanding of how many diseases are caused by microorganisms, such as bacteria, viruses, yeasts, and parasites.	
expanded standard	throughout history people have created explanations for disease	2-3, 6-4
	the introduction of germ theory by Pasteur led to the modern understanding of how diseases are caused by microorganisms	2-3, 6-4

	Academic Standards	Chapter-Section
7.6.2	Understand and explain that Louis Pasteur wanted to find out what caused milk and wine to spoil. Note that he demonstrated that spoilage and fermentation occur when microorganisms enter from the air, multiply rapidly, and produce waste products, with some desirable results, such as carbon dioxide in bread dough, and some undesirable, such as acetic acid in wine. Understand that after showing that spoilage could be avoided by keeping germs out or by destroying them with heat, Pasteur investigated animal diseases and showed that microorganisms were involved in many of them. Also note that other investigators later showed that specific kinds of germs caused specific diseases.	
expanded standard	Pasteur demonstrated that spoilage and fermentation occur from microorganisms with some desirable results and some undesirable results	3-3, 6-4
	after showing spoilage can be avoided by keeping germs out or by destroying them with heat, Pasteur showed that microorganisms are involved in many animal diseases	6-4
	other investigators showed that specific germs cause specific diseases	2-3, 6-4
7.6.3	Understand and explain that Louis Pasteur found that infection by disease organisms (germs) caused the body to build up an immunity against subsequent infection by the same organisms. Realize that Pasteur then demonstrated more widely what Edward Jenner had shown for smallpox without understanding the underlying mechanism: that it was possible to produce vaccines that would induce the body to build immunity to a disease without actually causing the disease itself.	
expanded standard	Pasteur found that infection by disease organisms caused the body to build up an immunity	6-4
	Edward Jenner had shown smallpox immunity without understanding the underlying mechanism	2-3
	Pasteur demonstrated that it was possible to produce vaccines that induce the body to build immunity without causing the disease	6-4
7.6.4	Understand and describe that changes in health practices have resulted from the acceptance of the germ theory of disease. Realize that before germ theory, illness was treated by appeals to supernatural powers or by trying to adjust body fluids through induced vomiting or bleeding. Note that the modern approach emphasizes sanitation, the safe handling of food and water, the pasteurization of milk, quarantine, and aseptic surgical techniques to keep germs out of the body; vaccinations to strengthen the body's immune system against subsequent infection by the same kind of microorganisms; and antibiotics and other chemicals and processes to destroy microorganisms.	
expanded standard	the modern approach to illness emphasizes sanitation, safe handling of food and water, pasteurization of milk, quarantine, aseptic surgical techniques to destroy microorganisms	2-3, 6-3, 6-4
	the modern approach to illness emphasizes vaccinations to destroy microorganisms	2-3, 6-3, 6-4
	the modern approach to illness emphasizes antibiotics, chemicals, and processes to destroy microorganisms	2-3, 6-3, 6-4

Standard 7 COMMON THEMES

Students analyze the relationships within systems. They investigate how different models can represent the same data, rates of change, cyclic changes, and changes that counterbalance one another.

	Academic Standards	Chapter-Section
7.7.1	Explain that the output from one part of a system, which can include material, energy, or information, can become the input to other parts and this feedback can serve to control what goes on in the system as a whole.	3-3
7.7.2	Use different models to represent the same thing, noting that the kind of model and its complexity should depend on its purpose.	4-3, 5-4, 6-3, 9-1
7.7.3	Describe how physical and biological systems tend to change until they reach equilibrium and remain that way unless their surroundings change.	
expanded standard	physical systems tend to change until they reach equilibrium and remain that way unless their surroundings change	3-2, 19-3
	biological systems tend to change until they reach equilibrium and remain that way unless their surroundings change	3-2
7.7.4	Use symbolic equations to show how the quantity of something changes over time or in response to changes in other quantities.	
expanded standard	use symbolic equations to show how the quantity of something changes over time	3-1, 11-1, 11-2
	use symbolic equations to show how the quantity of something changes in response to other quantities	3-1, 11-1, 11-2, 11-3, 12-1, 14-1

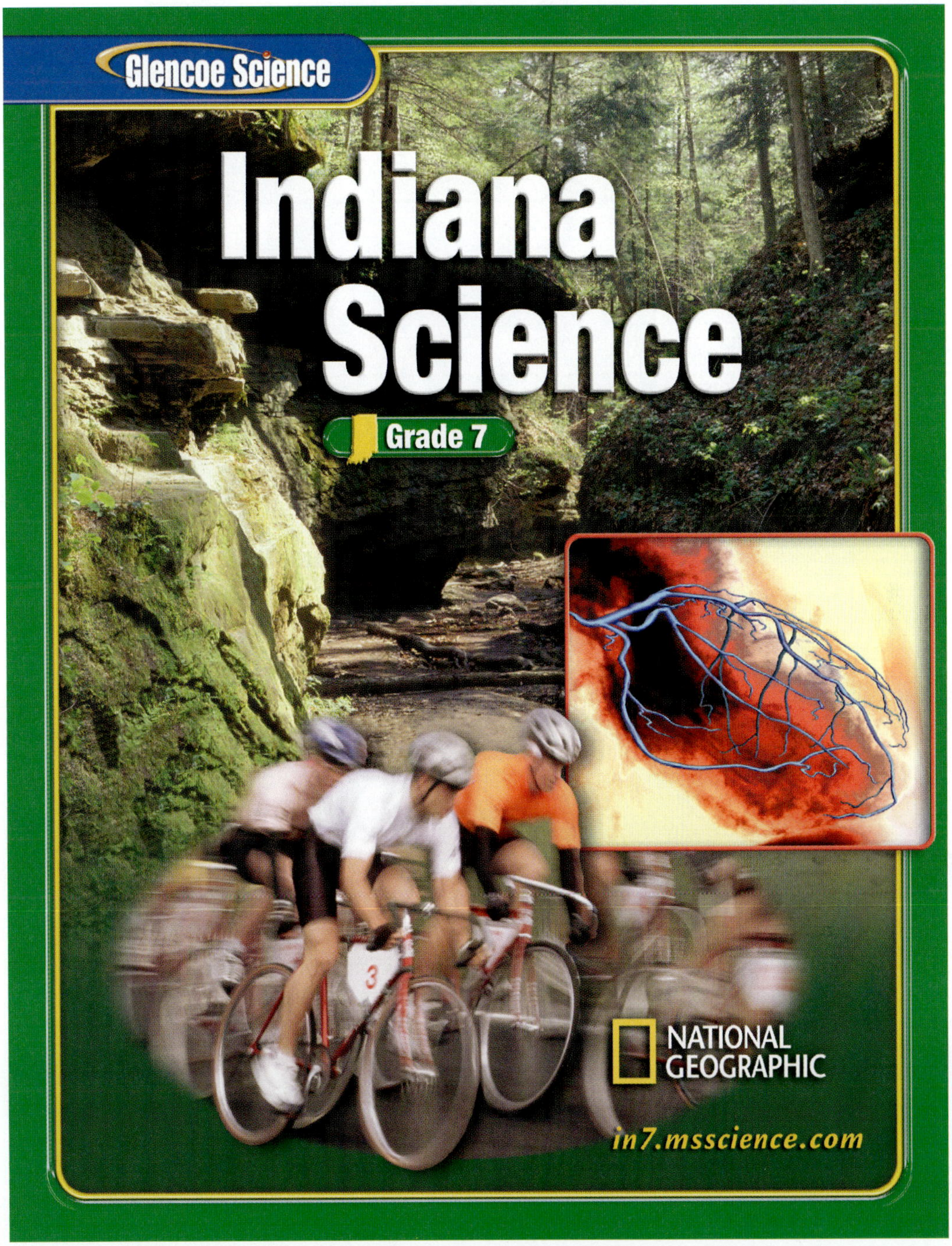

Glencoe Science

Indiana Science
Grade 7

NATIONAL GEOGRAPHIC

in7.msscience.com

Glencoe

New York, New York   Columbus, Ohio   Chicago, Illinois   Peoria, Illinois   Woodland Hills, California

Grade 7

Turkey Run State Park, located in western central Indiana, boasts sandstone features 300 to 600 million years old. The wheel bearings and the drive-train in these bikes cause friction resulting in a loss of efficiency, while the friction caused by the brakes helps stop the bike safely. The coronary artery supplies the heart muscle with oxygen-rich blood.

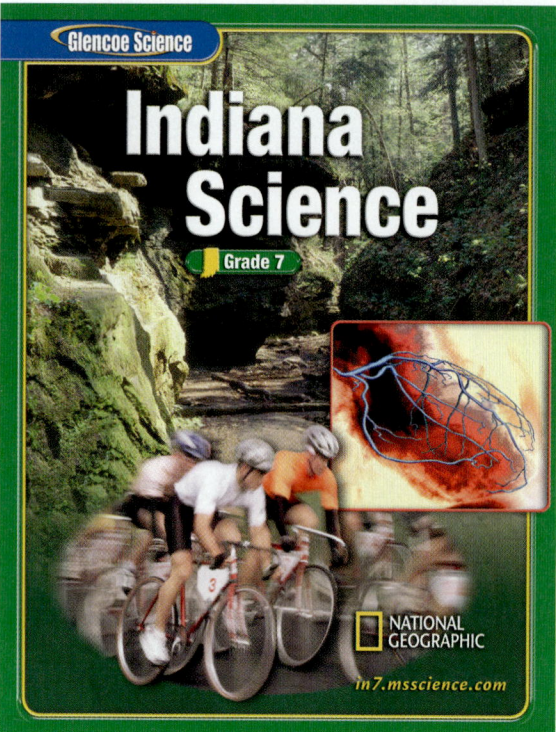

Copyright © 2005 by The McGraw-Hill Companies, Inc. All rights reserved. Except as permitted under the United States Copyright Act, no part of this publication may be reproduced or distributed in any form or by any means, or stored in a database or retrieval system, without prior written permission of the publisher.

The National Geographic features were designed and developed by the National Geographic Society's Education Division. Copyright © National Geographic Society. The name "National Geographic Society" and the Yellow Border Rectangle are trademarks of the Society, and their use, without prior written permission, is strictly prohibited.

The "Science and Society" and the "Science and History" features that appear in this book were designed and developed by TIME School Publishing, a division of TIME Magazine. TIME and the red border are trademarks of Time Inc. All rights reserved.

Send all inquiries to:
Glencoe/McGraw-Hill
8787 Orion Place
Columbus, OH 43240-4027

ISBN: 0-07-861781-2

2 3 4 5 6 7 8 9 10 079/111 09 08 07 06 05

Contents In Brief

Unit 1 — The Basis of Life 2
- **Chapter 1** Exploring and Classifying Life 4
- **Chapter 2** Cells 36
- **Chapter 3** Cell Processes 64
- **Chapter 4** Cell Reproduction 94

Unit 2 — The Interdependence of Life 124
- **Chapter 5** Digestion, Respiration, and Excretion 126
- **Chapter 6** Circulation and Immunity 160
- **Chapter 7** Interactions of Living Things 194
- **Chapter 8** Conserving Resources 222

Unit 3 — The Nature of Matter 254
- **Chapter 9** Atoms, Elements, and the Periodic Table ... 256
- **Chapter 10** Substances, Mixtures, and Solubility 286

Unit 4 — Motion, Forces, and Energy 318
- **Chapter 11** Motion and Momentum 320
- **Chapter 12** Force and Newton's Laws 348
- **Chapter 13** Energy and Energy Resources 378
- **Chapter 14** Waves, Sound, and Light 410
- **Chapter 15** Electronics and Computers 440

Unit 5 — Galaxies, Stars, and Earth 468
- **Chapter 16** Stars and Galaxies 470
- **Chapter 17** Minerals 502
- **Chapter 18** Rocks 530

Unit 6 — Processes that Shape Earth 560
- **Chapter 19** Forces Shaping Earth 562
- **Chapter 20** Earthquakes and Volcanoes 590
- **Chapter 21** Climate 622
- **Chapter 22** Clues to Earth's Past 652

Authors

Education Division
Washington, D.C.

Lucy Daniel, PhD
Teacher/Consultant
Rutherford County Schools
Rutherfordton, NC

Ralph M. Feather Jr., PhD
Assistant Professor
Geoscience Department
Indiana University of Pennsylvania
Indiana, PA

Edward Ortleb
Science Consultant
St. Louis, MO

Peter Rillero, PhD
Professor of Science Education
Arizona State University West
Phoenix, AZ

Susan Leach Snyder
Retired Earth Science Teacher, Consultant
Jones Middle School
Upper Arlington, OH

Dinah Zike
Educational Consultant
Dinah-Might Activities, Inc.
San Antonio, TX

Series Consultants

CONTENT

Alton J. Banks, PhD
Director of the Faculty Center
for Teaching and Learning
North Carolina State University
Raleigh, NC

Jack Cooper
Ennis High School
Ennis, TX

Sandra K. Enger, PhD
Associate Director,
Associate Professor
UAH Institute for Science Education
Huntsville, AL

David G. Haase, PhD
North Carolina State University
Raleigh, NC

Michael A. Hoggarth, PhD
Department of Life and
Earth Sciences
Otterbein College
Westerville, OH

Jerome A. Jackson, PhD
Whitaker Eminent Scholar in Science
Program Director
Center for Science, Mathematics,
and Technology Education
Florida Gulf Coast University
Fort Meyers, FL

William C. Keel, PhD
Department of Physics
and Astronomy
University of Alabama
Tuscaloosa, AL

Linda McGaw
Science Program Coordinator
Advanced Placement Strategies, Inc.
Dallas, TX

Madelaine Meek
Physics Consultant Editor
Lebanon, OH

Robert Nierste
Science Department Head
Hendrick Middle School, Plano ISD
Plano, TX

Connie Rizzo, MD, PhD
Department of Science/Math
Marymount Manhattan College
New York, NY

Dominic Salinas, PhD
Middle School Science Supervisor
Caddo Parish Schools
Shreveport, LA

Cheryl Wistrom, PhD
St. Joseph's College
Rensselaer, IN

Carl Zorn, PhD
Staff Scientist
Jefferson Laboratory
Newport News, VA

MATH

Michael Hopper, DEng
Manager of Aircraft Certification
L-3 Communications
Greenville, TX

Teri Willard, EdD
Mathematics Curriculum Writer
Belgrade, MT

READING

Elizabeth Babich
Special Education Teacher
Mashpee Public Schools
Mashpee, MA

Barry Barto
Special Education Teacher
John F. Kennedy Elementary
Manistee, MI

Carol A. Senf, PhD
School of Literature,
Communication, and Culture
Georgia Institute of Technology
Atlanta, GA

Rachel Swaters-Kissinger
Science Teacher
John Boise Middle School
Warsaw, MO

SAFETY

Aileen Duc, PhD
Science 8 Teacher
Hendrick Middle School, Plano ISD
Plano, TX

Sandra West, PhD
Department of Biology
Texas State University-San Marcos
San Marcos, TX

ACTIVITY TESTERS

Nerma Coats Henderson
Pickerington Lakeview Jr. High
School
Pickerington, OH

Mary Helen Mariscal-Cholka
William D. Slider Middle School
El Paso, TX

Science Kit and Boreal Laboratories
Tonawanda, NY

Reviewers

Deidre Adams
West Vigo Middle School
West Terre Haute, IN

Sharla Adams
IPC Teacher
Allen High School
Allen, TX

Maureen Barrett
Thomas E. Harrington Middle School
Mt. Laurel, NJ

John Barry
Seeger Jr.-Sr. High School
West Lebanon, IN

Desiree Bishop
Environmental Studies Center
Mobile County Public Schools
Mobile, AL

William Blair
Retired Teacher
J. Marshall Middle School
Billerica, MA

Tom Bright
Concord High School
Charlotte, NC

Nora M. Prestinari Burchett
Saint Luke School
McLean, VA

Lois Burdette
Green Bank Elementary-Middle School
Green Bank, WV

Marcia Chackan
Pine Crest School
Boca Raton, FL

Obioma Chukwu
J.H. Rose High School
Greenville, NC

Karen Curry
East Wake Middle School
Raleigh, NC
Merrilville, IN

Joanne Davis
Murphy High School
Murphy, NC

Robin Dillon
Hanover Central High School
Cedar Lake, IN

Anthony J. DiSipio, Jr.
8th Grade Science
Octorana Middle School
Atglen, PA

Sandra Everhart
Dauphin/Enterprise Jr. High Schools
Enterprise, AL

Mary Ferneau
Westview Middle School
Goose Creek, SC

Cory Fish
Burkholder Middle School
Henderson, NV

Linda V. Forsyth
Retired Teacher
Merrill Middle School
Denver, CO

George Gabb
Great Bridge Middle School
Chesapeake Public Schools
Chesapeake, VA

Annette D'Urso Garcia
Kearney Middle School
Commerce City, CO

Nerma Coats Henderson
Pickerington Lakeview Jr.
High School
Pickerington, OH

Lynne Huskey
Chase Middle School
Forest City, NC

Maria E. Kelly
Principal
Nativity School
Catholic Diocese of Arlington
Burke, VA

Michael Mansour
Board Member
National Middle Level Science
Teacher's Association
John Page Middle School
Madison Heights, MI

Mary Helen Mariscal-Cholka
William D. Slider Middle School
El Paso, TX

Michelle Mazeika-Simmons
Whiting Middle School
Whiting, IN

Joe McConnell
Speedway Jr. High School
Indianapolis, IN

Sharon Mitchell
William D. Slider Middle School
El Paso, TX

Amy Morgan
Berry Middle School
Hoover, AL

Norma Neely, EdD
Associate Director for Regional
Projects
Texas Rural Systemic Initiative
Austin, TX

Annette Parrott
Lakeside High School
Atlanta, GA

Mark Sailer
Pioneer Jr.-Sr. High School
Royal Center, IN

Joanne Stickney
Monticello Middle School
Monticello, NY

Dee Stout
Penn State University
University Park, PA

Darcy Vetro-Ravndal
Hillsborough High School
Tampa, FL

Karen Watkins
Perry Meridian Middle School
Indianapolis, IN

Clabe Webb
Permian High School
Ector County ISD
Odessa, TX

Alison Welch
William D. Slider Middle School
El Paso, TX

Kim Wimpey
North Gwinnett High School
Suwanee, GA

Kate Ziegler
Durant Road Middle School
Raleigh, NC

Teacher Advisory Board

The Teacher Advisory Board gave the editorial staff and design team feedback on the content and design of the Student Edition. They provided valuable input in the development of the 2005 editions of *Glencoe Science.*

John Gonzales
Challenger Middle School
Tucson, AZ

Rachel Shively
Aptakisic Jr. High School
Buffalo Grove, IL

Roger Pratt
Manistique High School
Manistique, MI

Kirtina Hile
Northmor Jr. High/High School
Galion, OH

Marie Renner
Diley Middle School
Pickerington, OH

Nelson Farrier
Hamlin Middle School
Springfield, OR

Jeff Remington
Palmyra Middle School
Palmyra, PA

Erin Peters
Williamsburg Middle School
Arlington, VA

Rubidel Peoples
Meacham Middle School
Fort Worth, TX

Kristi Ramsey
Navasota Jr. High School
Navasota, TX

Student Advisory Board

The Student Advisory Board gave the editorial staff and design team feedback on the design of the Student Edition. We thank these students for their hard work and creative suggestions in making the 2005 editions of *Glencoe Science* student friendly.

Jack Andrews
Reynoldsburg Jr. High School
Reynoldsburg, OH

Peter Arnold
Hastings Middle School
Upper Arlington, OH

Emily Barbe
Perry Middle School
Worthington, OH

Kirsty Bateman
Hilliard Heritage Middle School
Hilliard, OH

Andre Brown
Spanish Emersion Academy
Columbus, OH

Chris Dundon
Heritage Middle School
Westerville, OH

Ryan Manafee
Monroe Middle School
Columbus, OH

Addison Owen
Davis Middle School
Dublin, OH

Teriana Patrick
Eastmoor Middle School
Columbus, OH

Ashley Ruz
Karrar Middle School
Dublin, OH

The Glencoe middle school science Student Advisory Board taking a timeout at COSI, a science museum in Columbus, Ohio.

HOW TO...
Use Your Science Book

Why do I need my science book?

Have you ever been in class and not understood all of what was presented? Or, you understood everything in class, but at home, got stuck on how to answer a question? Maybe you just wondered when you were ever going to use this stuff?

These next few pages are designed to help you understand everything your science book can be used for . . . besides a paperweight!

Before You Read

- **Chapter Opener** Science is occurring all around you, and the opening photo of each chapter will preview the science you will be learning about. The **Chapter Preview** will give you an idea of what you will be learning about, and you can try the **Launch Lab** to help get your brain headed in the right direction. The **Foldables** exercise is a fun way to keep you organized.

- **Section Opener** Chapters are divided into two to four sections. The **As You Read** in the margin of the first page of each section will let you know what is most important in the section. It is divided into four parts. **What You'll Learn** will tell you the major topics you will be covering. **Why It's Important** will remind you why you are studying this in the first place! The **Review Vocabulary** word is a word you already know, either from your science studies or your prior knowledge. The **New Vocabulary** words are words that you need to learn to understand this section. These words will be in **boldfaced** print and highlighted in the section. Make a note to yourself to recognize these words as you are reading the section.

As You Read

- **Headings** Each section has a title in large red letters, and is further divided into blue titles and small red titles at the beginnings of some paragraphs. To help you study, make an outline of the headings and subheadings.

- **Margins** In the margins of your text, you will find many helpful resources. The **Science Online** exercises and **Integrate** activities help you explore the topics you are studying. **MiniLabs** reinforce the science concepts you have learned.

- **Building Skills** You also will find an **Applying Math** or **Applying Science** activity in each chapter. This gives you extra practice using your new knowledge, and helps prepare you for standardized tests.

- **Student Resources** At the end of the book you will find **Student Resources** to help you throughout your studies. These include **Science, Technology,** and **Math Skill Handbooks,** an **English/Spanish Glossary,** and an **Index.** Also, use your **Foldables** as a resource. It will help you organize information, and review before a test.

- **In Class** Remember, you can always ask your teacher to explain anything you don't understand.

FOLDABLES Study Organizer

Science Vocabulary Make the following Foldable to help you understand the vocabulary terms in this chapter.

STEP 1 **Fold** a vertical sheet of notebook paper from side to side.

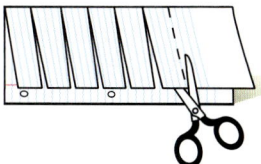

STEP 2 **Cut** along every third line of only the top layer to form tabs.

STEP 3 **Label** each tab with a vocabulary word from the chapter.

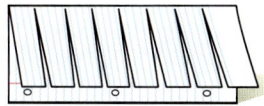

Build Vocabulary As you read the chapter, list the vocabulary words on the tabs. As you learn the definitions, write them under the tab for each vocabulary word.

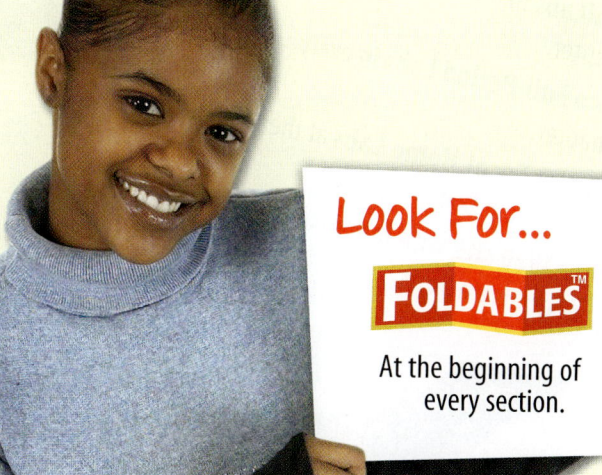

Look For... **FOLDABLES** At the beginning of every section.

In Lab

Working in the laboratory is one of the best ways to understand the concepts you are studying. Your book will be your guide through your laboratory experiences, and help you begin to think like a scientist. In it, you not only will find the steps necessary to follow the investigations, but you also will find helpful tips to make the most of your time.

- Each lab provides you with a **Real-World Question** to remind you that science is something you use every day, not just in class. This may lead to many more questions about how things happen in your world.

- Remember, experiments do not always produce the result you expect. Scientists have made many discoveries based on investigations with unexpected results. You can try the experiment again to make sure your results were accurate, or perhaps form a new hypothesis to test.

- Keeping a **Science Journal** is how scientists keep accurate records of observations and data. In your journal, you also can write any questions that may arise during your investigation. This is a great method of reminding yourself to find the answers later.

Look For...
- **Launch Labs** start every chapter.
- **MiniLabs** in the margin of each chapter.
- **Two Full-Period Labs** in every chapter.
- **EXTRA Try at Home Labs** at the end of your book.
- the **Web site** with **laboratory demonstrations**.

Before a Test

Admit it! You don't like to take tests! However, there *are* ways to review that make them less painful. Your book will help you be more successful taking tests if you use the resources provided to you.

- Review all of the **New Vocabulary** words and be sure you understand their definitions.
- Review the notes you've taken on your **Foldables,** in class, and in lab. Write down any question that you still need answered.
- Review the **Summaries** and **Self Check questions** at the end of each section.
- Study the concepts presented in the chapter by reading the **Study Guide** and answering the questions in the **Chapter Review.**

Look For...
- **Reading Checks** and **caption questions** throughout the text.
- the **Summaries** and **Self Check questions** at the end of each section.
- the **Study Guide** and **Review** at the end of each chapter.
- the **Standards Review** after each chapter.

Let's Get Started

To help you find the information you need quickly, use the Scavenger Hunt below to learn where things are located in Chapter 1.

1. What is the title of this chapter?
2. What will you learn in Section 1?
3. Sometimes you may ask, "Why am I learning this?" State a reason why the concepts from Section 2 are important.
4. What is the main topic presented in Section 2?
5. How many reading checks are in Section 1?
6. What is the Web address where you can find extra information?
7. What is the main heading above the sixth paragraph in Section 2?
8. There is an integration with another subject mentioned in one of the margins of the chapter. What subject is it?
9. List the new vocabulary words presented in Section 2.
10. List the safety symbols presented in the first Lab.
11. Where would you find a Self Check to be sure you understand the section?
12. Suppose you're doing the Self Check and you have a question about concept mapping. Where could you find help?
13. On what pages are the Chapter Study Guide and Chapter Review?
14. Look in the Table of Contents to find out on which page Section 2 of the chapter begins.
15. You complete the Chapter Review to study for your chapter test. Where could you find another quiz for more practice?

Contents

Unit 1: The Basis of Life—2

Chapter 1: Exploring and Classifying Life—4
- **Section 1** What is science? 6
- **Section 2** Living Things 14
- **Section 3** Where does life come from? 19
- **Section 4** How are living things classified? 22
  - Lab Classifying Seeds 27
  - Lab: Design Your Own
    Using Scientific Methods 28

In each chapter, look for these opportunities for review and assessment:
- Reading Checks
- Caption Questions
- Section Review
- Chapter Study Guide
- Chapter Review
- Standards Review
- Online practice at in7.msscience.com

Chapter 2: Cells—36
- **Section 1** Cell Structure 38
  - Lab Comparing Cells 46
- **Section 2** Viewing Cells 47
- **Section 3** Viruses 52
  - Lab: Design Your Own
    Comparing Light Microscopes 56

Chapter 3: Cell Processes—64
- **Section 1** Chemistry of Life 66
- **Section 2** Moving Cellular Materials 74
  - Lab Observing Osmosis 80
- **Section 3** Energy of Life 81
  - Lab Photosynthesis and Respiration 86

Chapter 4: Cell Reproduction—94
- **Section 1** Cell Division and Mitosis 96
  - Lab Mitosis in Plant Cells 103
- **Section 2** Sexual Reproduction and Meiosis 104
- **Section 3** DNA 110
  - Lab: Use the Internet
    Mutations 116

xiii

Contents

unit 2 — The Interdependence of Life—124

chapter 5 — Digestion, Respiration, and Excretion—126
- **Section 1** The Digestive System 128
- **Section 2** Nutrition 133
  - Lab Identifying Vitamin C Content 139
- **Section 3** The Respiratory System 140
- **Section 4** The Excretory System 147
  - Lab Particle Size and Absorption 152

chapter 6 — Circulation and Immunity—160
- **Section 1** Blood 162
- **Section 2** Circulation 167
- **Section 3** Immunity 173
- **Section 4** Diseases 177
  - Lab Microorganisms of Disease 185
  - **Lab: Design Your Own**
    Blood Types 186

chapter 7 — Interactions of Living Things—194
- **Section 1** The Environment 196
  - Lab Delicately Balanced Ecosystems 202
- **Section 2** Interactions Among Living Organisms 203
- **Section 3** Matter and Energy 208
  - **Lab: Design Your Own**
    Identifying a Limiting Factor 214

chapter 8 — Conserving Resources—222
- **Section 1** Resources 224
- **Section 2** Pollution 232
  - Lab The Greenhouse Effect 241
- **Section 3** The Three Rs of Conservation 242
  - **Lab: Model and Invent**
    Solar Cooking 246

Contents

unit 3 The Nature of Matter—254

chapter 9 Atoms, Elements, and the Periodic Table—256

Section 1	Structure of Matter	.258
Section 2	The Simplest Matter	.266
	Lab Elements and the Periodic Table	.272
Section 3	Compounds and Mixtures	.273
	Lab Mystery Mixture	.278

In each chapter, look for these opportunities for review and assessment:
- Reading Checks
- Caption Questions
- Section Review
- Chapter Study Guide
- Chapter Review
- Standards Review
- Online practice at in7.msscience.com

chapter 10 Substances, Mixtures, and Solubility—286

Section 1	What is a solution?	.288
Section 2	Solubility	.294
	Lab Growing Crystals	.301
Section 3	Acidic and Basic Solutions	.302
	Lab Testing pH Using Natural Indicators	.310

unit 4 Motion, Forces, and Energy—318

chapter 11 Motion and Momentum—320

Section 1	What is motion?	.322
Section 2	Acceleration	.328
Section 3	Momentum	.333
	Lab Collisions	.339
	Lab: Design Your Own Car Safety Testing	.340

xv

Contents

Chapter 12 — Force and Newton's Laws—348

- **Section 1** Newton's First Law 350
- **Section 2** Newton's Second Law 356
- **Section 3** Newton's Third Law 363
  - **Lab** Balloon Races 369
  - **Lab: Design Your Own**
    Modeling Motion in Two Directions 370

In each chapter, look for these opportunities for review and assessment:
- **Reading Checks**
- **Caption Questions**
- **Section Review**
- **Chapter Study Guide**
- **Chapter Review**
- **Standards Review**
- **Online practice at in7.msscience.com**

Chapter 13 — Energy and Energy Resources—378

- **Section 1** What is energy? 380
- **Section 2** Energy Transformations 385
  - **Lab** Hearing with Your Jaw 392
- **Section 3** Sources of Energy 393
  - **Lab: Use the Internet**
    Energy to Power Your Life 402

Chapter 14 — Waves, Sound, and Light—410

- **Section 1** Waves 412
- **Section 2** Sound Waves 419
  - **Lab** Sound Waves in Matter 424
- **Section 3** Light 425
  - **Lab** Bending Light 432

Chapter 15 — Electronics and Computers—440

- **Section 1** Electronics 442
  - **Lab** Investigating Diodes 448
- **Section 2** Computers 449
  - **Lab: Use the Internet**
    Does your computer have a virus? 460

Contents

Galaxies, Stars, and Earth—468

Stars and Galaxies—470

Section 1	Stars	472
Section 2	The Sun	477
	Lab Sunspots	481
Section 3	Evolution of Stars	482
Section 4	Galaxies and the Universe	489
	Lab: Design Your Own Measuring Parallax	494

Minerals—502

Section 1	Minerals	504
	Lab Crystal Formation	508
Section 2	Mineral Identification	509
Section 3	Uses of Minerals	515
	Lab Mineral Identification	522

Rocks—530

Section 1	The Rock Cycle	532
Section 2	Igneous Rocks	536
	Lab Igneous Rock Clues	540
Section 3	Metamorphic Rocks	541
Section 4	Sedimentary Rocks	545
	Lab Sedimentary Rocks	552

Contents

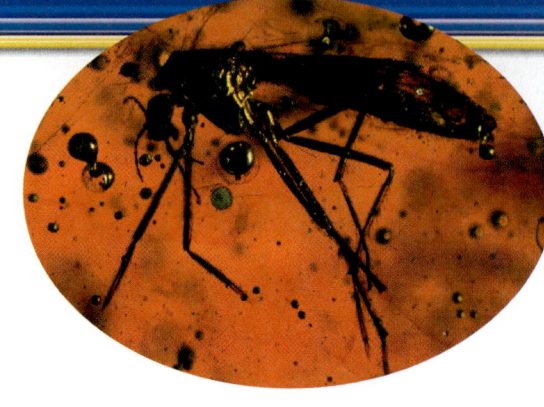

unit 6 Processes that Shape Earth—560

chapter 19 Forces Shaping Earth—562

- **Section 1** Earth's Moving Plates 564
  - Lab Earth's Moving Plates 574
- **Section 2** Uplift of Earth's Crust 575
  - Lab: Model and Invent
    Isostasy 582

chapter 20 Earthquakes and Volcanoes—590

- **Section 1** Earthquakes 592
- **Section 2** Volcanoes 601
  - Lab Disruptive Eruptions 607
- **Section 3** Earthquakes, Volcanoes, and
  Plate Tectonics 608
  - Lab Seismic Waves 614

chapter 21 Climate—622

- **Section 1** What is climate? 624
- **Section 2** Climate Types 628
- **Section 3** Climatic Changes 632
  - Lab The Greenhouse Effect 643
  - Lab Microclimates 644

chapter 22 Clues to Earth's Past—652

- **Section 1** Fossils 654
- **Section 2** Relative Ages of Rocks 662
  - Lab Relative Ages 668
- **Section 3** Absolute Ages of Rocks 669
  - Lab: Model and Invent
    Trace Fossils 674

xviii

Contents

Student Resources—682

Science Skill Handbook—684
Scientific Methods 684
Safety Symbols 693
Safety in the Science Laboratory 694

Extra Try at Home Labs—696

Technology Skill Handbook—707
Computer Skills 707
Presentation Skills 710

Math Skill Handbook—711
Math Review 711
Science Applications 721

Reference Handbooks—726
Use and Care of a Microscope 726
Rocks 727
Minerals 728
Physical Science Reference Tables 730
Periodic Table of the Elements 732

English/Spanish Glossary—734

Index—755

Credits—774

In each chapter, look for these opportunities for review and assessment:
- Reading Checks
- Caption Questions
- Section Review
- Chapter Study Guide
- Chapter Review
- Standards Review
- Online practice at in7.msscience.com

Cross-Curricular Readings

NATIONAL GEOGRAPHIC Unit Openers

Unit 1 How are Cargo Ships and Cancer Cells Connected?......2–3
Unit 2 How are Chickens and Rice Connected?...........124–125
Unit 3 How are Refrigerators and Frying Pans Connected? .254–255
Unit 4 How are Radar and Popcorn Connected?..........318–319
Unit 5 How are Canals and the Paleozoic Era Connected?..468–469
Unit 6 How are Rivers and Writing Connected?..........560–561

NATIONAL GEOGRAPHIC VISUALIZING

1. Origins of Life..20
2. Microscopes..48–49
3. Cell Membrane Transport..............................79
4. Polyploidy in Plants..................................108
5. Abdominal Thrusts...................................144
6. Koch's Rules..179
7. A Food Chain.......................................209
8. Solar Energy..231
9. The Periodic Table...................................268
10. Acid Precipitation...................................304
11. Conservation of Momentum..........................337
12. Newton's Laws in Sports.............................365
13. Energy Transformations..............................388
14. Common Vision Problems............................430
15. A Hard Disk..457
16. The Big Bang Theory.................................492
17. Crystal Systems.....................................506
18. The Rock Cycle.....................................534
19. Rift Valleys...570
20. Tsunamis..598
21. El Niño and La Niña.............................634–635
22. Unconformities.....................................665

Cross-Curricular Readings

TIME Science and Society

1	Monkey Business	30
12	Air Bag Safety	372
15	E-Lectrifying E-Books	462
18	Australia's Controversial Rock Star	554

TIME Science and History

2	Cobb Against Cancer	58
5	Overcoming the Odds	154
6	Have a Heart	188
9	Ancient Views of Matter	280
17	Dr. Dorothy Crawfoot Hodgkin	524
20	Quake	616
21	The Year There Was No Summer	646

Oops! Accidents in Science

4	A Tangled Tale	118
11	What Goes Around Comes Around	342
14	Jansky's Merry-Go-Round	434
22	The World's Oldest Fish Story	676

Science and Language Arts

3	"Tulip"	88
7	The Solace of Open Spaces	216
8	Beauty Plagiarized	248

Science Stats

10	Salty Solutions	312
13	Energy to Burn	404
16	Stars and Galaxies	496
19	Mountains	584

◧ available as a video lab

1	Classify Organisms	5
2	Magnifying Cells	37
3	Why does water enter and leave plant cells?	65
◧ 4	Infer About Seed Growth	95
5	Breathing Rate	127
6	Transportation by Road and Vessel	161
7	Space and Interactions	195
8	What happens when topsoil is left unprotected?	223
9	Observe Matter	257
10	Particle Size and Dissolving Rates	287
11	Motion After a Collision	321
12	Forces and Motion	349
◧ 13	Analyze a Marble Launch	379
14	Wave Properties	411
15	Electronic and Human Calculators	441
16	Why do clusters of galaxies move apart?	471
17	Distinguish Rocks from Minerals	503
18	Observe and Describe Rocks	531
19	Model Earth's Interior	563
◧ 20	Construct with Strength	591
21	Tracking World Climates	623
22	Clues to Life's Past	653

Mini LAB

◧ 1	Analyzing Data	9
2	Modeling Cytoplasm	40
3	Observing How Enzymes Work	71
4	Modeling Mitosis	101
5	Comparing the Fat Content of Foods	135
6	Modeling Scab Formation	164
7	Observing Symbiosis	206
8	Measuring Acid Rain	233
9	Investigating the Unseen	260
10	Observing a Nail in a Carbonated Drink	303
11	Modeling Acceleration	331
12	Measuring Force Pairs	367
13	Building a Solar Collector	397
14	Separating Wavelengths	428

	16	Measuring Distance in Space	490
	17	Observing Mineral Properties	514
	18	Classifying Sediments	546
	19	Modeling Mountains	577
	20	Observing Deformation	593
	21	Observing Solar Radiation	625
	22	Modeling Carbon-14 Dating	670

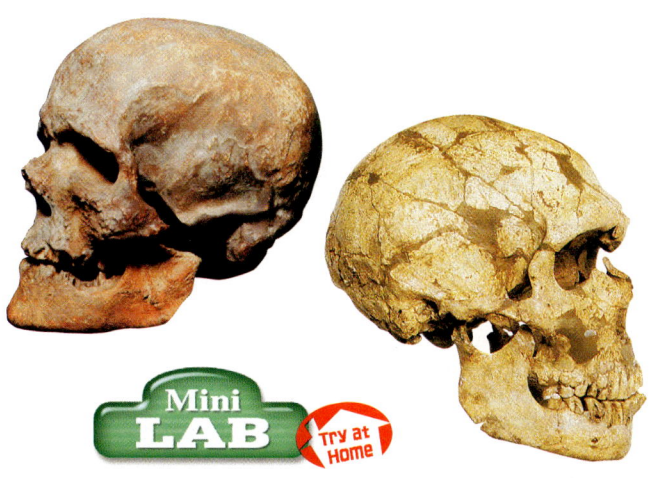

1	Communicating Ideas	25
2	Observing Magnified Objects	50
3	Observing Diffusion	75
4	Modeling DNA Replication	111
5	Comparing Surface Area	143
6	Determining Reproduction Rates	175
7	Modeling the Water Cycle	212
8	Observe Mineral Mining Effects	226
9	Comparing Compounds	274
10	Observing Chemical Processes	298
11	Measuring Average Speed	325
12	Observing Friction	354
13	Analyzing Energy Transformations	387
14	Refraction of Light	417
15	Using Binary Numbers	450
15	Observing Memory	453
16	Observing Star Patterns	473
17	Inferring Salt's Crystal System	505
18	Modeling Rock	533
19	Modeling Tension and Compression	571
20	Modeling an Eruption	602
21	Modeling El Niño	633
22	Predicting Fossil Preservation	655

xxiii

available as a video lab

One-Page Labs

	1	Classifying Seeds.................................27
▭	2	Comparing Cells..................................46
	3	Observing Osmosis...............................80
	4	Mitosis in Plant Cells............................103
▭	5	Identifying Vitamin C Content..................139
	6	Microorganisms and Disease....................185
	7	Delicately Balanced Ecosystems................202
▭	8	The Greenhouse Effect..........................241
	9	Elements and the Periodic Table................272
	10	Observing Gas Solubility.......................301
▭	11	Collisions.......................................339
▭	12	Balloon Races...................................369
	13	Hearing with Your Jaw.........................392
▭	14	Sound Waves in Matter........................424
	15	Investigating Diodess..........................448
	16	Sunspots.......................................481
	17	Crystal Formation..............................509

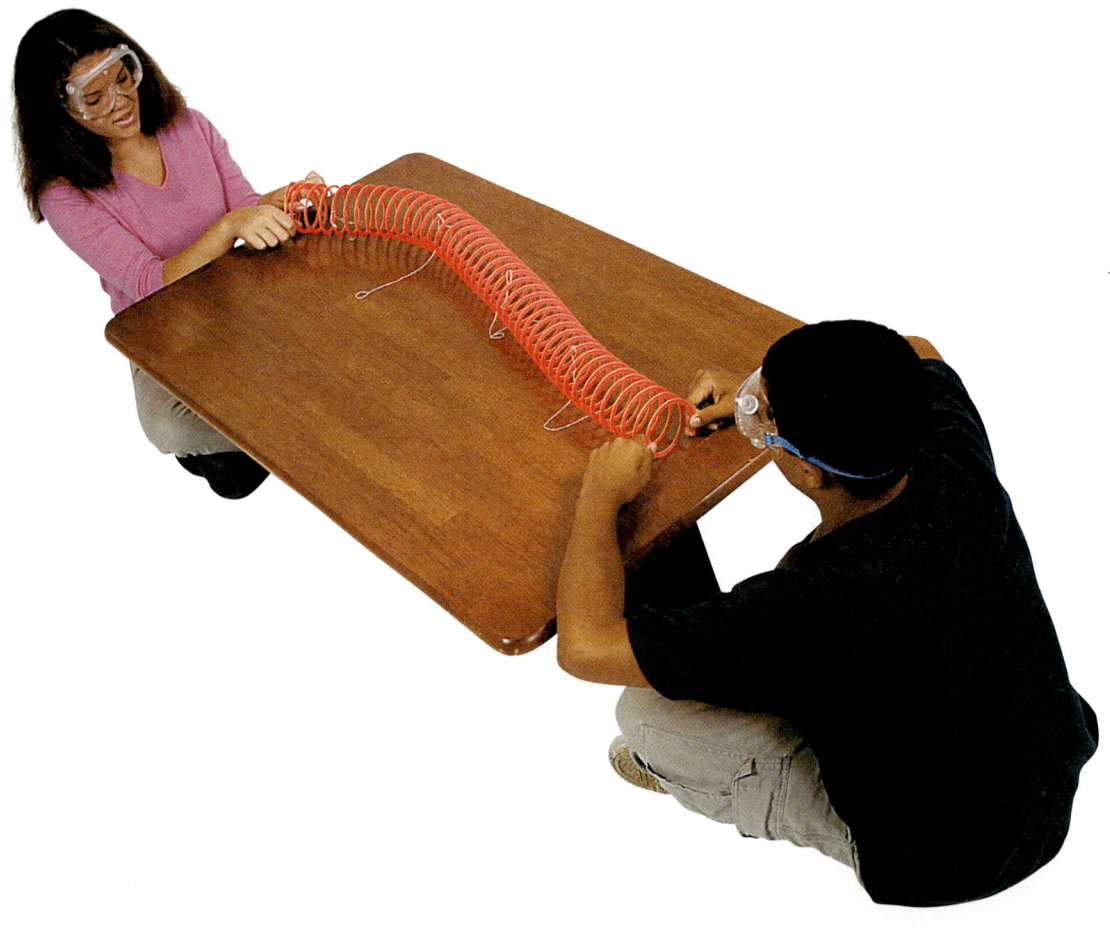

xxiv

18	Igneous Rock Clues	540
19	Earth's Moving Plates	574
20	Disruptive Eruptions	607
21	The Greenhouse Effect	643
22	Relative Ages	668

Two-Page Labs

3	Photosynthesis and Respiration	86–87
5	Particle Size and Absorption	152–153
9	Mystery Mixture	278–279
10	Testing pH Using Natural Indicators	310–311
14	Bending Light	432–433
17	Mineral Identification	522–523
18	Sedimentary Rocks	552–553
20	Seismic Waves	614–615
21	Microclimates	644–645

Design Your Own Labs

1	Using Scientific Methods	28–29
2	Comparing Light Microscopes	56–57
6	Blood Type Reactions	186–187
7	Identifying a Limiting Factor	214–215
11	Car Safety Testing	340–341
12	Modeling Motion in Two Directions	370–371
16	Measuring Parallax	494–495

Model and Invent Labs

8	Solar Cooking	246–247
19	Isostasy	582–583
22	Trace Fossils	674–675

Use the Internet Labs

4	Mutations	116–117
13	Energy to Power Your Life	402–403
15	Does your computer have a virus?	460–461

xxv

Activities

Applying Math

2	Cell Ratio	44
3	Calculate the Importance of Water	72
11	Speed of a Swimmer	324
11	Acceleration of a Bus	330
11	Momentum of a Bicycle	334
12	Acceleration of a Car	359
14	Speed of Sound	416
18	Coal Formation	550
20	P-wave Travel Time	612

Applying Science

1	Does temperature affect the rate of bacterial reproduction?	11
4	How can chromosome numbers be predicted?	107
5	How does your body gain and lose water?	150
6	Has the annual percentage of deaths from major diseases changed?	180
7	How do changes in Antarctic food webs affect populations?	210
8	What items are you recycling at home?	244
9	What's the best way to desalt ocean water?	275
10	How can you compare concentrations?	299
13	Is energy consumption outpacing production?	396
15	How much information can be stored?	451
16	Are distance and brightness related?	474
17	How can you identify minerals?	512
19	How can glaciers cause land to rise?	580
21	How do cities influence temperature?	626
22	When did the Iceman die?	672

Activities

INTEGRATE

Astronomy: 21
Career: 50, 83, 97, 198, 264, 299, 454, 548, 641
Chemistry: 105, 110, 211, 212, 233, 298, 446, 485, 519, 539, 566, 603, 610
Earth Science: 21, 277, 394, 414
Environment: 44, 291, 295, 456
Health: 77, 132, 145, 236, 421
History: 165, 259, 357, 389, 486
Language Arts: 580, 611
Life Science: 88, 216, 248, 276, 306, 324, 351, 364, 387, 629, 660
Physics: 42, 73, 170, 484, 507, 535, 564, 626, 669
Social Studies: 17, 136, 174, 227, 334, 519, 657

8, 15, 23, 53, 54, 70, 84, 113, 115, 134, 145, 163, 172, 178, 200, 204, 234, 244, 262, 267, 276, 289, 305, 308, 326, 336, 364, 386, 396, 426, 445, 452, 456, 458, 479, 484, 518, 538, 542, 569, 578, 597, 603, 639, 641, 663, 666, 672

Standards Review

34–35, 62–63, 92–93, 122–123, 158–159, 192–193, 220–221, 252–253, 284–285, 316–317, 346–347, 376–377, 408–409, 438–439, 466–467, 500–501, 528–529, 558–559, 588–589, 620–621, 650–651, 680–681

unit 1: The Basis of Life

How Are Cargo Ships & Cancer Cells Connected?

Below, a present-day cargo ship glides through a harbor in New Jersey. In 1943, during World War II, another cargo ship floated in an Italian harbor. The ship carried a certain type of chemical. When a bomb struck the ship, the chemical accidentally was released. Later, when doctors examined the sailors who were exposed to the chemical, they noticed that the sailors had low numbers of white blood cells. The chemical had interfered with the genetic material in certain cells, preventing the cells from reproducing. Since cancer cells (like the ones at lower left) are cells that reproduce without control, scientists wondered whether this chemical could be used to fight cancer. A compound related to the chemical became the first drug developed to fight cancer. Since then, many other cancer-fighting drugs have been developed.

unit projects

The assessed Indiana standard appears in blue.
To find project ideas and resources, visit in7.msscience.com/unit_project.
Projects include:
- **Career** Brainstorm a list of questions for a health professional about cell reproduction, or bacteria and virus resistance to drugs. **7.4.12**
- **Technology** Design a chart and graph that presents information on cell reproduction rate during specific time intervals. **7.4.4**
- **Model** Construct a thumb flip book that models mitosis. Complete a second book for meiosis to analyze and compare the two processes. **7.4.4**

WebQuest *New Research on Cells* provides an opportunity to explore current research on cells, and how different cells work in the human body. **7.4.5**

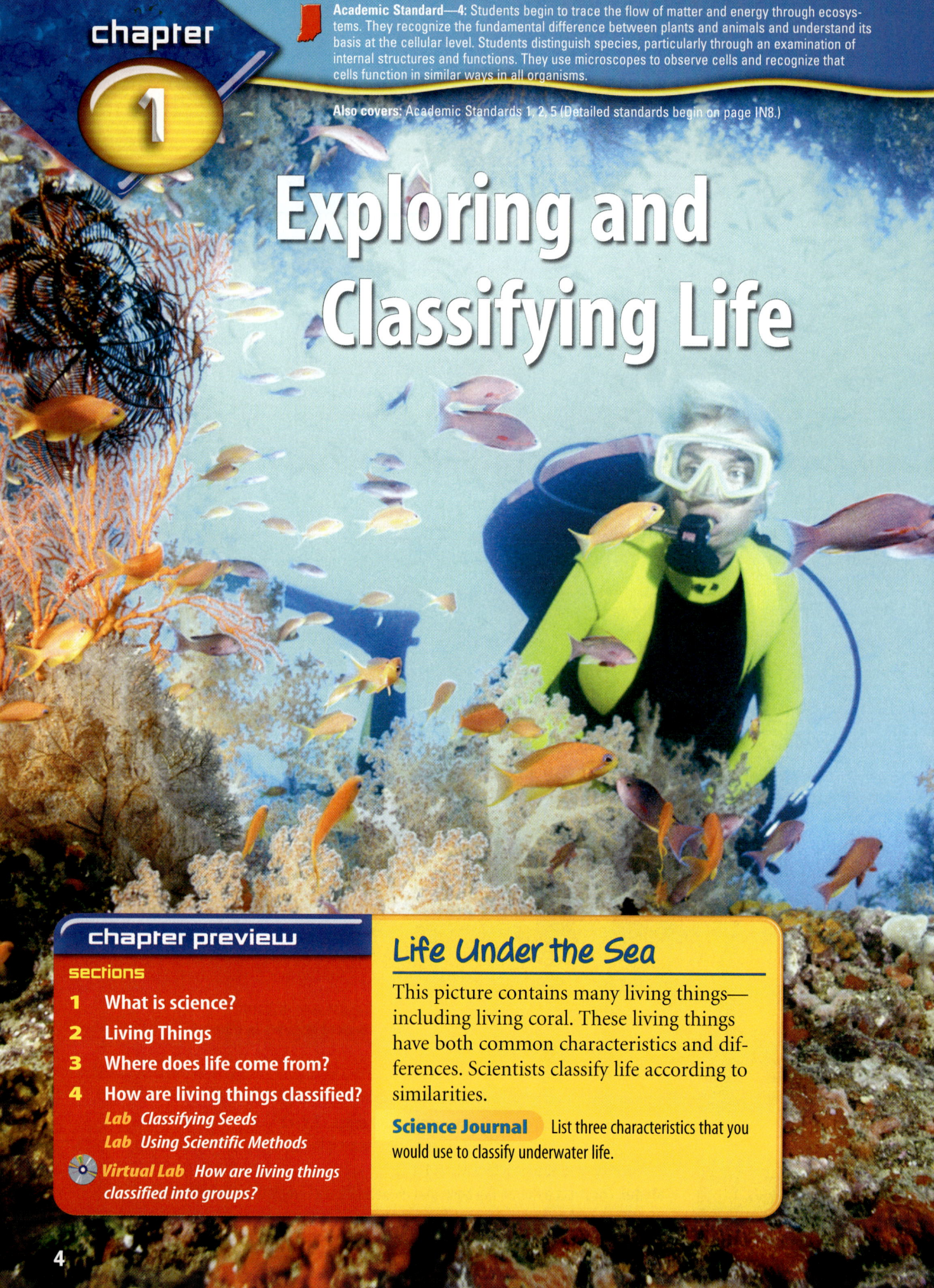

chapter 1

Academic Standard—4: Students begin to trace the flow of matter and energy through ecosystems. They recognize the fundamental difference between plants and animals and understand its basis at the cellular level. Students distinguish species, particularly through an examination of internal structures and functions. They use microscopes to observe cells and recognize that cells function in similar ways in all organisms.

Also covers: Academic Standards 1, 2, 5 (Detailed standards begin on page IN8.)

Exploring and Classifying Life

chapter preview

sections
1. What is science?
2. Living Things
3. Where does life come from?
4. How are living things classified?
   Lab Classifying Seeds
   Lab Using Scientific Methods
   Virtual Lab How are living things classified into groups?

Life Under the Sea

This picture contains many living things—including living coral. These living things have both common characteristics and differences. Scientists classify life according to similarities.

Science Journal List three characteristics that you would use to classify underwater life.

Start-Up Activities

Classify Organisms

Life scientists discover, describe, and name hundreds of organisms every year. How do they decide if a certain plant belongs to the iris or orchid family of flowering plants, or if an insect is more like a grasshopper or a beetle?

1. Observe the organisms on the opposite page or in an insect collection in your class.
2. Decide which feature could be used to separate the organisms into two groups, then sort the organisms into the two groups.
3. Continue to make new groups using different features until each organism is in a category by itself.
4. **Think Critically** How do you think scientists classify living things? List your ideas in your Science Journal.

Vocabulary Make the following Foldable to help you understand the vocabulary terms in this chapter.

STEP 1 Fold a vertical sheet of notebook paper from side to side.

STEP 2 Cut along every third line of only the top layer to form tabs.

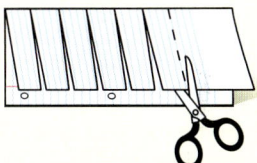

STEP 3 Label each tab.

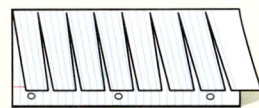

Build Vocabulary As you read the chapter, write the vocabulary words on the tabs. As you learn the definitions, write them under the tab for each vocabulary word.

 Preview this chapter's content and activities at in7.msscience.com

section 1

Standards—7.1.1: Recognize and explain that when similar investigations give different results, the scientific challenge is to judge whether the differences are trivial or significant, which often takes further studies to decide. **7.1.3:** Explain why it is important in science to keep honest, clear, and accurate records.

Also covers: 7.1.4, 7.1.8, 7.2.8 (Detailed standards begin on page IN8.)

What is science?

as you read

What You'll Learn
- **Apply** scientific methods to problem solving.
- **Demonstrate** how to measure using scientific units.

Why It's Important
Learning to use scientific methods will help you solve ordinary problems in your life.

Review Vocabulary
experiment: using controlled conditions to test a prediction

New Vocabulary
- scientific methods
- hypothesis
- control
- variable
- theory
- law

The Work of Science

Movies and popcorn seem to go together. So before you and your friends watch a movie, sometimes you pop some corn in a microwave oven. When the popping stops, you take out the bag and open it carefully. You smell the mouthwatering, freshly popped corn and avoid hot steam that escapes from the bag. What makes the popcorn pop? How do microwaves work and make things hot? By the way, what are microwaves anyway?

Asking questions like these is one way scientists find out about anything in the world and the universe. Science is often described as an organized way of studying things and finding answers to questions.

Types of Science Many types of science exist. Each is given a name to describe what is being studied. For example, energy and matter have a relationship. That's a topic for physics. A physicist could answer most questions about microwaves.

On the other hand, a life scientist might study any of the millions of different animals, plants, and other living things on Earth. Look at the objects in **Figure 1.** What do they look like to you? A life scientist could tell you that some of the objects are living plants and some are just rocks. Life scientists who study plants are botanists, and those who study animals are zoologists. What do you suppose a bacteriologist studies?

Figure 1 Examine the picture carefully. Some of these objects are actually *Lithops* plants. They commonly are called stone plants and are native to deserts in South Africa.

Critical Thinking

Whether or not you become a trained scientist, you are going to solve problems all your life. You probably solve many problems every day when you sort out ideas about what will or won't work. Suppose your CD player stops playing music. To figure out what happened, you have to think about it. That's called critical thinking, and it's the way you use skills to solve problems.

If you know that the CD player does not run on batteries and must be plugged in to work, that's the first thing you check to solve the problem. You check and the player is plugged in so you eliminate that possible solution. You separate important information from unimportant information—that's a skill. Could there be something wrong with the first outlet? You plug the player into a different outlet, and your CD starts playing. You now know that it's the first outlet that doesn't work. Identifying the problem is another skill you have.

Solving Problems

Scientists use the same types of skills that you do to solve problems and answer questions. Although scientists don't always find the answers to their questions, they always use critical thinking in their search. Besides critical thinking, solving a problem requires organization. In science, this organization often takes the form of a series of procedures called **scientific methods.** Figure 2 shows one way that scientific methods might be used to solve a problem.

State the Problem Suppose a veterinary technician wanted to find out whether different types of cat litter cause irritation to cats' skin. What would she do first? The technician begins by observing something she cannot explain. A pet owner brings his four cats to the clinic to be boarded while he travels. He leaves his cell phone number so he can be contacted if any problems arise. When they first arrive, the four cats seem healthy. The next day however, the technician notices that two of the cats are scratching and chewing at their skin. By the third day, these same two cats have bare patches of skin with red sores. The technician decides that something in the cats' surroundings or their food might be irritating their skin.

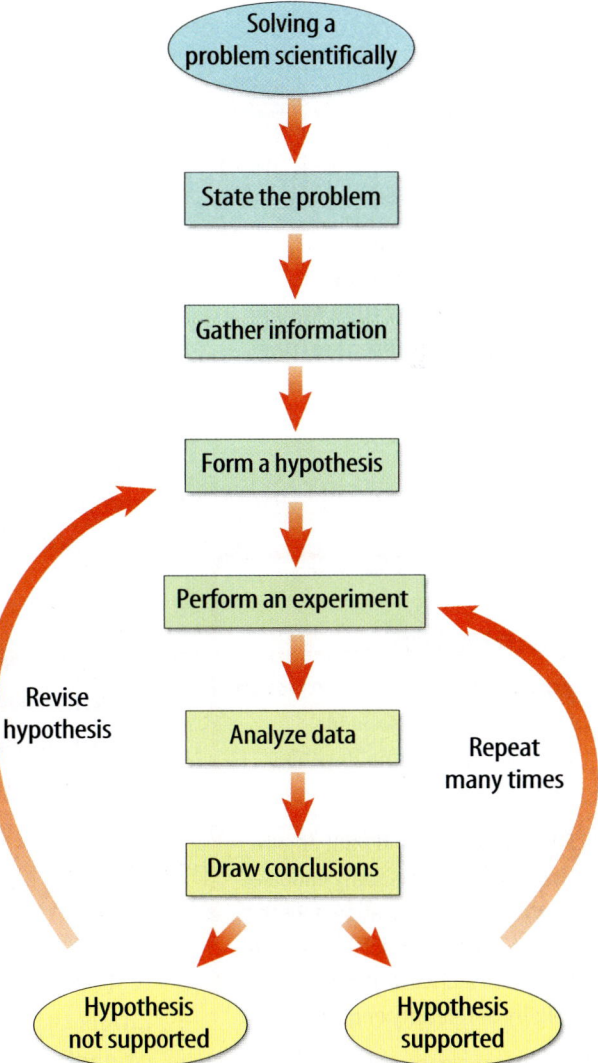

Figure 2 The series of procedures shown below is one way to use scientific methods to solve a problem.

SECTION 1   What is science?   **7**

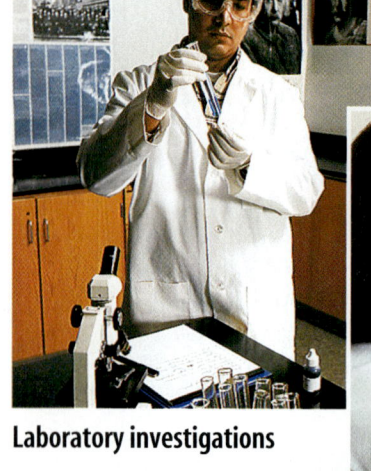
Laboratory investigations

Computer models

Fieldwork

Figure 3 Observations can be made in many different settings.
List *three other places where scientific observations can be made.*

Topic: Truth in Advertising
Visit in7.msscience.com for Web links to information about celebrity endorsements.

Activity Find and print an advertisement with a celebrity endorsement. What qualification does this person have for endorsing the product? Have a discussion about the validity of celebrity endorsements.

Gather Information Laboratory observations and experiments are ways to collect information. Some data also are gathered from fieldwork. Fieldwork includes observations or experiments that are done outside of the laboratory. For example, the best way to find out how a bird builds a nest is to go outside and watch it. **Figure 3** shows some ways data can be gathered.

The technician gathers information about the problem by watching the cats closely for the next two days. She knows that cats sometimes change their behavior when they are in a new place. She wants to see if the behavior of the cats with the skin sores seems different from that of the other two cats. Other than the scratching and chewing at their skin, all four cats' behavior seems to be the same.

The technician calls the owner and tells him about the problem. She asks him what brand of cat food he feeds his cats. Because his brand is the same one used at the clinic, she decides that food is not the cause of the skin irritation. She decides that the cats probably are reacting to something in their surroundings. There are many things in the clinic that the cats might react to. How does she decide what it is?

During her observations she notices that the cats seem to scratch and chew themselves most after using their litter boxes. The cat litter used by the clinic contains a deodorant. The technician calls the owner and finds out that the cat litter he buys does not contain a deodorant.

Form a Hypothesis Based on this information, the next thing the veterinary technician does is form a hypothesis. A **hypothesis** is a prediction that can be tested. After discussing her observations with the clinic veterinarian, she hypothesizes that something in the cat litter is irritating the cats' skin.

Test the Hypothesis with an Experiment The technician gets the owner's permission to test her hypothesis by performing an experiment. In an experiment, the hypothesis is tested using controlled conditions. The technician reads the labels on two brands of cat litter and finds that the ingredients of each are the same except that one contains a deodorant.

8 CHAPTER 1 Exploring and Classifying Life

Controls The technician separates the cats with sores from the other two cats. She puts each of the cats with sores in a cage by itself. One cat is called the experimental cat. This cat is given a litter box containing the cat litter without deodorant. The other cat is given a litter box that contains cat litter with deodorant. The cat with deodorant cat litter is the control.

A **control** is the standard to which the outcome of a test is compared. At the end of the experiment, the control cat will be compared with the experimental cat. Whether or not the cat litter contains deodorant is the variable. A **variable** is something in an experiment that can change. An experiment should have only one variable. Other than the difference in the cat litter, the technician treats both cats the same.

 *How many variables should an experiment have?*

Analyze Data The veterinary technician observes both cats for one week. During this time, she collects data on how often and when the cats scratch or chew, as shown in **Figure 4.** These data are recorded in a journal. The data show that the control cat scratches and chews more often than the experimental cat does. The sores on the skin of the experimental cat begin to heal, but those on the control cat do not.

Draw Conclusions The technician then draws the conclusion—a logical answer to a question based on data and observation—that the deodorant in the cat litter probably irritated the skin of the two cats. To accept or reject the hypothesis is the next step. In this case, the technician accepts the hypothesis. If she had rejected it, new experiments would have been necessary.

Although the technician decides to accept her hypothesis, she realizes that to be surer of her results she should continue her experiment. She should switch the experimental cat with the control cat to see what the results are a second time. If she did this, the healed cat might develop new sores. She makes an ethical decision and chooses not to continue the experiment. Ethical decisions, like this one, are important in deciding what science should be done.

Mini LAB

Analyzing Data
Procedure
1. Obtain a **pan balance.** Follow your teacher's instructions for using it.
2. Record all data in your **Science Journal.**
3. Measure and record the mass of a **dry sponge.**
4. Soak this sponge in **water.** Measure and record its mass.
5. Calculate how much water your sponge absorbed.
6. Combine the class data and calculate the average amount of water absorbed.

Analysis
What other information about the sponges might be important when analyzing the data from the entire class?

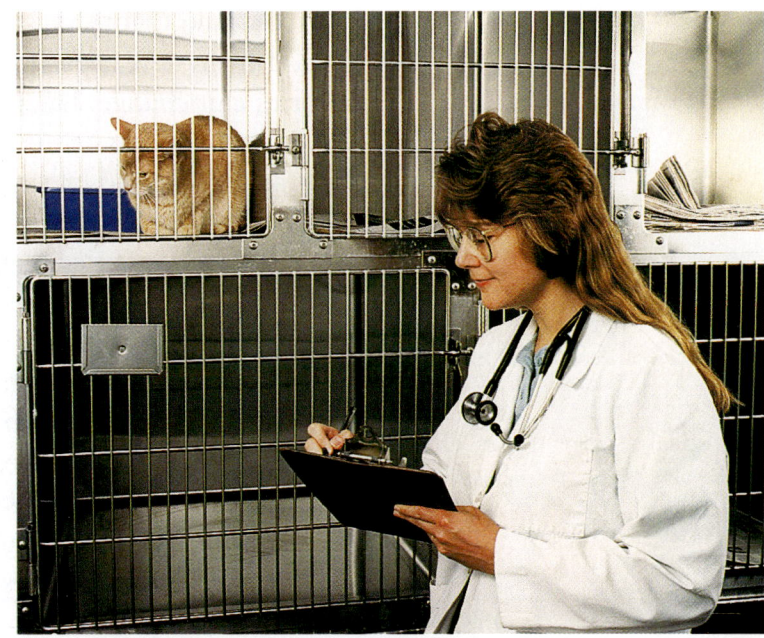

Figure 4 Collecting and analyzing data is part of scientific methods.

SECTION 1 What is science? **9**

Report Results When using scientific methods, it is important to share information. The veterinary technician calls the cats' owner and tells him the results of her experiment. She tells him she has stopped using the deodorant cat litter.

The technician also writes a story for the clinic's newsletter that describes her experiment and shares her conclusions. She reports the limits of her experiment and explains that her results are not final. In science it is important to explain how an experiment can be made better if it is done again.

Developing Theories

After scientists report the results of experiments supporting their hypotheses, the results can be used to propose a scientific theory. When you watch a magician do a trick you might decide you have an idea or "theory" about how the trick works. Is your idea just a hunch or a scientific theory? A scientific **theory** is an explanation of things or events based on scientific knowledge that is the result of many observations and experiments. It is not a guess or someone's opinion. Many scientists repeat the experiment. If the results always support the hypothesis, the hypothesis can be called a theory, as shown in **Figure 5**.

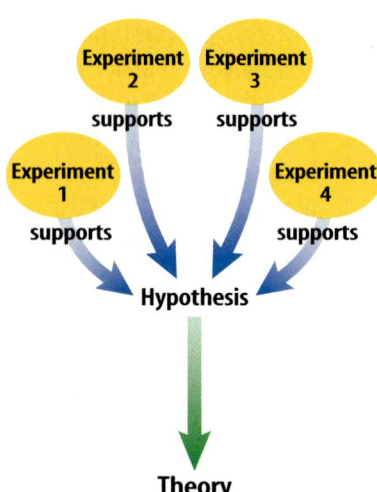

Figure 5 If data collected from several experiments over a period of time all support the hypothesis, it finally can be called a theory.

Reading Check *What is a theory based on?*

A theory usually explains many hypotheses. For example, an important theory in life sciences is the cell theory. Scientists made observations of cells and experimented for more than 100 years before enough information was collected to propose a theory. Hypotheses about cells in plants and animals are combined in the cell theory.

A valid theory raises many new questions. Data or information from new experiments might change conclusions and theories can change. Later in this chapter you will read about the theory of spontaneous generation and how this theory changed as scientists used experiments to study new hypotheses.

Laws A scientific **law** is a statement about how things work in nature that seems to be true all the time. Although laws can be modified as more information becomes known, they are less likely to change than theories. Laws tell you what will happen under certain conditions but do not necessarily explain why it happened. For example, in life science you might learn about laws of heredity. These laws explain how genes are inherited but do not explain how genes work. Due to the great variety of living things, laws that describe them are few. It is unlikely that a law about how all cells work will ever be developed.

Scientific Methods Help Answer Questions You can use scientific methods to answer all sorts of questions. Your questions may be as simple as "Where did I leave my house key?" or as complex as "Will global warming cause the polar ice caps to melt?" You probably have had to find the answer to the first question. Someday you might try to find the answer to the second question. Using these scientific methods does not guarantee that you will get an answer. Often scientific methods just lead to more questions and more experiments. That's what science is about—continuing to look for the best answers to your questions.

Applying Science

Does temperature affect the rate of bacterial reproduction?

Some bacteria make you sick. Other bacteria, however, are used to produce foods like cheese and yogurt. Understanding how quickly bacteria reproduce can help you avoid harmful bacteria and use helpful bacteria. It's important to know things that affect how quickly bacteria reproduce. How do you think temperature will affect the rate of bacterial reproduction? A student makes the hypothesis that bacteria will reproduce more quickly as the temperature increases.

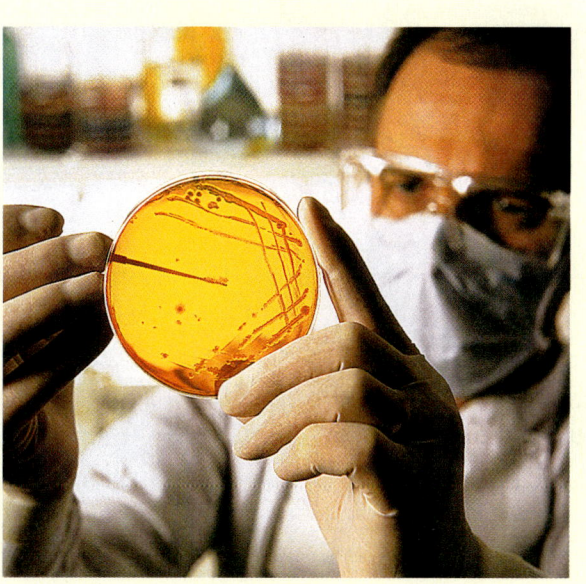

Identifying the Problem
The table below lists the reproduction-doubling rates at specific temperatures for one type of bacteria. A rate of 2.0 means that the number of bacteria doubled two times that hour (e.g., 100 to 200 to 400).

Bacterial Reproductive Rates	
Temperature (°C)	Doubling Rate per Hour
20.5	2.0
30.5	3.0
36.0	2.5
39.2	1.2

Look at the table. What conclusions can you draw from the data?

Solving the Problem
1. Do the data in the table support the student's hypothesis?
2. How would you write a hypothesis about the relationship between bacterial reproduction and temperature?
3. Make a list of other factors that might have influenced the results in the table.
4. Are you satisfied with these data? List other things that you wish you knew.
5. Describe an experiment that would help you test these other ideas.

Figure 6 Your food often is measured in metric units. Nutritional information on the label is listed in grams or milligrams.

Measuring with Scientific Units

An important part of most scientific investigations is making accurate measurements. Think about things you use every day that are measured. Ingredients in your hamburger, hot dog, potato chips, or soft drink are measured in units such as grams and milliliters, as shown in **Figure 6.** The water you drink, the gas you use, and the electricity needed for a CD player are measured, too.

The label of this juice bottle shows you that it contains 473 mL of juice.

Reading Check *Why is it important to make accurate measurements?*

In your classroom or laboratory this year, you will use the same standard system of measurement scientists use to communicate and understand each other's research and results. This system is called the International System of Units, or SI. For example, you may need to calculate the distance a bird flies in kilometers. Perhaps you will be asked to measure the amount of air your lungs can hold in liters or the mass of an automobile in kilograms. Some of the SI units are shown in **Table 1.**

Table 1 Common SI Measurements			
Measurement	**Unit**	**Symbol**	**Equal to**
Length	1 millimeter	mm	0.001 (1/1,000) m
	1 centimeter	cm	0.01 (1/100) m
	1 meter	m	100 cm
	1 kilometer	km	1,000 m
Volume	1 milliliter	mL	0.001 (1/1,000) L
	1 liter	L	1,000 mL
Mass	1 gram	g	1,000 mg
	1 kilogram	kg	1,000 g
	1 tonne	t	1,000 kg = 1 metric ton

Safety First

Doing science is usually much more interesting than just reading about it. Some of the scientific equipment that you will use in your classroom or laboratory is the same as what scientists use. Laboratory safety is important. In many states, a student can participate in a laboratory class only when wearing proper eye protection. Don't forget to wash your hands after handling materials. Following safety rules, as shown in **Figure 7,** will protect you and others from injury during your lab experiences. Symbols used throughout your text will alert you to situations that require special attention. Some of these symbols are shown below. A description of each symbol is in the Safety Symbols chart at the front of this book.

Figure 7 Proper eye protection should be worn whenever you see this safety symbol.
Predict what might happen if you do not wear eye protection in the lab.

section 1 review

Summary

The Work of Science
- Science is an organized way of studying things and finding answers to questions.

Solving Problems and Developing Theories
- Scientific methods are procedures used to solve problems and answer questions.
- A theory is an explanation based on many scientific observations.

Measuring with Scientific Units
- Scientists use the SI system for measurements.

Safety First
- Follow safety rules in the lab.

Self Check

1. **Describe** scientific methods.
2. **Infer** why it is important to test only one variable at a time during an experiment.
3. **Identify** the SI unit you would use to measure the width of your classroom.
4. **Compare and contrast** a theory with a hypothesis.
5. **Think Critically** Can the veterinary technician in this section be sure that deodorant caused the cats' skin problems? How could she improve her experiment?

Applying Skills

6. **Write a paper** that explains what the veterinary technician discovered from her experiment.

section 2

Standards—7.4.5: Explain that the basic functions of organisms . . . are carried out within the cell and understand that the way which cells function is similar in all organisms. **7.4.6:** Explain how food provides the fuel and the building material for all organisms. **7.4.8:** Describe how organisms that eat plants break down the plant structures to produce the materials and energy that they need to survive . . .

Also covers: 7.4.1, 7.4.4, 7.4.9 (Detailed standards begin on page IN8.)

Living Things

as you read

What You'll Learn
- **Distinguish** between living and nonliving things.
- **Identify** what living things need to survive.

Why It's Important
All living things, including you, have many of the same traits.

Review Vocabulary
raw materials: substances needed by organisms to make other necessary substances

New Vocabulary
- organism
- cell
- homeostasis

What are living things like?

What does it mean to be alive? If you walked down your street after a thunderstorm, you'd probably see earthworms on the sidewalk, birds flying, clouds moving across the sky, and puddles of water. You'd see living and nonliving things that are alike in some ways. For example, birds and clouds move. Earthworms and water feel wet when they are touched. Yet, clouds and water are nonliving things, and birds and earthworms are living things. Any living thing is called an **organism**.

Organisms vary in size from the microscopic bacteria in mud puddles to gigantic oak trees and are found just about everywhere. They have different behaviors and food needs. In spite of these differences, all organisms have similar traits. These traits determine what it means to be alive.

Living Things Are Organized If you were to look at almost any part of an organism, like a plant leaf or your skin, under a microscope, you would see that it is made up of small units called cells. A **cell** is the smallest unit of an organism that carries on the functions of life. Some organisms are composed of just one cell while others are composed of many cells. Cells take in materials from their surroundings and use them in complex ways. Each cell has an orderly structure and contains hereditary material. The hereditary material contains instructions for cellular organization and function. **Figure 8** shows some organisms that are made of many cells. All the things that these organisms can do are possible because of what their cells can do.

Muscle cells

Color-enhanced LM Magnification: 106×

Nerve cells

Figure 8 Your body is organized into many different types of cells. Two types are shown here.

Color-enhanced SEM Magnification: 2500×

Living Things Respond Living things interact with their surroundings. Watch your cat when you use your electric can opener. Does your cat come running to find out what's happening even when you're not opening a can of cat food? The cat in **Figure 9** ran in response to a stimulus—the sound of the can opener. Anything that causes some change in an organism is a stimulus (plural, *stimuli*). The reaction to a stimulus is a response. Often that response results in movement, such as when the cat runs toward the sound of the can opener. To carry on its daily activity and to survive, an organism must respond to stimuli.

Living things also respond to stimuli that occur inside them. For example, water or food levels in organisms' cells can increase or decrease. The organisms then make internal changes to keep the right amounts of water and food in their cells. Their temperature also must be within a certain range. An organism's ability to keep the proper conditions inside no matter what is going on outside the organism is called **homeostasis.** Homeostasis is a trait of all living things.

 *What are some internal stimuli living things respond to?*

Figure 9 Some cats respond to a food stimulus even when they are not hungry.
Infer *why a cat comes running when it hears a can opener.*

Living Things Use Energy Staying organized and carrying on activities like homeostasis require energy. The energy used by most organisms comes either directly or indirectly from the Sun. Plants and some other organisms use the Sun's energy and the raw materials carbon dioxide and water to make food. You and most other organisms can't use the energy of sunlight directly. Instead, you take in and use food as a source of energy. You get food by eating plants or other organisms that ate plants. Most organisms, including plants, also must take in oxygen in order to release the energy of foods.

Some bacteria live at the bottom of the oceans and in other areas where sunlight cannot reach. They can't use the Sun's energy to produce food. Instead, the bacteria use energy stored in some chemical compounds and the raw material carbon dioxide to make food. Unlike most other organisms, many of these bacteria do not need oxygen to release the energy that is found in their food.

Topic: Homeostasis
Visit in7.msscience.com for Web links to information about homeostasis.

Activity Describe the external stimuli and the corresponding internal changes for three different situations.

SECTION 2 Living Things **15**

Indiana Academic Standard Check

7.4.5: Explain that the basic functions of organisms . . . are carried out within the cell . . .

✓ How does a one-celled organism grow?

Living Things Grow and Develop When a puppy is born, it might be small enough to hold in one hand. After the same dog is fully grown, you might not be able to hold it at all. How does this happen? The puppy grows by taking in raw materials, like milk from its female parent, and making more cells. Growth of many-celled organisms, such as the puppy, is mostly due to an increase in the number of cells. In one-celled organisms, growth is due to an increase in the size of the cell.

Organisms change as they grow. Puppies can't see or walk when they are born. In eight or nine days, their eyes open, and their legs become strong enough to hold them up. All of the changes that take place during the life of an organism are called development. **Figure 10** shows how four different organisms changed as they grew.

The length of time an organism is expected to live is its life span. Dogs can live for 20 years and a cat for 25 years. Some organisms have a short life span. Mayflies live only one day, but a land tortoise can live for more than 180 years. Some bristlecone pine trees have been alive for more than 4,600 years. Your life span is about 80 years.

Figure 10 Complete development of an organism can take a few days or several years. The pictures below show the development of a dog, a human, a pea plant, and a butterfly.

16 CHAPTER 1 Exploring and Classifying Life

Figure 11 Living things reproduce themselves in many different ways. A *Paramecium* reproduces by dividing into two. Beetles, like most insects, reproduce by laying eggs. Every spore released by the puffballs can grow into a new fungus.

Beetle

Paramecium dividing
Color-enhanced LM
Magnification: 400×

Puffballs

Living Things Reproduce Cats, dogs, alligators, fish, birds, bees, and trees eventually reproduce. They make more of their own kind. Some bacteria reproduce every 20 minutes while it might take a pine tree two years to produce seeds. **Figure 11** shows some ways organisms reproduce.

Without reproduction, living things would not exist to replace those individuals that die. An individual cat can live its entire life without reproducing. However, if cats never reproduced, all cats soon would disappear.

 *Why is reproduction important?*

What do living things need?

What do you need to live? Do you have any needs that are different from those of other living things? To survive, all living things need a place to live and raw materials. The raw materials that they require and the exact place where they live can vary.

A Place to Live The environment limits where organisms can live. Not many kinds of organisms can live in extremely hot or extremely cold environments. Most cannot live at the bottom of the ocean or on the tops of mountains. All organisms also need living space in their surroundings. For example, thousands of penguins build their nests on an island. When the island becomes too crowded, the penguins fight for space and some may not find space to build nests. An organism's surroundings must provide for all of its needs.

INTEGRATE Social Studies

Social Development Human infants quickly develop their first year of life. Research to find out how infants interact socially at different stages of development. Make a chart that shows changes from birth to one year old.

SECTION 2 Living Things

Raw Materials Water is important for all living things. Plants and animals take in and give off large amounts of water each day, as shown in **Figure 12**. Organisms use homeostasis to balance the amounts of water lost with the amounts taken in. Most organisms are composed of more than 50 percent water. You are made of 60 to 70 percent water. Organisms use water for many things. For example, blood, which is about 90 percent water, transports digested food and wastes in animals. Plants have a watery sap that transports materials between roots and leaves.

Living things are made up of substances such as proteins, fats, and sugars. Animals take in most of these substances from the foods they eat. Plants and some bacteria make them using raw materials from their surroundings. These important substances are used over and over again. When organisms die, substances in their bodies are broken down and released into the soil or air. The substances can then be used again by other living organisms. Some of the substances in your body might once have been part of a butterfly or an apple tree.

At the beginning of this section, you learned that things such as clouds, sidewalks, and puddles of water are not living things. Now do you understand why? Clouds, sidewalks, and water do not reproduce, use energy, or have other traits of living things.

Figure 12 You and a corn plant each take in and give off about 2 L of water in a day. Most of the water you take in is from water you drink or from foods you eat. **Infer** *where plants get water to transport materials.*

section 2 review

Summary

What are living things like?
- A cell is the smallest unit of an organism that carries on the functions of life.
- Anything that causes some change in an organism is a stimulus.
- Organisms use energy to stay organized and perform activities like homeostasis.
- All of the changes that take place during an organism's life are called development.

What do living things need?
- Living things need a place to live, water, and food.

Self Check

1. **Identify** the source of energy for most organisms.
2. **List** five traits that most organisms have.
3. **Infer** why you would expect to see cells if you looked at a section of a mushroom cap under a microscope.
4. **Determine** what most organisms need to survive.
5. **Think Critically** Why is homeostasis important to organisms?

Applying Skills

6. **Use a Database** Use references to find the life span of ten animals. Use your computer to make a database. Then, graph the life spans from shortest to longest.

 in7.msscience.com/self_check_quiz

18 CHAPTER 1 Exploring and Classifying Life

section 3

Standards—7.1.2: Explain that what people expect to observe often affects what they actually do observe ... **7.1.4:** Describe that different explanations can be given for the same evidence, and it is not always possible to tell which one is correct without further inquiry.

Also covers: 7.1.5 (Detailed standards begin on page IN8.)

Where does life come from?

Life Comes from Life

You've probably seen a fish tank, like the one in **Figure 13**, that is full of algae. How did the algae get there? Before the seventeenth century, some people thought that insects and fish came from mud, that earthworms fell from the sky when it rained, and that mice came from grain. These were logical conclusions at that time, based on repeated personal experiences. The idea that living things come from nonliving things is known as **spontaneous generation.** This idea became a theory that was accepted for several hundred years. When scientists began to use controlled experiments to test this theory, the theory changed.

 *Why did the theory of spontaneous generation change?*

Spontaneous Generation and Biogenesis From the late seventeenth century through the middle of the eighteenth century, experiments were done to test the theory of spontaneous generation. Although these experiments showed that spontaneous generation did not occur in most cases, they did not disprove it entirely.

It was not until the mid-1800s that the work of Louis Pasteur, a French chemist, provided enough evidence to disprove the theory of spontaneous generation. It was replaced with **biogenesis** (bi oh JE nuh suss), which is the theory that living things come only from other living things.

as you read

What You'll Learn
- **Describe** experiments about spontaneous generation.
- **Explain** how scientific methods led to the idea of biogenesis.

Why It's Important
You can use scientific methods to try to find out about events that happened long ago or just last week. You can even use them to predict how something will behave in the future.

Review Vocabulary
contaminate: to make impure by coming into contact with an unwanted substance

New Vocabulary
- spontaneous generation
- biogenesis

Figure 13 The sides of this tank were clean and the water was clear when the aquarium was set up. Algal cells, which were not visible on plants and fish, reproduced in the tank. So many algal cells are present now that the water is cloudy.

SECTION 3 Where does life come from? **19**

NATIONAL GEOGRAPHIC VISUALIZING THE ORIGINS OF LIFE

Figure 14

For centuries scientists have theorized about the origins of life. As shown on this timeline, some examined spontaneous generation—the idea that nonliving material can produce life. More recently, scientists have proposed theories about the origins of life on Earth by testing hypotheses about conditions on early Earth.

1668 Francesco Redi put decaying meat in some jars, then covered half of them. When fly maggots appeared only on the uncovered meat (see below, left), Redi concluded that they had hatched from fly eggs and had not come from the meat.

1745 John Needham heated broth in sealed flasks. When the broth became cloudy with microorganisms, he mistakenly concluded that they developed spontaneously from the broth.

1768 Lazzaro Spallanzani boiled broth in sealed flasks for a longer time than Needham did. Only the ones he opened became cloudy with contamination.

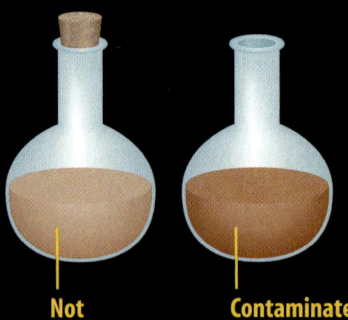

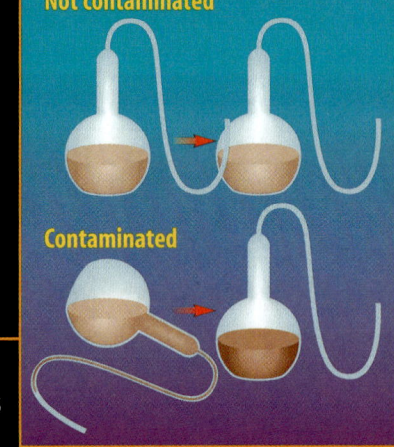

1859 Louis Pasteur disproved spontaneous generation by boiling broth in S-necked flasks that were open to the air. The broth became cloudy (see above, bottom right) only when a flask was tilted and the broth was exposed to dust in the S-neck.

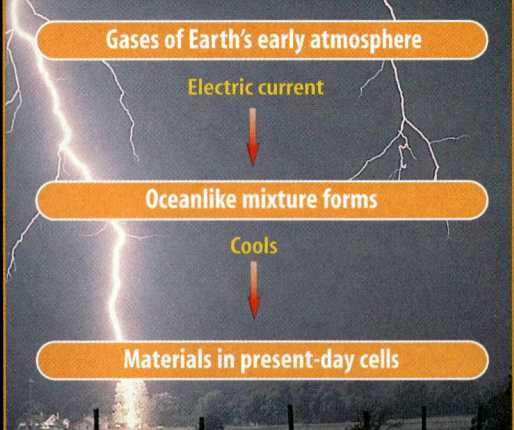

1953 Stanley Miller and Harold Urey sent electric currents through a mixture of gases like those thought to be in Earth's early atmosphere. When the gases cooled, they condensed to form an oceanlike liquid that contained materials such as amino acids, found in present-day cells.

1924 Alexander Oparin hypothesized that energy from the Sun, lightning, and Earth's heat triggered chemical reactions early in Earth's history. The newly-formed molecules washed into Earth's ancient oceans and became a part of what is often called the primordial soup.

20 CHAPTER 1 Exploring and Classifying Life

Life's Origins

If living things can come only from other living things, how did life on Earth begin? Some scientists hypothesize that about 5 billion years ago, Earth's solar system was a whirling mass of gas and dust. They hypothesize that the Sun and planets were formed from this mass. It is estimated that Earth is about 4.6 billion years old. Rocks found in Australia that are more than 3.5 billion years old contain fossils of once-living organisms. Where did these living organisms come from?

Oparin's Hypothesis In 1924, a Russian scientist named Alexander I. Oparin suggested that Earth's early atmosphere had no oxygen but was made up of the gases ammonia, hydrogen, methane, and water vapor. Oparin hypothesized that these gases could have combined to form the more complex compounds found in living things.

Using gases and conditions that Oparin described, American scientists Stanley L. Miller and Harold Urey set up an experiment to test Oparin's hypothesis in 1953. Although the Miller-Urey experiment showed that chemicals found in living things could be produced, it did not prove that life began in this way.

For many centuries, scientists have tried to find the origins of life, as shown in **Figure 14**. Although questions about spontaneous generation have been answered, some scientists still are investigating ideas about life's origins.

Oceans Scientists hypothesize that Earth's oceans originally formed when water vapor was released into the atmosphere from many volcanic eruptions. Once it cooled, rain fell and filled Earth's lowland areas. Identify five lowland areas on Earth that are now filled with water. Record your answer in your Science Journal.

section 3 review

Summary

Life Comes from Life
- Spontaneous generation is the idea that living things come from nonliving things.
- The work of Louis Pasteur in 1859 disproved the theory of spontaneous generation.
- Biogenesis is the theory that living things come only from other living things.

Life's Origins
- Alexander I. Oparin hypothesized about the origin of life.
- The Miller-Urey experiment did not prove that Oparin's hypothesis was correct.

Self Check

1. **Compare and contrast** spontaneous generation with biogenesis.
2. **Describe** three controlled experiments that helped disprove the theory of spontaneous generation and led to the theory of biogenesis.
3. **Summarize** the results of the Miller-Urey experiment.
4. **Think Critically** How do you think life on Earth began?

Applying Skills

5. **Draw Conclusions** Where could the organisms have come from in the 1768 broth experiment described in **Figure 14**?

Science online in7.msscience.com/self_check_quiz

SECTION 3 Where does life come from? **21**

section 4

Standards—7.4.1: Explain that similarities among organisms are found in external ... features ... Understand that these similarities are used to classify organisms since they may be used to infer the degree of relatedness among organisms. **7.4.5:** Explain that the basic functions of organisms ... are carried out within the cell and understand that the way which cells function is similar in all organisms.

Also covers: 7.1.3, 7.2.7, 7.5.3 (Detailed standards begin on page IN8.)

How are living things classified?

as you read

What You'll Learn
- **Describe** how early scientists classified living things.
- **Explain** how similarities are used to classify organisms.
- **Explain** the system of binomial nomenclature.
- **Demonstrate** how to use a dichotomous key.

Why It's Important
Knowing how living things are classified will help you understand the relationships that exist among all living things.

Review Vocabulary
common name: a nonscientific term that may vary from region to region

New Vocabulary
- phylogeny
- kingdom
- binomial nomenclature
- genus

Classification

If you go to a library to find a book about the life of Louis Pasteur, where do you look? Do you look for it among the mystery or sports books? You expect to find a book about Pasteur's life with other biography books. Libraries group similar types of books together. When you place similar items together, you classify them. Organisms also are classified into groups.

History of Classification When did people begin to group similar organisms together? Early classifications included grouping plants that were used in medicines. Animals were often classified by human traits such as courageous—for lions—or wise—for owls.

More than 2,000 years ago, a Greek named Aristotle observed living things. He decided that any organism could be classified as either a plant or an animal. Then he broke these two groups into smaller groups. For example, animal categories included hair or no hair, four legs or fewer legs, and blood or no blood. **Figure 15** shows some of the organisms Aristotle would have grouped together. For hundreds of years after Aristotle, no one way of classifying was accepted by everyone.

Figure 15 Using Aristotle's classification system, all animals without hair would be grouped together.
List other animals without hair that Aristotle would have put in this group.

22 CHAPTER 1 Exploring and Classifying Life

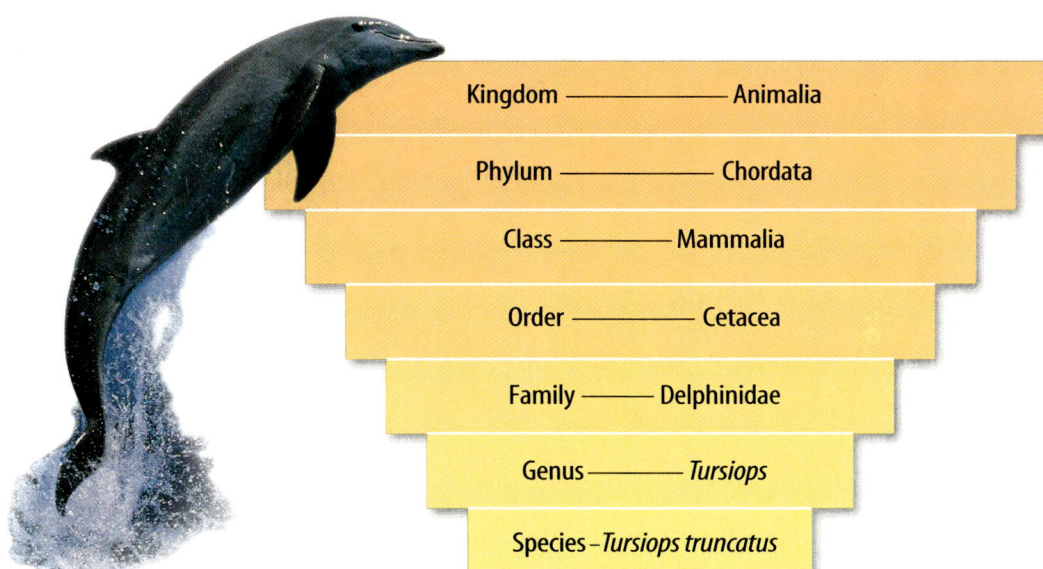

Figure 16 The classification of the bottle-nosed dolphin shows that it is in the order Cetacea. This order includes whales and porpoises.

Linnaeus In the late eighteenth century, Carolus Linnaeus, a Swedish naturalist, developed a new system of grouping organisms. His classification system was based on looking for organisms with similar structures. For example, plants that had similar flower structure were grouped together. Linnaeus's system eventually was accepted and used by most other scientists.

Modern Classification Like Linnaeus, modern scientists use similarities in structure to classify organisms. They also use similiarities in both external and internal features. Specific characteristics at the cellular level, such as the number of chromosomes, can be used to infer the degree of relatedness among organisms. In addition, scientists study fossils, hereditary information, and early stages of development. They use all of this information to determine an organism's phylogeny. **Phylogeny** (fi LAH juh nee) is the evolutionary history of an organism, or how it has changed over time. Today, it is the basis for the classification of many organisms.

 *What information would a scientist use to determine an organism's phylogeny?*

Six Kingdoms A classification system commonly used today groups organisms into six kingdoms. A **kingdom** is the first and largest category. Organisms are placed into kingdoms based on various characteristics. Kingdoms can be divided into smaller groups. The smallest classification category is a species. Organisms that belong to the same species can mate and produce fertile offspring. To understand how an organism is classified, look at the classification of the bottle-nosed dolphin in **Figure 16.** Some scientists propose that before organisms are grouped into kingdoms, they should be placed in larger groups called domains. One proposed system groups all organisms into three domains.

Indiana Academic Standard Check

7.4.1: Explain that similarities among organisms are found in external . . . features . . . Understand that these similarities are used to classify organisms . . .

✓ What plant feature did Linnaeus use for his classification system?

Topic: Domains
Visit in7.msscience.com for Web links to information about domains.

Activity List all the domains and give examples of organisms that are grouped in each domain.

SECTION 4 How are living things classified? **23**

Scientific Names

Using common names can cause confusion. Suppose that Diego is visiting Jamaal. Jamaal asks Diego if he would like a soda. Diego is confused until Jamaal hands him a soft drink. At Diego's house, a soft drink is called pop. Jamaal's grandmother, listening from the living room, thought that Jamaal was offering Diego an ice-cream soda.

What would happen if life scientists used only common names of organisms when they communicated with other scientists? Many misunderstandings would occur, and sometimes health and safety are involved. In **Figure 17,** you see examples of animals with common names that can be misleading. A naming system developed by Linnaeus helped solve this problem. It gave each species a unique, two-word scientific name.

Figure 17 Common names can be misleading.

Binomial Nomenclature The two-word naming system that Linnaeus used to name the various species is called **binomial nomenclature** (bi NOH mee ul • NOH mun klay chur). It is the system used by modern scientists to name organisms. The first word of the two-word name identifies the genus of the organism. A **genus** is a group of similar species. The second word of the name might tell you something about the organism—what it looks like, where it is found, or who discovered it.

In this system, the tree species commonly known as red maple has been given the name *Acer rubrum.* The maple genus is *Acer.* The word *rubrum* is Latin for red, which is the color of a red maple's leaves in the fall. The scientific name of another maple is *Acer saccharum.* The Latin word for sugar is *saccharum.* In the spring, the sap of this tree is sweet.

Sea lions are more closely related to seals than to lions. **Identify** another misleading common name.

Jellyfish are neither fish nor jelly.

24 CHAPTER 1 Exploring and Classifying Life

Figure 18 These two lizards have the same common name, iguana, but are two different species.

Uses of Scientific Names Two-word scientific names are used for four reasons. First, they help avoid mistakes. Both of the lizards shown in **Figure 18** have the name *iguana*. Using binomial nomenclature, the green iguana is named *Iguana iguana*. Someone who studied this *iguana*, shown in the left photo, would not be confused by information he or she read about *Dispsosaurus dorsalis*, the desert iguana, shown in the right photo. Second, organisms with similar evolutionary histories are classified together. Because of this, you know that organisms in the same genus are related. Third, scientific names give descriptive information about the species, like the maples mentioned earlier. Fourth, scientific names allow information about organisms to be organized easily and efficiently. Such information may be found in a book or a pamphlet that lists related organisms and gives their scientific names.

 *What are four functions of scientific names?*

Tools for Identifying Organisms

Tools used to identify organisms include field guides and dichotomous (di KAH tuh mus) keys. Using these tools is one way you and scientists solve problems scientifically.

Many different field guides are available. You will find some field guides at the back of this book. Most have descriptions and illustrations of organisms and information about where each organism lives. You can identify species from around the world using the appropriate field guide.

Mini LAB

Communicating Ideas

Procedure
1. Find a **magazine picture of a piece of furniture** that can be used as a place to sit and to lie down.
2. Show the picture to ten people and ask them to tell you what word they use for this piece of furniture.
3. Keep a record of the answers in your **Science Journal**.

Analysis
1. In your Science Journal, infer how using common names can be confusing.
2. How do scientific names make communication among scientists easier?

SECTION 4 How are living things classified?

Dichotomous Keys A dichotomous key is a detailed list of identifying characteristics that includes scientific names. Dichotomous keys are arranged in steps with two descriptive statements at each step. If you learn how to use a dichotomous key, you can identify and name a species.

Did you know many types of mice exist? You can use **Table 2** to find out what type of mouse is pictured to the left. Start by choosing between the first pair of descriptions. The mouse has hair on its tail, so you go to 2. The ears of the mouse are small, so you go on to 3. The tail of the mouse is less that 25 mm. What is the name of this mouse according to the key?

Table 2 Key to Some Mice of North America	
1. Tail hair	a. no hair on tail; scales show plainly; house mouse, *Mus musculus* b. hair on tail, go to 2
2. Ear size	a. ears small and nearly hidden in fur, go to 3 b. ears large and not hidden in fur, go to 4
3. Tail length	a. less than 25 mm; woodland vole, *Microtus pinetorum* b. more than 25 mm; prairie vole, *Microtus ochrogaster*
4. Tail coloration	a. sharply bicolor, white beneath and dark above; deer mouse, *Peromyscus maniculatus* b. darker above than below but not sharply bicolor; white-footed mouse, *Peromyscus leucopus*

section 4 review

Summary

Classification
- Organisms are classified into groups based on their similarities.
- Scientists today classify organisms into six kingdoms.
- Species is the smallest classification category.

Scientific Names
- Binomial nomenclature is the two-word naming system that gives organisms their scientific names.

Tools for Identifying Organisms
- Field guides and dichotomous keys are used to identify organisms.

Self Check

1. **State** Aristotle's and Linnaeus' contributions to classifying living things.
2. **Identify** a specific characteristic used to classify organisms.
3. **Describe** what each of the two words identifies in binomial nomenclature.
4. **Think Critically** Would you expect a field guide to have common names as well as scientific names? Why or why not?

Applying Skills

5. **Classify** Create a dichotomous key that identifies types of cars.

26 CHAPTER 1 Exploring and Classifying Life

 in7.msscience.com/self_check_quiz

Classifying Seeds

Scientists use classification systems to show how organisms are related. How do they determine which features to use to classify organisms? In this lab, you will observe seeds and use their features to classify them.

Real-World Question

How can the features of seeds be used to develop a key to identify the seed?

Goals
- **Observe** the seeds and notice their features.
- **Classify** seeds using these features.

Materials
packets of seeds (10 different kinds)
magnifying lens
metric ruler

Safety Precautions

WARNING: *Some seeds may have been treated with chemicals. Do not put them in your mouth.*

Procedure

1. Copy the following data table in your Science Journal and record the features of each seed. Your table will have a column for each different type of seed you observe.

Seed Data

Feature	Type of Seed		
Color			
Length (mm)	Do not write in this book.		
Shape			
Texture			

2. Use the features to develop a key.
3. Exchange keys with another group. Can you use their key to identify seeds?

Conclude and Apply

1. **Determine** how different seeds can be classified.
2. **Explain** how you would classify a seed you had not seen before using your data table.
3. **Explain** why it is an advantage for scientists to use a standardized system to classify organisms. What observations did you make to support your answer?

Communicating Your Data

Compare your conclusions with those of other students in your class. **For more help, refer to the** Science Skill Handbook.

Design Your Own

Using Scientific Methods

Goals
- **Design** and carry out an experiment using scientific methods to infer why brine shrimp live in the ocean.
- **Observe** the jars for one week and notice whether the brine shrimp eggs hatch.

Possible Materials
500-mL, widemouthed containers (3)
brine shrimp eggs
small, plastic spoon
distilled water (500 mL)
weak salt solution (500 mL)
strong salt solution (500 mL)
labels (3)
magnifying lens

Safety Precautions

WARNING: *Protect eyes and clothing. Be careful when working with live organisms.*

Real-World Question
Brine shrimp are relatives of lobsters, crabs, crayfish, and the shrimp eaten by humans. They are often raised as a live food source in aquariums. In nature, they live in the oceans where fish feed on them. They can hatch from eggs that have been stored in a dry condition for many years. How can you use scientific methods to determine whether salt affects the hatching and growth of brine shrimp?

Brine shrimp

Form a Hypothesis
Based on your observations, form a hypothesis to explain how salt affects the hatching and growth of brine shrimp.

Test Your Hypothesis
Make a Plan

1. As a group, agree upon the hypothesis and decide how you will test it. Identify what results will confirm the hypothesis.

28 CHAPTER 1 Exploring and Classifying Life

Using Scientific Methods

2. **List** steps that you need to test your hypothesis. Be specific. Describe exactly what you will do at each step.
3. **List** your materials.
4. **Prepare** a data table in your Science Journal to record your data.
5. Read over your entire experiment to make sure that all planned steps are in logical order.
6. **Identify** any constants, variables, and controls of the experiment.

Follow Your Plan

1. Make sure your teacher approves your plan before you start.
2. Carry out the experiment as planned by your group.
3. While doing the experiment, record any observations and complete the data table in your Science Journal.
4. Use a bar graph to plot your results.

Analyze Your Data

1. **Describe** the contents of each jar after one week.
2. **Identify** your control in this experiment.
3. **Identify** your variable in this experiment.

Conclude and Apply

1. **Explain** whether or not the results support your hypothesis.
2. **Predict** the effect that increasing the amount of salt in the water would have on the brine shrimp eggs.
3. **Compare** your results with those of other groups.

Communicating Your Data

Prepare a set of instructions on how to hatch brine shrimp to use to feed fish. Include diagrams and a step-by-step procedure.

TIME SCIENCE AND Society

SCIENCE ISSUES THAT AFFECT YOU!

Acari marmoset

Monkey Business

Manicore marmoset

In 2000, a scientist from Brazil's Amazon National Research Institute came across two squirrel-sized monkeys in a remote and isolated corner of the rain forest, about 2,575 km from Rio de Janeiro.

It turns out that the monkeys had never been seen before, or even known to exist.

Acari marmoset

The new species were spotted by a scientist who named them after two nearby rivers the Manicore and the Acari, where the animals were discovered. Both animals are marmosets, which is a type of monkey found only in Central and South America. Marmosets have claws instead of nails, live in trees, and use their extraordinarily long tail like an extra arm or leg. Small and light, both marmosets measure about 23 cm in length with a 38 cm tail, and weigh no more than 0.4 kg.

The Manicore marmoset has a silvery-white upper body, a light-gray cap on its head, a yellow-orange underbody, and a black tail.

The Acari marmoset's upper body is snowy white, its gray back sports a stripe running to the knee, and its black tail flashes a bright-orange tip.

Amazin' Amazon

The Amazon Basin is a treasure trove of unique species. The Amazon River is Earth's largest body of freshwater, with 1,100 smaller tributaries. And more than half of the world's plant and animal species live in its rain forest ecosystems.

Research and Report Working in small groups, find out more about the Amazon rain forest. Which plants and animals live there? What products come from the rain forest? How does what happens in the Amazon rain forest affect you? Prepare a multimedia presentation.

Science online
For more information, visit in7.msscience.com/time

Chapter 1 Study Guide

Reviewing Main Ideas

Section 1 — What is science?

1. Scientists use problem-solving methods to investigate observations about living and nonliving things.
2. Scientists use SI measurements to gather measurable data.
3. Safe laboratory practices help you learn more about science.

Section 2 — Living Things

1. Organisms are made of cells, use energy, reproduce, respond, grow, and develop.
2. Organisms need energy, water, food, and a place to live.

Section 3 — Where does life come from?

1. Controlled experiments finally disproved the theory of spontaneous generation.
2. Pasteur's experiment proved biogenesis.

Section 4 — How are living things classified?

1. Classification is the grouping of ideas, information, or objects based on their similar characteristics.
2. Scientists today use phylogeny to group organisms into six kingdoms.
3. All organisms are given a two-word scientific name using binomial nomenclature.

Visualizing Main Ideas

Copy and complete this events-chain concept map that shows the order in which you might use a scientific method. Use these terms: analyze data, perform an experiment, *and* form a hypothesis.

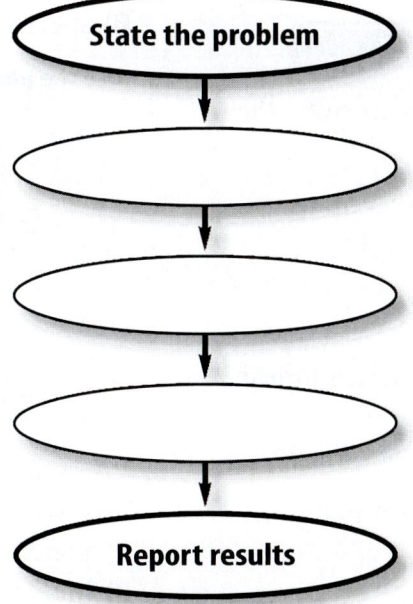

Science Online   in7.msscience.com/interactive_tutor

Chapter 1 Review

Using Vocabulary

binomial nomenclature p. 24
biogenesis p. 19
cell p. 14
control p. 9
genus p. 24
homeostasis p. 15
hypothesis p. 8
kingdom p. 23
law p. 10
organism p. 14
phylogeny p. 23
scientific methods p. 7
spontaneous generation p. 19
theory p. 10
variable p. 9

Explain the differences in the vocabulary words in each pair below. Then explain how they are related.

1. control—variable
2. law—theory
3. biogenesis—spontaneous generation
4. binomial nomenclature—phylogeny
5. organism—cell
6. kingdom—phylogeny
7. hypothesis—scientific methods
8. organism—homeostasis
9. kingdom—genus
10. theory—hypothesis

Checking Concepts

Choose the word or phrase that best answers the question.

11. What category of organisms can mate and produce fertile offspring?
    A) family   C) genus
    B) class   D) species

12. What is the closest relative of *Canis lupus*?
    A) *Quercus alba*   C) *Felis tigris*
    B) *Equus zebra*   D) *Canis familiaris*

13. What is the source of energy for plants?
    A) the Sun   C) water
    B) carbon dioxide D) oxygen

14. What makes up more than 50 percent of all living things?
    A) oxygen   C) minerals
    B) carbon dioxide D) water

15. Who finally disproved the theory of spontaneous generation?
    A) Oparin   C) Pasteur
    B) Aristotle   D) Miller

16. What gas do some scientists think was missing from Earth's early atmosphere?
    A) ammonia   C) methane
    B) hydrogen   D) oxygen

17. What is the length of time called that an organism is expected to live?
    A) life span   C) homeostasis
    B) stimulus   D) theory

18. What is the part of an experiment that can be changed called?
    A) conclusion   C) control
    B) variable   D) data

19. What does the first word in a two-word name of an organism identify?
    A) kingdom   C) phylum
    B) species   D) genus

Use the photo below to answer question 20.

20. What SI unit is used to measure the volume of soda shown above?
    A) meter   C) gram
    B) liter   D) degree

32 CHAPTER REVIEW

in7.msscience.com/vocabulary_puzzlemaker

chapter 1 Review

Thinking Critically

21. **Predict** what *Lathyrus odoratus*, the scientific name for a sweet pea plant, tells you about one of its characteristics.

Use the photo below to answer question 22.

22. **Determine** what problem-solving techniques this scientist would use to find how dolphins learn.

Use the graph below to answer question 23.

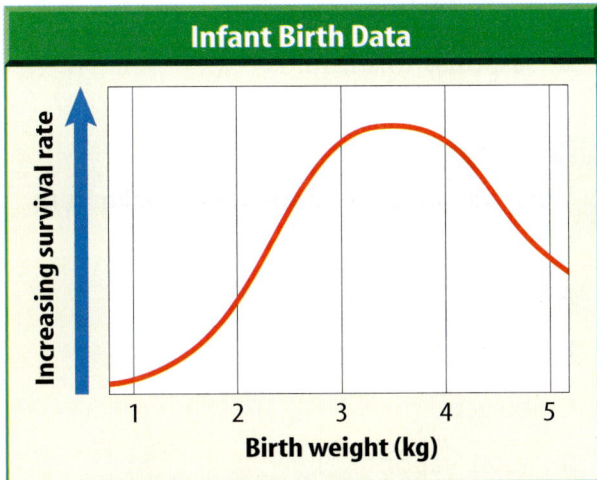

23. **Interpret Data** Do the data in the graph above support the hypothesis that babies with a birth weight of 2.5 kg have the best chance of survival? Explain.

24. **List** advantages of using SI units.

25. **Form a Hypothesis** A lima bean plant is placed under green light, another is placed under red light, and a third under blue light. Their growth is measured for four weeks to determine which light is best for plant growth. What are the variables in this experiment? State a hypothesis for this experiment.

Performance Activities

26. **Bulletin Board** Interview people in your community whose jobs require a knowledge of life science. Make a Life Science Careers bulletin board. Summarize each person's job and what he or she had to study to prepare for that job.

Applying Math

27. **Body Temperature** Normal human body temperature is 98.6°F. What is this temperature in degrees Celsius? Use the following expression, 5/9(°F−32), to find degrees Celsius.

Use the graph below to answer question 28.

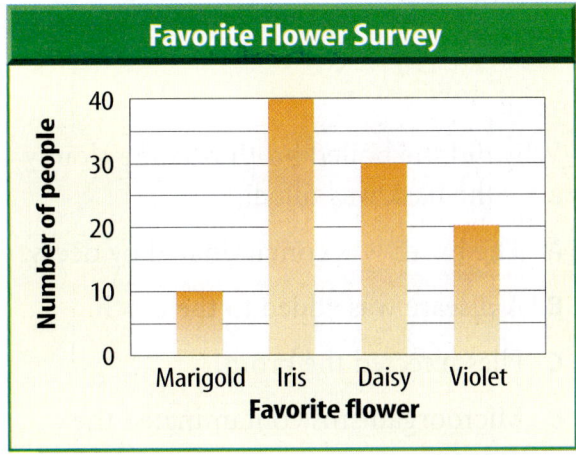

28. **Favorite Flower** The graph above shows how many people selected a certain type of flower as their favorite. According to the graph, what percentage of the people picked daisy as their favorite?

chapter 1 Indiana

The assessed Indiana standard appears above the question.

Record your answers on the answer sheet provided by your teacher or on a sheet of paper.

Part 1 Multiple Choice

7.1.3

1. Which unit might a biologist use when measuring the length of a mouse's tail?

    A gram

    B kilometer

    C milliliter

    D millimeter

2. The illustration below shows an experiment performed to support the theory of biogenesis.

    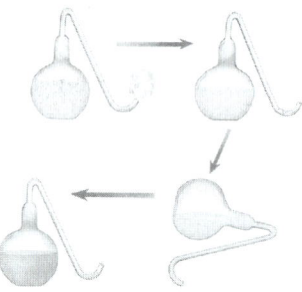

    Why did the boiled broth become cloudy after the flask was tilted?

    A The broth was contaminated by decay.

    B A disease was added to the broth.

    C Flies infected the broth.

    D Microorganisms contaminated the broth.

The photos below show two life stages of one dog species.

7.4.4

3. Which is responsible for most of the observable changes shown above?

    A an increase in the energy of cells

    B an increase in the number of cells

    C an increase in the size of cells

    D an increase in the water in cells

7.4.4

4. What characteristic of life do the photos above illustrate?

    A growth and development

    B use of energy

    C reproduction

    D response to stimulus

7.4.5 **7.4.6**

5. What gas must most organisms take in to release the energy in food?

    A carbon dioxide

    B hydrogen

    C oxygen

    D water vapor

Standards Review

6. The illustrations below show an experiment to study the response of plants to the stimulus of light.

Which hypothesis is likely being tested by this experiment?

A Plants do not grow in the dark.

B Plants do not grow in boxes.

C Plants grow away from light.

D Plants grow toward light.

Part 2 Constructed Response

7.1.4 7.1.5

7. Some scientists think that lightning might have caused chemicals in Earth's early atmosphere to combine and begin the origin of life. Explain how the experiment of Miller and Urey supports this hypothesis but does not prove this hypothesis.

7.4.1

8. What information would you need to write a field guide used to identify garden plants? What other information would you need if the guide included a dichotomous key?

The photo below shows beetles on a plant.

7.4.5

9. Describe the difference between the source of energy for the beetle and for the plant. In what similar ways would each of these organisms use energy?

7.4.6 7.4.8

10. How are the needs of these two organisms in the photo above alike? Explain why the plant is raw material for the beetle. When the beetle dies, how could it become raw material for the plant?

Test-Taking Tip

Practice Skills Remember that test-taking skills can improve with practice. If possible, take at least one practice test and familiarize yourself with the test format and instructions.

Science online in7.msscience.com/standards_review

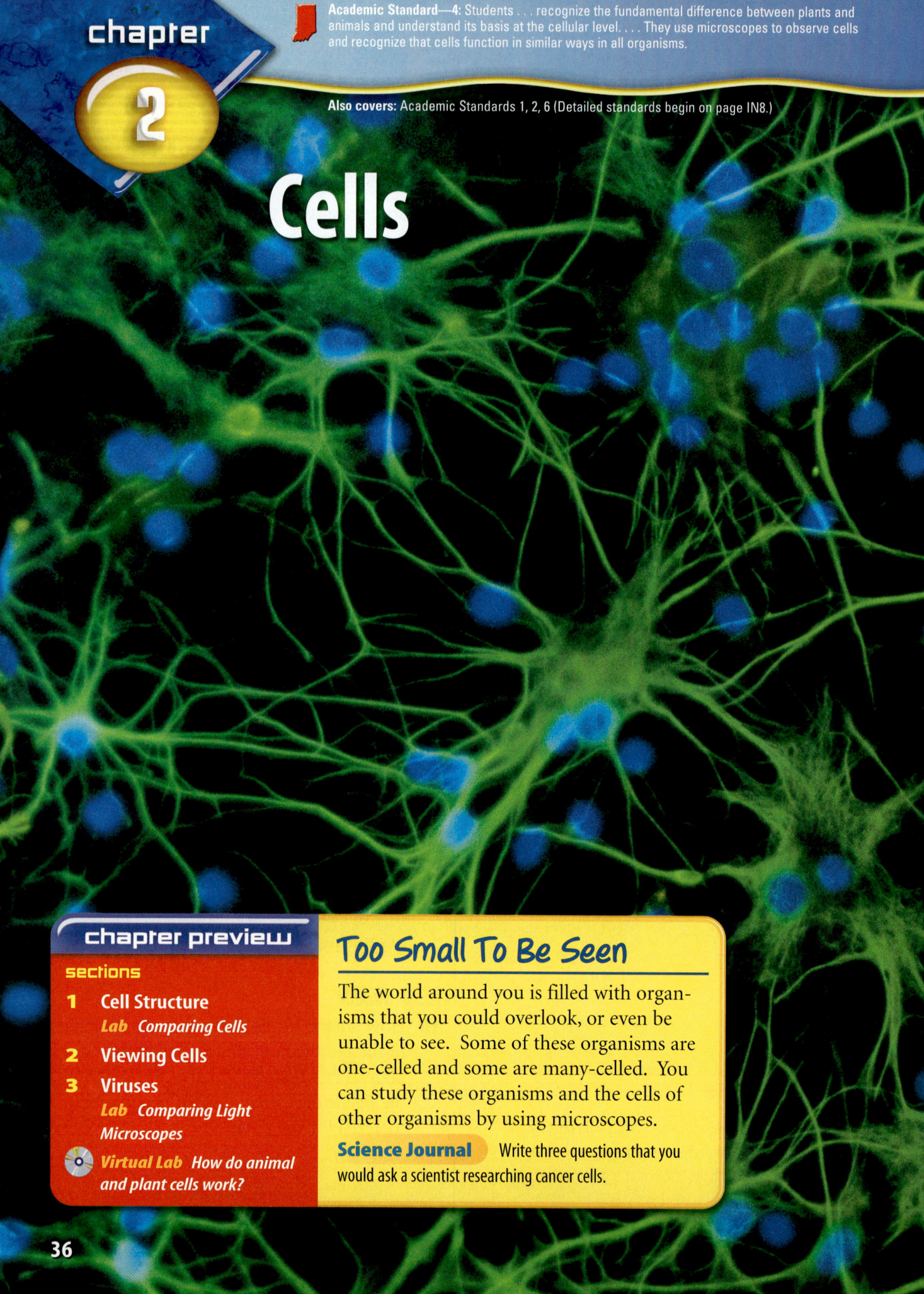

chapter 2

Academic Standard—4: Students... recognize the fundamental difference between plants and animals and understand its basis at the cellular level.... They use microscopes to observe cells and recognize that cells function in similar ways in all organisms.

Also covers: Academic Standards 1, 2, 6 (Detailed standards begin on page IN8.)

Cells

chapter preview

sections
1. **Cell Structure**
   Lab Comparing Cells
2. **Viewing Cells**
3. **Viruses**
   Lab Comparing Light Microscopes
   Virtual Lab How do animal and plant cells work?

Too Small To Be Seen

The world around you is filled with organisms that you could overlook, or even be unable to see. Some of these organisms are one-celled and some are many-celled. You can study these organisms and the cells of other organisms by using microscopes.

Science Journal Write three questions that you would ask a scientist researching cancer cells.

Start-Up Activities

Magnifying Cells

If you look around your classroom, you can see many things of all sizes. Using a magnifying lens, you can see more details. You might examine a speck of dust and discover that it is a living or dead insect. In the following lab, use a magnifying lens to search for the smallest thing you can find in the classroom.

1. Obtain a magnifying lens from your teacher. Note its power (the number followed by ×, shown somewhere on the lens frame or handle).
2. Using the magnifying lens, look around the room for the smallest object that you can find.
3. Measure the size of the image as you see it with the magnifying lens. To estimate the real size of the object, divide that number by the power. For example, if it looks 2 cm long and the power is 10×, the real length is about 0.2 cm.
4. **Think Critically** Write a paragraph that describes what you observed. Did the details become clearer? Explain.

Cells Make the following Foldable to help you illustrate the main parts of cells.

STEP 1 **Fold** a vertical sheet of paper in half from top to bottom.

STEP 2 **Fold** in half from side to side with the fold at the top.

STEP 3 **Unfold** the paper once. **Cut** only the fold of the top flap to make two tabs.

STEP 4 **Turn** the paper vertically and **write** on the front tabs as shown.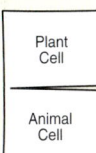

Illustrate and Label As you read the chapter, draw and identify the parts of plant and animal cells under the appropriate tab.

 Preview this chapter's content and activities at in7.msscience.com

section 1

Standards—7.4.4: ...various organs and tissues function to serve the needs of cells for food, air, and waste removal. **7.4.5:** Explain that the basic functions of organisms, such as extracting energy from food and getting rid of wastes, are carried out within the cell and understand that the way which cells function is similar in all organisms.

Also covers: 7.2.2, 7.4.7 (Detailed standards begin on page IN8.)

Cell Structure

as you read

What You'll Learn
- **Identify** names and functions of each part of a cell.
- **Explain** how important a nucleus is in a cell.
- **Compare** tissues, organs, and organ systems.

Why It's Important
If you know how organelles function, it's easier to understand how cells survive.

Review Vocabulary
photosynthesis: process by which most plants, some protists, and many types of bacteria make their own food

New Vocabulary
- cell membrane
- cytoplasm
- cell wall
- organelle
- nucleus
- chloroplast
- mitochondrion
- ribosome
- endoplasmic reticulum
- Golgi body
- tissue
- organ

Common Cell Traits

Living cells are dynamic and have several things in common. A cell is the smallest unit that is capable of performing life functions. All cells have an outer covering called a **cell membrane**. Inside every cell is a gelatinlike material called **cytoplasm** (SI tuh pla zum). In the cytoplasm of every cell is hereditary material that controls the life of the cell.

Comparing Cells Cells come in many sizes. A nerve cell in your leg could be a meter long. A human egg cell is no bigger than the dot on this *i*. A human red blood cell is about one-tenth the size of a human egg cell. A bacterium is even smaller—8,000 of the smallest bacteria can fit inside one of your red blood cells.

A cell's shape might tell you something about its function. The nerve cell in **Figure 1** has many fine extensions that send and receive impulses to and from other cells. Though a nerve cell cannot change shape, muscle cells and some blood cells can. In plant stems, some cells are long and hollow and have openings at their ends. These cells carry food and water throughout the plant.

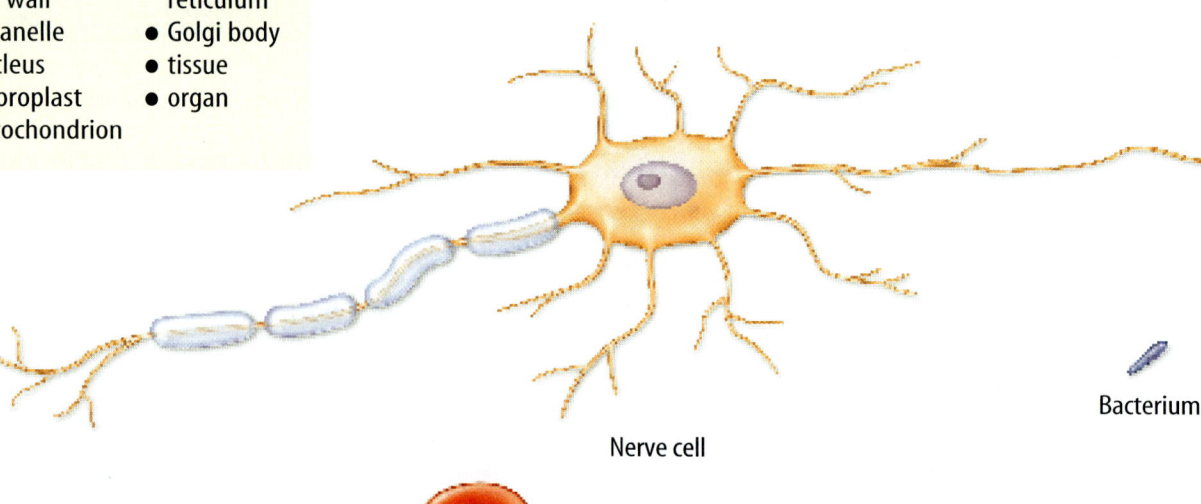

Figure 1 The shape of the cell can tell you something about its function. These cells are drawn 700 times their actual size.

Nerve cell
Bacterium
Red blood cell
Muscle cell

38 CHAPTER 2 Cells

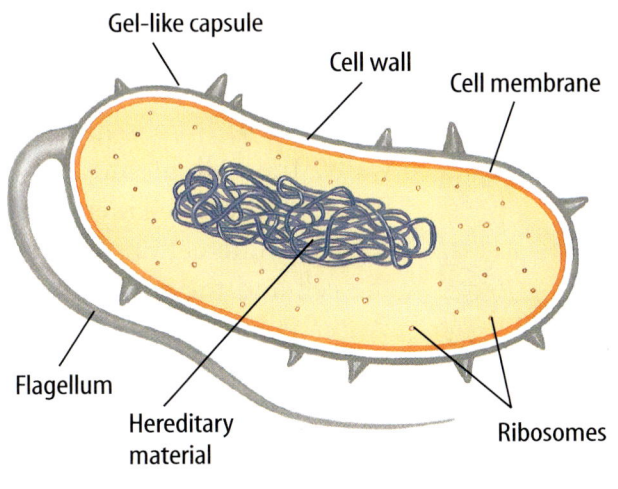
Prokaryotic cell

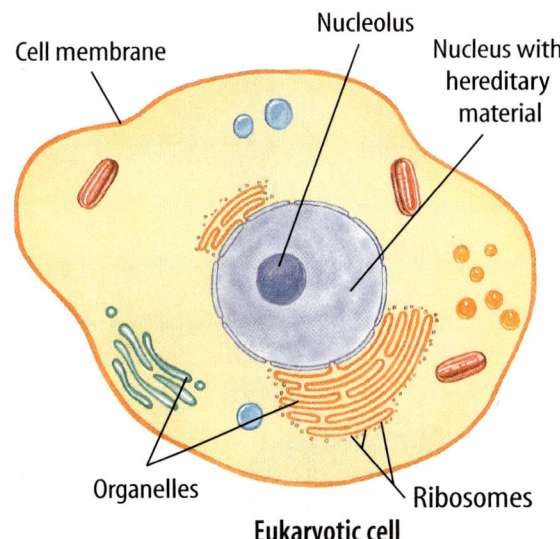
Eukaryotic cell

Cell Types Scientists have found that cells can be separated into two groups. One group has no membrane-bound structures inside the cell and the other group does, as shown in **Figure 2.** Cells without membrane-bound structures are called prokaryotic (proh KAYR ee yah tihk) cells. Cells with membrane-bound structures are called eukaryotic (yew KAYR ee yah tihk) cells.

Reading Check *Into what two groups can cells be separated?*

Cell Organization

Each cell in your body has a specific function. You might compare a cell to a busy delicatessen that is open 24 hours every day. Raw materials for the sandwiches are brought in often. Some food is eaten in the store, and some customers take their food with them. Sometimes food is prepared ahead of time for quick sale. Wastes are put into trash bags for removal or recycling. Similarly, your cells are taking in nutrients, secreting and storing chemicals, and breaking down substances 24 hours every day.

Cell Wall Just like a deli that is located inside the walls of a building, some cells are enclosed in a cell wall. The cells of plants, algae, fungi, and most bacteria are enclosed in a cell wall. **Cell walls** are tough, rigid outer coverings that protect the cell and give it shape.

A plant cell wall, as shown in **Figure 3,** mostly is made up of a carbohydrate called cellulose. The long, threadlike fibers of cellulose form a thick mesh that allows water and dissolved materials to pass through it. Cell walls also can contain pectin, which is used in jam and jelly, and lignin, which is a compound that makes cell walls rigid. Plant cells responsible for support have a lot of lignin in their walls.

Figure 2 Examine these drawings of cells. Prokaryotic cells are only found in one-celled organisms, such as bacteria. Protists, fungi, plants, and animals are made of eukaryotic cells.
Describe *differences you see between them.*

Figure 3 The protective cell wall of a plant cell is outside the cell membrane.

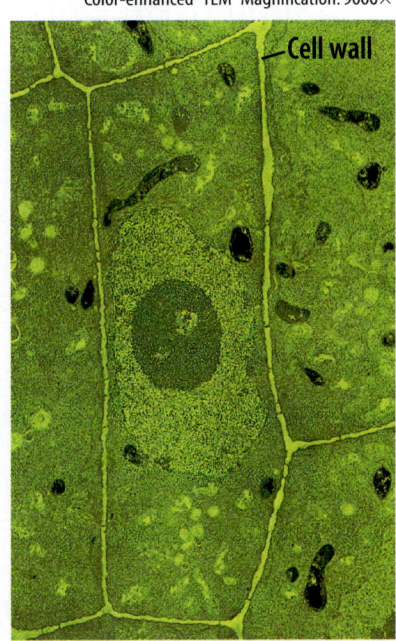
Color-enhanced TEM Magnification: 9000×

SECTION 1 Cell Structure **39**

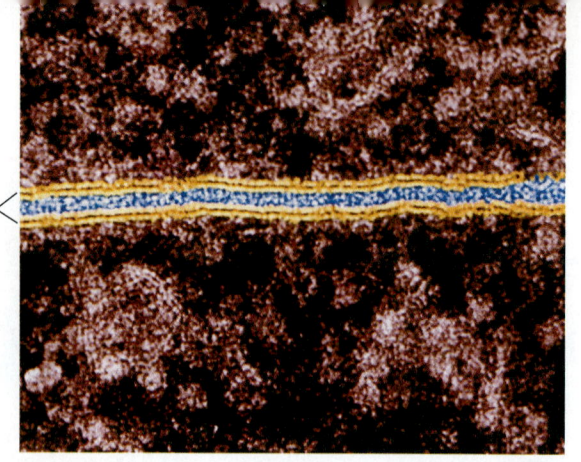

Figure 4 A cell membrane is made up of a double layer of fatlike molecules.

Cell membranes

Color-enhanced TEM Magnification: 125000×

Cell Membrane The protective layer around all cells is the cell membrane, as shown in **Figure 4.** If cells have cell walls, the cell membrane is inside of it. The cell membrane regulates interactions between the cell and the environment. Water is able to move freely into and out of the cell through the cell membrane. Food particles and some molecules enter and waste products leave through the cell membrane.

Cytoplasm Cells are filled with a gelatinlike substance called cytoplasm that constantly flows inside the cell membrane. Many important chemical reactions occur within the cytoplasm.

Throughout the cytoplasm is a framework called the cytoskeleton, which helps the cell maintain or change its shape. Cytoskeletons enable some cells to move. An amoeba, for example, moves by stretching and contracting its cytoskeleton. The cytoskeleton is made up of thin, hollow tubes of protein and thin, solid protein fibers, as shown in **Figure 5.** Proteins are organic molecules made up of amino acids.

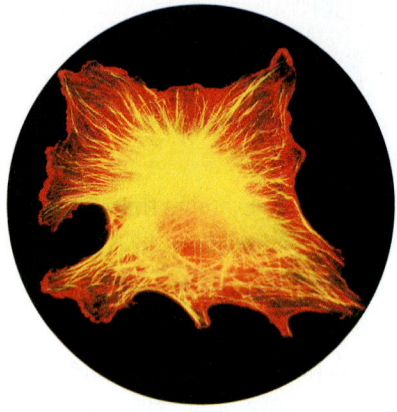

Stained LM Magnification: 700×

Figure 5 Cytoskeleton, a network of fibers in the cytoplasm, gives cells structure and helps them maintain shape.

Reading Check *What is the function of the cytoskeleton?*

Most of a cell's life processes occur in the cytoplasm. Within the cytoplasm of eukaryotic cells are structures called **organelles.** Some organelles process energy and others manufacture substances needed by the cell or other cells. Certain organelles move materials, while others act as storage sites. Most organelles are surrounded by membranes. The nucleus is usually the largest organelle in a cell.

Modeling Cytoplasm

Procedure
1. Add 100 mL of **water** to a **clear container.**
2. Add **unflavored gelatin** and stir.
3. Shine a **flashlight** through the solution.

Analysis
1. Describe what you see.
2. How does a model help you understand what cytoplasm might be like?

Nucleus The nucleus is like the deli manager who directs the store's daily operations and passes on information to employees. The **nucleus,** shown in **Figure 6,** directs all cell activities and is separated from the cytoplasm by a membrane. Materials enter and leave the nucleus through openings in the membrane. The nucleus contains the instructions for everything the cell does. These instructions are found on long, threadlike, hereditary material made of DNA. DNA is the chemical that contains the code for the cell's structure and activities. During cell division, the hereditary material coils tightly around proteins to form structures called chromosomes. A structure called a nucleolus also is found in the nucleus.

Figure 6 Refer to these diagrams of a typical animal cell (top) and plant cell (bottom) as you read about cell structures and their functions. **Determine** which structures a plant cell has that are not found in animal cells.

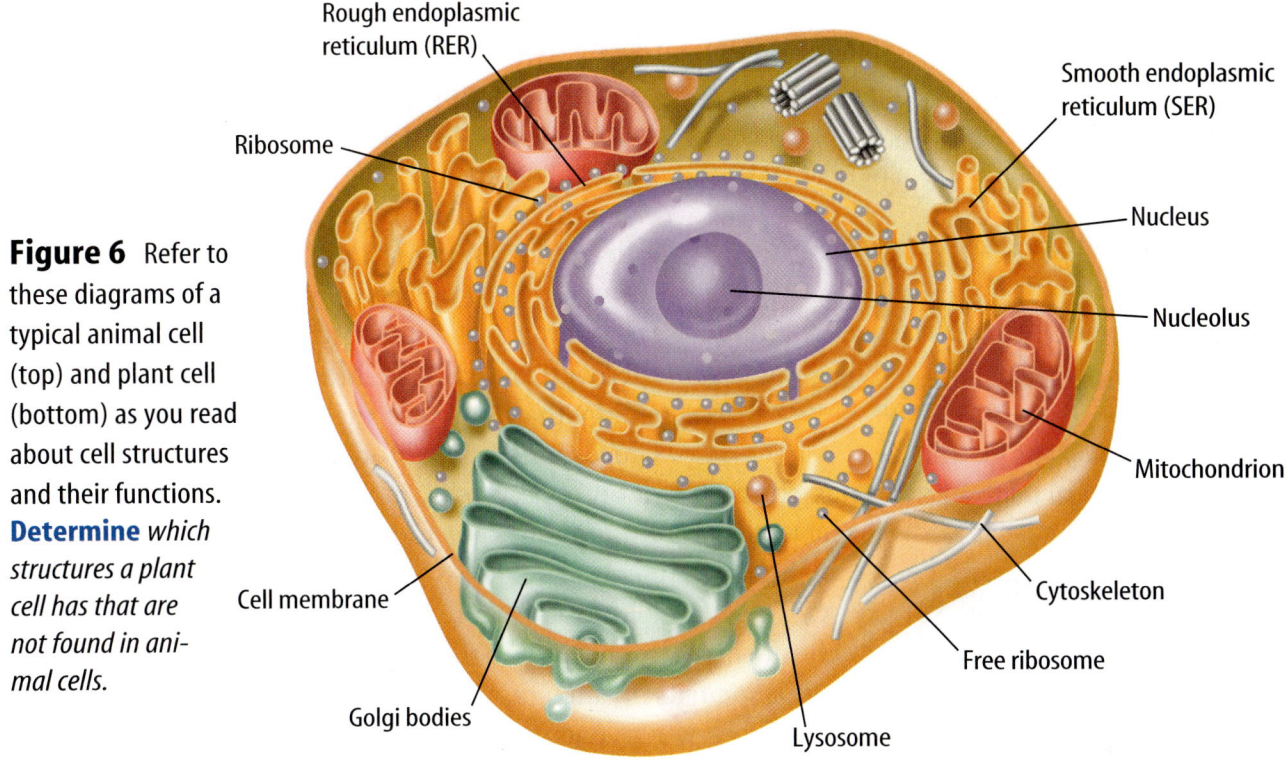

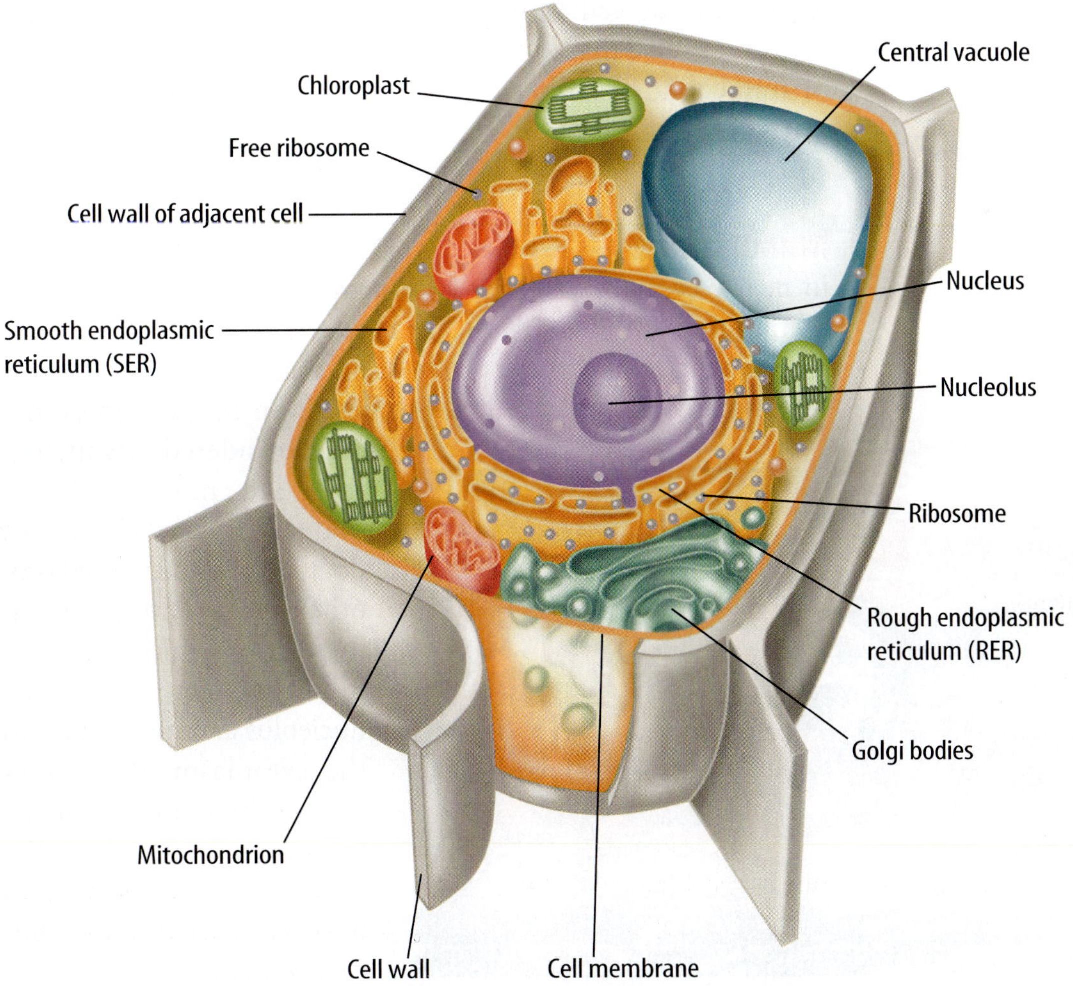

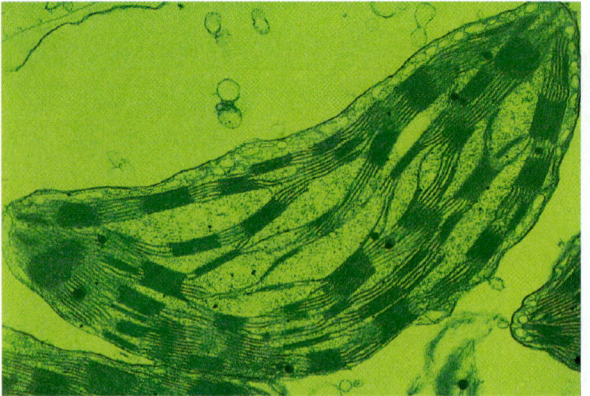

Color-enhanced TEM Magnification: 37000×

Figure 7 Chloroplasts use light energy to make sugar from carbon dioxide and water.

Energy-Processing Organelles Cells require a continuous supply of energy to process food, make new substances, eliminate wastes, and communicate with each other. In plant cells, food is made in green organelles in the cytoplasm called **chloroplasts** (KLOR uh plasts), as shown in **Figure 7**. Chloroplasts contain the green pigment chlorophyll, which gives many leaves and stems their green color. Chlorophyll captures light energy that is used to make a sugar called glucose. Glucose molecules store the captured light energy as chemical energy. Many cells, including animal cells, do not have chloroplasts for making food. They must get food from their environment.

The energy in food is stored until it is released by the mitochondria. **Mitochondria** (mi tuh KAHN dree uh) (singular, *mitochondrion*), such as the one shown in **Figure 8**, are organelles where energy is released from breaking down food into carbon dioxide and water. Just as the gas or electric company supplies fuel for the deli, a mitochondrion releases energy for use by the cell. Some types of cells, such as muscle cells, are more active than other cells. These cells have large numbers of mitochondria. Why would active cells have more or larger mitochondria?

Indiana Academic Standard Check

7.4.5: Explain how the basic functions of organisms . . . are carried out within the cell . . . .

✓ Why are ribosomes important to prokaryotic and eukaryotic cells?

Figure 8 Mitochondria release energy that is needed by the cell from food.

Manufacturing Organelles One substance that takes part in nearly every cell activity is protein. Proteins are part of cell membranes. Other proteins are needed for chemical reactions that take place in the cytoplasm. Cells make their own proteins on small structures called **ribosomes**. Even though ribosomes are considered organelles, they are not membrane bound. Some ribosomes float freely in the cytoplasm; others are attached to the endoplasmic reticulum. Ribosomes are made in the nucleolus and move out into the cytoplasm. Ribosomes receive directions from the hereditary material in the nucleus on how, when, and in what order to make specific proteins.

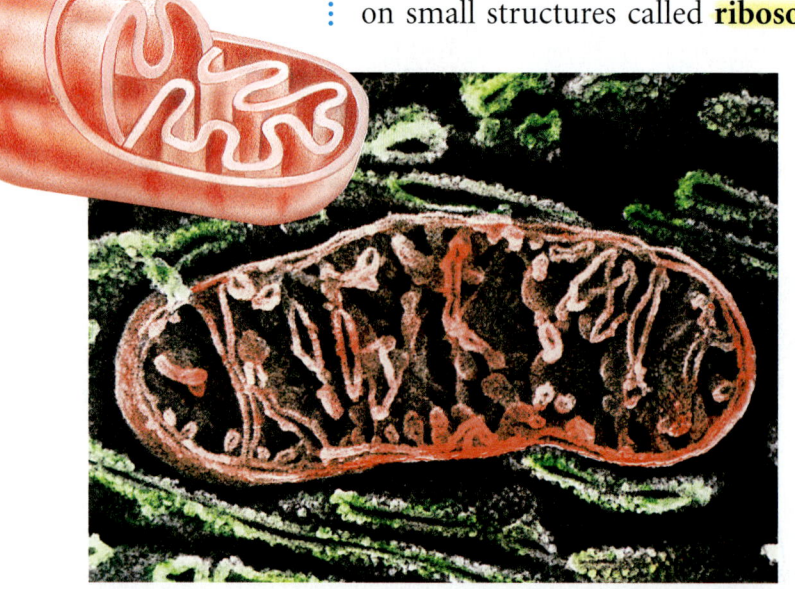

Color-enhanced SEM Magnification: 48000×

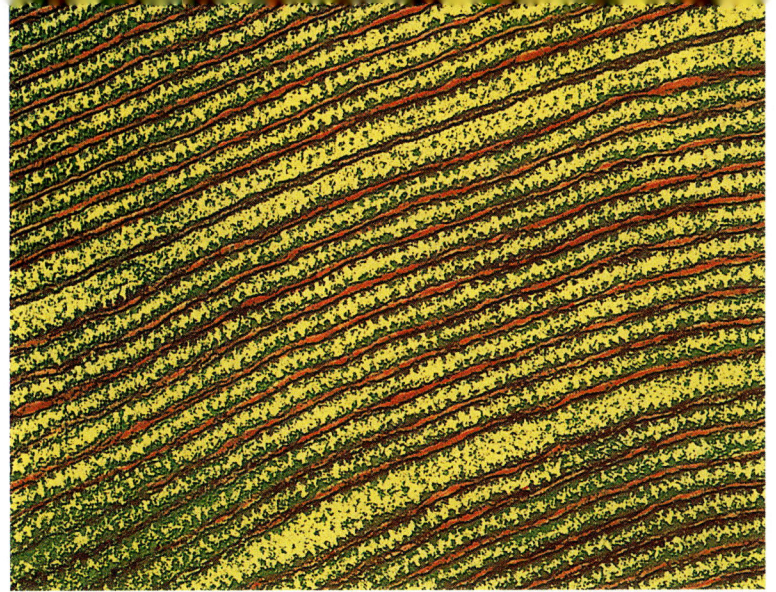

Figure 9 Endoplasmic reticulum (ER) is a complex series of membranes in the cytoplasm of the cell.
Infer what smooth ER would look like.

Color-enhanced TEM Magnification: 65000×

Processing, Transporting, and Storing Organelles

The **endoplasmic reticulum** (en duh PLAZ mihk • rih TIHK yuh lum) or ER, as shown in **Figure 9,** extends from the nucleus to the cell membrane. It is a series of folded membranes in which materials can be processed and moved around inside of the cell. The ER takes up a lot of space in some cells.

The endoplasmic reticulum may be "rough" or "smooth." ER that has no attached ribosomes is called smooth endoplasmic reticulum. This type of ER processes other cellular substances such as lipids that store energy. Ribosomes are attached to areas on the rough ER. There they carry out their job of making proteins that are moved out of the cell or used within the cell.

Reading Check What is the difference between rough ER and smooth ER?

After proteins are made in a cell, they are transferred to another type of cell organelle called the Golgi (GAWL jee) bodies. The **Golgi bodies,** as shown ion **Figure 10,** are stacked, flattened membranes. The Golgi bodies sort proteins and other cellular substances and package them into membrane-bound structures called vesicles. The vesicles deliver cellular substances to areas inside the cell. They also carry cellular substances to the cell membrane where they are released to the outside of the cell.

Just as a deli has refrigerators for temporary storage of some of its foods and ingredients, cells have membrane-bound spaces called vacuoles for the temporary storage of materials. A vacuole can store water, waste products, food, and other cellular materials. In plant cells, the vacuole may make up most of the cell's volume.

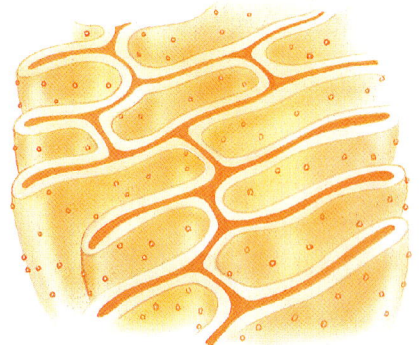

Figure 10 The Golgi body packages materials and moves them to the outside of the cell.
Explain why materials are removed from the cell.

Color-enhanced TEM Magnification: 28000×

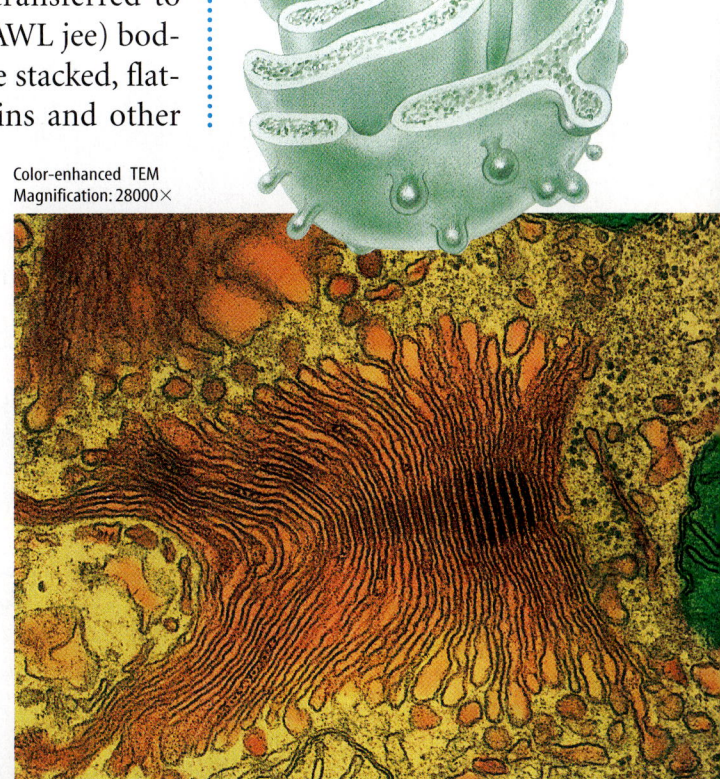

Recycling Just like a cell, you can recycle materials. Paper, plastics, aluminum, and glass are materials that can be recycled into usable items. Make a promotional poster to encourage others to recycle.

Recycling Organelles Active cells break down and recycle substances. Organelles called lysosomes (LI suh sohmz) contain digestive chemicals that help break down food molecules, cell wastes, and worn-out cell parts. In a healthy cell, chemicals are released into vacuoles only when needed. The lysosome's membrane prevents the digestive chemicals inside from leaking into the cytoplasm and destroying the cell. When a cell dies, a lysosome's membrane disintegrates. This releases digestive chemicals that allow the quick breakdown of the cell's contents.

 What is the function of the lysosome's membrane?

Applying Math — Calculate a Ratio

CELL RATIO Assume that a cell is like a cube with six equal sides. Find the ratio of surface area to volume for a cube that is 4 cm high.

Solution

1. *This is what you know:*   A cube has 6 equal sides of 4 cm × 4 cm.

2. *This is what you need to find out:*   What is the ratio (R) of surface area to volume for the cube?

3. *These are the equations you use:*
   - surface area (A) = width × length × 6
   - volume (V) = length × width × height
   - $R = A/V$

4. *This is the procedure you need to use:*
   - Substitute in known values and solve the equations
   $A = 4 \text{ cm} \times 4 \text{ cm} \times 6 = 96 \text{ cm}^2$
   $V = 4 \text{ cm} \times 4 \text{ cm} \times 4 \text{ cm} = 64 \text{ cm}^3$
   $R = 96 \text{ cm}^2 / 64 \text{ cm}^3 = 1.5 \text{ cm}^2/\text{cm}^3$

5. *Check your answer:*   Multiply the ratio by the volume. Did you calculate the surface area?

Practice Problems

1. Calculate the ratio of surface area to volume for a cube that is 2 cm high. What happens to this ratio as the size of the cube decreases?

2. If a 4-cm cube doubled just one of its dimensions, what would happen to the ratio of surface area to volume?

 For more practice, visit in7.msscience.com/math_practice

From Cell to Organism

Many one-celled organisms perform all their life functions by themselves. Cells in a many-celled organism, however, do not work alone. Each cell carries on its own life functions while depending in some way on other cells in the organism.

In **Figure 11,** you can see cardiac muscle cells grouped together to form a tissue. A **tissue** is a group of similar cells that work together to do one job. Each cell in a tissue does its part to keep the tissue alive.

Tissues are organized into organs. An **organ** is a structure made up of two or more different types of tissues that work together. Your heart is an organ made up of cardiac muscle tissue, nerve tissue, and blood tissues. The cardiac muscle tissue contracts, making the heart pump. The nerve tissue brings messages that tell the heart how fast to beat. The blood tissue is carried from the heart to other organs of the body.

 *What types of tissues make up your heart?*

A group of organs working together to perform a certain function is an organ system. Your heart, arteries, veins, and capillaries make up your cardiovascular system. In a many-celled organism, several systems work together in order to perform life functions efficiently. Your nervous, circulatory, respiratory, muscular, and other systems work together to keep you alive.

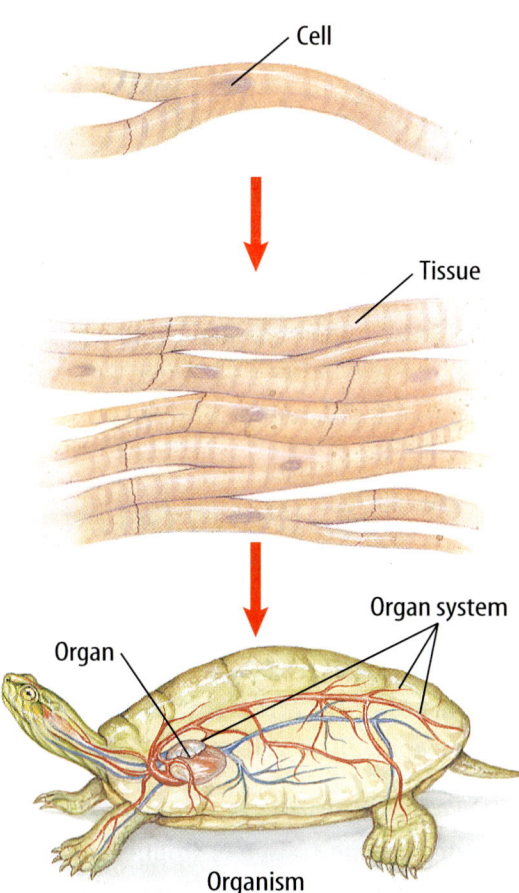

Figure 11 In a many-celled organism, cells are organized into tissues, tissues into organs, organs into systems, and systems into an organism.

section 1 review

Summary

Common Cell Traits
- All cells have an outer covering called a cell membrane.
- Cells can be classified as prokaryotic or eukaryotic.

Cell Organization
- Each cell in your body has a specific function.
- Most of a cell's life processes occur in the cytoplasm.

From Cell to Organism
- In a many-celled organism, several systems work together to perform life functions.

Self Check

1. **Explain** why the nucleus is important in the life of a cell.
2. **Determine** why digestive enzymes in a cell are enclosed in a membrane-bound organelle.
3. **Discuss** how cells, tissues, organs, and organ systems are related.
4. **Think Critically** How is the cell of a one-celled organism different from the cells in many-celled organisms?

Applying Skills

5. **Interpret Scientific Illustrations** Examine **Figure 6.** Make a list of differences and similarities between the animal cell and the plant cell.

in7.msscience.com/self_check_quiz

SECTION 1 Cell Structure

Comparing Cells

If you compared a goldfish to a rose, you would find them unlike each other. Are their individual cells different also?

Real-World Question
How do human cheek cells and plant cells compare?

Goals
- **Compare and contrast** an animal cell and a plant cell.

Materials
microscope
microscope slide
coverslip
forceps
tap water
dropper
Elodea plant
prepared slide of human cheek cells

Safety Precautions

Procedure

1. Copy the data table in your Science Journal. Check off the cell parts as you observe them.

Cell Observations		
Cell Part	**Cheek**	***Elodea***
Cytoplasm		
Nucleus		
Chloroplasts	Do not write in this book.	
Cell wall		
Cell membrane		

2. Using forceps, make a wet-mount slide of a young leaf from the tip of an *Elodea* plant.

3. **Observe** the leaf on low power. Focus on the top layer of cells.

4. Switch to high power and focus on one cell. In the center of the cell is a membrane-bound organelle called the central vacuole. Observe the chloroplasts—the green, disk-shaped objects moving around the central vacuole. Try to find the cell nucleus. It looks like a clear ball.

5. **Draw** the *Elodea* cell. Label the cell wall, cytoplasm, chloroplasts, central vacuole, and nucleus. Return to low power and remove the slide. Properly dispose of the slide.

6. **Observe** the prepared slide of cheek cells under low power.

7. Switch to high power and observe the cell nucleus. Draw and label the cell membrane, cytoplasm, and nucleus. Return to low power and remove the slide.

Conclude and Apply

1. **Compare and contrast** the shapes of the cheek cell and the *Elodea* cell.
2. **Draw conclusions** about the differences between plant and animal cells.

Communicating Your Data

Draw the two kinds of cells on one sheet of paper. Use a green pencil to label the organelles found only in plants, a red pencil to label the organelles found only in animals, and a blue pencil to label the organelles found in both. **For more help, refer to the Science Skill Handbook.**

section 2

Standard—7.4.5: Explain . . . and understand that the way which cells function is similar in all organisms.

Also covers: 7.1.5, 7.1.7, 7.4.4 (Detailed standards begin on page IN8.)

Viewing Cells

Magnifying Cells

The number of living things in your environment that you can't see is much greater than the number that you can see. Many of the things that you cannot see are only one cell in size. To see most cells, you need to use a microscope.

Trying to see separate cells in a leaf, like the ones in **Figure 12,** is like trying to see individual photos in a photo mosaic picture that is on the wall across the room. As you walk toward the wall, it becomes easier to see the individual photos. When you get right up to the wall, you can see details of each small photo. A microscope has one or more lenses that enlarge the image of an object as though you are walking closer to it. Seen through these lenses, the leaf appears much closer to you, and you can see the individual cells that carry on life processes.

Early Microscopes In the late 1500s, the first microscope was made by a Dutch maker of reading glasses. He put two magnifying glasses together in a tube and got an image that was larger than the image that was made by either lens alone.

In the mid 1600s, Antonie van Leeuwenhoek, a Dutch fabric merchant, made a simple microscope with a tiny glass bead for a lens, as shown in **Figure 13.** With it, he reported seeing things in pond water that no one had ever imagined. His microscope could magnify up to 270 times. Another way to say this is that his microscope could make the image of an object 270 times larger than its actual size. Today you would say his lens had a power of 270×. Early compound microscopes were crude by today's standards. The lenses would make an image larger, but it wasn't always sharp or clear.

as you read

What You'll Learn
- **Compare** the differences between the compound light microscope and the electron microscope.
- **Summarize** the discoveries that led to the development of the cell theory.

Why It's Important
Humans are like other living things because they are made of cells.

Review Vocabulary
magnify: to increase the size of something

New Vocabulary
• cell theory

Figure 12 Individual cells become visible when a plant leaf is viewed using a microscope with enough magnifying power.

Magnification: 250×

NATIONAL GEOGRAPHIC VISUALIZING MICROSCOPES

Figure 13

Microscopes give us a glimpse into a previously invisible world. Improvements have vastly increased their range of visibility, allowing researchers to study life at the molecular level. A selection of these powerful tools—and their magnification power—is shown here.

Up to 250× **LEEUWENHOEK MICROSCOPE** Held by a modern researcher, this historic microscope allowed Leeuwenhoek to see clear images of tiny freshwater organisms that he called "beasties."

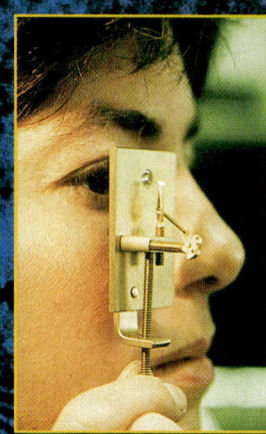

Up to 2,000× **BRIGHTFIELD / DARKFIELD MICROSCOPE** The light microscope is often called the brightfield microscope because the image is viewed against a bright background. A brightfield microscope is the tool most often used in laboratories to study cells. Placing a thin metal disc beneath the stage, between the light source and the objective lenses, converts a brightfield microscope to a darkfield microscope. The image seen using a darkfield microscope is bright against a dark background. This makes details more visible than with a brightfield microscope. Below are images of a *Paramecium* as seen using both processes.

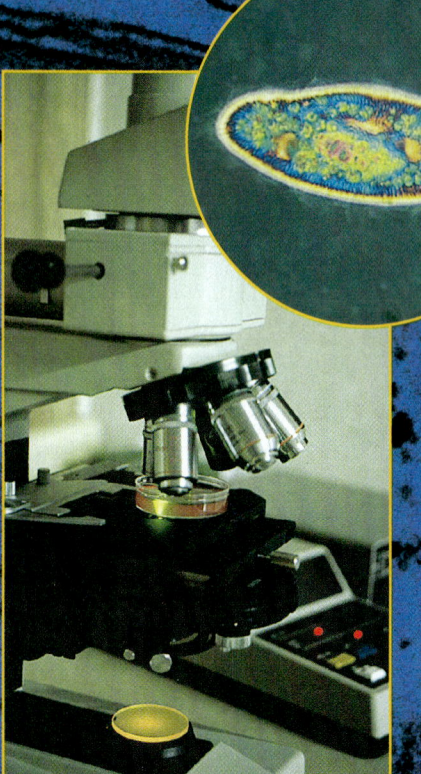

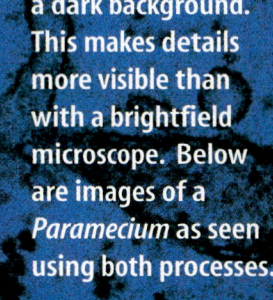
Darkfield

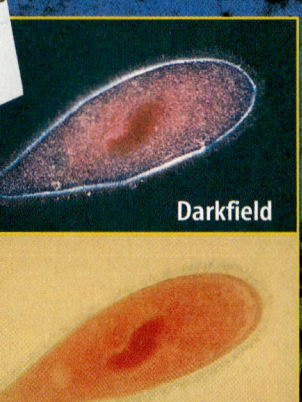
Brightfield

Up to 1,500× **FLUORESCENCE MICROSCOPE** This type of microscope requires that the specimen be treated with special fluorescent stains. When viewed through this microscope, certain cell structures or types of substances glow, as seen in the image of a *Paramecium* above.

▶ **Up to 1,000,000×** **TRANSMISSION ELECTRON MICROSCOPE** A TEM aims a beam of electrons through a specimen. Denser portions of the specimen allow fewer electrons to pass through and appear darker in the image. Organisms, such as the *Paramecium* at right, can only be seen when the image is photographed or shown on a monitor. A TEM can magnify hundreds of thousands of times.

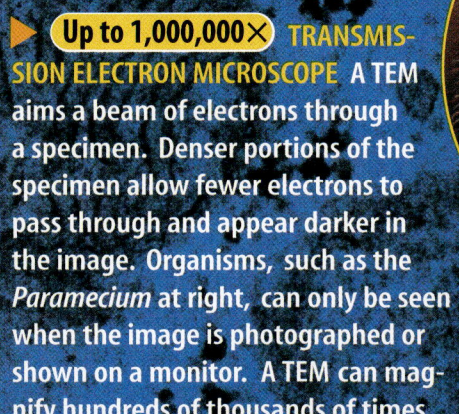

▶ **Up to 1,500×** **PHASE-CONTRAST MICROSCOPE** A phase-contrast microscope emphasizes slight differences in a specimen's capacity to bend light waves, thereby enhancing light and dark regions without the use of stains. This type of microscope is especially good for viewing living cells, like the *Paramecium* above left. The images from a phase-contrast microscope can only be seen when the specimen is photographed or shown on a monitor.

▶ **Up to 200,000×** **SCANNING ELECTRON MICROSCOPE** An SEM sweeps a beam of electrons over a specimen's surface, causing other electrons to be emitted from the specimen. SEMs produce realistic, three-dimensional images, which can only be viewed as photographs or on a monitor, as in the image of the *Paramecium* at right. Here a researcher compares an SEM picture to a computer monitor showing an enhanced image.

SECTION 2 Viewing Cells 49

Mini LAB

Observing Magnified Objects

Procedure
1. Look at a **newspaper** through the curved side and through the flat bottom of an **empty, clear glass**.
2. Look at the newspaper through a **clear glass bowl filled with water** and then with a **magnifying lens**.

Analysis
In your Science Journal, compare how well you can see the newspaper through each of the objects.

Try at Home

Cell Biologist Microscopes are important tools for cell biologists as they research diseases. In your Science Journal, make a list of diseases for which you think cell biologists are trying to find effective drugs.

Modern Microscopes Scientists use a variety of microscopes to study organisms, cells, and cell parts that are too small to be seen with the human eye. Depending on how many lenses a microscope contains, it is called simple or compound. A simple microscope is similar to a magnifying lens. It has only one lens. A microscope's lens makes an enlarged image of an object and directs light toward your eye. The change in apparent size produced by a microscope is called magnification. Microscopes vary in powers of magnification. Some microscopes can make images of individual atoms.

The microscope you probably will use to study life science is a compound light microscope, similar to the one in the Reference Handbook at the back of this book. The compound light microscope has two sets of lenses—eyepiece lenses and objective lenses. The eyepiece lenses are mounted in one or two tubelike structures. Images of objects viewed through two eyepieces, or stereomicroscopes, are three-dimensional. Images of objects viewed through one eyepiece are not. Compound light microscopes usually have two to four movable objective lenses.

Magnification The powers of the eyepiece and objective lenses determine the total magnifications of a microscope. If the eyepiece lens has a power of 10× and the objective lens has a power of 43×, then the total magnification is 430× (10× times 43×). Some compound microscopes, like those in **Figure 13**, have more powerful lenses that can magnify an object up to 2,000 times its original size.

Electron Microscopes Things that are too small to be seen with other microscopes can be viewed with an electron microscope. Instead of using lenses to direct beams of light, an electron microscope uses a magnetic field in a vacuum to direct beams of electrons. Some electron microscopes can magnify images up to one million times. Electron microscope images must be photographed or electronically produced.

Several kinds of electron microscopes have been invented, as shown in **Figure 13**. Scanning electron microscopes (SEM) produce a realistic, three-dimensional image. Only the surface of the specimen can be observed using an SEM. Transmission electron microscopes (TEM) produce a two-dimensional image of a thinly-sliced specimen. Details of cell parts can be examined using a TEM. Scanning tunneling microscopes (STM) are able to show the arrangement of atoms on the surface of a molecule. A metal probe is placed near the surface of the specimen and electrons flow from the tip. The hills and valleys of the specimen's surface are mapped.

Cell Theory

During the seventeenth century, scientists used their new invention, the microscope, to explore the newly discovered microscopic world. They examined drops of blood, scrapings from their own teeth, and other small things. Cells weren't discovered until the microscope was improved. In 1665, Robert Hooke cut a thin slice of cork and looked at it under his microscope. To Hooke, the cork seemed to be made up of empty little boxes, which he named cells.

In the 1830s, Matthias Schleiden used a microscope to study plants and concluded that all plants are made of cells. Theodor Schwann, after observing different animal cells, concluded that all animals are made up of cells. Eventually, they combined their ideas and became convinced that all living things are made of cells.

Several years later, Rudolf Virchow hypothesized that cells divide to form new cells. Virchow proposed that every cell came from a cell that already existed. His observations and conclusions and those of others are summarized in the **cell theory**, as described in **Table 1**.

Table 1 The Cell Theory

All organisms are made up of one or more cells.	An organism can be one cell or many cells like most plants and animals.
The cell is the basic unit of organization in organisms.	Even in complex organisms, the cell is the basic unit of structure and function.
All cells come from cells.	Most cells can divide to form two new, identical cells.

Indiana Academic Standard Check

7.4.5: Explain ... and understand that the way in which cells function is similar in all organisms.

✓ Which scientists concluded that the cell was the basic unit of structure in all organisms?

✓ **Reading Check** Who first concluded that all animals are made of cells?

section 2 review

Summary

Magnifying Cells
- The powers of the eyepiece and objective lenses determine the total magnification of a microscope.
- An electron microscope uses a magnetic field in a vacuum to direct beams of electrons.

Development of the Cell Theory
- In 1665, Robert Hooke looked at a piece of cork under his microscope and called what he saw cells.
- The conclusions of Rudolf Virchow and those of others are summarized in the cell theory.

Self Check

1. **Determine** why the invention of the microscope was important in the study of cells.
2. **State** the cell theory.
3. **Compare** a simple and a compound light microscope.
4. **Explain** Virchow's contribution to the cell theory.
5. **Think Critically** Why would it be better to look at living cells than at dead cells?

Applying Math

6. **Solve One-Step Equations** Calculate the magnifications of a microscope that has an $8\times$ eyepiece and $10\times$ and $40\times$ objectives.

section 3

Standards—7.4.12: Explain that viruses... may infect the human body... Recognize that a person can catch a cold many times.... **7.6.3:** ... Edward Jenner had shown for smallpox... that it was possible to produce vaccines that would induce the body to build immunity to a disease without actually causing the disease itself.

Also covers: 7.1.5, 7.1.6, 7.1.7, 7.4.7, 7.6.4 (Detailed standards begin on page IN8.)

Viruses

as you read

What You'll Learn
- **Explain** how a virus makes copies of itself.
- **Identify** the benefits of vaccines.
- **Investigate** some uses of viruses.

Why It's Important
Viruses infect nearly all organisms, usually affecting them negatively yet sometimes affecting them positively.

Review Vocabulary
disease: a condition that results from the disruption in function of one or more of an organism's normal processes

New Vocabulary
- virus
- host cell

What are viruses?

Cold sores, measles, chicken pox, colds, the flu, and AIDS are diseases caused by nonliving particles called viruses. A **virus** is a strand of hereditary material surrounded by a protein coating. Viruses don't have a nucleus or other organelles. They also lack a cell membrane. Viruses, as shown in **Figure 14**, have a variety of shapes. Because they are too small to be seen with a light microscope, they were discovered only after the electron microscope was invented. Before that time, scientists only hypothesized about viruses.

How do viruses multiply?

All viruses can do is make copies of themselves. However, they can't do that without the help of a living cell called a **host cell**. Crystalized forms of some viruses can be stored for years. Then, if they enter an organism, they can multiply quickly.

Once a virus is inside of a host cell, the virus can act in two ways. It can either be active or it can become latent, which is an inactive stage.

Figure 14 Viruses come in a variety of shapes.

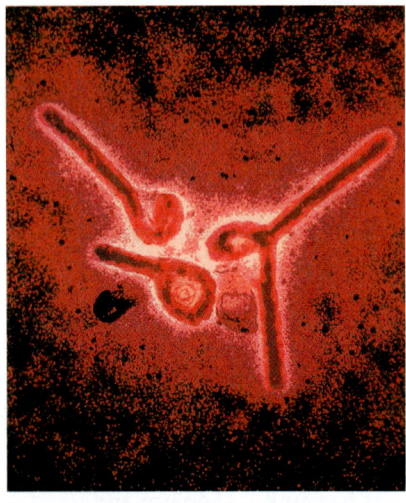

Color-enhanced TEM Magnification: 160000×

Filoviruses do not have uniform shapes. Some of these *Ebola* viruses have a loop at one end.

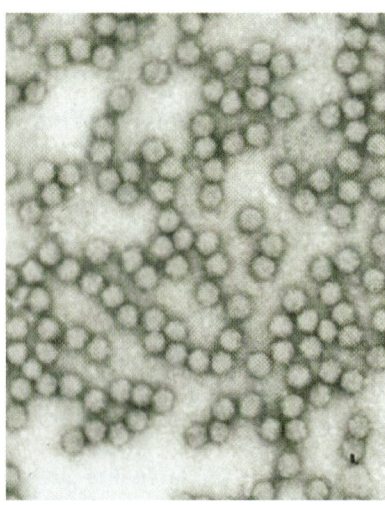

The potato leafroll virus, *Polervirus*, damages potato crops worldwide.

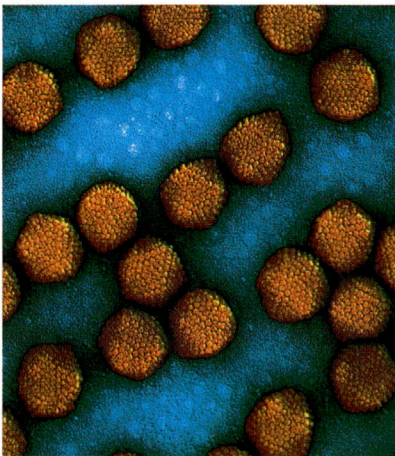

Color-enhanced SEM Magnification: 140000×

This is one of many adenoviruses that can cause a cold. Each time you have a cold, you've contacted a different adenovirus.

52 CHAPTER 2 Cells

Figure 15 An active virus multiplies and destroys the host cell.

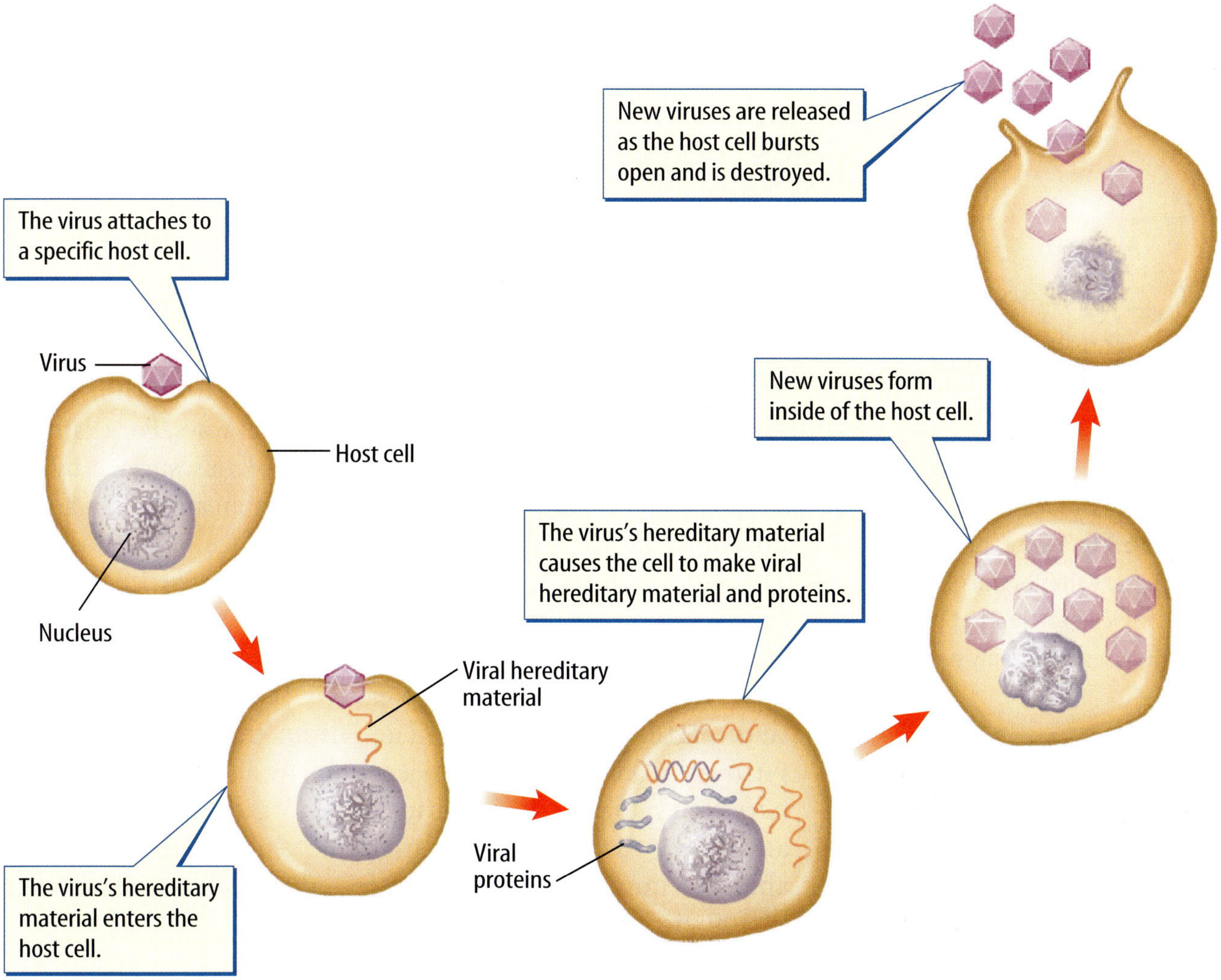

Active Viruses When a virus enters a cell and is active, it causes the host cell to make new viruses. This process destroys the host cell. Follow the steps in **Figure 15** to see one way that an active virus functions inside a cell.

Latent Viruses Some viruses can be latent. That means that after the virus enters a cell, its hereditary material can become part of the cell's hereditary material. It does not immediately make new viruses or destroy the cell. As the host cell reproduces, the viral DNA is copied. A virus can be latent for many years. Then, at any time, certain conditions, either inside or outside your body, can activate the virus.

If you have had a cold sore on your lip, a latent virus in your body has become active. The cold sore is a sign that the virus is active and destroying cells in your lip. When the cold sore disappears, the virus has become latent again. The virus is still in your body's cells, but it is hiding and doing no apparent harm.

Topic: Virus Reactivation
Visit in7.msscience.com for Web links to information about viruses.

Activity In your Science Journal, list five stimuli that might activate a latent virus.

SECTION 3 Viruses

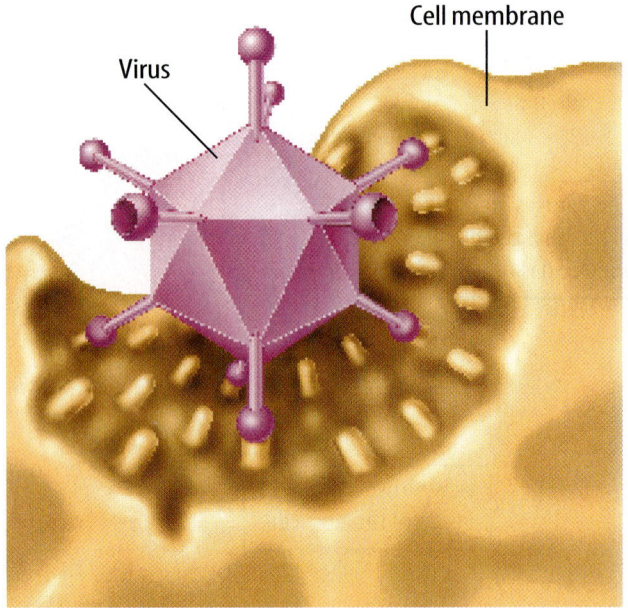

Figure 16 Viruses and the attachment sites of the host cell must match exactly. That's why most viruses infect only one kind of host cell.

Indiana Academic Standard Check

7.6.3: ...Edward Jenner,... without understanding the underlying mechanism,... produced a vaccine.

✓ What was the source of Jenner's vaccine?

Topic: Filoviruses
Visit in7.msscience.com for Web links to information about the virus family *Filoviridae*.

Activity Make a table that displays the virus name, location, and year of the initial outbreaks associated with the *Filoviridae* family.

How do viruses affect organisms?

Viruses attack animals, plants, fungi, protists, and all prokaryotes. Some viruses can infect only specific kinds of cells. For instance, many viruses, such as the potato leafroll virus, are limited to one host species or to one type of tissue within that species. A few viruses affect a broad range of hosts. An example of this is the rabies virus. Rabies can infect humans and many other animal hosts.

A virus cannot move by itself, but it can reach a host's body in several ways. For example, it can be carried onto a plant's surface by the wind or it can be inhaled by an animal. In a viral infection, the virus first attaches to the surface of the host cell. The virus and the place where it attaches must fit together exactly, as shown in **Figure 16.** Because of this, most viruses attack only one kind of host cell.

Viruses that infect bacteria are called bacteriophages (bak TIHR ee uh fay jihz). They differ from other kinds of viruses in the way that they enter bacteria and release their hereditary material. Bacteriophages attach to a bacterium and inject their hereditary material. The entire cycle takes about 20 min, and each virus-infected cell releases an average of 100 viruses.

Fighting Viruses

Vaccines are used to prevent disease. A vaccine is made from weakened virus particles that can't cause disease anymore. Vaccines have been made to prevent many diseases, including measles, mumps, smallpox, chicken pox, polio, and rabies.

 **Reading Check** *What is a vaccine?*

The First Vaccine Edward Jenner is credited with developing the first vaccine in 1796. He developed a vaccine for smallpox, a disease that was still feared in the early twentieth century. Jenner noticed that people who got a disease called cowpox didn't get smallpox. He prepared a vaccine from the sores of people who had cowpox. When injected into healthy people, the cowpox vaccine protected them from smallpox. Jenner didn't know he was fighting a virus. At that time, no one understood what caused disease or how the body fought disease.

Treating Viral Diseases Antibiotics treat bacterial infections but are not effective against viral diseases. One way your body can stop viral infections is by making interferons. Interferons are proteins that are produced rapidly by virus-infected cells and move to noninfected cells in the host. They cause the noninfected cells to produce protective substances.

Antiviral drugs can be given to infected patients to help fight a virus. A few drugs show some effectiveness against viruses but some have limited use because of their adverse side effects.

Preventing Viral Diseases Public health measures for preventing viral diseases include vaccinating people, improving sanitary conditions, quarantining patients, and controlling animals that spread disease. For example, annual rabies vaccinations of pets and farm animals protect them and humans from infection. To control the spread of rabies in wild animals such as coyotes and wolves, wildlife workers place bait containing an oral rabies vaccine, as shown in **Figure 17,** where wild animals will find it.

Figure 17 This oral rabies bait is being prepared for an aerial drop by the Texas Department of Health as part of their Oral Rabies Vaccination Program. This five-year program has prevented the expansion of rabies into Texas.

Research with Viruses

You might think viruses are always harmful. However, through research, scientists are discovering helpful uses for some viruses. One use, called gene therapy, substitutes normal hereditary material for a cell's defective hereditary material. The normal material is enclosed in viruses that "infect" targeted cells. The new hereditary material enters the cells and replaces the defective hereditary material. Using gene therapy, scientists hope to help people with genetic disorders and find a cure for cancer.

section 3 review

Summary

What are viruses?
- A virus is a strand of hereditary material surrounded by a protein coating.

How do viruses multiply?
- An active virus immediately destroys the host cell but a latent virus does not.

Fighting Viruses and Research with Viruses
- Antiviral drugs can be given to infected patients to help fight a virus.
- Scientists are discovering helpful uses for some viruses.

Self Check

1. **Describe** how viruses multiply.
2. **Explain** how vaccines are beneficial.
3. **Determine** how some viruses might be helpful.
4. **Discuss** how viral diseases might be prevented.
5. **Think Critically** Explain why a doctor might not give you any medication if you have a viral disease.

Applying Skills

6. **Concept Map** Make an events-chain concept map to show what happens when a latent virus becomes active.

LAB Design Your Own

Comparing Light Microscopes

Goals
- **Learn** how to correctly use a stereomicroscope and a compound light microscope.
- **Compare** the uses of the stereomicroscope and compound light microscope.

Possible Materials
compound light microscope
stereomicroscope
items from the classroom—include some living or once-living items (8)
microscope slides and coverslips
plastic petri dishes
distilled water
dropper

Safety Precautions

Real-World Question

You're a technician in a police forensic laboratory. You use a stereomicroscope and a compound light microscope in the laboratory. A detective just returned from a crime scene with bags of evidence. You must examine each piece of evidence under a microscope. How do you decide which microscope is the best tool to use? Will all of the evidence that you've collected be viewable through both microscopes?

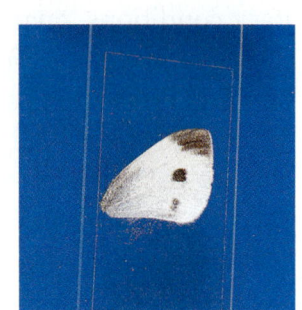

Form a Hypothesis

Compare the items to be examined under the microscopes. Form a hypothesis to predict which microscope will be used for each item and explain why.

56 CHAPTER 2 Cells

Using Scientific Methods

▶ Test Your Hypothesis

Make a Plan

1. As a group, decide how you will test your hypothesis.
2. **Describe** how you will carry out this experiment using a series of specific steps. Make sure the steps are in a logical order. Remember that you must place an item in the bottom of a plastic petri dish to examine it under the stereomicroscope and you must make a wet mount of any item to be examined under the compound light microscope. For more help, see the Reference Handbook.
3. If you need a data table or an observation table, design one in your Science Journal.

Follow Your Plan

1. Make sure your teacher approves the objects you'll examine, your plan, and your data table before you start.
2. Carry out the experiment.
3. While doing the experiment, record your observations and complete the data table.

▶ Analyze Your Data

1. **Compare** the items you examined with those of your classmates.
2. **Classify** the eight items you observed based on this experiment.

▶ Conclude and Apply

1. **Infer** which microscope a scientist might use to examine a blood sample, fibers, and live snails.
2. **List** five careers that require people to use a stereomicroscope. List five careers that require people to use a compound light microscope. Enter the lists in your Science Journal.
3. **Infer** how the images would differ if you examined an item under a compound light microscope and a stereomicroscope.
4. **Determine** which microscope is better for looking at large, or possibly live, items.

Communicating Your Data

In your Science Journal, **write** a short description of an imaginary crime scene and the evidence found there. Sort the evidence into two lists—items to be examined under a stereomicroscope and items to be examined under a compound light microscope. **For more help, refer to the Science Skill Handbook.**

LAB 57

TIME SCIENCE AND HISTORY

SCIENCE CAN CHANGE THE COURSE OF HISTORY!

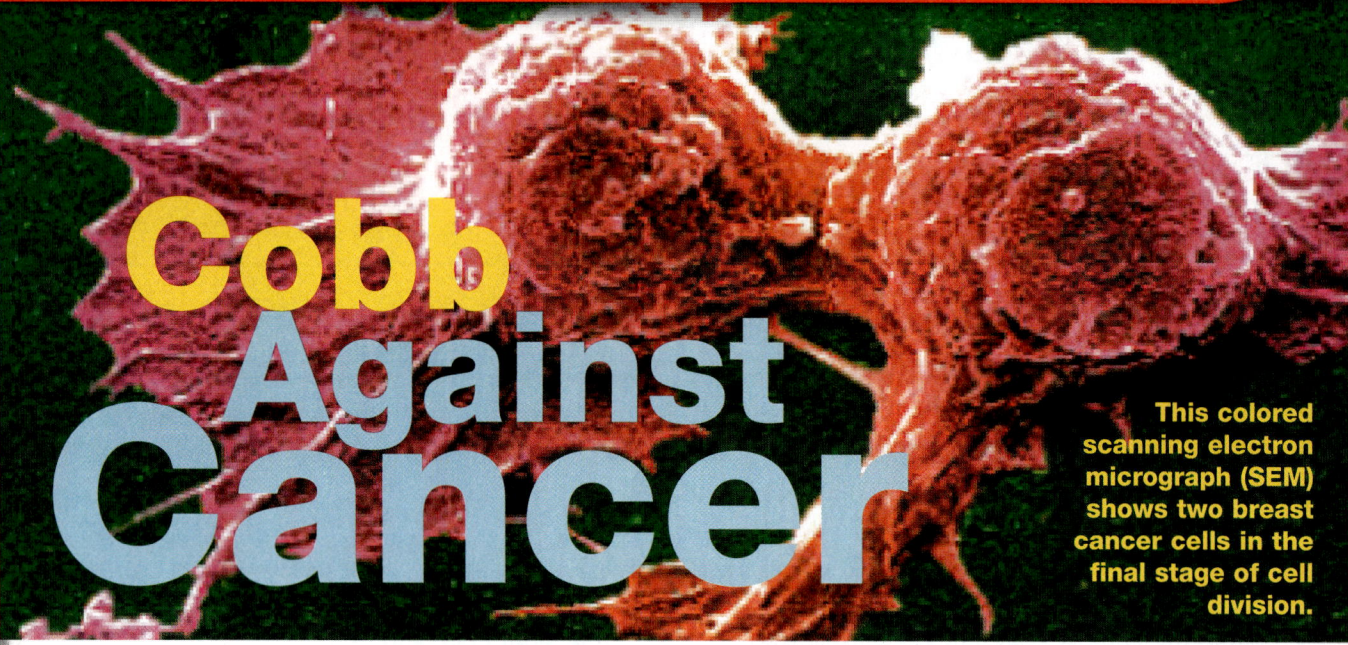

Cobb Against Cancer

This colored scanning electron micrograph (SEM) shows two breast cancer cells in the final stage of cell division.

Jewel Plummer Cobb is a cell biologist who did important background research on the use of drugs against cancer in the 1950s. She removed cells from cancerous tumors and cultured them in the lab. Then, in a controlled study, she tried a series of different drugs against batches of the same cells. Her goal was to find the right drug to cure each patient's particular cancer. Cobb never met that goal, but her research laid the groundwork for modern chemotherapy—the use of chemicals to treat cancer.

Jewel Cobb also influenced science in another way. She was a role model, especially in her role as dean or president of several universities. Cobb promoted equal opportunity for students of all backgrounds, especially in the sciences.

Light Up a Cure

Vancouver, British Columbia 2000. While Cobb herself was only able to infer what was going on inside a cell from its reactions to various drugs, her work has helped others go further. Building on Cobb's work, Professor Julia Levy and her research team at the University of British Columbia actually go inside cells, and even organelles, to work against cancer. One technique they are pioneering is the use of light to guide cancer drugs to the right cells. First, the patient is given a chemotherapy drug that reacts to light. Then, a fiber optic tube is inserted into the tumor. Finally, laser light is passed through the tube, which activates the light-sensitive drug—but only in the tumor itself. This will hopefully provide a technique to keep healthy cells healthy while killing sick cells.

Write Report on Cobb's experiments on cancer cells. What were her dependent and independent variables? What would she have used as a control? What sources of error did she have to guard against? Answer the same questions about Levy's work.

Science Online

For more information, visit in7.msscience.com/time

chapter 2 Study Guide

Reviewing Main Ideas

Section 1 Cell Structure

1. Prokaryotic and eukaryotic are the two cell types.
2. The DNA in the nucleus controls cell functions.
3. Organelles such as mitochondria and chloroplasts process energy.
4. Most many-celled organisms are organized into tissues, organs, and organ systems.

Section 2 Viewing Cells

1. A simple microscope has just one lens. A compound light microscope has an eyepiece and objective lenses.
2. To calculate the magnification of a microscope, multiply the power of the eyepiece by the power of the objective lens.
3. According to the cell theory, the cell is the basic unit of life. Organisms are made of one or more cells, and all cells come from other cells.

Section 3 Viruses

1. A virus is a structure containing hereditary material surrounded by a protein coating.
2. A virus can make copies of itself only when it is inside a living host cell.

Visualizing Main Ideas

Copy and complete the following concept map of the basic units of life.

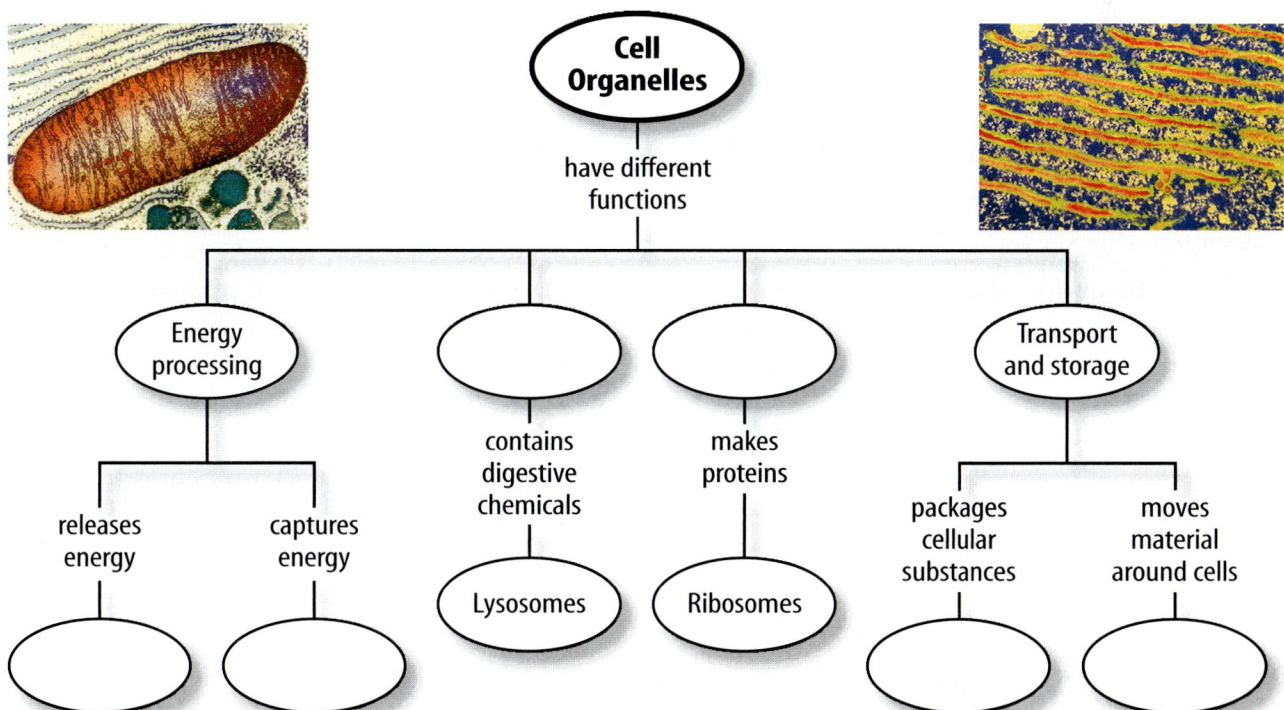

chapter 2 Review

Using Vocabulary

cell membrane p. 38	host cell p. 52
cell theory p. 51	mitochondrion p. 42
cell wall p. 39	nucleus p. 40
chloroplast p. 42	organ p. 45
cytoplasm p. 38	organelle p. 40
endoplasmic reticulum p. 43	ribosome p. 42
	tissue p. 45
Golgi body p. 43	virus p. 52

Using the vocabulary words, give an example of each of the following.

1. found in every organ
2. smaller than one cell
3. a plant-cell organelle
4. part of every cell
5. powerhouse of a cell
6. used by biologists
7. contains hereditary material
8. a structure that surrounds the cell
9. can be damaged by a virus
10. made up of cells

Checking Concepts

Choose the word or phrase that best answers the question.

11. What structure allows only certain things to pass in and out of the cell?
    A) cytoplasm   C) ribosomes
    B) cell membrane   D) Golgi body

12. What is the organelle to the right?
    A) nucleus
    B) cytoplasm
    C) Golgi body
    D) endoplasmic reticulum

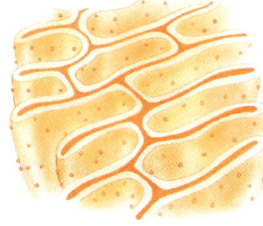

Use the illustration below to answer question 13.

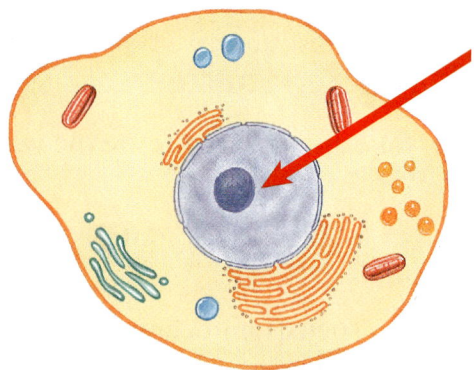

13. In the figure above, what is the function of the structure that the arrow is pointing to?
    A) recycles old cell parts
    B) controls cell activities
    C) protection
    D) releases energy

14. Which scientist gave the name *cells* to structures he viewed?
    A) Hooke   C) Schleiden
    B) Schwann   D) Virchow

15. Which of the following is a viral disease?
    A) tuberculosis   C) smallpox
    B) anthrax   D) tetanus

16. Which microscope can magnify up to a million times?
    A) compound light microscope
    B) stereomicroscope
    C) transmission electron microscope
    D) atomic force microscope

17. Which of the following is part of a bacterial cell?
    A) a cell wall   C) mitochondria
    B) lysosomes   D) a nucleus

18. Which of the following do groups of different tissues form?
    A) organ   C) organ system
    B) organelle   D) organism

60 CHAPTER REVIEW   Science Online in7.msscience.com/vocabulary_puzzlemaker

chapter 2 Review

Thinking Critically

19. **Infer** why it is difficult to treat a viral disease.

20. **Explain** which type of microscope would be best to view a piece of moldy bread.

21. **Predict** what would happen to a plant cell that suddenly lost its chloroplasts.

22. **Predict** what would happen if the animal cell shown to the right didn't have ribosomes.

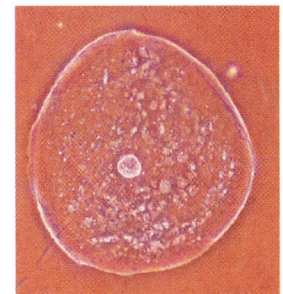

23. **Determine** how you would decide whether an unknown cell was an animal cell, a plant cell, or a bacterial cell.

24. **Concept Map** Make an events-chain concept map of the following from simple to complex: *small intestine, circular muscle cell, human,* and *digestive system.*

25. **Interpret Scientific Illustrations** Use the illustrations in **Figure 1** to describe how the shape of a cell is related to its function.

Use the table below to answer question 26.

Cell Structures		
Structure	Prokaryotic Cell	Eukaryotic Cell
Cell membrane		Yes
Cytoplasm	Yes	
Nucleus		Yes
Endoplasmic reticulum		
Golgi bodies		

26. **Compare and Contrast** Copy and complete the table above.

27. **Make a Model** Make and illustrate a time line about the development of the cell theory. Begin with the development of the microscope and end with Virchow. Include the contributions of Leeuwenhoek, Hooke, Schleiden, and Schwann.

Performance Activities

28. **Model** Use materials that resemble cell parts or represent their functions to make a model of a plant cell or an animal cell. Include a cell-parts key.

29. **Poster** Make a poster about the history of vaccinations. Contact your local Health Department for current information.

Applying Math

Use the illustration below to answer question 30.

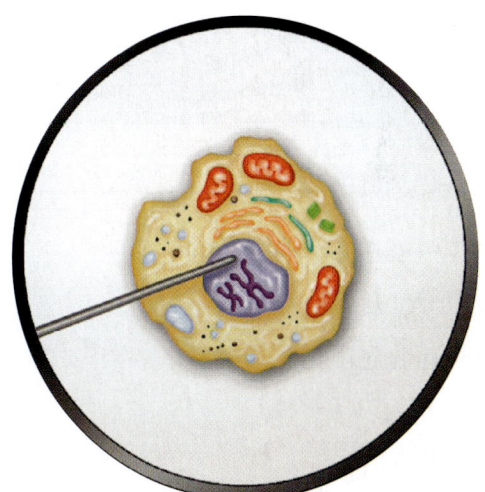

30. **Cell Width** If the pointer shown above with the cell is 10 micrometers (μm) in length, then about how wide is this cell?

    A) 20 μm   C) 5 μm
    B) 10 μm   D) 0.1 μm

31. **Magnification** Calculate the magnification of a microscope with a 20× eyepiece and a 40× objective.

chapter 2 Indiana

 The assessed Indiana standard appears above the question.

Record your answers on the answer sheet provided by your teacher or on a sheet of paper.

Part 1 Multiple Choice

1. Why is a virus **NOT** considered a living cell?
   - A It does not have a cell wall.
   - B It has defective hereditary material.
   - C It has few organelles.
   - D It cannot reproduce by itself.

The images below show the same organelle.

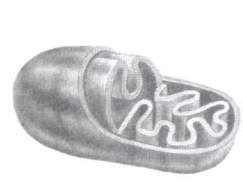 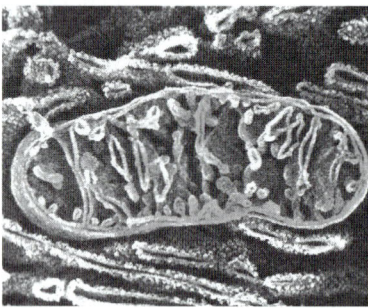

7.4.1
2. What organelle is shown?
   - A chloroplast
   - B mitochondrion
   - C nucleus
   - D ribosome

7.4.5
3. What is the primary function of the organelle shown above?
   - A capturing light energy
   - B directing cell processes
   - C releasing energy stored in food
   - D making proteins

7.4.5
4. Which organelle receives the directions from the DNA in the nucleus about which proteins to make?
   - A cytoplasm
   - B endoplasmic reticulum
   - C Golgi body
   - D ribosome

7.4.1
5. Which do a bacterial cell, a plant cell, and a nerve cell have in common?
   - A cell wall and nucleus
   - B cytoplasm and cell membrane
   - C endoplasmic reticulum
   - D flagella and chloroplasts

7.4.12
6. The illustration below shows a process that can occur in the human body.

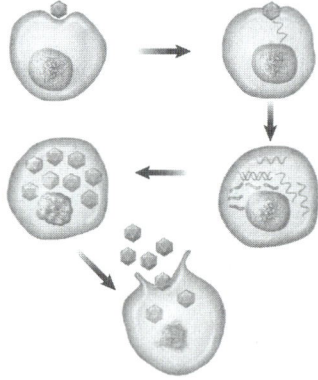

What does the illustration represent?
   - A cell reproduction
   - B bacterial reproduction
   - C active virus multiplication
   - D vaccination

62 INDIANA

Standards Review

7.4.5

7. Which is a **NOT** a function of an organelle?
   - A cell heredity
   - B cell protection
   - C energy release
   - D oxygen release

7.4.5

8. Where do most life processes occur in a cell?
   - A cell wall
   - B cytoplasm
   - C nucleus
   - D organ

7.4.1

9. The photo below shows Japanese beetles eating a plant.

Which statement is **TRUE** for both organisms?
   - A Carbon dioxide and water release energy that its cells use.
   - B DNA contains the code for its cells' structures.
   - C Organelles in its cells can transform light energy into chemical energy.
   - D Reproducing requires a host organism.

Part 2   Constructed Response

The illustration below is an interaction that can occur in the human body.

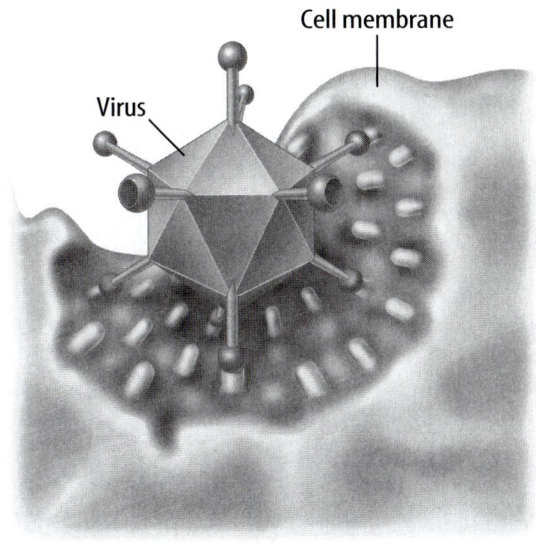

7.4.12

10. What interaction is taking place in the illustration above? What are two possible outcomes of this interaction?

11. Explain how Hooke, Schleiden, and Schwann contributed to the cell theory.

7.4.5

12. Discuss the importance of the structure and function of cytoplasm to a cell.

7.6.3

13. Describe the development of the first vaccine by Edward Jenner.

Test-Taking Tip

Read Carefully Read each question carefully for full understanding.

chapter 3

Academic Standard—4: Students begin to trace the flow of matter and energy through ecosystems. They recognize the fundamental difference between plants and animals and understand its basis at the cellular level... They use microscopes to observe cells and recognize that cells function in similar ways in all organisms.

Also covers: Academic Standards 2, 3, 6, 7 (Detailed standards begin on page IN8.)

Cell Processes

chapter preview

sections
1. **Chemistry of Life**
2. **Moving Cellular Material**
   Lab Observing Osmosis
3. **Energy for Life**
   Lab Photosynthesis and Respiration
   Virtual Lab Under what conditions do cells gain or lose water?

The Science of Gardening

Growing a garden is hard work for both you and the plants. Like you, plants need water and food for energy. How plants get food and water is different from you. Understanding how living things get the energy they need to survive will make a garden seem like much more than just plants and dirt.

Science Journal Describe two ways in which you think plants get food for energy.

Start-Up Activities

Why does water enter and leave plant cells?

If you forget to water a plant, it will wilt. After you water the plant, it probably will straighten up and look healthier. In the following lab, find out how water causes a plant to wilt and straighten.

1. Label a small bowl *Salt Water*. Pour 250 mL of water into the bowl. Then add 15 g of salt to the water and stir.
2. Pour 250 mL of water into another small bowl.
3. Place two carrot sticks into each bowl. Also, place two carrot sticks on the lab table.
4. After 30 min, remove the carrot sticks from the bowls and keep them next to the bowl they came from. Examine all six carrot sticks, then describe them in your Science Journal.
5. **Think Critically** Write a paragraph in your Science Journal that describes what would happen if you moved the carrot sticks from the plain water to the lab table, the ones from the salt water into the plain water, and the ones from the lab table into the salt water for 30 min. Now move the carrot sticks as described and write the results in your Science Journal.

FOLDABLES Study Organizer

How Living Things Survive Make the following vocabulary Foldable to help you understand the chemistry of living things and how energy is obtained for life.

STEP 1 Fold a vertical sheet of notebook paper from side to side.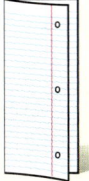

STEP 2 Cut along every third line of only the top layer to form tabs.

Build Vocabulary As you read this chapter, list the vocabulary words about cell processes on the tabs. As you learn the definitions, write them under the tab for each vocabulary word. Write a sentence about one of the cell processes using the vocabulary word on the tab.

 **Preview this chapter's content and activities at in7.msscience.com**

section 1

Standard—7.3.13: Explain that many substances dissolve in water....

Also covers: 7.2.1, 7.7.4 (Detailed standards begin on page IN8.)

Chemistry of Life

as you read

What You'll Learn
- **List** the differences among atoms, elements, molecules, and compounds.
- **Explain** the relationship between chemistry and life science.
- **Discuss** how organic compounds are different from inorganic compounds.

Why It's Important
You grow because of chemical reactions in your body.

Review Vocabulary
cell: the smallest unit of a living thing that can perform the functions of life

New Vocabulary
- mixture
- organic compound
- enzyme
- inorganic compound

The Nature of Matter

Think about everything that surrounds you—chairs, books, clothing, other students, and air. What are all these things made up of? You're right if you answer "matter and energy." Matter is anything that has mass and takes up space. Energy is anything that brings about change. Everything in your environment, including you, is made of matter. Energy can hold matter together or break it apart. For example, the food you eat is matter that is held together by chemical energy. When food is cooked, energy in the form of heat can break some of the bonds holding the matter in food together.

Atoms Whether it is solid, liquid, or gas, matter is made of atoms. **Figure 1** shows a model of an oxygen atom. At the center of an atom is a nucleus that contains protons and neutrons. Although they have nearly equal masses, a proton has a positive charge and a neutron has no charge. Outside the nucleus are electrons, each of which has a negative charge. It takes about 1,837 electrons to equal the mass of one proton. Electrons are important because they are the part of the atom that is involved in chemical reactions. Look at **Figure 1** again and you will see that an atom is mostly empty space. Energy holds the parts of an atom together.

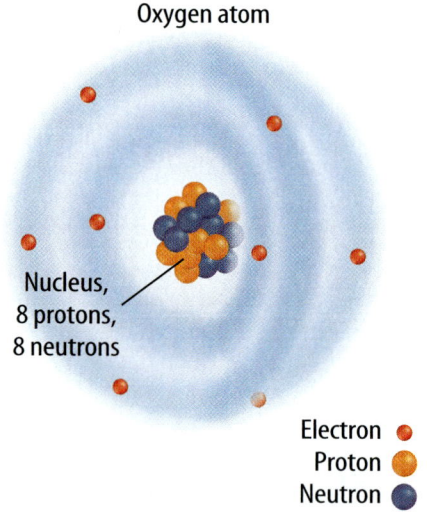

Figure 1 An oxygen atom model shows the placement of electrons, protons, and neutrons.

66   CHAPTER 3 Cell Processes

Table 1 Elements in the Human Body		
Symbol	Element	Percent
O	Oxygen	65.0
C	Carbon	18.5
H	Hydrogen	9.5
N	Nitrogen	3.2
Ca	Calcium	1.5
P	Phosphorus	1.0
K	Potassium	0.4
S	Sulfur	0.3
Na	Sodium	0.2
Cl	Chlorine	0.2
Mg	Magnesium	0.1
	Other elements	0.1

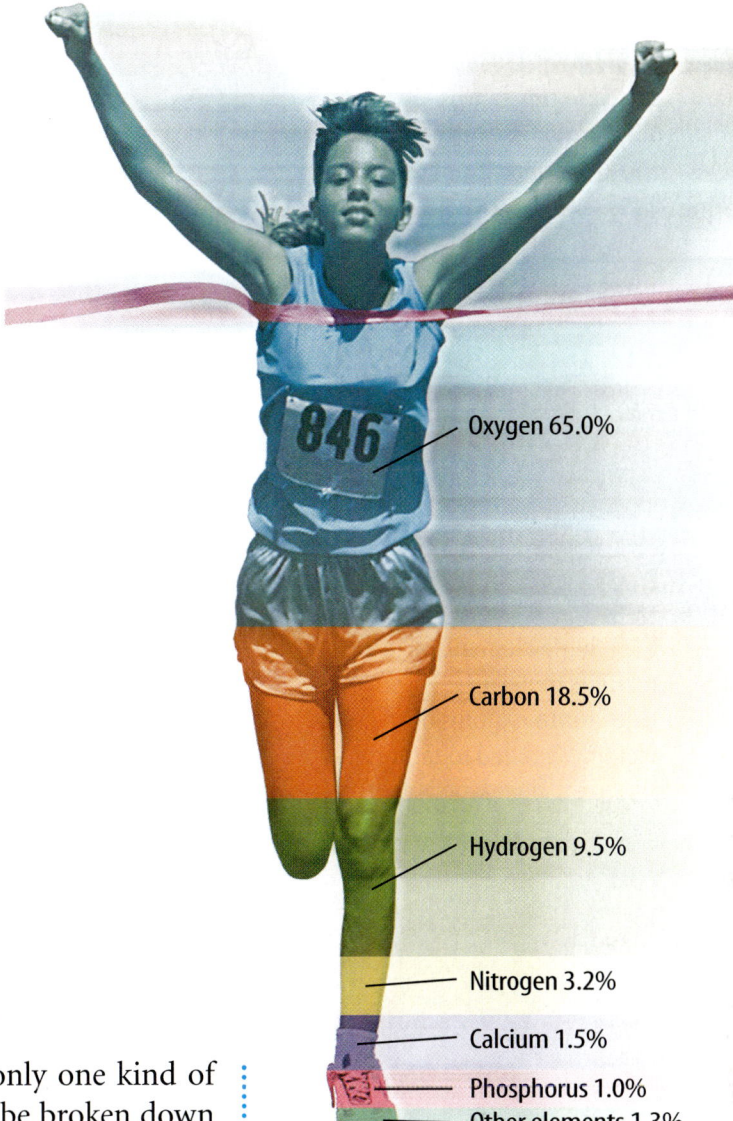

Elements When something is made up of only one kind of atom, it is called an element. An element can't be broken down into a simpler form by chemical reactions. The element oxygen is made up of only oxygen atoms, and hydrogen is made up of only hydrogen atoms. Scientists have given each element its own one- or two-letter symbol.

All elements are arranged in a chart known as the periodic table of elements. You can find this table at the back of this book. The table provides information about each element including its mass, how many protons it has, and its symbol.

Everything is made up of elements. Most things, including all living things, are made up of a combination of elements. Few things exist as pure elements. **Table 1** lists elements that are in the human body. What two elements make up most of your body?

Six of the elements listed in the table are important because they make up about 99 percent of living matter. The symbols for these elements are S, P, O, N, C, and H. Use **Table 1** to find the names of these elements.

 *What types of things are made up of elements?*

Figure 2 The words *atoms, molecules,* and *compounds* are used to describe substances.
Explain how these terms are related to each other.

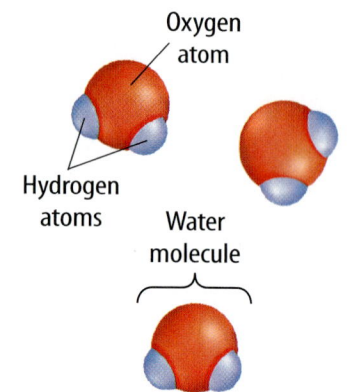

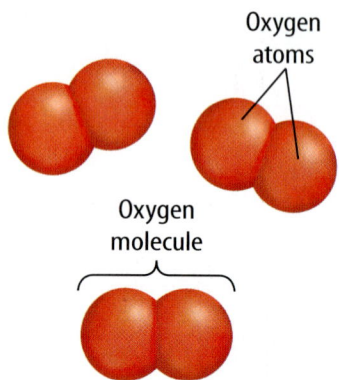

A Some elements, like oxygen, occur as molecules. These molecules contain atoms of the same element bonded together.

B Compounds also are composed of molecules. Molecules of compounds contain atoms of two or more different elements bonded together, as shown by these water molecules.

Compounds and Molecules

Suppose you make a pitcher of lemonade using a powdered mix and water. The water and the lemonade mix, which is mostly sugar, contain the elements oxygen and hydrogen. Yet, in one, they are part of a nearly tasteless liquid—water. In the other they are part of a sweet solid—sugar. How can the same elements be part of two materials that are so different? Water and sugar are compounds. Compounds are made up of two or more elements in exact proportions. For example, pure water, whether one milliliter of it or one million liters, is always made up of hydrogen atoms bonded to oxygen atoms in a ratio of two hydrogen atoms to one oxygen atom. Compounds have properties different from the elements they are made of. There are two types of compounds—molecular compounds and ionic compounds.

Molecular Compounds The smallest part of a molecular compound is a molecule. A molecule is a group of atoms held together by the energy of chemical bonds, as shown in **Figure 2**. When chemical reactions occur, chemical bonds break, atoms are rearranged, and new bonds form. The molecules produced are different from those that began the chemical reaction.

Molecular compounds form when different atoms share their outermost electrons. For example, two atoms of hydrogen each can share one electron on one atom of oxygen to form one molecule of water, as shown in **Figure 2B**. Water does not have the same properties as oxygen and hydrogen. Under normal conditions on Earth, oxygen and hydrogen are gases. Yet, water can be a liquid, a solid, or a gas. When hydrogen and oxygen combine, changes occur and a new substance forms.

Ions Atoms also combine because they've become positively or negatively charged. Atoms are usually neutral—they have no overall electric charge. When an atom loses an electron, it has more protons than electrons, so it becomes positively charged. When an atom gains an electron, it has more electrons than protons, so it becomes negatively charged. Electrically charged atoms—positive or negative—are called ions.

Ionic Compounds Ions of opposite charges attract one another to form electrically neutral compounds called ionic compounds. Table salt is made of sodium (Na) and chlorine (Cl) ions, as shown in **Figure 3B.** When they combine, a chlorine atom gains an electron from a sodium atom. The chlorine atom becomes a negatively charged ion, and the sodium atom becomes a positively charged ion. These oppositely charged ions then are attracted to each other and form the ionic compound sodium chloride, NaCl.

Ions are important in many life processes that take place in your body and in other organisms. For example, messages are sent along your nerves as potassium and sodium ions move in and out of nerve cells. Calcium ions are important in causing your muscles to contract. Ions also are involved in the transport of oxygen by your blood. The movement of some substances into and out of a cell would not be possible without ions.

A Magnified crystals of salt look like this.

B A salt crystal is held together by the attractions between sodium ions and chlorine ions.

Figure 3 Table salt crystals are held together by ionic bonds.

Mixtures

Some substances, such as a combination of sugar and salt, can't change each other or combine chemically. A **mixture** is a combination of substances in which individual substances retain their own properties. Mixtures can be solids, liquids, gases, or any combination of them.

 *Why is a combination of sugar and salt said to be a mixture?*

Most chemical reactions in living organisms take place in mixtures called solutions. You've probably noticed the taste of salt when you perspire. Sweat is a solution of salt and water. In a solution, two or more substances are mixed evenly. A cell's cytoplasm is a solution of dissolved molecules and ions.

Living things also contain mixtures called suspensions. A suspension is formed when a liquid or a gas has another substance evenly spread throughout it. Unlike solutions, the substances in a suspension eventually sink to the bottom. If blood, shown in **Figure 4,** is left undisturbed, the red blood cells and white blood cells will sink gradually to the bottom. However, the pumping action of your heart constantly moves your blood and the blood cells remain suspended.

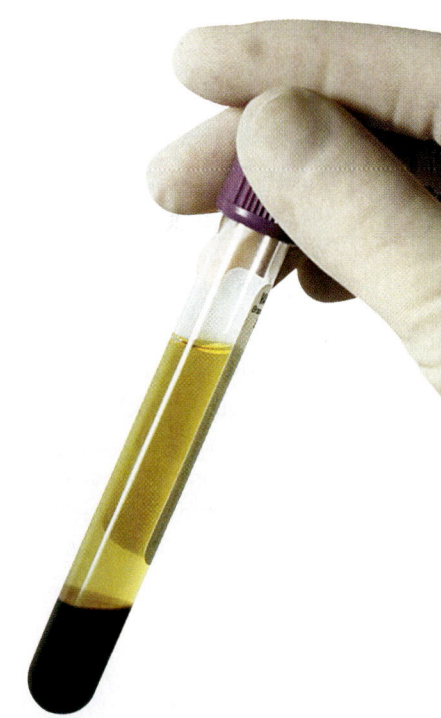

Figure 4 When a test tube of whole blood is left standing, the blood cells sink in the watery plasma.

SECTION 1 Chemistry of Life

Table 2 Organic Compounds Found in Living Things

	Carbohydrates	Lipids	Proteins	Nucleic Acids
Elements	carbon, hydrogen, and oxygen	carbon, oxygen, hydrogen, and phosphorus	carbon, oxygen, hydrogen, nitrogen, and sulfur	carbon, oxygen, hydrogen, nitrogen, and phosphorus
Examples	sugars, starch, and cellulose	fats, oils, waxes, phospholipids, and cholesterol	enzymes, skin, and hair	DNA and RNA
Function	supply energy for cell processes; form plant structures; short-term energy storage	store large amounts of energy long term; form boundaries around cells	regulate cell processes and build cell structures	carry hereditary information; used to make proteins

Topic: Air Quality
Visit in7.msscience.com for Web links to information about air quality.

Activity Organic compounds such as soot, smoke, and ash can affect air quality. Look up the air quality forecast for today. List three locations where the air quality forecast is good, and three locations where it is unhealthy.

Organic Compounds

You and all living things are made up of compounds that are classified as organic or inorganic. Rocks and other nonliving things contain inorganic compounds, but most do not contain large amounts of organic compounds. **Organic compounds** always contain carbon and hydrogen and usually are associated with living things. One exception would be nonliving things that are products of living things. For example, coal contains organic compounds because it was formed from dead and decaying plants. Organic molecules can contain hundreds or even thousands of atoms that can be arranged in many ways. **Table 2** compares the four groups of organic compounds that make up all living things—carbohydrates, lipids, proteins, and nucleic acids.

Carbohydrates Carbohydrates are organic molecules that supply energy for cell processes. Sugars and starches are carbohydrates that cells use for energy. Some carbohydrates also are important parts of cell structures. For example, a carbohydrate called cellulose is an important part of plant cells.

Lipids Another type of organic compound found in living things is a lipid. Lipids do not mix with water. Lipids such as fats and oils store and release even larger amounts of energy than carbohydrates do. One type of lipid, the phospholipid, is a major part of cell membranes.

 *What are three types of lipids?*

Proteins Organic compounds called proteins have many important functions in living organisms. They are made up of smaller molecules called amino acids. Proteins are the building blocks of many structures in organisms. Your muscles contain large amounts of protein. Proteins are scattered throughout cell membranes. Certain proteins called **enzymes** regulate nearly all chemical reactions in cells.

Nucleic Acids Large organic molecules that store important coded information in cells are called nucleic acids. One nucleic acid, deoxyribonucleic acid, or DNA—genetic material—is found in all cells at some point in their lives. It carries information that directs each cell's activities. Another nucleic acid, ribonucleic acid, or RNA, is needed to make enzymes and other proteins.

Inorganic Compounds

Most **inorganic compounds** are made from elements other than carbon. Generally, inorganic molecules contain fewer atoms than organic molecules. Inorganic compounds are the source for many elements needed by living things. For example, plants take up inorganic compounds from the soil. These inorganic compounds can contain the elements nitrogen, phosphorus, and sulfur. Many foods that you eat contain inorganic compounds. **Table 3** shows some of the inorganic compounds that are important to you. One of the most important inorganic compounds for living things is water.

Mini LAB

Observing How Enzymes Work

Procedure
1. Get two small cups of **prepared gelatin** from your teacher. Do not eat or drink anything in lab.
2. On the gelatin in one of the cups, place a piece of **fresh pineapple**.
3. Let both cups stand undisturbed overnight.
4. Observe what happens to the gelatin.

Analysis
1. What effect did the piece of fresh pineapple have on the gelatin?
2. What does fresh pineapple contain that caused it to have the effect on the gelatin you observed?
3. Why do the preparation directions on a box of gelatin dessert tell you not to mix it with fresh pineapple?

Table 3 Some Inorganic Compounds Important in Humans	
Compound	**Use in Body**
Water	makes up most of the blood; most chemical reactions occur in water
Calcium phosphate	gives strength to bones
Hydrochloric acid	breaks down foods in the stomach
Sodium bicarbonate	helps the digestion of food to occur
Salts containing sodium, chlorine, and potassium	important in sending messages along nerves

SECTION 1 Chemistry of Life

Indiana Academic Standard Check

7.3.13: Explain that many substances dissolve in water....

✓ Why are water solutions important to living things?

Importance of Water Some scientists hypothesize that life began in the water of Earth's ancient oceans. Chemical reactions might have occurred that produced organic molecules. Similar chemical reactions can take place in cells in your body.

Living things are composed of more than 50 percent water and depend on water to survive. You can live for weeks without food but only for a few days without water. **Figure 5** shows where water is found in your body. Although seeds and spores of plants, fungi, and bacteria can exist without water, they must have water if they are to grow and reproduce. All the chemical reactions in living things take place in water solutions, and most organisms use water to transport materials through their bodies. For example, many animals have blood that is mostly water and moves materials. Plants use water to move minerals and sugars between the roots and leaves.

Applying Math — Solve an Equation

CALCULATE THE IMPORTANCE OF WATER All life on Earth depends on water for survival. Water is the most vital part of humans and other animals. It is required for all of the chemical processes that keep us alive. At least 60 percent of an adult human body consists of water. If an adult man weighs 90 kg, how many kilograms of water does his body contain?

Solution

1 *This is what you know:*
- adult human body = 60% water
- man = 90 kg

2 *This is what you need to find:*
How many kilograms of water does the adult man have?

3 *This is the procedure you need to use:*
- Set up the ratio: 60/100 = x/90.
- Solve the equation for x: (60 × 90)/100.
- The adult man has 54 kg of water.

4 *Check your answer:*
Divide your answer by 90, then multiply by 100. You should get 60%.

Practice Problems

1. A human body at birth consists of 78 percent water. This gradually decreases to 60 percent in an adult. Assume a baby weighed 3.2 kg at birth and grew into an adult weighing 95 kg. Calculate the approximate number of kilograms of water the human gained.

2. Assume an adult woman weighs 65 kg and an adult man weighs 90 kg. Calculate how much more water, in kilograms, the man has compared to the woman.

For more practice, visit in7.msscience.com/math_practice

INTEGRATE Physics

Characteristics of Water The atoms of a water molecule are arranged in such a way that the molecule has areas with different charges. Water molecules are like magnets. The negative part of a water molecule is attracted to the positive part of another water molecule just like the north pole of a magnet is attracted to the south pole of another magnet. This attraction, or force, between water molecules is why a film forms on the surface of water. The film is strong enough to support small insects because the forces between water molecules are stronger than the force of gravity on the insect.

When heat is added to any substance, its molecules begin to move faster. Because water molecules are so strongly attracted to each other, the temperature of water changes slowly. The large percentage of water in living things acts like an insulator. The water in a cell helps keep its temperature constant, which allows life-sustaining chemical reactions to take place.

You've seen ice floating on water. When water freezes, ice crystals form. In the crystals, each water molecule is spaced at a certain distance from all the others. Because this distance is greater in frozen water than in liquid water, ice floats on water. Bodies of water freeze from the top down. The floating ice provides insulation from extremely cold temperatures and allows living things to survive in the cold water under the ice.

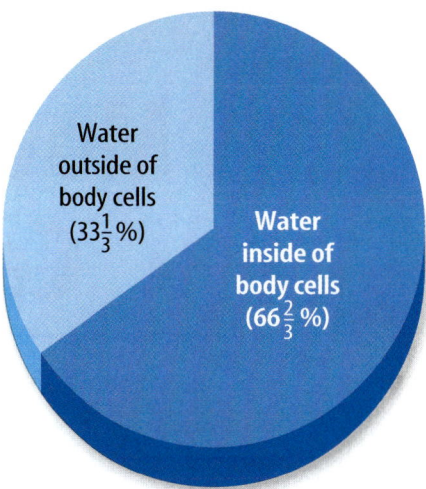

Figure 5 About two-thirds of your body's water is located within your body's cells. Water helps maintain the cells' shapes and sizes. One-third of your body's water is outside of your body's cells.

section 1 review

Summary

The Nature of Matter
- Atoms are made up of protons, neutrons, and electrons.
- Elements are made up of only one kind of atom.
- Compounds are made up of two or more elements.

Mixtures
- Solutions are made of two or more substances and are mixed evenly, whereas substances in suspension eventually will sink to the bottom.

Organic Compounds
- All living things contain organic compounds.

Inorganic Compounds
- Water is one of the most important inorganic compounds for living things.

Self Check

1. **Compare and contrast** atoms and molecules.
2. **Describe** the differences between an organic and an inorganic compound. Given an example of each type of compound.
3. **List** the four types of organic compounds found in all living things.
4. **Infer** why life as we know it depends on water.
5. **Think Critically** If you mix salt, sand, and sugar with water in a small jar, will the resulting mixture be a suspension, a solution, or both?

Applying Skills

6. **Interpret** Carefully observe **Figure 1** and determine how many protons, neutrons, and electrons an atom of oxygen has.

in7.msscience.com/self_check_quiz

SECTION 1 Chemistry of Life **73**

SECTION 2

Moving Cellular Materials

As You Read

What You'll Learn
- **Describe** the function of a selectively permeable membrane.
- **Explain** how the processes of diffusion and osmosis move molecules in living cells.
- **Explain** how passive transport and active transport differ.

Why It's Important
Cell membranes control the substances that enter and leave the cells in your body.

Review Vocabulary
cytoplasm: constantly moving gel-like mixture inside the cell membrane that contains hereditary material and is the location of most of a cell's life process

New Vocabulary
- passive transport
- diffusion
- equilibrium
- osmosis
- active transport
- endocytosis
- exocytosis

Passive Transport

"Close that window. Do you want to let in all the bugs and leaves?" How do you prevent unwanted things from coming through the window? As seen in **Figure 6,** a window screen provides the protection needed to keep unwanted things outside. It also allows some things to pass into or out of the room like air, unpleasant odors, or smoke.

Cells take in food, oxygen, and other substances from their environments. They also release waste materials into their environments. A cell has a membrane around it that works for a cell like a window screen does for a room. A cell's membrane is selectively permeable (PUR mee uh bul). It allows some things to enter or leave the cell while keeping other things outside or inside the cell. The window screen also is selectively permeable based on the size of its openings.

Things can move through a cell membrane in several ways. Which way things move depends on the size of the molecules or particles, the path taken through the membrane, and whether or not energy is used. The movement of substances through the cell membrane without the input of energy is called **passive transport**. Three types of passive transport can occur. The type depends on what is moving through the cell membrane.

Figure 6 A cell membrane, like a screen, will let some things through more easily than others. Air gets through a screen, but insects are kept out.

74 CHAPTER 3 Cell Processes

Figure 7 Like all other cells in your body, cells in your toes need oxygen.
Describe What is diffusion?

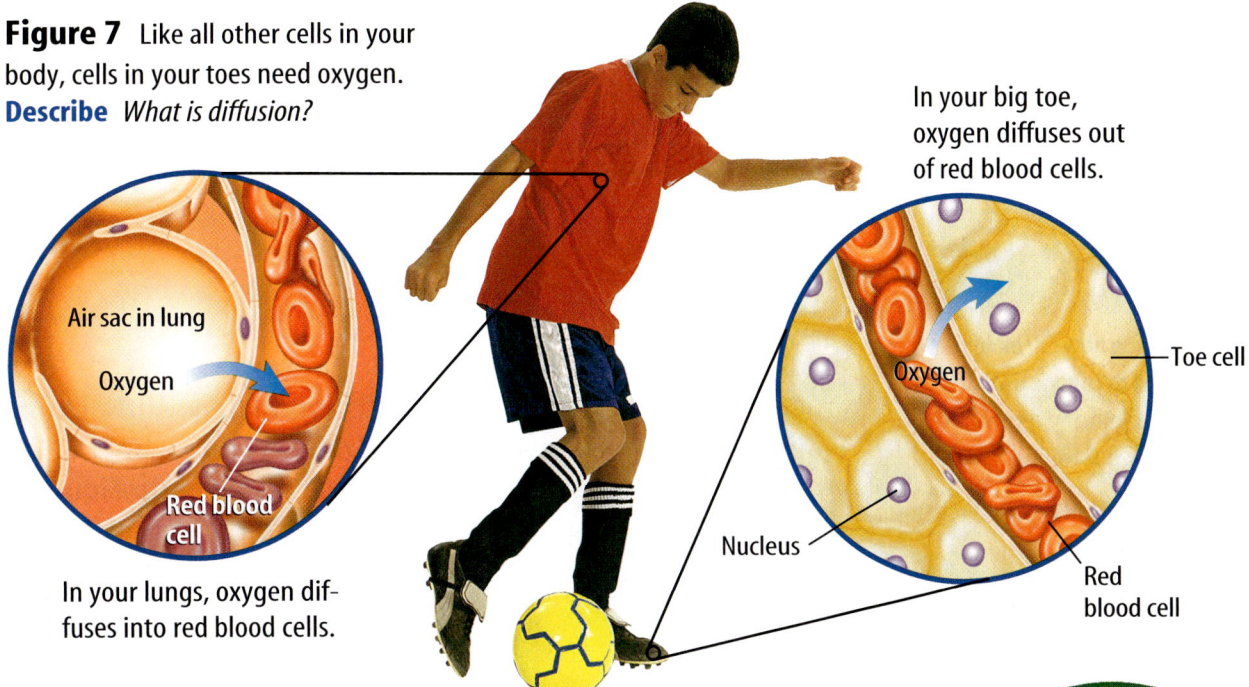

In your lungs, oxygen diffuses into red blood cells.

In your big toe, oxygen diffuses out of red blood cells.

Diffusion Molecules in solids, liquids, and gases move constantly and randomly. You might smell perfume when you sit near or as you walk past someone who is wearing it. This is because perfume molecules randomly move throughout the air. This random movement of molecules from an area where there is relatively more of them into an area where there is relatively fewer of them is called **diffusion**. Diffusion is one type of cellular passive transport. Molecules of a substance will continue to move from one area into another until the relative number of these molecules is equal in the two areas. When this occurs, **equilibrium** is reached and diffusion stops. After equilibrium occurs, it is maintained because molecules continue to move.

Reading Check What is equilibrium?

Every cell in your body uses oxygen. When you breathe, how does oxygen get from your lungs to cells in your big toe? Oxygen is carried throughout your body in your blood by the red blood cells. When your blood is pumped from your heart to your lungs, your red blood cells do not contain much oxygen. However, your lungs have more oxygen molecules than your red blood cells do, so the oxygen molecules diffuse into your red blood cells from your lungs, as shown in **Figure 7**. When the blood reaches your big toe, there are more oxygen molecules in your red blood cells than in your big toe cells. The oxygen diffuses from your red blood cells and into your big toe cells, as shown also in **Figure 7**.

Mini LAB

Observing Diffusion

Procedure
1. Use two clean glasses of equal size. Label one *Hot*, then fill it until half full with **very warm water**. Label the other *Cold*, then fill it until half full with **cold water**. **WARNING:** *Do not use boiling hot water.*
2. Add one drop of **food coloring** to each glass. Carefully release the drop just at the water's surface to avoid splashing the water.
3. Observe the water in the glasses. Record your observations immediately and again after 15 min.

Analysis
1. Describe what happens when food coloring is added to each glass.
2. How does temperature affect the rate of diffusion?

Try at Home

SECTION 2 Moving Cellular Materials

> **Indiana Academic Standard Check**
>
> **7.7.3:** Describe how . . . biological systems tend to change until they reach equilibrium and remain that way unless their surrounds change.
>
> ✓ How do molecules undergo diffusion?

Osmosis—The Diffusion of Water Remember that water makes up a large part of living matter. Cells contain water and are surrounded by water. Water molecules move by diffusion into and out of cells. The diffusion of water through a cell membrane is called **osmosis.**

If cells weren't surrounded by water that contains few dissolved substances, water inside of cells would diffuse out of them. This is why water left the carrot cells in this chapter's Launch Lab. Because there were relatively fewer water molecules in the salt solution around the carrot cells than in the carrot cells, water moved out of the cells and into the salt solution.

Losing water from a plant cell causes its cell membrane to come away from its cell wall, as shown on the left in **Figure 8.** This reduces pressure against its cell wall, and a plant cell becomes limp. If the carrot sticks were taken out of salt water and put in pure water, the water around the cells would move into them and they would fill with water. Their cell membranes would press against their cell walls, as shown on the right in **Figure 8,** pressure would increase, and the cells would become firm. That is why the carrot sticks would be crisp again.

✓ **Reading Check** *Why do carrots in salt water become limp?*

Osmosis also takes place in animal cells. If animal cells were placed in pure water, they too would swell up. However, animal cells are different from plant cells. Just like an overfilled water balloon, animal cells will burst if too much water enters the cell.

Figure 8 Cells respond to differences between the amount of water inside and outside the cell. **Define** *What is osmosis?*

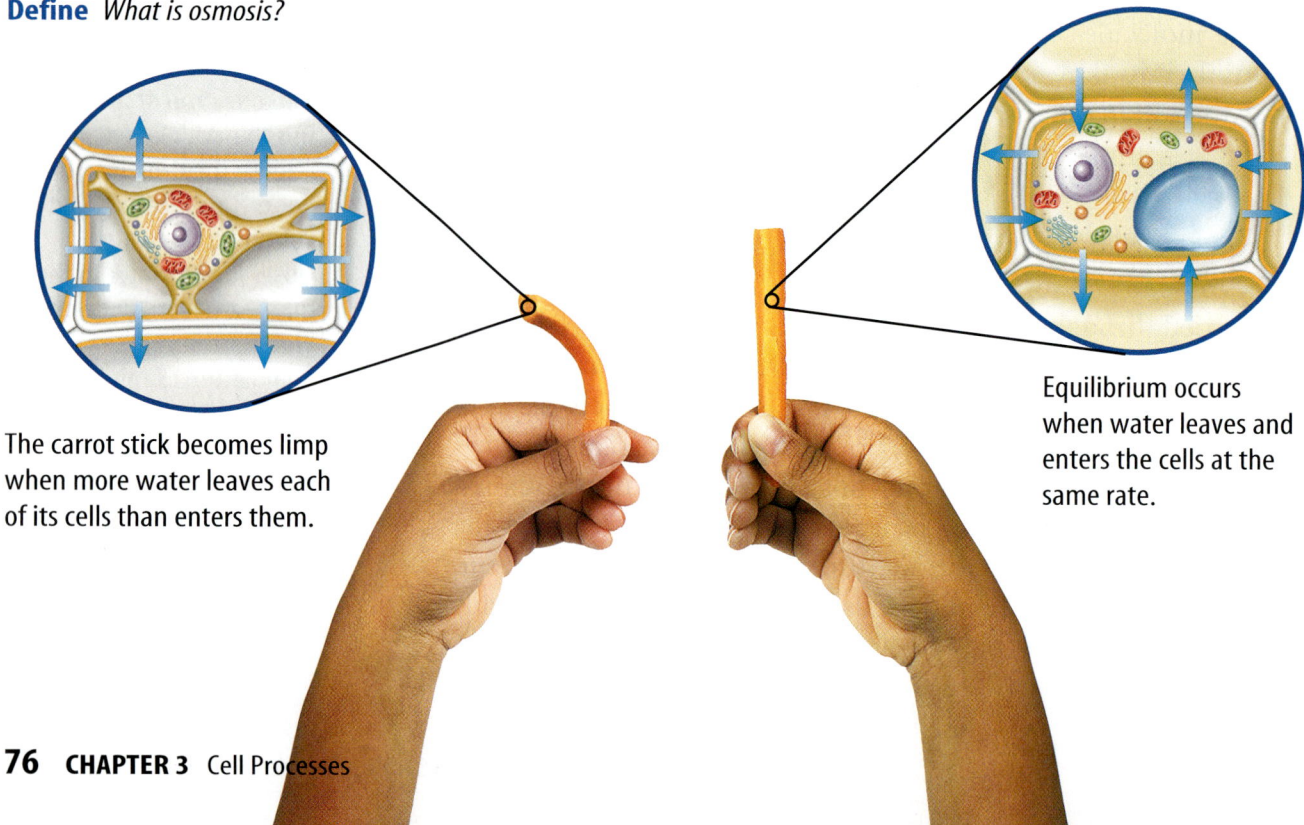

The carrot stick becomes limp when more water leaves each of its cells than enters them.

Equilibrium occurs when water leaves and enters the cells at the same rate.

Facilitated Diffusion Cells take in many substances. Some substances pass easily through the cell membrane by diffusion. Other substances, such as glucose molecules, are so large that they can enter the cell only with the help of molecules in the cell membrane called transport proteins. This process, a type of passive transport, is known as facilitated diffusion. Have you ever used the drive through at a fast-food restaurant to get your meal? The transport proteins in the cell membrane are like the drive-through window at the restaurant. The window lets you get food out of the restaurant and put money into the restaurant. Similarly, transport proteins are used to move substances into and out of the cell.

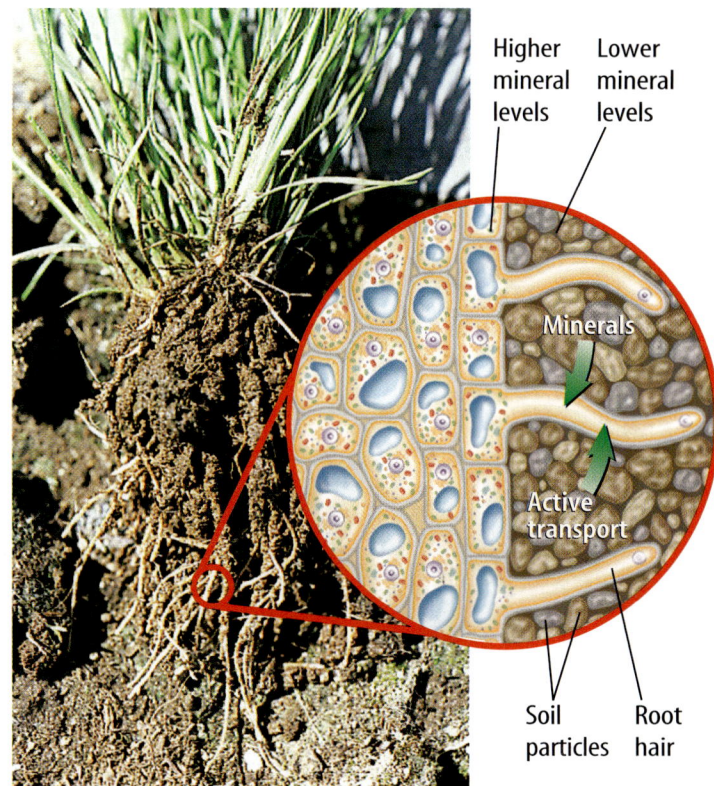

Active Transport

Imagine that a football game is over and you leave the stadium. As soon as you get outside of the stadium, you remember that you left your jacket on your seat. Now you have to move against the crowd coming out of the stadium to get back in to get your jacket. Which required more energy—leaving the stadium with the crowd or going back to get your jacket? Something similar to this happens in cells.

Sometimes, a substance is needed inside a cell even though the amount of that substance inside the cell is already greater than the amount outside the cell. For example, root cells require minerals from the soil. The roots of the plant in **Figure 9** already might contain more of those mineral molecules than the surrounding soil does. The tendency is for mineral molecules to move out of the root by diffusion or facilitated diffusion. But they need to move back across the cell membrane and into the cell just like you had to move back into the stadium. When an input of energy is required to move materials through a cell membrane, **active transport** takes place.

Active transport involves transport proteins, just as facilitated diffusion does. In active transport, a transport protein binds with the needed particle and cellular energy is used to move it through the cell membrane. When the particle is released, the transport protein can move another needed particle through the membrane.

Figure 9 Some root cells have extensions called root hairs that may be 5 mm to 8 mm long. Minerals are taken in by active transport through the cell membranes of root hairs.

Transport Proteins Your health depends on transport proteins. Sometimes transport proteins are missing or do not function correctly. What would happen if proteins that transport cholesterol across membranes were missing? Cholesterol is an important lipid used by your cells. Write your ideas in your Science Journal.

SECTION 2 Moving Cellular Materials

Endocytosis and Exocytosis

Some molecules and particles are too large to move by diffusion or to use the cell membrane's transport proteins. Large protein molecules and bacteria, for example, can enter a cell when they are surrounded by the cell membrane. The cell membrane folds in on itself, enclosing the item in a sphere called a vesicle. Vesicles are transport and storage structures in a cell's cytoplasm. The sphere pinches off, and the resulting vesicle enters the cytoplasm. A similar thing happens when you poke your finger into a partially inflated balloon. Your finger is surrounded by the balloon in much the same way that the protein molecule is surrounded by the cell membrane. This cell process that takes in a substance by surrounding it with the cell membrane is called **endocytosis** (en duh si TOH sus). Some one-celled organisms, as shown in **Figure 10,** take in food this way.

The contents of a vesicle can be released by a cell using the process called **exocytosis** (ek soh si TOH sus). Exocytosis occurs in the opposite way that endocytosis does. A vesicle's membrane fuses with a cell's membrane, and the vesicle's contents are released. Cells in your stomach use this process to release chemicals that help digest food. The ways that materials can enter or leave a cell are summarized in **Figure 11.**

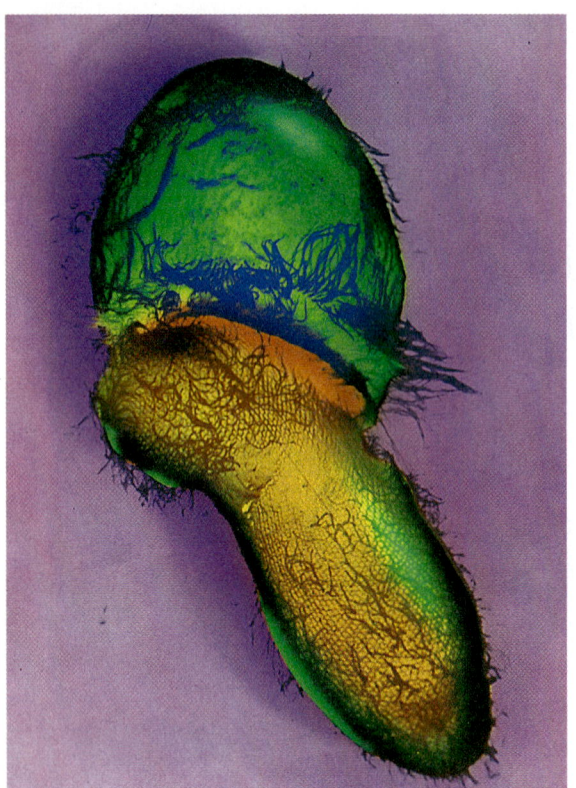

Color-enhanced TEM Magnification: 1,400×

Figure 10 One-celled organisms like this egg-shaped one can take in other one-celled organisms using endocytosis.

section 2 review

Summary

Passive Transport
- Cells take in substances and release waste through their cell membranes.
- Facilitated diffusion and osmosis are types of passive transport.

Active Transport
- Transport proteins are involved in active transport.
- Transport proteins can be reused many times.

Endocytosis and Exocytosis
- Vesicles are formed when a cell takes in a substance by endocytosis.
- Contents of a vesicle are released to the outside of a cell by exocytosis.

Self Check

1. **Describe** how cell membranes are selectively permeable.
2. **Compare and contrast** the processes of osmosis and diffusion.
3. **Infer** why endocytosis and exocytosis are important processes to cells.
4. **Think Critically** Why are fresh fruits and vegetables sprinkled with water at produce markets?

Applying Skills

5. **Communicate** Seawater is saltier than tap water. Explain why drinking large amounts of seawater would be dangerous for humans.

in7.msscience.com/self_check_quiz

NATIONAL GEOGRAPHIC VISUALIZING CELL MEMBRANE TRANSPORT

Figure 11

A flexible yet strong layer, the cell membrane is built of two layers of lipids (gold) pierced by protein "passageways" (purple). Molecules can enter or exit the cell by slipping between the lipids or through the protein passageways. Substances that cannot enter or exit the cell in these ways may be surrounded by the membrane and drawn into or expelled from the cell.

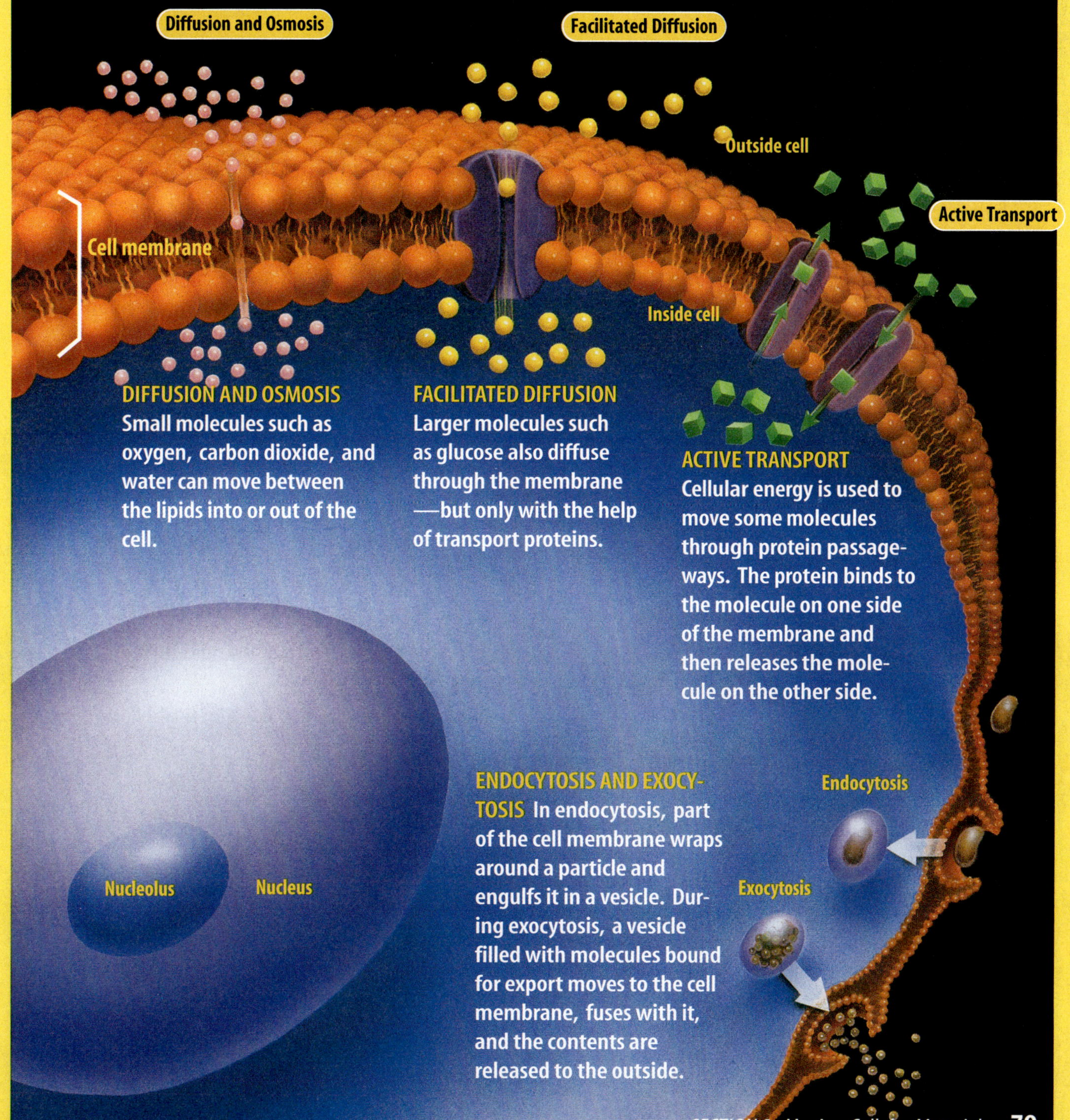

Diffusion and Osmosis

Facilitated Diffusion

Outside cell

Active Transport

Cell membrane

Inside cell

DIFFUSION AND OSMOSIS Small molecules such as oxygen, carbon dioxide, and water can move between the lipids into or out of the cell.

FACILITATED DIFFUSION Larger molecules such as glucose also diffuse through the membrane —but only with the help of transport proteins.

ACTIVE TRANSPORT Cellular energy is used to move some molecules through protein passageways. The protein binds to the molecule on one side of the membrane and then releases the molecule on the other side.

Nucleolus   Nucleus

ENDOCYTOSIS AND EXOCYTOSIS In endocytosis, part of the cell membrane wraps around a particle and engulfs it in a vesicle. During exocytosis, a vesicle filled with molecules bound for export moves to the cell membrane, fuses with it, and the contents are released to the outside.

Endocytosis

Exocytosis

SECTION 2 Moving Cellular Materials

Observing Osmosis

It is difficult to observe osmosis in cells because most cells are so small. However, a few cells can be seen without the aid of a microscope. Try this lab to observe osmosis.

Real-World Question

How does osmosis occur in an egg cell?

Materials

unshelled egg* distilled water (250 mL)
balance   light corn syrup (250 mL)
spoon   500-mL container

*an egg whose shell has been dissolved by vinegar

Goals
■ **Observe** osmosis in an egg cell.
■ **Determine** what affects osmosis.

Safety Precautions

WARNING: *Eggs may contain bacteria. Avoid touching your face.*

Procedure

1. Copy the table below into your Science Journal and use it to record your data.

Egg Mass Data		
	Beginning Egg Mass	Egg Mass After Two Days
Distilled water	Do not write in this book.	
Corn syrup		

2. Obtain an unshelled egg from your teacher. Handle the egg gently. Use a balance to find the egg's mass and record it in the table.

3. Place the egg in the container and add enough distilled water to cover it.

4. **Observe** the egg after 30 min, one day, and two days. After each observation, record the egg's appearance in your Science Journal.

5. After day two, remove the egg with a spoon and allow it to drain. Find the egg's mass and record it in the table.

6. Empty the container, then put the egg back in. Now add enough corn syrup to cover it. Repeat steps 4 and 5.

Conclude and Apply

1. **Explain** the difference between what happened to the egg in water and in corn syrup.
2. **Calculate** the mass of water that moved into and out of the egg.
3. **Hypothesize** why you used an unshelled egg for this investigation.
4. **Infer** what part of the egg controlled water's movement into and out of the egg.

Compare your conclusions with those of other students in your class. **For more help, refer to the Science Skill Handbook.**

section 3

Standards—7.4.5: Explain that the basic functions of organisms, such as extracting energy from food and getting rid of wastes, are carried out within the cell.... **7.4.7:** Describe how plants use the energy from light to make sugars from carbon dioxide and water to produce food that can be used immediately or stored for later use.

Also covers: 7.3.12, 7.3.14, 7.4.4, 7.4.8, 7.6.2, 7.7.1 (Detailed standards begin on page IN8.)

Energy for Life

Trapping and Using Energy

Think of all the energy that players use in a basketball game. Where does the energy come from? The simplest answer is "from the food they eat." The chemical energy stored in food molecules is changed inside of cells into forms needed to perform all the activities necessary for life. In every cell, these changes involve chemical reactions. All of the activities of an organism involve chemical reactions in some way. The total of all chemical reactions in an organism is called **metabolism**.

The chemical reactions of metabolism need enzymes. What do enzymes do? Suppose you are hungry and decide to open a can of spaghetti. You use a can opener to open the can. Without a can opener, the spaghetti is unusable. The can of spaghetti changes because of the can opener, but the can opener does not change. The can opener can be used again later to open more cans of spaghetti. Enzymes in cells work something like can openers. The enzyme, like the can opener, causes a change, but the enzyme is not changed and can be used again, as shown in **Figure 12.** Unlike the can opener, which can only cause things to come apart, enzymes also can cause molecules to join. Without the right enzyme, a chemical reaction in a cell cannot take place. Each chemical reaction in a cell requires a specific enzyme.

as you read

What You'll Learn
- **List** the differences between producers and consumers.
- **Explain** how the processes of photosynthesis and respiration store and release energy.
- **Describe** how cells get energy from glucose through fermentation.

Why It's Important
Because of photosynthesis and respiration, you use the Sun's energy.

Review Vocabulary
mitochondrion: cell organelle that breaks down lipids and carbohydrates and releases energy

New Vocabulary
- metabolism
- photosynthesis
- respiration
- fermentation

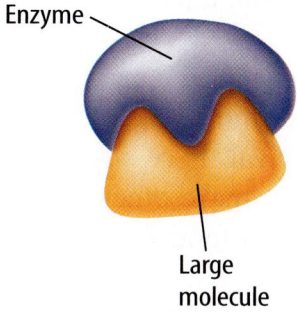
Large molecule

The enzyme attaches to the large molecule it will help change.

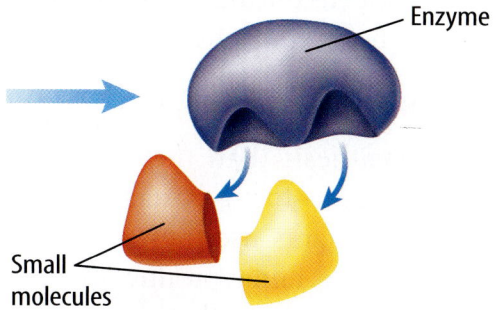
Small molecules

The enzyme causes the larger molecule to break down into two smaller molecules. The enzyme is not changed and can be used again.

Figure 12 Enzymes are needed for most chemical reactions that take place in cells.
Determine *What is the sum of all chemical reactions in an organism called?*

SECTION 3 Energy for Life **81**

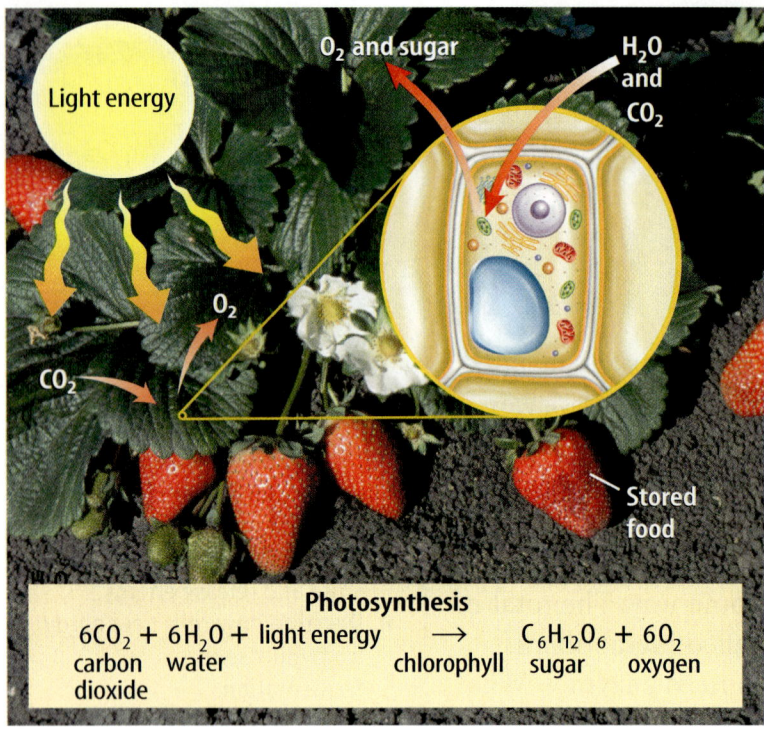

Photosynthesis Living things are divided into two groups—producers and consumers—based on how they obtain their food. Organisms that make their own food, such as plants, are called producers. Organisms that cannot make their own food are called consumers.

If you have ever walked barefoot across a sidewalk on a sunny summer day, you probably moved quickly because the sidewalk was hot. Sunlight energy was converted into thermal energy and heated the sidewalk. Plants and many other producers can convert light energy into another kind of energy—chemical energy. The process they use is called photosynthesis. During **photosynthesis,** producers use light energy to make sugars, which can be used as food.

Producing Carbohydrates Producers that use photosynthesis are usually green because they contain a green pigment called chlorophyll (KLOR uh fihl). Chlorophyll and other pigments are used in photosynthesis to capture light energy. In plant cells, these pigments are found in chloroplasts.

The captured light energy powers chemical reactions that produce sugar and oxygen from the raw materials, carbon dioxide and water. For plants, the raw materials come from air and soil. Some of the captured light energy is stored in the chemical bonds that hold the sugar molecules together. **Figure 13** shows what happens during photosynthesis in a plant. Enzymes also are needed before these reactions can occur.

Storing Carbohydrates Plants make more sugar during photosynthesis than they need for survival. Excess sugar is changed and stored as starches or used to make other carbohydrates. Plants use these carbohydrates as food for growth, maintenance, and reproduction.

Why is photosynthesis important to consumers? Do you eat apples? Apple trees use photosynthesis to produce apples. Do you like cheese? Some cheese comes from milk, which is produced by cows that eat plants. Consumers take in food by eating producers or other consumers. No matter what you eat, photosynthesis was involved directly or indirectly in its production.

Figure 13 Plants use photosynthesis to make food.
Determine According to the chemical equation, what raw materials would the plant in the photo need for photosynthesis?

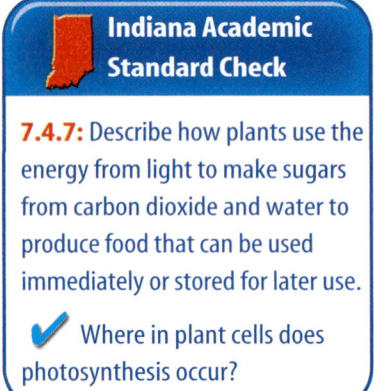

Indiana Academic Standard Check

7.4.7: Describe how plants use the energy from light to make sugars from carbon dioxide and water to produce food that can be used immediately or stored for later use.

✔ Where in plant cells does photosynthesis occur?

82 CHAPTER 3 Cell Processes

Respiration Imagine that you get up late for school. You dress quickly, then run three blocks to school. When you get to school, you feel hot and are breathing fast. Why? Your muscle cells use a lot of energy when you run. To get this energy, muscle cells break down food. Some of the energy from the food is used when you move and some of it becomes thermal energy, which is why you feel warm or hot. Most cells also need oxygen to break down food. You were breathing fast because your body was working to get oxygen to your muscles. Your muscle cells were using the oxygen for the process of respiration. During **respiration,** chemical reactions occur that break down food molecules into simpler substances and release their stored energy. Just as in photosynthesis, enzymes are needed for the chemical reactions of respiration.

 *What must happen to food molecules for respiration to take place?*

Breaking Down Carbohydrates The food molecules most easily broken down by cells are carbohydrates. Respiration of carbohydrates begins in the cytoplasm of the cell. The carbohydrates are broken down into glucose molecules. Each glucose molecule is broken down further into two simpler molecules. As the glucose molecules are broken down, energy is released.

The two simpler molecules are broken down again. This breakdown occurs in the mitochondria of the cells of plants, animals, fungi, and many other organisms. This process uses oxygen, releases much more energy, and produces carbon dioxide and water as wastes. When you exhale, you breathe out carbon dioxide and some of the water.

Respiration occurs in the cells of all living things. **Figure 14** shows how respiration occurs in one consumer. As you are reading this section of the chapter, millions of cells in your body are breaking down glucose, releasing energy, and producing carbon dioxide and water.

Microbiologist Dr. Harold Amos is a microbiologist who has studied cell processes in bacteria and mammals. He has a medical degree and a doctorate in bacteriology and immunology. He has also received many awards for his scientific work and his contributions to the careers of other scientists. Research microbiology careers, and write what you find in your Science Journal.

Figure 14 Producers and consumers carry on respiration that releases energy from foods.

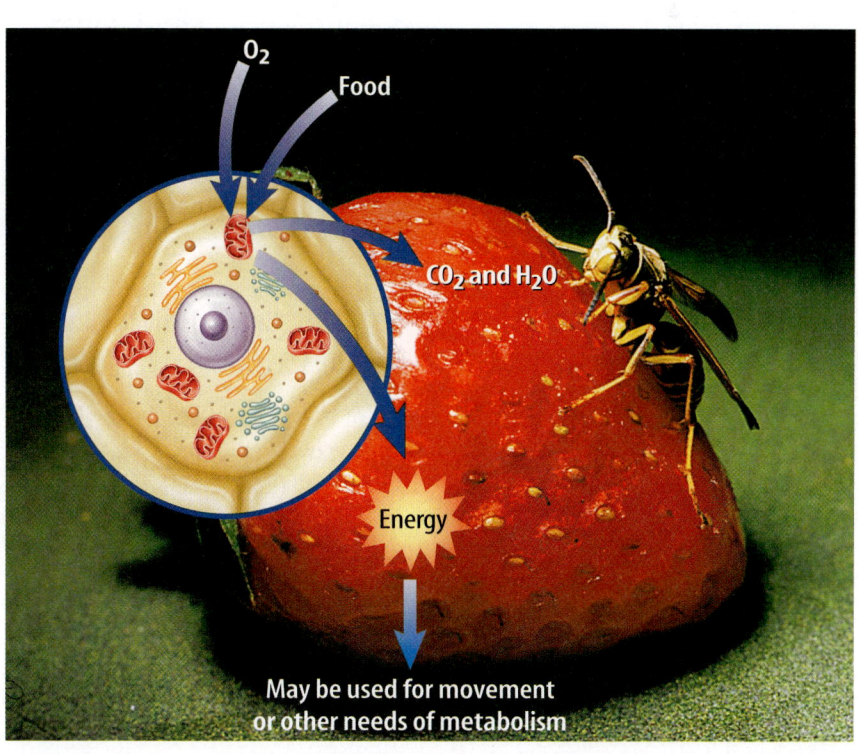

SECTION 3 Energy for Life **83**

Science Online

Topic: Beneficial Microorganisms

Visit in7.msscience.com for Web links to information about how microorganisms are used to produce many useful products.

Activity Find three other ways that microorganisms are beneficial.

Indiana Academic Standard Check

7.4.5: Explain that the basic functions of organisms, such as extracting energy from food....

✓ Where does fermentation occur in a cell?

Figure 15 Organisms that use fermentation produce several different wastes.

Fermentation Remember imagining you were late and had to run to school? During your run, your muscle cells might not have received enough oxygen, even though you were breathing rapidly. When cells do not have enough oxygen for respiration, they use a process called **fermentation** to release some of the energy stored in glucose molecules.

Like respiration, fermentation begins in the cytoplasm. Again, as the glucose molecules are broken down, energy is released. But the simple molecules from the breakdown of glucose do not move into the mitochondria. Instead, more chemical reactions occur in the cytoplasm. These reactions release some energy and produce wastes. Depending on the type of cell, the wastes may be lactic acid or alcohol and carbon dioxide, as shown in **Figure 15.** Your muscle cells can use fermentation to change the simple molecules into lactic acid while releasing energy. The presence of lactic acid is why your muscle cells might feel stiff and sore after you run to school.

✓ **Reading Check** Where in a cell does fermentation take place?

Some microscopic organisms, such as bacteria, carry out fermentation and make lactic acid. Some of these organisms are used to produce yogurt and some cheeses. These organisms break down a sugar in milk and release energy. The lactic acid produced causes the milk to become more solid and gives these foods some of their flavor.

Have you ever used yeast to make bread? Yeasts are one-celled living organisms. Yeast cells use fermentation and break down sugar in bread dough. They produce alcohol and carbon dioxide as wastes. The carbon dioxide waste is a gas that makes bread dough rise before it is baked. The alcohol is lost as the bread bakes.

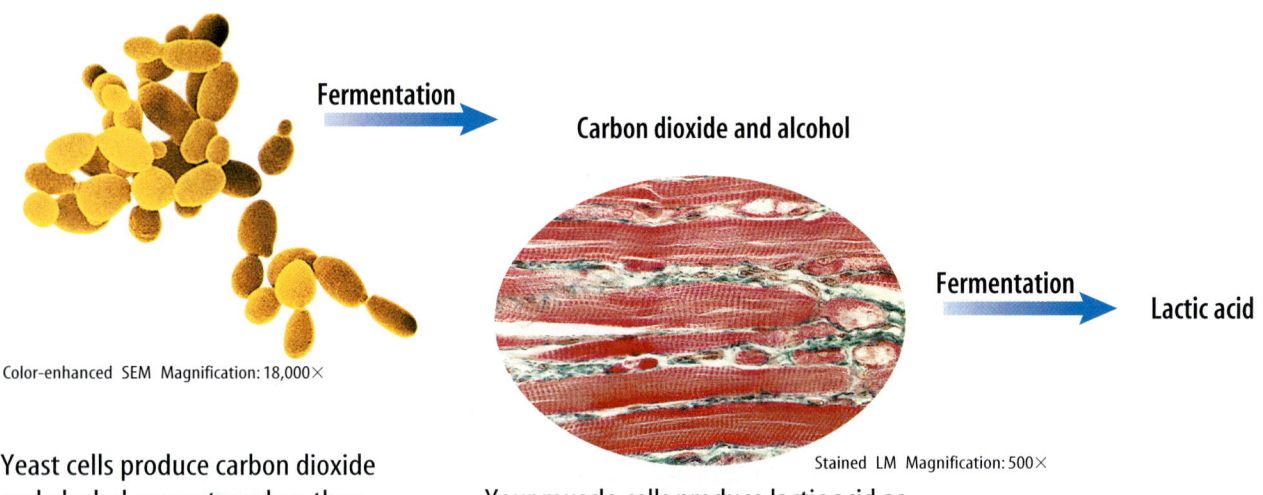

Color-enhanced SEM Magnification: 18,000×

Yeast cells produce carbon dioxide and alcohol as wastes when they undergo fermentation.

Stained LM Magnification: 500×

Your muscle cells produce lactic acid as a waste when they use fermentation.

Figure 16 The chemical reactions of photosynthesis and respiration could not take place without each other.

Related Processes How are photosynthesis, respiration, and fermentation related? Some producers use photosynthesis to make food. All living things use respiration or fermentation to release energy stored in food. If you think carefully about what happens during photosynthesis and respiration, you will see that what is produced in one is used in the other, as shown in **Figure 16**. These two processes are almost the opposite of each other. Photosynthesis produces sugars and oxygen, and respiration uses these products. The carbon dioxide and water produced during respiration are used during photosynthesis. Most life would not be possible without these important chemical reactions.

section 3 review

Summary

Trapping and Using Energy
- Metabolism is the total of all chemical reactions in an organism.
- During photosynthesis, light energy is used to make sugars.
- Chlorophyll and other pigments capture light energy.
- Consumers take in energy by eating producers and other consumers.
- Living cells break down glucose and release energy. This is called respiration.
- Fermentation changes simple molecules and releases energy.
- Without photosynthesis and respiration, most life would not be possible.

Self Check

1. **Explain** the difference between producers and consumers and give three examples of each.
2. **Infer** how the energy used by many living things on Earth can be traced back to sunlight.
3. **Compare and contrast** respiration and fermentation.
4. **Think Critically** How can some indoor plants help to improve the quality of air in a room?

Applying Math

5. **Solve** Refer to the chemical equation for photosynthesis. Calculate then compare the number of carbon, hydrogen, and oxygen atoms before and after photosynthesis.

Photosynthesis and Respiration

LM Magnification: 225×

Goals
- **Observe** green water plants in the light and dark.
- **Determine** whether plants carry on photosynthesis and respiration.

Materials
16-mm test tubes (3)
150-mm test tubes with stoppers (4)
*small, clear-glass baby food jars with lids (4)
test-tube rack
stirring rod
scissors
carbonated water (5 mL)
bromthymol blue solution in dropper bottle
aged tap water (20 mL)
*distilled water (20 mL)
sprigs of *Elodea* (2)
*other water plants
*Alternate materials

Safety Precautions

WARNING: *Wear splash-proof safety goggles to protect eyes from hazardous chemicals.*

Real-World Question

Every living cell carries on many chemical processes. Two important chemical processes are respiration and photosynthesis. All cells, including the ones in your body, carry on respiration. However, some plant cells can carry on both processes. In this experiment you will investigate when these processes occur in plant cells. How could you find out when plants were using these processes? Are the products of photosynthesis and respiration the same? When do plants carry on photosynthesis and respiration?

Procedure

1. In your Science Journal, copy and complete the test-tube data table as you perform this lab.

Test-Tube Data		
Test Tube	Color at Start	Color After 30 Minutes
1		
2	Do not write in this book.	
3		
4		

86 CHAPTER 3 Cell Processes

Using Scientific Methods

2. Label each test tube using the numbers *1, 2, 3,* and *4*. Pour 5 mL of aged tap water into each test tube.
3. Add 10 drops of carbonated water to test tubes *1* and *2*.
4. Add 10 drops of bromthymol blue to all of the test tubes. Bromthymol blue turns green to yellow in the presence of an acid.
5. Cut two 10-cm sprigs of *Elodea*. Place one sprig in test tube *1* and one sprig in test tube *3*. Stopper all test tubes.
6. Place test tubes *1* and *2* in bright light. Place tubes *3* and *4* in the dark. Observe the test tubes for 45 min or until the color changes. Record the color of each of the four test tubes.

Analyze Your Data

1. **Identify** what is indicated by the color of the water in all four test tubes at the start of the activity.
2. **Infer** what process occurred in the test tube or tubes that changed color after 30 min.

Conclude and Apply

1. **Describe** the purpose of test tubes *2* and *4* in this experiment.
2. **Explain** whether or not the results of this experiment show that photosynthesis and respiration occur in plants.

Communicating Your Data

Choose one of the following activities to **communicate** your data. Prepare an oral presentation that explains how the experiment showed the differences between products of photosynthesis and respiration. Draw a cartoon strip to **explain** what you did in this experiment. Use each panel to show a different step. **For more help, refer to the Science Skill Handbook.**

LAB **87**

Science and Language Arts

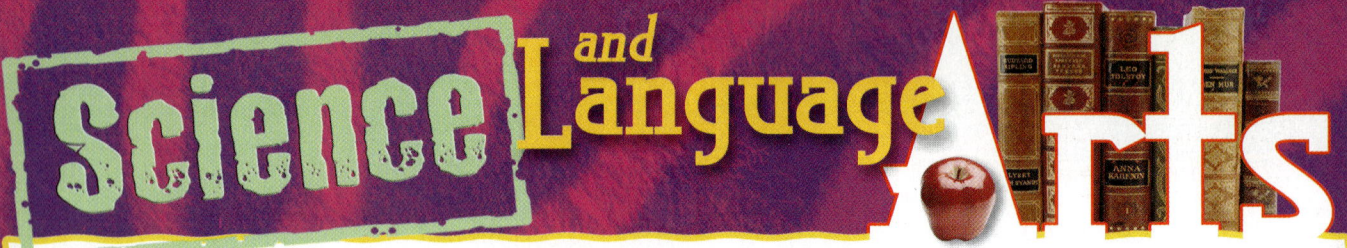

from "Tulip"
by Penny Harter

I watched its first green push
through bare dirt, where the builders
had dropped boards, shingles,
plaster—
killing everything.
    I could not recall what grew there,
what returned each spring,
but the leaves looked tulip,
and one morning it arrived,
a scarlet slash against the aluminum siding.
    Mornings, on the way to my car,
I bow to the still bell
of its closed petals; evenings,
it greets me, light ringing
at the end of my driveway.
    Sometimes I kneel
to stare into the yellow throat . . . .
It opens and closes my days.
It has made me weak with love . . . .

Understanding Literature

Personification Using human traits or emotions to describe an idea, animal, or inanimate object is called personification. When the poet writes that the tulip has a "yellow throat," she uses personification. Where else does the poet use personification?

Respond to the Reading

1. Why do you suppose the tulip survived the builders' abuse?
2. What is the yellow throat that the narrator is staring into?
3. **Linking Science and Writing** Keep a gardener's journal of a plant for a month, describing weekly the plant's condition, size, health, color, and other physical qualities.

 Because most chemical reactions in plants take place in water, plants must have water in order to grow. The water carries nutrients and minerals from the soil into the plant. The process of active transport allows needed nutrients to enter the roots. The cell membranes of root cells contain proteins that bind with the needed nutrients. Cellular energy is used to move these nutrients through the cell membrane.

Chapter 3 Study Guide

Reviewing Main Ideas

Section 1 — Chemistry of Life

1. Matter is anything that has mass and takes up space.
2. Energy in matter is in the chemical bonds that hold matter together.
3. All organic compounds contain the elements hydrogen and carbon. The organic compounds in living things are carbohydrates, lipids, proteins, and nucleic acids.
4. Organic and inorganic compounds are important to living things.

Section 2 — Moving Cellular Materials

1. The selectively permeable cell membrane controls which molecules can pass into and out of the cell.
2. In diffusion, molecules move from areas where there are relatively more of them to areas where there are relatively fewer of them.
3. Osmosis is the diffusion of water through a cell membrane.
4. Cells use energy to move molecules by active transport but do not use energy for passive transport.
5. Cells move large particles through cell membranes by endocytosis and exocytosis.

Section 3 — Energy for Life

1. Photosynthesis is the process by which some producers change light energy into chemical energy.
2. Respiration that uses oxygen releases the energy in food molecules and produces waste carbon dioxide and water.
3. Some one-celled organisms and cells that lack oxygen use fermentation to release small amounts of energy from glucose. Wastes such as alcohol, carbon dioxide, and lactic acid are produced.

Visualizing Main Ideas

Copy and complete the following table on energy processes.

Energy Processes	Photosynthesis	Respiration	Fermentation
Energy source		food (glucose)	food (glucose)
In plant and animal cells, occurs in			
Reactants are			
Products are			

Do not write in this book.

Science online in7.msscience.com/interactive_tutor

chapter 3 Review

Using Vocabulary

active transport p. 77
diffusion p. 75
endocytosis p. 78
enzyme p. 71
equilibrium p. 75
exocytosis p. 78
fermentation p. 84
inorganic compound p. 71
metabolism p. 81
mixture p. 69
organic compound p. 70
osmosis p. 76
passive transport p. 74
photosynthesis p. 82
respiration p. 83

Use what you know about the vocabulary words to answer the following questions.

1. What is the diffusion of water called?

2. What type of protein regulates nearly all chemical reactions in cells?

3. How do large food particles enter an amoeba?

4. What type of compound is water?

5. What process is used by some producers to convert light energy into chemical energy?

6. What type of compounds always contain carbon and hydrogen?

7. What process uses oxygen to break down glucose?

8. What is the total of all chemical reactions in an organism called?

Checking Concepts

Choose the word or phrase that best answers the question.

9. What is it called when cells use energy to move molecules?
   A) diffusion   C) active transport
   B) osmosis   D) passive transport

Use the photo below to answer question 10.

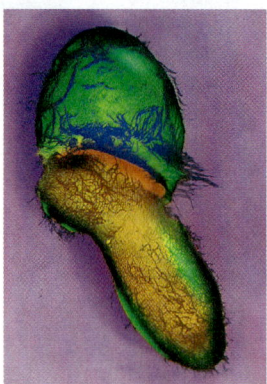

10. What cell process is occurring in the photo?
    A) osmosis   C) exocytosis
    B) endocytosis   D) diffusion

11. What occurs when the number of molecules of a substance is equal in two areas?
    A) equilibrium   C) fermentation
    B) metabolism   D) cellular respiration

12. Which of the following substances is an example of a carbohydrate?
    A) enzymes   C) waxes
    B) sugars   D) proteins

13. What is RNA an example of?
    A) carbon dioxide   C) lipid
    B) water   D) nucleic acid

14. What organic molecule stores the greatest amount of energy?
    A) carbohydrate   C) lipid
    B) water   D) nucleic acid

15. Which of these formulas is an example of an organic compound?
    A) $C_6H_{12}O_6$ C) H_2O
    B) NO_2 D) O_2

16. What are organisms that cannot make their own food called?
    A) biodegradables   C) consumers
    B) producers   D) enzymes

90 CHAPTER REVIEW   in7.msscience.com/vocabulary_puzzlemaker

Chapter 3 Review

Thinking Critically

17. **Concept Map** Copy and complete the events-chain concept map to sequence the following parts of matter from smallest to largest: *atom*, *electron*, and *compound*.

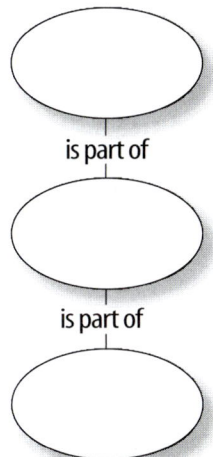

Use the table below to answer question 18.

Photosynthesis in Water Plants		
Beaker Number	Distance from Light (cm)	Bubbles per Minute
1	10	45
2	30	30
3	50	19
4	70	6
5	100	1

18. **Interpret Data** Water plants were placed at different distances from a light source. Bubbles coming from the plants were counted to measure the rate of photosynthesis. What can you say about how the distance from the light affected the rate?

19. **Infer** why, in snowy places, salt is used to melt ice on the roads. Explain what could happen to many roadside plants as a result.

20. **Draw a conclusion** about why sugar dissolves faster in hot tea than in iced tea.

21. **Predict** what would happen to the consumers in a lake if all the producers died.

22. **Explain** how meat tenderizers affect meat.

23. **Form a hypothesis** about what will happen to wilted celery when placed in a glass of plain water.

Performance Activities

24. **Puzzle** Make a crossword puzzle with words describing ways substances are transported across cell membranes. Use the following words in your puzzle: *diffusion*, *osmosis*, *facilitated diffusion*, *active transport*, *endocytosis*, and *exocytosis*. Make sure your clues give good descriptions of each transport method.

Applying Math

25. **Light and Photosynthesis** Using the data from question 18, make a line graph that shows the relationship between the rate of photosynthesis and the distance from light.

26. **Importance of Water** Assume the brain is 70% water. If the average adult human brain weighs 1.4 kg, how many kilograms of water does it contain?

Use the equation below to answer question 27.

Photosynthesis
$$6CO_2 + 6H_2O + \text{light energy} \xrightarrow{\text{chlorophyll}} C_6H_{12}O_6 + 6O_2$$
carbon water   chlorophyll sugar   oxygen
dioxide

27. **Photosynthesis** Refer to the chemical equation above. If 18 CO_2 molecules and 18 H_2O molecules are used with light energy to make sugar, how many sugar molecules will be produced? How many oxygen molecules will be produced?

chapter 3 Indiana

 The assessed Indiana standard appears above the question.

Record your answers on the answer sheet provided by your teacher or on a sheet of paper.

Part 1 Multiple Choice

1. Which describes a substance that is made up of only one kind of atom and cannot be broken down by chemical reactions?

   A carbohydrate

   B electron

   C element

   D molecule

2. The illustration below shows the crystal structure of salt, NaCl.

   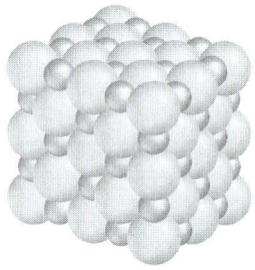

   What type of substance is salt?

   A element

   B ionic compound

   C mixture

   D molecular compound

7.7.3

3. A cell that contains 40% water is placed in a solution that is 20% water. Which percent represents equilibrium for the water and the cell?

   A 20%

   B 30%

   C 40%

   D 60%

4. Which is the sum of all the chemical reactions in an organism?

   A endocytosis

   B fermentation

   C metabolism

   D respiration

5. The table below shows the flexibility of cell substances.

Cell Substances		
Organic Compound	Flexibility	Found In
Keratin	Not very flexible	Hair and skin of mammals
Collagen	Not very flexible	Skin, bones, and tendons of mammals
Chitin	Very rigid	Tough outer shell of insects and crabs
Cellulose	Very flexible	Plant cell walls

   Which organic compound is least flexible?

   A cellulose

   B chitin

   C collagen

   D keratin

Test-Taking Tip

Diagrams Study a diagram carefully, being sure to read all labels and captions.

Standards Review

7.4.5

6. Which process has the carbon dioxide that you exhale as an end product?

   A DNA synthesis

   B osmosis

   C photosynthesis

   D respiration

7.4.5

7. Which process releases the most energy for an athlete's muscles?

   A fermentation

   B osmosis

   C photosynthesis

   D respiration

8. The table below shows how some substances in the body are classified.

Compound	Organic or Inorganic	Type of Substance
Fat	Organic	
Skin	Organic	
DNA	Organic	
Sugar	Organic	
Water	Inorganic	Molecular compound
Potassium	Inorganic	Element

Which correctly completes the table for *Fat*, *Skin*, *DNA*, and *Sugar*, in that order?

   A carbohydrate, lipid, nucleic acid, protein

   B carbohydrate, nucleic acid, protein, lipid

   C lipid, nucleic acid, carbohydrate, protein

   D lipid, protein, nucleic acid, carbohydrate

Part 2 Constructed Response

7.4.4

9. Compare and contrast endocytosis and exocytosis. List an example of how the body uses each process.

7.4.5

10. The illustration below shows a process that takes place in all organisms.

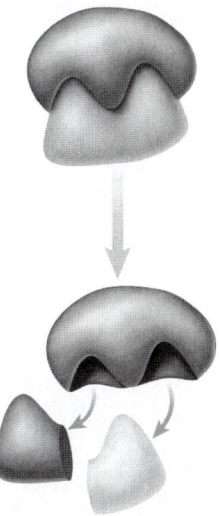

What process is taking place? What is the significance of this process for a cell?

7.4.5

11. Describe the chemical reaction for photosynthesis. What is the importance of the products of photosynthesis?

7.4.5

12. Why would plants need oxygen?

7.4.5

13. How do oxygen molecules get from plant cells to cells in your skin?

chapter 4

Academic Standard—4: Students . . . recognize the fundamental difference between plants and animals and understand its basis at the cellular level. Students distinguish species, particularly through an examination of internal structures and functions. They use microscopes to observe cells and recognize that cells function in similar ways in all organisms.

Also covers: Academic Standards 1, 2, 3, 5, 7 (Detailed standards begin on page IN8.)

Cell Reproduction

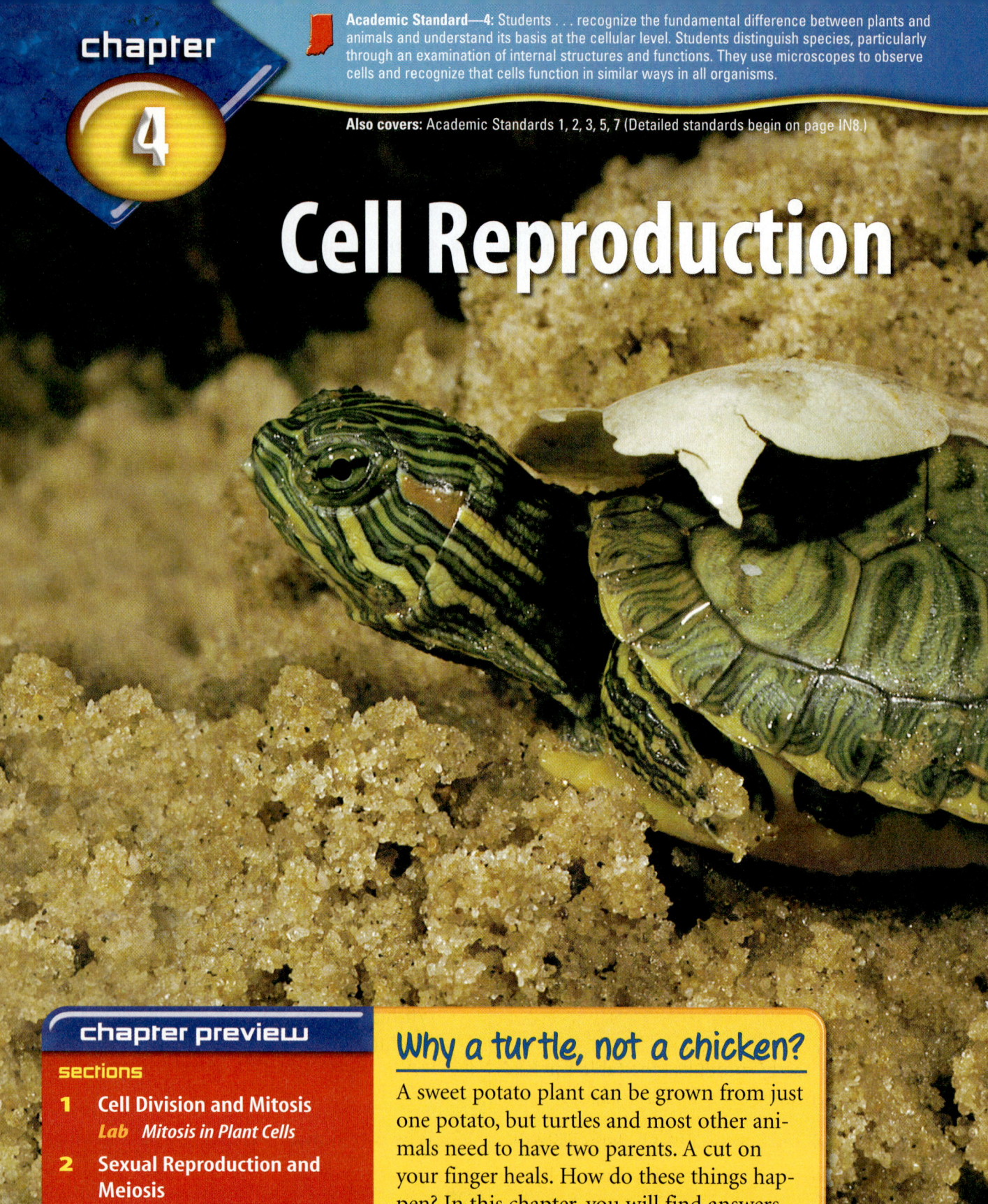

chapter preview

sections
1. **Cell Division and Mitosis**
   Lab Mitosis in Plant Cells
2. **Sexual Reproduction and Meiosis**
3. **DNA**
   Lab Mutations
   * Virtual Lab* What is the role of DNA and RNA in protein synthesis?

Why a turtle, not a chicken?
A sweet potato plant can be grown from just one potato, but turtles and most other animals need to have two parents. A cut on your finger heals. How do these things happen? In this chapter, you will find answers to these questions as you learn about cell reproduction.

Science Journal Write three things that you know about how and why cells reproduce.

Start-Up Activities

Infer About Seed Growth

Most flower and vegetable seeds sprout and grow into entire plants in just a few weeks. Although all of the cells in a seed have information and instructions to produce a new plant, only some of the cells in the seed use the information. Where are these cells in seeds? Do the following lab to find out.

1. Carefully split open two bean seeds that have soaked in water overnight.
2. Observe both halves and record your observations.
3. Wrap all four halves in a moist paper towel. Then put them into a self-sealing, plastic bag and seal the bag.
4. Make observations every day for a few days.
5. **Think Critically** Write a paragraph that describes what you observe. Hypothesize which cells in seeds use information about how plants grow.

Preview this chapter's content and activities at in7.msscience.com

How and Why Cells Divide
Make the following Foldable to help you organize information from the chapter about cell reproduction.

STEP 1 **Draw** a mark at the midpoint of a vertical sheet of paper along the side edge.

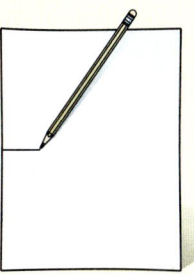

STEP 2 **Turn** the paper horizontally and **fold** the outside edges in to touch at the midpoint mark.

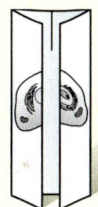

STEP 3 **Use** a pencil to draw a cell on the front of your Foldable as shown.

Analyze As you read the chapter, write under the flaps how cells divide. In the middle section, list why cells divide.

section 1

Standard—7.4.4: Explain that cells continually divide to make more cells for growth and repair …

Also covers: 7.2.7 (Detailed standards begin on page IN8.)

Cell Division and Mitosis

as you read

What You'll Learn
- **Explain** why mitosis is important.
- **Examine** the steps of mitosis.
- **Compare** mitosis in plant and animal cells.
- **List** two examples of asexual reproduction.

Why It's Important
Your growth, like that of many organisms, depends on cell division.

Review Vocabulary
nucleus: organelle that controls all the activities of a cell and contains hereditary material made of proteins and DNA

New Vocabulary
- mitosis
- chromosome
- asexual reproduction

Why is cell division important?

What do you, an octopus, and an oak tree have in common? You share many characteristics, but an important one is that you are all made of cells—trillions of cells. Where did all of those cells come from? As amazing as it might seem, many organisms start as just one cell. That cell divides and becomes two, two become four, four become eight, and so on. Many-celled organisms, including you, grow because cell division increases the total number of cells in an organism. Even after growth stops, cell division is still important. Every day, billions of red blood cells in your body wear out and are replaced. During the few seconds it takes you to read this sentence, your bone marrow produced about six million red blood cells. Cell division is important to one-celled organisms, too—it's how they reproduce themselves, as shown in **Figure 1**. Cell division isn't as simple as just cutting the cell in half, so how do cells divide?

The Cell Cycle

A living organism has a life cycle. A life cycle begins with the organism's formation, is followed by growth and development, and finally ends in death. Right now, you are in a stage of your life cycle called adolescence, which is a period of active growth and development. Individual cells also have life cycles.

Figure 1 All organisms use cell division. Many-celled organisms, such as this octopus, grow by increasing the numbers of their cells.

Like this dividing amoeba, a one-celled organism reaches a certain size and then reproduces.

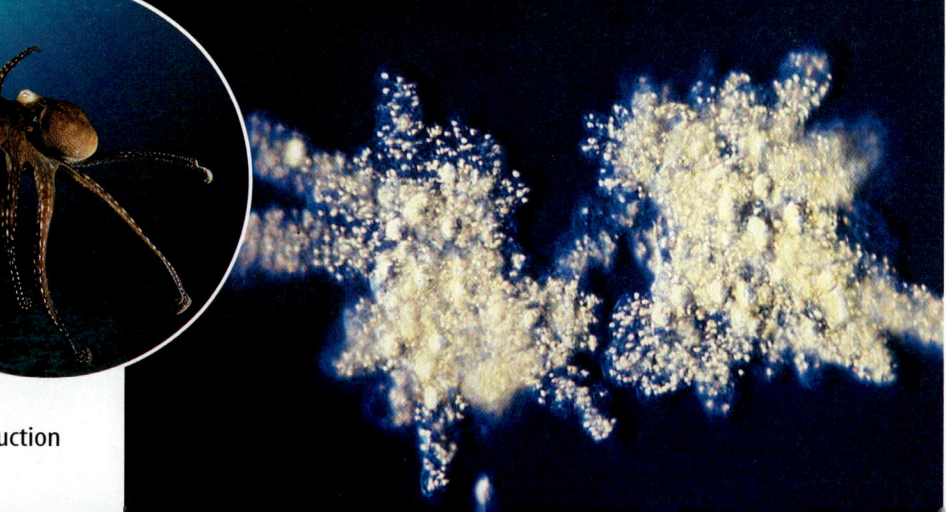

96 CHAPTER 4 Cell Reproduction

Figure 2 Interphase is the longest part of the cell cycle.
Identify When do chromosomes duplicate?

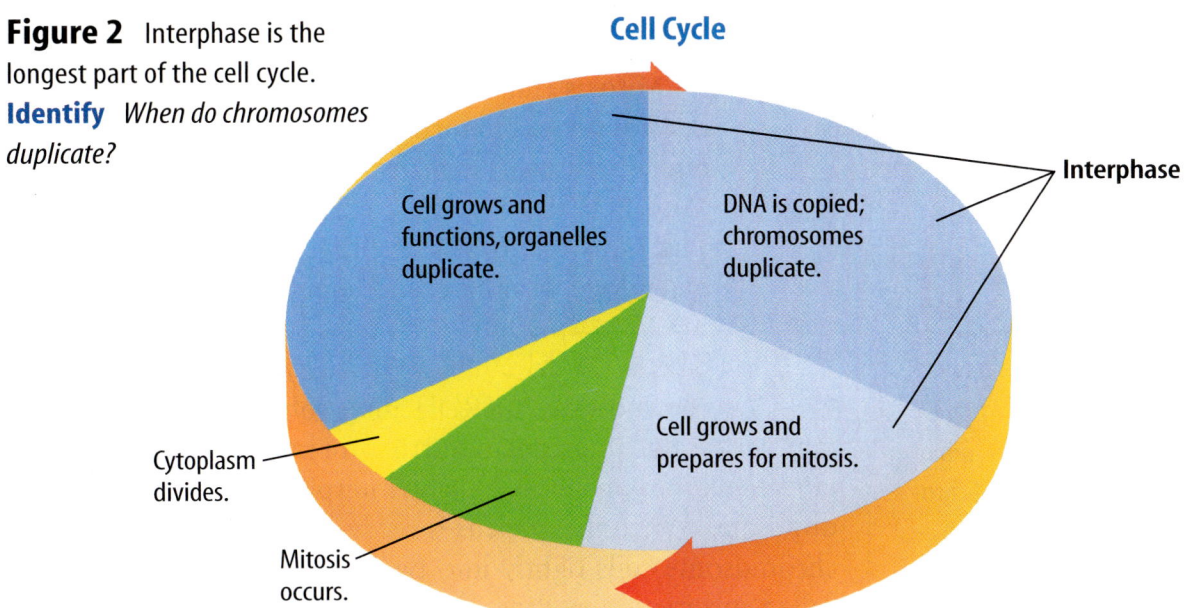

Length of Cycle The cell cycle, as shown in **Figure 2,** is a series of events that takes place from one cell division to the next. The time it takes to complete a cell cycle is not the same in all cells. For example, the cycle for cells in some bean plants takes about 19 h to complete. Cells in animal embryos divide rapidly and can complete their cycles in less than 20 min. In some human cells, the cell cycle takes about 16 h. Cells in humans that are needed for repair, growth, or replacement, like skin and bone cells, constantly repeat the cycle.

Interphase Most of the life of any eukaryotic cell—a cell with a nucleus—is spent in a period of growth and development called interphase. Cells in your body that no longer divide, such as nerve and muscle cells, are always in interphase. An actively dividing cell, such as a skin cell, copies its hereditary material and prepares for cell division during interphase.

Why is it important for a cell to copy its hereditary information before dividing? Imagine that you have a part in a play and the director has one complete copy of the script. If the director gave only one page to each person in the play, no one would have the entire script. Instead the director makes a complete, separate copy of the script for each member of the cast so that each one can learn his or her part. Before a cell divides, a copy of the hereditary material must be made so that each of the two new cells will get a complete copy. Just as the actors in the play need the entire script, each cell needs a complete set of hereditary material to carry out life functions.

After interphase, cell division begins. The nucleus divides, and then the cytoplasm separates to form two new cells.

Oncologist The cell cycle is well controlled in most cells, but cancer cells have uncontrolled cell division. Doctors who diagnose, study, and treat cancer are called oncologists. To be an oncologist, you must complete medical school, then have training in oncology. Research the subspecialties of oncology. List and describe them in your Science Journal.

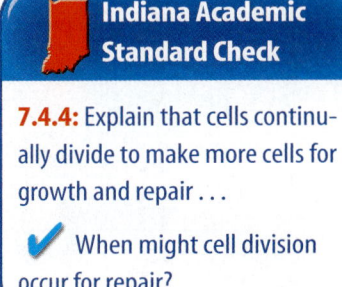

7.4.4: Explain that cells continually divide to make more cells for growth and repair...

✓ When might cell division occur for repair?

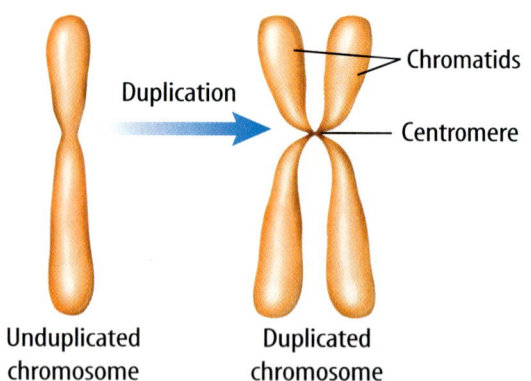

Figure 3 DNA is copied during interphase. An unduplicated chromosome has one strand of DNA. A duplicated chromosome has two identical DNA strands, called chromatids, that are held together at a region called the centromere.

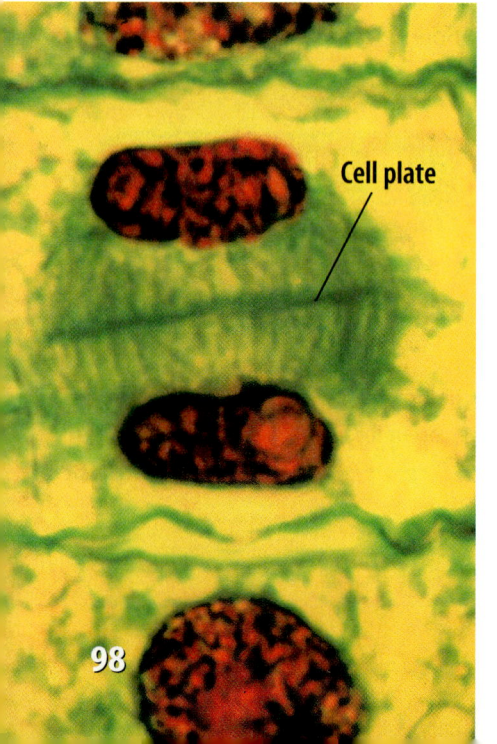

Figure 4 The cell plate shown in this plant cell appears when the cytoplasm is being divided.
Identify what phase of mitosis will be next.

Mitosis

Mitosis (mi TOH sus) is the process in which the nucleus divides to form two identical nuclei. Each new nucleus also is identical to the original nucleus. Mitosis is described as a series of phases, or steps. The steps of mitosis in order are named prophase, metaphase, anaphase, and telophase.

Steps of Mitosis When any nucleus divides, the chromosomes (KROH muh sohmz) play the important part. A **chromosome** is a structure in the nucleus that contains hereditary material. During interphase, each chromosome duplicates. When the nucleus is ready to divide, each duplicated chromosome coils tightly into two thickened, identical strands called chromatids, as shown in **Figure 3**.

Reading Check *How are chromosomes and chromatids related?*

During prophase, the pairs of chromatids are fully visible when viewed under a microscope. The nucleolus and the nuclear membrane disintegrate. Two small structures called centrioles (SEN tree olz) move to opposite ends of the cell. Between the centrioles, threadlike spindle fibers begin to stretch across the cell. Plant cells also form spindle fibers during mitosis but do not have centrioles.

In metaphase, the pairs of chromatids line up across the center of the cell. The centromere of each pair usually becomes attached to two spindle fibers—one from each side of the cell.

In anaphase, each centromere divides and the spindle fibers shorten. Each pair of chromatids separates, and chromatids begin to move to opposite ends of the cell. The separated chromatids are now called chromosomes. In the final step, telophase, spindle fibers start to disappear, the chromosomes start to uncoil, and a new nucleus forms.

Division of the Cytoplasm For most cells, after the nucleus has divided, the cytoplasm separates and two new cells are formed. In animal cells, the cell membrane pinches in the middle, like a balloon with a string tightened around it, and the cytoplasm divides. In plant cells, the appearance of a cell plate, as shown in **Figure 4,** tells you that the cytoplasm is being divided. New cell walls form along the cell plate, and new cell membranes develop inside the cell walls. Following division of the cytoplasm, most new cells begin the period of growth, or interphase, again. Review cell division for an animal cell using the illustrations in **Figure 5**.

Figure 5 Cell division for an animal cell is shown here. Each micrograph shown in this figure is magnified 600 times.

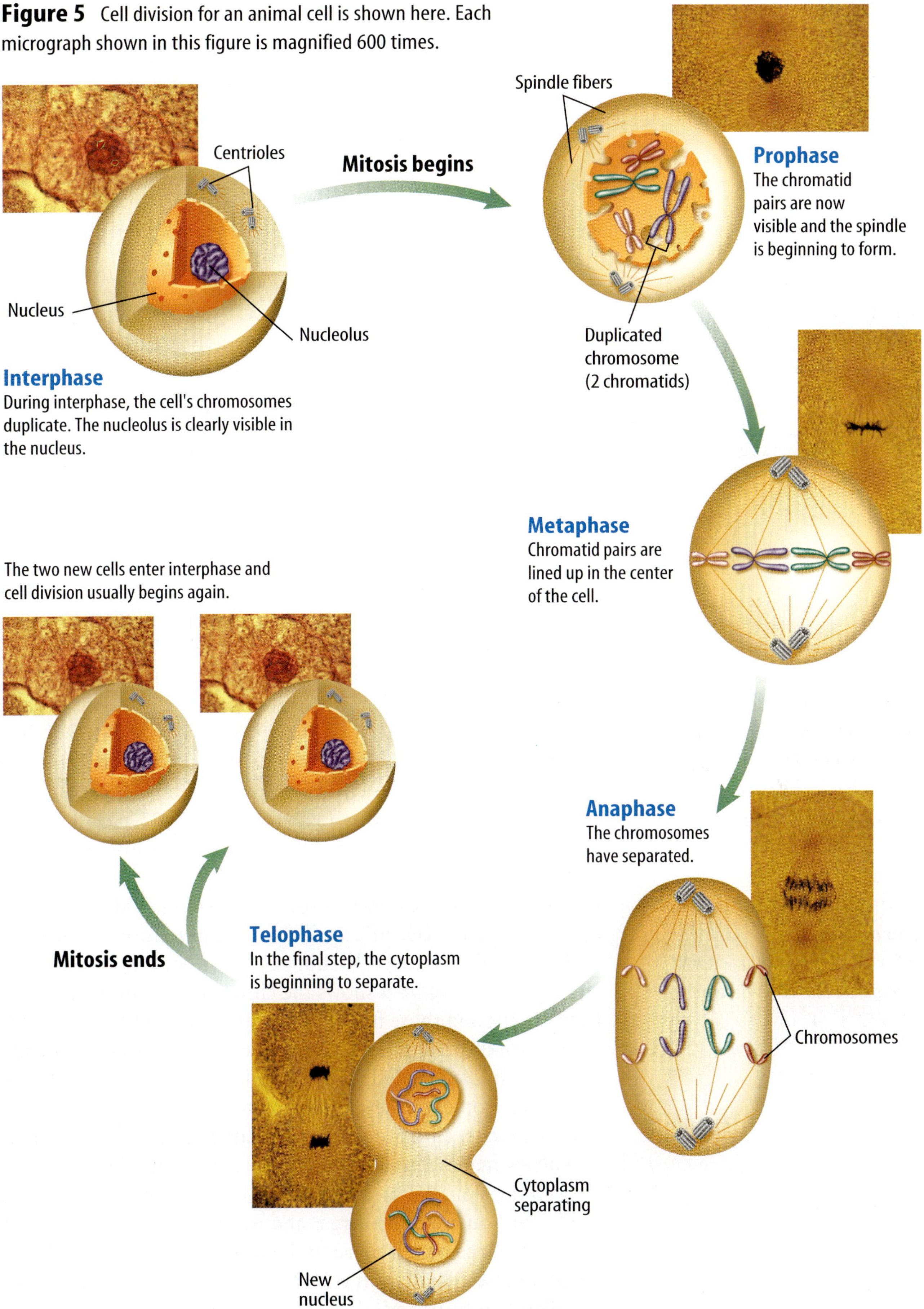

Interphase
During interphase, the cell's chromosomes duplicate. The nucleolus is clearly visible in the nucleus.

Labels: Nucleus, Centrioles, Nucleolus

Mitosis begins

Prophase
The chromatid pairs are now visible and the spindle is beginning to form.

Labels: Spindle fibers, Duplicated chromosome (2 chromatids)

Metaphase
Chromatid pairs are lined up in the center of the cell.

Anaphase
The chromosomes have separated.

Label: Chromosomes

Telophase
In the final step, the cytoplasm is beginning to separate.

Labels: Cytoplasm separating, New nucleus

Mitosis ends

The two new cells enter interphase and cell division usually begins again.

SECTION 1 Cell Division and Mitosis **99**

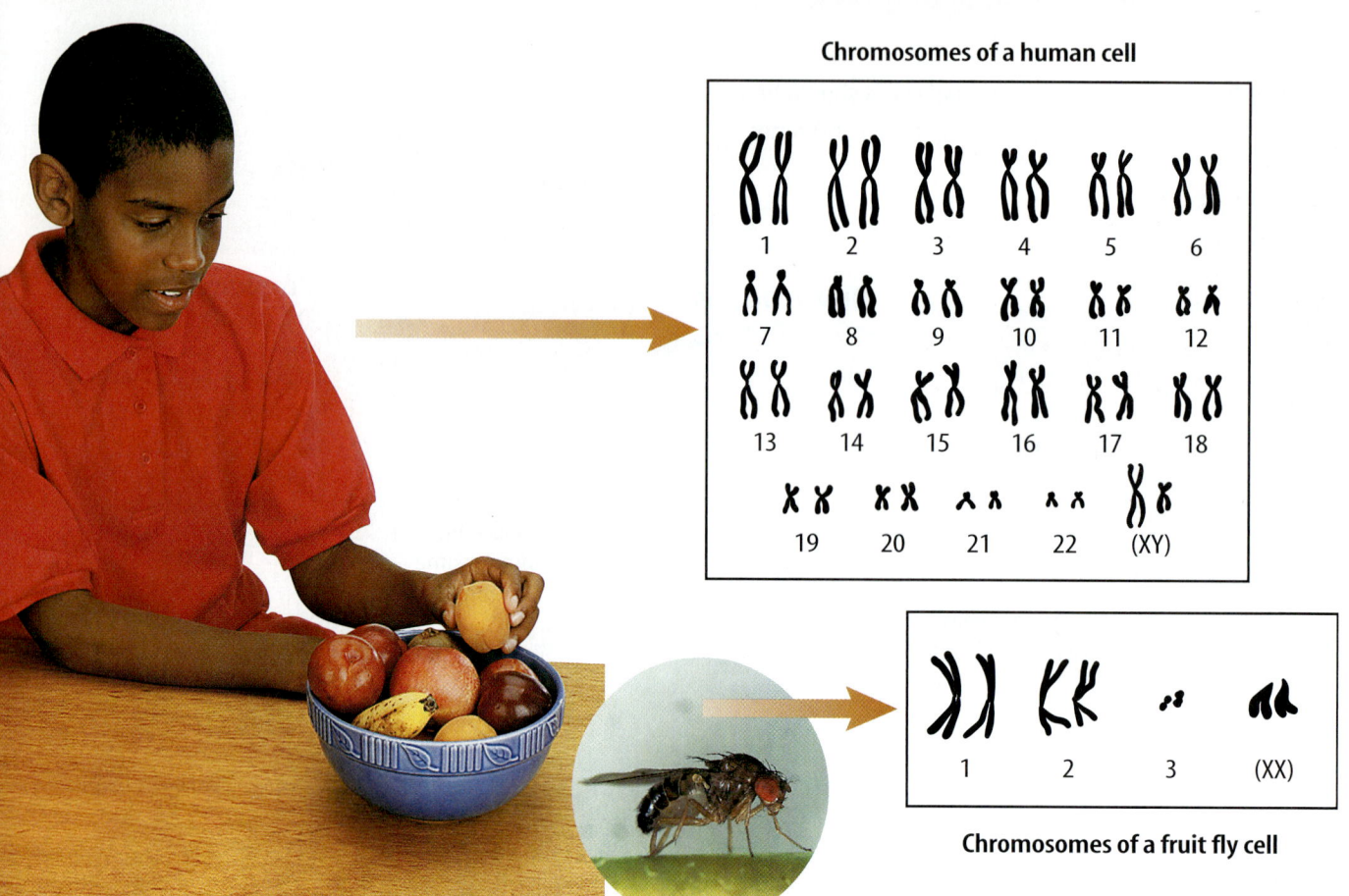

Figure 6 Pairs of chromosomes are found in the nucleus of most cells. All chromosomes shown here are in their duplicated form. Most human cells have 23 pairs of chromosomes including one pair of chromosomes that help determine sex such as the XY pair above. Most fruit fly cells have four pairs of chromosomes.

Infer What do you think the XX pair in fruit flies helps determine?

Results of Mitosis You should remember two important things about mitosis. First, it is the division of a nucleus. Second, it produces two new nuclei that are identical to each other and the original nucleus. Each new nucleus has the same number and type of chromosomes. Every cell in your body, except sex cells, has a nucleus with 46 chromosomes—23 pairs. This is because you began as one cell with 46 chromosomes in its nucleus. Skin cells, produced to replace or repair your skin, have the same 46 chromosomes as the original single cell you developed from. Each cell in a fruit fly has eight chromosomes, so each new cell produced by mitosis has a copy of those eight chromosomes. **Figure 6** shows the chromosomes found in most human cells and those found in most fruit fly cells.

Each of the trillions of cells in your body, except sex cells, has a copy of the same hereditary material. Even though all actors in a play have copies of the same script, they do not learn the same lines. Likewise, all of your cells use different parts of the same hereditary material to become different types of cells.

Cell division allows growth and replaces worn out or damaged cells. You are much larger and have more cells than a baby mainly because of cell division. If you cut yourself, the wound heals because cell division replaces damaged cells. Another way some organisms use cell division is to produce new organisms.

Asexual Reproduction

Reproduction is the process by which an organism produces others of its same kind. Among living organisms, there are two types of reproduction—sexual and asexual. Sexual reproduction usually requires two organisms. In **asexual reproduction,** a new organism (sometimes more than one) is produced from one organism. The new organism will have hereditary material identical to the hereditary material of the parent organism.

 *How many organisms are needed for asexual reproduction?*

Cellular Asexual Reproduction Organisms with eukaryotic cells asexually reproduce by cell division. A sweet potato growing in a jar of water is an example of asexual reproduction. All the stems, leaves, and roots that grow from the sweet potato have been produced by cell division and have the same hereditary material. New strawberry plants can be reproduced asexually from horizontal stems called runners. **Figure 7** shows asexual reproduction in a potato and a strawberry plant.

Recall that mitosis is the division of a nucleus. However, bacteria do not have a nucleus so they can't use mitosis. Instead, bacteria reproduce asexually by fission. During fission, an organism whose cells do not contain a nucleus copies its genetic material and then divides into two identical organisms.

Mini LAB

Modeling Mitosis

Procedure
1. Make models of cell division using **materials supplied by your teacher.**
2. Use four chromosomes in your model.
3. When finished, arrange the models in the order in which mitosis occurs.

Analysis
1. In which steps is the nucleus visible?
2. How many cells does a dividing cell form?

Figure 7 Many plants can reproduce asexually.

A new potato plant can grow from each sprout on this potato.

Infer *how the genetic material in the small strawberry plant above compares to the genetic material in the large strawberry plant.*

Figure 8 Some organisms use cell division for budding and regeneration.

B This sea star is regenerating four new arms.

A Hydra, a freshwater animal, can reproduce asexually by budding. The bud is a small exact copy of the adult.

Budding and Regeneration Look at **Figure 8A.** A new organism is growing from the body of the parent organism. This organism, called a hydra, is reproducing by budding. Budding is a type of asexual reproduction made possible because of cell division. When the bud on the adult becomes large enough, it breaks away to live on its own.

Could you grow a new finger? Some organisms can regrow damaged or lost body parts, as shown in **Figure 8B.** Regeneration is the process that uses cell division to regrow body parts. Sponges, planaria, sea stars, and some other organisms can use regeneration for asexual reproduction. If these organisms break into pieces, a whole new organism will grow from each piece. Because sea stars eat oysters, oyster farmers dislike them. What would happen if an oyster farmer collected sea stars, cut them into pieces, and threw them back into the ocean?

section 1 review

Summary

The Cell Cycle
- The cell cycle is a series of events from one cell division to the next.
- Most of a eukaryotic cell's life is interphase.

Mitosis
- Mitosis is a series of four phases or steps.
- Each new nucleus formed by mitosis has the same number and type of chromosomes.

Asexual Reproduction
- In asexual reproduction, a new organism is produced from one organism.
- Cellular, budding, and regeneration are forms of asexual reproduction.

Self Check

1. **Define** mitosis. How does it differ in plants and animals?
2. **Identify** two examples of asexual reproduction in many-celled organisms.
3. **Describe** what happens to chromosomes before mitosis.
4. **Compare and contrast** the two new cells formed after mitosis and cell division.
5. **Think Critically** Why is it important for the nuclear membrane to disintegrate during mitosis?

Applying Math

6. **Solve One-Step Equations** If a cell undergoes cell division every 5 min, how many cells will there be after 1 h?

in7.msscience.com/self_check_quiz

Mit☉sis in Plant Cells

Reproduction of most cells in plants and animals uses mitosis and cell division. In this lab, you will study mitosis in plant cells by examining prepared slides of onion root-tip cells.

◉ Real-World Question

How can plant cells in different stages of mitosis be distinguished from each other?

Goals
- **Compare** cells in different stages of mitosis and observe the location of their chromosomes.
- **Observe** what stage of mitosis is most common in onion root tips.

Materials
prepared slide of an onion root tip
microscope

Safety Precautions

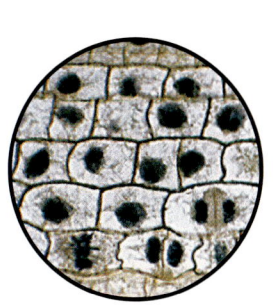
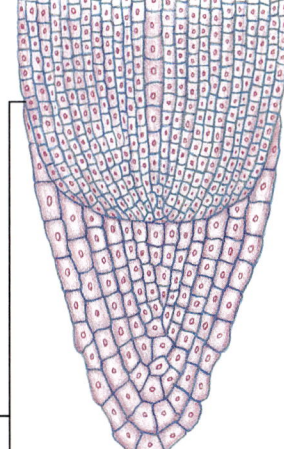

Zone of cell division   Root cap

3. Set your microscope on low power and examine the slide. The large, round cells at the root tip are called the root cap. Move the slide until you see the cells just behind the root cap. Turn to the high-power objective.

4. Find an area where you can see the most stages of mitosis. Count and record how many cells you see in each stage.

5. Return the nosepiece to low power. Remove the onion root-tip slide.

◉ Procedure

1. Copy the data table in your Science Journal.

Number of Root-Tip Cells Observed		
Stage of Mitosis	Number of Cells Observed	Percent of Cells Observed
Prophase		
Metaphase		
Anaphase	Do not write in this book.	
Telophase		
Total		

2. **Obtain** a prepared slide of cells from an onion root tip.

◉ Conclude and Apply

1. **Compare** the cells in the region behind the root cap to those in the root cap.
2. **Calculate** the percent of cells found in each stage of mitosis. Infer which stage of mitosis takes the longest period of time.

𝒞ommunicating Your Data

Write and illustrate a story as if you were a cell undergoing mitosis. Share your story with your class. **For more help, refer to the Science Skill Handbook.**

LAB **103**

section 2

Standard—7.4.3: Explain how, in sexual reproduction, a single specialized cell from a female merges with a specialized cell from a male and this fertilized egg carries genetic information from each parent and multiplies to form the complete organism.

Also covers: 7.4.1, 7.5.3 (Detailed standards begin on page IN8.)

Sexual Reproduction and Meiosis

as you read

What You'll Learn
- **Describe** the stages of meiosis and how sex cells are produced.
- **Explain** why meiosis is needed for sexual reproduction.
- **Name** the cells that are involved in fertilization.
- **Explain** how fertilization occurs in sexual reproduction.

Why It's Important
Meiosis and sexual reproduction are the reasons why no one else is exactly like you.

Review Vocabulary
organism: any living thing; uses energy, is made of cells, reproduces, responds, grows, and develops

New Vocabulary
- sexual reproduction
- sperm
- egg
- fertilization
- zygote
- diploid
- haploid
- meiosis

Sexual Reproduction

Sexual reproduction is another way that a new organism can be produced. During **sexual reproduction,** two sex cells, sometimes called an egg and a sperm, come together. Sex cells, like those in **Figure 9,** are formed from cells in reproductive organs. **Sperm** are formed in the male reproductive organs. **Eggs** are formed in the female reproductive organs. The joining of an egg and a sperm is called **fertilization,** and the cell that forms is called a **zygote** (ZI goht). Generally, the egg and the sperm come from two different organisms of the same species. Following fertilization, cell division begins. A new organism with a unique identity develops.

Diploid Cells Your body forms two types of cells—body cells and sex cells. Body cells far outnumber sex cells. Your brain, skin, bones, and other tissues and organs are formed from body cells. A typical human body cell has 46 chromosomes. Each chromosome has a mate that is similar to it in size and shape and has similar DNA. Human body cells have 23 pairs of chromosomes. When cells have pairs of similar chromosomes, they are said to be **diploid** (DIH ployd).

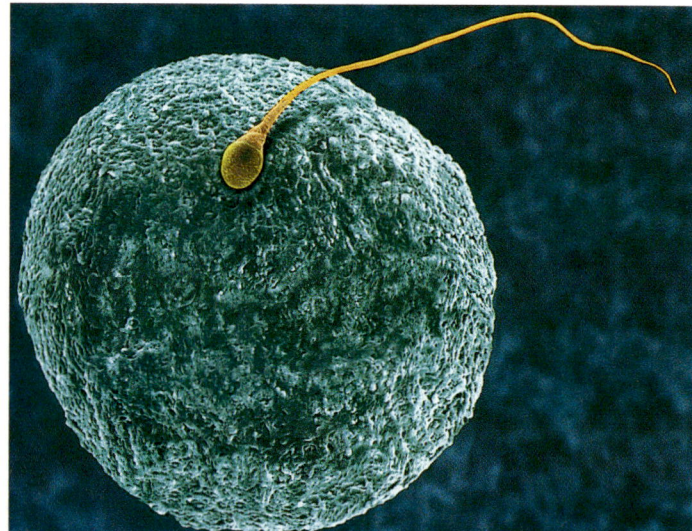

Figure 9 A human egg and a human sperm at fertilization.

Haploid Cells Because sex cells do not have pairs of chromosomes, they are said to be **haploid** (HA ployd). They have only half the number of chromosomes as body cells. *Haploid* means "single form." Human sex cells have only 23 chromosomes—one from each of the 23 pairs of similar chromosomes. Compare the chromosomes found in a sex cell, as shown in **Figure 9**, to the full set of human chromosomes seen in **Figure 6**.

 *How many chromosomes are usually in each human sperm?*

Meiosis and Sex Cells

A process called **meiosis** (mi OH sus) produces haploid sex cells. What would happen in sexual reproduction if two diploid cells combined? The offspring would have twice as many chromosomes as its parent. Although plants with twice the number of chromosomes as the parent plants are often produced, most animals do not survive with a double number of chromosomes. Meiosis ensures that the offspring will have the same diploid number as its parent, as shown in **Figure 10**. After two haploid sex cells combine, a diploid zygote is produced that develops into a new diploid organism.

During meiosis, two divisions of the nucleus occur. These divisions are called meiosis I and meiosis II. The steps of each division have names like those in mitosis and are numbered for the division in which they occur.

Diploid Zygote Usually, only one sperm fertilizes the egg. After the sperm nucleus enters the egg, the cell membrane of the egg changes in a way that prevents other sperm from entering. What adaptation in this process guarantees that the zygote will be diploid? Write a paragraph describing your ideas in your Science Journal.

7.4.3: Explain how . . . information . . . multiplies to form the complete organism.

How do the genetics of an organism compare to those of the zygote from which it developed?

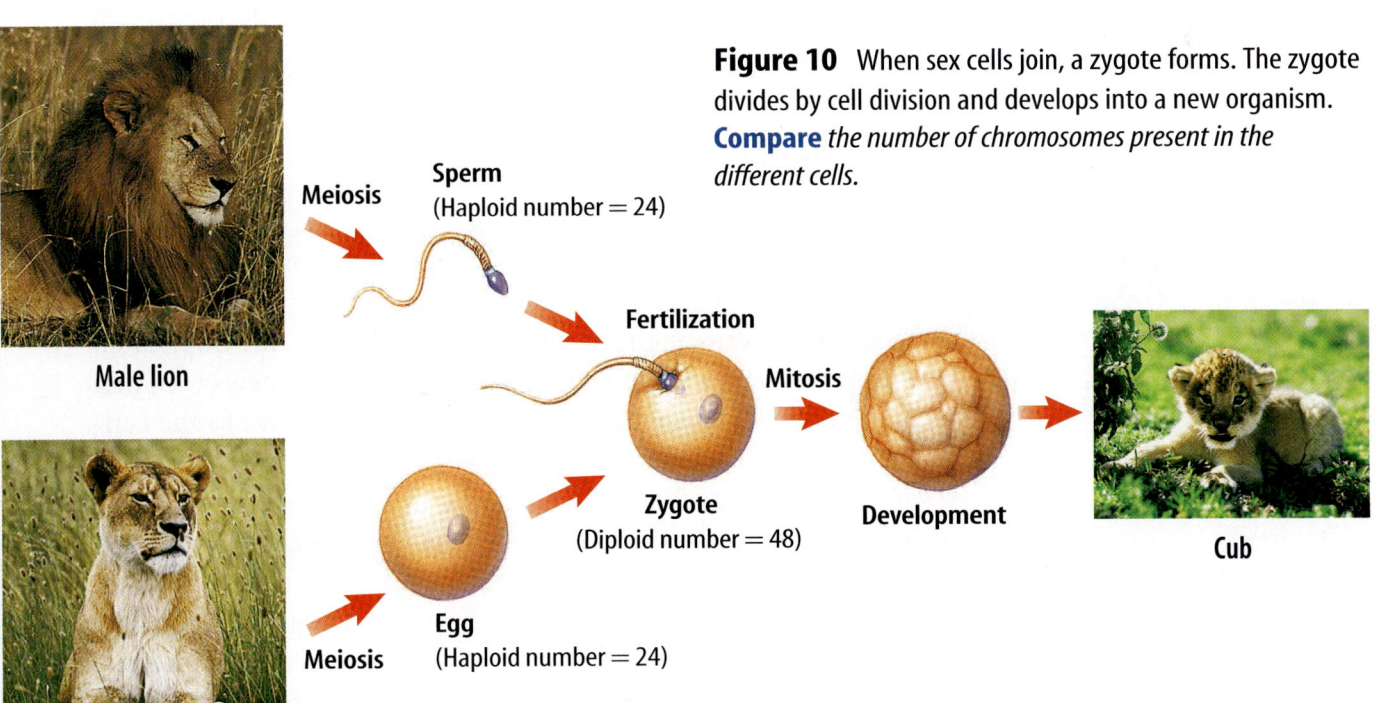

Figure 10 When sex cells join, a zygote forms. The zygote divides by cell division and develops into a new organism. **Compare** *the number of chromosomes present in the different cells.*

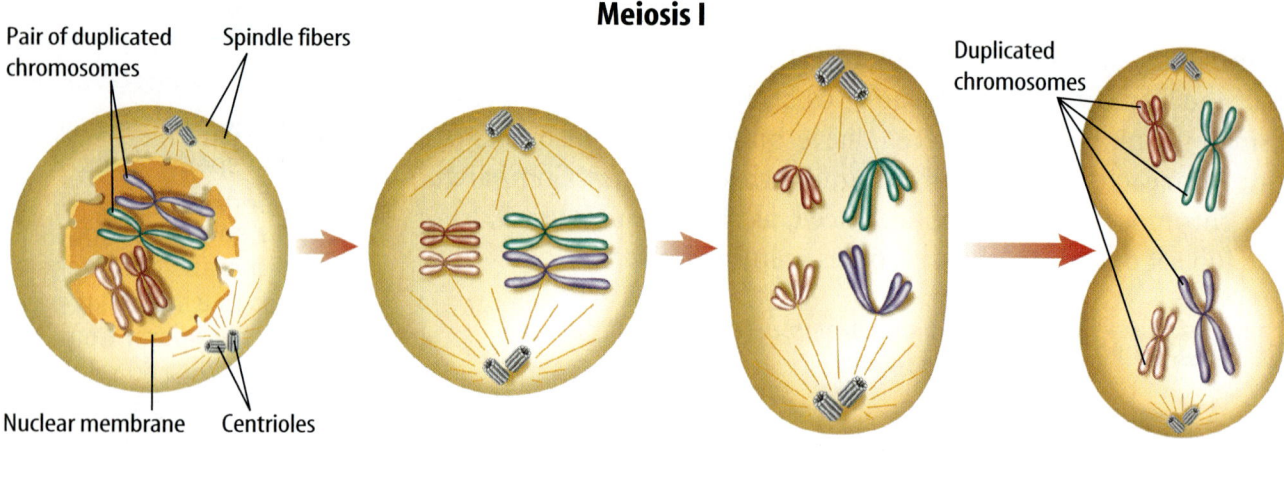

Meiosis I

Prophase I — Metaphase I — Anaphase I — Telophase I

Figure 11 Meiosis has two divisions of the nucleus—meiosis I and meiosis II.
Determine how many sex cells are finally formed after both divisions are completed.

Meiosis I Before meiosis begins, each chromosome is duplicated, just as in mitosis. When the cell is ready for meiosis, each duplicated chromosome is visible under the microscope as two chromatids. As shown in **Figure 11,** the events of prophase I are similar to those of prophase in mitosis. In meiosis, each duplicated chromosome comes near its similar duplicated mate. In mitosis they do not come near each other.

In metaphase I, the pairs of duplicated chromosomes line up in the center of the cell. The centromere of each chromatid pair becomes attached to one spindle fiber, so the chromatids do not separate in anaphase I. The two pairs of chromatids of each similar pair move away from each other to opposite ends of the cell. Each duplicated chromosome still has two chromatids. Then, in telophase I, the cytoplasm divides, and two new cells form. Each new cell has one duplicated chromosome from each similar pair.

 **What happens to duplicated chromosomes during anaphase I?**

Meiosis II The two cells formed during meiosis I now begin meiosis II. The chromatids of each duplicated chromosome will be separated during this division. In prophase II, the duplicated chromosomes and spindle fibers reappear in each new cell. Then in metaphase II, the duplicated chromosomes move to the center of the cell. Unlike what occurs in metaphase I, each centromere now attaches to two spindle fibers instead of one. The centromere divides during anaphase II, and the chromatids separate and move to opposite ends of the cell. Each chromatid now is an individual chromosome. As telophase II begins, the spindle fibers disappear, and a nuclear membrane forms around the chromosomes at each end of the cell. When meiosis II is finished, the cytoplasm divides.

Meiosis II

Prophase II → Metaphase II → Anaphase II → Telophase II

Unduplicated chromosomes

Summary of Meiosis Two cells form during meiosis I. In meiosis II, both of these cells form two cells. The two divisions of the nucleus result in four sex cells. Each has one-half the number of chromosomes in its nucleus that was in the original nucleus. From a human cell with 46 paired chromosomes, meiosis produces four sex cells each with 23 unpaired chromosomes.

Applying Science

How can chromosome numbers be predicted?

Offspring get half of their chromosomes from one parent and half from the other. What happens if each parent has a different diploid number of chromosomes?

Identifying the Problem

A zebra and a donkey can mate to produce a zonkey. Zebras have a diploid number of 46. Donkeys have a diploid number of 62.

Solving the Problem

1. How many chromosomes would the zonkey receive from each parent?
2. What is the chromosome number of the zonkey?
3. What would happen when meiosis occurs in the zonkey's reproductive organs?
4. Predict why zonkeys are usually sterile.

Donkey
62 chromosomes

Zonkey

Zebra
46 chromosomes

SECTION 2 Sexual Reproduction and Meiosis

NATIONAL GEOGRAPHIC VISUALIZING POLYPLOIDY IN PLANTS

Figure 12

You received a haploid (n) set of chromosomes from each of your parents, making you a diploid (2n) organism. In nature, however, many plants are polyploid—they have three (3n), four (4n), or more sets of chromosomes. We depend on some of these plants for food.

▲ **TRIPLOID** Bright yellow bananas typically come from triploid (3n) banana plants. Plants with an odd number of chromosome sets usually cannot reproduce sexually and have very small seeds or none at all.

▲ **TETRAPLOID** Polyploidy occurs naturally in many plants—including peanuts and daylilies—due to mistakes in mitosis or meiosis.

▼ **HEXAPLOID** Modern cultivated strains of oats have six sets of chromosomes, making them hexaploid (6n) plants.

▲ **OCTAPLOID** Polyploid plants often are bigger than nonpolyploid plants and may have especially large leaves, flowers, or fruits. Strawberries are an example of octaploid (8n) plants.

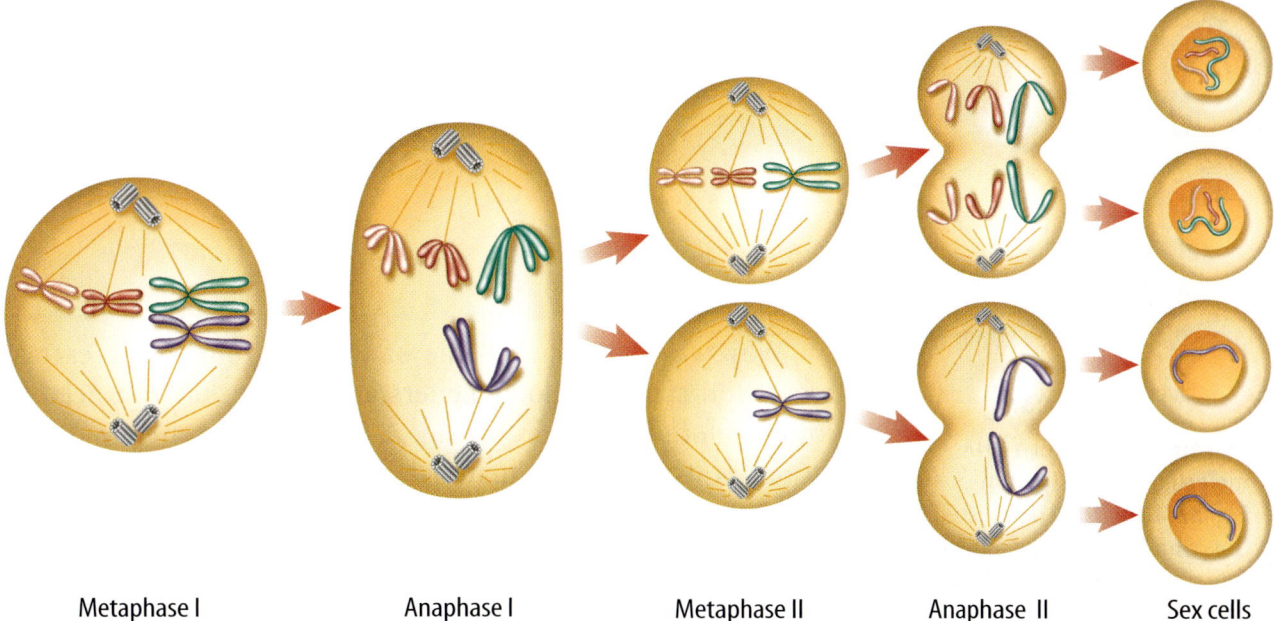

Metaphase I   Anaphase I   Metaphase II   Anaphase II   Sex cells

Mistakes in Meiosis Meiosis occurs many times in reproductive organs. Although mistakes in plants, as shown in **Figure 12,** are common, mistakes are less common in animals. These mistakes can produce sex cells with too many or too few chromosomes, as shown in **Figure 13**. Sometimes, zygotes produced from these sex cells die. If the zygote lives, every cell in the organism that grows from that zygote usually will have the wrong number of chromosomes. Organisms with the wrong number of chromosomes may not grow normally.

Figure 13 This diploid cell has four chromosomes. During anaphase I, one pair of duplicated chromosomes did not separate. **Infer** how many chromosomes each sex cell usually has.

section 2 review

Summary

Sexual Reproduction
- During sexual reproduction, two sex cells come together.
- Cell division begins after fertilization.
- A typical human body cell has 46 chromosomes, and a human sex cell has 23 chromosomes.

Meiosis and Sex Cells
- Each chromosome is duplicated before meiosis, then two divisions of the nucleus occur.
- During meiosis I, duplicated chromosomes are separated into new cells.
- Chromatids separate during meiosis II.
- Meiosis I and meiosis II result in four sex cells.

Self Check

1. **Describe** a zygote and how it is formed.
2. **Explain** where sex cells form.
3. **Compare** what happens to chromosomes during anaphase I and anaphase II.
4. **Think Critically** Plants grown from runners and leaf cuttings have the same traits as the parent plant. Plants grown from seeds can vary from the parent plants in many ways. Why can this happen?

Applying Skills

5. **Make and use a table** to compare mitosis and meiosis in humans. Vertical headings should include: *What Type of Cell (Body or Sex), Beginning Cell (Haploid or Diploid), Number of Cells Produced, End-Product Cell (Haploid or Diploid),* and *Number of Chromosomes in New Cells.*

SECTION 2 Sexual Reproduction and Meiosis

Standard—7.4.4: Explain that cells continually divide to make more cells for growth and repair…

section 3

DNA

Also covers: 7.1.5, 7.1.8, 7.1.10, 7.2.7, 7.7.2 (Detailed standards begin on page IN8.)

as you read

What You'll Learn
- **Identify** the parts of a DNA molecule and its structure.
- **Explain** how DNA copies itself.
- **Describe** the structure and function of each kind of RNA.

Why It's Important
DNA helps determine nearly everything your body is and does.

Review Vocabulary
heredity: the passing of traits from parents to offspring

New Vocabulary
- DNA
- gene
- RNA
- mutation

What is DNA?

Why was the alphabet one of the first things you learned when you started school? Letters are a code that you need to know before you learn to read. A cell also uses a code that is stored in its hereditary material. The code is a chemical called deoxyribonucleic (dee AHK sih ri boh noo klay ihk) acid, or **DNA**. It contains information for an organism's growth and function. **Figure 14** shows how DNA is stored in cells that have a nucleus. When a cell divides, the DNA code is copied and passed to the new cells. In this way, new cells receive the same coded information that was in the original cell. Every cell that has ever been formed in your body or in any other organism contains DNA.

INTEGRATE Chemistry

Discovering DNA Since the mid-1800s, scientists have known that the nuclei of cells contain large molecules called nucleic acids. By 1950, chemists had learned what the nucleic acid DNA was made of, but they didn't understand how the parts of DNA were arranged.

Figure 14 DNA is part of the chromosomes found in a cell's nucleus.

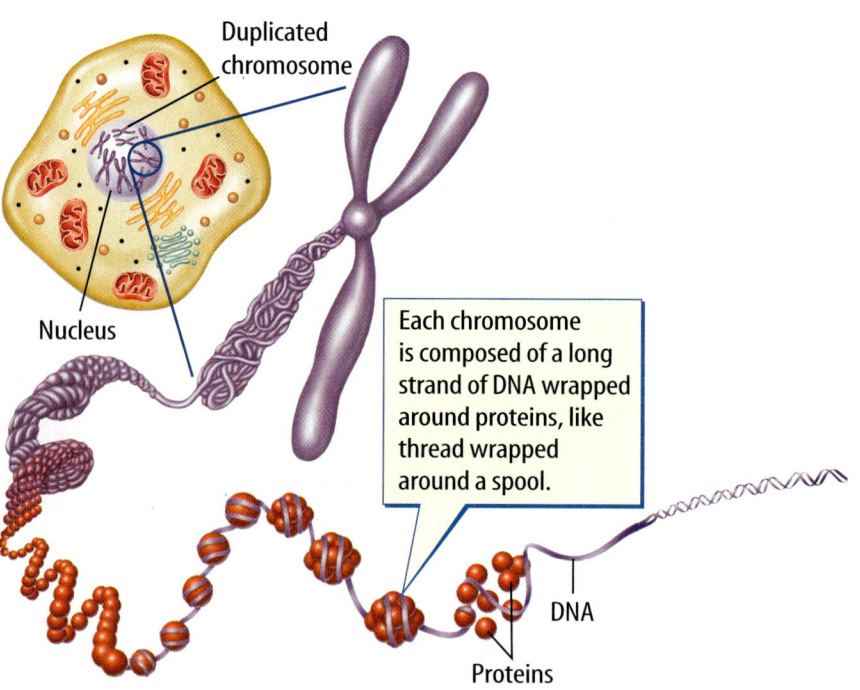

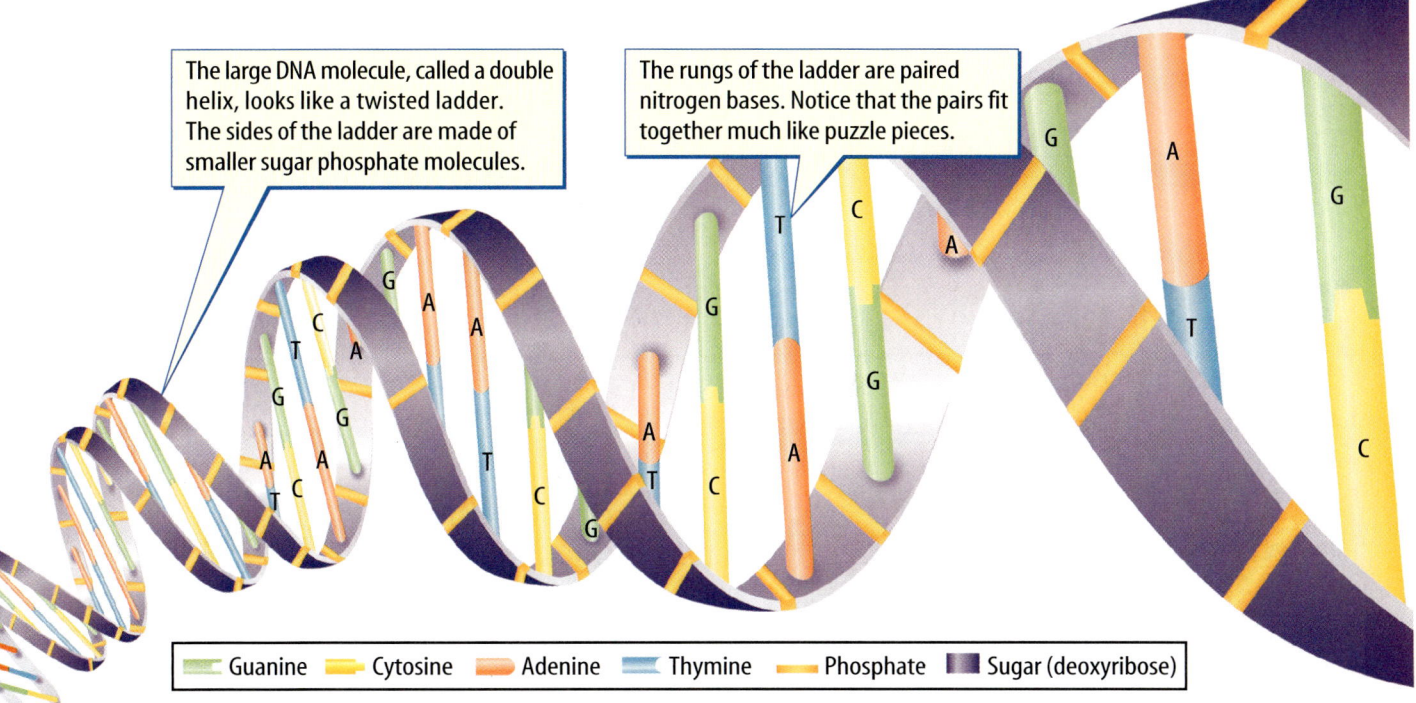

The large DNA molecule, called a double helix, looks like a twisted ladder. The sides of the ladder are made of smaller sugar phosphate molecules.

The rungs of the ladder are paired nitrogen bases. Notice that the pairs fit together much like puzzle pieces.

Guanine   Cytosine   Adenine   Thymine   Phosphate   Sugar (deoxyribose)

DNA's Structure In 1952, scientist Rosalind Franklin discovered that DNA is two chains of molecules in a spiral form. By using an X-ray technique, Dr. Franklin showed that the large spiral was probably made up of two spirals. As it turned out, the structure of DNA is similar to a twisted ladder. In 1953, using the work of Franklin and others, scientists James Watson and Francis Crick made a model of a DNA molecule.

A DNA Model What does DNA look like? According to the Watson and Crick DNA model, each side of the ladder is made up of sugar-phosphate molecules. Each molecule consists of the sugar called deoxyribose (dee AHK sih ri bohs) and a phosphate group. The rungs of the ladder are made up of other molecules called nitrogen bases. Four kinds of nitrogen bases are found in DNA—adenine (A duh neen), guanine (GWAH neen), cytosine (SI tuh seen), and thymine (THI meen). The bases are represented by the letters A, G, C, and T. The amount of cytosine in cells always equals the amount of guanine, and the amount of adenine always equals the amount of thymine. This led to the hypothesis that these bases occur as pairs in DNA. **Figure 14** shows that adenine always pairs with thymine, and guanine always pairs with cytosine. Like interlocking pieces of a puzzle, each base bonds only with its correct partner.

 *What are the nitrogen base pairs in a DNA molecule?*

Mini LAB

Modeling DNA Replication

Procedure
1. Suppose you have a segment of DNA that is six nitrogen base pairs in length. On **paper,** using the letters A, T, C, and G, write a combination of six pairs, remembering that A and T are always a pair and C and G are always a pair.
2. Duplicate your segment of DNA. On paper, diagram how this happens and show the new DNA segments.

Analysis
Compare the order of bases of the original DNA to the new DNA molecules.

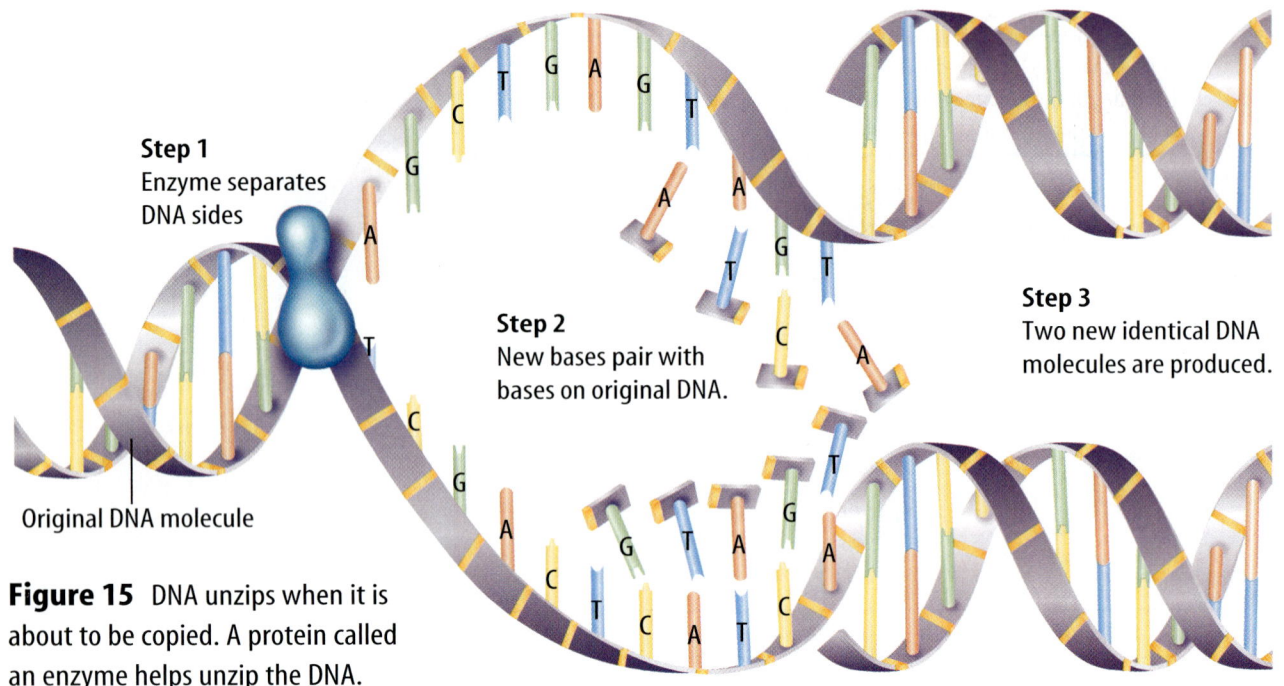

Figure 15 DNA unzips when it is about to be copied. A protein called an enzyme helps unzip the DNA.

Figure 16 This diagram shows just a few of the genes that have been identified on human chromosome 7. The bold print is the name that has been given to each gene.

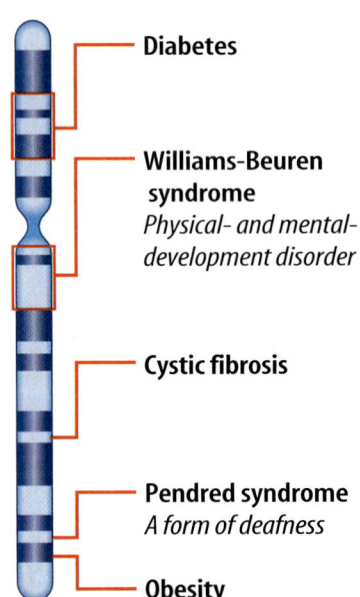

Copying DNA When chromosomes are duplicated before mitosis or meiosis, the amount of DNA in the nucleus is doubled. The Watson and Crick model shows how this takes place. The two sides of DNA unwind and separate. Each side then becomes a pattern on which a new side forms, as shown in **Figure 15**. The new DNA has bases that are identical to those of the original DNA and are in the same order.

Genes

Most of your characteristics, such as the color of your hair, your height, and even how things taste to you, depend on the kinds of proteins your cells make. DNA in your cells stores the instructions for making these proteins.

Proteins build cells and tissues or work as enzymes. The instructions for making a specific protein are found in a **gene** which is a section of DNA on a chromosome. As shown in **Figure 16,** each chromosome contains hundreds of genes. Proteins are made of chains of hundreds or thousands of amino acids. The gene determines the order of amino acids in a protein. Changing the order of the amino acids makes a different protein. What might occur if an important protein couldn't be made or if the wrong protein was made in your cells?

Making Proteins Genes are found in the nucleus, but proteins are made on ribosomes in cytoplasm. The codes for making proteins are carried from the nucleus to the ribosomes by another type of nucleic acid called ribonucleic acid, or **RNA.**

112 CHAPTER 4 Cell Reproduction

Ribonucleic Acid RNA is made in the nucleus on a DNA pattern. However, RNA is different from DNA. If DNA is like a ladder, RNA is like a ladder that has all its rungs sawed in half. Compare the DNA molecule in **Figure 14** to the RNA molecule in **Figure 17**. RNA has the bases A, G, and C like DNA but has the base uracil (U) instead of thymine (T). The sugar-phosphate molecules in RNA contain the sugar ribose, not deoxyribose.

The three main kinds of RNA made from DNA in a cell's nucleus are messenger RNA (mRNA), ribosomal RNA (rRNA), and transfer RNA (tRNA). Protein production begins when mRNA moves into the cytoplasm. There, ribosomes attach to it. Ribosomes are made of rRNA. Transfer RNA molecules in the cytoplasm bring amino acids to these ribosomes. Inside the ribosomes, three nitrogen bases on the mRNA temporarily match with three nitrogen bases on the tRNA. The same thing happens for the mRNA and another tRNA molecule, as shown in **Figure 17**. The amino acids that are attached to the two tRNA molecules bond. This is the beginning of a protein.

The code carried on the mRNA directs the order in which the amino acids bond. After a tRNA molecule has lost its amino acid, it can move about the cytoplasm and pick up another amino acid just like the first one. The ribosome moves along the mRNA. New tRNA molecules with amino acids match up and add amino acids to the protein molecule.

Science online

Topic: The Human Genome Project
Visit in7.msscience.com for Web links to information about the Human Genome Project.

Activity Find out when chromosomes 5, 16, 29, 21, and 22 were completely sequenced. Write about what scientists learned about each of these chromosomes.

Figure 17 Cells need DNA, RNA, and amino acids to make proteins.

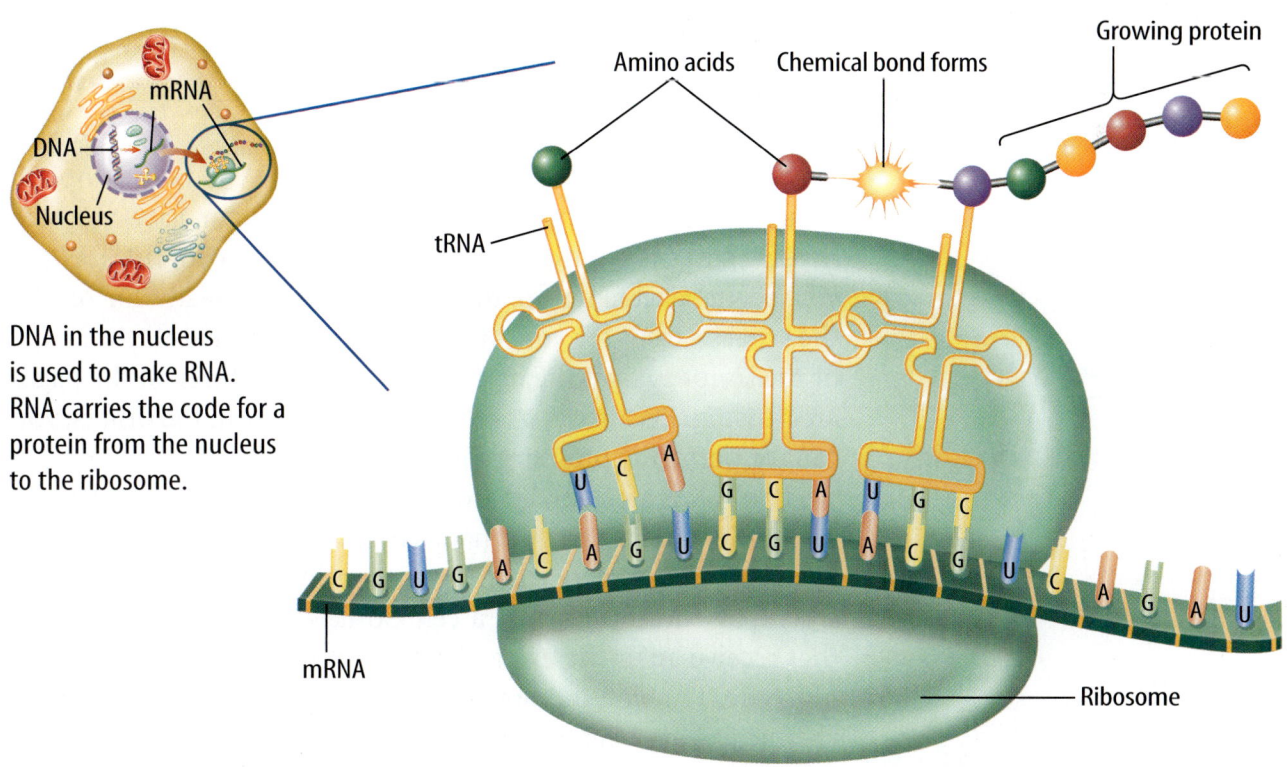

DNA in the nucleus is used to make RNA. RNA carries the code for a protein from the nucleus to the ribosome.

At the ribosome, the RNA's message is translated into a specific protein.

Controlling Genes You might think that because most cells in an organism have exactly the same chromosomes and the same genes, they would make the same proteins, but they don't. In many-celled organisms like you, each cell uses only some of the thousands of genes that it has to make proteins. Just as each actor uses only the lines from the script for his or her role, each cell uses only the genes that direct the making of proteins that it needs. For example, muscle proteins are made in muscle cells, as represented in **Figure 18,** but not in nerve cells.

Cells must be able to control genes by turning some genes off and turning other genes on. They do this in many different ways. Sometimes the DNA is twisted so tightly that no RNA can be made. Other times, chemicals bind to the DNA so that it cannot be used. If the incorrect proteins are produced, the organism cannot function properly.

Figure 18 Each cell in the body produces only the proteins that are necessary to do its job.

Mutations

Sometimes mistakes happen when DNA is being copied. Imagine that the copy of the script the director gave you was missing three pages. You use your copy to learn your lines. When you begin rehearsing for the play, everyone is ready for one of the scenes except for you. What happened? You check your copy of the script against the original and find that three of the pages are missing. Because your script is different from the others, you cannot perform your part correctly.

If DNA is not copied exactly, the proteins made from the instructions might not be made correctly. These mistakes, called **mutations,** are any permanent change in the DNA sequence of a gene or chromosome of a cell. Some mutations include cells that receive an entire extra chromosome or are missing a chromosome. Outside factors such as X rays, sunlight, and some chemicals have been known to cause mutations.

 *When are mutations likely to occur?*

Figure 19 Because of a defect on chromosome 2, the mutant fruit fly has short wings and cannot fly.
Predict Could this defect be transferred to the mutant's offspring? Explain.

Results of a Mutation Genes control the traits you inherit. Without correctly coded proteins, an organism can't grow, repair, or maintain itself. A change in a gene or chromosome can change the traits of an organism, as illustrated in **Figure 19**.

If the mutation occurs in a body cell, it might or might not be life threatening to the organism. However, if a mutation occurs in a sex cell, then all the cells that are formed from that sex cell will have that mutation. Mutations add variety to a species when the organism reproduces. Many mutations are harmful to organisms, often causing their death. Some mutations do not appear to have any effect on the organism, and some can even be beneficial. For example, a mutation to a plant might cause it to produce a chemical that certain insects avoid. If these insects normally eat the plant, the mutation will help the plant survive.

Topic: Fruit Fly Genes
Visit in7.msscience.com for Web links to information about what genes are present on the chromosomes of a fruit fly.

Activity Draw a picture of one of the chromosomes of a fruit fly and label some of its genes.

section 3 review

Summary

What is DNA?
- Each side of the DNA ladder is made up of sugar-phosphate molecules, and the rungs of the ladder are made up of nitrogenous bases.
- When DNA is copied, the new DNA has bases that are identical to those of the original DNA.

Genes
- The instructions for making a specific protein are found in genes in the cell nucleus. Proteins are made on ribosomes in the cytoplasm.
- There are three main kinds of RNA—mRNA, rRNA, and tRNA.

Mutations
- If DNA is not copied exactly, the resulting mutations may cause proteins to be made incorrectly.

Self Check

1. **Describe** how DNA makes a copy of itself.
2. **Explain** how the codes for proteins are carried from the nucleus to the ribosomes.
3. **Apply** A strand of DNA has the bases AGTAAC. Using letters, show a matching DNA strand.
4. **Determine** how tRNA is used when cells build proteins.
5. **Think Critically** You begin as one cell. Compare the DNA in your brain cells to the DNA in your heart cells.

Applying Skills

6. **Concept Map** Using a Venn diagram, compare and contrast DNA and RNA.
7. **Use a word processor** to make an outline of the events that led up to the discovery of DNA. Use library resources to find this information.

LAB Use the Internet

Mutations

▶ Real-World Question

Mutations can result in dominant or recessive genes. A recessive characteristic can appear only if an organism has two recessive genes for that characteristic. However, a dominant characteristic can appear if an organism has one or two dominant genes for that characteristic. Why do some mutations result in more common traits while others do not? Form a hypothesis about how a mutation can become a common trait.

Fantail pigeon

Goals
- **Observe** traits of various animals.
- **Research** how mutations become traits.
- Gather data about mutations.
- Make a frequency table of your findings and communicate them to other students.

Data Source

Visit **in7.msscience.com/ internet_lab** for more information on common genetic traits in different animals, recessive and dominant genes, and data from other students.

▶ Make a Plan

1. **Observe** common traits in various animals, such as household pets or animals you might see in a zoo.
2. **Learn** what genes carry these traits in each animal.
3. **Research** the traits to discover which ones are results of mutations. Are all mutations dominant? Are any of these mutations beneficial?

White tiger

116 CHAPTER 4 Cell Reproduction

Using Scientific Methods

Follow Your Plan

1. Make sure your teacher approves your plan before you start.
2. Visit the link shown below to access different Web sites for information about mutations and genetics.
3. **Decide** if a mutation is beneficial, harmful, or neither. Record your data in your Science Journal.

Analyze Your Data

1. **Record** in your Science Journal a list of traits that are results of mutations.
2. **Describe** an animal, such as a pet or an animal you've seen in the zoo. Point out which traits are known to be the result of a mutation.
3. **Make** a chart that compares recessive mutations to dominant mutations. Which are more common?
4. **Share** your data with other students by posting it at the link shown below.

Siberian Husky's eyes

Conclude and Apply

1. **Compare** your findings to those of your classmates and other data at the link shown below. What were some of the traits your classmates found that you did not? Which were the most common?
2. Look at your chart of mutations. Are all mutations beneficial? When might a mutation be harmful to an organism?
3. **Predict** how your data would be affected if you had performed this lab when one of these common mutations first appeared. Do you think you would see more or less animals with this trait?
4. Mutations occur every day but we only see a few of them. Infer how many mutations over millions of years can lead to a new species.

Find this lab using the link below. **Post** your data in the table provided. Combine your data with that of other students and make a chart that shows all of the data.

in7.msscience.com/internet_lab

LAB **117**

Oops! Accidents in SCIENCE

SOMETIMES GREAT DISCOVERIES HAPPEN BY ACCIDENT!

A Tangled Tale
How did a scientist get chromosomes to separate?

Thanks to chromosomes, each of us is unique!

Viewed under the microscope, chromosomes in cells sometimes look a lot like spaghetti. That's why scientists had such a hard time figuring out how many chromosomes are in each human cell. Imagine, then, how Dr. Tao-Chiuh Hsu (dow shew•SEW) must have felt when he looked into a microscope and saw "beautifully scattered chromosomes." The problem was, Hsu didn't know what he had done to separate the chromosomes into countable strands.

"I tried to study those slides and set up some more cultures to repeat the miracle," Hsu explained. "But nothing happened."

For three months Hsu tried changing every variable he could think of to make the chromosomes separate again. In April 1952, his efforts were finally rewarded. Hsu quickly realized that the chromosomes separated because of osmosis.

Osmosis is the movement of water molecules through cell membranes. This movement occurs in predictable ways. The water molecules move from areas with higher concentrations of water to areas with lower concentrations of water. In Hsu's case, the solution he used to prepare the cells had a higher concentration of water then the cell did. So water moved from the solution into the cell and the cell swelled until it finally exploded. The chromosomes suddenly were visible as separate strands.

What made the cells swell the first time? Apparently a technician had mixed the solution incorrectly. "Since nearly four months had elapsed, there was no way to trace who actually had prepared that particular [solution]," Hsu noted. "Therefore, this heroine must remain anonymous."

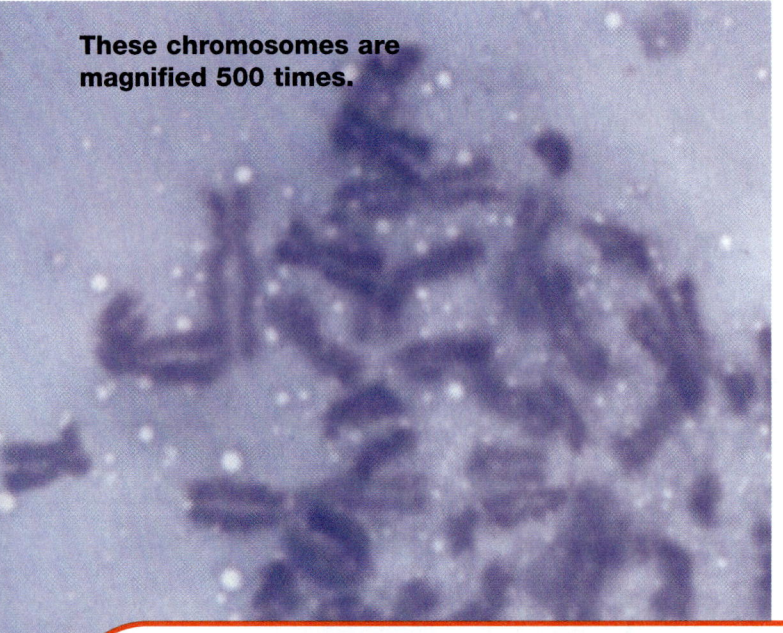

These chromosomes are magnified 500 times.

Research What developments led scientists to conclude that the human cell has 46 chromosomes? Visit the link shown to the right to get started.

Science online
For more information, visit
in7.msscience.com/oops

Chapter 4 Study Guide

Reviewing Main Ideas

Section 1 — Cell Division and Mitosis

1. The life cycle of a cell has two parts—growth and development, and cell division.

2. In mitosis, the nucleus divides to form two identical nuclei. Mitosis occurs in four continuous steps, or phases—prophase, metaphase, anaphase, and telophase.

3. Cell division in animal cells and plant cells is similar, but plant cells do not have centrioles and animal cells do not form cell walls.

4. Organisms use cell division to grow, to replace cells, and for asexual reproduction. Asexual reproduction produces organisms with DNA identical to the parent's DNA. Fission, budding, and regeneration can be used for asexual reproduction.

Section 2 — Sexual Reproduction and Meiosis

1. Sexual reproduction results when an egg and sperm join. This event is called fertilization, and the cell that forms is called the zygote.

2. Meiosis occurs in the reproductive organs, producing four haploid sex cells.

3. During meiosis, two divisions of the nucleus occur.

4. Meiosis ensures that offspring produced by fertilization have the same number of chromosomes as their parents.

Section 3 — DNA

1. DNA is a large molecule made up of two twisted strands of sugar-phosphate molecules and nitrogen bases.

2. All cells contain DNA. The section of DNA on a chromosome that directs the making of a specific protein is a gene.

3. DNA can copy itself and is the pattern from which RNA is made. Messenger RNA, ribosomal RNA, and transfer RNA are used to make proteins.

4. Permanent changes in DNA are called mutations.

Visualizing Main Ideas

Think of four ways that organisms can use mitosis. Copy and complete the spider diagram below.

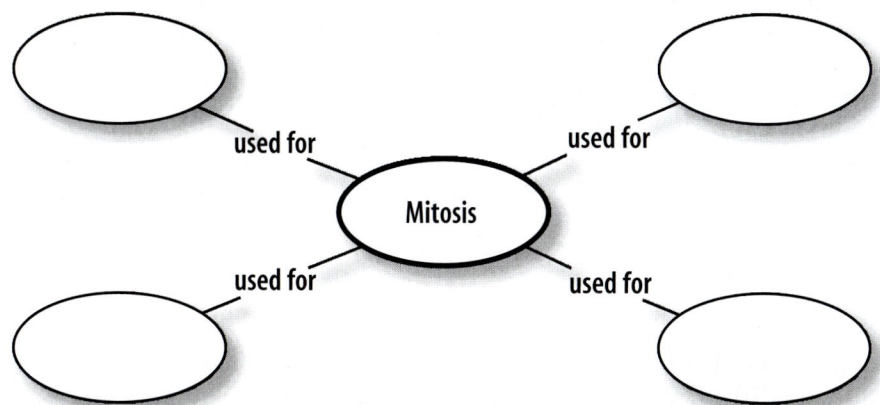

Chapter 4 Review

Using Vocabulary

asexual reproduction p. 101
chromosome p. 98
diploid p. 104
DNA p. 110
egg p. 104
fertilization p. 104
gene p. 112
haploid p. 105
meiosis p. 105
mitosis p. 98
mutation p. 114
RNA p. 112
sexual reproduction p. 104
sperm p. 104
zygote p. 104

Fill in the blanks with the correct vocabulary word or words.

1. _____ and _____ cells are sex cells.
2. _____ produces two identical cells.
3. An example of a nucleic acid is _____.
4. A(n) _____ is the code for a protein.
5. A(n) _____ sperm is formed during meiosis.
6. Budding is a type of _____.
7. A(n) _____ is a structure in the nucleus that contains hereditary material.
8. _____ produces four sex cells.
9. As a result of _____, a new organism develops that has its own unique identity.
10. An error made during the copying of DNA is called a(n) _____.

Checking Concepts

Choose the word or phrase that best answers the question.

11. Which of the following is a double spiral molecule with pairs of nitrogen bases?
    A) RNA   C) protein
    B) amino acid   D) DNA

12. What is in RNA but not in DNA?
    A) thymine   C) adenine
    B) thyroid   D) uracil

13. If a diploid tomato cell has 24 chromosomes, how many chromosomes will the tomato's sex cells have?
    A) 6   C) 24
    B) 12   D) 48

14. During a cell's life cycle, when do chromosomes duplicate?
    A) anaphase   C) interphase
    B) metaphase   D) telophase

15. When do chromatids separate during mitosis?
    A) anaphase   C) metaphase
    B) prophase   D) telophase

16. How is the hydra shown in the picture reproducing?
    A) asexually, by budding
    B) sexually, by budding
    C) asexually, by fission
    D) sexually, by fission

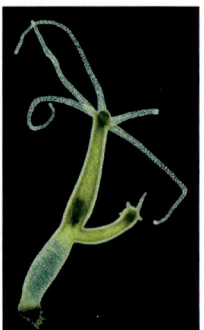

17. What is any permanent change in a gene or a chromosome called?
    A) fission   C) replication
    B) reproduction D) mutation

18. What does meiosis produce?
    A) cells with the diploid chromosome number
    B) cells with identical chromosomes
    C) sex cells
    D) a zygote

19. What type of nucleic acid carries the codes for making proteins from the nucleus to the ribosome?
    A) DNA   C) protein
    B) RNA   D) genes

chapter 4 Review

Thinking Critically

20. List the base sequence of a strand of RNA made using the DNA pattern ATCCGTC. Look at **Figure 14** for a hint.

21. Predict whether a mutation in a human skin cell can be passed on to the person's offspring. Explain.

22. Explain how a zygote could end up with an extra chromosome.

23. Classify Copy and complete this table about DNA and RNA.

DNA and RNA		
	DNA	**RNA**
Number of strands		
Type of sugar	Do not write in this book.	
Letter names of bases		
Where found		

24. Concept Map Make an events-chain concept map of what occurs from interphase in the parent cell to the formation of the zygote. Tell whether the chromosome's number at each stage is haploid or diploid.

25. Concept Map Copy and complete the events-chain concept map of DNA synthesis.

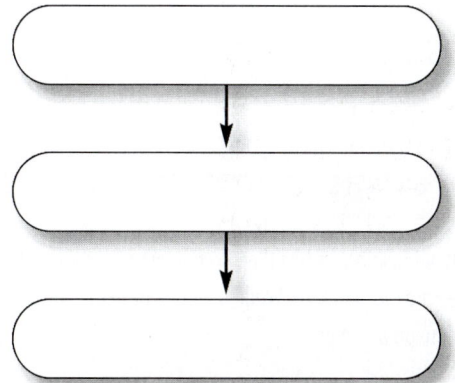

26. Compare and Contrast Meiosis is two divisions of a reproductive cell's nucleus. It occurs in a continuous series of steps. Compare and contrast the steps of meiosis I to the steps of meiosis II.

27. Describe what occurs in mitosis that gives the new cells identical DNA.

28. Form a hypothesis about the effect of an incorrect mitotic division on the new cells produced.

29. Determine how many chromosomes are in the original cell compared to those in the new cells formed by cell division. Explain.

Performance Activities

30. Flash Cards Make a set of 11 flash cards with drawings of a cell that show the different stages of meiosis. Shuffle your cards and then put them in the correct order. Give them to another student in the class to try.

Applying Math

31. Cell Cycle Assume an average human cell has a cell cycle of 20 hours. Calculate how many cells there would be after 80 hours.

Use the diagram below to answer question 32.

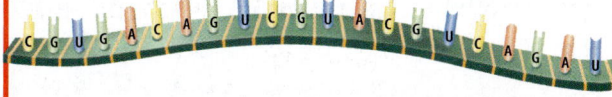

32. Amino Acids Sets of three nitrogen bases code for an amino acid. How many amino acids will make up the protein molecule that is coded for by the mRNA molecule above?

chapter 4 Indiana

The assessed Indiana standard appears above the question.

Record your answers on the answer sheet provided by your teacher or on a sheet of paper.

Part 1 Multiple Choice

The photo below shows a potato undergoing reproduction.

7.4.1

1. How does the genetic material of the new organism compare to the genetic material of the parent organism?

   A different genes

   B double the amount

   C half the amount

   D the same genes

7.4.4

2. What is the form of reproduction shown above?

   A asexual

   B meiosis

   C regeneration

   D sexual

The illustration below shows a model of genetic material.

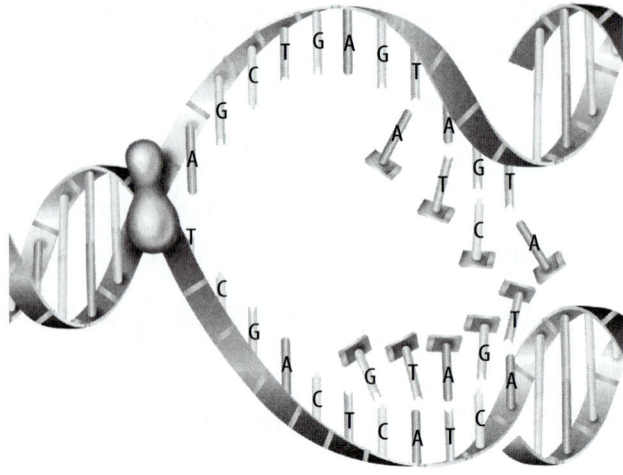

3. What does the illustration represent?

   A cell cycle

   B cell division

   C DNA duplication

   D RNA synthesis

4. When does the process shown above occur?

   A anaphase

   B interphase

   C metaphase

   D prophase

Test-Taking Tip

Prepare Avoid rushing on test day. Prepare your clothes and test supplies the night before. Wake up early and arrive at school on time on test day.

Standards Review

7.4.1

5. If an organism's sex cell has eight chromosomes, how many chromosomes are in the body cells of that organism?

   A 8 chromosomes

   B 16 chromosomes

   C 32 chromosomes

   D 64 chromosomes

The table below is about cell division.

Phase of Cell Cycle	Action
1	Chromosomes duplicate
2	Chromatid pairs are visible
Metaphase	
3	Chromosomes separate
4	Cytoplasm separates

6. What term correctly replaces phase 3?

   A anaphase

   B interphase

   C prophase

   D telephase

7. Which completes the action for metaphase in the table above?

   A cell organelles migrate

   B chromatid pairs line up

   C mitosis begins again

   D spindles form

Part 2 | Constructed Response

The photo below shows a cell undergoing cell division.

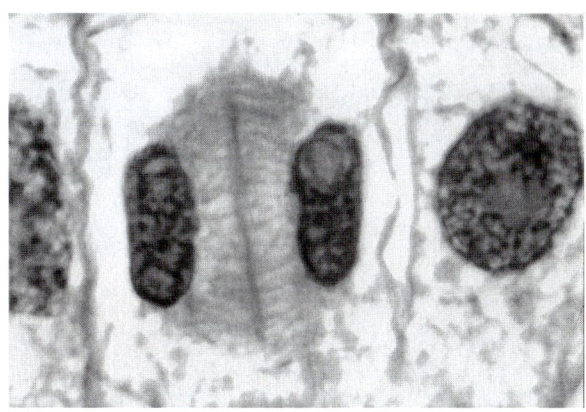

8. Is this cell an animal or a plant cell? Provide evidence to support your conclusion.

7.4.3

9. Describe the transfer of genetic information in sexual reproduction.

10. Compare and contrast DNA and RNA.

11. The diagram below shows protein synthesis.

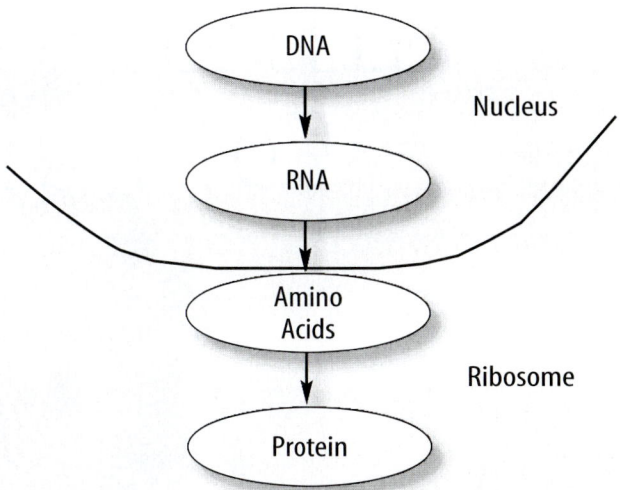

Give a detailed explanation of this diagram.

STANDARDS REVIEW 123

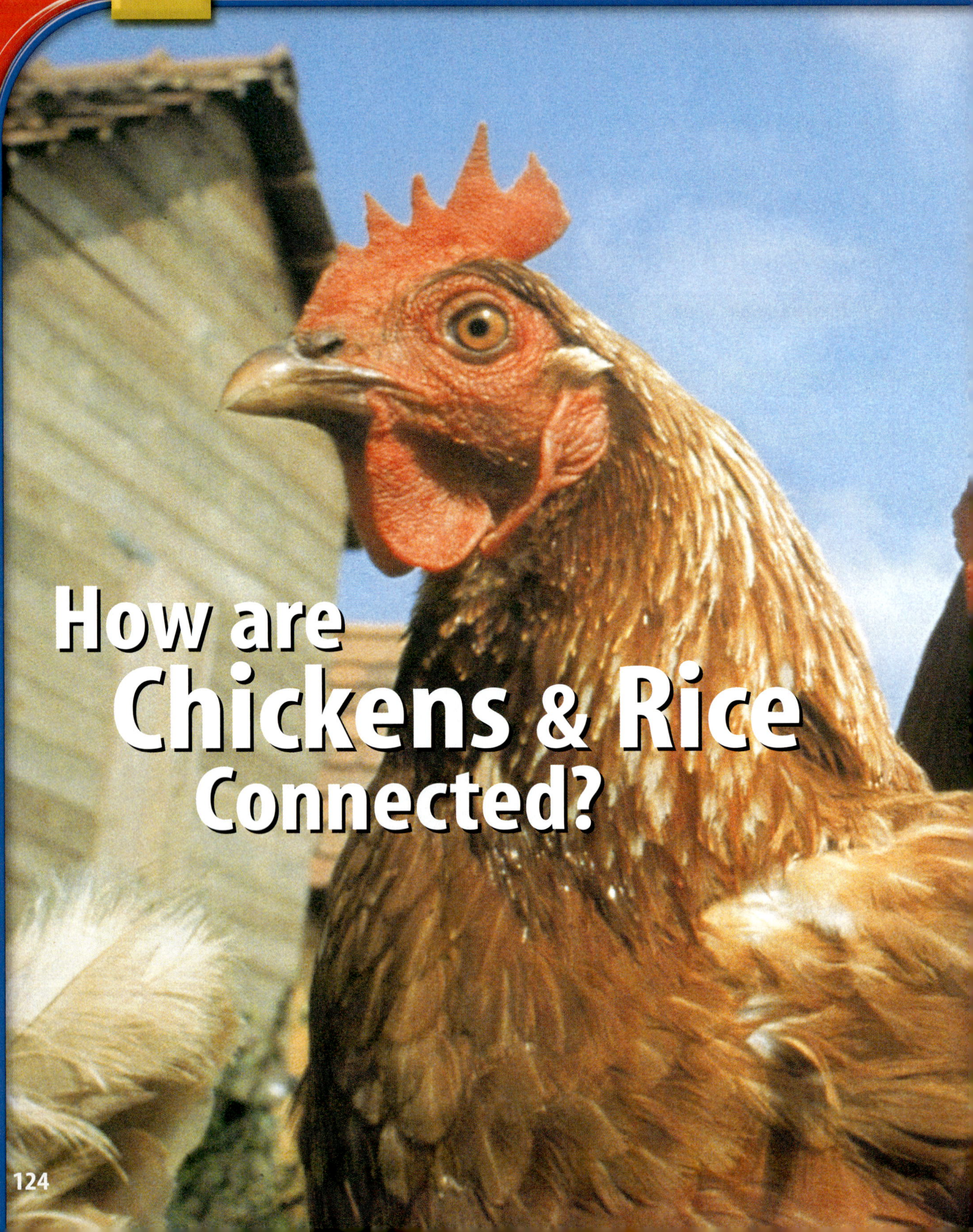

The Interdependence of Life

How are Chickens & Rice Connected?

Back in the 1800s, a mysterious disease called beriberi affected people in certain parts of Asia. One day, a doctor in Indonesia noticed some chickens staggering around, a symptom often seen in people with beriberi. It turned out that the chickens had been eating white rice—the same kind of rice that was being eaten by human beriberi sufferers. White rice has had the outer layers, including the bran, removed. When the sick chickens were fed rice that still had its bran, they quickly recovered. It turned out that the same treatment worked for people with beriberi! Research eventually showed that rice bran contains a vitamin, B_1, which is essential for good health. Today, white rice usually is "vitamin-enriched" to replace B_1 and other nutrients lost in processing.

unit projects

The assessed Indiana standard appears in blue.

To find project ideas and resources, visit in7.msscience.com/unit_project.
Projects include:

- **History** Contribute to a class "remedy journal" with interesting, out-dated medical treatments, and how techniques have improved. **7.6.1**
- **Technology** Investigate rare and interesting medical conditions, including their history, characteristics, and treatments. Present a colorful poster with photos and information for class display. **7.6.4**
- **Model** Gather data on hand span versus height for 20 people. Design a scatter plot to analyze trends and draw conclusions about growth, age, and gender relationships. **7.2.7**

 In *Investigating Disease and Prevention,* explore a variety of diseases and science through history, study one disease more in-depth, and then create a time line of new information. **7.6.1, 7.6.4**

chapter 5

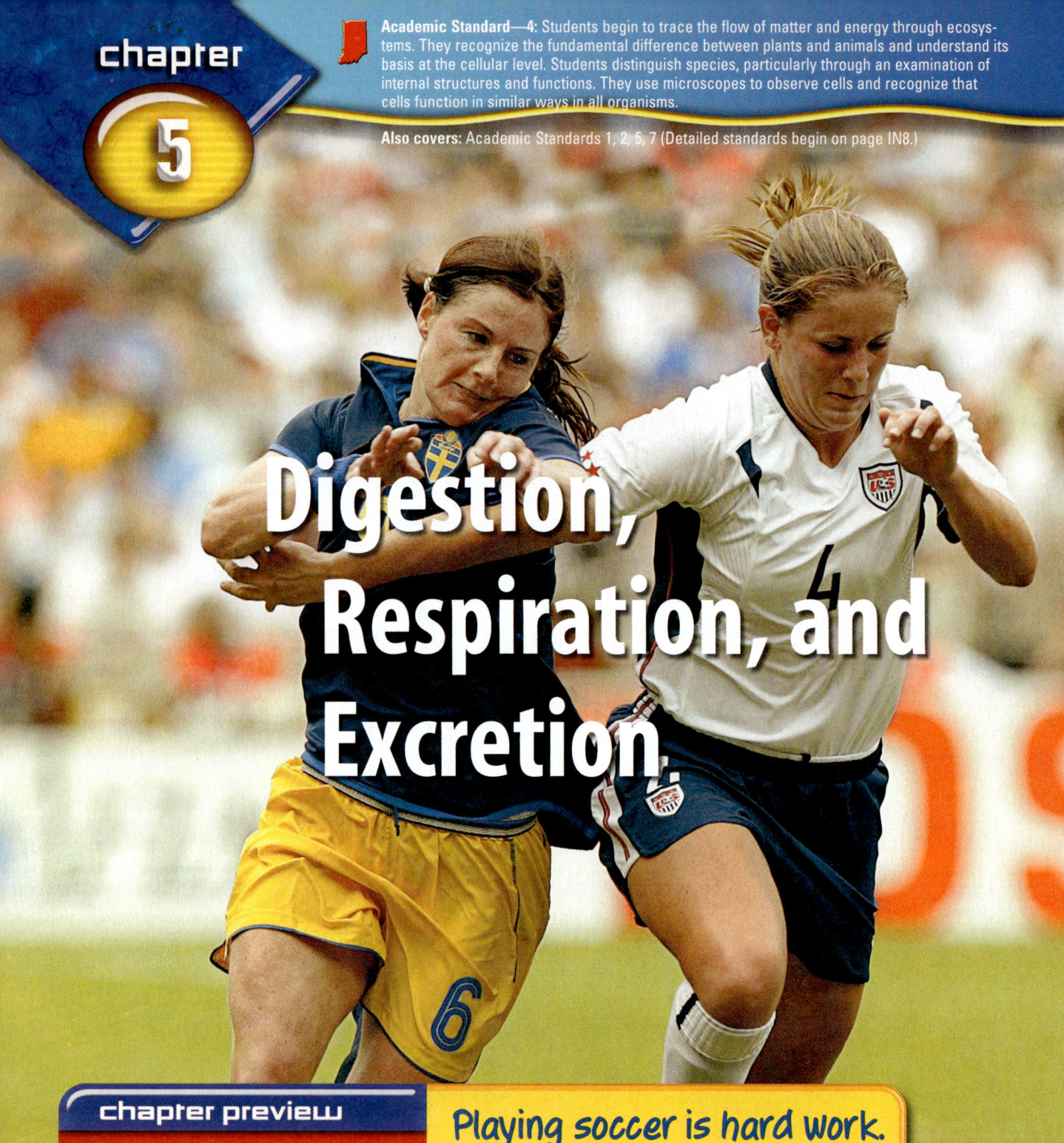

Academic Standard—4: Students begin to trace the flow of matter and energy through ecosystems. They recognize the fundamental difference between plants and animals and understand its basis at the cellular level. Students distinguish species, particularly through an examination of internal structures and functions. They use microscopes to observe cells and recognize that cells function in similar ways in all organisms.

Also covers: Academic Standards 1, 2, 5, 7 (Detailed standards begin on page IN8.)

Digestion, Respiration, and Excretion

chapter preview

sections
1. The Digestive System
2. Nutrition
   Lab Identifying Vitamin C Content
3. The Respiratory System
4. The Excretory System
   Lab Particle Size and Absorption
   Virtual Lab How do the parts of the respiratory system work together?

Playing soccer is hard work.
If you're like most people, when you play an active game like soccer you probably breathe hard and perspire. You need a constant supply of oxygen and energy to keep your body cells functioning. Your body is adapted to meet that need.

Science Journal Write a paragraph describing what you do to help your body recover after an active game.

Start-Up Activities

Breathing Rate

Your body can store food and water, but it cannot store much oxygen. Breathing brings oxygen into your body. In the following lab, find out about one factor that can change your breathing rate.

1. Put your hand on the side of your rib cage. Using a watch or clock with a second hand, count the number of breaths you take for 15 s. Multiply this number by four to calculate your normal breathing rate for one minute.
2. Repeat step 1 two more times, then calculate your average breathing rate.
3. Do a physical activity described by your teacher for one minute and repeat step 1 to determine your breathing rate now.
4. Time how long it takes for your breathing rate to return to normal.
5. **Think Critically** In your Science Journal, write a paragraph explaining how breathing rate appears to be related to physical activity.

Respiration Make the following Foldable to help identify what you already know, what you want to know, and what you learn about respiration.

STEP 1 **Fold** a vertical sheet of paper from side to side. Make the front edge about 1.25 cm shorter than the back edge.

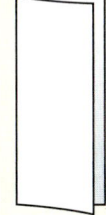

STEP 2 **Turn** lengthwise and **fold** into thirds.

STEP 3 **Unfold and cut** only the top layer along both folds to make three tabs. **Label** each tab.

Identify Questions Before you read the chapter, write *I breathe* under the left tab, and write *Why do I breathe?* under the center tab. As you read the chapter, write the answer you learn under the right tab.

Preview this chapter's content and activities at
in7.msscience.com

127

Standards—7.4.4: ... various organs and tissues function to serve the needs of cells for food ... **7.4.6:** Explain how food provides the fuel ... for all organisms. **7.4.8:** Describe how organisms that eat plants break down the plant structures to produce the materials and energy that they need to survive ...

section 1

The Digestive System

as you read

What You'll Learn
- **Distinguish** the differences between mechanical digestion and chemical digestion.
- **Identify** the organs of the digestive system and what takes place in each.
- **Explain** how homeostasis is maintained in digestion.

Why It's Important
The processes of the digestive system make the food you eat available to your cells.

Review Vocabulary
bacteria: one-celled organisms without membrane-bound organelles

New Vocabulary
- nutrient
- chyme
- enzyme
- villi
- peristalsis

Functions of the Digestive System

Food is processed in your body in four stages—ingestion, digestion, absorption, and elimination. Whether it is a piece of fruit or an entire meal, all the food you eat is treated to the same processes in your body. As soon as food enters your mouth, or is ingested, digestion begins. Digestion breaks down food so that nutrients (NEW tree unts) can be absorbed and moved into the blood. **Nutrients** are substances in food that provide energy and materials for cell development, growth, and repair. From the blood, these nutrients are transported across the cell membrane to be used by the cell. Unused substances pass out of your body as wastes.

Digestion is mechanical and chemical. Mechanical digestion takes place when food is chewed, mixed, and churned. Chemical digestion occurs when chemical reactions break down food.

Enzymes

Chemical digestion is possible only because of enzymes (EN zimez). An **enzyme** is a type of protein that speeds up the rate of a chemical reaction in your body. One way enzymes speed up reactions is by reducing the amount of energy necessary for a chemical reaction to begin. If enzymes weren't there to help, the rate of chemical reactions would be too slow. Some reactions might not even happen at all. As shown in **Figure 1,** enzymes work without being changed or used up.

Figure 1 Enzymes speed up the rate of certain body reactions.
Explain *what happens to the enzyme after it separates from the new molecule.*

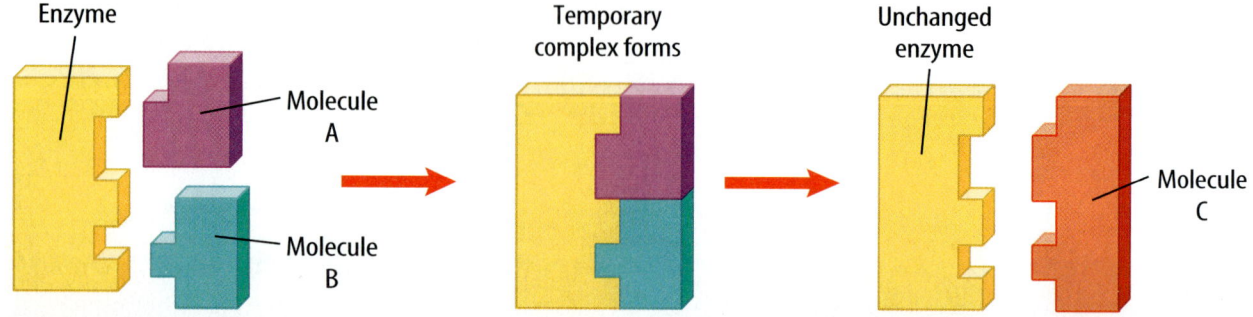

Enzymes in Digestion Many enzymes help you digest carbohydrates, proteins, and fats. These enzymes are produced in the salivary glands, stomach, small intestine, and pancreas.

Reading Check *What is the role of enzymes in the chemical digestion of food?*

Other Enzyme Actions Enzyme-aided reactions are not limited to the digestive process. Enzymes also help speed up chemical reactions responsible for building your body. They are involved in the energy-releasing activities of your muscle and nerve cells. Enzymes also aid in the blood-clotting process. Without enzymes, the chemical reactions in your body would happen too slowly for you to exist.

Organs of the Digestive System

Your digestive system has two parts—the digestive tract and the accessory organs. The major organs of your digestive tract—mouth, esophagus (ih SAH fuh gus), stomach, small intestine, large intestine, rectum, and anus—are shown in **Figure 2.** Food passes through all of these organs. The tongue, teeth, salivary glands, liver, gallbladder, and pancreas, also shown in **Figure 2,** are the accessory organs. Although food doesn't pass through them, they are important in mechanical and chemical digestion. Your liver, gallbladder, and pancreas produce or store enzymes and other chemicals that help break down food as it passes through the digestive tract.

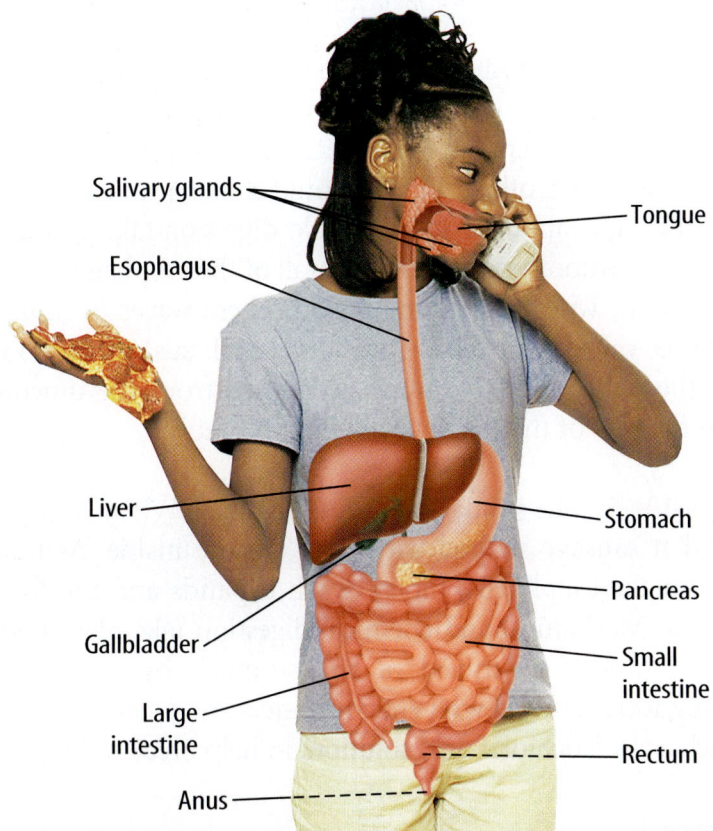

Figure 2 The human digestive system can be described as a tube divided into several specialized sections. If stretched out, an adult's digestive system is 6 m to 9 m long.

SECTION 1 The Digestive System

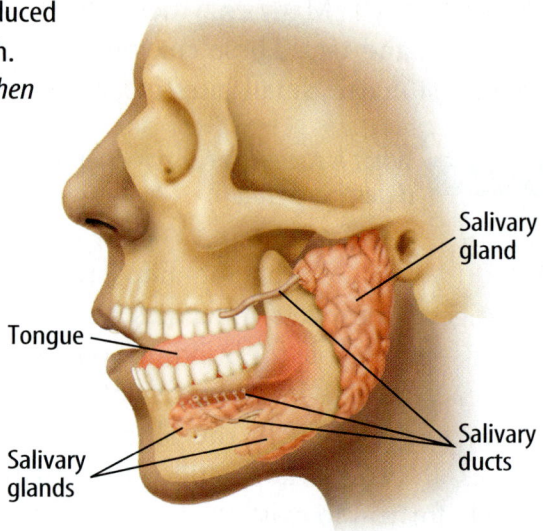

Figure 3 About 1.5 L of saliva are produced each day by salivary glands in your mouth. **Describe** what happens in your mouth when you think about a food you like.

The Mouth Mechanical and chemical digestion begin in your mouth. Mechanical digestion happens when you chew your food with your teeth and mix it with your tongue. Chemical digestion begins with the addition of a watery substance called saliva (suh LI vuh), which contains water, mucus, and an enzyme that aids in the breakdown of starch into sugar. Saliva is produced by three sets of glands near your mouth, shown in **Figure 3.** Food mixed with saliva becomes a soft mass and is moved to the back of your mouth by your tongue. It is swallowed and passes into your esophagus. Now ingestion is complete, but the process of digestion continues.

The Esophagus Food moving into the esophagus passes over a flap of tissue called the epiglottis (eh puh GLAH tus). This structure automatically covers the opening to the windpipe to prevent food from entering it, otherwise you would choke. Your esophagus is a muscular tube about 25 cm long. No digestion takes place in the esophagus. Smooth muscles in the wall of the esophagus move food downward with a squeezing action. These waves of muscle contractions, called **peristalsis** (per uh STAHL sus), move food through the entire digestive tract. Secretions from the mucous glands in the wall of the esophagus keep food moist.

The Stomach The stomach is a muscular bag. When empty, it is somewhat sausage shaped with folds on the inside. As food enters from the esophagus, the stomach expands and the folds smooth out. Mechanical and chemical digestion take place here. Mechanically, food is mixed in the stomach by peristalsis. Chemically, food is mixed with enzymes and strong digestive solutions, such as hydrochloric acid solution, to help break it down.

Specialized cells in the stomach's walls release about two liters of hydrochloric acid solution each day. This solution works with the enzyme pepsin to digest protein and destroys bacteria that are present in food. The stomach also produces mucus, which makes food more slippery and protects the stomach from the strong, digestive solutions. Food is changed in the stomach into a thin, watery liquid called **chyme** (KIME). Slowly, chyme moves out of your stomach and into your small intestine.

 **Why isn't your stomach digested by the acidic digestive solution?**

The Small Intestine Your small intestine, shown in **Figure 4,** is small in diameter, but it measures 4 m to 7 m in length. As chyme leaves your stomach, it enters the first part of your small intestine, called the duodenum (doo AH duh num). Most digestion takes place in your duodenum. Here, bile—a greenish fluid from the liver—is added. The acidic solution from the stomach makes large fat particles float to the top of the chyme. Bile breaks up the large fat particles, similar to the way detergent breaks up grease.

Chemical digestion of carbohydrates, proteins, and fats occurs when a digestive solution from the pancreas is mixed in. This solution contains bicarbonate ions and enzymes. The bicarbonate ions help neutralize the stomach acid that is mixed with chyme. Your pancreas also makes insulin, a hormone that allows glucose to pass from the bloodstream into your cells.

Absorption of broken down food takes place in the small intestine. The wall of the small intestine, shown in **Figure 4,** has many ridges and folds. These folds are covered with fingerlike projections called **villi** (VIH li). Villi increase the surface area of the small intestine, which allows more places for nutrients to be absorbed. Nutrients move into blood vessels within the villi. From here, blood transports the nutrients to all cells of your body. Peristalsis continues to force the remaining undigested and unabsorbed materials slowly into the large intestine.

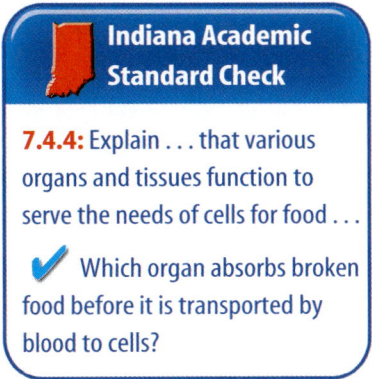

Indiana Academic Standard Check

7.4.4: Explain . . . that various organs and tissues function to serve the needs of cells for food . . .

✓ Which organ absorbs broken food before it is transported by blood to cells?

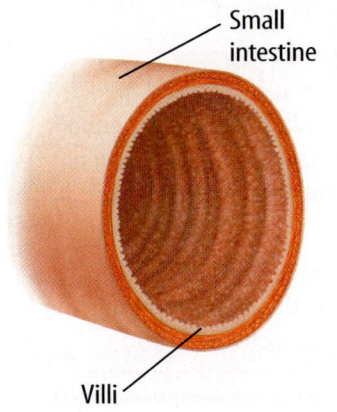
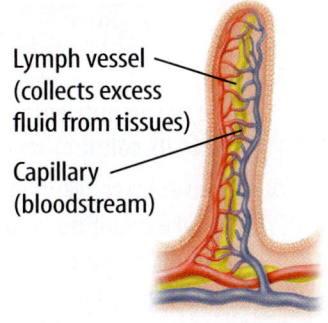

Figure 4 Hundreds of thousands of densely packed villi give the impression of a velvet cloth surface. If the surface area of your villi could be stretched out, it would cover an area the size of a tennis court.
Infer what would happen to a person's weight if the number of villi were drastically reduced. Why?

Large Intestine Bacteria
The species of bacteria that live in your large intestine are adapted to their habitat. What do you think would happen to the bacteria if their environment were to change? How would this affect your large intestine? Discuss your ideas with a classmate and write your answers in your Science Journal.

The Large Intestine When the chyme enters the large intestine, it is still a thin, watery mixture. The large intestine absorbs water from the undigested mass, which helps maintain homeostasis (hoh mee oh STAY sus). Peristalsis usually slows down in the large intestine. After the excess water is absorbed, the remaining undigested materials become more solid. Muscles in the rectum, which is the last section of the large intestine, and the anus control the release of semisolid wastes from the body in the form of feces (FEE seez).

Bacteria Are Important

Many types of bacteria live in your body. Some bacteria live in many of the organs of your digestive tract including your mouth and large intestine. Some of these bacteria live in a relationship that is beneficial to the bacteria and to your body. The bacteria in your large intestine feed on undigested material like cellulose and make vitamins you need—vitamin K and two B vitamins. Vitamin K is needed for blood clotting. The two B vitamins, niacin and thiamine, are important for your nervous system and for other body functions. Bacterial action also converts bile pigments into new compounds. The breakdown of intestinal materials by bacteria produces gas.

section 1 review

Summary

Functions of the Digestive System
- Food is processed in four stages—ingestion, digestion, absorption, and elimination.

Enzymes
- Enzymes make chemical digestion possible.
- Enzymes are used in other chemical reactions, including blood clotting.

Organs of the Digestive System
- In the digestive system, food passes through the mouth, esophagus, stomach, small intestine, large intestine, rectum, and anus.
- Accessory digestive organs help in mechanical and chemical digestion.

Bacteria Are Important
- Some bacteria that live in the organs of the digestive tract are helpful to your body.

Self Check

1. **Compare and contrast** mechanical digestion and chemical digestion.
2. **Describe** the function of each organ through which food passes as it moves through the digestive tract.
3. **Explain** how activities in the large intestine help maintain homeostasis.
4. **Describe** how the accessory organs aid digestion.
5. **Think Critically** Crackers contain starch. Explain why a cracker begins to taste sweet after it is in your mouth for five minutes without being chewed.

Applying Skills

6. **Recognize Cause and Effect** What would happen to some of the nutrients in chyme if the pancreas did not secrete its solution into the small intestine?
7. **Communicate** Write a paragraph in your Science Journal explaining what would happen to the mechanical and chemical digestion in a person missing a large portion of his or her stomach.

in7.msscience.com/self_check_quiz

section 2

Standards—7.4.6: Explain how food provides the fuel and the building material for all organisms.
7.4.8: Describe how organisms that eat plants break down the plant structures to produce the materials and energy that they need to survive, and in turn, how they are consumed by other organisms.

Also covers: 7.4.2, 7.4.4, 7.4.11 (Detailed standards begin on page IN8.)

Nutrition

Why do you eat?

You might choose a food because of its taste, because it's readily available, or quickly prepared. However, as much as you don't want to admit it, the nutritional value of and Calories in foods are more important. A Calorie is a measurement of the amount of energy available in food. The amount of food energy a person requires varies with body weight, age, sex, activity level, and natural body efficiency. A chocolate donut might be tasty, quick to eat, and provide plenty of Calories, but it has only some of the nutrients that your body needs.

Classes of Nutrients

Six kinds of nutrients are available in food—proteins, carbohydrates, fats, vitamins, minerals, and water. Proteins, carbohydrates, vitamins, and fats all contain carbon and are called organic nutrients. Inorganic nutrients, such as water and minerals, do not contain carbon. Foods containing carbohydrates, fats, and proteins need to be digested or broken down before your body can use them. Water, vitamins, and minerals don't require digestion and are absorbed directly into your bloodstream.

as you read

What You'll Learn
- **Distinguish** among the six classes of nutrients.
- **Identify** the importance of each type of nutrient.
- **Explain** the relationship between diet and health.

Why It's Important
You can make healthful food choices if you know what nutrients your body uses daily.

Review Vocabulary
molecule: the smallest particle of a substance that retains the properties of the substance and is composed of one or more atoms

New Vocabulary
- amino acid
- carbohydrate
- vitamin
- mineral

Proteins Your body uses proteins for replacement and repair of body cells and for growth. Proteins are large molecules that contain carbon, hydrogen, oxygen, nitrogen, and sometimes sulfur. A molecule of protein is made up of a large number of smaller units, or building blocks, called **amino acids**. You can see some sources of proteins in **Figure 5**.

Figure 5 Meats, poultry, eggs, fish, peas, beans, and nuts are all rich in protein.

SECTION 2 Nutrition **133**

Topic: Fiber
Visit in7.msscience.com for Web links to recent news or magazine articles about the importance of fiber in your diet.
Activity In your Science Journal, classify your favorite foods into two groups—*Good source of fiber* and *Little or no fiber.*

Indiana Academic Standard Check

7.4.8: Describe how organisms that eat plants break down plant structures to produce the materials and energy that they need to survive . . .

✔ What complex carbohydrate is in plant cell walls and what is its function in human diets?

Figure 6 These foods contain carbohydrates that provide energy for all the things that you do. **Describe** *the role of carbohydrates in your body.*

Protein Building Blocks Your body needs only 20 amino acids in various combinations to make the thousands of proteins used in your cells. Most of these amino acids can be made in your body's cells, but eight of them cannot. These eight are called essential amino acids. They have to be supplied by the foods you eat. Complete proteins provide all of the essential amino acids. Eggs, milk, cheese, and meat contain complete proteins. Incomplete proteins are missing one or more of the essential amino acids. If you are a vegetarian, you can get all of the essential amino acids by eating a wide variety of protein-rich vegetables, fruits, and grains.

Carbohydrates Study the nutrition label on several boxes of cereal. You'll notice that the number of grams of carbohydrates found in a typical serving of cereal is higher than the amounts of the other nutrients. **Carbohydrates** (kar boh HI drayts) usually are the main sources of energy for your body.

Three types of carbohydrates are sugar, starch, and fiber, shown in **Figure 6.** Sugars are called simple carbohydrates. You're probably most familiar with table sugar. However, fruits, honey, and milk also contain forms of sugar. Your cells break down glucose, a simple sugar.

The other two types of carbohydrates—starch and fiber—are called complex carbohydrates. Starch is found in potatoes and foods made from grains such as pasta. Starches are made up of many simple sugars. Fiber, such as cellulose, is found in the cell walls of plant cells. Foods like whole-grain breads and cereals, beans, peas, and other vegetables and fruits are good sources of fiber. Because different types of fiber are found in foods, you should eat a variety of fiber-rich plant foods. You cannot digest fiber, but it is needed to keep your digestive system running smoothly.

Fats The term *fat* has developed a negative meaning for some people. However, fats, also called lipids, are necessary because they provide energy and help your body absorb vitamins. Fat tissue cushions your internal organs. A major part of every cell membrane is made up of a type of fat.

134 CHAPTER 5 Digestion, Respiration, and Excretion

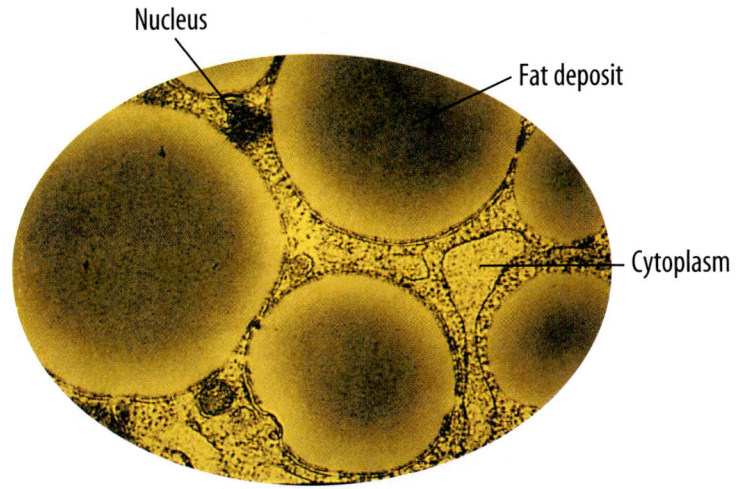

Figure 7 Fat is stored in certain cells in your body. Fat deposits push the cytoplasm and nucleus to the edge of the cell.

A gram of fat can release more than twice as much energy as a gram of carbohydrate can. Because fat is a good storage unit for energy, excess energy from the foods you eat is converted to fat and stored for later use, as shown in **Figure 7**.

Reading Check Why is fat a good storage unit for energy?

Fats are classified as unsaturated or saturated based on their chemical structure. Unsaturated fats are usually liquid at room temperature. Vegetable oils as well as fats found in seeds are unsaturated fats. Saturated fats are found in meats, animal products, and some plants and are usually solid at room temperature. Saturated fats have been associated with high levels of blood cholesterol. Your body makes cholesterol in your liver. Cholesterol is part of the cell membrane in all of your cells. However, a diet high in cholesterol may result in deposits forming on the inside walls of blood vessels. These deposits can block the blood supply to organs and increase blood pressure. This can lead to heart disease and strokes.

Vitamins Your bone cells need vitamin D to use calcium, and your blood needs vitamin K in order to clot. **Vitamins** are organic nutrients needed in small quantities for growth, regulating body functions, and preventing some diseases.

Vitamins are classified into two groups. Some vitamins dissolve easily in water and are called water-soluble vitamins. They are not stored by your body so you have to consume them daily. Other vitamins dissolve only in fat and are called fat-soluble vitamins. These vitamins are stored by your body. Although you eat or drink most vitamins, some are made by your body. Vitamin D is made when your skin is exposed to sunlight. Recall that vitamin K and two of the B vitamins are made in your large intestine with the help of bacteria that live there.

Mini LAB

Comparing the Fat Content of Foods

Procedure
1. Collect three pieces of each of the following foods: **potato chips; pretzels; peanuts;** and **small cubes of fruits, cheese, vegetables,** and **meat.**
2. Place the food items on a piece of **brown grocery bag.** Label the paper with the name of each food. Do not taste the foods.
3. Allow foods to sit for 30 min.
4. Remove the items, properly dispose of them, and observe the paper.

Analysis
1. Which items left a translucent (greasy) mark? Which left a wet mark?
2. How are the foods that left a greasy mark on the paper alike?
3. Use this test to determine which other foods contain fats. A greasy mark means the food contains fat. A wet mark means the food contains a lot of water.

SECTION 2 Nutrition

Table 1 Minerals

Mineral	Health Effect	Food Sources
Calcium	strong bones and teeth, blood clotting, muscle and nerve activity	dairy products, eggs, green leafy vegetables, soy
Phosphorus	strong bones and teeth, muscle contraction, stores energy	cheese, meat, cereal
Potassium	balance of water in cells, nerve impulse conduction, muscle contraction	bananas, potatoes, nuts, meat, oranges
Sodium	fluid balance in tissues, nerve impulse conduction	meat, milk, cheese, salt, beets, carrots, nearly all foods
Iron	oxygen is transported in hemoglobin by red blood cells	red meat, raisins, beans, spinach, eggs
Iodine (trace)	thyroid activity, metabolic stimulation	seafood, iodized salt

Salt Mines The mineral halite is processed to make table salt. In the United States, most salt comes from underground mines. Research to find the location of these mines, then label them on a map.

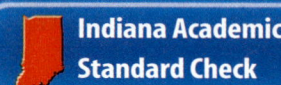

Indiana Academic Standard Check

7.4.6: Explain how food provides the fuel and the building material for all organisms.

✓ What mineral comes from seafood and is needed for thyroid activity?

Minerals Inorganic nutrients—nutrients that lack carbon and regulate many chemical reactions in your body—are called **minerals.** Of about 14 minerals that your body uses, calcium and phosphorus are used in the largest amounts for a variety of body functions. One of these functions is the formation and maintenance of bone. Some minerals, called trace minerals, are required only in small amounts. Copper and iodine usually are listed as trace minerals. Minerals are not used by the body as a source of energy. However, they do serve many different functions. Several minerals, their health effects, and some food sources for them are listed in **Table 1.**

 Why is copper considered a trace mineral?

Water Next to oxygen, water is the most important factor for survival. Different organisms need different amounts of water to survive. You could live for a few weeks without food but for only a few days without water because your cells need water to carry out their work. Most of the nutrients you have studied in this chapter can't be used by your body unless they are carried in a solution. This means that they have to be dissolved in water. In cells, chemical reactions take place in solutions.

The human body is about 60 percent water by mass. About two-thirds of your body water is located in your body cells. Water also is found around cells and in body fluids such as blood. **Table 2** shows how your body loses water every day. To replace water lost each day, you need to drink about 2 L of liquids. However, drinking liquids isn't the only way to supply cells with water. Most foods have more water than you realize. An apple is about 80 percent water, and many meats are 90 percent water.

Why do you get thirsty? Your body is made up of systems that operate together. When your body needs to replace lost water, messages are sent to your brain that result in a feeling of thirst. Drinking water satisfies your thirst and usually restores the body's homeostasis. When homeostasis is restored, the signal to the brain stops and you no longer feel thirsty.

Food Groups

Because no naturally occurring food has every nutrient, you need to eat a variety of foods. Nutritionists have developed a simple system, called the food pyramid, shown in **Figure 8,** to help people select foods that supply all the nutrients needed for energy and growth. The recommended daily amount for each food group will supply your body with the nutrients it needs for good health.

Table 2 Water Loss

Method of Loss	Amount (mL/day)
Exhaled air	350
Feces	150
Skin (mostly as sweat)	500
Urine	1,500

Figure 8 The pyramid shape reminds you that you should consume more servings from the bread and cereal group than from other groups.
Analyze *Where should the least number of servings come from?*

Fats, oils, and sweets

Milk, yogurt, and cheese

Meat, poultry, fish, dry beans, eggs, and nuts

Vegetables

Fruits

Bread, cereal, rice, and pasta

SECTION 2 Nutrition **137**

Figure 9 The information on a food label can help you decide what to eat.

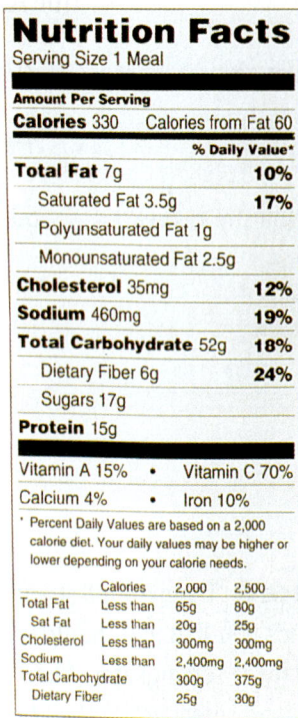

Daily Servings Each day you should eat six to eleven servings from the bread and cereal group, three to five servings from the vegetable group, two to four servings from the fruit group, two to three servings from the milk group, and two to three servings from the meat and beans group. Only small amounts of fats, oils, and sweets should be consumed.

The size of a serving is different for different foods. For example, a slice of bread or one ounce of ready-to-eat cereal is a bread and cereal group serving. One cup of raw leafy vegetables or one-half cup of cooked or chopped raw vegetables make a serving from the vegetable group. One medium apple, banana, or orange, one-half cup of canned fruit, or three-quarter cup of fruit juice is a fruit serving. A serving from the milk group can be one cup of milk or yogurt. Two ounces of cooked lean meat, one-half cup of cooked dry beans, one egg, or two tablespoons of peanut butter counts as a serving from the meat and beans group.

Food Labels The nutritional facts found on all packaged foods make it easier to make healthful food choices. These labels, as shown in **Figure 9,** can help you plan meals that supply the daily recommended amounts of nutrients and meet special dietary requirements (for example, a low-fat diet).

section 2 review

Summary

Why do you eat?
- Nutrients in food provide energy and materials for cell development, growth, and repair.

Classes of Nutrients
- Six kinds of nutrients are found in food—proteins, carbohydrates, fats, vitamins, minerals, and water.
- Proteins are used for growth and repair, carbohydrates provide energy, and fats store energy and cushion organs.
- Vitamins and minerals regulate body functions.
- Next to oxygen, water is the most important factor for your survival.

Food Groups
- The food pyramid and nutritional labels can help you choose foods that supply all the nutrients you need for energy and growth.

Self Check

1. **List** one example of a food source for each of the six classes of nutrients.
2. **Explain** how your body uses each class of nutrients.
3. **Discuss** how food choices can positively and negatively affect your health.
4. **Explain** the importance of water in the body.
5. **Think Critically** What foods from each food group would provide a balanced breakfast? Explain.

Applying Skills

6. **Interpret Data** Nutritional information can be found on the labels of most foods. Interpret the labels found on three different types of food products.
7. **Use a Spreadsheet** Make a spreadsheet of the minerals listed in **Table 1.** Use reference books to gather information about minerals and add these to the table: *sulfur, magnesium, copper, manganese, cobalt,* and *zinc.*

Identifying Vitamin C Content

Vitamin C is found in many fruits and vegetables. Oranges have a high vitamin C content. Try this lab to test the vitamin C content in different orange juices.

Real-World Question
Which orange juice contains the most vitamin C?

Goals
- **Observe** the vitamin C content of different orange juices.

Materials
test tube (4)
*paper cups
test-tube rack
masking tape
wooden stirrer (13)
graduated cylinder
*graduated container
2% tincture of iodine
dropper
cornstarch
triple-beam balance
weighing paper
water (50 mL)
glass-marking pencil
dropper bottles (4) containing orange juice that is:
  (1) freshly squeezed (3) canned
  (2) from frozen concentrate (4) in a carton

* Alternate materials

Safety Precautions

WARNING: *Do not taste any of the juices. Iodine is poisonous and can stain skin and clothing. It is an irritant and can cause damage if it comes in contact with your eyes. Notify your teacher if a spill occurs.*

Drops of Iodine Needed to Change Color

Juice	Trial 1	Trial 2	Trial 3	Average
1 Fresh juice				
2 Frozen juice		Do not write in this book.		
3 Canned juice				
4 Carton juice				

Procedure
1. Make a data table like the example shown to record your observations.
2. Label four test tubes 1 through 4 and place them in the test-tube rack.
3. Measure and pour 5 mL of juice from bottle 1 into test tube 1, 5 mL from bottle 2 into test tube 2, 5 mL from bottle 3 into test tube 3, and 5 mL from bottle 4 into test tube 4.
4. Measure 0.3 g of cornstarch, then put it in a container. Slowly mix in 50 mL of water until the cornstarch completely dissolves.
5. Add 5 mL of the cornstarch solution to each of the four test tubes. Stir well.
6. Add iodine to test tube 1, one drop at a time. Stir after each drop. Record the number of drops it takes for the juice to change to a purple color. The more vitamin C that is present, the more drops it takes to change color.
7. Repeat step 6 with test tubes 2, 3, and 4.
8. Empty and clean the test tubes. Repeat steps 3 through 7 two more times, then average your results.
9. Dispose of all materials as directed by your teacher. Wash your hands thoroughly.

Conclude and Apply
1. **Compare and contrast** the amount of vitamin C in the orange juices tested.
2. **Infer** why the amount of vitamin C varies in the orange juices.

LAB **139**

Standards—7.4.4: ... various organs and tissues function to serve the needs of cells for ... air ...
7.4.12: Explain that viruses, bacteria, fungi, and parasites may infect the human body and interfere with normal body functions.

section 3
The Respiratory System

as you read

What You'll Learn
- **Describe** the functions of the respiratory system.
- **Explain** how oxygen and carbon dioxide are exchanged in the lungs and in tissues.
- **Identify** the pathway of air in and out of the lungs.
- **Explain** the effects of smoking on the respiratory system.

Why It's Important
Your body's cells depend on your respiratory system to supply oxygen and remove carbon dioxide.

Review Vocabulary
diaphragm: muscle beneath the lungs that contracts and relaxes to move gases in and out of the body

New Vocabulary
- larynx
- trachea
- bronchi
- alveoli

Functions of the Respiratory System

Can you imagine an astronaut walking on the Moon without a space suit or a diver exploring the ocean without scuba gear? Of course not. They couldn't survive in either location under those conditions because humans need to breathe air.

People often confuse the terms *breathing* and *respiration.* Breathing is the movement of the chest that brings air into the lungs and removes waste gases. The air entering the lungs contains oxygen. It passes from the lungs into the circulatory system because there is less oxygen in blood when it enters the lungs than in cells of the lungs.

Blood carries oxygen and glucose from digested food to individual cells. In cells, they are raw materials for a series of chemical reactions called cellular respiration. Without oxygen, cellular respiration cannot occur. Cellular respiration results in the release of energy from glucose. Water and carbon dioxide are waste products of cellular respiration. Blood carries them back to the lungs. As shown in **Figure 10,** exhaling, or breathing out, eliminates waste carbon dioxide and some water molecules.

Reading Check *What is cellular respiration?*

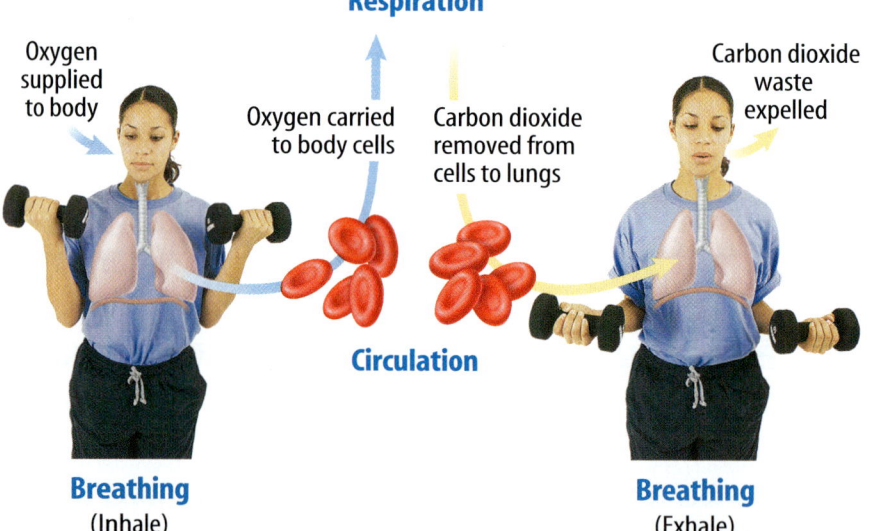

Figure 10 Several processes are involved in how the body obtains, transports, and uses oxygen.

140 CHAPTER 5 Digestion, Respiration, and Excretion

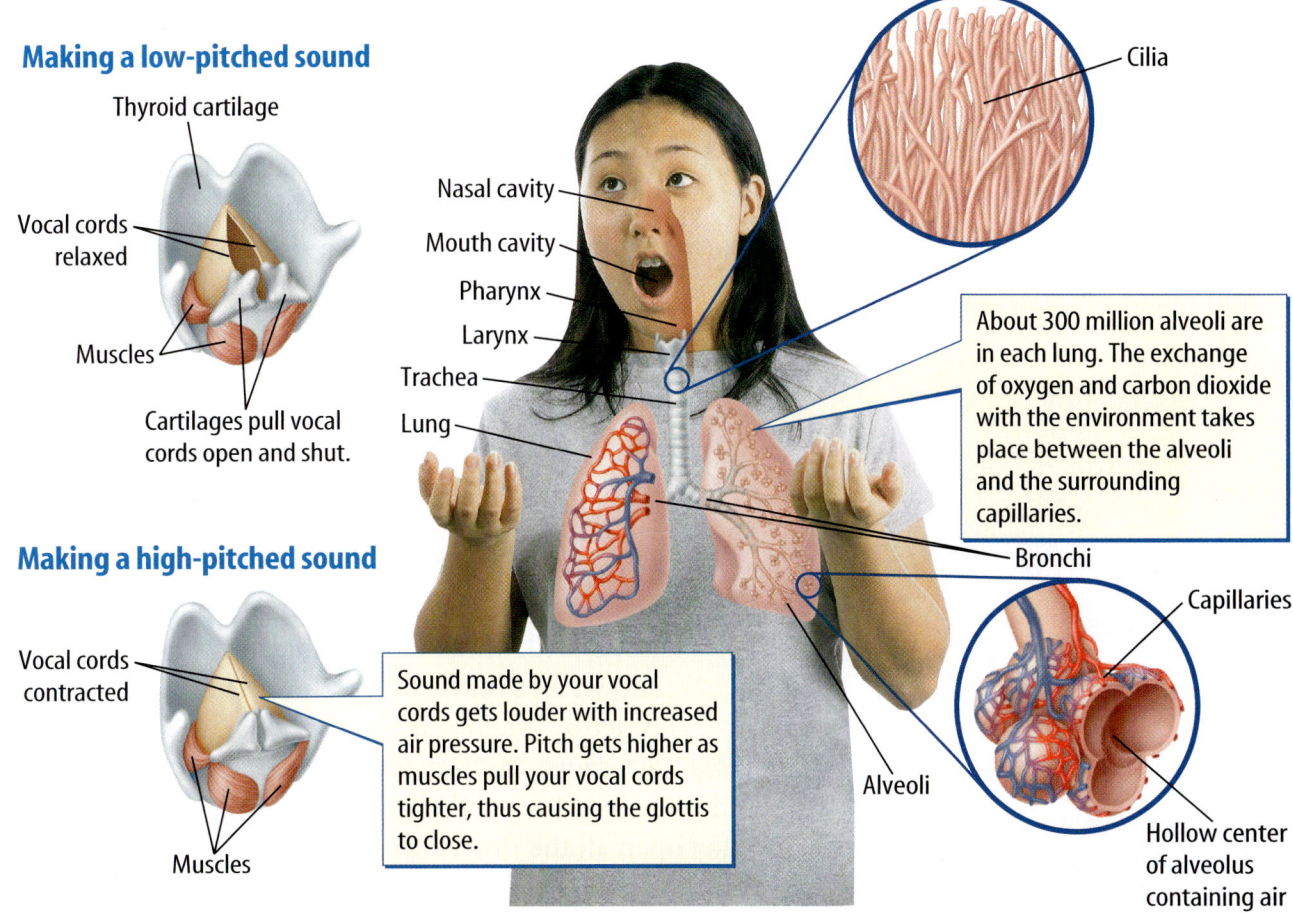

Figure 11 Air can enter the body through the nostrils and the mouth.
Explain *an advantage of having air enter through the nostrils.*

Organs of the Respiratory System

The respiratory system, shown in **Figure 11,** is made up of structures and organs that help move oxygen into the body and waste gases out of the body. Air enters your body through two openings in your nose called nostrils or through the mouth. Fine hairs inside the nostrils trap particles from the air. Air then passes through the nasal cavity, where it gets moistened and warmed by the body's heat. Glands that produce sticky mucus line the nasal cavity. The mucus traps particles that were not trapped by nasal hairs. This process helps filter and clean the air you breathe. Tiny, hairlike structures, called cilia (SIH lee uh), sweep mucus and trapped material to the back of the throat where it can be swallowed.

Pharynx Warmed, moist air then enters the pharynx (FER ingks), which is a tubelike passageway for food, liquids, and air. At the lower end of the pharynx is the epiglottis. When you swallow, your epiglottis folds down, which allows food or liquids to enter your esophagus instead of your airway. What do you think has happened if you begin to choke?

SECTION 3 The Respiratory System **141**

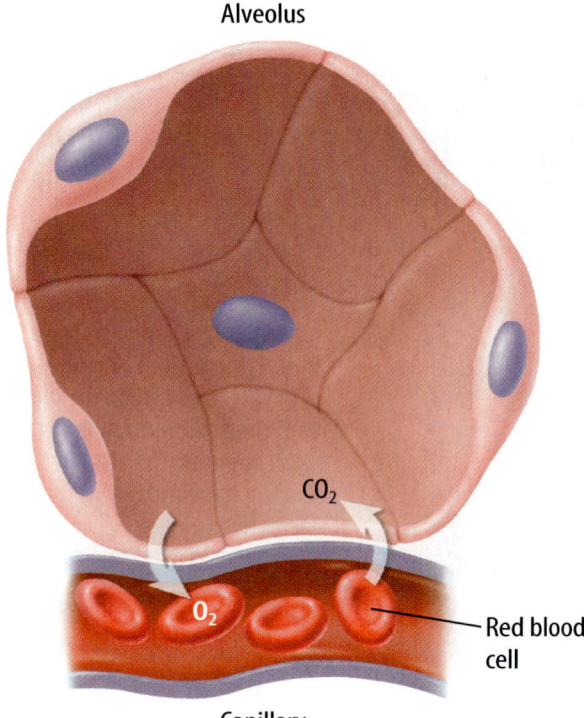

Figure 12 The thin capillary walls allow gases to be exchanged easily between the alveoli and the capillaries.

Name *the two gases that are exchanged by the capillaries and alveoli.*

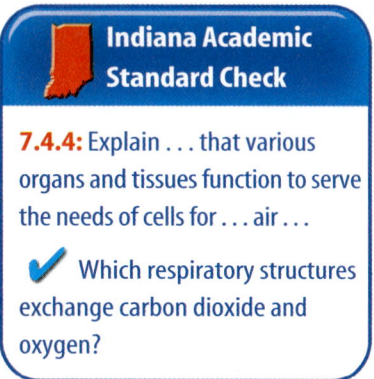

Indiana Academic Standard Check

7.4.4: Explain . . . that various organs and tissues function to serve the needs of cells for . . . air . . .

✔ Which respiratory structures exchange carbon dioxide and oxygen?

Larynx and Trachea Next, the air moves into your larynx (LER ingks). The **larynx** is the airway to which two pairs of horizontal folds of tissue, called vocal cords, are attached, as shown in **Figure 11** on the previous page. Forcing air between the cords causes them to vibrate and produce sounds. When you speak, muscles tighten or loosen your vocal cords, resulting in different sounds. Your brain coordinates the movement of the muscles in your throat, tongue, cheeks, and lips when you talk, sing, or just make noise. Your teeth also are involved in forming letter sounds and words.

From the larynx, air moves into the **trachea** (TRAY kee uh). Strong, C-shaped rings of cartilage prevent the trachea from collapsing. It is lined with mucous membranes and cilia, also shown in **Figure 11** on the previous page. The mucous membranes trap dust, bacteria, and pollen. The cilia move the mucus upward, where it is either swallowed or expelled from the nose or mouth. Why must the trachea stay open all the time?

Bronchi and the Lungs Air is carried into your lungs by two short tubes called **bronchi** (BRAHN ki) (singular, *bronchus*) at the lower end of the trachea. Within the lungs, the bronchi branch into smaller and smaller tubes. The smallest tubes are called bronchioles (BRAHN kee ohlz). At the end of each bronchiole are clusters of tiny, thin-walled sacs called **alveoli** (al VEE uh li) (singular, *alveolus*). Air passes into the bronchi, then into the bronchioles, and finally into the alveoli. Lungs are masses of alveoli, like the one shown in **Figure 12**, arranged in grapelike clusters. The capillaries surround the alveoli like a net.

The exchange of oxygen and carbon dioxide takes place between the alveoli and capillaries. The walls of the alveoli and capillaries are only one cell thick, as shown in **Figure 12.** Oxygen moves through the cell membranes of alveoli and through cell membranes of the capillaries into the blood. In blood, oxygen is picked up by hemoglobin (HEE muh gloh bun), a molecule in red blood cells, and carried to all body cells. At the same time, carbon dioxide and other cellular wastes leave the body cells and move into capillaries. Then they are carried by the blood to the lungs. In the lungs, waste gases move through cell membranes from capillaries into alveoli. Then waste gases leave the body when you exhale.

Why do you breathe?

Signals from your brain tell the muscles in your chest and abdomen to contract and relax. You don't have to think about breathing to breathe, just like your heart beats without you telling it to beat. Your brain can change your breathing rate depending on the amount of carbon dioxide present in your blood. If a lot of carbon dioxide is present, your breathing rate increases. It decreases if less carbon dioxide is in your blood. You do have some control over your breathing—you can hold your breath if you want to. Eventually, your brain will respond to the buildup of carbon dioxide in your blood and signal your chest and abdomen muscles to work automatically. You will breathe whether you want to or not.

Inhaling and Exhaling Breathing is partly the result of changes in volume and resulting air pressure. Under normal conditions, a gas moves from an area of higher pressure to an area of lower pressure. When you squeeze an empty, soft-plastic bottle, air is pushed out. This happens because air pressure outside the top of the bottle is less than the pressure you create inside the bottle when you changed its volume. As you release your grip on the bottle, the air pressure inside the bottle becomes less than it is outside the bottle because the bottle's volume changed. Air rushes back in, and the bottle returns to its original shape.

Your lungs work in a way similar to the squeezed bottle. Your diaphragm (DI uh fram) contracts and relaxes, changing the volume of the chest, which helps move gases into and out of your lungs. **Figure 13** illustrates breathing.

Reading Check *How does your diaphragm help you breathe?*

When a person's airway is blocked, a rescuer can use abdominal thrusts, as shown in **Figure 14,** to save the life of the choking victim.

Comparing Surface Area

Procedure
1. Stand a **bathroom-tissue cardboard tube** in an **empty bowl**.
2. Drop **marbles** into the tube, filling it to the top.
3. Count the number of marbles used.
4. Repeat steps 2 and 3 two more times. Calculate the average number of marbles needed to fill the tube.
5. The tube's inside surface area is approximately 161.29 cm^2. Each marble has a surface area of approximately 8.06 cm^2. Calculate the surface area of the average number of marbles.

Analysis
1. Compare the inside surface area of the tube with the surface area of the average number of marbles needed to fill the tube.
2. If the tube represents a bronchus, what do the marbles represent?
3. Using this model, explain what makes gas exchange in the lungs efficient.

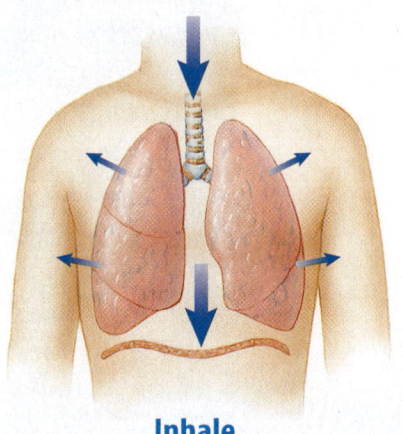

Inhale

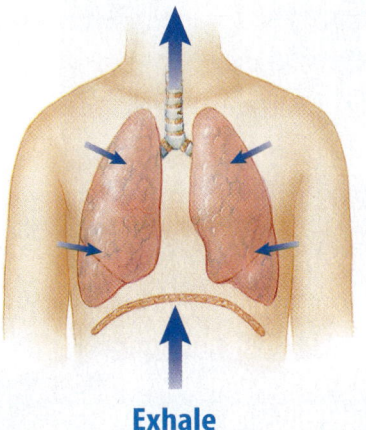

Exhale

Figure 13 Your lungs inhale and exhale about 500 mL of air with an average breath. This can increase to 2,000 mL of air per breath when you do strenuous activity.

NATIONAL GEOGRAPHIC VISUALIZING ABDOMINAL THRUSTS

Figure 14

When food or other objects become lodged in the trachea, airflow between the lungs and the mouth and nasal cavity is blocked. Death can occur in minutes. However, prompt action by someone can save the life of a choking victim. The rescuer uses abdominal thrusts to force the victim's diaphragm up. This decreases the volume of the chest cavity and forces air up in the trachea. The result is a rush of air that dislodges and expels the food or other object. The victim can breathe again. This technique is shown at right and should only be performed in emergency situations.

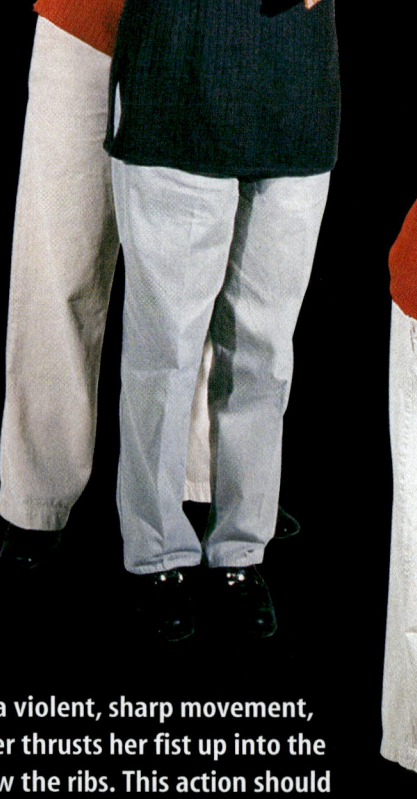

Food is lodged in the victim's trachea.

The rescuer places her fist against the victim's stomach.

The rescuer's second hand adds force to the fist.

An upward thrust dislodges the food from victim's trachea.

A The rescuer stands behind the choking victim and wraps her arms around the victim's upper abdomen. She places a fist (thumb side in) against the victim's stomach. The fist should be below the ribs and above the navel.

B With a violent, sharp movement, the rescuer thrusts her fist up into the area below the ribs. This action should be repeated as many times as necessary.

144 CHAPTER 5 Digestion, Respiration, and Excretion

Diseases and Disorders of the Respiratory System

INTEGRATE Health

If you were asked to make a list of some things that can harm your respiratory system, you probably would put smoking at the top. As you can see in **Table 3,** many serious diseases are related to smoking. The chemical substances in tobacco—nicotine and tars—are poisons and can destroy cells. The high temperatures, smoke, and carbon monoxide produced when tobacco burns also can injure a smoker's cells. Even if you are a nonsmoker, inhaling smoke from tobacco products—called secondhand smoke—is unhealthy and has the potential to harm your respiratory system. Smoking, polluted air, coal dust, and asbestos (as BES tus) have been related to respiratory problems such as asthma (AZ muh), bronchitis (brahn KI tus), emphysema (em fuh SEE muh), and cancer.

Table 3 Smokers' Risk of Death from Disease

Disease	Smokers' Risk Compared to Nonsmokers' Risk
Lung cancer	23 times higher for males; 11 times higher for females
Chronic bronchitis and emphysema	5 times higher
Heart disease	2 times higher

Respiratory Infections Bacteria, viruses, and other microorganisms can cause infections that affect any of the organs of the respiratory system. The common cold usually affects the upper part of the respiratory system—from the nose to the pharynx. The cold virus also can cause irritation and swelling in the larynx, trachea, and bronchi. The cilia that line the trachea and bronchi can be damaged. However, cilia usually heal rapidly.

Chronic Bronchitis When bronchial tubes are irritated and swell and too much mucus is produced, a disease called bronchitis develops. Many cases of bronchitis clear up within a few weeks, but the disease sometimes lasts for a long time. When this happens, it is called chronic (KRAH nihk) bronchitis.

Emphysema A disease in which the alveoli in the lungs enlarge is called emphysema. When cells in the alveoli are reddened and swollen, an enzyme is released that causes the walls of the alveoli to break down. As a result, alveoli can't push air out of the lungs, so less oxygen moves into the bloodstream from the alveoli. When blood becomes low in oxygen and high in carbon dioxide, shortness of breath occurs.

Science Online

Topic: Secondhand Smoke
Visit in7.msscience.com for Web links to information about the health aspects of secondhand smoke.

Activity Write a paragraph in your Science Journal summarizing the possible effects of secondhand smoke on your health.

Indiana Academic Standard Check

7.4.12: Explain that viruses... may infect the human body and interfere with normal body functions.

 What part of the respiratory system does a cold virus usually affect?

SECTION 3 The Respiratory System

Lung Cancer The third leading cause of death in men and women in the United States is lung cancer. Inhaling the tar in cigarette smoke is the greatest contributing factor to lung cancer. In the body, tar and other ingredients found in smoke act as carcinogens (kar SIH nuh junz). Carcinogens are substances that can cause an uncontrolled growth of cells. In the lungs, this is called lung cancer. Lung cancer is not easy to detect in its early stages. Smoking also has been linked to the development of cancers of the mouth, esophagus, larynx, pancreas, kidney, and bladder. See **Figure 15**.

Asthma Shortness of breath, wheezing, or coughing can occur in a lung disorder called asthma. When a person has an asthma attack, the bronchial tubes contract quickly. Inhaling medicine that relaxes the bronchial tubes is the usual treatment for an asthma attack. Asthma can be an allergic reaction. An allergic reaction occurs when the body overreacts to a foreign substance. An asthma attack can result from breathing certain substances such as cigarette smoke or certain plant pollen, eating certain foods, or stress in a person's life.

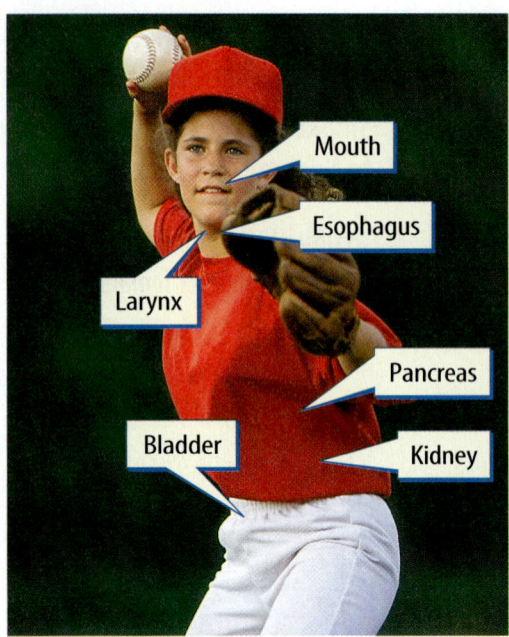

Figure 15 More than 85 percent of all lung cancer is related to smoking. Smoking also can play a part in the development of cancer in other body organs indicated above.

section 3 review

Summary

Functions of the Respiratory System
- Breathing moves the chest to bring air into and remove wastes from the lungs.
- Cellular respiration uses oxygen to release energy from glucose.

Organs of the Respiratory System
- Air flows from your nostrils or mouth through the pharynx, larynx, trachea, bronchi, and into the alveoli of your lungs.
- Alveoli and capillaries exchange oxygen and carbon dioxide.

Why do you breathe?
- Your brain sends signals to your chest and abdominal muscles to contract and relax, which controls breathing rate.

Diseases of the Respiratory System
- Problems of the respiratory system include chronic bronchitis, emphysema, and lung cancer.

Self Check

1. **State** the main function of the respiratory system.
2. **Describe** the exchange of oxygen, carbon dioxide, and other waste gases in the lungs and body tissues.
3. **Explain** how air moves into and out of the lungs.
4. **Describe** the effects of smoking on the respiratory and circulatory systems.
5. **Think Critically** How is the work of the digestive and circulatory systems related to the respiratory system?

Applying Skills

6. **Research Information** Nicotine in tobacco is a poison. Using library references, find out how nicotine affects the body.
7. **Communicate** Use references to find out about lung disease common among coal miners, stonecutters, and sandblasters. Find out what safety measures are required now for these trades. In your Science Journal, write a paragraph about these safety measures.

in7.msscience.com/self_check_quiz

section 4

Standards—7.1.6: Provide examples of people who overcame bias and/or limited opportunities in education and employment to excel in the fields of science. **7.4.4:** ... various organs and tissues function to serve the needs of cells for ... waste removal.

Also covers: 7.1.9, 7.2.7, 7.2.8, 7.4.6, 7.7.2 (Detailed standards begin on page IN8.)

The Excretory System

Functions of the Excretory System

It's your turn to take out the trash. You carry the bag outside and put it in the trash can. The next day, you bring out another bag of trash, but the trash can is full. When trash isn't collected, it piles up. Just as trash needs to be removed from your home to keep it livable, your body must eliminate wastes to remain healthy. Undigested material is eliminated by your large intestine. Waste gases are eliminated through the combined efforts of your circulatory and respiratory systems. Some salts are eliminated when you sweat. These systems function together as parts of your excretory system. If wastes aren't eliminated, toxic substances build up and damage organs. If not corrected, serious illness or death occurs.

The Urinary System

Figure 16 shows how the urinary system functions as a part of the excretory system. The urinary system rids the blood of wastes produced by the cells. It controls blood volume by removing excess water produced by body cells during cellular respiration. The urinary system also balances the amounts of certain salts and water that must be present for all cellular activities.

as you read

What You'll Learn
- **Distinguish** between the excretory and urinary systems.
- **Describe** how the kidneys work.
- **Explain** what happens when urinary organs don't work.

Why It's Important
The urinary system helps clean your blood of cellular wastes.

Review Vocabulary
capillary: blood vessel that connects arteries and veins

New Vocabulary
- nephron
- bladder
- ureter

Figure 16 The urinary, digestive, and respiratory systems, and the skin, make up the excretory system.

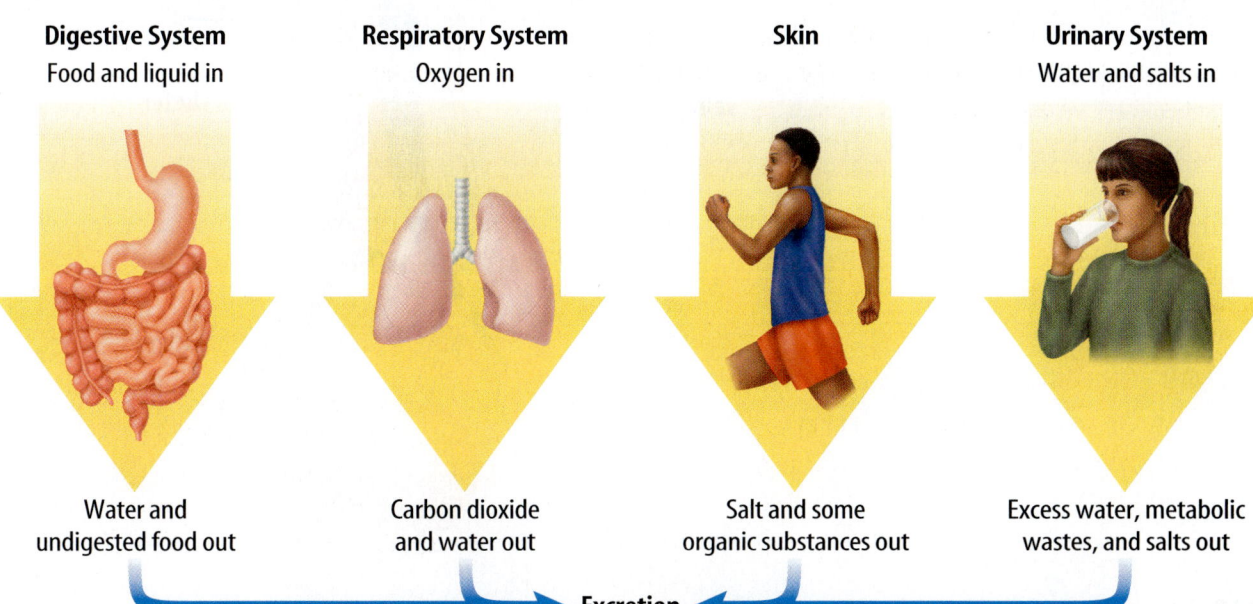

Regulating Fluid Levels To stay in good health, the fluid levels within the body must be balanced and normal blood pressure must be maintained. An area in the brain, the hypothalamus (hi poh THA luh mus), constantly monitors the amount of water in the blood. When the brain detects too much water in the blood, the hypothalamus releases a lesser amount of a specific hormone. This signals the kidneys to return less water to the blood and increase the amount of urine that is excreted.

Reading Check *How does the urinary system control the volume of water in the blood?*

Organs of the Urinary System Excretory organs is another name for the organs of the urinary system. The main organs of the urinary system are two bean-shaped kidneys. Kidneys are located on the back wall of the abdomen at about waist level. The kidneys filter blood that contains wastes collected from cells. In approximately 5 min, all of the blood in your body passes through the kidneys. The red-brown color of the kidneys is due to their enormous blood supply. In **Figure 17,** you can see that blood enters the kidneys through a large artery and leaves through a large vein.

Figure 17 The urinary system removes wastes from the blood. The urinary system includes the kidneys, the bladder, and the connecting tubes.
Explain *how the kidneys help the body balance its fluid levels.*

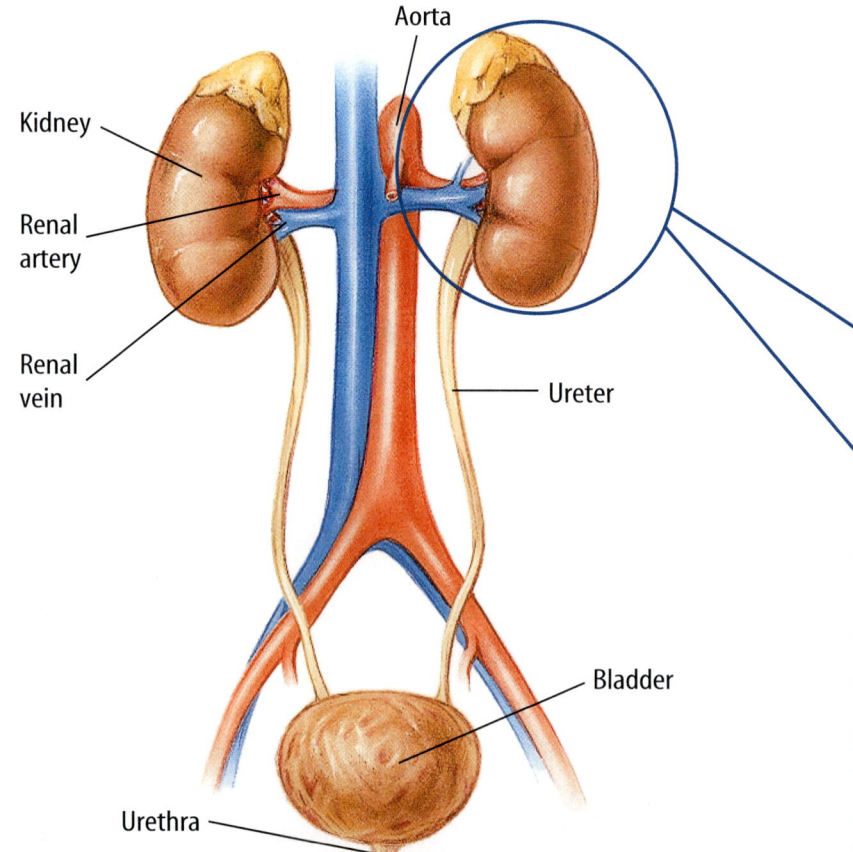

148 CHAPTER 5 Digestion, Respiration, and Excretion

Filtration in the Kidney A two-stage filtration system is an accurate description of a kidney, shown in **Figure 18.** It is made up of about one million tiny filtering units called **nephrons** (NE frahnz), also shown in **Figure 18.** Each nephron has a cuplike structure and a tubelike structure called a duct. Blood moves from a renal artery to capillaries in the cuplike structure. The first filtration occurs when water, sugar, salt, and wastes from the blood pass into the cuplike structure. Left behind in the blood are the red blood cells and proteins. Next, liquid in the cuplike structure is squeezed into a narrow tubule.

Capillaries that surround the tubule perform the second filtration. Most of the water, sugar, and salt are reabsorbed and returned to the blood. These collection capillaries merge to form small veins, which merge to form a renal vein in each kidney. Purified blood is returned to the main circulatory system. The liquid left behind flows into collecting tubules in each kidney. This wastewater, or urine, contains excess water, salts, and other wastes that are not reabsorbed by the body. An average-sized person produces about 1 L of urine per day.

Urine Collection and Release The urine in each collecting tubule drains into a funnel-shaped area of each kidney that leads to the **ureter** (YOO ruh tur). Ureters are tubes that lead from each kidney to the bladder. The **bladder** is an elastic, muscular organ that holds urine until it leaves the body. The elastic walls of the bladder can stretch to hold up to 0.5 L of urine. When empty, the bladder looks wrinkled and the cells lining the bladder are thick. When full, the bladder looks like an inflated balloon and the cells lining the bladder are stretched and thin. A tube called the urethra (yoo REE thruh) carries urine from the bladder to the outside of the body.

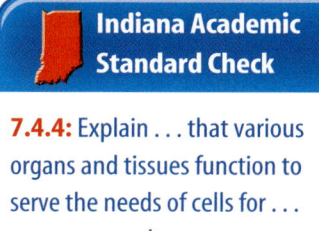

Indiana Academic Standard Check

7.4.4: Explain . . . that various organs and tissues function to serve the needs of cells for . . . waste removal.

✓ Which structures in a kidney filter wastes from the blood?

Figure 18 A single nephron is a complex structure.
Describe *the main function of a nephron.*

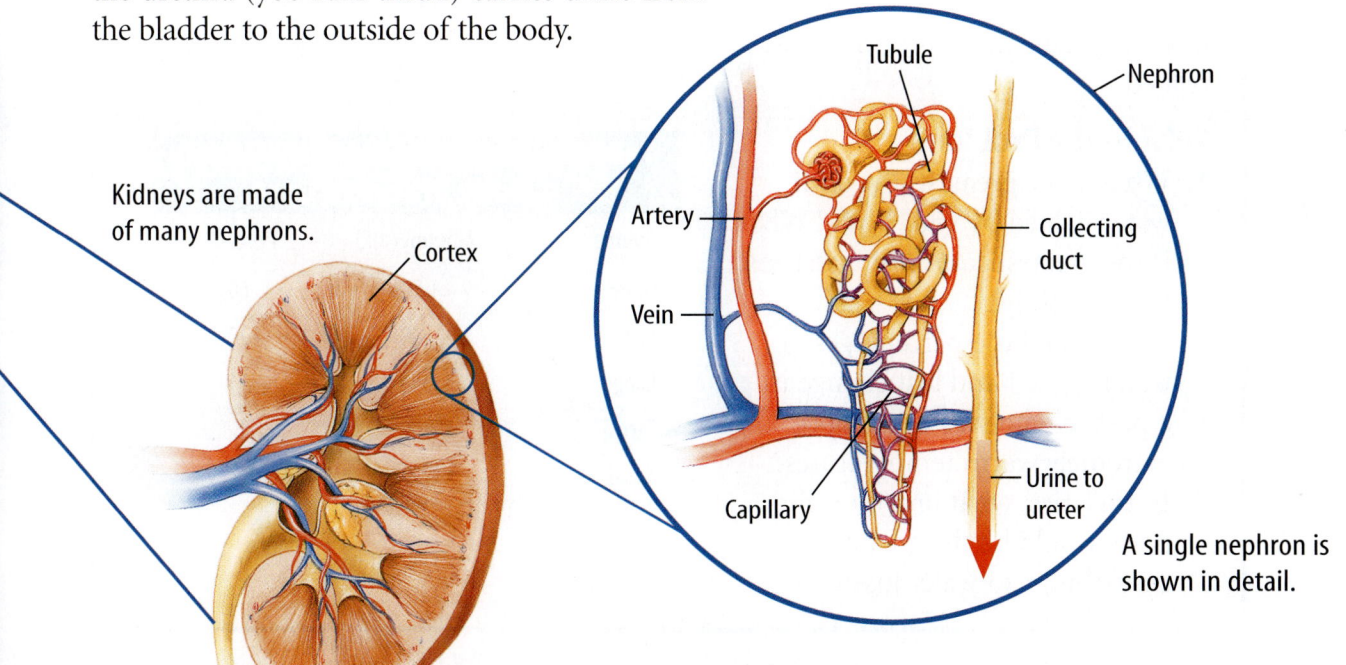

Kidneys are made of many nephrons.

Cortex

Artery
Vein
Capillary
Tubule
Nephron
Collecting duct
Urine to ureter

A single nephron is shown in detail.

Urinary Diseases and Disorders

What happens when someone's kidneys don't work properly or stop working? Waste products that are not removed build up and act as poisons in body cells. Without excretion, an imbalance of salts occurs. The body responds by trying to restore this balance. If the balance isn't restored, the kidneys and other organs can be damaged. Kidney failure occurs when the kidneys don't work as they should. This is always a serious problem because the kidneys' job is so important to the rest of the body.

Applying Science

How does your body gain and lose water?

Your body depends on water. Without water, your cells could not carry out their activities and body systems could not function. Water is so important to your body that your brain and other body systems are involved in balancing water gain and water loss.

Identifying the Problem

Table A shows the major sources by which your body gains water. Oxidation of nutrients occurs when energy is released from nutrients by your body's cells. Water is a waste product of these reactions. Table B lists the major sources by which your body loses water. The data show you how daily gain and loss of water are related.

Solving the Problem

1. What is the greatest source of water gained by your body? What is the greatest source of water lost by your body?
2. How would the percentages of water gained and lost change in a person who was working in extremely warm temperatures? In this case, what organ of the body would be the greatest contributor to water loss?

Table A Major Sources by Which Body Water Is Gained		
Source	Amount (mL)	Percent
Oxidation of nutrients	250	10
Foods	750	30
Liquids	1,500	60
Total	2,500	100

Table B Major Sources by Which Body Water Is Lost		
Source	Amount (mL)	Percent
Urine	1,500	60
Skin	500	20
Lungs	350	14
Feces	150	6
Total	2,500	100

Because the ureters and urethra are narrow tubes, they can be blocked easily in some disorders. A blockage can cause serious problems because urine cannot flow out of the body properly. If the blockage is not corrected, the kidneys can be damaged.

 Why is a blocked ureter or urethra a serious problem?

Dialysis A person who has only one kidney still can live normally. The remaining kidney increases in size and works harder to make up for the loss of the other kidney. However, if both kidneys fail, the person will need to have his or her blood filtered by an artificial kidney machine in a process called dialysis (di AH luh sus), as shown in **Figure 19**.

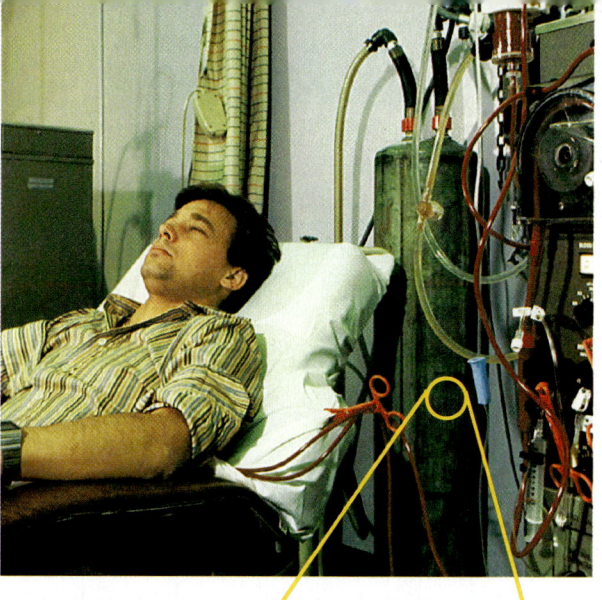

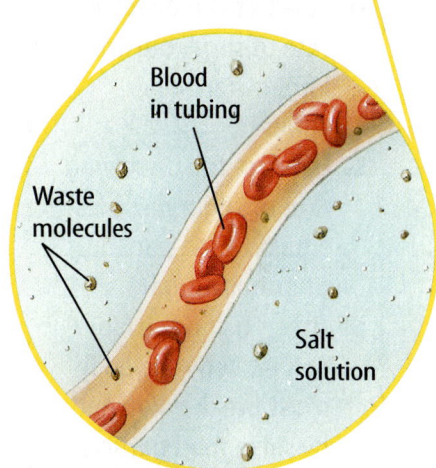

Figure 19 A dialysis machine can replace or help with some of the activities of the kidneys in a person with kidney failure. Like the kidney, the dialysis machine removes wastes from the blood.

section 4 review

Summary

Functions of the Excretory System
- The excretory system removes wastes from your body.
- The digestive, respiratory, and urinary systems and skin make up your excretory system.

The Urinary System
- The kidneys, which filter wastes from the blood, are the major organs of the urinary system.
- Urine moves from the kidneys through the ureters, into the bladder, then leaves the body through the urethra.

Urinary Diseases and Disorders
- Kidney failure can lead to a buildup of waste products in the body.
- An artificial kidney can be used to filter the blood in a process called dialysis.

Self Check

1. **List** the functions of a person's urinary system.
2. **Explain** how the kidneys remove wastes and keep fluids and salts in balance.
3. **Describe** what happens when the urinary system does not function properly.
4. **Compare** the excretory system and urinary system.
5. **Think Critically** Explain why reabsorption of certain materials in the kidneys is important to your health.

Applying Math

6. **Make and Use Graphs** Make a circle graph of major sources by which body water is gained. Use the data in **Table A** of the Applying Science activity.
7. **Concept Map** Using a network-tree concept map, compare the excretory functions of the kidneys and the lungs.

Particle Size and Absorption

Goals
- **Compare and contrast** the dissolving rates of different sized particles.
- **Predict** the dissolving rate of sugar particles larger than sugar cubes.
- **Predict** the dissolving rate of sugar particles smaller than particles of ground sugar.
- **Infer,** using the lab results, why the body must break down and dissolve food particles.

Materials
beakers or jars (3)
thermometers (3)
sugar granules
mortar and pestle
triple-beam balance
stirring rod
sugar cubes
weighing paper
warm water
stopwatch

Safety Precautions

WARNING: *Never taste, eat, or drink any materials used in the lab.*

Real-World Question

Before food reaches the small intestine, it is digested mechanically in the mouth and the stomach. The food mass is reduced to small particles. You can chew an apple into small pieces, but you would feed applesauce to a small child who didn't have teeth. What is the advantage of reducing the size of the food material? Does reducing the size of food particles aid the process of digestion?

Procedure

1. Copy the data table below into your Science Journal.

Dissolving Times of Sugar Particles		
Size of Sugar Particles	Mass	Time Until Dissolved
Sugar cube		
Sugar granules	*Do not write in this book.*	
Ground sugar particles		

2. Place a sugar cube into your mortar and grind up the cube with the pestle until the sugar becomes powder.

3. Using the triple-beam balance and weighing paper, measure the mass of the powdered sugar from your mortar. Using separate sheets of weighing paper, measure the mass of a sugar cube and the mass of a sample of the granular sugar. The masses of the powdered sugar, sugar cube, and granular sugar should be approximately equal to each other. Record the three masses in your data table.

4. Place warm water into the three beakers. Use the thermometers to be certain the water in each beaker is the same temperature.

152 CHAPTER 5 Digestion, Respiration, and Excretion

Using Scientific Methods

5. Place the sugar cube in a beaker, the powdered sugar in a second beaker, and the granular sugar in a third beaker. Place all the sugar samples in the beakers at the same time and start the stopwatch when you put the sugar samples in the beaker.
6. Stir each sample equally.
7. Measure the time it takes each sugar sample to dissolve and record the times in your data table.

Analyze Your Data

1. **Identify** the experiment's constants and variables.
2. **Compare** the rates at which the sugar samples dissolved. What type of sugar dissolved most rapidly? Which was the slowest to dissolve?

Conclude and Apply

1. **Predict** how long it would take sugar particles larger than the sugar cubes to dissolve. Predict how long it would take sugar particles smaller than the powdered sugar to dissolve.
2. **Infer** and explain the reason why small particles dissolve more rapidly than large particles.
3. **Infer** why you should thoroughly chew your food.
4. **Explain** how reducing the size of food particles aids the process of digestion.

Communicating Your Data

Write a news column for a health magazine explaining to health-conscious people what they can do to digest their food better.

LAB **153**

TIME SCIENCE AND HISTORY

SCIENCE CAN CHANGE THE COURSE OF HISTORY!

Overcoming the Odds

Overcoming the odds—especially when the odds seem stacked against you—is a challenge that many people face. Dr. Samuel Lee Kountz, Jr. (right) had the odds stacked against him. Thanks to his determination, however, he beat them.

Samuel Kountz decided at age eight to become a doctor. He faced his first challenge when he failed the entrance exam to his local Arkansas college. That didn't stop him, though. He asked the college president to give him another chance, and the president did. Kountz got into school and earned As and Bs. He went on to get a graduate degree in biochemistry and was admitted to the University of Arkansas's medical school. Kountz was especially interested in a process that was still brand new in the 1950s—the kidney transplant. At that time, a kidney transplant added months or a year to the lives of many patients. But then, a patient's body would reject the kidney, and the patient would die. Dr. Kountz was determined to see that kidney transplants saved lives and kept patients healthy for years.

Fixing the Problem

Kountz discovered the root of the problem—why and how a patient's body rejected the transplanted kidney. He and others at Stanford University developed a way for doctors to watch the flow of the kidney's blood supply following surgery. As a result, doctors can give patients the right kinds of drugs at the right time, so that their bodies can overcome the rejection process.

In 1959, Kountz performed the first successful kidney transplant. He went on to develop a procedure to keep body organs healthy for up to 60 hours after being taken from a donor. He also set up a system of organ donor cards through the National Kidney Foundation. And in his career, Dr. Kountz transplanted more than 1,000 kidneys himself—and paved the way for thousands more.

Research What kinds of medical breakthroughs has the last century brought? Locate an article that explains either a recent advance in medicine or the work that doctors and medical researchers are doing. Share your findings with your class.

Science Online
For more information, visit in7.msscience.com/time

chapter 5 Study Guide

Reviewing Main Ideas

Section 1 — The Digestive System

1. Mechanical digestion breaks down food through chewing and churning. Enzymes and other chemicals aid chemical digestion.
2. Food passes through the mouth, esophagus, stomach, small intestine, large intestine, and rectum and then out the anus.
3. The large intestine absorbs water, which helps the body maintain homeostasis.

Section 2 — Nutrition

1. Proteins, carbohydrates, fats, vitamins, minerals, and water are the six nutrients found in foods.
2. Health is affected by the combination of foods that make up a diet.

Section 3 — The Respiratory System

1. The respiratory system brings oxygen into the body and removes carbon dioxide.
2. Breathing is the movement of the chest that allows air to move into the lungs and waste gases to leave the lungs.
3. The chemical reaction in cells that needs oxygen to release energy and produces carbon dioxide and water as wastes is called cellular respiration.
4. Smoking causes many respiratory problems, including chronic bronchitis, emphysema, and lung cancer.

Section 4 — The Excretory System

1. The urinary system is part of the excretory system. The skin, lungs, liver, and large intestine are also excretory organs.
2. The kidneys are the major organs of the urinary system and have a two-stage filtration system that removes wastes.
3. When kidneys fail to work, an artificial kidney can be used to filter the blood in a process called dialysis.

Visualizing Main Ideas

Copy and complete the following table on the respiratory and excretory systems.

Human Body Systems	Respiratory System	Excretory System
Major Organs		
Wastes Eliminated	Do not write in this book.	
Disorders		

Science online in7.msscience.com/interactive_tutor

chapter 5 Review

Using Vocabulary

alveoli p. 142	mineral p. 136
amino acid p. 133	nephron p. 149
bladder p. 149	nutrient p. 128
bronchi p. 142	peristalsis p. 130
carbohydrate p. 134	trachea p. 142
chyme p. 131	ureter p. 149
enzyme p. 128	villi p. 131
larynx p. 142	vitamin p. 135

Fill in the blanks with the correct vocabulary word or words.

1. _____ is the muscular contractions of the esophagus.
2. The building blocks of proteins are _____.
3. The liquid product of digestion is called _____.
4. _____ are inorganic nutrients.
5. _____ are the filtering units of the kidney.
6. _____ are thin-walled sacs in the lungs.
7. The _____ is an elastic muscular organ that holds urine.

Checking Concepts

Choose the word or phrase that best answers the question.

8. Where in humans does most chemical digestion occur?
   A) duodenum   C) liver
   B) stomach   D) large intestine

9. In which organ is water absorbed?
   A) liver   C) small intestine
   B) esophagus   D) large intestine

10. Which of these organs is an accessory organ?
    A) mouth   C) small intestine
    B) stomach   D) liver

11. What beneficial substances are produced by bacteria in the large intestine?
    A) fats   C) vitamins
    B) minerals D) proteins

12. Which food group contains yogurt and cheese?
    A) dairy   C) meat
    B) grain   D) fruit

13. When you inhale, which of the following contracts and moves down?
    A) bronchioles C) nephrons
    B) diaphragm   D) kidneys

14. Exchange of gases occurs between capillaries and which of the following structures?
    A) alveoli   C) bronchioles
    B) bronchi   D) trachea

15. Which of the following conditions does smoking worsen?
    A) arthritis   C) excretion
    B) respiration D) emphysema

16. Urine is held temporarily in which of the following structures?

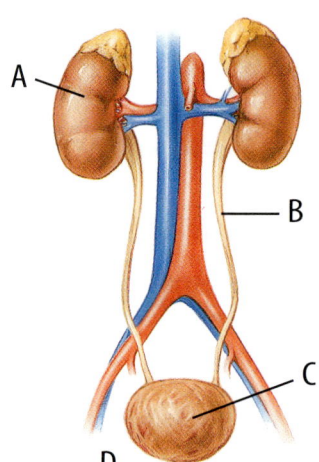

17. Which of the following substances is not reabsorbed by blood after it passes through the kidneys?
    A) salt   C) wastes
    B) sugar D) water

156 CHAPTER REVIEW

Chapter 5 Review

Thinking Critically

18. **Make and use a table** to sequence the order of organs in the digestive system through which food passes. Indicate whether ingestion, digestion, absorption, or elimination takes place in each.

19. **Compare and contrast** the three types of carbohydrates—sugar, starch, and fiber.

20. **Classify** the parts of your favorite sandwich into three of the nutrient categories—carbohydrates, proteins, and fats.

21. **Recognize cause and effect** by discussing how lack of oxygen is related to lack of energy.

22. **Form a hypothesis** about the number of breaths a person might take per minute in each of these situations: asleep, exercising, and on top of Mount Everest. Give a reason for each hypothesis.

23. **Concept Map** Make an events-chain concept map showing how urine forms in the kidneys. Begin with, "In the nephron …"

Use the table below to answer question 24.

Materials Filtered by the Kidneys

Substance Filtered in Urine	Amount Moving Through Kidney	Amount Excreted
Water	125 L	1 L
Salt	350 g	10 g
Urea	1 g	1 g
Glucose	50 g	0 g

24. **Interpret Data** Study the data above. How much of each substance is reabsorbed into the blood in the kidneys? What substance is excreted completely in the urine?

25. **Describe** how bile aids the diegestive process.

26. **Explain** how the bacteria that live in your large intestine help your body.

Performance Activities

27. **Questionnaire and Interview** Prepare a questionnaire that can be used to interview a health specialist who works with lung cancer patients. Include questions on reasons for choosing the career, new methods of treatment, and the most encouraging or discouraging part of the job.

Applying Math

28. **Kidney Blood Flow** In approximately 5 min, all 5 L of blood in the body pass through the kidneys. Calculate the average rate of flow through the kidneys in liters per minute.

Use the graph below to answer question 29.

Total Lung Capacity

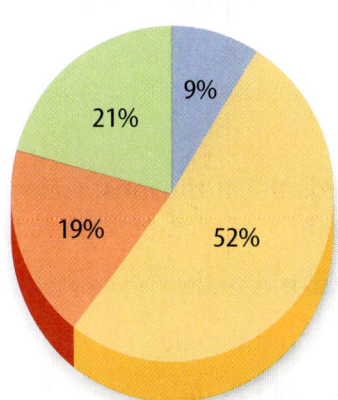

Total Lung Capacity = 5800 mL

- Volume of air normally inhaled or exhaled
- Volume of additional air that can be inhaled forcefully
- Volume of additional air that can be exhaled forcefully
- Volume of air left in lungs after forcefully exhaling

29. **Total Lung Capacity** What volume of air (mL) is left in the lungs after forcefully exhaling?

chapter 5 Indiana

The assessed Indiana standard appears above the question.

Record your answers on the answer sheet provided by your teacher or on a sheet of paper.

Part 1 Multiple Choice

The table below shows the recommended energy intake.

Recommended Energy Intake		Calories Per Day		
Gender	Age	Light Activity	Moderate Activity	Heavy Activity
Male	19–24	2,700	3,000	3,600
Male	25–50	3,000	3,200	4,000
Female	19–24	2,000	2,100	2,600
Female	25–50	2,200	2,300	2,800

Data from the National Academy of Sciences

7.4.11

1. Who needs to eat the most Calories per day to maintain a moderate activity level?
   - A 20-year-old male
   - B 20-year-old female
   - C 30-year-old male
   - D 30-year-old female

7.4.11

2. Using the table above, determine how many more Calories a 35-year-old female needs to eat if she increases her activity level from moderate to high?
   - A 500 Calories
   - B 600 Calories
   - C 700 Calories
   - D 800 Calories

7.4.8

3. Foods derived from grains usually contain large amounts of what type of nutrient?
   - A carbohydrate
   - B fat
   - C mineral
   - D protein

The illustration below shows a body system.

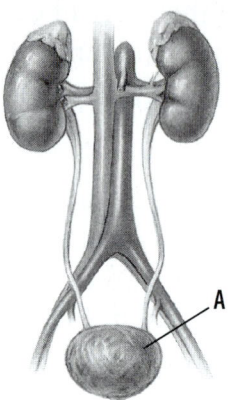

7.4.4

4. What is the organ labeled A?
   - A alveolus
   - B bladder
   - C gallbladder
   - D kidney

7.4.4

5. To which body system does the above organ labeled A belong?
   - A circulatory
   - B digestive
   - C respiratory
   - D urinary

Standards Review

6. Which disease is related to smoking?
   A bronchitis
   B diabetes
   C influenza
   D measles

7. For one week, research scientists collected and accurately measured the amount of body water lost and gained per day for four different patients. The table below lists results from their investigation.

Body Water Gained (+) and Lost (−)				
Patient	Day 1 (L)	Day 2 (L)	Day 3 (L)	Day 4 (L)
1	+0.15	+0.15	−0.35	+0.12
2	−0.01	0.00	−0.20	−0.01
3	0.00	+0.20	−0.28	+0.01
4	−0.50	−0.50	−0.55	−0.32

Which patient had the greatest total gain in body water over the four-day period?

A 1
B 2
C 3
D 4

Test-Taking Tip

Answer All Questions Never skip a question. If you are unsure of an answer, mark your best guess on another sheet of paper and mark the question in your test booklet to remind you to come back to it at the end of the test.

Part 2 Constructed Response

7.4.4
8. Explain the role of cilia in the respiratory system. In chronic bronchitis, cilia are damaged. What effects does this damage have on the respiratory system?

7.4.12
9. If a person is taking antibiotics to fight off a bacterial infection, what might happen to the normal bacteria living in the large intestine? How would this affect the body?

10. Compare and contrast the roles of mucus in the digestive and respiratory systems.

7.4.6
11. The illustration below shows the food pyramid.

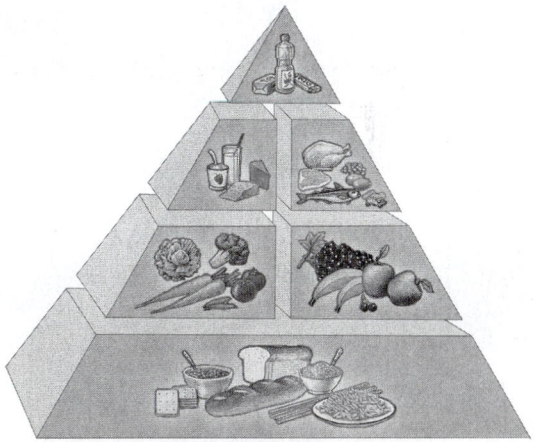

Explain why the greatest number of servings should come from the food group shown at the base of the food pyramid.

12. A person had a urine test that showed protein in the urine. Is protein normally present in the urine? How do you know? What might the results of this urine test mean?

chapter 6

Academic Standards—4: Students . . . recognize that cells function in similar ways in all organisms. **6:** Students gain understanding of how the scientific enterprise operates through examples of historical events . . . new ideas . . . grow or transform slowly through the contributions of many different investigators.
Also covers: Academic Standards 1, 5, 7 (Detailed standards begin on page IN8.)

Circulation and Immunity

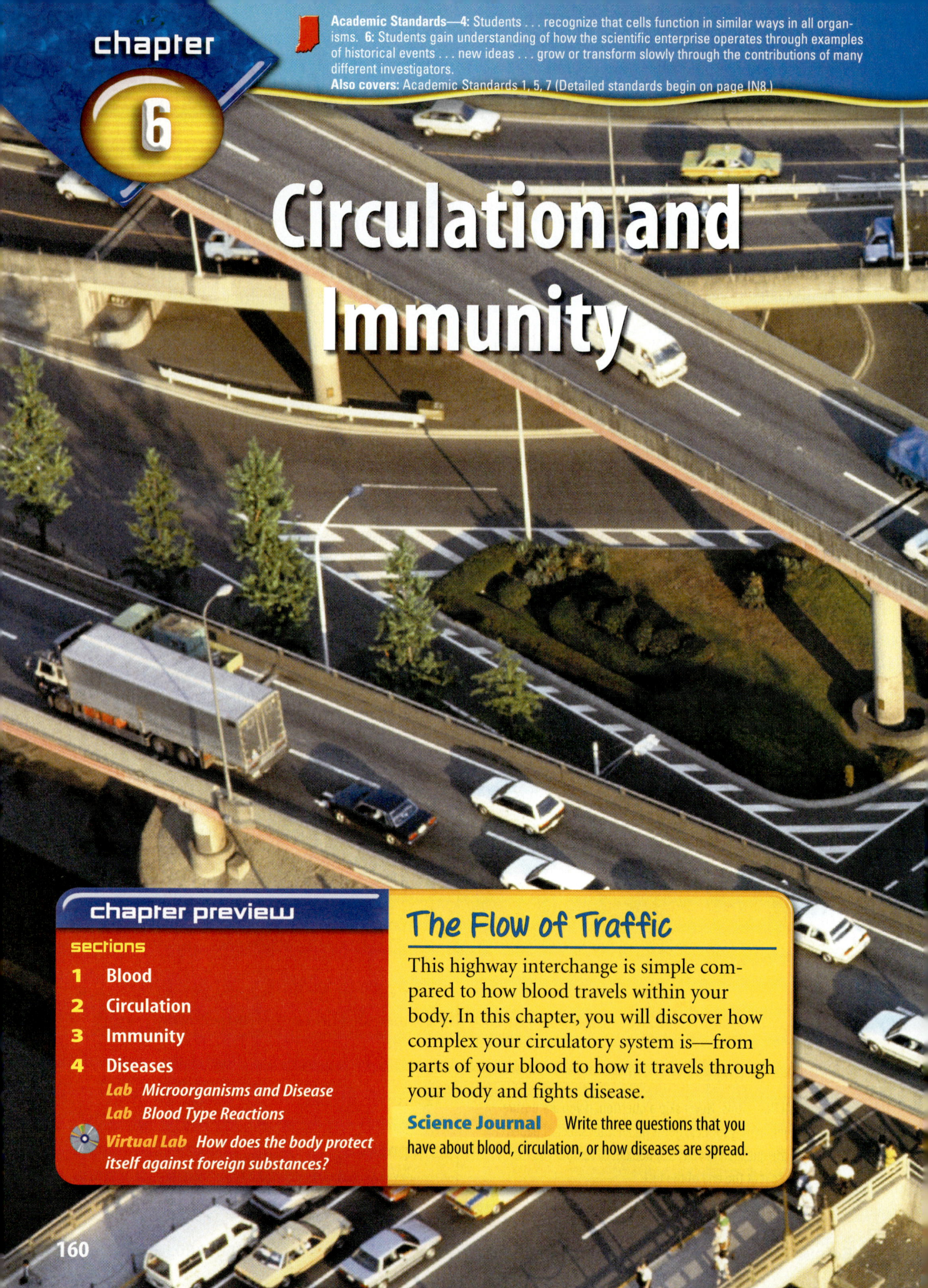

chapter preview

sections
1. Blood
2. Circulation
3. Immunity
4. Diseases
   Lab Microorganisms and Disease
   Lab Blood Type Reactions
   Virtual Lab How does the body protect itself against foreign substances?

The Flow of Traffic
This highway interchange is simple compared to how blood travels within your body. In this chapter, you will discover how complex your circulatory system is—from parts of your blood to how it travels through your body and fights disease.

Science Journal Write three questions that you have about blood, circulation, or how diseases are spread.

160

Start-Up Activities

Transportation by Road and Vessel

Your circulatory system is like a road system. Just as roads are used to transport goods to homes and factories, your blood vessels transport substances throughout your body. You'll find out how similar roads and blood vessels are in this lab.

1. Observe a map of your city, county, or state.
2. Identify roads that are interstates, as well as state and county roads, using the map key.
3. Plan a route to a destination that your teacher describes. Then plan a different return trip.
4. Draw a diagram in your Science Journal showing your routes to and from the destination.
5. **Think Critically** If the destination represents your heart, what do the routes represent? In your Science Journal, draw a comparison between a blocked road on your map and a clogged artery in your body.

Circulation Make the following Foldable to help you organize information and diagram ideas about circulation.

STEP 1 **Fold** a sheet of paper in half lengthwise. Make the back edge about 5 cm longer than the front edge.

STEP 2 **Turn** the paper so the fold is on the bottom. Then **fold** it into thirds.

STEP 3 **Unfold and cut** only the top layer along both folds to make three tabs.

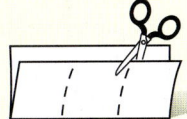

STEP 4 **Label** the Foldable as shown.

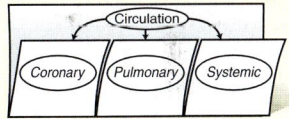

Read and Write As you read the chapter, write information about each circulatory system under the appropriate tab.

Preview this chapter's content and activities at
in7.msscience.com

section 1

Standards—7.4.4: Explain . . . that various organs and tissues function to serve the needs of cells for food, air, and waste removal. **7.4.13:** Explain that white blood cells engulf invaders or produce antibodies that attack invaders or mark the invaders for killing by other white blood cells. Know that the antibodies produced will remain and can fight off subsequent invaders of the same kind.

Also covers: 7.1.9 (Detailed standards begin on page IN8.)

Blood

as you read

What You'll Learn
- **Identify** the parts and functions of blood.
- **Explain** why blood types are checked before a transfusion.
- **Give** examples of diseases of blood.

Why It's Important
Blood plays a part in every major activity of your body.

Review Vocabulary
diffusion: a type of passive transport within cells in which molecules move from areas where there are more of them to areas where there are fewer of them

New Vocabulary
- plasma
- platelet
- hemoglobin

Functions of Blood

You take a last, deep, calming breath before plunging into a dark, vessel-like tube. Water is everywhere. You take a hard right turn, then left as you streak through a narrow tunnel of twists and turns. The water transports you down the slide much like the way blood carries substances to all parts of your body. Blood has four important functions.

1. Blood carries oxygen from your lungs to all your body cells. Carbon dioxide diffuses from your body cells into your blood. Your blood carries carbon dioxide to your lungs to be exhaled.
2. Blood carries waste products from your cells to your kidneys to be removed.
3. Blood transports nutrients and other substances to your body cells.
4. Cells and molecules in blood fight infections and help heal wounds.

Anything that disrupts or changes these functions affects all the tissues of your body. Can you understand why blood is sometimes called the tissue of life?

Parts of Blood

A close look at blood tells you that blood is not just a red-colored liquid. Blood is a tissue made of plasma (PLAZ muh), red and white blood cells, and platelets (PLAYT luts), shown in **Figure 1.** Blood makes up about eight percent of your body's total mass. If you weigh 45 kg, you have about 3.6 kg of blood moving through your body.

Plasma The liquid part of blood, which is made mostly of water, is called **plasma.** It makes up more than half the volume of blood. Nutrients, minerals, and oxygen are dissolved in plasma so that they can be carried to body cells. Wastes from body cells also are carried in plasma.

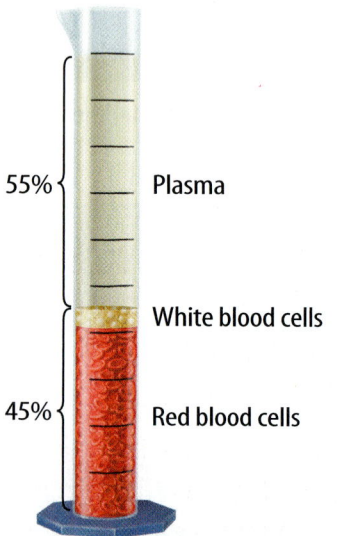

55% Plasma

White blood cells

45% Red blood cells

Figure 1 The blood in this graduated cylinder has separated into its parts. Each part plays a key role in body functions.

162 CHAPTER 6 Circulation and Immunity

Blood Cells Disk-shaped red blood cells, shown in **Figure 2**, are different from other cells in your body because they have no nuclei when they mature. They contain **hemoglobin** (HEE muh gloh bun), which is a molecule that carries oxygen and carbon dioxide. Hemoglobin carries oxygen from your lungs to your body cells. Then it carries some of the carbon dioxide from your body cells back to your lungs. The rest of the carbon dioxide is carried in the cytoplasm of red blood cells and in plasma.

Red blood cells have a life span of about 120 days. They are made at a rate of 2 million to 3 million per second in the center of long bones, like the femur in your thigh. Red blood cells wear out and are destroyed at about the same rate.

A cubic millimeter of blood, about the size of a grain of rice, has about 5 million red blood cells. In contrast, a cubic millimeter of blood has about 5,000 to 10,000 white blood cells. White blood cells fight bacteria, viruses, and other invaders of your body. Your body reacts to invaders by increasing the number of white blood cells. These cells leave the blood through capillary walls and go into the tissues that have been invaded. Here, they destroy bacteria and viruses and absorb dead cells. The life span of white blood cells varies from a few days to many months.

Circulating with the red and white blood cells are platelets. **Platelets** are irregularly shaped cell fragments that help clot blood. A cubic millimeter of blood can contain as many as 400,000 platelets. Platelets have a life span of five to nine days.

Science online

Topic: Human White Blood Cells

Visit in7.msscience.com for Web links to information about the types of human white blood cells and their functions.

Activity Make a table showing the functions of the various types of white blood cells.

Indiana Academic Standard Check

7.4.13: Explain that white blood cells engulf invaders or produce antibodies....

✔ How do white blood cells enter body tissues to attack pathogens?

Figure 2 Blood cells have different roles.

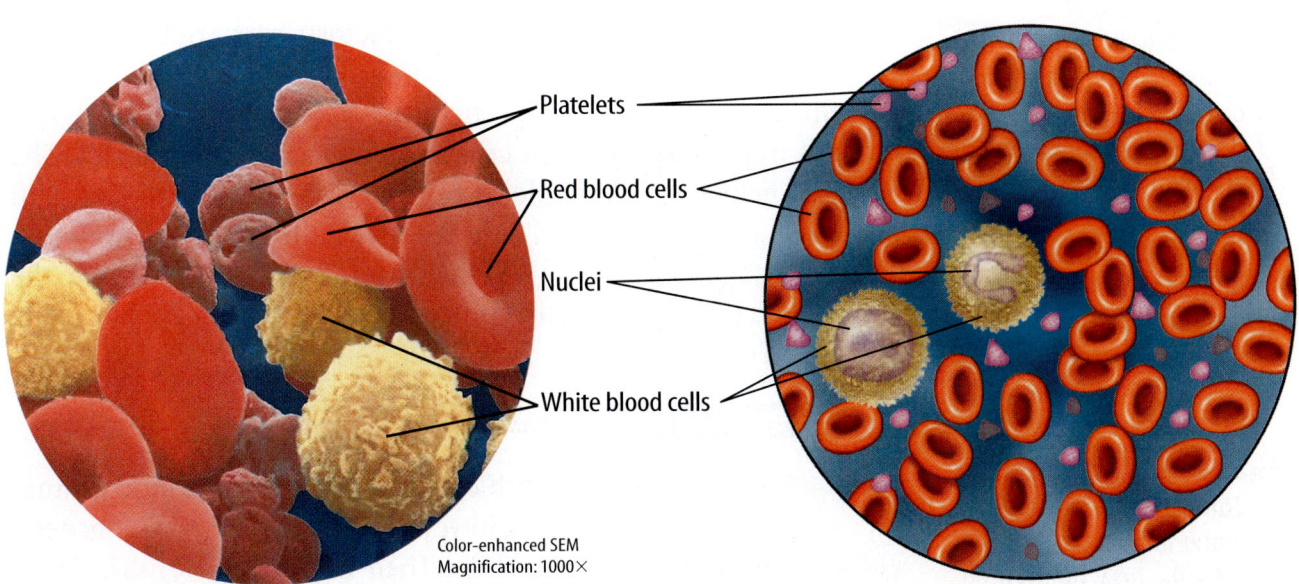

Red blood cells supply your body with oxygen. Platelets help stop bleeding and release chemicals that help form filaments of fibrin.

Several types, sizes, and shapes of white blood cells exist. These cells destroy bacteria, viruses, and foreign substances.

Figure 3 When the skin is damaged, a sticky blood clot seals the leaking blood vessel. Eventually, a scab forms to protect the wound from further damage and allow it to heal.

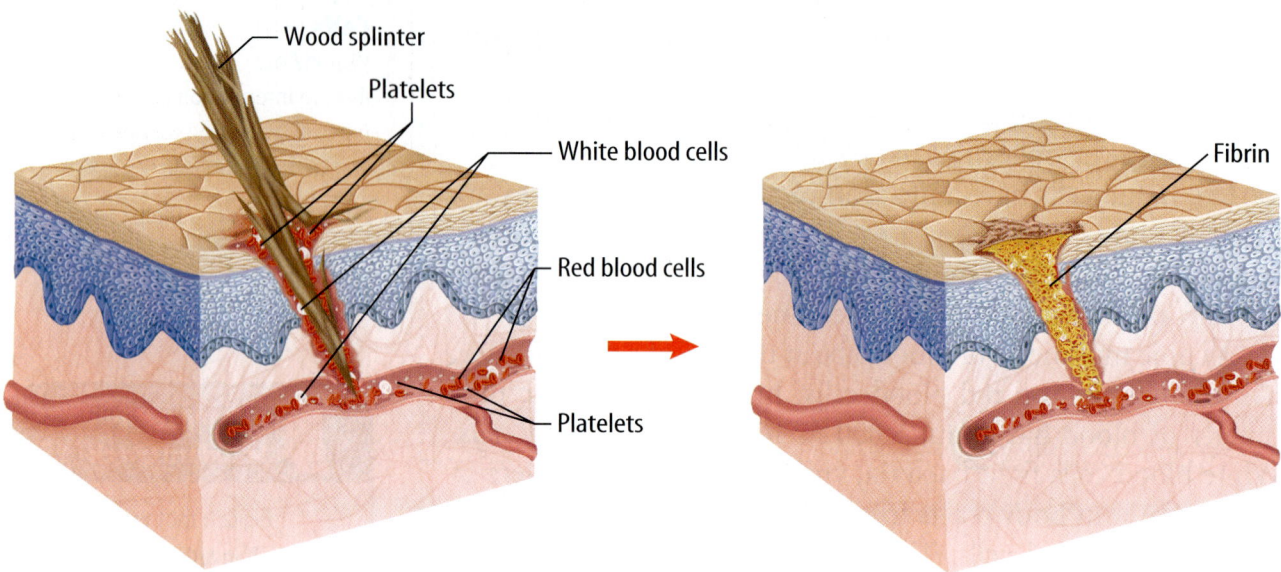

Modeling Scab Formation

Procedure
1. Place a 5-cm × 5-cm square of **gauze** on a piece of **aluminum foil**.
2. Place several drops of a **liquid bandage solution** onto the gauze and let it dry. Keep the liquid bandage away from eyes and mouth.
3. Use a **dropper** to place one drop of **water** onto the area of the liquid bandage. Place another drop of water in another area of the gauze.

Analysis
1. Compare the drops of water in both areas.
2. Describe how the treated area of the gauze is like a scab.

Blood Clotting

You're running with your dog in a park, when suddenly you trip and fall down. Your knee starts to bleed, but the bleeding stops quickly. Already the wounded area has begun to heal. Bleeding stops because platelets and clotting factors in your blood make a blood clot that plugs the wounded blood vessels.

A blood clot also acts somewhat like a bandage. When you cut yourself, platelets stick to the wound and release chemicals. Then substances, called clotting factors, carry out a series of chemical reactions. These reactions cause threadlike fibers called fibrin (FI brun) to form a sticky net, as shown in **Figure 3.** This net traps escaping blood cells and plasma and forms a clot. The clot helps stop more blood from escaping. After the clot is in place and becomes hard, skin cells begin the repair process under the scab. Eventually, the scab is lifted off. Bacteria that get into the wound during the healing process usually are destroyed by white blood cells.

Reading Check *What blood components help form blood clots?*

Most people will not bleed to death from a minor wound, such as a cut or scrape. However, some people have a genetic condition called hemophilia (hee muh FIH lee uh). Their plasma lacks one of the clotting factors that begins the clotting process. A minor injury can be a life-threatening problem for a person with hemophilia.

Blood Types

Blood clots stop blood loss quickly in a minor wound, but with a serious wound a person might lose a lot of blood. A blood transfusion might be necessary. During a blood transfusion, a person receives donated blood or parts of blood. The medical provider must be sure that the right type of blood is given. If the wrong type is given, the red blood cells will clump together. Then, clots form in the blood vessels and the person could die.

The ABO Identification System People can inherit one of four types of blood: A, B, AB, or O. Types A, B, and AB have chemical identification tags called antigens (AN tih junz) on their red blood cells. Type O red blood cells have no antigens.

Each blood type also has specific antibodies in its plasma. Antibodies are proteins that destroy or neutralize substances that do not belong in or are not part of your body. Because of these antibodies, certain blood types cannot be mixed. This limits blood transfusion possibilities, as shown in **Table 1**. If type A blood is mixed with type B blood, the antibodies in type A blood determine that type B blood does not belong there. The antibodies in type A blood cause the type B red blood cells to clump. In the same way, type B blood antibodies cause type A blood to clump. Type AB blood has no antibodies, so people with this blood type can receive blood from A, B, AB, and O types. Type O blood has both A and B antibodies.

 *Why are people with type O blood called universal donors?*

The Rh Factor Another inherited chemical identification tag in blood is the Rh factor. If the Rh factor is on red blood cells, the person has Rh-positive (Rh+) blood. If it is not present, the person has Rh-negative (Rh−) blood. If an Rh− person receives a blood transfusion from an Rh+ person, he or she will produce antibodies against the Rh factor. These antibodies can cause Rh+ cells to clump. Clots then form in the blood vessels and the person could die. In the same way, an Rh− mother can make antibodies against her Rh+ baby during pregnancy. If the antibodies pass into the baby's blood, they can destroy the baby's red blood cells. To prevent deadly results, blood groups and Rh factor are checked before transfusions and during pregnancies.

INTEGRATE History

Blood Transfusions In 1665, the first successful blood transfusion was performed between two dogs. The first successful human-to-human blood transfusion was performed in 1818. However, many failures followed. The different blood types and the problems that result when they are mixed were unknown at that time. Research the discovery of the four types of blood and write a summary in your Science Journal.

Table 1 Blood Transfusion Possibilities		
Type	Can Receive	Can Donate To
A	O, A	A, AB
B	O, B	B, AB
AB	all	AB
O	O	all

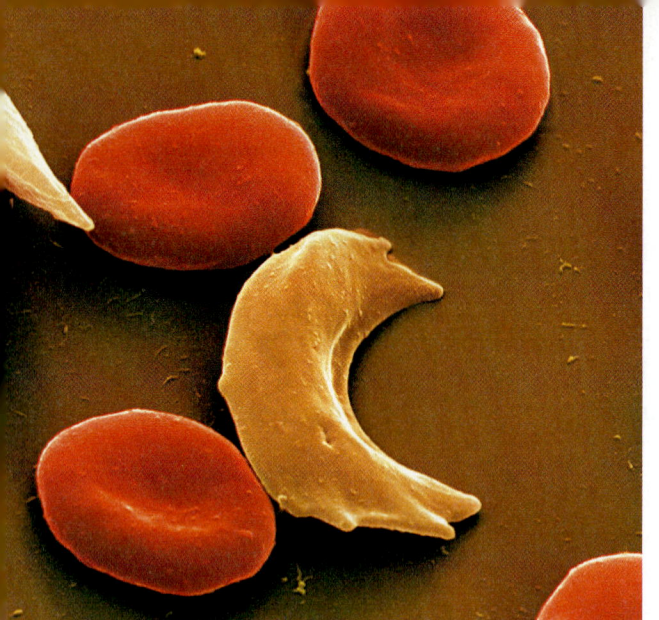

Figure 4 Persons with sickle-cell disease have misshapened red blood cells. The sickle-shaped cells clog the capillaries of a person with this disease. Oxygen cannot reach tissues served by the capillaries, and wastes cannot be removed. **Explain** how this damages the affected tissues.

Diseases of Blood

Because blood circulates to all parts of your body and performs so many important functions, any disease of the blood is a cause for concern. One common disease of the blood is anemia (uh NEE mee uh). In this disease of red blood cells, body tissues can't get enough oxygen and are unable to carry on their usual activities. Anemia has many causes. Sometimes, anemia is caused by the loss of large amounts of blood. A diet lacking iron or certain vitamins also might cause anemia. Still other types of anemia are inherited problems related to the structure of the red blood cells. Cells from one such type of anemia, sickle-cell disease, are shown in **Figure 4.**

Leukemia (lew KEE mee uh) is a disease in which one or more types of white blood cells are made in excessive numbers. These cells are immature and do not fight infections well. These immature cells fill the bone marrow and crowd out the normal, mature cells. Then not enough red blood cells, normal white blood cells, and platelets can be made. Some types of leukemia affect children. Other kinds are more common in adults. Medicines, blood transfusions, and bone marrow transplants are used to treat this disease. If the treatments are not successful, the person will eventually die from related complications.

section 1 review

Summary

Functions and Parts of Blood
- Blood carries oxygen, carbon dioxide, wastes, and nutrients.
- Blood contains cells that help fight infections and heal wounds.
- Blood is a tissue made of plasma, red and white blood cells, and platelets.

Blood Clotting and Blood Types
- Platelets and clotting factors form blood clots to stop bleeding from a wound.
- Blood type—A, B, AB, or O—must be identified before a person receives a transfusion.

Diseases of Blood
- Anemia affects red blood cells, while leukemia affects white blood cells.

Self Check

1. **List** the four functions of blood in the body.
2. **Compare and contrast** red blood cells, white blood cells, and platelets.
3. **Describe** how anemia and leukemia affect the blood.
4. **Explain** why blood type and Rh factor are checked before a transfusion.
5. **Think Critically** Think about the main job of your red blood cells. If red blood cells couldn't deliver oxygen to your cells, what would be the condition of your body tissues?

Applying Skills

6. **Interpret Data** Look at the data in **Table 1** about blood group interactions. To which group(s) can people with blood type AB donate blood?

in7.msscience.com/self_check_quiz

section 2

Circulation

The Body's Delivery System

It's time to get ready for school, but your younger sister is taking a long time in the shower. "Don't use up all the water," you shout. Water is carried throughout your house in pipes that are part of the plumbing system. The plumbing system supplies water for your needs and carries away wastes. Just as you expect water to flow when you turn on the faucet, your body needs a continuous supply of oxygen and nutrients and a way to remove wastes. In a similar way, materials are moved throughout your body by your cardiovascular (kar dee oh VAS kyuh lur) system. It includes your heart, kilometers of blood vessels, and blood. Blood vessels carry the blood to every part of your body, as shown in **Figure 5**. Recall that blood moves oxygen and nutrients to cells and carries carbon dioxide and other wastes away from the cells.

The Heart

Your heart is an organ made of cardiac muscle tissue. It is located behind your breastbone, called the sternum, and between your lungs. Your heart has four compartments called chambers. The two upper chambers are called the right and left atriums (AY tree umz). The two lower chambers are called the right and left ventricles (VEN trih kulz). A one-way valve separates each atrium from the ventricle below it. The blood flows from an atrium to a ventricle, then from a ventricle into a blood vessel. A wall between the two atriums or the two ventricles keeps blood rich in oxygen separate from blood low in oxygen.

as you read

What You'll Learn

- **Compare and contrast** arteries, veins, and capillaries.
- **Explain** how blood moves through the heart.
- **Identify** the functions of the pulmonary and systemic circulation systems.
- **Describe** functions of the lymphatic system.

Why It's Important

Your body's cells depend on blood vessels to deliver nutrients and remove wastes. The lymphatic system helps protect you from infections and disease.

Review Vocabulary
tissue: group of similar cells that work together to do one job

New Vocabulary
- capillary
- artery
- vein
- lymph

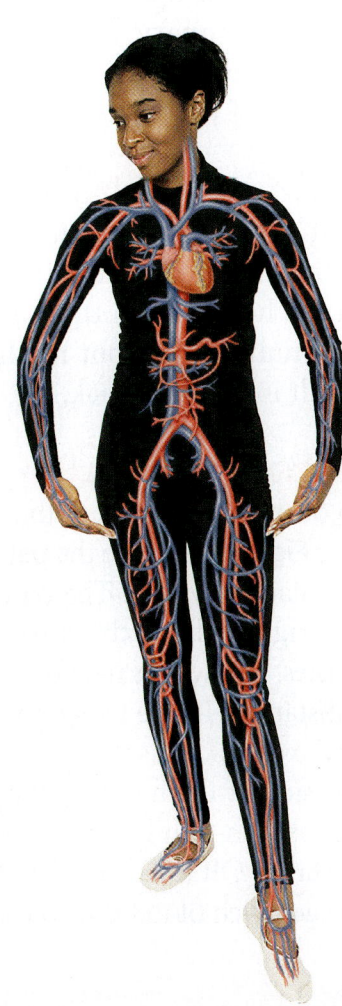

Figure 5 The blood is pumped by the heart to all the cells of the body and then back to the heart through a network of blood vessels.

SECTION 2 Circulation **167**

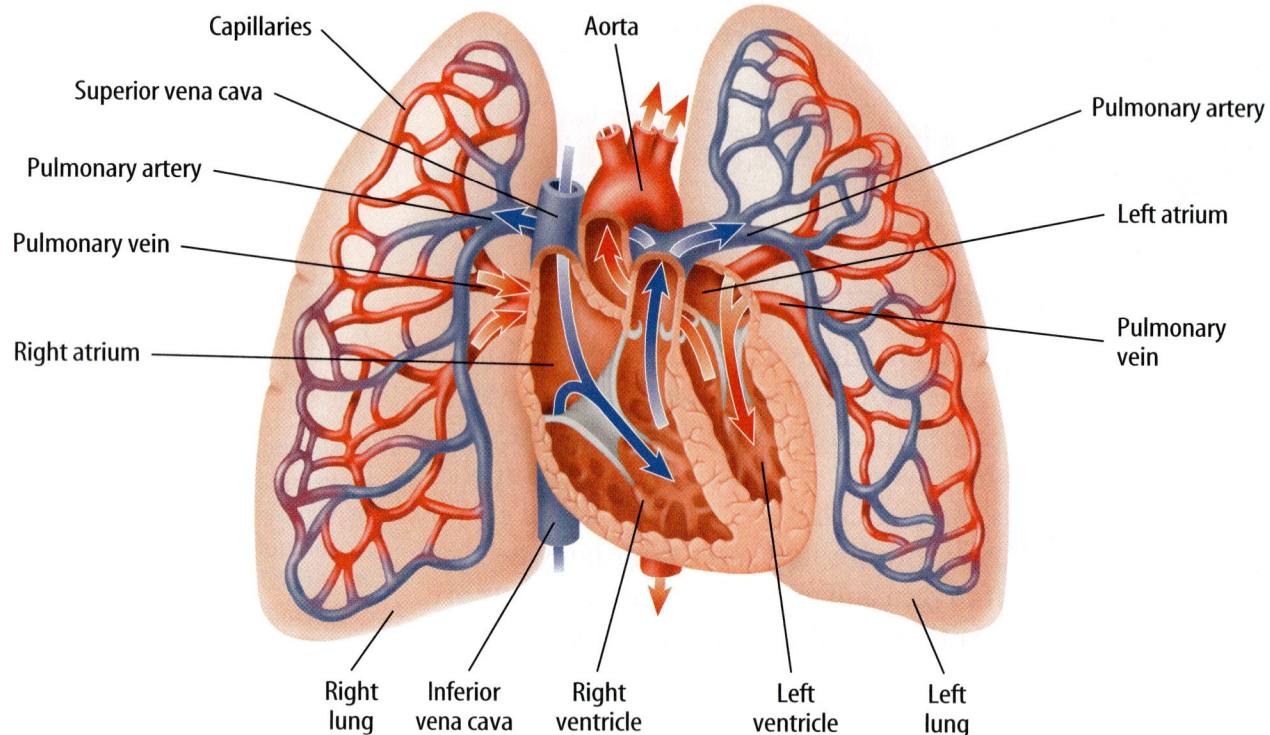

Figure 6 Pulmonary circulation moves blood between the heart and lungs.

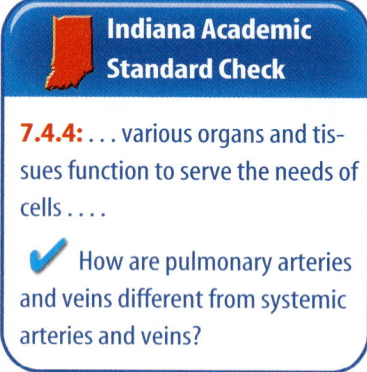

7.4.4: . . . various organs and tissues function to serve the needs of cells . . . .

✓ How are pulmonary arteries and veins different from systemic arteries and veins?

Types of Circulation

Scientists have divided the circulatory system into three sections—coronary (KOR uh ner ee) circulation, pulmonary (PUL muh ner ee) circulation, and systemic circulation. The beating of your heart controls blood flow through each section.

Coronary Circulation Your heart has its own blood vessels that supply it with nutrients and oxygen and remove wastes. Coronary circulation is the flow of blood to and from the tissues of the heart. When the coronary circulation is blocked, oxygen and nutrients cannot reach all the cells of the heart. This can result in a heart attack.

Pulmonary Circulation The flow of blood through the heart to the lungs and back to the heart is called pulmonary circulation. Use **Figure 6** to trace the path blood takes through this part of the circulatory system. The blood returning from the body through the right side of the heart and to the lungs contains cellular wastes. The wastes include molecules of carbon dioxide and other substances. In the lungs, gaseous wastes diffuse out of the blood, and oxygen diffuses into the blood. Then the blood returns to the left side of the heart. In the final step of pulmonary circulation, the oxygen-rich blood is pumped from the left ventricle into the aorta (ay OR tuh), the largest artery in your body. From there, the oxygen-rich blood flows to all parts of your body.

Systemic Circulation Oxygen-rich blood moves to all of your organs and body tissues, except the heart and lungs, and oxygen-poor blood returns to the heart by a process called systemic circulation. Systemic circulation is the largest of the three sections of your circulatory system. Oxygen-rich blood flows from your heart in the arteries of this system. Then nutrients and oxygen are delivered by blood to your body cells and exchanged for carbon dioxide and wastes. Finally, the blood returns to your heart in the veins of the systemic circulation system.

Blood Vessels

In the middle 1600s, scientists discovered that blood moves by the pumping of the heart and flows in one direction from arteries to veins. But they couldn't explain how blood gets from arteries to veins. Using a new invention of that time, the microscope, scientists discovered **capillaries** (KA puh ler eez), the blood vessels that connect arteries and veins.

Arteries As blood is pumped out of the heart, it travels through arteries, capillaries, and then veins, shown in **Figure 7**. **Arteries** are blood vessels that carry blood away from the heart. Arteries have thick, elastic walls made of connective tissue and smooth muscle tissue.

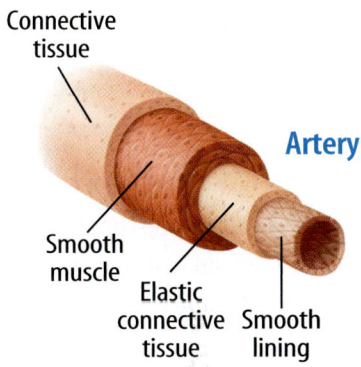

Artery

Veins The blood vessels that carry blood back to the heart are called **veins**. Veins have one-way valves that keep blood moving toward the heart. If blood flows backward, the pressure of the blood against the valves causes them to close. Blood flow in veins also is helped by your skeletal muscles. When skeletal muscles contract, this action squeezes veins and helps blood move toward the heart.

 *What are the similarities and differences between arteries and veins?*

Capillaries The walls of capillaries are only one cell thick. Nutrients and oxygen diffuse into body cells from capillaries. Waste materials and carbon dioxide diffuse from body cells into the capillaries.

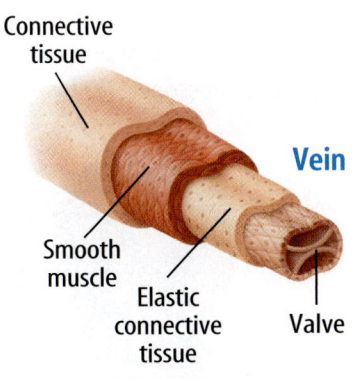

Vein

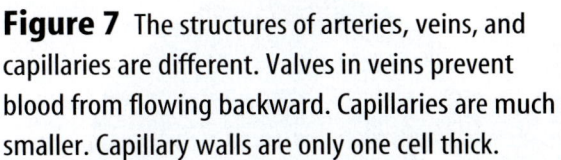

Capillary

Figure 7 The structures of arteries, veins, and capillaries are different. Valves in veins prevent blood from flowing backward. Capillaries are much smaller. Capillary walls are only one cell thick.

Blood Pressure

If you fill a balloon with water and then push on it, the pressure moves through the water in all directions, as shown in **Figure 8.** Your circulatory system is like the water balloon. When your heart pumps blood through the circulatory system, the pressure of the push moves through the blood. The force of the blood on the walls of the blood vessels is called blood pressure. This pressure is highest in arteries and lowest in veins. When you take your pulse, you can feel the waves of pressure. This rise and fall of pressure occurs with each heartbeat.

Controlling Blood Pressure Special nerve cells in the walls of some arteries sense changes in blood pressure. When pressure is higher or lower than normal, messages are sent to your brain. Then the brain sends messages that speed up or slow the heart rate. This helps keep blood pressure constant within your arteries so that enough blood reaches all organs and tissues in your body and delivers needed nutrients to every cell.

Cardiovascular Disease

Any disease that affects the cardiovascular system—the heart, blood vessels, and blood—can seriously affect the health of your entire body. Heart disease is the leading cause of death in humans.

Atherosclerosis One leading cause of heart disease is called atherosclerosis (ah thur oh skluh ROH sus). In this condition, fatty deposits build up on arterial walls. Atherosclerosis can occur in any artery in the body, but fatty deposits in coronary arteries are especially serious. If a coronary artery is blocked, a heart attack can occur. Open-heart surgery then may be needed to correct the problem.

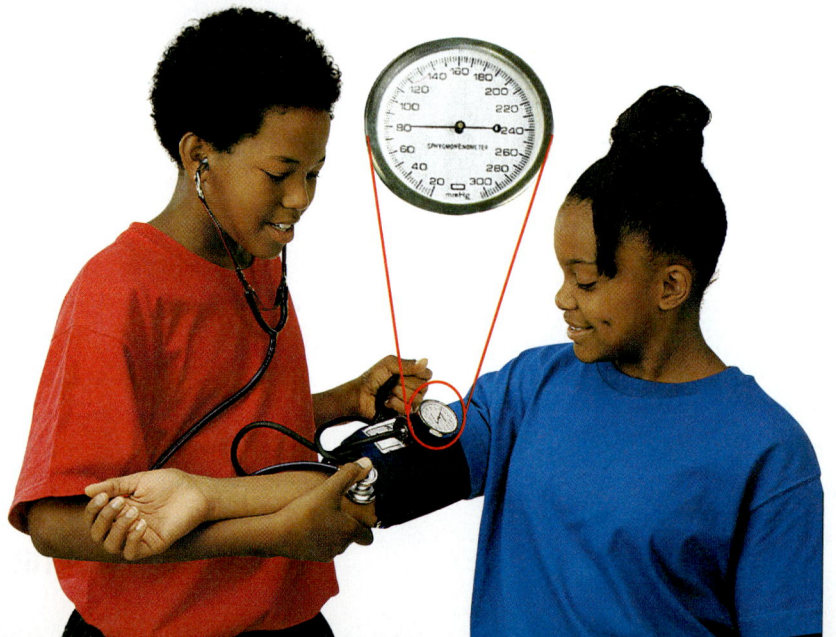

Figure 8 When pressure is exerted on a fluid in a closed container, the pressure is transmitted through the liquid in all directions. Your circulatory system is like a closed container. Blood pressure is measured using a blood pressure cuff and a stethoscope.

Hypertension Another condition of the cardiovascular system is called hypertension (hi pur TEN chun), or high blood pressure. When blood pressure is higher than normal most of the time, the heart must work harder to keep blood flowing. One cause of hypertension is atherosclerosis. A clogged artery can increase pressure within the vessel, causing the walls to become stiff and hard. The artery walls no longer contract and dilate easily because they have lost their elasticity.

Preventing Cardiovascular Disease

Having a healthy lifestyle is important for the health of your cardiovascular system. The choices you make now to maintain good health may reduce your risk of future serious illness. Regular checkups, a healthful diet, and exercise are all part of a heart-healthy lifestyle.

Another way to prevent cardiovascular disease is to not smoke. Smoking causes blood vessels to contract and makes the heart beat faster and harder. Smoking also increases carbon monoxide levels in the blood. Not smoking helps prevent heart disease and a number of respiratory system problems.

Indiana Academic Standard Check

7.4.11: Understand that regular exercise is important to maintain a healthy heart/lung system....

✓ Name three heart-healthy habits.

Functions of the Lymphatic System

You turn on the water faucet and fill a glass with water. The excess water runs down the drain. In a similar way, your body's tissue fluid is removed by the lymphatic (lihm FA tihk) system, shown in **Figure 9**. The nutrient, water, and oxygen molecules in blood diffuse through capillary walls to nearby cells. Water and other substances become part of the tissue fluid that is found between cells. This fluid is collected and returned to the blood by the lymphatic system.

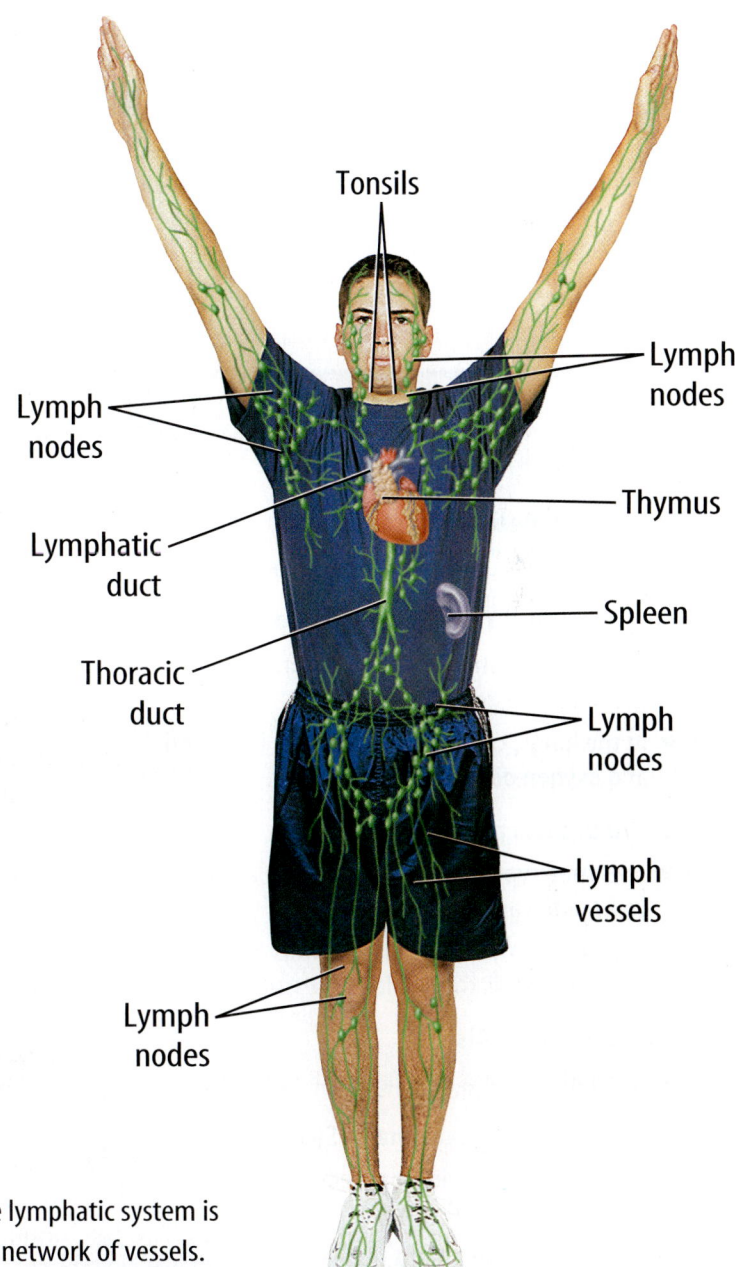

Figure 9 The lymphatic system is connected by a network of vessels.
Explain *how muscles help move lymph.*

SECTION 2 Circulation

Science Online

Topic: Hodgkin's Disease
Visit in7.msscience.com for Web links to information about Hodgkin's Disease.

Activity Create a brochure about Hodgkin's Disease, including what it is, its symptoms, risk factors, and treatment.

Lymph After tissue fluid diffuses into the lymphatic capillaries, it is called **lymph** (LIHMF). In addition to water and dissolved substances, lymph contains lymphocytes (LIHM fuh sites), a type of white blood cell. Lymphocytes help your body defend itself against disease-causing organisms. If the lymphatic system is not working properly, severe swelling occurs because the tissue fluid cannot get back to the blood.

Reading Check What is lymph?

Your lymphatic system carries lymph through a network of lymph capillaries and larger lymph vessels. Then, the lymph passes through lymph nodes, which are bean-shaped organs found throughout the body. Lymph nodes filter out microorganisms and foreign materials that have been taken up by lymphocytes. After it is filtered, lymph enters the bloodstream through large veins near the neck. No heartlike structure pumps the lymph through the lymphatic system. The movement of lymph depends on the contraction of smooth muscles in lymph vessels and skeletal muscles. Lymphatic vessels, like veins, have valves that keep lymph from flowing backward.

section 2 review

Summary

The Body's Delivery System
- Blood vessels carry blood to the body.

The Heart and Types of Circulation
- Your heart controls blood flow through the circulatory system.
- In the lungs, carbon dioxide leaves the blood and oxygen diffuses into the blood.

Blood Vessels and Blood Pressure
- The three types of blood vessels are arteries, veins, and capillaries.
- The force of the blood on the walls of the blood vessels is called blood pressure.

Cardiovascular Disease
- Heart disease is a leading cause of death.

Functions of the Lymphatic System
- Lymph is tissue fluid from cells that has entered the lymph vessels.
- Lymphocytes help fight disease.

Self Check

1. **Compare and contrast** veins, arteries, and capillaries.
2. **Identify** the vessels in the pulmonary and systemic circulation systems that carry oxygen-rich blood.
3. **Describe** the functions of the lymphatic system.
4. **Explain** how blood moves through the heart.
5. **Explain** why blood type and Rh factor are checked before a transfusion.
6. **Think Critically** What waste product builds up in blood and cells when the heart is unable to pump blood efficiently?

Applying Skills

7. **Use a Database** Research diseases of the circulatory system. Make a database showing what part of the circulatory system is affected by each disease. Categories should include the organs and vessels of the circulatory system.
8. **Concept Map** Make an events-chain concept map to show pulmonary circulation beginning at the right atrium and ending at the aorta.

 in7.msscience.com/self_check_quiz

section 3

Standards—7.4.10: Describe how technologies having to do with . . . disease prevention have . . . resulted in changes in factors that affect the growth of human population. **7.4.13:** . . . Know that the antibodies produced will remain and can fight off subsequent invaders of the same kind. **7.6.4:** Understand and describe that changes in health practices have resulted from the acceptance of the germ theory of disease. . . .

Also covers: 7.7.2 (Detailed standards begin on page IN8.)

Immunity

Lines of Defense

Your body has many ways to defend itself. Its first-line defenses work against harmful substances and all types of disease-causing organisms, called pathogens (PA thuh junz). Your second-line defenses are specific and work against specific pathogens. This complex group of defenses is called your immune system. Tonsils are one of the organs in the immune system that protect your body.

Reading Check What types of defenses does your body have?

First-Line Defenses Your skin and respiratory, digestive, and circulatory systems are first-line defenses against pathogens, like those in **Figure 10**. The skin is a barrier that prevents many pathogens from entering your body. However, pathogens can get into your body easily through a cut or through your mouth and the membranes in your nose and eyes. The conditions on the skin can affect pathogens. Perspiration contains substances that can slow the growth of some pathogens. At times, secretions from the skin's oil glands and perspiration are acidic. Some pathogens cannot grow in this acidic environment.

Internal First-Line Defenses Your respiratory system traps pathogens with hairlike structures, called cilia (SIH lee uh), and mucus. Mucus contains an enzyme that weakens the cell walls of some pathogens. When you cough or sneeze, you get rid of some of these trapped pathogens.

Your digestive system has several defenses against pathogens—saliva, enzymes, hydrochloric acid solution, and mucus. Saliva in your mouth contains substances that kill bacteria. Also, enzymes (EN zimez) in your stomach, pancreas, and liver help destroy pathogens. Hydrochloric acid solution in your stomach helps digest your food. It also kills some bacteria and stops the activity of some viruses that enter your body on the food that you eat. The mucus found on the walls of your digestive tract contains a chemical that coats bacteria and prevents them from binding to the inner lining of your digestive organs.

as you read

What You'll Learn
- **Explain** the difference between an antigen and an antibody.
- **Compare and contrast** active and passive immunity.

Why It's Important
Your body's defenses fight the pathogens that you are exposed to every day.

Review Vocabulary
enzyme: a type of protein that speeds up the rate of a chemical reaction in your body

New Vocabulary
- antigen
- antibody
- active immunity
- passive immunity

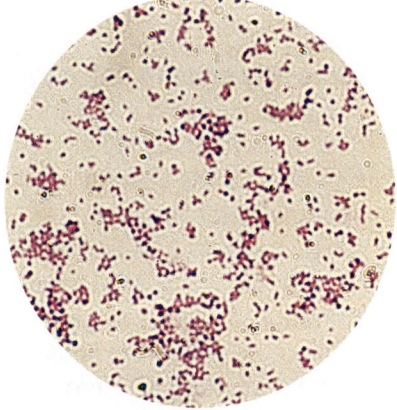

Stained LM Magnification: 1000×

Figure 10 Most pathogens, such as the staphylococci bacteria shown below, cannot get through unbroken skin.

SECTION 3 Immunity **173**

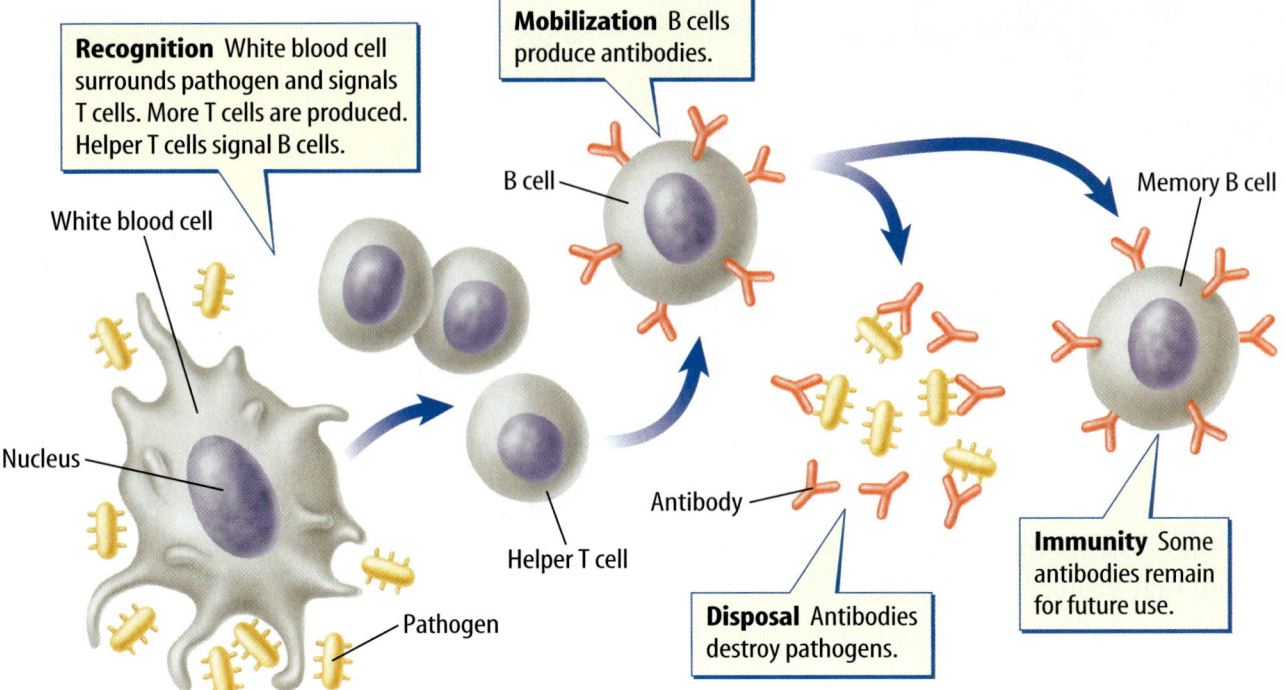

Figure 11 The response of your immune system to disease-causing organisms can be divided into four steps—recognition, mobilization, disposal, and immunity.
Describe the function of B cells.

White Blood Cells Your circulatory system contains white blood cells that surround and digest foreign organisms and chemicals. These white blood cells constantly patrol your body, sweeping up and digesting bacteria that invade.

Inflammation When tissue is damaged or infected by pathogens, it can become inflamed—becomes red, feels warm, swells, and hurts. Chemicals released by damaged cells expand capillary walls, allowing more blood to flow into the area. Other chemicals released by damaged tissue attract certain white blood cells that surround and take in pathogenic bacteria. If pathogens get past these first-line defenses, your body uses another line of defense called specific immunity.

Specific Immunity When your body fights disease, it is battling complex molecules called **antigens** that don't belong there. Antigens can be separate molecules or they can be found on the surface of a pathogen.

When your immune system recognizes foreign molecules, as in **Figure 11,** special lymphocytes called T cells respond. One type of T cells, called killer T cells, releases enzymes that help destroy invading foreign matter. Another type of T cells, called helper T cells, turns on the immune system. They stimulate other lymphocytes, known as B cells, to form antibodies. An **antibody** is a protein made in response to a specific antigen. The antibody attaches to the antigen and makes it useless.

Disease Immunity Edward Jenner discovered a vaccine that prevented smallpox. However, Louis Pasteur demonstrated that germs cause diseases and that vaccines, which contained small amounts of disease organisms, could cause the body to build immunity to that disease without causing it. Research and write a summary in your Science Journal about Jenner's discovery of the smallpox vaccine.

Memory B Cells Another type of lymphocyte, called memory B cells, also has antibodies for the specific pathogen. Memory B cells remain in the blood, ready to defend against an invasion by that same pathogen at another time.

Active Immunity Antibodies help your body build defenses in two ways—actively and passively. In **active immunity** your body makes its own antibodies in response to an antigen. **Passive immunity** results when antibodies that have been produced in another animal are introduced into your body.

When a pathogen invades your body, the pathogen quickly multiplies and you get sick. Your body immediately starts to make antibodies to attack the pathogen. After enough antibodies form, you usually get better. Some antibodies stay on duty in your blood, and more are produced rapidly if the pathogen enters your body again. Because of this defense system, you usually don't get certain diseases, such as chicken pox, more than once.

 *How does active immunity differ from passive immunity?*

Vaccination Another way to develop active immunity to a disease is to be inoculated with a vaccine, as shown in **Figure 12**. The process of giving a vaccine by injection or by mouth is called vaccination. A vaccine is a form of the antigen that gives you active immunity against a disease.

A vaccine can prevent a disease, but it is not a cure. As you grow older, you will be exposed to many more types of pathogens and will build a separate immunity to each one.

Determining Reproduction Rates

Procedure
1. Place **one penny** on a table. Imagine that the penny is a bacterium that can divide every 10 min.
2. Place **two pennies** below to form a triangle with the first penny. These indicate the two new bacteria present after a bacterium divides.
3. Repeat three more divisions, placing two pennies under each penny in the row above.
4. Calculate how many bacteria you would have after 5 h of reproduction. Graph your data.

Analysis
1. How many bacteria are present after 5 h?
2. Why is it important to take antibiotics promptly if you have an infection?

Indiana Academic Standard Check

7.4.10: Describe how technologies having to do with . . . disease prevention have dramatically changed how people live and work.

✔ What kind of immunity is acquired from a vaccination?

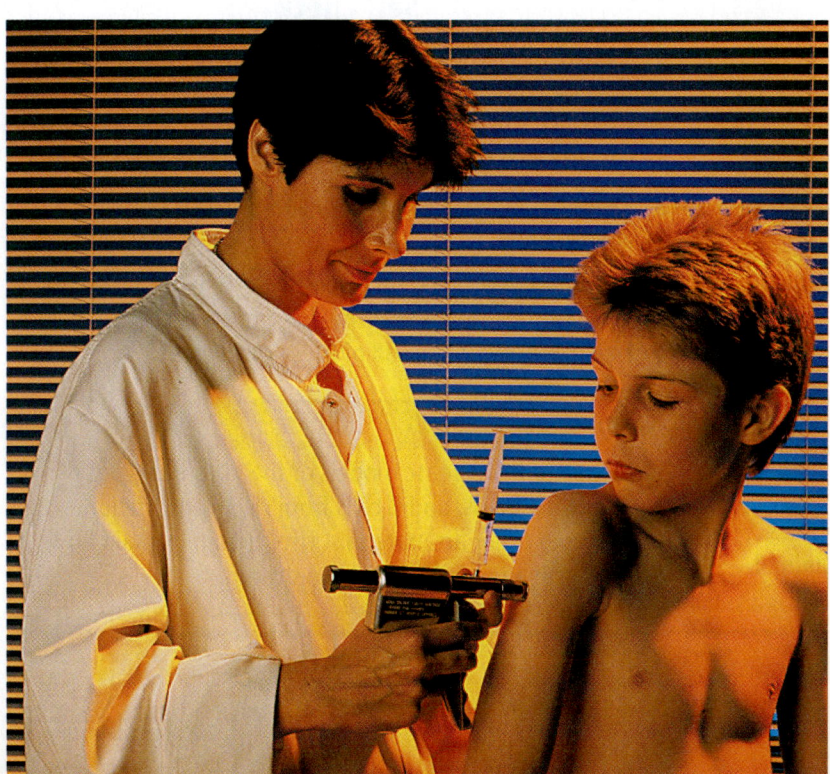

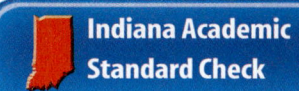

Figure 12 Many vaccines are injected into the arm.

SECTION 3 Immunity

Table 2 Cases of Disease Before and After Vaccine Availability in the U.S.

Disease	Average Number of Cases per Year Before Vaccine Available	Cases in 1998 After Vaccine Available
Measles	503,282	89
Diphtheria	175,885	1
Tetanus	1,314	34
Mumps	152,209	606
Rubella	47,745	345
Pertussis (whooping cough)	147,271	6,279

Data from the National Immunization Program, CDC

Passive Immunity Passive immunity does not last as long as active immunity does. For example, you were born with all the antibodies that your mother had in her blood. However, these antibodies stayed with you for only a few months. Because newborn babies lose their passive immunity in a few months, they need to be vaccinated to develop their own immunity. Vaccines have helped reduce the number of cases of many childhood diseases, as shown in **Table 2**.

section 3 review

Summary

Lines of Defense

- The purpose of the immune system is to fight disease.
- Your skin and your respiratory, digestive, and circulatory systems are first-line defenses against pathogens.
- Your body's second line of defense is called specific immunity.
- In active immunity, your body makes its own antibodies in response to an antigen.
- Vaccinations can give you active immunity against a disease.
- Passive immunity results when antibodies that have been produced in another animal are introduced into your body.

Self Check

1. **Describe** how harmful bacteria can cause infections in your body.
2. **List** the natural defenses that your body has against harmful substances and disease.
3. **Explain** how an active vaccine works to protect the human body.
4. **Think Critically** Several diseases have symptoms similar to those of measles. Why doesn't the measles vaccine protect you from all of these diseases?

Applying Skills

5. **Make Models** Create models of the different types of T cells, antigens, and B cells from clay, construction paper, or other art materials. Use them to explain how T cells function in the immune system.

section 4

Standards—7.4.10: Describe how technologies having to do with food production, sanitation . . . have dramatically changed how people live . . . **7.6.1–7.6.4:** Understand and explain that throughout history . . . introduction of germ theory by Louis Pasteur and others . . .

Also covers: 7.1.5, 7.4.4, 7.4.12, 7.4.14, 7.5.3 (Detailed standards begin on page IN8.)

Diseases

Disease in History

Throughout time, the plague, smallpox, and influenza have killed millions of people worldwide. Today, the causes of these diseases are known, and treatments can prevent or cure them. But even today, some diseases cannot be cured, and outbreaks of new diseases, such as severe acute respiratory syndrome (SARS), occur.

Discovering Disease Organisms With the invention of the microscope in the latter part of the seventeenth century, bacteria, yeast, and mold spores were seen for the first time. However, scientists did not make a connection between microorganisms and disease transmission until the late 1800s and early 1900s.

The French chemist Louis Pasteur learned that microorganisms cause disease in humans. Many scientists of his time did not believe that microorganisms could harm larger organisms, such as humans. However, Pasteur discovered that microorganisms could spoil wine and milk. He then realized that microorganisms could attack the human body in the same way. Pasteur invented **pasteurization** (pas chuh ruh ZAY shun), which is the process of heating a liquid to a temperature that kills most bacteria.

Disease Organisms Table 3 lists some of the diseases caused by various groups of pathogens. Bacteria and viruses cause many common diseases.

as you read

What You'll Learn
- **Describe** the work of Pasteur, Koch, and Lister in the discovery and prevention of disease.
- **Identify** diseases caused by viruses and bacteria.
- **Explain** how HIV affects the immune system.
- **Define** noninfectious diseases and list their causes.
- **Explain** what happens during an allergic reaction.

Why It's Important
You can help prevent certain illnesses if you know what causes disease and how disease spreads.

Review Vocabulary
virus: tiny piece of genetic material surrounded by a protein coating that infects and multiplies in host cells

New Vocabulary
- pasteurization
- infectious disease
- noninfectious disease
- allergen

Table 3 Human Diseases and Their Agents

Agent	Diseases
Bacteria	Tetanus, tuberculosis, typhoid fever, strep throat, bacterial pneumonia, plague
Protists	Malaria, sleeping sickness
Fungi	Athlete's foot, ringworm
Viruses	Colds, influenza, AIDS, measles, mumps, polio, smallpox, SARS

SECTION 4 Diseases

Science Online

Topic: Disease Theory
Visit in7.msscience.com for Web links to information about one of the historical theories of disease—the four body humors.

Activity Make a picture book describing the humoral theory of disease.

Indiana Academic Standard Check

7.6.1: Realize that the introduction of germ theory ... led to the modern understanding of how many diseases are caused by microorganisms....

✓ What is the first step of Koch's rules?

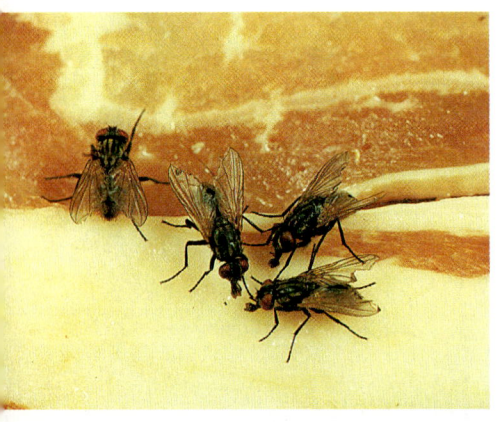

Figure 14 When flies land on food, they can transport pathogens from one location to another.

Pathogens The conditions in your body, such as temperature and available nutrients, help harmful bacteria that enter your body grow and multiply. Bacteria can slow down the normal growth and metabolic activities of body cells and tissues. Some bacteria even produce toxins that kill cells on contact.

A virus infects and multiplies in host cells. The host cells die when the viruses break out of them. These new viruses infect other cells, leading to the destruction of tissues or the interruption of vital body activities.

Reading Check What is the relationship between a virus and a host cell?

Pathogenic protists, such as the organisms that cause malaria, can destroy tissues and blood cells or interfere with normal body functions. In a similar manner, fungus infections can cause athlete's foot, nonhealing wounds, chronic lung disease, or inflammation of the membranes of the brain.

Koch's Rules Many diseases caused by pathogens can be treated with medicines. In many cases, these organisms need to be identified before specific treatment can begin. Today, a method developed in the nineteenth century by Robert Koch still is used to identify organisms, as shown in **Figure 13.**

Infectious Diseases

A disease that is caused by a virus, bacterium, protist, or fungus and is spread from an infected organism or the environment to another organism is called an **infectious disease.** Infectious diseases are spread by direct contact with the infected organism, through water and air, on food, by contact with contaminated objects, and by disease-carrying organisms called biological vectors. Examples of vectors that have been sources of disease are rats, birds, cats, dogs, mosquitoes, fleas, and flies, as shown in **Figure 14.**

Human Vectors People also can be carriers of disease. Colds and many other diseases are spread through contact. Each time you turn a doorknob or use a telephone, your skin comes in contact with bacteria and viruses, which is why washing your hands frequently should be part of your daily routine.

Joseph Lister, an English surgeon, recognized the relationship between infections and cleanliness. Lister dramatically reduced the number of deaths among his patients by washing their skin and his hands with carbolic (kar BAH lihk) acid, which is a liquid that kills pathogens.

NATIONAL GEOGRAPHIC VISUALIZING KOCH'S RULES

Figure 13

In the 1880s, German doctor Robert Koch developed a series of methods for identifying which organism was the cause of a particular disease. Koch's Rules are still in use today. Developed mainly for determining the cause of particular diseases in humans and other animals, these rules have been used for identifying diseases in plants as well.

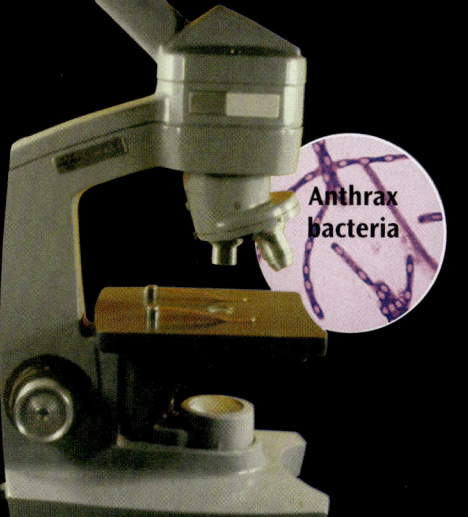

A In every case of a particular disease, the organism thought to cause the disease—the pathogen—must be present.

B The suspected pathogen must be separated from all other organisms and grown on agar gel with no other organisms present.

C When inoculated with the suspected pathogen, a healthy host must come down with the original illness.

D Finally, when the suspected pathogen is removed from the host and grown on agar gel again, it must be compared with the original organism. Only when they match can that organism be identified as the pathogen that causes the disease.

Indiana Academic Standard Check

7.4.12: Explain that viruses, bacteria... may infect the human body and interfere with normal body functions.

✔ Which STDs can be treated with antibodies?

Sexually Transmitted Diseases Infectious diseases that are passed from person to person during sexual contact are called sexually transmitted diseases (STDs). STDs are caused by bacteria or viruses.

Gonorrhea (gah nuh REE uh), chlamydia (kluh MIH dee uh), and syphilis (SIH fuh lus) are STDs caused by bacteria. Antibiotics are used to treat these diseases. If they are untreated, gonorrhea and chlamydia can leave a person sterile because the reproductive organs can be damaged permanently. Untreated syphilis may infect cardiovascular and nervous systems, resulting in damage to body organs that cannot be reversed.

Genital herpes, a lifelong viral disease, causes painful blisters on the sex organs. This type of herpes can be transmitted during sexual contact or from an infected mother to her child during birth. Herpes has no cure, and no vaccine can prevent it. However, the symptoms of herpes can be treated with antiviral medicines.

✔ **Reading Check** *Why should STDs be treated in the early stages?*

Applying Science

Has the annual percentage of deaths from major diseases changed?

Each year, many people die from diseases. Medical science has found numerous ways to treat and cure disease. Have new medicines, improved surgery techniques, and healthier lifestyles helped decrease the number of deaths from disease? By using your ability to interpret data tables, you can find out.

Percentage of Deaths Due to Major Diseases

Disease	Year			
	1950	1980	1990	2000
Heart	37.1	38.3	33.5	29.6
Cancer	14.6	20.9	23.5	23.0
Stroke	10.8	8.6	6.7	7.0
Diabetes	1.7	1.8	2.2	2.9
Pneumonia and flu	3.3	2.7	3.7	2.7

Identifying the Problem

The table above shows the percentage of total deaths due to six major diseases for a 50-year time period. Study the data for each disease. Can you see any trends in the percentage of deaths?

Solving the Problem

1. Has the percentage increased for any disease that is listed?
2. What factors could have contributed to this increase?

HIV and Your Immune System

Human immunodeficiency virus (HIV) can exist in blood and body fluids. This virus can hide in body cells, sometimes for years. You can become infected with HIV by having sex with an HIV-infected person or by reusing an HIV-contaminated hypodermic needle for an injection. However, a freshly unwrapped sterile needle cannot transmit infection. The risk of getting HIV through blood transfusion is small because all donated blood is tested for the presence of HIV. A pregnant woman with HIV can infect her child when the virus passes through the placenta. The child also may become infected from contacts with blood during the birth process or when nursing after birth.

HIV cannot multiply outside the body, and it does not survive long in the environment. The virus cannot be transmitted by touching an infected person, by handling objects used by the person unless they are contaminated with body fluids, or from contact with a toilet seat.

AIDS An HIV infection can lead to Acquired Immune Deficiency Syndrome (AIDS), which is a disease that attacks the body's immune system. HIV, as shown in **Figure 15,** is different from other viruses. It attacks the helper T cells in the immune system. The virus enters the T cell and multiplies. When the infected cell bursts open, it releases more HIV. These infect other T cells. Soon, so many T cells are destroyed that not enough B cells are stimulated to produce antibodies. The body no longer has an effective way to fight invading antigens. The immune system then is unable to fight HIV or any other pathogen.

In December 2003, it was estimateed that nearly 40 million people worldwide have HIV/AIDS. At this time the disease has no known cure. However, several medications help treat AIDS in some patients.

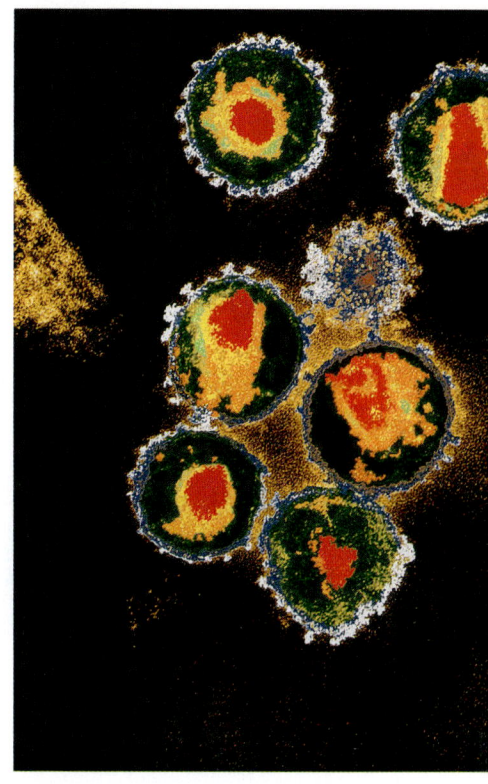

Figure 15 A person can be infected with HIV and not show any symptoms of the infection for several years.
Explain why this characteristic makes the spread of AIDS more likely.

Fighting Disease

Washing a small wound with soap and water is the first step in preventing an infection. Cleaning the wound with an antiseptic and covering it with a bandage are other steps. Is it necessary to wash your body to help prevent diseases? Yes! In addition to reducing body odor, washing your body removes and destroys some surface microorganisms.

In your mouth, microorganisms are responsible for mouth odor and tooth decay. Using dental floss and routine tooth brushing keep these organisms under control.

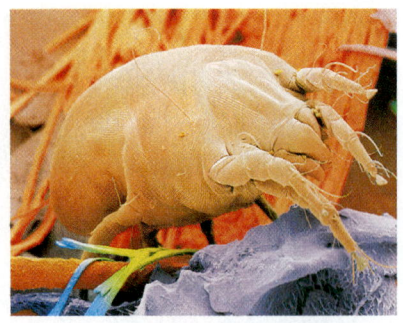

Figure 16 Dust mites are smaller than a period at the end of a sentence. They can live in pillows, mattresses, carpets, furniture, and other places.

Indiana Academic Standard Check

7.6.4: . . . the modern approach emphasizes sanitation . . . and aseptic surgical techniques to keep germs out of the body.

✓ How are airborne pathogens controlled in operating rooms?

Aseptic Surgical Techniques Every person involved with a surgery must help fight disease. Thorough washing of hands and wearing sterile gloves, gowns, and masks are standard practices. All surgical tools and operating room equipment must be sterilized. Even the operating room's air is filtered. Also, the patient's skin is cleaned where an incision is to be made, and then covered with sterile cloths.

Healthy Choices Exercise and good nutrition help the circulatory and respiratory systems work more effectively. Good health habits, including getting enough rest and eating well-balanced meals, can make you less susceptible to the actions of disease organisms such as those that cause colds and flu. Keeping up with recommended immunizations and having annual health checkups also can help you stay healthy.

Chronic Disease

Diseases and disorders such as diabetes, allergies, asthma, cancer, and heart disease are **noninfectious diseases**. They are not caused by pathogens and do not spread from one person to another. Many are chronic (KRAH nihk). This means that they can last for a long time.

Some infectious diseases can be chronic too. For example, deer ticks carry a bacterium that causes Lyme disease. This bacterium can affect the nervous system, heart, and joints for weeks to years. It can become chronic if not treated. Antibiotics will kill the bacteria, but some damage cannot be reversed.

Allergies Many people have allergies. An allergy is an overly strong reaction of the immune system to a foreign substance. Most allergic reactions are minor. However, severe allergic reactions can cause shock and even death if they aren't treated promptly.

Substances that cause an allergic response are called **allergens**. Some chemicals, certain foods, pollen, molds, some antibiotics, and dust are allergens for some people. Dust can contain cat and dog dander and dust mites, shown in **Figure 16.**

When you come in contact with an allergen, your immune system usually forms antibodies. Your body reacts by releasing chemicals called histamines (HIHS tuh meenz) that promote red, swollen tissues. Antihistamines are medications that can be used to treat allergic reactions and asthma, a lung disorder associated with reactions to allergens. Some severe allergies are treated with repeated injections of small doses of the allergen. This allows your body to become less sensitive to the allergen.

Diabetes A chronic disease associated with the levels of insulin produced by the pancreas is diabetes. Insulin is a hormone that enables glucose to pass from the bloodstream into your cells. Doctors recognize two types of diabetes—Type 1 and Type 2. Type 1 diabetes is the result of too little or no insulin production. In Type 2 diabetes, your body cannot properly process insulin. Symptoms of diabetes include fatigue, excessive thirst, frequent urination, and tingling sensations in the hands and feet.

If glucose levels in the blood remain high for a long time, other health problems can develop. These problems can include blurred vision, kidney failure, heart attack, stroke, loss of feeling in the feet, and the loss of consciousness (diabetic coma).

Cancer

Cancer is the name given to a group of closely related diseases that result from uncontrolled cell growth. It is a complicated disease, and no one fully understands how cancers form. Characteristics of cancer cells are shown in **Table 4.** Tumors can occur anywhere in your body. Cancerous cells can leave a tumor, spread throughout the body via blood and lymph vessels, and then invade other tissues.

 *How do cancers spread?*

Indiana Academic Standard Check

7.4.14: Explain that the environment may contain dangerous levels of substances that are harmful to human beings....

 What is a carcinogen?

Causes In the latter part of the eighteenth century, a British physician recognized the association of soot to cancer in chimney sweeps. Since that time, scientists have learned more about causes of cancer. Research done in the 1940s and 1950s first related genes to cancer.

Although not all the causes of cancer are known, many causes have been identified. Smoking has been linked to lung cancer—the leading cause of cancer deaths for males in the United States. Exposure to certain chemicals also can increase your chances of developing cancer. These substances, called carcinogens (kar SIH nuh junz), include asbestos, various solvents, heavy metals, alcohol, and home and garden chemicals. Exposure to X rays, nuclear radiation, and ultraviolet radiation of the Sun also increases your risk of cancer.

Table 4 Characteristics of Cancer Cells
Cell growth is uncontrolled.
These cells do not function as part of your body.
The cells take up space and interfere with normal body functions.
The cells travel throughout the body.
The cells produce tumors and abnormal growths anywhere in your body.

Table 5 Early Warning Signs of Cancer

Changes in bowel or bladder habits
A sore that does not heal
Unusual bleeding or discharge
Thickening or lump in the breast or elsewhere
Indigestion or difficulty swallowing
Obvious change in a wart or mole
Nagging cough or hoarseness

from the National Cancer Institute

Prevention Knowing some causes of cancer might help you prevent it. The first step is to know the early warning signs, shown in **Table 5.** Medical attention and treatments such as chemotherapy or surgery in the early stages of some cancers can cure or keep them inactive.

A second step in cancer prevention concerns lifestyle choices. Choosing not to use tobacco and alcohol products can help prevent mouth and lung cancers and the other associated respiratory and circulatory system diseases. Selecting a healthy diet without many foods that are high in fats, salt, and sugar also might reduce your chances of developing cancer. Using sunscreen and limiting the amount of time that you expose your skin to direct sunlight are good preventive measures against skin cancer. Careful handling of harmful home and garden chemicals will help you avoid the dangers connected with these substances.

section 4 review

Summary

Disease in History
- Pasteur, Koch, and Lister made important discoveries about the causes and how to prevent the spread of diseases.

Infectious Diseases and HIV
- Bacteria, fungi, protists, and viruses can cause infectious disease.
- STDs are passed during sexual contact and are caused by bacteria or viruses.
- HIV infection can lead to AIDS, a disease that attacks the immune system.

Fighting Disease
- Good health habits can help prevent the spread of disease.

Chronic Disease and Cancer
- Allergies, diabetes, and cancer are chronic noninfectious diseases.
- Early detection and lifestyle choices can help treat or prevent some cancers.

Self Check

1. **Name** an infectious disease caused by each of the following: a virus, a bacterium, a protist, and a fungus.
2. **Compare and contrast** how HIV and other viruses affect the immune system.
3. **Explain** why diabetes is classified as a noninfectious disease.
4. **Recognize** how poor hygiene is related to the spread of disease.
5. **Describe** how your body might respond to an allergen.
6. **Think Critically** In what ways does Koch's procedure demonstrate the use of scientific methods?

Applying Math

7. **Make and Use Graphs** Make a bar graph using the following data about the number of deaths from AIDS-related diseases for children younger than 13 years old: 1995, 536; 1996, 420; 1997, 209; 1998, 115; and 1999, 76.

CHAPTER 6 Circulation and Immunity

 in7.msscience.com/self_check_quiz

Microorganisms and Disease

Microorganisms are everywhere. Washing your hands and disinfecting items you use helps remove some of these organisms.

Real-World Question

How do microorganisms cause infection?

Goals
- **Observe** the transmission of microorganisms.
- **Relate** microorganisms to infections.

Materials
fresh apples (6)
rotting apple
rubbing alcohol (5 mL)
self-sealing plastic bags (6)
labels and pencil
gloves
paper towels
sandpaper
cotton ball
soap and water
newspaper

Safety Precautions

WARNING: *Do not eat the apples. Do not remove goggles until the lab and cleanup are completed. When you complete the experiment, give all bags to your teacher for disposal.*

Procedure

1. **Label** the plastic bags 1 through 6. Put on gloves. Place a fresh apple in bag 1.
2. Rub the rotting apple over the other five apples. This is your source of microorganisms. **WARNING:** *Don't touch your face.*
3. Put one apple in bag 2.
4. Hold one apple 1.5 m above the floor and drop it on a newspaper. Put it in bag 3.
5. Rub one apple with sandpaper. Place this apple in bag 4.
6. Wash one apple with soap and water. Dry it well. Put this apple in bag 5.
7. Use a cotton ball to spread alcohol over the last apple. Let it air-dry. Place it in bag 6.
8. Seal all bags and put them in a dark place.
9. On day 3 and day 7, compare all of the apples without removing them from the bags. Record your observations in a data table.

Apple Observations		
Condition	Day 3	Day 7
1. Fresh		
2. Untreated		
3. Dropped		
4. Rubbed with sandpaper	Do not write in this book.	
5. Washed with soap and water		
6. Covered with alcohol		

Conclude and Apply

1. **Infer** How does this experiment relate to infections on your skin?
2. **Explain** why it is important to clean a wound.

Communicating Your Data

Prepare a poster illustrating the advantages of washing hands to avoid the spread of disease. Get permission to put the poster near a school rest room. **For more help, refer to the** Science Skill Handbook.

LAB **185**

LAB Design Your Own

Blood Type Reactions

Goals
- **Design** an experiment that simulates the reactions between different blood types.
- **Identify** which blood types can donate to which other blood types.

Possible Materials
simulated blood (10 mL low-fat milk and 10 mL water plus red food coloring)
lemon juice as antigen A (for blood types B and O)
water as antigen A (for blood types A and AB)
droppers
small paper cups
marking pen
10-mL graduated cylinder

Safety Precautions

WARNING: *Do not taste, eat, or drink any materials used in the lab.*

Real-World Question
Human blood can be classified into four main blood types—A, B, AB, and O. These types are determined by the presence or absence of antigens on the red blood cells. After blood is collected into a transfusion bag, it is tested to determine the blood type. The type is labeled clearly on the bag. Blood is refrigerated to keep it fresh and available for transfusion. What happens when two different blood types are mixed?

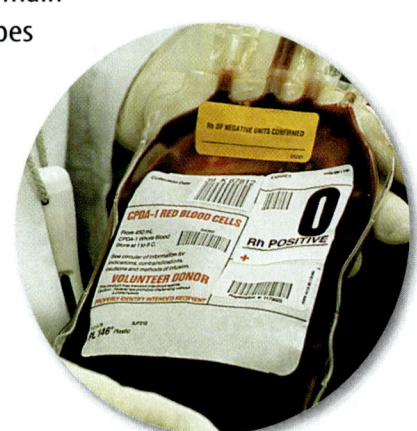

Form a Hypothesis
Based on your reading and observations, form a hypothesis to explain how different blood types will react to each other.

Test Your Hypothesis

Make a Plan
1. As a group, agree upon a hypothesis and decide how you will test it. Identify the results that will confirm the hypothesis.
2. **List** the steps you must take and the materials you will need to test your hypothesis. Be specific. Describe exactly what you will do in each step.
3. **Prepare** a data table like the one at the right in your Science Journal to record your observations.

Blood Type Reactions	
Blood Type	**Clumping (Yes or No)**
A	
B	Do not write in
AB	this book.
O	

186 CHAPTER 6 Circulation and Immunity

Using Scientific Methods

4. Reread the entire experiment to make sure all steps are in logical order.
5. **Identify** constants and variables. Blood type O will be the control.

Follow Your Plan

1. Make sure your teacher approves your plan before you start.
2. Carry out the experiment according to the approved plan.
3. While doing the experiment, record your observations and complete the data table in your Science Journal.

Analyze Your Data

1. **Compare** the reactions of each blood type (A, B, AB, and O) when antigen A was added to the blood.
2. **Observe** where clumping took place.
3. **Compare** your results with those of other groups.
4. What was the control factor in this experiment?
5. What were your variables?

Conclude and Apply

1. Did the results support your hypothesis? Explain.
2. **Predict** what might happen to a person if other antigens are not matched properly.
3. What would happen in an investigation with antigen B added to each blood type?

Write a brief report on how blood is tested to determine blood type. Describe why this is important to know before receiving a blood transfusion. **For more help, refer to the Science Skill Handbook.**

LAB **187**

TIME SCIENCE AND HISTORY

SCIENCE CAN CHANGE THE COURSE OF HISTORY!

Dr. Daniel Hale Williams was a pioneer in open-heart surgery.

Have a Heart

People didn't always know where blood came from or how it moved through the body.

You prick your finger, and when blood starts to flow out of the cut, you put on a bandage. But if you were a scientist living long ago, you might have also asked yourself some questions: How did your blood get to the tip of your finger? And why and how does it flow through (and sometimes out of!) your body?

As early as the 1500s, a Spanish scientist named Miguel Serveto (mee GEL • ser VEH toh) asked that question. His studies led him to the theory that blood circulated throughout the human body, but he didn't know how or why.

About 100 years later, William Harvey, an English doctor, explored Serveto's idea. Harvey studied animals to develop a theory about how the heart and the circulatory system work. Blood was pumped from the heart throughout the body, Harvey hypothesized. Then it returned to the heart and recirculated. He published his ideas in 1628 in his famous book, *On the Motion of the Heart and Blood in Animals.* His theories were correct, and Harvey's book became the basis for all modern research on heart and blood vessels.

Medical Pioneer

More than two centuries later, another pioneer, Dr. Daniel Hale Williams, stepped forward and used Harvey's ideas to change the science frontier again. He performed the first open-heart surgery by removing a knife from the heart of a stabbing victim. He stitched the wound in the fluid sac surrounding the heart, and the patient lived for several years afterward.

Report Identify a pioneer in science or medicine who has changed our lives for the better. Find out how this person started in the field, and how they came to make an important discovery. Give a presentation to the class.

For more information, visit in7.msscience.com/time

chapter 6 Study Guide

Reviewing Main Ideas

Section 1 Blood

1. Red blood cells carry oxygen and carbon dioxide, platelets form clots, and white blood cells fight infection.
2. A, B, AB, and O blood types are determined by the presence or absence of antigens on red blood cells.

Section 2 Circulation

1. Arteries carry blood away from the heart and veins return blood to the heart. Capillaries connect arteries to veins.
2. The circulatory system can be divided into three sections—coronary, pulmonary, and systemic circulation.
3. Lymph structures filter blood, produce white blood cells, and destroy worn out blood cells.

Section 3 Immunity

1. Your body is protected against most pathogens by the immune system.
2. Active immunity is long lasting, but passive immunity is not.

Section 4 Diseases

1. Pasteur and Koch discovered that microorganisms cause diseases. Lister learned that cleanliness helps control microorganisms.
2. Bacteria, viruses, fungi, and protists can cause infectious diseases.
3. HIV damages your body's immune system, which can cause AIDS.
4. Causes of noninfectious diseases, such as diabetes and cancer, include genetics, a poor diet, chemicals, and uncontrolled cell growth.

Visualizing Main Ideas

Copy and complete this concept map on the functions of the parts of the blood.

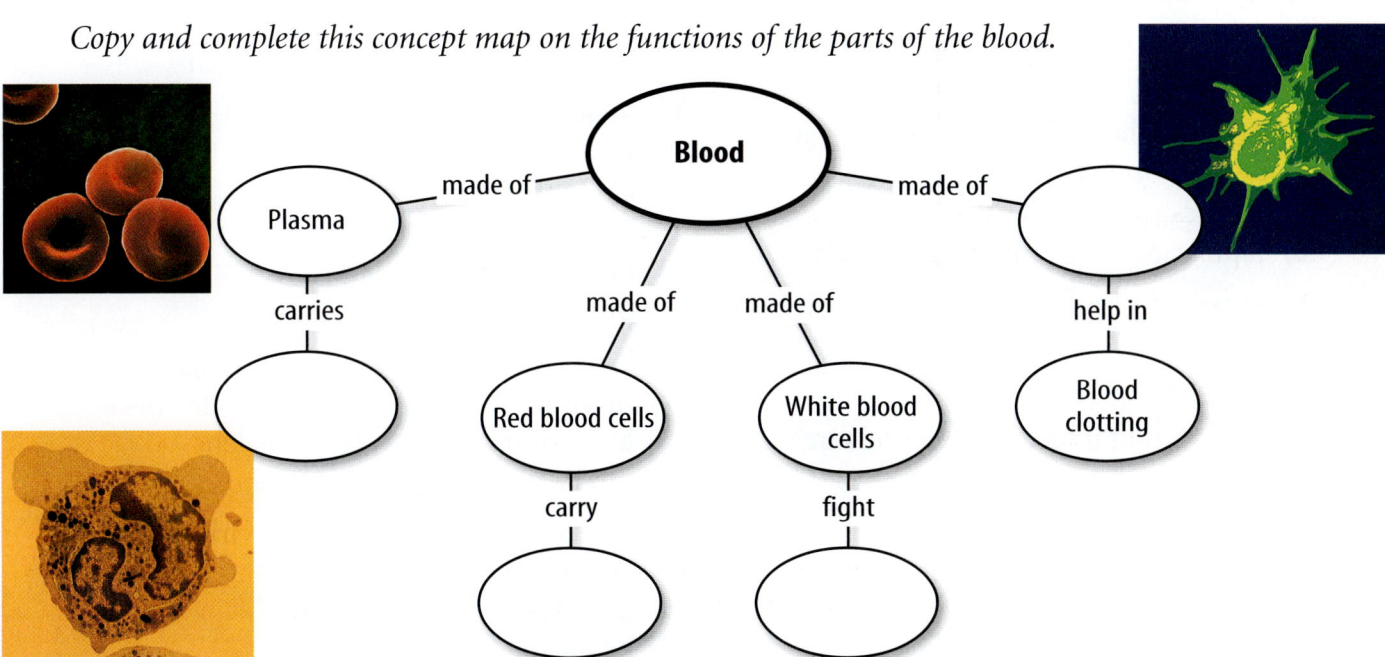

chapter 6 Review

Using Vocabulary

active immunity p. 175	lymph p. 172
allergen p. 182	noninfectious
antibody p. 174	disease p. 182
antigen p. 174	passive immunity p. 175
artery p. 169	pasteurization p. 177
capillary p. 169	plasma p. 162
hemoglobin p. 163	platelet p. 163
infectious disease p. 178	vein p. 169

Fill in the blanks with the correct vocabulary word or words.

1. _____ is the chemical in red blood cells.
2. _____ are cell fragments that help clot blood.
3. _____ occurs when your body makes its own antibodies.
4. A(n) _____ stimulates histamine release.
5. Heating a liquid to kill harmful bacteria is called _____.

Checking Concepts

Choose the word or phrase that best answers the question.

6. Where does the exchange of food, oxygen, and wastes occur?
   A) arteries   C) veins
   B) capillaries   D) lymph vessels

7. How can infectious diseases be caused?
   A) heredity   C) chemicals
   B) allergies   D) organisms

8. Where is blood under greatest pressure?
   A) arteries   C) veins
   B) capillaries   D) lymph vessels

9. Which cells fight off infection?
   A) red blood   C) white blood
   B) bone   D) nerve

10. Of the following, which carries oxygen in blood?
    A) red blood cells   C) white blood cells
    B) platelets   D) lymph

11. What is required to clot blood?
    A) plasma   C) platelets
    B) oxygen   D) carbon dioxide

Use the table below to answer question 12.

Table 1 Blood Types

Blood Type	Antigen	Antibody
A	A	Anti-B
B	B	Anti-A
AB	A, B	None
O	None	Anti-A, Anti-B

12. Using the table above, what kind of antigen does type O blood have?
    A) A   C) A and B
    B) B   D) no antigen

13. Where does oxygen-rich blood enter first?
    A) right atrium
    B) left atrium
    C) left ventricle
    D) right ventricle

14. What is formed in the blood to fight invading antigens?
    A) hormones   C) pathogens
    B) allergens   D) antibodies

15. Which disease is caused by a virus that attacks white blood cells?
    A) AIDS   C) flu
    B) measles   D) polio

190 CHAPTER REVIEW

Science online in7.msscience.com/vocabulary_puzzlemaker

chapter 6 Review

Thinking Critically

16. Compare and contrast the life spans of red blood cells, white blood cells, and platelets.

17. Sequence blood clotting from the wound to forming a scab.

18. Compare and contrast the functions of arteries, veins, and capillaries.

19. Analyze how antibodies, antigens, and antibiotics differ.

20. Recognize Cause and Effect Use library references to identify the cause—bacteria, virus, fungus, or protist—of each of these diseases: athlete's foot, AIDS, cold, dysentery, flu, pinkeye, acne, and strep throat.

21. Classify Using word processing software, make a table to classify the following diseases as infectious or noninfectious: diabetes, gonorrhea, herpes, strep throat, syphilis, cancer, and flu.

Use the graph below to answer question 22.

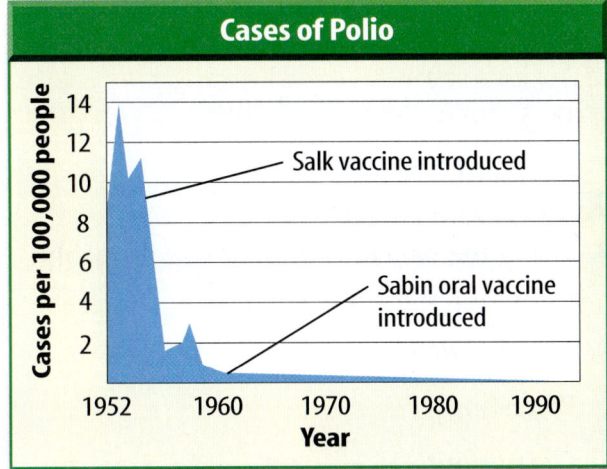

22. Explain the rate of polio cases between 1952 and 1965. What conclusions can you draw about the effectiveness of the polio vaccine?

Performance Activities

23. Scientific Drawing Prepare a drawing of the human heart and label its parts. Use arrows to show the flow of blood through the heart.

24. Poster Design and construct a poster to illustrate how a person with the flu could spread the disease to family members, classmates, and others.

25. Pamphlet Prepare a pamphlet describing heart transplants. Include an explanation of why the patient is given drugs that suppress the immune system and describe the patient's life after the operation.

Applying Math

26. Percentages of Blood Cells A cubic millimeter of blood has about five million red blood cells, 7,500 white blood cells, and 400,000 platelets. Find the total number of red blood cells, white blood cells, and platelets in 1 mm^3 of blood. Calculate what percentage of the total each type is.

Use the table below to answer question 27.

Gender and Heart Rate	
Sex	Pulse/Minute
Male 1	72
Male 2	64
Male 3	65
Female 1	67
Female 2	84
Female 3	74

27. Heart Rates Interpret the data listed in the table above. Find the average heart rate of the three males and the three females and compare the two averages.

chapter 6 Indiana

The assessed Indiana standard appears above the question.

Record your answers on the answer sheet provided by your teacher or on a sheet of paper.

Part 1 Multiple Choice

The graph below shows life expectancy data for some people.

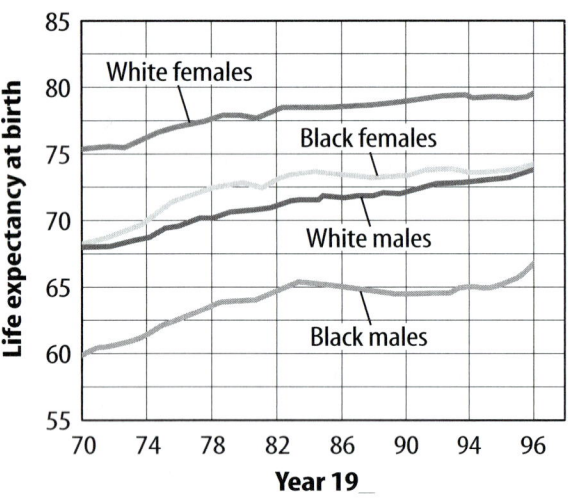

Life Expectancy by Race and Sex, 1970–1997

1. Which group had the lowest life expectancy in both 1975 and 1994?
   - A black females
   - B black males
   - C white females
   - D white males

Test-Taking Tip

Answer Bubbles For each question, double check that you are filling in the correct answer bubble for the question number you are working on.

7.4.4

2. Which is a function of blood?
   - A carries saliva to the mouth
   - B excretes salts from the body
   - C removes lymph from around cells
   - D transports substances to body cells

The table below lists recorded body data.

Results from Exercising			
Activity	Pulse Rate (beats/min)	Body Temperature	Degree of Sweating
1	80	98.6°F	None
2	90	98.8°F	Minimal
3	100	98.9°F	Little
4	120	99.1°F	Moderate
5	150	99.5°F	Considerable

7.4.11

3. Which activity caused a pulse of less than 100 beats per minute?
   - A 2
   - B 3
   - C 4
   - D 5

7.4.11

4. Using the data above, what was probably occurring during Activity 2?
   - A brisk walking
   - B resting
   - C running
   - D slow walking

Standards Review

7.4.4

5. This illustration shows part of a human's circulatory system.

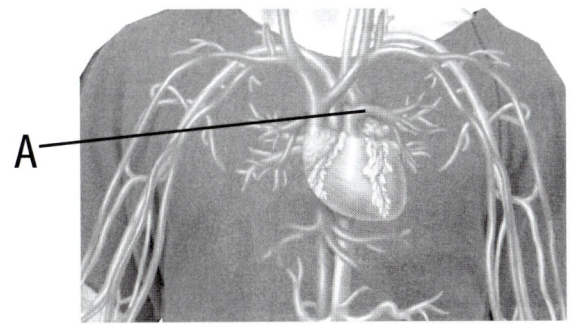

What might happen if vessel A became blocked?

A Blood could not flow to the lungs.

B Blood could not return to the heart from the body.

C Blood could not flow to the body.

D Blood could not return to the heart from the lungs.

7.4.12

6. Which is a noninfectious disease?

A diabetes

B malaria

C SARS

D tetanus

7.4.12

7. Which is **NOT** a biological vector?

A bird

B fly

C food

D human

Part 2 Constructed Response

7.4.4

8. How do the lymphatic and circulatory systems work together?

7.4.4

9. Below is an illustration of the interior of a human heart.

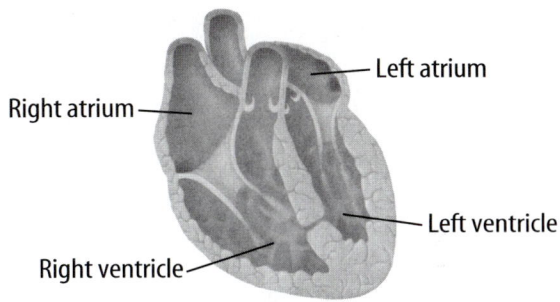

The left ventricle pumps blood under higher pressure than the right ventricle does. Compare the circulation in this heart with that of a normal heart.

7.4.11

10. What are some ways to prevent cardiovascular disease?

7.4.13

11. Which is longer lasting, active immunity or passive immunity? Why?

7.4.12   7.6.2

12. A scientist has isolated a bacterium that she thinks causes a recently discovered disease called red tree. How can she prove it? What steps should she follow?

7.4.12

13. Compare and contrast infectious and noninfectious diseases.

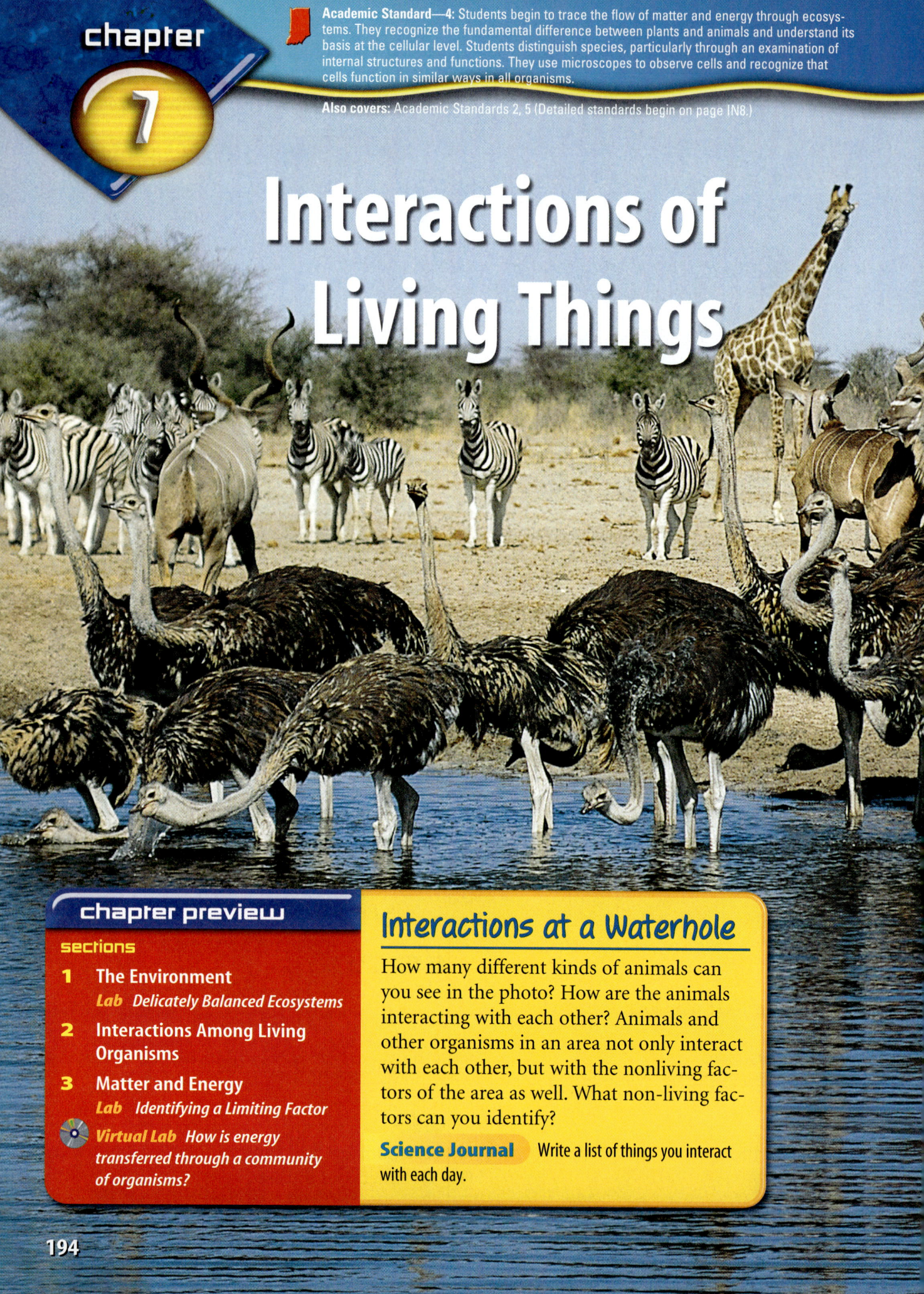

chapter 7

Academic Standard—4: Students begin to trace the flow of matter and energy through ecosystems. They recognize the fundamental difference between plants and animals and understand its basis at the cellular level. Students distinguish species, particularly through an examination of internal structures and functions. They use microscopes to observe cells and recognize that cells function in similar ways in all organisms.

Also covers: Academic Standards 2, 5 (Detailed standards begin on page IN8.)

Interactions of Living Things

chapter preview

sections
1. **The Environment**
   Lab Delicately Balanced Ecosystems
2. **Interactions Among Living Organisms**
3. **Matter and Energy**
   Lab Identifying a Limiting Factor
   Virtual Lab How is energy transferred through a community of organisms?

Interactions at a Waterhole
How many different kinds of animals can you see in the photo? How are the animals interacting with each other? Animals and other organisms in an area not only interact with each other, but with the nonliving factors of the area as well. What non-living factors can you identify?

Science Journal Write a list of things you interact with each day.

Start-Up Activities

Space and Interactions

Imagine that you are in a crowded elevator. Everyone jostles and bumps each other. The temperature increases and ordinary noises seem louder. Like people in an elevator, plants and animals in an area interact. How does the amount of space available to each organism affect its interaction with other organisms?

1. Use a meterstick to measure the length and width of the classroom.
2. Multiply the length by the width to find the area of the room in square meters.
3. Count the number of individuals in your class. Divide the area of the classroom by the number of individuals. In your Science Journal, record how much space each person has.
4. **Think Critically** Write a prediction in your Science Journal about what might happen if the number of students in your classroom doubled.

 Preview this chapter's content and activities at in7.msscience.com

 **Biotic and Abiotic** Make the following Foldable to help you understand the cause and effect relationship of biotic and abiotic things.

STEP 1 Fold a vertical sheet of paper in half from top to bottom.

STEP 2 Fold in half from side to side with the fold at the top.

STEP 3 Unfold the paper once. Cut only the fold of the top flap to make two tabs.

STEP 4 Turn the paper vertically and label the front tabs as shown.

Illustrate and Label Before you read the chapter, list examples of biotic and abiotic things around you on the tabs. As you read, write about each.

section 1

Standard—7.4.9: Understand and explain that as any population of organisms grows, it is held in check by one or more environmental factors. These factors could result in depletion of food or nesting sites and/or increase loss to increased numbers of predators or parasites. Give examples of some consequences of this.

Also covers: 7.1.7, 7.2.7 (Detailed standards begin on page IN8.)

The Environment

as you read

What You'll Learn
- **Identify** biotic and abiotic factors in an ecosystem.
- **Describe** the different levels of biological organization.
- **Explain** how ecology and the environment are related.

Why It's Important
Abiotic and biotic factors interact to make up your ecosystem. The quality of your ecosystem can affect your health. Your actions can affect the health of the ecosystem.

Review Vocabulary
climate: the average weather conditions of an area over time

New Vocabulary
- ecology
- abiotic factor
- biotic factor
- population
- community
- ecosystem
- biosphere

Ecology

All organisms, from the smallest bacteria to a blue whale, interact with their environment. **Ecology** is the study of the interactions among organisms and their environment. Ecologists, such as the one in **Figure 1,** are scientists who study these relationships. Ecologists organize the environmental factors that influence organisms into two groups—nonliving and living or once-living. **Abiotic (ay bi AH tihk) factors** are the nonliving parts of the environment. Living or once-living organisms in the environment are called **biotic (bi AH tihk) factors.**

 **Reading Check** Why is a rotting log considered a biotic factor in the environment?

Abiotic Factors

In any environment, birds, insects, and other living things, including humans, depend on one another for food and shelter. They also depend on the abiotic factors that surround them, such as water, sunlight, temperature, air, and soil. All of these factors and others are important in determining which organisms are able to live in a particular environment.

Figure 1 Ecologists study biotic and abiotic factors in an environment and the relationships among them. Many times, ecologists must travel to specific environments to examine the organisms that live there.

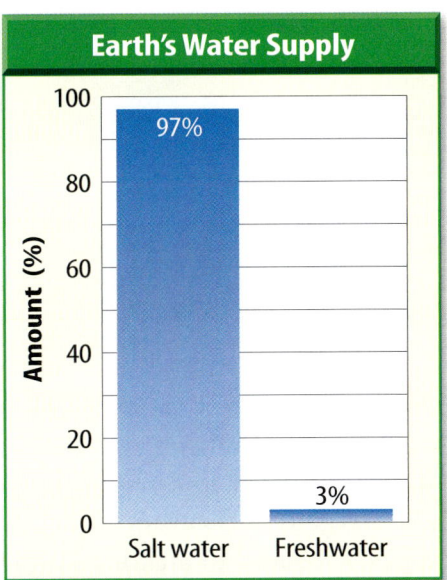

Figure 2 Salt water accounts for 97 percent of the water on Earth. It is found in the seas and oceans. Only three percent of Earth's water is freshwater.

Water All living organisms need water to survive. The bodies of most organisms are 50 percent to 95 percent water. Water is an important part of the cytoplasm in cells and the fluid that surrounds cells. Respiration, photosynthesis, digestion, and other important life processes can only occur in the presence of water.

More than 95 percent of Earth's surface water is found in the oceans. The saltwater environment in the oceans is home to a vast number of species. Freshwater environments, like the one in **Figure 2,** also support thousands of types of organisms.

Light and Temperature The abiotic factors of light and temperature also affect the environment. The availability of sunlight is a major factor in determining where green plants and other photosynthetic organisms live, as shown in **Figure 3.** By the process of photosynthesis, energy from the Sun is changed into chemical energy that is used for life processes. Most green algae live near the water's surface where sunlight can penetrate. In dense forests where little sunlight penetrates through to the forest floor, very few photosynthetic plants grow.

The temperature of a region also determines which plants and animals can live there. Some areas of the world have a fairly consistent temperature year round, but other areas have seasons during which temperatures vary. Water environments throughout the world also have widely varied temperatures. Living organisms are found in the freezing cold Arctic, in the extremely hot water near ocean vents, and at almost every temperature in between.

Figure 3 Flowers that grow on the forest floor, such as these bluebells, grow during the spring when they receive the most sunlight.
Infer why there is little sunlight on the forest floor during the summer.

SECTION 1 The Environment **197**

Figure 4 Air pollution can come from many different sources. Air quality in an area affects the health and survival of the species that live there.

Air Pollution Engineer
Have you ever wondered who monitors the air you breathe? Air pollution engineers are people who make sure air quality standards are being met. They also design new technologies to reduce air pollution, such as improved machinery, filters, and ventilation systems, to try and solve problems like "sick building syndrome."

Figure 5 Soil provides a home for many species of animals and other organisms.

Air Although you can't see the air that surrounds you, it has an impact on the lives of most species. Air is composed of a mixture of gases including nitrogen, oxygen, and carbon dioxide. Most plants and animals depend on the gases in air for respiration. The atmosphere is the layer of gases and airborne particles that surrounds Earth. Polluted air, like the air in **Figure 4,** can cause the species in an area to change, move, or die off.

Clouds and weather occur in the bottom 8 km to 16 km of the atmosphere. All species are affected by the weather in the area where they live. The ozone layer is 20 km to 50 km above Earth's surface and protects organisms from harmful radiation from the Sun. Air pressure, which is the weight of air pressing down on Earth, changes depending on altitude. Higher altitudes have less air pressure. Few organisms live at extreme air pressures.

 *How does pollution in the atmosphere affect the species in an area?*

Soil From one enviroment to another, soil, as shown in **Figure 5,** can vary greatly. Soil type is determined by the amounts of sand, silt, and clay it contains. Various kinds of soil contain different amounts of nutrients, minerals, and moisture. Different plants need different kinds of soil. Because the types of plants in an area help determine which other organisms can survive in that area, soil affects every organism in an environment.

Biotic Factors

Abiotic factors do not provide everything an organism needs for survival. Organisms depend on other organisms for food, shelter, protection, and reproduction. How organisms interact with one another and with abiotic factors can be described in an organized way.

Levels of Organization The living world is highly organized. Atoms are arranged into molecules, which in turn might be organized into cells. Cells form tissues, tissues form organs, and organs form organ systems. Together, organ systems form organisms. Biotic and abiotic factors also can be arranged into levels of biological organization, as shown in **Figure 6**.

Figure 6 The living world is organized in levels.

An organism is one individual from a population.

All of the individuals of one species that live in the same area at the same time make up a population.

The populations of different species that interact in some way are called a community.

All of the communities in an area and the abiotic factors they interact with make up an ecosystem.

A biome is a large region with plants and animals well adapted to the soil and climate of the region.

The level of biological organization that is made up of all the ecosystems on Earth is the biosphere.

SECTION 1 The Environment **199**

Populations All the members of one species that live together make up a **population**. For example, all of the humans living on Earth at the same time make up a population. Part of a population of penguins is shown in **Figure 7**. Members of a population compete for food, water, mates, and space. The resources of the environment and the ways the organisms use these resources determine how large a population can become.

Communities Most populations of organisms do not live alone. They live and interact with populations of other types of organisms. Groups of populations that interact with each other in a given area form a **community**. For example, a population of penguins and all of the species that they interact with form a community. Populations of organisms in a community depend on each other for food, shelter, and other needs.

Ecosystems In addition to interactions among populations, ecologists also study interactions among populations and their physical surroundings. An **ecosystem** is made up of a biotic community and the abiotic factors that affect it. Examples of ecosystems include coral reefs, forests, and ponds. You will learn more about the interactions that occur in ecosystems later in this chapter.

Figure 7 Members of a penguin population compete for resources. **Infer** *what resources these penguins might be using.*

Topic: Earth's Biomes
Visit in7.msscience.com for Web links to information about Earth's different biomes.

Activity Select one of Earth's biomes and research what plants, animals, and other organisms live there. Prepare a display that includes pictures and text about your selected biome.

Biomes Scientists divide Earth into different regions called biomes. A biome (BI ohm) is a large region with plant and animal groups that are well adapted to the soil and climate of the region. Many different ecosystems are found in a biome. Examples of biomes include tundra, as shown in **Figure 8,** tropical rain forests, and grasslands.

Figure 8 Biomes contain many different ecosystems. This mountaintop ecosystem is part of the alpine tundra biome.

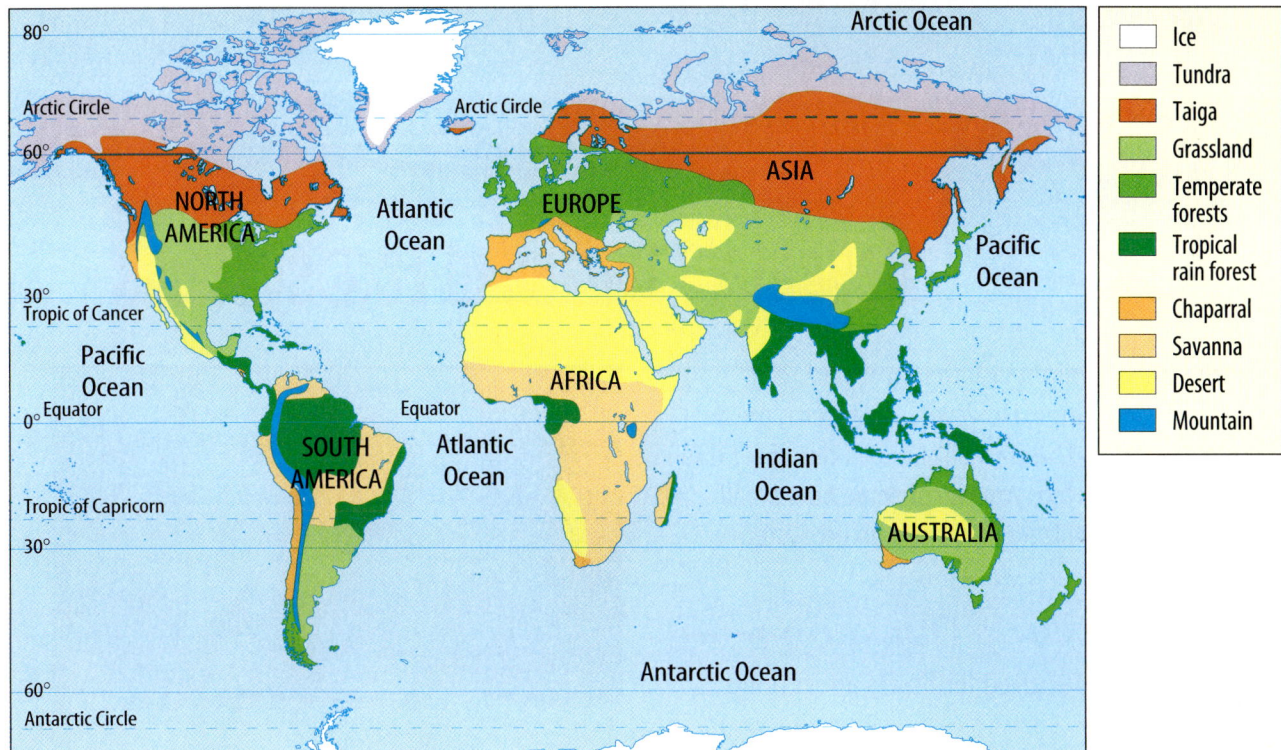

The Biosphere Where do all of Earth's organisms live? Living things can be found 11,000 m deep in the ocean, 9,000 m high on mountains, and 4.5 km high in Earth's atmosphere. The part of Earth that supports life is the **biosphere** (BI uh sfihr). It includes the top part of Earth's crust, all the waters that cover Earth's surface, the surrounding atmosphere, and all biomes, including those in **Figure 9**.

Figure 9 This map shows some of the major biomes of the world. **Determine** what biome you live in.

section 1 review

Summary

Abiotic Factors
- Organisms interact with and depend on factors in their environments.
- More than 95 percent of Earth's surface is water.
- The amount of sunlight determines where green plants can grow.
- Temperature determines which organisms can live in a region.
- Air is needed by most organisms. Polluted air can harm organisms.
- Soil can determine organisms in an area.

Biotic Factors
- Organisms depend on other organisms for food, shelter, protection, and reproduction.
- The living world is organized into levels.

Self Check

1. **Compare and contrast** abiotic factors and biotic factors. Give five examples of each that are in your ecosystem.
2. **Describe** a population and a community.
3. **Define** the term *ecosystem*.
4. **Explain** how the terms *ecology* and *environment* are related.
5. **Think Critically** Explain how biotic factors change in an ecosystem that has flooded.

Applying Skills

6. **Record Observations** Each person lives in a population as part of a community. Describe your population and community.
7. **Use a database** to research biomes. Find the name of the biome that best describes where you live.

Science online in7.msscience.com/self_check_quiz

SECTION 1 The Environment **201**

Delicately Balanced Ecosystems

Each year you might visit the same park, but notice little change. However, ecosystems are delicately balanced, and small changes can upset this balance. In this lab, you will observe how small amounts of fertilizer can disrupt an ecosystem.

Real-World Question

How do manufactured fertilizers affect pond systems?

Goals
- **Observe** the effects of manufactured fertilizer on water plants.
- **Predict** the effects of fertilizers on pond and stream ecosystems.

Materials

large glass jars of equal size (4)	rubber bands (4)
clear plastic wrap	pond water
stalks of *Elodea* (8)	triple-beam balance
*another aquatic plant	*electronic scale
garden fertilizer	weighing paper
*houseplant fertilizer	spoon
	metric ruler

*Alternate materials

Safety Precautions

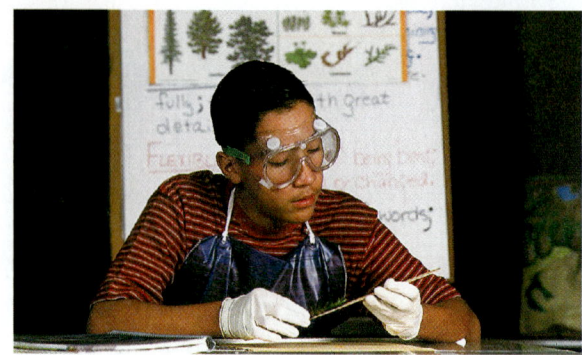

Procedure

1. Working in a group, label four jars *A, B, C,* and *D*.
2. **Measure** eight *Elodea* stalks to be certain that they are all about equal in length.
3. Fill the jars with equal volumes of pond water and place two stalks of *Elodea* in each jar.
4. Add 5 g of fertilizer to jar B, 10 g to jar C, and 30 g to jar D. Put no fertilizer in jar A.
5. Cover each jar with plastic wrap and secure it with a rubber band. Use your pencil to punch three small holes through the plastic wrap.
6. Place all jars in a well-lit area.
7. **Observe** the jars daily for three weeks. Record your observations in your Science Journal.
8. **Measure and record** the length of each *Elodea* stalk in your Science Journal.

Conclude and Apply

1. **List** the control and variables you used in this experiment.
2. **Compare** the growth of *Elodea* in each jar.
3. **Predict** what might happen to jar A if you added 5 g of fertilizer to it each week.
4. **Infer** what effects manufactured fertilizers might have on pond and stream ecosystems.

Compare your results with the results of other students. Research how fertilizer runoff from farms and lawns has affected aquatic ecosystems in your area.

202 CHAPTER 7 Interactions of Living Things

section 2

Standard—7.4.9: Understand and explain that as any population of organisms grows, it is held in check by one or more environmental factors. These factors could result in depletion of food or nesting sites and/or increase loss to increased numbers of predators or parasites. Give examples of some consequences of this.

Also covers: 7.4.8, 7.5.3 (Detailed standards begin on page IN8.)

Interactions Among Living Organisms

Characteristics of Populations

You, the person sitting next to you, everyone in your class, and every other organism on Earth is a member of a specific population. Populations can be described by their characteristics such as spacing and density.

Population Size The number of individuals in the population is the population's size, as shown in **Figure 10**. Population size can be difficult to measure. If a population is small and made up of organisms that do not move, the size can be determined by counting the individuals. Usually individuals are too widespread or move around too much to be counted. The population size then is estimated. The number of organisms of one species in a small section is counted and this value is used to estimate the population of the larger area.

Suppose you spent several months observing a population of field mice that live in a pasture. You probably would observe changes in the size of the population. Older mice die. Mice are born. Some are eaten by predators, and some mice move away to new nests. The size of a population is always changing. The rate of change in population size varies from population to population. In contrast to a mouse population, the number of pine trees in a mature forest changes slowly, but a forest fire or disease could reduce the pine tree population quickly.

as you read

What You'll Learn
- **Identify** the characteristics that describe populations.
- **Examine** the different types of relationships that occur among populations in a community.
- **Determine** the habitat and niche of a species in a community.

Why It's Important
You must interact with other organisms to survive.

Review Vocabulary
coexistence: living together in the same place at the same time

New Vocabulary
- population density
- limiting factor
- symbiosis
- niche
- habitat

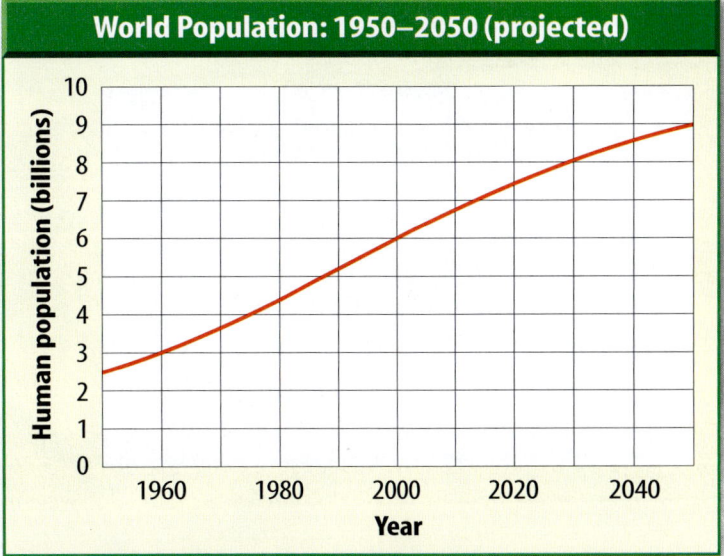

Figure 10 The size of the human population is increasing each year. By the year 2050, the human population is projected to be more than 9 billion.

Source: U.S. Census Bureau, International Data Base 5-10-00.

Figure 11 Population density can be shown on a map. This map uses different colors to show varying densities of a population of northern bobwhites, a type of bird.

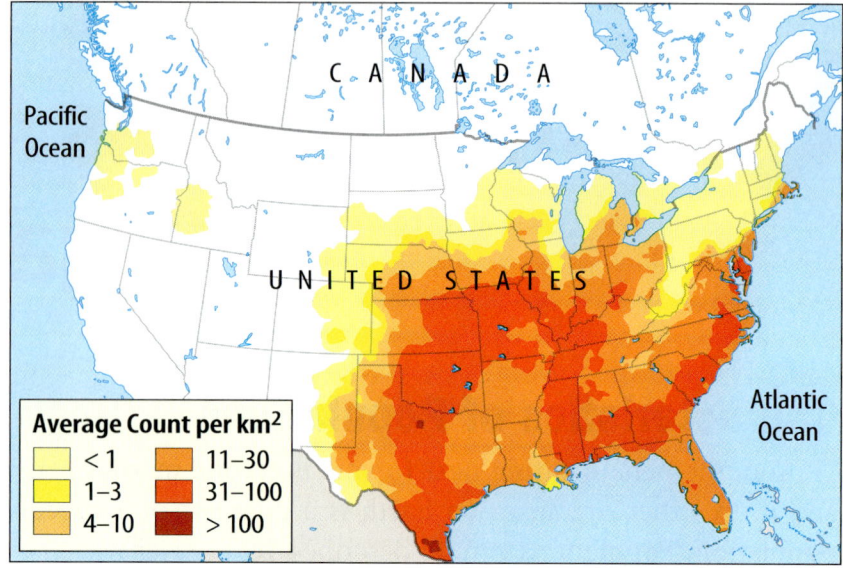

Topic: Human Population
Visit in7.msscience.com for Web links to information about human population and densities.

Activity Select at least three different areas of the world and prepare a bar graph to compare population density of each area. Compare the population density of where you live to the three areas of the world you select.

Population Density At the beginning of this chapter, when you figured out how much space is available to each student in your classroom, you were measuring another population characteristic. The number of individuals in a population that occupy a definite area is called **population density.** For example, if 100 mice live in an area of one square kilometer, the population density is 100 mice per square kilometer. When more individuals live in a given amount of space, as seen in **Figure 11,** the population is more dense.

Population Spacing Another characteristic of populations is spacing, or how the organisms are arranged in a given area. They can be evenly spaced, randomly spaced, or clumped together. If organisms have a fairly consistent distance between them, as shown in **Figure 12,** they are evenly spaced. In random spacing, each organism's location is independent of the locations of other organisms in the population. Random spacing of plants usually results when wind or birds disperse seeds. Clumped spacing occurs when resources such as food or living space are clumped. Clumping results when animals gather in groups or plants grow near each other in groups.

Figure 12 Some populations, such as creosote bushes in the desert, are evenly spaced throughout an area.

204 CHAPTER 7 Interactions of Living Things

Limiting Factors Populations, such as the antelopes in **Figure 13,** cannot continue to grow larger forever. All ecosystems have a limited amount of food, water, living space, mates, nesting sites, and other resources. A **limiting factor** is any biotic or abiotic factor that limits the number of individuals in a population. A limiting factor also can affect other populations in the community indirectly. For example, a drought might reduce the number of seed-producing plants in a forest clearing. Fewer plants means that food can become a limiting factor for deer that eat the plants and for a songbird population that feeds on the seeds of these plants. Food also could become a limiting factor for animals that feed on the songbirds.

Reading Check *What is an example of a limiting factor?*

Competition is the struggle among organisms to obtain the same resources needed to survive and reproduce, as shown in **Figure 14.** As population density increases, so does competition among individuals for the resources in their environment.

Carrying Capacity Suppose a population increases in size year after year. At some point, food, nesting space, or other resources become so scarce that some individuals are not able to survive or reproduce. When this happens, the environment has reached its carrying capacity. Carrying capacity is the largest number of individuals of a species that an environment can support and maintain for a long period of time. If a population gets bigger than the carrying capacity of the environment, some individuals are left without adequate resources. They will die or be forced to move elsewhere.

Figure 13 These antelope and zebra populations live in the grasslands of Africa.
Infer *what limiting factors might affect the plant and animal populations shown here.*

Indiana Academic Standard Check

7.4.9: Understand and explain that as any population of organisms grows, it is held in check by one or more environmental factors.... Give examples of some consequences of this.

✔ What can happen if the size of a population exceeds the carrying capacity of its environment?

Figure 14 During dry summers, the populations of animals at existing watering holes increase because some watering holes have dried up. This creates competition for water, a valuable resource.

Biotic Potential What would happen if a population's environment had no limiting factors? The size of the population would continue to increase. The maximum rate at which a population increases when plenty of food and water are available, the weather is ideal, and no diseases or enemies exist, is its biotic potential. Most populations never reach their biotic potential, or they do so for only a short period of time. Eventually, the carrying capacity of the environment is reached and the population stops increasing.

Symbiosis and Other Interactions

In ecosystems, many species of organisms have close relationships that are necessary for their survival. **Symbiosis** (sihm bee OH sus) is any close interaction between two or more different species. Symbiotic relationships can be identified by the type of interaction between organisms. Mutualism is a symbiotic relationship in which two different species of organisms cooperate and both benefit. **Figure 15** shows one example of mutualism.

Commensalism is a form of symbiosis that benefits one organism without affecting the other organism. For example, a species of flatworm benefits by living in the gills of horseshoe crabs, eating scraps of the horseshoe crab's meals. The horseshoe crab is unaffected by the flatworms.

Parasitism is a symbiotic relationship between two species in which one species benefits and the other species is harmed. Some species of mistletoe are parasites because their roots grow into a tree's tissue and take nutrients from the tree.

Reading Check What form of symbiosis exists between a bee and a flower?

Observing Symbiosis

Procedure

1. Carefully wash and examine the roots of a **legume plant** and a **nonlegume plant.**
2. Use a **magnifying lens** to examine the roots of the legume plant.

Analysis

1. What differences do you observe in the roots of the two plants?
2. Bacteria and legume plants help one another thrive. What type of symbiotic relationship is this?

The yucca depends on the moth to pollinate its flowers.

The moth depends on the yucca for a protected place to lay its eggs and a source of food for its larvae.

Figure 15 The partnership between the desert yucca plant and the yucca moth is an example of mutualism.

Predation One way that population size is regulated is by predation (prih DAY shun). Predation is the act of one organism hunting, killing, and feeding on another organism. Owls are predators of mice, as shown in **Figure 16.** Mice are their prey. Predators are biotic factors that limit the size of the prey population. Availability of prey is a biotic factor that can limit the size of the predator population. Because predators are more likely to capture old, ill, or young prey, the strongest individuals in the prey population are the ones that manage to reproduce. This improves the prey population over several generations.

Habitats and Niches In a community, every species plays a particular role. For example, some are producers and some are consumers. Each also has a particular place to live. The role, or job, of an organism in the ecosystem is called its niche (NICH). What a species eats, how it gets its food, and how it interacts with other organisms are all parts of its niche. The place where an organism lives is called its habitat. For example, an earthworm's habitat is soil. An earthworm's niche includes loosening, aerating, and enriching the soil.

Figure 16 Owls use their keen senses of sight and hearing to hunt for mice in the dark.

section 2 review

Summary

Characteristics of Populations
- Populations can be described by size, density, and spacing.
- Limiting factors affect population size.
- The number of individuals an environment can support and maintain over time is called the carrying capacity.
- The biotic potential is the rate a population would increase without limiting factors.

Symbiosis and Other Interactions
- A close interaction between two or more different species is called symbiosis.
- Mutualism, commensalism, and parasitism are types of symbiotic relationships that can exist between organisms.
- Predators are biotic limiting factors of prey.
- The role an organism plays is called its niche.

Self Check

1. **Determine** the population of students in your classroom.
2. **Describe** how limiting factors can affect a population.
3. **Explain** the difference between a habitat and a niche.
4. **Describe** and give an example of two symbiotic relationships that occur among populations in a community.
5. **Explain** how sound could be used to relate the size of the cricket population in one field to the cricket population in another field.
6. **Think Critically** A parasite obtains food from its host. Most parasites weaken but do not kill their hosts. Why?

Applying Math

7. **Solve One-Step Equations** A 15-m^2 wooded area has the following: 30 ferns, 150 grass plants, and 6 oak trees. What is the population density per m^2 of each of the above species?

SECTION 3

Standards—7.4.2: Describe that all organisms, including the human species, are part of and depend on two main interconnected global food webs, the ocean food web and the land food web. **7.4.8:** Describe how organisms that eat plants break down the plant structures to produce the materials and energy that they need to survive, and in turn, how they are consumed by other organisms.

Also covers: 7.4.6, 7.5.3 (Detailed standards begin on page IN8.)

Matter and Energy

as you read

What You'll Learn
- **Explain** the difference between a food chain and a food web.
- **Describe** how energy flows through ecosystems.
- **Examine** how materials such as water, carbon, and nitrogen are used repeatedly.

Why It's Important
You are dependent upon the recycling of matter and the transfer of energy for survival.

Review Vocabulary
consumer: organism that obtains energy by eating other organisms

New Vocabulary
- food chain
- food web
- water cycle

Energy Flow Through Ecosystems

Life on Earth is not simply a collection of independent organisms. Even organisms that seem to spend most of their time alone interact with other members of their species. They also interact with members of other species. Most of the interactions among members of different species occur when one organism feeds on another. Food contains nutrients and energy needed for survival. When one organism is food for another organism, some of the energy in the first organism (the food) is transferred to the second organism (the eater).

Producers are organisms that take in and use energy from the Sun or some other source to produce food. Some use the Sun's energy for photosynthesis to produce carbohydrates. For example, plants, algae, and some one-celled, photosynthetic organisms are producers. Consumers are organisms that take in energy when they feed on producers or other consumers. The transfer of energy does not end there. When organisms die, other organisms called decomposers, as shown in **Figure 17,** take in energy as they break down the remains of organisms. This movement of energy through a community can be diagrammed as a food chain or a food web.

Food Chains A **food chain,** as shown in **Figure 18,** is a model, a simple way of showing how energy, in the form of food, passes from one organism to another. When drawing a food chain, arrows between organisms indicate the direction of energy transfer. An example of a pond food chain follows.

aquatic plants → insects → bluegill → bass → humans

Food chains usually have only three or four links. This is because the available energy decreases from one link to the next link. At each transfer of energy, a portion of the energy is lost as heat due to the activities of the organisms. In a food chain, the amount of energy left for the last link is only a small portion of the energy in the first link.

Figure 17 These mushrooms are decomposers. They obtain needed energy for life when they break down organic material.

NATIONAL GEOGRAPHIC VISUALIZING A FOOD CHAIN

Figure 18

In nature, energy in food passes from one organism to another in a sequence known as a food chain. All living things are linked in food chains, and there are millions of different chains in the world. Each chain is made up of organisms in a community. The photographs here show a food chain in a North American meadow community.

E The last link in many food chains is a top carnivore, an animal that feeds on other animals, including other carnivores. This great horned owl is a top carnivore.

D The fourth link of this food chain is a garter snake, which feeds on toads.

A The first link in any food chain is a producer—in this case, grass. Grass gets its energy from sunlight.

B The second link of a food chain is usually an herbivore like this grasshopper. Herbivores are animals that feed only on producers.

C The third link of this food chain is a carnivore, an animal that feeds on other animals. This woodhouse toad feeds on grasshoppers.

SECTION 3 Matter and Energy

Indiana Academic Standard Check

7.4.2: Describe that all organisms ... are part of and depend on two main interconnected global food webs, the ocean food web and the land food web.

✓ Where might humans fit in the ocean food web shown below?

Food Webs Food chains are too simple to describe the many interactions among organisms in an ecosystem. A **food web** is a series of overlapping food chains that exist in an ecosystem. A food web provides a more complete model of the way energy moves through an ecosystem. They also are more accurate models because food webs show how many organisms, including humans, are part of more than one food chain in an ecosystem.

Humans are a part of many land and aquatic food webs. Most people eat foods from several different levels of a food chain. Every time you eat a hamburger, an apple, or other food, you have become a link in a food web. Can you picture the steps in the food web that led to the food in your lunch?

Applying Science

How do changes in Antarctic food webs affect populations?

The food webs in the icy Antarctic Ocean are based on phytoplankton, which are microscopic algae that float near the water's surface. The algae are eaten by tiny, shrimplike krill, which are consumed by baleen whales, squid, and fish. Toothed whales, seals, and penguins eat the fish and squid. How would changes in any of these populations affect the other populations?

Identifying the Problem

Worldwide, the hunting of most baleen whales has been illegal since 1986. It is hoped that the baleen whale population will increase. How will an increase in the whale population affect the food web illustrated below?

Solving the Problem

1. Populations of seals, penguins, and krill-eating fish increased in size as populations of baleen whales declined. Explain why this occurred.
2. What might happen if the number of baleen whales increases but the amount of krill does not?

210 CHAPTER 7 Interactions of Living Things

Ecological Pyramids Most of the energy in the biosphere comes from the Sun. Producers take in and transform only a small part of the energy that reaches Earth's surface. When an herbivore eats a plant, some of the energy in the plant passes to the herbivore. However, most of it is given off into the atmosphere as heat. The same thing happens when a carnivore eats an herbivore. An ecological pyramid models the number of organisms at each level of a food chain. The bottom of an ecological pyramid represents the producers of an ecosystem. The rest of the levels represent successive consumers.

Reading Check *What is an ecological pyramid?*

Energy Pyramid The flow of energy from grass to the hawk in **Figure 19** can be illustrated by an energy pyramid. An energy pyramid compares the energy available at each level of the food chain in an ecosystem. Just as most food chains have three or four links, a pyramid of energy usually has three or four levels. Only about ten percent of the energy at each level of the pyramid is available to the next level. By the time the top level is reached, the amount of energy available is greatly reduced.

Chemosynthesis Certain bacteria take in energy through a process called chemosynthesis. In chemosynthesis, the bacteria produce food using the energy in chemical compounds instead of light energy. In your Science Journal, predict where these bacteria are found.

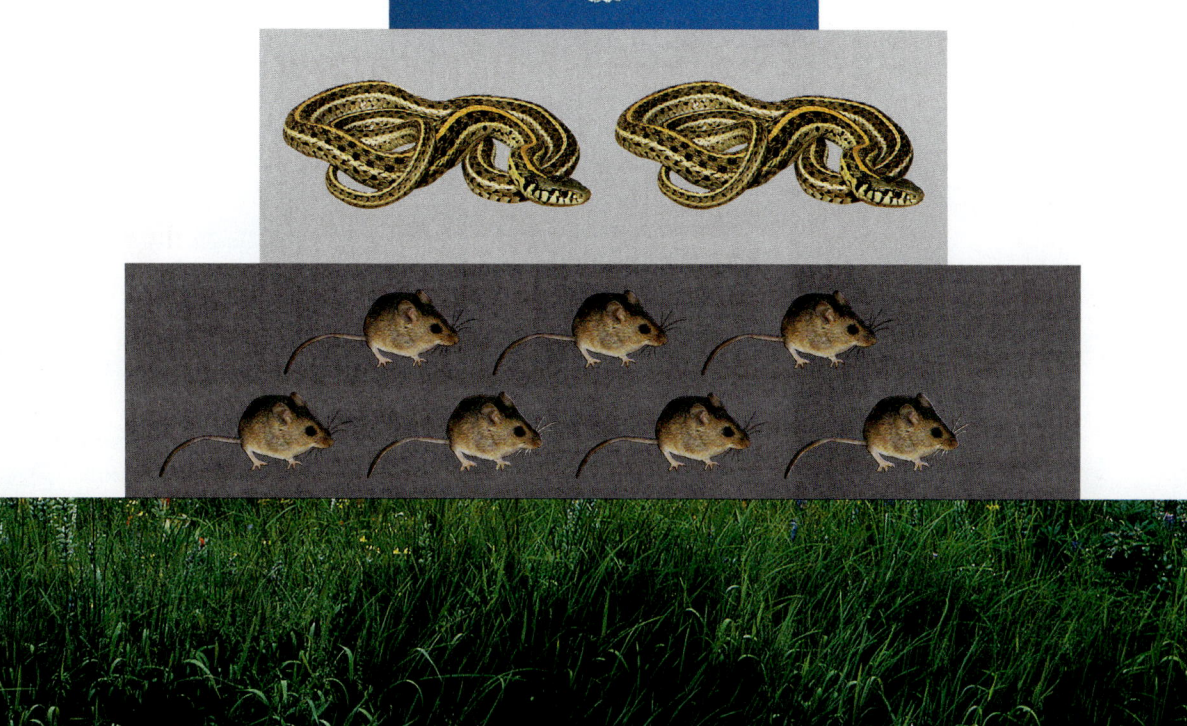

Figure 19 An energy pyramid illustrates that available energy decreases at each successive feeding step.
Determine *why an energy pyramid doesn't have more levels.*

SECTION 3 Matter and Energy   **211**

Modeling the Water Cycle

Procedure
1. With a **marker**, make a line halfway up on a **plastic cup**. Fill the cup to the mark with water.
2. Cover the top with **plastic wrap** and secure it with a **rubber band or tape**.
3. Put the cup in direct sunlight. Observe the cup for three days. Record your observations.
4. Remove the plastic wrap and observe the cup for seven more days.

Analysis
1. What parts of the water cycle did you observe during this activity?
2. How did the water level in the cup change after the plastic wrap was removed?

The Cycles of Matter

The energy available as food is constantly renewed by plants using sunlight. However, think about the matter that makes up the bodies of living organisms. The law of conservation of mass states that matter on Earth is never lost or gained. It is used over and over again. In other words, it is recycled. The carbon atoms in your body might have been on Earth since the planet formed billions of years ago. They have been recycled billions of times. Many important materials that make up your body cycle through the environment. Some of these materials are water, carbon, and nitrogen.

Water Cycle Water molecules on Earth constantly rise into the atmosphere, fall to Earth, and soak into the ground or flow into rivers and oceans. The **water cycle** involves the processes of evaporation, condensation, and precipitation.

Heat from the Sun causes water on Earth's surface to evaporate, or change from a liquid to a gas, and rise into the atmosphere as water vapor. As the water vapor rises, it encounters colder and colder air and the molecules of water vapor slow down. Eventually, the water vapor changes back into tiny droplets of water. It condenses, or changes from a gas to a liquid. These water droplets clump together to form clouds. When the droplets become large and heavy enough, they fall back to Earth as rain or other precipitation. This process is illustrated in **Figure 20.**

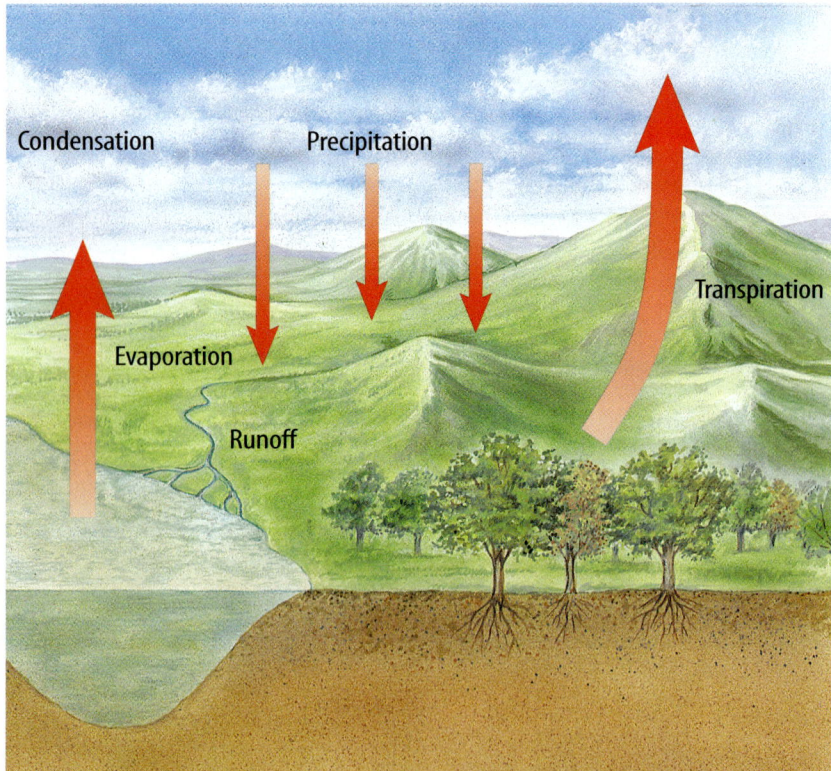

Figure 20 A water molecule that falls as rain can follow several paths through the water cycle. **Identify** these paths in this diagram.

212

Other Cycles in Nature You and all organisms contain carbon. Earth's atmosphere contains about 0.03 percent carbon in the form of carbon dioxide gas. The movement of carbon through Earth's biosphere is called the carbon cycle, as shown in **Figure 21.**

Nitrogen is an element found in proteins and nucleic acids. The nitrogen cycle begins with the transfer of nitrogen from the atmosphere to producers then to consumers. The nitrogen then moves back to the atmosphere or directly into producers again.

Phosphorus, sulfur, and other elements needed by living organisms also are used and returned to the environment. Just as you recycle aluminum, glass, and paper products, the matter that organisms need to live is recycled continuously in the biosphere.

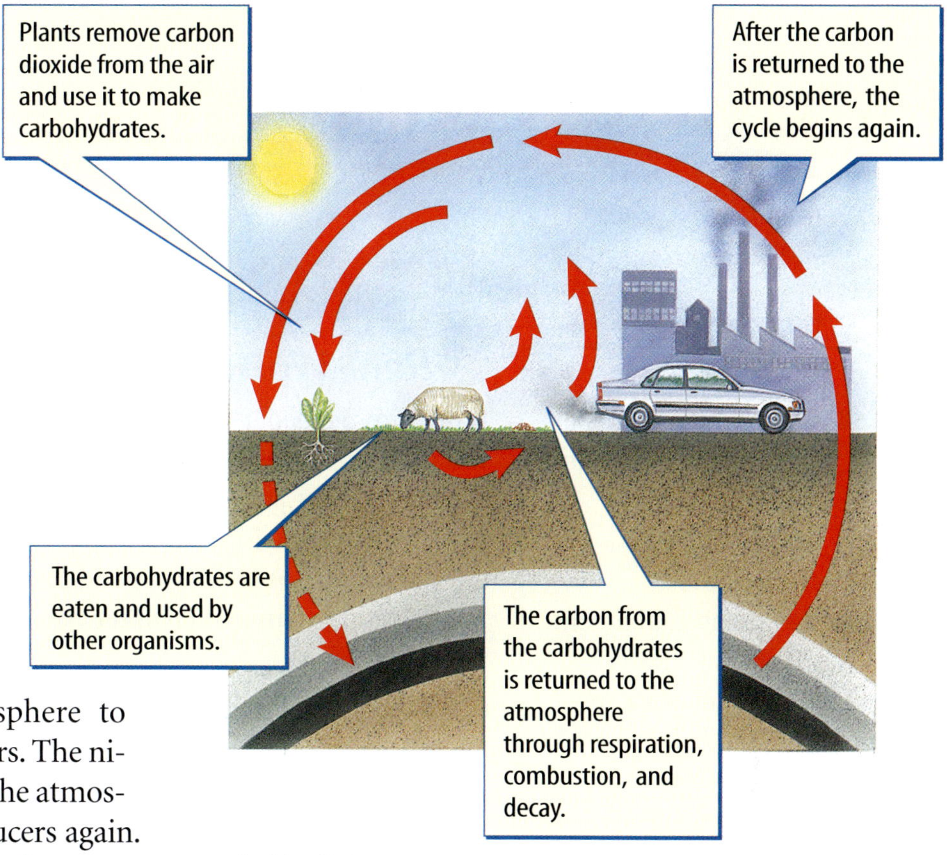

Plants remove carbon dioxide from the air and use it to make carbohydrates.

After the carbon is returned to the atmosphere, the cycle begins again.

The carbohydrates are eaten and used by other organisms.

The carbon from the carbohydrates is returned to the atmosphere through respiration, combustion, and decay.

Figure 21 Carbon can follow several different paths through the carbon cycle. Some carbon is stored in Earth's biomass.

section 3 review

Summary

Energy Flow Through Ecosystems
- A food chain models one pathway of energy through an ecosystem, and a food web is made of many food chains.
- Humans are part of different food webs.
- Ecological pyramids model the number of organisms at each level of a food chain.
- Energy pyramids illustrate the available energy at each level of a food chain.

The Cycles of Matter
- Energy is constantly renewed by the Sun, but matter must be recycled.
- The water cycle involves evaporation, condensation, and precipitation.
- Other matter that cycles includes carbon, nitrogen, phosphorus, and sulfur.

Self Check

1. **Draw and label** a food web that includes you and what you've eaten today.
2. **Compare and contrast** producers, consumers, and decomposers.
3. **Explain** how carbon flows through ecosystems.
4. **Think Critically** Use your knowledge of food chains and the energy pyramid to explain why fewer lions than gazelles live on the African plains.

Applying Skills

5. **Classify** Look at the food chain in **Figure 18.** Classify each organism as a producer or a consumer.
6. **Communicate** In your Science Journal, write a short essay about how the water cycle, carbon cycle, and nitrogen cycle are important to living organisms.

Science online in7.msscience.com/self_check_quiz

LAB Design Your Own

Identifying a Limiting Factor

Goals
- **Observe** the effects of an abiotic factor on the germination and growth of bean seedlings.
- **Design** an experiment that demonstrates whether or not a specific abiotic factor limits the germination of bean seeds.

Possible Materials
bean seeds
small planting containers
soil
water
label
trowel
*spoon
aluminum foil
sunny window
*other light source
refrigerator or oven
*Alternate materials

Safety Precautions

Real-World Question
Organisms depend upon many biotic and abiotic factors in their environment to survive. When these factors are limited or are not available, it can affect an organism's survival. How do abiotic factors such as light, water, and temperature affect the germination of seeds?

Form a Hypothesis
Based on what you have learned about limiting factors, make a hypothesis about how one specific abiotic factor might affect the germination of a bean seed. Be sure to consider factors that you can change easily.

Test Your Hypothesis

Make a Plan
1. As a group, agree upon and write out a hypothesis statement.
2. **Decide** on a way to test your group's hypothesis. Keep available materials in mind as you plan your procedure. List your materials.
3. **Design** a data table in your Science Journal for recording data.
4. Remember to test only one variable at a time and use suitable controls.

214

Using Scientific Methods

5. Read over your entire experiment to make sure that all steps are in logical order.
6. **Identify** any constants, variables, and controls in your experiment.
7. Be sure the factor that you will test is measurable.

Follow Your Plan

1. Make sure your teacher approves your plan before you start.
2. Carry out your approved plan.
3. While the experiment is going on, record any observations that you make and complete the data table in your Science Journal.

Analyze Your Data

1. **Compare** the results of this experiment with those of other groups in your class.
2. **Infer** how the abiotic factor you tested affected the germination of bean seeds.
3. **Graph** your results in a bar graph that compares the number of bean seeds that germinated in the experimental container with the number of seeds that germinated in the control container.

Conclude and Apply

1. **Identify** which factor had the greatest effect on the germination of the seeds.
2. **Determine** whether or not you could change more than one factor in this experiment and still have germination of seeds.

Write a set of instructions that could be included on a packet of this type of seeds. Describe the best conditions for seed germination.

LAB **215**

Science and Language Arts

The Solace of Open Spaces
a novel by Gretel Ehrlich

Animals give us their constant, unjaded[1] faces and we burden them with our bodies and civilized ordeals. We're both humbled by and imperious[2] with them. We're comrades who save each other's lives. The horse we pulled from a boghole this morning bucked someone off later in the day; one stock dog refuses to work sheep, while another brings back a calf we had overlooked. . . . What's stubborn, secretive, dumb, and keen[3] in us bumps up against those same qualities in them. . . .

Living with animals makes us redefine our ideas about intelligence. Horses are as mischievous as they are dependable. Stupid enough to let us use them, they are cunning enough to catch us off guard. . . .

We pay for their loyalty; They can be willful, hard to catch, dangerous to shoe and buck on frosty mornings. In turn, they'll work themselves into a lather cutting cows, not for the praise they'll get but for the simple glory of outdodging a calf or catching up with an errant steer. . . .

1 *Jaded* means "to be weary with fatigue," so *unjaded* means "not to be weary with fatigue."
2 domineering or overbearing
3 intellectually smart or sharp

Understanding Literature

Informative Writing This passage is informative because it describes the real relationship between people and animals on a ranch in Wyoming. The author speaks from her own point of view, not from the point of view of a disinterested party. How might this story have been different if it had been told from the point of view of a visiting journalist?

Respond to the Reading

1. Describe the relationship between people and animals in this passage.
2. What words does the author use to indicate that horses are intelligent?
3. **Linking Science and Writing** Write a short passage about an experience you have had with a pet. Put yourself in the passage without overusing the word "I".

Animals and ranchers are clearly dependent on each other. Ranchers provide nutrition and shelter for animals on the ranch and, in turn, animals provide food, companionship, and perform work for the ranchers. You might consider the relationship between horses and ranchers to be a symbiotic one. Symbiosis (sihm bee OH sus) is any close interaction among two or more different species.

chapter 7 Study Guide

Reviewing Main Ideas

Section 1 | The Environment

1. Ecology is the study of interactions among organisms and their environment.
2. The nonliving features of the environment are abiotic factors, and the organisms in the environment are biotic factors.
3. Ecosystems include biotic and abiotic factors.
4. The region of Earth and its atmosphere in which all organisms live is the biosphere.

Section 2 | Interactions Among Living Organisms

1. Characteristics that can describe populations include size, spacing, and density.
2. Any biotic or abiotic factor that limits the number of individuals in a population is a limiting factor.
3. A close relationship between two or more species is a symbiotic relationship.
4. The place where an organism lives is its habitat, and its role in the environment is its niche.

Section 3 | Matter and Energy

1. Food chains and food webs are models that describe the flow of energy.
2. At each level of a food chain, organisms lose energy as heat. Energy on Earth is renewed constantly by sunlight.
3. Matter on Earth is never lost or gained. It is used over and over again, or recycled.

Visualizing Main Ideas

Copy and complete the following concept map on the biosphere.

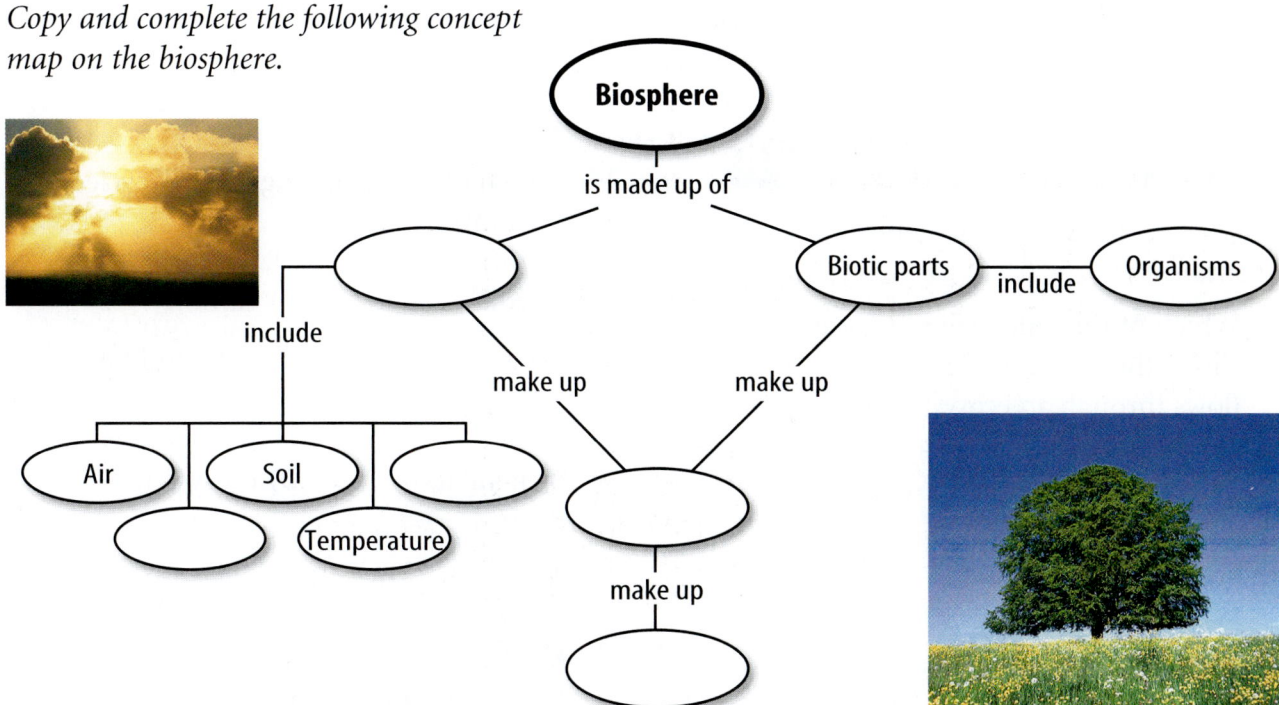

CHAPTER STUDY GUIDE 217

chapter 7 Review

Using Vocabulary

abiotic factor p. 196
biosphere p. 201
biotic factor p. 196
community p. 200
ecology p. 196
ecosystem p. 200
food chain p. 208
food web p. 210
habitat p. 207
limiting factor p. 205
niche p. 207
population p. 200
population density p. 204
symbiosis p. 206
water cycle p. 212

Fill in the blanks with the correct vocabulary word or words.

1. A(n) _____ is any living thing in the environment.
2. A series of overlapping food chains makes up a(n) _____.
3. The size of a population that occupies an area of definite size is its _____.
4. Where an organism lives in an ecosystem is its _____.
5. The part of Earth that supports life is the _____.
6. Any close relationship between two or more species is _____.

Checking Concepts

Choose the word or phrase that best answers the question.

7. Which of the following is a model that shows the amount of energy available as it flows through an ecosystem?
    A) niche
    B) energy pyramid
    C) carrying capacity
    D) food chain

8. Which of the following is a biotic factor?
    A) animals   C) sunlight
    B) air   D) soil

9. What is made up of all populations in an area?
    A) niche   C) community
    B) habitat   D) ecosystem

10. What is the term for the total number of individuals in a population occupying a certain area?
    A) clumping   C) spacing
    B) size   D) density

11. What is the tree to the right an example of?
    A) prey
    B) consumer
    C) producer
    D) predator

12. Which level of the food chain has the most energy?
    A) consumer   C) decomposers
    B) herbivores D) producers

13. What is the symbitotc relationship called in which one organism is helped and the other organism is harmed?
    A) mutualism
    B) parasitism
    C) commensalism
    D) consumer

14. Which of the following is NOT cycled in the biosphere?
    A) nitrogen   C) water
    B) soil   D) carbon

15. What are coral reefs, forests, and ponds examples of?
    A) niches   C) populations
    B) habitats   D) ecosystems

16. What are all of the individuals of one species that live in the same area at the same time called?
    A) community   C) biosphere
    B) population D) organism

218 CHAPTER REVIEW

chapter 7 Review

Thinking Critically

Use the illustration below to answer question 17.

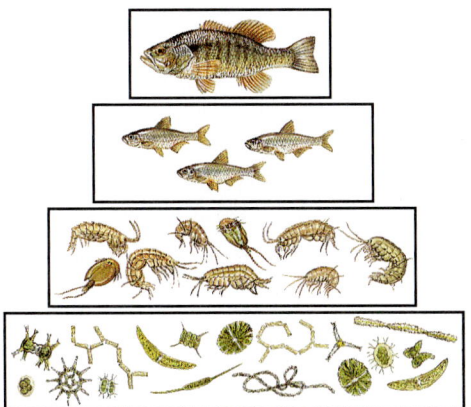

17. Infer why each level of the energy pyramid shown above is smaller than the one below it.

18. Compare and contrast the role of producers, consumers, and decomposers in an ecosystem.

19. Explain what carrying capacity has to do with whether or not a population reaches its biotic potential.

20. Infer why decomposers are vital to the cycling of matter in an ecosystem.

21. Write a paragraph that describes your own habitat and niche.

22. Classify the following as the result of either evaporation or condensation.
   a. A puddle disappears after a rainstorm.
   b. Rain falls.
   c. A lake becomes shallower.
   d. Clouds form.

23. Concept Map Use the following information to draw a food web of organisms living in a goldenrod field. *Aphids eat goldenrod sap, bees eat goldenrod nectar, beetles eat goldenrod pollen and goldenrod leaves, stinkbugs eat beetles, spiders eat aphids,* and *assassin bugs eat bees.*

24. Record Observations A home aquarium contains water, an air pump, a light, algae, a goldfish, and algae-eating snails. What are the abiotic factors in this environment?

25. Determine why viruses are considered parasites.

Performance Activities

26. Poster Use your own observations or the results of library research to develop a food web for a nearby park, pond, or other ecosystem. Make a poster display illustrating the food web.

27. Oral Presentation Research the steps in the phosphorous cycle. Find out what role phosphorus plays in the growth of algae in ponds and lakes. Present your findings to the class.

Applying Math

Use the table below to answer questions 28 and 29.

Arizona Deer Population	
Year	Deer Per 400 Hectares
1905	5.7
1915	35.7
1920	142.9
1925	85.7
1935	25.7

28. Deer Population Use the data above to graph the population density of a deer population over the years. Plot the number of deer on the y-axis and years on the x-axis. Predict what might have happened to cause the changes in the size of the population.

29. Population Trend What might the population of deer be in 1940 if the trend continued?

chapter 7 Indiana

 The assessed Indiana standard appears above the question.

Record your answers on the answer sheet provided by your teacher or on a sheet of paper.

Part 1 | Multiple Choice

The photo below shows a deciduous forest.

7.4.9

1. What is the limiting factor for plants on the forest floor?
   - A food
   - B soil
   - C sunlight
   - D water

7.4.9

2. When would the plants on the forest floor shown in the photo above grow best?
   - A spring
   - B summer
   - C fall
   - D winter

The photo below shows grassland animals.

3. Which describes the animals in the photo?
   - A carnivores
   - B detritivores
   - C herbivores
   - D omnivores

4. Which describes interactions between groups of antelope and zebras shown in the photo above?
   - A biome
   - B community
   - C ecosystem
   - D population

7.4.9

5. What helps determine the number of individuals that can survive in an area?
   - A biotic potential
   - B carrying capacity
   - C limiting factors
   - D population spacing

Standards Review

7.4.9

6. What would happen to a king penguin population if the fish in its habitat became scarce?

   A decrease, then stabilize

   B decrease, then increase

   C increase, then stabilize

   D increase, then decrease

7. What is any close interaction between two or more species?

   A commensalism

   B mutualism

   C parasitism

   D symbiosis

7.4.9

8. The photo below shows grassland animals in Africa.

   Which environmental factor is the reason for the competition among these animals?

   A food

   B mates

   C sunlight

   D water

Part 2 Constructed Response

The illustration below shows a cycle of matter.

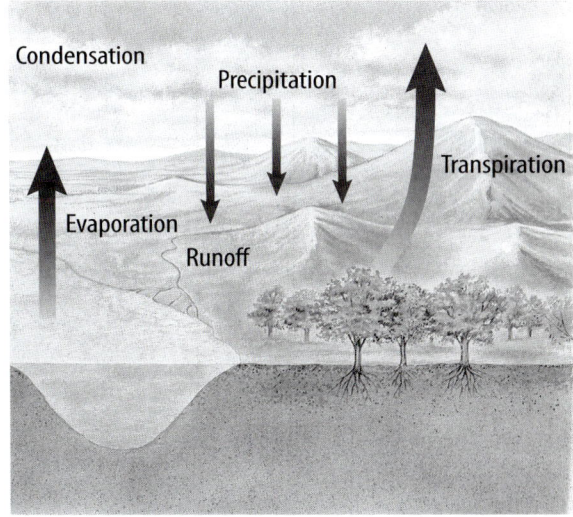

9. Name and describe the cycle shown above.

7.4.9

10. Why is the cycle shown above important for an organism's survival?

7.4.2

11. How do humans interact with land and aquatic food webs? What would happen if one part of this web were destroyed?

12. Describe how better food production, sanitation, and disease prevention have contributed to the yearly increase in the human population.

Test-Taking Tip

Answer All Parts of the Question Make sure each part of the question is answered when listing discussion points.

Question 12 Notice that this question asks you to describe how three things contribute to human population growth.

chapter 8

Academic Standard—3: Students collect and organize data to identify relationships between physical objects, events, and processes. They use logical reasoning to question their own ideas as new information challenges their conceptions of the natural world.

Also covers: Academic Standards 1, 2, 4, 5, 7 (Detailed standards begin on page IN8.)

Conserving Resources

chapter preview

sections
1. Resources
2. Pollution
   Lab The Greenhouse Effect
3. The Three Rs of Conservation
   Lab Solar Cooking
* *Virtual Lab* When is water safe to drink?

Resources Fuel Our Lives

Resources, such as clean water and air, are commonly taken for granted. We depend on water and air to survive. Fossil fuels are another type of resource, and we depend on them for energy. However, fossil fuels can pollute our air and water.

Science Journal List some other resources that we depend on and describe how we use them.

Start-Up Activities

What happens when topsoil is left unprotected?

Plants grow in the top, nutrient-rich layer, called topsoil. Plants help keep topsoil in place by protecting it from wind and rain. Try the following experiment to find out what happens when topsoil is left unprotected.

1. Use a mixture of moist sand and potting soil to create a miniature landscape in a plastic basin or aluminum-foil baking pan. Form hills and valleys in your landscape.
2. Use clumps of moss to cover areas of your landscape. Leave some sloping portions without plant cover.
3. Simulate a rainstorm over your landscape by spraying water on it from a spray bottle or by pouring a slow stream of water on it from a beaker.
4. **Think Critically** In your Science Journal, record your observations and describe what happened to the land that was not protected by plant cover.

Preview this chapter's content and activities at in7.msscience.com

Resources Make the following Foldable to help you organize information and diagram ideas about renewable and nonrenewable resources.

Fold a sheet of paper in half lengthwise. Make the back edge about 5 cm longer than the front edge.

Turn the paper so the fold is on the bottom. Then **fold** in half.

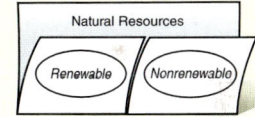
Unfold and cut only the top layer along the fold to make two tabs. **Label** the Foldable as shown.

Make a Concept Map Before you read the chapter, list examples of each type of natural resource you already know on the back of the appropriate tabs. As you read the chapter, add to your lists.

Standard—7.3.16: Recognize and explain that different ways of obtaining, transforming, and distributing energy have different environmental consequences.

section 1

Also covers: 7.1.8 (Detailed standards begin on page IN8.)

Resources

as you read

What You'll Learn
- **Compare** renewable and nonrenewable resources.
- **List** uses of fossil fuels.
- **Identify** alternatives to fossil fuel use.

Why It's Important
Wise use of natural resources is important for the health of all life on Earth.

Review Vocabulary
geyser: a spring that emits intermittent jets of heated water and steam

New Vocabulary
- natural resource
- renewable resource
- nonrenewable resource
- petroleum
- fossil fuel
- hydroelectric power
- nuclear energy
- geothermal energy

Natural Resources

An earthworm burrowing in moist soil eats decaying plant material. A robin catches the worm and flies to a tree. The leaves of the tree use sunlight during photosynthesis. Leaves fall to the ground, decay, and perhaps become an earthworm's meal. What do these living things have in common? They rely on Earth's **natural resources**—the parts of the environment that are useful or necessary for the survival of living organisms.

What kinds of natural resources do you use? Like other organisms, you need food, air, and water. You also use resources that are needed to make everything from clothes to cars. Natural resources supply energy for automobiles and power plants. Although some natural resources are plentiful, others are not.

Renewable Resources The Sun, an inexhaustible resource, provides a constant supply of heat and light. Rain fills lakes and streams with water. When plants carry out photosynthesis, they add oxygen to the air. Sunlight, water, air, and the crops shown in **Figure 1** are examples of renewable resources. A **renewable resource** is any natural resource that is recycled or replaced constantly by nature.

Figure 1 Cotton and wood are renewable resources. Cotton cloth is used for rugs, curtains, and clothing. A new crop of cotton can be grown every year. Wood is used for furniture, building materials, and paper. It will take 20 years for these young trees to grow large enough to harvest.

224 CHAPTER 8 Conserving Resources

Supply and Demand Even though renewable resources are recycled or replaced, they are sometimes in short supply. Rain and melted snow replace the water in streams, lakes, and reservoirs. Sometimes, there may not be enough rain or snowmelt to meet all the needs of people, plants, and animals. In some parts of the world, especially desert regions, water and other resources usually are scarce. Other resources can be used instead, as shown in **Figure 2.**

Nonrenewable Resources Natural resources that are used up more quickly than they can be replaced by natural processes are **nonrenewable resources.** Earth's supply of nonrenewable resources is limited. You use nonrenewable resources when you take home groceries in a plastic bag, paint a wall, or travel by car. Plastics, paints, and gasoline are made from an important nonrenewable resource called petroleum, or oil. **Petroleum** is formed mostly from the remains of microscopic marine organisms buried in Earth's crust. It is nonrenewable because it takes hundreds of millions of years for it to form.

Reading Check *What are nonrenewable resources?*

Minerals and metals found in Earth's crust are nonrenewable resources. Petroleum is a mineral. So are diamonds and the graphite in pencil lead. The aluminum used to make soft-drink cans is a metal. Iron, copper, tin, gold, silver, tungsten, and uranium also are metals. Many manufactured items, like the car shown in **Figure 3,** are made from nonrenewable resources.

Figure 2 In parts of Africa, firewood has become scarce. People in this village now use solar energy instead of wood for cooking.

Figure 3 Iron, a nonrenewable resource, is the main ingredient in steel. Steel is used to make cars, trucks, appliances, buildings, bridges, and even tires.
Infer *what other nonrenewable resources are used to build a car.*

SECTION 1 Resources **225**

Mini LAB

Observing Mineral Mining Effects

Procedure
1. Place a **chocolate-chip cookie** on a **paper plate**. Pretend the chips are mineral deposits and the rest of the cookie is Earth's crust.
2. Use a **toothpick** to locate and dig up the mineral deposits. Try to disturb the land as little as possible.
3. When mining is completed, try to restore the land to its original condition.

Analysis
1. How well were you able to restore the land?
2. Compare the difficulty of digging for mineral deposits found close to the surface with digging for those found deep in Earth's crust.
3. Describe environmental changes that might result from a mining operation.

Try at Home

Fossil Fuels

Coal, oil, and natural gas are nonrenewable resources that supply energy. Most of the energy you use comes from these fossil fuels, as the graph in **Figure 4** shows. **Fossil fuels** are fuels formed in Earth's crust over hundreds of millions of years. Cars, buses, trains, and airplanes are powered by gasoline, diesel fuel, and jet fuel, which are made from oil. Coal is used in many power plants to produce electricity. Natural gas is used in manufacturing, for heating and cooking, and sometimes as a vehicle fuel.

Fossil Fuel Conservation Billions of people all over the world use fossil fuels every day. Because fossil fuels are nonrenewable, Earth's supply of them is limited. In the future, they may become more expensive and difficult to obtain. Also, the use of fossil fuels can lead to environmental problems. For example, mining coal can require stripping away thick layers of soil and rock, as shown in **Figure 4,** which destroys ecosystems. Another problem is that fossil fuels must be burned to release the energy stored in them. The burning of fossil fuels produces waste gases that cause air pollution, including smog and acid rain. For these reasons, many people suggest reducing the use of fossil fuels and finding other sources of energy.

You can use simple conservation measures to help reduce fossil fuel use. Switch off the light when you leave a room and turn off the television when you're not watching it. These actions reduce your use of electricity, which often is produced in power plants that burn fossil fuels. Hundreds of millions of automobiles are in use in the United States. Riding in a car pool or taking public transportation uses fewer liters of gasoline than driving alone in a car. Walking or riding a bicycle uses even less fossil fuel. Reducing fossil fuel use has an added benefit—the less you use, the more money you save.

Figure 4 Coal is a fossil fuel. It often is obtained by strip mining, which removes all the soil above the coal deposit. The soil is replaced, but it takes many years for the ecosystem to recover.
Identify the resource that provided 84 percent of the energy used in the United States in 1999.

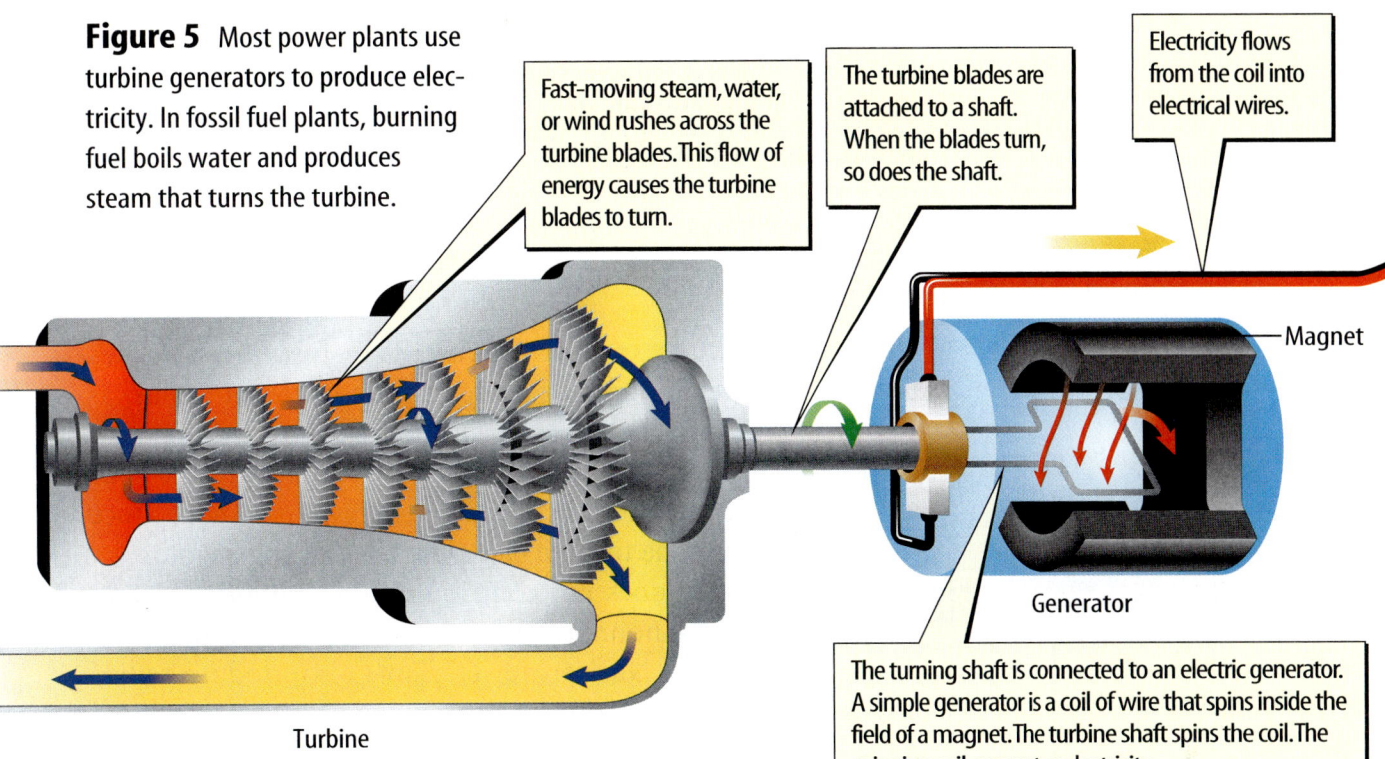

Figure 5 Most power plants use turbine generators to produce electricity. In fossil fuel plants, burning fuel boils water and produces steam that turns the turbine.

Fast-moving steam, water, or wind rushes across the turbine blades. This flow of energy causes the turbine blades to turn.

The turbine blades are attached to a shaft. When the blades turn, so does the shaft.

Electricity flows from the coil into electrical wires.

Magnet

Generator

The turning shaft is connected to an electric generator. A simple generator is a coil of wire that spins inside the field of a magnet. The turbine shaft spins the coil. The spinning coil generates electricity.

Turbine

Alternatives to Fossil Fuels

Another approach to reducing fossil fuel use is to develop other sources of energy. Much of the electricity used today comes from power plants that burn fossil fuels. As **Figure 5** shows, electricity is generated when a rotating turbine turns a coil of wires in the magnetic field of an electric generator. Fossil-fuel power plants boil water to produce steam that turns the turbine. Alternative energy sources, including water, wind, and atomic energy can be used instead of fossil fuels to turn turbines. Also, solar cells can produce electricity using only sunlight, with no turbines at all. Some of these alternative energy sources—particularly wind and solar energy—are so plentiful they could be considered inexhaustible resources.

Water Power Water is a renewable energy source that can be used to generate electricity. **Hydroelectric power** is electricity that is produced when the energy of falling water is used to turn the turbines of an electric generator. Hydroelectric power does not contribute to air pollution because no fuel is burned. However, it does present environmental concerns. Building a hydroelectric plant usually involves constructing a dam across a river. The dam raises the water level high enough to produce the energy required for electricity generation. Many acres behind the dam are flooded, destroying land habitats and changing part of the river into a lake.

INTEGRATE Social Studies

Energy Oil and natural gas are used to produce over 60 percent of the energy supply in the United States. Over half of the oil used is imported from other countries. Many scientists suggest that emissions from the burning of fossil fuels are principally responsible for global warming. In your Science Journal, write what you might do to persuade utility companies to increase their use of water, wind, and solar power.

SECTION 1 Resources **227**

Wind Power Wind power is another renewable energy source that can be used for electricity production. Wind turns the blades of a turbine, which powers an electric generator. When winds blow at least 32 km/h, energy is produced. Wind power does not cause air pollution, but electricity can be produced only when the wind is blowing. So far, wind power accounts for only a small percentage of the electricity used worldwide.

Nuclear Power Another alternative to fossil fuels makes use of the huge amounts of energy in the nuclei of atoms, as shown in **Figure 6**. Nuclear energy is released when billions of atomic nuclei from uranium, a radioactive element, are split apart in a nuclear fission reaction. This energy is used to produce steam that rotates the turbine blades of an electric generator.

Nuclear power does not contribute to air pollution. However, uranium is a nonrenewable resource, and mining it can disrupt ecosystems. Nuclear power plants also produce radioactive wastes that can seriously harm living organisms. Some of these wastes remain radioactive for thousands of years, and their safe disposal is a problem that has not yet been solved. Accidents also are a danger.

Figure 6 Nuclear power plants are designed to withstand the high energy produced by nuclear reactions.

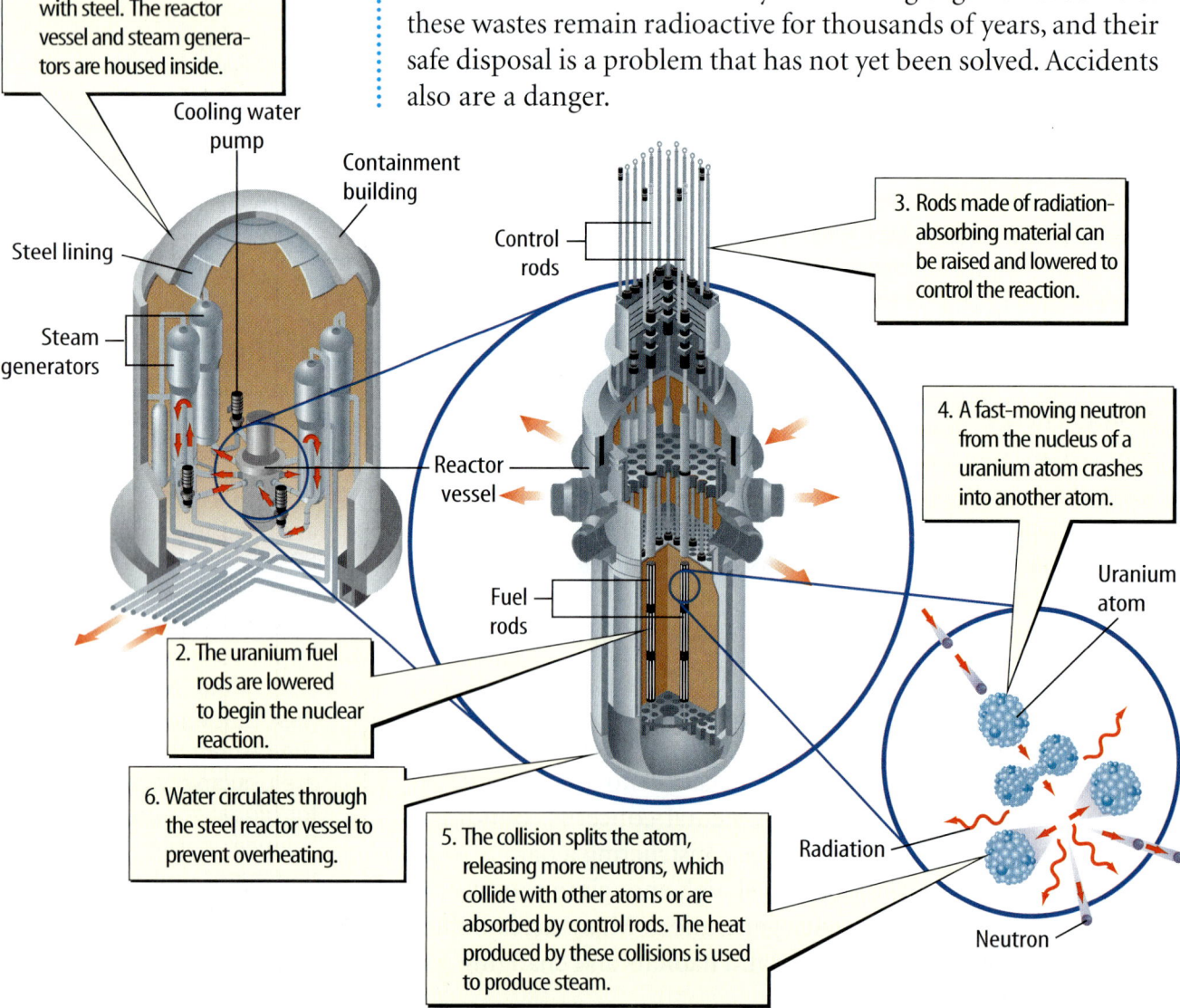

1. The containment building is made of concrete lined with steel. The reactor vessel and steam generators are housed inside.

2. The uranium fuel rods are lowered to begin the nuclear reaction.

3. Rods made of radiation-absorbing material can be raised and lowered to control the reaction.

4. A fast-moving neutron from the nucleus of a uranium atom crashes into another atom.

5. The collision splits the atom, releasing more neutrons, which collide with other atoms or are absorbed by control rods. The heat produced by these collisions is used to produce steam.

6. Water circulates through the steel reactor vessel to prevent overheating.

228 CHAPTER 8 Conserving Resources

Geothermal Energy The hot, molten rock that lies deep beneath Earth's surface is also a source of energy. You see the effects of this energy when lava and hot gases escape from an erupting volcano or when hot water spews from a geyser. The heat energy contained in Earth's crust is called **geothermal energy**. Most geothermal power plants use this energy to produce steam to generate electricity.

Geothermal energy for power plants is available only where natural geysers or volcanoes are found. A geothermal power plant in California uses steam produced by geysers. The island nation of Iceland was formed by volcanoes, and geothermal energy is plentiful there. Geothermal power plants supply heat and electricity to about 90 percent of the homes in Iceland. Outdoor swimming areas also are heated with geothermal energy, as shown in **Figure 7**.

Reading Check *Where does geothermal energy come from?*

Figure 7 In Iceland, a geothermal power plant pumps hot water out of the ground to heat buildings and generate electricity. Leftover hot water goes into this lake, making it warm enough for swimming even when the ground is covered with snow.

Solar Energy The most inexhaustible source of energy for all life on Earth is the Sun. Solar energy is an alternative to fossil fuels. One use of solar energy is in solar-heated buildings. During winter in the northern hemisphere, the parts of a building that face south receive the most sunlight. Large windows placed on the south side of a building help heat it by allowing warm sunshine into the building during the day. Floors and walls of most solar-heated buildings are made of materials that absorb heat during the day. During the night, the stored heat is released slowly, keeping the building warm. **Figure 8** shows how solar energy can be used.

Figure 8 The Zion National Park Visitor Center in Utah is a solar-heated building designed to save energy. The roof holds solar panels that are used to generate electricity. High windows can be opened to circulate air and help cool the building on hot days. The overhanging roof shades the windows during summer.

SECTION 1 Resources **229**

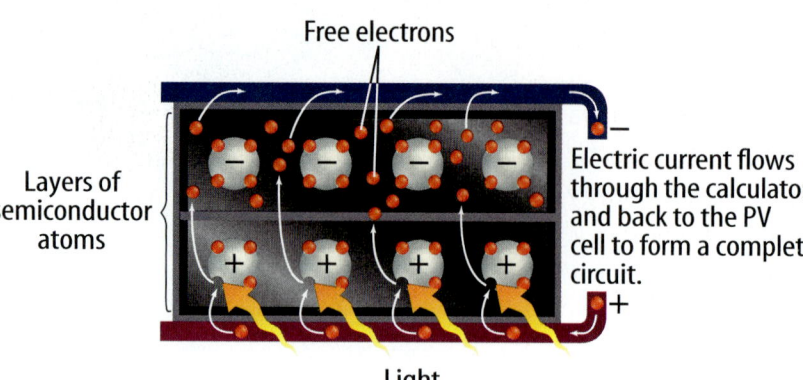

Figure 9 Light energy from the Sun travels in tiny packets of energy called photons. Photons crash into the atoms of PV cells, knocking electrons loose. These electrons create an electric current.

Solar Cells Do you know how a solar-powered calculator works? How do spacecraft use sunlight to generate electricity? These devices use photovoltaic (foh toh vohl TAY ihk) cells to turn sunlight into electric current, as shown in **Figure 9**. Photovoltaic (PV) cells are small and easy to use. However, they produce electricity only in sunlight, so batteries are needed to store electricity for use at night or on cloudy days. Also, PV cells presently are too expensive to use for generating large amounts of electricity. Improvements in this technology continue to be made, and prices probably will go down in the future. As **Figure 10** shows, solar buildings and PV cells are just two of the many ways solar energy can be used to replace fossil fuels.

section 1 review

Summary

Natural Resources
- All living things depend on natural resources to survive.
- Some resources are renewable, while other resources, such as petroleum, are nonrenewable.

Fossil Fuels
- Most of the energy that humans use comes from fossil fuels.
- Fossil fuels must be burned to release the energy stored in them, which causes air pollution.

Alternatives to Fossil Fuels
- Alternatives to fossil fuels include water power, wind power, nuclear power, geothermal energy, and solar energy.
- The Sun provides the most inexhaustible supply of energy for all life on Earth.

Self Check

1. **Summarize** What are natural resources?
2. **Compare and contrast** renewable and nonrenewable resources. Give five examples of each.
3. **Describe** the advantages and disadvantages of using nuclear power.
4. **Describe** two ways solar energy can be used to reduce fossil fuel use.
5. **Think Critically** Explain why the water that is used to cool the reactor vessel of a nuclear power plant is kept separate from the water that is heated to produce steam for the turbine generators.

Applying Math

6. **Solve One-Step Equations** Most cars in the U.S. are driven about 10,000 miles each year. If a car can travel 30 miles on one gallon of gasoline, how many gallons will it use in a year?

CHAPTER 8 Conserving Resources

in7.msscience.com/self_check_quiz

NATIONAL GEOGRAPHIC VISUALIZING SOLAR ENERGY

Figure 10

Sunlight is a renewable energy source that provides an alternative to fossil fuels. Solar technologies use the Sun's energy in many ways—from heating to electricity generation.

▼ **ELECTRICITY** Photovoltaic (PV) cells turn sunlight into electric current. They are commonly used to power small devices, such as calculators. Panels that combine many PV cells provide enough electricity for a home—or an orbiting satellite, such as the International Space Station, below.

▲ **POWER PLANTS** In California's Mojave Desert, an experimental solar power plant used hundreds of mirrors to focus sunlight on a water-filled tower. The steam produced by this system generates enough electricity to power 2,400 homes.

▼ **COOKING** In hot, sunny weather, a solar oven or panel cooker can be used to cook a pot of rice or heat water. The powerful solar cooker shown below reaches even higher temperatures. It is being used to fry food.

▼ **INDOOR HEATING** South-facing windows and heat-absorbing construction materials turn a room into a solar collector that can help heat an entire building, such as this Connecticut home.

▲ **WATER HEATING** Water is heated as it flows through small pipes in this roof-mounted solar heat collector. The hot water then flows into an insulated tank for storage.

SECTION 1 Resources **231**

section 2

Standard—7.4.14: Explain that the environment may contain dangerous levels of substances that are harmful to human beings. Understand, therefore, that the good health of individuals requires monitoring the soil, air, and water as well as taking steps to keep them safe.

Also covers: 7.1.8, 7.2.7, 7.3.16 (Detailed standards begin on page IN8.)

Pollution

as you read

What You'll Learn
- **Describe** types of air pollution.
- **Identify** causes of water pollution.
- **Explain** methods that can be used to prevent erosion.

Why It's Important
By understanding the causes of pollution, you can help solve pollution problems.

Review Vocabulary
atmosphere: the whole mass of air surrounding Earth

New Vocabulary
- pollutant
- acid precipitation
- greenhouse effect
- ozone depletion
- erosion
- hazardous waste

Keeping the Environment Healthy

More than six billion people live on Earth. This large human population puts a strain on the environment, but each person can make a difference. You can help safeguard the environment by paying attention to how your use of natural resources affects air, land, and water.

Air Pollution

On a still, sunny day in almost any large city, you might see a dark haze in the air, like that in **Figure 11.** The haze comes from pollutants that form when wood or fuels are burned. A **pollutant** is a substance that contaminates the environment. Air pollutants include soot, smoke, ash, and gases such as carbon dioxide, carbon monoxide, nitrogen oxides, and sulfur oxides. Wherever cars, trucks, airplanes, factories, homes, or power plants are found, air pollution is likely. Air pollution also can be caused by volcanic eruptions, wind-blown dust and sand, forest fires, and the evaporation of paints and other chemicals.

Smog is a form of air pollution created when sunlight reacts with pollutants produced by burning fuels. It can irritate the eyes and make breathing difficult for people with asthma or other lung diseases. Smog can be reduced if people take buses or trains instead of driving or if they use vehicles, such as electric cars, that produce fewer pollutants than gasoline-powered vehicles.

Figure 11 The term *smog* was used for the first time in the early 1900s to describe the mixture of smoke and fog that often covers large cities in the industrial world. **Infer** how smog can be reduced in large cities.

232   CHAPTER 8   Conserving Resources

Figure 12 Compare these two photographs of the same statue. The photo on the left was taken before acid rain became a problem. The photo on the right shows acid rain damage. The pH scale, shown below, indicates whether a solution is acidic or basic.

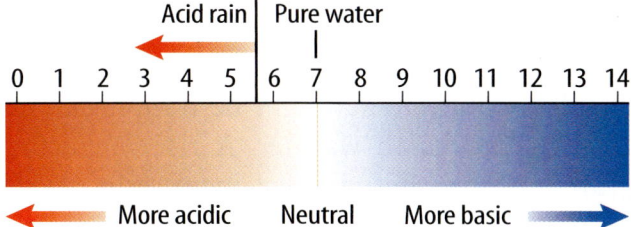

Acid Precipitation

Water vapor condenses on dust particles in the air to form droplets that combine to create clouds. Eventually, the droplets become large enough to fall to the ground as precipitation—mist, rain, snow, sleet, or hail. Air pollutants from the burning of fossil fuels can react with water in the atmosphere to form strong acids. Acidity is measured by a value called pH, as shown in **Figure 12**. **Acid precipitation** has a pH below 5.6.

Effects of Acid Rain Acid precipitation washes nutrients from the soil, which can lead to the death of trees and other plants. Runoff from acid rain that flows into a lake or pond can lower the pH of the water. If algae and microscopic organisms cannot survive in the acidic water, fish and other organisms that depend on them for food also die.

Preventing Acid Rain Sulfur from burning coal and nitrogen oxides from vehicle exhaust are the pollutants primarily responsible for acid rain. Using low-sulfur fuels, such as natural gas or low-sulfur coal, can help reduce acid precipitation. However, these fuels are less plentiful and more expensive than high-sulfur coal. Smokestacks that remove sulfur dioxide before it enters the atmosphere also help. Reducing automobile use and keeping car engines properly tuned can reduce acid rain caused by nitrogen oxide pollution. The use of electric cars, or hybrid-fuel cars that can run on electricity as well as gasoline, also could help.

Mini LAB

Measuring Acid Rain

Procedure
1. Collect **rainwater** by placing a clean **cup** outdoors. Do not collect rainwater that has been in contact with any object or organism.
2. Dip a piece of **pH indicator paper** into the sample.
3. Compare the color of the paper to the pH chart provided. Record the pH of the rainwater.
4. Use separate pieces of pH paper to test the pH of **tap water** and **distilled water**. Record these results.

Analysis
1. Is the rainwater acidic, basic, or neutral?
2. How does the pH of the rainwater compare with the pH of tap water? With the pH of distilled water?

SECTION 2 Pollution

Topic: Global Warming

Visit in7.msscience.com for Web links to information about global warming.

Activity Describe three possible impacts of global warming. Provide one fact that supports global warming and one fact that does not.

Greenhouse Effect

Sunlight travels through the atmosphere to Earth's surface. Some of this sunlight normally is reflected back into space. The rest is trapped by certain atmospheric gases, as shown in **Figure 13**. This heat-trapping feature of the atmosphere is the **greenhouse effect**. Without it, temperatures on Earth probably would be too cold to support life.

Atmospheric gases that trap heat are called greenhouse gases. One of the most important greenhouse gases is carbon dioxide (CO_2). CO_2 is a normal part of the atmosphere. It is also a waste product that forms when fossil fuels are burned. Over the past century, more fossil fuels have been burned than ever before, which is increasing the percentage of CO_2 in the atmosphere. The atmosphere might be trapping more of the Sun's heat, making Earth warmer. A rise in Earth's average temperature, possibly caused by an increase in greenhouse gases, is known as global warming.

Global Warming Temperature data collected from 1895 through 1995 indicate that Earth's average temperature increased about 1°C during that 100-year period. No one is certain whether this rise was caused by human activities or is a natural part of Earth's weather cycle. What kinds of changes might be caused by global warming? Changing rainfall patterns could alter ecosystems and affect the kinds of crops that can be grown in different parts of the world. The number of storms and hurricanes might increase. The polar ice caps might begin to melt, raising sea levels and flooding coastal areas. Warmer weather might allow tropical diseases, such as malaria, to become more widespread. Many people feel that the possibility of global warming is a good reason to reduce fossil fuel use.

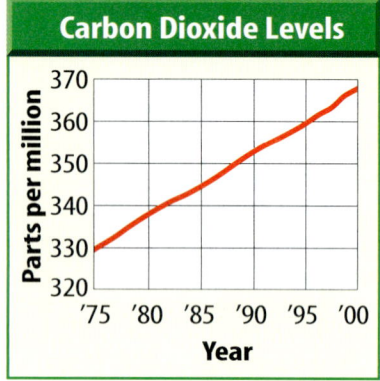

Figure 13 The moment you step inside a greenhouse, you feel the results of the greenhouse effect. Heat trapped by the glass walls warms the air inside. In a similar way, atmospheric greenhouse gases trap heat close to Earth's surface.

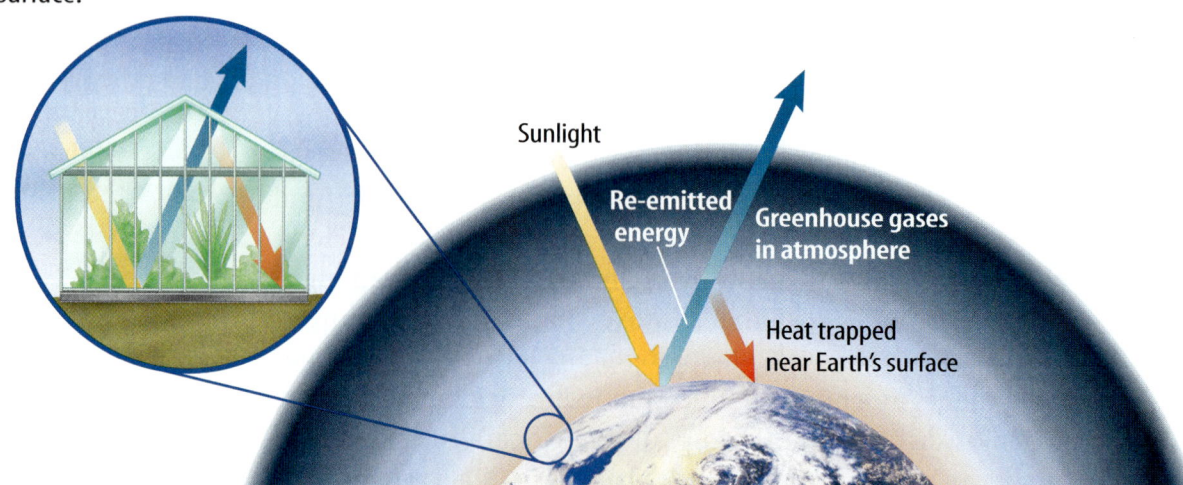

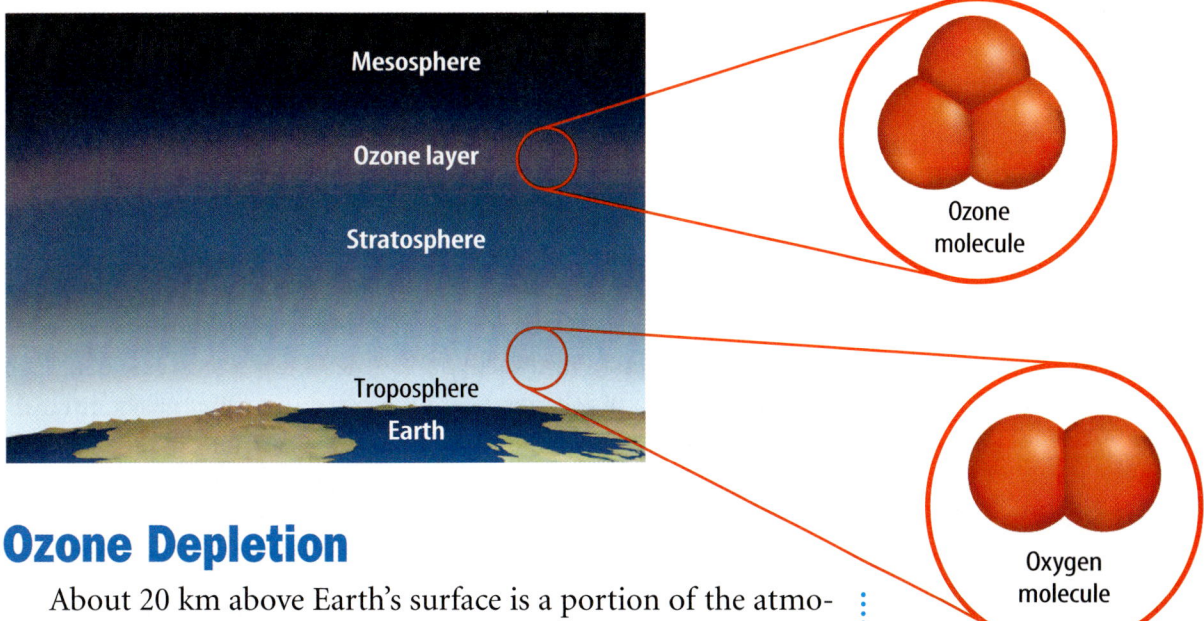

Ozone Depletion

About 20 km above Earth's surface is a portion of the atmosphere known as the ozone (OH zohn) layer. Ozone is a form of oxygen, as shown in **Figure 14.** The ozone layer absorbs some of the Sun's harmful ultraviolet (UV) radiation. UV radiation can damage living cells.

Every year, the ozone layer temporarily becomes thinner over each polar region during its spring season. The thinning of the ozone layer is called **ozone depletion.** This problem is caused by certain pollutant gases, especially chlorofluorocarbons (klor oh FLOR oh kar bunz) (CFCs). CFCs are used in the cooling systems of refrigerators, freezers, and air conditioners. When CFCs leak into the air, they slowly rise into the atmosphere until they arrive at the ozone layer. CFCs react chemically with ozone, breaking apart the ozone molecules.

UV Radiation Because of ozone depletion, the amount of UV radiation that reaches Earth's surface could be increasing. UV radiation could be causing a rise in the number of skin cancer cases in humans. It also might be harming other organisms. The ozone layer is so important to the survival of life on Earth that world governments and industries have agreed to stop making and using CFCs.

Ozone that is high in the upper atmosphere protects life on Earth. Near Earth's surface though, it can be harmful. Ozone is produced when fossil fuels are burned. This ozone stays in the lower atmosphere, where it pollutes the air. Ozone damages the lungs and other sensitive tissues of animals and plants. For example, it can cause the needles of a Ponderosa pine to drop, harming growth.

Figure 14 The atmosphere's ozone layer absorbs large amounts of UV radiation, preventing it from reaching Earth's surface. Ozone molecules are made of three oxygen atoms. They are formed in a chemical reaction between sunlight and oxygen. The oxygen you breathe has two oxygen atoms in each molecule.
Infer what will happen if the ozone layer continues to thin.

 *What is the difference between ozone in the upper atmosphere and ozone in the lower atmosphere?*

Air Quality Carbon monoxide enters the body through the lungs. It attaches to red blood cells, preventing the cells from absorbing oxygen. In your Science Journal, explain why heaters and barbecues designed for outdoor use never should be used indoors.

7.4.14: Explain that the environment may contain dangerous levels of substances... Understand, therefore, ... steps to keep them safe.

✓ How can radon pollution be controlled in a building?

Figure 15 The map shows the potential for radon exposure in different parts of the United States. **Identify** the area of the country with soils that produce the most radon gas.

Indoor Air Pollution

Air pollution can occur indoors. Today's buildings are better insulated to conserve energy. However, better insulation reduces the flow of air into and out of a building, so air pollutants can build up indoors. For example, burning cigarettes release hazardous particles and gases into the air. Even nonsmokers can suffer ill effects from secondhand cigarette smoke. As a result, smoking no longer is allowed in many public and private buildings. Paints, carpets, glues and adhesives, printers, and photocopy machines also give off dangerous gases, including formaldehyde. Like cigarette smoke, formaldehyde is a carcinogen, which means it can cause cancer.

Carbon Monoxide Carbon monoxide (CO) is a poisonous gas that is produced whenever charcoal, natural gas, kerosene, or other fuels are burned. CO poisoning can cause serious illness or death. Fuel-burning stoves and heaters must be designed to prevent CO from building up indoors. CO is colorless and odorless, so it is difficult to detect. Alarms that provide warning of a dangerous buildup of CO are being used in more and more homes.

Radon Radon is a naturally occurring, radioactive gas that is given off by some types of rock and soil, as shown in **Figure 15**. Radon has no color or odor. It can seep into basements and the lower floors of buildings. Radon exposure is the second leading cause of lung cancer in this country. A radon detector sounds an alarm when levels of the gas in indoor air become too high. If radon is present, increasing a building's ventilation can eliminate any damaging effects.

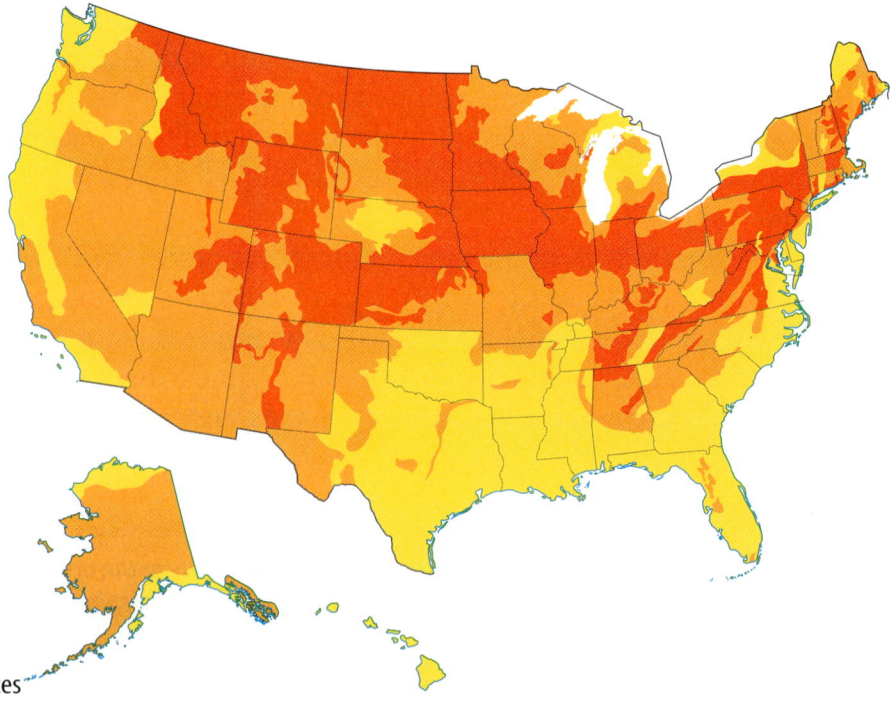

When rain falls on roads and parking lots, it can wash oil and grease onto the soil and into nearby streams.

Rain can wash agricultural pesticides and fertilizers into lakes, streams, or oceans.

Industrial wastes are sometimes released directly into surface waters.

Figure 16 Pollution of surface waters can occur in several ways, as shown above.

Water Pollution

Pollutants enter water, too. Air pollutants can drift into water or be washed out of the sky by rain. Rain can wash land pollutants into waterways, as shown in **Figure 16.** Wastewater from factories and sewage-treatment plants often is released into waterways. In the United States and many other countries, laws require that wastewater be treated to remove pollutants before it is released. But, in many parts of the world, wastewater treatment is not always possible. Pollution also enters water when people dump litter or waste materials into rivers, lakes, and oceans.

Surface Water Some water pollutants poison fish and other wildlife, and can be harmful to people who swim in or drink the water. For example, chemical pesticides sprayed on farmland can wash into lakes and streams. These chemicals can harm the insects that fish, turtles, or frogs rely on for food. Shortages of food can lead to deaths among water-dwelling animals. Some pollutants, especially those containing mercury and other metals, can build up in the tissues of fish. Eating contaminated fish and shellfish can transfer these metals to people, birds, and other animals. In some areas, people are advised not to eat fish or shellfish taken from polluted waterways.

Algal blooms are another water pollution problem. Raw sewage and excess fertilizer contain large amounts of nitrogen. If they are washed into a lake or pond, they can cause the rapid growth of algae. When the algae die, they are decomposed by huge numbers of bacteria that use up much of the oxygen in the water. Fish and other organisms can die from a lack of oxygen in the water.

Indiana Academic Standard Check

7.4.14: Explain that the environment may contain dangerous levels of substances that are harmful to human beings....

✓ How can surface water pollutants be harmful?

Figure 17 In 1996, the oil tanker *Sea Empress* spilled more than 72 million kg of oil into the sea along the coast of Wales. More than $40 million was spent on the cleanup effort, but thousands of ocean organisms were destroyed, including birds, fish, and shellfish.

Ocean Water Rivers and streams eventually flow into oceans, bringing their pollutants along. Also, polluted water can enter the ocean in coastal areas where factories, sewage-treatment plants, or shipping activities are located. Oil spills are a well-known ocean pollution problem. About 4 billion kg of oil are spilled into ocean waters every year. Much of that oil comes from ships that use ocean water to wash out their fuel tanks. Oil also can come from oil tanker wrecks, as shown in **Figure 17**.

Groundwater Pollution can affect water that seeps underground, as shown in **Figure 18**. Groundwater is water that collects between particles of soil and rock. It comes from precipitation and runoff that soaks into the soil. This water can flow slowly through permeable layers of rock called aquifers. If this water comes into contact with pollutants as it moves through the soil and into an aquifer, the aquifer could become polluted. Polluted groundwater is difficult—and sometimes impossible—to clean. In some parts of the country, chemicals leaking from underground storage tanks have created groundwater pollution problems.

Figure 18 Water from rainfall slowly filters through sand or soil until it is trapped in underground aquifers. Pollutants picked up by the water as it filters through the soil can contaminate water wells.

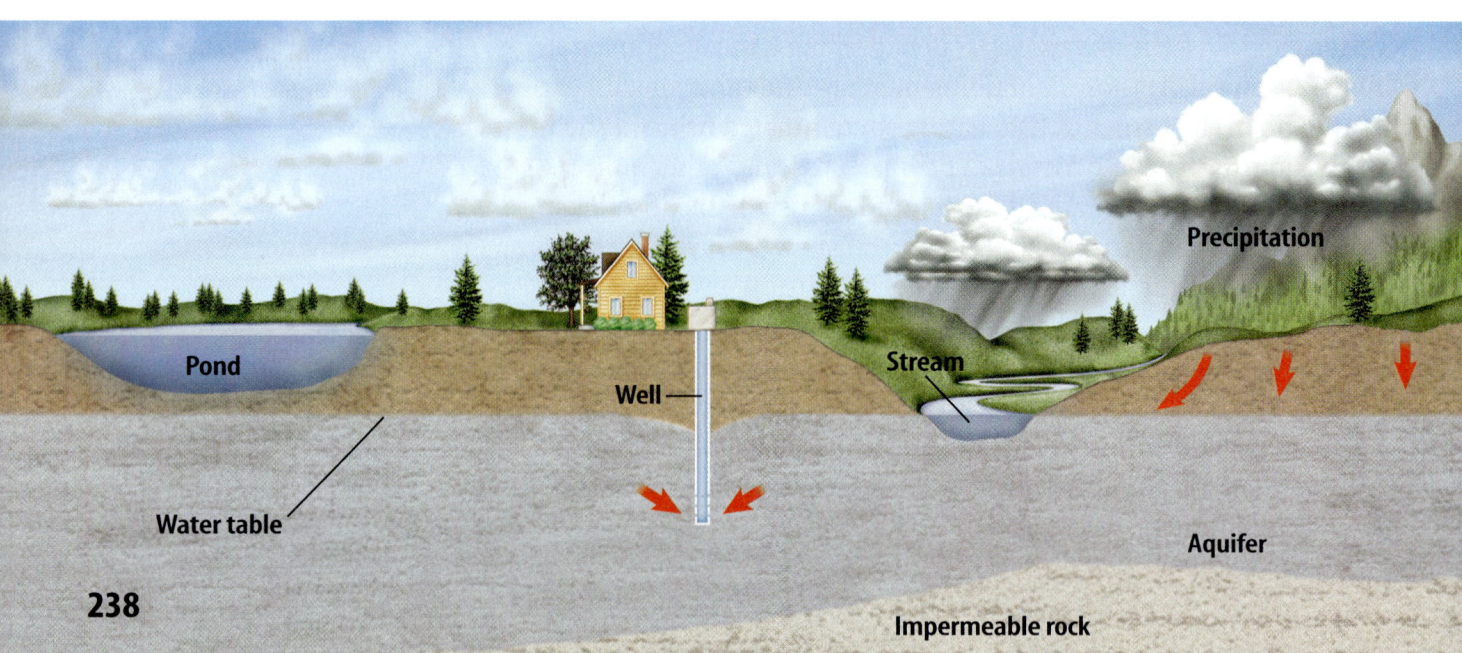

Contour plowing reduces the downhill flow of water.

Figure 19 The farming methods shown here help prevent soil erosion.
Infer *why soil erosion is a concern for farmers.*

On steep hillsides, flat areas called terraces reduce downhill flow.

Soil Loss

Fertile topsoil is important to plant growth. New topsoil takes hundreds or thousands of years to form. The Launch Lab at the beginning of this chapter shows that rain washes away loose topsoil. Wind also blows it away. The movement of soil from one place to another is called **erosion** (ih ROH zhun). Eroded soil that washes into a river or stream can block sunlight and slow photosynthesis. It also can harm fish, clams, and other organisms. Erosion is a natural process, but human activities increase it. When a farmer plows a field or a forest is cut down, soil is left bare. Bare soil is more easily carried away by rain and wind. **Figure 19** shows some methods farmers use to reduce soil erosion.

Soil Pollution

Soil can become polluted when air pollutants drift to the ground or when water leaves pollutants behind as it flows through the soil. Soil also can be polluted when people toss litter on the ground or dispose of trash in landfills.

In strip cropping, cover crops are planted between rows to reduce wind erosion.

Solid Wastes What happens to the trash you throw out every week? What do people do with old refrigerators, TVs, and toys? Most of this solid waste is dumped in landfills. Most landfills are designed to seal out air and water. This helps prevent pollutants from seeping into surrounding soil, but it slows normal decay processes. Even food scraps and paper, which usually break down quickly, can last for decades in a landfill. In populated areas, landfills fill up quickly. Reducing the amount of trash people generate can reduce the need for new landfills.

In no-till farming, soil is never left bare.

SECTION 2 Pollution   **239**

Figure 20 Leftover paints, batteries, pesticides, drain cleaners, and medicines are hazardous wastes that should not be discarded in the trash. They should never be poured down a drain, onto the ground, or into a storm sewer. Most communities have collection facilities where people can dispose of hazardous materials like these.

Hazardous Wastes Waste materials that are harmful to human health or poisonous to living organisms are **hazardous wastes.** They include dangerous chemicals, such as pesticides, oil, and petroleum-based solvents used in industry. They also include radioactive wastes from nuclear power plants, from hospitals that use radioactive materials to treat disease, and from nuclear weapons production. Many household items also are considered hazardous, such as those shown in **Figure 20.** If these materials are dumped into landfills, they could seep into the soil, surface water, or groundwater over time. Hazardous wastes usually are handled separately from trash. They are treated in ways that prevent environmental pollution.

 *What are hazardous wastes?*

section 2 review

Summary

Air Pollution and Acid Precipitation
- Vehicles, volcanoes, forest fires, and even wind-blown dust and sand can cause air pollution.
- Acid rain washes nutrients from the soil, which can harm plants.

Greenhouse Effect and Ozone Depletion
- CO_2 is a greenhouse gas that helps warm Earth.
- The ozone layer protects life on Earth.

Indoor Air Pollution, Water Pollution, Soil Loss, and Soil Pollution
- Pollutants can build up inside of buildings.
- There are many sources of water pollutants.
- Wind and rain can erode bare soil.
- Pollutants in soil decay more slowly than in air.

Self Check

1. **List** four ways that air pollution affects the environment.
2. **Explain** how an algal bloom can affect other pond organisms.
3. **Describe** possible causes and effects of ozone depletion.
4. **Think Critically** How could hazardous wastes in landfills eventually affect groundwater?

Applying Math

5. **Solve a One-Step Equation** A solution of pH 4 is 10 times more acidic than one of pH 5, and it is 10 times more acidic than a solution of pH 6. How many times more acidic is the solution of pH 4 than the one of pH 6?

 in7.msscience.com/self_check_quiz

The Greenhouse Effect

You can create models of Earth with and without heat-reflecting green-house gases. Then, experiment with the models to observe the greenhouse effect.

● Real-World Question

How does the greenhouse effect influence temperatures on Earth?

Goals
- **Observe** the greenhouse effect.
- **Describe** the effect that a heat source has on an environment.

Materials
1-L clear-plastic, soft-drink bottles with tops cut off and labels removed (2)
thermometers (2)
*temperature probe
potting soil
masking tape
plastic wrap
rubber band
lamp with 100-W lightbulb
watch or clock with second hand
*Alternate materials

Safety Precautions

Time (min)	Changes in Temperature	
	Open Container Temperature (°C)	Closed Container Temperature (°C)
0		
2	*Do not write in this book.*	
4		
6		

● Procedure

1. Copy the data table and use it to record your temperature measurements.
2. Put an equal volume of potting soil in the bottom of each container.
3. Use masking tape to attach a thermometer to the inside of each container. Place each thermometer at the same height above the soil. Shield each thermometer bulb by putting a double layer of masking tape over it.
4. Seal the top of one container with plastic wrap held in place with a rubber band.
5. Place the lamp with the exposed 100-W lightbulb between the two containers and exactly 1 cm away from each. Do not turn on the light.
6. Let the setup sit for 5 min, then record the temperature in each container.
7. Turn on the light. Record the temperature in each container every 2 min for 15 min to 20 min. Graph the results.

● Conclude and Apply

1. **Compare and contrast** temperatures in each container at the end of the experiment.
2. **Infer** What does the lightbulb represent in this experimental model? What does the plastic wrap represent?

Communicating Your Data

Average the data obtained in the experiments conducted by all the groups in your class. Prepare a line graph of these data. **For more help, refer to the Science Skill Handbook.**

LAB **241**

section 3

Standard—7.4.14: Explain that the environment may contain dangerous levels of substances that are harmful to human beings. Understand, therefore, that the good health of individuals requires monitoring the soil, air, and water as well as taking steps to keep them safe.

Also covers: 7.3.16 (Detailed standards begin on page IN8.)

The Three Rs of Conservation

as you read

What You'll Learn
- **Recognize** ways you can reduce your use of natural resources.
- **Explain** how you can reuse resources to promote conservation.
- **Describe** how many materials can be recycled.

Why It's Important
Conservation preserves resources and reduces pollution.

Review Vocabulary
reprocessing: to subject to a special process or treatment in preparation for reuse

New Vocabulary
- recycling

Figure 21 Worn-out automobile tires can have other useful purposes.

Conservation

A teacher travels to school in a car pool. In the school cafeteria, students place glass bottles and cans in separate containers from the rest of the garbage. Conservation efforts like these can help prevent shortages of natural resources, slow growth of landfills, reduce pollution levels, and save people money. Every time a new landfill is created, an ecosystem is disturbed. Reducing the need for landfills is a major benefit of conservation. The three Rs of conservation are reduce, reuse, and recycle.

Reduce

You contribute to conservation whenever you reduce your use of natural resources. You use less fossil fuel when you walk or ride a bicycle instead of taking the bus or riding in a car. If you buy a carton of milk, reduce your use of petroleum by telling the clerk you don't need a plastic bag to carry it in.

You also can avoid buying things you don't need. For example, most of the paper, plastic, and cardboard used to package items for display on store shelves is thrown away as soon as the product is brought home. You can look for products with less packaging or with packaging made from recycled materials. What are some other ways you can reduce your use of natural resources?

Reuse

Another way to help conserve natural resources is to use items more than once. Reusing an item means using it again without changing it or reprocessing it, as shown in **Figure 21.** Bring reusable canvas bags to the grocery store to carry home your purchases. Donate clothes you've outgrown to charity so that others can reuse them. Take reusable plates and utensils on picnics instead of disposable paper items.

Recycle

If you can't avoid using an item, and if you can't reuse it, the next best thing is to recycle it. **Recycling** is a form of reuse that requires changing or reprocessing an item or natural resource. If your city or town has a curbside recycling program, you already separate recyclables from the rest of your garbage. Materials that can be recycled include glass, metals, paper, plastics, and yard and kitchen waste.

✓ **Reading Check** How is recycling different from reusing?

Plastics Plastic is more difficult to recycle than other materials, mainly because several types of plastic are in use. A recycle code marked on every plastic container indicates the type of plastic it is made of. Plastic soft-drink bottles, like the one shown in **Figure 22,** are made of type 1 plastic and are the easiest to recycle. Most plastic bags are made of type 2 or type 4 plastic; they can be reused as well as recycled. Types 6 and 7 can't be recycled at all because they are made of a mixture of different plastics. Each type of plastic must be separated carefully before it is recycled because a single piece of a different type of plastic can ruin an entire batch.

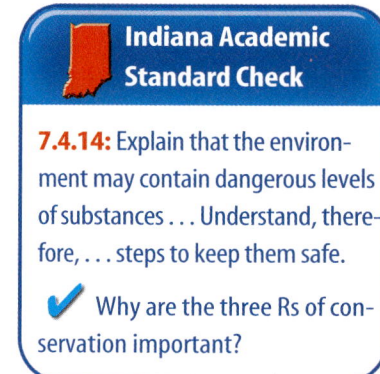

Indiana Academic Standard Check

7.4.14: Explain that the environment may contain dangerous levels of substances... Understand, therefore,... steps to keep them safe.

✓ Why are the three Rs of conservation important?

Figure 22 Many soft-drink bottles are made of PETE, which is the most common type of recyclable plastic. It can be melted down and spun into fibers to make carpets, paintbrushes, rope, and clothing. **Identify** other products made out of recycled materials.

SECTION 3 The Three Rs of Conservation **243**

Topic: Recycling

Visit in7.msscience.com for Web links to information about recycling bottles and cans.

Activity Write one argument in support of a money deposit for bottles and cans and one argument against it. Provide data to support one of your arguments.

Metals The manufacturing industry has been recycling all kinds of metals, especially steel, for decades. At least 25 percent of the steel in cans, appliances, and automobiles is recycled steel. Up to 100 percent of the steel in plates and beams used to build skyscrapers is made from reprocessed steel. About one metric ton of recycled steel saves about 1.1 metric tons of iron ore and 0.5 metric ton of coal. Using recycled steel to make new steel products reduces energy use by 75 percent. Other metals, including iron, copper, aluminum, and lead also can be recycled.

You can conserve metals by recycling food cans, which are mostly steel, and aluminum cans. It takes less energy to make a can from recycled aluminum than from raw materials. Also, remember that recycled cans do not take up space in landfills.

Glass When sterilized, glass bottles and jars can be reused. They also can be melted and re-formed into new bottles, especially those made of clear glass. Most glass bottles already contain at least 25 percent recycled glass. Glass can be recycled again and again. It never needs to be thrown away. Recycling about one metric ton of glass saves more than one metric ton of mineral resources and reduces the energy used to make new glass by 25 percent or more.

Applying Science

What items are you recycling at home?

Many communities have recycling programs. Recyclable items may be picked up at the curbside, taken to a collection site, or the resident may hire a licensed recycling handler to pick them up. What do you recycle in your home?

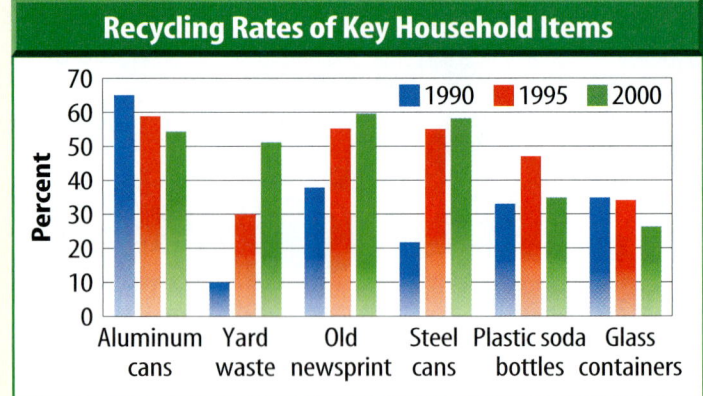

Source: U.S. EPA, 2003

Identifying the Problem

This bar graph shows the recycling rates in the U. S. of six types of household items for the years 1990, 1995, and 2000. What are you and your classmates' recycling rates?

Solving the Problem

For one week, list each glass, plastic, and aluminum item you use. Note which items you throw away and which ones you recycle. Calculate the percentage of glass, plastic, and aluminum you recycled. How do your percentages compare with those on the graph?

Paper Used paper is recycled into paper towels, insulation, newsprint, cardboard, and stationery. Ranchers and dairy farmers sometimes use shredded paper instead of straw for bedding in barns and stables. Used paper can be made into compost. Recycling about one metric ton of paper saves 17 trees, more than 26,000 L of water, close to 1,900 L of oil, and more than 4,000 kW of electric energy. You can do your part by recycling newspapers, notebook and printer paper, cardboard, and junk mail.

 What nonrenewable resource(s) do you conserve by recycling paper?

Compost Grass clippings, leaves, and fruit and vegetable scraps that are discarded in a landfill can remain there for decades without breaking down. The same items can be turned into soil-enriching compost in just a few weeks, as shown in **Figure 23**. Many communities distribute compost bins to encourage residents to recycle fruit and vegetable scraps and yard waste.

Buy Recycled People have become so good at recycling that recyclable materials are piling up, just waiting to be put to use. You can help by reading labels when you shop and choosing products that contain recycled materials. What other ways of recycling natural resources can you think of?

Figure 23 Composting is a way of turning plant material you would otherwise throw away into rich garden soil. Dry leaves and weeds, grass clippings, vegetable trimmings, and nonmeat food scraps can be composted.

section 3 review

Summary

Conservation
- The three Rs of conservation are reduce, reuse, and recycle.

Reduce
- You can contribute to conservation by reducing your use of natural resources.

Reuse
- Some items can be used more than once, such as reusable canvas bags for groceries.

Recycle
- Some items can be recycled, including some plastics, metal, glass, and paper.
- Grass clippings, leaves, and fruit and vegetable scraps can be composted into rich garden soil.

Self Check

1. **Describe** at least three actions you could take to reduce your use of natural resources.
2. **Describe** how you could reuse three items people usually throw away.
3. **Think Critically** Why is reusing something better than recycling it?

Applying Skills

4. **Make and Use Tables** Make a table of data of the number of aluminum cans thrown away in the United States: 2.7 billion in 1970; 11.1 billion in 1974; 21.3 billion in 1978; 22.7 billion in 1982; 35.0 billion in 1986; 33.8 billion in 1990; 38.5 billion in 1994; 45.5 billion in 1998; 50.7 billion in 2001.

in7.msscience.com/self_check_quiz

LAB Model and Invent

Solar Cooking

Goals
- **Research** designs for solar panel cookers or box cookers.
- **Design** a solar cooker that can be used to cook food.
- **Plan** an experiment to measure the effectiveness of your solar cooker.

Possible Materials
poster board
cardboard boxes
aluminum foil
string
wire coat hangers
clear plastic sheets
*oven bags
black cookware
thermometer
stopwatch
*timer
glue
tape
scissors
*Alternate materials

Safety Precautions

WARNING: *Be careful when cutting materials. Your solar cooker will get hot. Use insulated gloves or tongs to handle hot objects.*

◉ Real-World Question

The disappearance of forests in some places on Earth has made firewood extremely difficult and expensive to obtain. People living in these regions often have to travel long distances or sell some of their food to get firewood. This can be a serious problem for people who may not have much food to begin with. Is there a way they could cook food without using firewood? How would you design and build a cooking device that uses the Sun's energy?

◉ Make the Model

1. **Design** a solar cooker. In your Science Journal, explain why you chose this design and draw a picture of it.
2. **Write** a summary explaining how you will measure the effectiveness of your solar cooker. What will you measure? How will you collect and organize your data? How will you present your results?

246 CHAPTER 8 Conserving Resources

Using Scientific Methods

3. **Compare** your solar cooker design to those of other students.
4. **Share** your experimental plan with students in your class. Discuss the reasoning behind your plan. Be specific about what you intend to test and how you are going to test it.
5. **Make** sure your teacher approves your plan before you start working on your model.
6. **Using** all of the information you have gathered, construct a solar cooker that follows your design.

Test the Model

1. **Test** your design to determine how well it works. Try out a classmate's design. How do the two compare?

Analyze Your Data

1. Combine the results for your entire class and decide which type of solar cooker was most effective. How could you design a more effective solar cooker, based on what you learned from this activity?
2. **Infer** Do you think your results might have been different if you tested your solar cooker on a different day? Explain. Why might a solar cooker be more useful in some regions of the world than in others?

Conclude and Apply

1. **Infer** Based on what you've read and the results obtained by you and your classmates, do you think that your solar cooker could boil water? Explain.
2. **Compare** the amount of time needed to cook food with a solar cooker and with more traditional cooking methods. Assuming plenty of sunlight is available, would you prefer to use a solar cooker or a traditional oven? Explain.

Prepare a demonstration showing how to use a solar cooker. Present your demonstration to another class of students or to a group of friends or relatives. **For more help, refer to the Science Skill Handbook.**

LAB 247

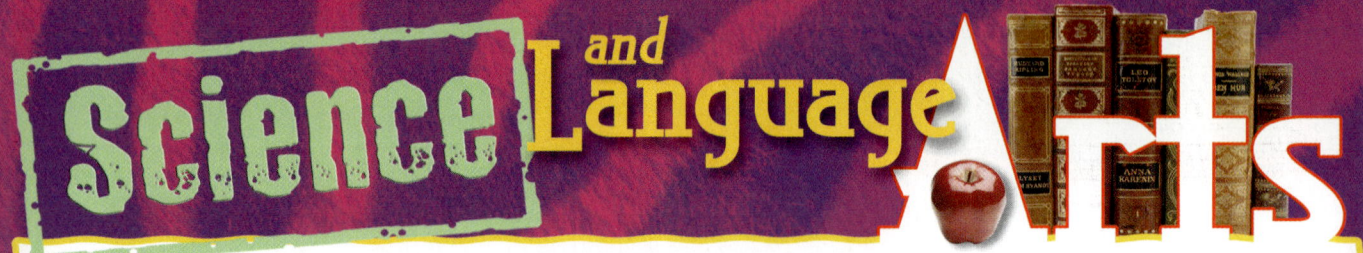

Science and Language Arts

Beauty Plagiarized
by Amitabha Mukerjee

I wandered lonely as a cloud –
Except for a motorboat,
Nary a soul in sight.
Beside the lake beneath the trees,
Next to the barbed wire fence,
There was a picnic table
And beer bottle caps from many years.
A boat ramp to the left,
And the chimney from a power station on the other side,
A summer haze hung in the air,
And the lazy drone of traffic far away.

Crimson autumn of mists and mellow fruitfulness
Blue plastic covers the swimming pools
The leaves fall so I can see
Dark glass reflections in the building
That came up
where the pine cones crunched underfoot . . .

And then it is snow
White lining on trees and rooftops . . .
And through my windshield wipers
The snow is piled dark and grey . . .
Next to my driveway where I check my mail
Little footprints on fresh snow —
A visiting rabbit.

I knew a bank where the wild thyme blew
Over-canopied with luscious woodbine
It is now a landfill —
Fermentation of civilization
Flowers on TV
Hyacinth rose tulip chrysanthemum
Acres of colour
Wind up wrapped in decorous plastic,
In this landfill where oxlips grew. . .

Understanding Literature

Cause and Effect Recognizing cause-and-effect relationships can help you make sense out of what you read. One event causes another event. The second event is the effect of the first event. In the poem, the author describes the causes and effects of pollution and waste. What effects do pollution and the use of nonrenewable resources have on nature in the poem?

Respond to the Reading

1. To plagiarize is to copy without giving credit to the source. In this poem, who or what has plagiarized beauty?
2. What do the four verses in the poem correspond to?
3. **Linking Science and Writing** Write a poem that shows how conservation methods could restore the beauty in nature.

The poet makes a connection between the four seasons of the year and the pollution and waste products created by human activity, or civilization. For example, in the spring, a landfill for dumping garbage replaces a field of wildflowers. Describing four seasons instead of one reinforces the poet's message that the beauty of nature has been stolen, or plagiarized.

chapter 8 Study Guide

Reviewing Main Ideas

Section 1 Resources

1. Natural resources are the parts of the environment that supply materials needed for the survival of living organisms.
2. Renewable resources are being replaced continually by natural processes.
3. Nonrenewable resources cannot be replaced or are replaced very slowly.
4. Energy sources include fossil fuels, wind, solar energy, geothermal energy, hydroelectric power, and nuclear power.

Section 2 Pollution

1. Most air pollution is made up of waste products from the burning of fossil fuels.
2. The greenhouse effect is the warming of Earth by a blanket of heat-reflecting gases in the atmosphere.
3. Water can be polluted by acid rain and by the spilling of oil or other wastes into waterways.
4. Solid wastes and hazardous wastes dumped on land or disposed of in landfills can pollute the soil. Erosion can cause the loss of fertile topsoil.

Section 3 The Three Rs of Conservation

1. You can reduce your use of natural resources in many ways.
2. Reusing items is an excellent way to practice conservation.
3. In recycling, materials are changed in some way so that they can be used again.
4. Materials that can be recycled include paper, metals, glass, plastics, yard waste, and nonmeat kitchen scraps.

Visualizing Main Ideas

Copy and complete the following concept map using the terms smog, acid precipitation, *and* ozone depletion.

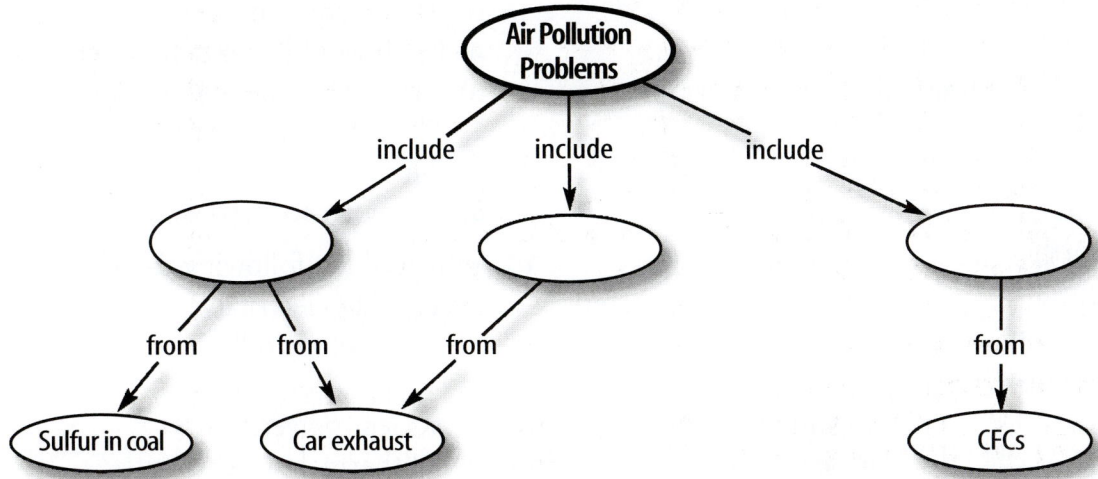

chapter 8 Review

Using Vocabulary

acid precipitation p. 233
erosion p. 239
fossil fuel p. 226
geothermal energy p. 229
greenhouse effect p. 234
hazardous waste p. 240
hydroelectric power p. 227
natural resource p. 224
nonrenewable resource p. 225
nuclear energy p. 228
ozone depletion p. 235
petroleum p. 225
pollutant p. 232
recycling p. 243
renewable resource p. 224

Explain the differences in the vocabulary words given below. Then explain how the words are related. Use complete sentences in your answers.

1. fossil fuel—petroleum
2. erosion—pollutant
3. ozone depletion—acid precipitation
4. greenhouse effect—fossil fuels
5. hazardous wastes—nuclear energy
6. hydroelectric power—fossil fuels
7. acid precipitation—fossil fuels
8. ozone depletion—pollutant
9. recycle—nonrenewable resources
10. geothermal energy—fossil fuels

Checking Concepts

Choose the word or phrase that best answers the question.

11. An architect wants to design a solar house in the northern hemisphere. For maximum warmth, which side of the house should have the most windows?
    A) north   C) east
    B) south   D) west

12. Of the following, which is considered a renewable resource?
    A) coal   C) sunlight
    B) oil   D) aluminum

Use the photo below to answer question 13.

13. Which energy resource is shown in the photo?
    A) solar energy
    B) geothermal energy
    C) hydroelectric energy
    D) photovoltaic energy

14. Which of the following is a fossil fuel?
    A) wood   C) nuclear power
    B) oil   D) photovoltaic cell

15. Which of the following contributes to ozone depletion?
    A) carbon dioxide   C) CFCs
    B) radon   D) carbon monoxide

16. What is a substance that contaminates the environment called?
    A) acid rain   C) pollutant
    B) pollution   D) ozone

17. If there were no greenhouse effect in Earth's atmosphere, which of the following statements would be true?
    A) Earth would be much hotter.
    B) Earth would be much colder.
    C) The temperature of Earth would be the same.
    D) The polar ice caps would melt.

18. Which of the following can change solar energy into electricity?
    A) photovoltaic cells
    B) smog
    C) nuclear power plants
    D) geothermal power plants

250 CHAPTER REVIEW   Science Online   in7.msscience.com/vocabulary_puzzlemaker

Chapter 8 Review

Thinking Critically

19. **Explain** how geothermal energy is used to produce electricity.

20. **Infer** why burning wood and burning fossil fuels produce similar pollutants.

Use the photos below to answer question 21.

21. **Draw a Conclusion** Which would make a better location for a solar power plant—a polar region (left) or a desert region (right)? Why?

22. **Explain** why it is beneficial to grow a different crop on soil after the major crop has been harvested.

23. **Infer** Is garbage a renewable resource? Why or why not?

24. **Summarize** Solar, nuclear, wind, water, and geothermal energy are alternatives to fossil fuels. Are they all renewable? Why or why not?

25. **Draw Conclusions** Would you save more energy by recycling or reusing a plastic bag?

26. **Recognize Cause and Effect** Forests use large amounts of carbon dioxide during photosynthesis. How might cutting down a large percentage of Earth's forests affect the greenhouse effect?

27. **Form a hypothesis** about why Americans throw away more aluminum cans each year.

28. **Compare and contrast** contour farming, terracing, strip cropping, and no-till farming.

Performance Activities

29. **Poster** Create a poster to illustrate and describe three things students at your school can do to conserve natural resources.

Applying Math

Use the table below to answer questions 30 and 31.

Estimated Recycling Rates	
Item	Percent Recycled
Aluminum cans	60
Glass beverage bottles	31
Plastic soft-drink containers	37
Newsprint	56
Magazines	23

30. **Recycling Rates** Make a bar graph of the data above.

31. **Bottle Recycling** For every 1,000 glass beverage bottles that are produced, how many are recycled?

32. **Nonrenewable Resources** 45.8 billion (45,800,000,000) cans were thrown away in 2000. If it takes 33.79 cans to equal one pound and the average scrap value is $0.58/lb, then what was the total dollar value of the discarded cans?

33. **Ozone Depletion** The thin ozone layer called the "ozone hole" over Antarctica reached nearly 27,000,000 km^2 in 1998. To conceptualize this, the United States has a geographical area of 9,363,130 km^2. How much larger is the "ozone hole" in comparison to the United States?

34. **Increased CO_2 Levels** To determine the effects of increased CO_2 levels in the atmosphere, scientists increased the CO_2 concentration by 70 percent in an enclosed rain forest environment. If the initial CO_2 concentration was 430 parts per million, what was it after the increase?

chapter 8 Indiana

The assessed Indiana standard appears above the question.

Record your answers on the answer sheet provided by your teacher or on a sheet of paper.

Part 1 Multiple Choice

1. Which natural resource is the source of plastics, paints, and gasoline?

   A coal

   B iron ore

   C natural gas

   D petroleum

The illustration below shows a turbine generator.

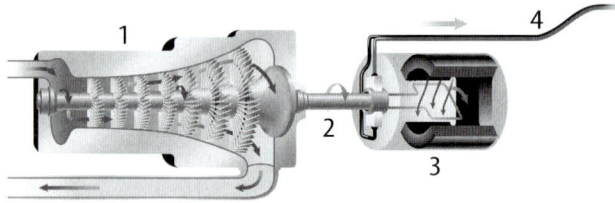

2. What does this machine produce?

   A electricity

   B microwaves

   C nuclear power

   D solar power

3. Where does a flow of water cause the blades to turn in the machine shown above?

   A 1

   B 2

   C 3

   D 4

The photo below shows a method of farming.

4. Which method of farming is shown?

   A contour plowing

   B no-till farming

   C strip cropping

   D terracing

5. What is the purpose of the farming method shown above?

   A to decrease effects of acid rain

   B to decrease nutrient loss from water erosion

   C to decrease nutrients returned to the soil

   D to decrease soil loss from wind erosion

7.3.16 **7.4.14**

6. What type of air pollution results when sunlight reacts with pollutants produced by burning fossil fuels?

   A acid rain

   B ozone

   C smog

   D UV radiation

Standards Review

7. The illustration below shows a type of alternative energy.

What type of alternative energy is being used?

A geothermal

B hydroelectric

C solar

D wind

7.1.8 **7.3.16**

8. What is one drawback to using the alternative energy shown above?

A available only when the Sun is shining

B available only where geysers or volcanoes are found

C available only when the wind is blowing

D available only where there is falling water

Part 2 Constructed Response

7.1.8

9. What is the cause of algal blooms in lakes and ponds? Suggest ways to limit algal blooms.

7.3.16 **7.4.14**

10. What are the possible worldwide effects of global warming? What causes global warming? Why do some people think that using fossil fuels less will decrease global warming?

7.3.16

11. The illustration below shows part of the process for an alternative form of energy.

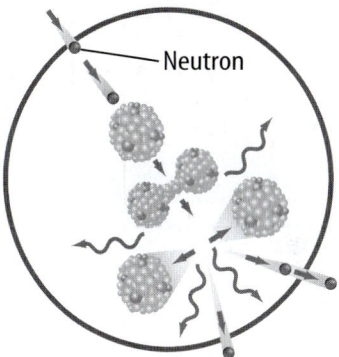

What does the illustration represent?

Test-Taking Tip

Qualifying Terms Look for qualifiers in a question. Such questions are not looking for absolute answers. Qualifiers could be words such as *most likely*, *most common*, or *least common*.

Question 10 The qualifier in this question is *possible*. This indicates that there is uncertainty about the effects of global warming.

The Nature of Matter

How Are Refrigerators & Frying Pans Connected?

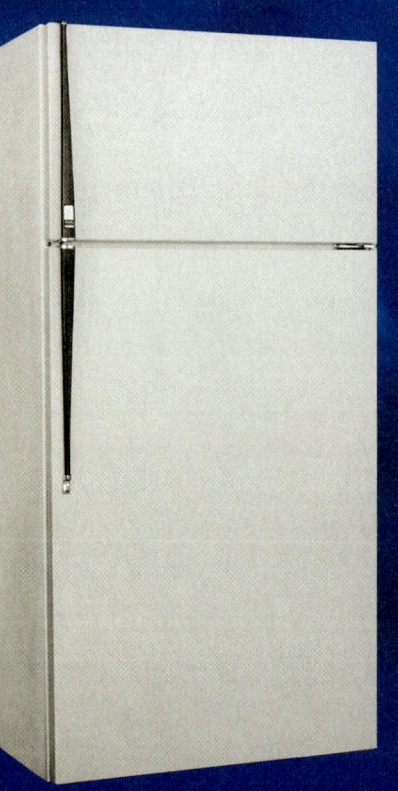

In the late 1930s, scientists were experimenting with a gas that they hoped would work as a new coolant in refrigerators. They filled several metal canisters with the gas and stored the canisters on dry ice. Later, when they opened the canisters, they were surprised to find that the gas had disappeared and that the inside of each canister was coated with a slick, powdery, white solid. The gas had undergone a chemical change. That is, the chemical bonds in its molecules had broken and new bonds had formed, turning one kind of matter into a completely different kind of matter. Strangely, the mysterious white powder proved to be just about the slipperiest substance that anyone had ever encountered. Years later, a creative Frenchman obtained some of the slippery stuff and tried applying it to his fishing tackle to keep the lines from tangling. His wife noticed what he was doing and suggested putting the substance on the inside of a frying pan to keep food from sticking. He did, and nonstick cookware was born!

NATIONAL GEOGRAPHIC

unit projects

The assessed Indiana standard appears in blue.

To find project ideas and resources, visit **in7.msscience.com/unit_project**.
Projects include:

- **History** Discover the chemistry related to airships. Investigate the design, voyages, and destruction of famous airships. Display your information on a creative mobile. **7.1.5**
- **Technology** Design a classroom periodic table wall mural. Use the information as a learning tool and review game.
- **Model** Demonstrate your knowledge of the characteristics of physical and chemical change by preparing a simple snack to share.

WebQuest *Art of Neon* is an investigation of the noble gases and how they are inserted into glass tubes to be used in art and signage.

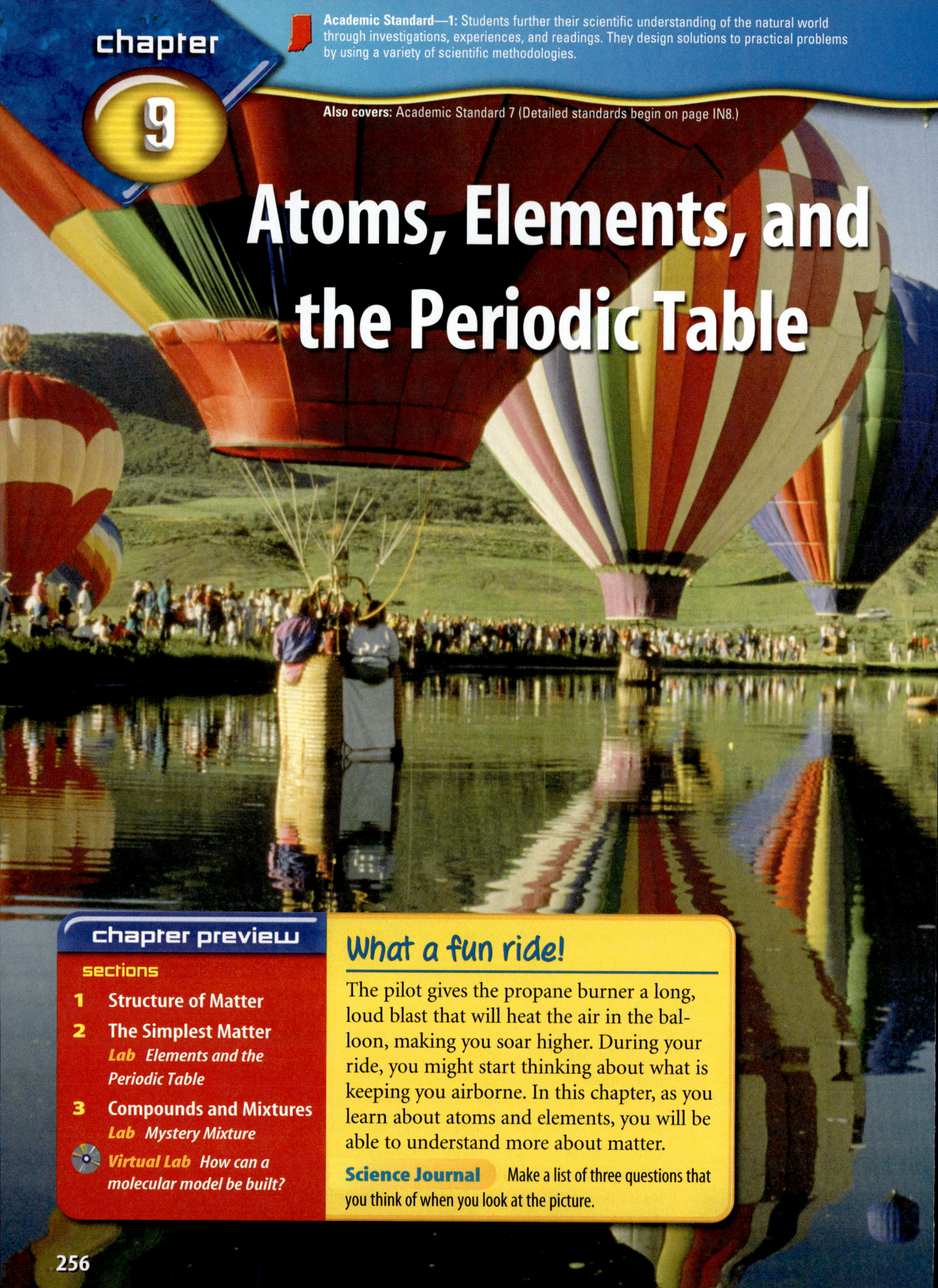

chapter 9

Atoms, Elements, and the Periodic Table

Academic Standard—1: Students further their scientific understanding of the natural world through investigations, experiences, and readings. They design solutions to practical problems by using a variety of scientific methodologies.

Also covers: Academic Standard 7 (Detailed standards begin on page IN8.)

chapter preview

sections
1. Structure of Matter
2. The Simplest Matter
   Lab Elements and the Periodic Table
3. Compounds and Mixtures
   Lab Mystery Mixture
   Virtual Lab How can a molecular model be built?

What a fun ride!

The pilot gives the propane burner a long, loud blast that will heat the air in the balloon, making you soar higher. During your ride, you might start thinking about what is keeping you airborne. In this chapter, as you learn about atoms and elements, you will be able to understand more about matter.

Science Journal Make a list of three questions that you think of when you look at the picture.

Start-Up Activities

Observe Matter

You've just finished playing basketball. You're hot and thirsty. You reach for your bottle of water and take a drink. Releasing your grip, you notice that the bottle is nearly empty. Is the bottle really almost empty? According to the dictionary, *empty* means "containing nothing." When you have finished all the water in the bottle, will it be empty or full?

1. Wad up a dry paper towel or tissue and tape it to the inside of a plastic cup as shown.
2. Fill a bowl or sink with water. Turn the cup upside down and slowly push the cup straight down into the water as far as you can.
3. Slowly raise the cup straight up and out of the water. Remove the paper towel or tissue paper and examine it.
4. **Think Critically** In your Science Journal, describe the lab and its results. Explain what you think happened. Was anything in the cup besides the paper? If so, what was it?

Atoms, Elements, and the Periodic Table Make the following Foldable to help you identify the main ideas about atoms, elements, compounds, and mixtures.

STEP 1 **Draw** a mark at the midpoint of a sheet of paper along the side edge. Then **fold** the top and bottom edges in to touch the midpoint.

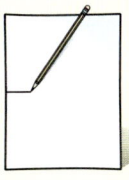

STEP 2 **Fold** in half from side to side.

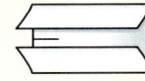

STEP 3 **Open and cut** along the inside fold lines to form four tabs.

STEP 4 **Label** each tab as shown.

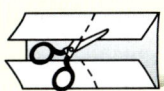

Read and Write As you read the chapter, list several everyday examples of atoms, elements, compounds, and mixtures on the back of the appropriate tab.

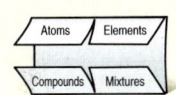

Preview this chapter's content and activities at in7.msscience.com

section 1

Standard—7.1.5: Identify some important contributions to the advancement of science . . . that have been made by different kinds of people, in different cultures, at different times.

Also covers: 7.1.1, 7.7.2 (Detailed standards begin on page IN8.)

Structure of Matter

as you read

What You'll Learn
- **Describe** characteristics of matter.
- **Identify** what makes up matter.
- **Identify** the parts of an atom.
- **Compare** the models that are used for atoms.

Why It's Important
Matter makes up almost everything we see—and much of what we can't see.

Review Vocabulary
density: the mass of an object divided by its volume

New Vocabulary
- matter
- atom
- law of conservation of matter
- electron
- nucleus
- proton
- neutron

What is matter?

Is a glass with some water in it half empty or half full? Actually, neither is correct. The glass is completely full—half full of water and half full of air. What is air? Air is a mixture of several gases, including nitrogen and oxygen, which are kinds of matter. **Matter** is anything that has mass and takes up space. So, even though you can't see it or hold it in your hand, air is matter. What about all the things you can see, taste, smell, and touch? Most are made of matter, too. Look at the things pictured in **Figure 1** and determine which of them are matter.

What isn't matter?

You can see the words on this page because of the light from the Sun or from a fixture in the room. Does light have mass or take up space? What about the warmth from the Sun or the heat from the heater in your classroom? Light and heat do not take up space, and they have no mass. Therefore, they are not forms of matter. Emotions, thoughts, and ideas are not matter either. Does this information change your mind about the items in **Figure 1?**

Reading Check *Why is air matter, but light is not?*

Figure 1 A rainbow is formed when light filters through the raindrops, a plant grows from a seed in the ground, and a statue is sculpted from bronze.
Identify which are matter.

258 **CHAPTER 9** Atoms, Elements, and the Periodic Table

Figure 2 Early Beliefs About the Composition of Matter

Many Indian Philosophers (1,000 B.C.)	Kashyapa, an Indian Philosopher (1,000 B.C.)	Many Greek Philosophers (500–300 B.C.)	Democritus (380 B.C.)	Aristotle (330 B.C.)	Chinese Philosophers (300 B.C.)
• Ether—an invisible substance that filled the heavens • Earth • Water • Air • Fire	• Five elements broken down into smaller units called parmanu • Parmanu of earth elements are heavier than air elements	• Earth • Water • Air • Fire	• Tiny individual particles he called *atomos* • Empty space through which atoms move • Each substance composed of one type of *atomos*	• Empty space could not exist • Earth • Water • Air • Fire	• Metal • Earth • Water • Air • Fire

What makes up matter?

Suppose you cut a chunk of wood into smaller and smaller pieces. Do the pieces seem to be made of the same matter as the large chunk you started with? If you could cut a small enough piece, would it still have the same properties as the first chunk? Would you reach a point where the last cut resulted in a piece that no longer resembled the first chunk? Is there a limit to how small a piece can be? For centuries, people have asked questions like these and wondered what matter is made of.

An Early Idea Democritus, who lived from about 460 B.C. to 370 B.C., was a Greek philosopher who thought the universe was made of empty space and tiny bits of stuff. He believed that the bits of stuff were so small they could no longer be divided into smaller pieces. He called these tiny pieces atoms. The term *atom* comes from a Greek word that means "cannot be divided." Today an **atom** is defined as a small particle that makes up most types of matter. **Figure 2** shows the difference between Democritus's ideas and those of other early scientists and philosophers. Democritus thought that different types of atoms existed for every type of matter and that the atom's identity explained the characteristics of each type of matter. Democritus's ideas about atoms were a first step toward understanding matter. However, his ideas were not accepted for over 2,000 years. It wasn't until the early 1800s that scientists built upon the concept of atoms to form the current atomic theory of matter.

Atomism Historians note that Leucippus developed the idea of the atom around 440 B.C. He and his student, Democritus, refined the idea of the atom years later. Their concept of the atom was based on five major points: (1) all matter is made of atoms, (2) there are empty spaces between atoms, (3) atoms are complete solids, (4) atoms do not have internal structure, and (5) atoms are different in size, shape, and weight.

Figure 3 When wood burns, matter is not lost. The total mass of the wood and the oxygen it combines with during a fire equals the total mass of the ash, water vapor, carbon dioxide, and other gases produced.
Infer *When you burn wood in a fireplace, what is the source of oxygen?*

wood + oxygen = ash + gases + water vapor

Investigating the Unseen

Procedure
1. Your teacher will give you a **sealed shoe box** that contains **one or more items**.
2. Try to find out how many and what kinds of items are inside the box. You cannot look inside the box. The only observations you can make are by handling the box.

Analysis
1. How many items do you infer are in the box? Sketch the apparent shapes of the items and identify them if you can.
2. Compare your procedure with how scientists perform experiments and make models to find out more about the atom.

Lavoisier's Contribution Lavoisier (la VWAH see ay), a French chemist who lived about 2,000 years after Democritus, also was curious about matter—especially when it changed form. Before Lavoisier, people thought matter could appear and disappear because of the changes they saw as matter burned or rusted. You might have thought that matter can disappear if you've ever watched wood burn in a fireplace or at a bonfire. Lavoisier showed that wood and the oxygen it combines with during burning have the same mass as the ash, water, carbon dioxide, and other gases that are produced, as shown in **Figure 3**. In a similar way, an iron bar, oxygen, and water have the same mass as the rust that forms when they interact. From Lavoisier's work came the **law of conservation of matter**, which states that matter is not created or destroyed—it only changes form.

Models of the Atom

Models are often used for things that are too small or too large to be observed or that are too difficult to be understood easily. One way to make a model is to make a smaller version of something large. If you wanted to design a new sailboat, would you build a full-sized boat and hope it would float? It would be more efficient, less expensive, and safer to build and test a smaller version first. Then, if it didn't float, you could change your design and build another model. You could keep trying until the model worked.

In the case of atoms, scientists use large models to explain something that is too small to be looked at. These models of the atom were used to explain data or facts that were gathered experimentally. As a result, these models are also theories.

Dalton's Atomic Model In the early 1800s, an English schoolteacher and chemist named John Dalton studied the experiments of Lavoisier and others. Dalton thought he could design an atomic model that explained the results of those experiments. Dalton's atomic model was a set of ideas—not a physical object. Dalton believed that matter was made of atoms that were too small to be seen by the human eye. He also thought that each type of matter was made of only one kind of atom. For example, gold atoms make up a gold nugget and give a gold ring its shiny appearance. Likewise, iron atoms make up an iron bar and give it unique properties, and so on. Because predictions using Dalton's model were supported by data, the model became known as the atomic theory of matter.

Indiana Academic Standard Check

7.1.5: Identify some important contributions to the advancement of science . . . that have been made by different kinds of people, in different cultures, at different times.

✓ How did Dalton's research build upon the work of Lavoisier?

Sizes of Atoms Atoms are so small it would take about 1 million of them lined up in a row to equal the thickness of a human hair. For another example of how small atoms are, look at **Figure 4.** Imagine you are holding an orange in your hand. If you wanted to be able to see the individual atoms on the orange's surface, the size of the orange would have to be increased to the size of Earth. Then, imagine the Earth-sized orange covered with billions and billions of marbles. Each marble would represent one of the atoms on the skin of the orange. No matter what kind of model you use to picture it, the result is the same—an atom is an extremely small particle of matter.

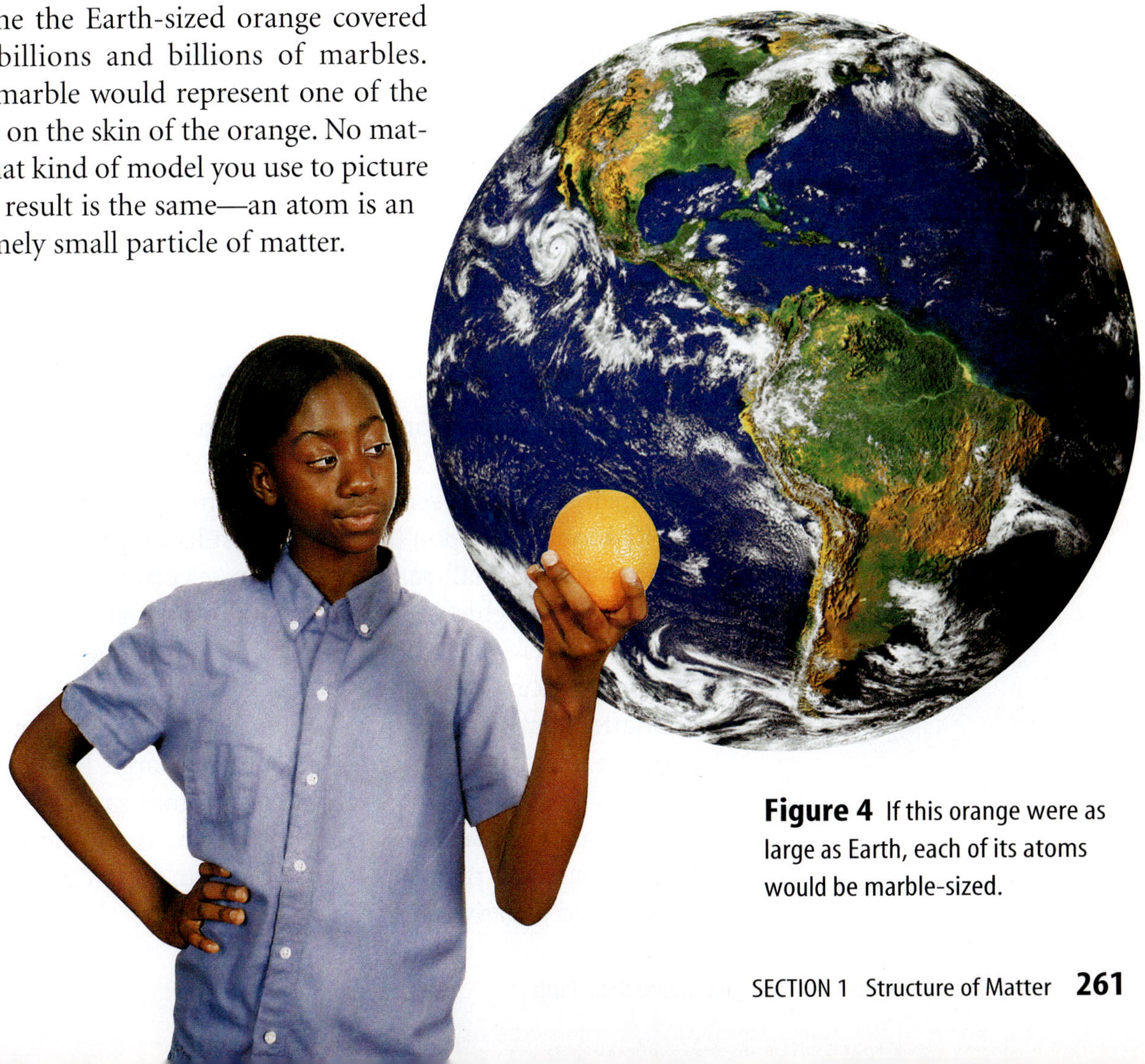

Figure 4 If this orange were as large as Earth, each of its atoms would be marble-sized.

SECTION 1 Structure of Matter **261**

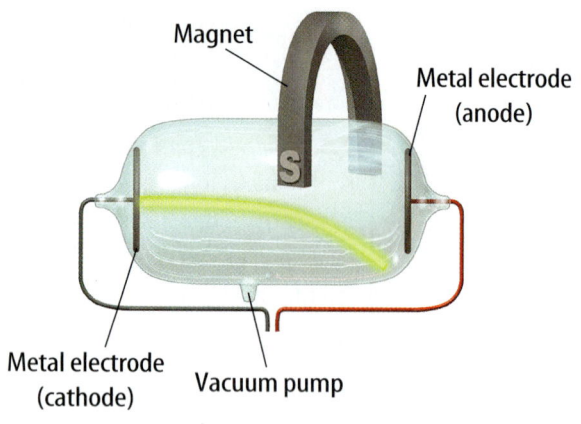

Figure 5 In Thomson's experiment, the magnet caused the cathode rays inside the tube to bend. **Describe** what you think would happen to the cathode rays if the magnet were removed.

Topic: Subatomic Particles
Visit in7.msscience.com for Web links to information about particles that make up atoms.

Activity Can any of the particles be divided further? Display your data in a table.

Discovering the Electron One of the many pioneers in the development of today's atomic model was J.J. Thomson, an English scientist. He conducted experiments using a cathode ray tube, which is a glass tube sealed at both ends out of which most of the air has been pumped. Thomson's tube had a metal plate at each end. The plates were connected to a high-voltage electrical source that gave one of the plates—the anode—a positive charge and the other plate—the cathode—a negative charge. During his experiments, Thomson observed rays that traveled from the cathode to the anode. These cathode rays were bent by a magnet, as seen in **Figure 5,** showing that they were made up of particles that had mass and charge. Thomson knew that like charges repel each other and opposite charges attract each other. When he saw that the rays traveled toward a positively charged plate, he concluded that the cathode rays were made up of negatively charged particles. These invisible, negatively charged particles are called **electrons**.

Reading Check *Why were the cathode rays in Thomson's cathode ray tube bent by a magnet?*

Try to imagine Thomson's excitement at this discovery. He had shown that atoms are not too tiny to divide after all. Rather, they are made up of even smaller subatomic particles. Other scientists soon built upon Thomson's results and found that the electron had a small mass. In fact, an electron is 1/1,837 the mass of the lightest atom, the hydrogen atom. In 1906, Thomson received the Nobel Prize in Physics for his work on the discovery of the electron.

Matter that has an equal amount of positive and negative charge is said to be neutral—it has no net charge. Because most matter is neutral, Thomson pictured the atom as a ball of positive charge with electrons embedded in it. It was later determined that neutral atoms contained an equal number of positive and negative charges.

Thomson's Model Thomson's model, shown in **Figure 6,** can be compared to chocolate chips spread throughout a ball of cookie dough. However, the model did not provide all the answers to the questions that puzzled scientists about atoms.

Rutherford—The Nucleus Scientists still had questions about how the atom was arranged and about the presence of positively charged particles. In about 1910, a team of scientists led by Ernest Rutherford worked on these questions. In their experiment, they bombarded an extremely thin piece of gold foil with alpha particles. Alpha particles are tiny, high-energy, positively charged particles that he predicted would pass through the foil. Most of the particles passed straight through the foil as if it were not there at all. However, other particles changed direction, and some even bounced back. Rutherford thought the result was so remarkable that he later said, "It was almost as incredible as if you had fired a 15-inch shell at a piece of tissue paper, and it came back and hit you."

Positive Center Rutherford concluded that because so many of the alpha particles passed straight through the gold foil, the atoms must be made of mostly empty space. However, because some of the positively charged alpha particles bounced off something, the gold atoms must contain some positively charged object concentrated in the midst of this empty space. Rutherford called the positively charged, central part of the atom the **nucleus** (NEW klee us). He named the positively charged particles in the nucleus **protons**. He also suggested that electrons were scattered in the mostly empty space around the nucleus, as shown in **Figure 7.**

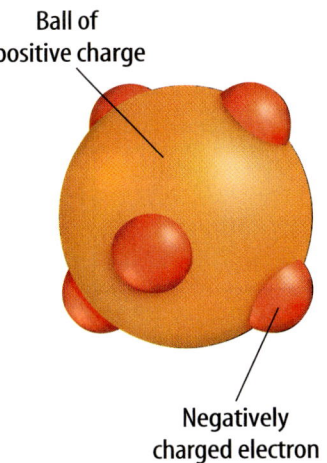

Figure 6 Thomson's model shows the atom as electrons embedded in a ball of positive charge.
Explain how Thomson knew atoms contained positive and negative charges.

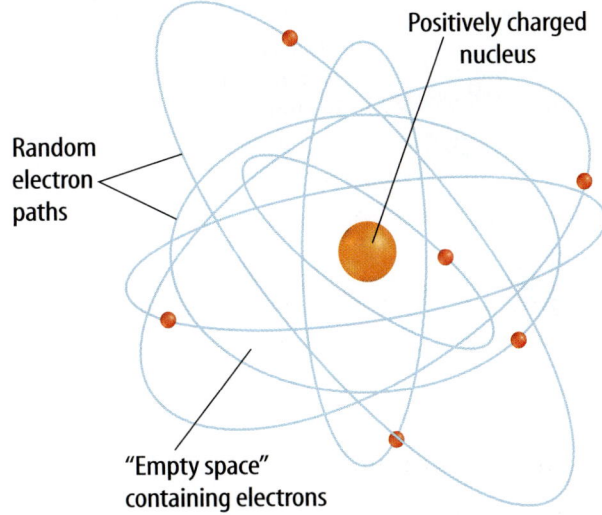

Figure 7 Rutherford concluded that the atom must be mostly empty space in which electrons travel in random paths around the nucleus. He also thought the nucleus of the atom must be small and positively charged.
Identify where most of the mass of an atom is concentrated.

SECTION 1 Structure of Matter **263**

Discovering the Neutron Rutherford had been puzzled by one observation from his experiments with nuclei. After the collisions, the nuclei seemed to be heavier. Where did this extra mass come from? James Chadwick, a student of Rutherford's, answered this question. The alpha particles themselves were not heavier. The atoms that had been bombarded had given off new particles. Chadwick experimented with these new particles and found that, unlike electrons, the paths of these particles were not affected by an electric field. To explain his observations, he said that these particles came from the nucleus and had no charge. Chadwick called these uncharged particles **neutrons** (NEW trahnz). His proton-neutron model of the atomic nucleus is still accepted today.

Improving the Atomic Model

Early in the twentieth century, a scientist named Niels Bohr found evidence that electrons in atoms are arranged according to energy levels. The lowest energy level is closest to the nucleus and can hold only two electrons. Higher energy levels are farther from the nucleus and can contain more electrons. To explain these energy levels, some scientists thought that the electrons might orbit an atom's nucleus in paths that are specific distances from the nucleus, as shown in **Figure 8.** This is similar to how the planets orbit the Sun.

The Modern Atomic Model As a result of continuing research, scientists now realize that because electrons have characteristics that are similar to waves and particles, their energy levels are not defined, planet-like orbits around the nucleus. Rather, it seems most likely that electrons move in what is called the atom's electron cloud, as shown in **Figure 9.**

Physicists and Chemists Physicists generally study the physical atom. The physical atom includes the inner components of an atom such as protons and neutrons, the forces that hold or change their positions in space and the bulk properties of elements such as melting point. Chemists, on the other hand, study the chemical atom. The chemical atom refers to the manner in which different elements relate to each other and the new substances formed by their union.

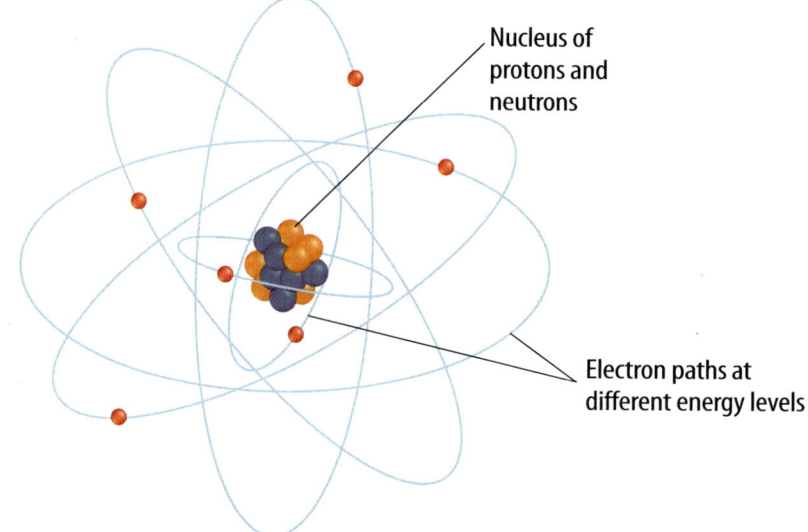

Figure 8 This simplified Bohr model shows a nucleus of protons and neutrons and electron paths based on energy levels.

The Electron Cloud The electron cloud is a spherical cloud of varying density surrounding the nucleus. The varying density shows where an electron is more or less likely to be. Atoms with electrons in higher energy levels have electron clouds of different shapes that also show where those electrons are likely to be. Generally, the electron cloud has a radius 10,000 times that of the nucleus.

Further Research By the 1930s, it was recognized that matter was made up of atoms, which were, in turn, made up of protons, neutrons, and electrons. But scientists, called physicists, continued to study the basic parts of this atom. Today, they have succeeded in breaking down protons and neutrons into even smaller particles called quarks. These particles can combine to make other kinds of tiny particles, too. The six types of quarks are *up, down, strange, charmed, top,* and *bottom*. Quarks have fractional electric charges of +2/3 or −1/3, unlike the +1 charge of a proton or the −1 charge of an electron. Research will continue as new discoveries are made about the structure of matter.

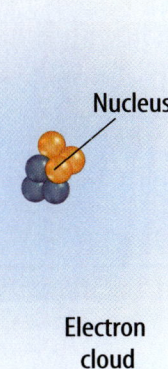

Figure 9 This model of the atom shows the electrons moving around the nucleus in a region called an electron cloud. The dark cloud of color represents the area where the electron is more likely to be found.
Infer *What does the intensity of color near the nucleus suggest?*

section 1 review

Summary

What is matter?
- Matter is anything that has mass and takes up space.
- Matter is composed of atoms.

Models of the Atom
- Democritus introduced the idea of an atom. Lavoisier showed matter is neither created nor destroyed, just changed.
- Dalton's ideas led to the atomic theory of matter.
- Thomson discovered the electron.
- Rutherford discovered protons exist in the nucleus.
- Chadwick discovered the neutron.

Improving the Atomic Model
- Niels Bohr suggested electrons move in energy levels.
- More recent physicists introduced the idea of the electron cloud and were able to break down protons and neutrons into smaller particles called quarks.

Self Check

1. **List** five examples of matter and five examples that are not matter. Explain your answers.
2. **Describe** and name the parts of the atom.
3. **Explain** why the word *atom* was an appropriate term for Democritus's idea.
4. **Think Critically** When neutrons were discovered, were these neutrons created in the experiment? How does Lavoisier's work help answer this question?
5. **Explain** the law of conservation of matter using your own examples.
6. **Think Critically** How is the electron cloud model different from Bohr's atomic model?

Applying Skills

7. **Classify** each scientist and his contribution according to the type of discovery each person made. Explain why you grouped certain scientists together.
8. **Evaluate Others' Data and Conclusions** Analyze, review, and critique the strengths and weaknesses of Thomson's "cookie dough" theory using the results of Rutherford's gold foil experiment.

section 2

Standard—7.1.5: Identify some important contributions to the advancement of science ... that have been made by different kinds of people, in different cultures, at different times.

The Simplest Matter

as you read

What You'll Learn
- **Describe** the relationship between elements and the periodic table.
- **Explain** the meaning of atomic mass and atomic number.
- **Identify** what makes an isotope.
- **Contrast** metals, metalloids, and nonmetals.

Why It's Important
Everything on Earth is made of the elements that are listed on the periodic table.

Review Vocabulary
mass: a measure of the amount of matter an object has

New Vocabulary
- element
- atomic number
- isotope
- mass number
- atomic mass
- metal
- nonmetal
- metalloid

The Elements

Have you watched television today? TV sets are common, yet each one is a complex system. The outer case is made mostly of plastic, and the screen is made of glass. Many of the parts that conduct electricity are metals or combinations of metals. Other parts in the interior of the set contain materials that barely conduct electricity. All of the different materials have one thing in common: they are made up of even simpler materials. In fact, if you had the proper equipment, you could separate the plastics, glass, and metals into these simpler materials.

One Kind of Atom Eventually, though, you would separate the materials into groups of atoms. At that point, you would have a collection of elements. An **element** is matter made of only one kind of atom. At least 115 elements are known and about 90 of them occur naturally on Earth. These elements make up gases in the air, minerals in rocks, and liquids such as water. Examples of naturally occurring elements include the oxygen and nitrogen in the air you breathe and the metals gold, silver, aluminum, and iron. The other elements are known as synthetic elements. These elements have been made in nuclear reactions by scientists with machines called particle accelerators, like the one shown in **Figure 10**. Some synthetic elements have important uses in medical testing and are found in smoke detectors and heart pacemaker batteries.

Figure 10 The Tevatron has a circumference of 6.3 km—a distance that allows particles to accelerate to high speeds. These high-speed collisions can create synthetic elements.

266

Figure 11 When you look for information in the library, a system of organization called the Dewey Decimal Classification System helps you find a book quickly and efficiently.

Dewey Decimal Classification System	
000	Computers, information and general reference
100	Philosophy and psychology
200	Religion
300	Social sciences
400	Languages
500	Science
600	Technology
700	Arts and recreation
800	Literature
900	History and geography

The Periodic Table

Suppose you go to a library, like the one shown in **Figure 11,** to look up information for a school assignment. How would you find the information? You could look randomly on shelves as you walk up and down rows of books, but the chances of finding your book would be slim. To avoid such haphazard searching, some libraries use the Dewey Decimal Classification System to categorize and organize their volumes and to help you find books quickly and efficiently.

Charting the Elements Chemists have created a chart called the periodic table of the elements to help them organize and display the elements. **Figure 12** shows how scientists changed their model of the periodic table over time.

On the inside back cover of this book, you will find a modern version of the periodic table. Each element is represented by a chemical symbol that contains one to three letters. The symbols are a form of chemical shorthand that chemists use to save time and space—on the periodic table as well as in written formulas. The symbols are an important part of an international system that is understood by scientists everywhere.

The elements are organized on the periodic table by their properties. There are rows and columns that represent relationships between the elements. The rows in the table are called periods. The elements in a row have the same number of energy levels. The columns are called groups. The elements in each group have similar properties related to their structure. They also tend to form similar bonds.

Topic: New Elements
Visit in7.msscience.com for Web links to information about new elements.

Activity Research physical properties of two synthetic elements.

SECTION 2 The Simplest Matter **267**

NATIONAL GEOGRAPHIC VISUALIZING THE PERIODIC TABLE

Figure 12

The familiar periodic table that adorns many science classrooms is based on a number of earlier efforts to identify and classify the elements. In the 1790s, one of the first lists of elements and their compounds was compiled by French chemist Antoine-Laurent Lavoisier, who is shown in the background picture with his wife and assistant, Marie Anne. Three other tables are shown here.

John Dalton (Britain, 1803) used symbols to represent elements. His table also assigned masses to each element.

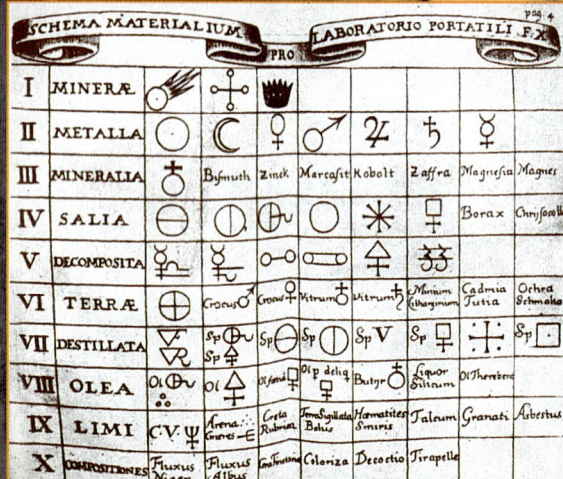

An early alchemist put together this table of elements and compounds. Some of the symbols have their origin in astrology.

Dmitri Mendeleev (Russia, 1869) arranged the 63 elements known to exist at that time into groups based on their chemical properties and atomic weights. He left gaps for elements he predicted were yet to be discovered.

Identifying Characteristics

Each element is different and has unique properties. These differences can be described in part by looking at the relationships between the atomic particles in each element. The periodic table contains numbers that describe these relationships.

Number of Protons and Neutrons Look up the element chlorine on the periodic table found on the inside back cover of your book. Cl is the symbol for chlorine, as shown in **Figure 13**, but what are the two numbers? The top number is the element's *atomic number*. It tells you the number of protons in the nucleus of each atom of that element. Every atom of chlorine, for example, has 17 protons in its nucleus.

 *What are the atomic numbers for Cs, Ne, Pb, and U?*

Isotopes Although the number of protons changes from element to element, every atom of the same element has the same number of protons. However, the number of neutrons can vary even for one element. For example, some chlorine atoms have 18 neutrons in their nucleus while others have 20. These two types of chlorine atoms are chlorine-35 and chlorine-37. They are called *isotopes* (I suh tohps), which are atoms of the same element that have different numbers of neutrons.

You can tell someone exactly which isotope you are referring to by using its mass number. An atom's *mass number* is the number of protons plus the number of neutrons it contains. The numbers 35 and 37, which were used to refer to chlorine, are mass numbers. Hydrogen has three isotopes with mass numbers of 1, 2, and 3. They are shown in **Figure 14**. Each hydrogen atom always has one proton, but in each isotope the number of neutrons is different.

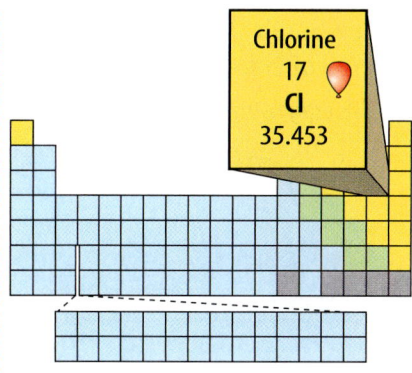

Figure 13 The periodic table block for chlorine shows its symbol, atomic number, and atomic mass.
Determine *if chlorine atoms are more or less massive than carbon atoms.*

Figure 14 Three isotopes of hydrogen are known to exist. They have zero, one, and two neutrons in addition to their one proton. Protium, with only the one proton, is the most abundant isotope.

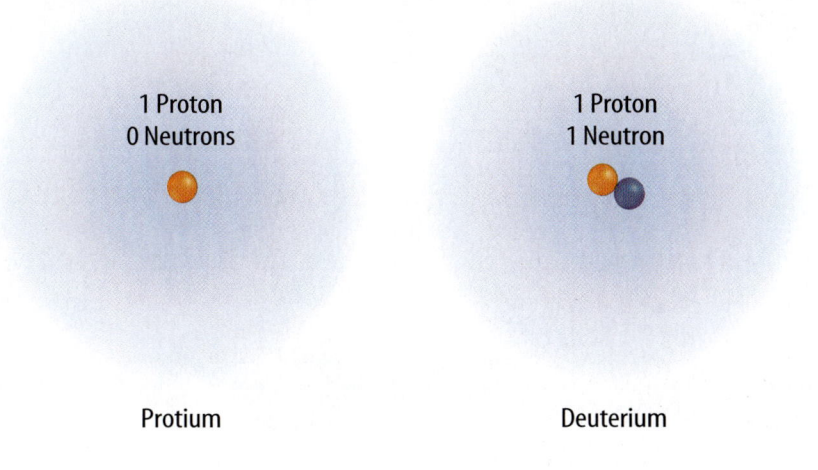
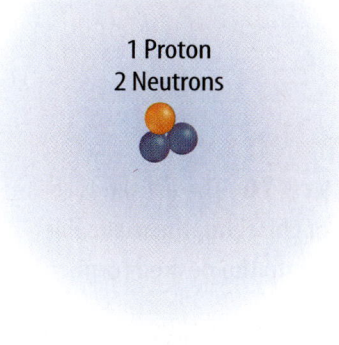

Protium   Deuterium   Tritium

SECTION 2 The Simplest Matter   **269**

Circle Graph Showing Abundance of Chlorine Isotopes
Average atomic mass = 35.45 u

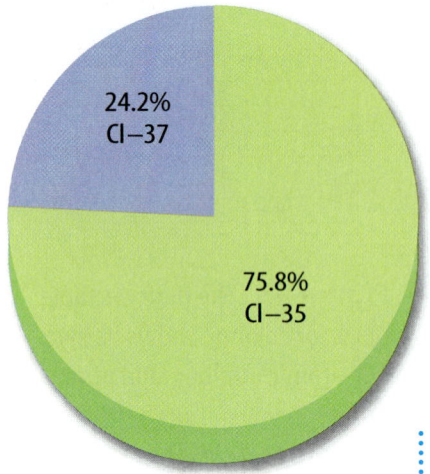

Figure 15 If you have 1,000 atoms of chlorine, about 758 will be chlorine-35 and have a mass of 34.97 u each. About 242 will be chlorine-37 and have a mass of 36.97 u each. The total mass of the 1,000 atoms is 35,454 u, so the average mass of one chlorine atom is about 35.45 u.

Atomic Mass The **atomic mass** is the weighted average mass of the isotopes of an element. The atomic mass is the number found below the element symbol in **Figure 13.** The unit that scientists use for atomic mass is called the atomic mass unit, which is given the symbol u. It is defined as 1/12 the mass of a carbon-12 atom.

The calculation of atomic mass takes into account the different isotopes of the element. Chlorine's atomic mass of 35.45 u could be confusing because there aren't any chlorine atoms that have that exact mass. About 76 percent of chlorine atoms are chlorine-35 and about 24 percent are chlorine-37, as shown in **Figure 15.** The weighted average mass of all chlorine atoms is 35.45 u.

Classification of Elements

Elements fall into three general categories—metals, metalloids (ME tuh loydz), and nonmetals. The elements in each category have similar properties.

Metals generally have a shiny or metallic luster and are good conductors of heat and electricity. All metals, except mercury, are solids at room temperature. Metals are malleable (MAL yuh bul), which means they can be bent and pounded into various shapes. The beautiful form of the shell-shaped basin in **Figure 16** is a result of this characteristic. Metals are also ductile, which means they can be drawn into wires without breaking. If you look at the periodic table, you can see that most of the elements are metals.

Figure 16 The artisan is chasing, or chiseling, the malleable metal into the desired form.

270 CHAPTER 9 Atoms, Elements, and the Periodic Table

Other Elements **Nonmetals** are elements that are usually dull in appearance. Most are poor conductors of heat and electricity. Many are gases at room temperature, and bromine is a liquid. The solid nonmetals are generally brittle, meaning they cannot change shape easily without breaking. The nonmetals are essential to the chemicals of life. More than 97 percent of your body is made up of various nonmetals, as shown in **Figure 17.** You can see that, except for hydrogen, the nonmetals are found on the right side of the periodic table.

Metalloids are elements that have characteristics of metals and nonmetals. On the periodic table, metalloids are found between the metals and nonmetals. All metalloids are solids at room temperature. Some metalloids are shiny and many are conductors, but they are not as good at conducting heat and electricity as metals are. Some metalloids, such as silicon, are used to make the electronic circuits in computers, televisions, and other electronic devices.

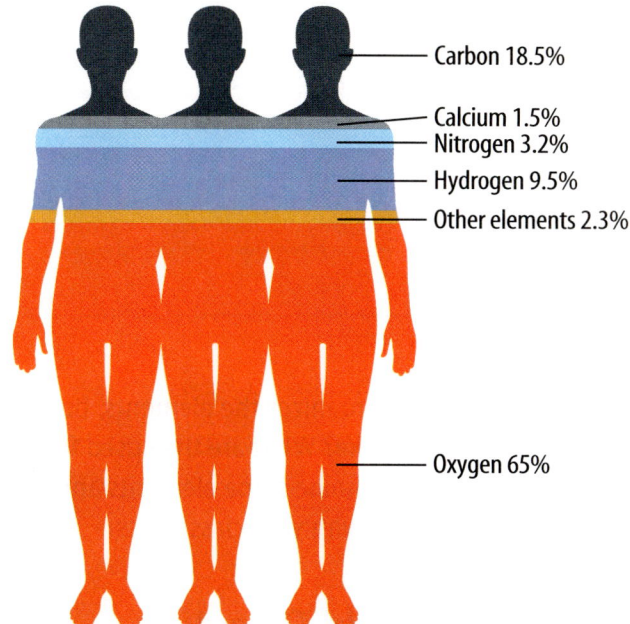

Figure 17 You are made up of mostly nonmetals.

 What is a metalloid?

section 2 review

Summary

The Elements
- An element is matter made of only one type of atom.
- Some elements occur naturally on Earth. Synthetic elements are made in nuclear reactions in particle accelerators.
- Elements are divided into three categories based on certain properties.

The Periodic Table
- The periodic table arranges and displays all known elements in an orderly way.
- Each element has a chemical symbol.

Identifying Characteristics
- Each element has a unique number of protons, called the atomic mass number.
- Isotopes of an element are important when determining the atomic mass of an element.

Self Check

1. **Explain** some of the uses of metals based on their properties.
2. **Describe** the difference between atomic number and atomic mass.
3. **Define** the term *isotope*. Explain how two isotopes of an element are different.
4. **Identify** the isotopes of hydrogen.
5. **Think Critically** Describe how to find the atomic number for the element oxygen. Explain what this information tells you about oxygen.

Applying Math

6. **Simple Equation** An atom of niobium has a mass number of 93. How many neutrons are in the nucleus of this atom? An atom of phosphorus has 15 protons and 15 neutrons in the nucleus. What is the mass number of this isotope?

Elements and the Periodic Table

The periodic table organizes the elements, but what do they look like? What are they used for? In this lab, you'll examine some elements and share your findings with your classmates.

Real-World Question
What are some of the characteristics and purposes of the chemical elements?

Goals
- **Classify** the chemical elements.
- **Organize** the elements into the groups and periods of the periodic table.

Materials
colored markers
large index cards
Merck Index
encyclopedia
*other reference materials
large bulletin board
8½-in × 14-in paper
thumbtacks
*pushpins

*Alternate materials

Safety Precaution

WARNING: *Use care when handling sharp objects.*

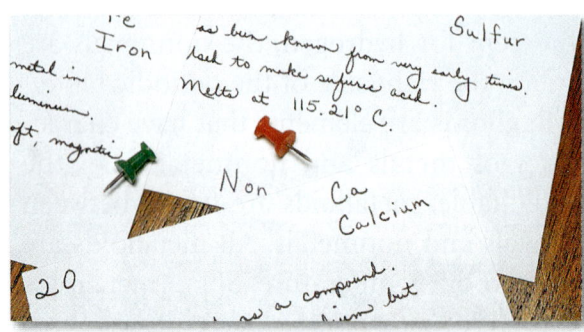

Procedure
1. Select the assigned number of elements from the list provided by your teacher.
2. **Design** an index card for each of your selected elements. On each card, mark the element's atomic number in the upper left-hand corner and write its symbol and name in the upper right-hand corner.
3. **Research** each of the elements and write several sentences on the card about its appearance, its other properties, and its uses.
4. **Classify** each of your elements as a metal, a metalloid, or a nonmetal based upon its properties.
5. **Write** the appropriate classification on each of your cards using the colored marker chosen by your teacher.
6. Work with your classmates to make a large periodic table. Use thumbtacks to attach your cards to a bulletin board in their proper positions on the periodic table.
7. **Draw** your own periodic table. Place the elements' symbols and atomic numbers in the proper locations on your table.

Conclude and Apply
1. **Interpret** the class data and classify the elements into the categories metal, metalloid, and nonmetal. Highlight each category in a different color on your periodic table.
2. **Predict** the properties of a yet-undiscovered element located directly under francium on the periodic table.

section 3

Standard—7.1.5: Identify some important contributions to the advancement of science... that have been made by different kinds of people, in different cultures, at different times.

Compounds and Mixtures

Substances

Scientists classify matter in several ways that depend on what it is made of and how it behaves. For example, matter that has the same composition and properties throughout is called a **substance**. Elements, such as a bar of gold or a sheet of aluminum, are substances. When different elements combine, other substances are formed.

Compounds What do you call the colorless liquid that flows from the kitchen faucet? You probably call it water, but maybe you've seen it written H_2O. The elements hydrogen and oxygen exist as separate, colorless gases. However, these two elements can combine, as shown in **Figure 18,** to form the compound water, which is different from the elements that make it up. A **compound** is a substance whose smallest unit is made up of atoms of more than one element bonded together.

Compounds often have properties that are different from the elements that make them up. Water is distinctly different from the elements that make it up. It is also different from another compound made from the same elements. Have you ever used hydrogen peroxide (H_2O_2) to disinfect a cut? This compound is a different combination of hydrogen and oxygen and has different properties from those of water.

Water is a nonirritating liquid that is used for bathing, drinking, cooking, and much more. In contrast, hydrogen peroxide carries warnings on its labels such as *Keep Hydrogen Peroxide Out of the Eyes*. Although it is useful in solutions for cleaning contact lenses, it is not safe for your eyes as it comes from the bottle.

as you read

What **You'll Learn**
- **Identify** the characteristics of a compound.
- **Compare and contrast** different types of mixtures.

Why **It's Important**
The food you eat, the materials you use, and all matter can be classified by compounds or mixtures.

Review Vocabulary
formula: shows which elements and how many atoms of each make up a compound

New Vocabulary
• substance • mixture
• compound

Figure 18 A space shuttle is powered by the reaction between liquid hydrogen and liquid oxygen. The reaction produces a large amount of energy and the compound water.
Explain *why a car that burns hydrogen rather than gasoline would be friendly to the environment.*

Figure 19 The elements hydrogen and oxygen can form two compounds—water and hydrogen peroxide. Note the differences in their structure.

Mini LAB

Comparing Compounds

Procedure

1. Collect the following substances—**granular sugar, rubbing alcohol,** and **salad oil.**
2. Observe the color, appearance, and state of each substance. Note the thickness or texture of each substance.
3. Stir a spoonful of each substance into separate **glasses** of **hot tap water** and observe.

Analysis

1. Compare the different properties of the substances.
2. The formulas of the three substances are made of only carbon, hydrogen, and oxygen. Infer how they can have different properties.

Compounds Have Formulas What's the difference between water and hydrogen peroxide? H_2O is the chemical formula for water, and H_2O_2 is the formula for hydrogen peroxide. The formula tells you which elements make up a compound as well as how many atoms of each element are present. Look at **Figure 19.** The subscript number written below and to the right of each element's symbol tells you how many atoms of that element exist in one unit of that compound. For example, hydrogen peroxide has two atoms of hydrogen and two atoms of oxygen. Water is made up of two atoms of hydrogen and one atom of oxygen.

Carbon dioxide, CO_2, is another common compound. Carbon dioxide is made up of one atom of carbon and two atoms of oxygen. Carbon and oxygen also can form the compound carbon monoxide, CO, which is a gas that is poisonous to all warm-blooded animals. As you can see, no subscript is used when only one atom of an element is present. A given compound always is made of the same elements in the same proportion. For example, water always has two hydrogen atoms for every oxygen atom, no matter what the source of the water is. No matter what quantity of the compound you have, the formula of the compound always remains the same. If you have 12 atoms of hydrogen and six atoms of oxygen, the compound is still written H_2O, but you have six molecules of H_2O (6 H_2O), not $H_{12}O_6$. The formula of a compound communicates its identity and makeup to any scientist in the world.

Reading Check *Propane has three carbon and eight hydrogen atoms. What is its chemical formula?*

274 CHAPTER 9 Atoms, Elements, and the Periodic Table

Mixtures

When two or more substances (elements or compounds) come together but don't combine to make a new substance, a **mixture** results. Unlike compounds, the proportions of the substances in a mixture can be changed without changing the identity of the mixture. For example, if you put some sand into a bucket of water, you have a mixture of sand and water. If you add more sand or more water, it's still a mixture of sand and water. Its identity has not changed. Air is another mixture. Air is a mixture of nitrogen, oxygen, and other gases, which can vary at different times and places. Whatever the proportion of gases, it is still air. Even your blood is a mixture that can be separated, as shown in **Figure 20,** by a machine called a centrifuge.

 *How do the proportions of a mixture relate to its identity?*

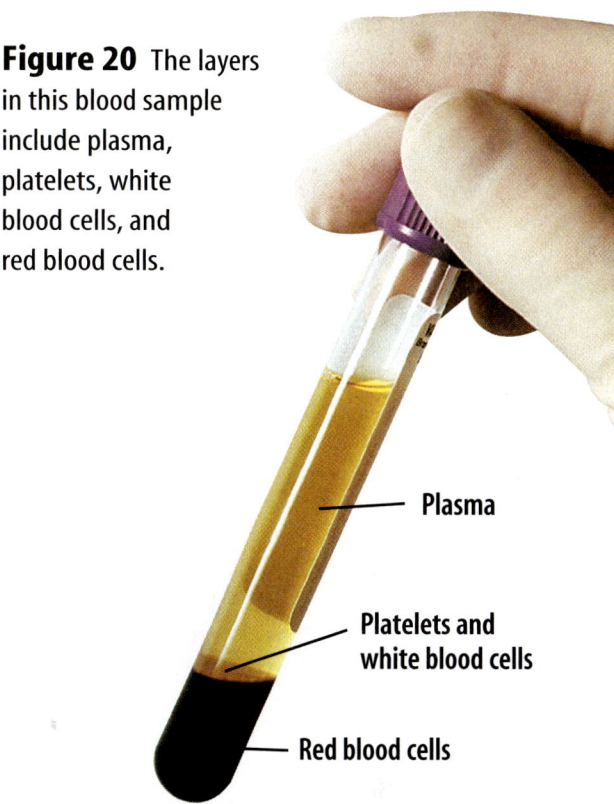

Figure 20 The layers in this blood sample include plasma, platelets, white blood cells, and red blood cells.

Applying Science

What's the best way to desalt ocean water?

You can't drink ocean water because it contains salt and other suspended materials. Or can you? In many areas of the world where drinking water is in short supply, methods for getting the salt out of salt water are being used to meet the demand for fresh water. Use your problem-solving skills to find the best method to use in a particular area.

Methods for Desalting Ocean Water

Process	Amount of Water a Unit Can Desalt in a Day (m^3)	Special Needs	Number of People Needed to Operate
Distillation	1,000 to 200,000	lots of energy to boil the water	many
Electrodialysis	10 to 4,000	stable source of electricity	1 to 2 persons

Identifying the Problem

The table above compares desalting methods. In distillation, the ocean water is heated. Pure water boils off and is collected, and the salt is left behind. Electrodialysis uses an electric current to pull salt particles out of water.

Solving the Problem

1. What method(s) might you use to desalt the water for a large population where energy is plentiful?
2. What method(s) would you choose to use in a single home?

SECTION 3 Compounds and Mixtures

Figure 21 Mixtures are part of your everyday life.

Your blood is a mixture made up of elements and compounds. It contains white blood cells, red blood cells, water, and a number of dissolved substances. The different parts of blood can be separated and used by doctors in different ways. The proportions of the substances in your blood change daily, but the mixture does not change its identity.

Separating Mixtures Sometimes you can use a liquid to separate a mixture of solids. For example, if you add water to a mixture of sugar and sand, only the sugar dissolves in the water. The sand then can be separated from the sugar and water by pouring the mixture through a filter. Heating the remaining solution will separate the water from the sugar.

At other times, separating a mixture of solids of different sizes might be as easy as pouring them through successively smaller sieves or filters. A mixture of marbles, pebbles, and sand could be separated in this way.

Topic: Mixtures
Visit in7.msscience.com for Web links to information about separating mixtures.

Activity Describe the difference between mixtures and compounds.

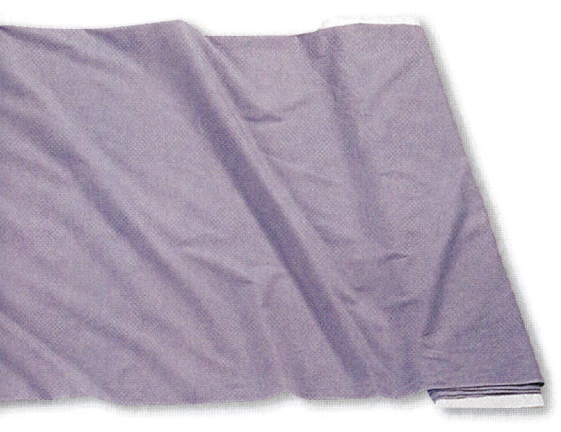

Homogeneous or Heterogeneous Mixtures, such as the ones shown in **Figure 21,** can be classified as homogeneous or heterogeneous. *Homogeneous* means "the same throughout." You can't see the different parts in this type of mixture. In fact, you might not always know that homogeneous mixtures are mixtures because you can't tell by looking. Which mixtures in **Figure 21** are homogeneous? No matter how closely you look, you can't see the individual parts that make up air or the parts of the mixture called brass in the lamp shown. Homogeneous mixtures can be solids, liquids, or gases.

A heterogeneous mixture has larger parts that are different from each other. You can see the different parts of a heterogeneous mixture, such as sand and water. How many heterogeneous mixtures are in **Figure 21?** A pepperoni and mushroom pizza is a tasty kind of heterogeneous mixture. Other examples of this kind of mixture include tacos, vegetable soup, a toy box full of toys, or a toolbox full of nuts and bolts.

Rocks and Minerals
Scientists called geologists study rocks and minerals. A mineral is composed of a pure substance. Rocks are mixtures and can be described as being homogeneous or heterogeneous. Research to learn more about rocks and minerals and note some examples of homogeneous and heterogeneous rocks in your Science Journal.

section 3 review

Summary

Substances
- A substance can be either an element or a compound.
- A compound contains more than one kind of element bonded together.
- A chemical formula shows which elements and how many atoms of each make up a compound.

Mixtures
- A mixture contains substances that are not chemically bonded together.
- There are many ways to separate mixtures, based on their physical properties.
- Homogeneous mixtures are those that are the same throughout. These types of mixtures can be solids, liquids, or gases.
- Heterogeneous mixtures have larger parts that are different from each other.

Self Check

1. **List** three examples of compounds and three examples of mixtures. Explain your choices.
2. **Determine** A container contains a mixture of sand, salt, and pebbles. How can each substance be separated from the others?
3. **Think Critically** Explain whether your breakfast was a compound, a homogeneous mixture, or a heterogeneous mixture.

Applying Skills

4. **Compare and contrast** compounds and mixtures based on what you have learned from this section.
5. **Use a Database** Use a computerized card catalog or database to find information about one element from the periodic table. Include information about the properties and uses of the mixtures and/or compounds in which the element is frequently found.

Mystery Mixture

Real-World Question

You will encounter many compounds that look alike. For example, a laboratory stockroom is filled with white powders. It is important to know what each is. In a kitchen, cornstarch, baking powder, and powdered sugar are compounds that look alike. To avoid mistaking one for another, you can learn how to identify them. Different compounds can be identified by using chemical tests. For example, some compounds react with certain liquids to produce gases. Other combinations produce distinctive colors. Some compounds have high melting points. Others have low melting points. How can the compounds in an unknown mixture be identified by experimentation?

Goals
- **Test** for the presence of certain compounds.
- **Decide** which of these compounds are present in an unknown mixture.

Materials
test tubes (4)
cornstarch
powdered sugar
baking soda
mystery mixture
small scoops (3)
dropper bottles (2)
iodine solution
white vinegar
hot plate
250-mL beaker
water (125 mL)
test-tube holder
small pie pan

Safety Precautions

WARNING: *Use caution when handling hot objects. Substances could stain or burn clothing. Be sure to point the test tube away from your face and your classmates while heating.*

278 CHAPTER 9 Atoms, Elements, and the Periodic Table

Using Scientific Methods

Procedure

1. Copy the data table into your Science Journal. Record your results carefully for each of the following steps.
2. Place a small scoopful of cornstarch on the pie pan. Do the same for the sugar and baking soda making separate piles. Add a drop of vinegar to each. Wash and dry the pan after you record your observations.
3. Again, place a small scoopful of cornstarch, sugar, and baking soda on the pie pan. Add a drop of iodine solution to each one. Wash and dry the pan after you record your observations.
4. Again place a small scoopful of each compound in a separate test tube. Hold the test tube with the test-tube holder and with an oven mitt. Gently heat the test tube in a beaker of boiling water on a hot plate.
5. Follow steps 2 through 4 to test your mystery mixture for each compound.

Identifying Presence of Compounds			
Substance to Be Tested	Fizzes with Vinegar	Turns Blue with Iodine	Melts When Heated
Cornstarch			
Sugar		Do not write in this book.	
Baking soda			
Mystery mix			

Analyze Your Data

Identify from your data table which compound(s) you have.

Conclude and Apply

1. **Describe** how you decided which substances were in your unknown mixture.
2. **Explain** how you would be able to tell if all three compounds were not in your mystery substance.
3. **Draw a Conclusion** What would you conclude if you tested baking powder from your kitchen and found that it fizzed with vinegar, turned blue with iodine, and did not melt when heated?

Make a different data table to display your results in a new way. **For more help, refer to the Science Skill Handbook.**

TIME SCIENCE AND HISTORY

SCIENCE CAN CHANGE THE COURSE OF HISTORY!

Ancient Views of Matter

Two cultures observed the world around them differently

The world's earliest scientists were people who were curious about the world around them and who tried to develop explanations for the things they observed. This type of observation and inquiry flourished in ancient cultures such as those found in India and China. Read on to see how the ancient Indians and Chinese defined matter.

Indian Ideas

To Indians living about 3,000 years ago, the world was made up of five elements: fire, air, earth, water, and ether, which they thought of as an unseen substance that filled the heavens. Building upon this concept, the early Indian philosopher Kashyapa (kah SHI ah pah) proposed that the five elements could be broken down into smaller units called parmanu (par MAH new). Parmanu were similar to atoms in that they were too small to be seen but still retained the properties of the original element. Kashyapa also believed that each type of parmanu had unique physical and chemical properties.

Parmanu of earth elements, for instance, were heavier than parmanu of air elements. The different properties of the parmanu determined the characteristics of a substance. Kashyapa's ideas about matter are similar to those of the Greek philosopher Democritus, who lived centuries after Kashyapa.

Chinese Ideas

The ancient Chinese also broke matter down into five elements: fire, wood, metal, earth, and water. Unlike the early Indians, however, the Chinese believed that the elements constantly changed form. For example, wood can be burned and thus changes to fire. Fire eventually dies down and becomes ashes, or earth. Earth gives forth metals from the ground. Dew or water collects on these metals, and the water then nurtures plants that grow into trees, or wood.

This cycle of constant change was explained in the fourth century B.C. by the philosopher Tsou Yen. Yen, who is known as the founder of Chinese scientific thought, wrote that all changes that took place in nature were linked to changes in the five elements.

Research Write a brief paragraph that compares and contrasts the ancient Indian and Chinese views of matter. How are they different? Similar? Which is closer to the modern view of matter? Explain.

For more information, visit in7.msscience.com/time

Chapter 9 Study Guide

Reviewing Main Ideas

Section 1 — Structure of Matter

1. Matter is anything that occupies space and has mass.
2. Matter is made up of atoms.
3. Atoms are made of smaller parts called protons, neutrons, and electrons.
4. Many models of atoms have been created as scientists try to discover and define the atom's internal structure. Today's model has a central nucleus with the protons and neutrons, and an electron cloud surrounding it.

Section 2 — The Simplest Matter

1. Elements are the building blocks of matter.

2. An element's atomic number tells how many protons its atoms contain, and its atomic mass tells the average mass of its atoms.
3. Isotopes are two or more atoms of the same element that have different numbers of neutrons.

Section 3 — Compounds and Mixtures

1. Compounds are substances that are produced when elements combine. Compounds contain specific proportions of the elements that make them up.
2. Mixtures are combinations of compounds and elements that have not formed new substances. Their proportions can change.

Visualizing Main Ideas

Copy and complete the following concept map.

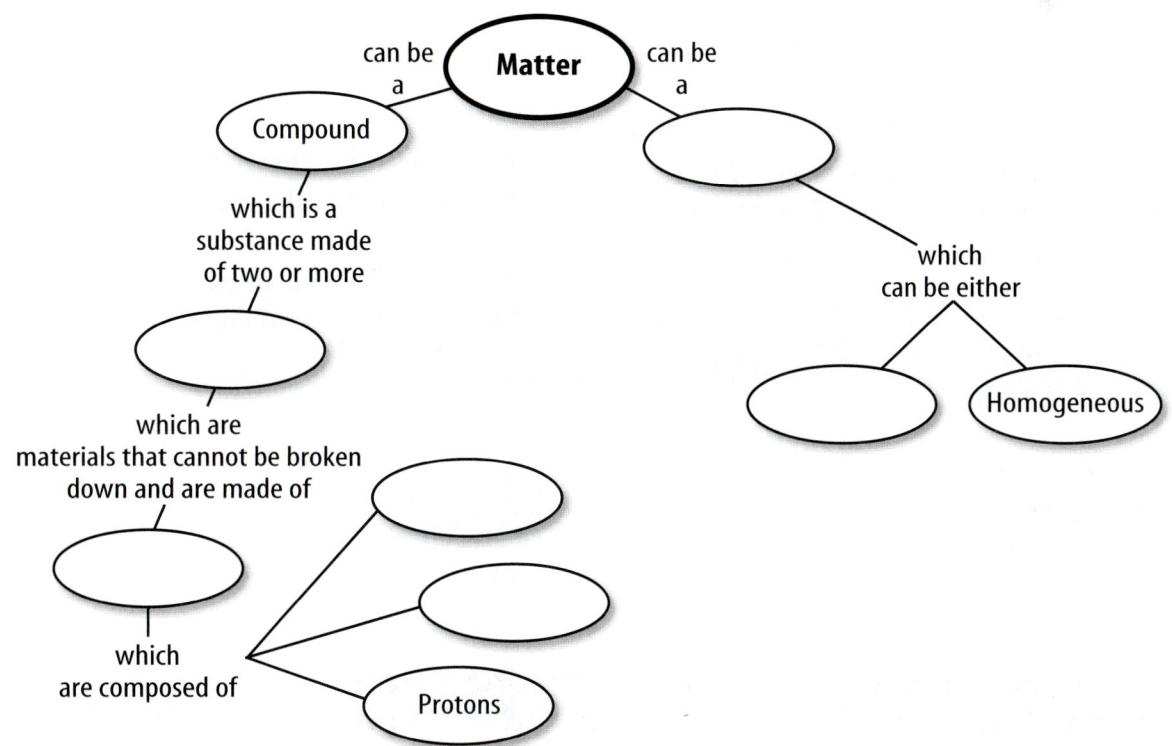

Science online in7.msscience.com/interactive_tutor

Chapter 9 Review

Using Vocabulary

atom p. 259
atomic mass p. 270
atomic number p. 269
compound p. 273
electron p. 262
element p. 266
isotope p. 269
law of conservation of matter p. 260
mass number p. 269
matter p. 258
metal p. 270
metalloid p. 271
mixture p. 275
neutron p. 264
nonmetal p. 271
nucleus p. 263
proton p. 263
substance p. 273

Fill in the blanks with the correct vocabulary word or words.

1. The _____ is the particle in the nucleus of the atom that carries a positive charge and is counted to identify the atomic number.

2. The new substance formed when elements combine chemically is a(n) _____.

3. Anything that has mass and takes up space is _____.

4. The particles in the atom that account for most of the mass of the atom are protons and _____.

5. Elements that are shiny, malleable, ductile, good conductors of heat and electricity, and make up most of the periodic table are _____.

Checking Concepts

Choose the word or phrase that best answers the question.

6. What is a solution an example of?
   A) element
   B) heterogeneous mixture
   C) compound
   D) homogeneous mixture

7. The nucleus of one atom contains 12 protons and 12 neutrons, while the nucleus of another atom contains 12 protons and 16 neutrons. What are the atoms?
   A) chromium atoms
   B) two different elements
   C) two isotopes of an element
   D) negatively charged

8. What is a compound?
   A) a mixture of chemicals and elements
   B) a combination of two or more elements
   C) anything that has mass and occupies space
   D) the building block of matter

9. What does the atom consist of?
   A) electrons, protons, and alpha particles
   B) neutrons and protons
   C) electrons, protons, and neutrons
   D) elements, protons, and electrons

10. In an atom, where is an electron located?
    A) in the nucleus with the proton
    B) on the periodic table of the elements
    C) with the neutron
    D) in a cloudlike formation surrounding the nucleus

11. How is matter defined?
    A) the negative charge in an atom
    B) anything that has mass and occupies space
    C) the mass of the nucleus
    D) sound, light, and energy

12. What are two atoms that have the same number of protons called?
    A) metals
    B) nonmetals
    C) isotopes
    D) metalloids

13. Which is a heterogeneous mixture?
    A) air
    B) brass
    C) a salad
    D) apple juice

282 CHAPTER REVIEW

in7.msscience.com/vocabulary_puzzlemaker

chapter 9 Review

Use the illustration below to answer questions 14 and 15.

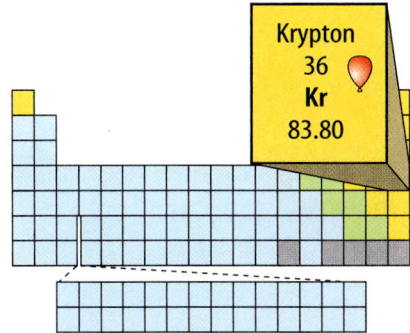

14. Using the figure above, krypton has
    A) an atomic number of 84.
    B) an atomic number of 36.
    C) an atomic mass of 36.
    D) an atomic mass of 72.

15. From the figure, the element krypton is
    A) a solid.   C) a mixture.
    B) a liquid.   D) a gas.

Thinking Critically

16. **Analyze Information** A chemical formula is written to indicate the makeup of a compound. What is the ratio of sulfur atoms to oxygen atoms in SO_2?

17. **Determine** which element contains seven protons.

18. **Describe** what happens to an element when it becomes part of a compound.

19. **Explain** how cobalt-60 and cobalt-59 can be the same element but have different mass numbers.

20. **Analyze Information** What did Rutherford's gold foil experiment tell scientists about atomic structure?

21. **Predict** Suppose Rutherford had bombarded aluminum foil with alpha particles instead of the gold foil he used in his experiment. What observations do you predict Rutherford would have made? Explain your prediction.

22. **Draw Conclusions** You are shown a liquid that looks the same throughout. You're told that it contains more than one type of element and that the proportion of each varies throughout the liquid. Is this an element, a compound, or a mixture?

Use the illustrations below to answer question 23.

23. **Interpret Scientific Illustrations** Look at the two carbon atoms above. Explain whether or not the atoms are isotopes.

24. **Explain** how the atomic mass of an element is determined.

Performance Activities

25. **Newspaper Article** Research the source, composition, and properties of asbestos. Why was it used in the past? Why is it a health hazard now? What is being done about it? Write a newspaper article to share your findings.

Applying Math

26. **Atomic Mass** Krypton has six naturally occurring isotopes with atomic masses of 78, 80, 82, 83, 84, and 86. Make a table of the number of protons, electrons, and neutrons in each isotope.

27. **Atomic Ratio** A researcher is analyzing two different compounds, sulfuric acid (H_2SO_4) and hydrogen peroxide (H_2O_2). What is the ratio of hydrogen to oxygen in sulfuric acid? What is the ratio of hydrogen to oxygen in hydrogen peroxide?

chapter 9 Indiana

 The assessed Indiana standard appears above the question.

Record your answers on the answer sheet provided by your teacher or on a sheet of paper.

Part 1 Multiple Choice

7.1.5

1. Which scientist introduced the idea that matter is made up of tiny, individual bits called atoms?

   A Chadwick
   B Democritus
   C Rutherford
   D Thomson

2. The periodic table block shown below lists properties of the element chlorine.

   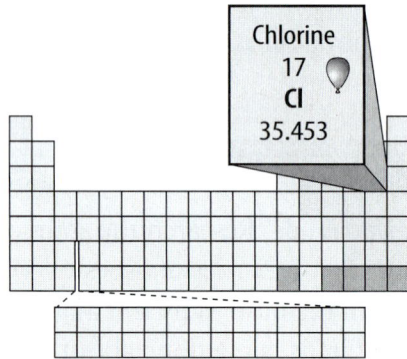

   What does the number 17 represent?

   A number of electrons
   B number of isotopes
   C number of neutrons
   D number of protons

Test-Taking Tip

Full Understanding Read each question carefully for full understanding.

7.1.5

3. Which scientist envisioned the atom as a ball of positive charge with electrons embedded in it?

   A Crookes
   B Dalton
   C Rutherford
   D Thomson

The illustrations below show three nuclei.

1 Proton   1 Proton   1 Proton
0 Neutrons   1 Neutron   2 Neutrons

4. Which correctly identifies the three nuclei?

   A hydrogen, lithium, sodium
   B hydrogen, helium, lithium
   C hydrogen, helium, helium
   D hydrogen, hydrogen, hydrogen

5. What is the mass number for each of the nuclei shown in the illustration above?

   A 0, 1, 2
   B 1, 1, 1
   C 1, 2, 2
   D 1, 2, 3

284 INDIANA

6. Which are found close to the right side of the periodic table?

   A nonmetals

   B metals

   C metalloids

   D lanthanides

7. Which is a characteristic that is typical of a solid, nonmetal element?

   A brittle

   B good electrical conductor

   C good heat conductor

   D shiny

8. The illustration below shows atoms of two compounds that are combined without making a new compound.

   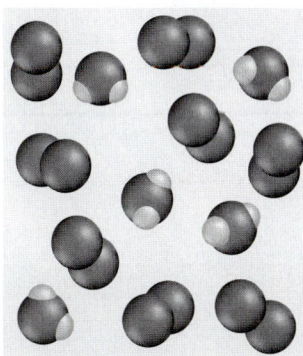

   What term describes this combination?

   A compound

   B element

   C mixture

   D substance

Part 2 Constructed Response

9. What are the rows and columns on the periodic table called? How are elements in the rows similar, and how are elements in the columns similar?

10. Describe three possible methods for separating mixtures. Give an example for each method.

The illustration below shows Rutherford's gold foil experiment.

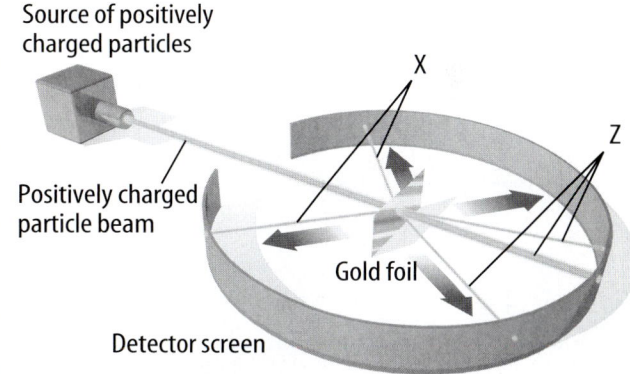

11. What has happened to the positively charged particles labeled Z? What has happened to the positively charged particles labeled X? How is this different from what Rutherford expected?

12. How does the structure of the atom explain why particles traveled in both paths Z and X above?

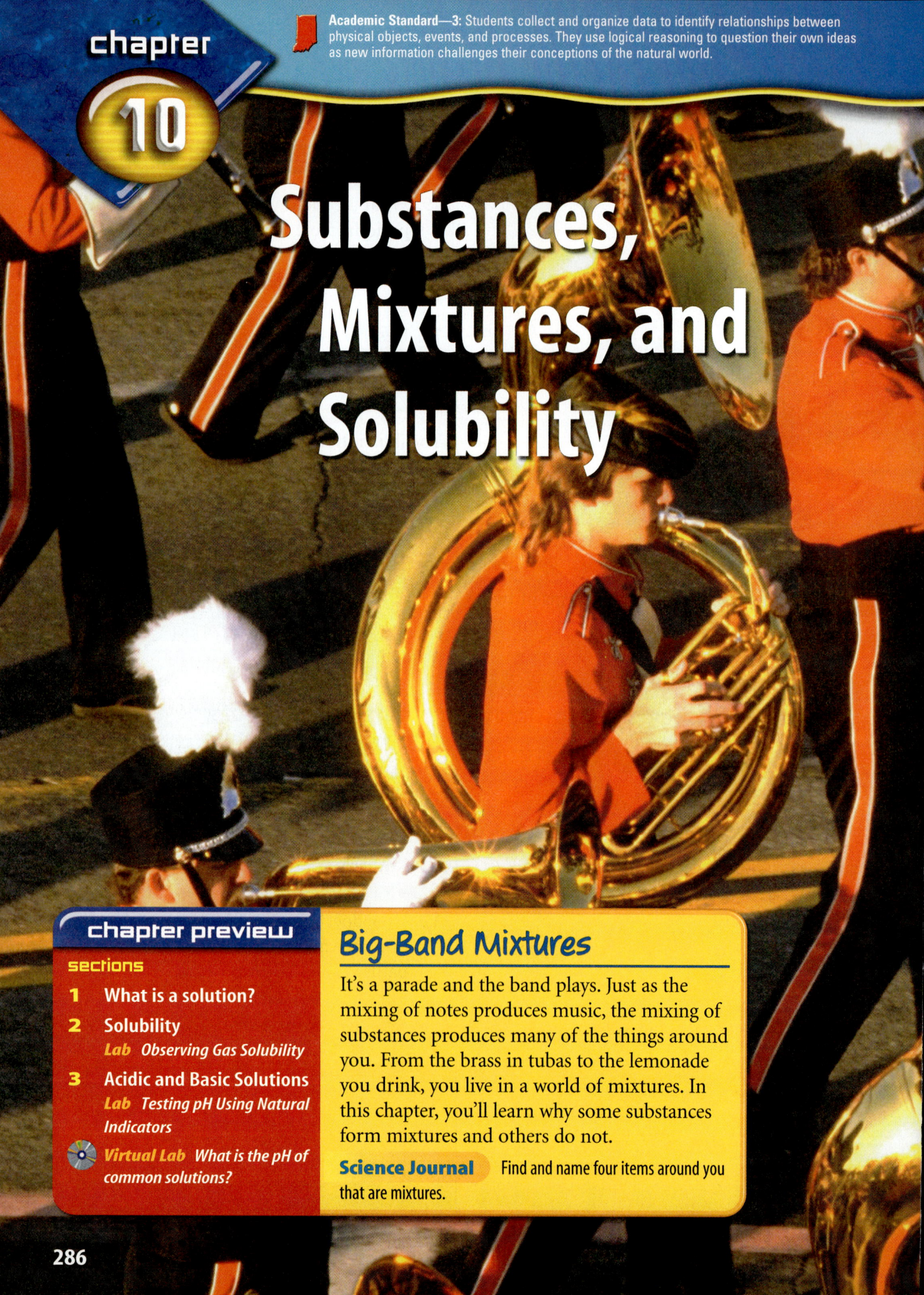

chapter 10

Academic Standard—3: Students collect and organize data to identify relationships between physical objects, events, and processes. They use logical reasoning to question their own ideas as new information challenges their conceptions of the natural world.

Substances, Mixtures, and Solubility

chapter preview

sections

1. What is a solution?
2. Solubility
   Lab Observing Gas Solubility
3. Acidic and Basic Solutions
   Lab Testing pH Using Natural Indicators
   Virtual Lab What is the pH of common solutions?

Big-Band Mixtures

It's a parade and the band plays. Just as the mixing of notes produces music, the mixing of substances produces many of the things around you. From the brass in tubas to the lemonade you drink, you live in a world of mixtures. In this chapter, you'll learn why some substances form mixtures and others do not.

Science Journal Find and name four items around you that are mixtures.

Start-Up Activities

Particle Size and Dissolving Rates

Why do drink mixes come in powder form? What would happen if you dropped a big chunk of drink mix into the water? Would it dissolve quickly? Powdered drink mix dissolves faster in water than chunks do because it is divided into smaller particles, exposing more of the mix to the water. See for yourself how particle size affects the rate at which a substance dissolves.

1. Pour 400 mL of water into each of two 600-mL beakers.
2. Carefully grind a bouillon cube into powder using a mortar and pestle.
3. Place the bouillon powder into one beaker and drop a whole bouillon cube into the second beaker.
4. Stir the water in each beaker for 10 s and observe.
5. **Think Critically** Write a paragraph in your Science Journal comparing the color of the two liquids and the amount of undissolved bouillon at the bottom of each beaker. How does the particle size affect the rate at which a substance dissolves?

Solutions Make the following Foldable to help classify solutions based on their common features.

STEP 1 **Fold** a vertical sheet of paper from side to side. Make the front edge about 1.25 cm shorter than the back edge.

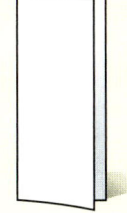

STEP 2 **Turn** lengthwise and **fold** into thirds.

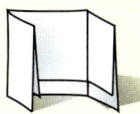

STEP 3 **Unfold and cut** only the top layer along both folds to make three tabs.

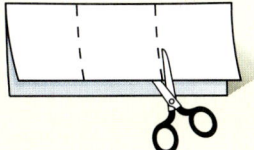

STEP 4 **Label** each tab as shown.

Find Main Ideas As you read the chapter, classify solutions based on their states and list them under the appropriate tabs. On your Foldable, circle the solutions that are acids and underline the solutions that are bases.

Preview this chapter's content and activities at
in7.msscience.com

287

section 1

Standard—7.3.13: Explain that many substances dissolve in water. Understand that the presence of these substances often affects the rates of reactions that are occurring in the water as compared to the same reactions occurring in the water in the absence of the substance.

What is a solution?

as you read

What You'll Learn
- **Distinguish** between substances and mixtures.
- **Describe** two different types of mixtures.
- **Explain** how solutions form.
- **Describe** different types of solutions.

Why It's Important
The air you breathe, the water you drink, and even parts of your body are all solutions.

Review Vocabulary
proton: positively charged particle located in the nucleus of an atom

New Vocabulary
- substance
- heterogeneous mixture
- homogeneous mixture
- solution
- solute
- solvent
- precipitate

Substances

Water, salt water, and pulpy orange juice have some obvious differences. These differences can be explained by chemistry. Think about pure water. No matter what you do to it physically—freeze it, boil it, stir it, or strain it—it still is water. On the other hand, if you boil salt water, the water turns to gas and leaves the salt behind. If you strain pulpy orange juice, it loses its pulp. How does chemistry explain these differences? The answer has to do with the chemical compositions of the materials.

Atoms and Elements Recall that atoms are the basic building blocks of matter. Each atom has unique chemical and physical properties which are determined by the number of protons it has. For example, all atoms that have eight protons are oxygen atoms. A **substance** is matter that has the same fixed composition and properties. It can't be broken down into simpler parts by ordinary physical processes, such as boiling, grinding, or filtering. Only a chemical process can change a substance into one or more new substances. **Table 1** lists some examples of physical and chemical processes. An element is an example of a pure substance; it cannot be broken down into simpler substances. The number of protons in an element, like oxygen, are fixed—it cannot change unless the element changes.

Compounds Water is another example of a substance. It is always water even when you boil it or freeze it. Water, however, is not an element. It is an example of a compound which is made of two or more elements that are chemically combined. Compounds also have fixed compositions. The ratio of the atoms in a compound is always the same. For example, when two hydrogen atoms combine with one oxygen atom, water is formed. All water—whether it's in the form of ice, liquid, or steam—has the same ratio of hydrogen atoms to oxygen atoms.

Table 1 Examples of Physical and Chemical Processes	
Physical Processes	**Chemical Processes**
Boiling	Burning
Changing pressure	Reacting with other chemicals
Cooling	Reacting with light
Sorting	

288 CHAPTER 10 Substances, Mixtures, and Solubility

Figure 1 Mixtures can be separated by physical processes.
Explain why the iron-sand mixture and the pulpy lemonade are not pure substances.

Separation by magnetism

Separation by straining

Mixtures

Imagine drinking a glass of salt water. You would know right away that you weren't drinking pure water. Like salt water, many things are not pure substances. Salt water is a mixture of salt and water. Mixtures are combinations of substances that are not bonded together and can be separated by physical processes. For example, you can boil salt water to separate the salt from the water. If you had a mixture of iron filings and sand, you could separate the iron filings from the sand with a magnet. **Figure 1** shows some mixtures being separated.

Unlike compounds, mixtures do not always contain the same proportions of the substances that they are composed of. Lemonade is a mixture that can be strong tasting or weak tasting, depending on the amounts of water and lemon juice that are added. It also can be sweet or sour, depending on how much sugar is added. But whether it is strong, weak, sweet, or sour, it is still lemonade.

Heterogeneous Mixtures It is easy to tell that some things are mixtures just by looking at them. A watermelon is a mixture of fruit and seeds. The seeds are not evenly spaced through the whole melon—one bite you take might not have any seeds in it and another bite might have several seeds. A type of mixture where the substances are not mixed evenly is called a **heterogeneous** (he tuh ruh JEE nee us) **mixture.** The different areas of a heterogeneous mixture have different compositions. The substances in a heterogeneous mixture are usually easy to tell apart, like the seeds from the fruit of a watermelon. Other examples of heterogeneous mixtures include a bowl of cold cereal with milk and the mixture of pens, pencils, and books in your backpack.

Science online

Topic: Desalination
Visit in7.msscience.com for Web links to information about how salt is removed from salt water to provide drinking water.

Activity Compare and contrast the two most common methods used for desalination.

SECTION 1 What is a solution? **289**

Homogeneous Mixtures Your shampoo contains many ingredients, but you can't see them when you look at the shampoo. It is the same color and texture throughout. Shampoo is an example of a homogeneous (hoh muh JEE nee us) mixture. A **homogeneous mixture** contains two or more substances that are evenly mixed on a molecular level but still are not bonded together. Another name for a homogeneous mixture is a **solution**. The sugar and water in the frozen pops shown in **Figure 2,** are a solution—the sugar is evenly distributed in the water, and you can't see the sugar.

Figure 2 Molecules of sugar and water are evenly mixed in frozen pops.

Reading Check What is another name for a homogeneous mixture?

How Solutions Form

How do you make sugar water for a hummingbird feeder? You might add sugar to water and heat the mixture until the sugar disappears. The sugar molecules would spread out until they were evenly spaced throughout the water, forming a solution. This is called dissolving. The substance that dissolves—or seems to disappear—is called the **solute**. The substance that dissolves the solute is called the **solvent**. In the hummingbird feeder solution, the solute is the sugar and the solvent is water. The substance that is present in the greatest quantity is the solvent.

Figure 3 Minerals and soap react to form soap scum, which comes out of the water solution and coats the tiles of a shower.

Forming Solids from Solutions Under certain conditions, a solute can come back out of its solution and form a solid. This process is called crystallization. Sometimes this occurs when the solution is cooled or when some of the solvent evaporates. Crystallization is the result of a physical change. When some solutions are mixed, a chemical reaction occurs, forming a solid. This solid is called a **precipitate** (prih SIH puh tayt). A precipitate is the result of a chemical change. Precipitates probably have formed in your sink or shower because of chemical reactions. Minerals that are dissolved in tap water react chemically with soap. The product of this reaction leaves the water as a precipitate called soap scum, shown in **Figure 3**.

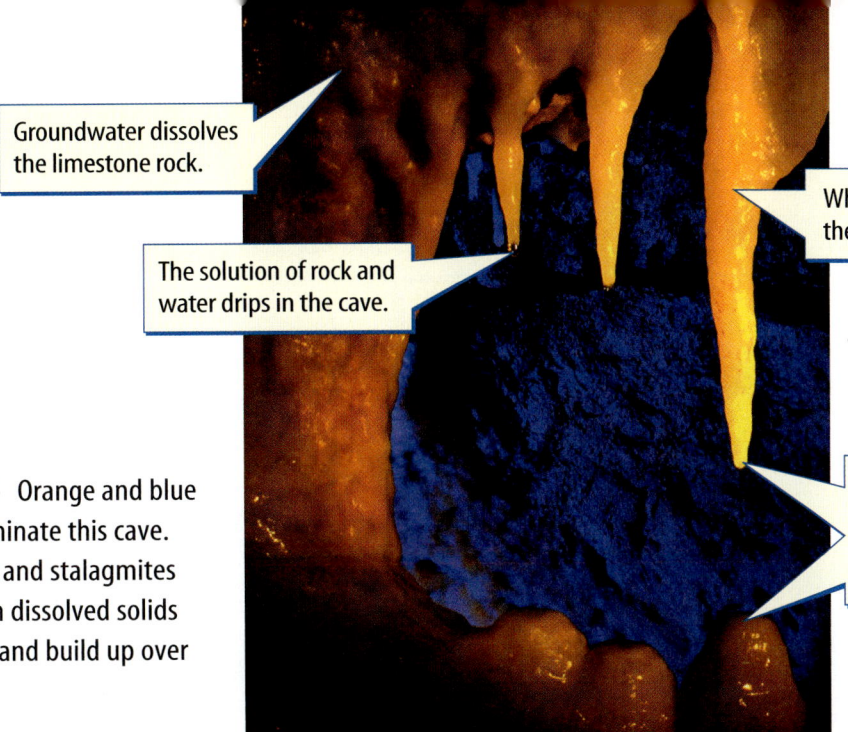

Figure 4 Orange and blue lights illuminate this cave. Stalactites and stalagmites form when dissolved solids crystallize and build up over time.

- Groundwater dissolves the limestone rock.
- The solution of rock and water drips in the cave.
- When the water evaporates, the limestone rock is left behind.
- Stalactites and stalagmites form as more rock accumulates.

INTEGRATE Environment

Stalactites and stalagmites in caves are formed from solutions, as shown in **Figure 4**. First, minerals dissolve in water as it flows through rocks at the top of the cave. This solution of water and dissolved minerals drips from the ceiling of the cave. When drops of the solution evaporate from the roof of the cave, the minerals are left behind. They create the hanging rock formations called stalactites. When drops of the solution fall onto the floor of the cave and evaporate, they form stalagmites. Very often, a stalactite develops downward while a stalagmite develops upward until the two meet. One continuous column of minerals is formed. This process will be discussed later.

Types of Solutions

So far, you've learned about types of solutions in which a solid solute dissolves in a liquid solvent. But solutions can be made up of different combinations of solids, liquids, and gases, as shown in **Table 2**.

Table 2 Examples of Common Solutions

	Solvent/State	Solute/State	State of Solution
Earth's atmosphere	nitrogen/gas	oxygen/gas carbon dioxide/gas argon/gas	gas
Ocean water	water/liquid	salt/solid oxygen/gas carbon dioxide/gas	liquid
Carbonated beverage	water/liquid	carbon dioxide/gas	liquid
Brass	copper/solid	zinc/solid	solid

SECTION 1 What is a solution?

Figure 5 Acetic acid (a liquid), carbon dioxide (a gas), and drink-mix crystals (a solid) can be dissolved in water (a liquid). **Determine** whether one liquid solution could contain all three different kinds of solute.

Liquid Solutions

You're probably most familiar with liquid solutions like the ones shown in **Figure 5,** in which the solvent is a liquid. The solute can be another liquid, a solid, or even a gas. You've already learned about liquid-solid solutions such as sugar water and salt water. When discussing solutions, the state of the solvent usually determines the state of the solution.

Liquid-Gas Solutions Carbonated beverages are liquid-gas solutions—carbon dioxide is the gaseous solute, and water is the liquid solvent. The carbon dioxide gas gives the beverage its fizz and some of its tartness. The beverage also might contain other solutes, such as the compounds that give it its flavor and color.

 *What are the solutes in a carbonated beverage?*

Liquid-Liquid Solutions In a liquid-liquid solution, both the solvent and the solute are liquids. Vinegar, which you might use to make salad dressing, is a liquid-liquid solution made of 95 percent water (the solvent) and 5 percent acetic acid (the solute).

Gaseous Solutions

In gaseous solutions, a smaller amount of one gas is dissolved in a larger amount of another gas. This is called a gas-gas solution because both the solvent and solute are gases. The air you breathe is a gaseous solution. Nitrogen makes up about 78 percent of dry air and is the solvent. The other gases are the solutes.

Figure 6 Metal alloys can contain either metal or nonmetal solutes dissolved in a metal solvent.

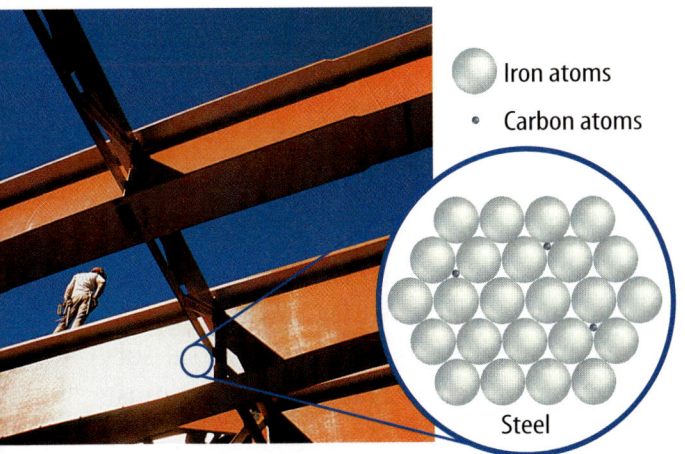

Steel is a solid solution of the metal iron and the nonmetal carbon.

Brass is a solid solution made of copper and zinc.

Solid Solutions In solid solutions, the solvent is a solid. The solute can be a solid, liquid, or gas. The most common solid solutions are solid-solid solutions—ones in which the solvent and the solute are solids. A solid-solid solution made from two or more metals is called an alloy. It's also possible to include elements that are not metals in alloys. For example, steel is an alloy that has carbon dissolved in iron. The carbon makes steel much stronger and yet more flexible than iron. Two alloys are shown in **Figure 6**.

section review

Summary

Substances
- Elements are substances that cannot be broken down into simpler substances.
- A compound is made up of two or more elements bonded together.

Mixtures and Solutions
- Mixtures are either heterogeneous or homogeneous.
- Solutions have two parts—solute and solvent.
- Crystallization and precipitation are two ways that solids are formed from solutions.

Types of Solutions
- The solutes and solvents can be solids, liquids, or gases.

Self Check

1. **Compare and contrast** substances and mixtures. Give two examples of each.
2. **Describe** how heterogeneous and homogeneous mixtures differ.
3. **Explain** how a solution forms.
4. **Identify** the common name for a solid-solid solution of metals.
5. **Think Critically** The tops of carbonated-beverage cans usually are made with a different aluminum alloy than the pull tabs are made with. Explain.

Applying Skills

6. **Compare and contrast** the following solutions: a helium-neon laser, bronze (a copper-tin alloy), cloudy ice cubes, and ginger ale.

Science online in7.msscience.com/self_check_quiz

SECTION 1 What is a solution? **293**

Standards—7.3.12: Investigate how the temperature and acidity of a solution influences reaction rates, such as those resulting in food spoilage. 7.3.13: Explain that many substances dissolve in water. Understand that the presence of these substances often affects the rates of reactions that are occurring in the water as compared to the same reactions occurring in the water in the absence of the substance.

section 2

Solubility

as you read

What You'll Learn

- **Explain** why water is a good general solvent.
- **Describe** how the structure of a compound affects which solvents it dissolves in.
- **Identify** factors that affect how much of a substance will dissolve in a solvent.
- **Describe** how temperature affects reaction rate.
- **Explain** how solute particles affect physical properties of water.

Why It's Important

How you wash your hands, clothes, and dishes depends on which substances can dissolve in other substances.

Review Vocabulary

polar bond: a bond resulting from the unequal sharing of electrons

New Vocabulary

- aqueous
- solubility
- saturated
- concentration

Water—The Universal Solvent

In many solutions, including fruit juice and vinegar, water is the solvent. A solution in which water is the solvent is called an **aqueous** (A kwee us) solution. Because water can dissolve so many different solutes, chemists often call it the universal solvent. To understand why water is such a great solvent, you must first know a few things about atoms and bonding.

Molecular Compounds When certain atoms form compounds, they share electrons. Sharing electrons is called covalent bonding. Compounds that contain covalent bonds are called molecular compounds, or molecules.

If a molecule has an even distribution of electrons, like the one in **Figure 7,** it is called nonpolar. The atoms in some molecules do not have an even distribution of electrons. For example, in a water molecule, two hydrogen atoms share electrons with a single oxygen atom. However, as **Figure 7** shows, the electrons spend more time around the oxygen atom than they spend around the hydrogen atoms. As a result, the oxygen portion of the water molecule has a partial negative charge and the hydrogen portions have a partial positive charge. The overall charge of the water molecule is neutral. Such a molecule is said to be polar, and the bonds between its atoms are called polar covalent bonds.

Figure 7 Some atoms share electrons to form covalent bonds.

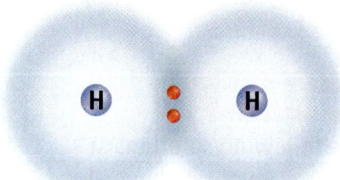

Two atoms of hydrogen share their electrons equally. Such a molecule is nonpolar.

The electrons spend more time around the oxygen atom than the hydrogen atoms. Such a molecule is polar.

(Partial negative charge)

(Partial positive charge)

294 CHAPTER 10 Substances, Mixtures, and Solubility

Ionic Bonds Some atoms do not share electrons when they join with other atoms to form compounds. Instead, these atoms lose or gain electrons. When they do, the number of protons and electrons within an atom are no longer equal, and the atom becomes positively or negatively charged. Atoms with a charge are called ions. Bonds between ions that are formed by the transfer of electrons are called ionic bonds, and the compound that is formed is called an ionic compound. Table salt is an ionic compound that is made of sodium ions and chloride ions. Each sodium atom loses one electron to a chlorine atom and becomes a positively charged sodium ion. Each chlorine atom gains one electron from a sodium atom, becoming a negatively charged chloride ion.

 *How does an ionic compound differ from a molecular compound?*

Solutions Seawater is a solution that contains nearly every element found on Earth. Most elements are present in tiny quantities. Sodium and chloride ions are the most common ions in seawater. Several gases, including oxygen, nitrogen, and carbon dioxide, also are dissolved in seawater.

How Water Dissolves Ionic Compounds Now think about the properties of water and the properties of ionic compounds as you visualize how an ionic compound dissolves in water. Because water molecules are polar, they attract positive and negative ions. The more positive part of a water molecule—where the hydrogen atoms are—is attracted to negatively charged ions. The more negative part of a water molecule—where the oxygen atom is—attracts positive ions. When an ionic compound is mixed with water, the different ions of the compound are pulled apart by the water molecules. **Figure 8** shows how sodium chloride dissolves in water.

Figure 8 Water dissolves table salt because its partial charges are attracted to the charged ions in the salt.

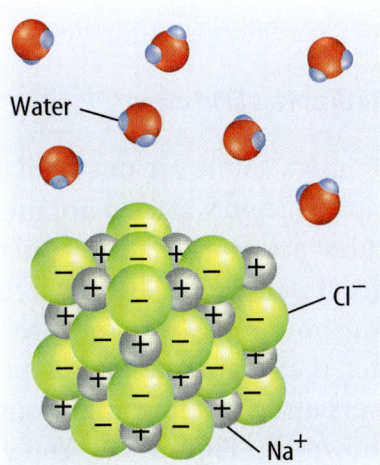
The partially negative oxygen in the water molecule is attracted to a positive sodium ion.

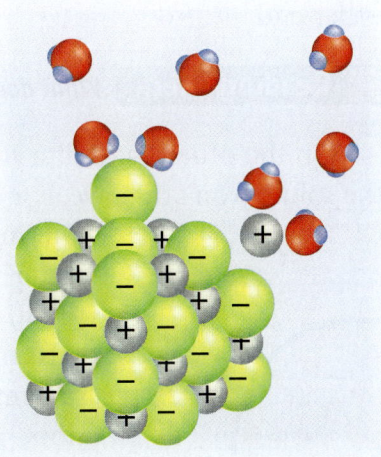
The partially positive hydrogen atoms in another water molecule are attracted to a negative chloride ion.

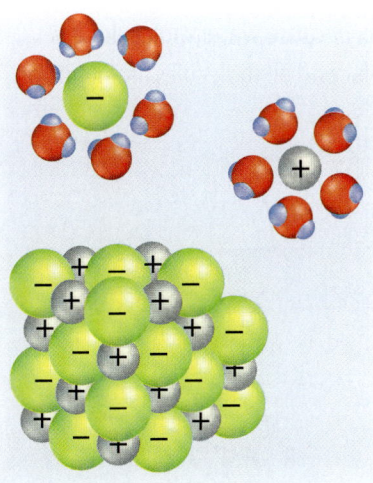
The sodium and chloride ions are pulled apart from each other, and more water molecules are attracted to them.

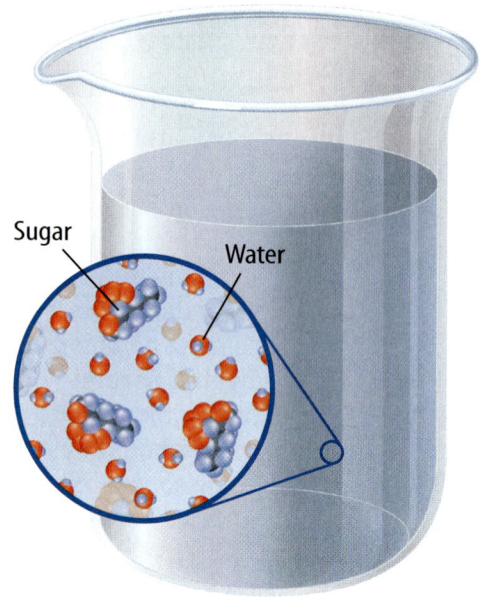

Figure 9 Sugar molecules that are dissolved in water spread out until they are spaced evenly in the water.

How Water Dissolves Molecular Compounds

Can water also dissolve molecular compounds that are not made of ions? Water does dissolve molecular compounds, such as sugar, although it doesn't break each sugar molecule apart. Water simply moves between different molecules of sugar, separating them. Like water, a sugar molecule is polar. Polar water molecules are attracted to the positive and negative portions of the polar sugar molecules. When the sugar molecules are separated by the water and spread throughout it, as **Figure 9** shows, they have dissolved.

What will dissolve?

When you stir a spoonful of sugar into iced tea, all of the sugar dissolves but none of the metal in the spoon does. Why does sugar dissolve in water, but metal does not? A substance that dissolves in another is said to be soluble in that substance. You would say that the sugar is soluble in water but the metal of the spoon is insoluble in water, because it does not dissolve readily.

Like Dissolves Like When trying to predict which solvents can dissolve which solutes, chemists use the rule of "like dissolves like." This means that polar solvents dissolve polar solutes and nonpolar solvents dissolve nonpolar solutes. In the case of sugar and water, both are made up of polar molecules, so sugar is soluble in water. In the case of salt and water, the sodium and chloride ion pair is like the water molecule because it has a positive charge at one end and a negative charge at the other end.

Reading Check *What does "like dissolves like" mean?*

On the other hand, if a solvent and a solute are not similar, the solute won't dissolve. For example, oil and water do not mix.

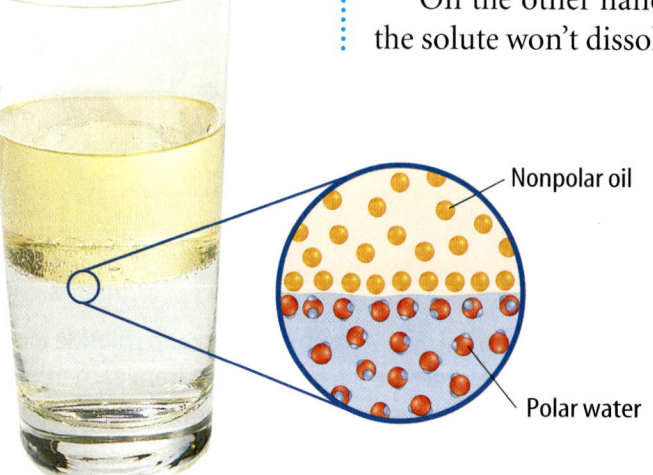

Figure 10 Water and oil do not mix because water molecules are polar and oil molecules are nonpolar.

Oil molecules are nonpolar, so polar water molecules are not attracted to them. If you pour vegetable oil into a glass of water, the oil and the water separate into layers instead of forming a solution, as shown in **Figure 10**. You've probably noticed the same thing about the oil-and-water mixtures that make up some salad dressings. The oil stays on the top. Oils generally dissolve better in solvents that have nonpolar molecules.

296 CHAPTER 10 Substances, Mixtures, and Solubility

How much will dissolve?

Even though sugar is soluble in water, if you tried to dissolve 1 kg of sugar into one small glass of water, not all of the sugar would dissolve. **Solubility** (sahl yuh BIH luh tee) is a measurement that describes how much solute dissolves in a given amount of solvent. The solubility of a material has been described as the amount of the material that can dissolve in 100 g of solvent at a given temperature. Some solutes are highly soluble, meaning that a large amount of solute can be dissolved in 100 g of solvent. For example, 63 g of potassium chromate can be dissolved in 100 g of water at 25°C. On the other hand, some solutes are not very soluble. For example, only 0.00025 g of barium sulfate will dissolve in 100 g of water at 25°C. When a substance has an extremely low solubility, like barium sulfate does in water, it usually is considered insoluble.

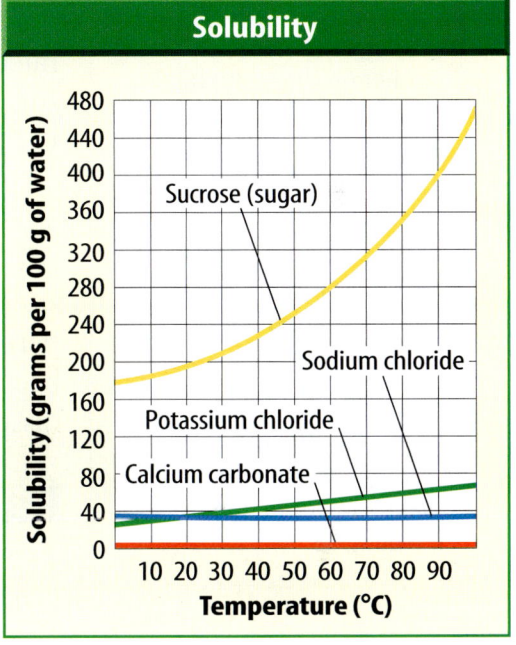

Figure 11 The solubility of some solutes changes as the temperature of the solvent increases.
Use a Graph According to the graph, is it likely that warm ocean water contains any more sodium chloride than cold ocean water does?

Reading Check *What is an example of a substance that is considered to be insoluble in water?*

Solubility in Liquid-Solid Solutions Did you notice that the temperature was included in the explanation about the amount of solute that dissolves in a quantity of solvent? The solubility of many solutes changes if you change the temperature of the solvent. For example, if you heat water, not only does the sugar dissolve at a faster rate, but more sugar can dissolve in it. However, some solutes, like sodium chloride and calcium carbonate, do not become more soluble when the temperature of water increases. The graph in **Figure 11** shows how the temperature of the solvent affects the solubility of some solutes.

Solubility in Liquid-Gas Solutions Unlike liquid-solid solutions, an increase in temperature decreases the solubility of a gas in a liquid-gas solution. You might notice this if you have ever opened a warm carbonated beverage and it bubbled up out of control while a chilled one barely fizzed. Carbon dioxide is less soluble in a warm solution. What keeps the carbon dioxide from bubbling out when it is sitting at room temperature on a supermarket shelf? When a bottle is filled, extra carbon dioxide gas is squeezed into the space above the liquid, increasing the pressure in the bottle. This increased pressure increases the solubility of gas and forces most of it into the solution. When you open the cap, the pressure is released and the solubility of the carbon dioxide decreases.

Reading Check *Why does a bottle of carbonated beverage go "flat" after it has been opened for a few days?*

Figure 12 The Dead Sea is a saturated solution. When the water evaporates, minerals are left behind as pillars.

Mini LAB

Observing Chemical Processes

Procedure

1. Pour **two small glasses of milk.**
2. Place one glass of milk in the **refrigerator.** Leave the other on the counter.
3. Allow the milk to sit overnight. **WARNING:** *Do not drink the milk that sat out overnight.*
4. On the following day, smell both glasses of milk. Record your observations.

Analysis

1. Compare and contrast the appearance and odor of both glasses of milk.
2. Explain why refrigeration is needed.

Indiana Academic Standard Check

7.3.12: Investigate how the temperature . . . of a solution influences reaction rates, such as those resulting in food spoilage.

✔ How do the movements of molecules affect food spoilage?

Saturated Solutions If you add calcium carbonate to 100 g of water at 25°C, only 0.0014 g of it will dissolve. Additional calcium carbonate will not dissolve. Such a solution—one that contains all of the solute that it can hold under the given conditions—is called a **saturated** solution. **Figure 12** shows a saturated solution. If a solution is a liquid-solid solution, the extra solute that is added will settle to the bottom of the container. Unsaturated solutions contain less solute than the maximum amount that will dissolve.

When a saturated solution cools, some of the solute usually falls out of the solution. But if a saturated solution is cooled slowly, sometimes the excess solute remains dissolved for a period of time. Such a solution is said to be supersaturated, because it contains more than the maximum amount that will dissolve.

Rate of Dissolving

Solubility does not tell you how fast a solute will dissolve—it tells you only how much of a solute will dissolve at a given temperature. Some solutes dissolve quickly, but others take a long time to dissolve. A solute dissolves faster when the solution is stirred or shaken or when the temperature of the solution is increased. These methods increase the rate at which the surfaces of the solute come into contact with the solvent. Increasing the area of contact between the solute and the solvent can also increase the rate of dissolving. This can be done by breaking up the solute into smaller pieces, which increases the surface area of the solute that is exposed to the solvent.

Molecules always are moving and colliding. Collisions must take place for chemical reactions to occur. The higher the temperature, the more collisions that occur and the higher the rate of reaction. The opposite also is true. The lower the temperature, the fewer collisions that occur and the lower the rate of reaction. Refrigerators slow reaction rates, preventing food spoilage.

Concentration

What makes strong lemonade strong and weak lemonade weak? The difference between the two drinks is the amount of water in each one compared to the amount of lemon. The lemon is present in different concentrations in the solution. The **concentration** of a solution tells you how much solute is present compared to the amount of solvent. You can give a simple description of a solution's concentration by calling it either concentrated or dilute. These terms are used when comparing the concentrations of two solutions with the same type of solute and solvent. A concentrated solution has more solute per given amount of solvent than a dilute solution.

Measuring Concentration Can you imagine a doctor ordering a dilute intravenous, or IV, solution for a patient? Because dilute is not an exact measurement, the IV could be made with a variety of amounts of medicine. The doctor would need to specify the exact concentration of the IV solution to make sure that the patient is treated correctly.

INTEGRATE Career

Pharmacist Doctors rely on pharmacists to formulate IV solutions. Pharmacists begin with a concentrated form of the drug, which is supplied by pharmaceutical companies. This is the solute of the IV solution. The pharmacist adds the correct amount of solvent to a small amount of the solute to achieve the concentration requested by the doctor. There may be more than one solute per IV solution in varying concentrations.

Applying Science

How can you compare concentrations?

A solute is a substance that can be dissolved in another substance called a solvent. Solutions vary in concentration, or strength, depending on the amount of solute and solvent being used. Fruit drinks are examples of such a solution. Stronger fruit drinks appear darker in color and are the result of more drink mix being dissolved in a given amount of water. What would happen if more water were added to the solution?

Glucose Solutions (g/100 mL)

Solute Glucose (g)	Solvent Water (mL)	Solution Concentration of Glucose (%)
2	100	2
4	100	4
10	100	10
20	100	20

Identifying the Problem

The table on the right lists different concentration levels of glucose solutions, a type of carbohydrate your body uses as a source of energy. The glucose is measured in grams, and the water is measured in milliliters.

Solving the Problem

A physician writes a prescription for a patient to receive 1,000 mL of a 20 percent solution of glucose. How many grams of glucose must the pharmacist add to 1,000 mL of water to prepare this 20 percent concentration level?

SECTION 2 Solubility

Figure 13 Concentrations can be stated in percentages.

>
> **Indiana Academic Standard Check**
>
> **7.3.13:** ... the presence of [dissolved] substances often affects the rates of reactions ... in the water as compared to the same reactions ... in the absence of the substance.
>
> ✔ How does a solute affect boiling point?

One way of giving the exact concentration is to state the percentage of the volume of the solution that is made up of solute. Labels on fruit drinks show their concentration like the one in **Figure 13.** When a fruit drink contains 15 percent fruit juice, the remaining 85 percent of the drink is water and other substances such as sweeteners and flavorings. This drink is more concentrated than another brand that contains 10 percent fruit juice, but it's more dilute than pure juice, which is 100 percent juice. Another way to describe the concentration of a solution is to give the percentage of the total mass that is made up of solute.

Effects of Solute Particles All solute particles affect the physical properties of the solvent, such as its boiling point and freezing point. The effect that a solute has on the freezing or boiling point of a solvent depends on the number of solute particles.

When a solvent such as water begins to freeze, its molecules arrange themselves in a particular pattern. When a solute, such as sodium chloride, is added, the solute particles interfere with the formation of the solid. To overcome this interference, a lower temperature is needed to freeze the solvent.

When a solvent such as water begins to boil, the solvent molecules are gaining enough energy to move from the liquid state to the gaseous state. When a solute such as sodium chloride is added to the solvent, fewer solvent particles escape the liquid's surface to the gas phase. More energy is needed for the solvent particles to escape from the liquid, and the boiling point of the solution will be higher.

section 2 review

Summary

The Universal Solvent
- Water is known as the universal solvent.
- A molecule that has an even distribution of electrons is a nonpolar molecule.
- A molecule that has an uneven distribution of electrons is a polar molecule.
- A compound that loses or gains electrons is an ionic compound.

Dissolving a Substance
- Chemists use the rule "like dissolves like."

Concentration
- Concentration is the quantity of solute present compared to the amount of solvent.

Self Check

1. **Identify** the property of water that makes it the universal solvent.
2. **Describe** the two methods to increase the rate at which a substance dissolves.
3. **Infer** why it is important to add sodium chloride to water when making homemade ice cream.
4. **Think Critically** Why can the fluids used to dry-clean clothing remove grease even when water cannot?

Applying Skills

5. **Recognize Cause and Effect** Why is it more important in terms of reaction rate to take groceries straight home from the store when it is 25°C than when it is 2°C?

 in7.msscience.com/self_check_quiz

Observing Gas Solubility

On a hot day, a carbonated beverage will cool you off. If you leave the beverage uncovered at room temperature, it quickly loses its fizz. However, if you cap the beverage and place it in the refrigerator, it will still have its fizz hours later. In this lab you will explore why this happens.

Real-World Question

What effect does temperature have on the fizz, or carbon dioxide, in your carbonated beverage?

Goals
- **Observe** the effect that temperature has on solubility.
- **Compare** the amount of carbon dioxide released at room temperature and in hot tap water.

Materials
carbonated beverages in plastic bottles, thoroughly chilled (2)
balloons (2)   *ruler
tape   container
fabric tape measure hot tap water
*string   *Alternative materials

Safety Precautions

WARNING: DO NOT point the bottles at anyone at any time during the lab.

Procedure

1. Carefully remove the caps from the thoroughly chilled plastic bottles one at a time. Create as little agitation as possible.
2. Quickly cover the opening of each bottle with an uninflated balloon.
3. Use tape to secure and tightly seal the balloons to the top of the bottles.
4. Gently agitate one bottle from side to side for two minutes. Measure the circumference of the balloon.

WARNING: *Contents under pressure can cause serious accidents. Be sure to wear safety goggles, and DO NOT point the bottles at anyone.*

5. Gently agitate the second bottle in the same manner as in step 4. Then, place the bottle in a container of hot tap water for ten minutes. Measure the circumference of the balloon.

Conclude and Apply

1. **Compare and contrast** the relative amounts of carbon dioxide gas released from the cold and the warm carbonated beverages.
2. **Infer** Why does the warmed carbonated beverage release a different amount of carbon dioxide than the chilled one?

Compare the circumferences of your balloons with those of members of your class. **For more help, refer to the** Science Skill Handbook.

LAB **301**

Standard—7.3.12: Investigate how the . . . acidity of a solution influences reaction rates . . .

section 3

Acidic and Basic Solutions

as you read

What You'll Learn
- **Compare** acids and bases and their properties.
- **Describe** practical uses of acids and bases.
- **Explain** how pH is used to describe the strength of an acid or base.
- **Describe** how acids and bases react when they are brought together.

Why It's Important
Many common products, such as batteries and bleach, work because of acids or bases.

Review Vocabulary
physical property: any characteristic of a material that can be seen or measured without changing the material

New Vocabulary
- acid
- hydronium ion
- base
- pH
- indicator
- neutralization

Acids

What makes orange juice, vinegar, dill pickles, and grapefruit tangy? Acids cause the sour taste of these and other foods. **Acids** are substances that release positively charged hydrogen ions, H^+, in water. When an acid mixes with water, the acid dissolves, releasing a hydrogen ion. The hydrogen ion then combines with a water molecule to form a hydronium ion, as shown in **Figure 14**. **Hydronium ions** are positively charged and have the formula H_3O^+.

Properties of Acidic Solutions Sour taste is one of the properties of acidic solutions. The taste allows you to detect the presence of acids in your food. However, even though you can identify acidic solutions by their sour taste, you should never taste anything in the laboratory, and you should never use taste to test for the presence of acids in an unknown substance. Many acids can cause serious burns to body tissues.

Another property of acidic solutions is that they can conduct electricity. The hydronium ions in an acidic solution can carry the electric charges in a current. This is why some batteries contain an acid. Acidic solutions also are corrosive, which means they can break down certain substances. Many acids can corrode fabric, skin, and paper. The solutions of some acids also react strongly with certain metals. The acid-metal reaction forms metallic compounds and hydrogen gas, leaving holes in the metal in the process.

$$H^+ \quad + \quad H_2O \quad \rightarrow \quad H_3O^+$$

Hydrogen ion   Water molecule   Hydronium ion

Figure 14 One hydrogen ion can combine with one water molecule to form one positively charged hydronium ion.
Identify *what kinds of substances are sources of hydrogen ions.*

302 CHAPTER 10 Substances, Mixtures, and Solubility

Figure 15 Each of these products contains an acid or is made with the help of an acid.
Describe how your life would be different if acids were not available to make these products.

Uses of Acids You're probably familiar with many acids. Vinegar, which is used in salad dressing, contains acetic acid. Lemons, limes, and oranges have a sour taste because they contain citric acid. Your body needs ascorbic acid, which is vitamin C. Ants that sting inject formic acid into their victims.

Figure 15 shows other products that are made with acids. Sulfuric acid is used in the production of fertilizers, steel, paints, and plastics. Acids often are used in batteries because their solutions conduct electricity. For this reason, it sometimes is referred to as battery acid. Hydrochloric acid, which is known commercially as muriatic acid, is used in a process called pickling. Pickling is a process that removes impurities from the surfaces of metals. Hydrochloric acid also can be used to clean mortar from brick walls. Nitric acid is used in the production of fertilizers, dyes, and plastics.

Acid in the Environment Carbonic acid plays a key role in the formation of caves and of stalactites and stalagmites. Carbonic acid is formed when carbon dioxide in soil is dissolved in water. When this acidic solution comes in contact with calcium carbonate—or limestone rock—it can dissolve it, eventually carving out a cave in the rock. A similar process occurs when acid rain falls on statues and eats away at the stone, as shown in **Figure 16.** When this acidic solution drips from the ceiling of the cave, water evaporates and carbon dioxide becomes less soluble, forcing it out of solution. The solution becomes less acidic and the limestone becomes less soluble, causing it to come out of solution. These solids form stalactites and stalagmites.

Mini LAB

Observing a Nail in a Carbonated Drink

Procedure
1. Observe the initial appearance of an **iron nail.**
2. Pour enough **carbonated soft drink** into a **cup or beaker** to cover the nail.
3. Drop the nail into the soft drink and observe what happens.
4. Leave the nail in the soft drink overnight and observe it again the next day.

Analysis
1. Describe what happened when you first dropped the nail into the soft drink and the appearance of the nail the following day.
2. Based upon the fact that the soft drink was carbonated, explain why you think the drink reacted with the nail as you observed.

SECTION 3 Acidic and Basic Solutions

NATIONAL GEOGRAPHIC VISUALIZING ACID PRECIPITATION

Figure 16

When fossil fuels such as coal and oil are burned, a variety of chemical compounds are produced and released into the air. In the atmosphere, some of these compounds form acids that mix with water vapor and fall back to Earth as acid precipitation—rain, sleet, snow, or fog. The effects of acid precipitation on the environment can be devastating. Winds carry these acids hundreds of miles from their source, damaging forests, corroding statues, and endangering human health.

B Sulfur dioxide and nitrogen oxides react with water vapor in the air to form highly acidic solutions of nitric acid (HNO_3) and sulfuric acid (H_2SO_4). These solutions eventually return to Earth as acid precipitation.

C Some acid rain in the United States has a pH as low as 2.3—close to the acidity of stomach acid.

A Power plants and cars burn fossil fuels to generate energy for human use. In the process, sulfur dioxide (SO_2) and nitrogen oxides are released into the atmosphere.

Bases

People often use ammonia solutions to clean windows and floors. These solutions have different properties from those of acidic solutions. Ammonia is called a base. **Bases** are substances that can accept hydrogen ions. When bases dissolve in water, some hydrogen atoms from the water molecules are attracted to the base. A hydrogen atom in the water molecule leaves behind the other hydrogen atom and oxygen atom. This pair of atoms is a negatively charged ion called a hydroxide ion. A hydroxide ion has the formula OH^-. Most bases contain a hydroxide ion, which is released when the base dissolves in water. For example, sodium hydroxide is a base with the formula NaOH. When NaOH dissolves in water, a sodium ion and the hydroxide ion separate.

Topic: Calcium Hydroxide
Visit in7.msscience.com for Web links to information about the uses for calcium hydroxide.

Activity Describe the chemical reaction that converts limestone (calcium carbonate) to calcium hydroxide.

Properties of Basic Solutions Most soaps are bases, so if you think about how soap feels, you can figure out some of the properties of basic solutions. Basic solutions feel slippery. Acids in water solution taste sour, but bases taste bitter—as you know if you have ever accidentally gotten soap in your mouth.

Like acids, bases are corrosive. Bases can cause burns and damage tissue. You should never touch or taste a substance to find out whether it is a base. Basic solutions contain ions and can conduct electricity. Basic solutions are not as reactive with metals as acidic solutions are.

Uses of Bases Many uses for bases are shown in **Figure 17**. Bases give soaps, ammonia, and many other cleaning products some of their useful properties. The hydroxide ions produced by bases can interact strongly with certain substances, such as dirt and grease.

Chalk and oven cleaner are examples of familiar products that contain bases. Your blood is a basic solution. Calcium hydroxide, often called lime, is used to mark the lines on athletic fields. It also can be used to treat lawns and gardens that have acidic soil. Sodium hydroxide, known as lye, is a strong base that can cause burns and other health problems. Lye is used to make soap, clean ovens, and unclog drains.

Figure 17 Many products, including soaps, cleaners, and plaster contain bases or are made with the help of bases.

pH Levels Most life-forms can't exist at extremely low pH levels. However, some bacteria thrive in acidic environments. Acidophils are bacteria that exist at low pH levels. These bacteria have been found in the Hot Springs of Yellowstone National Park in areas with pH levels ranging from 1 to 3.

What is pH?

You've probably heard of pH-balanced shampoo or deodorant, and you might have seen someone test the pH of the water in a swimming pool. **pH** is a measure of how acidic or basic a solution is. The pH scale ranges from 0 to 14. Acidic solutions have pH values below 7. A solution with a pH of 0 is very acidic. Hydrochloric acid can have a pH of 0. A solution with a pH of 7 is neutral, meaning it is neither acidic nor basic. Pure water is neutral. Basic solutions have pH values above 7. A solution with a pH of 14 is very basic. Sodium hydroxide can have a pH of 14. **Figure 18** shows where various common substances fall on the pH scale.

The pH of a solution is related directly to its concentrations of hydronium ions (H_3O^+) and hydroxide ions (OH^-). Acidic solutions have more hydronium ions than hydroxide ions. Neutral solutions have equal numbers of the two ions. Basic solutions have more hydroxide ions than hydronium ions.

In a neutral solution, how do the numbers of hydronium ions and hydroxide ions compare?

pH Scale The pH scale is not a simple linear scale like mass or volume. For example, if one book has a mass of 2 kg and a second book has a mass of 1 kg, the mass of the first book is twice that of the second. However, a change of 1 pH unit represents a tenfold change in the acidity of the solution. For example, if one solution has a pH of 1 and a second solution has a pH of 2, the first solution is not twice as acidic as the second—it is ten times more acidic. To determine the difference in pH strength, use the following calculation: 10^n, where n = the difference between pHs. For example: pH3 − pH1 = 2, 10^2 = 100 times more acidic.

Figure 18 The pH scale classifies a solution as acidic, basic, or neutral.

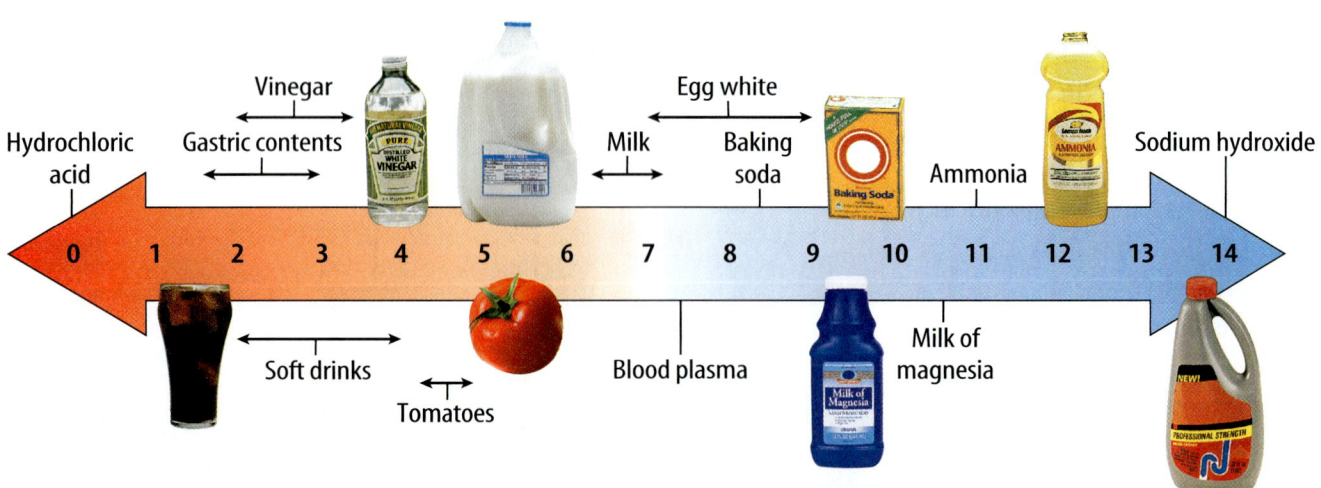

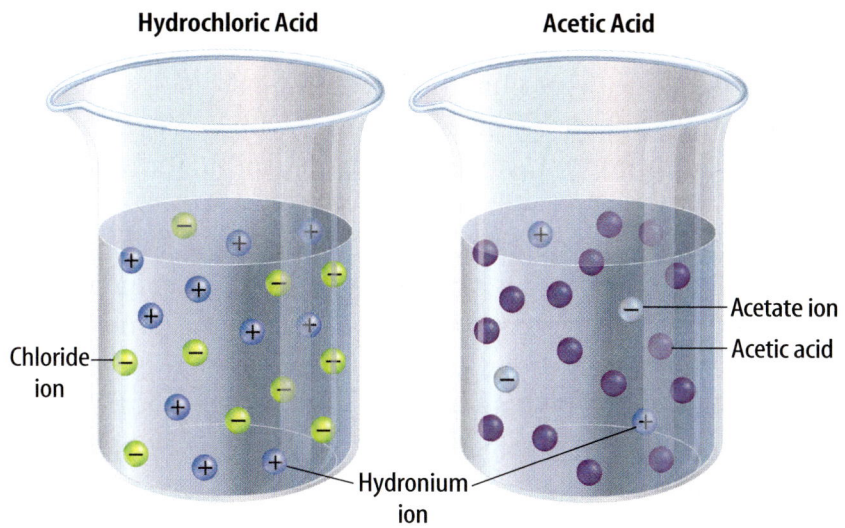

Figure 19 Hydrochloric acid separates into ions more readily than acetic acid does when it dissolves in water. Therefore, hydrochloric acid exists in water as separated ions. Acetic acid exists in water almost entirely as molecules.

Strengths of Acids and Bases You've learned that acids give foods a sour taste but also can cause burns and damage tissue. The difference between food acids and the acids that can burn you is that they have different strengths. The acids in food are fairly weak acids, while the dangerous acids are strong acids. The strength of an acid is related to how easily the acid separates into ions, or how easily a hydrogen ion is released, when the acid dissolves in water. Look at **Figure 19.** In the same concentration, a strong acid—like hydrochloric acid—forms more hydronium ions in solution than a weak acid does—like acetic acid. More hydronium ions means the strong-acid solution has a lower pH than the weak-acid solution. Similarly, the strength of a base is related to how easily the base separates into ions, or how easily a hydroxide ion is released, when the base dissolves in water. The relative strengths of some common acids and bases are shown in **Table 3.**

Reading Check What determines the strength of an acid or a base?

An acid containing more hydrogen atoms, such as carbonic acid, H_2CO_3, is not necessarily stronger than an acid containing fewer hydrogen atoms, such as nitric acid, HNO_3. An acid's strength is related to how easily a hydrogen ion separates—not to how many hydrogen atoms it has. For this reason, nitric acid is stronger than carbonic acid.

Table 3 Strengths of Some Acids and Bases

	Acid	Base
Strong	hydrochloric (HCl) sulfuric (H_2SO_4) nitric (HNO_3)	sodium hydroxide (NaOH) potassium hydroxide (KOH)
Weak	acetic (CH_3COOH) carbonic (H_2CO_3) ascorbic ($H_2C_6H_6O_6$)	ammonia (NH_3) aluminum hydroxide ($Al(OH)_3$) iron (III) hydroxide ($Fe(OH)_3$)

Topic: Indicators
Visit in7.msscience.com for Web links to information about the types of pH indicators.

Activity Describe how plants can act as indicators in acidic and basic solutions.

Indicators

What is a safe way to find out how acidic or basic a solution is? **Indicators** are compounds that react with acidic and basic solutions and produce certain colors, depending on the solution's pH.

Because they are different colors at different pHs, indicators can help you determine the pH of a solution. Some indicators, such as litmus, are soaked into paper strips. When litmus paper is placed in an acidic solution, it turns red. When placed in a basic solution, litmus paper turns blue. Some indicators can change through a wide range of colors, with each different color appearing at a different pH value.

Neutralization

Perhaps you've heard someone complain about heartburn or an upset stomach after eating spicy food. To feel better, the person might have taken an antacid. Think about the word *antacid* for a minute. How do antacids work?

Heartburn or stomach discomfort is caused by excess hydrochloric acid in the stomach. Hydrochloric acid helps break down the food you eat, but too much of it can irritate your stomach or digestive tract. An antacid product, often made from the base magnesium hydroxide, $Mg(OH)_2$, neutralizes the excess acid. **Neutralization** (new truh luh ZAY shun) is the reaction of an acid with a base. It is called this because the properties of both the acid and base are diminished, or neutralized. In most cases, the reaction produces a water and a salt. **Figure 20** illustrates the relative amounts of hydronium and hydroxide ions between pH 0 and pH 14.

 What are the products of neutralization?

Figure 20 The pH of a solution is more acidic when greater amounts of hydronium ions are present.
Define what makes a pH 7 solution neutral.

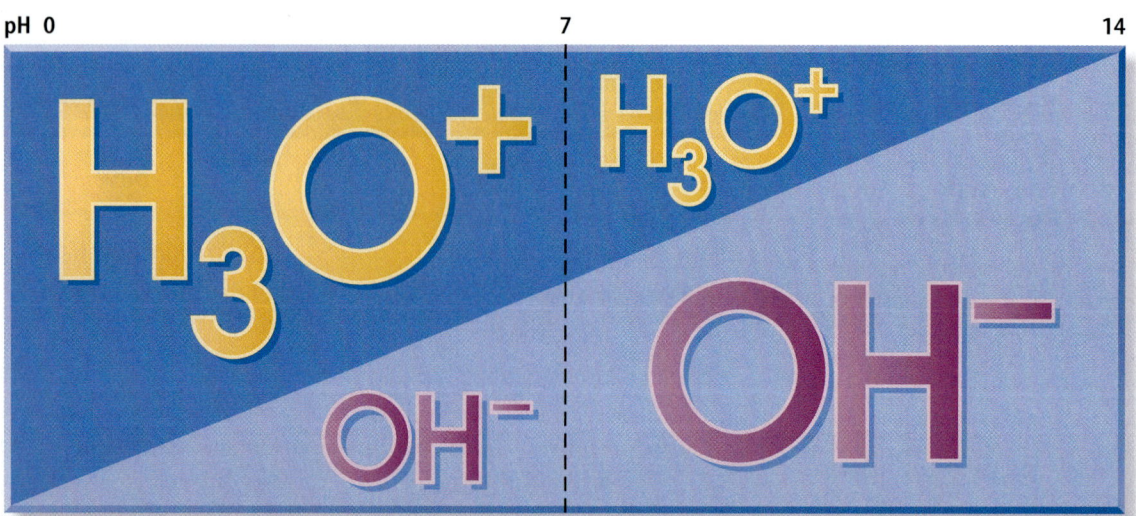

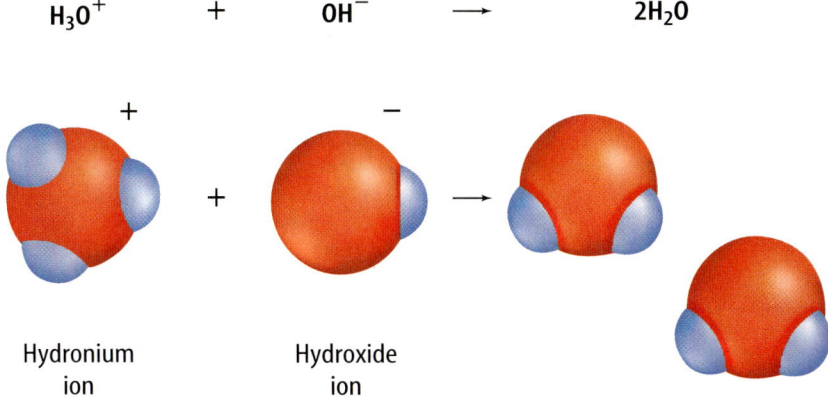

Figure 21 When acidic and basic solutions react, hydronium and hydroxide ions react to form water.
Determine why the pH of the solution changes.

How does neutralization occur?
Recall that every water molecule contains two hydrogen atoms and one oxygen atom. As **Figure 21** shows, when one hydronium ion reacts with one hydroxide ion, the product is two water molecules. This reaction occurs during acid-base neutralization. Equal numbers of hydronium ions from the acidic solution and hydroxide ions from the basic solution react to produce water. Pure water has a pH of 7, which means that it's neutral.

 **What happens to acids and bases during neutralization?**

section 3 review

Summary

Acids and Bases
- Acids are substances that release positively charged hydrogen ions in water.
- Substances that accept hydrogen ions in water are bases.
- Acidic and basic solutions can conduct electricity.

pH
- pH measures how acidic or basic a solution is.
- The scale ranges from 0 to 14.

Neutralization
- Neutralization is the interaction between an acid and a base to form water and a salt.

Self Check

1. **Identify** what ions are produced by acids in water and bases in water. Give two properties each of acids and bases.
2. **Name** three acids and three bases and list an industrial or household use of each.
3. **Explain** how the concentration of hydronium ions and hydroxide ions are related to pH.
4. **Think Critically** In what ways might a company that uses a strong acid handle an acid spill on the factory floor?

Applying Math

5. **Solve One-Step Equations** How much more acidic is a solution with a pH of 2 than one with a pH of 6? How much more basic is a solution with a pH of 13 than one with a pH of 10?

in7.msscience.com/self_check_quiz   SECTION 3 Acidic and Basic Solutions

Testing pH Using Natural Indicators

Goals
- **Determine** the relative acidity or basicity of several common solutions.
- **Compare** the strengths of several common acids and bases.

Materials
small test tubes (9)
test-tube rack
concentrated red cabbage juice in a dropper bottle
labeled bottles containing:
 household ammonia, baking soda solution, soap solution, 0.1M hydrochloric acid solution, white vinegar, colorless carbonated soft drink, borax soap solution, distilled water
grease pencil
droppers (9)

Safety Precautions

WARNING: *Many acids and bases are poisonous, can damage your eyes, and can burn your skin. Wear goggles and gloves AT ALL TIMES. Tell your teacher immediately if a substance spills. Wash your hands after you finish but before removing your goggles.*

Real-World Question

You have learned that certain substances, called indicators, change color when the pH of a solution changes. The juice from red cabbage is a natural indicator. How do the pH values of various solutions compare to each other? How can you use red cabbage juice to determine the relative pH of several solutions?

Procedure

1. **Design** a data table to record the names of the solutions to be tested, the colors caused by the added cabbage juice indicator, and the relative strengths of the solutions.
2. Mark each test tube with the identity of the acid or base solution it will contain.
3. Half-fill each test tube with the solution to be tested.
   WARNING: *If you spill any liquids on your skin, rinse the area immediately with water. Alert your teacher if any liquid spills in the work area or on your skin.*

310   CHAPTER 10 Substances, Mixtures, and Solubility

Using Scientific Methods

4. Add ten drops of the cabbage juice indicator to each of the solutions to be tested. Gently agitate or wiggle each test tube to mix the cabbage juice with the solution.
5. **Observe** and record the color of each solution in your data table.

Determining pH Values	
Cabbage Juice Color	Relative Strength of Acid or Base
(red)	strong acid
(dark red)	medium acid
(magenta)	weak acid
(purple)	neutral
(teal)	weak base
(green)	medium base
(yellow)	strong base

▶ Analyze Your Data

1. **Compare** your observations with the table above. Record in your data table the relative acid or base strength of each solution you tested.
2. **List** the solutions by pH value starting with the most acidic and finishing with the most basic.

▶ Conclude and Apply

1. **Classify** which solutions were acidic and which were basic.
2. **Identify** which solution was the weakest acid. The strongest base? The closest to neutral?
3. **Predict** what ion might be involved in the cleaning process based upon your data for the ammonia, soap, and borax soap solutions.

▶ Form a Hypothesis

Form a hypothesis that explains why the borax soap solution was less basic than an ammonia solution of approximately the same concentration.

Communicating Your Data

Use your data to create labels for the solutions you tested. Include the relative strength of each solution and any other safety information you think is important on each label. **For more help, refer to the Science Skill Handbook.**

LAB 311

Science Stats

Salty Solutions

Did you know...

...Seawater is certainly a salty solution. Ninety-nine percent of all salt ions in the sea are sodium, chlorine, sulfate, magnesium, calcium, and potassium. The major gases in the sea are nitrogen, oxygen, carbon dioxide, argon, neon, and helium.

...Tears and saliva have a lot in common. Both are salty solutions that protect you from harmful bacteria, keep tissues moist, and help spread nutrients. Bland-tasting saliva, however, is 99 percent water. The remaining one percent is a combination of many ions, including sodium and several proteins.

...The largest salt lake in the United States is the Great Salt Lake. It covers more than 4,000 km^2 in Utah and is up to 13.4 m deep. The Great Salt Lake and the Salt Lake Desert were once part of the enormous, prehistoric Lake Bonneville, which was 305 m deep at some points.

Applying Math At its largest, Lake Bonneville covered about 32,000 km^2. What percentage of that area does the Great Salt Lake now cover?

...Salt can reduce pain. Gargled salt water is a disinfectant; it fights the bacteria that cause some sore throats.

Graph It

Visit in7.msscience.com/science_stats to research and learn about other elements in seawater. **Create a graph that shows the amounts of the ten most common elements in 1 L of seawater.**

312 CHAPTER 10 Substances, Mixtures, and Solubility

Chapter 10 Study Guide

Reviewing Main Ideas

Section 1: What is a solution?

1. Elements and compounds are pure substances, because their compositions are fixed. Mixtures are not pure substances.
2. Heterogeneous mixtures are not mixed evenly. Homogeneous mixtures, also called solutions, are mixed evenly on a molecular level.
3. Solutes and solvents can be gases, liquids, or solids, combined in many different ways.

Section 2: Solubility

1. Because water molecules are polar, they can dissolve many different solutes. Like dissolves like.
2. Temperature and pressure can affect solubility.

3. Solutions can be unsaturated, saturated, or supersaturated, depending on how much solute is dissolved compared to the solubility of the solute in the solvent.
4. The concentration of a solution is the amount of solute in a particular volume of solvent.

Section 3: Acidic and Basic Solutions

1. Acids release H+ ions and produce hydronium ions when they are dissolved in water. Bases accept H+ ions and produce hydroxide ions when dissolved in water.
2. pH expresses the concentrations of hydronium ions and hydroxide ions in aqueous solutions.
3. In a neutralization reaction, an acid reacts with a base to form water and a salt.

Visualizing Main Ideas

Copy and complete the concept map on the classification of matter.

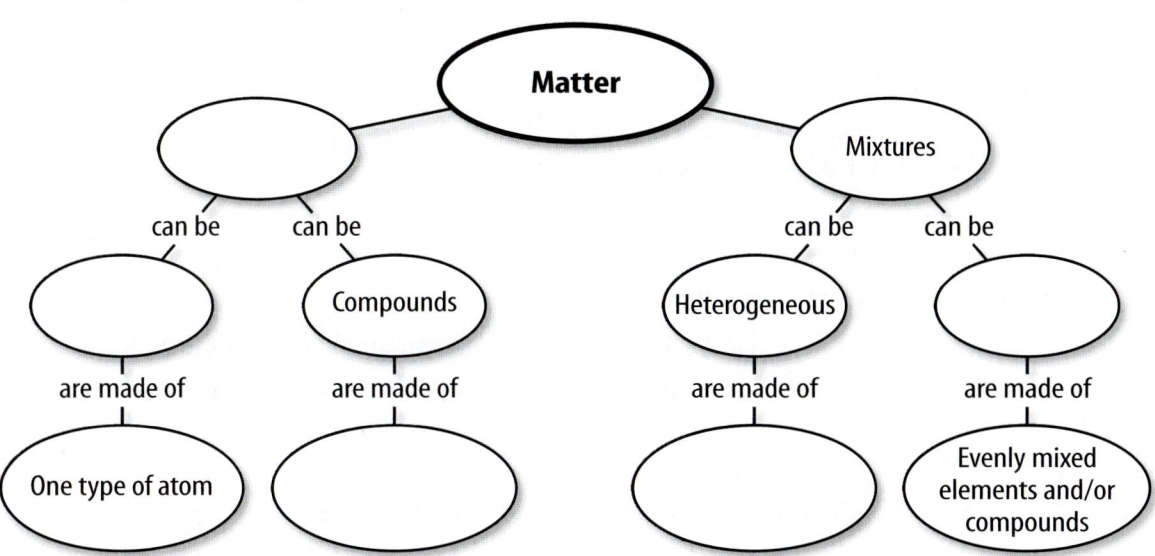

chapter 10 Review

Using Vocabulary

acid p. 302
aqueous p. 294
base p. 305
concentration p. 299
heterogeneous mixture p. 289
homogeneous mixture p. 290
hydronium ion p. 302
indicator p. 308
neutralization p. 308
pH p. 306
precipitate p. 290
saturated p. 298
solubility p. 297
solute p. 290
solution p. 290
solvent p. 290
substance p. 288

Fill in the blanks with the correct vocabulary word.

1. A base has a(n) _____ value above 7.
2. A measure of how much solute is in a solution is its _____.
3. The amount of a solute that can dissolve in 100 g of solvent is its _____.
4. The _____ is the substance that is dissolved to form a solution.
5. The reaction between an acidic and basic solution is called _____.
6. A(n) _____ has a fixed composition.

Checking Concepts

Choose the word or phrase that best answers the question.

7. Which of the following is a solution?
   A) pure water
   B) an oatmeal-raisin cookie
   C) copper
   D) vinegar

8. What type of compounds will not dissolve in water?
   A) polar   C) nonpolar
   B) ionic   D) charged

9. What type of molecule is water?
   A) polar   C) nonpolar
   B) ionic   D) precipitate

10. When chlorine compounds are dissolved in pool water, what is the water?
    A) the alloy
    B) the solvent
    C) the solution
    D) the solute

11. A solid might become less soluble in a liquid when you decrease what?
    A) particle size   C) temperature
    B) pressure   D) container size

12. Which acid is used in the industrial process known as pickling?
    A) hydrochloric   C) sulfuric
    B) carbonic   D) nitric

13. A solution is prepared by adding 100 g of solid sodium hydroxide, NaOH, to 1,000 mL of water. What is the solid NaOH called?
    A) solution   C) solvent
    B) solute   D) mixture

14. Given equal concentrations, which of the following will produce the most hydronium ions in an aqueous solution?
    A) a strong base   C) a strong acid
    B) a weak base   D) a weak acid

15. Bile, an acidic body fluid used in digestion, has a high concentration of hydronium ions. Predict its pH.
    A) 11   C) less than 7
    B) 7   D) greater than 7

16. When you swallow an antacid, what happens to your stomach acid?
    A) It is more acidic.
    B) It is concentrated.
    C) It is diluted.
    D) It is neutralized.

chapter 10 Review

Thinking Critically

17. **Infer** why deposits form in the steam vents of irons in some parts of the country.

18. **Explain** if it is possible to have a dilute solution of a strong acid.

19. **Draw Conclusions** Antifreeze is added to water in a car's radiator to prevent freezing in cold months. It also prevents overheating or boiling. Explain how antifreeze does both.

Use the illustration below to answer question 20.

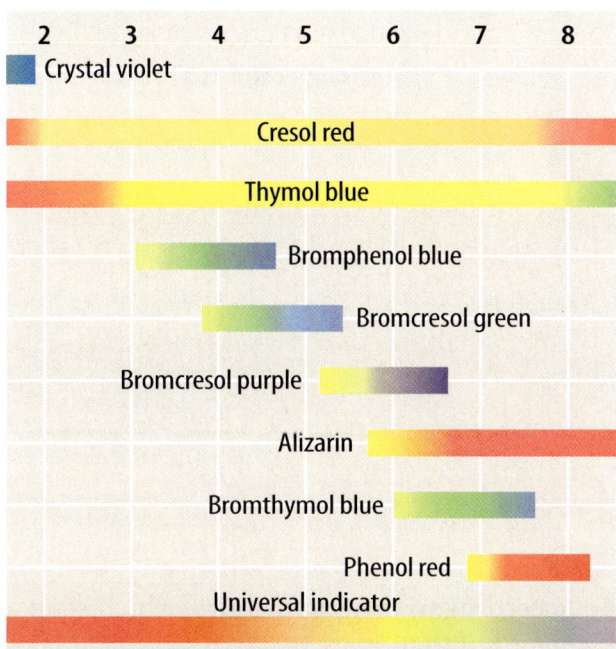

20. **Interpret** Chemists use a variety of indicators. Using the correct indicator is important. The color change must occur at the proper pH or the results could be misleading. Looking at the indicator chart, what indicators could be used to produce a color change at both pH 2 and pH 8?

21. **Explain** Water molecules can break apart to form H^+ ions and OH^- ions. Water is known as an amphoteric substance, which is something that can act as an acid or a base. Explain how this can be so.

22. **Describe** how a liquid-solid solution forms. How is this different from a liquid-gas solution? How are these two types of solutions different from a liquid-liquid solution? Give an example of each with your description.

23. **Compare and contrast** examples of heterogeneous and homogeneous mixtures from your daily life.

24. **Form a Hypotheses** A warm carbonated beverage seems to fizz more than a cold one when it is opened. Explain this based on the solubility of carbon dioxide in water.

Performance Activities

25. **Poem** Write a poem that explains the difference between a substance and a mixture.

Applying Math

Use the graph below to answer question 26.

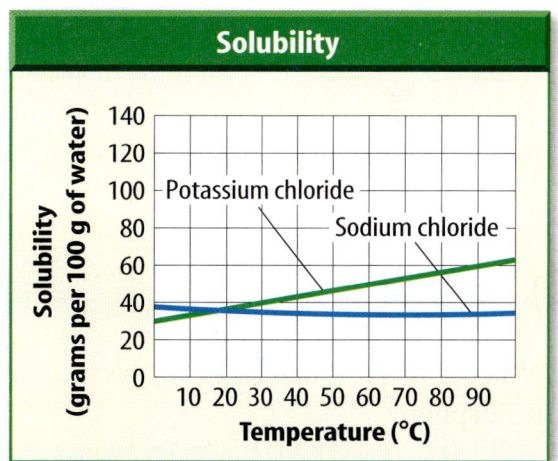

26. **Solubility** Using the solubility graph above, estimate the solubilities of potassium chloride and sodium chloride in grams per 100 g of water at 80°C.

27. **Juice Concentration** You made a one-liter (1,000 mL) container of juice. How much concentrate, in mL, did you add to make a concentration of 18 percent?

chapter 10 Indiana

 The assessed Indiana standard appears above the question.

Record your answers on the answer sheet provided by your teacher or on a sheet of paper.

Part 1 | Multiple Choice

1. The graph below displays the compostion of Earth's atmosphere.

Composition of Earth's Atmosphere

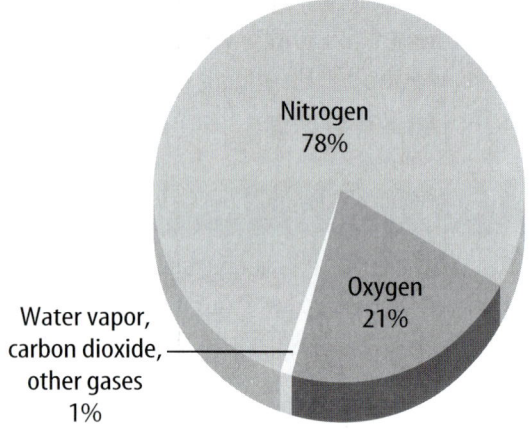

Which is the solvent in Earth's atmosphere?

A carbon dioxide

B nitrogen

C oxygen

D water vapor

2. Which term best describes Earth's atmosphere?

A atom

B element

C compound

D solution

The graph below shows the solubilities of two solids.

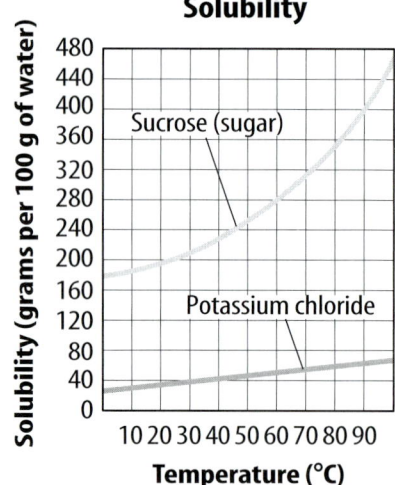

7.3.13

3. According to the graph, how many grams of sucrose will dissolve in water at 60°C?

A 50 g

B 80 g

C 280 g

D 320 g

7.3.13

4. According to the graph above, which statement is **TRUE**?

A Potassium chloride is more soluble in water than sucrose.

B As water temperature increases, the solubility of potassium chloride decreases.

C Sucrose is more soluble in water than potassium chloride.

D Temperature does not affect the solubility of either chemical.

316 INDIANA

Standards Review

5. Steel is composed of carbon and what other element?

A copper

B iron

C silicon

D zinc

6. Which is the symbol for a hydronium ion?

A H^+

B H_3O^+

C H_3O^-

D OH^-

7. The photo below shows a mixture of sand and iron filings being separated.

What physical property is used to separate the sand and iron?

A density

B ductility

C magnetism

D malleability

Part 2 Constructed Response

8. Explain why a carbonated beverage can be classified as a liquid-gas solution. Explain how the ratio of liquid solvent to gas solute changes when the container is opened.

9. The diagram below shows a water molecule.

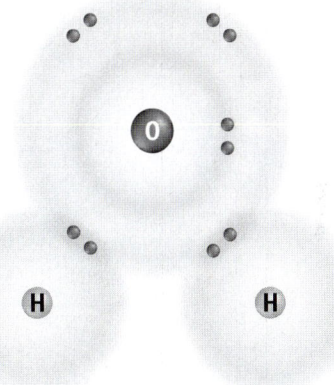

(Partial negative charge)

(Partial positive charge)

Use the distribution of electrons to describe this molecule's polarity. What type of bonds does water contain?

7.3.13

10. Explain how the polarity of water makes water effective in dissolving ionic compounds.

Test-Taking Tip

Start the Day Right The morning of the test, eat a healthy breakfast with a balanced amount of protein and carbohydrates.

unit 4
Motion, Forces, and Energy

How Are Radar & Popcorn Connected?

Radar systems—such as the one in this modern air traffic control room—use radio waves to detect objects. In the 1940s, the radio waves used for radar were generated by a device called a magnetron. One day, an engineer working on a radar project was standing near a magnetron when he noticed that the candy bar in his pocket had melted. Intrigued, the engineer got some unpopped popcorn and placed it next to the magnetron. Sure enough, the kernels began to pop. The engineer realized that the magnetron's short radio waves, called microwaves, caused the molecules in the food to move more quickly, increasing the food's temperature. Soon, magnetrons were being used in the first microwave ovens. Today, microwave ovens are used to pop popcorn—and heat many other kinds of food—in kitchens all over the world.

unit projects

The assessed Indiana standard appears in blue.

To find project ideas and resources, visit **in7.msscience.com/unit_project**.
Projects include:

- **History** Research tsunamis, their energy, and other characteristics. Graph and compare height, distance, and lives lost from past waves.
- **Technology** Discover how steel drums are made. Construct your own drum and experiment with sounds and patterns of vibrations.
- **Model** Create an original light show with colored lights and stick puppets expressing your new knowledge of light, mirrors, and lenses. **7.3.19**

WebQuest *Laser Eye Surgery* provides an opportunity to be an informed consumer of the advantages and disadvantages of laser eye surgery. **7.3.20**

chapter 11

Academic Standard—7: Students analyze the relationships within systems. They investigate how different models can represent the same data, rates of change, cyclic changes, and changes that counterbalance one another.

Also covers: Academic Standard 2 (Detailed standards begin on page IN8.)

Motion and Momentum

chapter preview

sections
1. What is motion?
2. Acceleration
3. Momentum
   - **Lab** Collisions
   - **Lab** Car Safety Testing
   - **Virtual Lab** How does horizontal motion affect vertical motion?

A Vanishing Act
You hear the crack of the bat and an instant later the ball disappears into a diving infielder's glove. Think of how the motion of the ball changed—it moved toward the batter, changed direction when it collided with the bat, and then stopped when it collided with the infielder's glove.

Science Journal Describe how your motion changed as you moved from your school's entrance to your classroom.

Start-Up Activities

Motion After a Collision

How is it possible for a 70-kg football player to knock down a 110-kg football player? The smaller player usually must be running faster. Mass makes a difference when two objects collide, but the speed of the objects also matters. Explore the behavior of colliding objects during this lab.

1. Space yourself about 2 m away from a partner. Slowly roll a baseball on the floor toward your partner, and have your partner roll a baseball quickly into your ball.
2. Have your partner slowly roll a baseball as you quickly roll a tennis ball into the baseball.
3. Roll two tennis balls toward each other at the same speed.
4. **Think Critically** In your Science Journal, describe how the motion of the balls changed after the collisions, including the effects of speed and type of ball.

Preview this chapter's content and activities at
in7.msscience.com

FOLDABLES Study Organizer

Motion and Momentum Make the following Foldable to help you understand the vocabulary terms in this chapter.

STEP 1 Fold a vertical sheet of notebook paper from side to side.

STEP 2 Cut along every third line of only the top layer to form tabs.

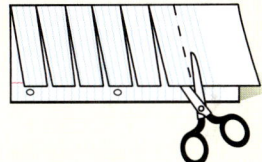

STEP 3 Label each tab.

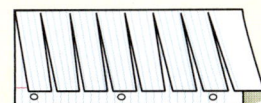

Build Vocabulary As you read the chapter, list the vocabulary words about motion and momentum on the tabs. As you learn the definitions, write them under the tab for each vocabulary word.

Standard—7.7.4: Use symbolic equations to show how the quantity of something changes over time or in response to changes in other quantities.

section 1

Also covers: 7.2.6, 7.2.7 (Detailed standards begin on page IN8.)

What is motion?

as you read

What You'll Learn
- **Define** distance, speed, and velocity.
- **Graph** motion.

Why It's Important
The different motions of objects you see every day can be described in the same way.

Review Vocabulary
meter: SI unit of distance, abbreviated m; equal to approximately 39.37 in

New Vocabulary
- speed
- average speed
- instantaneous speed
- velocity

Matter and Motion

All matter in the universe is constantly in motion, from the revolution of Earth around the Sun to electrons moving around the nucleus of an atom. Leaves rustle in the wind. Lava flows from a volcano. Bees move from flower to flower as they gather pollen. Blood circulates through your body. These are all examples of matter in motion. How can the motion of these different objects be described?

Changing Position

To describe an object in motion, you must first recognize that the object is in motion. Something is in motion if it is changing position. It could be a fast-moving airplane, a leaf swirling in the wind, or water trickling from a hose. Even your school, attached to Earth, is moving through space. When an object moves from one location to another, it is changing position. The runners shown in **Figure 1** sprint from the start line to the finish line. Their positions change, so they are in motion.

Figure 1 When running a race, you are in motion because your position changes.

322 CHAPTER 11 Motion and Momentum

Relative Motion Determining whether something changes position requires a point of reference. An object changes position if it moves relative to a reference point. To visualize this, picture yourself competing in a 100-m dash. You begin just behind the start line. When you pass the finish line, you are 100 m from the start line. If the start line is your reference point, then your position has changed by 100 m relative to the start line, and motion has occurred. Look at **Figure 2**. How can you determine that the dog has been in motion?

 *How do you know if an object has changed position?*

Distance and Displacement Suppose you are to meet your friends at the park in five minutes. Can you get there on time by walking, or should you ride your bike? To help you decide, you need to know the distance you will travel to get to the park. This distance is the length of the route you will travel from your house to the park.

Suppose the distance you traveled from your house to the park was 200 m. When you get to the park, how would you describe your location? You could say that your location was 200 m from your house. However, your final position depends on both the distance you travel and the direction. Did you go 200 m east or west? To describe your final position exactly, you also would have to tell the direction from your starting point. To do this, you would specify your displacement. Displacement includes the distance between the starting and ending points and the direction in which you travel. **Figure 3** shows the difference between distance and displacement.

Figure 2 Motion occurs when something changes position relative to a reference point.
Explain *whether the dog's position would depend on the reference point chosen.*

Figure 3 Distance is how far you have walked. Displacement is the direction and difference in position between your starting and ending points.

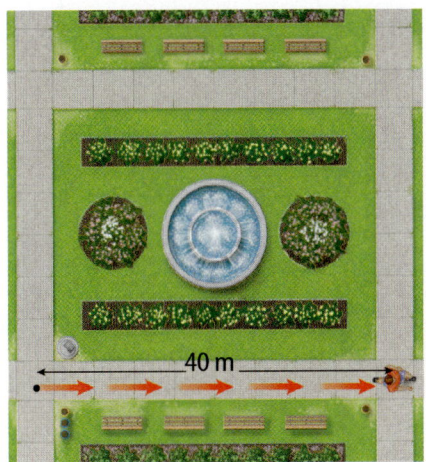

Distance: 40 m
Displacement: 40 m east

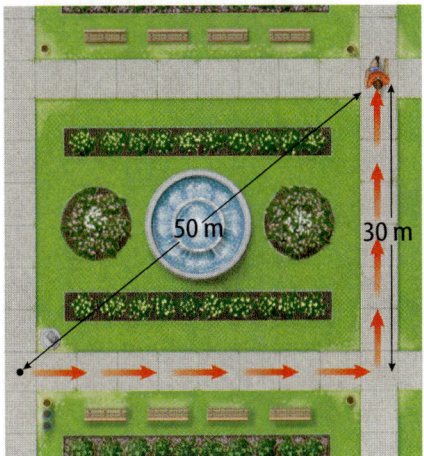

Distance: 70 m
Displacement: 50 m northeast

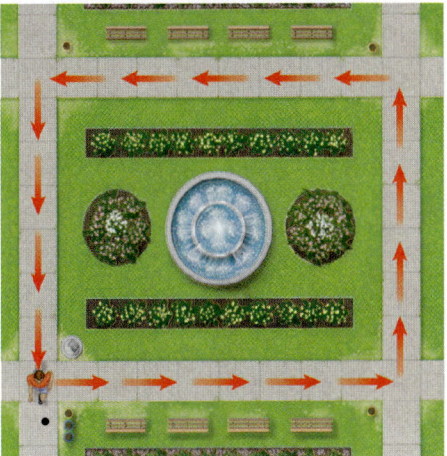

Distance: 140 m
Displacement: 0 m

SECTION 1 What is motion? **323**

Animal Speeds Different animals can move at different top speeds. What are some of the fastest animals? Research the characteristics that help animals run, swim, or fly at high speed.

Speed

To describe motion, you usually want to describe how fast something is moving. The faster something is moving, the less time it takes to travel a certain distance. **Speed** is the distance traveled divided by the time taken to travel the distance. Speed can be calculated from this equation:

Speed Equation

$$\text{speed (in meters/second)} = \frac{\text{distance (in meters)}}{\text{time (in seconds)}}$$

$$s = \frac{d}{t}$$

Because speed equals distance divided by time, the unit of speed is the unit of distance divided by the unit of time. In SI units, distance is measured in m and time is measured in s. As a result, the SI unit of speed is the m/s—the SI distance unit divided by the SI time unit.

Applying Math — Solve a Simple Equation

SPEED OF A SWIMMER Calculate the speed of a swimmer who swims 100 m in 56 s.

Solution

1 *This is what you know:*
- distance: $d = 100$ m
- time: $t = 56$ s

2 *This is what you need to know:*
speed: $s = ?$ m/s

3 *This is the procedure you need to use:*
Substitute the known values for distance and time into the speed equation and calculate the speed:

$$s = \frac{d}{t} = \frac{100 \text{ m}}{56 \text{ s}} = \frac{100}{56} \frac{\text{m}}{\text{s}} = 1.8 \text{ m/s}$$

4 *Check your answer:*
Multiply your answer by the time. You should get the distance that was given.

Practice Problems

1. A runner completes a 400-m race in 43.9 s. In a 100-m race, he finishes in 10.4 s. In which race was his speed faster?

2. A passenger train travels from Boston to New York, a distance of 350 km, in 3.5 h. What is the train's speed?

 For more practice, visit in7.msscience.com/math_practice

Average Speed If a sprinter ran the 100-m dash in 10 s, she probably couldn't have run the entire race with a speed of 10 m/s. Consider that when the race started, the sprinter wasn't moving. Then, as she started running, she moved faster and faster, which increased her speed. During the entire race, the sprinter's speed could have been different from instant to instant. However, the sprinter's motion for the entire race can be described by her average speed, which is 10 m/s. **Average speed** is found by dividing the total distance traveled by the time taken.

Reading Check *How is average speed calculated?*

An object in motion can change speeds many times as it speeds up or slows down. The speed of an object at one instant of time is the object's **instantaneous speed**. To understand the difference between average and instantaneous speeds, think about walking to the library. If it takes you 0.5 h to walk 2 km to the library, your average speed would be as follows:

$$s = \frac{d}{t}$$
$$= \frac{2 \text{ km}}{0.5 \text{ h}} = 4 \text{ km/h}$$

However, you might not have been moving at the same speed throughout the trip. At a crosswalk, your instantaneous speed might have been 0 km/h. If you raced across the street, your speed might have been 7 km/h. If you were able to walk at a steady rate of 4 km/h during the entire trip, you would have moved at a constant speed. Average speed, instantaneous speed, and constant speed are illustrated in **Figure 4.**

Measuring Average Speed

Procedure
1. Choose two points, such as two doorways, and mark each with a small piece of **masking tape.**
2. Measure the distance between the two points.
3. Use a **watch, clock,** or **timer** that indicates seconds to time yourself walking from one mark to the other.
4. Time yourself walking slowly, walking safely and quickly, and walking with a varying speed; for example, slow/fast/slow.

Analysis
1. Calculate your average speed in each case.
2. Predict how long it would take you to walk 100 m slowly, at your normal speed, and quickly.

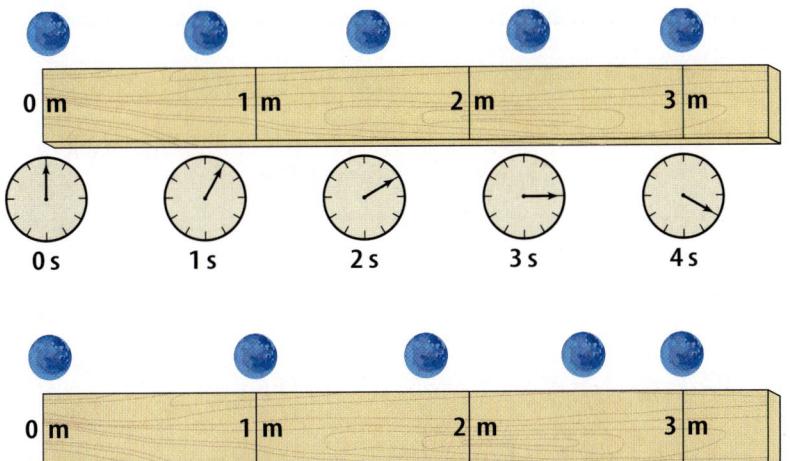

Figure 4 The average speed of each ball is the same from 0 s to 4 s.

The top ball is moving at a constant speed. In each second, the ball moves the same distance.

The bottom ball has a varying speed. Its instantaneous speed is fast between 0 s and 1 s, slower between 2 s and 3 s, and even slower between 3 s and 4 s.

SECTION 1 What is motion?

Science Online

Topic: Land Speed Record
Visit in7.msscience.com for Web links to information about how the land speed record has changed over the past century.

Activity Make a graph showing the increase in the land speed over time.

Graphing Motion

You can represent the motion of an object with a distance-time graph. For this type of graph, time is plotted on the horizontal axis and distance is plotted on the vertical axis. **Figure 5** shows the motion of two students who walked across a classroom plotted on a distance-time graph.

Distance-Time Graphs and Speed A distance-time graph can be used to compare the speeds of objects. Look at the graph shown in **Figure 5**. According to the graph, after 1 s student A traveled 1 m. Her average speed during the first second is as follows:

$$\text{speed} = \frac{\text{distance}}{\text{time}} = \frac{1 \text{ m}}{1 \text{ s}} = 1 \text{ m/s}$$

Student B, however, traveled only 0.5 m in the first second. His average speed is

$$\text{speed} = \frac{\text{distance}}{\text{time}} = \frac{0.5 \text{ m}}{1 \text{ s}} = 0.5 \text{ m/s}$$

So student A traveled faster than student B. Now compare the steepness of the lines on the graph in **Figure 5**. The line representing the motion of student A is steeper than the line for student B. A steeper line on the distance-time graph represents a greater speed. A horizontal line on the distance-time graph means that no change in position occurs. In that case, the speed, represented by the line on the graph, is zero.

Figure 5 The motion of two students walking across a classroom is plotted on this distance-time graph.

Use the graph to determine which student had the faster average speed.

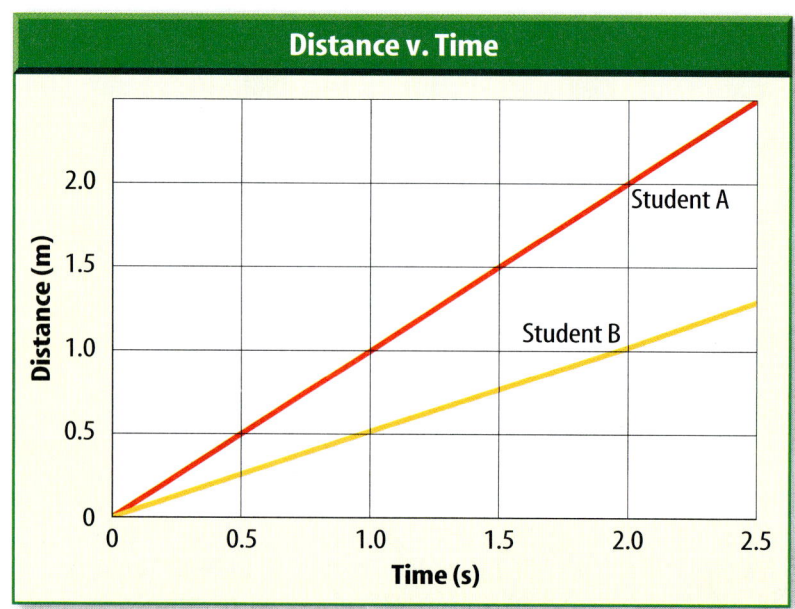

326 CHAPTER 11 Motion and Momentum

Velocity

If you are hiking in the woods, it is important to know in which direction you should walk in order to get back to camp. You want to know not only your speed, but also the direction in which you are moving. The **velocity** of an object is the speed of the object and the direction of its motion. This is why a compass and a map, like the one shown in **Figure 6,** are useful to hikers. The map and the compass help the hikers to determine what their velocity must be. Velocity has the same units as speed, but it includes the direction of motion.

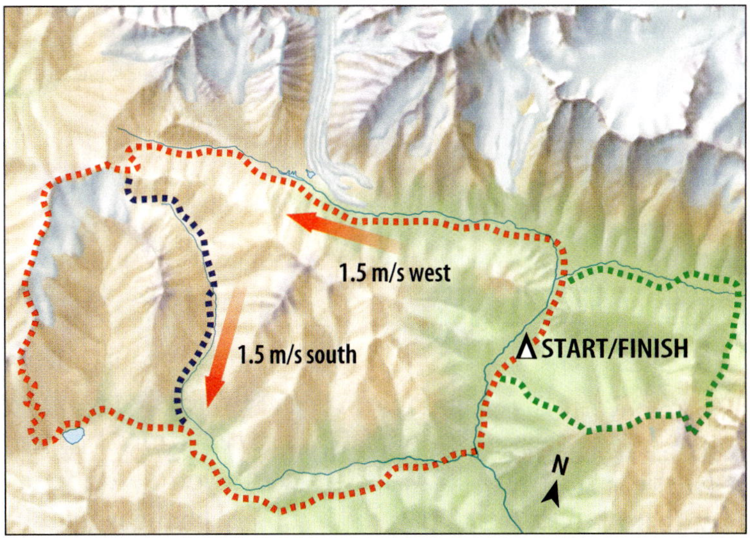

The velocity of an object can change if the object's speed changes, its direction of motion changes, or they both change. For example, suppose a car is traveling at a speed of 40 km/h north and then turns left at an intersection and continues on with a speed of 40 km/h. The speed of the car is constant at 40 km/h, but the velocity changes from 40 km/h north to 40 km/h west. Why can you say the velocity of a car changes as it comes to a stop at an intersection?

Figure 6 A map helps determine the direction in which you need to travel. Together with your speed, this gives your velocity.

section 1 review

Summary

Changing Position
- An object is in motion if it changes position relative to a reference point.
- Motion can be described by distance, speed, displacement, and velocity, where displacement and velocity also include direction.

Speed and Velocity
- The speed of an object can be calculated by dividing the distance traveled by the time needed to travel the distance.
- For an object traveling at constant speed, its average speed is the same as its instantaneous speed.
- The velocity of an object is the speed of the object and its direction of motion.

Graphing Motion
- A line on a distance-time graph becomes steeper as an object's speed increases.

Self Check

1. **Identify** the two pieces of information you need to know the velocity of an object.
2. **Make and Use Graphs** You walk forward at 1.5 m/s for 8 s. Your friend decides to walk faster and starts out at 2.0 m/s for the first 4 s. Then she slows down and walks forward at 1.0 m/s for the next 4 s. Make a distance-time graph of your motion and your friend's motion. Who walked farther?
3. **Think Critically** A bee flies 25 m north of the hive, then 10 m east, 5 m west, and 10 m south. How far north and east of the hive is it now? Explain how you calculated your answer.

Applying Math

4. **Calculate** the average velocity of a dancer who moves 5 m toward the left of the stage over the course of 15 s.
5. **Calculate Travel Time** An airplane flew a distance of 650 km at an average speed of 300 km/h. How much time did the flight take?

SECTION 2

Standard—This section builds a foundation for **Standard 7.3.17**.

Also covers: 7.2.7, 7.7.4 (Detailed standards begin on page IN8.)

Acceleration

as you read

What You'll Learn
- **Define** acceleration.
- **Predict** what effect acceleration will have on motion.

Why It's Important
Whenever the motion of an object changes, it is accelerating.

Review Vocabulary
kilogram: SI unit of mass, abbreviated kg; equal to approximately 2.2 lbs

New Vocabulary
- acceleration

Acceleration and Motion

When you watch the first few seconds of a liftoff, a rocket barely seems to move. With each passing second, however, you can see it move faster until it reaches an enormous speed. How could you describe the change in the rocket's motion? When an object changes its motion, it is accelerating. **Acceleration** is the change in velocity divided by the time it takes for the change to occur.

Like velocity, acceleration has a direction. If an object speeds up, the acceleration is in the direction that the object is moving. If an object slows down, the acceleration is opposite to the direction that the object is moving. What if the direction of the acceleration is at an angle to the direction of motion? Then the direction of motion will turn toward the direction of the acceleration.

Speeding Up You get on a bicycle and begin to pedal. The bike moves slowly at first, and then accelerates because its speed increases. When an object that is already in motion speeds up, it also is accelerating. Imagine that you are biking along a level path and you start pedaling harder. Your speed increases. When the speed of an object increases, it is accelerating.

Suppose a toy car is speeding up, as shown in **Figure 7**. Each second, the car moves at a greater speed and travels a greater distance than it did in the previous second. When the car stops accelerating, it will move in a straight line at the speed it had when the acceleration stopped.

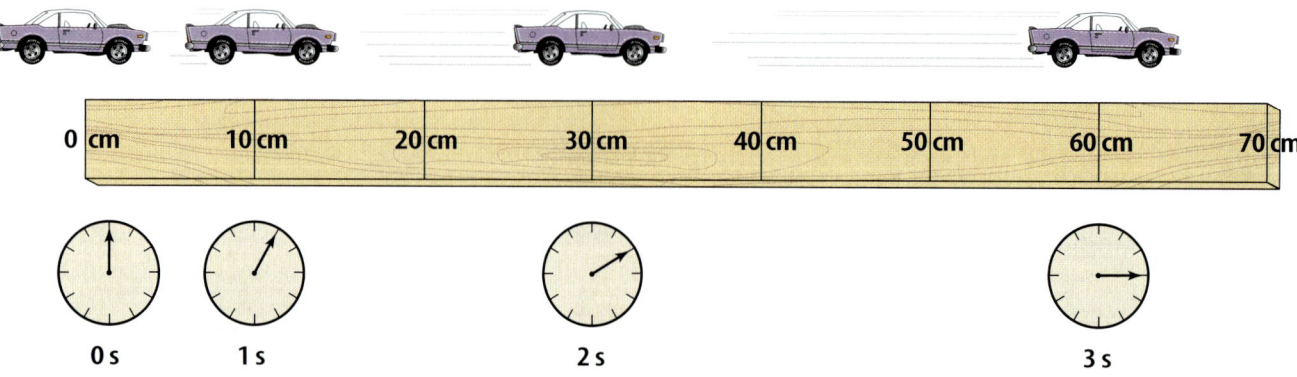

Figure 7 The toy car is accelerating to the right. Its speed is increasing.

328 CHAPTER 11 Motion and Momentum

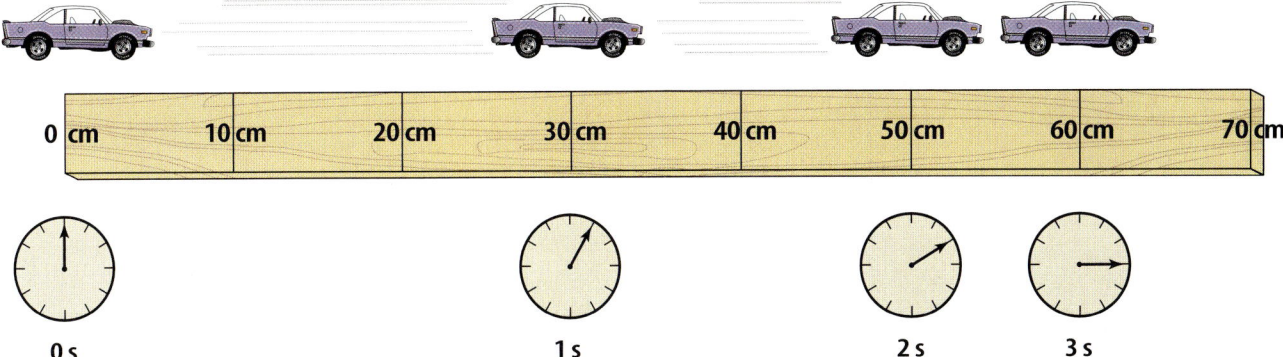

Slowing Down
Now suppose you are biking at a speed of 4 m/s and you apply the brakes. This causes you to slow down. It might sound odd, but because your speed is changing, you are accelerating. Acceleration occurs when an object slows down, as well as when it speeds up. The car in **Figure 8** is slowing down. During each time interval, the car travels a smaller distance, so its speed is decreasing.

In both of these examples, speed is changing, so acceleration is occurring. Because speed is decreasing in the second example, the direction of the acceleration is opposite to the direction of motion. Any time an object slows down, its acceleration is in the direction opposite to the direction of its motion.

Changing Direction
Motion is not always along a straight line. If the acceleration is at an angle to the direction of motion, the object will turn. At the same time, it might speed up, slow down, or not change speed at all.

Again imagine yourself riding a bicycle. When you lean to one side and turn the handlebars, the bike turns. Because the direction of the bike's motion has changed, the bike has accelerated. The acceleration is in the direction that the bicycle turned.

Figure 9 shows another example of an object that is accelerating. The ball starts moving upward, but its direction of motion changes as its path turns downward. Here the acceleration is downward. The longer the ball accelerates, the more its path turns toward the direction of acceleration.

 **What are three ways to accelerate?**

Figure 8 The car is moving to the right but accelerating to the left. In each time interval, it covers less distance and moves more slowly.
Determine *how the car's velocity is changing.*

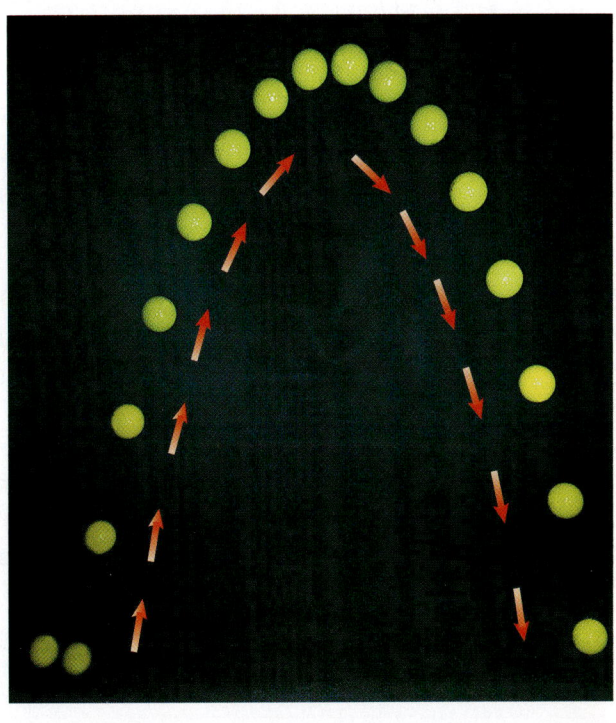

Figure 9 The ball starts out by moving forward and upward, but the acceleration is downward, so the ball's path turns in that direction.

SECTION 2 Acceleration **329**

Calculating Acceleration

If an object is moving in a straight line, its acceleration can be calculated using this equation.

Acceleration Equation

acceleration (in m/s²) =
$$\frac{(\text{final speed (in m/s)} - \text{initial speed (in m/s)})}{\text{time (in s)}}$$

$$a = \frac{(s_f - s_i)}{t}$$

In this equation, time is the length of time over which the motion changes. In SI units, acceleration has units of meters per second squared (m/s²).

Applying Math — Solve a Simple Equation

ACCELERATION OF A BUS Calculate the acceleration of a bus whose speed changes from 6 m/s to 12 m/s over a period of 3 s.

Solution

1 *This is what you know:*
- initial speed: s_i = 6 m/s
- final speed: s_f = 12 m/s
- time: t = 3 s

2 *This is what you need to know:*

acceleration: a = ? m/s²

3 *This is the procedure you need to use:*

Substitute the known values of initial speed, final speed and time in the acceleration equation and calculate the acceleration:

$$a = \frac{(s_f - s_i)}{t} = \frac{(12 \text{ m/s} - 6 \text{ m/s})}{3 \text{ s}} = 6\frac{\text{m}}{\text{s}} \times \frac{1}{3 \text{ s}} = 2 \text{ m/s}^2$$

4 *Check your answer:*

Multiply the calculated acceleration by the known time. Then add the known initial speed. You should get the final speed that was given.

Practice Problems

1. Find the acceleration of a train whose speed increases from 7 m/s to 17 m/s in 120 s.
2. A bicycle accelerates from rest to 6 m/s in 2 s. What is the bicycle's acceleration?

For more practice, visit in7.msscience.com/math_practice

CHAPTER 11 Motion and Momentum

Figure 10 When skidding to a stop, you are slowing down. This means you have a negative acceleration.

Positive and Negative Acceleration An object is accelerating when it speeds up, and the acceleration is in the same direction as the motion. An object also is accelerating when it slows down, but the acceleration is in the direction opposite to the motion, such as the bicycle in **Figure 10.** How else is acceleration different when an object is speeding up and slowing down?

Suppose you were riding your bicycle in a straight line and increased your speed from 4 m/s to 6 m/s in 5 s. You could calculate your acceleration from the equation on the previous page.

$$a = \frac{(s_f - s_i)}{t}$$
$$= \frac{(6 \text{ m/s} - 4 \text{ m/s})}{5 \text{ s}} = \frac{+2 \text{ m/s}}{5 \text{ s}}$$
$$= +0.4 \text{ m/s}^2$$

When you speed up, your final speed always will be greater than your initial speed. So subtracting your initial speed from your final speed gives a positive number. As a result, your acceleration is positive when you are speeding up.

Suppose you slow down from a speed of 4 m/s to 2 m/s in 5 s. Now the final speed is less than the initial speed. You could calculate your acceleration as follows:

$$a = \frac{(s_f - s_i)}{t}$$
$$= \frac{(2 \text{ m/s} - 4 \text{ m/s})}{5 \text{ s}} = \frac{-2 \text{ m/s}}{5 \text{ s}}$$
$$= -0.4 \text{ m/s}^2$$

Because your final speed is less than your initial speed, your acceleration is negative when you slow down.

Modeling Acceleration

Procedure
1. Use **masking tape** to lay a course on the floor. Mark a starting point and place marks along a straight path at 10 cm, 40 cm, 90 cm, 160 cm, and 250 cm from the start.
2. Clap a steady beat. On the first beat, the person walking the course should be at the starting point. On the second beat, the walker should be on the first mark, and so on.

Analysis
1. Describe what happens to your speed as you move along the course. Infer what would happen if the course were extended farther.
2. Repeat step 2, starting at the other end. Are you still accelerating? Explain.

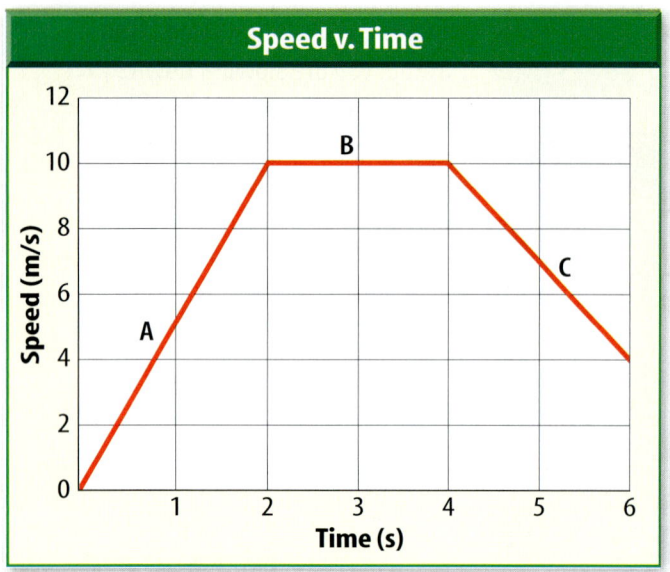

Figure 11 A speed-time graph can be used to find acceleration. When the line rises, the object is speeding up. When the line falls, the object is slowing down.
Infer what acceleration a horizontal line represents.

Graphing Accelerated Motion The motion of an object that is accelerating can be shown with a graph. For this type of graph, speed is plotted on the vertical axis and time on the horizontal axis. Take a look at **Figure 11.** On section A of the graph, the speed increases from 0 m/s to 10 m/s during the first 2 s, so the acceleration is +5 m/s². The line in section A slopes upward to the right. An object that is speeding up will have a line on a speed-time graph that slopes upward.

Now look at section C. Between 4 s and 6 s, the object slows down from 10 m/s to 4 m/s. The acceleration is −3 m/s². On the speed-time graph, the line in section C is sloping downward to the right. An object that is slowing down will have a line on a speed-time graph that slopes downward.

On section B, where the line is horizontal, the change in speed is zero. So a horizontal line on the speed-time graph represents an acceleration of zero or constant speed.

section 2 review

Summary

Acceleration and Motion
- Acceleration is the change in velocity divided by the time it takes to make the change. Acceleration has direction.
- Acceleration occurs whenever an object speeds up, slows down, or changes direction.

Calculating Acceleration
- For motion in a straight line, acceleration can be calculated from this equation:

$$a = \frac{s_f - s_i}{t}$$

- If an object is speeding up, its acceleration is positive; if an object is slowing down, its acceleration is negative.
- On a speed-time graph, a line sloping up represents positive acceleration, a line sloping down represents negative acceleration, and a horizontal line represents zero acceleration or constant speed.

Self Check

1. **Compare and contrast** speed, velocity, and acceleration.
2. **Infer** the motion of a car whose speed-time graph shows a horizontal line, followed by a straight line that slopes downward to the bottom of the graph.
3. **Think Critically** You start to roll backward down a hill on your bike, so you use the brakes to stop your motion. In what direction did you accelerate?

Applying Math

4. **Calculate** the acceleration of a runner who accelerates from 0 m/s to 3 m/s in 12 s.
5. **Calculate Speed** An object falls with an acceleration of 9.8 m/s². What is its speed after 2 s?
6. **Make and Use a Graph** A sprinter had the following speeds at different times during a race: 0 m/s at 0 s, 4 m/s at 2 s, 7 m/s at 4 s, 10 m/s at 6 s, 12 m/s at 8 s, and 10 m/s at 10 s. Plot these data on a speed-time graph. During what time intervals is the acceleration positive? Negative? Is the acceleration ever zero?

Standard—7.7.4: Use symbolic equations to show how the quantity of something changes over time or in response to changes in other quantities.

section 3

Also covers: 7.2.7 (Detailed standards begin on page IN8.)

Momentum

Mass and Inertia

The world you live in is filled with objects in motion. How can you describe these objects? Objects have many properties such as color, size, and composition. One important property of an object is its mass. The **mass** of an object is the amount of matter in the object. In SI units, the unit for mass is the kilogram.

The weight of an object is related to the object's mass. Objects with more mass weigh more than objects with less mass. A bowling ball has more mass than a pillow, so it weighs more than a pillow. However, the size of an object is not the same as the mass of the object. For example, a pillow is larger than a bowling ball, but the bowling ball has more mass.

Objects with different masses are different in an important way. Think about what happens when you try to stop someone who is rushing toward you. A small child is easy to stop. A large adult is hard to stop. The more mass an object has, the harder it is to start it moving, slow it down, speed it up, or turn it. This tendency of an object to resist a change in its motion is called **inertia**. Objects with more mass have more inertia, as shown in **Figure 12.** The more mass an object has, the harder it is to change its motion.

Reading Check *What is inertia?*

as you read

What You'll Learn
- **Explain** the relationship between mass and inertia.
- **Define** momentum.
- **Predict** motion using the law of conservation of momentum.

Why It's Important

Objects in motion have momentum. The motion of objects after they collide depends on their momentum.

Review Vocabulary
triple-beam balance: scientific instrument used to measure mass precisely by comparing the mass of a sample to known masses

New Vocabulary
- mass
- inertia
- momentum
- law of conservation of momentum

Figure 12 The more mass an object has, the greater its inertia is. A table-tennis ball responds to a gentle hit that would move a tennis ball only slightly.

SECTION 3 Momentum **333**

Forensics and Momentum
Forensic investigations of accidents and crimes often involve determining the momentum of an object. For example, the law of conservation of momentum sometimes is used to reconstruct the motion of vehicles involved in a collision. Research other ways momentum is used in forensic investigations.

Momentum

You know that the faster a bicycle moves, the harder it is to stop. Just as increasing the mass of an object makes it harder to stop, so does increasing the speed or velocity of the object. The **momentum** of an object is a measure of how hard it is to stop the object, and it depends on the object's mass and velocity. Momentum is usually symbolized by p.

Momentum Equation
momentum (in kg · m/s) = **mass** (in kg) × **velocity** (in m/s)
$$p = mv$$

Mass is measured in kilograms and velocity has units of meters per second, so momentum has units of kilograms multiplied by meters per second (kg · m/s). Also, because velocity includes a direction, momentum has a direction that is the same as the direction of the velocity.

 Explain how an object's momentum changes as its velocity changes.

Applying Math — Solve a Simple Equation

MOMENTUM OF A BICYCLE Calculate the momentum of a 14-kg bicycle traveling north at 2 m/s.

Solution

① *This is what you know:*
- mass: $m = 14$ kg
- velocity: $v = 2$ m/s north

② *This is what you need to find:*
momentum: $p = ?$ kg · m/s

③ *This is the procedure you need to use:*
Substitute the known values of mass and velocity into the momentum equation and calculate the momentum:
$p = mv = (14$ kg$)(2$ m/s north$) = 28$ kg · m/s north

④ *Check your answer:*
Divide the calculated momentum by the mass of the bicycle. You should get the velocity that was given.

Practice Problems

1. A 10,000-kg train is traveling east at 15 m/s. Calculate the momentum of the train.
2. What is the momentum of a car with a mass of 900 kg traveling north at 27 m/s?

 For more practice, visit in7.msscience.com/math_practice

Conservation of Momentum

If you've ever played billiards, you know that when the cue ball hits another ball, the motions of both balls change. The cue ball slows down and may change direction, so its momentum decreases. Meanwhile, the other ball starts moving, so its momentum increases. It seems as if momentum is transferred from the cue ball to the other ball.

In fact, during the collision, the momentum lost by the cue ball was gained by the other ball. This means that the total momentum of the two balls was the same just before and just after the collision. This is true for any collision, as long as no outside forces such as friction act on the objects and change their speeds after the collision. According to the **law of conservation of momentum,** the total momentum of objects that collide is the same before and after the collision. This is true for the collisions of the billiard balls shown in **Figure 13,** as well as for collisions of atoms, cars, football players, or any other matter.

Using Momentum Conservation

Outside forces, such as gravity and friction, are almost always acting on objects that are colliding. However, sometimes, the effects of these forces are small enough that they can be ignored. Then the law of conservation of momentum enables you to predict how the motions of objects will change after a collision.

There are many ways that collisions can occur. Two examples are shown in **Figure 14.** Sometimes, the objects that collide will bounce off of each other, like the bowling ball and bowling pins. In other collisions, objects will stick to each other after the collision, like the two football players. In both of these types of collisions, the law of conservation of momentum enables the speeds of the objects after the collision to be calculated.

Figure 13 When the cue ball hits the other billiard balls, it slows down because it transfers some of its momentum to the other billiard balls.
Predict *what would happen to the speed of the cue ball if all of its momentum were transferred to the other billiard balls.*

Figure 14 In these collisions, the total momentum before the collision equals the total momentum after the collision.

When the bowling ball hits the pins, some of its momentum is transferred to the pins. The ball slows down, and the pins speed up.

When one player tackles the other, they both change speeds, but momentum is conserved.

Before the student on skates and the backpack collide, she is not moving.

After the collision, the student and the backpack move together at a slower speed than the backpack had before the collision.

Figure 15 Momentum is conserved in the collision of the backpack and the student.

Sticking Together Imagine being on skates when someone throws a backpack to you, as in **Figure 15**. When you catch the backpack, you and the backpack continue to move in the same direction as the backpack was moving before the collision.

The law of conservation of momentum can be used to find your velocity after you catch the backpack. Suppose a 2-kg backpack is tossed at a speed of 5 m/s. Your mass is 48 kg, and initially you are at rest. Then the total initial momentum is

total momentum = momentum of backpack + your momentum
= 2 kg × 5 m/s + 48 kg × 0 m/s
= 10 kg · m/s

After the collision, the total momentum remains the same, and only one object is moving. Its mass is the sum of your mass and the mass of the backpack. You can use the equation for momentum to find the final velocity.

total momentum = (mass of backpack + your mass) × velocity
10 kg · m/s = (2 kg + 48 kg) × velocity
10 kg · m/s = (50 kg) × velocity
0.2 m/s = velocity

This is your velocity right after you catch the backpack. As you continue to move on your skates, the force of friction between the ground and the skates slows you down. Because of friction, the momentum of you and the backpack together continually decreases until you come to a stop. **Figure 16** shows the results of some collisions between two objects with various masses and velocities.

Topic: Collisions
Visit in7.msscience.com for Web links to information about collisions between objects with different masses.

Activity Draw diagrams showing the results of collisions between a bowling ball and a tennis ball if they are moving in the same direction and if they are in opposite directions.

NATIONAL GEOGRAPHIC
VISUALIZING CONSERVATION OF MOMENTUM

Figure 16

The law of conservation of momentum can be used to predict the results of collisions between different objects, whether they are subatomic particles smashing into each other at enormous speeds, or the collisions of marbles, as shown on this page. What happens when one marble hits another marble initially at rest? The results of the collisions depend on the masses of the marbles.

A Here, a less massive marble strikes a more massive marble that is at rest. After the collision, the smaller marble bounces off in the opposite direction. The larger marble moves in the same direction that the small marble was initially moving.

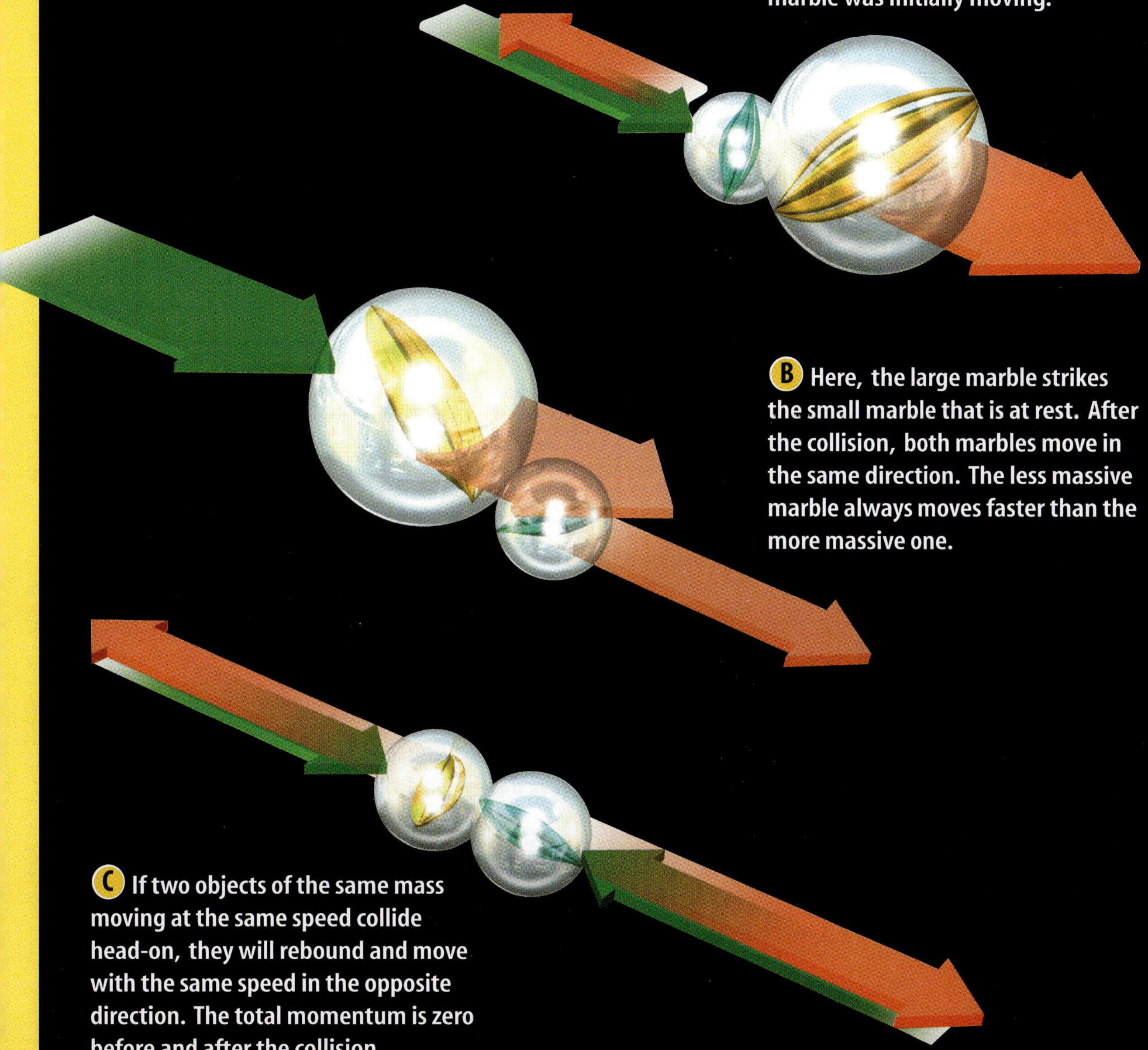

B Here, the large marble strikes the small marble that is at rest. After the collision, both marbles move in the same direction. The less massive marble always moves faster than the more massive one.

C If two objects of the same mass moving at the same speed collide head-on, they will rebound and move with the same speed in the opposite direction. The total momentum is zero before and after the collision.

SECTION 3 Momentum

Figure 17 When bumper cars collide, they bounce off each other, and momentum is transferred.

Colliding and Bouncing Off In some collisions, the objects involved, like the bumper cars in **Figure 17,** bounce off each other. The law of conservation of momentum can be used to determine how these objects move after they collide.

For example, suppose two identical objects moving with the same speed collide head on and bounce off. Before the collision, the momentum of each object is the same, but in opposite directions. So the total momentum before the collision is zero. If momentum is conserved, the total momentum after the collision must be zero also. This means that the two objects must move in opposite directions with the same speed after the collision. Then the total momentum once again is zero.

section 3 review

Summary

Mass, Inertia, and Momentum
- Mass is the amount of matter in an object.
- Inertia is the tendency of an object to resist a change in motion. Inertia increases as the mass of an object increases.
- The momentum of an object in motion is related to how hard it is to stop the object, and can be calculated from the following equation:
  $$p = mv$$
- Because velocity has a direction, momentum also has a direction.

The Law of Conservation of Momentum
- The law of conservation of momentum states that in a collision, the total momentum of the objects that collide is the same before and after the collision.

Self Check

1. **Explain** how momentum is transferred when a golfer hits a ball with a golf club.
2. **Determine** if the momentum of an object moving in a circular path at constant speed is constant.
3. **Explain** why the momentum of a billiard ball rolling on a billiard table changes.
4. **Think Critically** Two identical balls move directly toward each other with equal speeds. How will the balls move if they collide and stick together?

Applying Math

5. **Calculate Momentum** What is the momentum of a 0.1-kg mass moving with a speed of 5 m/s?
6. **Calculate Speed** A 1-kg ball moving at 3 m/s strikes a 2-kg ball and stops. If the 2-kg ball was initially at rest, find its speed after the collision.

Science online in7.msscience.com/self_check_quiz

Collisions

A collision occurs when a baseball bat hits a baseball or a tennis racket hits a tennis ball. What would happen if you hit a baseball with a table-tennis paddle or a table-tennis ball with a baseball bat? How do the masses of colliding objects change the results of collisions?

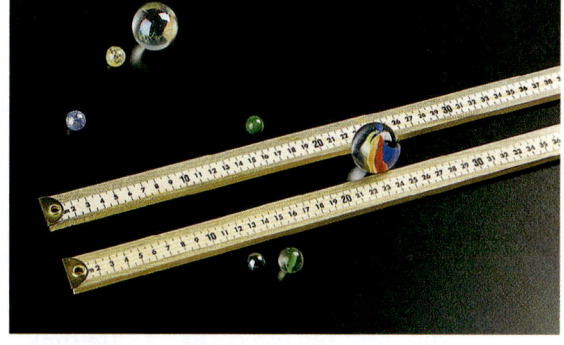

Real-World Question

How does changing the size and number of objects in a collision affect the collision?

Goals
- **Compare and contrast** different collisions.
- **Determine** how the speeds after a collision depend on the masses of the colliding objects.

Materials
small marbles (5)
large marbles (2)
metersticks (2)
tape

Safety Precautions

Procedure

1. Tape the metersticks next to each other, slightly farther apart than the width of the large marbles. This limits the motion of the marbles to nearly a straight line.
2. Place a small target marble in the center of the track formed by the metersticks. Place another small marble at one end of the track. Flick the small marble toward the target marble. Describe the collision.
3. Repeat step 2, replacing the two small marbles with the two large marbles.
4. Repeat step 2, replacing the small shooter marble with a large marble.
5. Repeat step 2, replacing the small target marble with a large marble.
6. Repeat step 2, replacing the small target marble with four small marbles that are touching.
7. Place two small marbles at opposite ends of the metersticks. Shoot the marbles toward each other and describe the collision.
8. Place two large marbles at opposite ends of the metersticks. Shoot the marbles toward each other and describe the collision.
9. Place a small marble and a large marble at opposite ends of the metersticks. Shoot the marbles toward each other and describe the collision.

Conclude and Apply

1. **Describe** In which collisions did the shooter marble change direction? How did the mass of the target marble compare with the mass of the shooter marble in these collisions?
2. **Explain** how momentum was conserved in these collisions.

Communicating Your Data

Make a chart showing your results. You might want to make before-and-after sketches, with short arrows to show slow movement and long arrows to show fast movement.

LAB **339**

LAB

Design Your Own

Car Safety Testing

Goals
- **Construct** a fast car.
- **Design** a safe car that will protect a plastic egg from the effects of inertia when the car crashes.

Possible Materials
insulated foam meat trays or fast food trays
insulated foam cups
straws, narrow and wide
straight pins
tape
plastic eggs

Safety Precautions

WARNING: *Protect your eyes from possible flying objects.*

🔸 Real-World Question

Imagine that you are a car designer. How can you create an attractive, fast car that is safe? When a car crashes, the passengers have inertia that can keep them moving. How can you protect the passengers from stops caused by sudden, head-on impacts?

🔸 Form a Hypothesis

Develop a hypothesis about how to design a car to deliver a plastic egg quickly and safely through a race course and a crash at the end.

🔸 Test Your Hypothesis

Make a Plan

1. Be sure your group has agreed on the hypothesis statement.
2. **Sketch** the design for your car. List the materials you will need. Remember that to make the car move smoothly, narrow straws will have to fit into the wider straws.

340 CHAPTER 11 Motion and Momentum

Using Scientific Methods

3. As a group, make a detailed list of the steps you will take to test your hypothesis.
4. Gather the materials you will need to carry out your experiment.

Follow Your Plan

1. Make sure your teacher approves your plan before you start. Include any changes suggested by your teacher in your plans.

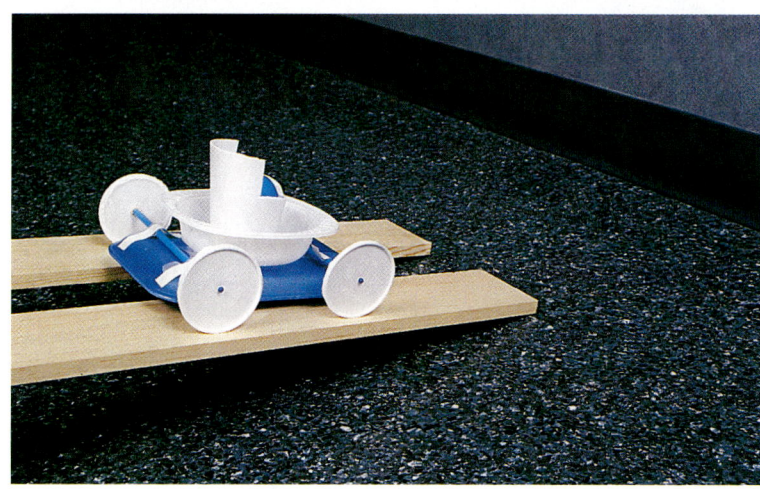

2. Carry out the experiment as planned.
3. **Record** any observations that you made while doing your experiment. Include suggestions for improving your design.

Analyze Your Data

1. **Compare** your car design to the designs of the other groups. What made the fastest car fast? What slowed the slowest car?
2. **Compare** your car's safety features to those of the other cars. What protected the eggs the best? How could you improve the unsuccessful designs?
3. **Predict** What effect would decreasing the speed of your car have on the safety of the egg?

Conclude and Apply

1. **Summarize** How did the best designs protect the egg?
2. **Apply** If you were designing cars, what could you do to better protect passengers from sudden stops?

Communicating Your Data

Write a descriptive paragraph about ways a car could be designed to protect its passengers effectively. Include a sketch of your ideas.

LAB **341**

Oops! Accidents in Science

SOMETIMES GREAT DISCOVERIES HAPPEN BY ACCIDENT!

What Goes Around Comes Around
The Story of Boomerangs

Imagine a group gathered on a flat, yellow plain on the Australian Outback. One youth steps forward and, with the flick of an arm, sends a long, flat, angled stick soaring and spinning into the sky. The stick's path curves until it returns right back into the thrower's hand. Thrower after thrower steps forward, and the contest goes on all afternoon.

This contest involved throwing boomerangs—elegantly curved sticks. Because of how boomerangs are shaped, they always return to the thrower's hand

This amazing design is over 15,000 years old. Scientists believe that boomerangs developed from simple clubs thrown to stun and kill animals for food. Differently shaped clubs flew in different ways. As the shape of the club was refined, people probably started throwing them for fun too. In fact, today, using boomerangs for fun is still a popular sport, as world-class throwers compete in contests of strength and skill.

Boomerangs come in several forms, but all of them have several things in common. First a boomerang is shaped like an airplane's wing: flat on one side and curved on the other. Second, boomerangs are angled, which makes them spin as they fly. These two features determine the aerodynamics that give the boomerang its unique flight path.

From its beginning as a hunting tool to its use in today's World Boomerang Championships, the boomerang has remained a source of fascination for thousands of years.

Design Boomerangs are made from various materials. Research to find instructions for making boomerangs. After you and your friends build some boomerangs, have a competition of your own.

Science online
For more information, visit in7.msscience.com/oops

chapter 11 Study Guide

Reviewing Main Ideas

Section 1 — What is motion?

1. The position of an object depends on the reference point that is chosen.
2. An object is in motion if the position of the object is changing.
3. The speed of an object equals the distance traveled divided by the time:
$$s = \frac{d}{t}$$
4. The velocity of an object includes the speed and the direction of motion.
5. The motion of an object can be represented on a speed-time graph.

Section 2 — Acceleration

1. Acceleration is a measure of how quickly velocity changes. It includes a direction.
2. An object is accelerating when it speeds up, slows down, or turns.
3. When an object moves in a straight line, its acceleration can be calculated by
$$a = \frac{(s_f - s_i)}{t}$$

Section 3 — Momentum

1. Momentum equals the mass of an object times its velocity:
$$p = mv$$
2. Momentum is transferred from one object to another in a collision.
3. According to the law of conservation of momentum, the total amount of momentum of a group of objects doesn't change unless outside forces act on the objects.

Visualizing Main Ideas

Copy and complete the following table on motion.

Describing Motion

Quantity	Definition	Direction
Distance	length of path traveled	no
Displacement	direction and change in position	
Speed		no
Velocity	rate of change in position and direction	
Acceleration		
Momentum		yes

chapter 11 Review

Using Vocabulary

acceleration p. 328
average speed p. 325
inertia p. 333
instantaneous speed p. 325
law of conservation of momentum p. 335
mass p. 333
momentum p. 334
speed p. 324
velocity p. 327

Explain the relationship between each pair of terms.

1. speed—velocity
2. velocity—acceleration
3. velocity—momentum
4. momentum—law of conservation of momentum
5. mass—momentum
6. mass—inertia
7. momentum—inertia
8. average speed—instantaneous speed

Checking Concepts

Choose the word or phrase that best answers the question.

9. What measures the quantity of matter?
   A) speed
   B) weight
   C) acceleration
   D) mass

10. Which of the following objects is NOT accelerating?
    A) a jogger moving at a constant speed
    B) a car that is slowing down
    C) Earth orbiting the Sun
    D) a car that is speeding up

11. Which of the following equals speed?
    A) acceleration/time
    B) (change in velocity)/time
    C) distance/time
    D) displacement/time

12. A parked car is hit by a moving car, and the two cars stick together. How does the speed of the combined cars compare to the speed of the car before the collision?
    A) The combined speed is the same.
    B) The combined speed is greater.
    C) The combined speed is smaller.
    D) Any of these could be true.

13. What is a measure of inertia?
    A) weight
    B) gravity
    C) momentum
    D) mass

14. What is 18 cm/h north an example of?
    A) speed
    B) velocity
    C) acceleration
    D) momentum

15. Ball A bumps into ball B. Which is the same before and after the collision?
    A) the momentum of ball A
    B) the momentum of ball B
    C) the sum of the momentums
    D) the difference in the momentums

16. Which of the following equals the change in velocity divided by the time?
    A) speed
    B) displacement
    C) momentum
    D) acceleration

17. You travel to a city 200 km away in 2.5 hours. What is your average speed in km/h?
    A) 180 km/h
    B) 12.5 km/h
    C) 80 km/h
    D) 500 km/h

18. Two objects collide and stick together. How does the total momentum change?
    A) Total momentum increases.
    B) Total momentum decreases.
    C) The total momentum doesn't change.
    D) The total momentum is zero.

chapter 11 Review

Thinking Critically

19. **Explain** You run 100 m in 25 s. If you later run the same distance in less time, explain if your average speed increase or decrease.

Use the graph below to answer questions 20 and 21.

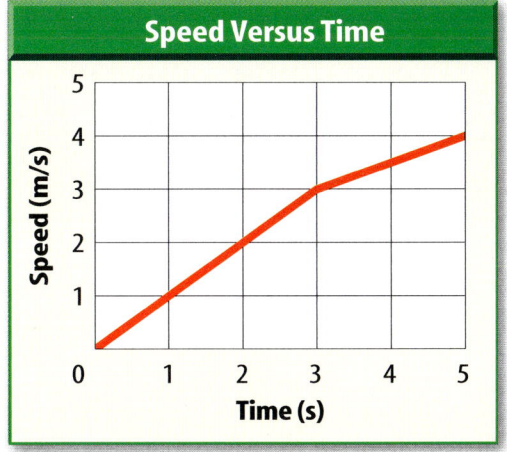

20. **Compare** For the motion of the object plotted on the speed-time graph above, how does the acceleration between 0 s and 3 s compare to the acceleration between 3 s and 5 s?

21. **Calculate** the acceleration of the object over the time interval from 0 s to 3 s.

22. **Infer** The molecules in a gas are often modeled as small balls. If the molecules all have the same mass, infer what happens if two molecules traveling at the same speed collide head on.

23. **Calculate** What is your displacement if you walk 100 m north, 20 m east, 30 m south, 50 m west, and then 70 m south?

24. **Infer** You are standing on ice skates and throw a basketball forward. Infer how your motion after you throw the basketball compares with the motion of the basketball.

25. **Determine** You throw a ball upward and then it falls back down. How does the velocity of the ball change as it rises and falls?

Use the graph below to answer question 26.

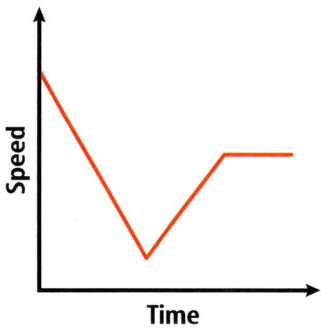

26. **Make and Use Graphs** The motion of a car is plotted on the speed-time graph above. Over which section of the graph is the acceleration of the car zero?

Performance Activities

27. **Demonstrate** Design a racetrack and make rules that specify the types of motion allowed. Demonstrate how to measure distance, measure time, and calculate speed accurately.

Applying Math

28. **Speed of a Ball** Calculate the speed of a 2-kg ball that has a momentum of 10 kg · m/s.

29. **Distance Traveled** A car travels for a half hour at a speed of 40 km/h. How far does the car travel?

Use the graph below to answer question 30.

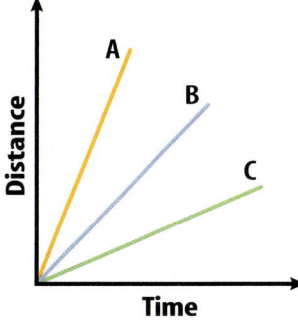

30. **Speed** From the graph determine which object is moving the fastest and which is moving the slowest.

chapter 11 Indiana

The assessed Indiana standard appears above the question.

Record your answers on the answer sheet provided by your teacher or on a sheet of paper.

Part 1 | Multiple Choice

The illustration below show the position of a ball at one-second time intervals.

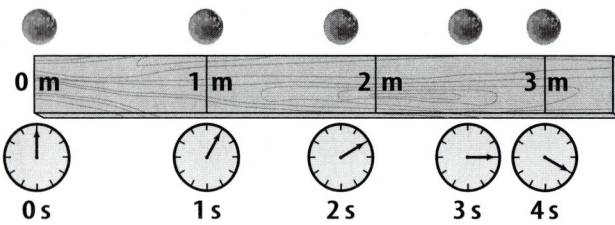

7.7.4

1. Over which time period is the ball's average speed largest?

   A 0 s to 1 s

   B 1 s to 2 s

   C 2 s to 3 s

   D 3 s to 4 s

7.7.4

2. What is the average speed of the ball over the 3-m distance in the illustration above?

   A 0.75 m/s

   B 1.0 m/s

   C 1.25 m/s

   D 1.5 m/s

7.7.4

3. A car's speed changes from 15 m/s to 30 m/s in 3.0 s. What is the car's acceleration?

   A 5 m/s^2

   B 10 m/s^2

   C 15 m/s^2

   D 45 m/s^2

The graph below shows a speed-time graph.

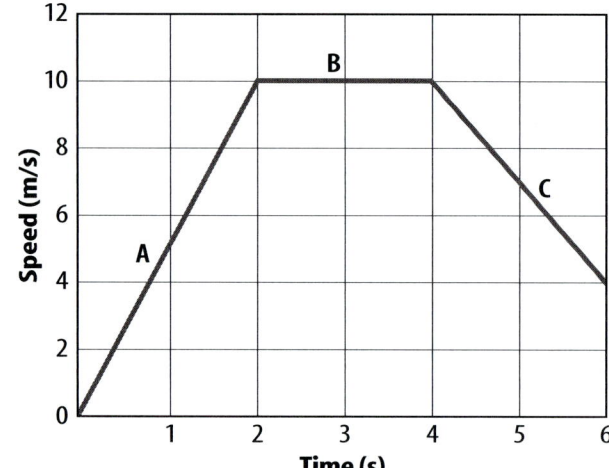

7.7.4

4. What is the acceleration over the time interval 4 s to 6 s?

   A -3 m/s^2

   B -1.5 m/s^2

   C 1.5 m/s^2

   D 3 m/s^2

7.7.4

5. Over what time interval is the speed of the object constant in the graph above?

   A 0 s to 1 s

   B 1 s to 2 s

   C 2 s to 3 s

   D 4 s to 5 s

Standards Review

7.7.4

6. A car travels for 5.5 h at an average speed of 75 km/h. How far did the car travel?

- A 13.6 km
- B 53.9 km
- C 75 km
- D 412.5 km

7. What is the momentum of a 21-kg bicycle traveling west at 3.0 m/s?

- A 7 kg · m/s west
- B 18 kg · m/s west
- C 24 kg · m/s west
- D 63 kg · m/s west

7.7.4

8. The graph below shows the motion of two students.

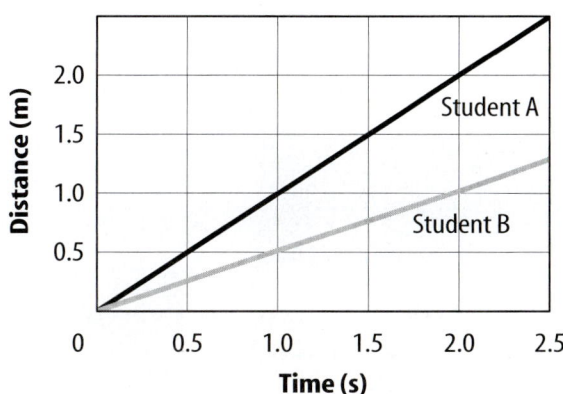

Distance v. Time

How does the speed of student A compare to the speed of student B?

- A It is half as large.
- B It is the same.
- C It is twice as large.
- D It is three times as large.

Part 2 Constructed Response

The illustration below shows the path of a ball.

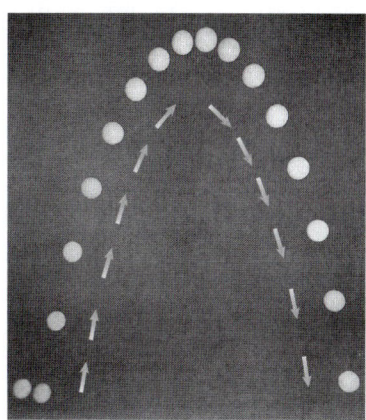

9. Describe the motion of the ball in terms of its speed, velocity, and acceleration.

10. During which part of its path does the ball have positive acceleration? During which part of its path does it have negative acceleration? Explain.

11. A girl leaves school at 3:00 and starts walking home. Her house is 2 km from school. She gets home at 3:30. What was her average speed? Do you know her instantaneous speed at 3:15? Why or why not?

12. If a car is moving with a constant speed, can you be certain the car is not accelerating? Explain.

Test-Taking Tip

Look for Missing Information Questions sometimes will ask about missing information. Notice what is missing as well as what is given.

chapter 12

Academic Standard—3: Students collect and organize data to identify relationships between physical objects, events, and processes. They use logical reasoning to question their own ideas as new information challenges their conceptions of the natural world.

Also covers: Academic Standards 1, 2, 7 (Detailed standards begin on page IN8.)

Force and Newton's Laws

chapter preview

sections
1. Newton's First Law
2. Newton's Second Law
3. Newton's Third Law
   Lab Balloon Races
   Lab Modeling Motion in Two Directions
   Virtual Labs What is Newton's second law of motion?

Moving at a Crawl
This enormous vehicle is a crawler that moves a space shuttle to the launch pad. The crawler and space shuttle together have a mass of about 7,700,000 kg. To move the crawler at a speed of about 1.5 km/h requires a force of about 10,000,000 N. This force is exerted by 16 electric motors in the crawler.

Science Journal Describe three examples of pushing or pulling an object. How did the object move?

Start-Up Activities

Forces and Motion

Imagine being on a bobsled team speeding down an icy run. Forces are exerted on the sled by the ice, the sled's brakes and steering mechanism, and gravity. Newton's laws predict how these forces cause the bobsled to turn, speed up, or slow down. Newton's Laws tell how forces cause the motion of any object to change.

1. Lean two metersticks parallel, less than a marble width apart on three books as shown on the left. This is your ramp.
2. Tap a marble so it rolls up the ramp. Measure how far up the ramp it travels before rolling back.
3. Repeat step 2 using two books, one book, and zero books. The same person should tap with the same force each time.
4. **Think Critically** Make a table to record the motion of the marble for each ramp height. What would happen if the ramp were perfectly smooth and level?

Newton's Laws Make the following Foldable to help you organize your thoughts about Newton's laws.

STEP 1 **Fold** a sheet of paper in half lengthwise. Make the back edge about 5 cm longer than the front edge.

STEP 2 **Turn** the paper so the fold is on the bottom. Then **fold** it into thirds.

STEP 3 **Unfold and cut** only the top layer along both folds to make three tabs.

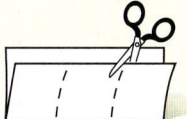

STEP 4 **Label** the foldable as shown.

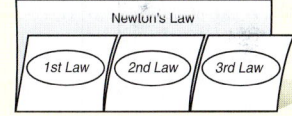

Make a Concept Map As you read the chapter, record what you learn about each of Newton's laws in your concept map.

Preview this chapter's content and activities at
in7.msscience.com

section 1

Standard—7.3.17: Investigate that an unbalanced force, acting on an object, changes its speed or path of motion or both, and know that if the force always acts toward the same center as the object moves, the object's path may curve into an orbit around the center.

Also covers: 7.1.5, 7.7.4 (Detailed standards begin on page IN8.)

Newton's First Law

as you read

What You'll Learn
- **Distinguish** between balanced and net forces.
- **Describe** Newton's first law of motion.
- **Explain** how friction affects motion.

Why It's Important
Newton's first law explains why objects change direction.

Review Vocabulary
velocity: the speed and direction of a moving object

New Vocabulary
- force
- net force
- balanced forces
- unbalanced forces
- Newton's first law of motion
- friction

Force

A soccer ball sits on the ground, motionless, until you kick it. Your science book sits on the table until you pick it up. If you hold your book above the ground, then let it go, gravity pulls it to the floor. In every one of these cases, the motion of the ball or book was changed by something pushing or pulling on it. An object will speed up, slow down, or turn only if something is pushing or pulling on it.

A **force** is a push or a pull. Examples of forces are shown in **Figure 1.** Think about throwing a ball. Your hand exerts a force on the ball, and the ball accelerates forward until it leaves your hand. After the ball leaves your hand, the force of gravity causes its path to curve downward. When the ball hits the ground, the ground exerts a force, stopping the ball.

A force can be exerted in different ways. For instance, a paper clip can be moved by the force a magnet exerts, the pull of Earth's gravity, or the force you exert when you pick it up. These are all examples of forces acting on the paper clip.

The magnet on the crane pulls the pieces of scrap metal upward.

Figure 1 A force is a push or a pull.

This golf club exerts a force by pushing on the golf ball.

350 CHAPTER 12 Force and Newton's Laws

This door is not moving because the forces exerted on it are equal and in opposite directions.

The door is closing because the force pushing the door closed is greater than the force pushing it open.

Figure 2 When the forces on an object are balanced, no change in motion occurs. A change in motion occurs only when the forces acting on an object are unbalanced.

Combining Forces More than one force can act on an object at the same time. If you hold a paper clip near a magnet, you, the magnet, and gravity all exert forces on the paper clip. The combination of all the forces acting on an object is the **net force**. When more than one force is acting on an object, the net force determines the motion of the object. In this example, the paper clip is not moving, so the net force is zero.

How do forces combine to form the net force? If the forces are in the same direction, they add together to form the net force. If two forces are in opposite directions, then the net force is the difference between the two forces, and it is in the direction of the larger force.

Balanced and Unbalanced Forces A force can act on an object without causing it to accelerate if other forces cancel the push or pull of the force. Look at **Figure 2**. If you and your friend push on a door with the same force in opposite directions, the door does not move. Because you both exert forces of the same size in opposite directions on the door, the two forces cancel each other. Two or more forces exerted on an object are **balanced forces** if their effects cancel each other and they do not cause a change in the object's motion. If the forces on an object are balanced, the net force is zero. If the forces are **unbalanced forces**, their effects don't cancel each other. Any time the forces acting on an object are unbalanced, the net force is not zero and the motion of the object changes.

Biomechanics Whether you run, jump, or sit, forces are being exerted on different parts of your body. Biomechanics is the study of how the body exerts forces and how it is affected by forces acting on it. Research how biomechanics has been used to reduce job-related injuries. Write a paragraph on what you've learned in your Science Journal.

Newton's First Law of Motion

If you stand on a skateboard and someone gives you a push, then you and your skateboard will start moving. You will begin to move when the force was applied. An object at rest—like you on your skateboard—remains at rest unless an unbalanced force acts on it and causes it to move.

Because a force had to be applied to make you move when you and your skateboard were at rest, you might think that a force has to be applied continually to keep an object moving. Surprisingly, this is not the case. An object can be moving even if the net force acting on it is zero.

The Italian scientist Galileo Galilei, who lived from 1564 to 1642, was one of the first to understand that a force doesn't need to be constantly applied to an object to keep it moving.

Galileo's ideas helped Isaac Newton to better understand the nature of motion. Newton, who lived from 1642 to 1727, explained the motion of objects in three rules called Newton's laws of motion.

Newton's first law of motion describes how an object moves when the net force acting on it is zero. According to **Newton's first law of motion,** if the net force acting on an object is zero, the object remains at rest, or if the object is already moving, continues to move in a straight line with constant speed.

Friction

Galileo realized the motion of an object doesn't change until an unbalanced force acts on it. Every day you see moving objects come to a stop. The force that brings nearly everything to a stop is **friction,** which is the force that acts to resist sliding between two touching surfaces, as shown in **Figure 3**. Friction is why you never see objects moving with constant velocity unless a net force is applied. Friction is the force that eventually brings your skateboard to a stop unless you keep pushing on it. Friction also acts on objects that are sliding or moving through substances such as air or water.

Figure 3 When two objects in contact try to slide past each other, friction keeps them from moving or slows them down.

Without friction, the rock climber would slide down the rock.

Friction slows down this sliding baseball player.

Friction Opposes Sliding Although several different forms of friction exist, they all have one thing in common. If two objects are in contact, frictional forces always try to prevent one object from sliding on the other object. If you rub your hand against a tabletop, you can feel the friction push against the motion of your hand. If you rub the other way, you can feel the direction of friction change so it is again acting against your hand's motion. Friction always will slow a moving object.

 *What do the different forms of friction have in common?*

Older Ideas About Motion It took a long time to understand motion. One reason was that people did not understand the behavior of friction and that friction was a force. Because moving objects eventually come to a stop, people thought the natural state of an object was to be at rest. For an object to be in motion, something always had to be pushing or pulling it to keep the object moving. As soon as the force stopped, the object would stop moving.

Galileo understood that an object in constant motion is as natural as an object at rest. It was usually friction that made moving objects slow down and eventually come to a stop. To keep an object moving, a force had to be applied to overcome the effects of friction. If friction could be removed, an object in motion would continue to move in a straight line with constant speed. **Figure 4** shows motion where there is almost no friction.

Topic: Galileo and Newton
Visit in7.msscience.com for Web links to information about the lives of Galileo and Newton.

Activity Make a time line showing important events in the lives of either Galileo or Newton.

Figure 4 In an air hockey game, the puck floats on a layer of air, so that friction is almost eliminated. As a result, the puck moves in a straight line with nearly constant speed after it's been hit.
Infer *how the puck would move if there was no layer of air.*

Observing Friction

Procedure
1. Lay a **bar of soap,** a **flat eraser,** and a **key** side by side on one end of a **hard-sided notebook.**
2. At a constant rate, slowly lift the end of notebook with objects on it. Note the order in which the objects start sliding.

Analysis
1. For which object was static friction the greatest? For which object was it the smallest? Explain, based on your observations.
2. Which object slid the fastest? Which slid the slowest? Explain why there is a difference in speed.
3. How could you increase and decrease the amount of friction between two materials?

Static Friction If you've ever tried pushing something heavy, like a refrigerator, you might have discovered that nothing happened at first. Then as you push harder and harder, the object suddenly will start to move. When you first start to push, friction between the heavy refrigerator and the floor opposes the force you are exerting and the net force is zero. The type of friction that prevents an object from moving when a force is applied is called static friction.

Static friction is caused by the attraction between the atoms on the two surfaces that are in contact. This causes the surfaces to stick or weld together where they are in contact. Usually, as the surface gets rougher and the object gets heavier, the force of static friction will be larger. To move the object, you have to exert a force large enough to break the bonds holding two surfaces together.

Sliding Friction While static friction keeps an object at rest, sliding friction slows down an object that slides. If you push an object across a room, you notice the sliding friction between the bottom of the object and the floor. You have to keep pushing to overcome the force of sliding friction. Sliding friction is due to the microscopic roughness of two surfaces, as shown in **Figure 5.** A force must be applied to move the rough areas of one surface past the rough areas of the other. A sliding friction force is produced when the brake pads in a car's brakes rub against the wheels. This force slows the car. Bicycle brakes, shown in **Figure 6,** work the same way.

 What is the difference between static friction and sliding friction?

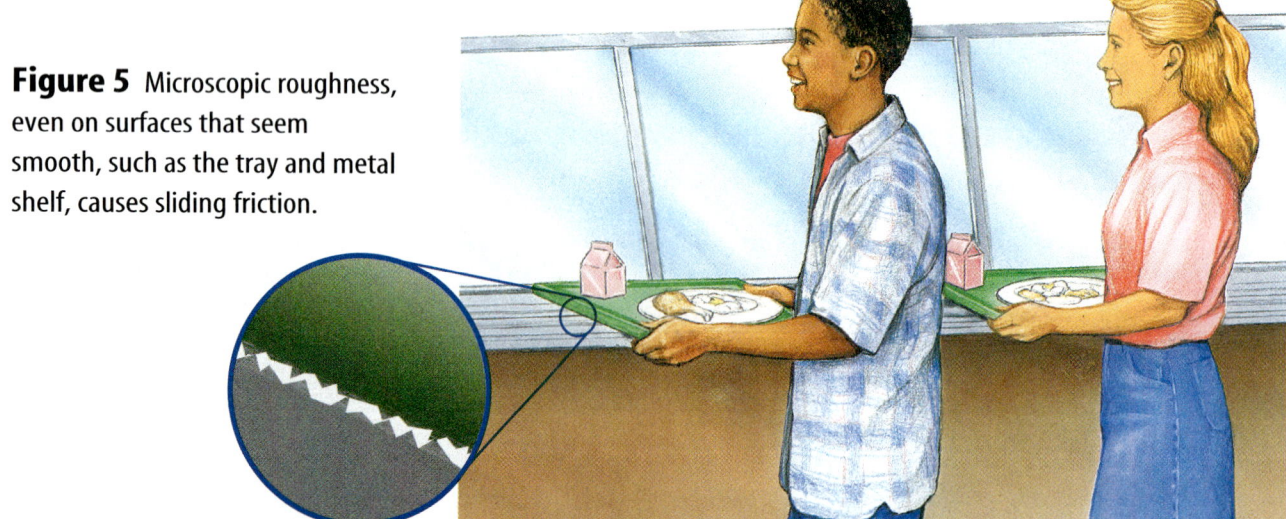

Figure 5 Microscopic roughness, even on surfaces that seem smooth, such as the tray and metal shelf, causes sliding friction.

Figure 6 A bicycle uses sliding friction and rolling friction.

Sliding friction is used to stop this bicycle tire. Friction between the brake pads and the wheel brings the wheel to a stop.

Rolling friction with the ground pushes the bottom of the bicycle tire, so it rolls forward.

Rolling Friction Another type of friction, rolling friction, is needed to make a wheel or tire turn. Rolling friction occurs between the ground and the part of the tire touching the ground, as shown in **Figure 6**. Rolling friction keeps the tire from slipping on the ground. If the bicycle tires are rolling forward, rolling friction exerts the force on the tires that pushes the bicycle forward.

It's usually easier to pull a load on a wagon or cart that has wheels rather than to drag the load along the ground. This is because rolling friction between the wheels and the ground is less than the sliding friction between the load and the ground.

section 1 review

Summary

Force
- A force is a push or a pull.
- The net force on an object is the combination of all the forces acting on the object.
- The forces acting on an object can be balanced or unbalanced. If the forces are balanced, the net force is zero.

Newton's First Law of Motion
- If the net force on an object at rest is zero, the object remains at rest, or if the object is moving, it continues moving in a straight line with constant speed.

Friction
- Friction is the force that acts to resist sliding between two surfaces that are touching.
- Three types of friction are static friction, sliding friction, and rolling friction.

Self Check

1. **Explain** whether a force is acting on a car that is moving at 20 km/h and turns to the left.
2. **Describe** the factors that cause static friction between two surfaces to increase.
3. **Discuss** why friction made it difficult to discover Newton's first law of motion.
4. **Discuss** whether an object can be moving if the net force acting on the object is zero.
5. **Think Critically** For the following actions, explain whether the forces involved are balanced or unbalanced.
   a. You push a box until it moves.
   b. You push a box but it doesn't move.
   c. You stop pushing a box and it slows down.

Applying Skills

6. **Compare and contrast** static, sliding, and rolling friction.

section 2

Newton's Second Law

Standard—7.3.17: Investigate that an unbalanced force, acting on an object, changes its speed or path of motion or both, and know that if the force always acts toward the same center as the object moves, the object's path may curve into an orbit around the center.

Also covers: 7.1.5 (Detailed standards begin on page IN8.)

as you read

What You'll Learn
- **Explain** Newton's second law of motion.
- **Explain** why the direction of force is important.

Why It's Important
Newton's second law of motion explains how any object, from a swimmer to a satellite, moves when acted on by forces.

Review Vocabulary
acceleration: the change in velocity divided by the time over which the change occurred

New Vocabulary
- Newton's second law of motion
- weight
- center of mass

Force and Acceleration

When you go shopping in a grocery store and push a cart, you exert a force to make the cart move. If you want to slow down or change the direction of the cart, a force is required to do this, as well. Would it be easier for you to stop a full or empty grocery cart suddenly, as in **Figure 7**? When the motion of an object changes, the object is accelerating. Acceleration occurs any time an object speeds up, slows down, or changes its direction of motion. Newton's second law describes how forces cause an object's motion to change.

Newton's second law of motion connects force, acceleration, and mass. According to the second law of motion, an object acted upon by a force will accelerate in the direction of the force. The acceleration is given by the following equation

Acceleration Equation

$$\text{acceleration (in meters/second}^2\text{)} = \frac{\text{net force (in newtons)}}{\text{mass (in kilograms)}}$$

$$a = \frac{F_{net}}{m}$$

In this equation, a is the acceleration, m is the mass, and F_{net} is the net force. If both sides of the above equation are multiplied by the mass, the equation can be written this way:

$$F_{net} = ma$$

Reading Check *What is Newton's second law?*

Figure 7 The force needed to change the motion of an object depends on its mass.
Predict *which grocery cart would be easier to stop.*

356 CHAPTER 12

Units of Force Force is measured in newtons, abbreviated N. Because the SI unit for mass is the kilogram (kg) and acceleration has units of meters per second squared (m/s²), 1 N also is equal to 1 kg·m/s². In other words, to calculate a force in newtons from the equation shown on the prior page, the mass must be given in kg and the acceleration in m/s².

Gravity

One force that you are familiar with is gravity. Whether you're coasting down a hill on a bike or a skateboard or jumping into a pool, gravity is at work pulling you downward. Gravity also is the force that causes Earth to orbit the Sun and the Moon to orbit Earth.

What is gravity? The force of gravity exists between any two objects that have mass. Gravity always is attractive and pulls objects toward each other. A gravitational attraction exists between you and every object in the universe that has mass. However, the force of gravity depends on the mass of the objects and the distance between them. The gravitational force becomes weaker the farther apart the objects are and also decreases as the masses of the objects involved decrease.

For example, there is a gravitational force between you and the Sun and between you and Earth. The Sun is much more massive than Earth, but is so far away that the gravitational force between you and the Sun is too weak to notice. Only Earth is close enough and massive enough to exert a noticeable gravitational force on you. The force of gravity between you and Earth is about 1,650 times greater than between you and the Sun.

Newton and Gravity
Isaac Newton was the first to realize that gravity—the force that made objects fall to Earth—was also the force that caused the Moon to orbit Earth and the planets to orbit the Sun. In 1687, Newton published a book that included the law of universal gravitation. This law showed how to calculate the gravitational force between any two objects. Using the law of universal gravitation, astronomers were able to explain the motions of the planets in the solar system, as well as the motions of distant stars and galaxies.

Weight The force of gravity causes all objects near Earth's surface to fall with an acceleration of 9.8 m/s². By Newton's second law, the gravitational force on any object near Earth's surface is:

$$F = ma = m \times (9.8 \text{ m/s}^2)$$

This gravitational force also is called the weight of the object. Your **weight** on Earth is the gravitational force between you and Earth. Your weight would change if you were standing on a planet other than Earth, as shown in **Table 1**. Your weight on a different planet would be the gravitational force between you and the planet.

Table 1 Weight of 60-kg Person on Different Planets		
Place	Weight in Newtons if Your Mass were 60 kg	Percent of Your Weight on Earth
Mars	221	37.6
Earth	588	100.0
Jupiter	1,387	235.9
Pluto	39	6.6

Figure 8 The girl on the sled is speeding up because she is being pushed in the same direction that she is moving.

Figure 9 The boy is slowing down because the force exerted by his feet is in the opposite direction of his motion.

Weight and Mass Weight and mass are different. Weight is a force, just like the push of your hand is a force, and is measured in newtons. When you stand on a bathroom scale, you are measuring the pull of Earth's gravity—a force. However, mass is the amount of matter in an object, and doesn't depend on location. Weight will vary with location, but mass will remain constant. A book with a mass of 1 kg has a mass of 1 kg on Earth or on Mars. However, the weight of the book would be different on Earth and Mars. The two planets would exert a different gravitational force on the book.

Using Newton's Second Law

How does Newton's second law determine how an object moves when acted upon by forces? The second law tells how to calculate the acceleration of an object if its mass and the forces acting on it are known. You may remember that the motion of an object can be described by its velocity. The velocity tells how fast an object is moving and in what direction. Acceleration tells how velocity changes. If the acceleration of an object is known, then the change in velocity can be determined.

Speeding Up Think about a soccer ball sitting on the ground. If you kick the ball, it starts moving. You exert a force on the ball, and the ball accelerates only while your foot is in contact with the ball. If you look back at all of the examples of objects speeding up, you'll notice that something is pushing or pulling the object in the direction it is moving, as in **Figure 8**. The direction of the push or pull is the direction of the force. It also is the direction of the acceleration.

358 CHAPTER 12 Force and Newton's Laws

Slowing Down If you wanted to slow down an object, you would have to push or pull it against the direction it is moving. An example is given in **Figure 9.**

Suppose you push a book across a tabletop. When you start pushing, the book speeds up. Sliding friction also acts on the book. After you stop pushing, sliding friction causes the book to slow down and stop.

Calculating Acceleration Newton's second law of motion can be used to calculate acceleration. For example, suppose you pull a 10-kg sled so that the net force on the sled is 5 N. The acceleration can be found as follows:

$$a = \frac{F_{net}}{m} = \frac{5 \text{ N}}{10 \text{ kg}} = 0.5 \text{ m/s}^2$$

The sled keeps accelerating as long as you keep pulling on it. The acceleration does not depend on how fast the sled is moving. It depends only on the net force and the mass of the sled.

Applying Math — Solving a Simple Equation

ACCELERATION OF A CAR A net force of 4,500 N acts on a car with a mass of 1,500 kg. What is the acceleration of the car?

Solution

1 *This is what you know:*
- net force: $F_{net} = 4,500 \text{ N}^2$
- mass: $m = 1,500 \text{ kg}$

2 *This is what you need to find:* acceleration: $a = ? \text{ m/s}^2$

3 *This is the procedure you need to use:* Substitute the known values for net force and mass into the equation for Newton's second law of motion to calculate the acceleration:

$$a = \frac{F_{net}}{m} = \frac{4,500 \text{ N}}{1,500 \text{ kg}} = 3.0 \frac{\text{N}}{\text{kg}} = 3.0 \text{ m/s}^2$$

4 *Check your answer:* Multiply your answer by the mass, 1,500 kg. The result should be the given net force, 4,500 N.

Practice Problems

1. A book with a mass of 2.0 kg is pushed along a table. If the net force on the book is 1.0 N, what is the book's acceleration?

2. A baseball has a mass of 0.15 kg. What is the net force on the ball if its acceleration is 40 m/s²?

For more practice visit in7.msscience.com/math_practice

SECTION 2 Newton's Second Law

Figure 10 When the ball is thrown, it doesn't keep moving in a straight line. Gravity exerts a force downward that makes it move in a curved path.
Infer *how the ball would move if it were thrown horizontally.*

Turning Sometimes forces and motion are not in a straight line. If a net force acts at an angle to the direction an object is moving, the object will follow a curved path. The object might be going slower, faster, or at the same speed after it turns.

For example, when you shoot a basketball, the ball doesn't continue to move in a straight line after it leaves your hand. Instead it starts to curve downward, as shown in **Figure 10**. The force of gravity pulls the ball downward. The ball's motion is a combination of its original motion and the downward motion due to gravity. This causes the ball to move in a curved path.

Circular Motion

A rider on a merry-go-round ride moves in a circle. This type of motion is called circular motion. If you are in circular motion, your direction of motion is constantly changing. This means you are constantly accelerating. According to Newton's second law of motion, if you are constantly accelerating, there must be a force acting on you the entire time.

Think about an object on the end of a string whirling in a circle. The force that keeps the object moving in a circle is exerted by the string. The string pulls on the object to keep it moving in a circle. The force exerted by the string is the centripetal force and always points toward the center of the circle. In circular motion the centripetal force is always perpendicular to the motion.

Indiana Academic Standard Check

7.3.17: Investigate that an unbalanced force . . . may curve into an orbit around the center.

✔ In circular motion, how does the direction of the centripetal force compare to the direction of an object's motion?

360 CHAPTER 12 Force and Newton's Laws

Satellite Motion Objects that orbit Earth are satellites of Earth. Satellites go around Earth in nearly circular orbits, with the centripetal force being gravity. Why doesn't a satellite fall to Earth like a baseball does? Actually, a satellite is falling to Earth just like a baseball.

Suppose Earth were perfectly smooth and you throw a baseball horizontally. Gravity pulls the baseball downward so it travels in a curved path. If the baseball is thrown faster, its path is less curved, and it travels farther before it hits the ground. If the baseball were traveling fast enough, as it fell, its curved path would follow the curve of Earth's surface as shown in **Figure 11.** Then the baseball would never hit the ground. Instead, it would continue to fall around Earth.

Satellites in orbit are being pulled toward Earth just as baseballs are. The difference is that satellites are moving so fast horizontally that Earth's surface curves downward at the same rate that the satellites are falling downward. The speed at which a object must move to go into orbit near Earth's surface is about 8 km/s, or about 29,000 km/h.

To place a satellite into orbit, a rocket carries the satellite to the desired height. Then the rocket fires again to give the satellite the horizontal speed it needs to stay in orbit.

Figure 11 The faster a ball is thrown, the farther it travels before gravity pulls it to Earth. If the ball is traveling fast enough, Earth's surface curves away from it as fast as it falls downward. Then the ball never hits the ground.

Air Resistance

Whether you are walking, running, or biking, air is pushing against you. This push is air resistance. Air resistance is a form of friction that acts to slow down any object moving in the air. Air resistance is a force that gets larger as an object moves faster. Air resistance also depends on the shape of an object. A piece of paper crumpled into a ball falls faster than a flat piece of paper falls.

When an object falls it speeds up as gravity pulls it downward. At the same time, the force of air resistance pushing up on the object is increasing as the object moves faster. Finally, the upward air resistance force becomes large enough to equal the downward force of gravity.

When the air resistance force equals the weight, the net force on the object is zero. By Newton's second law, the object's acceleration then is zero, and its speed no longer increases. When air resistance balances the force of gravity, the object falls at a constant speed called the terminal velocity.

Figure 12 The wrench is spinning as it slides across the table. The center of mass of the wrench, shown by the dots, moves as if the force of friction is acting at that point.

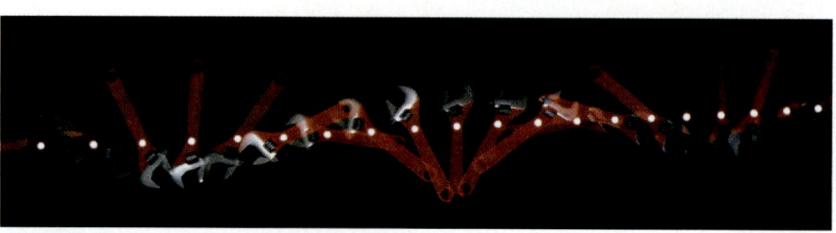

Center of Mass

When you throw a stick, the motion of the stick might seem to be complicated. However, there is one point on the stick, called the center of mass, that moves in a smooth path. The **center of mass** is the point in an object that moves as if all the object's mass were concentrated at that point. For a symmetrical object, such as a ball, the center of mass is at the object's center. However, for any object the center of mass moves as if the net force is being applied there.

Figure 12 shows how the center of mass of a wrench moves as it slides across a table. The net force on the wrench is the force of friction between on the wrench and the table. This causes the center of mass to move in a straight line with decreasing speed.

section 2 review

Summary

Force and Acceleration
- According to Newton's second law, the net force on an object, its mass, and its acceleration are related by
$$F_{net} = ma$$

Gravity
- The force of gravity between any two objects is always attractive and depends on the masses of the objects and the distance between them.

Using Newton's Second Law
- A moving object speeds up if the net force is in the direction of the motion.
- A moving object slows down if the net force is in the direction opposite to the motion.
- A moving object turns if the net force is at an angle to the direction of motion.

Circular Motion
- A centripetal force exerted toward the center of the circle keeps an object moving in circular motion.

Self Check

1. **Make a diagram** showing the forces acting on a coasting bike rider traveling at 25 km/h on a flat roadway.
2. **Analyze** how your weight would change with time if you were on a space ship traveling away from Earth toward the Moon.
3. **Explain** how the force of air resistance depends on an object's speed.
4. **Infer** the direction of the net force acting on a car as it slows down and turns right.
5. **Think Critically** Three students are pushing on a box. Under what conditions will the motion of the box change?

Applying Math

6. **Calculate Net Force** A car has a mass of 1,500 kg. If the car has an acceleration of 2.0 m/s^2, what is the net force acting on the car?
7. **Calculate Mass** During a softball game, a softball is struck by a bat and has an acceleration of 1,500 m/s^2. If the net force exerted on the softball by the bat is 300 N, what is the softball's mass?

 in7.msscience.com/self_check_quiz

Standard—7.3.17: Investigate that an unbalanced force, acting on an object, changes its speed or path of motion or both, and know that if the force always acts toward the same center as the object moves, the object's path may curve into an orbit around the center.

Also covers: 7.2.6 (Detailed standards begin on page IN8.)

section 3
Newton's Third Law

Action and Reaction

Newton's first two laws of motion explain how the motion of a single object changes. If the forces acting on the object are balanced, the object will remain at rest or stay in motion with constant velocity. If the forces are unbalanced, the object will accelerate in the direction of the net force. Newton's second law tells how to calculate the acceleration, or change in motion, of an object if the net force acting on it is known.

Newton's third law describes something else that happens when one object exerts a force on another object. Suppose you push on a wall. It may surprise you to learn that if you push on a wall, the wall also pushes on you. According to **Newton's third law of motion**, forces always act in equal but opposite pairs. Another way of saying this is for every action, there is an equal but opposite reaction. This means that when you push on a wall, the wall pushes back on you with a force equal in strength to the force you exerted. When one object exerts a force on another object, the second object exerts the same size force on the first object, as shown in **Figure 13**.

as you read

What You'll Learn
- **Identify** the relationship between the forces that objects exert on each other.

Why It's Important
Newton's third law can explain how birds fly and rockets move.

Review Vocabulary
force: a push or a pull

New Vocabulary
● Newton's third law of motion

Figure 13 The car jack is pushing up on the car with the same amount of force with which the car is pushing down on the jack. **Identify** the other force acting on the car.

SECTION 3 Newton's Third Law **363**

Figure 14 In this collision, the first car exerts a force on the second. The second exerts the same force in the opposite direction on the first car.
Explain whether both cars will have the same acceleration.

Action and Reaction Forces Don't Cancel The forces exerted by two objects on each other are often called an action-reaction force pair. Either force can be considered the action force or the reaction force. You might think that because action-reaction forces are equal and opposite that they cancel. However, action and reaction force pairs don't cancel because they act on different objects. Forces can cancel only if they act on the same object.

For example, imagine you're driving a bumper car and are about to bump a friend in another car, as shown in **Figure 14.** When the two cars collide, your car pushes on the other car. By Newton's third law, that car pushes on your car with the same force, but in the opposite direction. This force causes you to slow down. One force of the action-reaction force pair is exerted on your friend's car, and the other force of the force pair is exerted on your car. Another example of an action-reaction pair is shown in **Figure 15.**

You constantly use action-reaction force pairs as you move about. When you jump, you push down on the ground. The ground then pushes up on you. It is this upward force that pushes you into the air. **Figure 16** shows some examples of how Newton's laws of motion are demonstrated in sporting events.

Science Online

Topic: How Birds Fly
Visit in7.msscience.com for Web links to information about how birds and other animals fly.

Activity Make a diagram showing the forces acting on a bird as it flies.

Figure 15 When the child pushes against the wall, the wall pushes against the child.

INTEGRATE Life Science Birds and other flying creatures also use Newton's third law. When a bird flies, its wings push in a downward and a backward direction. This pushes air downward and backward. By Newton's third law, the air pushes back on the bird in the opposite directions—upward and forward. This force keeps a bird in the air and propels it forward.

NATIONAL GEOGRAPHIC
VISUALIZING NEWTON'S LAWS IN SPORTS

Figure 16

Although it is not obvious, Newton's laws of motion are demonstrated in sports activities all the time. According to the first law, if an object is in motion, it moves in a straight line with constant speed unless a net force acts on it. If an object is at rest, it stays at rest unless a net force acts on it. The second law states that a net force acting on an object causes the object to accelerate in the direction of the force. The third law can be understood this way—for every action force, there is an equal and opposite reaction force.

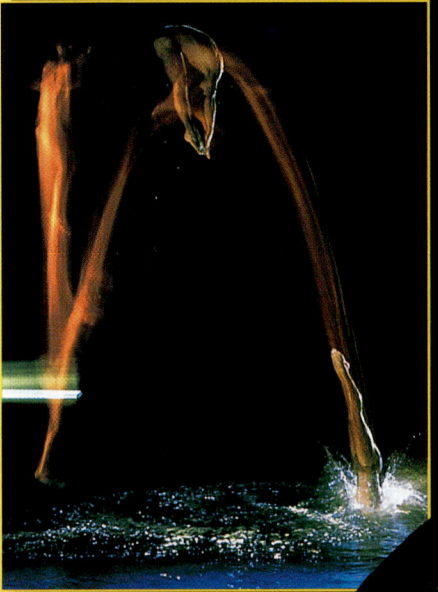

▲ **NEWTON'S FIRST LAW** According to Newton's first law, the diver does not move in a straight line with constant speed because of the force of gravity.

◀ **NEWTON'S SECOND LAW** As Tiger Woods hits a golf ball, he applies a force that will drive the ball in the direction of that force—an example of Newton's second law.

▶ **NEWTON'S THIRD LAW** Newton's third law applies even when objects do not move. Here a gymnast pushes downward on the bars. The bars push back on the gymnast with an equal force.

SECTION 3 Newton's Third Law **365**

Figure 17 The force of the ground on your foot is equal and opposite to the force of your foot on the ground. If you push back harder, the ground pushes forward harder.

Determine *In what direction does the ground push on you if you are standing still?*

Large and Small Objects Sometimes it's easy not to notice an action-reaction pair is because one of the objects is often much more massive and appears to remain motionless when a force acts on it. It has so much inertia, or tendency to remain at rest, that it hardly accelerates. Walking is a good example. When you walk forward, you push backward on the ground. Your shoe pushes Earth backward, and Earth pushes your shoe forward, as shown in **Figure 16.** Earth has so much mass compared to you that it does not move noticeably when you push it. If you step on something that has less mass than you do, like a skateboard, you can see it being pushed back.

A Rocket Launch The launching of a space shuttle is a spectacular example of Newton's third law. Three rocket engines supply the force, called thrust, that lifts the rocket. When the rocket fuel is ignited, a hot gas is produced. As the gas molecules collide with the inside engine walls, the walls exert a force that pushes them out of the bottom of the engine, as shown in **Figure 18.** This downward push is the action force. The reaction force is the upward push on the rocket engine by the gas molecules. This is the thrust that propels the rocket upward.

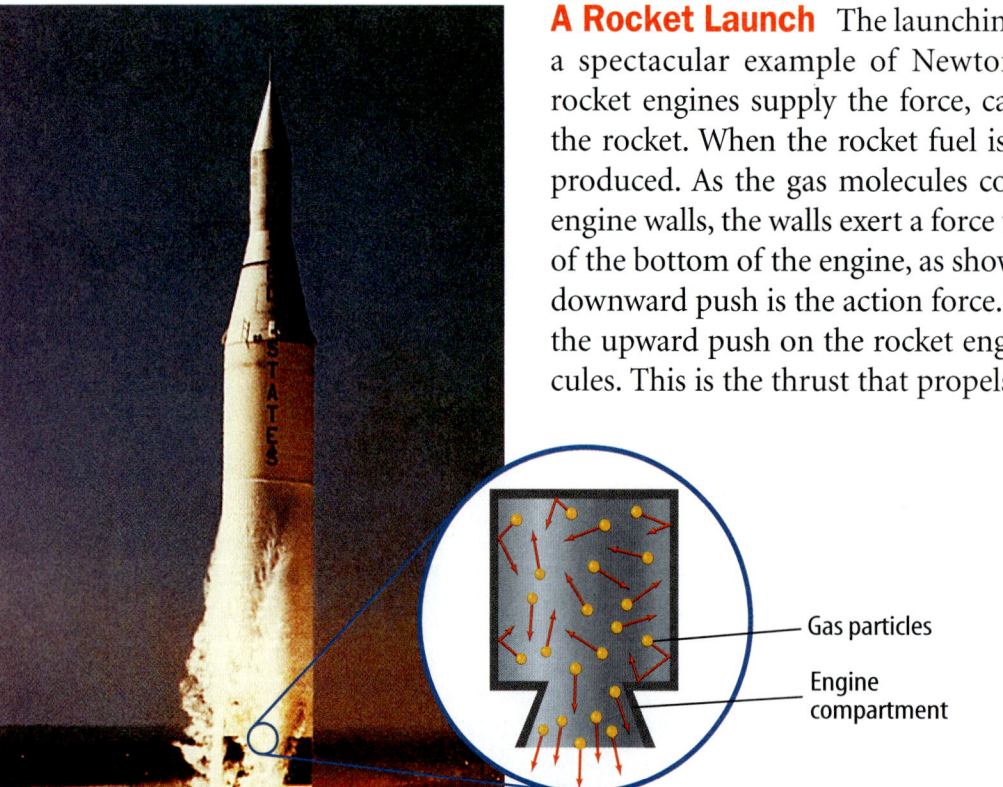

Figure 18 Newton's third law enables a rocket to fly. The rocket pushes the gas molecules downward, and the gas molecules push the rocket upward.

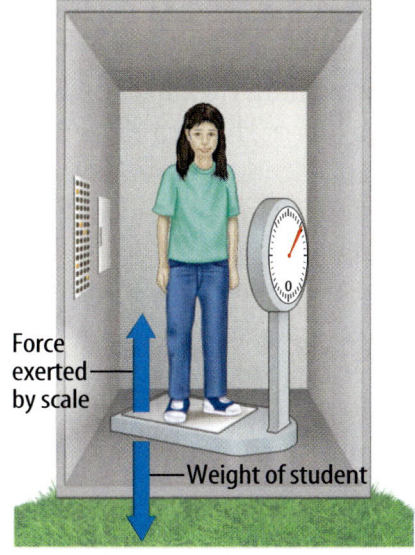
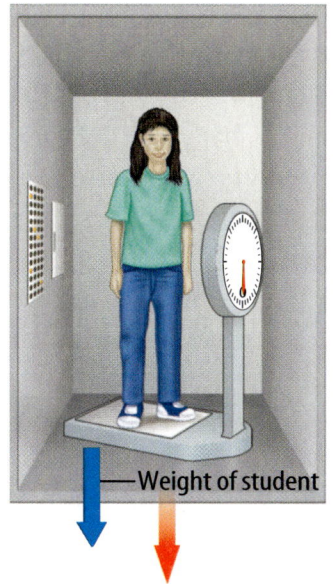

Figure 19 Whether you are standing on Earth or falling, the force of Earth's gravity on you doesn't change. However, your weight measured by a scale would change.

Weightlessness

You might have seen pictures of astronauts floating inside a space shuttle as it orbits Earth. The astronauts are said to be weightless, as if Earth's gravity were no longer pulling on them. Yet the force of gravity on the shuttle is almost 90 percent as large as at Earth's surface. Newton's laws of motion can explain why the astronauts float as if there were no forces acting on them.

Measuring Weight Think about how you measure your weight. When you stand on a scale, your weight pushes down on the scale. This causes the scale pointer to point to your weight. At the same time, by Newton's third law the scale pushes up on you with a force equal to your weight, as shown in **Figure 19.** This force balances the downward pull of gravity on you.

Free Fall and Weightlessness Now suppose you were standing on a scale in an elevator that is falling, as shown in **Figure 19.** A falling object is in free fall when the only force acting on the object is gravity. Inside the free-falling elevator, you and the scale are both in free fall. Because the only force acting on you is gravity, the scale no longer is pushing up on you. According to Newton's third law, you no longer push down on the scale. So the scale pointer stays at zero and you seem to be weightless. Weightlessness is the condition that occurs in free fall when the weight of an object seems to be zero.

However, you are not really weightless in free fall because Earth is still pulling down on you. With nothing to push up on you, such as your chair, you would have no sensation of weight.

Measuring Force Pairs

Procedure
1. Work in pairs. Each person needs a **spring scale**.
2. Hook the two scales together. Each person should pull back on a scale. Record the two readings. Pull harder and record the two readings.
3. Continue to pull on both scales, but let the scales move toward one person. Do the readings change?
4. Try to pull in such a way that the two scales have different readings.

Analysis
1. What can you conclude about the pair of forces in each situation?
2. Explain how this experiment demonstrates Newton's third law.

SECTION 3 Newton's Third Law

Figure 20 These oranges seem to be floating because they are falling around Earth at the same speed as the space shuttle and the astronauts. As a result, they aren't moving relative to the astronauts in the cabin.

Weightlessness in Orbit To understand how objects move in the orbiting space shuttle, imagine you were holding a ball in the free-falling elevator. If you let the ball go, the position of the ball relative to you and the elevator wouldn't change, because you, the ball, and the elevator are moving at the same speed.

However, suppose you give the ball a gentle push downward. While you are pushing the ball, this downward force adds to the downward force of gravity. According to Newton's second law, the acceleration of the ball increases. So while you are pushing, the acceleration of the ball is greater than the acceleration of both you and the elevator. This causes the ball to speed up relative to you and the elevator. After it speeds up, it continues moving faster than you and the elevator, and it drifts downward until it hits the elevator floor.

When the space shuttle orbits Earth, the shuttle and all the objects in it are in free fall. They are falling in a curved path around Earth, instead of falling straight downward. As a result, objects in the shuttle appear to be weightless, as shown in **Figure 20**. A small push causes an object to drift away, just as a small downward push on the ball in the free-falling elevator caused it to drift to the floor.

section 3 review

Summary

Action and Reaction

- According to Newton's third law, when one object exerts a force on another object, the second object exerts the same size force on the first object.
- Either force in an action-reaction force pair can be the action force or the reaction force.
- Action and reaction force pairs don't cancel because they are exerted on different objects.
- When action and reaction forces are exerted by two objects, the accelerations of the objects depend on the masses of the objects.

Weightlessness

- A falling object is in free fall if the only force acting on it is gravity.
- Weightlessness occurs in free fall when the weight of an object seems to be zero.
- Objects orbiting Earth appear to be weightless because they are in free fall in a curved path around Earth.

Self Check

1. **Evaluate** the force a skateboard exerts on you if your mass is 60 kg and you push on the skateboard with a force of 60 N.
2. **Explain** why you move forward and a boat moves backward when you jump from a boat to a pier.
3. **Describe** the action and reaction forces when a hammer hits a nail.
4. **Infer** You and a child are on skates and you give each other a push. If the mass of the child is half your mass, who has the greater acceleration? By what factor?
5. **Think Critically** Suppose you are walking in an airliner in flight. Use Newton's third law to describe the effect of your walk on the motion on the airliner.

Applying Math

6. **Calculate Acceleration** A person standing in a canoe exerts a force of 700 N to throw an anchor over the side. Find the acceleration of the canoe if the total mass of the canoe and the person is 100 kg.

368 CHAPTER 12 Force and Newton's Laws   in7.msscience.com/self_check_quiz

BALLOON RACES

Real-World Question

The motion of a rocket lifting off a launch pad is determined by Newton's laws of motion. Here you will make a balloon rocket that is powered by escaping air. How do Newton's laws of motion explain the motion of balloon rockets?

Goals
- **Measure** the speed of a balloon rocket.
- **Describe** how Newton's laws explain a rocket's motion.

Materials
balloons	meterstick
drinking straws	stopwatch
string	*clock
tape	*Alternate materials

Safety Precautions

Procedure

1. Make a rocket path by threading a string through a drinking straw. Run the string across the classroom and fasten at both ends.
2. Blow up a balloon and hold it tightly at the end to prevent air from escaping. Tape the balloon to the straw on the string.
3. Release the balloon so it moves along the string. Measure the distance the balloon travels and the time it takes.
4. Repeat steps 2 and 3 with different balloons.

Conclude and Apply

1. **Compare and contrast** the distances traveled. Which rocket went the greatest distance?
2. **Calculate** the average speed for each rocket. Compare and contrast them. Which rocket has the greatest average speed?
3. **Infer** which aspects of these rockets made them travel far or fast.
4. **Draw** a diagram showing all the forces acting on a balloon rocket.
5. Use Newton's laws of motion to explain the motion of a balloon rocket from launch until it comes to a stop.

Communicating Your Data

Discuss with classmates which balloon rocket traveled the farthest. Why? **For more help, refer to the** Science Skill Handbook.

LAB **369**

LAB Design Your Own

MODELING MOTION IN TWO DIRECTIONS

Goals
- **Move** the skid across the ground using two forces.
- **Measure** how fast the skid can be moved.
- **Determine** how smoothly the direction can be changed.

Possible Materials
masking tape
stopwatch
*watch or clock with a second hand
meterstick
*metric tape measure
spring scales marked in newtons (2)
plastic lid
golf ball
*tennis ball
*Alternate materials

Safety Precautions

Real-World Question
When you move a computer mouse across a mouse pad, how does the rolling ball tell the computer cursor to move in the direction that you push the mouse? Inside the housing for the mouse's ball are two or more rollers that the ball rubs against as you move the mouse. They measure up-and-down and back-and-forth motions. The motion of the cursor on the screen is based on the movement of the up-and-down rollers and the back-and-forth rollers. Can any object be moved along a path by a series of motions in only two directions?

Form a Hypothesis
How can you combine forces to move in a straight line, along a diagonal, or around corners? Place a golf ball on something that will slide, such as a plastic lid. The plastic lid is called a skid. Lay out a course to follow on the floor. Write a plan for moving your golf ball along the path without having the golf ball roll away.

Test Your Hypothesis
Make a Plan

1. Lay out a course that involves two directions, such as always moving forward or left.

2. Attach two spring scales to the skid. One always will pull straight forward. One always will pull to one side. You cannot turn the skid. If one scale is pulling toward the door of your classroom, it always must pull in that direction. (It can pull with zero force if needed, but it can't push.)

3. How will you handle movements along diagonals and turns?

4. How will you measure speed?

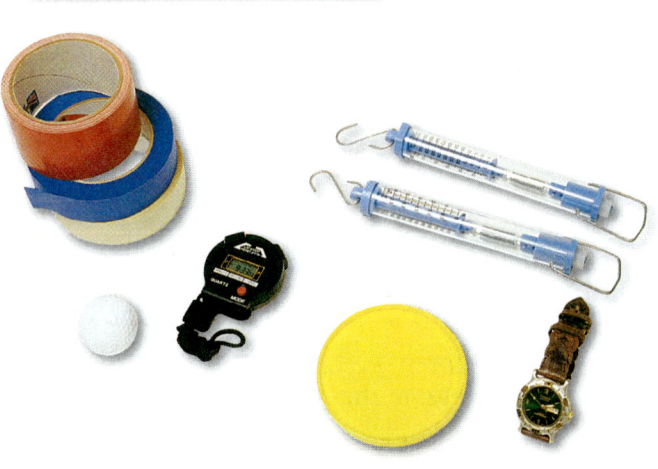

370 CHAPTER 12 Force and Newton's Laws

Using Scientific Methods

5. **Experiment** with your skid. How hard do you have to pull to counteract sliding friction at a given speed? How fast can you accelerate? Can you stop suddenly without spilling the golf ball, or do you need to slow down?

6. **Write** a plan for moving your golf ball along the course by pulling only forward or to one side. Be sure you understand your plan and have considered all the details.

Follow Your Plan

1. Make sure your teacher approves your plan before you start.
2. Move your golf ball along the path.
3. Modify your plan, if needed.
4. **Organize** your data so they can be used to run your course and write them in your Science Journal.
5. **Test** your results with a new route.

Analyze Your Data

1. What was the difference between the two routes? How did this affect the forces you needed to use on the golf ball?
2. How did you separate and control variables in this experiment?
3. Was your hypothesis supported? Explain.

Conclude and Apply

1. What happens when you combine two forces at right angles?
2. If you could pull on all four sides (front, back, left, right) of your skid, could you move anywhere along the floor? Make a hypothesis to explain your answer.

Communicating Your Data

Compare your conclusions with those of other students in your class. **For more help, refer to the Science Skill Handbook.**

LAB **371**

TIME SCIENCE AND Society

SCIENCE ISSUES THAT AFFECT YOU!

Air Bag Safety

After complaints and injuries, air bags in cars are helping all passengers

The car in front of yours stops suddenly. You hear the crunch of car against car and feel your seat belt grab you. Your mom is covered with, not blood, thank goodness, but with a big white cloth. Your seat belts and air bags worked perfectly.

Popcorn in the Dash

Air bags have saved more than a thousand lives since 1992. They are like having a giant popcorn kernel in the dashboard that pops and becomes many times its original size. But unlike popcorn, an air bag is triggered by impact, not heat. In a crash, a chemical reaction produces a gas that expands in a split second, inflating a balloonlike bag to cushion the driver and possibly the front-seat passenger. The bag deflates quickly so it doesn't trap people in the car.

Newton and the Air Bag

When you're traveling in a car, you move with it at whatever speed it is going. According to Newton's first law, you are the object in motion, and you will continue in motion unless acted upon by a force, such as a car crash.

Unfortunately, a crash stops the car, but it doesn't stop you, at least, not right away. You continue moving forward if your car doesn't have air bags or if you haven't buckled your seat belt. You stop when you strike the inside of the car. You hit the dashboard or steering wheel while traveling at the speed of the car. When an air bag inflates, you come to a stop move slowly, which reduces the force that is exerted on you.

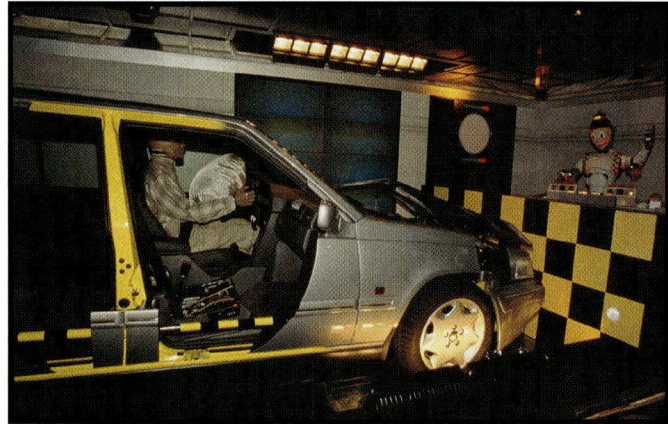

A test measures the speed at which an air bag deploys.

Measure Hold a paper plate 26 cm in front of you. Use a ruler to measure the distance. That's the distance drivers should have between the chest and the steering wheel to make air bags safe. Inform adult drivers in your family about this safety distance.

For more information, visit in7.msscience.com/time

chapter 12 Study Guide

Reviewing Main Ideas

Section 1 — Newton's First Law

1. A force is a push or a pull.
2. Newton's first law states that objects in motion tend to stay in motion and objects at rest tend to stay at rest unless acted upon by a nonzero net force.
3. Friction is a force that resists motion between surfaces that are touching each other.

Section 2 — Newton's Second Law

1. Newton's second law states that an object acted upon by a net force will accelerate in the direction of this force.
2. The acceleration due to a net force is given by the equation $a = F_{net}/m$.

3. The force of gravity between two objects depends on their masses and the distance between them.
4. In circular motion, a force pointing toward the center of the circle acts on an object.

Section 3 — Newton's Third Law

1. According to Newton's third law, the forces two objects exert on each other are always equal but in opposite directions.
2. Action and reaction forces don't cancel because they act on different objects.
3. Objects in orbit appear to be weightless because they are in free fall around Earth.

Visualizing Main Ideas

Copy and complete the following concept map on Newton's laws of motion.

- Newton's Laws of Motion
  - (First) — An object at rest will remain at rest until a force is applied
  - (Third)
  - Second

Science online in7.msscience.com/interactive_tutor

chapter 12 Review

Using Vocabulary

balanced forces p. 351
center of mass p. 362
force p. 350
friction p. 352
net force p. 351
Newton's first law of motion p. 352
Newton's second law of motion p. 356
Newton's third law of motion p. 363
unbalanced forces p. 351
weight p. 357

Explain the differences between the terms in the following sets.

1. force—inertia—weight
2. Newton's first law of motion—Newton's third law of motion
3. friction—force
4. net force—balanced forces
5. weight—weightlessness
6. balanced forces—unbalanced forces
7. friction—weight
8. Newton's first law of motion—Newton's second law of motion
9. friction—unbalanced force
10. net force—Newton's third law of motion

Checking Concepts

Choose the word or phrase that best answers the question.

11. Which of the following changes when an unbalanced force acts on an object?
    A) mass
    B) motion
    C) inertia
    D) weight

12. Which of the following is the force that slows a book sliding on a table?
    A) gravity
    B) static friction
    C) sliding friction
    D) inertia

Use the illustration below to answer question 13.

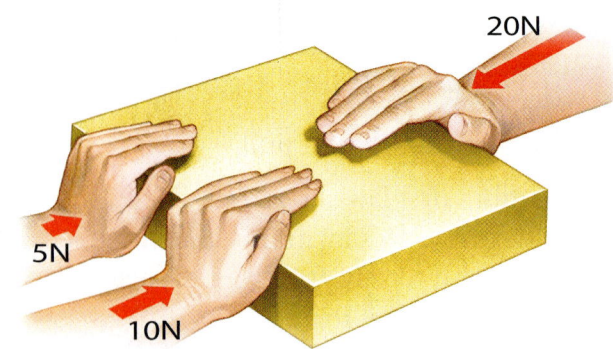

13. Two students are pushing on the left side of a box and one student is pushing on the right. The diagram above shows the forces they exert. Which way will the box move?
    A) up   C) down
    B) left   D) right

14. What combination of units is equivalent to the newton?
    A) m/s^2 C) kg·m/s^2
    B) kg·m/s   D) kg/m

15. Which of the following is a push or a pull?
    A) force   C) acceleration
    B) momentum   D) inertia

16. An object is accelerated by a net force in which direction?
    A) at an angle to the force
    B) in the direction of the force
    C) in the direction opposite to the force
    D) Any of these is possible.

17. You are riding on a bike. In which of the following situations are the forces acting on the bike balanced?
    A) You pedal to speed up.
    B) You turn at constant speed.
    C) You coast to slow down.
    D) You pedal at constant speed.

18. Which of the following has no direction?
    A) force   C) weight
    B) acceleration D) mass

chapter 12 Review

Thinking Critically

19. **Explain** why the speed of a sled increases as it moves down a snow-covered hill, even though no one is pushing on the sled.

20. **Explain** A baseball is pitched east at a speed of 40 km/h. The batter hits it west at a speed of 40 km/h. Did the ball accelerate?

21. **Form a Hypothesis** Frequently, the pair of forces acting between two objects are not noticed because one of the objects is Earth. Explain why the force acting on Earth isn't noticed.

22. **Identify** A car is parked on a hill. The driver starts the car, accelerates until the car is driving at constant speed, drives at constant speed, and then brakes to put the brake pads in contact with the spinning wheels. Explain how static friction, sliding friction, rolling friction, and air resistance are acting on the car.

23. **Draw Conclusions** You hit a hockey puck and it slides across the ice at nearly a constant speed. Is a force keeping it in motion? Explain.

24. **Infer** Newton's third law describes the forces between two colliding objects. Use this connection to explain the forces acting when you kick a soccer ball.

25. **Recognize Cause and Effect** Use Newton's third law to explain how a rocket accelerates upon takeoff.

26. **Predict** Two balls of the same size and shape are dropped from a helicopter. One ball has twice the mass of the other ball. On which ball will the force of air resistance be greater when terminal velocity is reached?

Use the figure below to answer question 27.

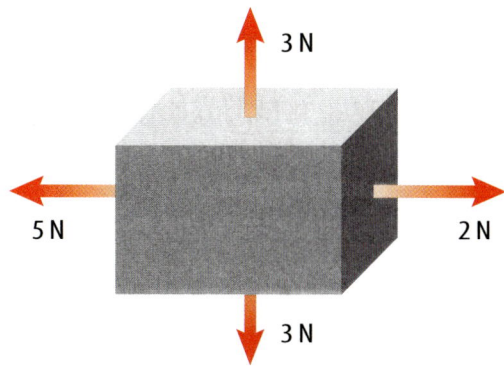

27. **Interpreting Scientific Illustrations** Is the force on the box balanced? Explain.

Performance Activities

28. **Oral Presentation** Research one of Newton's laws of motion and compose an oral presentation. Provide examples of the law. You might want to use a visual aid.

29. **Writing in Science** Create an experiment that deals with Newton's laws of motion. Document it using the following subject heads: *Title of Experiment, Partners' Names, Hypothesis, Materials, Procedures, Data, Results,* and *Conclusion*.

Applying Math

30. **Acceleration** If you exert a net force of 8 N on a 2-kg object, what will its acceleration be?

31. **Force** You push against a wall with a force of 5 N. What is the force the wall exerts on your hands?

32. **Net Force** A 0.4-kg object accelerates at 2 m/s². Find the net force.

33. **Friction** A 2-kg book is pushed along a table with a force of 4 N. Find the frictional force on the book if the book's acceleration is 1.5 m/s².

chapter 12 Indiana

The assessed Indiana standard appears above the question.

Record your answers on the answer sheet provided by your teacher or on a sheet of paper.

Part 1 Multiple Choice

1. Which description of the gravitational force is **FALSE**?

   A It depends on the distance between objects.

   B It depends on the masses of objects.

   C It exists between all objects.

   D It is a repulsive force.

7.3.17

2. The table below shows the mass of some objects.

Mass of Common Objects	
Object	Mass (g)
Cup	380
Book	1,100
Can	240
Ruler	25
Stapler	620

   Which object has an acceleration of 0.50 m/s² if you push it with a force of 0.31 N?

   A book

   B can

   C ruler

   D stapler

> **Test-Taking Tip**
>
> **Check Symbols** Be sure you understand all symbols on a table or graph before answering any questions about the table or graph.

The illustration below shows the forces acting on a box.

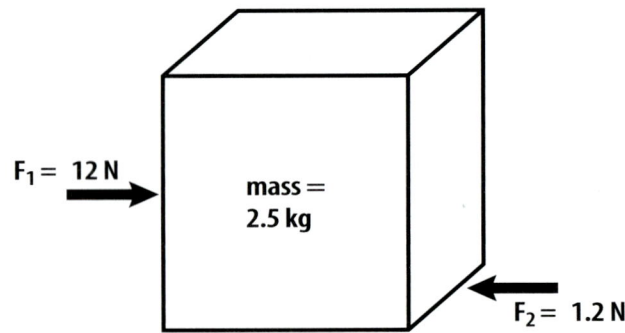

7.3.17

3. What is the acceleration of the box?

   A 0.48 m/s²

   B 4.3 m/s²

   C 4.8 m/s²

   D 27 m/s²

7.3.17

4. If you are pushing the box in the illustration above along the floor with a force of 12 N, what is the force of friction acting on the box?

   A 1.2 N

   B 10.8 N

   C 12 N

   D 13.2 N

7.3.17

5. Which best describes why astronauts in orbit seem to float in the space shuttle?

   A The gravitational force on the astronauts in orbit is nearly zero.

   B The astronauts are in free fall.

   C The astronauts are not accelerating.

   D The space shuttle exerts a reaction force that balances the force of gravity.

Standards Review

6. What is the weight of a book that has a mass of 0.35 kg?

   A 0.036 N

   B 3.4 N

   C 28 N

   D 34 N

7.3.17

7. Which best describes the force that pushes a rocket forward?

   A The exhaust gases pushing on the air.

   B The exhaust gases pushing on the rocket.

   C The rocket pushing on the exhaust gases.

   D The rocket pushing on the air.

8. The table below shows the acceleration of gravity at the surface of various planets.

Acceleration of Gravity on Different Planets	
Planet	Gravitational acceleration (m/s^2)
Mars	3.69
Saturn	8.96
Neptune	11.00
Pluto	0.65

   On which planet would your weight be greatest?

   A Mars

   B Neptune

   C Pluto

   D Saturn

Part 2 Constructed Response

7.3.17

9. A skater is coasting along the ice. Which law of motion explains the skater's ability to continue moving?

7.3.17

10. Describe how satellites are able to remain in orbit around Earth.

7.3.17

11. The illustration below shows the path of a ball thrown into the air.

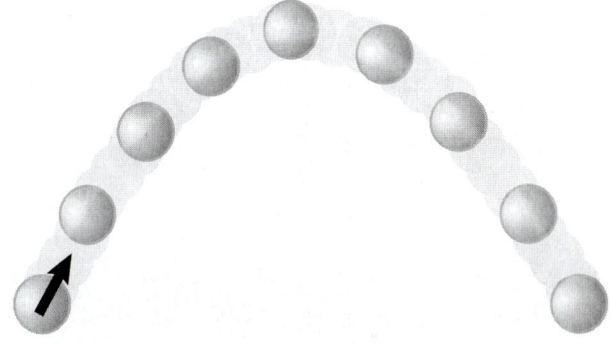

    What causes the ball to move along a curved path?

7.3.17

12. How does Newton's second law determine the motion of a book as you push it across a desktop?

7.3.17

13. According to Newton's third law of motion, a rock sitting on the ground pushes against the ground, and the ground pushes back against the rock with an equal force. Explain why this force doesn't cause the rock to accelerate upward from the ground according to Newton's second law.

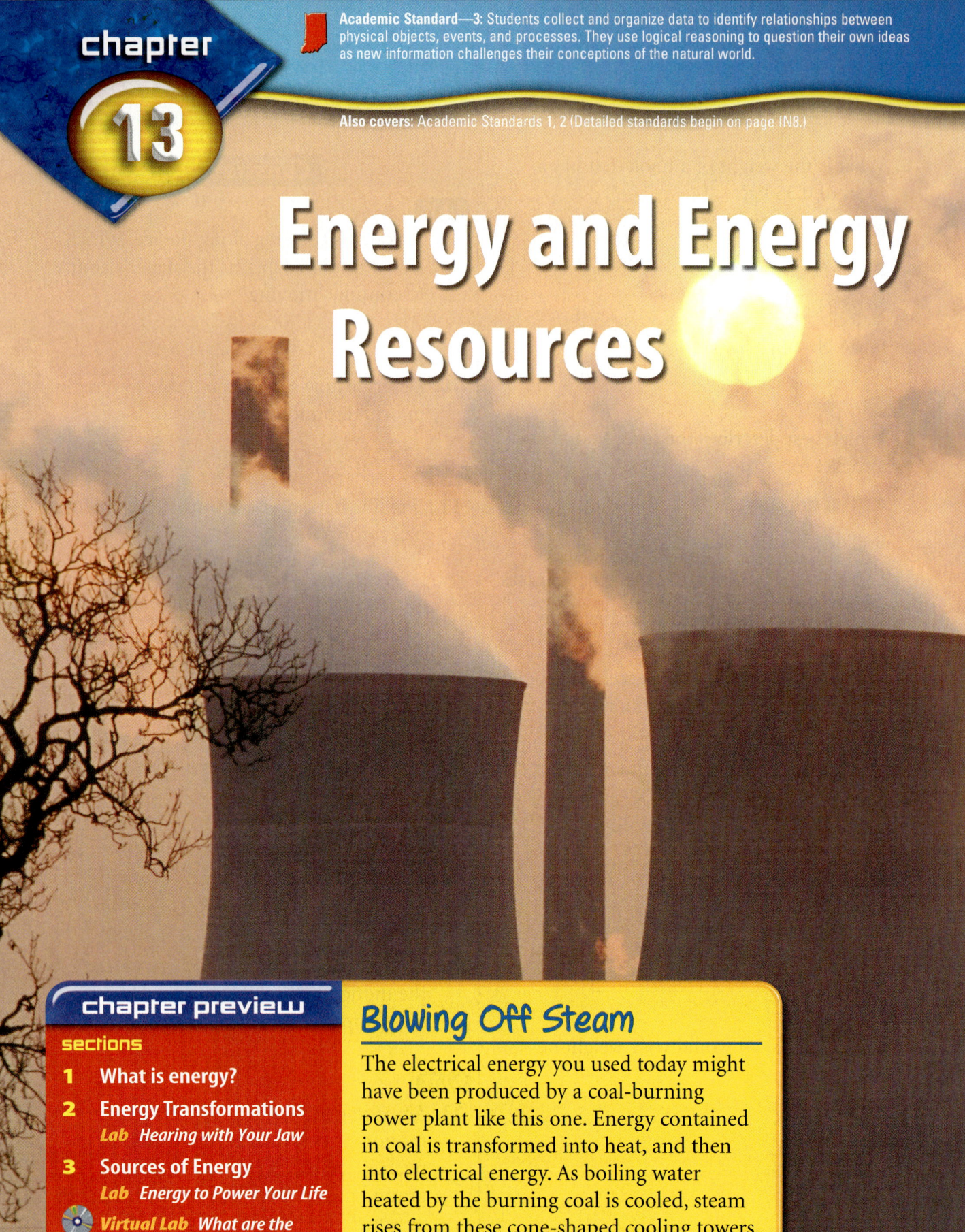

chapter 13

Academic Standard—3: Students collect and organize data to identify relationships between physical objects, events, and processes. They use logical reasoning to question their own ideas as new information challenges their conceptions of the natural world.

Also covers: Academic Standards 1, 2 (Detailed standards begin on page IN8.)

Energy and Energy Resources

chapter preview

sections
1. What is energy?
2. Energy Transformations
   Lab Hearing with Your Jaw
3. Sources of Energy
   Lab Energy to Power Your Life
   Virtual Lab What are the relationships between kinetic energy and potential energy?

Blowing Off Steam
The electrical energy you used today might have been produced by a coal-burning power plant like this one. Energy contained in coal is transformed into heat, and then into electrical energy. As boiling water heated by the burning coal is cooled, steam rises from these cone-shaped cooling towers.

Science Journal Choose three devices that use electricity, and identify the function of each device.

Start-Up Activities

Analyze a Marble Launch

What's the difference between a moving marble and one at rest? A moving marble can hit something and cause a change to occur. How can a marble acquire energy—the ability to cause change?

1. Make a track on a table by slightly separating two metersticks placed side by side.
2. Using a book, raise one end of the track slightly and measure the height.
3. Roll a marble down the track. Measure the distance from its starting point to where it hits the floor. Repeat. Calculate the average of the two measurements.
4. Repeat steps 2 and 3 for three different heights. Predict what will happen if you use a heavier marble. Test your prediction and record your observations.
5. **Think Critically** In your Science Journal, describe how the distance traveled by the marble is related to the height of the ramp. How is the motion of the marble related to the ramp height?

FOLDABLES Study Organizer

Energy Make the following Foldable to help identify what you already know, what you want to know, and what you learned about energy.

STEP 1 **Fold** a vertical sheet of paper from side to side. Make the front edge about 1 cm shorter than the back edge.

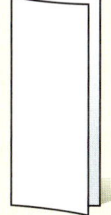

STEP 2 **Turn** lengthwise and **fold** into thirds.

STEP 3 **Unfold, cut, and label** each tab for only the top layer along both folds to make three tabs.

Identify Questions Before you read the chapter, write what you know and what you want to know about the types, sources, and transformation of energy under the appropriate tabs. As you read the chapter, correct what you have written and add more questions under the *Learned* tab.

Preview this chapter's content and activities at in7.msscience.com

Standard—7.3.14: Explain that energy in the form of heat is almost always one of the products of an energy transformation, such as in the examples of exploding stars, biological growth, the operation of machines, and the motion of people.

section 1

What is energy?

as you read

What You'll Learn
- **Explain** what energy is.
- **Distinguish** between kinetic energy and potential energy.
- **Identify** the various forms of energy.

Why It's Important
Energy is involved whenever a change occurs.

Review Vocabulary
mass: a measure of the amount of matter in an object

New Vocabulary
- energy
- kinetic energy
- potential energy
- thermal energy
- chemical energy
- radiant energy
- electrical energy
- nuclear energy

The Nature of Energy

What comes to mind when you hear the word *energy?* Do you picture running, leaping, and spinning like a dancer or a gymnast? How would you define energy? When an object has energy, it can make things happen. In other words, **energy** is the ability to cause change. What do the items shown in **Figure 1** have in common?

Look around and notice the changes that are occurring—someone walking by or a ray of sunshine that is streaming through the window and warming your desk. Maybe you can see the wind moving the leaves on a tree. What changes are occurring?

Transferring Energy You might not realize it, but you have a large amount of energy. In fact, everything around you has energy, but you notice it only when a change takes place. Anytime a change occurs, energy is transferred from one object to another. You hear a footstep because energy is transferred from a foot hitting the ground to your ears. Leaves are put into motion when energy in the moving wind is transferred to them. The spot on the desktop becomes warmer when energy is transferred to it from the sunlight. In fact, all objects, including leaves and desktops, have energy.

Figure 1 Energy is the ability to cause change.
Explain how these objects cause change.

380 CHAPTER 13 Energy and Energy Resources

Energy of Motion

Things that move can cause change. A bowling ball rolls down the alley and knocks down some pins, as in **Figure 2A.** Is energy involved? A change occurs when the pins fall over. The bowling ball causes this change, so the bowling ball has energy. The energy in the motion of the bowling ball causes the pins to fall. As the ball moves, it has a form of energy called kinetic energy. **Kinetic energy** is the energy an object has due to its motion. If an object isn't moving, it doesn't have kinetic energy.

Kinetic Energy and Speed If you roll the bowling ball so it moves faster, what happens when it hits the pins? It might knock down more pins, or it might cause the pins to go flying farther. A faster ball causes more change to occur than a ball that is moving slowly. Look at **Figure 2B.** The professional bowler rolls a fast-moving bowling ball. When her ball hits the pins, pins go flying faster and farther than for a slower-moving ball. All that action signals that her ball has more energy. The faster the ball goes, the more kinetic energy it has. This is true for all moving objects. Kinetic energy increases as an object moves faster.

Reading Check How does kinetic energy depend on speed?

Kinetic Energy and Mass Suppose, as shown in **Figure 2C,** you roll a volleyball down the alley instead of a bowling ball. If the volleyball travels at the same speed as a bowling ball, do you think it will send pins flying as far? The answer is no. The volleyball might not knock down any pins. Does the volleyball have less energy than the bowling ball even though they are traveling at the same speed?

An important difference between the volleyball and the bowling ball is that the volleyball has less mass. Even though the volleyball is moving at the same speed as the bowling ball, the volleyball has less kinetic energy because it has less mass. Kinetic energy also depends on the mass of a moving object. Kinetic energy increases as the mass of the object increases.

Figure 2 The kinetic energy of an object depends on the mass and speed of the object.

 **A** This ball has kinetic energy because it is rolling down the alley.

B This ball has more kinetic energy because it has more speed.

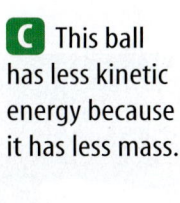 **C** This ball has less kinetic energy because it has less mass.

Figure 3 The potential energy of an object depends on its mass and height above the ground.
Determine which vase has more potential energy, the red one or the blue one.

Energy of Position

An object can have energy even though it is not moving. For example, a glass of water sitting on the kitchen table doesn't have any kinetic energy because it isn't moving. If you accidentally nudge the glass and it falls on the floor, changes occur. Gravity pulls the glass downward, and the glass has energy of motion as it falls. Where did this energy come from?

When the glass was sitting on the table, it had potential (puh TEN chul) energy. **Potential energy** is the energy stored in an object because of its position. In this case, the position is the height of the glass above the floor. The potential energy of the glass changes to kinetic energy as the glass falls. The potential energy of the glass is greater if it is higher above the floor. Potential energy also depends on mass. The more mass an object has, the more potential energy it has. Which object in **Figure 3** has the most potential energy?

Forms of Energy

Food, sunlight, and wind have energy, yet they seem different because they contain different forms of energy. Food and sunlight contain forms of energy different from the kinetic energy in the motion of the wind. The warmth you feel from sunlight is another type of energy that is different from the energy of motion or position.

Thermal Energy The feeling of warmth from sunlight signals that your body is acquiring more thermal energy. All objects have **thermal energy** that increases as its temperature increases. A cup of hot chocolate has more thermal energy than a cup of cold water, as shown in **Figure 4**. Similarly, the cup of water has more thermal energy than a block of ice of the same mass. Your body continually produces thermal energy. Many chemical reactions that take place inside your cells produce thermal energy. Where does this energy come from? Thermal energy released by chemical reactions comes from another form of energy called chemical energy.

Figure 4 The hotter an object is, the more thermal energy it has. A cup of hot chocolate has more thermal energy than a cup of cold water, which has more thermal energy than a block of ice with the same mass.

Figure 5 Complex chemicals in food store chemical energy. During activity, the chemical energy transforms into kinetic energy.

Chemical Energy When you eat a meal, you are putting a source of energy inside your body. Food contains chemical energy that your body uses to provide energy for your brain, to power your movements, and to fuel your growth. As in **Figure 5,** food contains chemicals, such as sugar, which can be broken down in your body. These chemicals are made of atoms that are bonded together, and energy is stored in the bonds between atoms. **Chemical energy** is the energy stored in chemical bonds. When chemicals are broken apart and new chemicals are formed, some of this energy is released. The flame of a candle is the result of chemical energy stored in the wax. When the wax burns, chemical energy is transformed into thermal energy and light energy.

Reading Check *When is chemical energy released?*

Light Energy Light from the candle flame travels through the air at an incredibly fast speed of 300,000 km/s. This is fast enough to circle Earth almost eight times in 1 s. When light strikes something, it can be absorbed, transmitted, or reflected. When the light is absorbed by an object, the object can become warmer. The object absorbs energy from the light and this energy is transformed into thermal energy. Then energy carried by light is called **radiant energy**. **Figure 6** shows a coil of wire that produces radiant energy when it is heated. To heat the metal, another type of energy can be used—electrical energy.

Figure 6 Electrical energy is transformed into thermal energy in the metal heating coil. As the metal becomes hotter, it emits more radiant energy.

SECTION 1 What is energy? **383**

Electrical Energy Electrical lighting is one of the many ways electrical energy is used. Look around at all the devices that use electricity. Electric current flows in these devices when they are connected to batteries or plugged into an electric outlet. **Electrical energy** is the energy that is carried by an electric current. An electric device uses the electrical energy provided by the current flowing in the device. Large electric power plants generate the enormous amounts of electrical energy used each day. In the United States, about 20 percent of the electrical energy used is generated by nuclear power plants.

Figure 7 Complex power plants are required to obtain useful energy from the nucleus of an atom.

Nuclear Energy Nuclear power plants use the energy stored in the nucleus of an atom to generate electricity. Every atomic nucleus contains energy—**nuclear energy**—that can be transformed into other forms of energy. However, releasing the nuclear energy is a difficult process. It involves the construction of complex power plants, shown in **Figure 7**. In contrast, all that is needed to release chemical energy from wood is a lighted match.

section 1 review

Summary

The Nature of Energy
- Energy is the ability to cause change.
- Kinetic energy is the energy an object has due to its motion. Kinetic energy depends on an object's speed and mass.
- Potential energy is the energy an object has due to its position. Potential energy depends on an object's height and mass.

Forces of Energy
- Thermal energy increases as temperature increases.
- Chemical energy is the energy stored in chemical bonds in molecules.
- Light energy, also called radiant energy, is the energy contained in light.
- Electrical energy is the energy carried by electric current.
- Nuclear energy is the energy contained in the nucleus of an atom.

Self Check

1. **Explain** why a high-speed collision between two cars would cause more damage than a low-speed collision between the same two cars.
2. **Describe** the energy transformations that occur when a piece of wood is burned.
3. **Identify** the form of energy that is converted into thermal energy by your body.
4. **Explain** how, if two vases are side by side on a shelf, one could have more potential energy.
5. **Think Critically** A golf ball and a bowling ball are moving and both have the same kinetic energy. Which one is moving faster? If they move at the same speed, which one has more kinetic energy?

Applying Skills

6. **Communicate** In your Science Journal, record different ways the word *energy* is used. Which ways of using the word *energy* are closest to the definition of energy given in this section?

 in7.msscience.com/self_check_quiz

384 CHAPTER 13 Energy and Energy Resources

section 2

Standards—7.3.14: Explain that energy in the form of heat is almost always one of the products of an energy transformation, such as in the examples of exploding stars, biological growth, the operation of machines, and the motion of people. **7.3.15:** Describe how electrical energy can be produced from a variety of energy sources and can be transformed into almost any other form of energy, such as light or heat.

Also covers: 7.1.10, 7.2.7 (Detailed standards begin on page IN8.)

Energy Transformations

Changing Forms of Energy

Chemical, thermal, radiant, and electrical are some of the forms that energy can have. In the world around you, energy is transforming continually between one form and another. You observe some of these transformations by noticing a change in your environment. Forest fires are a dramatic example of an environmental change that can occur naturally as a result of lightning strikes. A number of changes occur that involve energy as the mountain biker in **Figure 8** pedals up a hill. What energy transformations cause these changes to occur?

Tracking Energy Transformations As the mountain biker pedals, his leg muscles transform chemical energy into kinetic energy. The kinetic energy of his leg muscles transforms into kinetic energy of the bicycle as he pedals. Some of this energy transforms into potential energy as he moves up the hill. Also, some energy is transformed into thermal energy. His body is warmer because chemical energy is being released. Because of friction, the mechanical parts of the bicycle are warmer, too. Energy in the form of heat is almost always one of the products of an energy transformation. The energy transformations that occur when people exercise, when cars run, when living things grow and even when stars explode, all produce heat.

as you read

What You'll Learn
- **Apply** the law of conservation of energy to energy transformations.
- **Identify** how energy changes form.
- **Describe** how electric power plants produce energy.

Why It's Important
Changing energy from one form to another is what makes cars run, furnaces heat, telephones work, and plants grow.

Review Vocabulary
transformation: a change in composition or structure

New Vocabulary
- law of conservation of energy
- generator
- turbine

Figure 8 The ability to transform energy allows the biker to climb the hill.
Identify all the forms of energy that are represented in the photograph.

SECTION 2 Energy Transformations **385**

The Law of Conservation of Energy

It can be a challenge to track energy as it moves from object to object. However, one extremely important principle can serve as a guide as you trace the flow of energy. According to the **law of conservation of energy,** energy is never created or destroyed. The only thing that changes is the form in which energy appears. When the biker is resting at the summit, all his original energy is still around. Some of the energy is in the form of potential energy, which he will use as he coasts down the hill. Some of this energy was changed to thermal energy by friction in the bike. Chemical energy was also changed to thermal energy in the biker's muscles, making him feel hot. As he rests, this thermal energy moves from his body to the air around him. No energy is missing—it can all be accounted for.

Reading Check *Can energy ever be lost? Why or why not?*

Changing Kinetic and Potential Energy

The law of conservation of energy can be used to identify the energy changes in a system. For example, tossing a ball into the air and catching it is a simple system. As shown in **Figure 9,** as the ball leaves your hand, most of its energy is kinetic. As the ball rises, it slows and its kinetic energy decreases. But, the total energy of the ball hasn't changed. The decrease in kinetic energy equals the increase in potential energy as the ball flies higher in the air. The total amount of energy always remains constant. Energy moves from place to place and changes form, but it never is created or destroyed.

Topic: Energy Transformations

Visit in7.msscience.com for Web links to information about energy transformations that occur during different activities and processes.

Activity Choose an activity or process and make a graph showing how the kinetic and potential energy change during it.

Indiana Academic Standard Check

7.3.14: Explain that energy in the form of heat is almost always one of the products of an energy transformation . . .

✓ What type of force converts mechanical energy into heat?

Figure 9 During the flight of the baseball, energy is transforming between kinetic and potential energy.
Determine where the ball has the most kinetic energy. Where does the ball have the most total energy?

Figure 10 Hybrid cars that use an electric motor and a gasoline engine for power are now available. Hybrid cars make energy transformations more efficient.

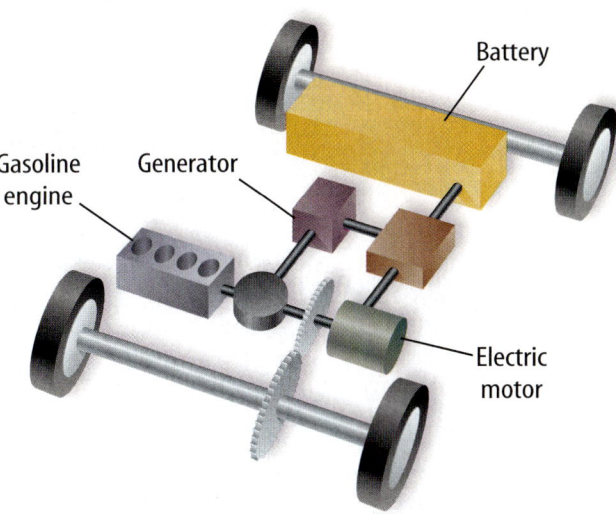

Energy Changes Form

Energy transformations occur constantly all around you. Many machines are devices that transform energy from one form to another. For example, an automobile engine transforms the chemical energy in gasoline into energy of motion. However, not all of the chemical energy is converted into kinetic energy. Instead, some of the chemical energy is converted into thermal energy, and the engine becomes hot. An engine that converts chemical energy into more kinetic energy is a more efficient engine. New types of cars, like the one shown in **Figure 10**, use an electric motor along with a gasoline engine. These engines are more efficient so the car can travel farther on a gallon of gas.

Transforming Chemical Energy Inside your body, chemical energy also is transformed into kinetic energy. Look at **Figure 11**. The transformation of chemical to kinetic energy occurs in muscle cells. There, chemical reactions take place that cause certain molecules to change shape. Your muscle contracts when many of these changes occur, and a part of your body moves.

The matter contained in living organisms, also called biomass, contains chemical energy. When organisms die, chemical compounds in their biomass break down. Bacteria, fungi, and other organisms help convert these chemical compounds to simpler chemicals that can be used by other living things.

Thermal energy also is released as these changes occur. For example, a compost pile can contain plant matter, such as grass clippings and leaves. As the compost pile decomposes, chemical energy is converted into thermal energy. This can cause the temperature of a compost pile to reach 60°C.

Mini LAB

Analyzing Energy Transformations

Procedure
1. Place soft **clay** on the floor and smooth out its surface.
2. Hold a **marble** 1.5 m above the clay and drop it. Measure the depth of the crater made by the marble.
3. Repeat this procedure using a **golf ball** and a **plastic golf ball.**

Analysis
1. Compare the depths of the craters to determine which ball had the most kinetic energy as it hit the clay.
2. Explain how potential energy was transformed into kinetic energy during your activity.

SECTION 2 Energy Transformations **387**

NATIONAL GEOGRAPHIC VISUALIZING ENERGY TRANSFORMATIONS

Figure 11

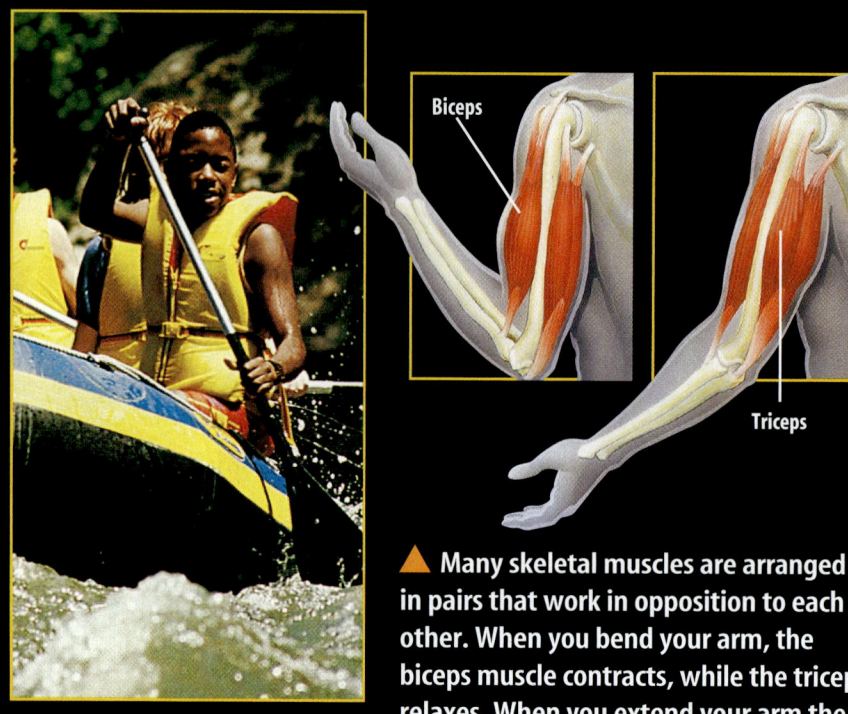

Paddling a raft, throwing a baseball, playing the violin — your skeletal muscles make these and countless other body movements possible. Muscles work by pulling, or contracting. At the cellular level, muscle contractions are powered by reactions that transform chemical energy into kinetic energy.

▶ Energy transformations taking place in your muscles provide the power to move.

▲ Many skeletal muscles are arranged in pairs that work in opposition to each other. When you bend your arm, the biceps muscle contracts, while the triceps relaxes. When you extend your arm the triceps contracts, and the biceps relaxes.

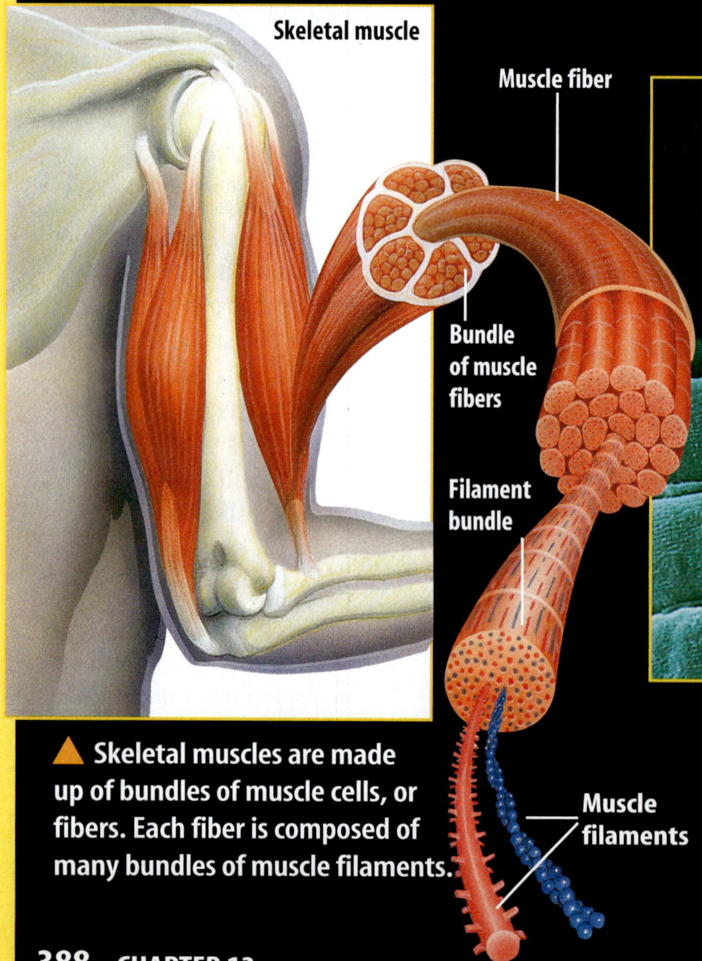

▲ Skeletal muscles are made up of bundles of muscle cells, or fibers. Each fiber is composed of many bundles of muscle filaments.

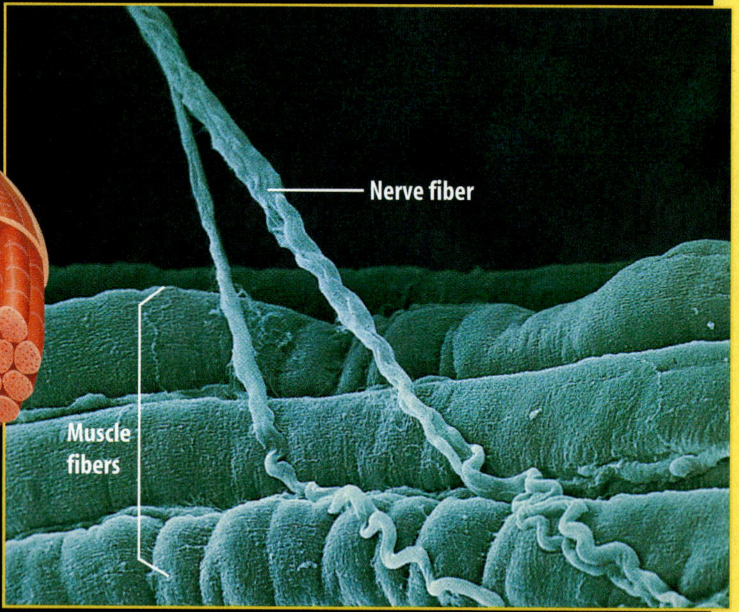

▲ A signal from a nerve fiber starts a chemical reaction in the muscle filament. This causes molecules in the muscle filament to gain energy and move. Many filaments moving together cause the muscle to contract.

Figure 12 The simple act of listening to a radio involves many energy transformations. A few are diagrammed here.

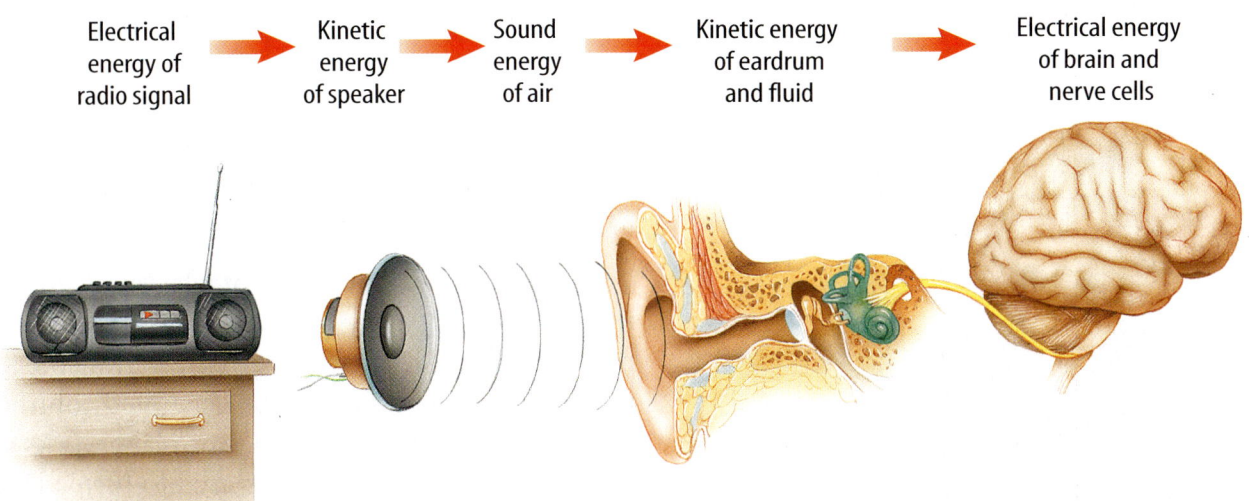

Electrical energy of radio signal → Kinetic energy of speaker → Sound energy of air → Kinetic energy of eardrum and fluid → Electrical energy of brain and nerve cells

Transforming Electrical Energy Every day you use electrical energy. When you flip a light switch, or turn on a radio or television, or use a hair drier, you are transforming electrical energy to other forms of energy. Every time you plug something into a wall outlet, or use a battery, you are using electrical energy. **Figure 12** shows how electrical energy is transformed into other forms of energy when you listen to a radio. A loudspeaker in the radio converts electrical energy into sound waves that travel to your ear—energy in motion. The energy that is carried by the sound waves causes parts of the ear to move also. This energy of motion is transformed again into chemical and electrical energy in nerve cells, which send the energy to your brain. After your brain interprets this energy as a voice or music, where does the energy go? The energy finally is transformed into thermal energy.

Transforming Thermal Energy Different forms of energy can be transformed into thermal energy. For example, chemical energy changes into thermal energy when something burns. Electrical energy changes into thermal energy when a wire that is carrying an electric current gets hot. Thermal energy can be used to heat buildings and keep you warm. Thermal energy also can be used to heat water. If water is heated to its boiling point, it changes to steam. This steam can be used to produce kinetic energy by steam engines, like the steam locomotives that used to pull trains. Thermal energy also can be transformed into radiant energy. For example, when a bar of metal is heated to a high temperature, it glows and gives off light.

INTEGRATE History

The Industrial Revolution Beginning in the 18th century, machines began to be used widely to replace manual labor. This change is called the industrial revolution. The steam engine provided the source of energy for factories to manufacture various goods, such as cloth, that used to be made by hand. As the number of factory jobs increased, workers moved from rural areas to cities. This caused many cities to grow much larger, not only in Great Britain, but also in other countries such as the United States. Research the history of the steam engine. What other changes to society did the steam engine help bring about?

SECTION 2 Energy Transformations

Figure 13 Thermal energy moves from the hot chocolate to the cooler surroundings.
Explain *what happens to the hot chocolate as it loses thermal energy.*

Figure 14 A coal-burning power plant transforms the chemical energy in coal into electrical energy.
List *some of the other energy sources that power plants use.*

How Thermal Energy Moves Thermal energy can move from one place to another. Look at **Figure 13.** The hot chocolate has thermal energy that moves from the cup to the cooler air around it, and to the cooler spoon. Thermal energy only moves from something at a higher temperature to something at a lower temperature.

Generating Electrical Energy

The enormous amount of electrical energy that is used every day is too large to be stored in batteries. The electrical energy that is available for use at any wall socket must be generated continually by power plants. Every power plant works on the same principle—energy is used to turn a large generator. A **generator** is a device that transforms kinetic energy into electrical energy. In fossil fuel power plants, coal, oil, or natural gas is burned to boil water. As the hot water boils, the steam rushes through a **turbine,** which contains a set of narrowly spaced fan blades. The steam pushes on the blades and turns the turbine, which in turn rotates a shaft in the generator to produce the electrical energy, as shown in **Figure 14.**

Reading Check *What does a generator do?*

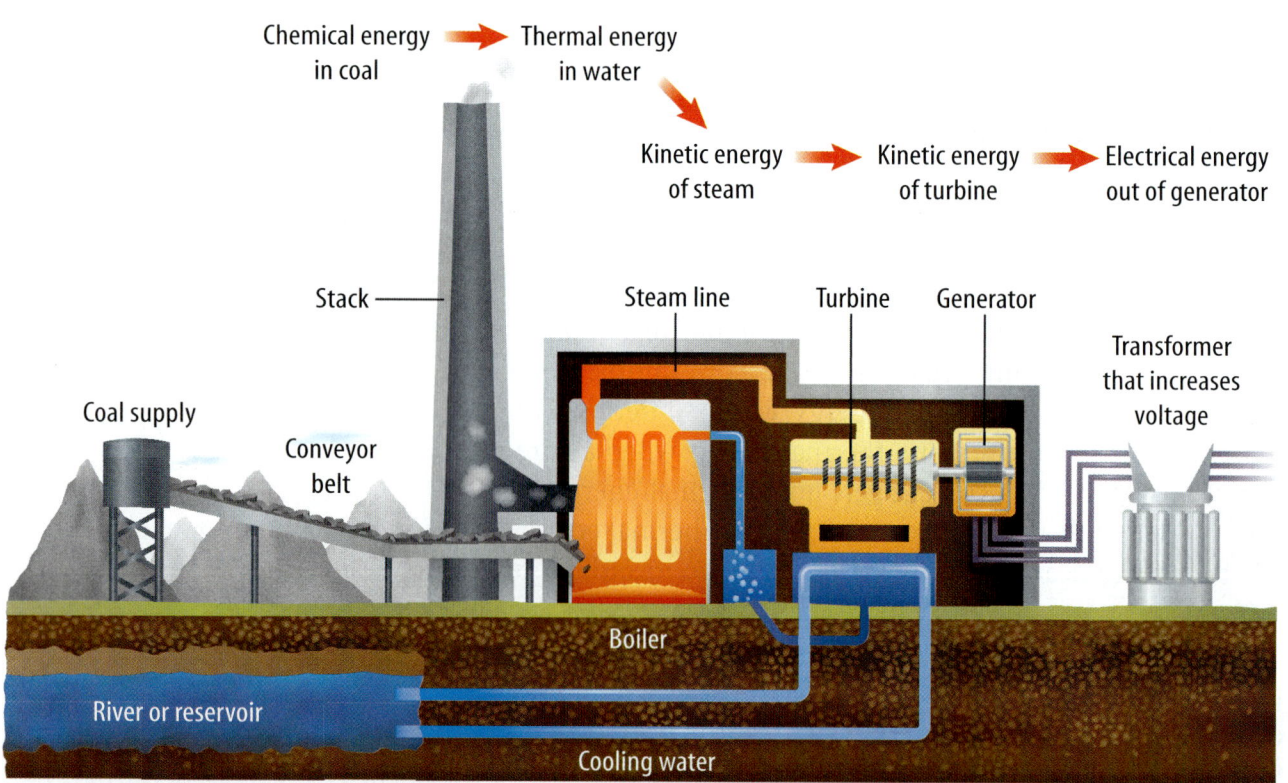

390 CHAPTER 13 Energy and Energy Resources

Power Plants Almost 90 percent of the electrical energy generated in the United States is produced by nuclear and fossil fuel power plants, as shown in **Figure 15.** Other types of power plants include hydroelectric (hi droh ih LEK trihk) and wind. Hydroelectric power plants transform the kinetic energy of moving water into electrical energy. Wind power plants transform the kinetic energy of moving air into electrical energy. In these power plants, a generator converts the kinetic energy of moving water or wind to electrical energy.

To analyze the energy transformations in a power plant, you can diagram the energy changes using arrows. A coal-burning power plant generates electrical energy through the following series of energy transformations.

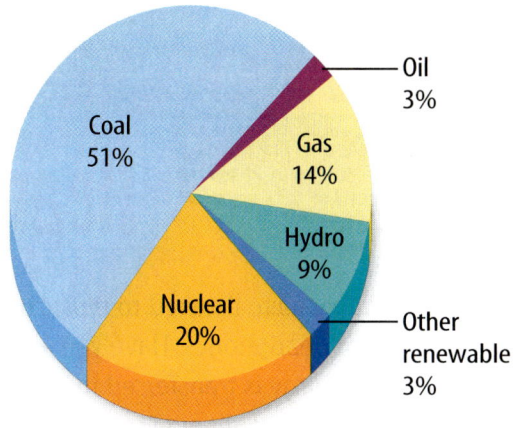

Figure 15 The graph shows sources of electrical energy in the United States.
Name the energy source that you think is being used to provide the electricity for the lights overhead.

chemical energy of coal → thermal energy of water → kinetic energy of steam → kinetic energy of turbine → electrical energy out of generator

Nuclear power plants use a similar series of transformations. Hydroelectric plants, however, skip the steps that change water into steam because the water strikes the turbine directly.

section 2 review

Summary

Changing Forms of Energy
- Heat usually is one of the forms of energy produced in energy transformations.
- The law of conservation of energy states that energy cannot be created or destroyed; it can only change form.
- The total energy doesn't change when an energy transformation occurs.
- As an object rises and falls, kinetic and potential energy are transformed into each other, but the total energy doesn't change.

Generating Electrical Energy
- A generator converts kinetic energy into electrical energy.
- Burning fossil fuels produces thermal energy that is used to boil water and produce steam.
- In a power plant, steam is used to spin a turbine which then spins an electric generator.

Self Check

1. **Describe** the conversions between potential and kinetic energy that occur when you shoot a basketball at a basket.
2. **Explain** whether your body gains or loses thermal energy if your body temperature is 37°C and the temperature around you is 25°C.
3. **Describe** a process that converts chemical energy to thermal energy.
4. **Think Critically** A lightbulb converts 10 percent of the electrical energy it uses into radiant energy. Make a hypothesis about the other form of energy produced.

Applying Math

5. **Use a Ratio** How many times greater is the amount of electrical energy produced in the United States by coal-burning power plants than the amount produced by nuclear power plants?

SECTION 2 Energy Transformations

Hearing with Your Jaw

You probably have listened to music using speakers or headphones. Have you ever considered how energy is transferred to get the energy from the radio or CD player to your brain? What type of energy is needed to power the radio or CD player? Where does this energy come from? How does that energy become sound? How does the sound get to you? In this activity, the sound from a radio or CD player is going to travel through a motor before entering your body through your jaw instead of your ears.

Real-World Question

How can energy be transferred from a radio or CD player to your brain?

Goals
- **Identify** energy transfers and transformations.
- **Explain** your observations using the law of conservation of energy.

Materials
radio or CD player
small electrical motor
headphone jack

Procedure

1. Go to one of the places in the room with a motor/radio assembly.
2. Turn on the radio or CD player so that you hear the music.
3. Push the headphone jack into the headphone plug on the radio or CD player.
4. Press the axle of the motor against the side of your jaw.

Conclude and Apply

1. **Describe** what you heard in your Science Journal.
2. **Identify** the form of energy produced by the radio or CD player.
3. **Draw** a diagram to show all of the energy transformations taking place.
4. **Evaluate** Did anything get hotter as a result of this activity? Explain.
5. **Explain** your observations using the law of conservation of energy.

Compare your conclusions with those of other students in your class. **For more help, refer to the Science Skill Handbook.**

392 CHAPTER 13 Energy and Energy Resources

Standards—7.3.15: Describe how electrical energy can be produced from a variety of energy sources and can be transformed into almost any other form of energy, such as light or heat. **7.3.16:** Recognize and explain that different ways of obtaining, transforming, and distributing energy have different environmental consequences.

section 3

Also covers: 7.1.8, 7.2.6, 7.2.7 (Detailed standards begin on page IN8.)

Sources of Energy

Using Energy

Every day, energy is used to provide light and to heat and cool homes, schools, and workplaces. According to the law of conservation of energy, energy can't be created or destroyed. Energy only can change form. If a car or refrigerator can't create the energy they use, then where does this energy come from?

Energy Resources

Energy cannot be made, but must come from the natural world. As you can see in **Figure 16,** the surface of Earth receives energy from two sources—the Sun and radioactive atoms in Earth's interior. The amount of energy Earth receives from the Sun is far greater than the amount generated in Earth's interior. Nearly all the energy you used today can be traced to the Sun, even the gasoline used to power the car or school bus you came to school in.

as you read

What You'll Learn
- **Explain** what renewable, non-renewable, and alternative resources are.
- **Describe** the advantages and disadvantages of using various energy sources.

Why It's Important
Energy is vital for survival and making life comfortable. Developing new energy sources will improve modern standards of living.

Review Vocabulary
resource: a natural feature or phenomenon that enhances the quality of life

New Vocabulary
- nonrenewable resource
- renewable resource
- alternative resource
- inexhaustible resource
- photovoltaic

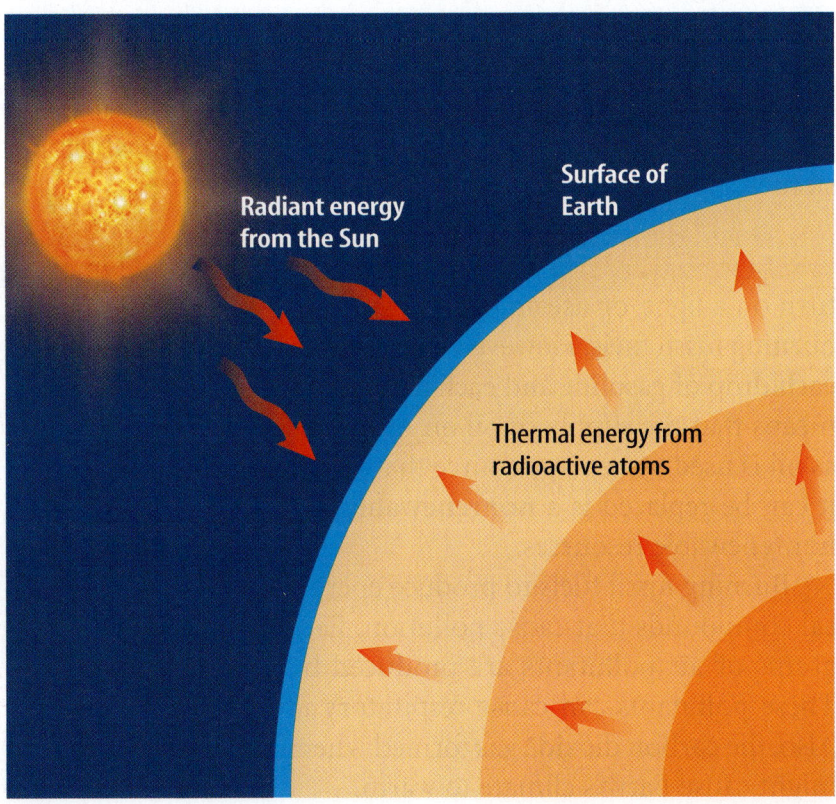

Figure 16 All the energy you use can be traced to one of two sources—the Sun or radioactive atoms in Earth's interior.

SECTION 3 Sources of Energy **393**

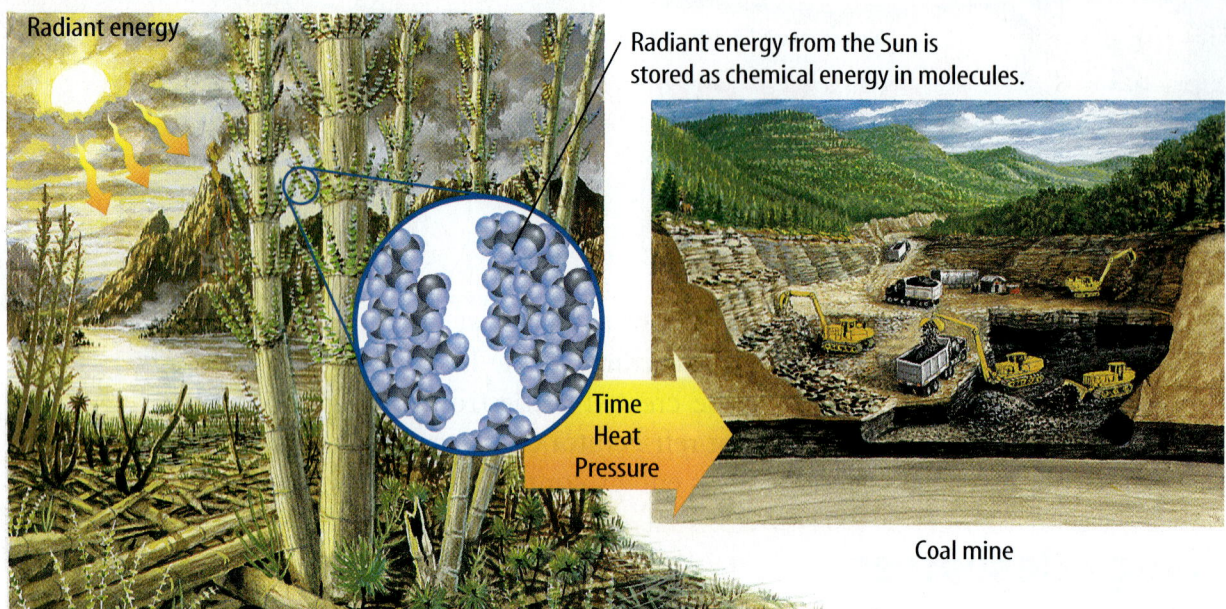

Figure 17 Coal is formed after the molecules in ancient plants are heated under pressure for millions of years. The energy stored by the molecules in coal originally came from the Sun.

Energy Source Origins The kinds of fossil fuels found in the ground depend on the kinds of organisms (animal or plant) that died and were buried in that spot. Research coal, oil, and natural gas to find out what types of organisms were primarily responsible for producing each.

Fossil Fuels

Fossil fuels are coal, oil, and natural gas. Oil and natural gas were made from the remains of microscopic organisms that lived in Earth's oceans millions of years ago. Heat and pressure gradually turned these ancient organisms into oil and natural gas. Coal was formed by a similar process from the remains of ancient plants that once lived on land, as shown in **Figure 17.**

Through the process of photosynthesis, ancient plants converted the radiant energy in sunlight to chemical energy stored in various types of molecules. Heat and pressure changed these molecules into other types of molecules as fossil fuels formed. Chemical energy stored in these molecules is released when fossil fuels are burned.

Using Fossil Fuels The energy used when you ride in a car, turn on a light, or use an electric appliance usually comes from burning fossil fuels. However, it takes millions of years to replace each drop of gasoline and each lump of coal that is burned. This means that the supply of oil on Earth will continue to decrease as oil is used. An energy source that is used up much faster than it can be replaced is a **nonrenewable resource.** Fossil fuels are nonrenewable resources.

Burning fossil fuels to produce energy also generates chemical compounds that cause pollution. Each year billions of kilograms of air pollutants are produced by burning fossil fuels. These pollutants can cause respiratory illnesses and acid rain. Also, the carbon dioxide gas formed when fossil fuels are burned might cause Earth's climate to warm.

Nuclear Energy

Can you imagine running an automobile on 1 kg of fuel that releases almost 3 million times more energy than 1 L of gas? What could supply so much energy from so little mass? The answer is the nuclei of uranium atoms. Some of these nuclei are unstable and break apart, releasing enormous amounts of energy in the process. This energy can be used to generate electricity by heating water to produce steam that spins an electric generator, as shown in **Figure 18.** Because no fossil fuels are burned, generating electricity using nuclear energy helps make the supply of fossil fuels last longer. Also, unlike fossil fuel power plants, nuclear power plants produce almost no air pollution. In one year, a typical nuclear power plant generates enough energy to supply 600,000 homes with power and produces only 1 m³ of waste.

Nuclear Wastes Like all energy sources, nuclear energy has its advantages and disadvantages. One disadvantage is the amount of uranium in Earth's crust is nonrenewable. Another is that the waste produced by nuclear power plants is radioactive and can be dangerous to living things. Some of the materials in the nuclear waste will remain radioactive for many thousands of years. As a result the waste must be stored so no radioactivity is released into the environment for a long time. One method is to seal the waste in a ceramic material, place the ceramic in protective containers, and then bury the containers far underground. However, the burial site would have to be chosen carefully so underground water supplies aren't contaminated. Also, the site would have to be safe from earthquakes and other natural disasters that might cause radioactive material to be released.

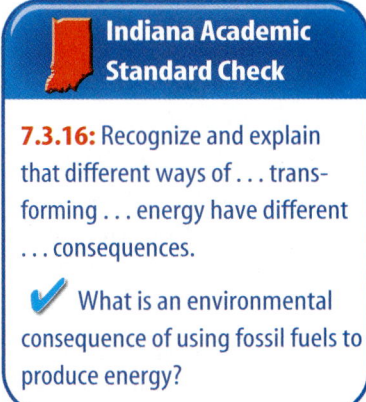

Indiana Academic Standard Check

7.3.16: Recognize and explain that different ways of . . . transforming . . . energy have different . . . consequences.

✔ What is an environmental consequence of using fossil fuels to produce energy?

Figure 18 To obtain electrical energy from nuclear energy, a series of energy transformations must occur.

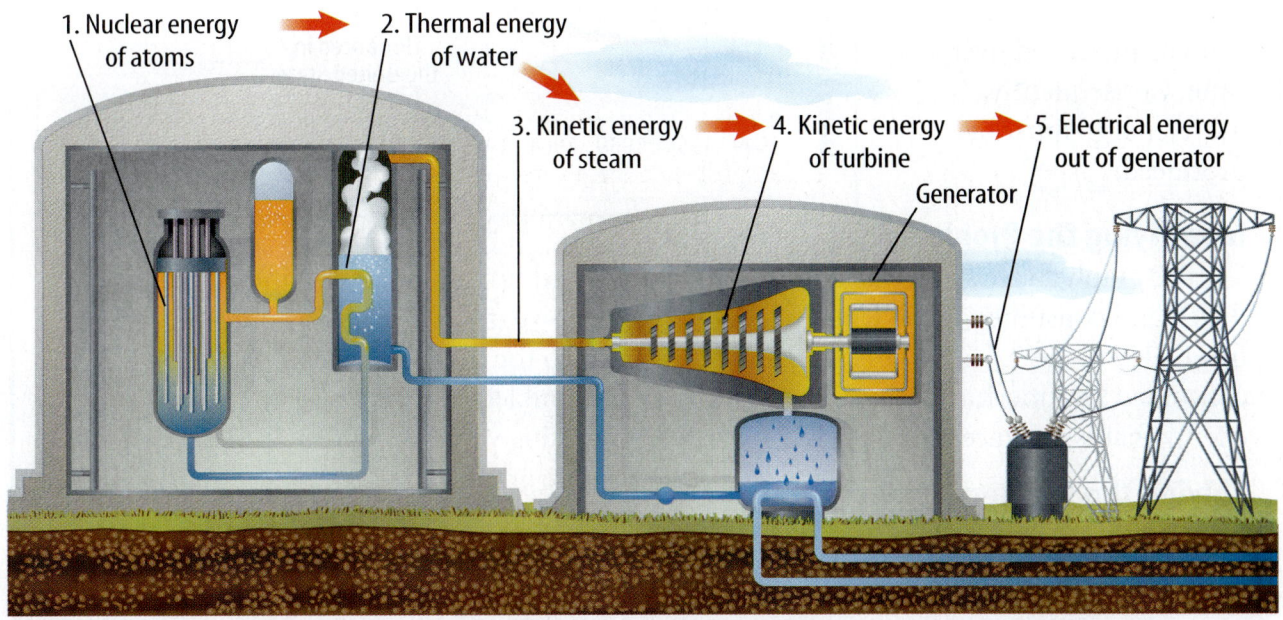

1. Nuclear energy of atoms
2. Thermal energy of water
3. Kinetic energy of steam
4. Kinetic energy of turbine
5. Electrical energy out of generator

Generator

SECTION 3 Sources of Energy 395

Hydroelectricity

Currently, transforming the potential energy of water that is trapped behind dams supplies the world with almost 20 percent of its electrical energy. Hydroelectricity is the largest renewable source of energy. A **renewable resource** is an energy source that is replenished continually. As long as enough rain and snow fall to keep rivers flowing, hydroelectric power plants can generate electrical energy, as shown in **Figure 19**.

Although production of hydroelectricity is largely pollution free, it has one major problem. It disrupts the life cycle of aquatic animals, especially fish. This is particularly true in the Northwest where salmon spawn and run. Because salmon return to the spot where they were hatched to lay their eggs, the development of dams has hindered a large fraction of salmon from reproducing. This has greatly reduced the salmon population. Efforts to correct the problem have resulted in plans to remove a number of dams. In an attempt to help fish bypass some dams, fish ladders are being installed. Like most energy sources, hydroelectricity has advantages and disadvantages.

Topic: Hydroelectricity
Visit in7.msscience.com for Web links to information about the use of hydroelectricity in various parts of the world.

Activity On a map of the world, show where the use of hydroelectricity is the greatest.

Applying Science

Is energy consumption outpacing production?

You use energy every day—to get to school, to watch TV, and to heat or cool your home. The amount of energy consumed by an average person has increased over time. Consequently, more energy must be produced.

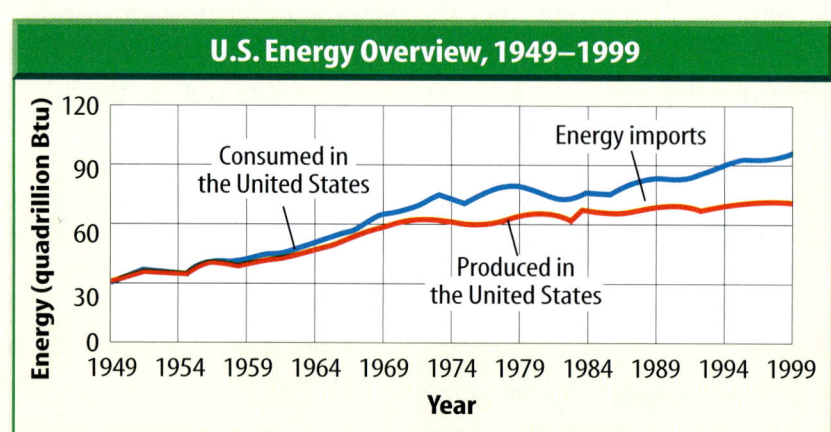

Identifying the Problem

The graph above shows the energy produced and consumed in the United States from 1949 to 1999. How does energy that is consumed by Americans compare with energy that is produced in the United States?

Solving the Problem

1. Determine the approximate amount of energy produced in 1949 and in 1999 and how much it has increased in 50 years. Has it doubled or tripled?
2. Do the same for consumption. Has it doubled or tripled?
3. Using your answers for steps 1 and 2 and the graph, where does the additional energy that is needed come from? Give some examples.

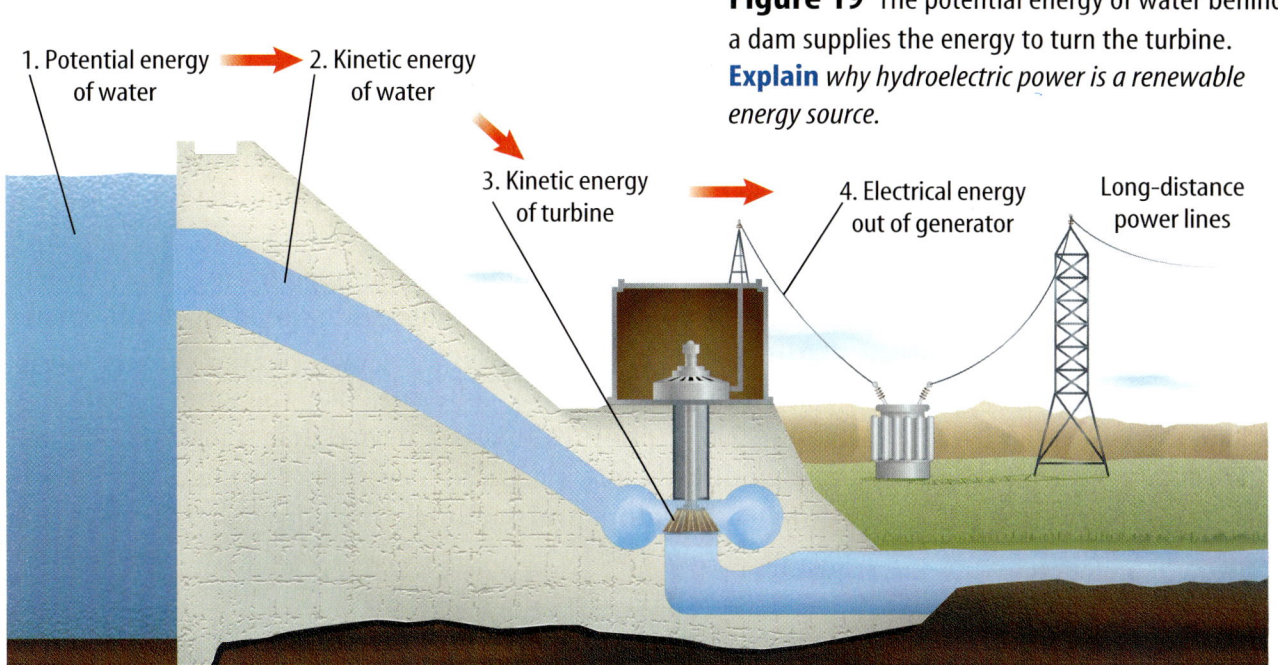

Figure 19 The potential energy of water behind a dam supplies the energy to turn the turbine. **Explain** why hydroelectric power is a renewable energy source.

Alternative Sources of Energy

Electrical energy can be generated in several ways. However, each has disadvantages that can affect the environment and the quality of life for humans. Research is being done to develop new sources of energy that are safer and cause less harm to the environment. These sources often are called **alternative resources**. These alternative resources include solar energy, wind, and geothermal energy.

Solar Energy

The Sun is the origin of almost all the energy that is used on Earth. Because the Sun will go on producing an enormous amount of energy for billions of years, the Sun is an inexhaustible source of energy. An **inexhaustible resource** is an energy source that can't be used up by humans.

Each day, on average, the amount of solar energy that strikes the United States is more than the total amount of energy used by the entire country in a year. However, less than 0.1 percent of the energy used in the United States comes directly from the Sun. One reason is that solar energy is more expensive to use than fossil fuels. However, as the supply of fossil fuels decreases, the cost of finding and mining these fuels might increase. Then, it may be cheaper to use solar energy or other energy sources to generate electricity and heat buildings than to use fossil fuels.

 *What is an inexhaustible energy source?*

Building a Solar Collector

Procedure
1. Line a **large pot** with **black plastic** and fill with **water**.
2. Stretch **clear-plastic wrap** over the pot and tape it taut.
3. Make a slit in the top and slide a **thermometer** or a **computer probe** into the water.
4. Place your solar collector in direct sunlight and monitor the temperature change every 3 min for 15 min.
5. Repeat your experiment without using any black plastic.

Analysis
1. Graph the temperature changes in both setups.
2. Explain how your solar collector works.

SECTION 3 Sources of Energy

Collecting the Sun's Energy Two types of collectors capture the Sun's rays. If you look around your neighborhood, you might see large, rectangular panels attached to the roofs of buildings or houses. If, as in **Figure 20,** pipes come out of the panel, it is a thermal collector. Using a black surface, a thermal collector heats water by directly absorbing the Sun's radiant energy. Water circulating in this system can be heated to about 70°C. The hot water can be pumped through the house to provide heat. Also, the hot water can be used for washing and bathing. If the panel has no pipes, it is a photovoltaic (foh toh vol TAY ihk) collector, like the one pictured in **Figure 20.** A **photovoltaic** is a device that transforms radiant energy directly into electrical energy. Photovoltaics are used to power calculators and satellites, including the *International Space Station.*

Figure 20 Solar energy can be collected and utilized by individuals using thermal collectors or photovoltaic collectors.

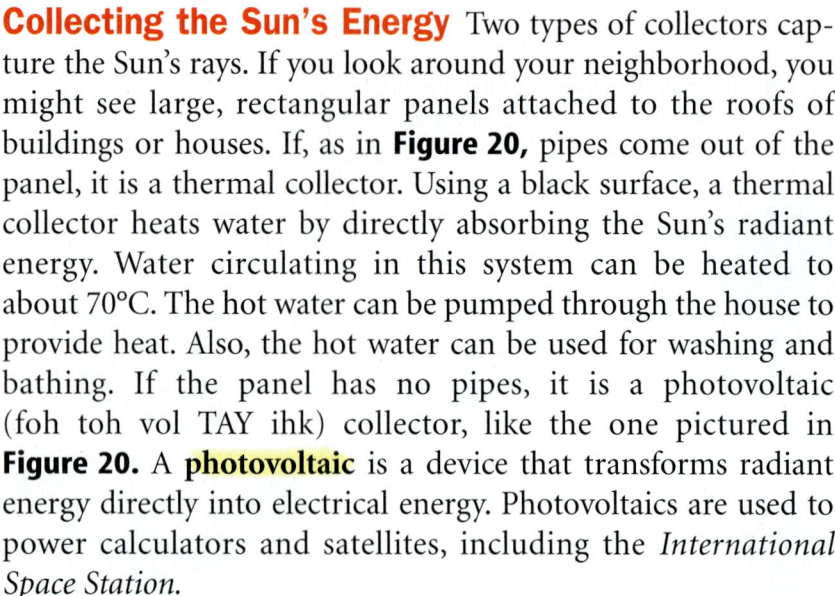

Reading Check *What does a photovoltaic do?*

Geothermal Energy

Imagine you could take a journey to the center of Earth—down to about 6,400 km below the surface. As you went deeper and deeper, you would find the temperature increasing. In fact, after going only about 3 km, the temperature could have increased enough to boil water. At a depth of 100 km, the temperature could be over 900°C. The heat generated inside Earth is called geothermal energy. Some of this heat is produced when unstable radioactive atoms inside Earth decay, converting nuclear energy to thermal energy.

At some places deep within Earth the temperature is hot enough to melt rock. This molten rock, or magma, can rise up close to the surface through cracks in the crust. During a volcanic eruption, magma reaches the surface. In other places, magma gets close to the surface and heats the rock around it.

Geothermal Reservoirs In some regions where magma is close to the surface, rainwater and water from melted snow can seep down to the hot rock through cracks and other openings in Earth's surface. The water then becomes hot and sometimes can form steam. The hot water and steam can be trapped under high pressure in cracks and pockets called geothermal reservoirs. In some places, the hot water and steam are close enough to the surface to form hot springs and geysers.

Geothermal Power Plants In places where the geothermal reservoirs are less than several kilometers deep, wells can be drilled to reach them. The hot water and steam produced by geothermal energy then can be used by geothermal power plants, like the one in **Figure 21,** to generate electricity.

Most geothermal reservoirs contain hot water under high pressure. **Figure 22** shows how these reservoirs can be used to generate electricity. While geothermal power is an inexhaustible source of energy, geothermal power plants can be built only in regions where geothermal reservoirs are close to the surface, such as in the western United States.

Heat Pumps Geothermal heat helps keep the temperature of the ground at a depth of several meters at a nearly constant temperature of about 10° to 20°C. This constant temperature can be used to cool and heat buildings by using a heat pump.

A heat pump contains a water-filled loop of pipe that is buried to a depth where the temperature is nearly constant. In summer the air is warmer than this underground temperature. Warm water from the building is pumped through the pipe down into the ground. The water cools and then is pumped back to the house where it absorbs more heat, and the cycle is repeated. During the winter, the air is cooler than the ground below. Then, cool water absorbs heat from the ground and releases it into the house.

Figure 21 This geothermal power plant in Nevada produces enough electricity to power about 50,000 homes.

Figure 22 The hot water in a geothermal reservoir is used to generate electricity in a geothermal power plant.

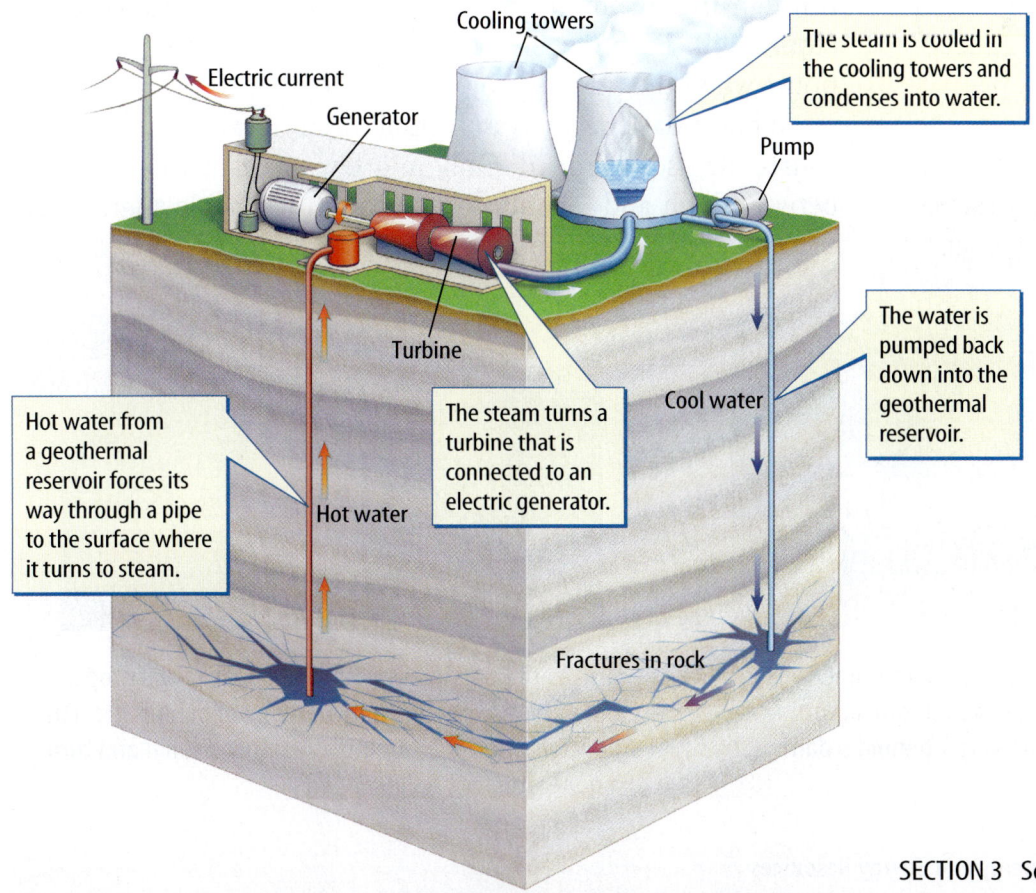

SECTION 3 Sources of Energy **399**

Energy from the Oceans

The ocean is in constant motion. If you've been to the seashore you've seen waves roll in. You may have seen the level of the ocean rise and fall over a period of about a half day. This rise and fall in the ocean level is called a tide. The constant movement of the ocean is an inexhaustible source of mechanical energy that can be converted into electric energy. While methods are still being developed to convert the motion in ocean waves to electric energy, several electric power plants using tidal motion have been built.

Figure 23 This tidal power plant in Annapolis Royal, Nova Scotia, is the only operating tidal power plant in North America.

Using Tidal Energy A high tide and a low tide each occur about twice a day. In most places the level of the ocean changes by less than a few meters. However, in some places the change is much greater. In the Bay of Fundy in Eastern Canada, the ocean level changes by 16 m between high tide and low tide. Almost 14 trillion kg of water move into or out of the bay between high and low tide.

Figure 23 shows an electric power plant that has been built along the Bay of Fundy. This power plant generates enough electric energy to power about 12,000 homes. The power plant is constructed so that as the tide rises, water flows through a turbine that causes an electric generator to spin, as shown in **Figure 24A.** The water is then trapped behind a dam. When the tide goes out, the trapped water behind the dam is released through the turbine to generate more electricity, as shown in **Figure 24B.** Each day electric power is generated for about ten hours when the tide is rising and falling.

While tidal energy is a nonpolluting, inexhaustible energy source, its use is limited. Only in a few places is the difference between high and low tide large enough to enable a large electric power plant to be built.

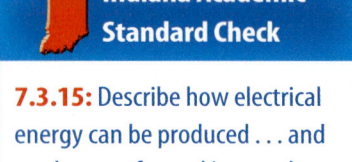

Indiana Academic Standard Check

7.3.15: Describe how electrical energy can be produced . . . and can be transformed into . . . heat or light.

✔ What form of energy is converted to electrical energy by a windmill?

Figure 24 A tidal power plant can generate electricity when the tide is coming in and going out.

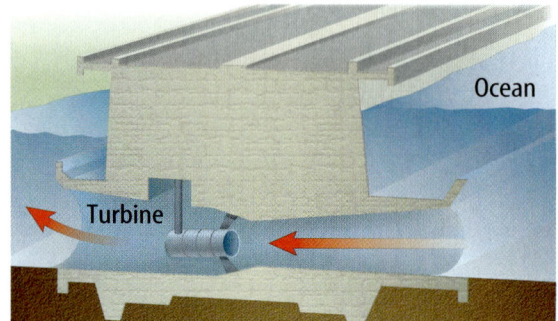

A As the tide comes in, it turns a turbine connected to a generator. When high tide occurs, gates are closed that trap water behind a dam.

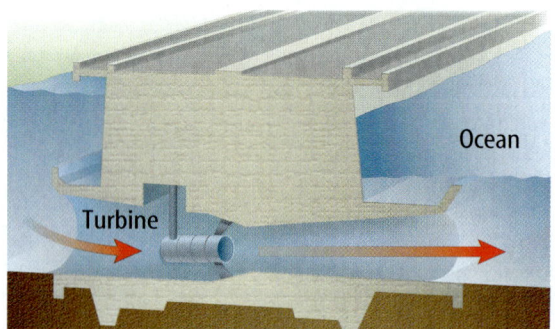

B As the tide goes out and the ocean level drops, the gates are opened and water from behind the dam flows through the turbine, causing it to spin and turn a generator.

Wind

Wind is another inexhaustible supply of energy. Modern windmills, like the ones in **Figure 25,** convert the kinetic energy of the wind to electrical energy. The propeller is connected to a generator so that electrical energy is generated when wind spins the propeller. These windmills produce almost no pollution. Some disadvantages are that windmills produce noise and that large areas of land are needed. Also, studies have shown that birds sometimes are killed by windmills.

Conserving Energy

Fossil fuels are a valuable resource. Not only are they burned to provide energy, but oil and coal also are used to make plastics and other materials. One way to make the supply of fossil fuels last longer is to use less energy. Reducing the use of energy is called conserving energy.

You can conserve energy and also save money by turning off lights and appliances such as televisions when you are not using them. Also keep doors and windows closed tightly when it's cold or hot to keep heat from leaking out of or into your house. Energy could also be conserved if buildings are properly insulated, especially around windows. The use of oil could be reduced if cars were used less and made more efficient, so they went farther on a liter of gas. Recycling materials such as aluminum cans and glass also helps conserve energy.

Figure 25 Windmills work on the same basic principles as a power plant. Instead of steam turning a turbine, wind turns the rotors. **Describe** *some of the advantages and disadvantages of using windmills.*

section 3 review

Summary

Nonrenewable Resources

- All energy resources have advantages and disadvantages.
- Nonrenewable energy resources are used faster than they are replaced.
- Fossil fuels include oil, coal, and natural gas and are nonrenewable resources. Nuclear energy is a nonrenewable resource.

Renewable and Alternative Resources

- Renewable energy resources, such as hydroelectricity, are resources that are replenished continually.
- Alternative energy sources include solar energy, wind energy, and geothermal energy.

Self Check

1. **Diagram** the energy conversions that occur when coal is formed, and then burned to produce thermal energy.
2. **Explain** why solar energy is considered an inexhaustible source of energy.
3. **Explain** how a heat pump is used to both heat and cool a building.
4. **Think Critically** Identify advantages and disadvantages of using fossil fuels, hydroelectricity, and solar energy as energy sources.

Applying Math

5. **Use a Ratio** Earth's temperature increases with depth. Suppose the temperature increase inside Earth is 500°C at a depth of 50 km. What is the temperature increase at a depth of 10 km?

LAB

Use the Internet

Energy to Power Your Life

Goals
- **Identify** how energy you use is produced and delivered.
- **Investigate** alternative sources for the energy you use.
- **Outline** a plan for how these alternative sources of energy could be used.

Data Source

Visit **in7.msscience.com/ internet_lab** for more information about sources of energy and for data collected by other students.

Real-World Question

Over the past 100 years, the amount of energy used in the United States and elsewhere has greatly increased. Today, a number of energy sources are available, such as coal, oil, natural gas, nuclear energy, hydroelectric power, wind, and solar energy. Some of these energy sources are being used up and are nonrenewable, but others are replaced as fast as they are used and, therefore, are renewable. Some energy sources are so vast that human usage has almost no effect on the amount available. These energy sources are inexhaustible.

Think about the types of energy you use at home and school every day. In this lab, you will investigate how and where energy is produced, and how it gets to you. You will also investigate alternative ways energy can be produced, and whether these sources are renewable, nonrenewable, or inexhaustible. What are the sources of the energy you use every day?

Local Energy Information	
Energy Type	
Where is that energy produced?	
How is that energy produced?	**Do not write in this book.**
How is that energy delivered to you?	
Is the energy source renewable, nonrenewable, or inexhaustible?	
What type of alternative energy source could you use instead?	

402 CHAPTER 13 Energy and Energy Resources

Using Scientific Methods

⏵ Make a Plan

1. Think about the activities you do every day and the things you use. When you watch television, listen to the radio, ride in a car, use a hair drier, or turn on the air conditioning, you use energy. Select one activity or appliance that uses energy.
2. **Identify** the type of energy that is used.
3. **Investigate** how that energy is produced and delivered to you.
4. **Determine** if the energy source is renewable, nonrenewable, or inexhaustible.
5. If your energy source is nonrenewable, describe how the energy you use could be produced by renewable sources.

⏵ Follow Your Plan

1. Make sure your teacher approves your plan before you start.
2. Organize your findings in a data table, similar to the one that is shown.

⏵ Analyze Your Data

1. **Describe** the process for producing and delivering the energy source you researched. How is it created, and how does it get to you?
2. How much energy is produced by the energy source you investigated?
3. Is the energy source you researched renewable, nonrenewable, or inexhaustible? Why?

⏵ Conclude and Apply

1. **Describe** If the energy source you investigated is nonrenewable, how the use of this energy source be reduced?
2. **Organize** What alternative sources of energy could you use for everyday energy needs? On the computer, create a plan for using renewable or inexhaustible sources.

Your Data

Find this lab using the link below. Post your data in the table that is provided. **Compare** your data to those of other students. **Combine** your data with those of other students and make inferences using the combined data.

in7.msscience.com/internet_lab

LAB 403

SCIENCE Stats

Energy to Burn

Did you know...

... The energy released by the average hurricane is equal to about 200 times the total energy produced by all of the world's power plants. Almost all of this energy is released as heat when raindrops form.

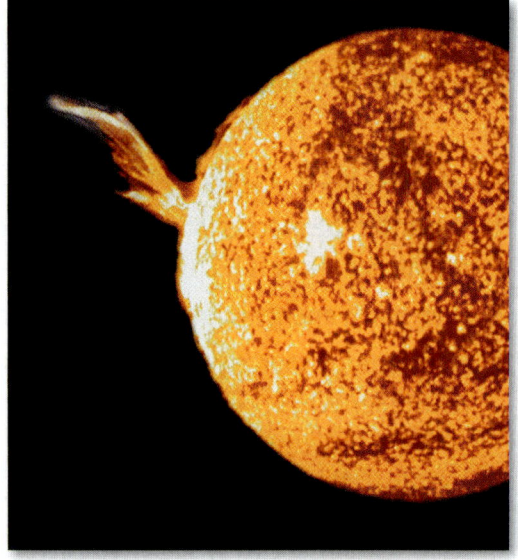

... The energy Earth gets each half hour from the Sun is enough to meet the world's demands for a year. Renewable and inexhaustible resources, including the Sun, account for only 18 percent of the energy that is used worldwide.

... The Calories in one medium apple will give you enough energy to walk for about 15 min, swim for about 10 min, or jog for about 9 min.

Applying Math If walking for 15 min requires 80 Calories of fuel (from food), how many Calories would someone need to consume to walk for 1 h?

Write About It

Where would you place solar collectors in the United States? Why? For more information on solar energy, go to in7.msscience.com/science_stats.

404 CHAPTER 13 Energy and Energy Resources

chapter 13 Study Guide

Reviewing Main Ideas

Section 1 What is energy?

1. Energy is the ability to cause change.
2. A moving object has kinetic energy that depends on the object's mass and speed.
3. Potential energy is energy due to position and depends on an object's mass and height.
4. Light carries radiant energy, electric current carries electrical energy, and atomic nuclei contain nuclear energy.

Section 2 Energy Transformations

1. Energy can be transformed from one form to another. Thermal energy is usually produced when energy transformations occur.
2. The law of conservation of energy states that energy cannot be created or destroyed.

3. Electric power plants convert a source of energy into electrical energy. Steam spins a turbine which spins an electric generator.

Section 3 Sources of Energy

1. The use of an energy source has advantages and disadvantages.
2. Fossil fuels and nuclear energy are nonrenewable energy sources that are consumed faster than they can be replaced.
3. Hydroelectricity is a renewable energy source that is continually being replaced.
4. Alternative energy sources include solar, wind, and geothermal energy. Solar energy is an inexhaustible energy source.

Visualizing Main Ideas

Copy and complete the concept map using the following terms: fossil fuels, hydroelectric, solar, wind, oil, coal, photovoltaic, *and* nonrenewable resources.

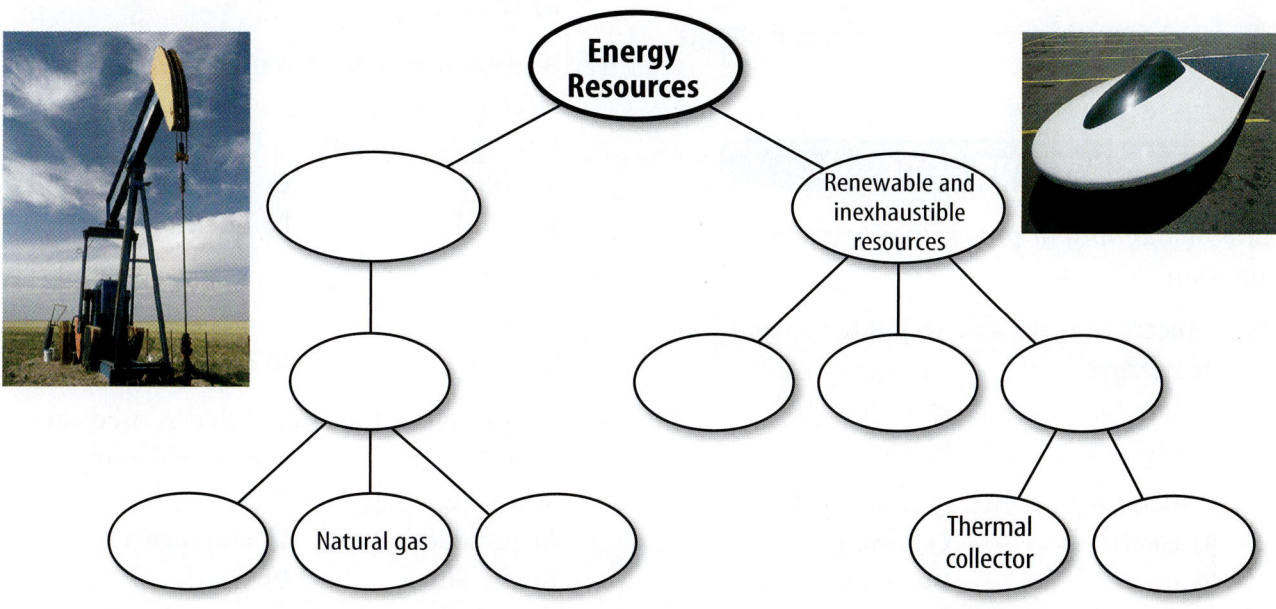

chapter 13 Review

Using Vocabulary

alternative resource p. 397	nonrenewable
chemical energy p. 383	resource p. 394
electrical energy p. 384	nuclear energy p. 384
energy p. 380	photovoltaic p. 398
generator p. 390	potential energy p. 382
inexhaustible	radiant energy p. 383
resource p. 397	renewable resource p. 396
kinetic energy p. 381	thermal energy p. 382
law of conservation	turbine p. 390
of energy p. 386	

For each of the terms below, explain the relationship that exists.

1. electrical energy—nuclear energy
2. turbine—generator
3. photovoltaic—radiant energy—electrical energy
4. renewable resource—inexhaustible resource
5. potential energy—kinetic energy
6. kinetic energy—electrical energy—generator
7. thermal energy—radiant energy
8. law of conservation of energy—energy transformations
9. nonrenewable resource—chemical energy

Checking Concepts

Choose the word or phrase that best answers the question.

10. Objects that are able to fall have what type of energy?
    A) kinetic   C) potential
    B) radiant   D) electrical

11. Which form of energy does light have?
    A) electrical C) kinetic
    B) nuclear   D) radiant

12. Muscles perform what type of energy transformation?
    A) kinetic to potential
    B) kinetic to electrical
    C) thermal to radiant
    D) chemical to kinetic

13. Photovoltaics perform what type of energy transformation?
    A) thermal to radiant
    B) kinetic to electrical
    C) radiant to electrical
    D) electrical to thermal

14. The form of energy that food contains is which of the following?
    A) chemical   C) radiant
    B) potential   D) electrical

15. Solar energy, wind, and geothermal are what type of energy resource?
    A) inexhaustible C) nonrenewable
    B) inexpensive   D) chemical

16. Which of the following is a nonrenewable source of energy?
    A) hydroelectricity
    B) nuclear
    C) wind
    D) solar

17. A generator is NOT required to generate electrical energy when which of the following energy sources is used?
    A) solar   C) hydroelectric
    B) wind   D) nuclear

18. Which of the following are fossil fuels?
    A) gas   C) oil
    B) coal   D) all of these

19. Almost all of the energy that is used on Earth's surface comes from which of the following energy sources?
    A) radioactivity C) chemicals
    B) the Sun   D) wind

in7.msscience.com/vocabulary_puzzlemaker

Chapter 13 Review

Thinking Critically

20. **Explain** how the motion of a swing illustrates the transformation between potential and kinetic energy.

21. **Explain** what happens to the kinetic energy of a skateboard that is coasting along a flat surface, slows down, and comes to a stop.

22. **Describe** the energy transformations that occur in the process of toasting a bagel in an electric toaster.

23. **Compare and contrast** the formation of coal and the formation of oil and natural gas.

24. **Explain** the difference between the law of conservation of energy and conserving energy. How can conserving energy help prevent energy shortages?

25. **Make a Hypothesis** about how spacecraft that travel through the solar system obtain the energy they need to operate. Do research to verify your hypothesis.

26. **Concept Map** Copy and complete this concept map about energy.

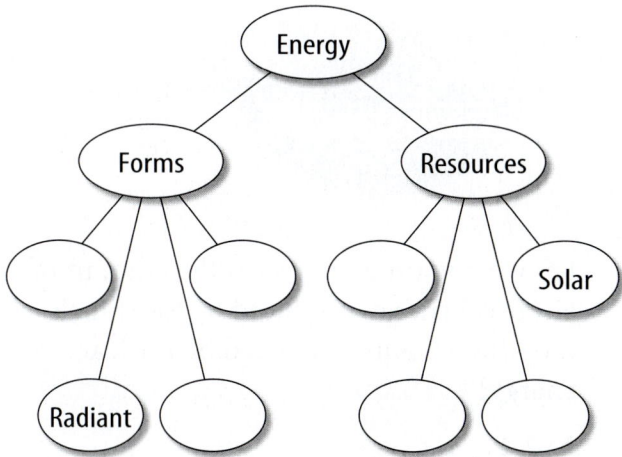

27. **Diagram** the energy transformations that occur when you rub sandpaper on a piece of wood and the wood becomes warm.

Performance Activities

28. **Multimedia Presentation** Alternative sources of energy that weren't discussed include biomass energy, wave energy, and hydrogen fuel cells. Research an alternative energy source and then prepare a digital slide show about the information you found. Use the concepts you learned from this chapter to inform your classmates about the future prospects of using such an energy source on a large scale.

Applying Math

29. **Calculate Number of Power Plants** A certain type of power plant is designed to provide energy for 10,000 homes. How many of these power plants would be needed to provide energy for 300,000 homes?

Use the table below to answer questions 30 and 31.

Energy Sources Used in the United States	
Energy Source	Percent of Energy Used
Coal	23%
Oil	39%
Natural gas	23%
Nuclear	8%
Hydroelectric	4%
Other	3%

30. **Use Percentages** According to the data in the table above, what percentage of the energy used in the United States comes from fossil fuels?

31. **Calculate a Ratio** How many times greater is the amount of energy that comes from fossil fuels than the amount of energy from all other energy sources?

in7.msscience.com/chapter_review

chapter 13 Indiana

 The assessed Indiana standard appears above the question.

Record your answers on the answer sheet provided by your teacher or on a sheet of paper.

Part 1 Multiple Choice

7.3.16

1. The graph below shows global energy use from 1970 to 2000.

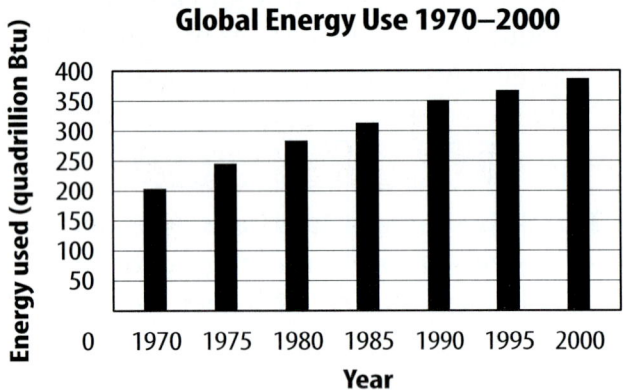

By about how many times did the global use of energy increase from 1970 to 2000?

A 1.5
B 2.0
C 2.5
D 3.0

7.3.15

2. Which is **TRUE** when chemical energy is transformed into thermal energy?

A Only the amount of chemical energy changes.
B Only the amount of thermal energy changes.
C The total amount of energy changes.
D The total amount of energy doesn't change.

7.3.16

3. Which energy source is being used faster than it can be replaced?

A hydroelectric
B oil
C tidal
D wind

4. Which energy conversion occurs as a ball falls?

A kinetic to potential
B potential to kinetic
C thermal to potential
D thermal to kinetic

5. The circle graph below shows the sources of electrical energy in the United States.

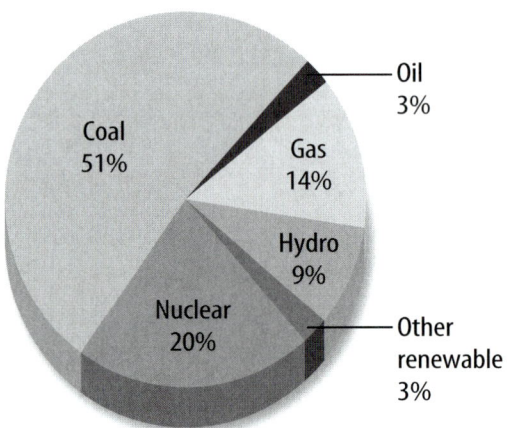

How many times greater is the amount of electrical energy produced by fossil fuels than the amount produced by nuclear energy?

A 2.4
B 3.0
C 3.4
D 4.0

Standards Review

6. The kinetic energy of an object increases if which increases?

   A its height

   B its speed

   C its temperature

   D its volume

7. The graph below shows actual global oil production from 1930 to 2000 and estimated global oil production from 2000 to 2050.

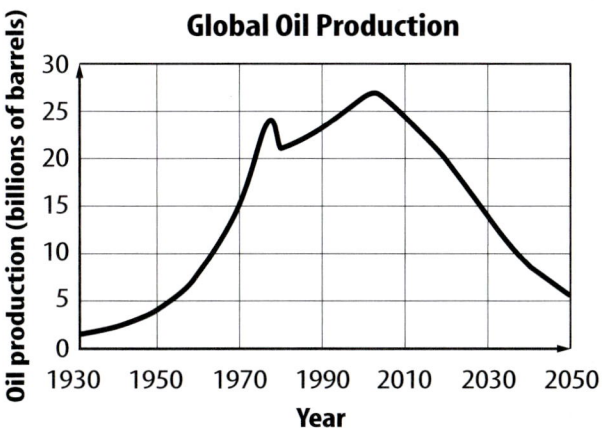

   In approximately what year will estimated global oil production equal the actual oil production in 1970?

   A 2005

   B 2010

   C 2020

   D 2030

Test-Taking Tip

Don't Panic Stay calm during the test. If you feel yourself getting nervous, close your eyes and take five slow, deep breaths.

Part 2 Constructed Response

7.3.14

8. When you drop a tennis ball, it hits the floor and bounces back up. It does not reach the same height as released, and each successive upward bounce is smaller than the one previous. However, you notice the tennis ball is slightly warmer after it finishes bouncing. Explain how the law of conservation of energy is obeyed.

9. The graph below shows how the potential energy of a batted ball changes as the distance from the batter increases.

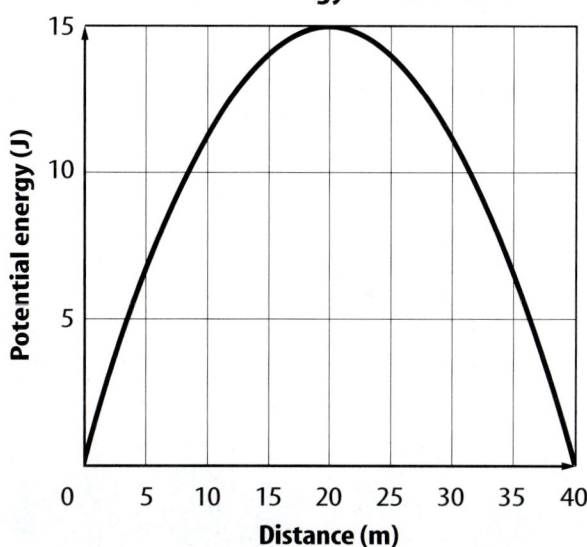

   At what distances is the kinetic energy of the ball greatest?

7.3.16

10. List advantages and disadvantages of the following energy sources: fossil fuels, nuclear energy, and geothermal energy.

Academic Standard—3: Students collect and organize data to identify relationships between physical objects, events, and processes. They use logical reasoning to question their own ideas as new information challenges their conceptions of the natural world.

Also covers: Academic Standards 1, 7 (Detailed standards begin on page IN8.)

Waves, Sound, and Light

chapter preview

sections
1. **Waves**
2. **Sound Waves**
   Lab Sound Waves in Matter
3. **Light**
   Lab Bending Light

Virtual Lab What are some characteristics of waves?

Ups and Downs
This wind surfer is riding high for now, but that will change soon. The energy carried by ocean waves makes this a thrilling ride, but other waves carry energy, too. Sound waves and light waves carry energy that enable you to hear and see the world around you.

Science Journal Write a short paragraph describing water waves you have seen.

Start-Up Activities

Wave Properties

If you drop a pebble into a pool of water, you notice how the water rises and falls as waves spread out in all directions. How could you describe the waves? In this lab you'll make a model of one type of wave. By describing the model, you'll learn about some properties of all waves.

1. Make a model of a wave by forming a piece of thick string about 50-cm long into a series of *S* shapes with an up and down pattern.
2. Compare the wave you made with those of other students. Notice how many peaks you have in your wave.
3. Reform your wave so that you have a different number of peaks.
4. **Think Critically** Write a description of your wave model. How did the distance between the peaks change as the number of peaks increased?

Preview this chapter's content and activities at in7.msscience.com

Waves Make the following Foldable to compare and contrast the characteristics of transverse and compressional waves.

STEP 1 **Fold** one sheet of lengthwise paper in half.

STEP 2 **Fold** into thirds.

STEP 3 **Unfold and draw** overlapping ovals. **Cut** the top sheet along the folds.

STEP 4 **Label** the ovals as shown.

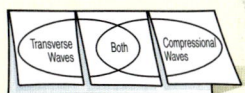

Construct a Venn Diagram As you read the chapter, list the characteristics unique to transverse waves under the left tab, those unique to compressional waves under the right tab, and those characteristics common to both under the middle tab.

Standards—7.3.18: Describe that light waves, sound waves, and other waves move at different speeds in different materials. **7.7.4:** Use symbolic equations to show how the quantity of something changes . . . in response to changes in other quantities.

section 1

Waves

as you read

What You'll Learn
- **Explain** how waves transport energy.
- **Distinguish** among transverse, compressional, and electromagnetic waves.
- **Describe** the properties of waves.
- **Describe** reflection, refraction, and diffraction of waves.

Why It's Important
Devices such as televisions, radios, and cell phones receive and transmit information by waves.

Review Vocabulary
density: the mass per cubic meter of a substance

New Vocabulary
- wave
- transverse wave
- compressional wave
- wavelength
- frequency
- law of reflection
- refraction
- diffraction

What are waves?

When you float in the pool on a warm summer day, the up-and-down movement of the water tells you waves are moving past. Sometimes the waves are so strong they almost push you over. Other times, the waves just gently rock you. You know about water waves because you can see and feel their movement, but there are other types of waves, also. Different types of waves carry signals to televisions and radios. Sound and light waves move all around you and enable you to hear and see. Waves are even responsible for the damage caused by earthquakes.

Waves Carry Energy, not Matter A **wave** is a disturbance that moves through matter or space. Waves carry energy from one place to another. You can see that the waves in **Figure 1** carry energy by the way they crash against the rocks. In water waves, the energy is transferred by water molecules. When a wave moves, it may seem that the wave carries matter from place to place as the wave moves.

But that's not what really happens. When waves travel through solids, liquids, and gases, matter is not carried along with the waves. The movement of the fishing bob in **Figure 1** transfers energy to nearby water molecules. The energy is then passed from molecule to molecule as the wave spreads out. The wave disturbance moves outward, but the locations of the water molecules hardly change at all.

Figure 1 Waves carry energy from place to place without carrying matter.

The energy carried by ocean waves can break rocks.

The movement of the fishing bob produces water waves that carry energy through the water.

412 CHAPTER 14 Waves, Sound, and Light

Types of Waves

Waves usually are produced by something moving back and forth, or vibrating. It is the energy of the vibrating object that waves carry outward. This energy can spread out from the vibrating object in different types of waves. Some waves, known as mechanical waves, can travel only through matter. Other waves called electromagnetic waves can travel either through matter or through empty space.

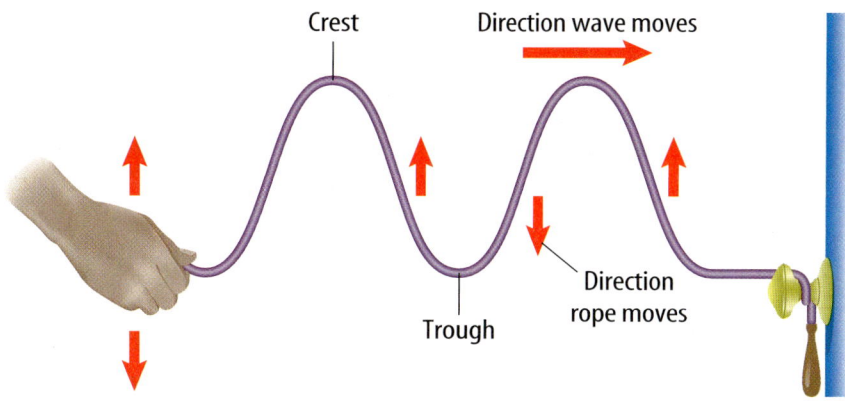

Figure 2 You make a transverse wave when you shake the end of a rope up and down.

Transverse Waves One type of mechanical wave is a transverse wave, shown in **Figure 2**. A **transverse wave** causes particles in matter to move back and forth at right angles to the direction in which the wave travels. If you tie a rope to a door handle and shake the end of the rope up and down, transverse waves travel through the rope.

High points in the wave are called crests. Low points are called troughs. The series of crests and troughs forms a transverse wave. The crests and troughs travel along the rope, but the particles in the rope move only up and down.

Compressional Waves Another type of mechanical wave is a compressional wave. **Figure 3** shows a compressional wave traveling along a spring coil. A **compressional wave** causes particles in matter to move back and forth along the same direction in which the wave travels.

In **Figure 3** the places where the coils are squeezed together are called compressions. The places where the coils are spread apart are called rarefactions. The series of compressions and rarefactions forms a compressional wave. The compressions and rarefactions travel along the spring, but the coils move only back and forth.

 *How does matter move in a compressional wave?*

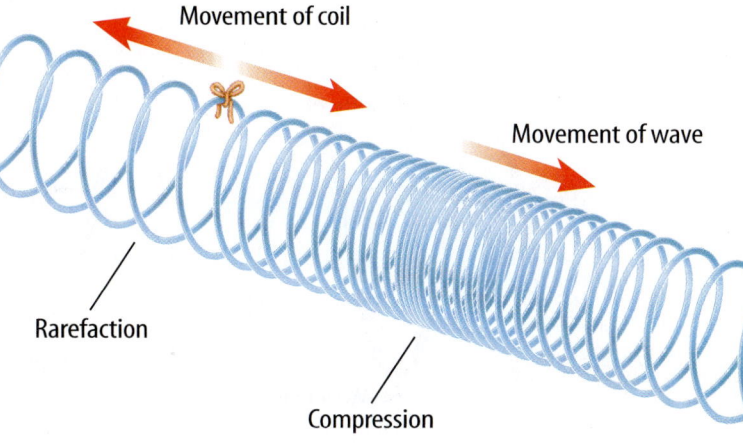

Figure 3 A wave on a spring coil is an example of a compressional wave.

INTEGRATE Earth Science Seismic waves move through the ground during an earthquake. Some of these waves are compressional, and others are transverse. The seismic waves that cause most damage to buildings are a kind of rolling waves. These rolling waves are a combination of compressional and transverse waves.

Electromagnetic Waves Light, radio waves, and X rays are examples of electromagnetic waves. Just like waves on a rope, electromagnetic waves are transverse waves. However, electromagnetic waves contain electric and magnetic parts that vibrate up and down perpendicular to the direction the wave travels.

Properties of Waves

The properties that waves have depend on the vibrations that produce the waves. For example, if you move a pencil slowly up and down in a bowl of water, the waves produced by the pencil's motion will be small and spread apart. If you move the pencil rapidly, the waves will be larger and close together.

Wavelength The distance between one point on a wave and the nearest point moving with the same speed and direction is the **wavelength**. **Figure 4** shows how the wavelengths of transverse and compressional waves are measured. The wavelength of a transverse wave is the distance between two adjacent crests or two adjacent troughs. The wavelength of a compressional wave is the distance between two adjacent compressions or rarefactions.

Frequency The **frequency** of a wave is the number of wavelengths that pass by a point each second. If you were watching a transverse wave on a rope, the frequency of the wave would be the number of crests or troughs that pass you each second. In the same way, the frequency of a compressional wave is the number of compressions or rarefactions that would pass by each second.

Figure 4 The wavelength of a transverse wave is the distance from crest to crest or from trough to trough. The wavelength of a compressional wave is the distance from compression to compression or rarefaction to rarefaction.

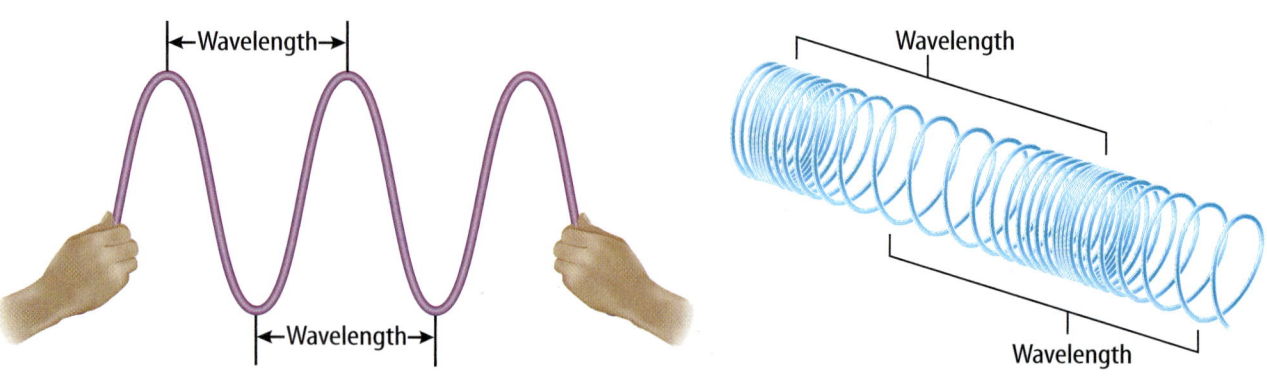

Amplitude of a Transverse Wave Waves have another property called amplitude. Suppose you shake the end of a rope by moving your hand up and down a large distance. Then you make a transverse wave with high crests and deep troughs. The wave you've made has a large amplitude. The amplitude of a transverse wave is half the distance between a crest and trough as shown in **Figure 5**. As the distance between crests and troughs increases, the amplitude of a transverse wave increases.

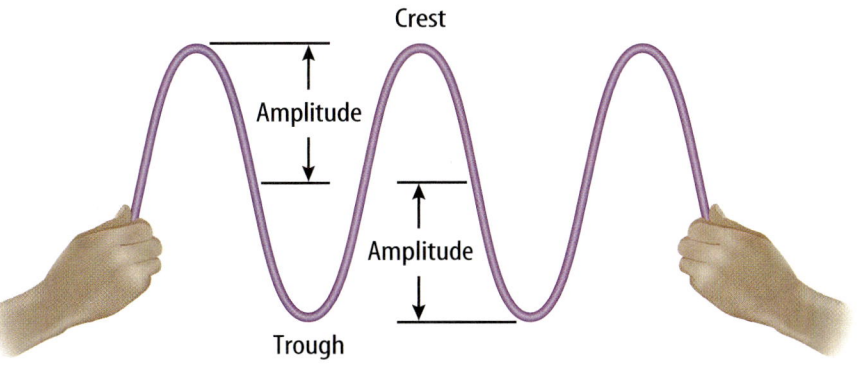

Figure 5 The amplitude of a transverse wave depends on the height of the crests or the depth of the troughs.

Amplitude of a Compressional Wave The amplitude of a compressional wave depends on the density of material in compressions and rarefactions as shown in **Figure 6**. Compressional waves with greater amplitude have compressions that are more squeezed together and rarefactions that are more spread apart. For example, in a spring, squeezing some coils together more tightly causes the nearby coils to be more spread apart.

Reading Check What is the amplitude of a compressional wave?

Amplitude and Energy The vibrations that produce a wave transfer energy to the wave. The more energy a wave carries, the larger its amplitude. By moving your hand up and down a larger distance in making a wave on a rope, you transfer more energy to the wave. Seismic waves are produced by vibrations in Earth's crust that cause earthquakes. The more energy these waves have, the larger their amplitudes and the more damage they cause as they travel along Earth's surface.

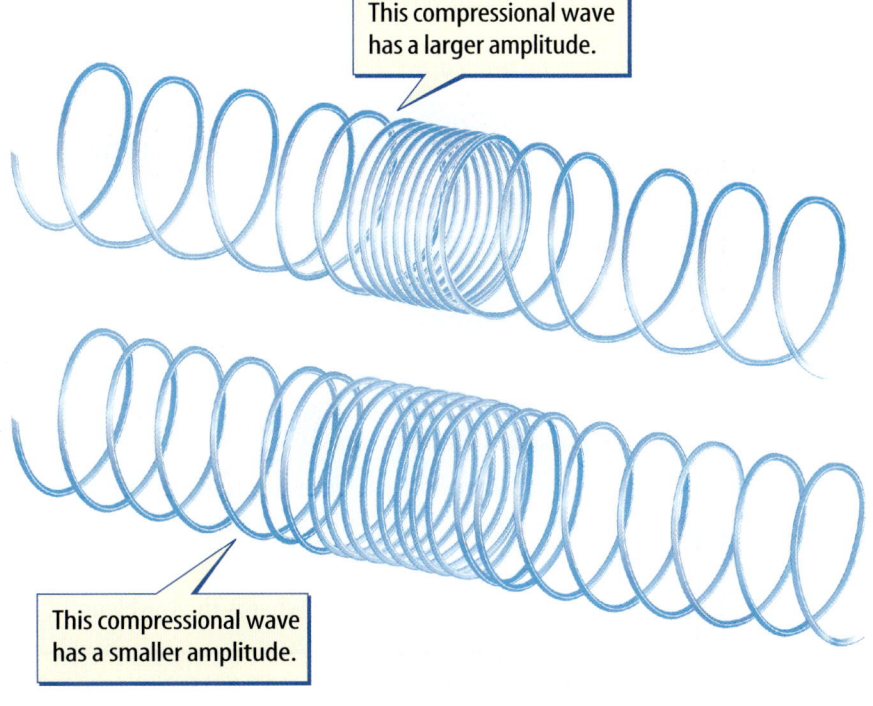

Figure 6 The amplitude of a compressional wave depends on the density of the material in the compressions and rarefactions.

SECTION 1 Waves **415**

Indiana Academic Standard Check

7.3.18: Describe that...waves move at different speeds in different materials.

✓ How does the speed of a light wave change when it travels from air into water?

Wave Speed The speed of a wave depends on the medium in which the wave travels. The faster waves travel, the more crests or compressions pass by you each second. You can calculate the speed of a wave if you know its wavelength and frequency using the equation below.

Wave Speed Equation

wave speed (in m/s) = **wavelength** (in m) × **frequency** (in Hz)

$$v = \lambda f$$

In this equation, v is the symbol for wave speed and f is the symbol for frequency. The SI unit for frequency is the hertz, abbreviated Hz. One hertz equals one vibration per second, or one wavelength passing a point in one second. One hertz is equal to the unit 1/s. The wavelength is represented by the Greek letter lambda, λ, and is measured in meters.

Applying Math — Solve a Simple Equation

SPEED OF SOUND A sound wave produced by a lightning bolt has a frequency of 34 Hz and a wavelength of 10.0 m. What is the speed of the sound wave?

Solution

1 *This is what you know:*
- wavelength: λ = 10 m
- frequency: f = 34 Hz

2 *This is what you need to find:* wave speed: v = ? m/s

3 *This is the procedure you need to use:* Substitute the known values for wavelength and frequency into the wave speed equation and calculate the wave speed:

$v = \lambda f$ = (10.0 m)(34 Hz)

= 340 m × Hz = 340 m × (1/s) = 340 m/s

4 *Check your answer:* Divide your answer by the wavelength 10.0 m. The result should be the given frequency 34 Hz.

Practice Problems

1. Waves on a string have a wavelength of 0.55 m. If the frequency of the waves is 6.0 Hz, what is the wave speed?

2. If the frequency of a sound wave in water is 15,000 Hz, and the sound wave travels through water at a speed of 1,500 m/s, what is the wavelength?

For more practice, visit in7.msscience.com/math_practice

Waves Can Change Direction

Waves don't always travel in a straight line. When you look into a mirror, you use the mirror to make light waves change direction. Waves can change direction when they travel from one material to another. The waves can reflect (bounce off a surface), refract (change direction), or diffract (bend around an obstacle).

The Law of Reflection When waves reflect off a surface, they always obey the law of reflection, as shown in **Figure 7.** A line that makes an angle of 90 degrees with a surface is called the normal to the surface. According to **law of reflection,** the angle that the incoming wave makes with the normal equals the angle that the outgoing wave makes with the normal.

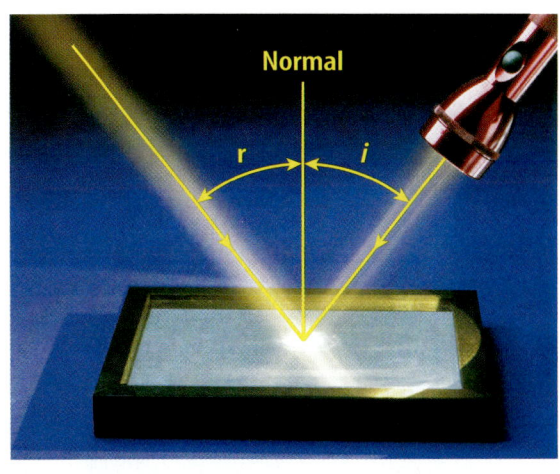

Figure 7 All waves obey the law of reflection. The angle of reflection, r, always equals the angle of incidence, i.

Refraction The speed of the wave depends on properties of the material through which it travels. A light wave, for example, travels faster through air than it does through water. **Figure 8** shows that a change in a wave's speed changes the direction in which the wave travels. When the light wave moves from air to water, it slows down. This change in speed causes the light wave to bend. **Refraction** is the change in direction of a wave when it changes speed as it travels from one material to another.

Figure 8 Refraction occurs when a wave changes speed. Light waves change direction when they slow down as they pass from air to water.

Refraction of Light

Procedure
1. Fill a **drinking glass** about half full with water.
2. Place a **pencil** in the glass. Describe the appearance of the pencil.
3. Slowly add water to the glass. Describe how the appearance of the pencil changes.

Analysis
1. How does the appearance of the pencil depend on the level of water in the glass?
2. Where do the light waves coming from the pencil change speed?
3. **Infer** how the appearance of the pencil and the change in speed of the light waves are related.

Diffraction Waves can change direction by **diffraction**, which is the bending of waves around an object. In **Figure 9**, the water waves are not completely blocked by the obstacle, but instead bend around the obstacle.

The amount of diffraction or bending of the wave depends on the size of the obstacle the wave encounters. If the size of the obstacle is much larger than the wavelength, very little diffraction occurs. Then there is a shadow behind the object where there are no waves.

As the wavelength increases compared with the size of the obstacle, the amount of diffraction increases. The amount of diffraction is greatest if the wavelength is much larger than the obstacle.

Figure 9 The amount of diffraction or bending around an obstacle depends on the size of the obstacle and the wavelength of the wave.

Diffraction of Sound and Light The wavelengths of sound waves are similar to the size of objects around you, but the wavelength of light waves are much shorter. As a result, you can hear people talking in a room with an open door even though you can't see them.

section 1 review

Summary

Wave Energy
- Waves transport energy without transporting matter.

Types of Waves
- Transverse waves cause particles in a material to move back and forth at right angles to the direction the waves travel.
- Compressional waves cause particles in a material to move back and forth along the same direction the waves travel.
- Electromagnetic waves are transverse waves that can travel through empty space.

Wave Properties
- A wave can be described by its wavelength, frequency, and amplitude.
- The energy carried by a wave increases as the amplitude of the wave increases.
- The speed of a wave, v, equals its wavelength, λ, multiplied by its frequency, f:
$$v = \lambda f$$
- Reflection, refraction, or diffraction can cause waves to change direction.

Self Check

1. **Analyze** How can waves transport energy without transporting matter from place to another?
2. **Explain** how the spacing between coils of a spring changes if the amplitude of compressional waves traveling along the spring increases.
3. **Predict** how the wavelength of waves traveling with the same speed would change if the frequency of the waves increases.
4. **Apply** Two similar-sized stones, one heavy and one light, are dropped from the same height into a pond. Explain why the impact of the heavy stone would produce waves with higher amplitude than the impact of the light stone would.
5. **Think Critically** Water waves produced by a speed boat strike a floating inner tube. Describe the motion of the inner tube as the waves pass by.

Applying Math

6. **Calculate Wave Speed** Find the speed of a wave with a wavelength of 0.2 m and a frequency of 1.5 Hz.
7. **Calculate Wavelength** Find the wavelength of a wave with a speed of 3.0 m/s and a frequency of 0.5 Hz.

in7.mssscience.com/self_check_quiz

Standards—7.3.18: Describe that . . . sound waves . . . move at different speeds in different materials
7.3.20: Describe that something . . . can be "heard" when sound waves from it enter the ear.

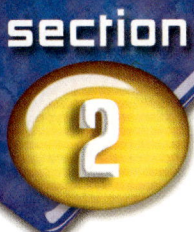

section 2
Sound Waves

Making Sound Waves

How does the motion of a drummer's drumsticks produce sound waves? The impact of the sticks on the head of a drum causes the drum head to vibrate. These vibrations transfer energy to nearby air particles, producing sound waves in air. You can hear the sound because energy from the drums travels as sound waves to your ears. Every sound you hear is caused by something vibrating. For example, when you talk, tissues in your throat vibrate in different ways to form sounds.

Sound Waves are Compressional Waves Sound waves produced by a vibrating object are compressional waves. **Figure 10** shows how the vibrating drum produces compressional waves. When the drummer hits the drum, the head of the drum vibrates. Nearby air particles vibrate with the same frequency as the frequency of vibrations. The drum head moving outward compresses nearby air particles. The drum head moving inward causes rarefactions in nearby air particles. The inward and outward movement of the drum head produces the same pattern of compressions and rarefactions in the air particles.

Sound waves can only travel through matter. The energy carried by a sound wave is transferred by the collisions between the particles in the material the wave is traveling in. A spaceship traveling outside Earth's atmosphere, for example, does not make any sound outside the ship.

as you read

What You'll Learn
- **Describe** how sound waves are produced.
- **Explain** how sound waves travel through matter.
- **Describe** the relationship between loudness and sound intensity.
- **Explain** how humans hear sound.

Why It's Important
A knowledge of sound helps you understand how to protect your hearing.

Review Vocabulary
perception: a recognition, sense, or understanding of something

New Vocabulary
- intensity
- pitch
- reverberation

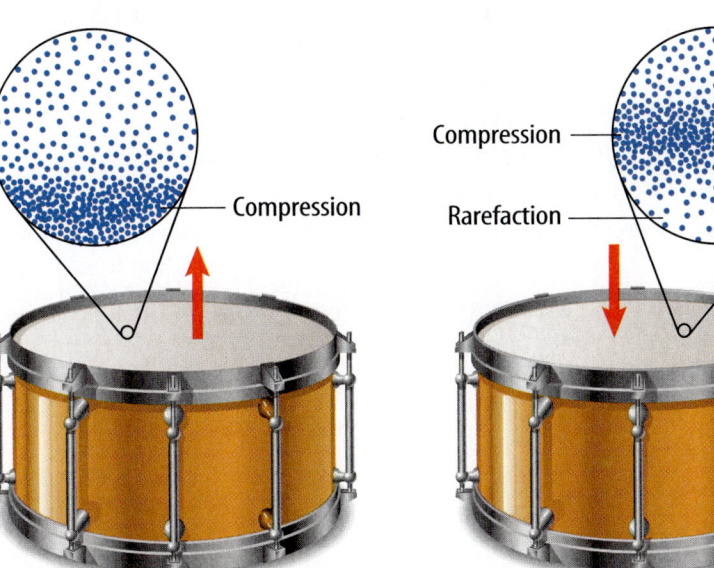

Figure 10 A vibrating drumhead produces a sound wave. The drum head produces a compression each time it moves upward and a rarefaction each time it moves downward.

Table 1 Speed of Sound in Different Materials	
Material	Speed (m/s)
Air (20°C)	343
Glass	5,640
Steel	5,940
Water (25°C)	1,493
Seawater (25°C)	1,533
Rubber	1,600
Diamond	12,000
Iron	5,130

The Speed of Sound

Like all waves, the speed of sound depends on the matter through which it travels. Sound waves travel faster through solids and liquids. **Table 1** shows the speed of sound in different materials.

The speed of sound through a material increases as the temperature of the material increases. The effect of temperature is greatest in gases. For example, the speed of sound in air increases from about 330 m/s to about 350 m/s as the air temperature increases from 0° to 30°C.

Reading Check *How does temperature affect the speed of sound through a material?*

The Loudness of Sound

What makes a sound loud or soft? The girl in **Figure 11** can make a loud sound by clapping the cymbals together sharply. She can make a soft sound by clapping the cymbals together gently. The difference is the amount of energy the girl gives to the cymbals. Loud sounds have more energy than soft sounds.

Intensity The amount of energy that a wave carries past a certain area each second is the **intensity** of the sound. **Figure 12** shows how the intensity of sound from the cymbals decreases with distance. A person standing close when the girl claps the cymbals would hear an intense sound. The sound would be less intense for someone standing farther away. The intensity of sound waves is related to the amplitude. Sound with a greater amplitude also has a greater intensity.

Figure 11 The loudness of a sound depends on the amount of energy the sound waves carry.

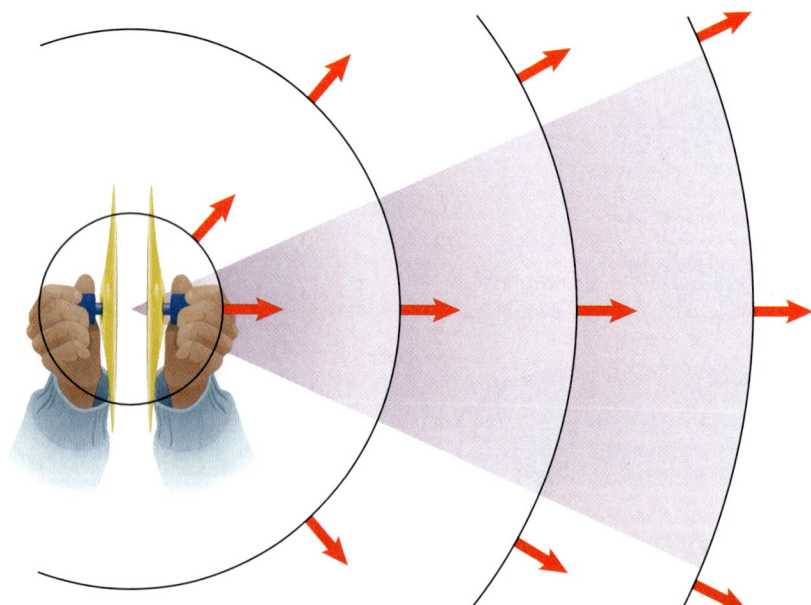

Figure 12 The intensity of a sound wave decreases as the wave spreads out from the source of the sound. The energy the wave carries is spread over a larger area.

420 CHAPTER 14 Waves, Sound, and Light

Loudness in Decibels

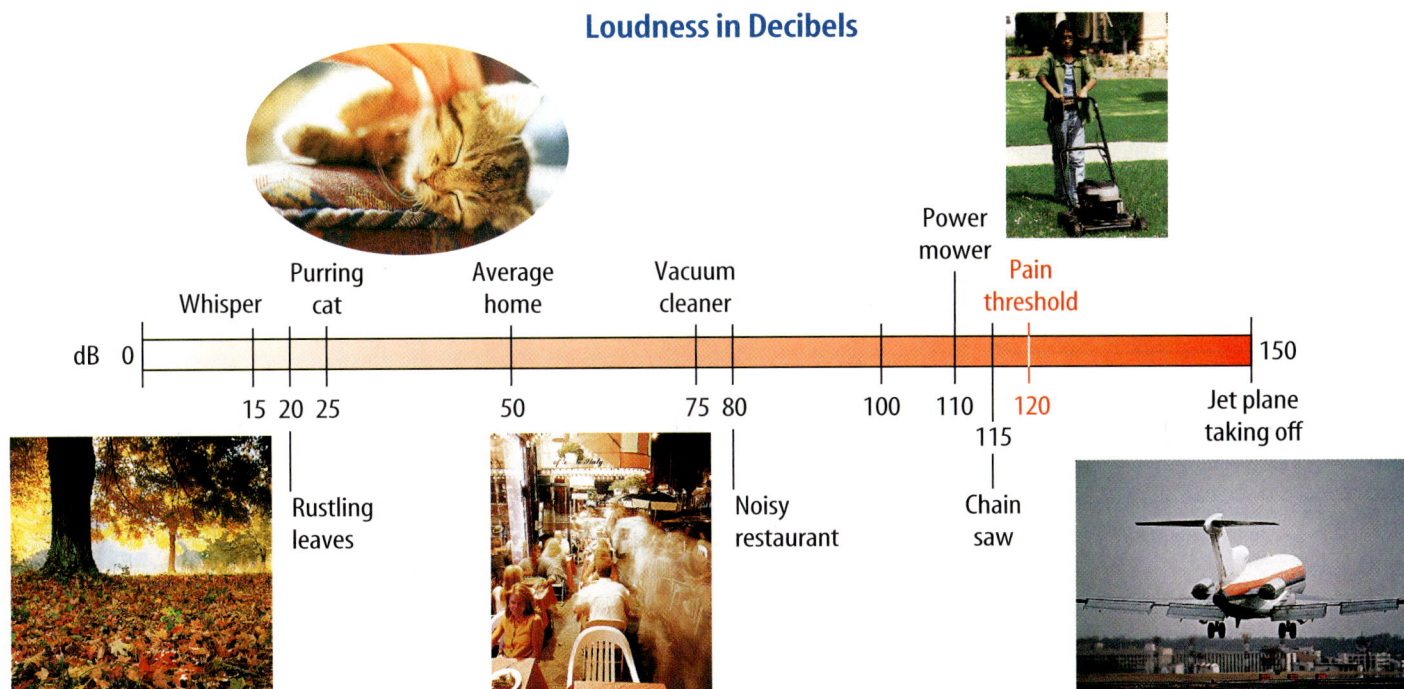

The Decibel Scale and Loudness The intensity of sound waves is measured in units of decibels (dB), as shown in **Figure 13**. The softest sound a person can hear has an intensity of 0 dB. Normal conversation has an intensity of about 50 dB. Sound with intensities of about 120 dB or higher are painful to people.

Loudness is the human perception of the intensity of sound waves. Each increase of 10 dB in intensity multiplies the energy of the sound waves ten times. Most people perceive this as a doubling of the loudness of the sound. An intensity increase of 20 dB corresponds to a hundred times the energy and an increase in loudness of about four times.

Figure 13 The intensity of sound is measured on the decibel scale.
Infer *how many times louder a power mower is compared to a noisy restaurant.*

 *How much has the energy of a sound wave changed if its intensity has increased by 30 dB?*

Frequency and Pitch

The frequency of sound waves is determined by the frequency of the vibrations that produce the sound. Recall that wave frequency is measured in units of hertz (Hz), which is the number of vibrations each second. On the musical scale, the note C has a frequency of 262 Hz. The note E has a frequency of 330 Hz. People are usually able to hear sounds with frequencies between about 20 Hz and 20,000 Hz.

Pitch is the human perception of the frequency of sound. The sounds from a tuba have a low pitch and the sounds from a flute have a high pitch. Sounds with low frequencies have low pitch and sounds with high frequencies have high pitch.

Hearing Damage
Prolonged exposure to sounds above 85 dB can damage your hearing. Research to find out the danger of noise levels you might experience at activities such as loud music concerts or basketball games.

SECTION 2 Sound Waves **421**

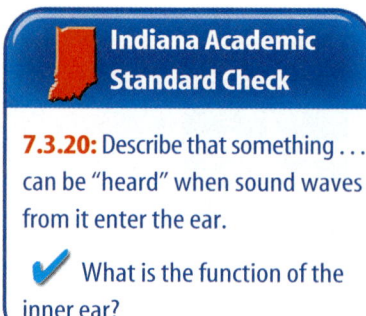

Indiana Academic Standard Check

7.3.20: Describe that something . . . can be "heard" when sound waves from it enter the ear.

✓ What is the function of the inner ear?

Hearing and the Ear

The ear is a complex organ that can detect a wide range of sounds. You may think that the ear is just the structure that you see on the side of your head. However, the ear can be divided into three parts—the outer ear, the middle ear, and the inner ear. **Figure 14** shows the different parts of the human ear.

The Outer Ear The outer ear is a sound collector. It consists of the part that you can see and the ear canal. The visible part is shaped somewhat like a funnel. This shape helps the visible part collect sound waves and direct them into the ear canal.

The Middle Ear The middle air is a sound amplifier. It consists of the ear drum and three tiny bones called the hammer, the anvil, and the stirrup. Sound waves that pass through the ear canal cause the eardrum to vibrate. Theses vibrations are transmitted to the three small bones, which amplify the vibrations.

The Inner Ear The inner ear contains the cochlea. The cochlea is filled with fluid and is lined with tiny hair-like cells. Vibrations of the stirrup bone are transmitted to the hair cells. The movement of the hair cells produce signals that travel to your brain, where they are interpreted as sound.

Figure 14 The human ear can be divided into three parts. The outer ear is the sound collector, the middle ear is the sound amplifier, and the inner ear is the sound interpreter.

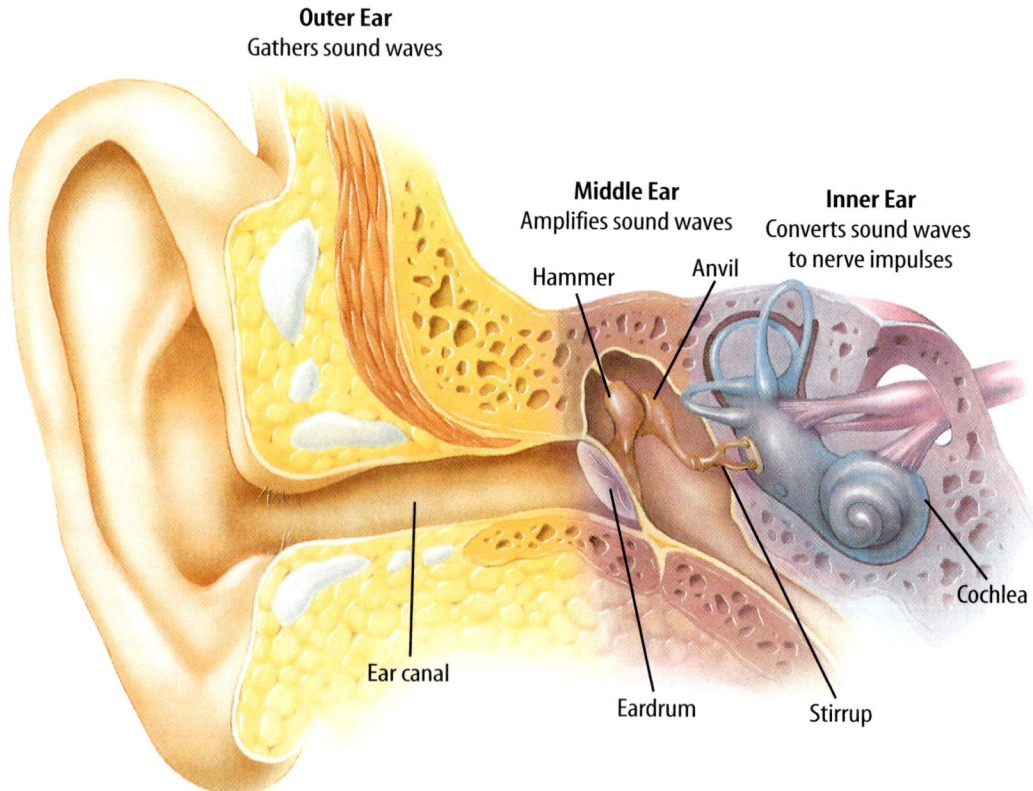

422 CHAPTER 14 Waves, Sound, and Light

The Reflection of Sound

Have you ever stood in an empty room and heard echoes when you talked very loudly? Echoes are sounds that reflect off surfaces. Repeated echoes are called **reverberation.** Concert halls and auditoriums are designed with soft materials on the ceilings and walls to avoid too much reverberation. Theaters like the one in **Figure 15** often have curtains on the walls because sounds won't reflect off soft surfaces. The curtains absorb the energy of the sound waves.

The reflection of sound can be used to locate or identify objects. Echolocation is the process of locating objects by bouncing sounds off them. Bats, dolphins, and other animals emit short, high-frequency sound waves toward a certain area. By interpreting the reflected waves, the animals can locate and determine properties of other animals. Doctors use reflection of sound waves in medicine. Computers can analyze ultrasonic waves that reflect off body parts to produce an internal picture of the body. These pictures help doctors monitor pregnancies, heart problems, and other medical conditions.

Figure 15 A modern concert hall contains materials that absorb sound waves to control reverberation and other sound reflections.

section 2 review

Summary

Making Sound Waves
- Sound waves are compressional waves produced by something vibrating.
- The speed of sound waves depends on the material in which the waves travel and its temperature.

Loudness and Pitch
- The intensity of a wave is the amount of energy the wave transports each second across a unit surface.
- The intensity of sound waves is measured in units of decibels.
- Loudness is the human perception of sound intensity.
- Pitch is the human perception of the frequency of a sound.

Hearing Sound
- You hear a sound when a sound wave reaches your ear and causes structures in your ear to vibrate.

Self Check

1. **Explain** why you hear a sound when you clap your hands together.
2. **Predict** whether sound will would travel faster in air in the summer or in the winter.
3. **Compare and contrast** the sound waves produced by someone whispering and someone shouting.
4. **Describe** how vibrations produced in your ear by a sound wave enable you to hear the sound.
5. **Think Critically** Vibrations cause sounds, yet if you move your hand back and forth through the air, you don't hear a sound. Explain.

Applying Math

6. **Calculate a Ratio** How many times louder is a sound wave with an intensity of 50 dB than a sound wave with an intensity of 20 dB?
7. **Calculate Increase in Intensity** If the energy carried by a sound wave is multiplied by a thousand times, by what factor does the intensity of the sound wave increase?

in7.msscience.com/self_check_quiz

Sound Waves in Matter

In this lab you can hear differences in sound when the sound waves travel through various materials.

Real-World Question
How does the movement of sound waves through different materials affect the sounds we hear?

Goals
- **Notice** the variations in sound when sound waves travel through different materials.
- **Infer** what property of the materials cause the sound waves to produce a different sound.

Materials
150-mL beakers (4)   corn syrup
water   pencil
vegetable oil

Safety Precautions

Procedure
1. Fill a beaker to the 140-mL line with water. Fill another beaker with 140 mL of vegetable oil. Fill a third beaker with 140 mL of corn syrup. Leave the fourth beaker empty.
2. Hold the pencil securely and tap the side of the beaker about halfway down from its rim. Use the metal band near the end of the pencil to make a clear sound.
3. Pay careful attention to the pitch of the sound. Notice whether the sound continues for a moment after the tap or if it stops suddenly. Write a description of the sound you hear in your data table.
4. Repeat steps 3 and 4 for the remaining beakers. You may wish to tap each beaker several times to be sure you hear the sound well.
5. **Compare** the sounds made by the beaker filled with air and the beaker filled with the different liquids.

Conclude and Apply
1. **List** the materials in the beakers in order of increasing density.
2. **Infer** how the pitch of the sound changes as the density of the material in the beaker increases.
3. How does the density of the material in the beaker affect how long the sound continued to be heard after the beaker was tapped?

Communicating Your Data
Compare your results with other students in your class.

section 3

Standards—7.3.19: Explain that human eyes respond to a narrow range of wavelengths of the electromagnetic spectrum. **7.3.20:** Describe that something can be "seen" when light waves emitted or reflected by it enter the eye . . . .

Also covers: 7.1.5, 7.3.2, 7.3.11, 7.3.18 (Detailed standards begin on page IN8.)

Light

Waves in Empty Space

On a clear night you might see the Moon shining brightly, as in **Figure 16**. Like other waves, light waves can travel through matter, but light waves are different from water waves and sound waves. Light from the Moon has traveled through space that contains almost no matter. You can see light from the moon, distant stars, and galaxies because light is an electromagnetic wave. **Electromagnetic waves** are waves that can travel through matter or through empty space.

The Speed of Light Have you ever seen a movie where a spaceship travels faster than the speed of light? In reality, nothing travels faster than the speed of light. In empty space, light travels at a speed of about 300,000 km/s. Light travels so fast that light emitted from the Sun travels 150 million km to Earth in only about eight and a half minutes.

However, when light travels in matter, it interacts with the atoms and molecules in the material and slows down. As a result, light travels fastest in empty space, and travels slowest in solids. In glass, for example, light travels about 197,000 km/s.

Wavelength and Frequency of Light Can you guess how long a wavelength of light is? Wavelengths of light are usually expressed in units of nanometers (nm). One nanometer is equal to one billionth of a meter. For example, green light has a wavelength of about 500 nm, or 500 billionths of a meter. A light wave with this wavelength has a frequency of 600 trillion Hz.

as you read

What You'll Learn
- **Identify** the properties of light waves.
- **Describe** the electromagnetic spectrum.
- **Describe** the types of electromagnetic waves that travel from the Sun to Earth.
- **Explain** human vision and color perception.

Why It's Important
Light is necessary for vision. Other electromagnetic waves are used in devices such as cell phones and microwave ovens.

Review Vocabulary
spectrum: a range of values or properties

New Vocabulary
- electromagnetic waves
- electromagnetic spectrum
- infrared waves
- ultraviolet waves

Figure 16 The Moon reflects light from the Sun. These light waves travel through space to reach your eyes.
Infer *whether a sound wave could travel from the Moon to Earth.*

SECTION 3 Light **425**

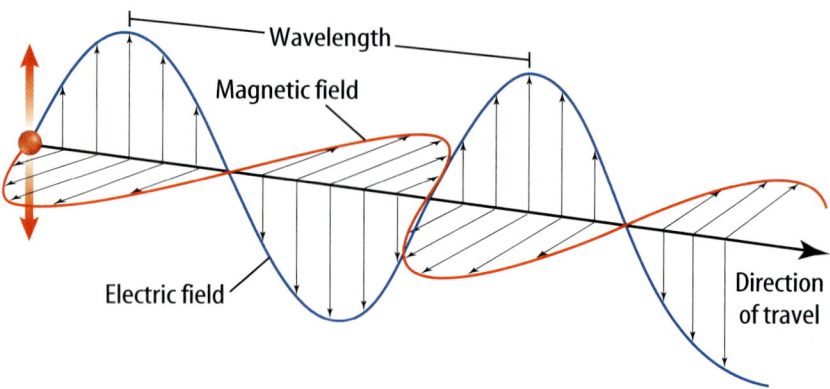

Figure 17 A light wave is a transverse wave that contains vibrating electric and magnetic fields. The fields vibrate at right angles to the direction the wave travels.

Properties of Light Waves

Light waves, and all electromagnetic waves, are transverse waves. Recall that a wave on a rope is a transverse wave that causes the rope to move at right angles to the direction the wave is traveling. An electromagnetic wave traveling through matter also can cause matter to move at right angles to the direction the wave is moving.

An electromagnetic wave contains an electric part and a magnetic part, as shown in **Figure 17.** Both parts are called fields and vibrate at right angles to the wave motion. The number of times the electric and magnetic parts vibrate each second is the frequency of the wave. The wavelength is the distance between the crests or troughs of the vibrating electric or magnetic parts.

Intensity of Light Waves The intensity of waves is a measure of the amount of energy that the waves carry. For light waves, the intensity determines the brightness of the light. A dim light has lower intensity because the waves carry less energy. However, as you move away from a light source, the energy spreads out and the intensity decreases.

 What determines the intensity of light waves?

The Electromagnetic Spectrum

Light waves aren't the only kind of electromagnetic waves. In fact, there is an entire spectrum of electromagnetic waves, as shown in **Figure 18.** The **electromagnetic spectrum** is the complete range of electromagnetic wave frequencies and wavelengths. At one end of the spectrum the waves have low frequency, long wavelength, and low energy. At the other end of the spectrum the waves have high frequency, short wavelength, and high energy. All of the waves—from radio waves to visible light to gamma rays—are the same kind of waves. They differ from each other only by their frequencies, wavelengths, and energy.

Topic: Lasers
Visit in7.msscience.com for Web links to information about why the intensity of light emitted by lasers makes them useful.

Activity Write a short paragraph describing three uses for lasers.

Indiana Academic Standard Check

7.3.19: Explain that human eyes respond to a narrow range of wavelengths of the electromagnetic spectrum.

✓ What range of wavelengths in the electromagnetic spectrum does the human eye detect?

426 CHAPTER 14 Waves, Sound, and Light

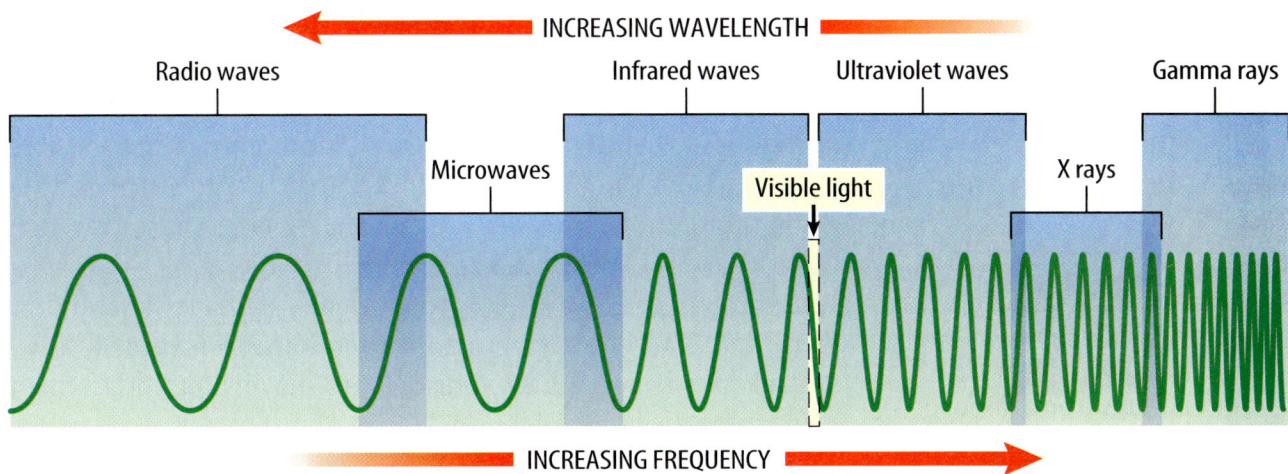

Radio Waves and Microwaves The waves that carry radio and television signals to your home are radio waves. The wavelengths of radio waves are greater than about 0.3 meters. Some are even thousands of meters long. The shortest radio waves are called microwaves. These waves have a wavelength between about 0.3 meters and 0.001 meters. You use these waves when you cook food in a microwave oven. Microwaves are also used to transmit information to and from cell phones.

Infrared Waves When you use a remote control, infrared waves travel from the remote to a receiver on your television. Infrared waves have wavelengths between 0.001 meters and 700 billionths of a meter. All warm bodies emit infrared waves. Because of this, law enforcement officials and military personnel sometimes use special night goggles that are sensitive to infrared waves. These goggles can be used to help locate people in the dark.

Visible Light and Color The range of electromagnetic waves between 700 and 400 billionths of a meter is special, because that is the range of wavelengths people can see. Electromagnetic waves in this range are called visible light. **Figure 19** shows how different wavelengths correspond to different colors of light. White light, like the light from the Sun or a flashlight, is really a combination of different colors. You can see this by using a prism to separate white light into different colors. When the light passes through the prism, the different wavelengths of light are bent different amounts. Violet light is bent the most because it has the shortest wavelength. Red light is bent the least.

 *What range of wavelengths of electromagnetic waves can people see?*

Figure 18 Electromagnetic waves have a range of frequencies and wavelengths called the electromagnetic spectrum.
Infer *how the frequency of electromagnetic waves change as their wavelength decreases.*

Figure 19 Visible light waves are electromagnetic waves with a narrow range of wavelengths from about 700 to 400 billionths of a meter. The color of visible light waves depends on their wavelength.
Determine *the color of the visible light waves with the highest frequency.*

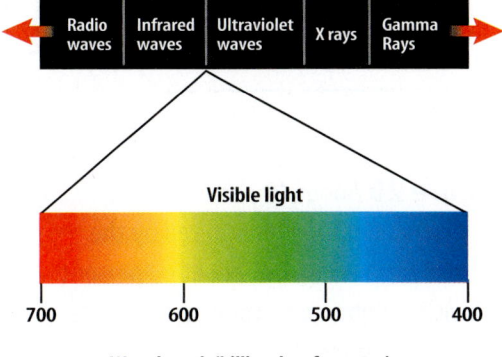

SECTION 3 Light

Mini LAB

Separating Wavelengths

Procedure
1. Place a **prism** in sunlight. Adjust its position until a color spectrum is produced.
2. Place the prism on a **desktop**. Dim the lights and shine a **flashlight** on the prism.
3. Shine a **laser pointer** on the prism.

WARNING: *Do not shine the laser pointer into anyone's eyes.*

Analysis
1. Determine whether sunlight and the light emitted from the flashlight contain more than one wavelength.
2. Determine whether the light emitted from the laser pointer contains more than one wavelength.

Indiana Academic Standard Check

7.3.11: Explain that . . . only a tiny fraction of . . . the Sun's energy arrives as light . . . consisting of . . . untraviolet radiation.

✔ Which waves from the Sun are blocked by Earth's atmosphere?

Figure 20 About 49 percent of the electromagnetic waves emitted by the Sun are infrared waves, about 43 percent are visible light, and about 7 percent are ultraviolet waves.

Ultraviolet Waves Electromagnetic waves with wavelengths between about 400 billionths and 10 billionths of a meter are **ultraviolet waves**. These wavelengths are shorter than those of visible light. Ultraviolet waves carry more energy than visible light waves. Sunlight that reaches Earth's surface contains a small fraction of ultraviolet waves. These waves can cause sunburn if skin is exposed to sunlight for too long. Excessive exposure to ultraviolet waves can permanently damage skin, and in some cases cause skin cancer. However, some exposure to ultraviolet waves is needed for your body to make vitamin D, which helps form healthy bones and teeth.

X Rays and Gamma Rays The electromagnetic waves with the highest energy, highest frequency, and shortest wavelengths are X rays and gamma rays. If you've ever broken a bone, the doctor probably took an X ray to examine the injured area. X rays are energetic enough to pass through the body. X rays pass through soft tissues, but are blocked by denser body parts, such as bones. This enables images to be made of internal body parts. Gamma rays are even more energetic than X rays. One use of gamma rays is in the food industry to kill bacteria that might increase the rate of spoilage of food.

Electromagnetic Waves from the Sun Most of the energy emitted by the Sun is in the form of ultraviolet, visible, and infrared waves, as shown in **Figure 20**. These waves carry energy away from the Sun and spread out in all directions. Only a tiny fraction of this energy reaches Earth. Most of the ultraviolet waves from the Sun are blocked by Earth's atmosphere. As a result, almost all energy from the Sun that reaches Earth's surface is carried by infrared and visible electromagnetic waves.

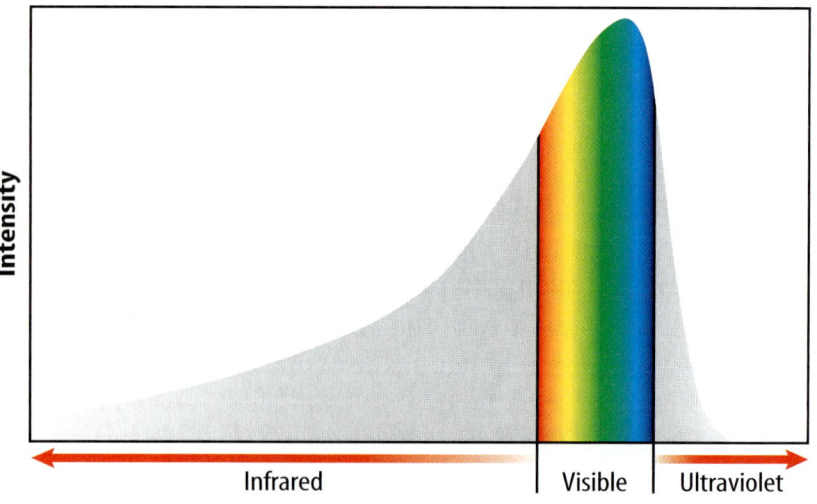

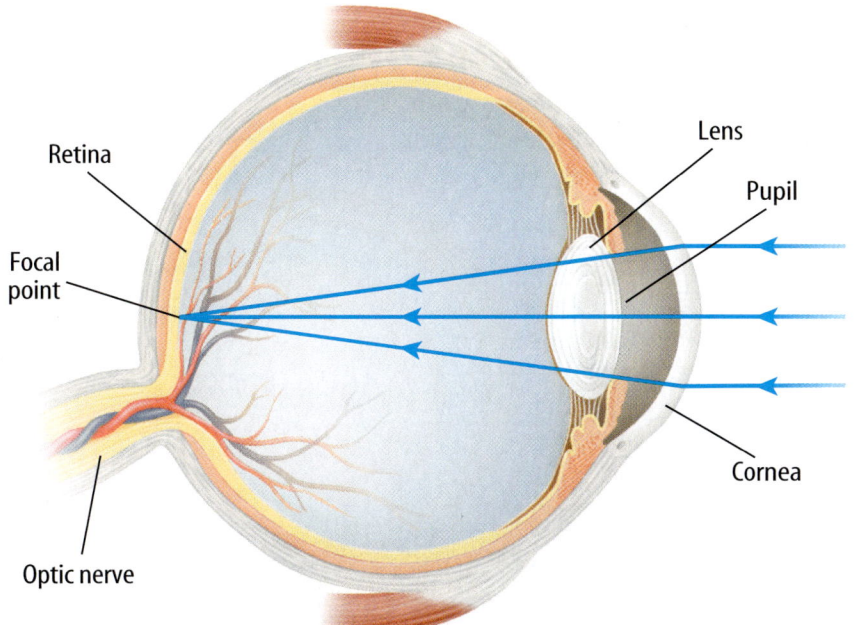

Figure 21 The cornea and the lens focus light waves that enter your eye so that a sharp image is formed on the retina. Special cells in the retina cause signals to be sent to the brain when they are struck by light.

The Eye and Seeing Light

You see an object when light emitted or reflected from the object enters your eye, as shown in **Figure 21**. Light waves first pass through a transparent layer called the cornea (KOR nee uh), and then the transparent lens. The lens is flexible and changes shape to enable you to focus on objects that are nearby and far away, as shown in **Figure 22**. However, sometimes the eye is unable to form sharp images of both nearby and distant objects, as shown in **Figure 23** on the next page.

Why do objects have color? When light waves strike an object, some of the light waves are reflected. The wavelengths of the light waves that are reflected determine the object's color. For example, a red rose reflects light waves that have wavelengths in the red part of the visible spectrum. The color of objects that emit light is determined by the wavelengths of light that they emit. A neon sign appears to be red because it emits red light waves.

Indiana Academic Standard Check

7.3.20: Describe something that can be "seen" when light waves emitted or reflected by it enter the eye....

✓ Which parts of the eye focus the light waves that enter the eye?

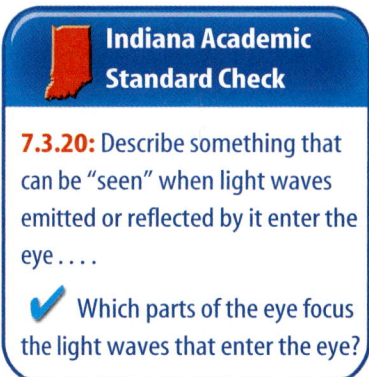

Figure 22 The shape of the lens changes when you focus on nearby and distant objects.

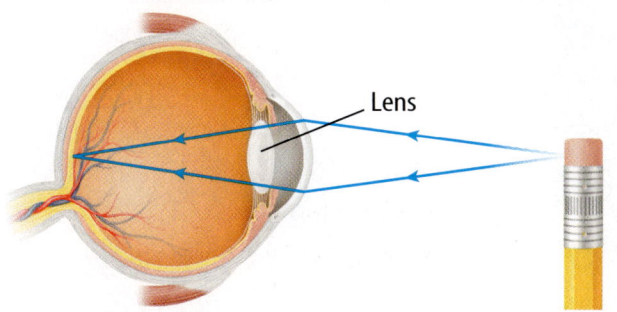

The lens becomes flatter when you focus on a distant object.

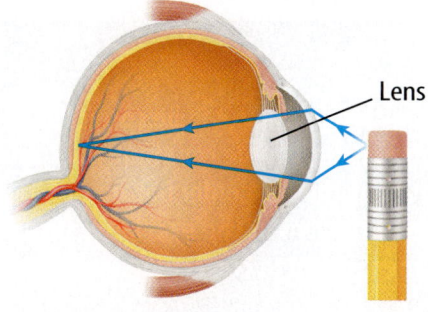

The lens becomes more curved when you focus on an object nearby.

NATIONAL GEOGRAPHIC VISUALIZING COMMON VISION PROBLEMS

Figure 23

In a human eye, light waves pass through the transparent cornea and the lens of the eye. The cornea and the lens cause light waves from an object to be focused on the retina, forming a sharp image. However, vision problems result when a sharp image is not formed on the retina. The two most common vision problems are farsightedness and nearsightedness.

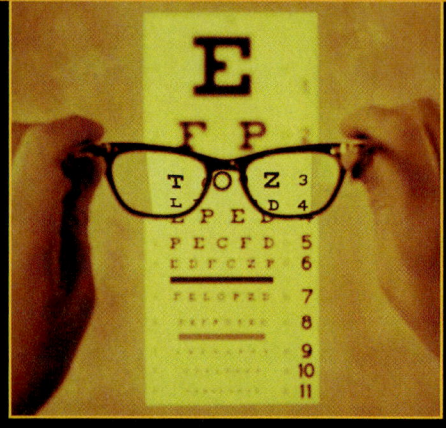

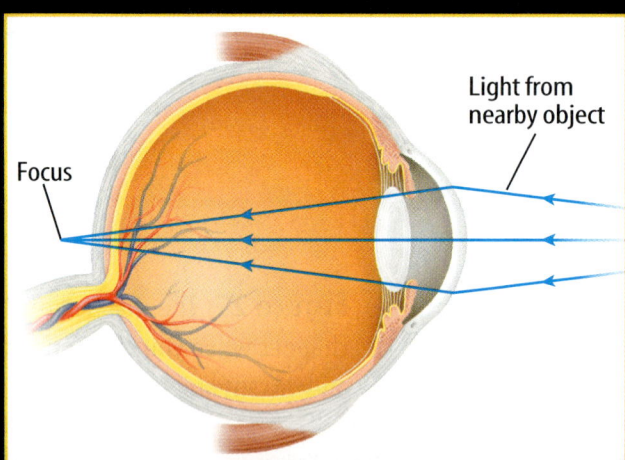

◀ **Nearsightedness** A person that is nearsighted can see nearby objects clearly, but distant objects seem blurry. Nearsightedness results if the eyeball is too long, so that light waves from far away objects are brought to a focus before they reach the retina. This vision problem usually is corrected by wearing glasses or contact lenses. Laser surgery also is used to correct nearsightedness by reshaping the cornea.

◀ **Farsightedness** A farsighted person can see distant objects clearly, but cannot focus clearly on nearby objects. Farsightedness results if the eyeball is too short, so light waves from nearby objects have not been brought to a focus when they strike the retina.

▶ Farsightedness also can be corrected by wearing glasses. People commonly become farsighted as they get older because of changes in the lens of the eye. Laser surgery sometimes is used to correct farsightedness.

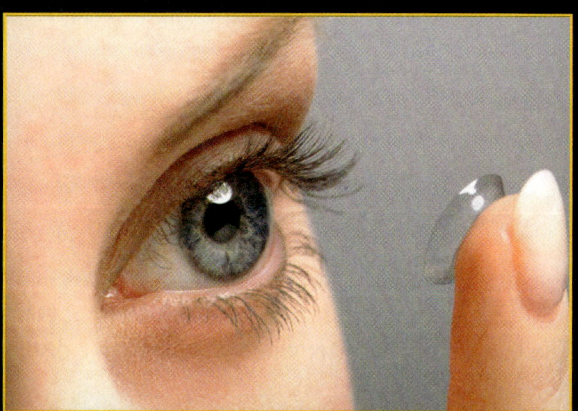

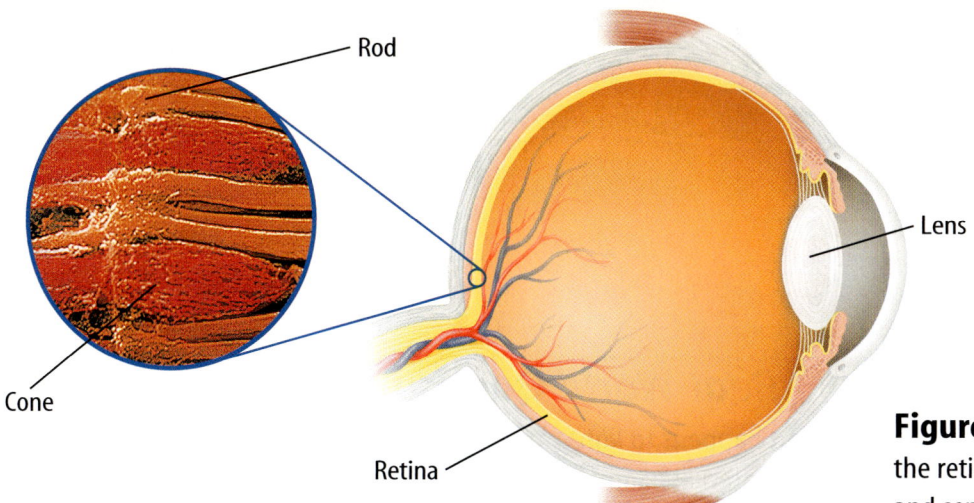

Figure 24 Rod and cone cells in the retina of the eye detect light and send signals to the brain.

Rod and Cone Cells The retina contains over a hundred million light-sensitive cells called rods and cones, shown in **Figure 24.** Rod cells are sensitive to dim light, and cone cells enable you to see colors. There are three types of cone cells. One type is sensitive to red and yellow light, another type is sensitive to green and yellow light, and the third type is sensitive to blue and violet light. The combination of the signals sent to the brain by all three types of cone cells forms the color image that you see.

section 3 review

Summary

Light and Electromagnetic Waves
- Light waves are electromagnetic waves. These waves travel through empty space at a speed of 300,000 km/s.
- Electromagnetic waves are transverse waves made of vibrating electric and magnetic fields.
- Radio waves, infrared waves, visible light, ultraviolet waves, X rays, and gamma rays form the electromagnetic spectrum.
- Most of the electromagnetic waves emitted by the Sun are infrared waves, visible light, and ultraviolet waves.

Color and Vision
- The color of an object is the color of the light the object emits or reflects.
- You see an object when light waves emitted or reflected by the object enter your eye and strike the retina.
- Rod cells and cone cells in the retina of the eye are light-sensitive cells that send signals to the brain when light strikes them.

Self Check

1. **Identify** the electromagnetic waves with the longest wavelengths and the electromagnetic waves with the shortest wavelengths.
2. **Describe** the difference between radio waves, visible light, and gamma rays.
3. **Compare and contrast** the rod cells and the cone cells in the retina of the human eye.
4. **Explain** why most of the electromagnetic waves emitted by the Sun that strike Earth's surface are infrared and visible light waves.
5. **Think Critically** Explain why the brightness of the light emitted by a flashlight decreases as the flashlight moves farther away from you.

Applying Skills

6. **Make a Concept Map** Design a concept map to show the sequence of events that occurs when you see a blue object.
7. **Recognize Cause and Effect** Why does light travel faster through empty space than it does through matter?

Bending Light

Real-World Question

What happens to light waves when they strike the boundary between two materials? Some of the light waves might be reflected from the boundary and some of the waves might travel into the second material. These light waves can change direction and be refracted in the second material. Transmission occurs when the light waves finally pass through the second material. What happens to light waves when they strike a boundary between air and other materials?

Goals
- **Compare and contrast** the reflection, refraction, and transmission of light.
- **Observe** how the refraction of white light can produce different colors of light.

Materials
small piece of cardboard
scissors
tape
flashlight
flat mirror
clear plastic CD case
250-mL beaker
prism

Safety Precautions

Procedure

1. Make a data table similar to the one shown below.

Bending of Light by Different Surfaces		
Surface	How Beam is Affected	Colors Formed
Mirror		
CD case	Do not write in this book.	
Water		
Prism		

2. Cut a slit about 3 cm long and 2 mm wide in a circular piece of cardboard. Tape the cardboard to the face of the flashlight.

3. In a darkened room, shine the flashlight at an angle toward the mirror. Determine whether the flashlight beam is reflected, refracted, or transmitted. Look at the color of the light beam after it strikes the mirror. Has the white light been changed into differenet colors of light? Record your observations on the chart.

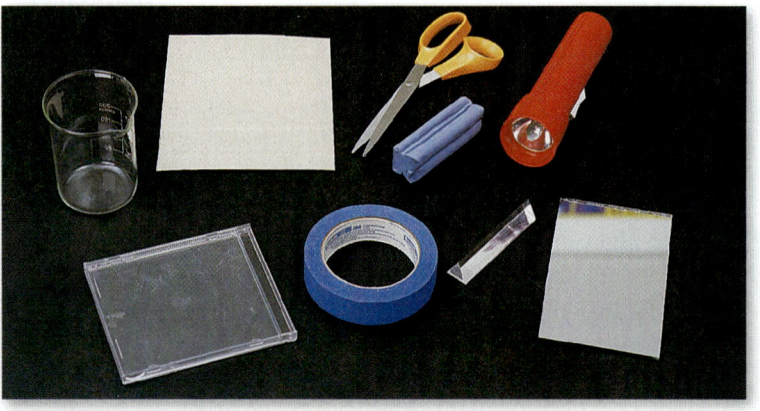

Using Scientific Methods

4. Remove the clear plastic front from an empty CD case. Shine the flashlight at an angle toward the plastic. Does transmission occur? Record your observations about how the direction of the beam changes and colors of the light.
5. Fill the beaker with water. Shine the flashlight toward the side of the beaker so that the light shines through the water. Move the light beam from side to side. Record your observations.
6. Shine the flashlight toward a side of the prism. Move the light beam around until you see the outgoing beam spread into different colors. Record your observations.

Analyze Your Data

1. For which objects did reflection occur? For which objects did refraction occur? For which objects did transmission occur?
2. For which objects did refraction cause the flashlight beam to be separated into different colors?

Conclude and Apply

1. **Compare and contrast** the behavior of light waves when they strike the mirror and the CD case.
2. **Explain** why the beam that passes through the CD case does or does not change direction.
3. **Describe** how the light beam changes after it passes through the prism.

Communicating Your Data

Create a sketch showing how light refracts in a prism and divides into different colors.

Oops! Accidents in SCIENCE

SOMETIMES GREAT DISCOVERIES HAPPEN BY ACCIDENT!

Jansky's Merry-Go-Round

Before the first radio signals were sent across the Atlantic Ocean in 1902, ships could only communicate if they could see one another. Being able to communicate using radio waves was a real breakthrough. But it wasn't without its problems—namely lots of static. Around 1930, Bell Labs was trying to improve radio communication by using radio waves with shorter wavelengths—between 10 and 20 m. They put Karl Jansky to work finding out what might be causing the static.

Karl Jansky built the first radiotelescope.

An Unexpected Discovery

This antenna built by Janksy detected radio waves from the Milky Way galaxy.

Jansky built an antenna to receive radio waves with a wavelength of about 14.5 m. He mounted it on a turntable so that he could rotate it in any direction. His coworkers called it "Jansky's merry-go-round."

After recording signals for several months, Jansky found that there were three types of static. Two were caused by nearby and distant thunderstorms.

But the third was totally unexpected. It seemed to come from the center of our Milky Way galaxy! Jansky wanted to follow up on this unexpected discovery, but Bell Labs had the information it wanted. They were in the telephone business, not astronomy!

A New Branch of Astronomy

Fortunately, other scientists were fascinated with Jansky's find. Grote Reber built a "radiotelescope" in his Illinois backyard. He confirmed Jansky's discovery and did the first systematic survey of radio waves from space. The field of radioastronomy was born.

Previously, astronomers could observe distant galaxies only by gathering the light arriving from their stars. But they couldn't see past the clouds of gas and small particles surrounding the galaxies. Radio waves emitted by a galaxy can penetrate much of the gas and dust in space. This allows radio astronomers to make images of galaxies and other objects they can't see. As a result, Radio astronomy has revealed previously invisible objects such as quasars and pulsars.

The blue-white colors in this image are all you could see without radio waves.

Experiment Research how astronomers convert the radio waves received by radio telescopes into images of galaxies and stars.

Science online

For more information, visit in7.msscience.com/oops

Chapter 14 Study Guide

Reviewing Main Ideas

Section 1 Waves

1. Waves carry energy from place to place without transporting matter.
2. Transverse waves move particles in matter at right angles to the direction in which the waves travel.
3. Compressional waves move particles back and forth along the same direction in which the waves travel.
4. The speed of a wave equals its wavelength multiplied by its frequency.

Section 2 Sound Waves

1. Sound waves are compressional waves produced by something vibrating.
2. The intensity of sound waves is measured in units of decibels.
3. You hear sound when sound waves reach your ear and cause parts of the ear to vibrate.

Section 3 Light

1. Electromagnetic waves are transverse waves that can travel in matter or empty space.
2. Light waves are electromagnetic waves.
3. The range of frequencies and wavelengths of electromagnetic waves forms the electromagnetic spectrum.
4. You see an object when light waves emitted or reflected by the object enter your eye and strike light-sensitive cells inside the eye.

Visualizing Main Ideas

Copy and complete the following concept map on waves.

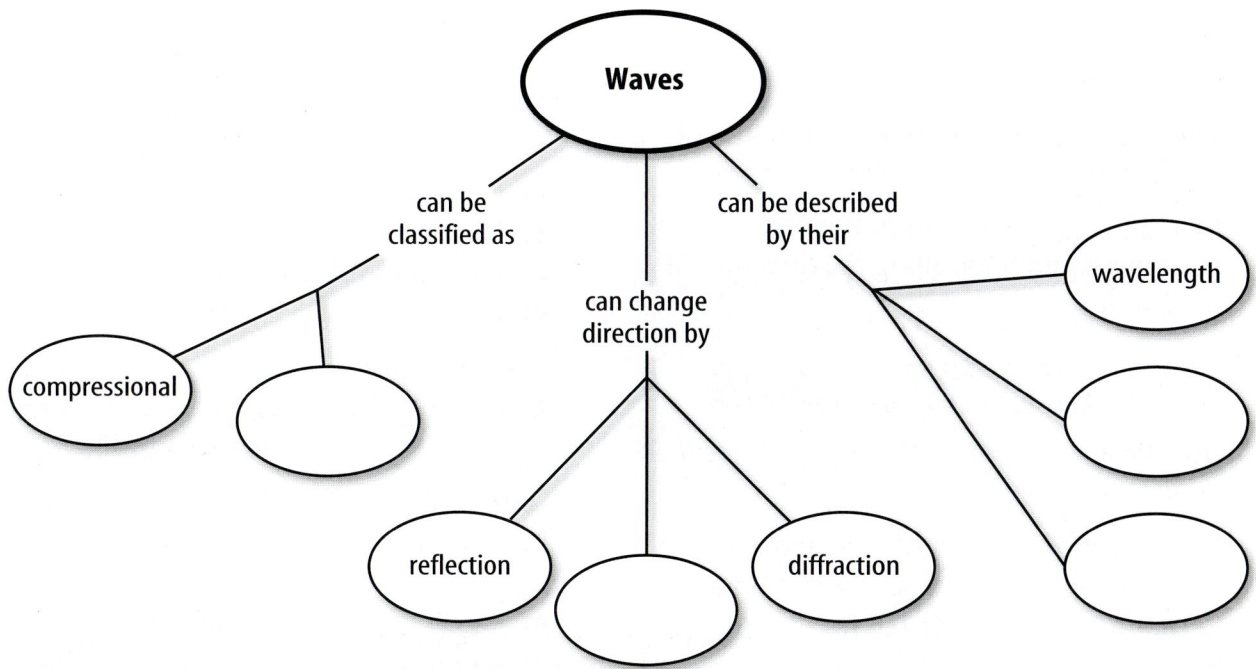

chapter 14 Review

Using Vocabulary

compressional wave p. 413
diffraction p. 418
electromagnetic spectrum p. 426
electromagnetic waves p. 425
frequency p. 414
infrared waves p. 427
intensity p. 420
law of reflection p. 417
pitch p. 421
refraction p. 417
reverberation p. 423
transverse wave p. 413
ultraviolet waves p. 428
wave p. 412
wavelength p. 414

Complete each statement using a word(s) from the vocabulary list above.

1. The bending of a wave when it moves from one material into another is _____.
2. The bending of waves around an object is due to _____.
3. The _____ is the complete range of electromagnetic wave frequencies and wavelengths.
4. The amount of energy that a wave carries past a certain area each second is the _____.
5. In a(n) _____, the particles in the material move at right angles to the direction the wave moves.
6. The _____ of a wave is the number of wavelengths that pass a point each second.
7. In a _____, particles in the material move back and forth along the direction of wave motion.

Checking Concepts

Choose the word or phrase that best answers the question.

8. If the distance between the crest and trough of a wave is 0.6 m, what is the wave's amplitude?
   A) 0.3 m   C) 0.6 m
   B) 1.2 m   D) 2.4

9. Which of the following are units for measuring frequency?
   A) decibels   C) meters
   B) hertz   D) meters/second

10. Through which of these materials does sound travel fastest?
    A) empty space C) steel
    B) water   D) air

11. An increase in a sound's pitch corresponds to an increase in what other property?
    A) intensity   C) wavelength
    B) frequency   D) loudness

12. Soft materials are sometimes used in concert halls to prevent what effect?
    A) refraction   C) compression
    B) diffraction D) reverberation

13. Which of the following are not transverse waves?
    A) radio waves C) sound waves
    B) infrared waves D) visible light

14. Which of the following wave properties determines the energy carried by a wave?
    A) amplitude   C) wavelength
    B) frequency   D) wave speed

15. Which of the following best describes why refraction of a wave occurs when the wave travels from one material into another?
    A) The wavelength increases.
    B) The speed of the wave changes.
    C) The amplitude increases.
    D) The frequency decreases.

16. What produces waves?
    A) sound   C) transfer of energy
    B) heat   D) vibrations

17. Which of the following has wavelengths longer than the wavelengths of visible light?
    A) X rays   C) radio waves
    B) gamma rays   D) ultraviolet waves

Chapter 14 Review

Thinking Critically

18. Infer Radio waves broadcast by a radio station strike your radio and your ear. Infer whether the human ear can hear radio waves. What evidence supports your conclusion?

19. Solve an Equation Robotic spacecraft on Mars have sent radio signals back to Earth. The distance from Mars to Earth, at its greatest, is about 401,300,000 km. About how many minutes would it take a signal to reach Earth from that distance?

20. Recognize Cause and Effect When a musician plucks a string on a guitar it produces sound with a certain pitch. If the musician then presses down on the string and plucks it, the sound produced has a shorter wavelength. How does the pitch of the sound change?

21. Interpret Scientific Illustrations One way that radio waves can carry signals to radios is by varying the amplitude of the wave. This is known as amplitude modulation (AM). Another way is by varying the frequency. This is called frequency modulation (FM). Which of the waves below shows AM, and which shows FM? Explain.

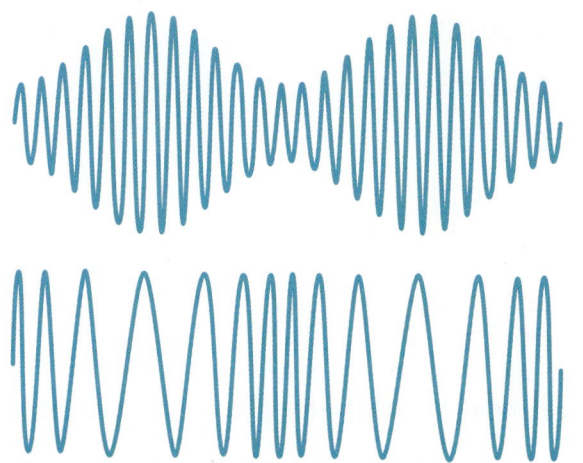

22. Infer When light passes through a prism, infer how the amount of bending of a light wave depends on the frequency of the light wave. How does the amount of bending depend on the wavelength of the light wave?

23. Describe how the lenses in your eyes change shape when you first look at your wristwatch to read the time, and then look at a mountain in the distance.

Performance Activities

24. Poster Investigate a musical instrument to find out how it produces sound. Make a poster showing the instrument and describing how it works.

25. Model Make an instrument out of common materials. Present the instrument to the class, and explain how it can produce different pitches.

Applying Math

26. Noise Levels A noisy restaurant has an intensity of about 80 dB, and a lawn mower has an intensity of about 110 dB. How many times louder does the lawn mower noise seem?

27. Wavelength of Sound Sound waves with a frequency of 150 Hz travel at a speed of 340 m/s. What is the wavelength of the sound waves?

28. Ultrasound Physicians sometimes use high-frequency sound waves to diagnose and monitor medical conditions. A typical frequency for the sound waves is about 5,000,000.0 Hz. Sound travels through soft body tissue at about 1500.0 m/s. What is the wavelength of the sound waves?

29. Frequency of Radio Waves Find the frequency of radio waves that have a wavelength of 15 m if they are traveling at a speed of 300,000,000 m/s.

chapter 14 Indiana

 The assessed Indiana standard appears above the question.

Record your answers on the answer sheet provided by your teacher or on a sheet of paper.

Part 1 Multiple Choice

7.3.18

1. The table below shows the speed of sound in different materials.

Speed of Sound in Different Materials	
Material	Speed (m/s)
Air (20°C)	343
Glass	5,640
Steel	5,940
Water (25°C)	1,493
Seawater (25°C)	1,533

If sound travels 2,146 m through a material in 1.4 s, what is the material?

- A air
- B glass
- C seawater
- D water

2. Which term refers to the bending of waves around obstacles?

- A diffraction
- B reflection
- C refraction
- D transmission

3. Which is a **TRUE** statement?

- A Waves do not transport the matter in which they travel.
- B Waves can transport matter through solids, liquids, and gases, but not through empty space.
- C Waves can transport matter through liquids and solids, but not through gases or empty space.
- D Sound and water waves can transport matter, but light waves can't.

7.3.20

4. The table below shows various sound intensity levels on the decibel scale.

Decibel Scale	
Sound Source	Loudness (dB)
Jet plane taking off	150
Running lawn mower	100
Average home	50
Whisper	15

What would be the approximate sound intensity level of a noisy restaurant?

- A 20 dB
- B 40 dB
- C 80 dB
- D 120 dB

Test-Taking Tip

Be Well-Rested Get plenty of sleep—at least eight hours every night—during test week and the week before the test.

438 INDIANA

Standards Review

5. Which do not travel through empty space?

   A infrared waves

   B light waves

   C sound waves

   D ultraviolet waves

6. What is the maximum range of sound frequencies that humans can hear?

   A 0 Hz to 3,300 Hz

   B 0 Hz to 20,000 Hz

   C 20 Hz to 20,000 Hz

   D 50 Hz to 50,000 Hz

7.3.11

7. The graph below shows the intensity of electromagnetic waves emitted by the Sun.

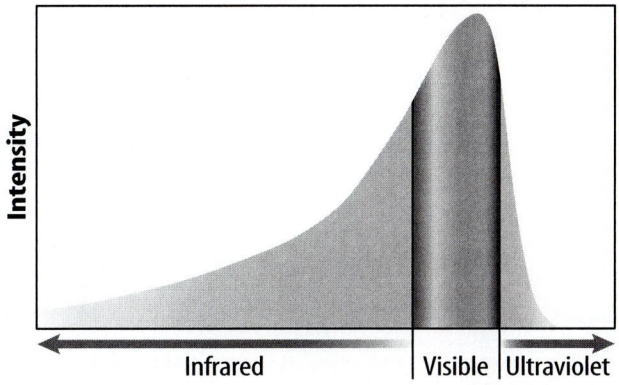

What waves emitted by the Sun have the greatest intensity?

   A infrared

   B visible

   C visible and infrared

   D visible and ultraviolet

Part 2 Constructed Response

7.3.18

8. Compare and contrast light waves and sound waves.

7.3.20

9. The illustration below shows a cross section of the human eye.

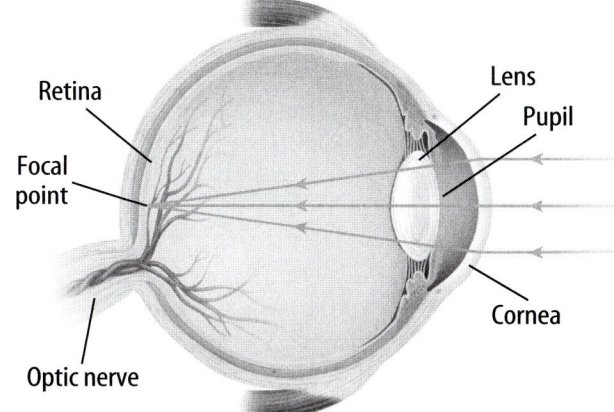

Describe the process that occurs when light waves enter your eye and produce a signal in the optic nerve.

10. Name the different types of electromagnetic waves from longest to shortest wavelength. Give an example of each type.

11. Describe compressional and transverse waves. Explain the difference between them.

7.3.18

12. Explain why sound travels faster through some types of matter than through others. How does temperature affect the speed of sound through a material?

Academic Standard—1: Students further their scientific understanding of the natural world through investigations, experiences, and readings. They design solutions to practical problems by using a variety of scientific methodologies.

Also covers: Academic Standard 2 (Detailed standards begin on page IN8.)

chapter 15

Electronics and Computers

chapter preview

sections
1 **Electronics**
   Lab Investigating Diodes
2 **Computers**
   Lab Does your computer have a virus?
   Virtual Lab How can a decision tree be used to generate binary numbers?

Deep in Thought?

You are looking at a brain—the brain of a computer. This is a microprocessor—a device that controls a computer. Even though this microprocessor is only a few cm on a side, it contains over a million microscopic circuits that enable it to store and process information very quickly.

Science Journal Describe three activities that you do using a computer.

Start-Up Activities

Electronic and Human Calculators

Imagine how your life would be different if you had been born before the invention of electronic devices. You could not watch television or use a computer. Besides providing entertainment, electronic devices and computers can make many tasks easier. For example, how much quicker is an electronic calculator than a human calculator?

1. Use a stopwatch to time how long it takes a volunteer to add the numbers 423, 21, 84, and 1,098.
2. Time how long it takes another volunteer to add these numbers using a calculator.
3. Repeat steps 1 and 2 this time asking the competitors to multiply 149 and 876.
4. Divide the time needed by the student calculator by the time needed by the calculator to solve each problem. How many times faster is the calculator?
5. **Think Critically** Write a paragraph describing which step in each calculation takes the most time.

Preview this chapter's content and activities at in7.msscience.com

FOLDABLES Study Organizer

Electronics and Computers Make the following Foldable to help you identify what you already know and what you want to learn about electronics and computers.

STEP 1 Fold a vertical sheet of paper from side to side. Make the front edge about 1 cm shorter than the back edge.

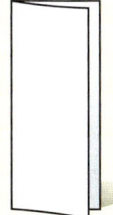

STEP 2 Turn lengthwise and fold into thirds.

STEP 3 Unfold and cut only the top layer along both folds to make three tabs.

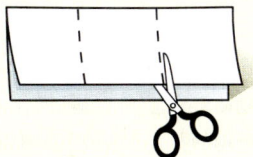

STEP 4 Label the tabs as shown.

Identify Questions Before you read the chapter, write what you know under the left tab and what you want to know under the middle tab. As you read the chapter, add to and correct what you have written. After you read the chapter, write what you have learned under the right tab of your Foldable.

section 1

This section builds a foundation for Standard 7.1.11.

Electronics

as you read

What You'll Learn
- **Compare and contrast** analog and digital signals.
- **Explain** how semiconductors are used in electronic devices.

Why It's Important
You use electronic devices every day to make your life easier and more enjoyable.

Review Vocabulary
crystal: a solid substance which has a regularly repeating internal arrangement of atoms

New Vocabulary
- electronic signal
- analog signal
- digital signal
- semiconductor
- diode
- transistor
- integrated circuit

Electronic Signals

You've popped some popcorn, put a video in the VCR, and turned off the lights. Now you're ready to watch a movie. The VCR, television, and lamp shown in **Figure 1** use electricity to operate. However, unlike the lamp, the VCR and the TV are electronic devices. An electronic device uses electricity to store, process, and transfer information.

The VCR and the TV use information recorded on the videotape to produce the images and sounds you see as a movie. As the videotape moves inside the VCR, it produces a changing electric current. This changing electric current is the information the VCR uses to send signals to the TV. The TV then uses these signals to produce the images you see and the sounds you hear.

A changing electric current that carries information is an **electronic signal**. The information can be used to produce sounds, images, printed words, numbers, or other data. For example, a changing electric current causes a loudspeaker to produce sound. If the electric current didn't change, no sound would be produced by the loudspeaker. There are two types of electronic signals—analog and digital.

Analog Signals Most TVs, VCRs, radios, and telephones process and transmit information that is in the form of analog electronic signals. An **analog signal** is a signal that varies smoothly in time. In an analog electronic signal the electric current increases or decreases smoothly in time, just as your hand can move smoothly up and down.

Electronic signals are not the only types of analog signals. An analog signal can be produced by something that varies in a smooth, continuous way and contains information. For example, a person's temperature changes smoothly and contains information about a person's health.

Figure 1 A VCR sends electronic signals to the TV, which uses the information in these signals to produce images and sound.

Figure 2 Clocks can be analog or digital devices.

The information displayed on an analog device such as this clock changes continuously.

On this digital clock, the displayed time jumps from one number to another.

Analog Devices The clock with hands shown in **Figure 2** is an example of an analog device. The hands move smoothly from one number to the next to represent the time of day. Fluid-filled and dial thermometers also are analog devices. In a fluid-filled thermometer, the height of the fluid column smoothly rises or falls as the temperature changes. In a dial thermometer, a spring smoothly expands or contracts as the temperature changes.

You have used another analog device if you ever have made a recording on a magnetic tape recorder. When voices or music are recorded on magnetic tape, the tape stores an analog signal of the sounds. When you play the tape, the tape recorder converts the analog signal to an electric current. This current changes smoothly with time and causes a loudspeaker to vibrate, recreating the sounds for you to hear.

Digital Signals Some devices, such as CD players, use a different kind of electronic signal called a digital signal. Unlike an analog signal, a **digital signal** does not vary smoothly, but changes in jumps or steps. If each jump is represented by a number, a digital signal can be represented by a series of numbers.

 *How is a digital signal different from an analog signal?*

You might have a digital clock or watch similar to the one shown on the right in **Figure 2** that displays the time as numbers. The display changes from 6:29 to 6:30 in a single jump, rather than sweeping smoothly from second to second. You might have seen digital thermometers that display temperature as a number. Some digital thermometers display temperature to the nearest whole degree, such as 23°C. The displayed temperature changes by jumps of 1°C. As a result, temperatures between two whole degrees, such as 22.7°C, are not displayed.

SECTION 1 Electronics **443**

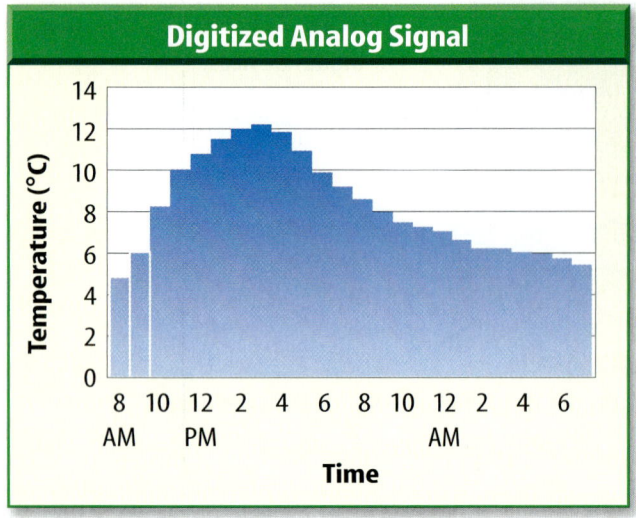

Making Digital Signals A smoothly varying analog signal can be converted to a digital signal. For example, suppose you wish to create a record of how the temperature outside changed over a day. One way to do this would be read an outdoor thermometer every hour and record the temperature and time. At the end of the day your temperature record would be a series of numbers. If you used these numbers to make a graph of the temperature record, it might look like the one shown in **Figure 3.** The temperature information shown by the graph changes in steps and is a digital signal.

Figure 3 A temperature record made by recording the temperature every hour changes in steps and is a digital signal.

Sampling an Analog Signal By recording the temperature every hour, you have sampled the smoothly varying outdoor temperature. When an analog signal is sampled, a value of the signal is read and recorded at some time interval, such as every hour or every second. An example is shown in **Figure 4.** As a result, a smoothly changing analog signal is converted to a series of numbers. This series of numbers is a digital signal.

The process of converting an analog signal to a digital signal is called digitization. The analog signal on a magnetic tape can be converted to a digital signal by sampling. In this way, a song can be represented by a series of numbers.

Figure 4 An analog signal can be converted to a digital signal. At a fixed time interval, the strength of the analog signal is measured and recorded. The resulting digital signal changes in steps.

Using Digital Signals It might seem that analog signals would be more useful than digital signals. After all, when an analog signal is converted to a digital signal, some information is lost. However, think about how analog and digital signals might be stored. Suppose a song that is stored as an analog signal on a small cassette tape were digitized and converted into a series of numbers. It might take millions of numbers to digitize a song, so how could these numbers be stored? As you will see later in this chapter, there is one electronic device that can store these numbers easily—a computer.

Once a digital signal is stored on a computer as a series of numbers, the computer can change these numbers using mathematical formulas. This process changes the signal and is called signal processing. For example, background noise can be removed from a digitized song using signal processing.

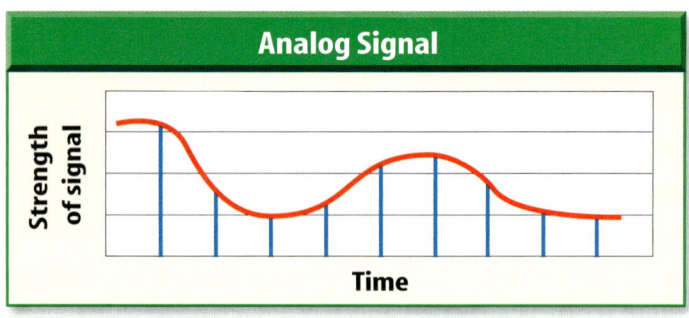

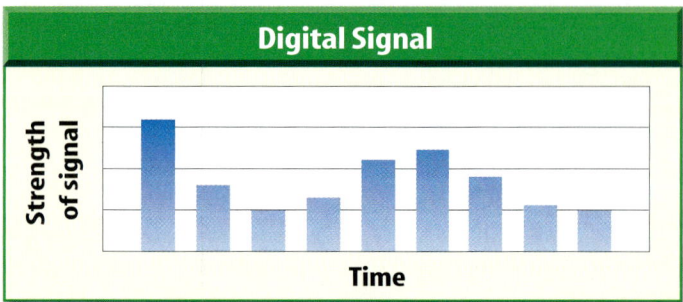

Early Television

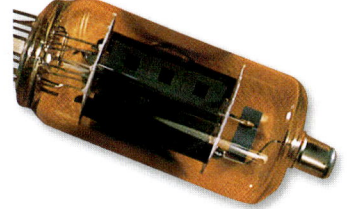
Vacuum Tube

Modern Television

Electronic Devices

An electronic device, such as a calculator or a CD player, uses the information contained in electronic signals to do a job. For example, the job can be adding two numbers together or making sounds and images. The electronic signals are electric currents that flow through circuits in the electronic device. An electronic device, such as a calculator or a VCR, may contain hundreds or thousands of complex electric circuits.

Electronic Components The electric circuits in an electronic device usually contain electronic components. These electronic components are small devices that use the information in the electronic signals to control the flow of current in the circuits.

Early electronic devices, such as the early television shown in **Figure 5,** used electronic components called vacuum tubes, such as the one shown in the middle of **Figure 5,** to help create sounds and images. Vacuum tubes were bulky and generated a great deal of heat. As a result, early electronic devices used more electric power and were less dependable than those used today, such as the modern television shown in **Figure 5.** Today, televisions and radios no longer use vacuum tubes. Instead, they contain electronic components made from semiconductors.

Semiconductors

On the periodic table, the small number of elements found between the metals and nonmetals are called metalloids. Some metalloids, such as silicon and germanium, are semiconductors. A **semiconductor** is an element that is a poorer conductor of electricity than metals but a better conductor than nonmetals. However, semiconductors have a special property that ordinary conductors and insulators lack—their electrical conductivity can be controlled by adding impurities.

Figure 5 Because early televisions used vacuum tubes, they used more electrical power and were less reliable than their modern versions.

Topic: Semiconductor Devices
Visit in7.msscience.com for Web links to information about semiconductor devices.

Activity Choose one semiconductor device and write a paragraph explaining one way that it is used.

SECTION 1 Electronics

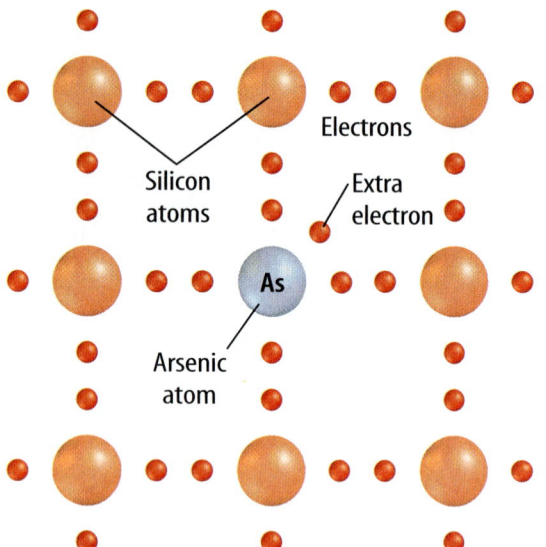

Figure 6 When arsenic atoms are added to a silicon crystal, they add extra electrons that are free to move about. This causes the electrical conductivity of the silicon crystal to increase.

Adding Impurities Adding even a single atom of an element such as gallium or arsenic to a million silicon atoms significantly changes the conductivity. This process of adding impurities is called doping.

Doping can produce two different kinds of semiconductors. One type of semiconductor can be created by adding atoms like arsenic to a silicon crystal, as shown in **Figure 6.** Then the silicon crystal contains extra electrons. A semiconductor with extra electrons is an n-type semiconductor.

A p-type semiconductor is produced when atoms like gallium are added to a silicon crystal. Then the silicon crystal has fewer electrons than it had before. An n-type semiconductor can give, or donate, electrons and a p-type semiconductor can take, or accept, electrons.

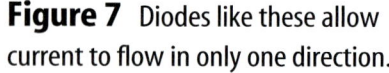 *How are n-type and p-type semiconductors different?*

Solid-State Components

The two types of semiconductors can be put together to form electronic components that can control the flow of electric current in a circuit. Combinations of n-type and p-type semiconductors can form components that behave like switches that can be turned off and on. Other combinations can form components that can increase, or amplify, the change in an electric current or voltage. Electronic components that are made from combinations of semiconductors are called solid-state components. Diodes and transistors are examples of solid-state components that often are used in electric circuits.

Figure 7 Diodes like these allow current to flow in only one direction.

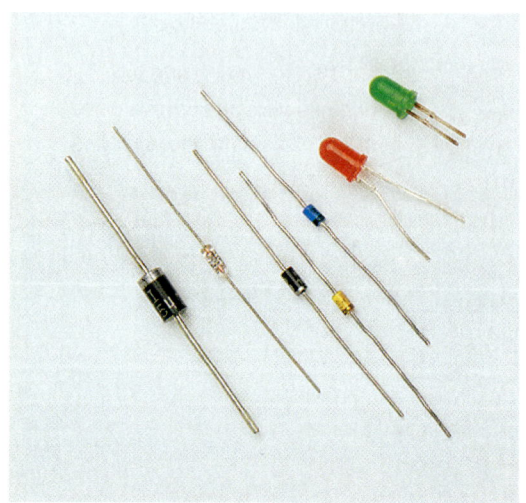

Diodes A **diode** is a solid-state component that, like a one-way street, allows current to flow only in one direction. In a diode, a p-type semiconductor is connected to an n-type semiconductor. Because an n-type semiconductor gives electrons and a p-type semiconductor accepts electrons, current can flow from the n-type to the p-type semiconductor, but not in the opposite direction. **Figure 7** shows common types of diodes. Diodes are useful for converting alternating current (AC) to direct current (DC). Recall that an alternating current constantly changes direction. When an alternating current reaches a diode, the diode allows the current to flow in only one direction. The result is direct current.

446 CHAPTER 15 Electronics and Computers

Transistors A **transistor** is a solid-state component that can be used to amplify signals in an electric circuit. A transistor also is used as an electronic switch. Electronic signals can cause a transistor to allow current to pass through it or to block the flow of current. **Figure 8** shows examples of transistors that are used in many electronic devices. Unlike a diode, a transistor is made from three layers of n-type and p-type semiconductor material sandwiched together.

Figure 8 Transistors such as these are used in electric circuits to amplify signals or to act as switches.

Integrated Circuits Personal computers usually contain millions of transistors, and would be many times larger if they used transistors the size of those shown in **Figure 8**. Instead, computers and other electronic devices use integrated circuits. An **integrated circuit** contains large numbers of interconnected solid-state components and is made from a single chip of semiconductor material such as silicon. An integrated circuit, like the one shown in **Figure 9,** may be smaller than 1 mm on each side and still can contain millions of transistors, diodes, and other components.

Figure 9 This tiny integrated circuit contains thousands of diodes and transistors.

section 1 review

Summary

Electronic Signals
- An electronic signal is a changing electric current that carries information.
- Analog electronic signals change continuously and digital electronic signals change in steps.
- An analog signal can be converted to a digital signal that is a series of numbers.

Solid-State Components
- Adding impurities to silicon can produce n-type semiconductors that donate electrons and p-type semiconductors that accept electrons.
- Solid-state components are electronic devices, such as diodes and transistors, made from n-type and p-type semiconductors.
- An integrated circuit contains a large number of solid-state components on a single semiconductor chip.

Self Check

1. **Explain** why the electric current that flows in a lamp is not an electronic signal.
2. **Describe** two advantages of using integrated circuits instead of vacuum tubes in electronic devices.
3. **Explain** why a digital signal can be stored on a computer.
4. **Compare and contrast** diodes and transistors.
5. **Think Critically** When an analog signal is sampled, what are the advantages and disadvantages of decreasing the time interval?

Applying Math

6. **Digital Signal** A song on a cassette tape is sampled and converted to a digital signal that is stored on a computer. The strength of the analog signal produced by the tape is sampled every 0.1 s. If the song is 3 min and 20 s long, how many numbers are in the digital signal stored on the computer?

Investigating Diodes

Diodes are found in most electronic devices. They are used to control the flow of electrons through a circuit. Electrons will flow through a diode in only one direction, from the n-type semiconductor to the p-type semiconductor. In this lab you will use a type of diode called an LED (light-emitting diode) to observe how a diode works.

▶ Real-World Question

How does electric current flow through a diode?

Goals
- **Create** an electronic circuit.
- **Observe** how an LED works.

Materials
light-emitting diode   D-cell battery and holder
lightbulb and holder   wire

Safety Precautions

▶ Procedure

1. Set up the circuit shown below. Record your observations. Then reverse the connections so each wire is connected to the other battery terminals. Record your observations.

2. Disconnect the wires from the lightbulb and attach one wire to each end of an LED. Observe whether the LED lights up when you connect the battery.

3. Reverse the connections on the LED so the current goes into the opposite end. Observe whether the LED lights up this time. Record your observation.

▶ Conclude and Apply

1. **Explain** why the bulb did or did not light up each time.
2. **Explain** why the LED did or did not light up each time.
3. **Describe** how the behavior of the lightbulb is different from that of the LED.
4. **Infer** which wire on the LED is connected to the n-type semiconductor and which is connected to the p-type semiconductor based on your observations.

 ommunicating
Your Data

Discuss your results with other students in your class. Did their LEDs behave in the same way? **For more help, refer to the Science Skill Handbook.**

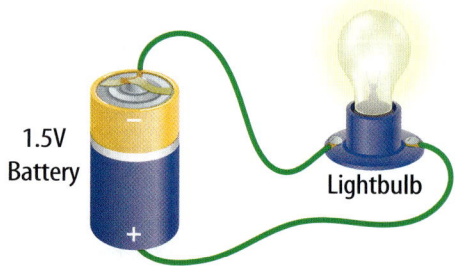

1.5V Battery   Lightbulb

448 CHAPTER 15 Electronics and Computers

section 2

Standard—7.1.11: Illustrate how numbers can be represented using sequences of only two symbols, such as 1 and 0 or on and off, and how that affects the storage of information in our society.

Also covers: 7.1.8, 7.2.7 (Detailed standards begin on page IN8.)

Computers

What are computers?

When was the last time you used a computer? Computers are found in libraries, grocery stores, banks, and gas stations. Computers seem to be everywhere. A computer is an electronic device that can carry out a set of instructions, or a program. By changing the program, the same computer can be made to do a different job.

Compared to today's desktop and laptop computers, the first electronic computers, like the one shown in **Figure 10,** were much bigger and slower. Several of the first electronic computers were built in the United States between 1946 and 1951. Solid-state components and the integrated circuit had not been developed yet. So these early computers contained thousands of vacuum tubes that used a great deal of electric power and produced large amounts of heat.

Computers became much smaller, faster, and more efficient after integrated circuits became available in the 1960s. Today, even a game system, like the one in **Figure 10,** can carry out many more operations each second than the early computers.

as you read

What You'll Learn
- **Describe** the different parts of a computer.
- **Compare** computer hardware with computer software.
- **Discuss** the different types of memory and storage in a computer.

Why It's Important
You can do more with computers if you understand how they work.

Review Vocabulary
laser: a device that produces a concentrated beam of light

New Vocabulary
- binary system
- random-access memory
- read-only memory
- computer software
- microprocessor

Figure 10 One of the first electronic computers was ENIAC, which was built in 1946 and weighed more than 30 tons. ENIAC could do 5,000 additions per second.

This handheld game system can do millions of operations per second.

SECTION 2 Computers **449**

Mini LAB

Using Binary Numbers

Procedure
1. Cut out **8 small paper squares.**
2. On four of the squares, draw the number zero, and on the other four, draw the number one.
3. Use the numbered squares to help determine the number of different combinations possible from four binary digits. List the combinations.

Analysis
1. From **Table 1** and your results from this MiniLAB, what happens to the number of combinations each time the number of binary digits is increased by one?
2. Infer how many combinations would be possible using five binary digits.

Try at Home

Table 1 Combinations of Binary Digits	
Number of of Binary Digits	Possible Combinations
1	0 1
2	00 01 10 11
3	000 001 010 011 100 101 110 111

Computer Information

How does a computer display images, generate sounds, and manipulate numbers and words? Every piece of information that is stored in or used by a computer must be converted to a series of numbers. The words you write with a word processor, or the numbers in a spreadsheet are stored in the computer's memory as numbers. An image or a sound file also is stored as a series of numbers. Information stored in this way is sometimes called digital information.

Binary Numbers Imagine what it would be like if you had to communicate with just two words—on and off. Could you use these words to describe your favorite music or to read a book out loud? Communication with just two words seems impossible, but that's exactly what a computer does.

All the digital information in a computer is converted to a type of number that is expressed using only two digits—0 and 1. This type of number is called a binary (BI nuh ree) number. Each 0 or 1 is called a binary digit, or bit. Because this number system uses only two digits, it is called the **binary system**, or base-2 number system.

✓ **Reading Check** *Which digits are used in the binary system?*

Combining Binary Digits You might think that using only two digits would limit the amount of information you can represent. However, a small number of binary digits can be used to generate a large number of combinations, as shown in **Table 1**.

While one binary digit has only two possible combinations—0 or 1—there are four possible combinations for a group of two binary digits, as shown in **Table 1**. By using just one more binary digit the possible number of combinations is increased to eight. The number of combinations increases quickly as more binary digits are added to the group. For example, there are 65,536 combinations possible for a group of 16 binary digits.

Representing Information with Binary Digits
Combinations of binary digits can be used to represent information. For example, the English alphabet has 26 letters. Suppose each letter was represented by one combination of binary digits. To represent both lowercase and uppercase letters would require a total of 52 different combinations of binary digits. Would a group of five binary digits have enough possible combinations?

450 CHAPTER 15 Electronics and Computers

Representing Letters and Numbers A common system that is used by computers represents each letter, number, or other text character by eight binary digits, or one byte. There are 256 combinations possible for a group of eight binary digits. In this system, the letter "A" is represented by the byte 01000001, while the letter "a" is represented by the byte 01100001, and a question mark is represented by 00111111.

Computer Memory

Why are digital signals stored in a computer as binary numbers? A binary number is a series of bits that can have only one of two values—0 and 1. A switch, such as a light switch on a wall, can have two positions: on or off. A switch could be used to represent the two values of a bit. A switch in the "off" position could represent a 0, and a switch in the "on" position could represent a 1. **Table 2** shows how switches could be used to represent combinations of binary digits.

Table 2 Representing Binary Digits

Binary Number	Switches
0000	↓ ↓ ↓ ↓
0001	↓ ↓ ↓ ↑
0010	↓ ↓ ↑ ↓
0011	↓ ↓ ↑ ↑
0100	↓ ↑ ↓ ↓
1010	↑ ↓ ↑ ↓

Applying Science

How much information can be stored?

Information can be stored in a computer's memory or in storage devices such as hard disks or CDs. The amount of information that can be stored is so large that special units, shown in the table on the right, are used. Desktop computers often have hard disks that can store many gigabytes of information. How much information can be stored in one gigabyte of storage?

Size of Information Storage Units

Information Storage Unit	Number of Bytes
kilobyte	1,024
megabyte	1,048,576
gigabyte	1,073,741,824

Identifying the Problem

When words are stored on a computer, every letter, punctuation mark, and space between words is represented by one byte. A page of text, such as this page, might contain as many as 2,900 characters. So to store a page of text on a computer might require 2,900 bytes.

If you write a page of text using a word-processing program, more bytes might be needed to store the page. This is because when the page is stored, some word-processing programs include other information along with the text.

Solving the Problem

1. If it takes 2,900 bytes to store one page of text on a computer, how many pages can be stored in 1 gigabyte of storage?
2. Suppose a book contains 400 pages of text. How many books could be stored on a 1-gigabyte hard disk?
3. A CD can hold 650 megabytes of information. How many 400-page books could be stored on a CD?

SECTION 2 Computers

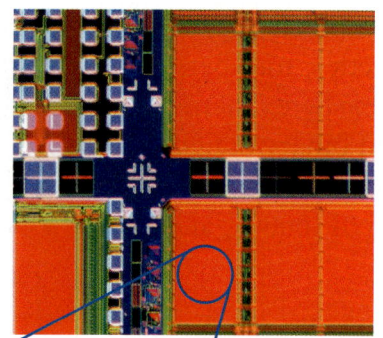

Figure 11 Computer memory is made of integrated circuits like this one. This integrated circuit can contain millions of microscopic circuits, shown here under high magnification.

Storing Information The memory in a computer is an integrated circuit that contains millions of tiny electronic circuits, as shown in **Figure 11.** In the most commonly used type of computer memory, each circuit is able to store electric charge and can be either charged or uncharged. If the circuit is charged, it represents the bit 1 and if it is uncharged it represents the bit 0. Because computer memory contains millions of these circuits, it can store tremendous amounts of information using only the numbers 1 and 0.

What is your earliest memory? When you remember something from long ago, you use your long-term memory. On the other hand, when you work on a math problem, you may keep the numbers in your head long enough to find the answer. Like you, a computer has a long-term memory and a short-term memory that are used for different purposes.

Random-Access Memory A computer's **random-access memory,** or RAM, is short-term memory that stores documents, programs, and data while they are being used. Program instructions and data are temporarily stored in RAM while you are using a program or changing the data.

For example, a computer game is kept in RAM while you are playing it. If you are using a word-processing program to write a report, the report is temporarily held in RAM while you are working on it. Because information stored in RAM is lost when the computer is turned off, this type of memory cannot store anything that you want to use later.

The amount of RAM depends on the number of binary digits it can store. Recall that eight bits is called a byte. A megabyte is more than one million bytes. A computer that has 128 megabytes of memory can store more than 128 million bytes of information in its RAM, or nearly one billion bits.

 **Reading Check** *What happens to information in RAM when the computer is turned off?*

Indiana Academic Standard Check

7.1.11: Illustrate how numbers can be represented using sequences of only two symbols . . .

✓ How many microscopic circuits in a computer's memory are needed to store 1 byte?

Topic: Computer Software
Visit in7.msscience.com for Web links to information about types of computer software.

Activity Choose one type of software application and write a paragraph explaining why it is useful. Create a chart that summarizes what the software does.

Read-Only Memory Some information that is needed to enable the computer to operate is stored in its permanent memory. The computer can read this memory, but it cannot be changed. Memory that can't be changed and is permanently stored inside the computer is called **read-only memory,** or ROM. ROM is not lost when the computer is turned off.

452 CHAPTER 15 Electronics and Computers

Computer Programs

It's your mother's birthday and you decide to surprise her by baking a chocolate cake. You find a recipe for chocolate cake in a cookbook and follow the directions in the order the recipe tells you to. However, if the person who wrote the recipe left out any steps or put them in the wrong order, the cake probably will not turn out the way you expected. A computer program is like a recipe. A program is a series of instructions that tell the computer how to do a job. Unlike the recipe for a cake, some computer programs contain millions of instructions that tell the computer how to do many different jobs.

All the functions of a computer, such as displaying an image on the computer monitor or doing a math calculation, are controlled by programs. These instructions tell the computer how to add two numbers, how to display a word, or how to change an image on the monitor when you move a joystick. Many different programs can be stored in a computer's memory.

Computer Software When you type a report, play a video game, draw a picture, or look through an encyclopedia on a computer, you are using computer software. **Computer software** is any list of instructions for the computer. The instructions that are part of the software tell the computer what to display on the monitor. If you respond to what you see, for example by moving the mouse, the software instructions tell the computer how to respond to your action.

Computer Programming

The process of writing computer software is called computer programming. To write a computer program, you must decide what you want the computer to do, plan the best way to organize the instructions, write the instructions, and test the program to be sure it works. A person who writes computer programs is called a computer programmer. Computer programmers write software in computer languages such as Basic, C++, and Java.

Figure 12 shows part of a computer program. After the program is written, it is converted into binary digits to enable it to be stored in the computer's memory. Then the computer can carry out the program's instructions.

Mini LAB

Observing Memory

Procedure
1. Write a different five-digit number on six 3 × 5 cards.
2. Show a card to a partner for 3 s. Turn the card over and ask your partner to repeat the number. Repeat with two other cards.
3. Repeat this procedure with the last three cards, but wait 20 s before asking your partner to repeat each number.

Analysis
Is your partner's memory of the five-digit numbers more like computer RAM or ROM? Explain.

Try at Home

Figure 12 The text below is part of a computer program that directs the operation of a computer.

```
int request_dma(unsigned int dmanr, const char * device_id)
{
    if (dmanr > = MAX_DMA_CHANNELS)
        return -EINVAL;

    if (xchg(&dma_chan_busy[dmanr].lock, 1) != 0)
        return -EBUSY;

    dma_chan_busy[dmanr].device_id = device_id;

    /* old flag was 0, now contains 1 to indicate busy */
    return 0;
} /* request_dma */

void free_dma(unsigned int dmanr)
{
    if (dmanr > = MAX_DMA_CHANNELS) {
        printk("Trying to free DMA%d\n", dmanr);
        return;
    }
```

SECTION 2 Computers **453**

Computer Programmers
Computer software is written by computer programmers. It may take from a few hours to more than a year to write a program, and involve a single programmer or a team of programmers. A programmer usually must know several computer languages, such as COBOL, Java, and C++. Training in computer languages is required, and most jobs also require a college degree. Research to find the schools in your area that offer training as a computer programmer.

Computer Hardware

When you press a key on a computer's keyboard, a letter appears on the screen. This seems to occur all at once, but actually three steps are involved. In the first step, the computer receives information from an input device, such as a keyboard or mouse. For example, when you press a key on the keyboard, the computer receives and stores an electronic signal from the keyboard.

The next step is to process the input signal from the keyboard. This means to change the input signal into an electronic signal that can be understood by the computer monitor. The computer does this by following instructions contained in the programs stored in the computer's memory. The third step is to send the processed signal to the monitor.

All three steps can be carried out with a combination of hardware and software components. Computer hardware consists of input devices, output devices, storage devices, and integrated circuits for storing information. A keyboard and a mouse are examples of input devices, while a monitor, a printer, and loudspeakers are examples of output devices. Storage devices, such as floppy disks, hard disks, and CDs, are used to store information outside of the computer memory. A computer also contains a microprocessor that controls the computer hardware. Examples of computer hardware are shown in **Figure 13**.

Figure 13 Computer hardware includes input devices, output devices, and storage devices.

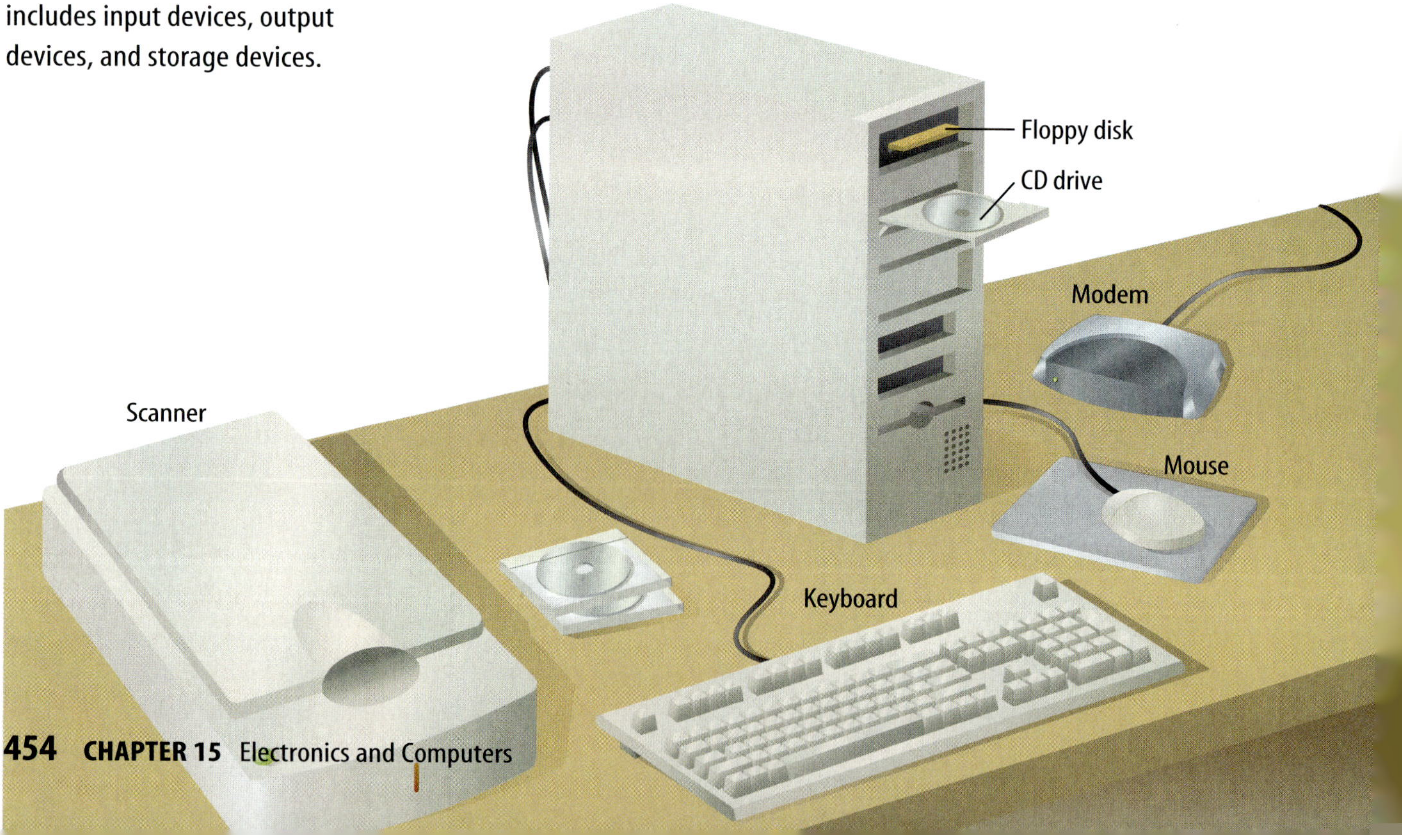

The Microprocessor Modern computers contain a microprocessor, like the one shown in **Figure 14,** that serves as the brain of the computer. A **microprocessor,** which is also called the central processing unit, or CPU, is an integrated circuit that controls the flow of information between different parts of the computer. A microprocessor can contain millions of interconnected transistors and other components. The microprocessor receives electronic signals from various parts of the computer, processes these signals, and sends electronic signals to other parts of the computer. For example, the microprocessor might tell the hard-disk drive to write data to the hard disk or the monitor to change the image on the screen. The microprocessor does this by carrying out instructions that are contained in computer programs stored in the computer's memory.

The microprocessor was developed in the late 1970s as the result of a process that made it possible to fit thousands of electronic components on a silicon chip. In the 1980s, the number of components on a silicon chip increased to hundreds of thousands. In the 1990s, microprocessors were developed that contained several million components on a single chip.

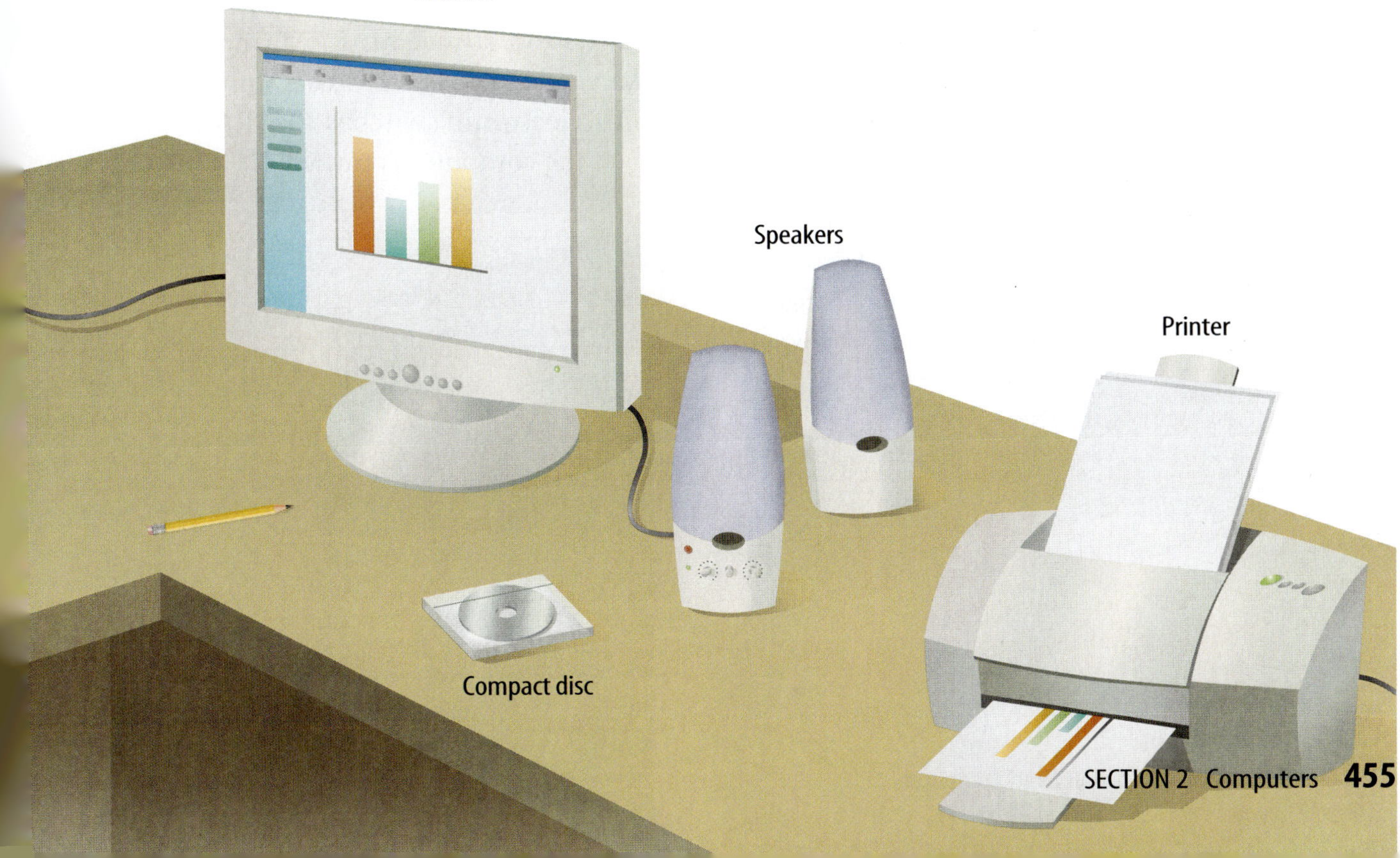

Figure 14 The pencil points to the microprocessor in the photo above. This microprocessor has dimensions of about one centimeter on a side, but contains millions of transistors and other solid-state components.

SECTION 2 Computers **455**

Recycling Computers
Changes in computer technology occur so rapidly that computers are often replaced after being used for only a few years. What happens to old computers? Some computer parts contain lead, mercury, and other toxic substances. Research how toxic materials can be recovered from old computers, and disposed of safely. Summarize your findings in your Science Journal.

Topic: Magnetic Disks
Visit in7.msscience.com for Web links to information about storing data on magnetic disks.

Activity Write a paragraph explaining why hard disks can store more information than floppy disks.

Storing Information

You have decided to type your homework assignment on a computer. The resulting paper is quite long and you make many changes to it each time you read it. How does the computer make it possible for you to store your information and make changes to it?

Both RAM and ROM are integrated circuits inside the computer. You might wonder, then, why other types of information storage are needed. Information stored in RAM is lost when the computer is turned off, and information stored in ROM can only be read—it can't be changed. If you want to store information that can be changed but isn't lost when the computer is off, you must store that information on a storage device, such as a disk. Several different types of disks are available.

Hard Disks A hard disk is a device that stores computer information magnetically. A hard disk is usually located inside a computer. **Figure 15** shows the inside of a hard disk, and **Figure 16** shows how a hard disk stores data. The hard disk contains one or more metal disks that have magnetic particles on one surface. When you save information on a hard disk, a device called a read/write head inside the disk drive changes the orientation of the magnetic particles on the disk's surface. Orientation in one direction represents 0 and orientation in the opposite direction represents 1. When a magnetized disk is read, the read/write head converts the digital information on the disk to pulses of electric current.

Information stored magnetically cannot be read by the computer as quickly as information stored on RAM and ROM. However, because the information on a hard disk is stored magnetically rather than with electronic switches like RAM, the information isn't lost when the computer is turned off.

Figure 15 A hard disk contains a disk or platter that is coated with magnetic particles. A read/write head moves over the surface of the disk.

NATIONAL GEOGRAPHIC VISUALIZING A HARD DISK

Figure 16

Computers are useful because they can process large amounts of information quickly. Almost all desktop computers use a hard disk to store information. A hard disk is an electronic filing cabinet that can store enormous amounts of information and retrieve them quickly.

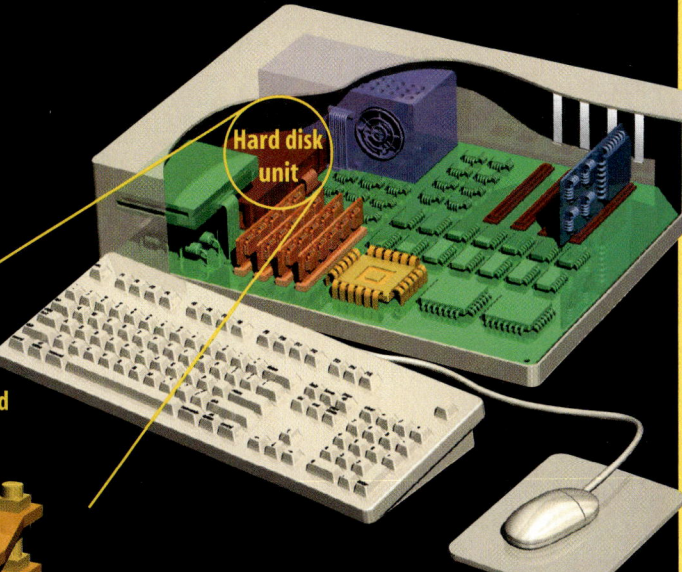

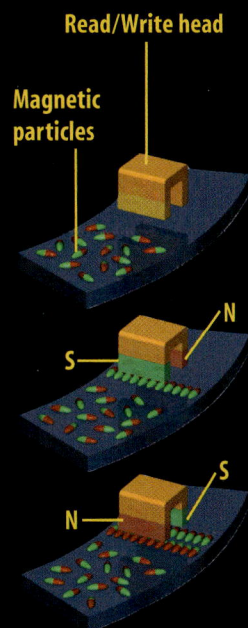

A A hard-disk drive is made of a stack of aluminum disks, called platters, that are coated with a thin layer that contains magnetic particles. Like tiny compasses, these particles will line up along magnetic field lines. The hard disk also contains read/write heads that contain electromagnets. When the hard disk is turned on, the platters spin under the heads.

B To write information on the disk, a magnetic field is created around the head by an electric current. As the platter rotates past the head, this magnetic field causes the magnetic particles on the platter to line up in bands. One direction of the bands corresponds to the digital bit 0, the other to the digital bit 1.

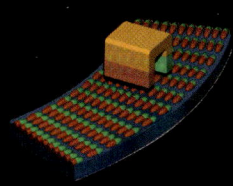

C To read information on the disk, no current is sent to the heads. Instead, the magnetized bands create a changing current in the head as it passes over the platter. This current is the electronic signal that represents the needed information.

SECTION 2 Computers   **457**

Floppy Disks Storing information on a hard disk is convenient, but sometimes you might want to store information that you can carry with you. The original storage device of this type was the floppy disk. A floppy disk is a thin, flexible, plastic disk. You might be confused by the term *floppy* if you have heard it used to describe disks that seem quite rigid. That is because you don't actually hold the floppy disk. Instead, you hold the harder plastic case in which the floppy disk is encased. Just as for a hard disk, the floppy disk is coated with a magnetic material that is magnetized and read by a read/write head. Floppy disks have lower storage capacity than hard disks. Also, compared to hard disks, information is read from and written to floppy disks much more slowly.

Optical Disks An optical storage disk, such as a CD, is a thin, plastic disk that has information digitally stored on it. The disk contains a series of microscopic pits and flat spots as shown on the left in **Figure 17**. A tiny laser beam shines on the surface of the disk. The information on the disk is read by measuring the intensity of the laser light reflected from the surface of the disk. This intensity will depend on whether the laser beam strikes a pit or a flat spot. The original optical storage disks, laser discs, CD-ROMs, and DVD-ROMs, were read-only. Several of these are shown on the right in **Figure 17**. However, CD-RW disks can be erased and rewritten many times. Information is written by a CD burner that causes a metal alloy in the disk to change form when heated by a laser. When the disk is read, the intensity of reflected laser light depends on which form of the alloy the beam strikes.

Science Online

Topic: Optical Disks
Visit in7.msscience.com for Web links to information about storing data on optical disks.

Activity Make a table that shows the similarities and differences between CDs and DVDs.

Figure 17 An optical storage disk stores information that is read by a laser.
Explain *the difference between a read-only disk and a reusable disk.*

Information is stored on an optical disk by a series of pits and flat spots, representing a binary 1 or 0.

CDs, laser disks, and DVDs are all examples of optical storage disks.

458 CHAPTER 15 Electronics and Computers

Computer Networks

People can communicate using a computer if it is part of a computer network. A computer network is two or more computers that are connected to share files or other information. The computers might be linked by cables, telephone lines, or radio signals.

The Internet is a collection of computer networks from all over the world. The Internet is linked together by cable or satellite. The Internet itself has no information. No documents or files exist on the Internet, but you can use the Internet to access a tremendous amount of information by linking to other computers.

The World Wide Web is part of the Internet. The World Wide Web is the ever-changing collection of information (text, graphics, audio, and video) on computers all over the world. The computers that store these documents are called servers. When you connect with a server through the Internet, you can view any of the Web documents that are stored there, like the Web page shown in **Figure 18**. A particular collection of information that is stored in one place is known as a Web site.

Figure 18 When you connect to the Internet, you can be linked with other computers that are part of the World Wide Web. Then you can have access to the information stored at millions of Web sites.

section 2 review

Summary

Computer Information
- A binary digit can be a 0 or a 1.
- Computers store information as groups of binary digits.
- Computers use tiny electronic circuits to represent binary digits and store information.

Computer Software and Hardware
- Computer software and computer programs are lists of instructions for a computer.
- Computer programs are written in special computer languages.
- Computer hardware, such as keyboards and hard disks, is controlled by a microprocessor.

Storing Information
- Hard disks and floppy disks store information on disks coated with magnetic particles.
- Optical disks store information as a series of pits and flat spots that is read by a laser.

Self Check

1. **Explain** why the binary number system is used for storing information in computers.
2. **Compare and contrast** the Internet and the World Wide Web.
3. **Describe** what a microprocessor does with the signals it receives from various parts of a computer.
4. **Compare and contrast** three different computer information storage devices.
5. **Think Critically** Why can't computer information be stored only in RAM and ROM, making storage devices such as hard disks and optical disks unnecessary?

Applying Skills

6. **Make a Concept Map** Develop a spider map about computers. Include the following terms in your spider map: *keyboard, monitor, microprocessor, software, printer, RAM, ROM, floppy disk, hard disk, CD, Internet,* and *World Wide Web*.

in7.msscience.com/self_check_quiz

LAB
Use the Internet

Does your computer have a virus?

Goals
- **Understand** what a computer virus is.
- **Identify** different types of computer viruses.
- **Describe** how a computer virus is spread.
- **Create** a plan for protecting electronic files and computers from computer viruses.

Data Source

Science Online

Visit **in7.msscience.com/ internet_lab** to get more information about computer viruses and for data collected by other students.

Real-World Question

The Internet has provided many ways to share information and become connected with people near and far. People can communicate ideas and information quickly and easily. Unfortunately, some people use computers and the Internet as an opportunity to create and spread computer viruses. Many new viruses are created each year that can damage information and programs on a computer. Viruses create problems for computers in homes and schools. Computer problems caused by viruses can be costly for business and government computers as well. How can acquiring and transmitting computer viruses be prevented?

Make a Plan

People share information and ideas by exchanging electronic files with one another. Perhaps you send email to your friends and family. Many people send word processing or spreadsheet files to friends and associates. What happens if a computer file is infected with a virus? How is that virus spread among different users? How can you protect your computer and your information from being attacked by a virus?

460 CHAPTER 15 Electronics and Computers

Using Scientific Methods

⊙ Follow Your Plan

1. Do research to find out what a computer virus is and the difference between various types of viruses. Also research the ways that a computer virus can damage computer files and programs.
2. After you know what a computer virus is, make a list of different types of viruses and how they are passed from computer to computer. For example, some viruses can be passed through attachments to email. Others can be passed by sharing spreadsheet files. Be specific about how a virus is passed.
3. Discover how you can protect yourself from viruses that attack your computer. Make a list of steps to follow to avoid infection.
4. Make sure your teacher approves your plan before you start.
5. Visit the link below to post your data.

⊙ Analyze Your Data

1. **Explain** how computer viruses are transferred from one computer to another.
2. **Explain** how you can prevent your computer from becoming infected by a virus.
3. **Explain** how you can prevent other people from getting computer viruses.
4. **Describe** what steps you should take to make sure you do not spread viruses to the computers of people you share information with.
5. **Describe** the different ways computer viruses can damage computer files and programs.

⊙ Conclude and Apply

1. **List** five to eight steps a computer user should follow to prevent getting a computer virus or passing a computer virus to another computer.
2. **Discuss** how antivirus software can keep viruses from spreading. Could antivirus software always prevent you from getting a computer virus? Why or why not?

Communicating Your Data

Find this lab using the link below. Post your data in the table that is provided. **Compare** your data on types of viruses and how they infect computers with that of other students.

Science online
in7.msscience.com/internet_lab

LAB **461**

TIME SCIENCE AND Society
SCIENCE ISSUES THAT AFFECT YOU!

E-Lectrifying E-Books

Here's a look at how computers and the Internet are changing what—and how—you read

All of these stacked books can fit into one e-book.

In recent years, people have been using their computers to order books from online bookstores. That's no big deal. What might become a big deal is the ordering of electronic books—books that you download to your own computer and read on the screen or print out to read later. Some famous authors are writing books just for that purpose. Some of the books are published only online—you can't find them anywhere else.

Many other Web sites, however, are selling any book anybody wishes to write—including students like you. In fact, you could start your own online bookstore with your own stories and reports. It will be up to readers to pick and choose what's good from the huge number of e-books that will be on the Web.

Curling Up with a Good Disk

Downloading books to your home computer is just one way to get an e-book. You can also buy versions of books to read on hand-held devices that are about the size of a paperback book. With one device, the books come on CD-ROM disks. With another, the books download to the device over a modem.

Current e-book devices are expensive, heavy, and awkward, and the number of books you can get for them is small. But if improvements come quickly, it might not be long before you check out of the library with a pocketful of disks instead of a heavy armload of books!

Will Traditional Books Disappear?

Most people think that the traditional printed book will never disappear. Publishers will still be printing books on paper with soft and hard covers. But publishers also predict there will be more and more kinds of formats for books. E-books, for example, might be best for interactive works that blend video, sound, and words the way many Web sites already do. For example, an e-book biography might allow the reader to click on photos and videos of the subject, and even provide links to other sources of information.

Interview Talk to a bookstore employee to find out how book publishing and selling has changed in the last five years. Can he or she predict how people will read books in the future? Report to the class.

For more information, visit in7.msscience.com/time

chapter 15 Study Guide

Reviewing Main Ideas

Section 1 Electronics

1. A changing electric current used to carry information is an electronic signal. Electronic signals can be either analog or digital.

2. Semiconductor elements, such as silicon and germanium, conduct electricity better than nonmetals but not as well as metals. If a small amount of some impurities is added to a semiconductor, its conductivity can be controlled.

3. Diodes and transistors are solid-state components. Diodes allow current to flow in one direction only. Transistors are used as switches or amplifiers.

Section 2 Computers

1. The binary system consists of two digits, 0 and 1. Switches within electronic devices such as computers can store information by turning on (1) and off (0).

2. Electronic memory within a computer can be random-access (RAM) or read-only (ROM).

3. Computer hardware consists of the physical parts of a computer. Computer software is a list of instructions for a computer.

4. A microprocessor is a complex integrated circuit that receives signals from various parts of the computer, processes these signals, and then sends instructions to various parts of the computer.

5. Floppy disks, hard disks, and optical disks are types of computer information storage devices.

6. The Internet is a collection of linked computer networks from all over the world. The World Wide Web is part of the Internet.

Visualizing Main Ideas

Copy and complete the following concept map on computers.

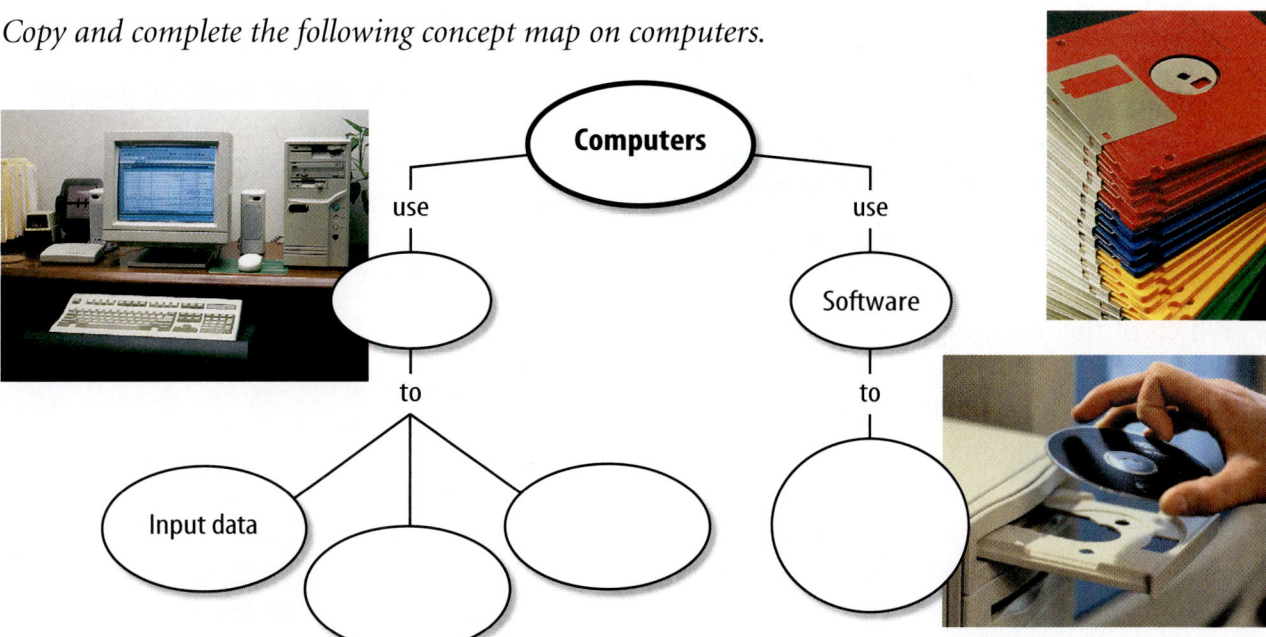

chapter 15 Review

Using Vocabulary

analog signal p. 442
binary system p. 450
computer software p. 453
digital signal p. 443
diode p. 446
electronic signal p. 442
integrated circuit p. 447
microprocessor p. 455
random access memory p. 452
read-only memory p. 452
semiconductor p. 445
transistor p. 447

Fill in the blanks with the correct vocabulary word or words.

1. _____ is a base-2 number system.

2. A(n) _____ can change AC current to DC current.

3. A(n) _____ is made from a single piece of semiconductor material and can contain thousands of solid-state components.

4. The information in a computer's _____ changes each time the computer is used.

5. An electronic device that can be used as a switch or to amplify electronic signals is a(n) _____.

6. A(n) _____ is also called a CPU.

7. An electronic signal that varies smoothly with time is a(n) _____.

Checking Concepts

Choose the word or phrase that best answers the question.

8. Which of the following best describes integrated circuits?
   A) They can be read with a laser.
   B) They use vacuum tubes as transistors and diodes.
   C) They contain pits and flat areas.
   D) They can be small and contain a large number of solid-state components.

9. Which type of elements are semiconductors?
   A) metals   C) metalloids
   B) nonmetals   D) gases

10. How is a digital signal different from an analog signal?
    A) It uses electric current.
    B) It varies continuously.
    C) It changes in steps.
    D) It is used as a switch.

11. Which of the following uses magnetic materials to store digital information.
    A) DVD   C) RAM
    B) hard disk   D) compact disk

12. Which part of a computer carries out the instructions contained in computer programs and software?
    A) RAM   C) hard disk
    B) ROM   D) microprocessor

13. Which type of computer memory is used when a computer is first turned on?
    A) ROM   C) DVD
    B) RAM   D) floppy disk

14. The instructions contained in a computer program are stored in which type of computer memory while the program is being used?
    A) ROM   C) CD
    B) RAM   D) floppy disk

Use the figure below to answer question 15.

15. What binary number is represented by the positions of the switches?
    A) 1110   C) 0101
    B) 0010   D) 0001

464 CHAPTER REVIEW   in7.msscience.com/vocabulary_puzzlemaker

chapter 15 Review

Thinking Critically

16. **Compare and contrast** an analog device and a digital device.

17. **Make and Use Tables** Copy and complete the following table that describes solid-state components.

Solid-State Components		
Component	Description	Use
Diode		
Transistor	Do not write in this book.	
Integrated circuit		

18. **Explain** why the binary number system is used to store digital information in computers, instead of the decimal number system you use every day.

19. **Concept Map** Copy and complete the following events-chain map showing the sequence of events that occurs when a computer mouse is moved.

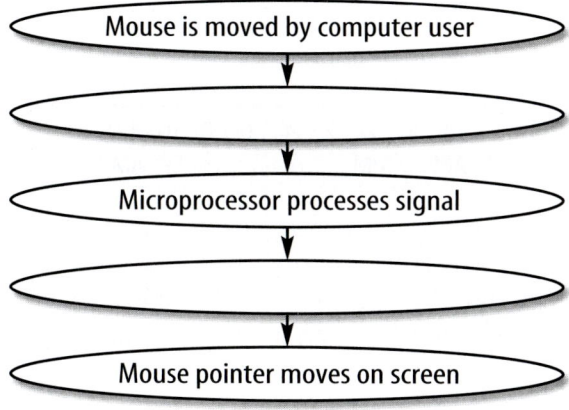

20. **Discuss** how the development of solid-state components and integrated circuits affected devices such as TVs and computers.

21. **Make a table** to classify the different types of internal and external computer memory and storage.

Performance Activities

22. **Make a Poster** Microprocessors continue to be developed that are more complex and contain an ever-increasing number of solid state components. Visit **in7.msscience.com** for links to information about different microprocessors and how they have changed. Make a poster that summarizes what you have learned.

Applying Math

Students at a middle school researched the storage capacity of different computer storage devices. The information is summarized in the table below. The storage capacity is listed in units of gigabytes. A gigabyte is 1,074,000,000 bytes.

Use the table below to answer questions 23–25.

Computer Storage Devices	
Device	Capacity (Gb)
Floppy disk	0.00144
Compact disc	0.650
DVD	4.7
Hard Disk A	8.60
Hard Disk B	120.2

23. **Music Files Storage** In a certain format, to store 1 min of music as a digital signal requires 10,584,000 bytes. How many minutes of music in this format can be stored on the compact disc?

24. **Digital Pictures Storage** A certain digital camera produces digital images that require 921,600 bytes to store. How many of these images could be stored on hard disk A?

25. **Documents Storage** Seven documents produced by word processing software are stored on a floppy disk. If there are 40,000 bytes of storage still available on the disk, what is the average amount of storage used by each of the documents?

in7.msscience.com/chapter_review   CHAPTER REVIEW **465**

chapter 15 Indiana

 The assessed Indiana standard appears above the question.

Record your answers on the answer sheet provided by your teacher or on a sheet of paper.

Part 1 Multiple Choice

The table below shows the number of combinations for different numbers of binary digits.

Number of Binary Digit Combinations	
Number of Binary Digits	Total Number of Combinations
1	2
2	4
3	8
4	?
5	32

7.1.11

1. What is the total number of combinations of four binary digits?
   - A 8
   - B 16
   - C 32
   - D 64

7.1.11

2. Based on the trend in the table above, what is the total number of combinations of six binary digits?
   - A 40
   - B 44
   - C 64
   - D 96

3. What materials are used to make solid-state components?
   - A conductors
   - B insulators
   - C semiconductors
   - D superconductors

4. Which best describes computer software?
   - A It is the central processing unit.
   - B It is a list of instructions.
   - C It is a type of magnetic disk.
   - D It is a type of optical disk.

5. The graph below shows a digitized signal.

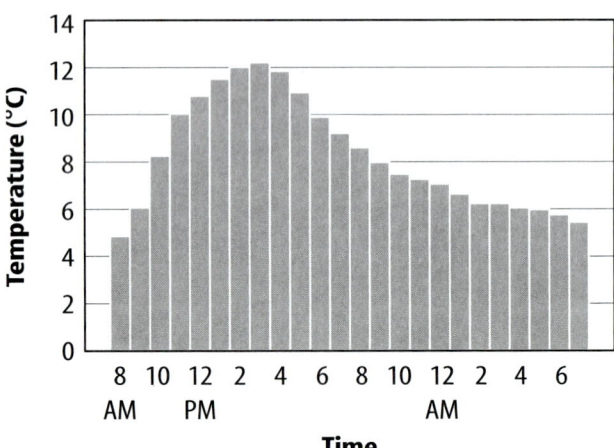

What is the process that produces this digital signal from an analog signal?
   - A doping
   - B programming
   - C sampling
   - D switching

Standards Review

6. Which is **NOT** an electronic device?

   A calculator

   B CD player

   C lightbulb

   D television

7. The illustration below shows arsenic atoms in a silicon crystal.

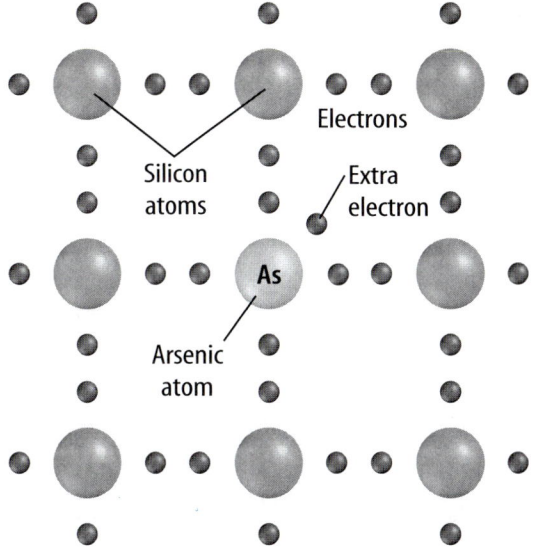

   Adding atoms of other elements to a semiconductor material mainly affects which physical property?

   A density

   B electrical conductivity

   C heat generated

   D weight

Test-Taking Tip

Some Questions Have Qualifiers Look for qualifiers in a question. Such questions are not looking for absolute answers. Qualifiers could be words such as *best describes*, *most common*, or *least common*.

Part 2 | Constructed Response

7.1.11

8. Classify each of the following as an input, output, or storage device: monitor, keyboard, printer, hard disk. Explain the function of each device if you are using a word processing program to write a report.

7.1.11

9. Compare and contrast a floppy disk with an optical disk, such as a CD.

7.1.11

10. Explain why electric circuits that can be charged or uncharged are used as the components of computer memory.

The photo below shows a hard disk drive.

7.1.11

11. Describe how the read/write heads write information on a platter in the hard disk drive.

7.1.11

12. Describe how the read/write heads read information that is stored on the platters in the hard disk drive shown in the photo above.

unit 5
Galaxies, Stars, and Earth

How Are Canals & the Paleozoic Era Connected?

Before the invention of the locomotive, canals, such as the one at upper right, were an important means of transportation. In the 1790s, an engineer traveled around England to study new canals. The engineer noticed something odd: All across the country, certain types of rocks seemed to lie in predictable layers, or strata. And the same strata always had the same kinds of fossils in them. Since each layer of sedimentary rock typically forms on top of the previous one, scientists realized that the strata recorded the history of life on Earth. By the mid-1800s, the known rock strata had been organized into a system that we now know as the geologic time scale. In this system, Earth's history is divided into units called eras, which in turn are divided into periods. Many of the rock layers in the Grand Canyon (background) date from the Paleozoic, or "ancient life," Era.

unit projects

The assessed Indiana standard appears in blue.

To find project ideas and resources, visit **in7.msscience.com/unit_project**.
Projects include:

- **History** Discover some of Earth's inhabitants of different time periods using the fossil record. Create a drawing of a scene in Earth's history. **7.3.10, 7.7.2**
- **Technology** Research the history and physical characteristics of an astronomical body. Write a newspaper article about your new "discovery." **7.1.5**
- **Model** As a group, design a wall mural or diorama depicting the layers of the geologic time scale, or a particular scene of interest from an era. **7.3.10, 7.7.2**

WebQuest *Created Gemstones: The Real Thing* offers an opportunity to evaluate the process and value of manufactured gems. **7.1.8**

chapter 16

Stars and Galaxies

Academic Standard—3: Students collect and organize data to identify relationships between physical objects, events, and processes. They use logical reasoning to question their own ideas as new information challenges their conceptions of the natural world.

Also covers: Academic Standard 1 (Detailed standards begin on page IN8.)

chapter preview

sections
1 Stars
2 The Sun
   Lab Sunspots
3 Evolution of Stars
4 Galaxies and the Universe
   Lab Measuring Parallax
   Virtual Lab How does the chemical composition of stars determine their classification?

What's your address?

You know your address at home. You also know your address at school. But do you know your address in space? You live on a planet called Earth that revolves around a star called the Sun. Earth and the Sun are part of a galaxy called the Milky Way. It looks similar to galaxy M83, shown in the photo.

Science Journal Write a description in your Science Journal of the galaxy shown on this page.

Start-Up Activities

Why do clusters of galaxies move apart?

Astronomers know that most galaxies occur in groups of galaxies called clusters. These clusters are moving away from each other in space. The fabric of space is stretching like an inflating balloon.

1. Partially inflate a balloon. Use a piece of string to seal the neck.
2. Draw six evenly spaced dots on the balloon with a felt-tipped marker. Label the dots A through F.
3. Use string and a ruler to measure the distance, in millimeters, from dot A to each of the other dots.
4. Inflate the balloon more.
5. Measure the distances from dot A again.
6. Inflate the balloon again and make new measurements.
7. **Think Critically** Imagine that each dot represents a cluster of galaxies and that the balloon represents the universe. Describe the motion of the clusters in your Science Journal.

 **Preview this chapter's content and activities at** in7.msscience.com

 **Stars, Galaxies, and the Universe** Make the following Foldable to show what you know about stars, galaxies, and the universe.

STEP 1 Fold a sheet of paper from side to side. Make the front edge about 1.25 cm shorter than the back edge.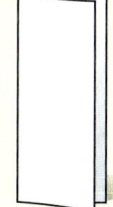

STEP 2 Turn lengthwise and fold into thirds.

STEP 3 Unfold and cut only the top layer along both folds to make three tabs.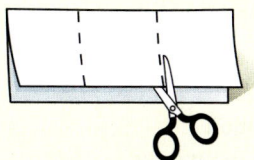

STEP 4 Label the tabs *Stars, Galaxies,* and *Universe.*

Read and Write Before you read the chapter, write what you already know about stars, galaxies, and the universe. As you read the chapter, add to or correct what you have written under the tabs.

Standard—7.1.5: Identify some important contributions to the advancement of science...that have been made by different kinds of people in different cultures at different times.

section 1
Stars

as you read

What You'll Learn
- **Explain** why some constellations are visible only during certain seasons.
- **Distinguish** between absolute magnitude and apparent magnitude.

Why It's Important
The Sun is a typical star.

Review Vocabulary
star: a large, spherical mass of gas that gives off light and other types of radiation

New Vocabulary
- constellation
- absolute magnitude
- apparent magnitude
- light-year

Constellations

It's fun to look at clouds and find ones that remind you of animals, people, or objects that you recognize. It takes more imagination to play this game with stars. Ancient Greeks, Romans, and other early cultures observed patterns of stars in the night sky called **constellations.** They imagined that the constellations represented mythological characters, animals, or familiar objects.

From Earth, a constellation looks like spots of light arranged in a particular shape against the dark night sky. **Figure 1** shows how the constellation of the mythological Greek hunter Orion appears from Earth. It also shows that the stars in a constellation often have no relationship to each other in space.

Stars in the sky can be found at specific locations within a constellation. For example, you can find the star Betelgeuse (BEE tul jooz) in the shoulder of the mighty hunter Orion. Orion's faithful companion is his dog, Canis Major. Sirius, the brightest star that is visible from the northern hemisphere, is in Canis Major.

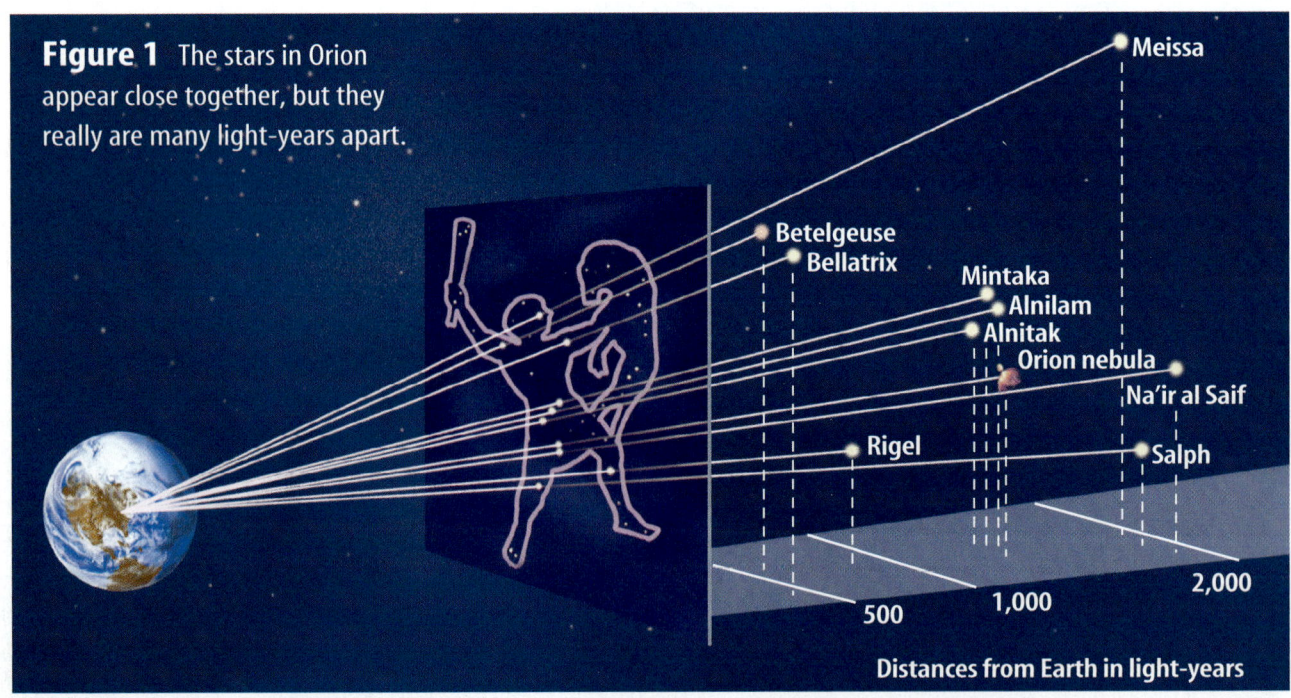

Figure 1 The stars in Orion appear close together, but they really are many light-years apart.

472 CHAPTER 16 Stars and Galaxies

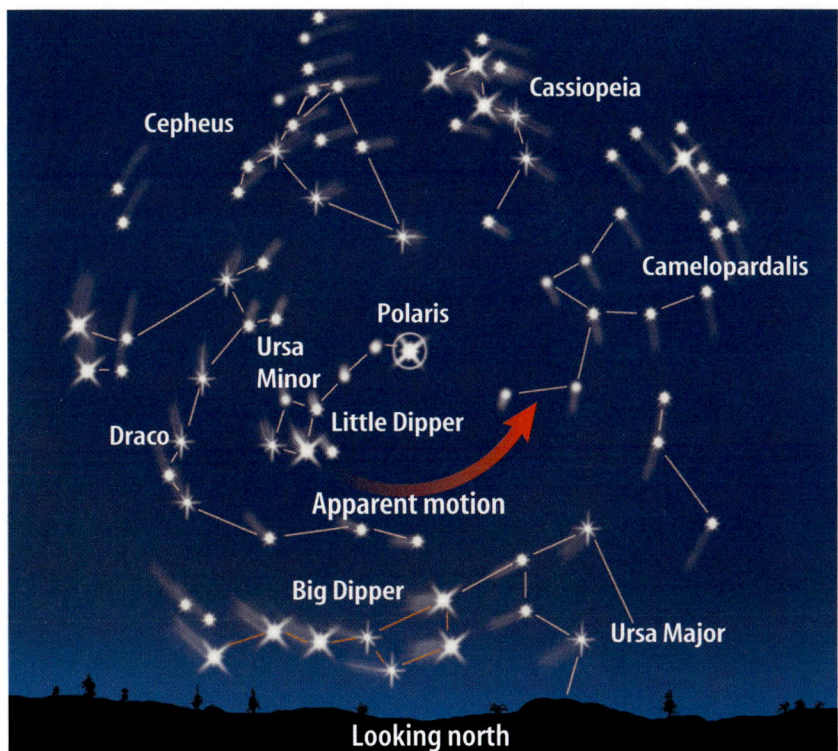

Figure 2 The Big Dipper, in red, is part of the constellation Ursa Major. It is visible year-round in the northern hemisphere. Constellations close to Polaris rotate around Polaris, which is almost directly over the north pole.

Modern Constellations Modern astronomy divides the sky into 88 constellations, many of which were named by early astronomers. You probably know some of them. Can you recognize the Big Dipper? It's part of the constellation Ursa Major, shown in **Figure 2.** Notice how the front two stars of the Big Dipper point almost directly at Polaris, which often is called the North Star. Polaris is located at the end of the Little Dipper in the constellation Ursa Minor. It is positioned almost directly over Earth's north pole.

Circumpolar Constellations As Earth rotates, Ursa Major, Ursa Minor, and other constellations in the northern sky circle around Polaris. Because of this, they are called circumpolar constellations. The constellations appear to move, as shown in **Figure 2,** because Earth is in motion. The stars appear to complete one full circle in the sky in about 24 h as Earth rotates on its axis. One circumpolar constellation that's easy to find is Cassiopeia (ka see uh PEE uh). You can look for five bright stars that form a big W or a big M in the northern sky, depending on the season.

As Earth orbits the Sun, different constellations come into view while others disappear. Because of their unique position, circumpolar constellations are visible all year long. Other constellations are not. Orion, which is visible in the winter in the northern hemisphere, can't be seen there in the summer because the daytime side of Earth is facing it.

Observing Star Patterns

Procedure
1. On a clear night, go outside after dark and study the stars. Take an adult with you.
2. Let your imagination flow to find patterns of stars that look like something familiar.
3. Draw the stars you see, note their positions, and include a drawing of what you think each star pattern resembles.

Analysis
1. Which of your constellations match those observed by your classmates?
2. How can recognizing star patterns be useful?

SECTION 1 Stars **473**

Absolute and Apparent Magnitudes

When you look at constellations, you'll notice that some stars are brighter than others. For example, Sirius looks much brighter than Rigel. Is Sirius a brighter star, or is it just closer to Earth, making it appear to be brighter? As it turns out, Sirius is 100 times closer to Earth than Rigel is. If Sirius and Rigel were the same distance from Earth, Rigel would appear much brighter in the night sky than Sirius would.

When you refer to the brightness of a star, you can refer to its absolute magnitude or its apparent magnitude. The **absolute magnitude** of a star is a measure of the amount of light it gives off. A measure of the amount of light received on Earth is the **apparent magnitude.** A star that's dim can appear bright in the sky if it's close to Earth, and a star that's bright can appear dim if it's far away. If two stars are the same distance away, what might cause one of them to be brighter than the other?

 What is the difference between absolute and apparent magnitude?

Applying Science

Are distance and brightness related?

The apparent magnitude of a star is affected by its distance from Earth. This activity will help you determine the relationship between distance and brightness.

Identifying the Problem

Luisa conducted an experiment to determine the relationship between distance and the brightness of stars. She used a meterstick, a light meter, and a lightbulb. She placed the bulb at the zero end of the meterstick, then placed the light meter at the 20-cm mark and recorded the distance and the light-meter reading in her data table. Readings are in luxes, which are units for measuring light intensity. Luisa then increased the distance from the bulb to the light meter and took more readings. By examining the data in the table, can you see a relationship between the two variables?

Effect of Distance on Light

Distance (cm)	Meter Reading (luxes)
20	4150.0
40	1037.5
60	461.1
80	259.4

Solving the Problem

1. What happened to the amount of light recorded when the distance was increased from 20 cm to 40 cm? When the distance was increased from 20 cm to 60 cm?
2. What does this indicate about the relationship between light intensity and distance? What would the light intensity be at 100 cm? Would making a graph help you visualize the relationship?

Measurement in Space

How do scientists determine the distance from Earth to nearby stars? One way is to measure parallax—the apparent shift in the position of an object when viewed from two different positions. Extend your arm and look at your thumb first with your left eye closed and then with your right eye closed, as the girl in **Figure 3A** is doing. Your thumb appears to change position with respect to the background. Now do the same experiment with your thumb closer to your face, as shown in **Figure 3B.** What do you observe? The nearer an object is to the observer, the greater its parallax is.

Astronomers can measure the parallax of relatively close stars to determine their distances from Earth. **Figure 4** shows how a close star's position appears to change. Knowing the angle that the star's position changes and the size of Earth's orbit, astronomers can calculate the distance of the star from Earth.

Because space is so vast, a special unit of measure is needed to record distances. Distances between stars and galaxies are measured in light-years. A **light-year** is the distance that light travels in one year. Light travels at 300,000 km/s, or about 9.5 trillion km in one year. The nearest star to Earth, other than the Sun, is Proxima Centauri. Proxima Centauri is a mere 4.2 light-years away, or about 40 trillion km.

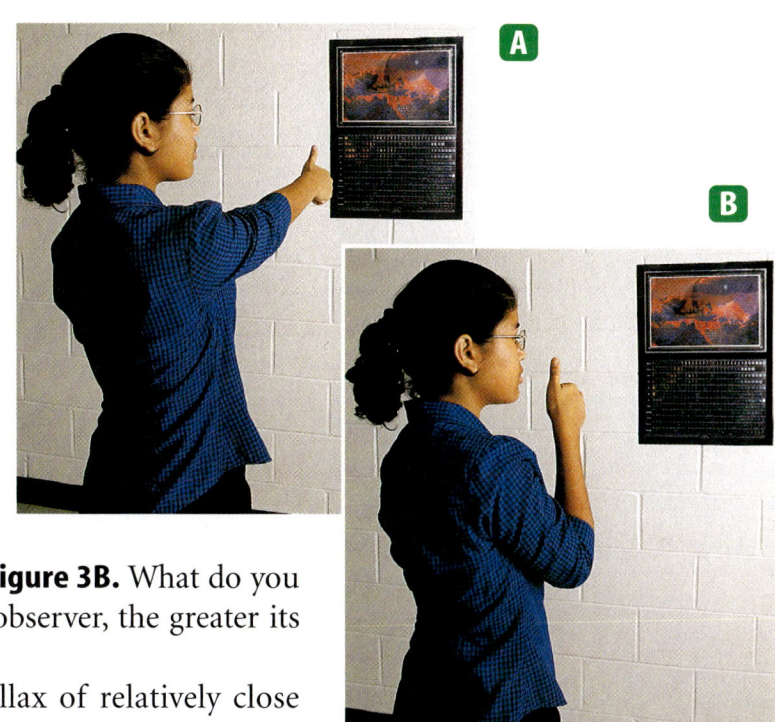

Figure 3 **A** Your thumb appears to move less against the background when it is farther away from your eyes. **B** It appears to move more when it is closer to your eyes.

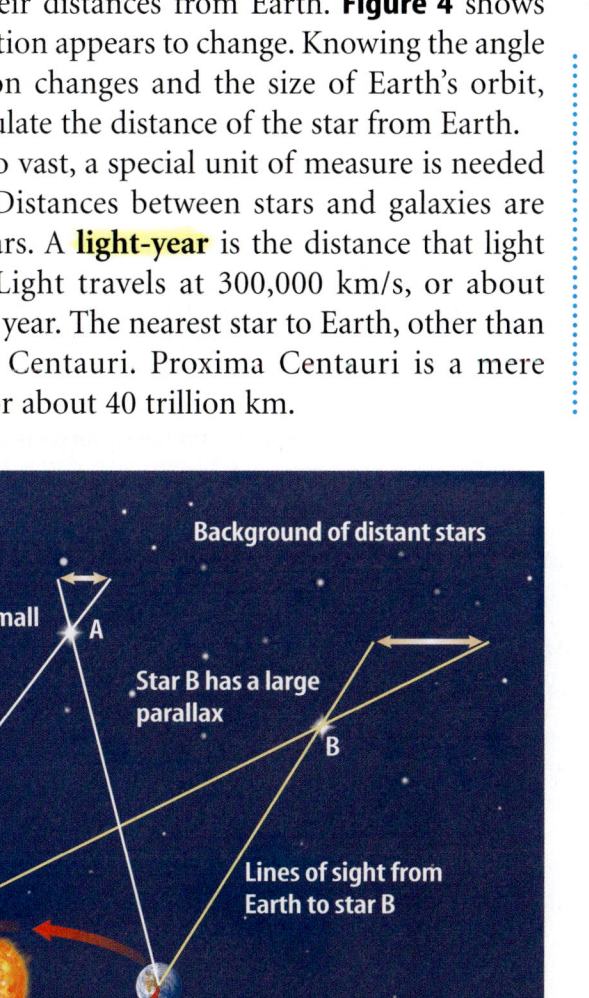

Figure 4 Parallax is determined by observing the same star when Earth is at two different points in its orbit around the Sun. The star's position relative to more distant background stars will appear to change.
Infer whether star **A** or **B** is farther from Earth.

SECTION 1 Stars **475**

Figure 5 This star spectrum was made by placing a diffraction grating over a telescope's objective lens. A diffraction grating produces a spectrum by causing interference of light waves. **Explain** what causes the lines in spectra.

Properties of Stars

The color of a star indicates its temperature. For example, hot stars are a blue-white color. A relatively cool star looks orange or red. Stars that have the same temperature as the Sun have a yellow color.

Astronomers study the composition of stars by observing their spectra. When fitted into a telescope, a spectroscope acts like a prism. It spreads light out in the rainbow band called a spectrum. When light from a star passes through a spectroscope, it breaks into its component colors. Look at the spectrum of a star in **Figure 5.** Notice the dark lines caused by elements in the star's atmosphere. Light radiated from a star passes through the star's atmosphere. As it does, elements in the atmosphere absorb some of this light. The wavelengths of visible light that are absorbed appear as dark lines in the spectrum. Each element absorbs certain wavelengths, producing a unique pattern of dark lines. Like a fingerprint, the patterns of lines can be used to identify the elements in a star's atmosphere.

section 1 review

Summary

Constellations
- Constellations are patterns of stars in the night sky.
- The stars in a constellation often have no relationship to each other in space.

Absolute and Apparent Magnitudes
- Absolute magnitude is a measure of how much light is given off by a star.
- Apparent magnitude is a measure of how much light from a star is received on Earth.

Measurement in Space
- Distances between stars are measured in light-years.

Properties of Stars
- Astronomers study the composition of stars by observing their spectra.

Self Check

1. **Describe** circumpolar constellations.
2. **Explain** why some constellations are visible only during certain seasons.
3. **Infer** how two stars could have the same apparent magnitude but different absolute magnitudes.
4. **Explain** how a star is similar to the Sun if it has the same absorption lines in its spectrum that occur in the Sun's spectrum.
5. **Think Critically** If a star's parallax angle is too small to measure, what can you conclude about the star's distance from Earth?

Applying Skills

6. **Recognize Cause and Effect** Suppose you viewed Proxima Centauri, which is 4.2 light-years from Earth, through a telescope. How old were you when the light that you see left this star?

476   CHAPTER 16   Stars and Galaxies

in7.msscience.com/self_check_quiz

section 2

Standard—7.3.2: Recognize and describe that the Sun is many thousands of times closer to Earth than any other star, allowing light from the Sun to reach Earth in a few minutes. Note that this may be compared to time spans of longer than a year for all other stars.

Also covers: 7.3.11 (Detailed standards begin on page IN8.)

The Sun

The Sun's Layers

The Sun is an ordinary star, but it's important to you. The Sun is the center of the solar system, and the closest star to Earth. Almost all of the life on Earth depends on energy from the Sun.

Notice the different layers of the Sun, shown in **Figure 6,** as you read about them. Like other stars, the Sun is an enormous ball of gas that produces energy by fusing hydrogen into helium in its core. This energy travels outward through the radiation zone and the convection zone. In the convection zone, gases circulate in giant swirls. Finally, energy passes into the Sun's atmosphere.

The Sun's Atmosphere

The lowest layer of the Sun's atmosphere and the layer from which light is given off is the **photosphere.** The photosphere often is called the surface of the Sun, although the surface is not a smooth feature. Temperatures there are about 6,000 K. Above the photosphere is the **chromosphere.** This layer extends upward about 2,000 km above the photosphere. A transition zone occurs between 2,000 km and 10,000 km above the photosphere. Above the transition zone is the **corona.** This is the largest layer of the Sun's atmosphere and extends millions of kilometers into space. Temperatures in the corona are as high as 2 million K. Charged particles continually escape from the corona and move through space as solar wind.

as you read

What You'll Learn
- **Explain** that the Sun is the closest star to Earth.
- **Describe** the structure of the Sun.
- **Describe** sunspots, prominences, and solar flares.

Why It's Important
The Sun is the source of most energy on Earth.

Review Vocabulary
cycle: a repeating sequence of events, such as the sunspot cycle

New Vocabulary
- photosphere
- chromosphere
- corona
- sunspot

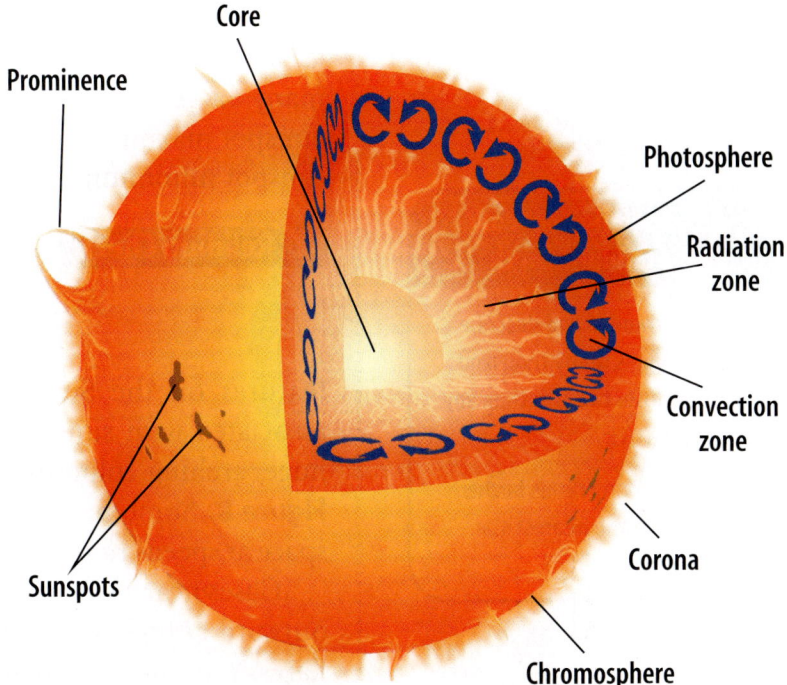

Figure 6 Energy produced in the Sun's core by fusion travels outward by radiation and convection. The Sun's atmosphere shines by the energy produced in the core.

SECTION 2 The Sun **477**

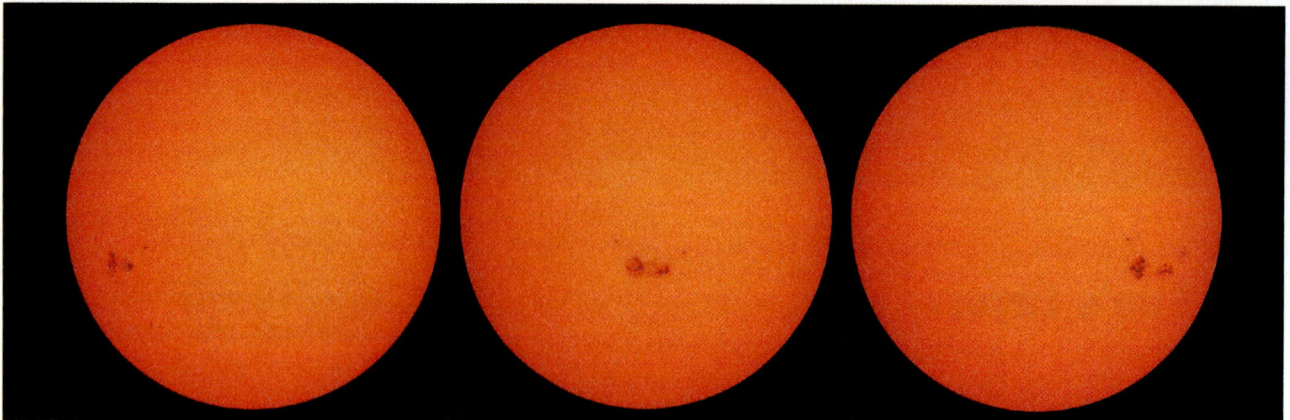

Figure 7 Sunspots are bright, but when viewed against the rest of the photosphere, they appear dark. Notice how these sunspots move as the Sun rotates.
Describe the Sun's direction of rotation.

Surface Features

From the viewpoint that you observe the Sun, its surface appears to be a smooth layer. But the Sun's surface has many features, including sunspots, prominences, flares, and CMEs.

Sunspots Areas of the Sun's surface that appear dark because they are cooler than surrounding areas are called **sunspots.** Ever since Galileo Galilei made drawings of sunspots, scientists have been studying them. Because scientists could observe the movement of individual sunspots, shown in **Figure 7,** they concluded that the Sun rotates. However, the Sun doesn't rotate as a solid body, as Earth does. It rotates faster at its equator than at its poles. Sunspots at the equator take about 25 days to complete one rotation. Near the poles, they take about 35 days.

Sunspots aren't permanent features on the Sun. They appear and disappear over a period of several days, weeks, or months. The number of sunspots increases and decreases in a fairly regular pattern called the sunspot, or solar activity, cycle. Times when many large sunspots occur are called sunspot maximums. Sunspot maximums occur about every 10 to 11 years. Periods of sunspot minimum occur in between.

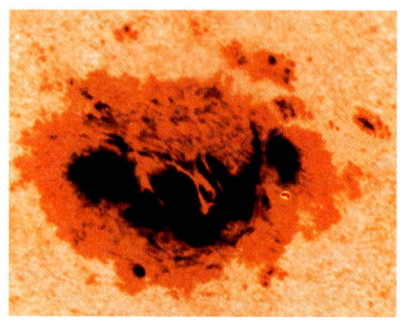

This is a close-up photo of a large sunspot.

Reading Check What is a sunspot cycle?

Prominences and Flares Sunspots are related to several features on the Sun's surface. The intense magnetic fields associated with sunspots might cause prominences, which are huge, arching columns of gas. Notice the huge prominence in **Figure 8.** Some prominences blast material from the Sun into space at speeds ranging from 600 km/s to more than 1,000 km/s.

Gases near a sunspot sometimes brighten suddenly, shooting outward at high speed. These violent eruptions are called solar flares. You can see a solar flare in **Figure 8.**

Indiana Academic Standard Check

7.3.2: Recognize and describe that the Sun is many thousands of times closer to Earth than any other star, ...

✓ How many times farther from Earth is the nearest star compared to the Sun?

CMEs Coronal mass ejections (CMEs) occur when large amounts of electrically charged gas are ejected suddenly from the Sun's corona. CMEs can occur as often as two or three times each day during a sunspot maximum.

CMEs present little danger to life on Earth, but they do have some effects. CMEs can damage satellites in orbit around Earth. They also can interfere with radio and power distribution equipment. CMEs often cause auroras. High-energy particles contained in CMEs and the solar wind are carried past Earth's magnetic field. This generates electric currents that flow toward Earth's poles. These electric currents ionize gases in Earth's atmosphere. When these ions recombine with electrons, they produce the light of an aurora, shown in **Figure 8.**

Topic: Space Weather
Visit in7.msscience.com for Web links to information about space weather and its effects.

Activity Record space weather conditions for several weeks. How does space weather affect Earth?

Figure 8 Features such as solar prominences and solar flares can reach hundreds of thousands of kilometers into space. CMEs are generated as magnetic fields above sunspot groups rearrange. CMEs can trigger events that produce auroras.

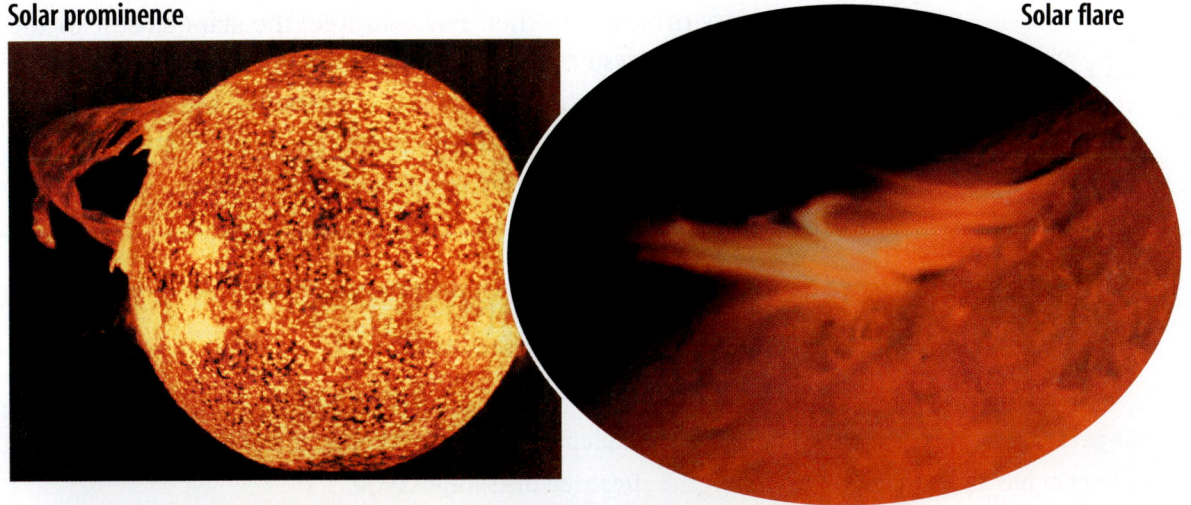

Solar prominence

Solar flare

Aurora borealis, or northern lights

SECTION 2 The Sun

The Age of the Sun

The nuclear fusion reactions in the Sun that convert hydrogen to helium have been going on for about five billion years. As these reactions occur, the Sun emits energy. As a result, the Sun continually loses energy as nuclear energy in the Sun's interior is converted to other forms of energy that are radiated into space. However, it is estimated that the Sun still has enough hydrogen to keep these nuclear reactions going for another five billion years.

The Sun in Space

In some ways the Sun is an average star. Compared to other stars, its mass, absolute magnitude, and age are about average. However, the Sun is unusual in one way—it is relatively far from any other stars. As a result, the Sun is much closer to Earth than any other star. The next closest star, Proxima Centauri, is about 270,000 times farther from Earth than the Sun. Light from this star takes over four years to reach Earth while light from the Sun reaches Earth in only about 8 min.

Unlike the Sun, most stars are part of a system in which two or more stars orbit each other. For example, the stars closest to the Sun form a star system in which three stars orbit each other. Larger groups of stars sometimes form star clusters that are held together by the gravitational attraction between the stars. **Figure 9** shows the double star cluster in the constellation Perseus.

Figure 9 Most stars originally formed in large clusters containing hundreds, or even thousands, of stars.
Draw and label *a sketch of the double cluster.*

---

section 2 review

Summary

The Sun's Layers
- The Sun's interior has layers that include the core, radiation zone, and convection zone.

The Sun's Atmosphere
- The Sun's atmosphere includes the photosphere, chromosphere, and corona.

Surface Features
- The number of sunspots on the Sun varies in a 10- to 11-year cycle.
- Auroras occur when charged particles from the Sun interact with Earth's magnetic field.

The Sun—An Average Star
- The Sun is an average star, but it is much closer to Earth than any other star.

Self Check

1. **Explain** why the Sun is important for life on Earth.
2. **Describe** the sunspot cycle.
3. **Explain** why sunspots appear dark.
4. **Explain** why the Sun, which is an average star, appears so much brighter from Earth than other stars do.
5. **Think Critically** When a CME occurs on the Sun, it takes a couple of days for effects to be noticed on Earth. Explain.

Applying Skills

6. **Communicate** Make a sketch that shows the Sun's layers in your Science Journal. Write a short description of each layer.

in7.msscience.com/self_check_quiz

480 CHAPTER 16 Stars and Galaxies

Sunspots

Sunspots can be observed moving across the face of the Sun as it rotates. Measure the movement of sunspots, and use your data to determine the Sun's period of rotation.

Real-World Question

Can sunspot motion be used to determine the Sun's period of rotation?

Goals

- **Observe** sunspots and estimate their size.
- **Estimate** the rate at which sunspots move across the face of the Sun.

Materials

several books
piece of cardboard
drawing paper
refracting telescope
clipboard
small tripod
scissors

Safety Precautions

WARNING: *Handle scissors with care.*

Procedure

1. Find a location where the Sun can be viewed at the same time of day for a minimum of five days. **WARNING:** *Do not look directly at the Sun. Do not look through the telescope at the Sun. You could damage your eyes.*
2. If the telescope has a small finder scope attached, remove it or keep it covered.
3. Set up the telescope with the eyepiece facing away from the Sun, as shown. Align the telescope so that the shadow it casts on the ground is the smallest size possible. Cut and attach the cardboard as shown in the photo.
4. Use books to prop the clipboard upright. Point the eyepiece at the drawing paper.
5. Move the clipboard back and forth until you have the largest image of the Sun on the paper. Adjust the telescope to form a clear image. Trace the outline of the Sun on the paper.
6. Trace any sunspots that appear as dark areas on the Sun's image. Repeat this step at the same time each day for a week.
7. Using the Sun's diameter (approximately 1,390,000 km), estimate the size of the largest sunspots that you observed.
8. **Calculate** how many kilometers the sunspots move each day.
9. **Predict** how many days it will take for the same group of sunspots to return to the same position in which they appeared on day 1.

Conclude and Apply

1. What was the estimated size and rate of motion of the largest sunspots?
2. **Infer** how sunspots can be used to determine that the Sun's surface is not solid like Earth's surface.

Communicating Your Data

Compare your conclusions with those of other students in your class. **For more help, refer to the Science Skill Handbook.**

Standard—7.3.11: Explain that the Sun loses energy by emitting light. Note that only a tiny fraction of that light reaches Earth. Understand that the Sun's energy arrives as light with a wide range of wavelengths, consisting of visible light, infrared, and ultraviolet radiation.

Also covers: 7.1.5 (Detailed standards begin on page IN8.)

section 3
Evolution of Stars

as you read

What You'll Learn
- **Describe** how stars are classified.
- **Compare** the Sun to other types of stars on the H-R diagram.
- **Describe** how stars evolve.

Why It's Important
Earth and your body contain elements that were made in stars.

Review Vocabulary
gravity: an attractive force between objects that have mass

New Vocabulary
- nebula
- giant
- white dwarf
- supergiant
- neutron star
- black hole

Classifying Stars

When you look at the night sky, all stars might appear to be similar, but they are quite different. Like people, they vary in age and size, but stars also vary in temperature and brightness.

In the early 1900s, Ejnar Hertzsprung and Henry Russell made some important observations. They noticed that, in general, stars with higher temperatures also have brighter absolute magnitudes.

Hertzsprung and Russell developed a graph, shown in **Figure 10,** to show this relationship. They placed temperatures across the bottom and absolute magnitudes up one side. A graph that shows the relationship of a star's temperature to its absolute magnitude is called a Hertzsprung-Russell (H-R) diagram.

The Main Sequence As you can see, stars seem to fit into specific areas of the graph. Most stars fit into a diagonal band that runs from the upper left to the lower right of the graph. This band, called the main sequence, contains hot, blue, bright stars in the upper left and cool, red, dim stars in the lower right. Yellow main sequence stars, like the Sun, fall in between.

Figure 10 The relationships among a star's color, temperature, and brightness are shown in this H-R diagram. Stars in the upper left are hot, bright stars, and stars in the lower right are cool, dim stars.
Classify Which type of star shown in the diagram is the hottest, dimmest star?

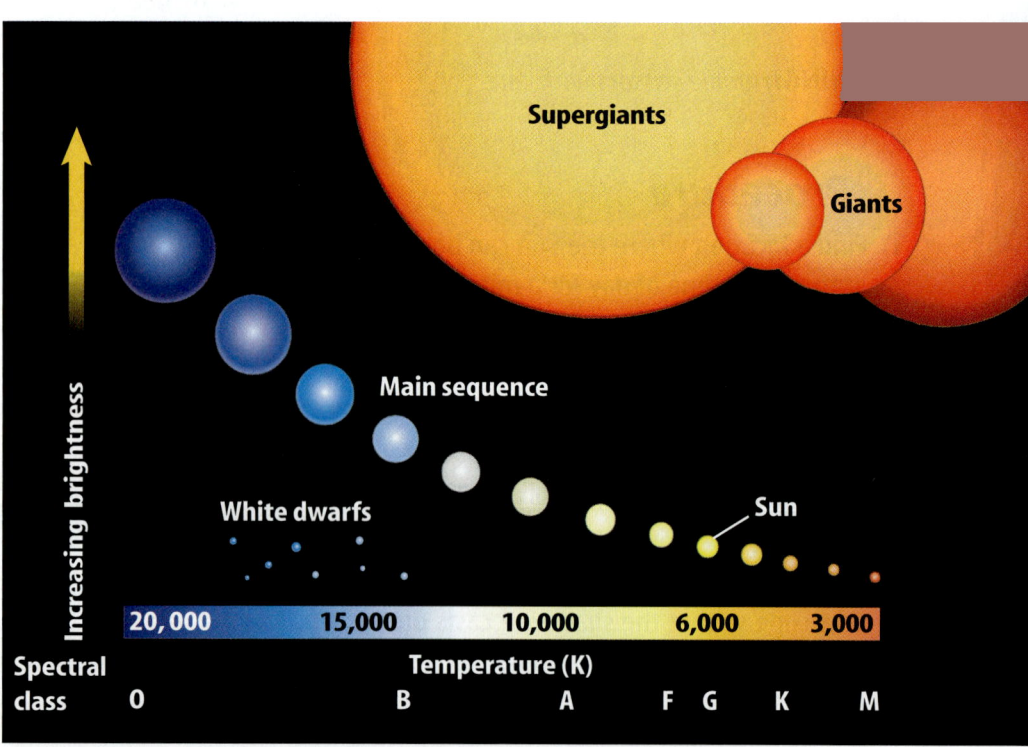

482 CHAPTER 16 Stars and Galaxies

Dwarfs and Giants About 90 percent of all stars are main sequence stars. Most of these are small, red stars found in the lower right of the H-R diagram. Among main sequence stars, the hottest stars generate the most light and the coolest ones generate the least. What about the ten percent of stars that are not part of the main sequence? Some of these stars are hot but not bright. These small stars are located on the lower left of the H-R diagram and are called white dwarfs. Other stars are extremely bright but not hot. These large stars on the upper right of the H-R diagram are called giants, or red giants, because they are usually red in color. The largest giants are called supergiants. **Figure 11** shows the supergiant, Antares—a star 300 times the Sun's diameter—in the constellation Scorpius. It is more than 11,000 times as bright as the Sun.

 *What kinds of stars are on the main sequence?*

How do stars shine?

For centuries, people were puzzled by the questions of what stars were made of and how they produced light. Many people had estimated that Earth was only a few thousand years old. The Sun could have been made of coal and shined for that long. However, when people realized that Earth was much older, they wondered what material possibly could burn for so many years. Early in the twentieth century, scientists began to understand the process that keeps stars shining for billions of years.

Generating Energy In the 1930s, scientists discovered reactions between the nuclei of atoms. They hypothesized that temperatures in the center of the Sun must be high enough to cause hydrogen to fuse to make helium. This nuclear fusion reaction releases tremendous amounts of energy. Much of this energy is emitted as different wavelengths of light, including visible, infrared, and ultraviolet light. Only a tiny fraction of this light comes to Earth. During the nuclear fusion reaction, four hydrogen nuclei combine to create one helium nucleus. The mass of one helium nucleus is less than the mass of four hydrogen nuclei, so some mass is lost in the reaction.

Years earlier, in 1905, Albert Einstein had proposed a theory stating that mass can be converted into energy. This was stated as the famous equation $E = mc^2$. In this equation, E is the energy produced, m is the mass, and c is the speed of light. A small amount of mass is converted to a large amount of energy when hydrogen atoms fuse to form a helium atom.

Figure 11 Antares is a bright supergiant located 400 light-years from Earth. Although its temperature is only about 3,500 K, it is the 16th brightest star in the sky.

Indiana Academic Standard Check

7.3.11: Explain that the Sun loses energy by emitting light ... consisting of visible light, infrared, and ultraviolet radiation.

 What type of reaction in the Sun converts a small amount of mass into a large amount of energy?

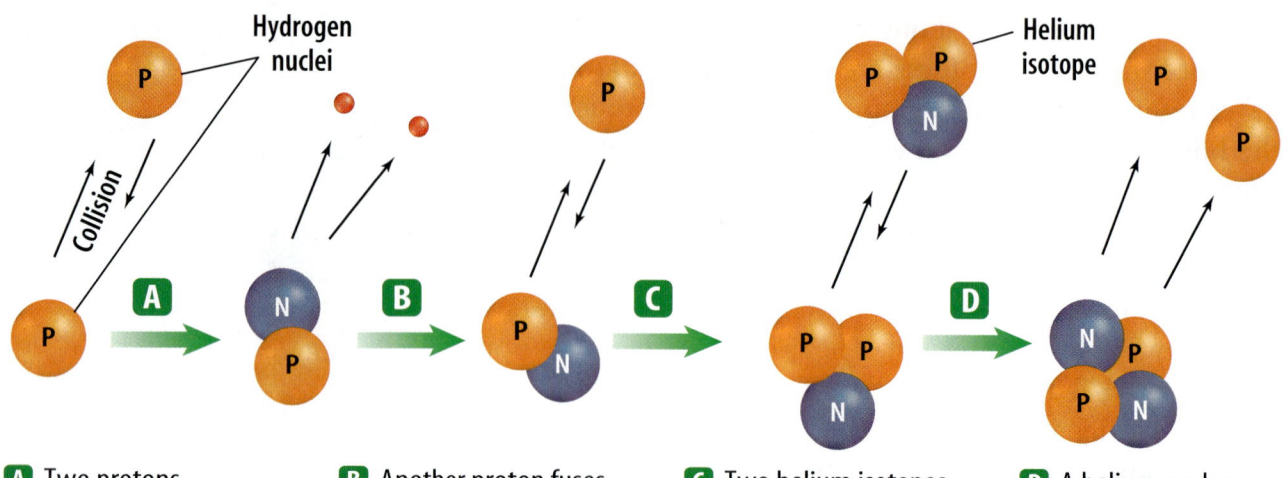

A Two protons (hydrogen nuclei) collide. One proton decays to a neutron, releasing subatomic particles and some energy.

B Another proton fuses with a proton and neutron to form an isotope of helium. Energy is given off again.

C Two helium isotopes collide with enough energy to fuse.

D A helium nucleus (two protons and two neutrons) forms as two protons break away. During the process, still more energy is released.

Figure 12 Fusion of hydrogen into helium occurs in a star's core. **Infer** why nuclear reactions occur only in the core of a star.

Fusion Shown in **Figure 12,** fusion occurs in the cores of stars. Only in the core are temperatures high enough to cause atoms to fuse. Normally, they would repel each other, but in the core of a star where temperatures can exceed 15,000,000 K, atoms can move so fast that some of them fuse upon colliding.

Evolution of Stars

The H-R diagram explained a lot about stars. However, it also led to more questions. Many wondered why some stars didn't fit in the main sequence group and what happened when a star depleted its supply of hydrogen fuel. Today, scientists have theories about how stars evolve, what makes them different from one another, and what happens when they die. **Figure 13** illustrates the lives of different types of stars.

When hydrogen fuel is depleted, a star loses its main sequence status. This can take less than 1 million years for the brightest stars to many billions of years for the dimmest stars. The Sun has a main sequence life span of about 10 billion years. Half of its life span is still in the future.

Nebula Stars begin as a large cloud of gas and dust called a **nebula.** As the particles of gas and dust exert a gravitational force on each other, the nebula begins to contract. Gravitational forces cause instability within the nebula. The nebula can break apart into smaller and smaller pieces. Each piece eventually might collapse to form a star.

Topic: Evolution of Stars
Visit in7.msscience.com for Web links to information about the evolution of stars.

Activity Make a three-circle Venn diagram to compare and contrast white dwarfs, neutron stars, and black holes.

484 CHAPTER 16 Stars and Galaxies

A Star Is Born As the particles in the smaller pieces of nebula move closer together, the temperatures in each nebula piece increase. When the temperature inside the core of a nebula piece reaches 10 million K, fusion begins. The energy released radiates outward through the condensing ball of gas. As the energy radiates into space, stars are born.

 *How are stars born?*

Main Sequence to Giant Stars In the newly formed star, the heat from fusion causes pressure to increase. This pressure balances the attraction due to gravity. The star becomes a main sequence star. It continues to use its hydrogen fuel.

When hydrogen in the core of the star is depleted, a balance no longer exists between pressure and gravity. The core contracts, and temperatures inside the star increase. This causes the outer layers of the star to expand and cool. In this late stage of its life cycle, a star is called a **giant**.

After the core temperature reaches 100 million K, helium nuclei fuse to form carbon in the giant's core. By this time, the star has expanded to an enormous size, and its outer layers are much cooler than they were when it was a main sequence star. In about 5 billion years, the Sun will become a giant.

White Dwarfs After the star's core uses much of its helium, it contracts even more and its outer layers escape into space. This leaves behind the hot, dense core. At this stage in a star's evolution, it becomes a **white dwarf**. A white dwarf is about the size of Earth. Eventually, the white dwarf will cool and stop giving off light.

White Dwarf Matter The matter in white dwarf stars is more than 500,000 times as dense as the matter in Earth. In white dwarf matter, there are free electrons and atomic nuclei. The resistance of the electrons to pack together more provides pressure that keeps the star from collapsing. This state of matter is called electron degeneracy.

Figure 13 The life of a star depends on its mass. Massive stars eventually become neutron stars or black holes.
Explain *what happens to stars that are the size of the Sun.*

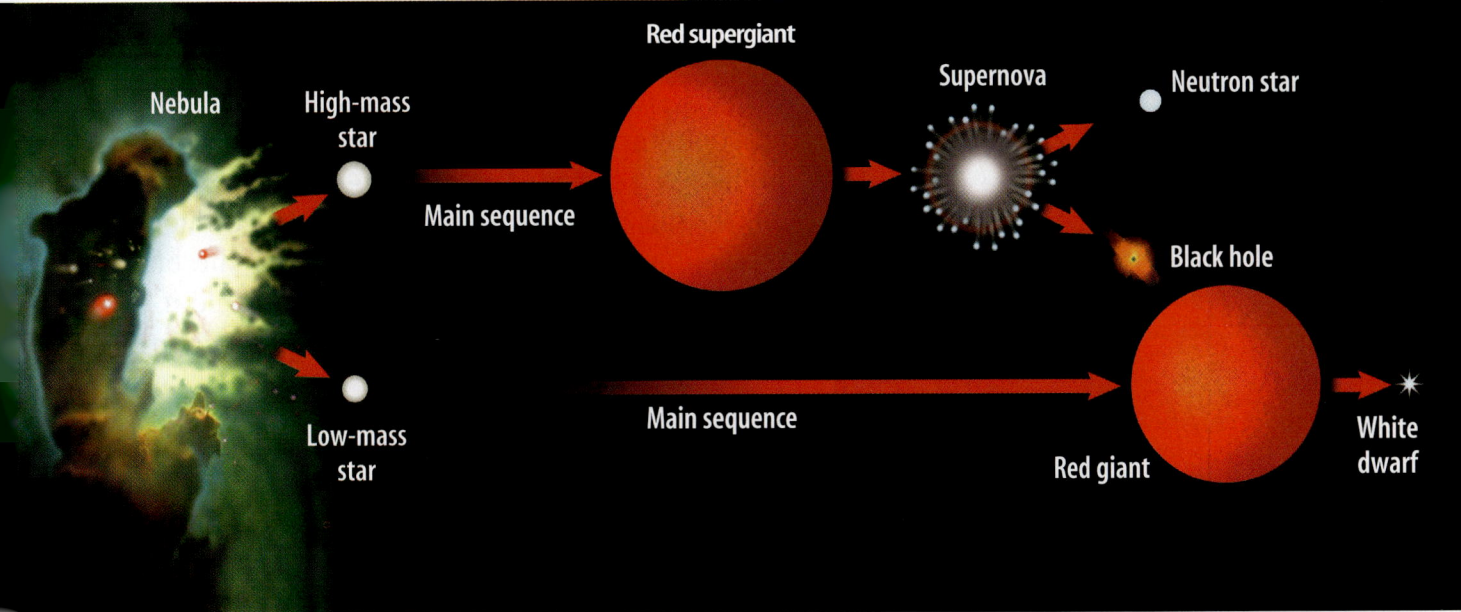

386 Supernova In 386 A.D., Chinese observers described a new star—a supernova—in the night sky. More recently, astronomers using the *Chandra X-ray Observatory* found evidence of a spinning neutron star, called a pulsar, in exactly the same location. Because of the Chinese account, astronomers better understand how neutron stars form and evolve.

Supergiants and Supernovas In stars that are more than about eight times more massive than the Sun, the stages of evolution occur more quickly and more violently. Look back at **Figure 13**. In massive stars, the core heats up to much higher temperatures. Heavier and heavier elements form by fusion, and the star expands into a **supergiant**. Eventually, iron forms in the core. Because of iron's atomic structure, it cannot release energy through fusion. The core collapses violently, and a shock wave travels outward through the star. The outer portion of the star explodes, producing a supernova. A supernova can be millions of times brighter than the original star was.

Neutron Stars If the collapsed core of a supernova is between about 1.4 and 3 times as massive as the Sun, it will shrink to approximately 20 km in diameter. Only neutrons can exist in the dense core, and it becomes a **neutron star.** Neutron stars are so dense that a teaspoonful would weigh more than 600 million metric tons in Earth's gravity. As dense as neutron stars are, they can contract only so far because the neutrons resist the inward pull of gravity.

Black Holes If the remaining dense core from a supernova is more than about three times more massive than the Sun, probably nothing can stop the core's collapse. Under these conditions, all of the core's mass collapses to a point. The gravity near this mass is so strong that nothing can escape from it, not even light. Because light cannot escape, the region is called a **black hole.** If you could shine a flashlight on a black hole, the light simply would disappear into it.

Reading Check *What is a black hole?*

Black holes, however, are not like giant vacuum cleaners, sucking in distant objects. A black hole has an event horizon, which is a region inside of which nothing can escape. If something—including light—crosses the event horizon, it will be pulled into the black hole. Beyond the event horizon, the black hole's gravity pulls on objects just as it would if the mass had not collapsed. Stars and planets can orbit around a black hole.

The photograph in **Figure 14** was taken by the *Hubble Space Telescope.* It shows a jet of gas streaming out of the center of galaxy M87. This jet of gas formed as matter flowed toward a black hole, and some of the gas was ejected along the polar axis.

Figure 14 The black hole at the center of galaxy M87 pulls matter into it at extremely high velocities. Some matter is ejected to produce a jet of gas that streams away from the center of the galaxy at nearly light speed.

Recycling Matter A star begins its life as a nebula, such as the one shown in **Figure 15.** Where does the matter in a nebula come from? Nebulas form partly from the matter that was once in other stars. A star ejects enormous amounts of matter during its lifetime. Some of this matter is incorporated into nebulas, which can evolve to form new stars. The matter in stars is recycled many times.

What about the matter created in the cores of stars and during supernova explosions? Are elements such as carbon and iron also recycled? These elements can become parts of new stars. In fact, spectrographs have shown that the Sun contains some carbon, iron, and other heavier elements. Because the Sun is an average, main sequence star, it is too young and its mass is too small to have formed these elements itself. The Sun condensed from material that was created in stars that died many billions of years ago.

Some elements condense to form planets and other bodies rather than stars. In fact, your body contains many atoms that were fused in the cores of ancient stars. Evidence suggests that the first stars formed from hydrogen and helium and that all the other elements have formed in the cores of stars or as stars explode.

Figure 15 Stars are forming in the Orion Nebula and other similar nebulae.
Describe a star-forming nebula.

section 3 review

Summary

Classifying Stars
- Most stars plot on the main sequence of an H-R diagram.
- As stars near the end of their lives, they move off of the main sequence.

How do stars shine?
- Stars shine because of a process called fusion.
- During fusion, nuclei of a lighter element merge to form a heavier element.

Evolution of Stars
- Stars form in regions of gas and dust called nebulae.
- Stars evolve differently depending on how massive they are.

Self Check

1. **Explain** how the Sun is different from other stars on the main sequence. How is it different from a giant star? How is it different from a white dwarf?
2. **Describe** how stars release energy.
3. **Outline** the past and probable future of the Sun.
4. **Define** a black hole.
5. **Think Critically** How can white dwarf stars be both hot and dim?

Applying Math

6. **Convert Units** A neutron star has a diameter of 20 km. One kilometer equals 0.62 miles. What is the neutron star's diameter in miles?

Standard—7.3.1: Recognize and describe that the Sun is a medium-sized star located near the edge of a disk-shaped galaxy of stars and that the universe contains many billions of galaxies and each galaxy contains many billions of stars.

section 4

Galaxies and the Universe

as you read

What You'll Learn
- **Describe** the Sun's position in the Milky Way Galaxy.
- **Explain** that the same natural laws that apply to our solar system also apply in other galaxies.

Why It's Important
Studying the universe could determine whether life exists elsewhere.

Review Vocabulary
universe: the space that contains all known matter and energy

New Vocabulary
- galaxy
- big bang theory

Galaxies

If you enjoy science fiction, you might have read about explorers traveling through the galaxy. On their way, they visit planets around other stars and encounter strange alien beings. Although this type of space exploration is futuristic, it is possible to explore galaxies today. Using a variety of telescopes, much is being learned about the Milky Way and other galaxies.

A **galaxy** is a large group of stars, gas, and dust held together by gravity. Earth and the solar system are in a galaxy called the Milky Way. It might contain as many as one trillion stars. The universe contains many billions of galaxies. Most of these galaxies contain billions of stars. Some, like the Milky Way, might contain a trillion stars or more. Galaxies are separated by huge distances—often millions of light-years.

In the same way that stars are grouped together within galaxies, galaxies are grouped into clusters. The cluster that the Milky Way belongs to is called the Local Group. It contains about 45 galaxies of various sizes and types. The three major types of galaxies are spiral, elliptical, and irregular.

Spiral Galaxies Spiral galaxies are galaxies that have spiral arms that wind outward from the center. The arms consist of bright stars, dust, and gas. The Milky Way Galaxy, shown in **Figure 16,** is a spiral galaxy. The Sun and the rest of the solar system are located near the outer edge of the Milky Way Galaxy.

Spiral galaxies can be normal or barred. Arms in a normal spiral start close to the center of the galaxy. Barred spirals have spiral arms extending from a large bar of stars and gas that passes through the center of the galaxy.

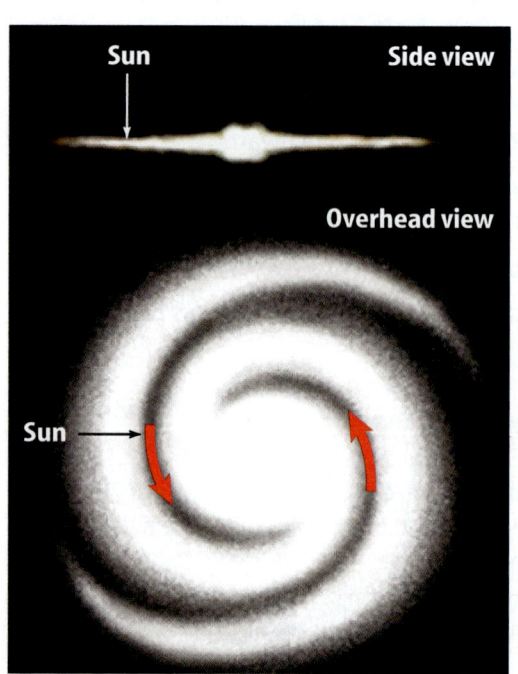

Figure 16 This illustration shows a side view and an overhead view of the Milky Way.
Describe where the Sun is in the Milky Way.

488 CHAPTER 16 Stars and Galaxies

Elliptical Galaxies A common type of galaxy is the elliptical galaxy. **Figure 17** shows an elliptical galaxy in the constellation Andromeda. These galaxies are shaped like large, three-dimensional ellipses. Many are football shaped, but others are round. Some elliptical galaxies are small, while others are so large that several galaxies the size of the Milky Way would fit inside one of them.

Irregular Galaxies The third type—an irregular galaxy—includes most of those galaxies that don't fit into the other categories. Irregular galaxies have many different shapes. They are smaller than the other types of galaxies. Two irregular galaxies called the Clouds of Magellan orbit the Milky Way. The Large Magellanic Cloud is shown in **Figure 18**.

 *How do the three different types of galaxies differ?*

Figure 17 This photo shows an example of an elliptical galaxy. **Identify** *the two other types of galaxies.*

The Milky Way Galaxy

The Milky Way might contain one trillion stars. The visible disk of stars shown in **Figure 16** is about 100,000 light-years across. Find the location of the Sun. Notice that it is located about 26,000 light-years from the galaxy's center in one of the spiral arms. In the galaxy, all stars orbit around a central region, or core. It takes about 225 million years for the Sun to orbit the center of the Milky Way.

The Milky Way often is classified as a normal spiral galaxy. However, recent evidence suggests that it might be a barred spiral. It is difficult to know for sure because astronomers have limited data about how the galaxy looks from the outside.

You can't see the shape of the Milky Way because you are located within one of its spiral arms. You can, however, see the Milky Way stretching across the sky as a misty band of faint light. You can see the brightest part of the Milky Way if you look low in the southern sky on a moonless summer night. All the stars you can see in the night sky belong to the Milky Way.

Like many other galaxies, the Milky Way has a supermassive black hole at its center. This black hole might be more than 2.5 million times as massive as the Sun. Evidence for the existence of the black hole comes from observing the orbit of a star near the galaxy's center. Additional evidence includes X-ray emissions detected by the *Chandra X-ray Observatory*. X rays are produced when matter spirals into a black hole.

Figure 18 The Large Magellanic Cloud is an irregular galaxy. It's a member of the Local Group, and it orbits the Milky Way.

Mini LAB

Measuring Distance in Space

Procedure
1. On a large sheet of **paper**, draw an overhead view of the Milky Way. If necessary, refer to **Figure 16.** Choose a scale to show distance in light-years.
2. Mark the approximate location of the solar system, which is about two-thirds of the way out on one of the spiral arms.
3. Now, draw a side view of the Milky Way Galaxy. Mark the position of the solar system.

Analysis
1. What scale did you use to represent distance on your model of the Milky Way?
2. The Andromeda Galaxy is about 2.9 million light-years from Earth. What scale distance would this represent?

Origin of the Universe

People long have wondered how the universe formed. Several models of its origin have been proposed. One model is the steady state theory. It suggests that the universe always has been the same as it is now. The universe always existed and always will. As the universe expands, new matter is created to keep the overall density of the universe the same or in a steady state. However, evidence indicates that the universe was much different in the past.

A second idea is called the oscillating model. In this model, the universe began with expansion. Over time, the expansion slowed and the universe contracted. Then the process began again, oscillating back and forth. Some scientists still hypothesize that the universe expands and contracts in a cycle.

A third model of how the universe formed is called the big bang theory. The universe started with a big bang and has been expanding ever since. This theory will be described later.

Expansion of the Universe

What does it sound like when a train is blowing its whistle while it travels past you? The whistle has a higher pitch as the train approaches you. Then the whistle seems to drop in pitch as the train moves away. This effect is called the Doppler shift. The Doppler shift occurs with light as well as with sound. **Figure 19** shows how the Doppler shift causes changes in the light coming from distant stars and galaxies. If a star is moving toward Earth, its wavelengths of light are compressed. If a star is moving away from Earth, its wavelengths of light are stretched.

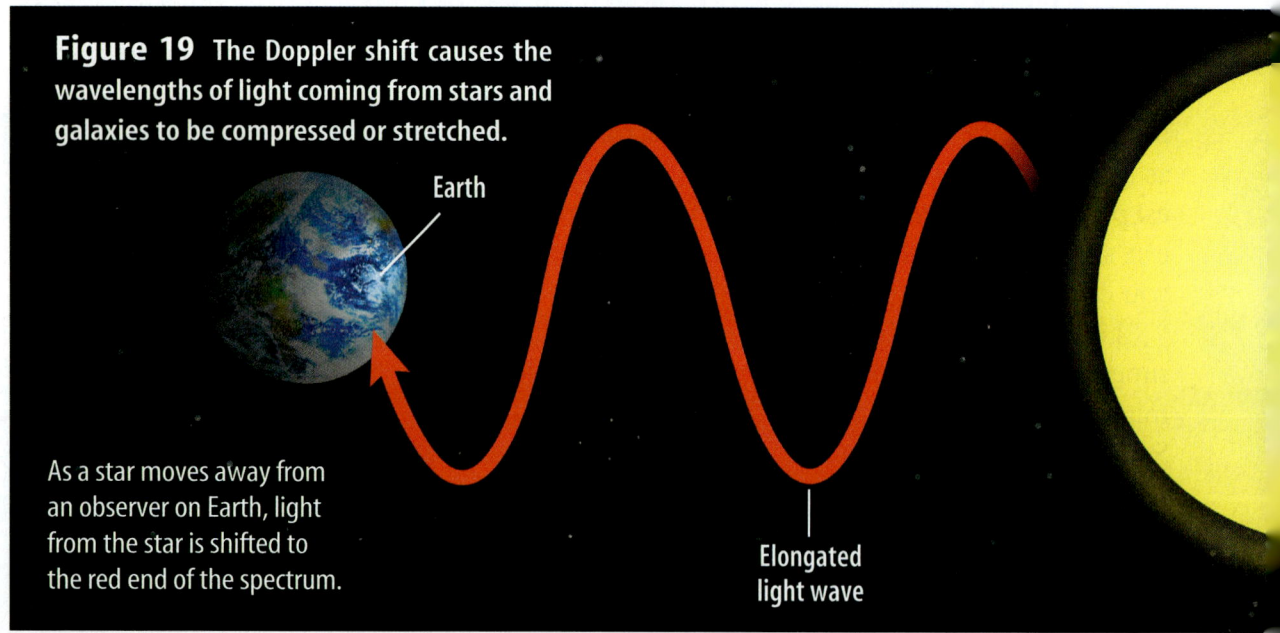

Figure 19 The Doppler shift causes the wavelengths of light coming from stars and galaxies to be compressed or stretched.

As a star moves away from an observer on Earth, light from the star is shifted to the red end of the spectrum.

490 CHAPTER 16 Stars and Galaxies

The Doppler Shift Look at the spectrum of a star in **Figure 20A**. Note the position of the dark lines. How do they compare with the lines in **Figures 20B** and **20C**? They have shifted in position. What caused this shift? As you just read, when a star is moving toward Earth, its wavelengths of light are compressed, just as the sound waves from the train's whistle are. This causes the dark lines in the spectrum to shift toward the blue-violet end of the spectrum. A red shift in the spectrum occurs when a star is moving away from Earth. In a red shift, the dark lines shift toward the red end of the spectrum.

Red Shift In 1929, Edwin Hubble published an interesting fact about the light coming from most galaxies. When a spectrograph is used to study light from galaxies beyond the Local Group, a red shift occurs in the light. What does this red shift tell you about the universe?

Because all galaxies beyond the Local Group show a red shift in their spectra, they must be moving away from Earth. If all galaxies outside the Local Group are moving away from Earth, then the entire universe must be expanding. Remember the Launch Lab at the beginning of the chapter? The dots on the balloon moved apart as the model universe expanded. Regardless of which dot you picked, all the other dots moved away from it. In a similar way, galaxies beyond the Local Group are moving away from Earth.

Figure 20 **A** This spectrum shows dark absorption lines. **B** The dark lines shift toward the blue-violet end for a star moving toward Earth. **C** The lines shift toward the red end for a star moving away from Earth.

Indiana Academic Standard Check

7.3.1: Recognize and describe that . . . each galaxy contains many billions of stars.

✓ In which galaxy is the Sun located?

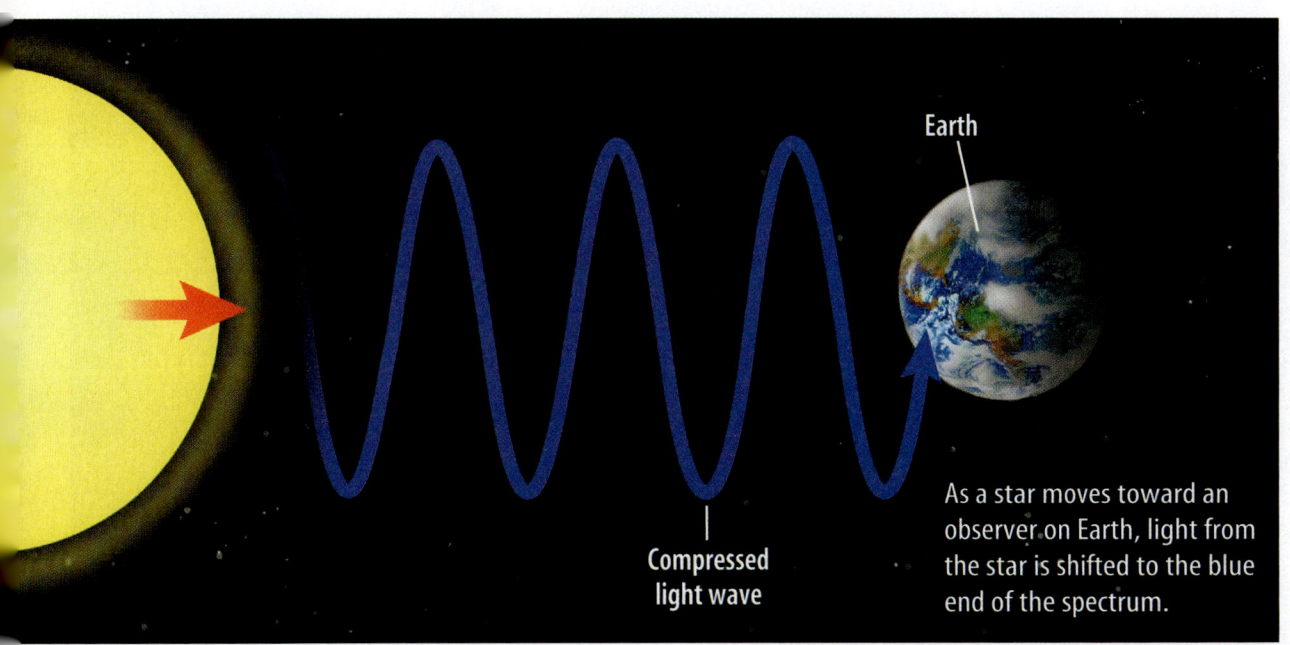

Compressed light wave

As a star moves toward an observer on Earth, light from the star is shifted to the blue end of the spectrum.

SECTION 4 Galaxies and the Universe **491**

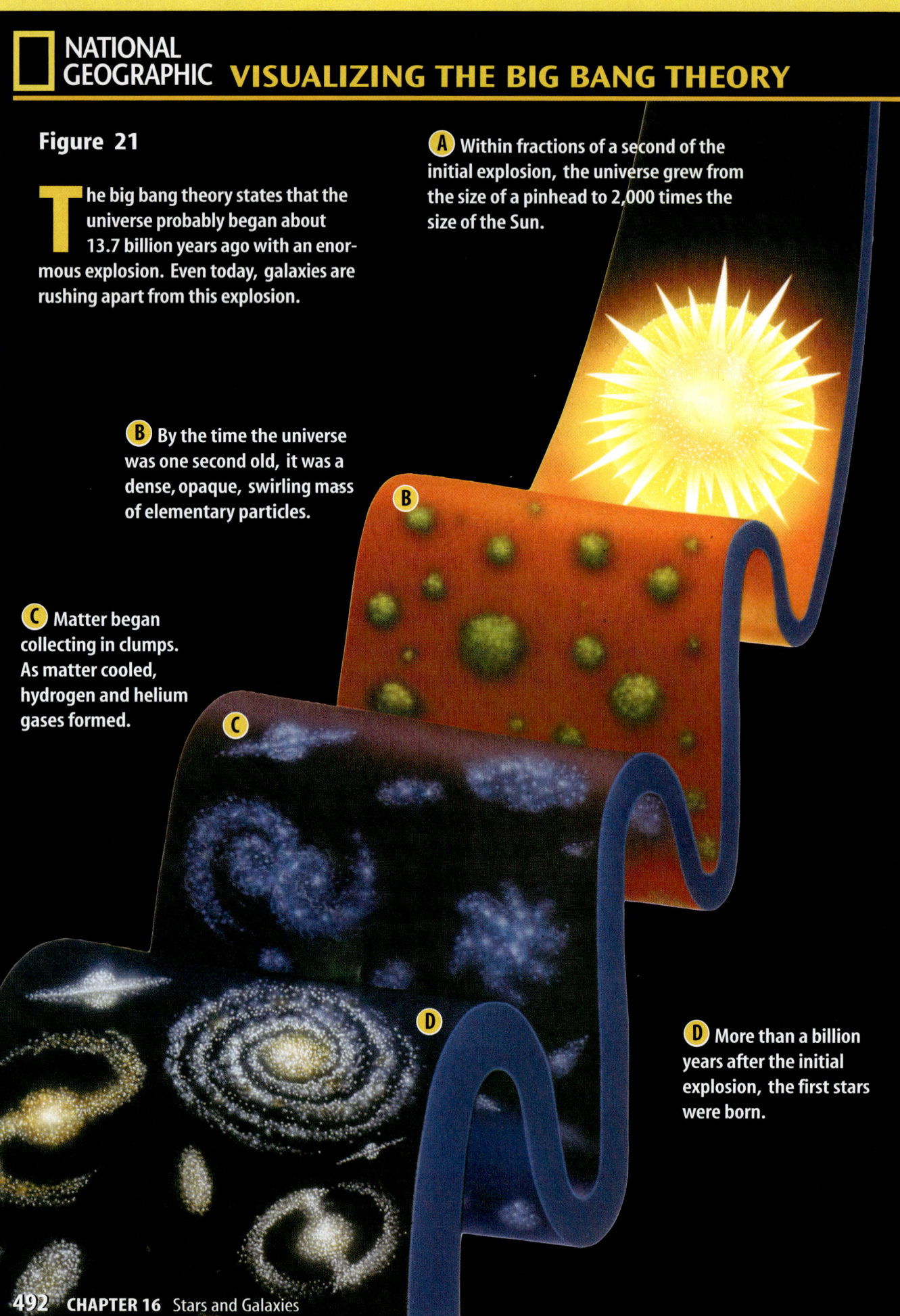

NATIONAL GEOGRAPHIC VISUALIZING THE BIG BANG THEORY

Figure 21

The big bang theory states that the universe probably began about 13.7 billion years ago with an enormous explosion. Even today, galaxies are rushing apart from this explosion.

A Within fractions of a second of the initial explosion, the universe grew from the size of a pinhead to 2,000 times the size of the Sun.

B By the time the universe was one second old, it was a dense, opaque, swirling mass of elementary particles.

C Matter began collecting in clumps. As matter cooled, hydrogen and helium gases formed.

D More than a billion years after the initial explosion, the first stars were born.

492 CHAPTER 16 Stars and Galaxies

The Big Bang Theory

When scientists determined that the universe was expanding, they developed a theory to explain their observations. The leading theory about the formation of the universe is called the **big bang theory**. **Figure 21** illustrates the big bang theory. According to this theory, approximately 13.7 billion years ago, the universe began with an enormous explosion. The entire universe began to expand everywhere at the same time.

Looking Back in Time The time-exposure photograph shown in **Figure 22** was taken by the *Hubble Space Telescope*. It shows more than 1,500 galaxies at distances of more than 10 billion light-years. These galaxies could date back to when the universe was no more than 1 billion years old. The galaxies are in various stages of development. One astronomer says that humans might be looking back to a time when the Milky Way was forming.

Whether the universe will expand forever or stop expanding is still unknown. If enough matter exists, gravity might halt the expansion, and the universe will contract until everything comes to a single point. However, studies of distant supernovae indicate that an energy, called dark energy, is causing the universe to expand faster. Scientists are trying to understand how dark energy might affect the fate of the universe.

Figure 22 The light from the galaxies in this photo mosaic took billions of years to reach Earth.

section 4 review

Summary

Galaxies
- The three main types of galaxies are spiral, elliptical, and irregular.

The Milky Way Galaxy
- The Milky Way is a spiral galaxy and the Sun is about 26,000 light-years from its center.

Origin of the Universe
- Theories about how the universe formed include the steady state theory, the oscillating universe theory, and the big bang theory.

The Big Bang Theory
- This theory states that the universe began with an explosion about 13.7 billion years ago.

Self Check

1. **Describe** elliptical galaxies. How are they different from spiral galaxies?
2. **Identify** the galaxy that you live in.
3. **Explain** the Doppler shift.
4. **Explain** how all galaxies are similar.
5. **Think Critically** All galaxies outside the Local Group show a red shift. Within the Local Group, some show a red shift and some show a blue shift. What does this tell you about the galaxies in the Local Group?

Applying Skills

6. **Compare and contrast** the theories about the origin of the universe.

Design Your Own

Measuring Parallax

Goals
- **Design** a model to show how the distance from an observer to an object affects the object's parallax shift.
- **Describe** how parallax can be used to determine the distance to a star.

Possible Materials
meterstick
masking tape
metric ruler
pencil

Safety Precautions

WARNING: *Be sure to wear goggles to protect your eyes.*

Real-World Question
Parallax is the apparent shift in the position of an object when viewed from two locations. How can you build a model to show the relationship between distance and parallax?

Form a Hypothesis
State a hypothesis about how parallax varies with distance.

Test Your Hypothesis
Make a Plan
1. As a group, agree upon and write your hypothesis statement.
2. **List** the steps you need to take to build your model. Be specific, describing exactly what you will do at each step.
3. **Devise** a method to test how distance from an observer to an object, such as a pencil, affects the parallax of the object.
4. **List** the steps you will take to test your hypothesis. Be specific, describing exactly what you will do at each step.
5. Read over your plan for the model to be used in this experiment.

494 CHAPTER 16 Stars and Galaxies

Using Scientific Methods

6. How will you determine changes in observed parallax? Remember, these changes should occur when the distance from the observer to the object is changed.
7. You should measure shifts in parallax from several different positions. How will these positions differ?
8. How will you measure distances accurately and compare relative position shift?

Follow Your Plan

1. Make sure your teacher approves your plan before you start.
2. **Construct** the model your team has planned.
3. Carry out the experiment as planned.
4. While conducting the experiment, record any observations that you or other members of your group make in your Science Journal.

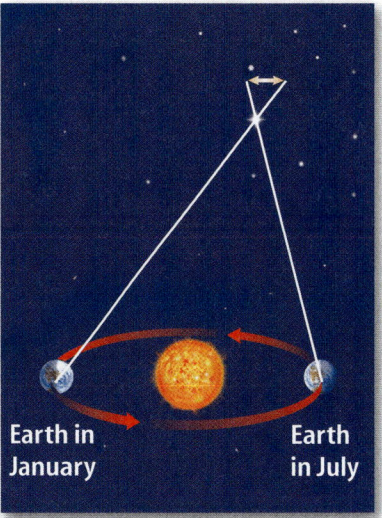

Earth in January   Earth in July

Analyze Your Data

1. **Compare** what happened to the object when it was viewed with one eye closed, then the other.
2. At what distance from the observer did the object appear to shift the most?
3. At what distance did it appear to shift the least?

Conclude and Apply

1. **Infer** what happened to the apparent shift of the object's location as the distance from the observer was increased or decreased.
2. **Describe** how astronomers might use parallax to study stars.

Prepare a chart showing the results of your experiment. Share the chart with members of your class. **For more help, refer to the** Science Skill Handbook.

LAB **495**

SCIENCE Stats

Stars and Galaxies

Did you know...

...A star in Earth's galaxy explodes as a supernova about once a century. The most famous supernova of this galaxy occurred in 1054 and was recorded by the ancient Chinese and Koreans. The explosion was so powerful that it could be seen during the day, and its brightness lasted for weeks. Other major supernovas in the Milky Way that were observed from Earth occurred in 185, 386, 1006, 1181, 1572, and 1604.

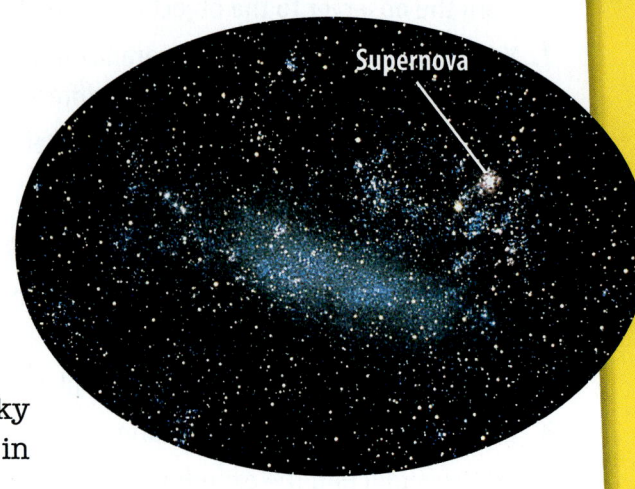

...The large loops of material called solar prominences can extend more than 320,000 km above the Sun's surface. This is so high that two Jupiters and three Earths could fit under the arch.

...The red giant star Betelgeuse has a diameter larger than that of Earth's Sun. This gigantic star measures 450,520,000 km in diameter, while the Sun's diameter is a mere 1,390,176 km.

Applying Math Use words to express the number 450,520,000.

Write About It

Visit **in7.msscience.com/science_stats** to learn whether it might be possible for Earth astronauts to travel to the nearest stars. How long would such a trip take? What problems would have to be overcome? Write a brief report about what you find.

chapter 16 Study Guide

Reviewing Main Ideas

Section 1 Stars

1. Constellations are patterns of stars in the night sky. Some constellations can be seen all year. Other constellations are visible only during certain seasons.

2. Parallax is the apparent shift in the position of an object when viewed from two different positions. Parallax is used to find the distance to nearby stars.

Section 2 The Sun

1. The Sun is the closest star to Earth.

2. Sunspots are areas on the Sun's surface that are cooler and less bright than surrounding areas.

Section 3 Evolution of Stars

1. Stars are classified according to their position on the H-R diagram.

2. Low-mass stars end their lives as white dwarfs. High-mass stars become neutron stars or black holes.

Section 4 Galaxies and the Universe

1. A galaxy consists of stars, gas, and dust held together by gravity.

2. Earth's solar system is in the Milky Way, a spiral galaxy.

3. The universe is expanding. Scientists don't know whether the universe will expand forever or contract to a single point.

Visualizing Main Ideas

Copy and complete the following concept map that shows the evolution of a main sequence star with a mass similar to that of the Sun.

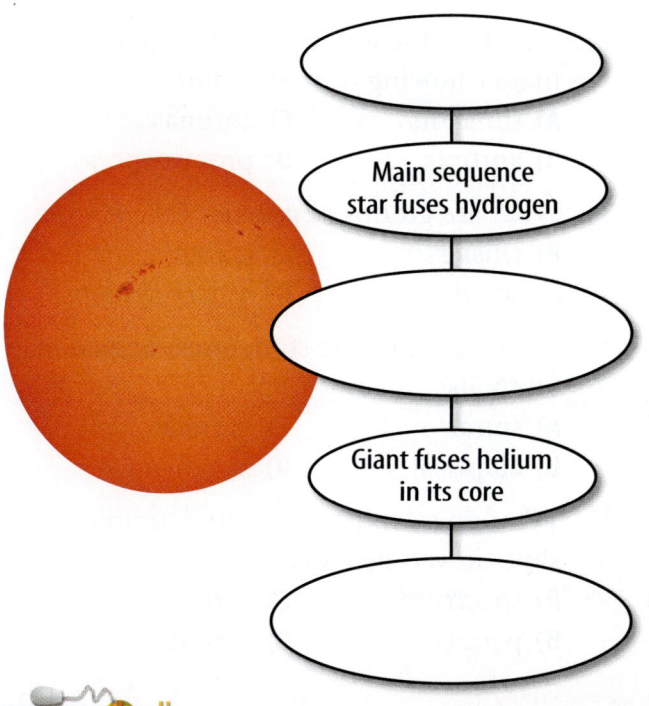

chapter 16 Review

Using Vocabulary

absolute magnitude p. 474	giant p. 485
apparent magnitude p. 474	light-year p. 475
big bang theory p. 493	nebula p. 484
black hole p. 486	neutron star p. 486
chromosphere p. 477	photosphere p. 477
constellation p. 472	sunspot p. 478
corona p. 477	supergiant p. 486
galaxy p. 488	white dwarf p. 485

Explain the difference between the terms in each of the following sets.

1. absolute magnitude—apparent magnitude
2. galaxy—constellation
3. giant—supergiant
4. chromosphere—photosphere
5. black hole—neutron star

Checking Concepts

Choose the word or phrase that best answers the question.

6. What is a measure of the amount of a star's light that is received on Earth?
    A) absolute magnitude
    B) apparent magnitude
    C) fusion
    D) parallax

7. What is higher for closer stars?
    A) absolute magnitude
    B) red shift
    C) parallax
    D) blue shift

8. What happens after a nebula contracts and its temperature increases to 10 million K?
    A) a black hole forms
    B) a supernova occurs
    C) fusion begins
    D) a white dwarf forms

9. Which of these has an event horizon?
    A) giant
    B) white dwarf
    C) black hole
    D) neutron star

10. What forms when the Sun fuses hydrogen?
    A) carbon
    B) oxygen
    C) iron
    D) helium

Use the illustration below to answer question 11.

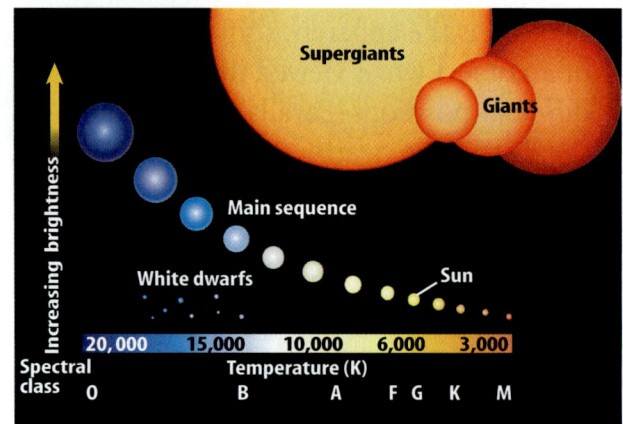

11. Which of the following best describes giant stars?
    A) hot, dim stars
    B) cool, dim stars
    C) hot, bright stars
    D) cool, bright stars

12. Which of the following are loops of matter flowing from the Sun?
    A) sunspots
    B) auroras
    C) coronas
    D) prominences

13. What are groups of galaxies called?
    A) clusters
    B) supergiants
    C) giants
    D) binary systems

14. Which galaxies are sometimes shaped like footballs?
    A) spiral
    B) elliptical
    C) barred
    D) irregular

15. What do scientists study to determine shifts in wavelengths of light?
    A) spectrum
    B) parallax
    C) corona
    D) nebula

498 CHAPTER REVIEW

Science online in7.msscience.com/vocabulary_puzzlemaker

chapter 16 Review

Thinking Critically

Use the table below to answer question 16.

Magnitude and Distance of Stars			
Star	Apparent Magnitude	Absolute Magnitude	Distance in Light-Years
A	−26	4.8	0.00002
B	−1.5	1.4	8.7
C	0.1	4.4	4.3
D	0.1	−7.0	815
E	0.4	−5.9	520
F	1.0	−0.6	45

16. Interpret Data Use the table above to answer the following questions. *Hint: lower magnitude values are brighter than higher magnitude values.*
   a. Which star appears brightest from Earth?
   b. Which star would appear brightest from a distance of 10 light-years?
   c. Infer which star in the table above is the Sun.

17. Infer How do scientists know that black holes exist if these objects don't emit visible light?

18. Recognize Cause and Effect Why can parallax only be used to measure distances to stars that are relatively close to Earth?

19. Compare and contrast the Sun with other stars on the H-R diagram.

20. Concept Map Make a concept map showing the life history of a very large star.

21. Make Models Make a model of the Sun. Include all of the Sun's layers in your model.

Performance Activities

22. Story Write a short science-fiction story about an astronaut traveling through the universe. In your story, describe what the astronaut observes. Use as many vocabulary words as you can.

23. Photomontage Gather photographs of the aurora borealis from magazines and other sources. Use the photographs to create a photomontage. Write a caption for each photo.

Applying Math

24. Travel to Vega Vega is a star that is 26 light-years away. If a spaceship could travel at one-tenth the speed of light, how long would it take to reach this star?

Use the illustration below to answer question 25.

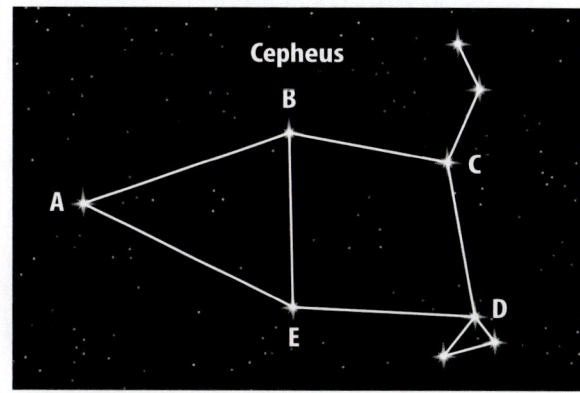

25. Constellation Cepheus The illustration above shows the constellation Cepheus. Answer the following questions about this contellation.
   a. Which of the line segments are nearly parallel?
   b. Which line segments are nearly perpendicular?
   c. Which angles are oblique?
   d. What geometric shape do the three stars at the left side of the drawing form?

Science online in7.msscience.com/chapter_review

chapter 16 Indiana

 The assessed Indiana standard appears above the question.

Record your answers on the answer sheet provided by your teacher or on a sheet of paper.

Part 1 Multiple Choice

The illustration below shows parts of the Sun.

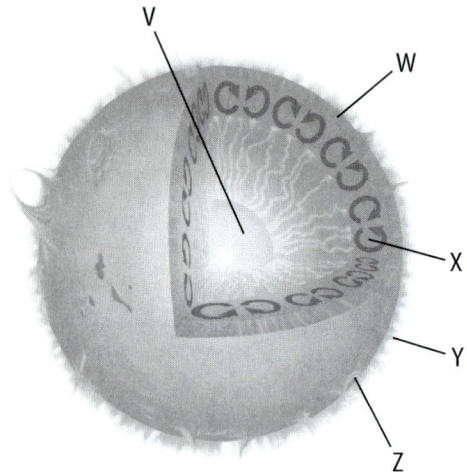

7.3.11

1. In which layer of the Sun is energy produced?
   - A V
   - B X
   - C Y
   - D Z

2. In the illustration above, which layer of the Sun is the source of solar wind?
   - A V
   - B W
   - C Y
   - D Z

3. Which is the most abundant element in the Sun?
   - A carbon
   - B helium
   - C hydrogen
   - D oxygen

7.3.1

4. The illustration below shows a side view of the Milky Way Galaxy.

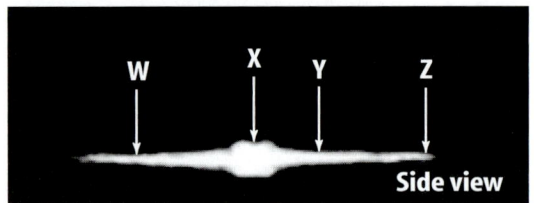

Where is the Sun located?
   - A W
   - B X
   - C Y
   - D Z

7.3.2

5. About how long does it take light from the Sun to reach Earth?
   - A 8 seconds
   - B 8 minutes
   - C 8 hours
   - D 8 days

Test-Taking Tip

Process of Elimination If you don't know the answer to a multiple-choice question, eliminate as many incorrect choices as possible. Mark your best guess from the remaining answers before moving on to the next question.

500 INDIANA

Standards Review

6. What type of object do the most massive stars become at the end of their lives?

   A black hole

   B neutron star

   C red giant

   D white dwarf

7. The illustration below shows the distance between Earth and the nearest star besides the Sun, Proxima Centauri.

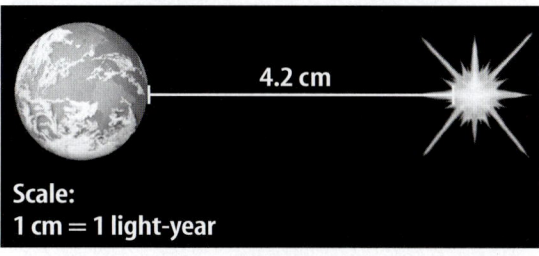

How far away from Earth is Proxima Centauri?

   A 8.4 AU's

   B 8.4 light-years

   C 4.2 AU's

   D 4.2 light-years

7.3.1

8. Which series is ordered from smallest to largest?

   A universe, galaxy clusters, galaxies, stars

   B stars, galaxies, galaxy clusters, universe

   C galaxies, stars, star clusters, universe

   D galaxy clusters, galaxies, stars, universe

Part 2 Constructed Response

7.3.11

9. Why do nuclear fusion reactions cause the amount of hydrogen in the Sun to decrease?

10. The graph below shows how the brightness of a supernova changed over time.

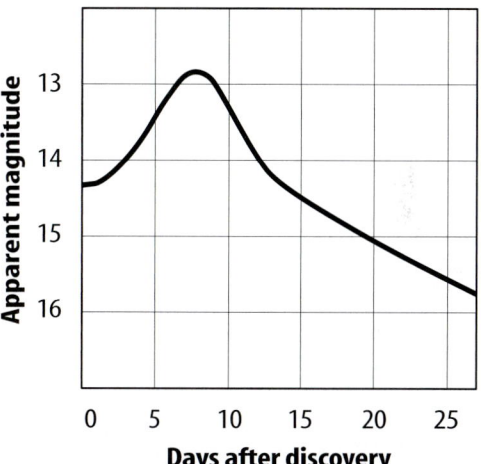

On what day after discovery was the supernova brightest? Describe how the brightness changed after that day.

11. Explain why the constellations appear to move. Why are some visible all year and others only visible during certain seasons?

7.3.2

12. Explain how parallax is used to measure the distance to nearby stars.

13. What can be learned by studying the dark lines in a star's spectrum?

chapter 17

Minerals

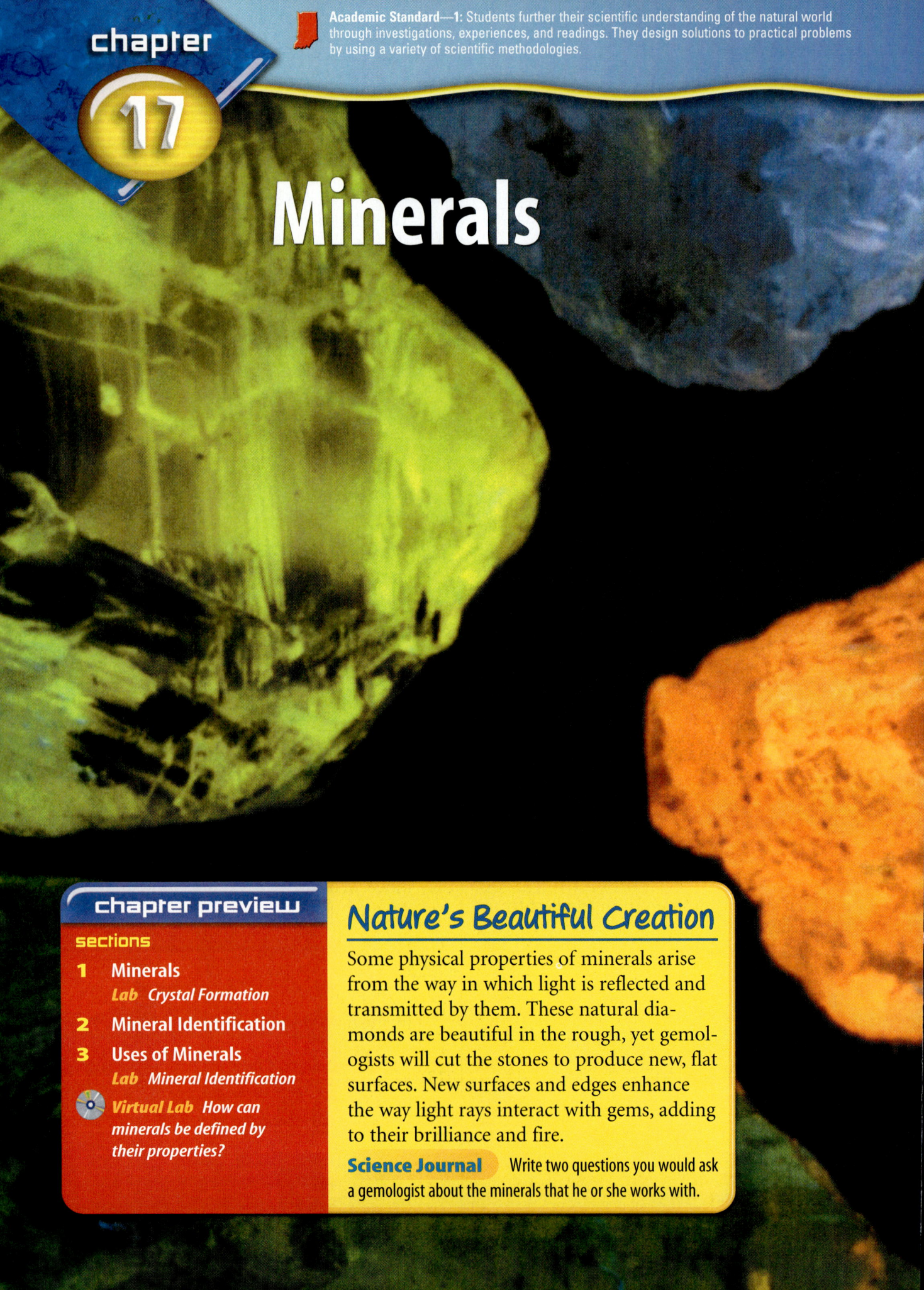

chapter preview

sections
1. **Minerals**
   Lab Crystal Formation
2. **Mineral Identification**
3. **Uses of Minerals**
   Lab Mineral Identification
   Virtual Lab How can minerals be defined by their properties?

Nature's Beautiful Creation

Some physical properties of minerals arise from the way in which light is reflected and transmitted by them. These natural diamonds are beautiful in the rough, yet gemologists will cut the stones to produce new, flat surfaces. New surfaces and edges enhance the way light rays interact with gems, adding to their brilliance and fire.

Science Journal Write two questions you would ask a gemologist about the minerals that he or she works with.

Academic Standard—1: Students further their scientific understanding of the natural world through investigations, experiences, and readings. They design solutions to practical problems by using a variety of scientific methodologies.

Start-Up Activities

Distinguish Rocks from Minerals

When examining rocks, you'll notice that many of them are made of more than one material. Some rocks are made of many different crystals of mostly the same mineral. A mineral, however, will appear more like a pure substance and will tend to look the same throughout. Can you tell a rock from a mineral?

1. Use a magnifying lens to observe a quartz crystal, salt grains, and samples of sandstone, granite, calcite, mica, and schist (SHIHST).
2. Draw a sketch of each sample.
3. Infer which samples are made of one type of material and should be classified as minerals.
4. Infer which samples should be classified as rocks.
5. **Think Critically** In your Science Journal, compile a list of descriptions for the minerals you examined and a second list of descriptions for the rocks. Compare and contrast your observations of minerals and rocks.

Minerals Make the following Foldable to help you better understand minerals.

STEP 1 Fold a vertical sheet of notebook paper from side to side.

STEP 2 Cut along every third line of only the top layer to form tabs.

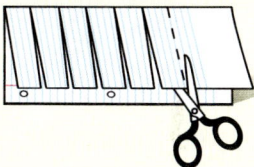

STEP 3 Label each tab with a question.

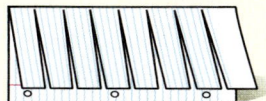

Ask Questions Before you read the chapter, write questions you have about minerals on the front of the tabs. As you read the chapter, add more questions and write answers under the appropriate tabs.

 Preview this chapter's content and activities at in7.msscience.com

Standards—This section builds a foundation for **standards 7.3.8 and 7.3.9.**

section 1
Minerals

as you read

What You'll Learn
- **Describe** characteristics that all minerals share.
- **Explain** how minerals form.

Why It's Important
You use minerals and products made from them every day.

Review Vocabulary
atoms: tiny particles that make up matter; composed of protons, electrons, and neutrons

New Vocabulary
- mineral
- crystal
- magma
- silicate

Figure 1 You probably use minerals or materials made from minerals every day without thinking about it.
Infer *How many objects in this picture might be made from minerals?*

What is a mineral?

How important are minerals to you? Very important? You actually own or encounter many things made from minerals every day. Ceramic, metallic, and even some paper items are examples of products that are derived from or include minerals. **Figure 1** shows just a few of these things. Metal bicycle racks, bricks, and the glass in windows would not exist if it weren't for minerals. A **mineral** is a naturally occurring, inorganic solid with a definite chemical composition and an orderly arrangement of atoms. About 4,000 different minerals are found on Earth, but they all share these four characteristics.

Mineral Characteristics First, all minerals are formed by natural processes. These are processes that occur on or inside Earth with no input from humans. For example, salt formed by the natural evaporation of seawater is the mineral halite, but salt formed by evaporation of saltwater solutions in laboratories is not a mineral. Second, minerals are inorganic. This means that they aren't made by life processes. Third, every mineral is an element or compound with a definite chemical composition. For example, halite's composition, NaCl, gives it a distinctive taste that adds flavor to many foods. Fourth, minerals are crystalline solids. All solids have a definite volume and shape. Gases and liquids like air and water have no definite shape, and they aren't crystalline. Only a solid can be a mineral, but not all solids are minerals.

Atom Patterns The word *crystalline* means that atoms are arranged in a pattern that is repeated over and over again. For example, graphite's atoms are arranged in layers. Opal, on the other hand, is not a mineral in the strictest sense because its atoms are not all arranged in a definite, repeating pattern, even though it is a naturally occurring, inorganic solid.

504 CHAPTER 17 Minerals

Figure 2 More than 200 years ago, the smooth, flat surfaces on crystals led scientists to infer that minerals had an orderly structure inside.

Even though this rose quartz looks uneven on the outside, its atoms have an orderly arrangement on the inside.

The well-formed crystal shapes exhibited by these clear quartz crystals suggest an orderly structure.

The Structure of Minerals

Do you have a favorite mineral sample or gemstone? If so, perhaps it contains well-formed crystals. A **crystal** is a solid in which the atoms are arranged in orderly, repeating patterns. You can see evidence for this orderly arrangement of atoms when you observe the smooth, flat outside surfaces of crystals. A crystal system is a group of crystals that have similar atomic arrangements and therefore similar external crystal shapes.

Reading Check *What is a crystal?*

Crystals Not all mineral crystals have smooth surfaces and regular shapes like the clear quartz crystals in **Figure 2**. The rose quartz in the smaller photo of **Figure 2** has atoms arranged in repeating patterns, but you can't see the crystal shape on the outside of the mineral. This is because the rose quartz crystals developed in a tight space, while the clear quartz crystals developed freely in an open space. The six-sided, or hexagonal crystal shape of the clear quartz crystals in **Figure 2,** and other forms of quartz can be seen in some samples of the mineral. **Figure 3** illustrates the six major crystal systems, which classify minerals according to their crystal structures. The hexagonal system to which quartz belongs is one example of a crystal system.

Crystals form by many processes. Next, you'll learn about two of these processes—crystals that form from magma and crystals that form from solutions of salts.

Mini LAB

Inferring Salt's Crystal System

Procedure
1. Use a **magnifying lens** to observe grains of common **table salt** on a dark sheet of **construction paper**. Sketch the shape of a salt grain. WARNING: *Do not taste or eat mineral samples. Keep hands away from your face.*
2. Compare the shapes of the salt crystals with the shapes of crystals shown in **Figure 3**.

Analysis
1. Which characteristics do all the grains have in common?
2. Research another mineral with the same crystal system as salt. What is this crystal system called?

SECTION 1 Minerals

NATIONAL GEOGRAPHIC VISUALIZING CRYSTAL SYSTEMS

Figure 3

A crystal's shape depends on how its atoms are arranged. Crystal shapes can be organized into groups known as crystal systems—shown here in 3-D with geometric models (in blue). Knowing a mineral's crystal system helps researchers understand its atomic structure and physical properties.

▶ **CUBIC** Fluorite is an example of a mineral that forms cubic crystals. Minerals in the cubic crystal system are equal in size along all three principal dimensions.

▲ **HEXAGONAL** (hek SA guh nul) In hexagonal crystals, horizontal distances between opposite crystal surfaces are equal. These crystal surfaces intersect to form 60° or 120° angles. The vertical length is longer or shorter than the horizontal lengths.

◀ **TETRAGONAL** (te TRA guh nul) Zircon crystals are tetragonal. Tetragonal crystals are much like cubic crystals, except that one of the principal dimensions is longer or shorter than the other two dimensions.

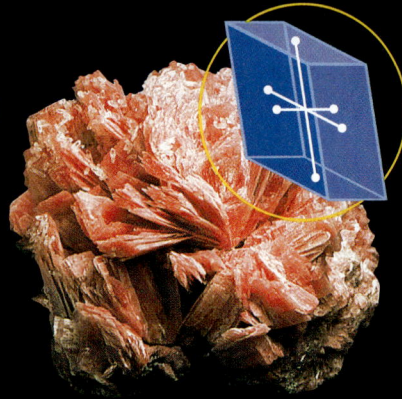

▲ **ORTHORHOMBIC** (awr thuh RAHM bihk) Minerals with orthorhombic structure, such as barite, have dimensions that are unequal in length, resulting in crystals with a brick-like shape.

▲ **MONOCLINIC** (mah nuh KLIH nihk) Minerals in the monoclinic system, such as orthoclase, also exhibit unequal dimensions in their crystal structure. Only one right angle forms where crystal surfaces meet. The other angles are oblique, which means they don't form 90° angles where they intersect.

▲ **TRICLINIC** (tri KLIH nihk) The triclinic crystal system includes minerals exhibiting the least symmetry. Triclinic crystals, such as rhodonite (ROH dun ite), are unequal in all dimensions, and all angles where crystal surfaces meet are oblique.

Figure 4 Minerals form by many natural processes.

A This rock formed as magma cooled slowly, allowing large mineral grains to form.

Labradorite

B Some minerals form when salt water evaporates, such as these white crystals of halite in Death Valley, California.

Crystals from Magma Natural processes form minerals in many ways. For example, hot melted rock material, called **magma,** cools when it reaches Earth's surface, or even if it's trapped below the surface. As magma cools, its atoms lose heat energy, move closer together, and begin to combine into compounds. During this process, atoms of the different compounds arrange themselves into orderly, repeating patterns. The type and amount of elements present in a magma partly determine which minerals will form. Also, the size of the crystals that form depends partly on how rapidly the magma cools.

When magma cools slowly, the crystals that form are generally large enough to see with the unaided eye, as shown in **Figure 4A.** This is because the atoms have enough time to move together and form into larger crystals. When magma cools rapidly, the crystals that form will be small. In such cases, you can't easily see individual mineral crystals.

Crystals from Solution Crystals also can form from minerals dissolved in water. When water evaporates, as in a dry climate, ions that are left behind can come together to form crystals like the halite crystals in **Figure 4B.** Or, if too much of a substance is dissolved in water, ions can come together and crystals of that substance can begin to form in the solution. Minerals can form from a solution in this way without the need for evaporation.

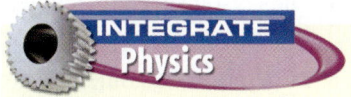

Crystal Formation Evaporites commonly form in dry climates. Research the changes that take place when a saline lake or shallow sea evaporates and halite or gypsum forms.

SECTION 1 Minerals

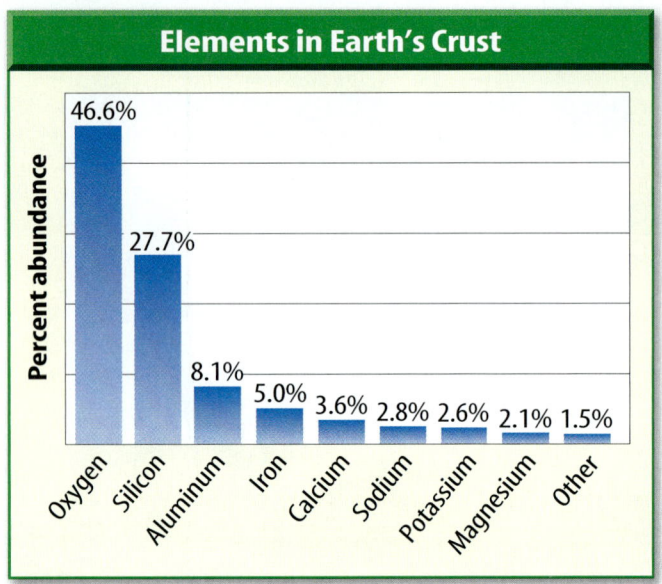

Figure 5 Most of Earth's crust is composed of eight elements.

Mineral Compositions and Groups

Ninety elements occur naturally in Earth's crust. Approximately 98 percent (by weight) of the crust is made of only eight of these elements, as shown in **Figure 5.** Of the thousands of known minerals, only a few dozen are common, and these are mostly composed of the eight most common elements in Earth's crust.

Most of the common rock-forming minerals belong to a group called the silicates. **Silicates** (SIH luh kayts) are minerals that contain silicon (Si) and oxygen (O) and usually one or more other elements. Silicon and oxygen are the two most abundant elements in Earth's crust. These two elements alone combine to form the basic building blocks of most of the minerals in Earth's crust and mantle. Feldspar and quartz, which are silicates, and calcite, which is a carbonate, are examples of common, rock-forming minerals. Other mineral groups also are defined according to their compositions.

section 1 review

Summary

What is a mineral?
- Many products used by humans are made from minerals.
- Minerals are defined by four main characteristics.

The Structure of Minerals
- The crystal shape of a mineral reflects the way in which its atoms are arranged.
- Minerals are classified according to the types of atoms in their structures and the way that the atoms are arranged.

Mineral Compositions and Groups
- Only eight elements form approximately 98 percent (by weight) of Earth's crust.
- The majority of Earth's crust is composed of silicate minerals.

Self Check

1. **List** four characteristics that all minerals share.
2. **Describe** two ways that minerals can form from solution.
3. **Explain** whether diamonds made in the laboratory are considered to be minerals.
4. **Describe** how crystals of minerals are classified.
5. **Think Critically** The mineral dolomite, a rock-forming mineral, contains oxygen, carbon, magnesium, and calcium. Is dolomite a silicate? Explain.

Applying Skills

6. **Graph** Make a graph of your own design that shows the relative percentages of the eight most common elements in Earth's crust. Then determine the approximate percentage of the crust that is made up of iron and aluminum. If one is available, you may use an electronic spreadsheet program to make your graph and perform the calculation.

Crystal Formation

In this lab, you'll have a chance to learn how crystals form from solutions.

▶ Real-World Question
How do crystals form from solution?

Goals
- **Compare and contrast** the crystals that form from salt and sugar solutions.
- **Observe** crystals and infer how they formed.

Materials
250-mL beakers (2)	cotton string
cardboard	hot plate
large paper clip	magnifying lens
table salt	thermal mitt
flat wooden stick	shallow pan
granulated sugar	spoon

Safety Precautions

WARNING: *Never taste or eat any lab materials.*

▶ Procedure

1. Gently mix separate solutions of salt in water and sugar in water in the two beakers. Keep stirring the solutions as you add salt or sugar to the water. Stop mixing when no more salt or sugar will dissolve in the solutions. Label each beaker.
2. Place the sugar solution beaker on a hot plate. Use the hot plate to heat the sugar solution gently. **WARNING:** *Do not touch the hot beaker without protecting your hands.*
3. Tie one end of the thread to the middle of the wooden stick. Tie a large paper clip to the free end of the string for weight. Place the stick across the opening of the sugar beaker so the thread dangles in the sugar solution.
4. Remove the beaker from the hot plate and cover it with cardboard. Place it in a location where it won't be disturbed.
5. Pour a thin layer of the salt solution into the shallow pan.
6. Leave the beaker and the shallow pan undisturbed for at least one week.
7. After one week, examine each solution with a magnifying lens to see whether crystals have formed.

▶ Conclude and Apply

1. **Compare and contrast** the crystals that formed from the salt and the sugar solutions. How do they compare with samples of table salt and sugar?
2. **Describe** what happened to the saltwater solution in the shallow pan.
3. Did this same process occur in the sugar solution? Explain.

Make a poster that describes your methods of growing salt and sugar crystals. Present your results to your class.

section 2

Standards—This section builds a foundation for **standards 7.3.8 and 7.3.9.**

Mineral Identification

as you read

What You'll Learn
- **Describe** physical properties used to identify minerals.
- **Identify** minerals using physical properties such as hardness and streak.

Why It's Important
Identifying minerals helps you recognize valuable mineral resources.

Review Vocabulary
physical property: any characteristic of a material that you can observe without changing the identity of the material

New Vocabulary
- hardness
- luster
- specific gravity
- streak
- cleavage
- fracture

Physical Properties

Why can you recognize a classmate when you see him or her in a crowd away from school? A person's height or the shape of his or her face helps you tell that person from the rest of your class. Height and facial shape are two properties unique to individuals. Individual minerals also have unique properties that distinguish them.

Mineral Appearance Just like height and facial characteristics help you recognize someone, mineral properties can help you recognize and distinguish minerals. Color and appearance are two obvious clues that can be used to identify minerals.

However, these clues alone aren't enough to recognize most minerals. The minerals pyrite and gold are gold in color and can appear similar, as shown in **Figure 6**. As a matter of fact, pyrite often is called fool's gold. Gold is worth a lot of money, whereas pyrite has little value. You need to look at other properties of minerals to tell them apart. Some other properties to study include how hard a mineral is, how it breaks, and its color when crushed into a powder. Every property you observe in a mineral is a clue to its identity.

Figure 6 The general appearance of a mineral often is not enough to identify it.

Pyrite   **Gold**

Using only color, observers can be fooled when trying to distinguish between pyrite and gold.

Azurite

The mineral azurite is identified readily by its striking blue color.

510 CHAPTER 17 Minerals

Hardness A measure of how easily a mineral can be scratched is its **hardness.** The mineral talc is so soft you can scratch it loose with your fingernail. Talcum powder is made from this soft mineral. Diamonds, on the other hand, are the hardest mineral. Some diamonds are used as cutting tools, as shown in **Figure 7.** A diamond can be scratched only by another diamond. Diamonds can be broken, however.

 *Why is hardness sometimes referred to as scratchability?*

Sometimes the concept of hardness is confused with whether or not a mineral will break. It is important to understand that even though a diamond is extremely hard, it can shatter if given a hard enough blow in the right direction along the crystal.

Mohs Scale In 1824, the Austrian scientist Friedrich Mohs developed a list of common minerals to compare their hardnesses. This list is called Mohs scale of hardness, as seen in **Table 1.** The scale lists the hardness of ten minerals. Talc, the softest mineral, has a hardness value of one, and diamond, the hardest mineral, has a value of ten.

Here's how the scale works. Imagine that you have a clear or whitish-colored mineral that you know is either fluorite or quartz. You try to scratch it with your fingernail and then with an iron nail. You can't scratch it with your fingernail but you can scratch it with the iron nail. Because the hardness of your fingernail is 2.5 and that of the iron nail is 4.5, you can determine the unknown mineral's hardness to be somewhere around 3 or 4. Because it is known that quartz has a hardness of 7 and fluorite has a hardness of 4, the mystery mineral must be fluorite.

Some minerals have a hardness range rather than a single hardness value. This is because atoms are arranged differently in different directions in their crystal structures.

Figure 7 Some saw blades have diamonds embedded in them to help slice through materials, such as this limestone. Blades are kept cool by running water over them.

Table 1 Mineral Hardness

Mohs Scale	Hardness	Hardness of Common Objects	
Talc (softest)	1		
Gypsum	2	fingernail	(2.5)
Calcite	3	piece of copper	(2.5 to 3.0)
Fluorite	4	iron nail	(4.5)
Apatite	5	glass	(5.5)
Feldspar	6	steel file	(6.5)
Quartz	7	streak plate	(7.0)
Topaz	8		
Corundum	9		
Diamond (hardest)	10		

Graphite

Fluorite

Figure 8 Luster is an important physical property that is used to distinguish minerals. Graphite has a metallic luster. Fluorite has a nonmetallic, glassy luster.

Luster The way a mineral reflects light is known as **luster**. Luster can be metallic or nonmetallic. Minerals with a metallic luster, like the graphite shown in **Figure 8,** shine like metal. Metallic luster can be compared to the shine of a metal belt buckle, the shiny chrome trim on some cars, or the shine of metallic cooking utensils. When a mineral does not shine like metal, its luster is nonmetallic. Examples of terms for nonmetallic luster include dull, pearly, silky, and glassy. Common examples of minerals with glassy luster are quartz, calcite, halite, and fluorite.

Specific Gravity Minerals also can be distinguished by comparing the weights of equal-sized samples. The **specific gravity** of a mineral is the ratio of its weight compared with the weight of an equal volume of water. Like hardness, specific gravity is expressed as a number. If you were to research the specific gravities of gold and pyrite, you'd find that gold's specific gravity is about 19, and pyrite's is 5. This means that gold is about 19 times heavier than water and pyrite is 5 times heavier than water. You could experience this by comparing equal-sized samples of gold and pyrite in your hands—the pyrite would feel much lighter. The term *heft* is sometimes used to describe how heavy a mineral sample feels.

Applying Science

How can you identify minerals?

Properties of Minerals

Mineral	Hardness	Streak
Copper	2.5–3	copper-red
Galena	2.5	dark gray
Gold	2.5–3	yellow
Hematite	5.5–6.5	red to brown
Magnetite	6–6.5	black
Silver	2.5–3	silver-white

You have learned that minerals are identified by their physical properties, such as streak, hardness, cleavage, and color. Use your knowledge of mineral properties and your ability to read a table to solve the following problems.

Identifying the Problem

The table includes hardnesses and streak colors for several minerals. How can you use these data to distinguish minerals?

Solving the Problem

1. What test would you perform to distinguish hematite from copper? How would you carry out this test?
2. How could you distinguish copper from galena? What tool would you use?
3. What would you do if two minerals had the same hardness and the same streak color?

Streak When a mineral is rubbed across a piece of unglazed porcelain tile, as in **Figure 9,** a streak of powdered mineral is left behind. **Streak** is the color of a mineral when it is in a powdered form. The streak test works only for minerals that are softer than the streak plate. Gold and pyrite can be distinguished by a streak test. Gold has a yellow streak and pyrite has a greenish-black or brownish-black streak.

Some soft minerals will leave a streak even on paper. The last time you used a pencil to write on paper, you left a streak of the mineral graphite. One reason that graphite is used in pencil lead is because it is soft enough to leave a streak on paper.

 *Why do gold and pyrite leave a streak, but quartz does not?*

Figure 9 Streak is more useful for mineral identification than is mineral color. Hematite, for example, can be dark red, gray, or silver in color. However, its streak is always dark reddish-brown.

Cleavage and Fracture The way a mineral breaks is another clue to its identity. Minerals that break along smooth, flat surfaces have **cleavage** (KLEE vihj). Cleavage, like hardness, is determined partly by the arrangement of the mineral's atoms. Mica is a mineral that has one perfect cleavage. **Figure 10** shows how mica breaks along smooth, flat planes. If you were to take a layer cake and separate its layers, you would show that the cake has cleavage. Not all minerals have cleavage. Minerals that break with uneven, rough, or jagged surfaces have **fracture**. Quartz is a mineral with fracture. If you were to grab a chunk out of the side of that cake, it would be like breaking a mineral that has fracture.

Mica

Halite

Figure 10 Weak or fewer bonds within the structures of mica and halite allow them to be broken along smooth, flat cleavage planes. *Infer If you broke quartz, would it look the same?*

SECTION 2 Mineral Identification

Mini LAB

Observing Mineral Properties

Procedure
1. Obtain samples of some of the following clear minerals: **gypsum, muscovite mica, halite,** and **calcite.**
2. Place each sample over the print on this page and observe the letters.

Analysis
1. Which mineral can be identified by observing the print's double image?
2. What other special property is used to identify this mineral?

Figure 11 Some minerals are natural magnets, such as this lodestone, which is a variety of magnetite.

Other Properties Some minerals have unique properties. Magnetite, as you can guess by its name, is attracted to magnets. Lodestone, a form of magnetite, will pick up iron filings like a magnet, as shown in **Figure 11.** Light forms two separate rays when it passes through calcite, causing you to see a double image when viewed through transparent specimens. Calcite also can be identified because it fizzes when hydrochloric acid is put on it.

Now you know that you sometimes need more information than color and appearance to identify a mineral. You also might need to test its streak, hardness, luster, and cleavage or fracture. Although the overall appearance of a mineral can be different from sample to sample, its physical properties remain the same.

section 2 review

Summary

Physical Properties
- Minerals are identified by observing their physical properties.
- Hardness is a measure of how easily a mineral can be scratched.
- Luster describes how a mineral reflects light.
- Specific gravity is the ratio of the weight of a mineral sample compared to the weight of an equal volume of water.
- Streak is the color of a powdered mineral.
- Minerals with cleavage break along smooth, flat surfaces in one or more directions.
- Fracture describes any uneven manner in which a mineral breaks.
- Some minerals react readily with acid, form a double image, or are magnetic.

Self Check

1. **Compare and contrast** a mineral fragment that has one cleavage direction with one that has only fracture.
2. **Explain** how an unglazed porcelain tile can be used to identify a mineral.
3. **Explain** why streak often is more useful for mineral identification than color.
4. **Determine** What hardness does a mineral have if it does not scratch glass but it scratches an iron nail?
5. **Think Critically** What does the presence of cleavage planes within a mineral tell you about the chemical bonds that hold the mineral together?

Applying Skills

6. **Draw Conclusions** A large piece of the mineral halite is broken repeatedly into several perfect cubes. How can this be explained?

 in7.msscience.com/self_check_quiz

section 3

Standards—7.1.5: Identify some important contributions to the advancement of science ... and technology that have been made by different kinds of people, in different cultures, at different times. **7.1.6:** Provide examples of people who overcame bias and/or limited opportunities in education and employment to excel in the fields of science.

Uses of Minerals

Gems

Walking past the window of a jewelry store, you notice a large selection of beautiful jewelry—a watch sparkling with diamonds, a necklace holding a brilliant red ruby, and a gold ring. For thousands of years, people have worn and prized minerals in their jewelry. What makes some minerals special? What unusual properties do they have that make them so valuable?

Properties of Gems As you can see in **Figure 12,** gems or gemstones are highly prized minerals because they are rare and beautiful. Most gems are special varieties of a particular mineral. They are clearer, brighter, or more colorful than common samples of that mineral. The difference between a gem and the common form of the same mineral can be slight. Amethyst is a gem form of quartz that contains just traces of iron in its structure. This small amount of iron gives amethyst a desirable purple color. Sometimes a gem has a crystal structure that allows it to be cut and polished to a higher quality than that of a non-gem mineral. **Table 2** lists popular gems and some locations where they have been collected.

as you read

What You'll Learn
- **Describe** characteristics of gems that make them more valuable than other minerals.
- **Identify** useful elements that are contained in minerals.

Why It's Important
Minerals are necessary materials for decorative items and many manufactured products.

Review Vocabulary
metal: element that typically is a shiny, malleable solid that conducts heat and electricity well

New Vocabulary
• gem   • ore

Figure 12 It is easy to see why gems are prized for their beauty and rarity. Shown here is The Imperial State Crown, made for Queen Victoria of England in 1838. It contains thousands of jewels, including diamonds, rubies, sapphires, and emeralds.

SECTION 3 Uses of Minerals **515**

Table 2 Minerals and Their Gems

Fun Facts	Mineral	Gem Example	Some Important Locations
Beryl is named for the element beryllium, which it contains. Some crystals reach several meters in length.	Beryl	Emerald	Colombia, Brazil, South Africa, North Carolina
A red spinel in the British crown jewels has a mass of 352 carats. A carat is 0.2 g.	Spinel	Ruby spinel	Sri Lanka, Thailand, Myanmar (Burma)
Purplish-blue examples of zoisite were discovered in 1967 near Arusha, Tanzania.	Zoisite	Tanzanite	Tanzania
The most valuable examples are yellow, pink, and blue varieties.	Topaz (uncut)	Topaz (gem)	Siberia, Germany, Japan, Mexico, Brazil, Colorado, Utah, Texas, California, Maine, Virginia, South Carolina

Fun Facts	Mineral	Gem Example	Some Important Locations
Olivine composes a large part of Earth's upper mantle. It is also present in moon rocks.	Olivine	Peridot	Myanmar (Burma), Zebirget (Saint John's Island, located in the Red Sea), Arizona, New Mexico
Garnet is a common mineral found in a wide variety of rock types. The red color of the variety almandine is caused by iron in its crystal structure.	Garnet	Almandine	Ural Mountains, Italy, Madagascar, Czech Republic, India, Sri Lanka, Brazil, North Carolina, Arizona, New Mexico
Quartz makes up about 30 percent of Earth's continental crust.	Quartz	Amethyst	Colorless varieties in Hot Springs, Arkansas; Amethyst in Brazil, Uruguay, Madagascar, Montana, North Carolina, California, Maine
The blue color of sapphire is caused by iron or titanium in corundum. Chromium in corundum produces the red color of ruby.	Corundum	Blue sapphire	Thailand, Cambodia, Sri Lanka, Kashmir

Important Gems All gems are prized, but some are truly spectacular and have played an important role in history. For example, the Cullinan diamond, found in South Africa in 1905, was the largest uncut diamond ever discovered. Its mass was 3,106.75 carats (about 621 g). The Cullinan diamond was cut into 9 main stones and 96 smaller ones. The largest of these is called the Cullinan 1 or Great Star of Africa. Its mass is 530.20 carats (about 106 g), and it is now part of the British monarchy's crown jewels, shown in **Figure 13A.**

Another well-known diamond is the blue Hope diamond, shown in **Figure 13B.** This is perhaps the most notorious of all diamonds. It was purchased by Henry Philip Hope around 1830, after whom it is named. Because his entire family as well as a later owner suffered misfortune, the Hope diamond has gained a reputation for bringing its owner bad luck. The Hope diamond's mass is 45.52 carats (about 9 g). Currently it is displayed in the Smithsonian Institution in Washington, D.C.

Useful Gems In addition to their beauty, some gems serve useful purposes. You learned earlier that diamonds have a hardness of 10 on Mohs scale. They can scratch almost any material—a property that makes them useful as industrial abrasives and cutting tools. Other useful gems include rubies, which are used to produce specific types of laser light. Quartz crystals are used in electronics and as timepieces. When subjected to an electric field, quartz vibrates steadily, which helps control frequencies in electronic devices and allows for accurate timekeeping.

Most industrial diamonds and other gems are synthetic, which means that humans make them. However, the study of natural gems led to their synthesis, allowing the synthetic varieties to be used by humans readily.

Science Online

Topic: Gemstone Data
Visit in7.msscience.com for Web links to information about gems at the Smithsonian Museum of Natural History.

Activity List three important examples of gems other than those described on this page. Prepare a data table with the heads *Gem Name/Type, Weight (carats/grams), Mineral,* and *Location.* Fill in the table entries for the gemstones you selected.

Figure 13 These gems are among the most famous examples of precious stones.

A The Great Star of Africa is part of a sceptre in the collection of British crown jewels.

B Beginning in 1668, the Hope diamond was part of the French crown jewels. Then known as the French Blue, it was stolen in 1792 and later surfaced in London, England in 1812.

Figure 14 Bauxite, an ore of aluminum, is processed to make pure aluminum metal for useful products.

Bauxite

Useful Elements in Minerals

Gemstones are perhaps the best-known use of minerals, but they are not the most important. Look around your home. How many things made from minerals can you name? Can you find anything made from iron?

Ores Iron, used in everything from frying pans to ships, is obtained from its ore, hematite. A mineral or rock is an **ore** if it contains a useful substance that can be mined at a profit. Magnetite is another mineral that contains iron.

 *When is a mineral also an ore?*

 Aluminum sometimes is refined, or purified, from the ore bauxite, shown in **Figure 14.** In the process of refining aluminum, aluminum oxide powder is separated from unwanted materials that are present in the original bauxite. After this, the aluminum oxide powder is converted to molten aluminum by a process called smelting.

During smelting, a substance is melted to separate it from any unwanted materials that may remain. Aluminum can be made into useful products like bicycles, soft-drink cans, foil, and lightweight parts for airplanes and cars. The plane flown by the Wright brothers during the first flight at Kitty Hawk had an engine made partly of aluminum.

Historical Mineralogy An early scientific description of minerals was published by Georgius Agricola in 1556. Use print and online resources to research the mining techniques discussed by Agricola in his work *De Re Metallica*.

SECTION 3 Uses of Minerals **519**

Figure 15 The mineral sphalerite (greenish when nearly pure) is an important source of zinc. Iron often is coated with zinc to prevent rust in a process called galvanization.

Vein Minerals Under certain conditions, metallic elements can dissolve in fluids. These fluids then travel through weaknesses in rocks and form mineral deposits. Weaknesses in rocks include natural fractures or cracks, faults, and surfaces between layered rock formations. Mineral deposits left behind that fill in the open spaces created by the weaknesses are called vein mineral deposits.

Reading Check *How do fluids move through rocks?*

Sometimes vein mineral deposits fill in the empty spaces after rocks collapse. An example of a mineral that can form in this way is shown in **Figure 15**. This is the shiny mineral sphalerite, a source of the element zinc, which is used in batteries. Sphalerite sometimes fills spaces in collapsed limestone.

Minerals Containing Titanium You might own golf clubs with titanium shafts or a racing bicycle containing titanium. Perhaps you know someone who has a titanium hip or knee replacement. Titanium is a durable, lightweight, metallic element derived from minerals that contain this metal in their crystal structures. Two minerals that are sources of the element titanium are ilmenite (IHL muh nite) and rutile (rew TEEL), shown in **Figure 16**. Ilmenite and rutile are common in rocks that form when magma cools and solidifies. They also occur as vein mineral deposits and in beach sands.

Figure 16 Rutile and ilmenite are common ore minerals of the element titanium.

Rutile

Ilmenite

Uses for Titanium Titanium is used in automobile body parts, such as connecting rods, valves, and suspension springs. Low density and durability make it useful in the manufacture of aircraft, eyeglass frames, and sports equipment such as tennis rackets and bicycles. Wheelchairs used by people who want to race or play basketball often are made from titanium, as shown in **Figure 17**. Titanium is one of many examples of useful materials that come from minerals and that enrich humans' lives.

Figure 17 Wheelchairs used for racing and playing basketball often have parts made from titanium.

section 3 review

Summary

Gems
- Gems are highly prized mineral specimens often used as decorative pieces in jewelry or other items.
- Some gems, especially synthetic ones, have industrial uses.

Useful Elements in Minerals
- Economically important quantities of useful elements or compounds are present in ores.
- Ores generally must be processed to extract the desired material.
- Iron, aluminum, zinc, and titanium are common metals that are extracted from minerals.

Self Check

1. **Explain** why the Cullinan diamond is an important gem.
2. **Identify** Examine **Table 2**. What do rubies and sapphires have in common?
3. **Describe** how vein minerals form.
4. **Explain** why bauxite is considered to be a useful rock.
5. **Think Critically** Titanium is nontoxic. Why is this important in the manufacture of artificial body parts?

Applying Skills

6. **Use Percentages** Earth's average continental crust contains 5 percent iron and 0.007 percent zinc. How many times more iron than zinc is present in average continental crust?

Mineral Identification

Real-World Question
Although certain minerals can be identified by observing only one property, others require testing several properties to identify them. How can you identify unknown minerals?

Goals
- **Hypothesize** which properties of each mineral are most useful for identification purposes.
- **Test** your hypothesis as you attempt to identify unknown mineral samples.

Materials
mineral samples
magnifying lens
pan balance
graduated cylinder
water
piece of copper
*copper penny
glass plate
small iron nail
steel file
streak plate
5% HCl with dropper
Mohs scale of hardness
Minerals Appendix
*minerals field guide
safety goggles
*Alternate materials

Safety Precautions

WARNING: *If an HCl spill occurs, notify your teacher and rinse with cool water until you are told to stop. Do not taste, eat, or drink any lab materials.*

Procedure
1. Copy the data table into your Science Journal. Obtain a set of unknown minerals.
2. Observe a numbered mineral specimen carefully. Write a star in the table entry that represents what you hypothesize is an important physical property. Choose one or two properties that you think will help most in identifying the sample.
3. Perform tests to observe your chosen properties first.
    a. To estimate hardness:
        - Rub the sample firmly against objects of known hardness and observe whether it leaves a scratch on the objects.
        - Estimate a hardness range based on which items the mineral scratches.
    b. To estimate specific gravity: Perform a density measurement.
        - Use the pan balance to determine the sample's mass, in grams.

522 CHAPTER 17 Minerals

Using Scientific Methods

- Measure its volume using a graduated cylinder partially filled with water. The amount of water displaced by the immersed sample, in mL, is an estimate of its volume in cm³.
- Divide mass by volume to determine density. This number, without units, is comparable to specific gravity.

4. With the help of the Mineral Appendix or a field guide, attempt to identify the sample using the properties from step 2. Perform more physical property observations until you can identify the sample. Repeat steps 2 through 4 for each unknown.

Physical Properties of Minerals

Sample Number	Hardness	Cleavage or Fracture	Color	Specific Gravity	Luster and Streak	Crystal Shape	Other Properties	Mineral Name
1								
2			Do not write in this book.					
etc.								

Analyze Your Data

1. Which properties were most useful in identifying your samples? Which properties were least useful?
2. **Compare** the properties that worked best for you with those that worked best for other students.

Conclude and Apply

1. **Determine** two properties that distinguish clear, transparent quartz from clear, transparent calcite. Explain your choice of properties.
2. Which physical properties would be easiest to determine if you found a mineral specimen in the field?

For three minerals, list physical properties that were important for their identification. **For more help, refer to the Science Skill Handbook.**

TIME SCIENCE AND HISTORY

SCIENCE CAN CHANGE THE COURSE OF HISTORY!

Dr. Dorothy Crowfoot Hodgkin

Like X rays, electrons are diffracted by crystalline substances, revealing information about their internal structures and symmetry. This electron diffraction pattern of titanium was obtained with an electron beam focused along a specific direction in the crystal.

Trailblazing scientist and humanitarian

What contributions did Dorothy Crowfoot Hodgkin make to science?

Dr. Hodgkin used a method called X-ray crystallography (kris tuh LAH gruh fee) to figure out the structures of crystalline substances, including vitamin B^{12}, vitamin D, penicillin, and insulin.

What's X-ray crystallography?

Scientists expose a crystalline sample to X rays. As X rays travel through a crystal, the crystal diffracts, or scatters, the X rays into a regular pattern. Like an individual's fingerprints, each crystalline substance has a unique diffraction pattern. Crystallography has applications in the life, Earth, and physical sciences. For example, geologists use X-ray crystallography to identify and study minerals found in rocks.

What were some obstacles Hodgkin overcame?

During the 1930s, there were few women scientists. Hodgkin was not even allowed to attend meetings of the chemistry faculty where she taught because she was a woman. Eventually, she won over her colleagues with her intelligence and tenacity.

How does Hodgkin's research help people today?

Dr. Hodgkin's discovery of the structure of insulin helped scientists learn how to control diabetes, a disease that affects more than 15 million Americans. Diabetics' bodies are unable to process sugar efficiently. Diabetes can be fatal. Fortunately, Dr. Hodgkin's research with insulin has saved many lives.

1910–1994

Research Look in reference books or go to the Glencoe Science Web site for information on how X-ray crystallography is used to study minerals. Write your findings and share them with your class.

Science online
For more information, visit
in7.msscience.com/time

chapter 17 Study Guide

Reviewing Main Ideas

Section 1 Minerals

1. Much of what you use each day is made at least in some part from minerals.
2. All minerals are formed by natural processes and are inorganic solids with definite chemical compositions and orderly arrangements of atoms.
3. Minerals have crystal structures in one of six major crystal systems.

Section 2 Mineral Identification

1. Hardness is a measure of how easily a mineral can be scratched.
2. Luster describes how light reflects from a mineral's surface.
3. Streak is the color of the powder left by a mineral on an unglazed porcelain tile.
4. Minerals that break along smooth, flat surfaces have cleavage. When minerals break with rough or jagged surfaces, they are displaying fracture.
5. Some minerals have special properties that aid in identifying them. For example, magnetite is identified by its attraction to a magnet.

Section 3 Uses of Minerals

1. Gems are minerals that are more rare and beautiful than common minerals.
2. Minerals are useful for their physical properties and for the elements they contain.

Visualizing Main Ideas

Copy and complete the following concept map about minerals. Use the following words and phrases: the way a mineral breaks, the way a mineral reflects light, ore, a rare and beautiful mineral, how easily a mineral is scratched, streak, and a useful substance mined for profit.

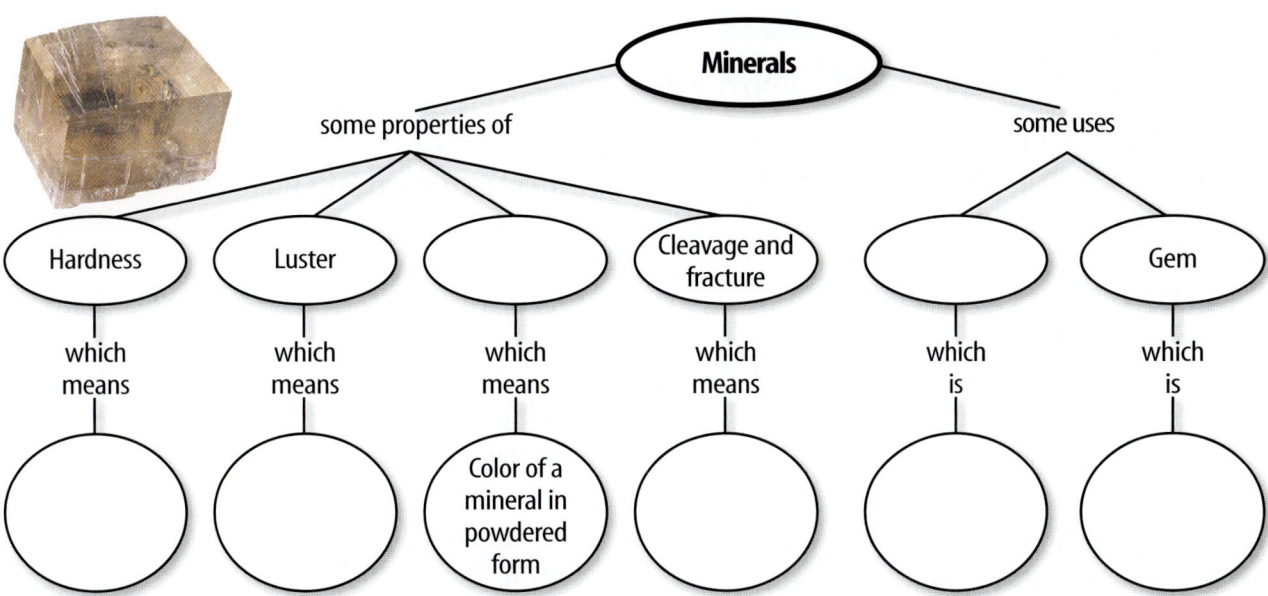

chapter 17 Review

Using Vocabulary

cleavage p. 513
crystal p. 505
fracture p. 513
gem p. 515
hardness p. 511
luster p. 512
magma p. 507
mineral p. 504
ore p. 519
silicate p. 508
specific gravity p. 512
streak p. 513

Explain the difference between the vocabulary words in each of the following sets.

1. cleavage—fracture
2. crystal—mineral
3. luster—streak
4. magma—crystal
5. hardness—specific gravity
6. ore—mineral
7. crystal—luster
8. mineral—silicate
9. gem—crystal
10. streak—specific gravity

Checking Concepts

Choose the word or phrase that best answers the question.

11. Which is a characteristic of a mineral?
    A) It can be a liquid.
    B) It is organic.
    C) It has no crystal structure.
    D) It is inorganic.

12. What must all silicates contain?
    A) magnesium
    B) silicon and oxygen
    C) silicon and aluminum
    D) oxygen and carbon

13. What is the measure of how easily a mineral can be scratched?
    A) luster
    B) hardness
    C) cleavage
    D) fracture

Use the photo below to answer question 14.

14. Examine the photo of quartz above. In what way does quartz break?
    A) cleavage   C) luster
    B) fracture   D) flat planes

15. Which of the following must crystalline solids have?
    A) carbonates
    B) cubic structures
    C) orderly arrangement of atoms
    D) cleavage

16. What is the color of a powdered mineral formed when rubbing it against an unglazed porcelain tile?
    A) luster
    B) density
    C) hardness
    D) streak

17. Which is hardest on Mohs scale?
    A) talc
    B) quartz
    C) diamond
    D) feldspar

Science online in7.msscience.com/vocabulary_puzzlemaker

chapter 17 Review

Thinking Critically

18. **Classify** Water is an inorganic substance that is formed by natural processes on Earth. It has a unique composition. Sometimes water is a mineral and other times it is not. Explain.

19. **Determine** how many sides a perfect salt crystal has.

20. **Apply** Suppose you let a sugar solution evaporate, leaving sugar crystals behind. Are these crystals minerals? Explain.

21. **Predict** Will a diamond leave a streak on a streak plate? Explain.

22. **Collect Data** Make an outline of how at least seven physical properties can be used to identify unknown minerals.

23. **Explain** how you would use **Table 1** to determine the hardness of any mineral.

24. **Concept Map** Copy and complete the concept map below, which includes two crystal systems and two examples from each system. Use the following words and phrases: *hexagonal, corundum, halite, fluorite,* and *quartz*.

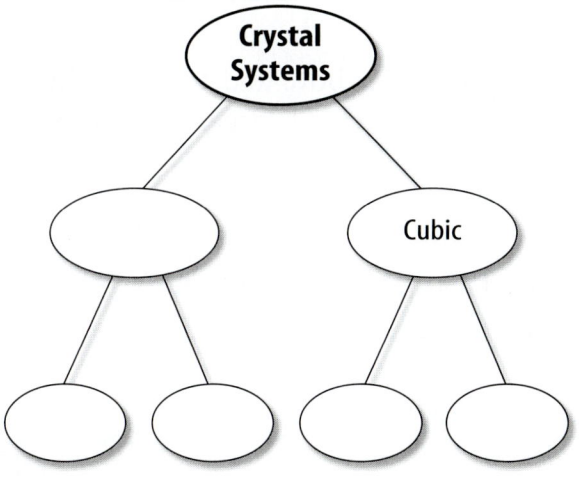

Performance Activities

25. **Display** Make a display that shows the six crystal systems of minerals. Research the crystal systems of minerals and give three examples for each crystal system. Indicate whether any of the minerals are found in your state. Describe any important uses of these minerals. Present your display to the class.

Applying Math

26. **Mineral Volume** Recall that 1 mL = 1 cm^3. Suppose that the volume of water in a graduated cylinder is 107.5 mL. A specimen of quartz, tied to a piece of string, is immersed in the water. The new water level reads 186 mL. What is the volume, in cm^3, of the piece of quartz?

Use the graph below to answer questions 27 and 28.

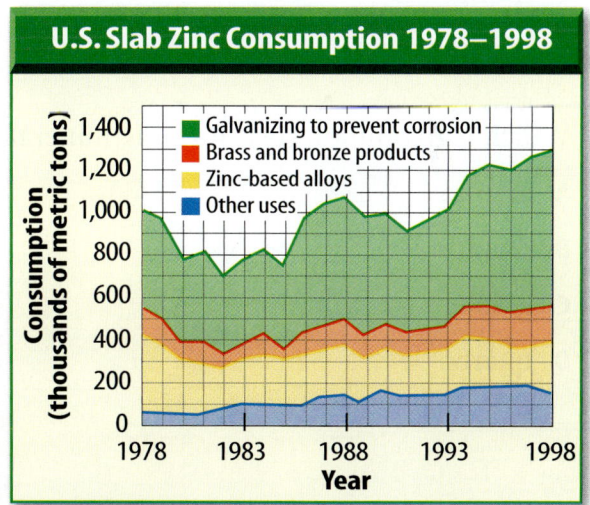

27. **Zinc Use** According to the graph above, what was the main use of zinc consumed in the United States between 1978 and 1998?

28. **Metal Products** According to the graph, approximately how many thousand metric tons of zinc were used to make brass and bronze products in 1998?

chapter 17 Indiana

 The assessed Indiana standard appears above the question.

Record your answers on the answer sheet provided by your teacher or on a sheet of paper.

Part 1 Multiple Choice

1. The photo below shows a crystal of pyrite.

   To which crystal system does the crystal shown above belong?
   - A cubic
   - B hexagonal
   - C monoclinic
   - D triclinic

2. Which is a common rock-forming mineral?
   - A azurite
   - B diamond
   - C gold
   - D quartz

3. Which term refers to the resistance of a mineral to scratching?
   - A fracture
   - B hardness
   - C luster
   - D streak

4. Which is the most abundant element in Earth's crust?
   - A iron
   - B manganese
   - C oxygen
   - D silicon

5. The table below is the Mohs hardness scale.

Mineral	Hardness
Talc	1
Gypsum	2
Calcite	3
Fluorite	4
Apatite	5
Feldspar	6
Quartz	7
Topaz	8
Corundum	9
Diamond	10

   Use the table above to determine which mineral scratches feldspar but not topaz.
   - A apatite
   - B calcite
   - C diamond
   - D quartz

> **Test-Taking Tip**
>
> **Pace Yourself** If you are taking a timed test, keep track of time during the test. If you find that you're spending too much time on a multiple-choice question, mark your best guess and move on.

Standards Review

The table below contains facts about selected diamonds and diamond production.

1.0 carat = 0.2 grams

Diamond	Carats	Grams
Uncle Sam: largest diamond found in United States	40.4	?
Punch Jones: second largest U.S. diamond; named after boy who discovered it	?	6.89
Theresa: discovered in Wisconsin in 1888	21.5	4.3
2001 diamond production from western Australia	21,679,930	?

6. How many grams is the *Uncle Sam* diamond?

   A 4.30 g

   B 6.89 g

   C 8.08 g

   D 202 g

7. Using the table above, how many grams, to the nearest million, were produced in western Australia in 2001?

   A 7,000,000 g

   B 6,000,000 g

   C 5,000,000 g

   D 4,000,000 g

Part 2 Constructed Response

8. The photo below shows a sample of granite.

The mineral crystals in the granite formed when magma cooled and are visible with the unaided eye. Hypothesize about how fast the magma cooled.

9. What is the source of most of the diamonds that are used for industrial purposes?

10. Explain how minerals are useful to society. Describe some of their uses.

11. Are gases that are given off by volcanoes minerals? Why or why not?

12. What is the most abundant mineral group in Earth's crust? What elements always are found in the minerals included in this group?

13. Several layers are peeled from a piece of muscovite mica. What property of minerals does this illustrate? Describe this property in mica.

Science online   in7.msscience.com/standards_review

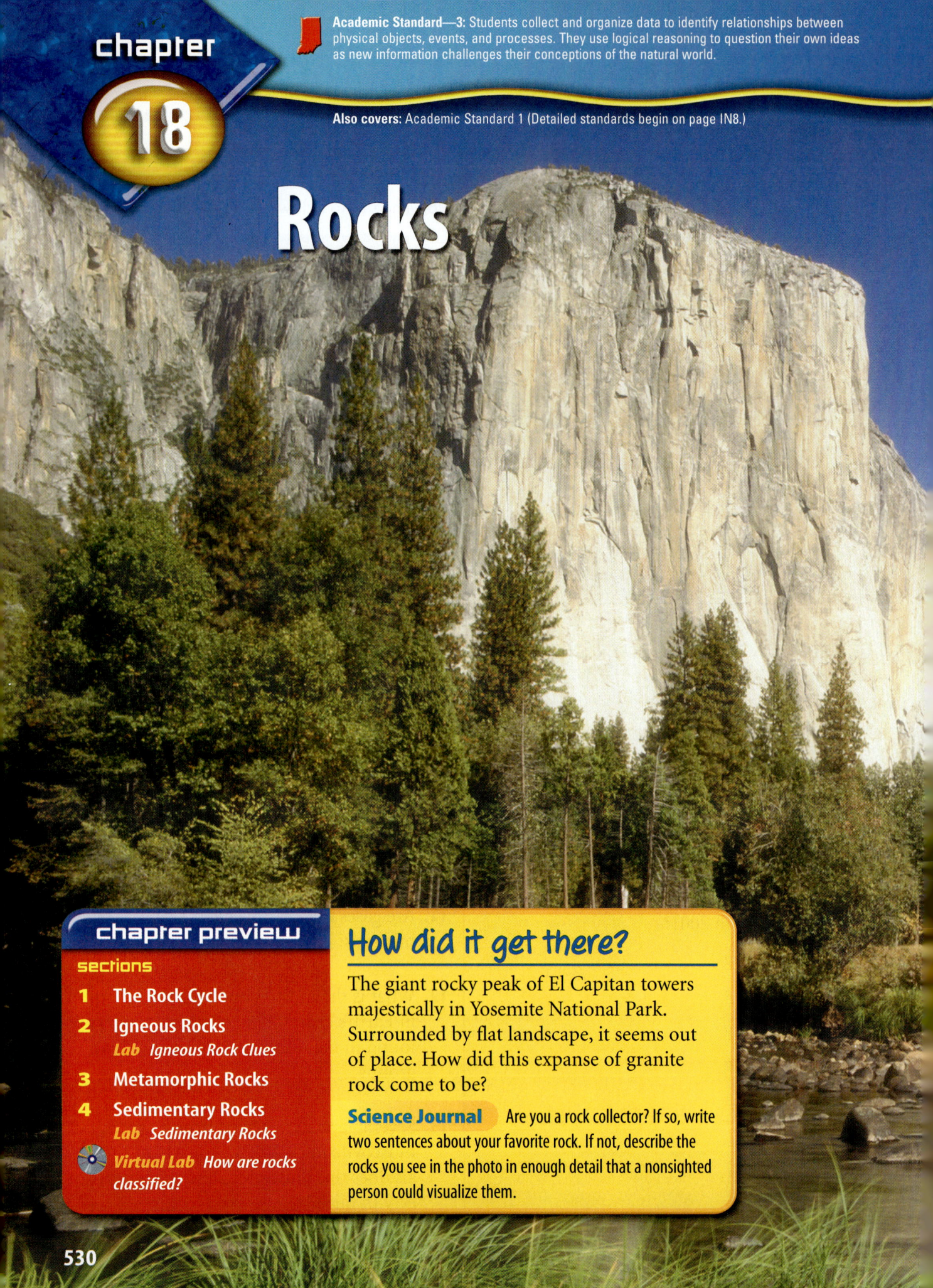

chapter 18

Academic Standard—3: Students collect and organize data to identify relationships between physical objects, events, and processes. They use logical reasoning to question their own ideas as new information challenges their conceptions of the natural world.

Also covers: Academic Standard 1 (Detailed standards begin on page IN8.)

Rocks

chapter preview

sections
1. **The Rock Cycle**
2. **Igneous Rocks**
   Lab Igneous Rock Clues
3. **Metamorphic Rocks**
4. **Sedimentary Rocks**
   Lab Sedimentary Rocks
   Virtual Lab How are rocks classified?

How did it get there?

The giant rocky peak of El Capitan towers majestically in Yosemite National Park. Surrounded by flat landscape, it seems out of place. How did this expanse of granite rock come to be?

Science Journal Are you a rock collector? If so, write two sentences about your favorite rock. If not, describe the rocks you see in the photo in enough detail that a nonsighted person could visualize them.

Start-Up Activities

Observe and Describe Rocks

Some rocks are made of small mineral grains that lock together, like pieces of a puzzle. Others are grains of sand tightly held together or solidified lava that once flowed from a volcano. If you examine rocks closely, you sometimes can tell what they are made of.

1. Collect three different rock samples near your home or school.
2. Draw a picture of the details you see in each rock.
3. Use a magnifying lens to look for different types of materials within the same rock.
4. Describe the characteristics of each rock. Compare your drawings and descriptions with photos, drawings, and descriptions in a rocks and minerals field guide.
5. Use the field guide to try to identify each rock.
6. **Think Critically** Decide whether you think your rocks are mixtures. If so, infer or suggest what these mixtures might contain. Write your explanations in your Science Journal.

Major Rock Types Make the following Foldable to help you organize facts about types of rocks.

STEP 1 **Fold** a sheet of paper in half lengthwise. Make the back edge about 5 cm longer than the front edge.

STEP 2 **Turn** the paper so the fold is on the bottom. Then fold it into thirds.

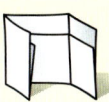

STEP 3 **Unfold and cut** only the top layer along both folds to make three tabs.

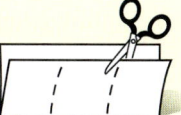

STEP 4 **Label** the Foldable as shown.

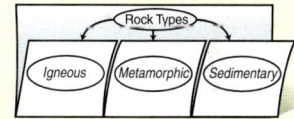

Make an Organizational Study Fold As you read the chapter, write and illustrate what you learn about the three main types of rocks in your study fold.

Preview this chapter's content and activities at in7.msscience.com

531

Standard—7.1.5: Identify some important contributions to the advancement of science, mathematics, and technology that have been made by different kinds of people, in different cultures, at different times.

section 1
The Rock Cycle

as you read

What You'll Learn
- **Distinguish** between a rock and a mineral.
- **Describe** the rock cycle and some changes that a rock could undergo.

Why It's Important
Rocks exist everywhere, from under deep oceans and in high mountain ranges, to the landscape beneath your feet.

Review Vocabulary
mineral: a naturally occurring, inorganic solid with a definite chemical composition and an orderly arrangement of atoms

New Vocabulary
- rock
- rock cycle

What is a rock?

Imagine you and some friends are exploring a creek. Your eye catches a glint from a piece of rock at the edge of the water. As you wander over to pick up the rock, you notice that it is made of different-colored materials. Some of the colors reflect light, while others are dull. You put the rock in your pocket for closer inspection in science lab.

Common Rocks The next time you walk past a large building or monument, stop and take a close look at it. Chances are that it is made out of common rock. In fact, most rock used for building stone contains one or more common minerals, called rock-forming minerals, such as quartz, feldspar, mica, or calcite. When you look closely, the sparkles you see are individual crystals of minerals. A **rock** is a mixture of such minerals, rock fragments, volcanic glass, organic matter, or other natural materials. **Figure 1** shows minerals mixed together to form the rock granite. You might even find granite near your home.

Figure 1 Mount Rushmore, in South Dakota, is made of granite. Granite is a mixture of feldspar, quartz, mica, hornblende, and other minerals.

532 CHAPTER 18 Rocks

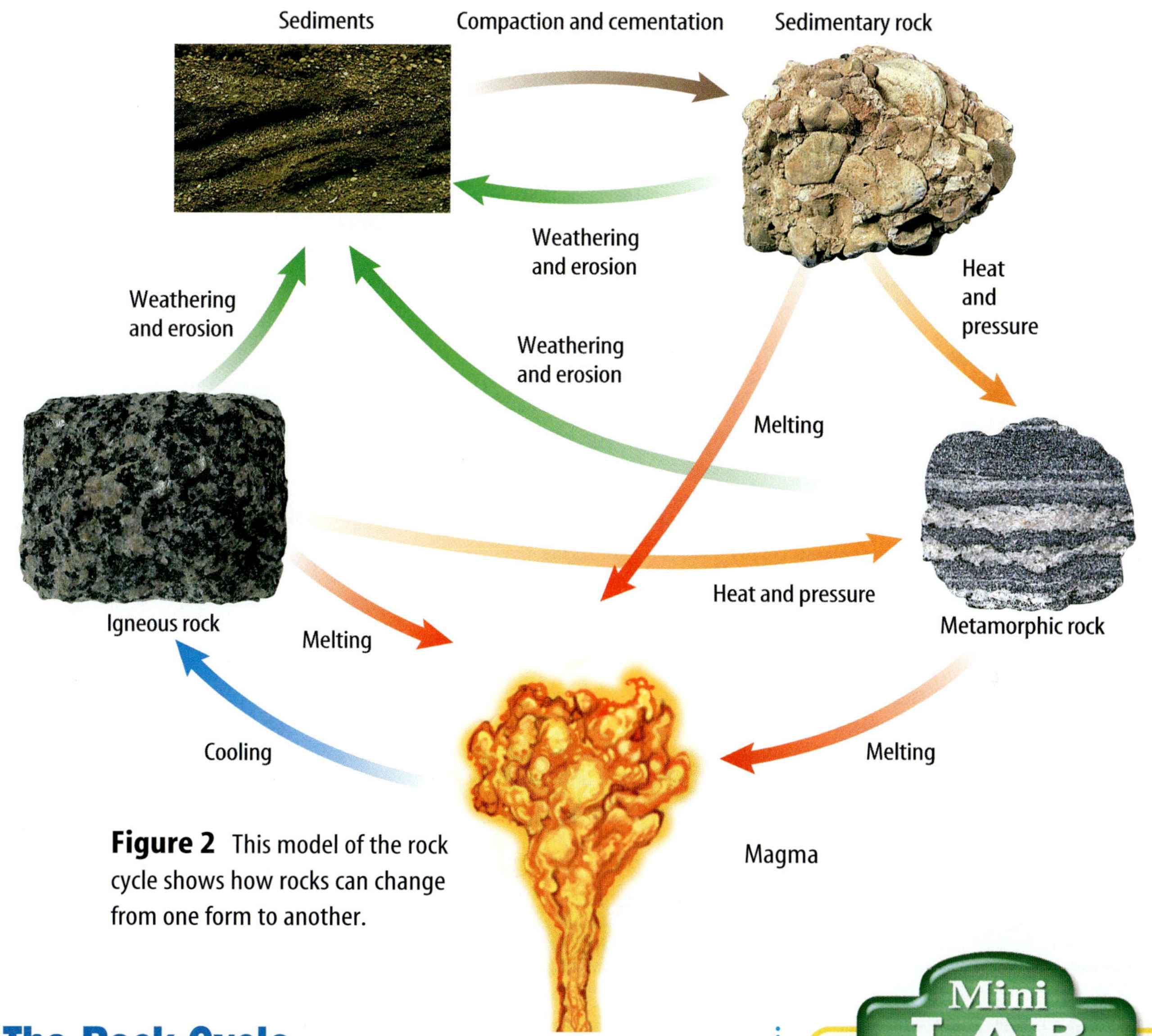

Figure 2 This model of the rock cycle shows how rocks can change from one form to another.

The Rock Cycle

To show how rocks slowly change through time, scientists have created a model called the **rock cycle,** shown in **Figure 2.** It illustrates the processes that create and change rocks. The rock cycle shows the three types of rock—igneous, metamorphic, and sedimentary—and the processes that form them.

Look at the rock cycle and notice that rocks change by many processes. For example, a sedimentary rock can change by heat and pressure to form a metamorphic rock. The metamorphic rock then can melt and later cool to form an igneous rock. The igneous rock then could be broken into fragments by weathering and erode away. The fragments might later compact and cement together to form another sedimentary rock. Any given rock can change into any of the three major rock types. A rock even can transform into another rock of the same type.

 *What is illustrated by the rock cycle?*

Mini LAB

Modeling Rock

Procedure
1. Mix about 10 mL of **white glue** with about 7 g of **dirt** or **sand** in a **small paper cup.**
2. Stir the mixture and then allow it to harden overnight.
3. Tear away the paper cup carefully from your mixture.

Analysis
1. Which rock type is similar to your hardened mixture?
2. Which part of the rock cycle did you model?

Try at Home

SECTION 1 The Rock Cycle **533**

NATIONAL GEOGRAPHIC VISUALIZING THE ROCK CYCLE

Figure 3

Rocks continuously form and transform in a process that geologists call the rock cycle. For example, molten rock—from volcanoes such as Washington's Mount Rainier, background—cools and solidifies to form igneous rock. It slowly breaks down when exposed to air and water to form sediments. These sediments are compacted or cemented into sedimentary rock. Heat and pressure might transform sedimentary rock into metamorphic rock. When metamorphic rock melts and hardens, igneous rock forms again. There is no distinct beginning, nor is there an end, to the rock cycle.

▲ The black sand beach of this Polynesian island is sediment weathered and eroded from the igneous rock of a volcano nearby.

▲ This alluvial fan on the edge of Death Valley, California, was formed when gravel, sand, and finer sediments were deposited by a stream emerging from a mountain canyon.

▲ Layers of shale and chalk form Kansas's Monument Rocks. They are remnants of sediments deposited on the floor of the ancient sea that once covered much of this region.

▲ Heat and pressure deep below Earth's surface can change rock into metamorphic rock, like this banded gneiss.

Matter and the Rock Cycle

The rock cycle, illustrated in **Figure 3**, shows how rock can be weathered to small rock and mineral grains. This material then can be eroded and carried away by wind, water, or ice. When you think of erosion, it might seem that the material is somehow destroyed and lost from the cycle. This is not the case. The chemical elements that make up minerals and rocks are not destroyed. This fact illustrates the principle of conservation of matter. The changes that take place in the rock cycle never destroy or create matter. The elements are just redistributed in other forms.

Figure 4 The rock formations at Siccar Point, Scotland, show that rocks undergo constant change.

 *What is the principle of conservation of matter?*

Discovering the Rock Cycle James Hutton, a Scottish physician and naturalist, first recognized in 1788 that rocks undergo profound changes. Hutton noticed, among other things, that some layers of solid rock in Siccar Point, shown in **Figure 4,** had been altered since they formed. Instead of showing a continuous pattern of horizontal layering, some of the rock layers at Siccar Point are tilted and partly eroded. However, the younger rocks above them are nearly horizontal.

Hutton published these and other observations, which proved that rocks are subject to constant change. Hutton's early recognition of the rock cycle continues to influence geologists.

section 1 review

Summary

What is a rock?
- Rocks are mixtures of minerals, rock fragments, organic matter, volcanic glass, and other materials found in nature.

The Rock Cycle
- The three major types of rock are igneous, metamorphic, and sedimentary.
- Rock cycle processes do not create or destroy matter.
- Processes that are part of the rock cycle change rocks slowly over time.
- In the late eighteenth century, James Hutton recognized some rock cycle processes by observing rocks in the field.
- Some of Hutton's ideas continue to influence geologic thinking today.

Self Check

1. **Explain** how rocks differ from minerals.
2. **Compare and contrast** igneous and metamorphic rock formation.
3. **Describe** the major processes of the rock cycle.
4. **Explain** one way that the rock cycle can illustrate the principle of conservation of matter.
5. **Think Critically** How would you define magma based on the illustration in **Figure 2**? How would you define sediment and sedimentary rock?

Applying Skills

6. **Communicate** Review the model of the rock cycle in **Figure 2.** In your Science Journal, write a story or poem that explains what can happen to a sedimentary rock as it changes throughout the rock cycle.

section 2

This section builds a foundation for **Standards 7.3.8 and 7.3.9.**

Igneous Rocks

as you read

What You'll Learn
- **Recognize** magma and lava as the materials that cool to form igneous rocks.
- **Contrast** the formation of intrusive and extrusive igneous rocks.
- **Contrast** granitic and basaltic igneous rocks.

Why It's Important
Igneous rocks are the most abundant kind of rock in Earth's crust. They contain many valuable resources.

Review Vocabulary
element: substance made of one type of atom that cannot be broken down by ordinary chemical or physical means

New Vocabulary
- igneous rock
- lava
- intrusive
- extrusive
- basaltic
- granitic

Formation of Igneous Rocks

Perhaps you've heard of recent volcanic eruptions in the news. When some volcanoes erupt, they eject a flow of molten rock material, as shown in **Figure 5.** Molten rock material, called magma, flows when it is hot and becomes solid when it cools. When hot magma cools and hardens, it forms **igneous (IHG nee us) rock.** Why do volcanoes erupt, and where does the molten material come from?

Magma In certain places within Earth, the temperature and pressure are just right for rocks to melt and form magma. Most magmas come from deep below Earth's surface. Magma is located at depths ranging from near the surface to about 150 km below the surface. Temperatures of magmas range from about 650°C to 1,200°C, depending on their chemical compositions and pressures exerted on them.

The heat that melts rocks comes from sources within Earth's interior. One source is the decay of radioactive elements within Earth. Some heat is left over from the formation of the planet, which originally was molten. Radioactive decay of elements contained in rocks balances some heat loss as Earth continues to cool.

Because magma is less dense than surrounding solid rock, it is forced upward toward the surface, as shown in **Figure 6.** When magma reaches Earth's surface and flows from volcanoes, it is called **lava.**

Figure 5 Some lava is highly fluid and free-flowing, as shown by this spectacular lava fall in Volcano National Park, East Rift, Kilauea, Hawaii.

536 CHAPTER 18 Rocks

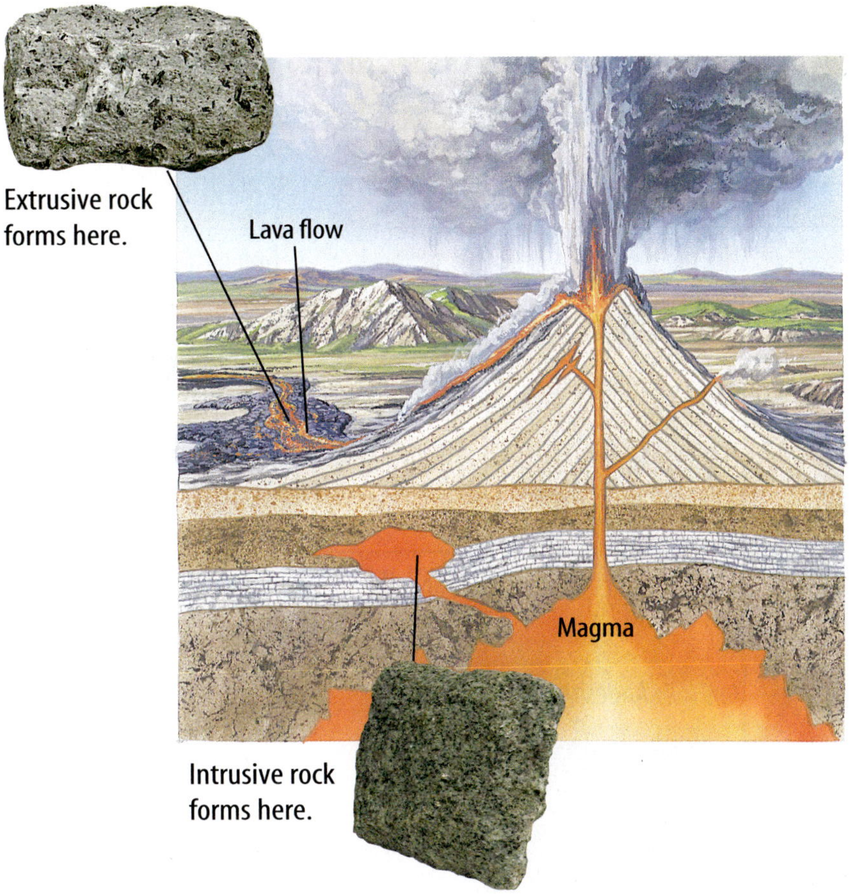

Figure 6 Intrusive rocks form from magma trapped below Earth's surface. Extrusive rocks form from lava flowing at the surface.

Intrusive Rocks Magma is melted rock material composed of common elements and fluids. As magma cools, atoms and compounds in the liquid rearrange themselves into new crystals called mineral grains. Rocks form as these mineral grains grow together. Rocks that form from magma below the surface, as illustrated in **Figure 6,** are called **intrusive** igneous rocks. Intrusive rocks are found at the surface only after the layers of rock and soil that once covered them have been removed by erosion. Erosion occurs when the rocks are pushed up by forces within Earth. Because intrusive rocks form at depth and they are surrounded by other rocks, it takes a long time for them to cool. Slowly cooled magma produces individual mineral grains that are large enough to be observed with the unaided eye.

Extrusive Rocks **Extrusive** igneous rocks are formed as lava cools on the surface of Earth. When lava flows on the surface, as illustrated in **Figure 6,** it is exposed to air and water. Lava, such as the basaltic lava shown in **Figure 5,** cools quickly under these conditions. The quick cooling rate keeps mineral grains from growing large, because the atoms in the liquid don't have the time to arrange into large crystals. Therefore, extrusive igneous rocks are fine grained.

 *What controls the grain size of an igneous rock?*

Table 1 Common Igneous Rocks

Magma Type	Basaltic	Andesitic	Granitic
Intrusive	Gabbro	Diorite	Granite
Extrusive	Basalt, Scoria	Andesite	Rhyolite, Obsidian, Pumice

Topic: Rock Formation
Visit in7.msscience.com for Web links to information about intrusive and extrusive rocks.

Activity List several geographic settings where intrusive or extrusive rocks are found. Select one setting for intrusive rocks, and one for extrusive rocks. Describe how igneous rocks form in the two settings, and locate an example of each on a map.

Volcanic Glass Pumice, obsidian, and scoria are examples of volcanic glass. These rocks cooled so quickly that few or no mineral grains formed. Most of the atoms in these rocks are not arranged in orderly patterns, and few crystals are present.

In the case of pumice and scoria, gases become trapped in the gooey molten material as it cools. Some of these gases eventually escape, but holes are left behind where the rock formed around the pockets of gas.

Classifying Igneous Rocks

Igneous rocks are intrusive or extrusive depending on how they are formed. A way to further classify these rocks is by the magma from which they form. As shown in **Table 1,** an igneous rock can form from basaltic, andesitic, or granitic magma. The type of magma that cools to form an igneous rock determines important chemical and physical properties of that rock. These include mineral composition, density, color, and melting temperature.

 *Name two ways igneous rocks are classified.*

Basaltic Rocks Basaltic (buh SAWL tihk) igneous rocks are dense, dark-colored rocks. They form from magma that is rich in iron and magnesium and poor in silica, which is the compound SiO_2. The presence of iron and magnesium in minerals in basalt gives basalt its dark color. Basaltic lava is fluid and flows freely from volcanoes in Hawaii, such as Kilauea. How does this explain the black beach sand common in Hawaii?

Granitic Rocks Granitic igneous rocks are light-colored rocks of a lower density than basaltic rocks. Granitic magma is thick and stiff and contains lots of silica but lesser amounts of iron and magnesium. Because granitic magma is stiff, it can build up a great deal of gas pressure, which is released explosively during violent volcanic eruptions.

Andesitic Rocks Andesitic igneous rocks have mineral compositions between those of basaltic and granitic rocks. Many volcanoes around the rim of the Pacific Ocean formed from andesitic magmas. Like volcanoes that erupt granitic magma, these volcanoes also can erupt violently.

Take another look at **Table 1.** Basalt forms at the surface of Earth because it is an extrusive rock. Granite forms below Earth's surface from magma with a high concentration of silica. When you identify an igneous rock, you can infer how it formed and the type of magma that it formed from.

Melting Rock Inside Earth, materials contained in rocks can melt. In your Science Journal, describe what is happening to the atoms and molecules to cause this change of state.

section 2 review

Summary

Formation of Igneous Rocks
- When molten rock material, called magma, cools and hardens, igneous rock forms.
- Intrusive igneous rocks form as magma cools and hardens slowly, beneath Earth's surface.
- Extrusive igneous rocks form as lava cools and hardens rapidly, at or above Earth's surface.

Classifying Igneous Rocks
- Igneous rocks are further classified according to their mineral compositions.
- The violent nature of some volcanic eruptions is partly explained by the composition of the magma that feeds them.

Self Check

1. **Explain** why some types of magma form igneous rocks that are dark colored and dense.
2. **Identify** the property of magma that causes it to be forced upward toward Earth's surface.
3. **Explain** The texture of obsidian is best described as glassy. Why does obsidian contain few or no mineral grains?
4. **Think Critically** Study the photos in **Table 1.** How are granite and rhyolite similar? How are they different?

Applying Skills

5. **Make and Use Graphs** Four elements make up most of the rocks in Earth's crust. They are: *oxygen—46.6 percent, aluminum—8.1 percent, silicon—27.7 percent,* and *iron—5.0 percent.* Make a bar graph of these data. What might you infer from the low amount of iron?

in7.msscience.com/self_check_quiz

Igneous Rock Clues

You've learned how color often is used to estimate the composition of an igneous rock. The texture of an igneous rock describes its overall appearance, including mineral grain sizes and the presence or absence of bubble holes, for example. In most cases, grain size relates to how quickly the magma or lava cooled. Crystals you can see without a magnifying lens indicate slower cooling. Smaller, fine-grained crystals indicate quicker cooling, possibly due to volcanic activity. Rocks with glassy textures cooled so quickly that there was no time to form mineral grains.

Real-World Question

What does an igneous rock's texture and color indicate about its formation history?

Goals

- **Classify** different samples of igneous rocks by color and infer their composition.
- **Observe** the textures of igneous rocks and infer how they formed.

Materials

rhyolite   granite
basalt   obsidian
vesicular basalt gabbro
pumice   magnifying lens

Safety Precautions

WARNING: *Some rock samples might have sharp edges. Always use caution while handling samples.*

Procedure

1. **Arrange** rocks according to color (light or dark). Record your observations in your Science Journal.
2. **Arrange** rocks according to similar texture. Consider grain sizes and shapes, presence of holes, etc. Use your magnifying lens to see small features more clearly. Record your observations.

Conclude and Apply

1. **Infer** which rocks are granitic based on color.
2. **Infer** which rocks cooled quickly. What observations led you to this inference?
3. **Identify** any samples that suggest gases were escaping from them as they cooled.
4. **Describe** Which samples have a glassy appearance? How did these rocks form?
5. **Infer** which samples are not volcanic. Explain.

Communicating Your Data

Research the compositions of each of your samples. Did the colors of any samples lead you to infer the wrong compositions? Communicate to your class what you learned.

Standard—7.3.9: Explain that sedimentary rock, when buried deep enough, may be reformed by pressure and heat, perhaps melting and recrystallizing into different kinds of rock. Describe that these reformed rock layers may be forced up again to become land surface and even mountains, and subsequently erode.

section 3

Metamorphic Rocks

Formation of Metamorphic Rocks

Have you ever packed your lunch in the morning and not been able to recognize it at lunchtime? You might have packed a sandwich, banana, and a large bottle of water. You know you didn't smash your lunch on the way to school. However, you didn't think about how the heavy water bottle would damage your food if the bottle was allowed to rest on the food all day. The heat in your locker and the pressure from the heavy water bottle changed your sandwich. Like your lunch, rocks can be affected by changes in temperature and pressure.

Metamorphic Rocks Rocks that have changed because of changes in temperature and pressure or the presence of hot, watery fluids are called **metamorphic rocks**. Changes that occur can be in the form of the rock, shown in **Figure 7,** the composition of the rock, or both. Metamorphic rocks can form from igneous, sedimentary, or other metamorphic rocks. What Earth processes can change these rocks?

as you read

What You'll Learn
- **Describe** the conditions in Earth that cause metamorphic rocks to form.
- **Classify** metamorphic rocks as foliated or nonfoliated.

Why It's Important
Metamorphic rocks are useful because of their unique properties.

Review Vocabulary
pressure: the amount of force exerted per unit of area

New Vocabulary
- metamorphic rock
- foliated
- nonfoliated

+ pressure →

Figure 7 The mineral grains in granite are flattened and aligned when heat and pressure are applied to them. As a result, gneiss is formed.
Describe other conditions that can cause metamorphic rocks to form.

Topic: Shale Metamorphism

Visit in7.msscience.com for Web links to information about the metamorphism of shale. Communicate to your class what you learn.

Activity Make a table with headings that are major rock types that form from shale metamorphism. Under each rock heading, make a list of minerals that can occur in the rock.

Indiana Academic Standard Check

7.3.9: Explain that sedimentary rock, when buried deep enough, may be reformed by pressure and heat, perhaps . . . recrystallizing into different kinds of rock. . . .

✓ Beginning with shale, name the sequence of rock types as increasing temperature and pressure are applied.

Heat and Pressure Rocks beneath Earth's surface are under great pressure from rock layers above them. Temperature also increases with depth in Earth. In some places, the heat and pressure are just right to cause rocks to melt and magma to form. In other areas where melting doesn't occur, some mineral grains can change by dissolving and recrystallizing—especially in the presence of fluids. Sometimes, under these conditions, minerals exchange atoms with surrounding minerals and new, bigger minerals form.

Depending upon the amount of pressure and temperature applied, one type of rock can change into several different metamorphic rocks, and each type of metamorphic rock can come from several kinds of parent rocks. For example, the sedimentary rock shale will change into slate. As increasing pressure and temperature are applied, the slate can change into phyllite, then schist, and eventually gneiss. Schist also can form when basalt is metamorphosed, or changed, and gneiss can come from granite.

 *How can one type of rock change into several different metamorphic rocks?*

Hot Fluids Did you know that fluids can move through rock? These fluids, which are mostly water with dissolved elements and compounds, can react chemically with a rock and change its composition, especially when the fluids are hot. That's what happens when rock surrounding a hot magma body reacts with hot fluids from the magma, as shown in **Figure 8**. Most fluids that transform rocks during metamorphic processes are hot and mainly are comprised of water and carbon dioxide.

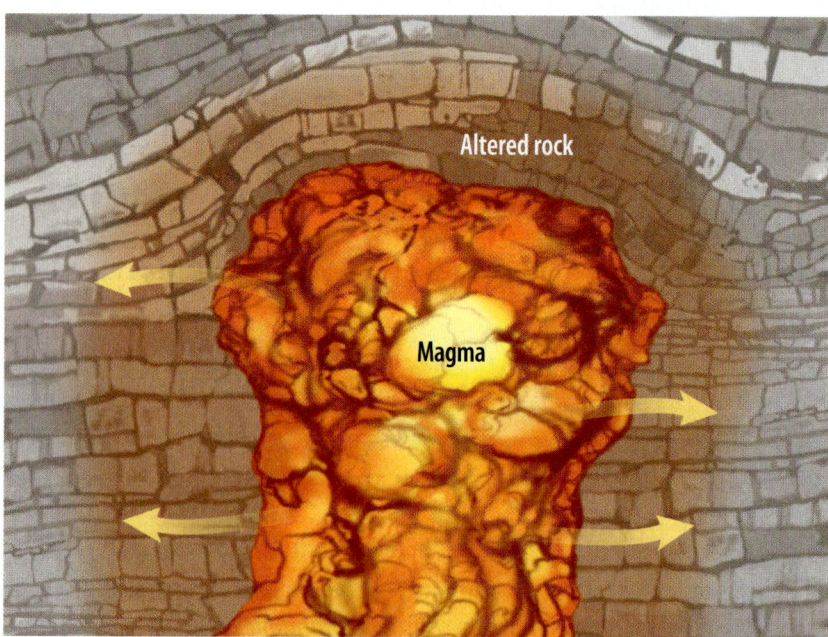

Figure 8 In the presence of hot, water-rich fluids, solid rock can change in mineral composition without having to melt.

Classifying Metamorphic Rocks

Metamorphic rocks form from igneous, sedimentary, or other metamorphic rocks. Heat, pressure, and hot fluids trigger the changes. Each resulting rock can be classified according to its composition and texture.

Foliated Rocks When mineral grains line up in parallel layers, the metamorphic rock is said to have a **foliated** texture. Two examples of foliated rocks are slate and gneiss. Slate forms from the sedimentary rock shale. The minerals in shale arrange into layers when they are exposed to heat and pressure. As **Figure 9** shows, slate separates easily along these foliation layers.

The minerals in slate are pressed together so tightly that water can't pass between them easily. Because it's watertight, slate is ideal for paving around pools and patios. The naturally flat nature of slate and the fact that it splits easily make it useful for roofing and tiling many surfaces.

Gneiss (NISE), another foliated rock, forms when granite and other rocks are changed. Foliation in gneiss shows up as alternating light and dark bands. Movement of atoms has separated the dark minerals, such as biotite mica, from the light minerals, which are mainly quartz and feldspar.

Figure 9 Slate often is used as a building or landscaping material. **Identify** *the properties that make slate so useful for these purposes.*

 *What type of metamorphic rock is composed of mineral grains arranged in parallel layers?*

Figure 10 This exhibit in Vermont shows the beauty of carved marble.

Nonfoliated Rocks In some metamorphic rocks, layering does not occur. The mineral grains grow and rearrange, but they don't form layers. This process produces a **nonfoliated** texture.

Sandstone is a sedimentary rock that's often composed mostly of quartz grains. When sandstone is heated under a lot of pressure, the grains of quartz grow in size and become interlocking, like the pieces of a jigsaw puzzle. The resulting rock is called quartzite.

Marble is another nonfoliated metamorphic rock. Marble forms from the sedimentary rock limestone, which is composed of the mineral calcite. Usually, marble contains several other minerals besides calcite. For example, hornblende and serpentine give marble a black or greenish tone, whereas hematite makes it red. As **Figure 10** shows, marble is a popular material for artists to sculpt because it is not as hard as other rocks.

So far, you've investigated only a portion of the rock cycle. You still haven't observed how sedimentary rocks are formed and how igneous and metamorphic rocks evolve from them. The next section will complete your investigation of the rock cycle.

section 3 review

Summary

Formation of Metamorphic Rocks
- Changes in pressure, temperature, or the presence of fluids can cause metamorphic rocks to form.
- Rock, altered by metamorphic processes at high temperatures and pressures, changes in the solid state without melting.
- Hot fluids that move through and react with preexisting rock are composed mainly of water and carbon dioxide.
- One source of hot, watery fluids is magma bodies close to the changing rock.
- Any parent rock type—igneous, metamorphic, or sedimentary—can become a metamorphic rock.

Classifying Metamorphic Rocks
- Texture and mineral composition determine how a metamorphic rock is classified.
- Physical properties of metamorphic rocks, such as the watertight nature of slate, make them useful for many purposes.

Self Check

1. **Explain** what role fluids play in rock metamorphism.
2. **Describe** how metamorphic rocks are classified. What are the characteristics of rocks in each of these classifications?
3. **Identify** Give an example of a foliated and a nonfoliated metamorphic rock. Name one of their possible parent rocks.
4. **Think Critically** Marble is a common material used to make sculptures, but not just because it's a beautiful stone. What properties of marble make it useful for this purpose?

Applying Skills

5. **Concept Map** Put the following events in an events-chain concept map that explains how a metamorphic rock might form from an igneous rock. *Hint:* Start with "Igneous Rock Forms." Use each event just once.

   Events: *sedimentary rock forms, weathering occurs, heat and pressure are applied, igneous rock forms, metamorphic rock forms, erosion occurs, sediments are formed, deposition occurs*

Standard—7.3.8: Describe how sediments of sand and smaller particles, sometimes containing the remains of organisms, are gradually buried and are cemented together by dissolved minerals to form solid rock again.

section 4

Also covers: 7.3.9, 7.3.10 (Detailed standards begin on page IN8.)

Sedimentary Rocks

Formation of Sedimentary Rocks

Igneous rocks are the most common rocks on Earth, but because most of them exist below the surface, you might not have seen too many of them. That's because 75 percent of the rocks exposed at the surface are sedimentary rocks.

Sediments are loose materials such as rock fragments, mineral grains, and bits of shell that have been moved by wind, water, ice, or gravity. If you look at the model of the rock cycle, you will see that sediments come from already-existing rocks that are weathered and eroded. **Sedimentary rock** forms when sediments are pressed and cemented together, or when minerals form from solutions.

Stacked Rocks Sedimentary rocks often form as layers. The older layers are on the bottom because they were deposited first. Sedimentary rock layers are a lot like the books and papers in your locker. Last week's homework is on the bottom, and today's notes will be deposited on top of the stack. However, if you disturb the stack, the order in which the books and papers are stacked will change, as shown in **Figure 11.** Sometimes, forces within Earth such as folding and faulting overturn or displace layers of rock, so that oldest are no longer on the bottom.

as you read

What You'll Learn
- **Explain** how sedimentary rocks form from sediments.
- **Classify** sedimentary rocks as detrital, chemical, or organic in origin.
- **Summarize** the rock cycle.

Why It's Important
Some sedimentary rocks, like coal, are important sources of energy.

Review Vocabulary
weathering: surface processes that work to break down rock mechanically or chemically

New Vocabulary
- sediment
- sedimentary rock
- compaction
- cementation

Figure 11 Like sedimentary rock layers, the oldest paper is at the bottom of the stack. If the stack is disturbed, then it is no longer in order.

SECTION 4 Sedimentary Rocks **545**

Mini LAB

Classifying Sediments

Procedure

WARNING: *Use care when handling sharp objects.*

1. Collect different samples of **sediment.**
2. Spread them on a sheet of **paper.**
3. Use **Table 2** to determine the size range of gravel-sized sediment.
4. Use **tweezers or a dissecting probe** and a **magnifying lens** to separate the gravel-sized sediments.
5. Separate the gravel into piles—rounded or angular.

Analysis

1. Describe the grains in both piles.
2. Determine what rock could form from each type of sediment you have.

Figure 12 During compaction, pore space between sediments decreases, causing them to become packed together more tightly.

Classifying Sedimentary Rocks

Sedimentary rocks can be made of just about any material found in nature. Sediments come from weathered and eroded igneous, metamorphic, and sedimentary rocks. Sediments also come from the remains of some organisms. The composition of a sedimentary rock depends upon the composition of the sediments from which it formed.

Like igneous and metamorphic rocks, sedimentary rocks are classified by their composition and by the manner in which they formed. Sedimentary rocks usually are classified as detrital, chemical, or organic.

Detrital Sedimentary Rocks

The word *detrital* (dih TRI tul) comes from the Latin word *detritus,* which means "to wear away." Detrital sedimentary rocks, such as those shown in **Table 2,** are made from the broken fragments of other rocks. These loose sediments are compacted and cemented together to form solid rock.

Weathering and Erosion When rock is exposed to air, water, or ice, it is unstable and breaks down chemically and mechanically. This process, which breaks rocks into smaller pieces, is called weathering. **Table 2** shows how these pieces are classified by size. The movement of weathered material is called erosion.

Compaction Erosion moves sediments to a new location, where they then are deposited. Here, layer upon layer of sediment builds up. Pressure from the upper layers pushes down on the lower layers. If the sediments are small, they can stick together and form solid rock. This process, shown in **Figure 12,** is called **compaction.**

Reading Check *How do rocks form through compaction?*

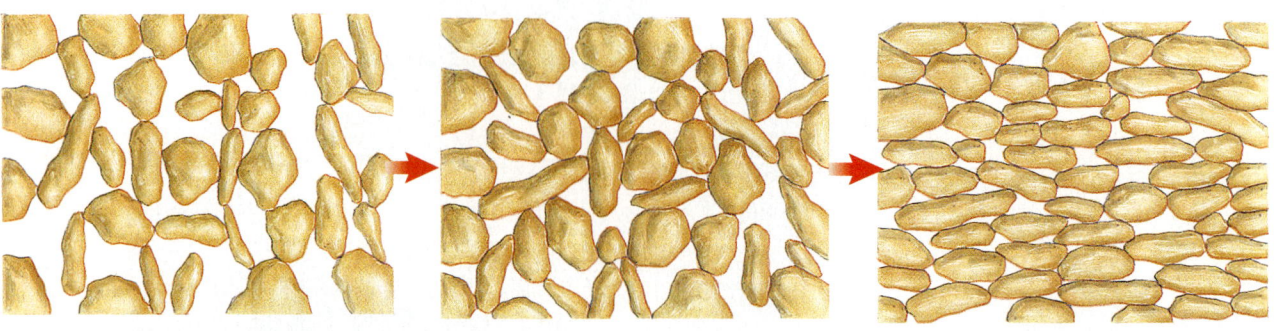

546 CHAPTER 18 Rocks

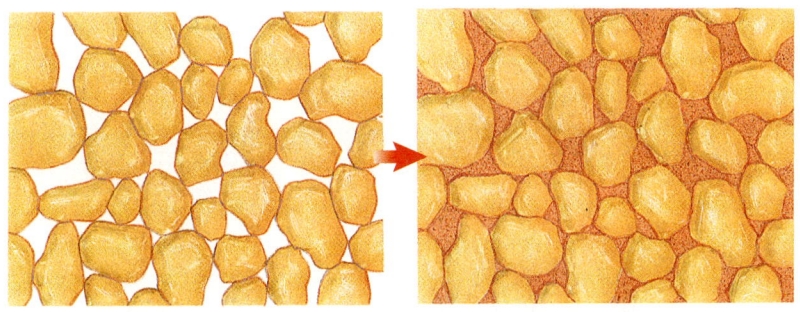

Figure 13 Sediments are cemented together as minerals crystallize between grains.

Cementation If sediments are large, like sand and pebbles, pressure alone can't make them stick together. Large sediments have to be cemented together. As water moves through soil and rock, it picks up materials released from minerals during weathering. The resulting solution of water and dissolved materials moves through open spaces between sediments. **Cementation**, which is shown in **Figure 13,** occurs when minerals such as quartz, calcite, and hematite are deposited between the pieces of sediment. These minerals, acting as natural cements, hold the sediment together like glue, making a detrital sedimentary rock.

Shape and Size of Sediments Detrital rocks have granular textures, much like granulated sugar. They are named according to the shapes and sizes of the sediments that form them. For example, conglomerate and breccia both form from large sediments, as shown in **Table 2.** If the sediments are rounded, the rock is called conglomerate. If the sediments have sharp angles, the rock is called breccia. The roundness of sediment particles depends on how far they have been moved by wind or water.

Table 2 Sediment Sizes and Detrital Rocks				
Sediment	Clay	Silt	Sand	Gravel
Size Range	<0.004 mm	0.004–0.063 mm	0.063–2 mm	>2 mm
Example	Shale	Siltstone	Sandstone	Conglomerate (shown) or Breccia

SECTION 4 Sedimentary Rocks

Conglomerate

Figure 14 Although concrete strongly resembles conglomerate, concrete is not a rock because it does not occur in nature.

Sedimentary Petrology Research the work done by sedimentary petrologists. Include examples of careers in academia and in industry.

Materials Found in Sedimentary Rocks The gravel-sized sediments in conglomerate and breccia can consist of any type of rock or mineral. Often, they are composed of chunks of the minerals quartz and feldspar. They also can be pieces of rocks such as gneiss, granite, or limestone. The cement that holds the sediments together usually is made of quartz or calcite.

Have you ever looked at the concrete in sidewalks, driveways, and stepping stones? The concrete in **Figure 14** is made of gravel and sand grains that have been cemented together. Although the structure is similar to that of naturally occurring conglomerate, it cannot be considered a rock.

Sandstone is formed from smaller particles than conglomerates and breccias. Its sand-sized sediments can be just about any mineral, but they are usually grains of minerals such as quartz and feldspar that are resistant to weathering. Siltstone is similar to sandstone except it is made of smaller, silt-sized particles. Shale is a detrital sedimentary rock that is made mainly of clay-sized particles. Clay-sized sediments are compacted together by pressure from overlying layers.

Chemical Sedimentary Rocks

Chemical sedimentary rocks form when dissolved minerals come out of solution. You can show that salt is deposited in the bottom of a glass or pan when saltwater solution evaporates. In a similar way, minerals collect when seas or lakes evaporate. The deposits of minerals that come out of solution form sediments and rocks. For example, the sediment making up New Mexico's White Sands desert consists of pieces of a chemical sedimentary rock called rock gypsum. Chemical sedimentary rocks are different. They are not made from pieces of preexisting rocks.

 *How do chemical sedimentary rocks form?*

Limestone Calcium carbonate is carried in solution in ocean water. When calcium carbonate ($CaCO_3$) comes out of solution as calcite and its many crystals grow together, limestone forms. Limestone also can contain other minerals and sediments, but it must be at least 50 percent calcite. Limestone usually is deposited on the bottom of lakes or shallow seas. Large areas of the central United States have limestone bedrock because seas covered much of the country for millions of years. It is hard to imagine Kansas being covered by ocean water, but it has happened several times throughout geological history.

Rock Salt When water that is rich in dissolved salt evaporates, it often deposits the mineral halite. Halite forms rock salt, shown in **Figure 15**. Rock salt deposits can range in thickness from a few meters to more than 400 m. Companies mine these deposits because rock salt is an important resource. It's used in the manufacturing of glass, paper, soap, and dairy products. The halite in rock salt is processed and used as table salt.

Figure 15 Rock salt is extracted from this mine in Germany.

Organic Sedimentary Rocks

Rocks made of the remains of once-living things are called organic sedimentary rocks. One of the most common organic sedimentary rocks is fossil-rich limestone. Like chemical limestone, fossil-rich limestone is made of the mineral calcite. However, fossil-rich limestone mostly contains remains of once-living ocean organisms instead of only calcite that formed directly from ocean water.

Animals such as mussels, clams, corals, and snails make their shells from $CaCO_3$ that eventually becomes calcite. When they die, their shells accumulate on the ocean floor. When these shells are cemented together, fossil-rich limestone forms. If a rock is made completely of shell fragments that you can see, the rock is called coquina (koh KEE nuh).

Chalk Chalk is another organic sedimentary rock that is made of microscopic shells. When you write with naturally occurring chalk, you're crushing and smearing the calcite-shell remains of once-living ocean organisms.

> **Indiana Academic Standard Check**
>
> **7.3.8:** Describe how sediments ... sometimes containing the remains of organisms, are ... buried and cemented together ... to form solid rock again.
>
> ✔ Name the three classifications of sedimentary rocks and describe how they are formed.

Coal Another useful organic sedimentary rock is coal, shown in **Figure 16.** Coal forms when pieces of dead plants are buried under other sediments in swamps. These plant materials are chemically changed by microorganisms. The resulting sediments are compacted over millions of years to form coal, an important source of energy. Much of the coal in North America and Europe formed during a period of geologic time that is so named because of this important reason. The Carboniferous Period, which spans from approximately 360 to 286 million years ago, was named in Europe. So much coal formed during this interval of time that coal's composition—primarily carbon—was the basis for naming a geologic period.

Applying Math — Calculate Thickness

COAL FORMATION It took 300 million years for a layer of plant matter about 0.9 m thick to produce a bed of bituminous coal 0.3 m thick. Estimate the thickness of plant matter that produced a bed of coal 0.15 m thick.

Solution

1. *This is what you know:*
   - original thickness of plant matter = 0.9 m
   - original coal thickness = 0.3 m
   - new coal thickness = 0.15 m

2. *This is what you need to know:* thickness of plant matter needed to form 0.15 m of coal

3. *This is the equation you need to use:* (thickness of plant matter)/(new coal thickness) = (original thickness of plant matter)/(original coal thickness)

4. *Substitute the known values:* (? m plant matter)/(0.15 m coal) = (0.9 m plant matter)/(0.3 m coal)

5. *Solve the equation:* (? m plant matter) = (0.9 m plant matter)(0.15 m coal)/(0.3 m coal) = 0.45 m plant matter

6. *Check your answer:* Multiply your answer by the original coal thickness. Divide by the original plant matter thickness to get the new coal thickness.

Practice Problems

1. Estimate the thickness of plant matter that produced a bed of coal 0.6 m thick.
2. About how much coal would have been produced from a layer of plant matter 0.50 m thick?

For more practice, visit in7.msscience.com/math_practice

Figure 16 This coal layer in Alaska is easily identified by its jet-black color, as compared with other sedimentary layers.

Another Look at the Rock Cycle

You have seen that the rock cycle has no beginning and no end. Rocks change continually from one form to another. Sediments can become so deeply buried that heat and pressure can reform them to become metamorphic or igneous rocks. These reformed rocks later can be uplifted and exposed to the surface—possibly as mountains to be worn away again by erosion.

All of the rocks that you've learned about in this chapter formed through some process within the rock cycle. All of the rocks around you, including those used to build houses and monuments, are part of the rock cycle. Slowly, they are all changing, because the rock cycle is a continuous, dynamic process.

Indiana Academic Standard Check

7.3.9: . . . Describe that these reformed rock layers may be forced up again to become land surface and even mountains, and subsequently erode.

✓ Does the rock cycle end when the rocks erode into sediment?

section 4 review

Summary

Formation of Sedimentary Rocks
- Sedimentary rocks form as layers, with older layers near the bottom of an undisturbed stack.

Classifying Sedimentary Rocks
- To classify a sedimentary rock, determine its composition and texture.

Detrital Sedimentary Rocks
- Rock and mineral fragments make up detrital rocks.

Chemical Sedimentary Rocks
- Chemical sedimentary rocks form from solutions of dissolved minerals.

Organic Sedimentary Rocks
- The remains of once-living organisms make up organic sedimentary rocks.

Self Check

1. **Identify** where sediments come from.
2. **Explain** how compaction is important in the formation of coal.
3. **Compare and contrast** detrital and chemical sedimentary rock.
4. **List** chemical sedimentary rocks that are essential to your health or that are used to make life more convenient. How is each used?
5. **Think Critically** Explain how pieces of granite and slate could both be found in the same conglomerate. How would the granite and slate pieces be held together?

Applying Math

6. **Calculate Ratios** Use information in **Table 2** to estimate how many times larger the largest grains of silt and sand are compared to the largest clay grains.

Sedimentary Rocks

Sedimentary rocks are formed by compaction and cementation of sediment. Because sediment is found in all shapes and sizes, do you think these characteristics could be used to classify detrital sedimentary rocks? Sedimentary rocks also can be classified as chemical or organic.

Real-World Question

How are rock characteristics used to classify sedimentary rocks as detrital, chemical, or organic?

Procedure

1. **Make** a Sedimentary Rock Samples chart in your Science Journal similar to the one shown on the next page.
2. **Determine** the sizes of sediments in each sample, using a magnifying lens and a metric ruler. Using **Table 2,** classify any grains of sediment in the rocks as gravel, sand, silt, or clay. In general, the sediment is silt if it is gritty and just barely visible, and clay if it is smooth and if individual grains are not visible.
3. Place a few drops of 5% HCl solution on each rock sample. Bubbling on a rock indicates the presence of calcite.
4. **Examine** each sample for fossils and describe any that are present.
5. **Determine** whether each sample has a granular or nongranular texture.

Goals
- **Observe** sedimentary rock characteristics.
- **Compare and contrast** sedimentary rock textures.
- **Classify** sedimentary rocks as detrital, chemical, or organic.

Materials
unknown sedimentary rock samples
marking pen
5% hydrochloric acid (HCl) solution
dropper
paper towels
water
magnifying lens
metric ruler

Safety Precautions

WARNING: *HCl is an acid and can cause burns. Wear goggles and a lab apron. Rinse spills with water and wash hands afterward.*

552 CHAPTER 18 Rocks

Using Scientific Methods

Sedimentary Rock Samples

Sample	Observations	Minerals or Fossils Present	Sediment Size	Detrital, Chemical, or Organic	Rock Name
A					
B					
C		Do not write in this book.			
D					
E					

Analyze Your Data

1. **Classify** your samples as detrital, chemical, or organic.
2. **Identify** each rock sample.

Conclude and Apply

1. **Explain** why you tested the rocks with acid. What minerals react with acid?
2. **Compare and contrast** sedimentary rocks that have a granular texture with sedimentary rocks that have a nongranular texture.

Compare your conclusions with those of other students in your class. **For more help, refer to the** Science Skill Handbook.

LAB 553

TIME SCIENCE AND Society

SCIENCE ISSUES THAT AFFECT YOU!

Australia's controversial rock star

One of the most famous rocks in the world is causing serious problems for Australians

Uluru (yew LEW rew), also known as Ayers Rock, is one of the most popular tourist destinations in Australia. This sandstone skyscraper is more than 8 km around, over 300 m high, and extends as much as 4.8 km below the surface. One writer describes it as an iceberg in the desert. Geologists hypothesize that the mighty Uluru rock began forming 550 million years ago during Precambrian time. That's when large mountain ranges started to form in Central Australia.

For more than 25,000 years, this geological wonder has played an important role in the lives of the Aboriginal peoples, the Anangu (a NA noo). These native Australians are the original owners of the rock and have spiritual explanations for its many caves, holes, and scars.

Athlete Nova Benis-Kneebone had the honor of receiving the Olympic torch near the sacred Uluru and carried it partway to the Olympic stadium.

Tourists Take Over

In the 1980s, some 100,000 tourists visited—and many climbed—Uluru. In 2000, the rock attracted about 400,000 tourists. The Anangu take offense at anyone climbing their sacred rock. However, if climbing the rock were outlawed, tourism would be seriously hurt. That would mean less income for Australians.

To respect the Anangu's wishes, the Australian government returned Ayers Rock to the Anangu in 1985 and agreed to call it by its traditional name. The Anangu leased back the rock to the Australian government until the year 2084, when its management will return to the Anangu. Until then, the Anangu will collect 25 percent of the money people pay to visit the rock.

The Aboriginal people encourage tourists to respect their beliefs. They offer a walking tour around the rock, and they show videos about Aboriginal traditions. The Anangu sell T-shirts that say "I *didn't* climb Uluru." They hope visitors to Uluru will wear the T-shirt with pride and respect.

Write Research a natural landmark or large natural land or water formation in your area. What is the geology behind it? When was it formed? How was it formed? Write a folktale that explains its formation. Share your folktale with the class.

For more information, visit in7.msscience.com/time

chapter 18 Study Guide

Reviewing Main Ideas

Section 1 — The Rock Cycle

1. A rock is a mixture of one or more minerals, rock fragments, organic matter, or volcanic glass.
2. The rock cycle includes all processes by which rocks form.

Section 2 — Igneous Rocks

1. Magma and lava are molten materials that harden to form igneous rocks.
2. Intrusive igneous rocks form when magma cools slowly below Earth's surface. Extrusive igneous rocks form when lava cools rapidly at the surface.
3. The compositions of most igneous rocks range from granitic to andesitic to basaltic.

Section 3 — Metamorphic Rocks

1. Heat, pressure, and fluids can cause metamorphic rocks to form.
2. Slate and gneiss are examples of foliated metamorphic rocks. Quartzite and marble are examples of nonfoliated metamorphic rocks.

Section 4 — Sedimentary Rocks

1. Detrital sedimentary rocks form when fragments of rocks and minerals are compacted and cemented together.
2. Chemical sedimentary rocks come out of solution or are left behind by evaporation.
3. Organic sedimentary rocks contain the remains of once-living organisms.

Visualizing Main Ideas

Copy and complete the following concept map on rocks. Use the following terms: organic, metamorphic, foliated, extrusive, igneous, *and* chemical.

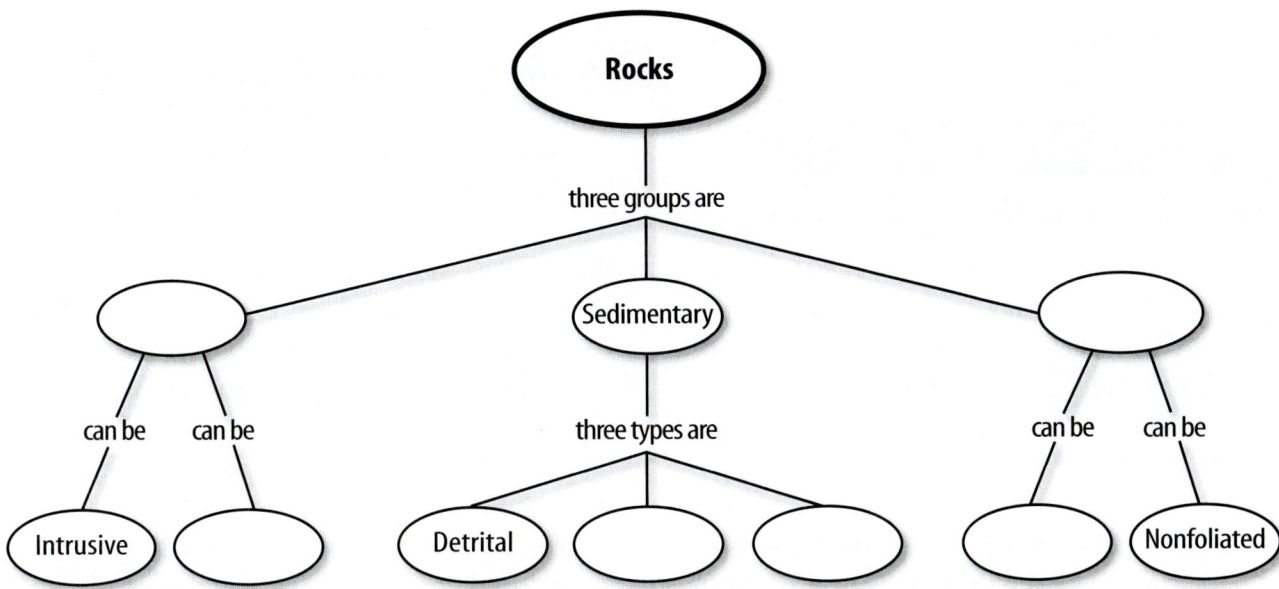

CHAPTER STUDY GUIDE 555

Chapter 18 Review

Using Vocabulary

basaltic p. 539
cementation p. 547
compaction p. 546
extrusive p. 537
foliated p. 543
granitic p. 539
igneous rock p. 536
intrusive p. 537
lava p. 536
metamorphic rock p. 541
nonfoliated p. 544
rock p. 532
rock cycle p. 533
sediment p. 545
sedimentary rock p. 545

Explain the difference between the vocabulary words in each of the following sets.

1. foliated—nonfoliated
2. cementation—compaction
3. sediment—lava
4. extrusive—intrusive
5. rock—rock cycle
6. metamorphic rock—igneous rock—sedimentary rock
7. sediment—sedimentary rock
8. lava—igneous rock
9. rock—sediment
10. basaltic—granitic

Checking Concepts

Choose the word or phrase that best answers the question.

11. Why does magma tend to rise toward Earth's surface?
    A) It is more dense than surrounding rocks.
    B) It is more massive than surrounding rocks.
    C) It is cooler than surrounding rocks.
    D) It is less dense than surrounding rocks.

12. During metamorphism of granite into gneiss, what happens to minerals?
    A) They partly melt.
    B) They become new sediments.
    C) They grow smaller.
    D) They align into layers.

13. Which rock has large mineral grains?
    A) granite   C) obsidian
    B) basalt   D) pumice

14. Which type of rock is shown in this photo?
    A) foliated
    B) nonfoliated
    C) intrusive
    D) extrusive

15. What do igneous rocks form from?
    A) sediments   C) gravel
    B) mud   D) magma

16. What sedimentary rock is made of large, angular pieces of sediments?
    A) conglomerate   C) limestone
    B) breccia   D) chalk

17. Which of the following is an example of a detrital sedimentary rock?
    A) limestone   C) breccia
    B) evaporite   D) chalk

18. What is molten material at Earth's surface called?
    A) limestone   C) breccia
    B) lava   D) granite

19. Which of these is an organic sedimentary rock?
    A) coquina   C) rock salt
    B) sandstone   D) conglomerate

556 CHAPTER REVIEW

in7.msscience.com/vocabulary_puzzlemaker

chapter 18 Review

Thinking Critically

20. **Infer** Granite, pumice, and scoria are igneous rocks. Why doesn't granite have airholes like the other two?

21. **Infer** why marble rarely contains fossils.

22. **Predict** Would you expect quartzite or sandstone to break more easily? Explain your answer.

23. **Compare and contrast** basaltic and granitic magmas.

24. **Form Hypotheses** A geologist was studying rocks in a mountain range. She found a layer of sedimentary rock that had formed in the ocean. Hypothesize how this could happen.

25. **Concept Map** Copy and complete the concept map shown below. Use the following terms and phrases: *magma, sediments, igneous rock, sedimentary rock, metamorphic rock*. Add and label any missing arrows.

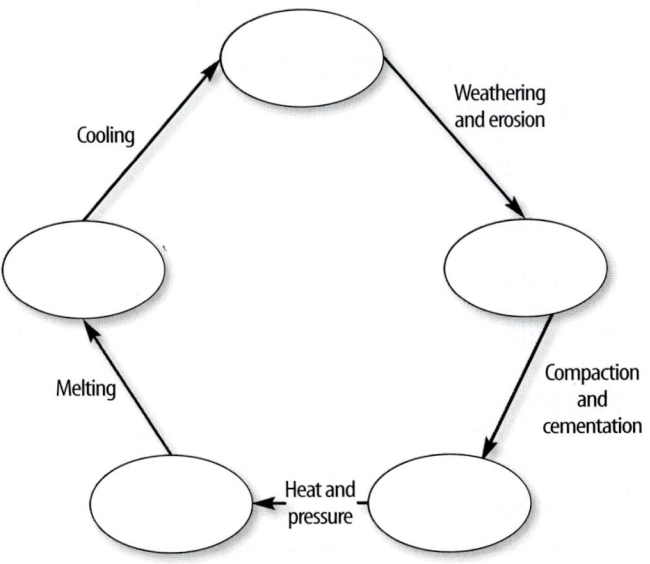

Performance Activities

26. **Poster** Collect a group of rocks. Make a poster that shows the classifications of rocks, and glue your rocks to the poster under the proper headings. Describe your rocks and explain where you found them.

Applying Math

27. **Grain Size** Assume that the conglomerate shown on the second page of the "Sedimentary Rocks" lab is one-half of its actual size. Determine the average length of the gravel in the rock.

28. **Plant Matter** Suppose that a 4-m layer of plant matter was compacted to form a coal layer 1 m thick. By what percent has the thickness of organic material been reduced?

Use the graph below to answer questions 29 and 30.

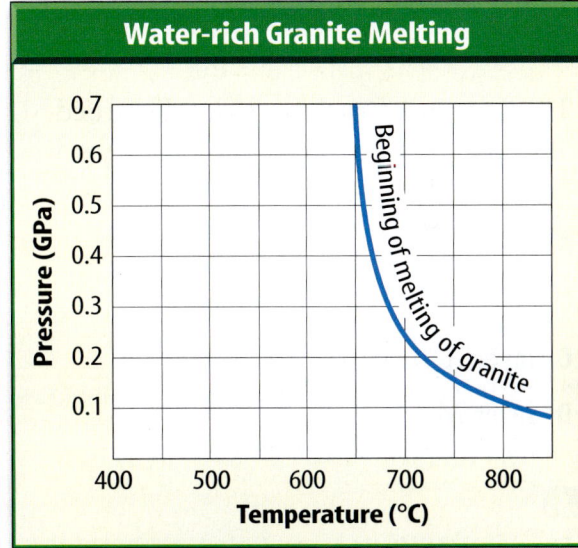

29. **Melting Granite** Determine the melting temperature of a water-rich granite at a pressure of 0.2 GPa.

    Pressure conversions:
    1 GPa, or gigapascal, = 10,000 bars
    1 bar = 0.9869 atmospheres

30. **Melting Pressure** At about what pressure will a water-rich granite melt at 680°C?

chapter 18 Indiana

The assessed Indiana standard appears above the question.

Record your answers on the answer sheet provided by your teacher or on a sheet of paper.

Part 1 Multiple Choice

7.3.10

1. The illustration below shows layers of sedimentary rock.

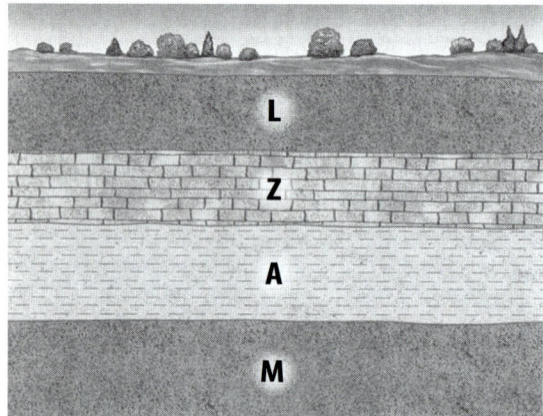

These layers of rock were not disturbed after they were deposited. Which layer was deposited first?

- **A** layer L
- **B** layer Z
- **C** layer A
- **D** layer M

7.3.8

2. During which process do minerals precipitate in the spaces between sediment grains?

- **A** cementation
- **B** compaction
- **C** conglomerate
- **D** weathering

7.3.8

3. Which rock consists mostly of pieces of seashell?

- **A** coquina
- **B** granite
- **C** pumice
- **D** sandstone

The illustration below shows processes of the rock cycle.

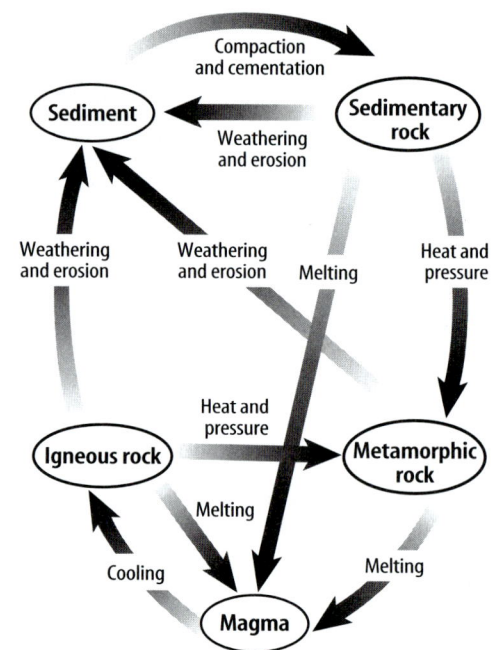

4. Which process in the rock cycle causes magma to form?

- **A** cooling
- **B** erosion
- **C** melting
- **D** weathering

Test-Taking Tip

Careful Reading Read each question carefully for full understanding.

Standards Review

The graph below shows how temperature changes with depth beneath the continents.

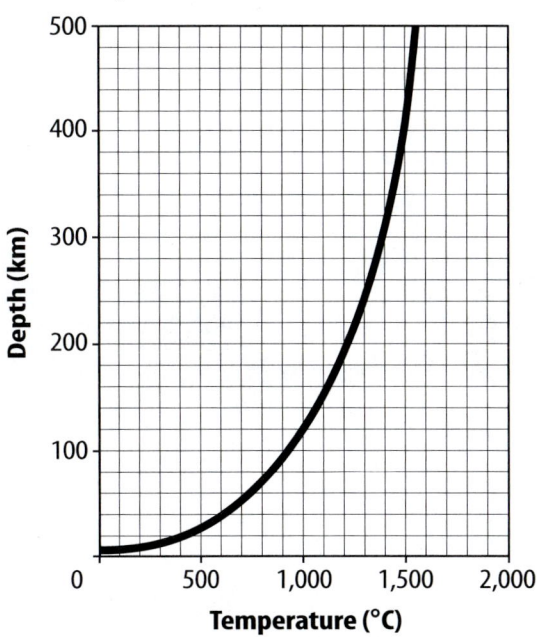

5. About how deep below a continent does the temperature reach 1000°C?

   A 100 km

   B 120 km

   C 140 km

   D 160 km

6. Using the graph above, what is the approximate temperature at a depth of about 60 km beneath a continent?

   A 500°C

   B 750°C

   C 1000°C

   D 1250°C

Part 2 Constructed Response

7.3.8

7. How is the formation of chemical sedimentary rocks similar to the formation of cement in detrital sedimentary rocks?

7.3.8

8. Explain how loose sediment can become sedimentary rock. Describe two processes that hold sediments together when forming sedimentary rock.

9. Why does pressure increase with depth in Earth? How does higher pressure affect rocks?

10. The table below shows an igneous rock classification.

Magma Type	Basaltic	Andesitic	Granitic
Intrusive	Gabbro	Diorite	Granite
Extrusive	Basalt or scoria	Andesite	Rhyolite, pumice, or obsidian

Explain how igneous rocks are classified.

7.3.10

11. A geologist found a sequence of rocks in which 200-million-year-old shales were on top of 100-million-year-old sandstones. Hypothesize how this could happen.

STANDARDS REVIEW

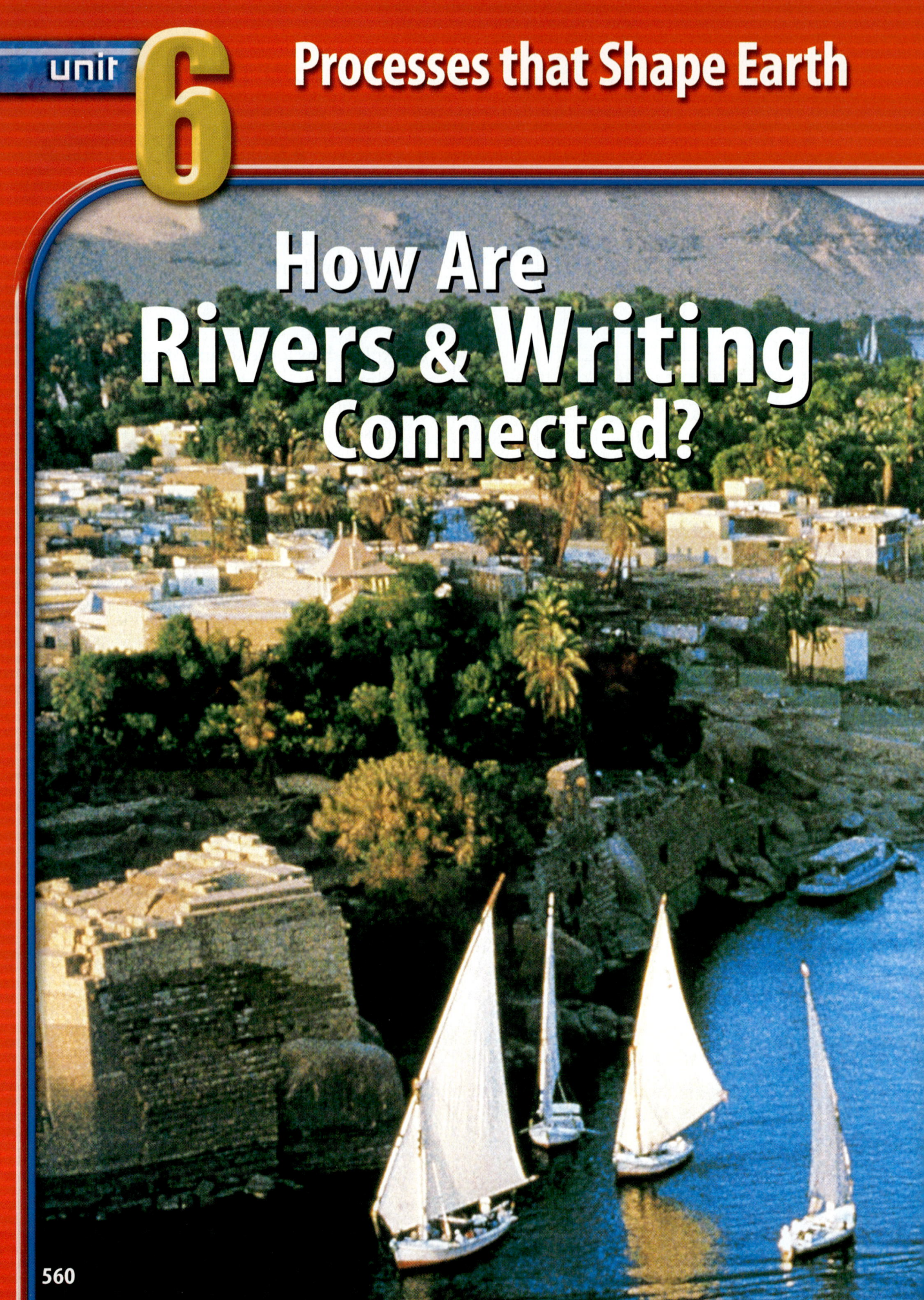

unit 6
Processes that Shape Earth

How Are Rivers & Writing Connected?

Rivers change the surface of Earth by moving material from place to place. In the process, rivers help build up fertile soil. Thousands of years ago, the Egyptian civilization took root in the extremely fertile soil along the Nile River (seen here as it looks today). Agriculture flourished, society grew more complex, and people needed a way to keep track of everything from harvests to history. Around 3100 B.C., the Egyptians developed one of the first systems of writing—a type of picture writing called hieroglyphics (left). Later peoples probably borrowed from the Egyptian system to create their own writing systems. By about 1000 B.C., the Phoenicians had developed an alphabet, with symbols that stood for individual sounds. The Phoenician alphabet was adopted and modified by other peoples, eventually giving rise to the alphabet we use today.

unit projects

The assessed Indiana objective appears in blue.

To find project ideas and resources, visit in7.msscience.com/unit_project. Projects include:

- **History** Discover the characteristics of a variety of landforms and then design a tourist brochure about your specific feature. 7.3.7
- **Career** Explore a geology-related career, learn the tools of the trade, and present your career at a class job fair. 7.1.2, 7.1.7, 7.1.9
- **Model** Create a picture book with adventurous characters to demonstrate your new knowledge of Earth's changing surface. 7.7.2
- **WebQuest** Investigate the *Fossils of Antarctica* and what they could tell us about its ancient climate and location on Earth. 7.1.2, 7.1.4, 7.1.5, 7.1.6, 7.1.7, 7.1.10

chapter 19

Academic Standard—3: Students collect and organize data to identify relationships between physical objects, events, and processes. They use logical reasoning to question their own ideas as new information challenges their conceptions of the natural world.

Also covers: Academic Standards 1, 2 (Detailed standards begin on page IN8.)

Forces Shaping Earth

chapter preview

sections
1. **Earth's Moving Plates**
   Lab Earth's Moving Plates
2. **Uplift of Earth's Crust**
   Lab Isostasy
   Virtual Lab How do glaciers shape the land?

Young or Old Mountains?

These majestic, snow-capped mountains are in their infancy. It would take a few hundred million years of erosion for their sharp, jagged peaks to become smooth. In this chapter, you'll learn how the movement of plates formed these mountains and about other Earth forces that shape mountains.

Science Journal Use descriptive adjectives to describe these mountains in a short paragraph.

562

Start-Up Activities

Model Earth's Interior

Geologists know many things about the interior of Earth even though its center is over 6,000 km deep. Use modeling clay to make a model of Earth's interior.

1. Obtain four pieces of different-colored clay.
2. Roll one piece of clay into a ball. This clay represents the inner core.
3. Wrap another piece of clay around the first ball of clay, making an even bigger ball. This clay represents the outer core.
4. Repeat step 3 with the third piece of clay, which represents Earth's mantle. Wrap your model with a thin layer of the fourth piece of clay to represent the crust.
5. Use a plastic knife to cut the ball of clay in half.
6. **Think Critically** Make a sketch of your model and label each of Earth's layers.

FOLDABLES Study Organizer

Earth's Interior and Surface Make the following cause and effect Foldable to help you understand the relationship between Earth's interior and surface.

STEP 1 **Collect** 2 sheets of paper and layer them about 2.5 cm apart vertically. Keep the edges level.

STEP 2 **Fold** up the bottom edges of the paper to form 4 equal tabs.

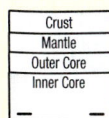

STEP 3 **Fold** the papers and crease well to hold the tabs in place. Staple along the fold. **Label** each tab as shown.

Cause and Effect As you read the chapter, record information about each layer and how it is related to the layer above it under the tabs.

Preview this chapter's content and activities at in7.msscience.com

Standard—7.3.4: Explain how heat flow and movement of material within Earth causes earthquakes and volcanic eruptions and creates mountains and ocean basins.

section 1

Also covers: 7.1.1, 7.1.4, 7.3.7, 7.3.18 (Detailed standards begin on page IN8.)

Earth's Moving Plates

as you read

What You'll Learn
- **Describe** how Earth's interior is divided into layers.
- **Explain** how plates of Earth's lithosphere move.
- **Discuss** why Earth's plates move.

Why It's Important
Forces that cause Earth's plates to move apart, together, or past each other cause events that shape Earth's surface, such as mountain building, volcanoes, and earthquakes.

Review Vocabulary
magma: melted rock material found beneath Earth's surface

New Vocabulary
- inner core
- outer core
- mantle
- crust
- lithosphere
- plate
- fault
- subduction

Figure 1 Waves carry energy across water just like seismic waves carry energy through Earth.

Clues to Earth's Interior

If someone gives you a wrapped present, how could you figure out what was in it? You might hold it, shake it gently, or weigh it. You'd look for clues that could help you identify the contents of the box. Even though you can't see what's inside the package, these types of clues can help you figure out what it might be. Because you can't see what's inside, the observations you make are known as indirect observations.

Geologists do the same thing when they try to learn about Earth's interior. Although the best way to find out what's inside Earth might be to dig a tunnel to its center, that isn't possible. The deepest mines in the world only scratch Earth's surface. A tunnel would need to be more than 6,000 km deep to reach the center, so geologists must use indirect observations to gather clues about what Earth's interior is made of and how it is structured. This indirect evidence includes information learned by studying earthquakes and rocks that are exposed at Earth's surface.

Waves When you throw a rock into a calm puddle or pond, you observe waves like those shown in **Figure 1.** Waves are disturbances that carry energy through matter or space. When a rock hits water, waves carry some of the rock's kinetic energy, or energy of motion, away from where it hit the water. When an earthquake occurs, as shown in **Figure 2,** energy is carried through objects by waves. The speed of these waves depends on the density and nature of the material they are traveling through. For example, a wave travels faster in solid rock than it does in a liquid. By studying the speed of these waves and the paths they take, geologists uncover clues as to how the planet is put together. In fact, these waves, called seismic waves, speed up in some areas, slow down in other areas, and can be bent or stopped.

Figure 2 As seismic waves travel across Earth's surface, the ground shakes and damage occurs.

Rock Clues Another clue to what's inside Earth comes in the form of certain rocks found in different places on Earth's surface. These rocks are made of material similar to what is thought to exist deep inside Earth. The rocks formed far below the surface. Forces inside Earth pushed them closer to the surface, where they eventually were exposed by erosion. The seismic clues and the rock clues suggest that Earth is made up of layers of different kinds of materials.

Earth's Layers

Based on evidence from earthquake waves and exposed rocks, scientists have produced a model of Earth's interior. The model shows that Earth's interior has at least four distinct layers—the inner core, the outer core, the mantle, and the crust. Earth's structure is similar in some ways to the structure of a peach, shown in **Figure 3.** A peach has a thin skin covering the thick, juicy part that you eat. Under that is a large pit that surrounds a seed.

Inner Core The pit and seed are similar to Earth's core. Earth's core is divided into two distinct parts—one that is liquid and one that is solid. The innermost layer of Earth's interior is the solid **inner core.** This part of the core is dense and composed mostly of solid iron. When seismic waves produced by earthquakes reach this layer they speed up, indicating that the inner core is solid.

Conditions in the inner core are extreme compared to those at the surface. At about 5,000°C, the inner core is the hottest part of Earth. Also, because of the weight of the surrounding rock, the core is under tremendous pressure. Pressure, or the force pushing on an area, increases the deeper you go beneath Earth's surface. Pressure increases because more material is pushing toward Earth's center as a result of gravity. The inner core, at the center of Earth, experiences the greatest amount of pressure.

Figure 3 The structure of Earth can be compared to a peach.
Explain *If the part of Earth that you live on is like the skin of the peach, what does that tell you about this layer of Earth?*

SECTION 1 Earth's Moving Plates **565**

INTEGRATE Chemistry

Iron Core Earth's crust is composed of about five percent iron. However, geologists theorize that Earth's core is composed mostly of iron. Research the theory that Earth's core is composed mostly of iron. Analyze, review, and critique the strengths and weaknesses of this theory using scientific evidence and information.

Outer Core The **outer core** lies above the inner core and is thought to be composed mostly of molten metal. The outer core stops one type of seismic wave and slows down another. Because of this, scientists have concluded that the outer core is a liquid. The location of the outer core is similar to the location of the pit in the peach model. Even the wrinkled surface of the pit resembles the uneven nature of the boundary between Earth's outer core and its mantle as indicated by seismic studies.

✓ **Reading Check** *What peach layer is similar to the outer core?*

Mantle The layer in Earth's interior above the outer core is the mantle. In the peach model, the mantle would be the juicy part of the peach that you would eat. The **mantle** is the largest layer of Earth's interior. Even though it's solid, the mantle flows slowly, similar to putty.

Crust Earth's outermost layer is the **crust.** In the model of the peach, this layer would be the fuzzy skin of the peach. Earth's crust is thin when compared to the other layers, though its thickness does vary. It is thinnest under the oceans and thickest through the continents. All features on Earth's surface are part of the crust.

Figure 4 Earth is made up of many layers.
Identify *geologic events that have allowed scientists to study Earth's interior.*

The lithosphere is composed of crust and uppermost mantle. The asthenosphere is a plasticlike layer upon which the plates of the lithosphere float and move.

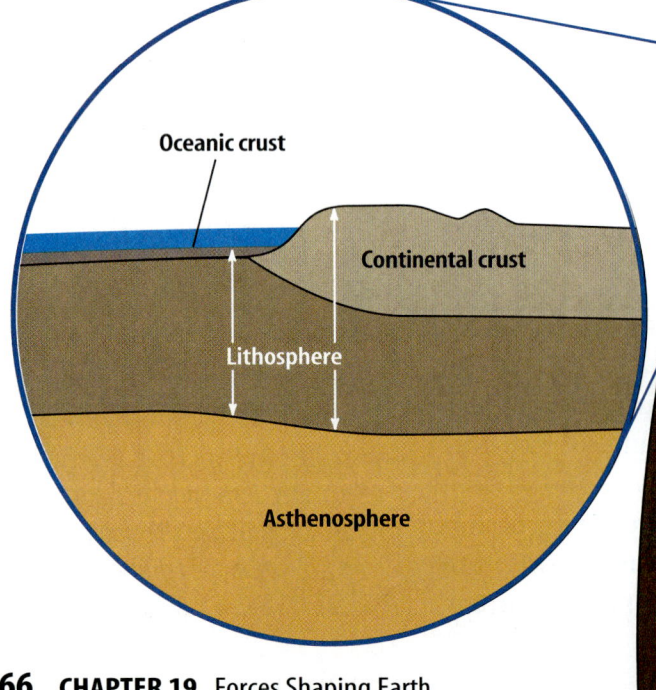

566 CHAPTER 19 Forces Shaping Earth

Earth's Structure

Although Earth's structure can be divided into four basic layers, it also can be divided into other layers based on physical properties that change with depth beneath the surface. **Figure 4** shows the structure of Earth and describes some of the properties of its layers. Density, temperature, and pressure are properties that are lowest in the crust and greatest in the inner core.

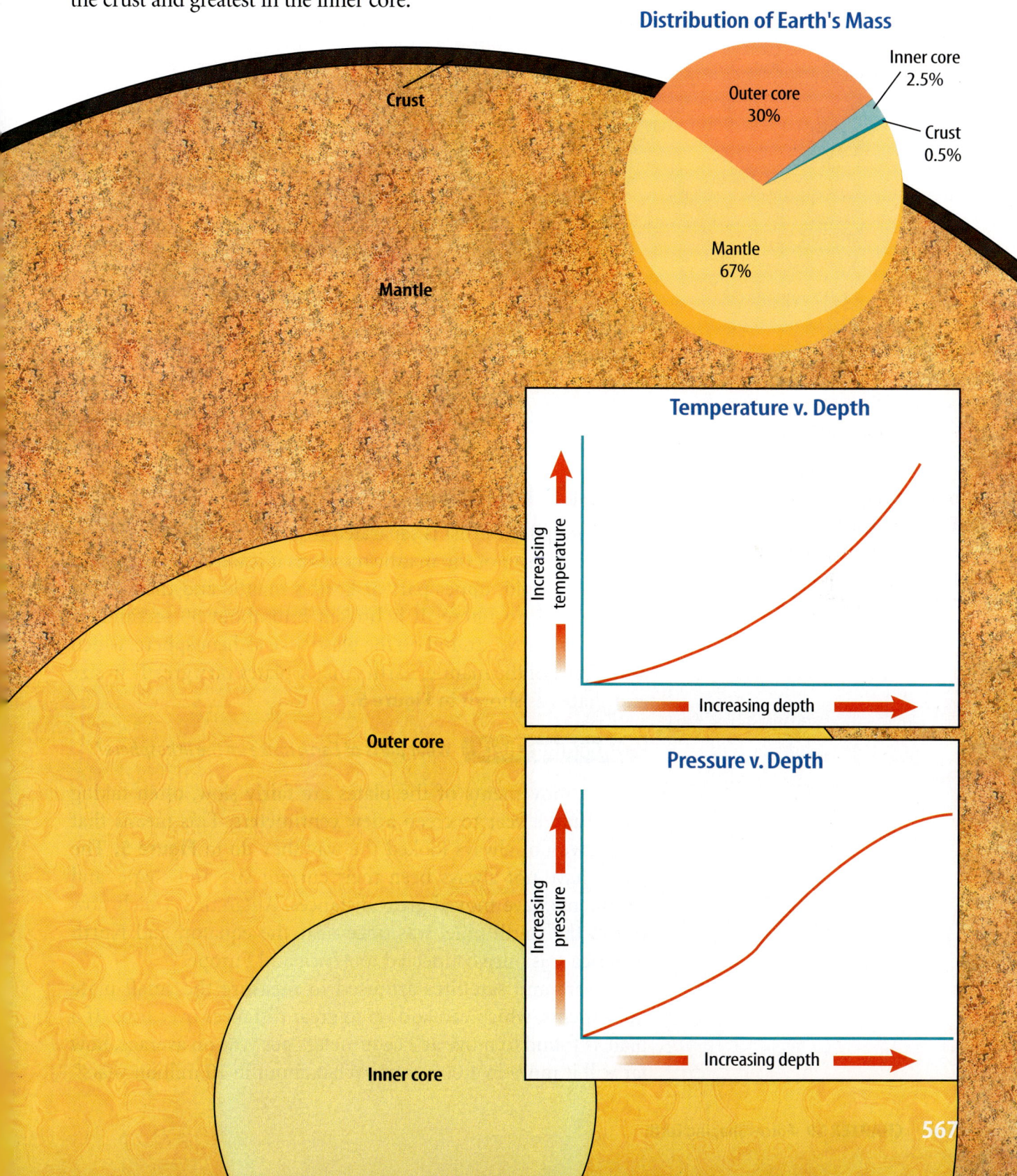

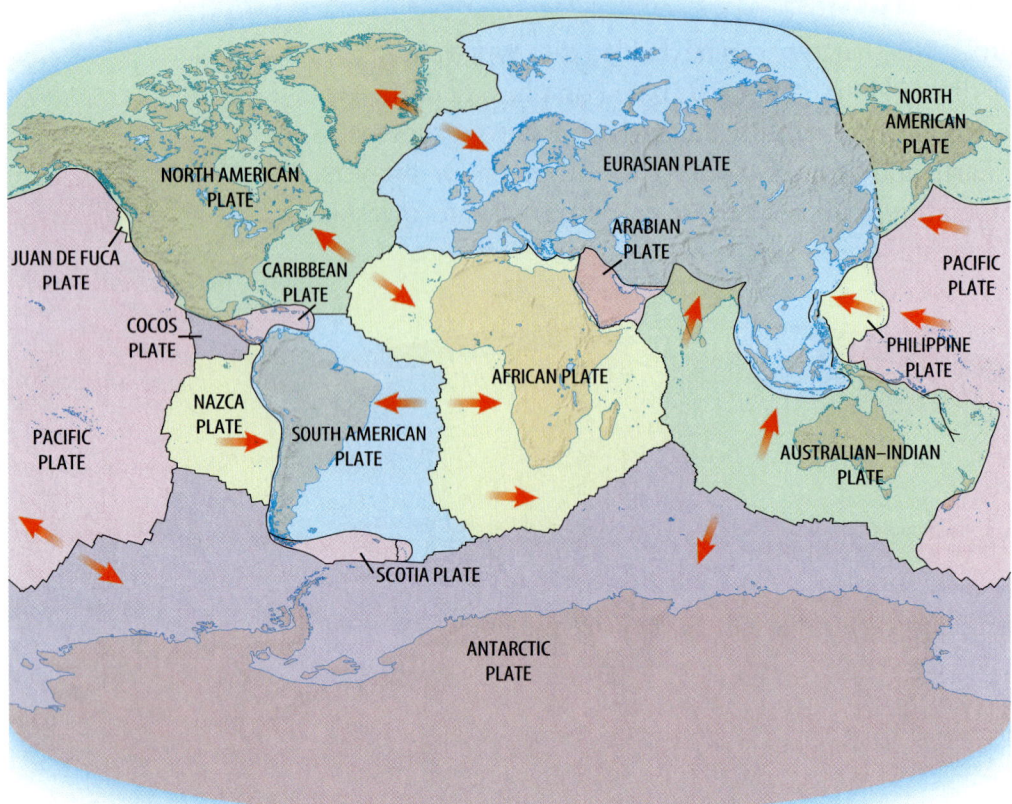

Figure 5 Earth's plates fit together like the pieces of a jigsaw puzzle.
Draw Conclusions *If the plates are moving, what do you suppose happens at the plate boundaries?*

Earth's Plates

Although the crust is separated from the mantle, the uppermost, rigid layer of the mantle moves as if it were part of Earth's crust. The rigid, upper part of Earth's mantle and the crust is called the **lithosphere**. It is broken into about 30 sections or **plates** that move around on the plasticlike asthenosphere, which also is part of the mantle. Earth's major plates vary greatly in size and shape, as shown in **Figure 5**.

Reading Check *What parts of Earth make up the lithosphere?*

The movements of the plates are fairly slow, often taking more than a year to creep a few centimeters. This means that they have not always looked the way they do in **Figure 5**. The plates have not always been their current size and shape, and continents have moved great distances. Antarctica, which now covers the south pole, was once near the equator, and North America was once connected to Africa and Europe.

Lasers and satellites are used to measure the small plate movements, which can add up to great distances over time. If a plate is found to move at 2 centimeters per year on average, how far will it move in 1,000 years? What about in 10 million years?

Plate Boundaries

The places where the edges of different plates meet are called plate boundaries. The constant movement of plates creates forces that affect Earth's surface at the boundaries of the plates. At some boundaries, these forces are large enough to cause mountains to form. Other boundaries form huge rift valleys with active volcanoes. At a third type of boundary, huge faults form. **Faults** are large fractures in rocks along which movement occurs. The movement can cause earthquakes. **Figure 6** shows the different plate motions.

Plates That Move Apart Plates move apart as a result of pulling forces that act in opposite directions on each plate. This pulling force is called tension. **Figure 7** shows what happens as tension continues to pull two plates apart.

One important result of plates separating is the formation of new crust. New crust forms in gaps where the plates pull apart. As tension continues along these boundaries, new gaps form and are filled in by magma that is pushed up from the mantle. Over time, the magma in the gaps cools to become new crust. This process of plate separation and crust formation takes place under the oceans at places called mid-ocean ridges. As new crust moves away from the mid-ocean ridges, it cools and becomes denser.

Science Online

Topic: Plate Boundaries
Visit in7.msscience.com for Web links to information about Earth's plates and the different boundaries that they form.

Activity Create a table of the information on plates and plate boundaries. Try to include specific plates and boundary locations. Share your findings with your classmates.

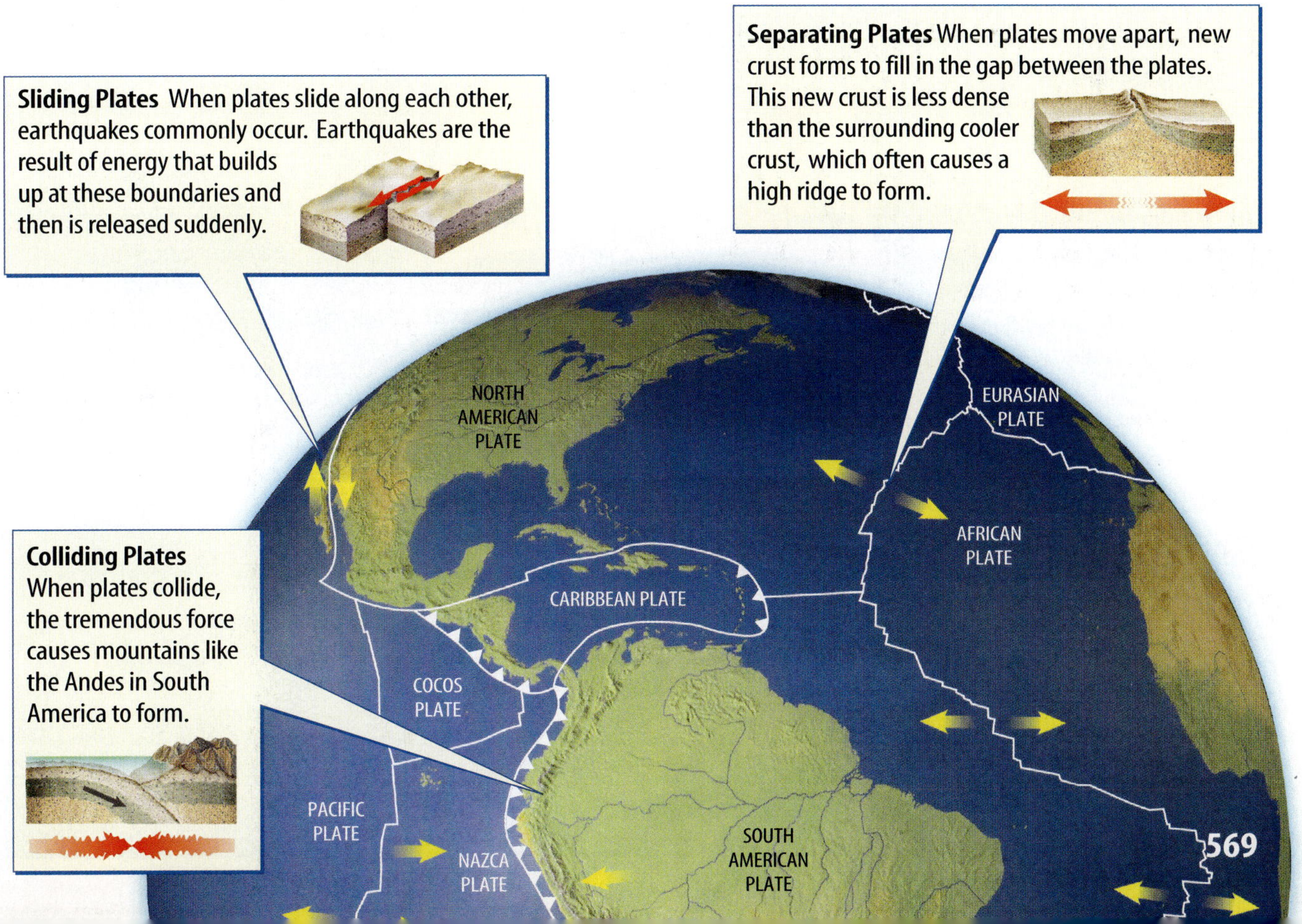

Figure 6 Earth's plates can collide, move away from each other, or slide past each other.

Sliding Plates When plates slide along each other, earthquakes commonly occur. Earthquakes are the result of energy that builds up at these boundaries and then is released suddenly.

Separating Plates When plates move apart, new crust forms to fill in the gap between the plates. This new crust is less dense than the surrounding cooler crust, which often causes a high ridge to form.

Colliding Plates When plates collide, the tremendous force causes mountains like the Andes in South America to form.

NATIONAL GEOGRAPHIC VISUALIZING RIFT VALLEYS

Figure 7

When two continental plates pull apart, rift valleys may form. If spreading continues and the growing rift reaches a coastline, seawater floods in. Beneath the waves, molten rock, or magma, oozes from the weakened and fractured valley floor. In time, the gap between the two continental slabs may widen into a full-fledged ocean. The four steps associated with this process are shown here. Africa's Great Rift Valley, which cuts across the eastern side of Africa for 5,600 km (right), represents the second of these four steps. If rifting processes continue in the Great Rift Valley, East Africa eventually will part from the mainland.

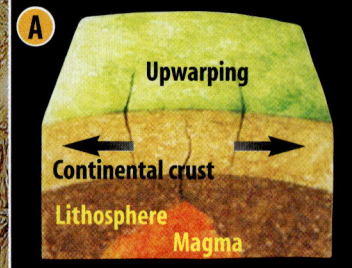

A Rising magma forces the crust upward, causing numerous cracks in the rigid crust.

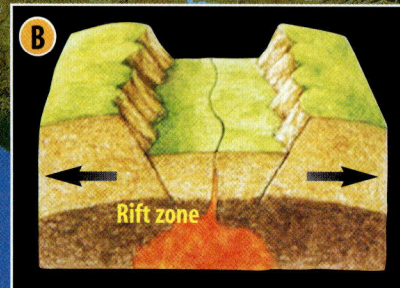

B As the crust is pulled apart, large slabs of rock sink, generating a rift zone.

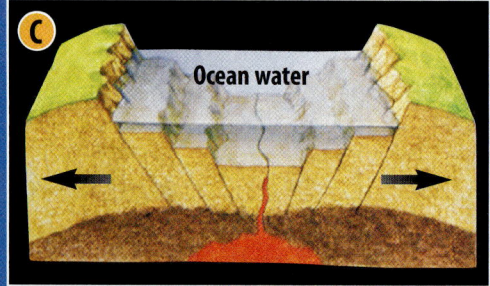

C Further spreading generates a narrow sea or lake.

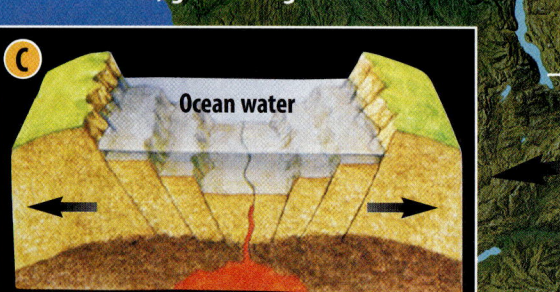

D Eventually, an expansive ocean basin and ridge system are created.

570 CHAPTER 19 Forces Shaping Earth

Plates That Collide When plates move toward each other, they collide, causing several different things to occur. As you can see in **Figure 8,** the outcome depends on the density of the two plates involved. The crust that forms the ocean floors, called oceanic crust, is more dense than the continental crust, which forms continents.

If two continental plates collide, they have a similar density which is less than the mantle underneath. Therefore, the collision causes the crust to pile up. When rock converges like this, the force is called compression. Compression causes the rock layers on both plates to crumple and fold. Imagine laying a piece of fabric flat on your desk. If you push the edges of the cloth toward each other, the fabric will crumple and fold over on itself. A similar process occurs when plates crash into each other, causing mountains to form.

Flat rock layers are pushed up into folds. Sometimes the folding is so severe that rock layers bend completely over on themselves, turning upside down. As rock layers are folded and faulted, they pile up and form mountains. The tallest mountains in the world, the Himalaya in Asia, are still rising as two continental plates collide.

Plate Subduction When an oceanic plate collides with another oceanic plate or a continental plate, the more dense one plunges underneath the other, forming a deep trench. When one plate sinks underneath another plate, it's called **subduction**. When a plate subducts, it sinks into the mantle. In this way, Earth's crust does not continue to grow larger. As new crust material is generated at a rift, older crustal material subducts into the mantle.

Mini LAB

Modeling Tension and Compression

Procedure
1. Obtain two bars of **taffy.**
2. Hold one bar of taffy between your hands and push your hands together.
3. Record your observations in your **Science Journal.**
4. Hold the other bar of taffy between your hands and pull gently on both ends.
5. Record your observations in your Science Journal.

Analysis
1. On which bar of taffy did you apply tension? Compression?
2. Explain how this applies to plate boundaries.

Try at Home

Figure 8 There are three types of convergent plate boundaries.

Continental-continental collisions Two continental plates have similar densities, which are less than underlying mantle rock. As a result, they buckle and fold when they collide, piling up into high mountain ranges, such as the Himalaya.

Oceanic-oceanic collisions The collision of two oceanic plates causes subduction of the denser plate, which forms a deep ocean trench where the plates meet. Erupting lava forms islands near the trench.

Continental-oceanic collisions When a continental plate collides with an oceanic plate, the more dense oceanic plate slides underneath the continental plate, forming volcanoes.

Figure 9 As two plates slide past each other, their edges grind and scrape. The jerky movement that results causes earthquakes like those frequently felt in California along the San Andreas Fault.

Plates That Slide Past In addition to moving toward and away from one another, plates also can slide past one another. For example, one plate might be moving north while the plate next to it is moving south. The boundary where these plates meet is called a transform boundary. When a force pushes something in two different directions, it's called shearing. Shearing causes the area between the plates to form faults and experience many earthquakes. **Figure 9** shows part of the San Andreas Fault near Taft, California, which is an example of the features that form along a transform boundary.

Why do plates move?

As you can see, Earth's plates are large. To move something so massive requires a tremendous amount of energy. Where does the energy that drives plate movement come from? The reason plates move is complex, and geologists still are trying to understand it fully. So far, scientists have come up with several possible explanations about what is happening inside Earth to cause plate movement. Most of these theories suggest that gravity is the driving force behind it. However, gravity pulls things toward the center of Earth, and plates move sideways across the globe. How does gravity make something move across the surface of Earth?

One theory that could explain plate movement is convection of the mantle. Convection in any material is driven by differences in density. In the mantle, density differences are caused by uneven heating, which results in a cycling of material, as shown in **Figure 10.** The theory suggests that the plates move as part of this circulation of mantle material.

Indiana Academic Standard Check

7.3.4: Explain how heat flow ... within Earth causes earthqakes and volcanic eruptions and creates mountains and ocean basins.

✓ What causes convection currents in Earth's mantle?

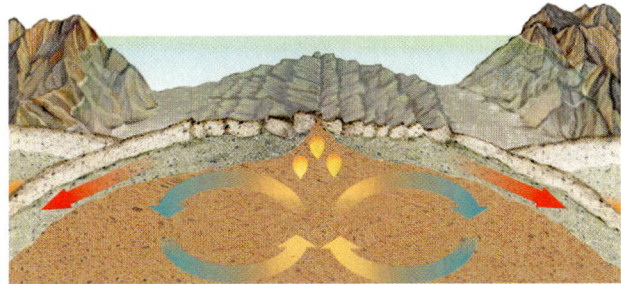

Figure 10 Convection, ridge-push, and slab-pull might all contribute to the motions of Earth's plates.

Uneven heating of the upper mantle could cause convection.

Ridge-push could occur at mid-ocean ridges.

Ridge-push and Slab-pull Other factors, as shown in **Figure 10,** that could play a role in plate movement are ridge-push and slab-pull. Ridge-push occurs at mid-ocean ridges, which are higher than surrounding ocean floor. The plates respond to gravity by sliding down the slope. Slab-pull occurs as the plates move away from the mid-ocean ridges and become cooler, which makes them more dense. A plate can get so dense that it sinks when it collides with another plate. When the more dense plate begins to sink, it becomes easier for it to move across Earth's surface because resistance to movement is reduced.

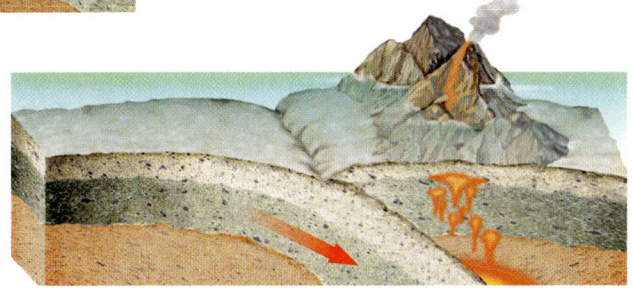

Slab-pull could occur where oceanic plates meet other oceanic or continental plates.

section 1 review

Summary

Clues to Earth's Interior
- Earth's interior has been explored using information from seismic waves and rocks.

Earth's Layers
- The interior of Earth is made of the inner core, outer core, mantle, and crust.

Plate Boundaries
- Plates can move apart, collide, subduct, or slide past each other.
- Plates probably move by convection and factors such as ridge-push and slab-pull.

Self Check

1. **Explain** How are earthquake waves used to provide information about Earth's interior?
2. **Identify** Give examples of where the three types of plate movements occur.
3. **Describe** the layer of Earth's interior that is the largest.
4. **List** the layers of Earth's interior in order of density.
5. **Think Critically** How can slab-pull and ridge-push contribute to the movement of a plate at the same time?

Applying Skills

6. **Compare and contrast** the following pairs of terms: *inner core, outer core; ridge-push, slab-pull.*

SECTION 1 Earth's Moving Plates

EARTH'S MOVING PLATES

You have learned that Earth's surface is separated into plates that move apart, move together, or slide past each other. In this lab, you will observe a process that is thought to cause this plate movement.

Real-World Question
What process inside Earth provides the energy for plate motion?

Goals
- **Observe** movement of solid plates on a liquid.
- **Identify** the cause of plate movement on Earth's surface.

Materials
1-L beakers (2)
food coloring
aluminum foil
pencil
rubber band
water (warm and cold)
2-cm paper squares (3)
small, clear-plastic cup

Safety Precautions

WARNING: *Handle the warm water with care. Water from the tap should be warm enough.*

Procedure

1. Fill one of the 1-L beakers with cold water.
2. Fill the small cup with warm water.
3. Add four drops of food coloring to the cup of warm water and cover the top with aluminum foil. Secure the aluminum foil with a rubber band. No air should be underneath the foil.
4. Carefully place the cup of colored, warm water in the bottom of the second 1-L beaker.
5. Carefully pour the cold water from the first 1-L beaker into the second 1-L beaker. Take care not to disturb the cup of colored water.
6. Place the pieces of paper on the surface of the water in the second 1-L beaker.

7. Use a long pencil to make two small holes in the aluminum foil covering the cup.
8. **Observe** what happens to the contents of the cup and to the pieces of paper. Record your observations in your Science Journal.

Conclude and Apply

1. **Describe** What happened to the colored, warm water originally located in the cup?
2. **Infer** What effect, if any, does the warm water have on the positions of the floating paper?
3. **Compare and Contrast** How is what happens to the warm water similar to processes that occur inside Earth? How is it different?
4. **Explain** After observing the pieces of paper floating on the cold water, explain what features on Earth's surface they are similar to.

Communicating Your Data

Compare your conclusions with those of other students in your class. **For more help, refer to the Science Skill Handbook.**

section 2

Standards—7.3.4: Explain how heat flow and movement of material within Earth causes earthquakes and volcanic eruptions and creates mountains and ocean basins. **7.3.7:** Give examples of some changes in Earth's surface that are abrupt, such as earthquakes and volcanic eruptions, and some changes that happen very slowly, such as uplift and wearing down of mountains and the action of glaciers.

Also covers: 7.2.7 (Detailed standards begin on page IN8.)

Uplift of Earth's Crust

Building Mountains

One popular vacation that people enjoy is a trip to the mountains. Mountains tower over the surrounding land, often providing spectacular views from their summits or from surrounding areas. The highest mountain peak in the world is Mount Everest in the Himalaya in Tibet. Its elevation is more than 8,800 m above sea level. In the United States, the highest mountains reach an elevation of more than 6,000 m. There are four main types of mountains—fault-block, folded, upwarped, and volcanic. Each type forms in a different way and can produce mountains that vary greatly in size.

Age of a Mountain As you can see in **Figure 11,** mountains can be rugged with high, snowcapped peaks, or they can be rounded and forested with gentle valleys and babbling streams. The ruggedness of a mountain chain depends largely on whether or not it is still forming. Mountains like the Himalaya are currently forming at a rate of several centimeters per year, while much older mountains like the Ouachita Mountains in Arkansas stopped forming millions of years ago and are now being eroded by geological processes.

Figure 11 Mountains can be high and rugged like the mountains of the Himalaya shown on the left, or they can be large, gently rolling hills like the Ouachita Mountains in Arkansas, shown above.
Infer *What determines how rugged and high a mountain chain is?*

as you read

What You'll Learn
- **Describe** how Earth's mountains form and erode.
- **Compare** types of mountains.
- **Identify** the forces that shape Earth's mountains.

Why It's Important
The forces inside Earth that cause Earth's plates to move around also are responsible for forming Earth's mountains.

Review Vocabulary
erosion: process by which products of weathering are moved

New Vocabulary
- fault-block mountain
- folded mountain
- upwarped mountain
- volcanic mountain
- isostasy

SECTION 2 Uplift of Earth's Crust **575**

Figure 12 Before tension is applied, the layers of rock are even and fairly level. After tension is applied, huge blocks of rock separate and slip downward. This leaves large, tilted blocks that become mountains.

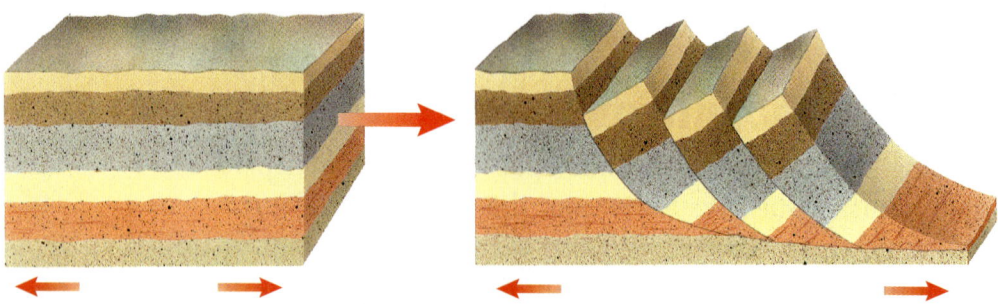

Indiana Academic Standard Check

7.3.7: Give examples of some changes in Earth's surface that . . . happen very slowly. . . .

✔ How rapidly are the Himalaya being uplifted?

Fault-Block Mountains The first mountains you'll study are fault-block mountains. Some examples are the Sierra Nevada in California and the Teton Range in Wyoming. Recall that pulling, or tension, forces that occur at the boundaries of plates moving apart, work to create surface features such as rift valleys and faults. Fault-block mountains also form from pulling forces. **Fault-block mountains** are made of huge, tilted blocks of rock that are separated from surrounding rock by faults. When rock layers are pulled from opposite directions, large blocks slide downward, creating peaks and valleys, as shown in **Figure 12**.

Models of Mountain Building If you hold a candy bar between your hands and then begin to pull it apart, cracks might form within the chocolate. Similarly, when rocks are pulled apart, faults form. Unlike rocks deep in Earth, rocks at Earth's surface are hard and brittle. When they are pulled apart, large blocks of rock can move along the faults. The Teton Range of Wyoming formed when a block of crust was tilted as one side of the range was uplifted above the neighboring valley. As shown in **Figure 13**, if you travel to the Grand Teton National Park, you will see sharp, jagged peaks that are characteristic of fault-block mountains.

Now, hold a flat piece of clay between your hands and then push your hands together gently. What happens? As you push your hands together, the clay begins to bend and fold over on itself. A similar process causes rocks to fold and bend, causing folded mountains to form on Earth's surface.

Figure 13 The Teton Range in the Grand Teton National Park has sharp, jagged peaks that are characteristic of fault-block mountains.

576 CHAPTER 19 Forces Shaping Earth

Folded Mountains Traveling along a road that is cut into the side of the Appalachian Mountains, you can see that rock layers were folded just as the clay was when it was squeezed, or compressed. Tremendous pushing forces exerted by two of Earth's plates moving together squeezed rock layers from opposite sides. This caused the rock layers to buckle and fold, forming folded mountains. **Folded mountains** are mountains formed by the folding of rock layers caused by compression forces.

Reading Check *What type of force causes folded mountains to form?*

The Appalachian Mountains are folded mountains that formed about 250 million to 300 million years ago. A small part of the folded Appalachians is shown in **Figure 14.** The compression occurred as the North American Plate and the African Plate moved together. The Appalachians are the oldest mountain range in North America, and also one of the longest. They extend from Alabama northward to Quebec, Canada. Erosion has been acting on these mountains since they were formed. As a result, the Appalachians are small compared to other mountain ranges. At one time, the Appalachian Mountains were higher than the Rocky Mountains are today.

Upwarped Mountains The Adirondack Mountains in New York, the southern Rocky Mountains in Colorado and New Mexico, and the Black Hills in South Dakota are examples of upwarped mountains. **Upwarped mountains** form when forces inside Earth push up the crust. With time, sedimentary rock layers on top will erode, exposing the igneous or metamorphic rocks underneath. The igneous and metamorphic rocks can erode further to form sharp peaks and ridges.

Mini LAB

Modeling Mountains

Procedure

1. Use layers of **clay** to build a model of each major type of mountain.
2. For fault-block mountains, cut the layers of clay with a **plastic knife** to show how one block moves upward and another moves downward.
3. For folded mountains, push on the layers of clay from directly opposite directions.
4. For upwarped mountains, push a large, round object, such as a **ball,** upward from below, forcing the layers of clay to warp.
5. For volcanic mountains, place layer upon layer of clay to form a cone-shaped feature.

Analysis

1. Do any of the mountains you have modeled look similar? Explain.
2. How could you recognize the different types of mountains?

Figure 14 This roadcut in Maryland exposes folded rock layers that formed when the North American Plate and the African Plate collided.

Science Online

Topic: Volcanic Mountains
Visit in7.msscience.com for Web links to information about volcanic mountains.

Activity Collect as many photographs of volcanic mountains as possible. Create a large map of the world with the photographs in their proper locations. Include some information about the volcanic mountains and the impact they have had on the environment around there.

Volcanic Mountains Occasionally, magma from inside Earth reaches the surface. When this happens, the magma is called lava. When hot, molten lava flows onto Earth's surface, volcanic mountains can form. Over time, layer upon layer of lava piles up until a cone-shaped feature called a **volcanic mountain** forms. Washington's Mount St. Helens and Mexico's Mount Popocateptl, shown in **Figure 15**, are examples. Next, you will take a closer look at how volcanic mountains form.

Some volcanic mountains form when large plates of Earth's lithosphere sink into Earth's mantle at subduction zones. As the plates sink deeper into the mantle, they cause melting to occur. The magma produced is less dense than the surrounding rock, so it is forced slowly upward to Earth's surface. If the magma reaches the surface, it can erupt as lava and ash. Layers of these materials can pile up over time to form volcanic mountains.

Figure 15 Volcanic mountains form when lava and ash build up in one area over time.

Crater This bowl-shaped part of the volcano surrounds the vent. Lava often collects here before it flows down the slope.

Vent As magma flows up the pipe, it reaches the surface at an opening called the vent. Side vents often branch off of the main pipe.

Pipe Magma flows through this nearly vertical crack in the rock called the pipe.

Magma Chamber Magma that has been forced upward forms and fills a large pocket underneath the volcano. This pocket is called the magma chamber. In some cases, one magma chamber feeds several volcanoes.

Magma The hot, molten mixture of rock material and gases is called magma.

Figure 16 The Hawaiian Islands are a series of volcanic mountains that have been built upward from the seafloor. They began to form as lava erupted onto the ocean floor. Over time, the mountain grew so large that it rose above sea level.

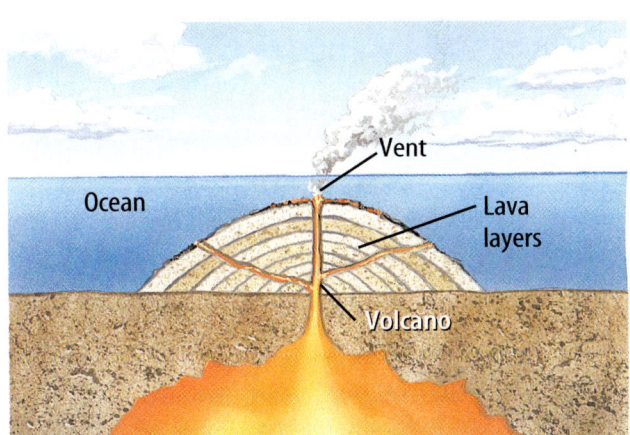

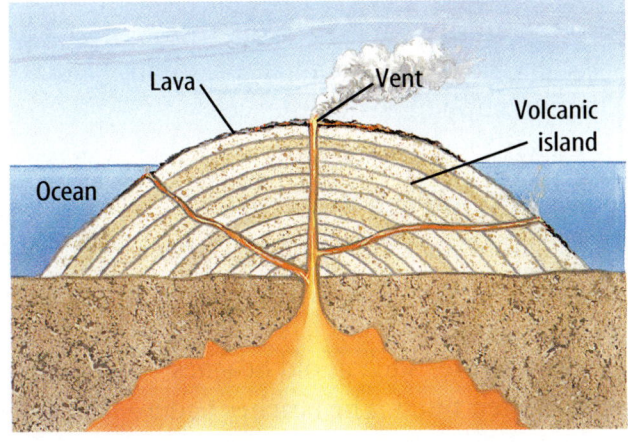

Underwater Volcanic Mountains You know that volcanic mountains form on land, but did you know that these mountains also form on the ocean floor? Underwater eruptions can produce mountains beneath the sea. Eventually, if enough lava is erupted, these mountains grow above sea level. For example, Hawaii, shown above in **Figure 16,** is the peak of a huge volcanic mountain that extends above the surface of the water of the Pacific Ocean. **Figure 16** also illustrates how the Hawaiian Islands formed.

Volcanic mountains like the Hawaiian Islands are different from the volcanic mountains that form where one plate subducts beneath another. The Hawaiian Islands formed from material that came from near the boundary between Earth's core and mantle. Hot rock is forced upward through the mantle as a plume and melts to form a hot spot in Earth's crust. As plates travel over the hot spot, a series of volcanoes, as seen in Hawaii, forms. Magma from subduction volcanoes forms much closer to Earth's surface. Hot spot volcanoes also are much larger and have more gently sloping sides than subduction volcanoes.

 *What type of mountains make up the Hawaiian Islands?*

SECTION 2 Uplift of Earth's Crust   **579**

INTEGRATE Language Arts

The Isostasy Story
Using the principle of isostasy, explain in your Science Journal why large features on Earth's surface, such as mountains, float on the layers of Earth beneath them.

Other Types of Uplift

You have learned about the origin of the pushing forces that bend crustal rocks during mountain-building processes. However, another force also works to keep mountains elevated above the surrounding land. If you place wooden blocks of various thicknesses in a container of water, you will notice that different blocks of wood float in the water at different heights. Also, the thicker blocks of wood float higher in the water than the thinner blocks do. The buoyant force of the water is balancing the force of gravity. A similar process called isostasy occurs in Earth. According to the principle of **isostasy** (i SAHS tuh see), Earth's lithosphere floats on a plasticlike upper part of the mantle, the asthenosphere.

The effects of isostasy were first noticed near large mountain ranges. Earth's crust is thicker under mountains than it is elsewhere. Also, if mountains continue to get uplifted, the crust under the mountains will become thicker and will extend farther down into the mantle. This is similar to the floating wooden blocks. If you pile another wooden block on a block that is already floating in the water, you will see that the new, larger block will sink down into the water farther than before. You also will see that the new block floats higher than it did before.

Applying Science

How can glaciers cause land to rise?

About 20,000 years ago, much of North America was covered by a large glacial ice sheet. How do you think an ice sheet can affect Earth's crust? What do you think happens when the ice melts?

Identifying the Problem

More than 100 years ago, people living in areas that once had been covered by glaciers noticed that features such as old beaches had been tilted. The beaches had a higher elevation in some places and a lower elevation in others. How do you think old beaches could be tilted?

Solving the Problem

1. The weight of glaciers pushes down Earth's crust. What do you think happens after the glacier melts?
2. How could rising crust cause beaches to be tilted? Do you think the crust would rise the same amount everywhere? Explain.

Figure 17 Isostasy makes Earth's crust behave in a similar way to these icebergs. As an iceberg melts and becomes smaller, ice from below the water's surface is forced up.

Adjusting to Gravity Similar to the wooden blocks, if mountains continue to grow larger, they will sink even farther into the mantle. Once mountains stop forming, erosion lowers the mountains and the crust rises again because weight has been removed. If the process continues, the once-thick crust under the mountains will be reduced to the thickness of the crust where no mountains exist.

Icebergs behave in much the same way, as shown in **Figure 17**. The iceberg is largest when it first breaks off of a glacier. As the iceberg floats, it melts and starts to lose mass. This causes the iceberg to rise in the water. Eventually, the iceberg will be much smaller and will not extend as deeply into the water. How is this similar to what happens to mountains?

section 2 review

Summary

Building Mountains
- A rugged, tall mountain is geologically young. An old mountain is rounded and lower in elevation.
- There are four main types of mountains: fault block, folded, upwarped, and volcanic.
- Volcanic mountains can form on the surface of the continents or under the ocean at ridges.

Other Types of Uplift
- The principle of isostasy explains how the lithosphere floats on the asthenosphere.
- The crust will also adjust to gravity as erosion and weathering wear away older mountains.

Self Check

1. **Predict** If compression were exerted on rock layers, what type of mountains would form?
2. **Describe** how fault-block mountains form.
3. **Explain** how a volcano forms.
4. **Think Critically** Put the Appalachian, Himalaya, and Rocky Mountains in order from youngest to oldest knowing that the Himalaya are most rugged and the Appalachians are the least rugged.

Applying Skills

5. **Concept Map** Make a chain-of-events concept map that describes how folded mountains form.

Model and Invent

Isostasy

Goals
- **Observe** the results of isostasy.
- **Predict** what will happen to floating objects when mass is removed or added.

Possible Materials
5-cm × 5-cm × 2-cm wooden blocks (3)
10-cm × 35-cm × 15-cm clear-plastic storage box or other bin
water
permanent marker
ruler

Safety Precautions

Real-World Question
The principle of isostasy states that Earth's crust floats on the more dense mantle beneath. This is similar to the way objects float in water. What do you think will happen when you add mass to a floating object? What if you take away mass? How does adding or removing mass affect the way an object floats in a fluid?

Make the Model

1. **Decide** what object(s) you will float in the water initially. How will you remove mass from that object? How will you add mass?
2. What will you observe as the mass changes? How will you record the effects of adding or removing mass?
3. How much water will you use? What problems might you encounter if you have too much or too little water?

Using Scientific Methods

4. Will you make any additional measurements or record any other data?
5. **List** all the steps that you plan to do in this activity. Are the steps in a logical order?
6. **Compare** your model plans to those of other students.
7. Make sure your teacher approves your plans before you start.

Test the Model

1. Fill the storage box or bin with an appropriate amount of water.
2. Start by floating the initial object you planned to use in the water. Observe and record relevant data.
3. Follow the list of steps you planned in order to obtain data for removing and adding mass. Observe your model and record all relevant data in your Science Journal.

Conclude and Apply

1. **Describe** What did your initial object look like? What level did the water rise to when your initial object was placed in the bin? How did you add and remove mass?
2. **Summarize** What happened to the amount of the object that was submerged and the amount sticking out of the water when mass was removed from the object?
3. **Summarize** What happened to the amount of the object that was submerged and the amount sticking out of the water when mass was added?
4. **Explain** How can you explain your observations about how much of the object was submerged and how much was sticking out of the water? How is this similar to processes that occur in Earth?

Communicating Your Data

Make a poster that illustrates what you have learned about isostasy. **For more help, refer to the Science Skill Handbook.**

LAB **583**

SCIENCE Stats

Mountains

Did you know...

...The world's longest mountain range is underwater. The mid-ocean ridge that winds around Earth beneath the Arctic, Atlantic, and Pacific Oceans is 65,000 km long. That's four times longer than the combined lengths of the Andes Mountains, the Rocky Mountains, and the Himalaya.

...The beautiful Appalachian Mountains are among the oldest in the world. By 250 million years ago, their formation was complete. Today, the mountains aren't among the tallest because they have been worn down by many millions of years of erosion.

...In 1963, Surtsey, a small island, formed when an underwater volcano erupted off the coast of Iceland. The 1.6-km-long island rose to the height of 183 m—about as tall as a 55-story building.

Applying Math Using this relationship, how many meters would there be in a one-story building?

Find Out About It

Research a mountain on **in7.msscience.com/science_stats**. Pinpoint its location on a map, and then accurately draw the mountain and the view from its top.

Chapter 19 Study Guide

Reviewing Main Ideas

Section 1 — Earth's Moving Plates

1. Earth's interior is divided into four layers, the inner core, the outer core, the mantle, and the crust.

2. Earth's inner and outer cores are thought to be composed mostly of iron. The outer core is thought to be liquid and the inner core is solid.

3. Plates composed of sections of Earth's crust and rigid upper mantle move around on the plasticlike asthenosphere.

4. Earth's plates move together, move apart, and slide past each other.

5. Convection in Earth's mantle, ridge-push, and slab-pull might all contribute to plate movement.

Section 2 — Uplift of Earth's Crust

1. Uplift causes mountains to form. Faulting, folding, upwarping, and volcanic eruptions are all processes that build mountains.

2. Four main types of mountains are fault-block, folded, upwarped, and volcanic.

3. As erosion removes material, the mass of the mountains is reduced. Isostasy, then forces the crust upward.

Visualizing Main Ideas

Copy and complete the following table comparing examples and causes of the four types of mountains.

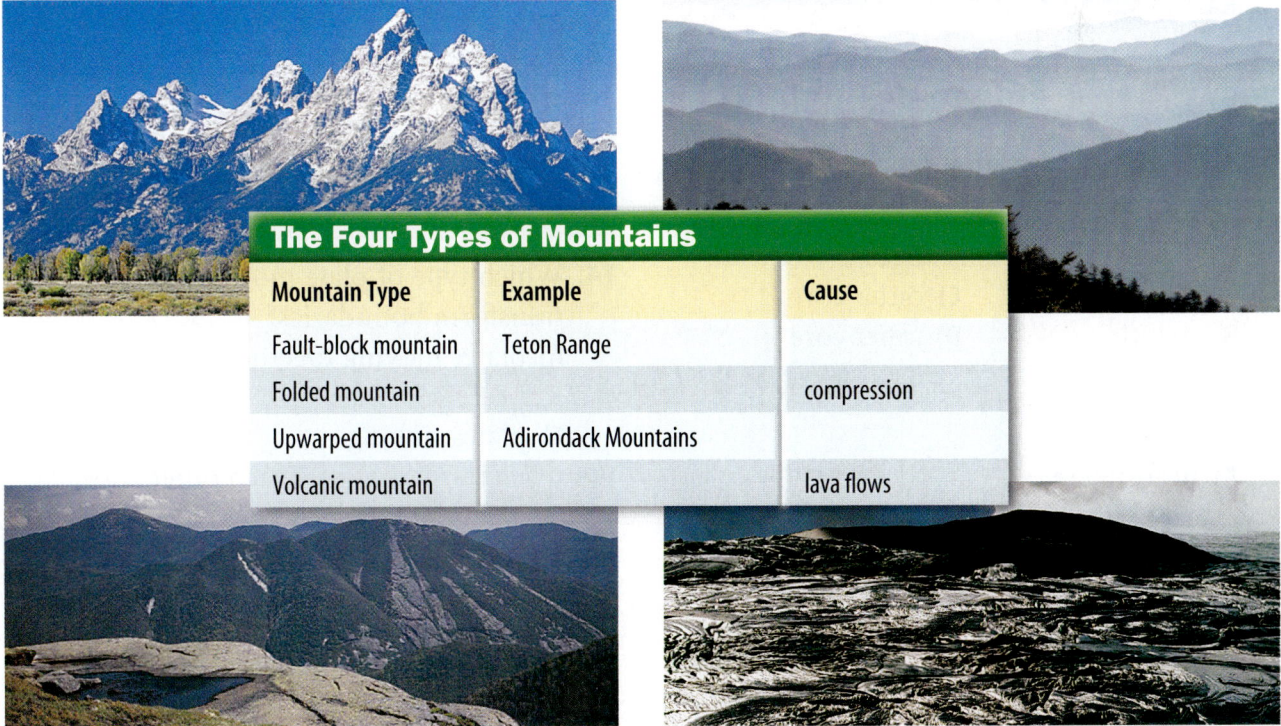

The Four Types of Mountains

Mountain Type	Example	Cause
Fault-block mountain	Teton Range	
Folded mountain		compression
Upwarped mountain	Adirondack Mountains	
Volcanic mountain		lava flows

chapter 19 Review

Using Vocabulary

crust p. 566
fault p. 569
fault-block mountain p. 576
folded mountain p. 577
inner core p. 565
isostasy p. 580
lithosphere p. 568
mantle p. 566
outer core p. 566
plate p. 568
subduction p. 571
upwarped mountain p. 577
volcanic mountain p. 578

Answer the following questions with complete sentences.

1. Which part of Earth's core do scientists think is liquid?
2. The Sierra Nevada mountains in California are which type of mountain?
3. What type of mountains form in areas where rocks are being pushed together?
4. What process occurs when a more dense plate sinks beneath a less dense plate?
5. Which type of mountain forms when magma is forced upward and flows onto Earth's surface?

Checking Concepts

Choose the word or phrase that best answers the question.

6. Which part of Earth is largest?
   A) crust
   B) mantle
   C) outer core
   D) inner core

7. Earth's plates are pieces of which layer of Earth?
   A) lithosphere
   B) asthenosphere
   C) inner core
   D) mantle

8. Which force pushes plates together?
   A) tension
   B) compression
   C) shearing
   D) isostasy

9. Which force occurs where Earth's plates are moving apart?
   A) tension
   B) compression
   C) shear
   D) isostasy

10. Which layer of Earth is thought to be solid and composed mostly of the metal iron?
    A) crust
    B) mantle
    C) outer core
    D) inner core

11. Which suggests that Earth's lithosphere floats on the asthenosphere?
    A) tension
    B) compression
    C) shear
    D) isostasy

12. Which type of mountain forms because of compression forces?
    A) fault-block mountains
    B) folded mountains
    C) upwarped mountains
    D) volcanic mountains

13. Which type of mountain forms because forces inside Earth push up overlying rock layers?
    A) fault-block mountains
    B) folded mountains
    C) upwarped mountains
    D) volcanic mountains

14. Which type of plate movement occurs at transform boundaries?
    A) plates moving together
    B) plates moving apart
    C) plates sinking
    D) plates sliding past each other

15. Which type of plate movement produces deep rifts such as the mid-ocean rift?
    A) plates moving together
    B) plates moving apart
    C) plates sliding past each other
    D) plates sinking

586 CHAPTER REVIEW

in7.msscience.com/vocabulary_puzzlemaker

chapter 19 Review

Thinking Critically

16. **Explain** Which is older, the Great Rift Valley in East Africa, or the Mid-Atlantic Ridge in the Atlantic Ocean?

17. **Explain** how you can determine whether or not a mountain is still forming.

18. **Infer** Seismic waves slow down when entering the asthenosphere. What does this tell you about the nature of the asthenosphere?

19. **Predict** what would happen to the elevation of the island of Greenland if the ice sheet were to melt away.

20. **Describe** If you wanted to know whether a certain mountain was formed by compression, what would you look for?

21. **Compare and contrast** volcanic and folded mountains. Draw a diagram of each type of mountain. Label important features.

22. **Make Models** Use layers of clay to make a model of fault-block mountains. Draw a diagram of your model.

23. **Draw Conclusions** The speed of seismic waves suddenly increases when they go from the upper mantle into the lower mantle. What does this indicate about the comparative densities of the rock in both layers?

24. **Use graphics software** to generate a scale illustration of Earth's interior. Include the thickness of each layer in kilometers.

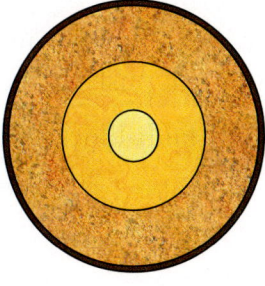

25. **Recognize Cause and Effect** What is the effect of subduction at the boundary of two plates?

Performance Activities

26. **Poem** Write a poem in a style of your choosing about the spectacular view often associated with mountains. You may wish to write about the scene from the top of a mountain or the one you see from the bottom of the mountain looking up to its peak.

Applying Math

27. **Mountain Climbing** The most standard climb for climbers of Mount Everest is up to Base Camp, an elevation of 5400 m. If the summit is 8850 m high, what percentage of Mount Everest's elevation is the Base Camp?

Use the map below to answer question 28.

28. **Moving Cities** The distance between San Francisco and Los Angeles is 616 km. If the San Andreas fault is moving at an average rate of 2.0 cm per year, how long will it be before Los Angeles is next to San Francisco?

chapter 19 Indiana

 The assessed Indiana standard appears above the question.

Record your answers on the answer sheet provided by your teacher or on a sheet of paper.

Part 1 | Multiple Choice

7.3.4

1. The graph below shows how temperature varies with depth.

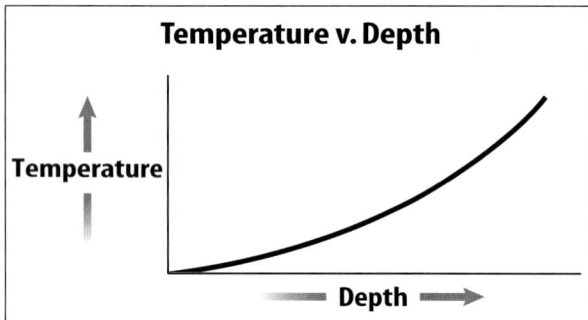

What happens to temperature as you go deeper into Earth?

- A decreases
- B decreases then increases
- C increases
- D increases then decreases

7.3.4

2. Which is believed to cause tectonic plate movement?

- A compression
- B convection
- C isostasy
- D tension

7.3.4

3. Which mountains form when forces pull from opposite directions?

- A fault-block
- B folded
- C upwarped
- D volcanic

7.3.7

4. The illustration below shows relative tectonic plate movement.

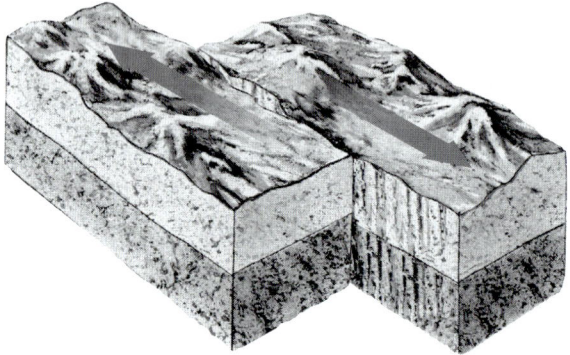

Which force is involved when Earth's plates slide past each other?

- A compression
- B isostasy
- C shear
- D tension

7.3.7

5. Which mountains form when forces inside Earth push up the crust?

- A fault-block
- B folded
- C upwarped
- D volcanic

Standards Review

7.3.4

6. Which is produced by differences in density in Earth's mantle?

   A compression

   B convection

   C shear

   D tension

7.3.4

7. The illustration below shows a type of mountain.

   Which type of mountain is shown above?

   A fault-block

   B folded

   C upwarped

   D volcanic

8. Which lists the layers of Earth's interior from the inside out?

   A crust, mantle, outer core, inner core

   B inner core, outer core, crust, mantle

   C inner core, outer core, mantle, crust

   D mantle, crust, outer core, inner core

Part 2 Constructed Response

7.3.4

9. The photo below shows folded mountains.

Explain how compression causes folded mountains to form. How must this force be applied for folded mountains to form?

7.3.4

10. Where does ridge-push occur? How is it involved in the movement of Earth's tectonic plates?

7.3.4

11. Compare and contrast mountains formed by volcanic activity and those formed by upwarping. Describe how characteristics of a volcanic mountain differ from the characteristics of mountains formed in other ways.

Test-Taking Tip

Check Never leave any critical-response answer blank. Answer each question as best as you can. You can receive partial credit for partially correct answers.

Standard—7.3.18: Describe that ... waves move at different speeds in different materials.

Also covers: 7.3.7 (Detailed standards begin on page IN8.)

section 1

Earthquakes

as you read

What You'll Learn
- **Explain** how earthquakes are caused by a buildup of strain in Earth's crust.
- **Compare and contrast** primary, secondary, and surface waves.
- **Recognize** earthquake hazards and how to prepare for them.

Why It's Important
Studying earthquakes will help you learn where they might occur and how you can prepare for their hazards.

Review Vocabulary
energy: the ability to cause change

New Vocabulary
- earthquake
- fault
- seismic wave
- focus
- epicenter
- seismograph
- magnitude
- tsunami
- seismic safe

What causes earthquakes?

If you've gone for a walk in the woods lately, maybe you picked up a stick along the way. If so, did you try to bend or break it? If you've ever bent a stick slowly, you might have noticed that it changes shape but usually springs back to normal form when you stop bending it. If you continue to bend the stick, you can do it for only so long before it changes permanently. When this elastic limit is passed, the stick may break, as shown in **Figure 1.** When the stick snaps, you can feel vibrations in the stick.

Elastic Rebound As hard as they seem, rocks act in much the same way when forces push or pull on them. If enough force is applied, rocks become strained, which means they change shape. They may even break, and the ends of the broken pieces may snap back. This snapping back is called elastic rebound.

Rocks usually change shape, or deform, slowly over long periods of time. As they are strained, potential energy builds up in them. This energy is released suddenly by the action of rocks breaking and moving. Such breaking, and the movement that follows, causes vibrations that move through rock or other earth materials. If they are large enough, these vibrations are felt as **earthquakes**.

Reading Check *What is an earthquake?*

Figure 1 A stick can bend only so far before it breaks.

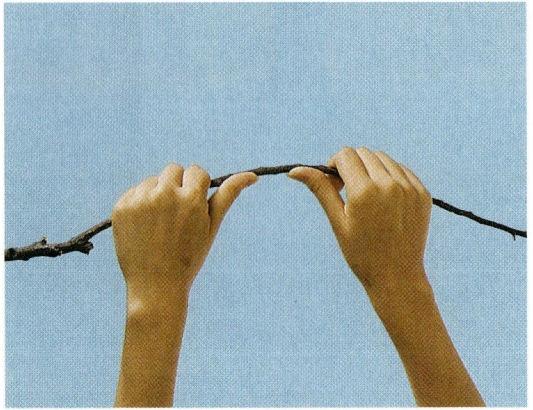

When a stick is bent, potential energy is stored in the stick.

The energy is released as vibrations when the stick breaks.

592 CHAPTER 20 Earthquakes and Volcanoes

Standards Review

7.3.4

6. Which is produced by differences in density in Earth's mantle?

- A compression
- B convection
- C shear
- D tension

7.3.4

7. The illustration below shows a type of mountain.

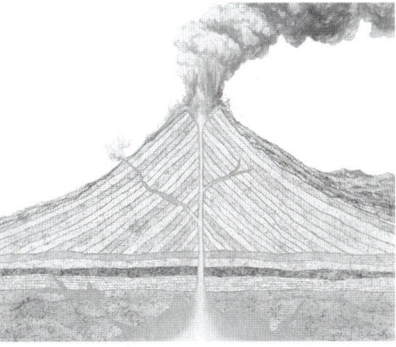

Which type of mountain is shown above?

- A fault-block
- B folded
- C upwarped
- D volcanic

8. Which lists the layers of Earth's interior from the inside out?

- A crust, mantle, outer core, inner core
- B inner core, outer core, crust, mantle
- C inner core, outer core, mantle, crust
- D mantle, crust, outer core, inner core

Part 2 Constructed Response

7.3.4

9. The photo below shows folded mountains.

Explain how compression causes folded mountains to form. How must this force be applied for folded mountains to form?

7.3.4

10. Where does ridge-push occur? How is it involved in the movement of Earth's tectonic plates?

7.3.4

11. Compare and contrast mountains formed by volcanic activity and those formed by upwarping. Describe how characteristics of a volcanic mountain differ from the characteristics of mountains formed in other ways.

Test-Taking Tip

Check Never leave any critical-response answer blank. Answer each question as best as you can. You can receive partial credit for partially correct answers.

chapter 20

Academic Standard—3: Students collect and organize data to identify relationships between physical objects, events, and processes. They use logical reasoning to question their own ideas as new information challenges their conceptions of the natural world.

Earthquakes and Volcanoes

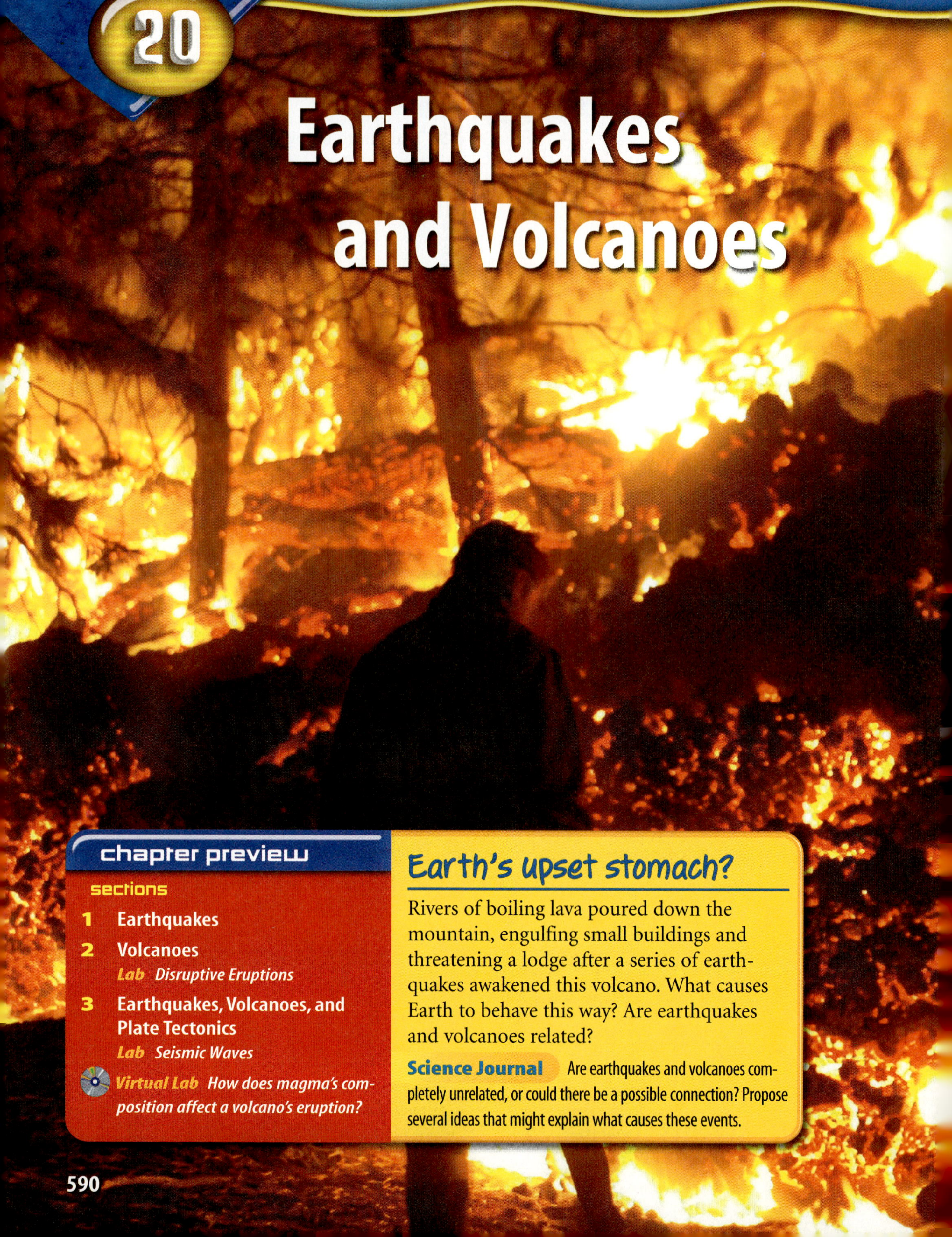

chapter preview

sections

1. **Earthquakes**
2. **Volcanoes**
   Lab Disruptive Eruptions
3. **Earthquakes, Volcanoes, and Plate Tectonics**
   Lab Seismic Waves

Virtual Lab How does magma's composition affect a volcano's eruption?

Earth's upset stomach?

Rivers of boiling lava poured down the mountain, engulfing small buildings and threatening a lodge after a series of earthquakes awakened this volcano. What causes Earth to behave this way? Are earthquakes and volcanoes related?

Science Journal Are earthquakes and volcanoes completely unrelated, or could there be a possible connection? Propose several ideas that might explain what causes these events.

Start-Up Activities

Construct with Strength

One of the greatest dangers associated with an earthquake occurs when people are inside buildings during the event. In the following lab, you will see how construction materials can be used to help strengthen a building.

1. Using wooden blocks, construct a building with four walls. Place a piece of cardboard over the four walls as a ceiling.
2. Gently shake the table under your building. Describe what happens.
3. Reconstruct the building. Wrap large rubber bands around each section, or wall, of blocks. Then wrap large rubber bands around the entire building.
4. Gently shake the table again.
5. **Think Critically** In your Science Journal, note any differences you observed as the two buildings were shaken. Hypothesize how the construction methods you used in this activity might be applied to the construction of real buildings.

 **Preview this chapter's content and activities at in7.msscience.com**

FOLDABLES Study Organizer

Earthquakes and Volcanoes Make the following Foldable to help you compare and contrast the characteristics of earthquakes and volcanoes.

STEP 1 Draw a mark at the midpoint of a vertical sheet of paper.

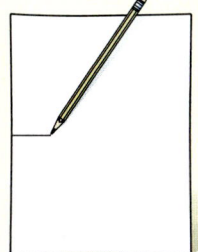

STEP 2 Turn the paper horizontally and **fold** the outside edges in to touch at the midpoint mark.

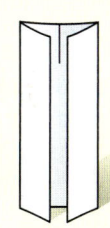

STEP 3 Draw a volcano on one flap and label the flap *Volcanoes*. Draw an earthquake on the other flap and label it *Earthquakes*. The inside portion should be labeled *Both* and include characteristics that both events share.

Analyze and Critique Before you read the chapter, write what you know about earthquakes and volcanoes on the back of each flap. As you read the chapter, add more information about earthquakes and volcanoes.

Standard—7.3.18: Describe that ... waves move at different speeds in different materials.

section 1

Also covers: 7.3.7 (Detailed standards begin on page IN8.)

Earthquakes

as you read

What You'll Learn
- **Explain** how earthquakes are caused by a buildup of strain in Earth's crust.
- **Compare and contrast** primary, secondary, and surface waves.
- **Recognize** earthquake hazards and how to prepare for them.

Why It's Important
Studying earthquakes will help you learn where they might occur and how you can prepare for their hazards.

Review Vocabulary
energy: the ability to cause change

New Vocabulary
- earthquake
- fault
- seismic wave
- focus
- epicenter
- seismograph
- magnitude
- tsunami
- seismic safe

What causes earthquakes?

If you've gone for a walk in the woods lately, maybe you picked up a stick along the way. If so, did you try to bend or break it? If you've ever bent a stick slowly, you might have noticed that it changes shape but usually springs back to normal form when you stop bending it. If you continue to bend the stick, you can do it for only so long before it changes permanently. When this elastic limit is passed, the stick may break, as shown in **Figure 1.** When the stick snaps, you can feel vibrations in the stick.

Elastic Rebound As hard as they seem, rocks act in much the same way when forces push or pull on them. If enough force is applied, rocks become strained, which means they change shape. They may even break, and the ends of the broken pieces may snap back. This snapping back is called elastic rebound.

Rocks usually change shape, or deform, slowly over long periods of time. As they are strained, potential energy builds up in them. This energy is released suddenly by the action of rocks breaking and moving. Such breaking, and the movement that follows, causes vibrations that move through rock or other earth materials. If they are large enough, these vibrations are felt as **earthquakes**.

Reading Check *What is an earthquake?*

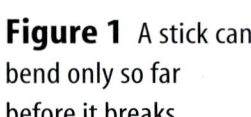

Figure 1 A stick can bend only so far before it breaks.

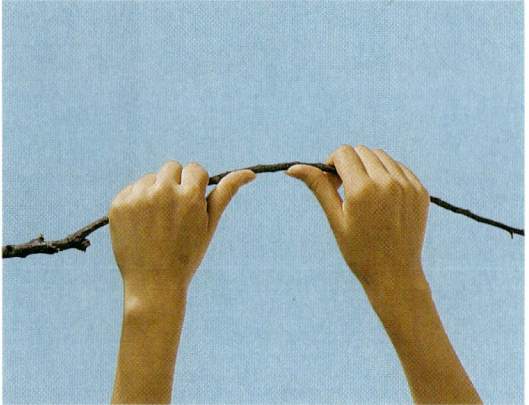

When a stick is bent, potential energy is stored in the stick.

The energy is released as vibrations when the stick breaks.

Figure 2 When rocks change shape by breaking, faults form. The type of fault formed depends on the type of stress exerted on the rock.

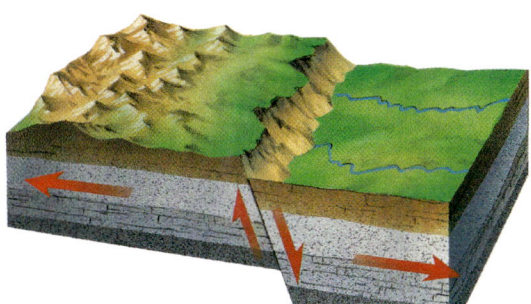

A When rocks are pulled apart, a normal fault may form.

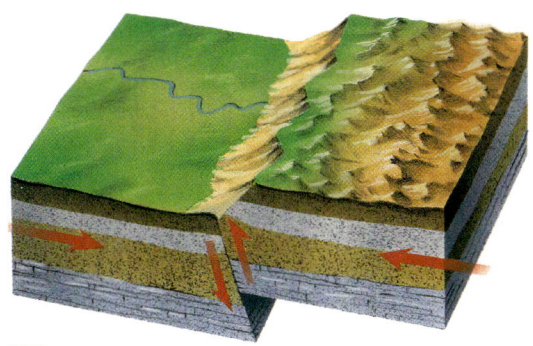

B When rocks are compressed, a reverse fault may form.

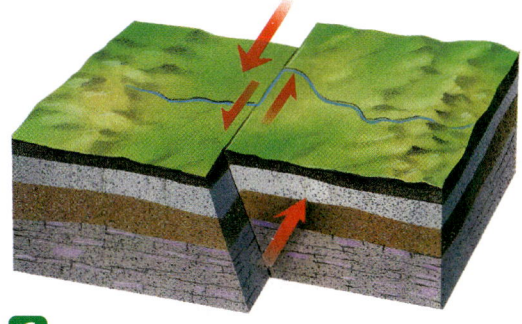

C When rocks are sheared, a strike-slip fault may form.

Types of Faults When a section of rock breaks, rocks on either side of the break along which rocks move might move as a result of elastic rebound. The surface of such a break along which rocks move is called a **fault**. Several types of faults exist. The type that forms depends on how forces were applied to the rocks.

When rocks are pulled apart under tension forces, normal faults form, as shown in **Figure 2A**. Along a normal fault, rock above the fault moves down compared to rock below the fault. Compression forces squeeze rocks together, like an accordion. Compression might cause rock above a fault to move up compared to rock below the fault. This movement forms reverse faults, as shown in **Figure 2B**. As illustrated in **Figure 2C**, rock experiencing shear forces can break to form a strike-slip fault. Shear forces cause rock on either side of a strike-slip fault to move past one another in opposite directions along Earth's surface. You could infer the motion of a strike-slip fault while walking along and observing an offset feature, such as a displaced fence line, on Earth's surface.

Where do the forces come from that cause rocks to deform by bending or breaking? Why do faults form and why do earthquakes occur in certain areas? As you'll learn later in this chapter, forces inside Earth are caused by the constant motion of plates, or sections, of Earth's crust and upper mantle.

Mini LAB

Observing Deformation

WARNING: *Do not taste or eat any lab materials. Wash hands when finished.*

Procedure
1. Remove the wrapper from three bars of **taffy**.
2. Hold a bar of taffy lengthwise between your hands and gently push on it from opposite directions.
3. Hold another bar of taffy and pull it in opposite directions.

Analysis
1. Which of the procedures that you performed on the taffy involved applying tension? Which involved applying compression?
2. Infer how to apply a shear stress to the third bar of taffy.

Making Waves

Do you recall the last time you shouted for a friend to save you a seat on the bus? When you called out, energy was transmitted through the air to your friend, who interpreted the familiar sound of your voice as belonging to you. These sound waves were released by your vocal cords and were affected by your tongue and mouth. They traveled outward through the air. Earthquakes also release waves. Earthquake waves are transmitted through materials in Earth and along Earth's surface. Earthquake waves are called **seismic waves**. In the two-page activity, you'll make waves similar to seismic waves by moving a coiled spring toy.

Earthquake Focus and Epicenter Movement along a fault releases strain energy. Strain energy is potential energy that builds up in rock when it is bent. When this potential energy is released, it moves outward from the fault in the form of seismic waves. The point inside Earth where this movement first occurs and energy is released is called the **focus** of an earthquake, as shown in **Figure 3**. The point on Earth's surface located directly above the earthquake focus is called the **epicenter** of the earthquake.

Reading Check *Where is the focus of an earthquake located?*

Figure 3 During an earthquake, several types of seismic waves form. Primary and secondary waves travel in all directions from the focus and can travel through Earth's interior. Surface waves travel at shallow depths and along Earth's surface.
Infer *Which seismic waves are the most destructive?*

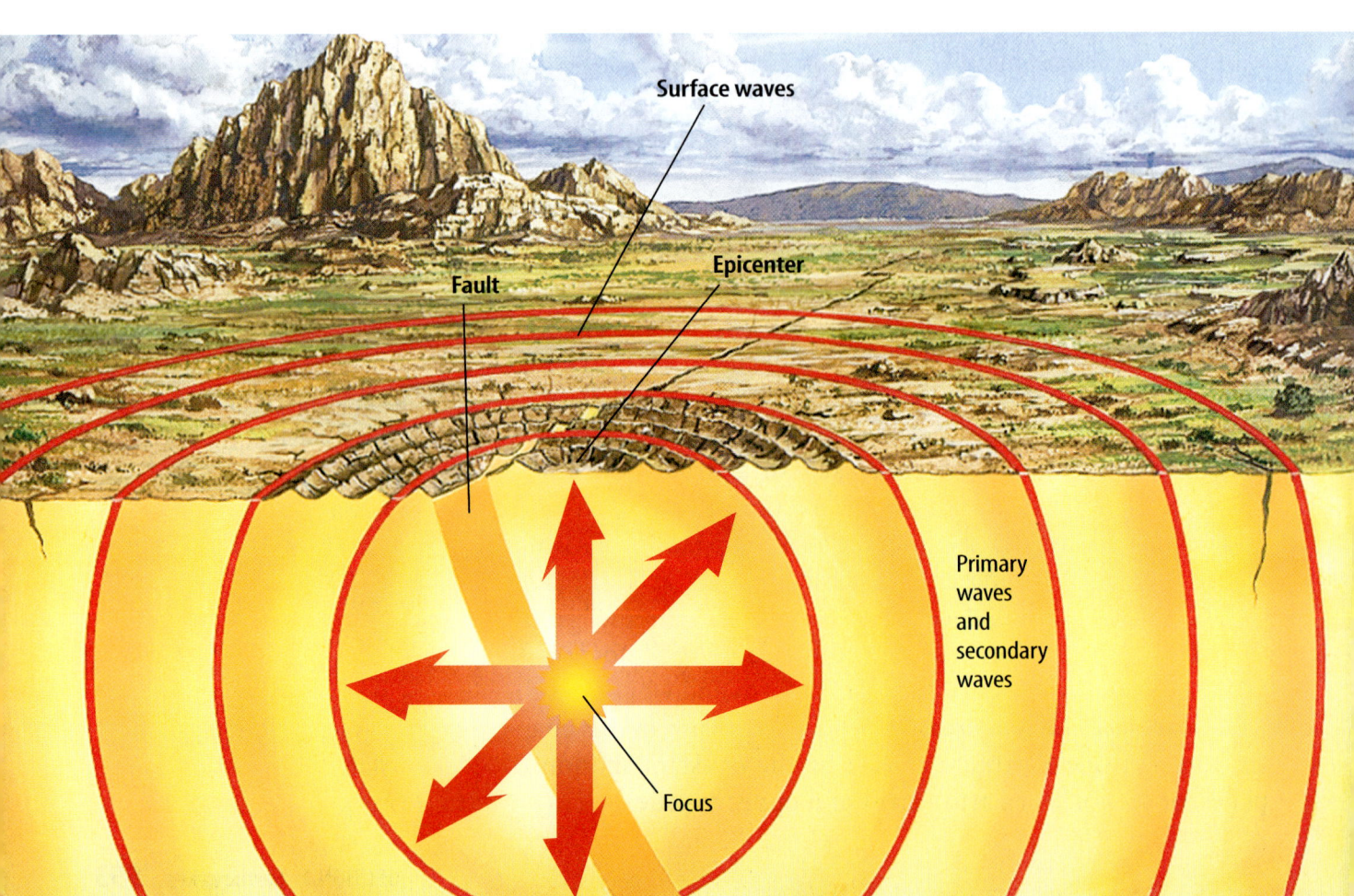

Seismic Waves After they are produced at the focus, seismic waves travel away from the focus in all directions, as illustrated in **Figure 3**. Some seismic waves travel throughout Earth's interior, and others travel along Earth's surface. The surface waves cause the most damage during an earthquake event.

Primary waves, also known as P-waves, travel the fastest through rock material by causing particles in the rock to move back and forth, or vibrate, in the same direction as the waves are moving. Secondary waves, known as S-waves, move through rock material by causing particles in the rock to vibrate at right angles to the direction in which the waves are moving. P- and S-waves travel through Earth's interior. Studying them has revealed much information about Earth's interior.

Surface waves are the slowest and largest of the seismic waves, and they cause most of the destruction during an earthquake. The movements of surface waves are complex. Some surface waves move along Earth's surface in a manner that moves rock and soil in a backward rolling motion. They have been observed moving across the land like waves of water. Some surface waves vibrate in a side-to-side, or swaying, motion parallel to Earth's surface. This motion can be particularly devastating to human-built structures.

Learning from Earthquakes

On your way to lunch tomorrow, suppose you were to walk twice as fast as your friend does. What would happen to the distance between the two of you as you walked to the lunchroom? The distance between you and your friend would become greater the farther you walked, and you would arrive first. Using this same line of reasoning, scientists use the different speeds of seismic waves and their differing arrival times to calculate the distance to an earthquake epicenter.

Earthquake Measurements Seismologists are scientists who study earthquakes and seismic waves. The instrument they use to obtain a record of seismic waves from all over the world is called a **seismograph**, shown in the top photo of **Figure 4**.

One type of seismograph has a drum holding a roll of paper on a fixed frame. A pendulum with an attached pen is suspended from the frame. When seismic waves are received at the station, the drum vibrates but the pendulum remains at rest. The pen on the pendulum traces a record of the vibrations on the paper. The height of the lines traced on the paper is a measure of the energy released by the earthquake, also known as its **magnitude**.

Figure 4 Scientists study seismic waves using seismographs located around the world.

This seismograph records incoming seismic waves using a fixed mass.

Some seismographs collect and store data on a computer.

Indiana Academic Standard Check

7.3.18: Describe that light waves, sound waves, and other waves move at different speeds in different materials.

✔ Which seismic waves travel fastest through Earth's interior?

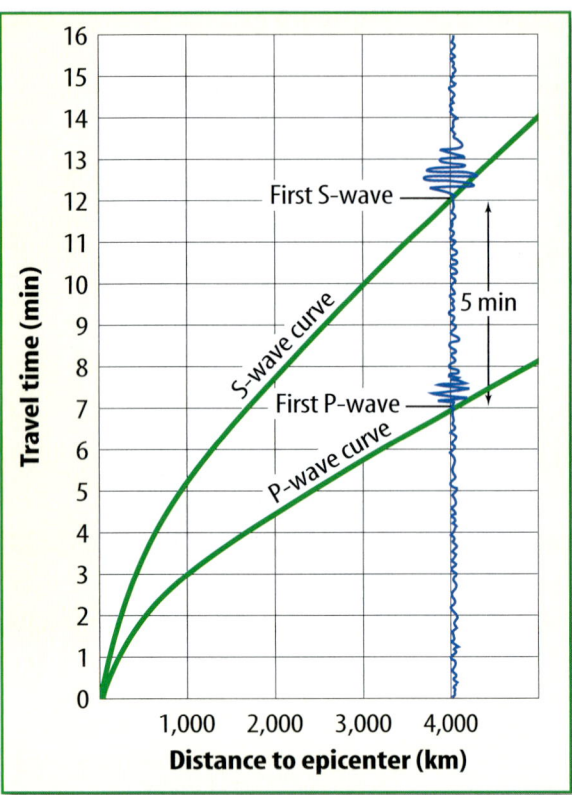

Figure 5 P-waves and S-waves travel at different speeds. These speeds are used to determine how close a seismograph station is to an earthquake.

Figure 6 After distances from at least three seismograph stations are determined, they are plotted as circles with radii equal to these distances on a map. The epicenter is the point at which the circles intersect.

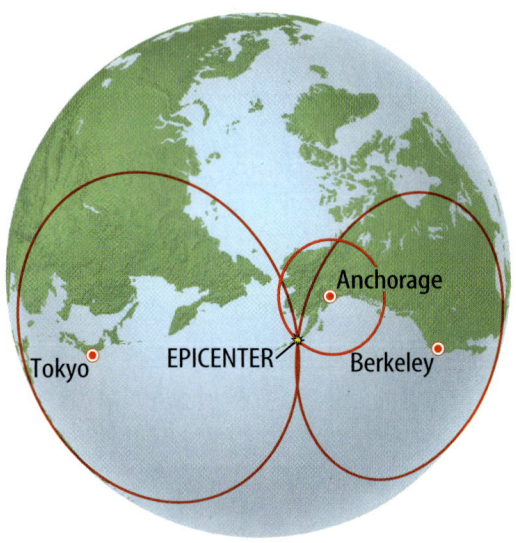

Epicenter Location When seismic-wave arrival times are recorded at a seismograph station, the distance from that station to the epicenter can be determined. The farther apart the arrival times for the different waves are, the farther away the earthquake epicenter is. This difference is shown by the graph in **Figure 5.** Using this information, scientists draw a circle with a radius equal to the distance from the earthquake for each of at least three seismograph stations, as illustrated in **Figure 6.** The point where the three circles meet is the location of the earthquake epicenter. Data from many stations normally are used to determine an epicenter location.

How strong are earthquakes?

As shown in **Table 1,** major earthquakes cause much loss of life. For example, on September 20, 1999, a major earthquake struck Taiwan, leaving more than 2,400 people dead, more than 8,700 injured, and at least 100,000 homeless. Sometimes earthquakes are felt and can cause destruction in areas hundreds of kilometers away from their epicenters. The Mexico City earthquake in 1985 is an example of this. The movement of the soft sediment underneath Mexico City caused extensive damage to this city, even though the epicenter was nearly 400 km away.

The Richter Scale Richter (RIHK tur) magnitude is based on measurements of amplitudes, or heights, of seismic waves as recorded on seismographs. Richter magnitude describes how much energy an earthquake releases. For each increase of 1.0 on the Richter scale, the amplitude of the highest recorded seismic wave increases by 10. However, about 32 times more energy is released for every increase of 1.0 on the scale. For example, an earthquake with a magnitude of 7.5 releases about 32 times more energy than one with a magnitude of 6.5, and the wave height for a 7.5-magnitude quake is ten times higher than for a quake with a magnitude of 6.5.

Earthquake Damage Another way to measure earthquakes is available. The modified Mercalli intensity scale measures the intensity of an earthquake. Intensity is a measure of the amount of structural and geologic damage done by an earthquake in a specific location. The range of intensities spans Roman numerals I through XII. The amount of damage done depends on several factors—the strength of the earthquake, the nature of the surface material, the design of structures, and the distance from the epicenter. An intensity-I earthquake would be felt only by a few people under ideal conditions. An intensity-VI earthquake would be felt by everyone. An intensity-XII earthquake would cause major destruction to human-built structures and Earth's surface. The 1994 earthquake in Northridge, California was a Richter magnitude 6.7, and its intensity was listed at IX. An intensity-IX earthquake causes considerable damage to buildings and could cause cracks in the ground.

Table 1 Strong Earthquakes

Year	Location	Magnitude	Deaths
1989	Loma Prieta, CA	7.1	62
1990	Iran	7.7	50,000
1993	Guam	8.1	none
1993	Maharashtra, India	6.4	30,000
1994	Northridge, CA	6.7	61
1995	Kobe, Japan	6.8	5,378
1999	Taiwan	7.7	2,400
2000	Indonesia	7.9	103
2001	India	7.7	20,000
2003	Iran	6.6	30,000

Tsunamis Most damage from an earthquake is caused by surface waves. Buildings can crack or fall down. Elevated bridges and highways can collapse. However, people living near the seashore must protect themselves against another hazard from earthquakes. When an earthquake occurs on the ocean floor, the sudden movement pushes against the water and powerful water waves are produced. These waves can travel outward from the earthquake thousands of kilometers in all directions.

When these seismic sea waves, or **tsunamis,** are far from shore, their energy is spread out over large distances and great water depths. The wave heights of tsunamis are less than a meter in deep water, and large ships can ride over them and not even know it. In the open ocean, the speed of tsunamis can reach 950 km/h. However, when tsunamis approach land, the waves slow down and their wave heights increase as they encounter the bottom of the seafloor. This creates huge tsunami waves that can be as much as 30 m in height. Just before a tsunami crashes to shore, the water near a shoreline may move rapidly out toward the sea. If this should happen, there is immediate danger that a tsunami is about to strike. **Figure 7** illustrates the behavior of a tsunami as it approaches the shore.

Topic: Earthquake Magnitude
Visit in7.msscience.com for Web links to information about determining earthquake magnitudes.

Activity Create a table that compares the damage in dollars, the magnitude, and the general location of six recent earthquakes.

NATIONAL GEOGRAPHIC VISUALIZING TSUNAMIS

Figure 7

The diagram below shows stages in the development of a tsunami. A tsunami is an ocean wave that is usually generated by an earthquake and is capable of inflicting great destruction.

▶ **TSUNAMI ALERT** The red dots on this map show the tide monitoring stations that make up part of the Tsunami Warning System for the Pacific Ocean. The map shows approximately how long it would take for tsunamis that originate at different places in the Pacific to reach Hawaii. Each ring represents two hours of travel time.

Displacement

B The waves travel across the ocean at speeds ranging from about 500 to 950 km/h.

C When a tsunami wave reaches shallow water, friction slows it down and causes it to roll up into a wall of water—sometimes 30 m high—before it breaks against the shore.

A The vibrations set off by a sudden movement along a fault in Earth's crust are transferred to the water's surface and spread across the ocean in a series of long waves.

Tsunami Warning System buoy

Earthquake Safety

You've just read about the destruction that earthquakes cause. Fortunately, there are ways to reduce the damage and the loss of life associated with earthquakes.

Learning the earthquake history of an area is one of the first things to do to protect yourself. If the area you are in has had earthquakes before, chances are it will again and you can prepare for that.

Is your home seismic safe? What could you do to make your home earthquake safe? As shown in **Figure 8,** it's a good idea to move all heavy objects to lower shelves so they can't fall on you. Make sure your gas hot-water heater and appliances are well secured. A new method of protecting against fire is to place sensors on your gas line that would shut off the gas when the vibrations of an earthquake are felt.

In the event of an earthquake, keep away from all windows and avoid anything that might fall on you. Watch for fallen power lines and possible fire hazards. Collapsed buildings and piles of rubble can contain many sharp edges, so keep clear of these areas.

Seismic-Safe Structures If a building is considered seismic safe, it will be able to stand up against the vibrations caused by most earthquakes. Residents in earthquake-prone areas are constantly improving the way structures are built. Since 1971, stricter building codes have been enforced in California. Older buildings have been reinforced. Many high-rise office buildings now stand on huge steel-and-rubber supports that could enable them to ride out the vibrations of an earthquake. Underground water and gas pipes are replaced with pipes that will bend during an earthquake. This can help prevent broken gas lines and therefore reduce damage from fires.

Seismic-safe highways have cement pillars with spiral reinforcing rods placed within them. One structure that was severely damaged in the 1989 Loma Prieta, California earthquake was Interstate Highway 880. The collapsed highway was due to be renovated to make it seismic safe. It was built in the 1950s and did not have spiral reinforcing rods in its concrete columns. When the upper highway went in one direction, the lower one went in the opposite direction. The columns collapsed and the upper highway came down onto the lower one.

Figure 8 You can minimize your risk of getting hurt by preparing for an earthquake in advance.

Placing heavy or breakable objects on lower shelves means they won't fall too far during an earthquake.

Vibration sensors on gas lines shut off the supply of gas automatically during an earthquake.
Draw Conclusions What hazard can be prevented if the gas is turned off?

Predicting Earthquakes Imagine how many lives could be saved if only the time and location of a major earthquake could be predicted. Because most injuries from earthquakes occur when structures fall on top of people, it would help if people could be warned to move outside of buildings.

Researchers try to predict earthquakes by noting changes that precede them. That way, if such changes are observed again, an earthquake warning may be issued.

For example, movement along faults is monitored using laser-equipped, distance-measuring devices, such as the one shown in **Figure 9**. Changes in groundwater level or in electrical properties of rocks under stress have been measured by some scientists. Some people even study rock layers that have been affected by ancient earthquakes. Whether any of these studies will lead to the accurate and reliable prediction of earthquakes, no one knows. A major problem is that no single change in Earth occurs for all earthquakes. Each earthquake is unique.

Long-range forecasts predict whether an earthquake of a certain magnitude is likely to occur in a given area within 30 to 100 years. Forecasts of this nature are used to update building codes to make a given area more seismic safe.

Figure 9 One way to monitor changes along a fault is to detect any movement that occurs.

section 1 review

Summary

What causes earthquakes?
- The sudden release of energy in rock and the resulting movement causes an earthquake.
- Faults are breaks in rocks along which movement occurs.

Making Waves
- The focus is where an earthquake occurs. The epicenter is directly above it.
- Earthquakes generate seismic waves.

How strong are earthquakes?
- The Richter Scale measures magnitude.
- The modified Mercalli scale measures intensity.

Earthquake Safety
- Structures can be made seismic safe.

Self Check

1. **Explain** what happens to rocks after their elastic limit is passed.
2. **Identify** Which seismic waves cause most of the damage during an earthquake?
3. **Apply** What has been done to make structures more seismic safe?
4. **Summarize** How can seismic waves be used to determine an earthquake's epicenter?
5. **Think Critically** Explain how a magnitude-8.0 earthquake could be classified as a low-intensity earthquake.

Applying Skills

6. **Make and Use Tables** Use **Table 1** to research the earthquakes that struck Indonesia in 2000, Loma Prieta, California in 1989, and Iran in 1990. Why was there such a great difference in the number of deaths?

in7.msscience.com/self_check_quiz

Standard—7.3.7: Give examples of some changes in Earth's surface that are abrupt, such as earthquakes and volcanic eruptions....

section 2

Volcanoes

How do volcanoes form?

Much like air bubbles that are forced upward toward the bottom of an overturned bottle of denser syrup, molten rock material, or magma, is forced upward toward Earth's surface by denser surrounding rock. Rising magma eventually can lead to an eruption, where magma, solids, and gas are spewed out to form cone-shaped mountains called **volcanoes.** As magma flows onto Earth's surface through a vent, or opening, it is called **lava.** Volcanoes have circular holes near their summits called craters. Lava and other volcanic materials can be expelled through a volcano's crater.

Some explosive eruptions throw lava and rock thousands of meters into the air. Bits of rock or solidified lava dropped from the air are called tephra. Tephra varies in size from volcanic ash to cinders to larger rocks called bombs or blocks.

Where Plates Collide Some volcanoes form because of collision of large plates of Earth's crust and upper mantle. This process has produced a string of volcanic islands, much like those illustrated in **Figure 10,** which includes Montserrat. These islands are forming as plates made up of oceanic crust and mantle collide. The older and denser oceanic plate subducts, or sinks beneath, the less dense plate, as shown in **Figure 10.** When one plate sinks under another plate, rock in and above the sinking plate melts, forming chambers of magma. This magma is the source for volcanic eruptions that have formed the Caribbean Islands.

as you read

What You'll Learn
- **Explain** how volcanoes can affect people.
- **Describe** how types of materials are produced by volcanoes.
- **Compare** how three different volcano forms develop.

Why It's Important
Volcanic eruptions can cause serious consequences for humans and other organisms.

Review Vocabulary
plate: a large section of Earth's crust and rigid upper mantle that moves around on the asthenosphere

New Vocabulary
- volcano
- lava
- shield volcano
- cinder cone volcano
- composite volcano

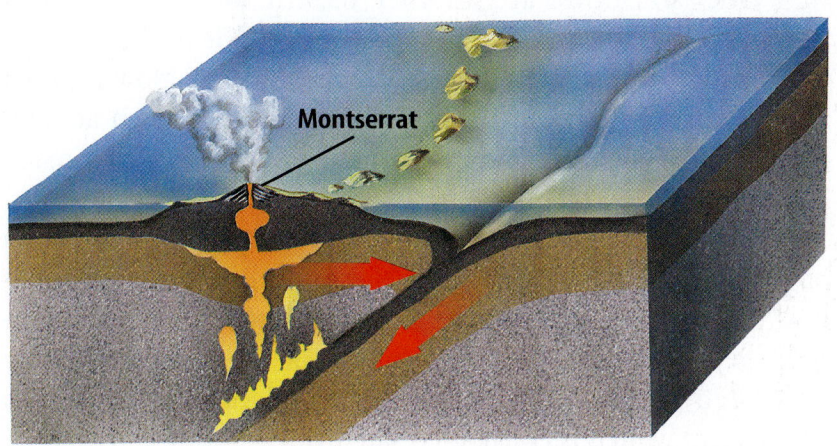

Figure 10 A string of Caribbean Islands known as the Lesser Antilles formed because of subduction. The island of Montserrat is among these.

SECTION 2 Volcanoes **601**

Figure 11 Several volcanic hazards are associated with explosive activity.

Volcanic ash blanketing an area can cause collapse of structures or—when mixed with precipitation—mudflows.

Objects in the path of a pyroclastic flow are subject to complete destruction.

Mini LAB

Modeling an Eruption

Procedure

1. Place **red-colored gelatin** into a **self-sealing plastic bag** until the bag is half full.
2. Seal the bag and press the gelatin to the bottom of the bag.
3. Put a hole in the bottom of the bag with a **pin**.

Analysis

1. What parts of a volcano do the gelatin, the plastic bag, and the hole represent?
2. What force in nature did you mimic as you moved the gelatin to the bottom of the bag?
3. What factors in nature cause this force to increase and lead to an eruption?

Try at Home

Eruptions on a Caribbean Island Soufrière (soo free UR) Hills volcano on the island of Montserrat was considered dormant until recently. However, in 1995, Soufrière Hills volcano surprised its inhabitants with explosive activity. In July 1995, plumes of ash soared to heights of more than 10,000 m. This ash covered the capital city of Plymouth and many other villages, as shown at left in **Figure 11**.

Every aspect of a once-calm tropical life changed when the volcano erupted. Glowing avalanches and hot, boiling mudflows destroyed villages and shut down the main harbor of the island and its airport. During activity on July 3, 1998, volcanic ash reached heights of more than 14,000 m. This ash settled over the entire island and was followed by mudflows brought on by heavy rains.

Pyroclastic flows are another hazard for inhabitants of Montserrat. They can occur anytime on any side of the volcano. Pyroclastic flows are massive avalanches of hot, glowing rock flowing on a cushion of intensely hot gases, as shown at right in **Figure 11**. Speeds at which these flows travel can reach 200 km/h.

More than one half of Montserrat has been converted to a barren wasteland by the volcano. Virtually all of the farmland is now unusable, and most of the island's business and leisure centers are gone. Many of the inhabitants of the island have been evacuated to England, surrounding islands, or northern Montserrat, which is considered safe from volcanic activity.

Volcanic Risks According to the volcanic-risk map shown in **Figure 12,** inactive volcanic centers exist at Silver Hill, Centre Hill, and South Soufrière Hills. The active volcano, Soufrière Hills volcano, is located just north of South Soufrière Hills. The risk map shows different zones of the island where inhabitants still are able to stay and locations from which they have been evacuated. Twenty people who had ignored evacuation orders were killed by pyroclastic flows from the June 25, 1997, event. These are the first and only deaths that have occurred since July 1995.

Forms of Volcanoes

As you have learned, volcanoes can cause great destruction. However, volcanoes also add new rock to Earth's crust with each eruption. The way volcanoes add this new material to Earth's surface varies greatly. Different types of eruptions produce different types of volcanoes.

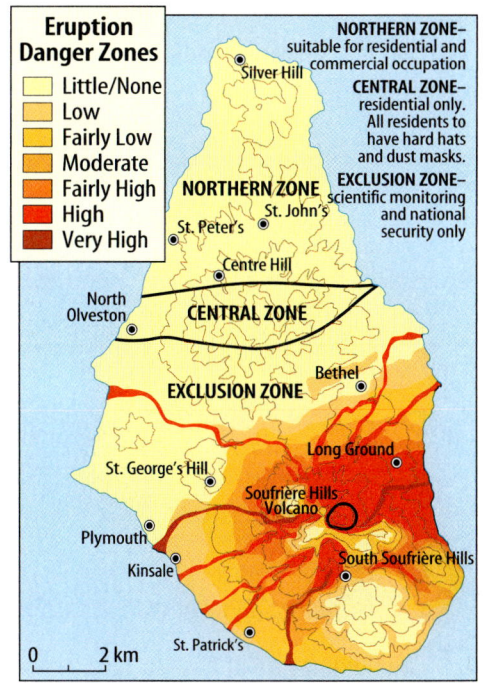

Figure 12 A volcanic risk map for Montserrat was prepared to warn inhabitants and visitors about unsafe areas on the island.

What determines how a volcano erupts? Some volcanic eruptions are violent, while during others lava flows out quietly around a vent. The composition of the magma plays a big part in determining the manner in which energy is released during a volcanic eruption. Lava that contains more silica, which is a compound consisting of silicon and oxygen, tends to be thicker and is more resistant to flow. Lava containing more iron and magnesium and less silica tends to flow easily. The amount of water vapor and other gases trapped in the lava also influences how lava erupts.

When you shake a bottle of carbonated soft drink before opening it, the pressure from the gas in the drink builds up and is released suddenly when the container is opened. Similarly, steam builds pressure in magma. This pressure is released as magma rises toward Earth's surface and eventually erupts. Sticky, silica-rich lava tends to trap water vapor and other gases.

Water is carried down from the surface of Earth into the mantle when one plate subducts beneath another, as in the case of the Lesser Antilles volcanoes. In hotter regions of Earth's interior, part of a descending plate and nearby rock will melt to form magma. The magma produced is more silica rich than the rock that melts to form the magma. Superheated steam produces tremendous pressure in such thick, silica-rich magmas. After enough pressure builds up, an eruption occurs. The type of lava and the gases contained in that lava determine the type of eruption that occurs.

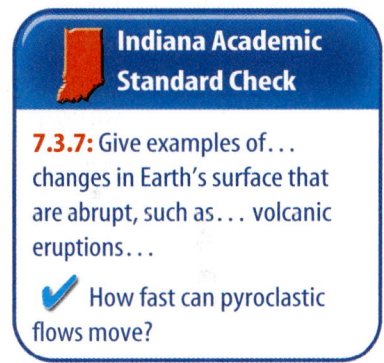

Indiana Academic Standard Check

7.3.7: Give examples of... changes in Earth's surface that are abrupt, such as... volcanic eruptions...

✓ How fast can pyroclastic flows move?

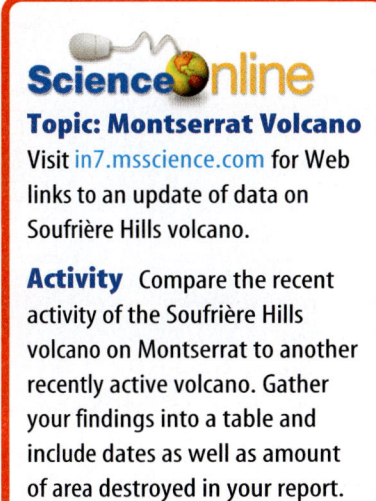

Topic: Montserrat Volcano
Visit in7.msscience.com for Web links to an update of data on Soufrière Hills volcano.

Activity Compare the recent activity of the Soufrière Hills volcano on Montserrat to another recently active volcano. Gather your findings into a table and include dates as well as amount of area destroyed in your report.

SECTION 2 Volcanoes **603**

Figure 13 Volcanic landforms vary greatly in size and shape.

A The fluid nature of basaltic lava has produced extensive flows at Mauna Loa, Hawaii—the largest active volcano on Earth.

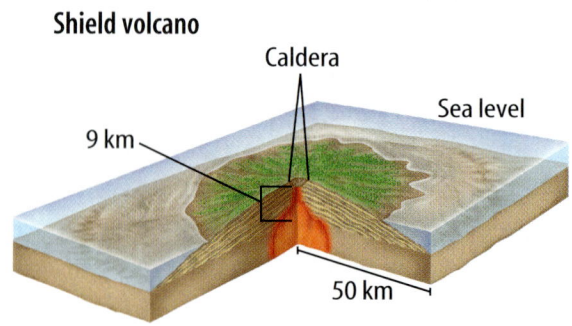

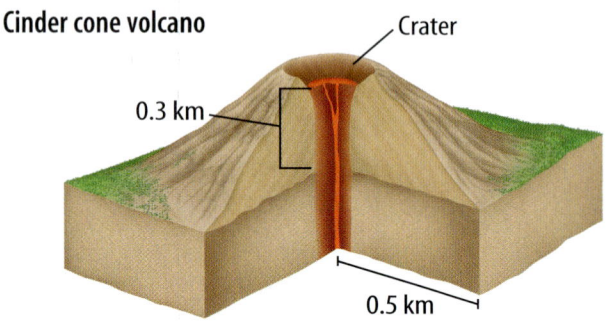

B Sunset Crater is small and steep along its flanks—typical of a cinder cone. Compare the scale given for Sunset Crater with that shown in Figure 13A.

Shield Volcanoes Basaltic lava, which is high in iron and magnesium and low in silica, flows in broad, flat layers. The buildup of basaltic layers forms a broad volcano with gently sloping sides called a **shield volcano**. Shield volcanoes, shown in **Figure 13A**, are the largest type of volcano. They form where magma is being forced up from extreme depths within Earth, or in areas where Earth's plates are moving apart. The separation of plates enables magma to be forced upward to Earth's surface.

 *What materials are shield volcanoes composed of?*

Cinder Cone Volcanoes Rising magma accumulates gases on its way to the surface. When the gas builds up enough pressure, it erupts. Moderate to violent eruptions throw volcanic ash, cinders, and lava high into the air. The lava cools quickly in midair and the particles of solidified lava, ash, and cinders fall back to Earth. This tephra forms a relatively small cone of volcanic material called a **cinder cone volcano**. Cinder cones are usually less than 300 m in height and often form in groups near other larger volcanoes. Because the eruption is powered by the high gas content, it usually doesn't last long. After the gas is released, the force behind the eruption is gone. Sunset Crater, an example of a cinder cone near Flagstaff, Arizona, is shown in **Figure 13B**.

Composite Volcanoes Steep-sided mountains composed of alternating layers of lava and tephra are ==composite volcanoes==. They sometimes erupt violently, releasing large quantities of ash and gas. This forms a tephra layer of solid materials. Then a quieter eruption forms a lava layer.

Composite volcanoes form where one plate sinks beneath another. Soufrière Hills volcano is an example of a composite volcano. Another volcanic eruption from a composite volcano was the May 1980 eruption of Mount St. Helens in the state of Washington. It erupted explosively, spewing ash that fell on regions hundreds of kilometers away from the volcano. A composite volcano is shown in **Figure 13C.**

Fissure Eruptions Magma that is highly fluid can ooze from cracks or fissures in Earth's surface. This is the type of magma that usually is associated with fissure eruptions. The lava that erupts has a low viscosity, which means it can flow freely across the land to form flood basalts. Flood basalts that have been exposed to erosion for millions of years can become large, relatively flat landforms known as lava plateaus, as shown in **Figure 13D.** The Columbia River Plateau in the northwestern United States was formed about 15 million years ago when several fissures erupted and the flows built up layer upon layer.

C Composite cones are intermediate in size and shape compared to shield volcanoes and cinder cone volcanoes.

Mount Rainier, Washington

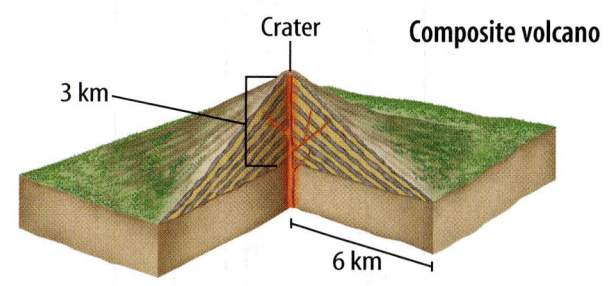

Composite volcano

D No modern example compares with the extensive flood basalts making up the Columbia River Plateau.

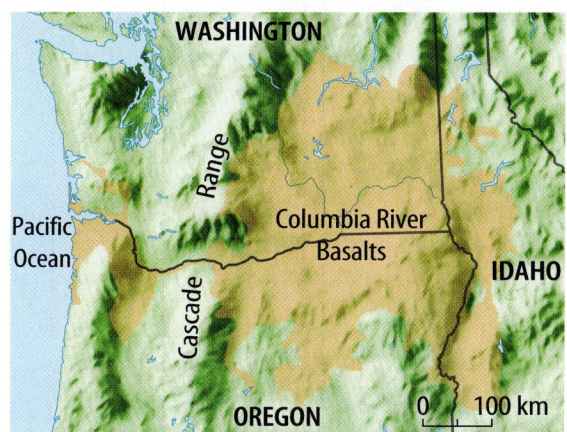

SECTION 2 Volcanoes **605**

Table 2 Seven Selected Eruptions in History

Volcano (Year)	Type	Eruptive Force	Silica Content	Gas Content	Eruption Products
Krakatau, Indonesia (1883)	composite	high	high	high	gas, cinders, ash
Katmai, Alaska (1912)	composite	high	high	high	lava, ash, gas
Paricutín, Mexico (1943)	cinder cone	moderate	high	low	gas, cinders, ash
Helgafell, Iceland (1973)	cinder cone	moderate	low	high	gas, ash
Mount St. Helens, Washington (1980)	composite	high	high	high	gas, ash
Kilauea Iki, Hawaii (1989)	shield	low	low	low	gas, lava
Soufrière Hills, Montserrat (1995–)	composite	high	high	high	gas, ash, rocks

You have read about some variables that control the type of volcanic eruption that will occur. Examine **Table 2** for a summary of these important factors. In the next section, you'll learn that the type of magma produced is associated with properties of Earth's plates and how these plates interact.

section 2 review

Summary

How do volcanoes form?
- Some volcanoes form as two or more large plates collide.
- The Caribbean Islands formed from volcanic eruptions as one plate sinks under another plate.

Forms of volcanoes
- Lava high in silica produces explosive eruptions, lava low in silica but high in iron and magnesium produces more fluid eruptions.
- The amount of water vapor and gases impacts how volcanoes erupt.
- The types of volcanoes include shield, cinder cone and composite volcanoes, and fissure eruptions.

Self Check

1. **Identify** Which types of lava eruptions cover the largest area on Earth's surface?
2. **Describe** the processes that have led to the formation of the Soufrière Hills volcano.
3. **Explain** why a cinder cone has steep sides?
4. **List** What types of materials are volcanoes like Mount St. Helens made of?
5. **Think Critically** Why is silica-rich magma explosive?

Applying Math

6. **Solve One-Step Equations** Mauna Loa in Hawaii rises 9 km above the seafloor. Sunset Crater in Arizona rises to an elevation of 300 m. How many times higher is Mauna Loa than Sunset Crater?

 in7.msscience.com/self_check_quiz

606 CHAPTER 20 Earthquakes and Volcanoes

Disruptive Eruptions

A volcano's structure can influence how it erupts. Some volcanoes have only one central vent, while others have numerous fissures that allow lava to escape. Materials in magma influence its viscosity, or how it flows. If magma is a thin fluid—not viscous—gases can escape easily. But if magma is thick—viscous—gases cannot escape as easily. This builds up pressure within a volcano.

Real-World Question

What determines the explosiveness of a volcanic eruption?

Goals
- **Infer** how a volcano's opening contributes to how explosive an eruption might be.
- **Hypothesize** how the viscosity of magma can influence an eruption.

Materials
plastic film canisters
baking soda ($NaHCO_3$)
vinegar (CH_3COOH)
50-mL graduated cylinder
teaspoon

Safety Precautions

This lab should be done outdoors. Goggles must be worn at all times. The caps of the film canisters fly off due to the chemical reaction that occurs inside them. Never put anything in your mouth while doing the experiment.

Procedure

1. Watch your teacher demonstrate this lab before attempting to do it yourself.
2. Add 15 mL of vinegar to a film canister.
3. Place 1 teaspoon of baking soda in the film canister's lid, using it as a type of plate.
4. Place the lid on top of the film canister, but do not cap it. The baking soda will fall into the vinegar. Move a safe distance away. Record your observations in your Science Journal.
5. Clean out your film canister and repeat the lab, but this time cap the canister quickly and tightly. Record your observations.

Conclude and Apply

1. **Identify** Which of the two labs models a more explosive eruption?
2. **Explain** Was the pressure greater inside the canister during the first or second lab? Why?
3. **Explain** What do the bubbles have to do with the explosion? How do they influence the pressure in the container?
4. **Infer** If the vinegar were a more viscous substance, how would the eruption be affected?

Communicating Your Data

Research three volcanic eruptions that have occurred in the past five years. Compare each eruption to one of the eruption styles you modeled in this lab. Communicate to your class what you learn.

section 3

Standard—7.3.7: Give examples of some changes in Earth's surface that are abrupt, such as earthquakes and volcanic eruptions. . . .

Also covers: 7.3.4, 7.3.18 (Detailed standards begin on page IN8.)

Earthquakes, Volcanoes, and Plate Tectonics

as you read

What You'll Learn
- **Explain** how the locations of volcanoes and earthquake epicenters are related to tectonic plate boundaries.
- **Explain** how heat within Earth causes Earth's plates to move.

Why It's Important
Most volcanoes and earthquakes are caused by the motion and interaction of Earth's plates.

Review Vocabulary
asthenosphere: plasticlike layer of mantle under the lithosphere

New Vocabulary
- rift
- hot spot

Earth's Moving Plates

At the beginning of class, your teacher asks for volunteers to help set up the cafeteria for a special assembly. You and your classmates begin to move the tables carefully, like the students shown in **Figure 14.** As you move the tables, two or three of them crash into each other. Think about what could happen if the students moving those tables kept pushing on them. For a while one or two of the tables might keep another from moving. However, if enough force were used, the tables would slide past one another. One table might even slide up on top of another. It is because of this possibility that your teacher has asked that you move the tables carefully.

The movement of the tables and the possible collisions among them is like the movement of Earth's crust and uppermost mantle, called the lithosphere. Earth's lithosphere is broken into separate sections, or plates. When these plates move around, they collide, move apart, or slide past each other. The movement of these plates can cause vibrations known as earthquakes and can create conditions that cause volcanoes to form.

Figure 14 Like the tables pictured here, Earth's plates are in contact with one another and can slide beneath each other. The way Earth's plates interact at boundaries is an important factor in the locations of earthquakes and volcanoes.

608 CHAPTER 20 Earthquakes and Volcanoes

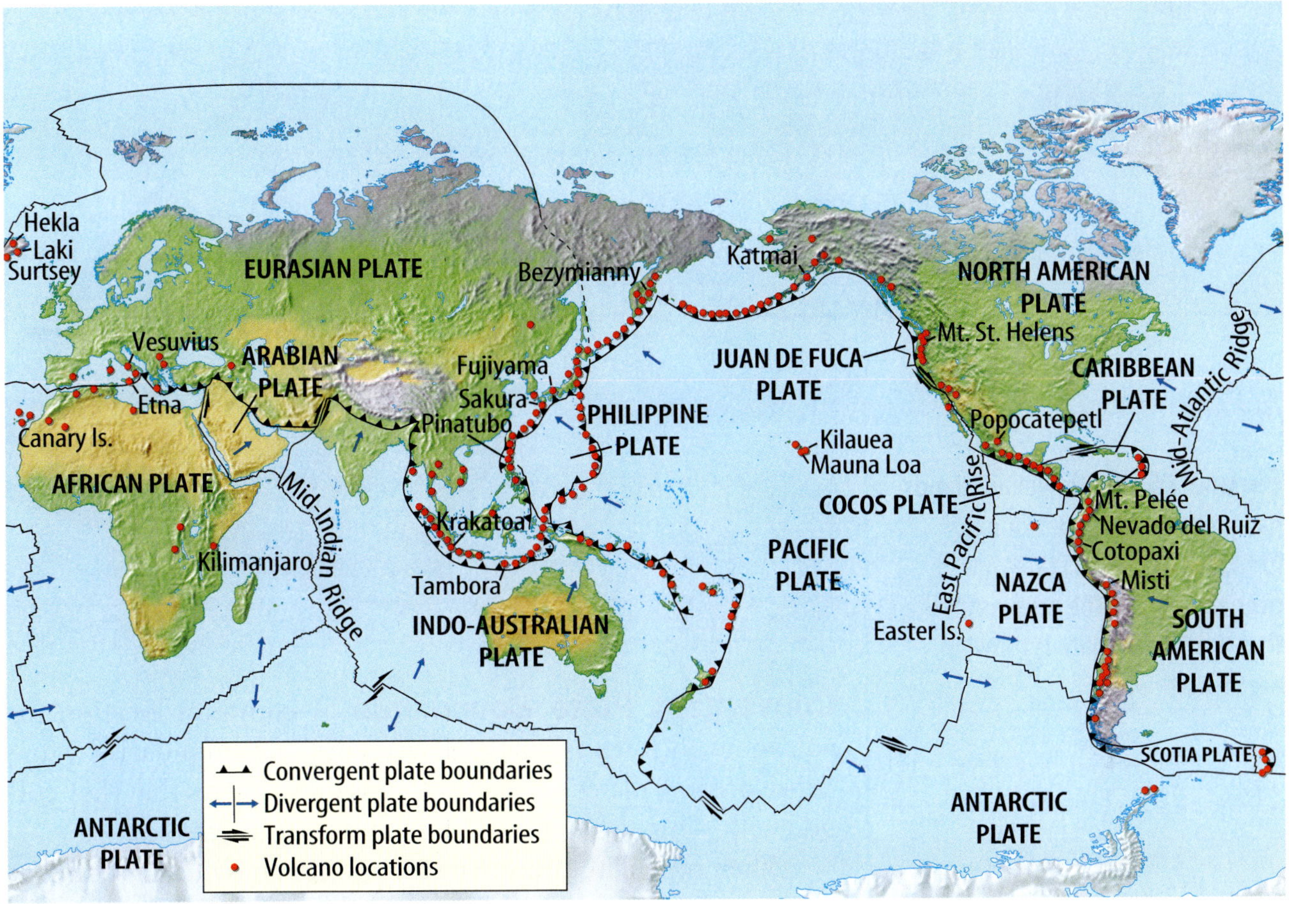

Figure 15 Earth's lithosphere is divided into about 13 major plates. Where plates collide, separate, and slip past one another at plate boundaries, interesting geological activity results.

Where Volcanoes Form

A plot of the location of plate boundaries and volcanoes on Earth shows that most volcanoes form along plate boundaries. Examine the map in **Figure 15**. Can you see how this indicates that plate tectonics and volcanic activity are related? Perhaps the energy involved in plate tectonics is causing magma to form deep under Earth's surface. You'll recall that the Soufrière Hills volcano formed where plates converge. Plate movement often explains why volcanoes form in certain areas.

Divergent Plate Boundaries Tectonic plates move apart at divergent plate boundaries. As the plates separate, long cracks called **rifts** form between them. Rifts contain fractures that serve as passageways for magma originating in the mantle. Rift zones account for most of the places where lava flows onto Earth's surface. Fissure eruptions often occur along rift zones. These eruptions form lava that cools and solidifies into basalt, the most abundant type of rock in Earth's crust.

 *Where does magma along divergent boundaries originate?*

SECTION 3 Earthquakes, Volcanoes, and Plate Tectonics **609**

Figure 16 The Hawaiian Islands have formed, and continue to form, as the Pacific Plate moves over a hot spot. The arrow shows that the Pacific Plate is moving north-northwest.

INTEGRATE Chemistry

Melting Points The melting point of a substance is the temperature at which a solid changes to a liquid. Depending on the substance, a change in pressure can raise or lower the melting point. Do research to find out how pressure affects the formation of magma in a mantle plume in a process called decompression melting.

Convergent Plate Boundaries A common location for volcanoes to form is along convergent plate boundaries. More dense oceanic plates sink beneath less dense plates that they collide with. This sets up conditions that form volcanoes.

When one plate sinks beneath another, basalt and sediment on an oceanic plate move down into the mantle. Water from the sediment and altered basalt lowers the melting point of the surrounding rock. Heat in the mantle causes part of the sinking plate and overlying mantle to melt. This melted material then is forced upward. Volcanoes have formed in this way all around the Pacific Ocean, where the Pacific Plate, among others, collides with several other plates. This belt of volcanoes surrounding the Pacific Ocean is called the Pacific Ring of Fire.

Hot Spots The Hawaiian Islands are volcanic islands that have not formed along a plate boundary. In fact, they are located well within the Pacific Plate. What process causes them to form? Large bodies of magma, called **hot spots,** are forced upward through Earth's mantle and crust, as shown in **Figure 16.** Scientists suggest that this is what is occurring at a hot spot that exists under the present location of Hawaii.

Reading Check *What is a hot spot?*

Volcanoes on Earth usually form along rift zones, subduction zones (where one plate sinks beneath another), or over hot spots. At each of these locations, magma from deep within Earth is forced upward toward the surface. Lava breaks through and flows out, where it piles up into layers or forms a volcanic cone.

Moving Plates Cause Earthquakes

Place two notebooks on your desk with the page edges facing each other. Then push them together slowly. The individual sheets of paper gradually will bend upward from the stress. If you continue to push on the notebooks, one will slip past the other suddenly. This sudden movement is like an earthquake.

Now imagine what would happen if tectonic plates were moving like the notebooks. What would happen if the plates collided and stopped moving? Forces generated by the locked-up plates would cause strain to build up. Both plates would begin to deform until the elastic limit was passed. The breaking and elastic rebound of the deformed material would produce vibrations felt as earthquakes.

Earthquakes often occur where tectonic plates come together at a convergent boundary, where tectonic plates move apart at a divergent boundary, and where tectonic plates grind past each other, called a transform boundary.

Friction Friction is a force that opposes the motion of two objects in contact. Do research to find out different types of friction in a literary and figurative sense.

Earthquake Locations If you look at a map of earthquakes, you'll see that most occur in well-known belts. About 80 percent of them occur in the Pacific Ring of Fire—the same belt in which many of Earth's volcanoes occur. If you compare **Figure 17** with **Figure 15,** you will notice a definite relationship between earthquake epicenters and tectonic plate boundaries. Movement of the plates produces forces that generate the energy to cause earthquakes.

Figure 17 Locations of earthquakes that have occurred between 1990 and 2000 are plotted below.

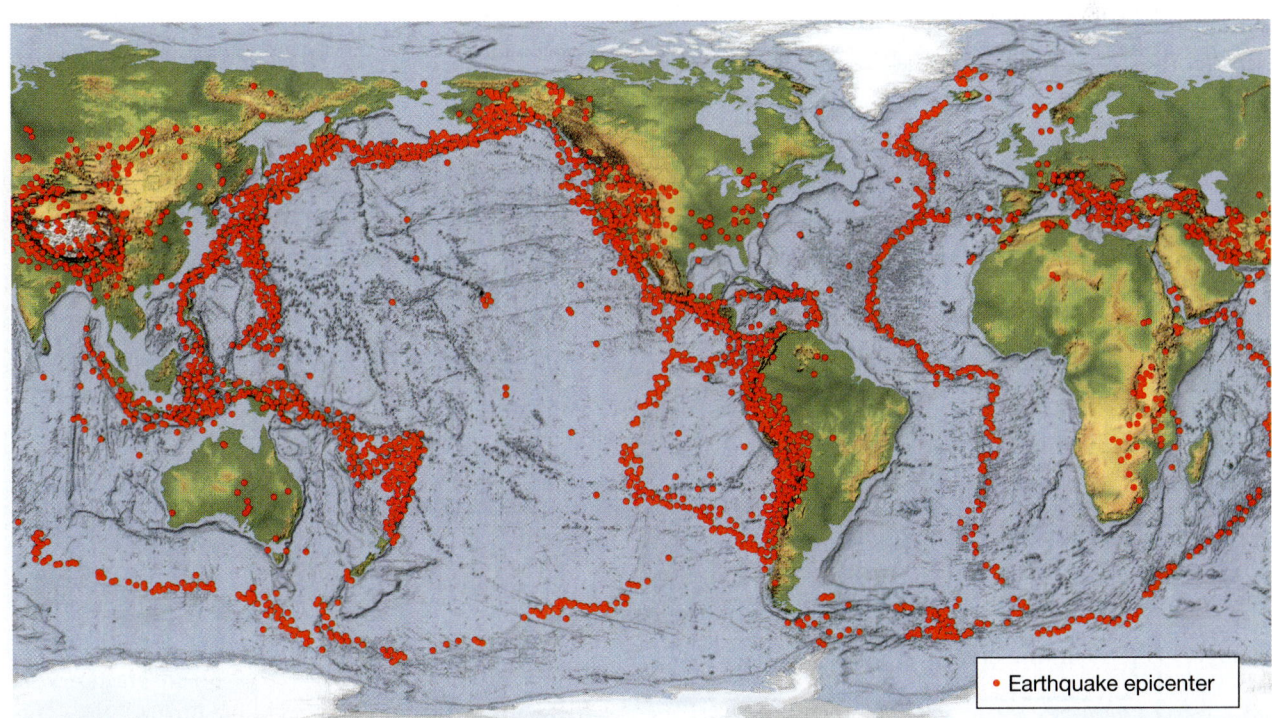

• Earthquake epicenter

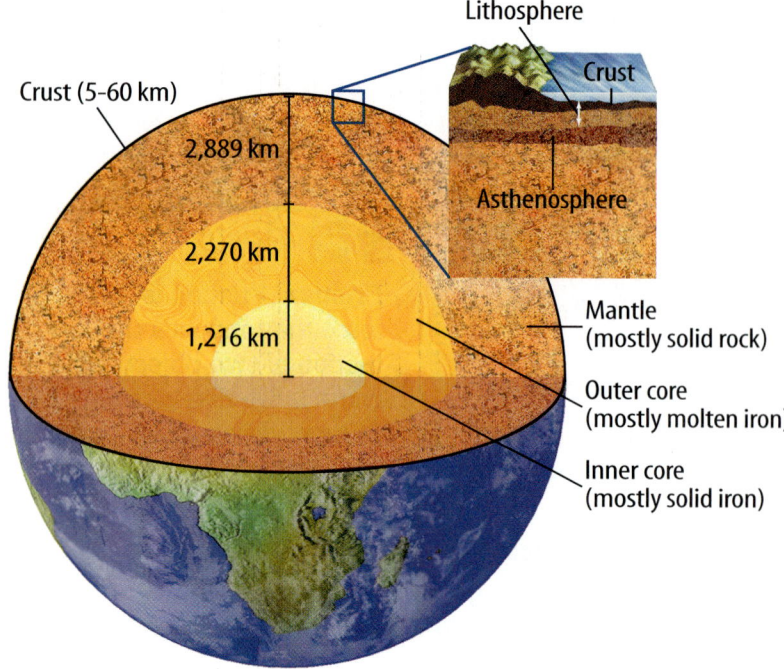

Figure 18 Seismic waves generated by earthquakes allow researchers to figure out the structure and composition of Earth's layers.

Earth's Plates and Interior

Researchers have learned much about Earth's interior and plate tectonics by studying seismic waves. The way in which seismic waves pass through a material depends on the properties of that material. Seismic wave speeds, and how they travel through different levels in the interior, have allowed scientists to map out the major layers of Earth, as shown in **Figure 18**.

For example, the asthenosphere was discovered when seismologists noted that seismic waves slowed when they reached the base of the lithosphere of the Earth. This partially molten layer forms a warmer, softer layer over which the colder, brittle, rocky plates move.

Applying Math Calculate

P-WAVE TRAVEL TIME There is a relationship between the density of a region in Earth and the velocity of P-waves. How can you calculate the time it would take P-waves to travel 100 km in the crust of Earth?

Density and Wave Velocity

Region	Density	P-Wave Velocity
Crust	2.8 g/cm^3	6 km/s
Upper mantle	3.3 g/cm^3	8 km/s

Solution

1. *This is what you know:*
   - velocity: v = 6 km/s
   - distance: d = 100 km

2. *This is what you need to find:* How long would it take a P wave to travel?

3. *This is the procedure you need to use:*
   - $t = d/v$
   - t = (100 km)/(6 km/s) = 16.7 s

4. *Check your answer:* Solve $v = d/t$ = (100 km)/(16.7 s) = 6 km/s

Practice Problems

1. Calculate the time it takes P-waves to travel 300 km in the upper mantle.
2. How long will it take a P-wave to travel 500 km in the crust?

For more practice, visit in7.msscience.com/math_practice

What is driving Earth's plates? There are several hypotheses about where all the energy comes from to power the movement of Earth's plates.

In one case, mantle material deep inside Earth is heated by Earth's core. This hot, less dense rock material is forced toward the surface. The hotter, rising mantle material eventually cools. The cooler material then sinks into the mantle toward Earth's core, completing the convection current. Convection currents inside Earth, shown in **Figure 19,** provide the mechanism for plate motion, which then produces the conditions that cause volcanoes and earthquakes. Sometimes magma is forced up directly within a plate. Volcanic activity in Yellowstone National Park is caused by a hot spot beneath the North American Plate. Such hot spots might be related to larger-scale convection in Earth's mantle.

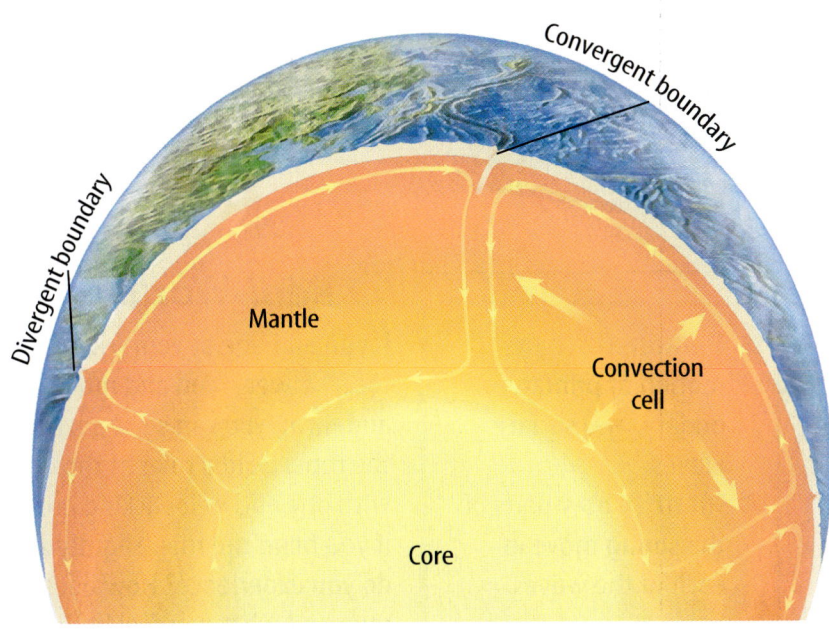

Figure 19 Convection of material in Earth's interior drives the motion of tectonic plates.

section 3 review

Summary

Earth's Moving Plates
- Earth's lithosphere is broken into plates that move around the planet.

Where Volcanoes Form
- Plates move apart at divergent plate boundaries, creating fissure eruptions.
- Plates collide at convergent plate boundaries.
- Many volcanoes form at convergent plate boundaries.
- Volcanoes may also form along rift zones, subduction zones, or over hot spots.

Moving Plates Cause Earthquakes
- Earthquakes often form at plate boundaries.
- Seismic waves have been used to determine the characteristics of Earth's interior.
- Convection currently may drive tectonic plate movement.

Self Check

1. **Identify** Along which type of plate boundary has the Soufrière Hills volcano formed?
2. **Predict** At which type of plate boundary does rift-volcanism occur?
3. **Explain** how volcanoes in Hawaii form.
4. **Recognize Cause and Effect** Why do most deep earthquakes occur at convergent boundaries?
5. **Think Critically** Subduction occurs where plates converge. This causes water-rich sediment and altered rock to be forced down to great depths. Explain how water can help form a volcano.

Applying Skills

6. **Form Hypotheses** Write a hypothesis concerning the type of lava that will form a hot spot volcano. Consider that magma in a hot spot comes from deep inside Earth's mantle.

Science Online in7.msscience.com/self_check_quiz

Seismic Waves

Real-World Question

If you and one of your friends hold a long piece of rope between you and move one end of the rope back and forth, you can send a wave through the length of the rope. Hold a ruler at the edge of a table securely with one end of it sticking out from the table's edge. If you bend the ruler slightly and then release it, what do you experience? How does what you see in the rope and what you feel in the ruler relate to seismic waves? How do seismic waves differ?

Goals
- **Demonstrate** the motion of primary, secondary, and surface waves.
- **Identify** how parts of the spring move in each of the waves.

Materials
coiled spring toy
yarn or string
metric ruler

Safety Precautions

Procedure

1. Copy the following data table in your Science Journal.
2. Tie a small piece of yarn or string to every tenth coil of the spring.
3. Place the spring on a smooth, flat surface. Stretch it so it is about 2 m long (1 m for shorter springs).
4. Hold your end of the spring firmly. Make a wave by having your partner snap the spring from side to side quickly.
5. **Record** your observations in your Science Journal and draw the wave you and your partner made in the data table.
6. Have your lab partner hold his or her end of the spring firmly. Make a wave by quickly pushing your end of the spring toward your partner and bringing it back to its original position.

Comparing Seismic Waves			
Observation of Wave	Observation of Yarn or String	Drawing	Wave Type
	Do not write in this book.		

614 CHAPTER 20 Earthquakes and Volcanoes

Using Scientific Methods

7. **Record** your observations of the wave and of the yarn or string and draw the wave in the data table.

8. Have your lab partner hold his or her end of the spring firmly. Move the spring off of the table. Gently move your end of the spring side to side while at the same time moving it in a rolling motion, first up and away and then down and toward your partner.

9. **Record** your observations and draw the wave in the data table.

◉ Conclude and Apply

1. Based on your observations, determine which of the waves that you and your partner have generated demonstrates a primary, or pressure, wave. Record in your data table and explain why you chose the wave you did.

2. Do the same for the secondary, or shear wave, and for the surface wave. Explain why you chose the wave you did.

3. **Explain** Based on your observations of wave motion, which of the waves that you and your partner generated probably would cause the most damage during an earthquake?

4. **Observe** What was the purpose of the yarn or string?

5. **Compare and contrast** the motion of the yarn or string when primary and secondary waves travel through the spring. Which of these waves is a compression wave? Explain your answer.

6. **Compare and Contrast** Which wave most closely resembled wave motion in a body of water? How was it different? Explain.

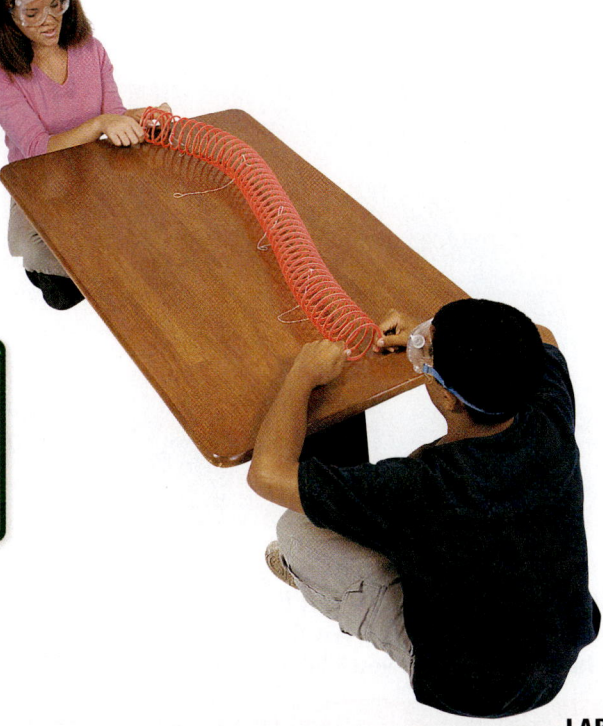

Compare your conclusions with those of other students in your class. **For more help, refer to the** Science Skill Handbook.

TIME SCIENCE AND HISTORY

SCIENCE CAN CHANGE THE COURSE OF HISTORY!

quake

The 1906 San Francisco earthquake taught people valuable lessons

It struck without warning. "We found ourselves staggering and reeling. It was as if the earth was slipping gently from under our feet. Then came the sickening swaying of the earth that threw us flat upon our faces. We struggled in the street. We could not get on our feet. Then it seemed as though my head were split with the roar that crashed into my ears. Big buildings were crumbling as one might crush a biscuit in one's hand."

That's how survivor P. Barrett described the San Francisco earthquake of 1906. Duration of the quake on the morning of April 18—one minute. Yet, in that short time, Earth opened a gaping hole stretching more than 430 km. The tragic result was one of the worst natural disasters in U.S. history.

Fires caused by falling chimneys and fed by broken gas mains raged for three days. Despite the estimated 3,000 deaths and enormous devastation to San Francisco, the earthquake did have a positive effect. It led to major building changes that would help protect people and property from future quakes.

Computers analyze information from seismographs that have helped to map the San Andreas Fault—the area along which many California earthquakes take place. This information is helping scientists better understand how and when earthquakes might strike.

The 1906 quake also has led to building codes that require stronger construction materials for homes, offices, and bridges. Laws have been passed saying where hospitals, homes, and nuclear power plants can be built—away from soft ground and away from the San Andreas Fault.

Even today, scientists can't predict an earthquake. But thanks to what they learned from the 1906 quake—and others—people are safer today than ever before.

Write Prepare a diary entry pretending to be a person who experienced the 1906 San Francisco earthquake. Possible events to include in your entry: What were you doing at 5:15 A.M.? What began to happen around you? What did you see and hear?

Science online

For more information, visit in7.msscience.com/time

Chapter 20 Study Guide

Reviewing Main Ideas

Section 1 — Earthquakes

1. Earthquakes occur whenever rocks inside Earth pass their elastic limit, break, and experience elastic rebound.
2. Seismic waves are vibrations inside Earth. P- and S-waves travel in all directions away from the earthquake focus. Surface waves travel along the surface.
3. Earthquakes are measured by their magnitudes—the amount of energy they release—and by their intensity—the amount of damage they produce.

Section 2 — Volcanoes

1. The Soufrière Hills volcano is a composite volcano formed by converging plates.
2. The way a volcano erupts is determined by the composition of the lava and the amount of water vapor and other gases in the lava.
3. Three different forms of volcanoes are shield volcanoes, cinder cone volcanoes, and composite volcanoes.

Section 3 — Earthquakes, Volcanoes, and Plate Tectonics

1. The locations of volcanoes and earthquake epicenters are related to the locations of plate boundaries.
2. Volcanoes occur along rift zones, subduction zones, and at hot spots.
3. Most earthquakes occur at convergent, divergent, and transform plate boundaries.

Visualizing Main Ideas

Copy and complete the following table comparing characteristics of shield, composite, and cinder cone volcanoes.

Volcanoes			
Characteristic	Shield Volcano	Cinder Cone Volcano	Composite Volcano
Relative size	large		
Nature of eruption			moderate to high eruptive force
Materials extruded	lava, gas	cinders, gas	
Composition of lava			high silica
Ability of lava to flow		low	variable

chapter 20 Review

Using Vocabulary

cinder cone volcano p. 604
composite volcano p. 605
earthquake p. 592
epicenter p. 594
fault p. 593
focus p. 594
hot spot p. 610
lava p. 601
magnitude p. 595
rift p. 609
seismic safe p. 599
seismic wave p. 594
seismograph p. 595
shield volcano p. 604
tsunami p. 597
volcano p. 601

Explain the differences between the vocabulary words in each of the following sets.

1. fault—earthquake
2. shield volcano—composite volcano
3. focus—epicenter
4. seismic wave—seismograph
5. tsunami—seismic wave
6. epicenter—earthquake
7. cinder cone volcano—shield volcano

Checking Concepts

Choose the word or phrase that best answers the question.

8. Which type of plate boundary caused the formation of the Soufrière Hills volcano?
   A) divergent   C) rift
   B) transform   D) convergent

9. What is a cone-shaped mountain that is built from layers of lava?
   A) volcano   C) vent
   B) lava flow   D) crater

10. What is the cause of the volcanoes on Hawaii?
    A) rift zone
    B) hot spot
    C) divergent plate boundary
    D) convergent plate boundary

11. Which type of lava flows easily?
    A) silica-rich   C) basaltic
    B) composite   D) smooth

12. Which type of volcano is built from alternating layers of lava and tephra?
    A) shield   C) lava dome
    B) cinder cone   D) composite

13. Which type of volcano is relatively small with steep sides?
    A) shield   C) lava dome
    B) cinder cone   D) composite

14. Which seismic wave moves through Earth at the fastest speed?
    A) primary wave
    B) secondary wave
    C) surface wave
    D) tsunami

15. Which of the following is a wave of water caused by an earthquake under the ocean?
    A) primary wave
    B) secondary wave
    C) surface wave
    D) tsunami

Use the illustration below to answer question 16.

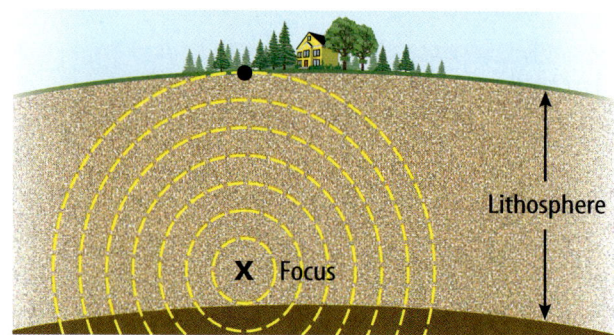

16. What is the point on Earth's surface directly above an earthquake's focus?
    A) earthquake center
    B) epicenter
    C) fault
    D) focus

618 CHAPTER REVIEW   in7.msscience.com/vocabulary_puzzlemaker

Chapter 20 Review

Thinking Critically

17. Infer Why does the Soufrière Hills volcano erupt so explosively?

18. Compare and contrast composite and cinder cone volcanoes.

19. Explain how the composition of magma can affect the way a volcano erupts.

20. Evaluate What factors determine an earthquake's intensity on the modified Mercalli scale?

21. Compare and contrast magnitude and intensity.

22. Make Models Select one of the three forms of volcanoes and make a model, using appropriate materials.

23. Draw Conclusions You are flying over an area that has just experienced an earthquake. You see that most of the buildings are damaged or destroyed and much of the surrounding countryside is disrupted. What level of intensity would you conclude for this earthquake?

24. Concept Map Copy and complete this concept map on examples of features produced along plate boundaries. Use the following terms: *Mid-Atlantic Ridge, Soufrière Hills volcano, divergent, San Andreas Fault, convergent,* and *transform*.

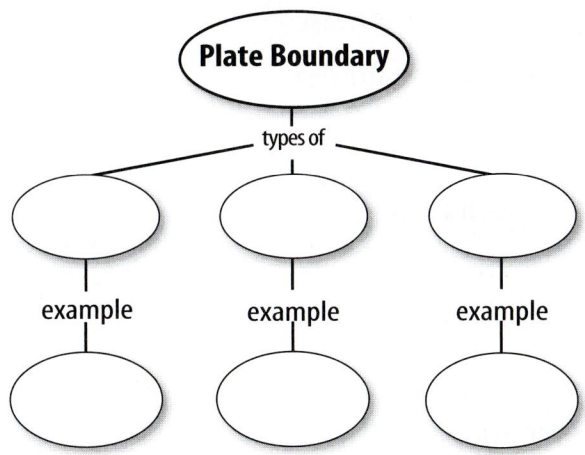

Performance Activities

25. Oral Presentation Research the earthquake or volcano history of your state or community. Find out how long ago your area experienced earthquake- or volcano-related problems. Present your findings in a speech to your class.

Applying Math

Use the graph below to answer questions 26 and 27.

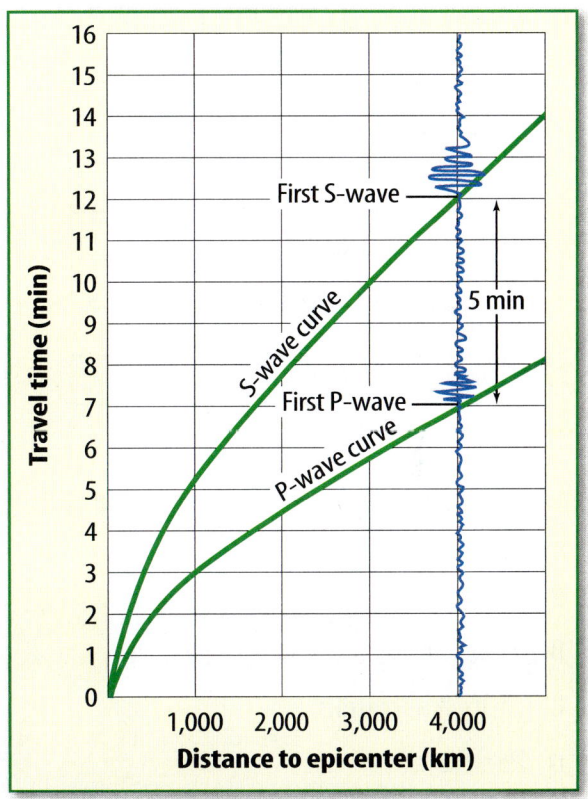

26. Earthquake Epicenter If a P-wave arrives at a seismograph station at 9:07 AM and the S-wave arrives at the same seismograph station at 9:09 AM, about how far is that station from the epicenter of the earthquake?

27. Arrival Time A seismograph station is 2,500 km from the epicenter of an earthquake. What is the difference in time between the P-wave arrival time and the S-wave arrival time?

chapter 20 Indiana

 The assessed Indiana standard appears above the question.

Record your answers on the answer sheet provided by your teacher or on a sheet of paper.

Part 1 Multiple Choice

The table below shows the number of convergent and divergent boundaries for different plates in Earth's crust.

Plate Boundaries		
Plate	Number of convergent boundaries	Number of divergent boundaries
African	1	4
Antarctic	1	2
Indo-Australian	4	2
Eurasian	4	1
North American	2	1
Pacific	6	2
South American	2	1

1. Determine which plate has the most spreading boundaries.
   - A African
   - B Antarctic
   - C Indo-Australian
   - D Pacific

7.3.4

2. Use the table above to predict which plate will be surrounded by the most volcanoes.
   - A Antarctic
   - B Eurasian
   - C Indo-Australian
   - D Pacific

7.3.8

3. Which are created by earthquakes, and travel through Earth's interior at various speeds?
   - A energy waves
   - B light waves
   - C seismic waves
   - D sound waves

The illustration below shows the Hawaiian Islands and its active volcanoes.

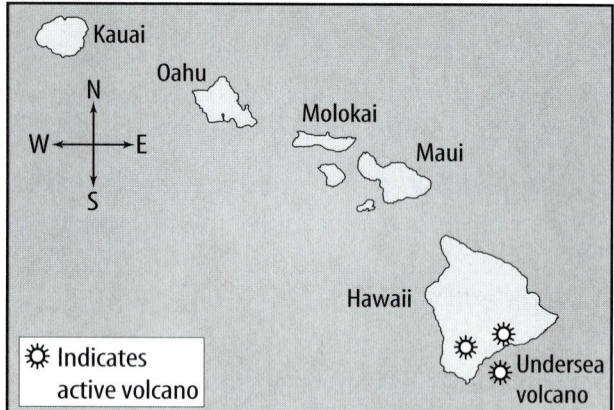

4. In which direction is the Pacific Plate moving?
   - A north-northeast
   - B north-northwest
   - C south-southeast
   - D south-southwest

5. Which island is the oldest?
   - A Hawaii
   - B Kauai
   - C Maui
   - D Molokai

Standards Review

6. Which instrument is used to study the waves produced by earthquakes?

   A lithograph

   B seismograph

   C creepmeter

   D tiltmeter

The illustration below shows a fault in Earth's crust.

7. Identify the type of fault shown.

   A normal fault

   B reverse fault

   C strike-slip fault

   D thrust fault

8. Which force creates this type of fault?

   A compression

   B deformation

   C extension

   D shear

Test-Taking Tip

Watch the Time If you are taking a timed test, keep track of time during the test. If you find you're spending too much time on a multiple-choice question, mark your best guess and move on.

Part 2 Constructed Response

7.3.7

9. What is an earthquake? Explain the relationship between faults and earthquakes.

7.3.7

10. The lava of a particular volcano is high in silica and water vapor and other gases. What kind of eruptive force will likely result from this volcano?

7.3.7

11. The illustration below shows Earth's interior.

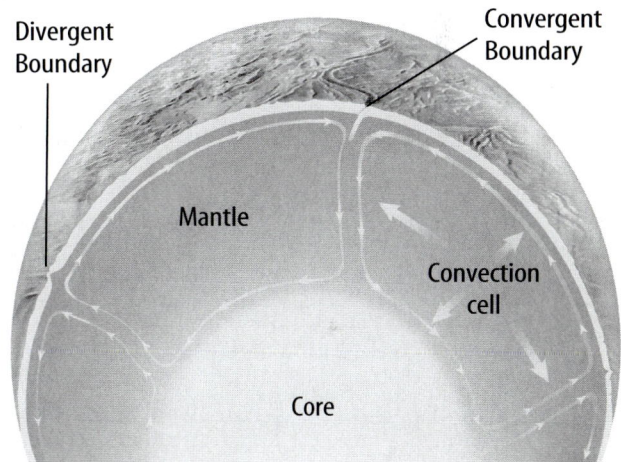

Explain how convection currents may be related to plate tectonics. How is plate tectonics related to earthquakes and volcanoes?

7.3.4

12. Name three types of volcanoes. Describe how each volcano forms.

7.3.4

13. Some surface waves vibrate in a side-to-side, or swaying, motion parallel to Earth's surface. Why is this type of motion so devastating to human-built structures?

chapter 21

Academic Standard—3: Students collect and organize data to identify relationships between physical objects, events, and processes. They use logical reasoning to question their own ideas as new information challenges their conceptions of the natural world.

Also covers: Academic Standards 1, 2, 4, 5 (Detailed standards begin on page IN8.)

Climate

chapter preview

sections
1. What is climate?
2. Climate Types
3. Climatic Changes
   - **Lab** The Greenhouse Effect
   - **Lab** Microclimates
   - **Virtual Lab** How can locations be identified by their climate and topography?

Why do seasons change?

Why do some places have four distinct seasons, while others have only a wet and dry season? In this chapter, you will learn what climate is and how climates are classified. You will also learn what causes climate changes and how humans and animals adapt to different climates.

Science Journal Write a paragraph explaining what you already know about the causes of seasons.

Start-Up Activities

Tracking World Climates

You wouldn't go to Alaska to swim or to Jamaica to snow ski. You know the climates in these places aren't suited for these sports. In this lab, you'll explore the climates in different parts of the world.

1. Obtain a world atlas, globe, or large classroom map. Select several cities from different parts of the world.
2. Record the longitude and latitude of your cities. Note if they are near mountains or an ocean.
3. Research the average temperature of your cities. In what months are they hottest? Coldest? What is the average yearly rainfall? What kinds of plants and animals live in the region? Record your findings.
4. Compare your findings with those of the rest of your class. Can you see any relationship between latitude and climate? Do cities near an ocean or a mountain range have different climatic characteristics?
5. **Think Critically** Keep track of the daily weather conditions in your cities. Are these representative of the kind of climates your cities are supposed to have? Suggest reasons why day-to-day weather conditions may vary.

Classifying Climates Make the following Foldable to help you compare climatic types.

STEP 1 Fold two pieces of paper lengthwise into thirds.

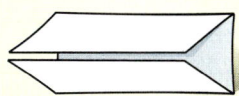

STEP 2 Fold the papers widthwise into fourths.

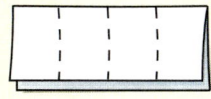

STEP 3 Unfold, lay the papers lengthwise, and draw lines along the folds as shown.

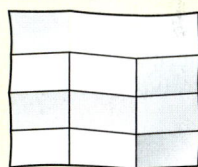

STEP 4 Label your tables as shown.

Climate Classification		
Tropical		
Mild		
Dry		

Climate Classification		
Continental		
Polar		
High elevation		

Make a Table As you read the chapter, define each type of climate and write notes on its weather characteristics.

 **Preview this chapter's content and activities at in7.msscience.com**

section 1

Standard—7.3.5: Recognize and explain that heat energy carried by ocean currents has a strong influence on climate around the world.

Also covers: 7.5.1 (Detailed standards begin on page IN8.)

What is climate?

as you read

What You'll Learn
- **Describe** what determines climate.
- **Explain** how latitude, oceans, and other factors affect the climate of a region.

Why It's Important
Climate affects the way you live.

Review Vocabulary
latitudes: distance in degrees north or south of the equator

New Vocabulary
- climate
- tropics
- polar zone
- temperate zone

Climate

If you wandered through a tropical rain forest, you would see beautiful plants flowering in shades of pink and purple beneath a canopy of towering trees. A variety of exotic birds and other animals would dart among the tree branches and across the forest floor. The sounds of singing birds and croaking frogs would surround you. All of these organisms thrive in hot temperatures and abundant rainfall. Rain forests have a hot, wet climate. **Climate** is the pattern of weather that occurs in an area over many years. It determines the types of plants or animals that can survive, and it influences how people live.

Climate is determined by averaging the weather of a region over a long period of time, such as 30 years. Scientists average temperature, precipitation, air pressure, humidity, and number of days of sunshine to determine an area's climate. Some factors that affect the climate of a region include latitude, landforms, location of lakes and oceans, and ocean currents.

Latitude and Climate

As you can see in **Figure 1,** regions close to the equator receive the most solar radiation. Latitude, a measure of distance north or south of the equator, affects climate. **Figure 2** compares cities at different latitudes. The **tropics**—the region between latitudes 23.5°N and 23.5°S—receive the most solar radiation because the Sun shines almost directly over these areas. The tropics have temperatures that are always hot, except at high elevations. The **polar zones** extend from 66.5°N and 66.5°S latitude to the poles. Solar radiation hits these zones at a low angle, spreading energy over a large area. During winter, polar regions receive little or no solar radiation. Polar regions are never warm.

Reading Check *How does latitude affect climate?*

Between the tropics and the polar zones are the **temperate zones.** Temperatures here are moderate. Most of the United States is in a temperate zone.

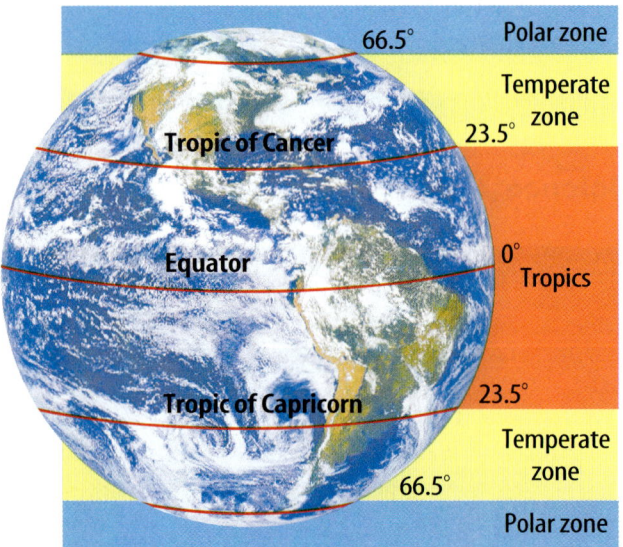

Figure 1 The tropics are warmer than the temperate zones and the polar zones because the tropics receive the most direct solar energy.

624 CHAPTER 21 Climate

Other Factors

In addition to the general climate divisions of polar, temperate, and tropical, natural features such as large bodies of water, ocean currents, and mountains affect climate within each zone. Large cities also change weather patterns and influence the local climate.

Large Bodies of Water If you live or have vacationed near an ocean, you may have noticed that water heats up and cools down more slowly than land does. This is because it takes a lot more heat to increase the temperature of water than it takes to increase the temperature of land. In addition, water must give up more heat than land does for it to cool. Large bodies of water can affect the climate of coastal areas by absorbing or giving off heat. This causes many coastal regions to be warmer in the winter and cooler in the summer than inland areas at similar latitude. Look at **Figure 2** again. You can see the effect of an ocean on climate by comparing the average temperatures in a coastal city and an inland city, both located at 37°N latitude.

Figure 2 This map shows average daily low temperatures in four cities during January and July. It also shows average yearly precipitation.

Observing Solar Radiation

Procedure
1. Darken the room.
2. Hold a **flashlight** about 30 cm from a **globe.** Shine the light directly on the equator. With your finger, trace around the light.
3. Now, tilt the flashlight to shine on 30°N latitude. The size of the lighted area should increase. Repeat at 60°N latitude.

Analysis
1. How did the size and shape of the light beam change as you directed the light toward higher latitudes?
2. How does Earth's tilt affect the solar radiation received by different latitudes?

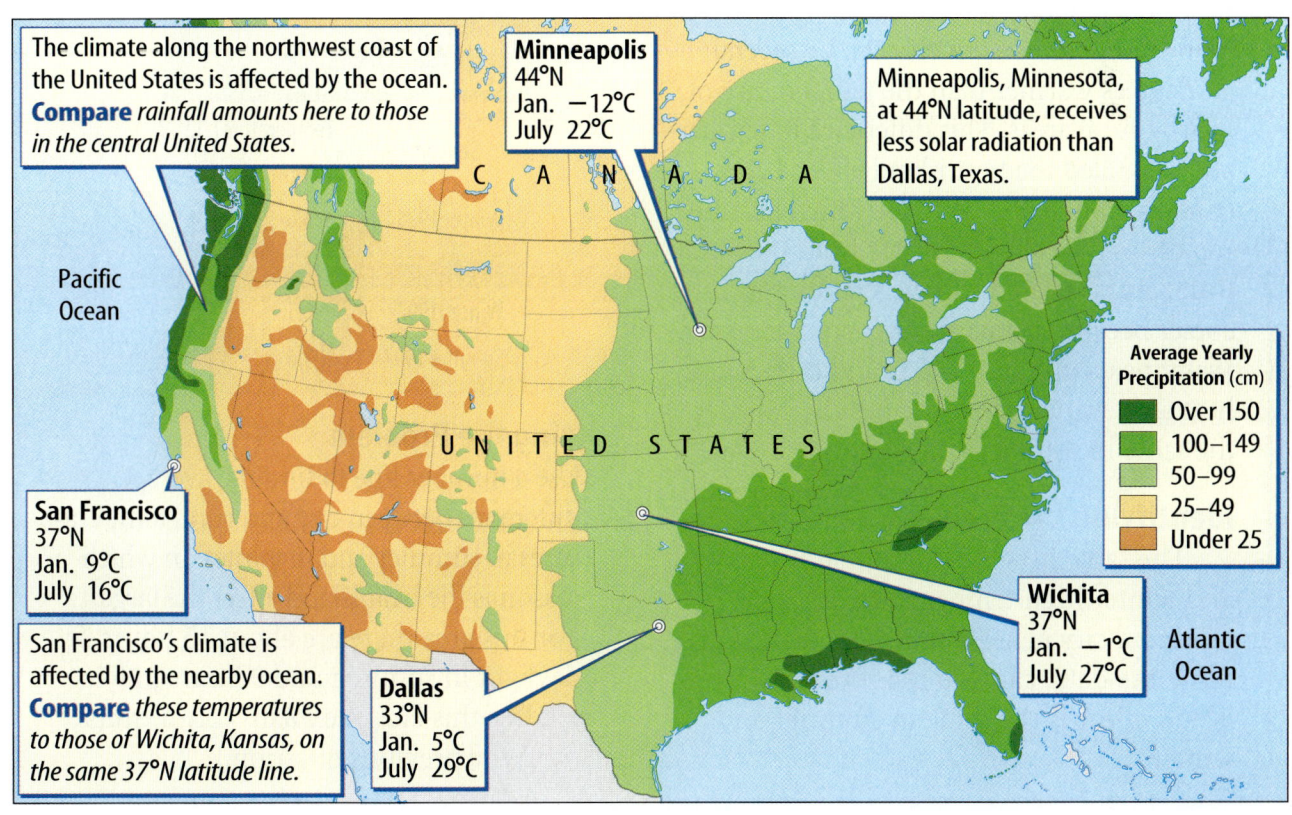

SECTION 1 What is climate? **625**

Indiana Academic Standard Check

7.3.5: Recognize and explain that heat energy carried by ocean currents has a strong influence on climate around the world.

✓ Describe how coastal climates are affected by ocean currents flowing from the equator toward higher latitudes.

Mountain Air When air rises over a mountain, the air expands and its temperature decreases, causing water vapor to condense and form rain.

Ocean Currents Ocean currents affect coastal climates. Warm currents begin near the equator and flow toward higher latitudes, warming the land regions they pass. When the currents cool off and flow back toward the equator, they cool the air and climates of nearby land.

Reading Check *How do ocean currents affect climate?*

Winds blowing from the sea are often moister than those blowing from land. Therefore, some coastal areas have wetter climates than places farther inland. Look at the northwest coast of the United States shown in **Figure 2.** The large amounts of precipitation in Washington, Oregon, and northern California can be explained by this moist ocean air.

Mountains At the same latitude, the climate is colder in the mountains than at sea level. When radiation from the Sun is absorbed by Earth's surface, it heats the land. Heat from Earth then warms the atmosphere. Because Earth's atmosphere gets thinner at higher altitudes, the air in the mountains has fewer molecules to absorb heat.

Applying Science

How do cities influence temperature?

The temperature in a city can be several degrees warmer than the temperature of nearby rural areas. This difference in temperature is called the heat island effect. Cities contain asphalt and concrete which heat up rapidly as they absorb energy from the Sun. Rural areas covered with vegetation stay cooler because plants and soil contain water. Water heats up more slowly and carries away heat as it evaporates. Is the heat island effect the same in summer and winter?

Identifying the Problem

The table lists the average summer and winter high temperatures in and around a city in 1996 and 1997. By examining the data, can you tell if the heat island effect is the same in summer and winter?

Average Seasonal Temperatures

Season	Temperature (°C)	
	City	Rural
Winter 1996	−3.0	−4.4
Summer 1996	23.5	20.9
Winter 1997	−0.1	−1.8
Summer 1997	23.6	21.2

Solving the Problem

1. Use a number line to find the average difference between city and rural temperatures in summer and in winter. In which season is the heat island effect the largest?
2. For this area there are about 15 hours of daylight in summer and 9 hours in winter. Use this fact to explain your results from the previous question.

Rain Shadows Mountains also affect regional climates, as shown in **Figure 3**. On the windward side of a mountain range, air rises, cools, and drops its moisture. On the leeward side of a mountain range air descends, heats up, and dries the land. Deserts are common on the leeward sides of mountains.

Cities Large cities affect local climates. Streets, parking lots, and buildings heat up, in turn heating the air. Air pollution traps this heat, creating what is known as the heat-island effect. Temperatures in a city can be 5°C higher than in surrounding rural areas.

Figure 3 Large mountain ranges can affect climate by forcing air to rise over the windward side, cooling and bringing precipitation. The air descends with little or no moisture, creating desertlike conditions on the leeward side.

section 1 review

Summary

Latitude and Climate

- Climate is the pattern of weather that occurs in an area over many years.
- The tropics receive the most solar radiation because the Sun shines most directly there.
- The polar zones receive the least solar energy due to the low-angled rays.
- Temperate zones, located between the tropics and the polar zones, have moderate temperatures.

Other Factors

- Natural features such as large bodies of water, ocean currents, and mountains can affect local and regional climates.
- Large cities can change weather patterns and influence local climates.

Self Check

1. **Explain** how two cities located at the same latitude can have different climates.
2. **Describe** how mountains affect climate.
3. **Define** the heat island effect.
4. **Compare and contrast** tropical and polar climates.
5. **Think Critically** Explain why plants found at different elevations on a mountain might differ. How can latitude affect the elevation at which some plants are found?

Applying Math

6. **Solve One-Step Equations** The coolest average summer temperature in the United States is 2°C at Barrow, Alaska, and the warmest is 37°C at Death Valley, California. Calculate the range of average summer temperatures in the United States.

SECTION 1 What is climate?

section 2
Climate Types

Standard—7.1.5: Identify some important contributions to the advancement of science ... that have been made by different kinds of people, in different cultures, at different times.

as you read

What You'll Learn
- **Describe** a climate classification system.
- **Explain** how organisms adapt to particular climates.

Why It's Important
Many organisms can survive only in climates to which they are adapted.

Review Vocabulary
regions: places united by specific characteristics

New Vocabulary
- adaptation
- hibernation

Figure 4 The type of vegetation in a region depends on the climate. **Describe** what these plants tell you about the climate shown here.

Classifying Climates

What is the climate like where you live? Would you call it generally warm? Usually wet and cold? Or different depending on the time of year? How would you classify the climate in your region? Life is full of familiar classification systems—from musical categories to food groups. Classifications help to organize your thoughts and to make your life more efficient. That's why Earth's climates also are classified and are organized into the various types that exist. Climatologists—people who study climates—usually use a system developed in 1918 by Wladimir Köppen to classify climates. Köppen observed that the types of plants found in a region depended on the climate of the area. **Figure 4** shows one type of region Köppen might have observed. He classified world climates by using the annual and monthly averages of temperature and precipitation of different regions. He then related the types and distribution of native vegetation to the various climates.

The climate classification system shown in **Figure 5** separates climates into six groups—tropical, mild, dry, continental, polar, and high elevation. These groups are further separated into types. For example, the dry climate classification is separated into semiarid and arid.

Adaptations

Climates vary around the world, and as Köppen observed, the type of climate that exists in an area determines the vegetation found there. Fir trees aren't found in deserts, nor are cacti found in rain forests. In fact, all organisms are best suited for certain climates. Organisms are adapted to their environment. An **adaptation** is any structure or behavior that helps an organism survive in its environment. Structural adaptations are inherited. They develop in a population over a long period of time. Once adapted to a particular climate, organisms may not be able to survive in other climates.

628

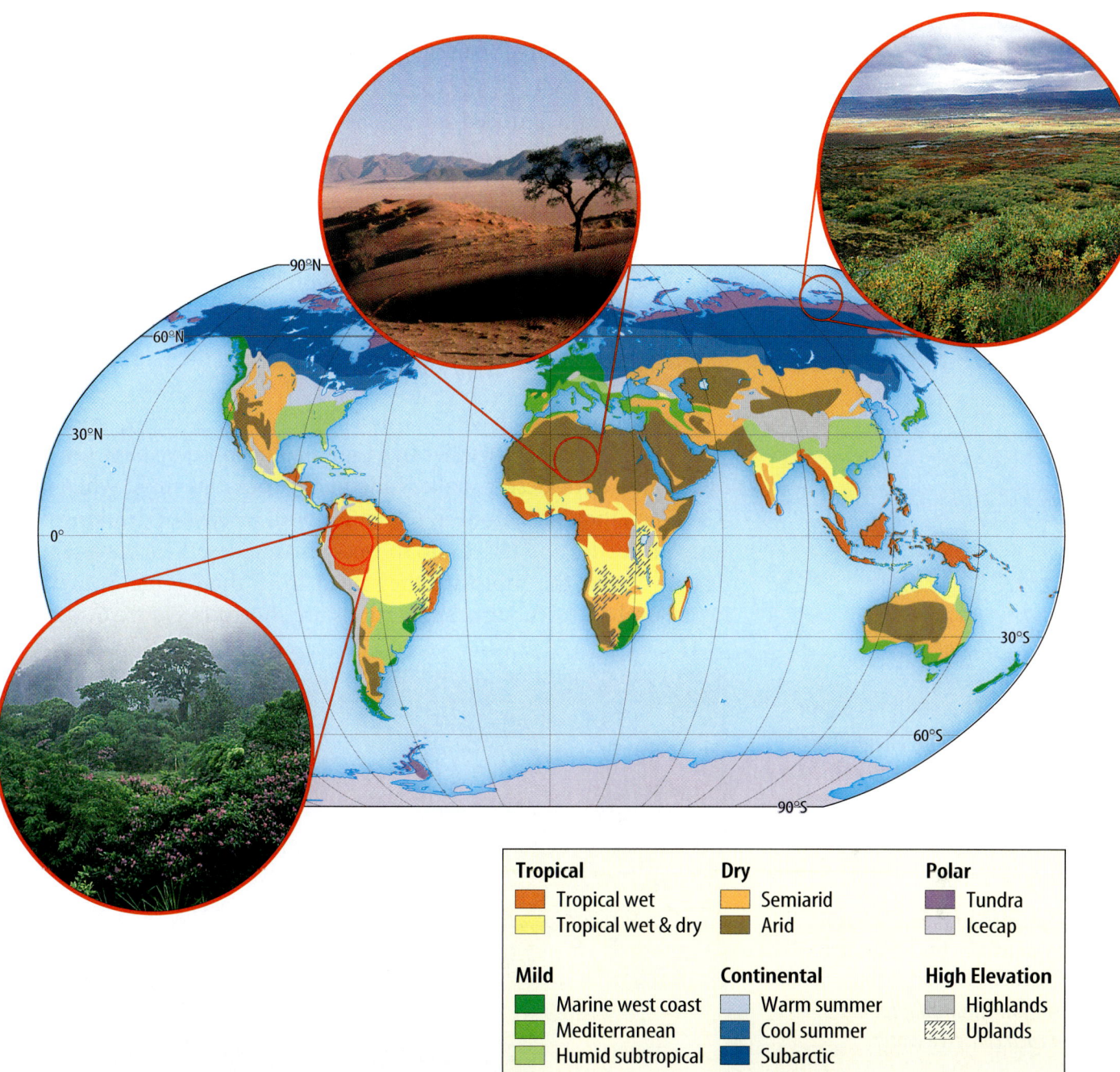

Figure 5 This map shows a climate classification system similar to the one developed by Köppen. **Describe** the patterns you can see in the locations of certain climate types.

Structural Adaptations Some organisms have body structures that help them survive in certain climates. The fur of mammals is really hair that insulates them from cold temperatures. A cactus has a thick, fleshy stem. This structural adaptation helps a cactus hold water. The waxy stem covering prevents water inside the cactus from evaporating. Instead of broad leaves, these plants have spiny leaves, called needles, that further reduce water loss.

Reading Check How do cacti conserve water?

Behavioral Adaptations Some organisms display behavioral adaptations that help them survive in a particular climate. For example, rodents and certain other mammals undergo a period of greatly reduced activity in winter called **hibernation**. During hibernation, body temperature drops and body processes are reduced to a minimum. Some of the factors thought to trigger hibernation include cooler temperatures, shorter days, and lack of adequate food. The length of time that an animal hibernates varies depending on the particular species of animal and the environmental conditions.

Reading Check *What is hibernation?*

Other animals have adapted differently. During cold weather, bees cluster together in a tight ball to conserve heat. On hot, sunny days, desert snakes hide under rocks. At night when it's cooler, they slither out in search of food. Instead of drinking water as turtles and lizards do in wet climates, desert turtles and lizards obtain the moisture they need from their food. Some behavioral and structural adaptations are shown in **Figure 6.**

Figure 6 Organisms have structural and behavioral adaptations that help them survive in particular climates.

The needles and the waxy skin of a cactus are structural adaptations to a desert climate. **Infer** *how these adaptations help cacti conserve water.*

These hibernating bats have adapted their behavior to survive winter.

Polar bears have structural adaptations to keep them warm. The hairs of their fur trap air and heat.

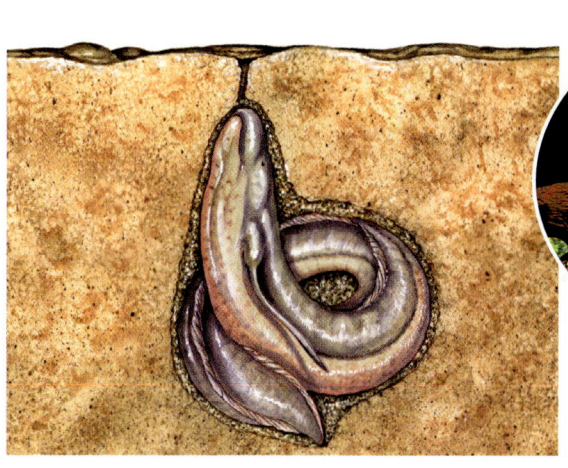

Figure 7 Lungfish survive periods of intense heat and drought by going into an inactive state called estivation. During the dry season when water evaporates, lungfish dig into the mud and curl up in a small chamber they make at the lake's bottom. During the wet season, lungfish reemerge to live in small lakes and pools.

Estivation Lungfish, shown in **Figure 7,** survive periods of intense heat by entering an inactive state called estivation (es tuh VAY shun). As the weather gets hot and water evaporates, the fish burrows into mud and covers itself in a leathery mixture of mud and mucus. It lives this way until the warm, dry months pass.

Like other organisms, you have adaptations that help you adjust to climate. In hot weather, your sweat glands release water onto your skin. The water evaporates, taking some heat with it. As a result, you become cooler. In cold weather, you may shiver to help your body stay warm. When you shiver, the rapid muscle movements produce some heat. What other adaptations to climate do people have?

section 2 review

Summary

Classifying Climates
- Climatologists classify climates into six main groups: tropical, mild, dry, continental, polar, and high elevation.

Adaptations
- Adaptations are any structures or behaviors that help an organism to survive.
- Structural adaptations such as fur, hair, and spiny needles help an organism to survive in certain climates.
- Behavioral adaptations include hibernation, a period of greatly reduced activity in winter; estivation, an inactive state during intense heat; clustering together in the cold; and obtaining water from food when water is not found elsewhere.

Self Check

1. **List** Use **Figure 5** and a world map to identify the climate type for each of the following locations: Cuba, North Korea, Egypt, and Uruguay.
2. **Compare and contrast** hibernation and estivation.
3. **Think Critically** What adaptations help dogs keep cool during hot weather?

Applying Skills

4. **Form Hypotheses** Some scientists have suggested that Earth's climate is getting warmer. What effects might this have on vegetation and animal life in various parts of the United States?
5. **Communicate** Research the types of vegetation found in the six climate regions shown in **Figure 5.** Write a paragraph in your Science Journal describing why vegetation can be used to help define climate boundaries.

Science online in7.msscience.com/self_check_quiz

SECTION 2 Climate Types

Standards—7.3.6: Describe how gas and dust from large volcanoes can change the atmosphere. **7.3.3:** Describe how climates have changed abruptly in the past as a result of changes in Earth's crust, such as volcanic eruptions or impacts of huge rocks from space.

Also covers: 7.1.4, 7.2.6, 7.2.7, 7.3.5, 7.4.14 (Detailed standards begin on page IN8.)

section 3
Climatic Changes

as you read

What You'll Learn
- **Explain** what causes seasons.
- **Describe** how El Niño affects climate.
- **Explore** possible causes of climatic change.

Why It's Important
Changing climates could affect sea level and life on Earth.

Review Vocabulary
solar radiation: energy from the Sun transferred by waves or rays

New Vocabulary
- season
- El Niño
- greenhouse effect
- global warming
- deforestation

Earth's Seasons

In temperate zones, you can play softball under the summer Sun and in the winter go sledding with friends. Weather changes with the season. **Seasons** are short periods of climatic change caused by changes in the amount of solar radiation an area receives. **Figure 8** shows Earth revolving around the Sun. Because Earth is tilted, different areas of Earth receive changing amounts of solar radiation throughout the year.

Seasonal Changes Because of fairly constant solar radiation near the equator, the tropics do not have much seasonal temperature change. However, they do experience dry and rainy seasons. The middle latitudes, or temperate zones, have warm summers and cool winters. Spring and fall are usually mild.

Reading Check What are seasons like in the tropics?

Figure 8 As Earth revolves around the Sun, different areas of Earth are tilted toward the Sun, which causes different seasons.
Identify During which northern hemisphere season is Earth closer to the Sun?

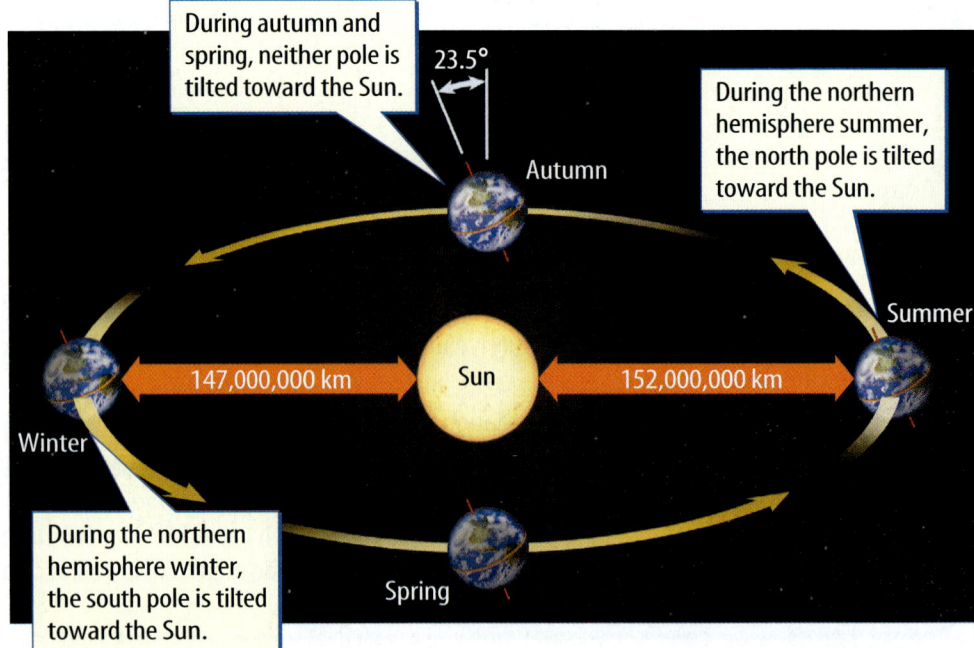

Figure 9 A strong El Niño, like the one that occurred in 1998, can affect weather patterns around the world.

A severe drought struck Indonesia, contributing to forest fires.

California was plagued by large storms that produced pounding surf and shoreline erosion.

High Latitudes During the year, the high latitudes near the poles have great differences in temperature and number of daylight hours. As shown in **Figure 8,** during summer in the northern hemisphere, the north pole is tilted toward the Sun. During summer at the north pole, the Sun doesn't set for nearly six months. During that same time, the Sun never rises at the south pole. At the equator days are about the same length all year long.

El Niño and La Niña

El Niño (el NEEN yoh) is a climatic event that involves the tropical Pacific Ocean and the atmosphere. During normal years, strong trade winds that blow east to west along the equator push warm surface water toward the western Pacific Ocean. Cold, deep water then is forced up from below along the coast of South America. During El Niño years, these winds weaken and sometimes reverse. The change in the winds allows warm, tropical water in the upper layers of the Pacific to flow back eastward to South America. Cold, deep water is no longer forced up from below. Ocean temperatures increase by 1°C to 7°C off the coast of Peru.

El Niño can affect weather patterns. It can alter the position and strength of one of the jet streams. This changes the atmospheric pressure off California and wind and precipitation patterns around the world. This can cause drought in Australia and Africa. This also affects monsoon rains in Indonesia and causes storms in California, as shown in **Figure 9.**

The opposite of El Niño is La Niña, shown in **Figure 10.** During La Niña, the winds blowing across the Pacific are stronger than normal, causing warm water to accumulate in the western Pacific. The water in the eastern Pacific near Peru is cooler than normal. La Niña may cause droughts in the southern United States and excess rainfall in the northwestern United States.

Mini LAB

Modeling El Niño

Procedure
1. During El Niño, trade winds blowing across the Pacific Ocean from east to west slacken or even reverse. Surface waters move back toward the coast of Peru.
2. Add **warm water** to a **9-in × 13-in baking pan** until it is two-thirds full. Place the pan on a smooth countertop.
3. Blow as hard as you can across the surface of the water along the length of the pan. Next, blow with less force. Then, blow in the opposite direction.

Analysis
1. What happened to the water as you blew across its surface? What was different when you blew with less force and when you blew from the opposite direction?
2. Explain how this is similar to what happens during an El Niño event.

Try at Home

SECTION 3 Climatic Changes

NATIONAL GEOGRAPHIC VISUALIZING EL NIÑO AND LA NIÑA

Figure 10

Weather in the United States can be affected by changes that occur thousands of kilometers away. Out in the middle of the Pacific Ocean, periodic warming and cooling of a huge mass of seawater—phenomena known as El Niño and La Niña, respectively—can impact weather across North America. During normal years (right), when neither El Niño nor La Niña is in effect, strong winds tend to keep warm surface waters contained in the western Pacific while cooler water wells up to the surface in the eastern Pacific.

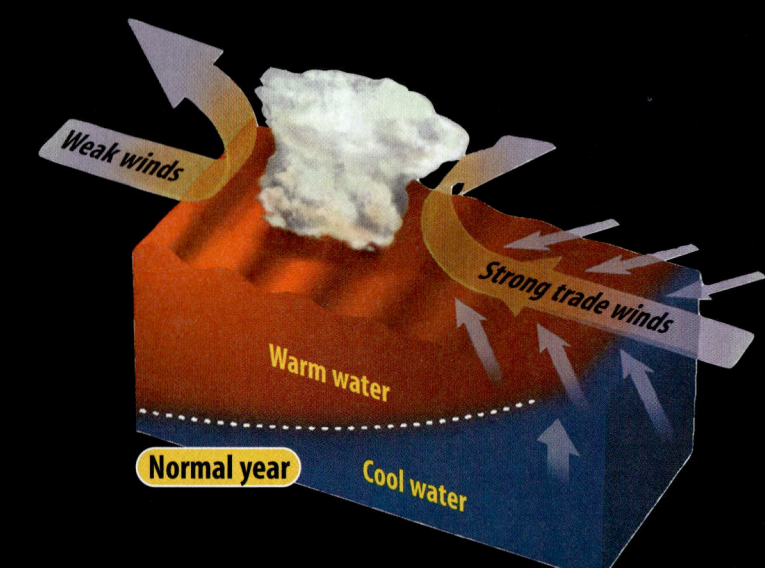

EL NIÑO During El Niño years, winds blowing west weaken and may even reverse. When this happens, warm waters in the western Pacific move eastward, preventing cold water from upwelling. These changes can alter global weather patterns and trigger heavier-than-normal precipitation across much of the United States.

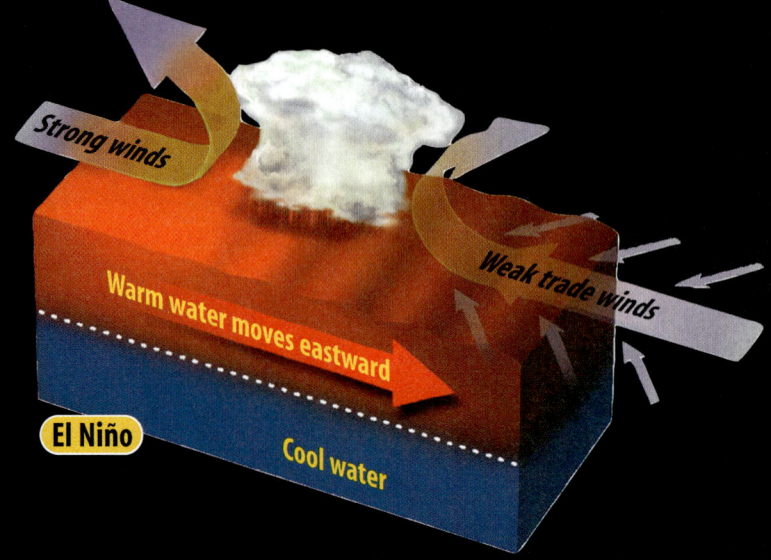

LA NIÑA During La Niña years, stronger-than-normal winds push warm Pacific waters farther west, toward Asia. Cold, deep-sea waters then well up strongly in the eastern Pacific, bringing cooler and often drier weather to many parts of the United States.

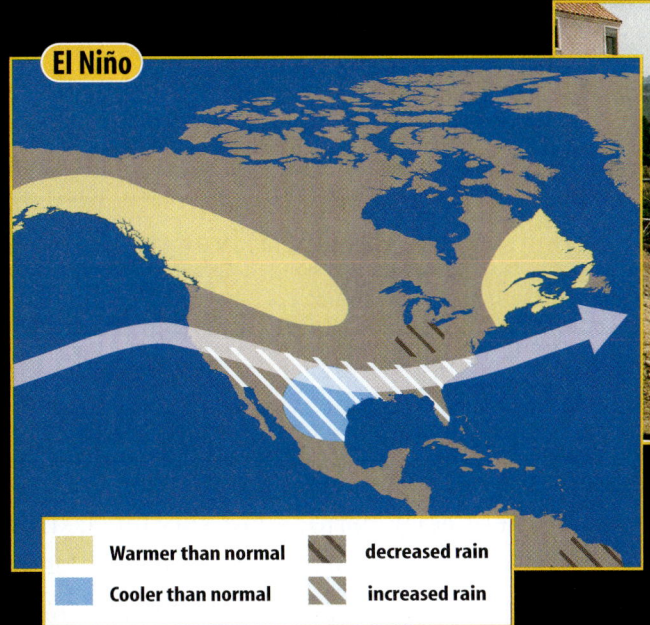

El Niño

Warmer than normal — decreased rain
Cooler than normal — increased rain

Sun-warmed surface water spans the Pacific Ocean during El Niño years. Clouds form above the warm ocean, carrying moisture aloft. The jet stream, shown by the white arrow above, helps bring some of this warm, moist air to the United States.

▲ **LANDSLIDE** Heavy rains in California resulting from El Niño can lead to landslides. This upended house in Laguna Niguel, California, took a ride downhill during the El Niño storms of 1998.

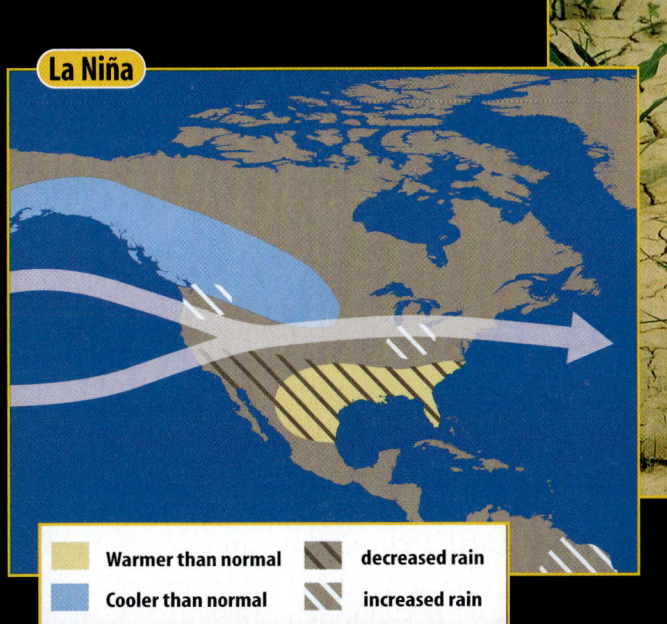

La Niña

Warmer than normal — decreased rain
Cooler than normal — increased rain

During a typical La Niña year, warm ocean waters, clouds, and moisture are pushed away from North America. A weaker jet stream often brings cooler weather to the northern parts of the continent and hot, dry weather to southern areas.

▲ **PARCHED LAND** The Southeast may experience drought conditions, like those that struck the cornfields of Montgomery County, Maryland, during the La Niña summer of 1988.

SECTION 3 Climatic Changes **635**

Climatic Change

If you were exploring in Antarctica near Earth's south pole and found a 3-million-year-old fossil of a warm-weather plant or animal, what would it tell you? You might conclude that the climate of that region changed because Antarctica is much too cold for similar plants and animals to survive today. Some warm-weather fossils found in polar regions indicate that at times in Earth's past, worldwide climate was much warmer than at present. At other times Earth's climate has been much colder than it is today.

Sediments in many parts of the world show that at several different times in the past 2 million years, glaciers covered large parts of Earth's surface. These times are called ice ages. During the past 2 million years, ice ages have alternated with warm periods called interglacial intervals. Ice ages seem to last 60,000 to 100,000 years. Most interglacial periods are shorter, lasting 10,000 to 15,000 years. We are now in an interglacial interval that began about 11,500 years ago. Additional evidence suggests that climate can change even more quickly. Ice cores record climate in a way similar to tree rings. Cores drilled in Greenland show that during the last ice age, colder times lasting 1,000 to 2,000 years changed quickly to warmer spells that lasted about as long. **Figure 11** shows a scientist working with ice cores.

Figure 11 Some ice cores consist of layers of ice that record detailed climate information for individual years. These ice cores can cover more than 300,000 years. **Describe** how this is helpful.

What causes climatic change?

Climatic change has many varied causes. These causes of climatic change can operate over short periods of time or very long periods of time. Catastrophic events, including meteorite collisions and large volcanic eruptions, can affect climate over short periods of time, such as a year or several years. These events add solid particles and liquid droplets to the upper atmosphere, which can change climate. Another factor that can alter Earth's climate is short- or long-term changes in solar output, which is the amount of energy given off by the Sun. Changes in Earth's movements in space affect climate over many thousands of years, and movement of Earth's crustal plates can change climate over millions of years. All of these things can work separately or together to alter Earth's climate.

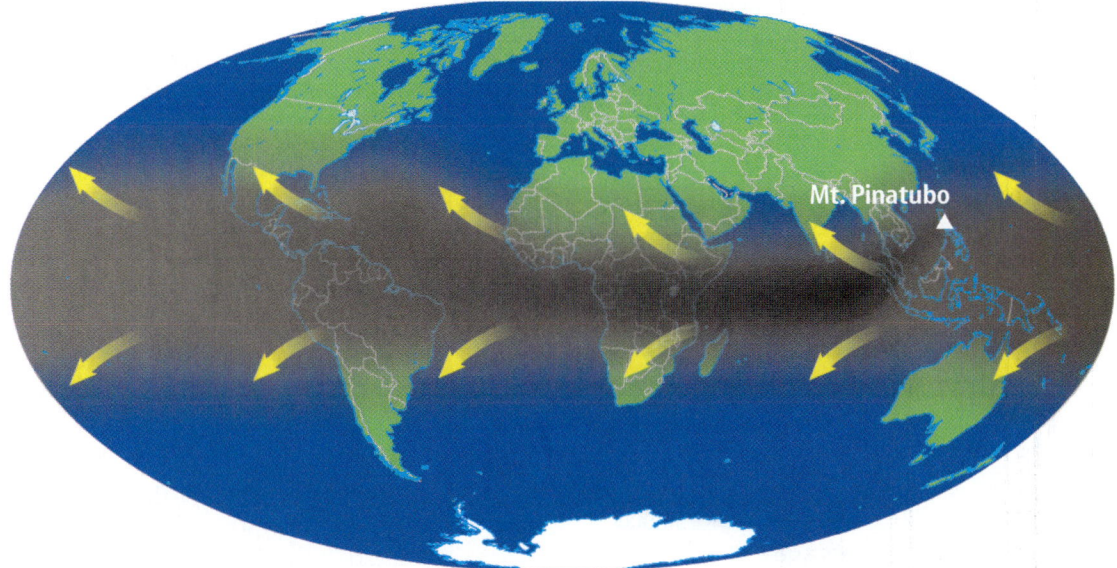

Atmospheric Solids and Liquids Small solid and liquid particles always are present in Earth's atmosphere. These particles can enter the atmosphere naturally or be added to the atmosphere by humans as pollution. Some ways that particles enter the atmosphere naturally include volcanic eruptions, soot from fires, and wind erosion of soil particles. Humans add particles to the atmosphere through automobile exhaust and smokestack emissions. These small particles can affect climate.

Catastrophic events such as meteorite collisions and volcanic eruptions put enormous volumes of dust, ash, and other particles into the atmosphere. These particles block so much solar radiation that they can cool the planet. **Figure 12** shows how a major volcanic eruption affected Earth's atmosphere.

In cities, particles put into the atmosphere as pollution can change the local climate. These particles can increase the amount of cloud cover downwind from the city. Some studies have even suggested that rainfall amounts can be reduced in these areas. This may happen because many small cloud droplets form rather than larger droplets that could produce rain.

Energy from the Sun Solar radiation provides Earth's energy. If the output of radiation from the Sun varies, Earth's climate could change. Some changes in the amount of energy given off by the Sun seem to be related to the presence of sunspots. Sunspots are dark spots on the surface of the Sun. **WARNING:** *Never look directly at the Sun.* Evidence supporting the link between sunspots and climate includes an extremely cold period in Europe between 1645 and 1715. During this time, very few sunspots appeared on the Sun.

Figure 12 Mount Pinatubo in the Philippines erupted in 1991. During the eruption, particles were spread high into the atmosphere and circled the globe. Over time, particles spread around the world, blocking some of the Sun's energy from reaching Earth. The gray areas show how particles from the eruption moved around the world.

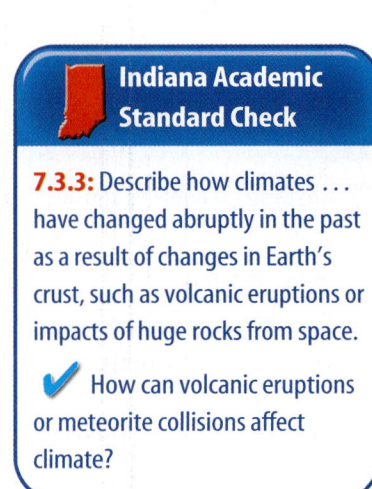

Indiana Academic Standard Check

7.3.3: Describe how climates . . . have changed abruptly in the past as a result of changes in Earth's crust, such as volcanic eruptions or impacts of huge rocks from space.

✔ How can volcanic eruptions or meteorite collisions affect climate?

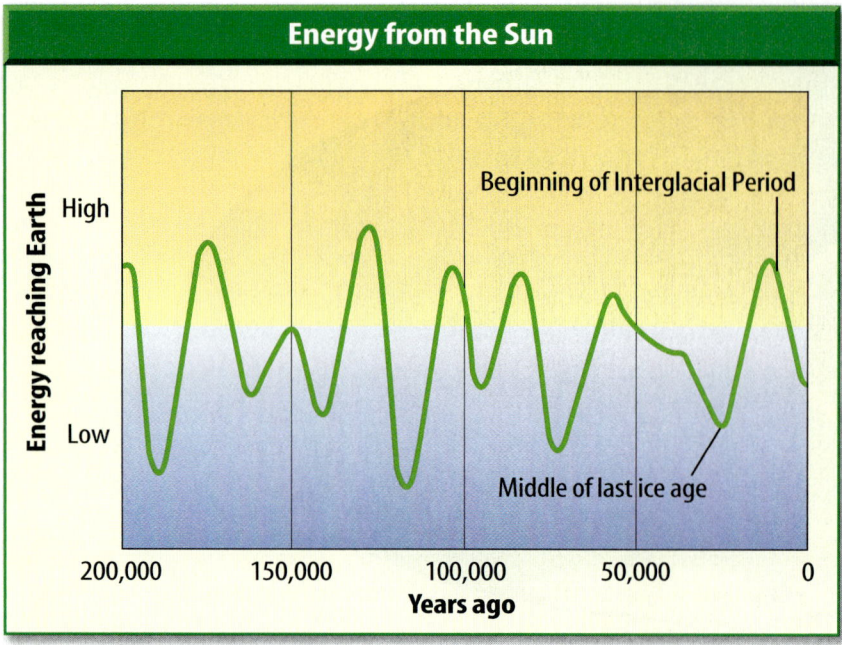

Figure 13 The curving line shows how the amount of the Sun's energy that strikes the northern hemisphere changed over the last 200,000 years.
Describe *the amount of energy that reached the northern hemisphere during the last ice age.*

Indiana Academic Standard Check

7.3.6: Describe how gas and dust from large volcanoes can change the atmosphere.

✓ Why can gas and dust from large volcanic eruptions cause Earth to cool?

Earth Movements Another explanation for some climatic changes involves Earth's movements in space. Earth's axis currently is tilted 23.5° from perpendicular to the plane of its orbit around the Sun. In the past, this tilt has increased to 24.5° and has decreased to 21.5°. When this tilt is at its maximum, the change between summer and winter is probably greater. Earth's tilt changes about every 41,000 years. Some scientists hypothesize that the change in tilt affects climate.

Two additional Earth movements also cause climatic change. Earth's axis wobbles in space just like the axis of a top wobbles when it begins to spin more slowly. This can affect the amount of solar energy received by different parts of Earth. Also, the shape of Earth's orbit changes. Sometimes it is more circular than at present and sometimes it is more flattened. The shape of Earth's orbit changes over a 100,000-year cycle.

Amount of Solar Energy These movements of Earth cause the amount of solar energy reaching different parts of Earth to vary over time, as shown in **Figure 13.** These changes might have caused glaciers to grow and shrink over the last few million years. However, they do not explain why glaciers have occurred so rarely over long spans of geologic time.

Crustal Plate Movement Another explanation for major climatic change over tens or hundreds of millions of years concerns the movement of Earth's crustal plates. The movement of continents and oceans affects the transfer of heat on Earth, which in turn affects wind and precipitation patterns. Through time, these altered patterns can change climate. One example of this is when movement of Earth's plates created the Himalaya about 40 million years ago. The growth of these mountains changed climate over much of Earth.

As you've learned, many theories attempt to answer questions about why Earth's climate has changed through the ages. Probably all of these things play some role in changing climates. More study needs to be done before all the factors that affect climate will be understood.

Climatic Changes Today

Beginning in 1992, representatives from many countries have met to discuss the greenhouse effect and global climate change. These subjects also have appeared frequently in the headlines of newspapers and magazines. Some people are concerned that the greenhouse effect could be responsible for some present-day warming of Earth's atmosphere and oceans.

The **greenhouse effect** is a natural heating process that occurs when certain gases in Earth's atmosphere trap heat. Radiation from the Sun strikes Earth's surface and causes it to warm. Some of this heat then is radiated back toward space. Some gases in the atmosphere, known as greenhouse gases, absorb a portion of this heat and then radiate heat back toward Earth, as shown in **Figure 14.** This keeps Earth warmer than it would be otherwise.

There are many natural greenhouse gases in Earth's atmosphere. Water vapor, carbon dioxide, and methane are some of the most important ones. Without these greenhouse gases, life would not be possible on Earth. Like Mars, Earth would be too cold. However, if the greenhouse effect is too strong, Earth could get too warm. High levels of carbon dioxide in its atmosphere indicate that this has happened on the planet Venus.

Topic: Greenhouse Effect
Visit in7.msscience.com for Web links to information about the greenhouse effect.

Activity Research changes in the greenhouse effect over the last 200 years. Infer what might be causing the changes.

Figure 14 The Sun's radiation travels through Earth's atmosphere and heats the surface. Gases in our atmosphere trap the heat.
Compare and contrast this to the way a greenhouse works.

Global Warming

Over the past 100 years, the average global surface temperature on Earth has increased by about 0.6°C. This increase in temperature is known as **global warming**. Over the same time period, atmospheric carbon dioxide has increased by about 20 percent. As a result, researchers hypothesize that the increase in global temperatures may be related to the increase in atmospheric carbon dioxide. Other hypotheses include the possibility that global warming might be caused by changes in the energy emitted by the Sun.

If Earth's average temperature continues to rise, many glaciers could melt. When glaciers melt, the extra water causes sea levels to rise. Low-lying coastal areas could experience increased flooding. Already some ice caps and small glaciers are beginning to melt and recede, as shown in **Figure 15**. Sea level is rising in some places. Some scientific studies show that these events are related to Earth's increased temperature.

You learned in the previous section that organisms are adapted to their environments. When environments change, can organisms cope? In some tropical waters around the world, corals are dying. Many people think these deaths are caused by warmer water to which the corals are not adapted.

Some climate models show that in the future, Earth's temperatures will increase faster than they have in the last 100 years. However, these predictions might change because of uncertainties in the climate models and in estimating future increases in atmospheric carbon dioxide.

Figure 15 This glacier in Greenland might have receded from its previous position because of global warming. The pile of sediment in front shows how far the glacier once reached.

Figure 16 When forests are cleared or burned, carbon dioxide levels increase in the atmosphere.

Human Activities

Human activities affect the air in Earth's atmosphere. Burning fossil fuels and removing vegetation increase the amount of carbon dioxide in the atmosphere. Because carbon dioxide is a greenhouse gas, it might contribute to global warming. Each year, the amount of carbon dioxide in the atmosphere continues to increase.

Burning Fossil Fuels When natural gas, oil, and coal are burned for energy, the carbon in these fossil fuels combines with atmospheric oxygen to form carbon dioxide. This increases the amount of carbon dioxide in Earth's atmosphere. Studies indicate that humans have increased carbon dioxide levels in the atmosphere by about 25 percent over the last 150 years.

Deforestation Destroying and cutting down trees, called **deforestation**, also affects the amount of carbon dioxide in the atmosphere. Forests, such as the one shown in **Figure 16,** are cleared for mining, roads, buildings, and grazing cattle. Large tracts of forest have been cleared in every country on Earth. Tropical forests have been decreasing at a rate of about one percent each year for the past two decades.

As trees grow, they take in carbon dioxide from the atmosphere. Trees use this carbon dioxide to produce wood and leaves. When trees are cut down, the carbon dioxide they could have removed from the atmosphere remains in the atmosphere. Cut-down trees often are burned for fuel or to clear the land. Burning trees produces even more carbon dioxide.

 *What can humans do to slow carbon dioxide increases in the atmosphere?*

Air Quality Control/Monitor Atmospheric particles from pollution can affect human health as well as climate. These small particles, often called particulates, can enter the lungs and cause tissue damage. The Department of Environmental Protection employs people to monitor air pollution and its causes. Research what types of laws air quality control monitors must enforce.

Topic: Deforestation
Visit in7.msscience.com for Web links to information about deforestation.

Activity Collect data on the world's decline in forests. Infer what the world's forests will be like in 100 years.

SECTION 3 Climatic Changes

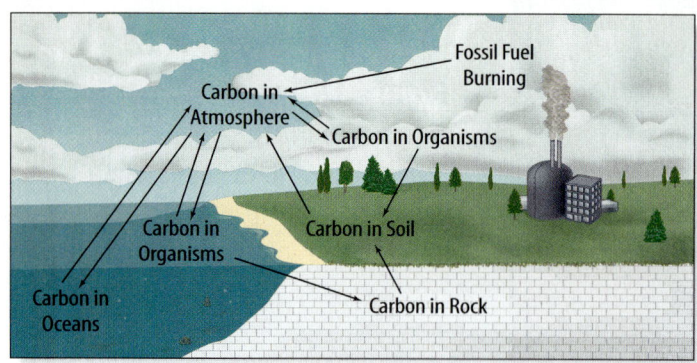

Figure 17 Carbon constantly is cycled among the atmosphere, oceans, solid earth, and biosphere.

The Carbon Cycle

Carbon, primarily as carbon dioxide, is constantly recycled in nature among the atmosphere, Earth's oceans, and organisms that inhabit the land. Organisms that undergo photosynthesis on land and in the water take in carbon dioxide and produce and store carbon-based food. This food is consumed by non-photosynthetic organisms. Carbon dioxide is released as food is broken down to release energy. When organisms die and decay, some carbon is stored as humus in soil and some carbon is released as carbon dioxide. This carbon cycle is illustrated in **Figure 17.**

Some carbon dioxide in the atmosphere dissolves in the oceans, and is used by algae and other photosynthetic, aquatic organisms. Just as on land, aquatic organisms give off carbon dioxide. However, Earth's oceans currently absorb more carbon dioxide from the atmosphere than they give off.

When Earth's climate changes, the amount of carbon dioxide that cycles among atmosphere, ocean, and land also can change. Some people hypothesize that if Earth's climate continues to warm, more carbon dioxide may be absorbed by oceans and land. Scientists continue to collect data to study any changes in the global carbon cycle.

section 3 review

Summary

Earth's Seasons
- Seasons are short periods of climatic changes due to Earth's tilt on its axis while revolving around the Sun, causing differing amounts of solar energy to reach areas of Earth.

El Niño and La Niña
- El Niño begins in the tropical Pacific Ocean when trade winds weaken or reverse directions, disrupting the normal temperature and precipitation patterns around the globe.

Climatic Changes Today
- The greenhouse effect is a natural heating process that occurs when certain gases in Earth's atmosphere trap heat.
- Burning fossil fuels increases the amount of carbon dioxide in the air.
- Deforestation increases the amount of carbon dioxide in the atmosphere.

Self Check

1. **Explain** how Earth's tilted axis is responsible for seasons.
2. **Compare and contrast** El Niño and La Niña. What climate changes do they demonstrate?
3. **List** factors that can cause Earth's climate to change.
4. **Explain** how people are adding carbon dioxide to the atmosphere.
5. **Think Critically** If Earth's climate continues to warm, how might your community be affected?

Applying Skills

6. **Use Models** Using a globe, model the three movements of Earth in space that can cause climatic change.
7. **Use a word processor** to make a table that lists the different processes that might cause Earth's climate to change. Include in your table a description of the process and how it causes climate to change.

642 CHAPTER 21 Climate

in7.msscience.com/self_check_quiz

The Greenhouse Effect

Do you remember climbing into the car on a warm, sunny day? Why was it so hot inside the car when it wasn't that hot outside? It was hotter in the car because the car functioned like a greenhouse. You experienced the greenhouse effect.

Real-World Question

How can you demonstrate the greenhouse effect?

Goals
- **Model** the greenhouse effect.
- **Measure and graph** temperature changes.

Materials
identical large, empty glass jars (2)
lid for one jar
nonmercury thermometers (3)

Safety Precautions

WARNING: *Be careful when you handle glass thermometers. If a thermometer breaks, do not touch it. Have your teacher dispose of the glass safely.*

Procedure

1. Lay a thermometer inside each jar.
2. Place the jars next to each other by a sunny window. Lay the third thermometer between the jars.
3. **Record** the temperatures of the three thermometers. They should be the same.
4. Place the lid on one jar.
5. **Record** the temperatures of all three thermometers at the end of 5, 10, and 15 min.
6. Make a line graph that shows the temperatures of the three thermometers for the 15 min of the experiment.

Conclude and Apply

1. **Explain** why you placed a thermometer between the two jars.
2. **List** the constants in this experiment. What was the variable?
3. **Identify** which thermometer showed the greatest temperature change during your experiment.
4. **Analyze** what occurred in this experiment. How was the lid in this experiment like the greenhouse gases in the atmosphere?
5. **Infer** from this experiment why you should never leave a pet inside a closed car in warm weather.

Communicating Your Data

Give a brief speech describing your conclusions to your class.

MICROCLIMATES

Goals
- **Observe** temperature, wind speed, relative humidity, and precipitation in areas outside your school.
- **Identify** local microclimates.

Materials
thermometers
psychrometer
paper strip or wind sock
large cans (4 or 5)
* beakers or rain gauges (4 or 5)
unlined paper
*Alternate materials

Safety Precautions

WARNING: *If a thermometer breaks, do not touch it. Have your teacher dispose of the glass safely.*

Real-World Question

A microclimate is a localized climate that differs from the main climate of a region. Buildings in a city, for instance, can affect the climate of the surrounding area. Large buildings, such as the Bank of America Plaza in Dallas, Texas, can create microclimates by blocking the Sun or changing wind patterns. Does your school create microclimates?

Procedure

1. Select four or five sites around your school building. Also, select a control site well away from the school.
2. Attach a thermometer to an object near each of the locations you selected. Set up a rain gauge, beaker, or can to collect precipitation.
3. Visit each site at two predetermined times, one in the morning and one in the afternoon, each day for a week. Record the temperature and measure any precipitation that might have fallen. Use a wind sock or paper strip to determine wind direction.

Relative Humidity

Dry Bulb Temperature (°C)	Dry Bulb Temperature Minus Wet Bulb Temperature (°C)									
	1	2	3	4	5	6	7	8	9	10
14	90	79	70	60	51	42	34	26	18	10
15	90	80	71	61	53	44	36	27	20	13
16	90	81	71	63	54	46	38	30	23	15
17	90	81	72	64	55	47	40	32	25	18
18	91	82	73	65	57	49	41	34	27	20
19	91	82	74	65	58	50	43	36	29	22
20	91	83	74	66	59	51	44	37	31	24
21	91	83	75	67	60	53	46	39	32	26
22	92	83	76	68	61	54	47	40	34	28
23	92	84	76	69	62	55	48	42	36	30
24	92	84	77	69	62	56	49	43	37	31
25	92	84	77	70	63	57	50	44	39	33

Using Scientific Methods

4. To find relative humidity, you'll need to use a psychrometer. A psychrometer is an instrument with two thermometers—one wet and one dry. As moisture from the wet thermometer evaporates, it takes heat energy from its environment, and the environment immediately around the wet thermometer cools. The thermometer records a lower temperature. Relative humidity can be found by finding the difference between the wet thermometer and the dry thermometer and by using the chart on the previous page. Record all of your weather data.

◉ Analyze Your Data

1. **Make** separate line graphs for temperature, relative humidity, and precipitation for your morning and afternoon data. Make a table showing wind direction data.
2. **Compare and contrast** weather data for each of your sites. What microclimates did you identify around your school building? How did these climates differ from the control site? How did they differ from each other?

◉ Conclude and Apply

1. **Explain** Why did you take weather data at a control site away from the school building? How did the control help you analyze and interpret your data?
2. **Infer** what conditions could have caused the microclimates that you identified. Are your microclimates similar to those that might exist in a large city? Explain.

Communicating Your Data

Use your graphs to make a large poster explaining your conclusions. Display your poster in the school building. **For more help, refer to the Science Skill Handbook.**

TIME SCIENCE AND HISTORY

SCIENCE CAN CHANGE THE COURSE OF HISTORY!

The Year there was No Summer

You've seen pictures of erupting volcanoes. One kind of volcano sends smoke, rock, and ash high into the air above the crater. Another kind of volcano erupts with fiery, red-hot rivers of lava snaking down its sides. Erupting volcanoes are nature's forces at their mightiest, causing destruction and death. But not everyone realizes how far-reaching the destruction can be. Large volcanic eruptions can affect people thousands of kilometers away. In fact, major volcanic eruptions can have effects that reach around the globe.

An erupting volcano can temporarily change Earth's climate. The ash a volcano ejects into the atmosphere can create day after day without sunshine. Other particles move high into the atmosphere and are carried all the way around Earth, sometimes causing global temperatures to drop for several months.

The Summer That Never Came

An example of a volcanic eruption with wide-ranging effects occurred in 1783 in Iceland, an island nation in the North Atlantic Ocean. Winds carried a black cloud of ash from an erupting volcano in Iceland westward across northern Canada, Alaska, and across the Pacific Ocean to Japan. The summer turned bitterly cold in these places. Water froze, and heavy snowstorms pelted the land. Sulfurous gases from the erupting volcano combined with water to form particles of acid that reflected solar energy back into space. This "blanket" in the atmosphere kept the Sun's rays from heating up part of Earth.

The most tragic result of this eruption was the death of many Kauwerak people, who lived in western Alaska. Only a handful of Kauwerak survived the summer that never came. They had no opportunity to catch needed foods to keep them alive through the following winter.

Locate Using an atlas, locate Indonesia and Iceland. Using reference materials, find five facts about each place. Make a map of each nation and illustrate the map with your five facts.

For more information, visit in7.msscience.com/time

Chapter 21 Study Guide

Reviewing Main Ideas

Section 1 — What is climate?

1. An area's climate is the average weather over a long period of time, such as 30 years.
2. The three main climate zones are tropical, polar, and temperate.
3. Features such as oceans, mountains, and even large cities affect climate.

Section 2 — Climate Types

1. Climates can be classified by various characteristics, such as temperature, precipitation, and vegetation. World climates commonly are separated into six major groups.
2. Organisms have structural and behavioral adaptations that help them survive in particular climates. Many organisms can survive only in the climate they are adapted to.
3. Adaptations develop in a population over a long period of time.

Section 3 — Climatic Changes

1. Seasons are caused by the tilt of Earth's axis as Earth revolves around the Sun.
2. El Niño disrupts normal temperature and precipitation patterns around the world.
3. Geological records show that over the past few million years, Earth's climate has alternated between ice ages and warmer periods.
4. The greenhouse effect occurs when certain gases trap heat in Earth's atmosphere.
5. Carbon dioxide enters the atmosphere when fossil fuels such as oil and coal are burned.

Visualizing Main Ideas

Copy and complete the following concept map on climate.

Climate
- affected by: Latitude, ___, Mountains
- changes over: Short time (caused by Seasons, caused by Volcanoes, caused by ___), due to Earth movement, due to ___

chapter 21 Review

Using Vocabulary

adaptation p. 628
climate p. 624
deforestation p. 641
El Niño p. 633
global warming p. 640
greenhouse effect p. 639
hibernation p. 630
polar zone p. 624
season p. 632
temperate zone p. 624
tropics p. 624

Fill in the blanks with the correct vocabulary word or words.

1. Earth's north pole is in the _____.

2. _____ causes the Pacific Ocean to become warmer off the coast of Peru.

3. During _____, an animal's body temperature drops.

4. _____ is the pattern of weather that occurs over many years.

5. _____ means global temperatures are rising.

Checking Concepts

Choose the word or phrase that best answers the question.

6. Which of the following is a greenhouse gas in Earth's atmosphere?
   A) helium   C) hydrogen
   B) carbon dioxide D) oxygen

7. During which of the following is the eastern Pacific warmer than normal?
   A) El Niño   C) summer
   B) La Niña   D) spring

8. Which latitude receives the most direct rays of the Sun year-round?
   A) 60°N   C) 30°S
   B) 90°N   D) 0°

9. What happens as you climb a mountain?
   A) temperature decreases
   B) temperature increases
   C) air pressure increases
   D) air pressure remains constant

10. Which of the following is true of El Niño?
    A) It cools the Pacific Ocean near Peru.
    B) It causes flooding in Australia.
    C) It cools the waters off Alaska.
    D) It may occur when the trade winds slacken or reverse.

11. What do changes in Earth's orbit affect?
    A) Earth's shape   C) Earth's rotation
    B) Earth's climate D) Earth's tilt

12. The Köppen climate classification system includes categories based on precipitation and what other factor?
    A) temperature   C) winds
    B) air pressure D) latitude

13. Which of the following is an example of structural adaptation?
    A) hibernation   C) fur
    B) migration   D) estivation

14. Which of these can people do in order to help reduce global warming?
    A) burn coal   C) conserve energy
    B) remove trees D) produce methane

Use the illustration below to answer question 15.

15. What would you most likely find on the leeward side of this mountain range?
    A) lakes   C) deserts
    B) rain forests D) glaciers

chapter 21 Review

Thinking Critically

16. **Draw a Conclusion** How could climate change cause the types of organisms in an area to change?

17. **Infer** What might you infer if you find fossils of tropical plants in a desert?

18. **Describe** On a summer day, why would a Florida beach be cooler than an orange grove that is 2 km inland?

19. **Infer** what would happen to global climates if the Sun emitted more energy.

20. **Explain** why it will be cooler if you climb to a higher elevation in a desert.

21. **Communicate** Explain how atmospheric pressure over the Pacific Ocean might affect how the trade winds blow.

22. **Predict** Make a chain-of-events chart to explain the effect of a major volcanic eruption on climate.

23. **Form Hypotheses** A mountain glacier in South America has been getting smaller over several decades. What hypotheses should a scientist consider to explain why this is occurring?

24. **Concept Map** Copy and complete the concept map using the following: *tropics, 0°–23.5° latitude, polar, temperate, 23.5°–66.5° latitude,* and *66.5° latitude to poles.*

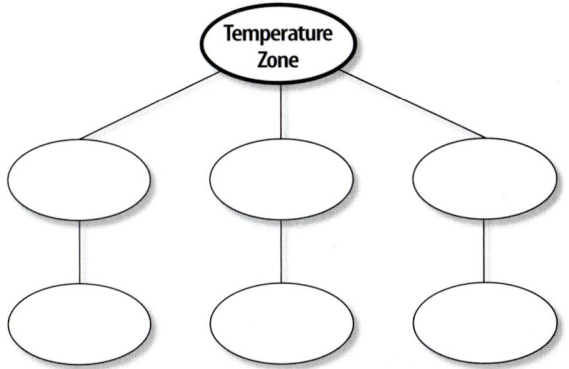

25. **Explain** how global warming might lead to the extinction of some organisms.

26. **Describe** how dust and ash from large volcanoes can change the atmosphere.

27. **Explain** how heat energy carried by ocean currents influences climate.

28. **Describe** how sediments, fossils, and ice cores record Earth's geologic history.

29. **Describe** how volcanic eruptions or meteorite collisions have changed past climates.

Performance Activities

30. **Science Display** Make a display illustrating different factors that can affect climate. Be sure to include detailed diagrams and descriptions for each factor in your display. Present your display to the class.

Applying Math

Use the table below to answer questions 31 and 32.

Precipitation in Phoenix, Arizona	
Season	Precipitation (cm)
Winter	5.7
Spring	1.2
Summer	6.7
Autumn	5.9
Total	19.5

31. **Precipitation Amounts** The following table gives average precipitation amounts for Phoenix, Arizona. Make a bar graph of these data. Which climate type do you think Phoenix represents?

32. **Local Precipitation** Use the table above to help estimate seasonal precipitation for your city or one that you choose. Create a bar graph for that data.

chapter 21 Indiana

 The assessed Indiana standard appears above the question.

Record your answers on the answer sheet provided by your teacher or on a sheet of paper.

Part 1 Multiple Choice

1. The graph below shows the levels of carbon dioxide in the atmosphere along with changes in temperature for the last 160,000 years.

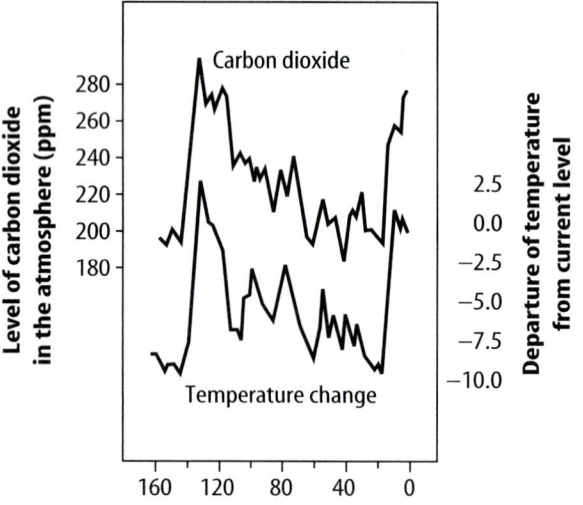

Which statement best describes the data in the graph above?

A As CO_2 levels have increased, global temperature has decreased.

B As CO_2 levels have increased, global temperature increased.

C As global temperature has decreased, CO_2 levels have increased.

D As global temperature has increased, CO_2 levels have decreased.

2. The table below shows the apparent temperature for a given air temperature and relative humidity.

Apparent Temperature Index					
		Relative Humidity (%)			
Air Temperature (°F)		80	85	90	95
	85	97	99	102	105
	80	86	87	88	89
	75	78	78	79	79
	70	71	71	71	71

If the relative humidity is 85% and the temperature is 75°F, what is the apparent temperature?

A 78°F

B 79°F

C 88°F

D 89°F

3. The temperature of a city can be up to 5°C warmer than in surrounding rural areas. What is this phenomenon called?

A the Coriolis effect

B the greenhouse effect

C the heat island effect

D the rain shadow effect

Test-Taking Tip

Fill In The Blanks Never leave any answer blank.

4. What is global warming?

   A the average difference in temperature between tropical regions and polar regions

   B the daily change in temperature as the Sun heats Earth's surface

   C the increase in average surface temperature on Earth over the past 100 years

   D the natural heating process that occurs when certain gases in the atmosphere trap heat

5. The illustration below shows what happens as the Sun's radiation passes through Earth's atmosphere.

   What specific process does this illustration depict?

   A El Niño

   B global warming

   C greenhouse effect

   D La Niña

Part 2 Constructed Response

6. The illustration below shows the carbon cycle.

   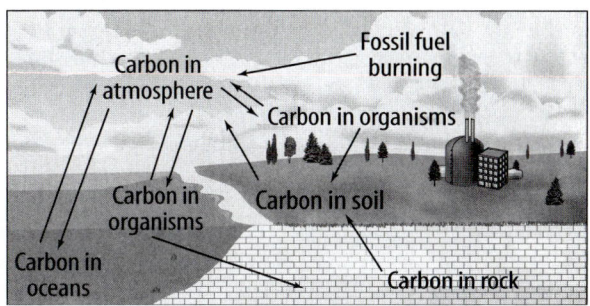

   Describe the carbon cycle. How does the burning of fossil fuels affect the amount of carbon dioxide entering the carbon cycle? How does deforestation affect the amount of carbon dioxide entering the carbon cycle?

   7.3.3 7.3.6

7. In 1991, Mt. Pinatubo erupted, releasing volcanic particulates into the atmosphere. Temperatures around the world fell by as much as 0.7°C below average during 1992. How was this global temperature change related to the volcanic eruption?

   7.3.5

8. Explain how a large body of water can affect the climate of a nearby area.

   7.3.5

9. Describe the relationship between ocean currents and precipitation in a coastal region.

chapter 22

Academic Standard—3: Students collect and organize data to identify relationships between physical objects, events, and processes. They use logical reasoning to question their own ideas as new information challenges their conceptions of the natural world.

Also covers: Academic Standard 4 (Detailed standards begin on page IN8.)

Clues to Earth's Past

chapter preview

sections
1. Fossils
2. Relative Ages of Rocks
   Lab Relative Ages
3. Absolute Ages of Rocks
   Lab Trace Fossils
   Virtual Lab How can fossil and rock data determine when an organism lived?

Reading the Past

The pages of Earth's history, much like the pages of human history, can be read if you look in the right place. Unlike the pages of a book, the pages of Earth's past are written in stone. In this chapter you will learn how to read the pages of Earth's history to understand what the planet was like in the distant past.

Science Journal List three fossils that you would expect to find a million years from now in the place you live today.

Start-Up Activities

Clues to Life's Past

Fossil formation begins when dead plants or animals are buried in sediment. In time, if conditions are right, the sediment hardens into sedimentary rock. Parts of the organism are preserved along with the impressions of parts that don't survive. Any evidence of once-living things contained in the rock record is a fossil.

1. Fill a small jar (about 500 mL) one-third full of plaster of paris. Add water until the jar is half full.
2. Drop in a few small shells.
3. Cover the jar and shake it to model a swift, muddy stream.
4. Now model the stream flowing into a lake by uncovering the jar and pouring the contents into a paper or plastic bowl. Let the mixture sit for an hour.
5. Crack open the hardened plaster to locate the model fossils.
6. **Think Critically** Remove the shells from the plaster and study the impressions they made. In your Science Journal, list what the impressions would tell you if found in a rock.

Age of Rocks Make the following Foldable to help you understand how scientists determine the age of a rock.

STEP 1 Fold a sheet of paper in half lengthwise.

STEP 2 Fold paper down 2.5 cm from the top. (Hint: From the tip of your index finger to your middle knuckle is about 2.5 cm.)

STEP 3 Open and draw lines along the 2.5-cm fold. Label as shown.

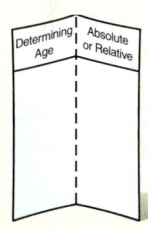

Summarize in a Table As you read the chapter, in the left column, list four different ways in which one could determine the age of a rock. In the right column, note whether each method gives an absolute or a relative age.

Preview this chapter's content and activities at
in7.msscience.com

section 1

Standards—7.3.8: Describe how sediments of sand and smaller particles, sometimes containing the remains of organisms, are gradually buried and are cemented together by dissolved minerals to form solid rock again. **7.3.10:** Explain how the thousands of layers of sedimentary rock can confirm the long history of the changing surface of Earth and the changing life forms whose remains are found in successive layers....

Fossils

as you read

What You'll Learn
- **List** the conditions necessary for fossils to form.
- **Describe** several processes of fossil formation.
- **Explain** how fossil correlation is used to determine rock ages.
- **Determine** how fossils can be used to explain changes in Earth's surface, life forms, and environments.

Why It's Important
Fossils help scientists find oil and other sources of energy necessary for society.

Review Vocabulary
paleontologist: a scientist who studies fossils

New Vocabulary
- fossil
- permineralized remains
- carbon film
- mold
- cast
- index fossil

Traces of the Distant Past

A giant crocodile lurks in the shallow water of a river. A herd of *Triceratops* emerges from the edge of the forest and cautiously moves toward the river. The dinosaurs are thirsty, but danger waits for them in the water. A large bull *Triceratops* moves into the river. The others follow.

Does this scene sound familiar to you? It's likely that you've read about dinosaurs and other past inhabitants of Earth. But how do you know that they really existed or what they were like? What evidence do humans have of past life on Earth? The answer is fossils. Paleontologists, scientists who study fossils, can learn about extinct animals from their fossil remains, as shown in **Figure 1.**

Figure 1 Scientists can learn how dinosaurs looked and moved using fossil remains. A skeleton can then be reassembled and displayed in a museum.

654

Formation of Fossils

Fossils are the remains, imprints, or traces of prehistoric organisms. Fossils have helped scientists determine approximately when life first appeared, when plants and animals first lived on land, and when organisms became extinct. Fossils are evidence of not only when and where organisms once lived, but also how they lived.

For the most part, the remains of dead plants and animals disappear quickly. Scavengers eat and scatter the remains of dead organisms. Fungi and bacteria invade, causing the remains to rot and disappear. If you've ever left a banana on the counter too long, you've seen this process begin. In time, compounds within the banana cause it to break down chemically and soften. Microorganisms, such as bacteria, cause it to decay. What keeps some plants and animals from disappearing before they become fossils? Which organisms are more likely to become fossils?

Figure 2 These fossil shark teeth are hard parts. Soft parts of animals do not become fossilized as easily.

Conditions Needed for Fossil Formation Whether or not a dead organism becomes a fossil depends upon how well it is protected from scavengers and agents of physical destruction, such as waves and currents. One way a dead organism can be protected is for sediment to bury the body quickly. If a fish dies and sinks to the bottom of a lake, sediment carried into the lake by a stream can cover the fish rapidly. As a result, no waves or scavengers can get to it and tear it apart. The body parts then might be fossilized and included in a sedimentary rock like shale. However, quick burial alone isn't always enough to make a fossil.

Organisms have a better chance of becoming fossils if they have hard parts such as bones, shells, or teeth. One reason is that scavengers are less likely to eat these hard parts. Hard parts also decay more slowly than soft parts do. Most fossils are the hard parts of organisms, such as the fossil teeth in **Figure 2**.

Types of Preservation

Perhaps you've seen skeletal remains of *Tyrannosaurus rex* towering above you in a museum. You also have some idea of what this dinosaur looked like because you've seen illustrations. Artists who draw *Tyrannosaurus rex* and other dinosaurs base their illustrations on fossil bones. What preserves fossil bones?

Mini LAB

Predicting Fossil Preservation

Procedure
1. Take a brief walk outside and observe your neighborhood.
2. Look around and notice what kinds of plants and animals live nearby.

Analysis
1. Predict what remains from your time might be preserved far into the future.
2. Explain what conditions would need to exist for these remains to be fossilized.

SECTION 1 Fossils

Figure 3 Opal and various minerals have replaced original materials and filled the hollow spaces in this permineralized dinosaur bone.
Explain why this fossil retained the shape of the original bone.

Mineral Replacement Most hard parts of organisms such as bones, teeth, and shells have tiny spaces within them. In life, these spaces can be filled with cells, blood vessels, nerves, or air. When the organism dies and the soft materials inside the hard parts decay, the tiny spaces become empty. If the hard part is buried, groundwater can seep in and deposit minerals in the spaces. **Permineralized remains** are fossils in which the spaces inside are filled with minerals from groundwater. In permineralized remains, some original material from the fossil organism's body might be preserved—encased within the minerals from groundwater. It is from these original materials that DNA, the chemical that contains an organism's genetic code, can sometimes be recovered.

Sometimes minerals replace the hard parts of fossil organisms. For example, a solution of water and dissolved silica (the compound SiO_2) might flow into and through the shell of a dead organism. If the water dissolves the shell and leaves silica in its place, the original shell is replaced.

Often people learn about past forms of life from bones, wood, and other remains that became permineralized or replaced with minerals from groundwater, as shown in **Figure 3**, but many other types of fossils can be found.

Figure 4 Graptolites lived hundreds of millions of years ago and drifted on currents in the oceans. These organisms often are preserved as carbon films.

Carbon Films The tissues of organisms are made of compounds that contain carbon. Sometimes fossils contain only carbon. Fossils usually form when sediments bury a dead organism. As sediment piles up, the organism's remains are subjected to pressure and heat. These conditions force gases and liquids from the body. A thin film of carbon residue is left, forming a silhouette of the original organism called a **carbon film**. **Figure 4** shows the carbonized remains of graptolites, which were small marine animals. Graptolites have been found in rocks as old as 500 million years.

Coal In swampy regions, large volumes of plant matter accumulate. Over millions of years, these deposits become completely carbonized, forming coal. Coal is an important fuel source, but since the structure of the original plant is usually lost, it cannot reveal as much about the past as other kinds of fossils.

Reading Check *In what sort of environment does coal form?*

Molds and Casts In nature, impressions form when seashells or other hard parts of organisms fall into a soft sediment such as mud. The object and sediment are then buried by more sediment. Compaction, together with cementation, which is the deposition of minerals from water into the pore spaces between sediment particles, turns the sediment into rock. Other open pores in the rock then let water and air reach the shell or hard part. The hard part might decay or dissolve, leaving behind a cavity in the rock called a **mold.** Later, mineral-rich water or other sediment might enter the cavity, form new rock, and produce a copy or **cast** of the original object, as shown in **Figure 5.**

Coal Mining Many of the first coal mines in the United States were located in eastern states like Pennsylvania and West Virginia. In your Science Journal, discuss how the environments of the past relate to people's lives today.

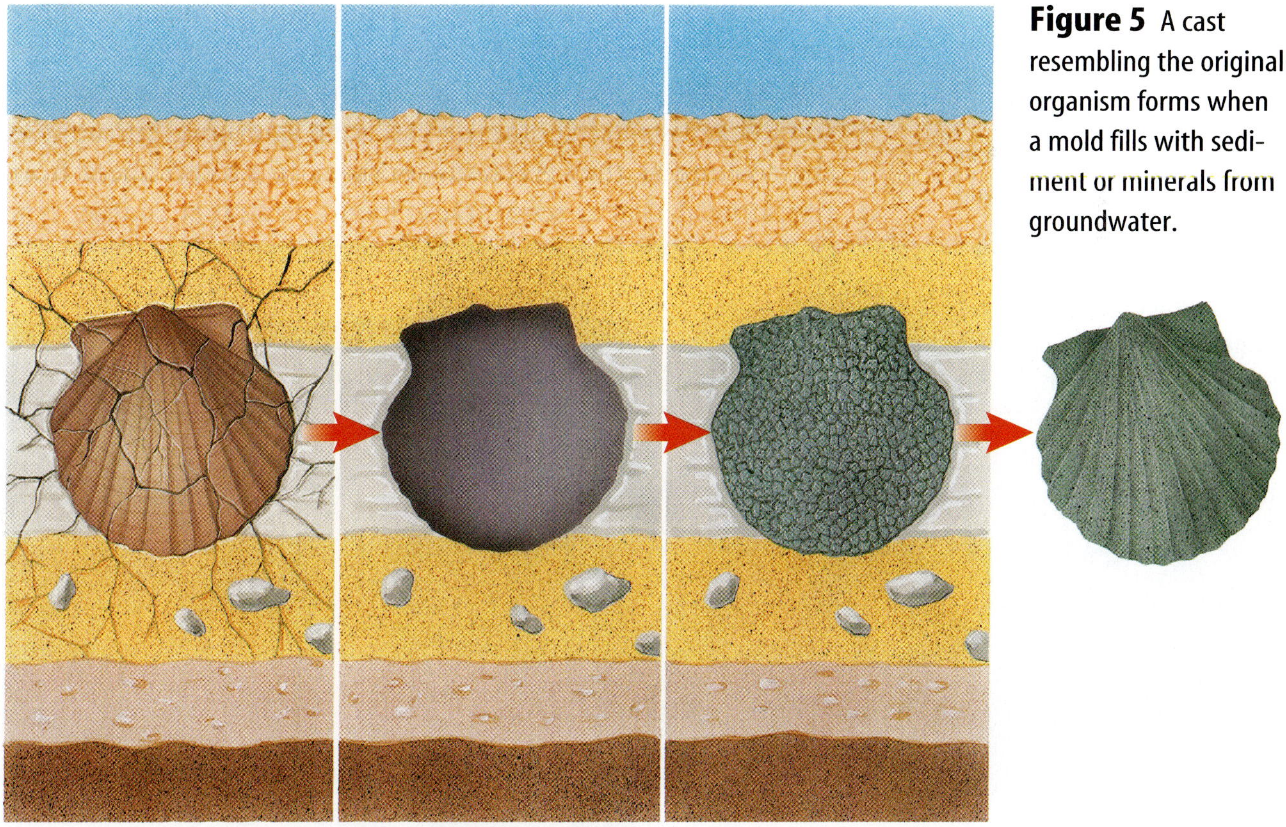

Figure 5 A cast resembling the original organism forms when a mold fills with sediment or minerals from groundwater.

The fossil begins to dissolve as water moves through spaces in the rock layers.

The fossil has been dissolved away. The harder rock once surrounding it forms a mold.

Sediment washes into the mold and is deposited, or mineral crystals form.

A cast results.

SECTION 1 Fossils **657**

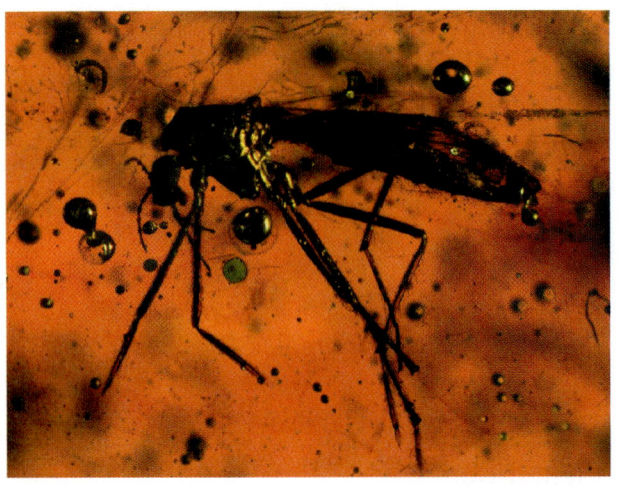

Original Remains Sometimes conditions allow original soft parts of organisms to be preserved for thousands or millions of years. For example, insects can be trapped in amber, a hardened form of sticky tree resin. The amber surrounds and protects the original material of the insect's exoskeleton from destruction, as shown in **Figure 6.** Some organisms, such as the mammoth, have been found preserved in frozen ground in Siberia. Original remains also have been found in natural tar deposits, such as the La Brea tar pits in California.

Figure 6 The original soft parts of this mosquito have been preserved in amber for millions of years.

Trace Fossils Do you have a handprint in plaster that you made when you were in kindergarten? If so, it's a record that tells something about you. From it, others can guess your size and maybe your weight at that age. Animals walking on Earth long ago left similar tracks, such as those in **Figure 7.** Trace fossils are fossilized tracks and other evidence of the activity of organisms. In some cases, tracks can tell you more about how an organism lived than any other type of fossil. For example, from a set of tracks at Davenport Ranch, Texas, you might be able to learn something about the social life of sauropods, which were large, plant-eating dinosaurs. The largest tracks of the herd are on the outer edges and the smallest are on the inside. These tracks led some scientists to hypothesize that adult sauropods surrounded their young as they traveled—perhaps to protect them from predators. A nearby set of tracks might mean that another type of dinosaur, an allosaur, was stalking the herd.

Figure 7 Tracks made in soft mud, and now preserved in solid rock, can provide information about animal size, speed, and behavior.

The dinosaur track below is from the Glen Rose Formation in north-central Texas.

The tracks to the right are located on a Navajo reservation in Arizona.

658 CHAPTER 22 Clues to Earth's Past

Trails and Burrows Other trace fossils include trails and burrows made by worms and other animals. These, too, tell something about how these animals lived. For example, by examining fossil burrows you can sometimes tell how firm the sediment the animals lived in was. As you can see, fossils can tell a great deal about the organisms that have inhabited Earth.

 *How are trace fossils different from fossils that are the remains of an organism's body?*

7.3.10: Explain how thousands of layers of sedimentary rock can confirm . . . the changing life forms whose remains are found in successive layers.

✓ What is the importance of index fossils?

Index Fossils

One thing you can learn by studying fossils is that species of organisms have changed over time. Some species of organisms inhabited Earth for long periods of time without changing. Other species changed a lot in comparatively short amounts of time. It is these organisms that scientists use as index fossils.

Index fossils are the remains of species that existed on Earth for relatively short periods of time, were abundant, and were widespread geographically. Because the organisms that became index fossils lived only during specific intervals of geologic time, geologists can estimate the ages of rock layers based on the particular index fossils they contain. However, not all rocks contain index fossils. Another way to approximate the age of a rock layer is to compare the spans of time, or ranges, over which more than one fossil appears. The estimated age is the time interval where fossil ranges overlap, as shown in **Figure 8.**

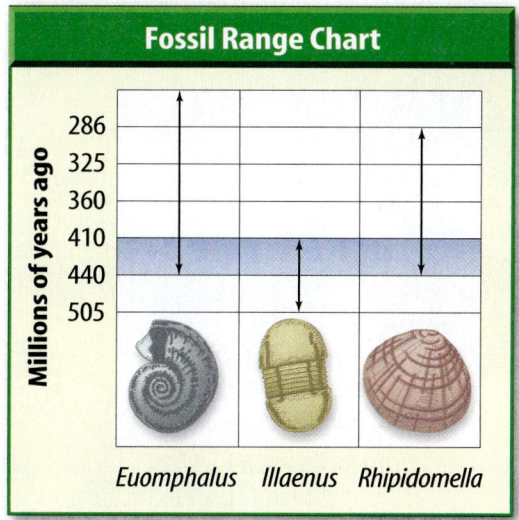

Figure 8 The fossils in a sequence of sedimentary rock can be used to estimate the ages of each layer. The chart shows when each organism inhabited Earth.
Explain why it is possible to say that the middle layer of rock was deposited between 440 million and 410 million years ago.

Ancient Ecology
Ecology is the study of how organisms interact with each other and with their environment. Some paleontologists study the ecology of ancient organisms. Discuss the kinds of information you could use to determine how ancient organisms interacted with their environment.

Fossils and Ancient Environments

Scientists can use fossils to determine what the environment of an area was like long ago. Using fossils, you might be able to find out whether an area was land or whether it was covered by an ocean at a particular time. If the region was covered by ocean, it might even be possible to learn the depth of the water. What clues about the depth of water do you think fossils could provide?

Fossils also are used to determine the past climate of a region. For example, rocks in parts of the eastern United States contain fossils of tropical plants. The environment of this part of the United States today isn't tropical. However, because of the fossils, scientists know that it was tropical when these plants were living. **Figure 9** shows that North America was located near the equator when these fossils formed.

Figure 9 The equator passed through North America 310 million years ago. At this time, warm, shallow seas and coal swamps covered much of the continent, and ferns like the *Neuropteris,* below, were common.

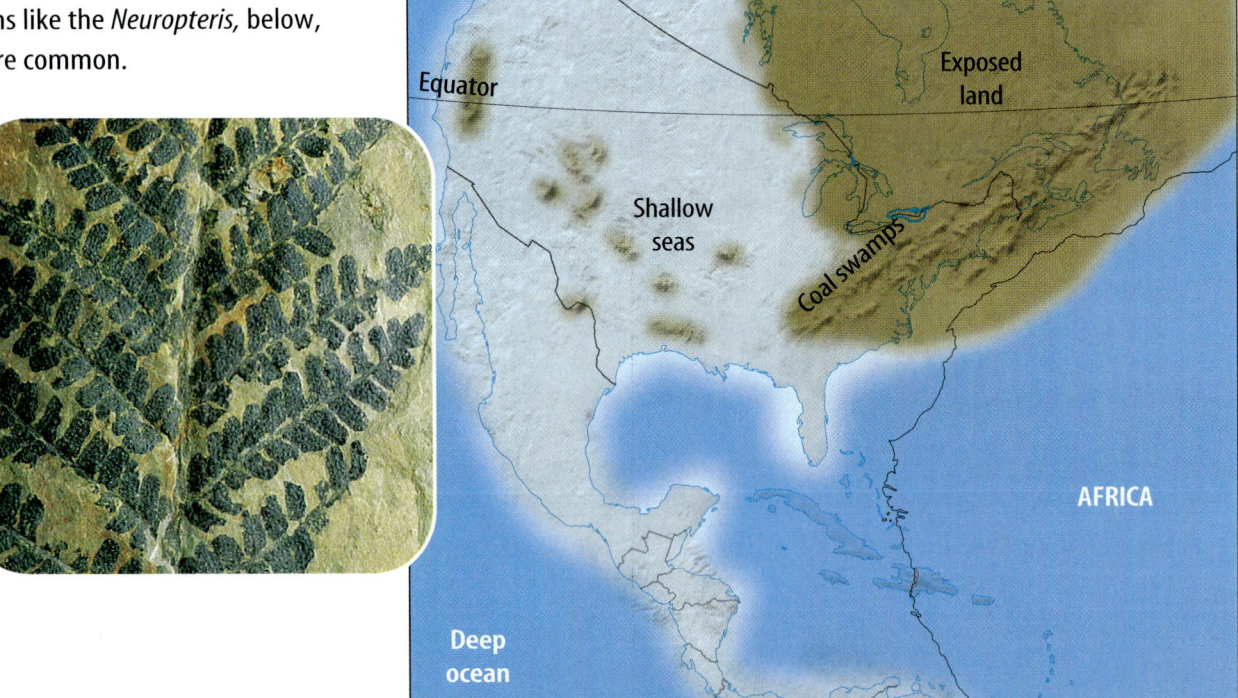

Shallow Seas How would you explain the presence of fossilized crinoids—animals that lived in shallow seas—in rocks found in what is today a desert? **Figure 10** shows a fossil crinoid and a living crinoid. When the fossil crinoids were alive, a shallow sea covered much of western and central North America. The crinoid hard parts were included in rocks that formed from the sediments at the bottom of this sea. Fossils provide information about past life on Earth and also about the history of the rock layers that contain them. Fossils can provide information about the ages of rocks and the climate and type of environment that existed when the rocks formed.

Figure 10 The crinoid on the left lived in warm, shallow seas that once covered part of North America. Crinoids like the one on the right typically live in warm, shallow waters in the Pacific Ocean.

section 1 review

Summary

Formation of Fossils
- Fossils are the remains, imprints, or traces of past organisms.
- Fossilization is most likely if the organism had hard parts and was buried quickly.

Fossil Preservation
- Permineralized remains have open spaces filled with minerals from groundwater.
- Thin carbon films remain in the shapes of dead organisms.
- Hard parts dissolve to leave molds.
- Trace fossils are evidence of past activity.

Index Fossils
- Index fossils are from species that were abundant briefly, but over wide areas.
- Scientists can estimate the ages of rocks containing index fossils.

Fossils and Ancient Environments
- Fossils tell us about the environment in which the organisms lived.

Self Check

1. **Describe** the typical conditions necessary for fossil formation.
2. **Explain** how a fossil mold is different from a fossil cast.
3. **Discuss** how the characteristics of an index fossil are useful to geologists.
4. **Describe** how carbon films form.
5. **Think Critically** What can you say about the ages of two widely separated layers of rock that contain the same type of fossil?

Applying Skills

6. **Communicate** what you learn about fossils. Visit a museum that has fossils on display. Make an illustration of each fossil in your Science Journal. Write a brief description, noting key facts about each fossil and how each fossil might have formed.
7. **Compare and contrast** original remains with other kinds of fossils. What kinds of information would only be available from original remains? Are there any limitations to the use of original remains?

Science online in7.msscience.com/self_check_quiz

Standard—7.3.10: ... although the youngest layers are not always found on top, because of folding, breaking, and uplift of layers.

section 2

Relative Ages of Rocks

as you read

What You'll Learn
- **Describe** methods used to assign relative ages to rock layers.
- **Interpret** gaps in the rock record.
- **Give** an example of how rock layers can be correlated with other rock layers.

Why It's Important
Being able to determine the age of rock layers is important in trying to understand a history of Earth.

Review Vocabulary
sedimentary rock: rock formed when sediments are cemented and compacted or when minerals are precipitated from solution

New Vocabulary
- principle of superposition
- relative age
- unconformity

Superposition

Imagine that you are walking to your favorite store and you happen to notice an interesting car go by. You're not sure what kind it is, but you remember that you read an article about it. You decide to look it up. At home you have a stack of magazines from the past year, as seen in **Figure 11.**

You know that the article you're thinking of came out in the January edition, so it must be near the bottom of the pile. As you dig downward, you find magazines from March, then February. January must be next. How did you know that the January issue of the magazine would be on the bottom? To find the older edition under newer ones, you applied the principle of superposition.

Oldest Rocks on the Bottom According to the **principle of superposition,** in undisturbed layers of rock, the oldest rocks are on the bottom and the rocks become progressively younger toward the top. Why is this the case?

Figure 11 The pile of magazines illustrates the principle of superposition. According to this principle, the oldest rock layer (or magazine) is on the bottom.

Rock Layers Sediment accumulates in horizontal beds, forming layers of sedimentary rock. The first layer to form is on the bottom. The next layer forms on top of the previous one. Because of this, the oldest rocks are at the bottom. However, forces generated by mountain formation sometimes can turn layers over. When layers have been turned upside down, it's necessary to use other clues in the rock layers to determine their original positions and relative ages.

Relative Ages

Now you want to look for another magazine. You're not sure how old it is, but you know it arrived after the January issue. You can find it in the stack by using the principle of relative age.

The **relative age** of something is its age in comparison to the ages of other things. Geologists determine the relative ages of rocks and other structures by examining their places in a sequence. For example, if layers of sedimentary rock are offset by a fault, which is a break in Earth's surface, you know that the layers had to be there before a fault could cut through them. The relative age of the rocks is older than the relative age of the fault. Relative age determination doesn't tell you anything about the age of rock layers in actual years. You don't know if a layer is 100 million or 10,000 years old. You only know that it's younger than the layers below it and older than the fault cutting through it.

Other Clues Help Determination of relative age is easy if the rocks haven't been faulted or turned upside down. For example, look at **Figure 12**. Which layer is the oldest? In cases where rock layers have been disturbed you might have to look for fossils and other clues to date the rocks. If you find a fossil in the top layer that's older than a fossil in a lower layer, you can hypothesize that layers have been turned upside down by folding during mountain building.

Topic: Relative Dating
Visit in7.msscience.com for Web links to information about relative dating of rocks and other materials.

Activity You have found a rare artifact. Make a list of clues you might look for to provide a relative date and explain how each would allow you to approximate the artifact's age.

Indiana Academic Standard Check

7.3.10: ...although the youngest layers are not always found on top, because of folding, breaking, and uplift of layers.

 What are clues that a geologist might use to determine the relative age of a rock?

Figure 12 In a stack of undisturbed sedimentary rocks, the oldest rocks are at the bottom. This stack of rocks can be folded by forces within Earth.

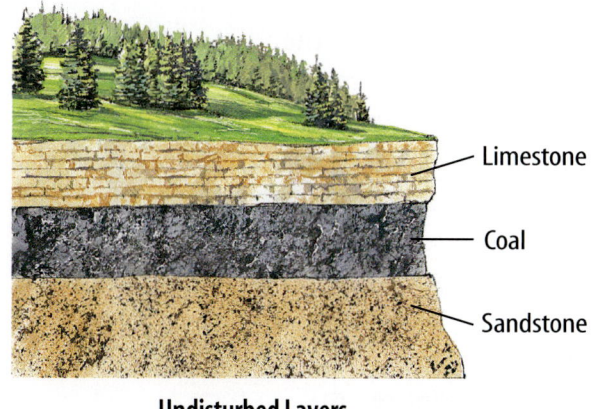

Undisturbed Layers — Limestone, Coal, Sandstone

Folded Layers — Limestone, Coal, Sandstone

Figure 13 An angular unconformity results when horizontal layers cover tilted, eroded layers.

A Sedimentary rocks are deposited originally as horizontal layers.

B The horizontal rock layers are tilted as forces within Earth deform them.

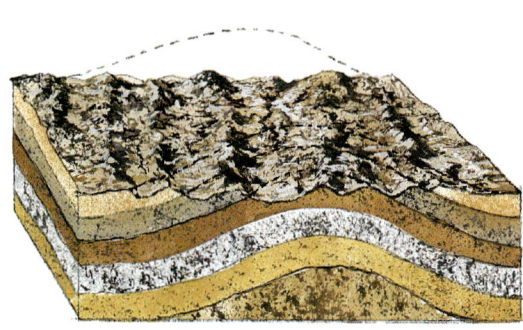

C The tilted layers erode.

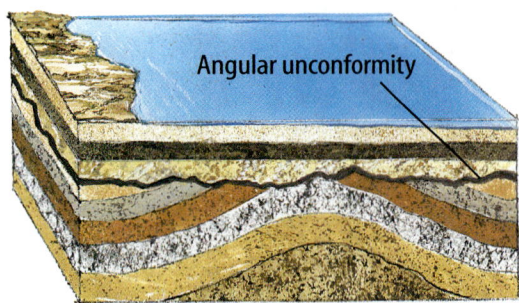

D An angular unconformity results when new layers form on the tilted layers as deposition resumes.

Unconformities

A sequence of rock is a record of past events. But most rock sequences are incomplete—layers are missing. These gaps in rock sequences are called **unconformities** (un kun FOR muh teez). Unconformities develop when agents of erosion such as running water or glaciers remove rock layers by washing or scraping them away.

Reading Check *How do unconformities form?*

Angular Unconformities Horizontal layers of sedimentary rock often are tilted and uplifted. Erosion and weathering then wear down these tilted rock layers. Eventually, younger sediment layers are deposited horizontally on top of the tilted and eroded layers. Geologists call such an unconformity an angular unconformity. **Figure 13** shows how angular unconformities develop.

Disconformity Suppose you're looking at a stack of sedimentary rock layers. They look complete, but layers are missing. If you look closely, you might find an old surface of erosion. This records a time when the rocks were exposed and eroded. Later, younger rocks formed above the erosion surface when deposition of sediment began again. Even though all the layers are parallel, the rock record still has a gap. This type of unconformity is called a disconformity. A disconformity also forms when a period of time passes without any new deposition occurring to form new layers of rock.

Nonconformity Another type of unconformity, called a nonconformity, occurs when metamorphic or igneous rocks are uplifted and eroded. Sedimentary rocks are then deposited on top of this erosion surface. The surface between the two rock types is a nonconformity. Sometimes rock fragments from below are incorporated into sediments deposited above the nonconformity. All types of unconformities are shown in **Figure 14.**

664 CHAPTER 22 Clues to Earth's Past

NATIONAL GEOGRAPHIC VISUALIZING UNCONFORMITIES

Figure 14

An unconformity is a gap in the rock record caused by erosion or a pause in deposition. There are three major kinds of unconformities—nonconformity, angular unconformity, and disconformity.

▲ In a nonconformity, horizontal layers of sedimentary rock overlie older igneous or metamorphic rocks. A nonconformity in Big Bend National Park, Texas, is shown above.

▲ An angular unconformity develops when new horizontal layers of sedimentary rock form on top of older sedimentary rock layers that have been folded by compression. An example of an angular unconformity at Siccar Point in southeastern Scotland is shown above.

▼ A disconformity develops when horizontal rock layers are exposed and eroded, and new horizontal layers of rock are deposited on the eroded surface. The disconformity shown below is in the Grand Canyon.

SECTION 2 Relative Ages of Rocks

Science Online

Topic: Correlating with Index Fossils

Visit in7.msscience.com for Web links to information about using index fossils to match up layers of rock.

Activity Make a chart that shows the rock layers of both the Grand Canyon and Capitol Reef National Park in Utah. For each layer that appears in both parks, list an index fossil you could find to correlate the layers.

Matching Up Rock Layers

Suppose you're studying a layer of sandstone in Bryce Canyon in Utah. Later, when you visit Canyonlands National Park, Utah, you notice that a layer of sandstone there looks just like the sandstone in Bryce Canyon, 250 km away. Above the sandstone in the Canyonlands is a layer of limestone and then another sandstone layer. You return to Bryce Canyon and find the same sequence—sandstone, limestone, and sandstone. What do you infer? It's likely that you're looking at the same layers of rocks in two different locations. **Figure 15** shows that these rocks are parts of huge deposits that covered this whole area of the western United States. Geologists often can match up, or correlate, layers of rocks over great distances.

Evidence Used for Correlation It's not always easy to say that a rock layer exposed in one area is the same as a rock layer exposed in another area. Sometimes it's possible to walk along the layer for kilometers and prove that it's continuous. In other cases, such as at the Canyonlands area and Bryce Canyon as seen in **Figure 16,** the rock layers are exposed only where rivers have cut through overlying layers of rock and sediment. How can you show that the limestone sandwiched between the two layers of sandstone in Canyonlands is likely the same limestone as at Bryce Canyon? One way is to use fossil evidence. If the same types of fossils were found in the limestone layer in both places, it's a good indication that the limestone at each location is the same age, and, therefore, one continuous deposit.

 *How do fossils help show that rocks at different locations belong to the same rock layer?*

Figure 15 These rock layers, exposed at Hopi Point in Grand Canyon National Park, Arizona, can be correlated, or matched up, with rocks from across large areas of the western United States.

666

Canyonlands National Park

Bryce Canyon National Park

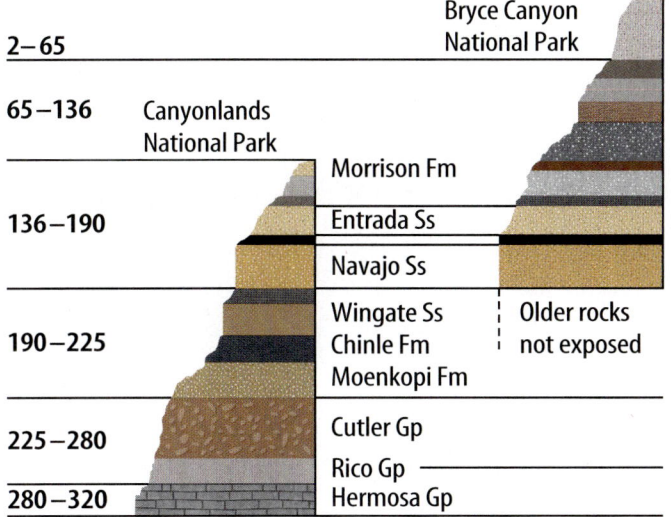

Figure 16 Geologists have named the many rock layers, or formations, in Canyonlands and in Bryce Canyon, Utah. They also have correlated some formations between the two canyons.
List *the labeled layers present at both canyons.*

Can layers of rock be correlated in other ways? Sometimes determining relative ages isn't enough and other dating methods must be used. In Section 3, you'll see how the numerical ages of rocks can be determined and how geologists have used this information to estimate the age of Earth.

section 2 review

Summary

Superposition
- Superposition states that in undisturbed rock, the oldest layers are on the bottom.

Relative Ages
- Rock layers can be ranked by relative age.

Unconformities
- Angular unconformities are new layers deposited over tilted and eroded rock layers.
- Disconformities are gaps in the rock record.
- Nonconformities divide uplifted igneous or metamorphic rock from new sedimentary rock.

Matching Up Rock Layers
- Rocks from different areas may be correlated if they are part of the same layer.

Self Check

1. **Discuss** how to find the oldest paper in a stack of papers.
2. **Explain** the concept of relative age.
3. **Illustrate** a disconformity.
4. **Describe** one way to correlate similar rock layers.
5. **Think Critically** Explain the relationship between the concept of relative age and the principle of superposition.

Applying Skills

6. **Interpret data** to determine the oldest rock bed. A sandstone contains a 400-million-year-old fossil. A shale has fossils that are over 500 million years old. A limestone, below the sandstone, contains fossils between 400 million and 500 million years old. Which rock bed is oldest? Explain.

in7.msscience.com/self_check_quiz

Relative Ages

Which of your two friends is older? To answer this question, you'd need to know their relative ages. You wouldn't need to know the exact age of either of your friends—just who was born first. The same is sometimes true for rock layers.

Real-World Question
Can you determine the relative ages of rock layers?

Goals
- **Interpret** illustrations of rock layers and other geological structures and determine the relative order of events.

Materials
paper   pencil

Procedure
1. **Analyze** Figures **A** and **B**.
2. Make a sketch of **Figure A**. On it, identify the relative age of each rock layer, igneous intrusion, fault, and unconformity. For example, the shale layer is the oldest, so mark it with a 1. Mark the next-oldest feature with a 2, and so on.
3. Repeat step 2 for **Figure B**.

Conclude and Apply

Figure A
1. **Identify** the type of unconformity shown. Is it possible that there were originally more layers of rock than are shown?
2. **Describe** how the rocks above the fault moved in relation to rocks below the fault.
3. **Hypothesize** how the hill on the left side of the figure formed.

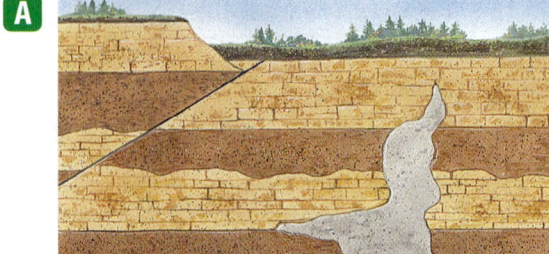

Granite   Limestone
Sandstone   Shale

Figure B
4. Is it possible to conclude if the igneous intrusion on the left is older or younger than the unconformity nearest the surface?
5. **Describe** the relative ages of the two igneous intrusions. How did you know?
6. **Hypothesize** which two layers of rock might have been much thicker in the past.

Compare your results with other students' results. **For more help, refer to the Science Skill Handbook.**

668   CHAPTER 22   Clues to Earth's Past

Standard—7.1.5: Identify some important contributions to the advancement of science…and technology that have been made by different kinds of people, in different cultures, at different times.

section 3
Absolute Ages of Rocks

Absolute Ages

As you sort through your stack of magazines looking for that article about the car you saw, you decide that you need to restack them into a neat pile. By now, they're in a jumble and no longer in order of their relative age, as shown in **Figure 17**. How can you stack them so the oldest are on the bottom and the newest are on top? Fortunately, magazine dates are printed on the cover. Thus, stacking magazines in order is a simple process. Unfortunately, rocks don't have their ages stamped on them. Or do they? **Absolute age** is the age, in years, of a rock or other object. Geologists determine absolute ages by using properties of the atoms that make up materials.

Radioactive Decay

INTEGRATE Physics

Atoms consist of a dense central region called the nucleus, which is surrounded by a cloud of negatively charged particles called electrons. The nucleus is made up of protons, which have a positive charge, and neutrons, which have no electric charge. The number of protons determines the identity of the element, and the number of neutrons determines the form of the element, or isotope. For example, every atom with a single proton is a hydrogen atom. Hydrogen atoms can have no neutrons, a single neutron, or two neutrons. This means that there are three isotopes of hydrogen.

Reading Check What particles make up an atom's nucleus?

Some isotopes are unstable and break down into other isotopes and particles. Sometimes a lot of energy is given off during this process. The process of breaking down is called **radioactive decay.** In the case of hydrogen, atoms with one proton and two neutrons are unstable and tend to break down. Many other elements have stable and unstable isotopes.

as you read

What You'll Learn
- **Identify** how absolute age differs from relative age.
- **Describe** how the half-lives of isotopes are used to determine a rock's age.

Why It's Important
Events in Earth's history can be better understood if their absolute ages are known.

Review Vocabulary
isotopes: atoms of the same element that have different numbers of neutrons

New Vocabulary
- absolute age
- radioactive decay
- half-life
- radiometric dating
- uniformitarianism

Figure 17 The magazines that have been shuffled through no longer illustrate the principle of superposition.

SECTION 3 Absolute Ages of Rocks **669**

Mini LAB

Modeling Carbon-14 Dating

Procedure
1. Count out 80 **red jelly beans.**
2. Remove half the red jelly beans and replace them with **green jelly beans.**
3. Continue replacing half the red jelly beans with green jelly beans until only 5 red jelly beans remain. Count the number of times you replace half the red jelly beans.

Analysis
1. How did this activity model the decay of carbon-14 atoms?
2. How many half lives of carbon-14 did you model during this activity?
3. If the atoms in a bone experienced the same number of half lives as your jelly beans, how old would the bone be?

Alpha and Beta Decay In some isotopes, a neutron breaks down into a proton and an electron. This type of radioactive decay is called beta decay because the electron leaves the atom as a beta particle. The nucleus loses a neutron but gains a proton. When the number of protons in an atom is changed, a new element forms. Other isotopes give off two protons and two neutrons in the form of an alpha particle. Alpha and beta decay are shown in **Figure 18.**

Half-Life In radioactive decay reactions, the parent isotope undergoes radioactive decay. The daughter product is produced by radioactive decay. Each radioactive parent isotope decays to its daughter product at a certain rate. Based on this decay rate, it takes a certain period of time for one half of the parent isotope to decay to its daughter product. The **half-life** of an isotope is the time it takes for half of the atoms in the isotope to decay. For example, the half-life of carbon-14 is 5,730 years. So it will take 5,730 years for half of the carbon-14 atoms in an object to change into nitrogen-14 atoms. You might guess that in another 5,730 years, all of the remaining carbon-14 atoms will decay to nitrogen-14. However, this is not the case. Only half of the atoms of carbon-14 remaining after the first 5,730 years will decay during the second 5,730 years. So, after two half-lives, one fourth of the original carbon-14 atoms still remain. Half of them will decay during another 5,730 years. After three half-lives, one eighth of the original carbon-14 atoms still remain. After many half-lives, such a small amount of the parent isotope remains that it might not be measurable.

Figure 18 In beta decay, a neutron changes into a proton by giving off an electron. This electron has a lot of energy and is called a beta particle.

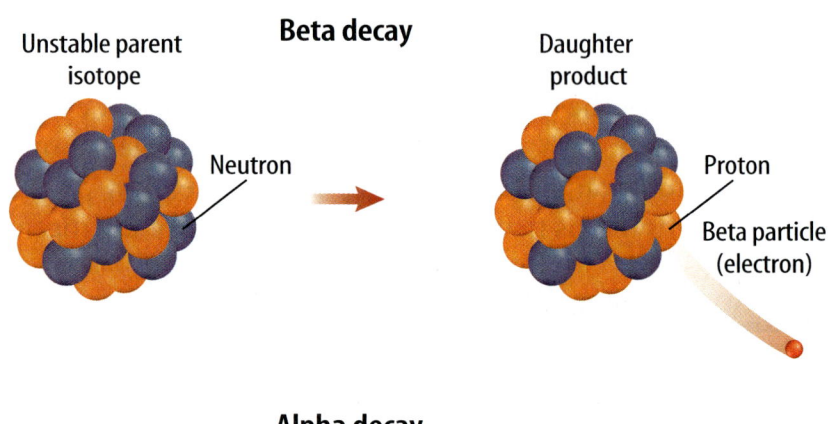

In the process of alpha decay, an unstable parent isotope nucleus gives off an alpha particle and changes into a new daughter product. Alpha particles contain two neutrons and two protons.

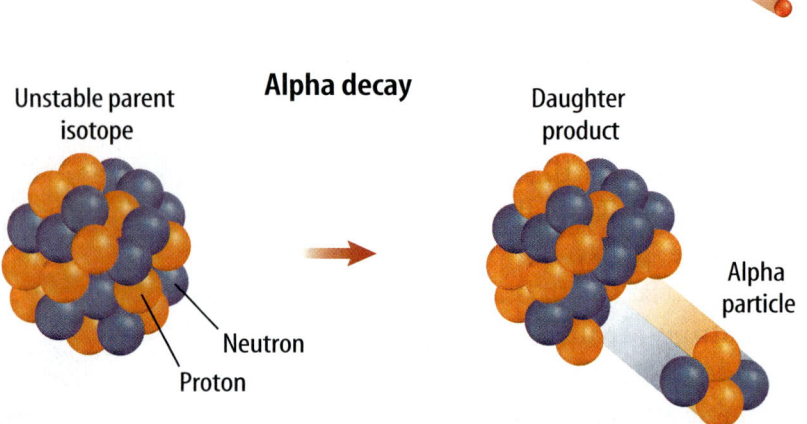

670 CHAPTER 22 Clues to Earth's Past

Radiometric Ages

Decay of radioactive isotopes is like a clock keeping track of time that has passed since rocks have formed. As time passes, the amount of parent isotope in a rock decreases as the amount of daughter product increases, as in **Figure 19**. By measuring the ratio of parent isotope to daughter product in a mineral and by knowing the half-life of the parent, in many cases you can calculate the absolute age of a rock. This process is called **radiometric dating**.

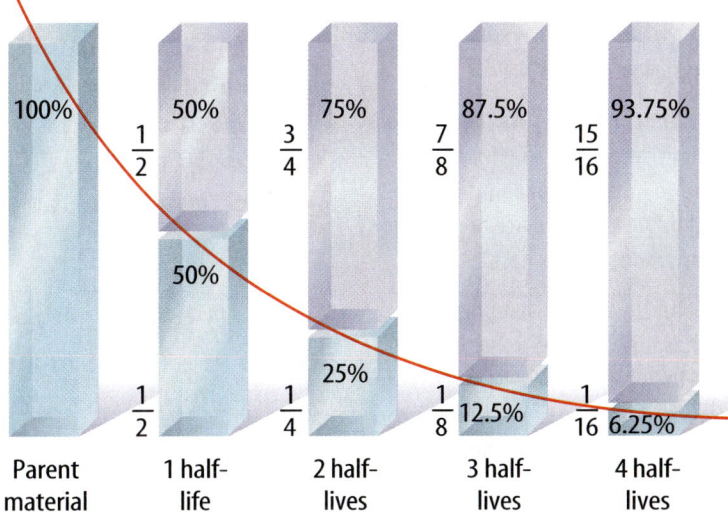

A scientist must decide which parent isotope to use when measuring the age of a rock. If the object to be dated seems old, then the geologist will use an isotope with a long half-life. The half-life for the decay of potassium-40 to argon-40 is 1.25 billion years. As a result, this isotope can be used to date rocks that are many millions of years old. To avoid error, conditions must be met for the ratios to give a correct indication of age. For example, the rock being studied must still retain all of the argon-40 that was produced by the decay of potassium-40. Also, it cannot contain any contamination of daughter product from other sources. Potassium-argon dating is good for rocks containing potassium, but what about other things?

Figure 19 During each half-life, one half of the parent material decays to the daughter product. **Explain** how one uses both parent and daughter material to estimate age.

Radiocarbon Dating Carbon-14 is useful for dating bones, wood, and charcoal up to 75,000 years old. Living things take in carbon from the environment to build their bodies. Most of that carbon is carbon-12, but some is carbon-14, and the ratio of these two isotopes in the environment is always the same. After the organism dies, the carbon-14 slowly decays. By determining the amounts of the isotopes in a sample, scientists can evaluate how much the isotope ratio in the sample differs from that in the environment. For example, during much of human history, people built campfires. The wood from these fires often is preserved as charcoal. Scientists can determine the amount of carbon-14 remaining in a sample of charcoal by measuring the amount of radiation emitted by the carbon-14 isotope in labs like the one in **Figure 20**. Once they know the amount of carbon-14 in a charcoal sample, scientists can determine the age of the wood used to make the fire.

Figure 20 Radiometric ages are determined in labs like this one.

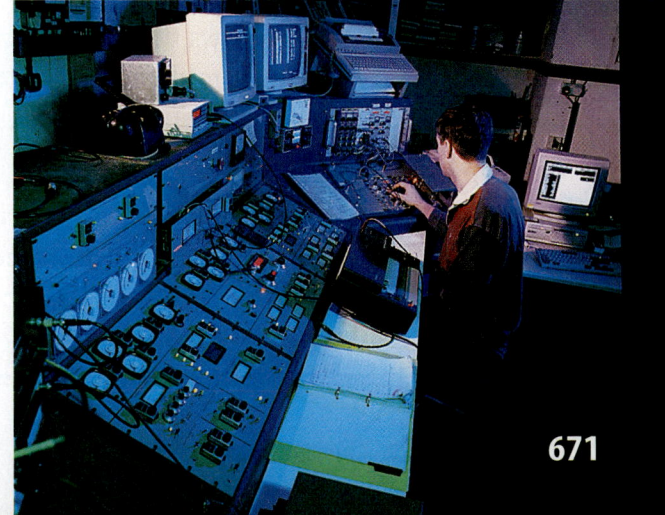

Topic: Isotopes in Ice Cores
Visit in7.msscience.com for Web links to information about ice cores and how isotopes in ice are used to learn about Earth's past.

Activity Prepare a report that shows how isotopes in ice cores can tell us about past Earth environments. Include how these findings can help us understand today's climate.

Age Determinations Aside from carbon-14 dating, rocks that can be radiometrically dated are mostly igneous and metamorphic rocks. Most sedimentary rocks cannot be dated by this method. This is because many sedimentary rocks are made up of particles eroded from older rocks. Dating these pieces only gives the age of the preexisting rock from which it came.

The Oldest Known Rocks Radiometric dating has been used to date the oldest rocks on Earth. These rocks are about 3.96 billion years old. By determining the age of meteorites, and using other evidence, scientists have estimated the age of Earth to be about 4.5 billion years. Earth rocks greater than 3.96 billion years old probably were eroded or changed by heat and pressure.

 Why can't most sedimentary rocks be dated radiometrically?

Applying Science

When did the Iceman die?

Carbon-14 dating has been used to date charcoal, wood, bones, mummies from Egypt and Peru, the Dead Sea Scrolls, and the Italian Iceman. The Iceman was found in 1991 in the Italian Alps, near the Austrian border. Based on carbon-14 analysis, scientists determined that the Iceman is 5,300 years old. Determine approximately in what year the Iceman died.

Half-Life of Carbon-14

Percent Carbon-14	Years Passed
100	0
50	5,730
25	11,460
12.5	17,190
6.25	22,920
3.125	

Reconstruction of Iceman

Identifying the Problem

The half-life chart shows the decay of carbon-14 over time. Half-life is the time it takes for half of a sample to decay. Fill in the years passed when only 3.125 percent of carbon-14 remain. Is there a point at which no carbon-14 would be present? Explain.

Solving the Problem

1. Estimate, using the data table, how much carbon-14 still was present in the Iceman's body that allowed scientists to determine his age.
2. If you had an artifact that originally contained 10.0 g of carbon-14, how many grams would remain after 17,190 years?

672 CHAPTER 22 Clues to Earth's Past

Uniformitarianism

Can you imagine trying to determine the age of Earth without some of the information you know today? Before the discovery of radiometric dating, many people estimated that Earth is only a few thousand years old. But in the 1700s, Scottish scientist James Hutton estimated that Earth is much older. He used the principle of **uniformitarianism.** This principle states that Earth processes occurring today are similar to those that occurred in the past. Hutton's principle is often paraphrased as "the present is the key to the past."

Hutton observed that the processes that changed the landscape around him were slow, and he inferred that they were just as slow throughout Earth's history. Hutton hypothesized that it took much longer than a few thousand years to form the layers of rock around him and to erode mountains that once stood kilometers high. **Figure 21** shows Hutton's native Scotland, a region shaped by millions of years of geologic processes.

Today, scientists recognize that Earth has been shaped by two types of change: slow, everyday processes that take place over millions of years, and violent, unusual events such as the collision of a comet or asteroid about 65 million years ago that might have caused the extinction of the dinosaurs.

Figure 21 The rugged highlands of Scotland were shaped by erosion and uplift.

section 3 review

Summary

Absolute Ages
- The absolute age is the actual age of an object.

Radioactive Decay
- Some isotopes are unstable and decay into other isotopes and particles.
- Decay is measured in half-lives, the time it takes for half of a given isotope to decay.

Radiometric Ages
- By measuring the ratio of parent isotope to daughter product, one can determine the absolute age of a rock.
- Living organisms less than 75,000 years old can be dated using carbon-14.

Uniformitarianism
- Processes observable today are the same as the processes that took place in the past.

Self Check

1. **Evaluate** the age of rocks. You find three undisturbed rock layers. The middle layer is 120 million years old. What can you say about the ages of the layers above and below it?
2. **Determine** the age of a fossil if it had only one eighth of its original carbon-14 content remaining.
3. **Explain** the concept of uniformitarianism.
4. **Describe** how radioactive isotopes decay.
5. **Think Critically** Why can't scientists use carbon-14 to determine the age of an igneous rock?

Applying Math

6. **Make and use a table** that shows the amount of parent material of a radioactive element that is left after four half-lives if the original parent material had a mass of 100 g.

Model and Invent

Trace Fossils

Goals
- **Construct** a model of trace fossils.
- **Describe** the information that you can learn from looking at your model.

Possible Materials
construction paper
wire
plastic (a fairly rigid type)
scissors
plaster of paris
toothpicks
sturdy cardboard
clay
pipe cleaners
glue

Safety Precautions

Real-World Question

Trace fossils can tell you a lot about the activities of organisms that left them. They can tell you how an organism fed or what kind of home it had. How can you model trace fossils that can provide information about the behavior of organisms? What materials can you use to model trace fossils? What types of behavior could you show with your trace fossil model?

Make a Model

1. **Decide** how you are going to make your model. What materials will you need?
2. **Decide** what types of activities you will demonstrate with your model. Were the organisms feeding? Resting? Traveling? Were they predators? Prey? How will your model indicate the activities you chose?
3. What is the setting of your model? Are you modeling the organism's home? Feeding areas? Is your model on land or water? How can the setting affect the way you build your model?
4. Will you only show trace fossils from a single species or multiple species? If you include more than one species, how will you provide evidence of any interaction between the species?

Check the Model Plans

1. Compare your plans with those of others in your class. Did other groups mention details that you had forgotten to think about? Are there any changes you would like to make to your plan before you continue?
2. Make sure your teacher approves your plan before you continue.

674 **CHAPTER 22** Clues to Earth's Past

Using Scientific Methods

⏵ Test Your Model

1. Following your plan, construct your model of trace fossils.
2. Have you included evidence of all the behaviors you intended to model?

⏵ Analyze Your Data

1. **Evaluate** Now that your model is complete, do you think that it adequately shows the behaviors you planned to demonstrate? Is there anything that you think you might want to do differently if you were going to make the model again?
2. **Describe** how using different kinds of materials might have affected your model. Can you think of other materials that would have allowed you to show more detail than you did?

⏵ Conclude and Apply

1. **Compare and contrast** your model of trace fossils with trace fossils left by real organisms. Is one more easily interpreted than the other? Explain.
2. **List** behaviors that might not leave any trace fossils. Explain.

Communicating Your Data

Ask other students in your class or another class to look at your model and describe what information they can learn from the trace fossils. Did their interpretations agree with what you intended to show?

LAB **675**

Oops! Accidents in SCIENCE

SOMETIMES GREAT DISCOVERIES HAPPEN BY ACCIDENT!

The World's Oldest Fish Story
A catch-of-the-day set science on its ears

[Coelacanth image with labels: Camouflage marks, First dorsal fin, Second dorsal fin, Pectoral fin, Anal fin, Pelvic fin]

Some scientists call the coelacanth "Old Four Legs." It got its nickname because the fish has paired fins that look something like legs.

On a December day in 1938, just before Christmas, Marjorie Courtenay-Latimer went to say hello to her friends on board a fishing boat that had just returned to port in South Africa. Courtenay-Latimer, who worked at a museum, often went aboard her friends' ship to check out the catch. On this visit, she received a surprise Christmas present—an odd-looking fish. As soon as the woman spotted its strange blue fins among the piles of sharks and rays, she knew it was special.

Courtenay-Latimer took the fish back to her museum to study it. "It was the most beautiful fish I had ever seen, five feet long, and a pale mauve blue with iridescent silver markings," she later wrote. Courtenay-Latimer sketched it and sent the drawing to a friend of hers, J. L. B. Smith.

Smith was a chemistry teacher who was passionate about fish. After a time, he realized it was a coelacanth (SEE luh kanth). Fish experts knew that coelacanths had first appeared on Earth 400 million years ago. But the experts thought the fish were extinct. People had found fossils of coelacanths, but no one had seen one alive. It was assumed that the last coelacanth species had died out 65 million years ago. They were wrong. The ship's crew had caught one by accident.

Smith figured there might be more living coelacanths. So he decided to offer a reward for anyone who could find a living specimen. After 14 years of silence, a report came in that a coelacanth had been caught off the east coast of Africa.

Today, scientists know that there are at least several hundred coelacanths living in the Indian Ocean, just east of central Africa. Many of these fish live near the Comoros Islands. The coelacanths live in underwater caves during the day but move out at night to feed. The rare fish are now a protected species. With any luck, they will survive for another hundred million years.

Write a short essay describing the discovery of the coelacanths and describe the reaction of scientists to this discovery.

Science online
For more information, visit in7.msscience.com/oops

chapter 22 Study Guide

Reviewing Main Ideas

Section 1 Fossils

1. Fossils are more likely to form if hard parts of the dead organisms are buried quickly.

2. Some fossils form when original materials that made up the organisms are replaced with minerals. Other fossils form when remains are subjected to heat and pressure, leaving only a carbon film behind. Some fossils are the tracks or traces left by ancient organisms.

Section 2 Relative Ages of Rocks

1. The principle of superposition states that, in undisturbed layers, older rocks lie underneath younger rocks.

2. Unconformities, or gaps in the rock record, are due to erosion or periods of time during which no deposition occurred.

3. Rock layers can be correlated using rock types and fossils.

Section 3 Absolute Ages of Rocks

1. Absolute dating provides an age in years for the rocks.

2. The half-life of a radioactive isotope is the time it takes for half of the atoms of the isotope to decay into another isotope.

Visualizing Main Ideas

Copy and complete the following concept map on fossils.

```
                        Fossils
            remains of  /    \  evidence of activities
            organisms  /      \  of organisms
                      /        \
                Body fossils    Trace fossils
               /  |    |  \      /         \
    types of remains  types of remains   kinds of evidence  kinds of evidence
      /        |          |        \         |                 |
  Original   Molds    Carbon films  ___    ___              Trails      Burrows
   parts   and casts
     |        |           |          |
  preserved preserved  preserved  preserved
     by       by          by        by
     |                               |
  Frozen                          Hollow
  in ice or                       spaces
  trapped in                      filled with
  amber                           minerals
```

CHAPTER STUDY GUIDE

chapter 22 Review

Using Vocabulary

absolute age p. 669
carbon film p. 656
cast p. 657
fossil p. 655
half-life p. 670
index fossil p. 659
mold p. 657
permineralized remains p. 656
principle of superposition p. 662
radioactive decay p. 669
radiometric dating p. 671
relative age p. 663
unconformity p. 664
uniformitarianism p. 673

Write an original sentence using the vocabulary word to which each phrase refers.

1. thin film of carbon preserved as a fossil
2. older rocks lie under younger rocks
3. processes occur today as they did in the past
4. gap in the rock record
5. time needed for half the atoms to decay
6. fossil organism that lived for a short time
7. gives the age of rocks in years
8. minerals fill spaces inside fossil
9. a copy of a fossil produced by filling a mold with sediment or crystals

Checking Concepts

Choose the word or phrase that best answers the question.

10. What is any evidence of ancient life called?
    A) half-life C) unconformity
    B) fossil D) disconformity

11. Which of the following conditions makes fossil formation more likely?
    A) buried slowly
    B) attacked by scavengers
    C) made of hard parts
    D) composed of soft parts

12. What are cavities left in rocks when a shell or bone dissolves called?
    A) casts C) original remains
    B) molds D) carbon films

13. To say "the present is the key to the past" is a way to describe which of the following principles?
    A) superposition C) radioactivity
    B) succession D) uniformitarianism

14. A fault can be useful in determining which of the following for a group of rocks?
    A) absolute age C) radiometric age
    B) index age D) relative age

15. Which of the following is an unconformity between parallel rock layers?
    A) angular unconformity
    B) fault
    C) disconformity
    D) nonconformity

Use the illustration below to answer question 16.

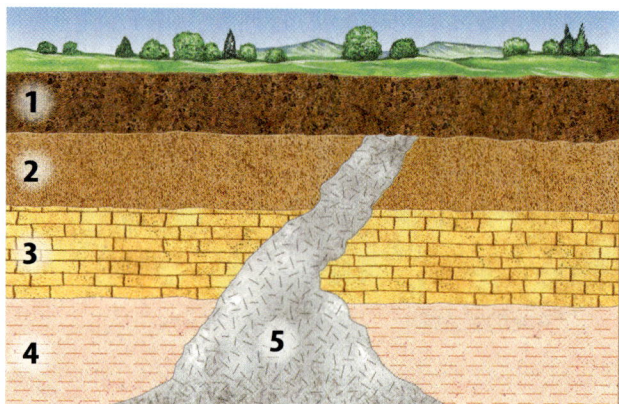

16. Which of the following puts the layers in order from oldest to youngest?
    A) 5-4-3-2-1 C) 2-3-4-5-1
    B) 1-2-3-4-5 D) 4-3-2-5-1

17. Which process forms new elements?
    A) superposition
    B) uniformitarianism
    C) permineralization
    D) radioactive decay

678 CHAPTER REVIEW

chapter 22 Review

Thinking Critically

18. **Explain** why the fossil record of life on Earth is incomplete. Give some reasons why.

19. **Infer** Suppose a lava flow was found between two sedimentary rock layers. How could you use the lava flow to learn about the ages of the sedimentary rock layers? (Hint: Most lava contains radioactive isotopes.)

20. **Infer** Suppose you're correlating rock layers in the western United States. You find a layer of volcanic ash deposits. How can this layer help you in your correlation over a large area?

21. **Recognize Cause and Effect** Explain how some woolly mammoths could have been preserved intact in frozen ground. What conditions must have persisted since the deaths of these animals?

22. **Classify** each of the following fossils in the correct category in the table below: *dinosaur footprint, worm burrow, dinosaur skull, insect in amber, fossil woodpecker hole,* and *fish tooth.*

Types of Fossils	
Trace Fossils	Body Fossils
Do not write in this book.	

23. **Compare and contrast** the three different kinds of unconformities. Draw sketches of each that illustrate the features that identify them.

24. **Describe** how relative and absolute ages differ. How might both be used to establish ages in a series of rock layers?

25. **Discuss** uniformitarianism in the following scenario. You find a shell on the beach, and a friend remembers seeing a similar fossil while hiking in the mountains. What does this suggest about the past environment of the mountain?

Performance Activities

26. **Illustrate** Create a model that allows you to explain how to establish the relative ages of rock layers.

27. **Use a Classification System** Start your own fossil collection. Label each find as to type, approximate age, and the place where it was found. Most state geological surveys can provide you with reference materials on local fossils.

Applying Math

28. **Calculate** how many half lives have passed in a rock containing one-eighth the original radioactive material and seven-eighths of the daughter product.

Use the graphs below to answer question 29.

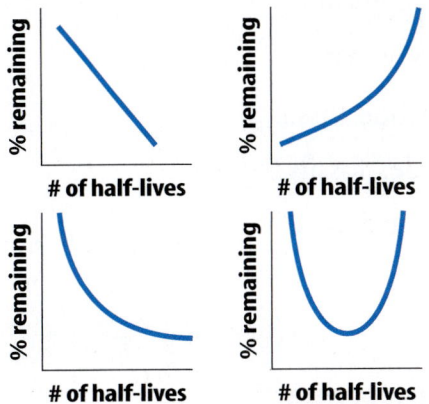

29. **Interpret Data** Which of the above curves best illustrates radioactive decay?

chapter 22 Indiana

 The assessed Indiana standard appears above the question.

Record your answers on the answer sheet provided by your teacher or on a sheet of paper.

Part 1 Multiple Choice

1. The photo below shows a kind of fossil.

   Which type of fossil preservation is this?
   A carbon film
   B original remain
   C permineralized remain
   D trace fossil

7.3.10

2. Which are the remains of species that existed on Earth for relatively short periods, and were abundant and widespread geographically?
   A body fossils
   B carbon fossils
   C index fossils
   D trace fossils

Test-Taking Tip

Check It Again Double check your answers before turning in the test.

3. Which separates tilted rocks below from horizontal rocks above?
   A angular unconformity
   B conformity
   C disconformity
   D nonconformity

The illustration below shows the strata at a certain locale.

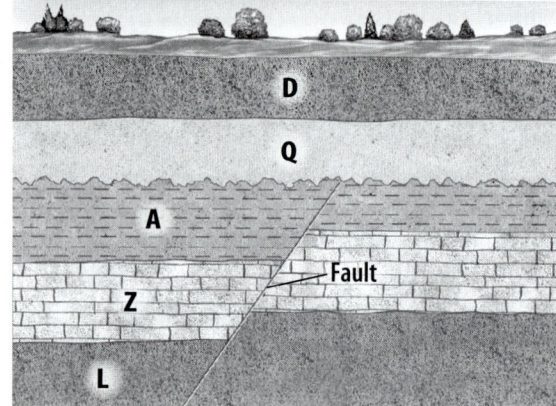

4. Which sequence of letters describes the rock layers from oldest to youngest?
   A D, Q, A, Z, L
   B L, Z, A, Q, D
   C Q, D, L, Z, A
   D Z, L, A, D, Q

5. What does the wavy line between layers A and Q in the illustration above represent?
   A an angular unconformity
   B a disconformity
   C an erosion
   D a fault

680 INDIANA

Standards Review

7.3.10

6. Which means matching up rock layers in different places?

- A absolute dating
- B correlation
- C relative dating
- D uniformitarianism

The table below shows the percent remaining parent isotope per half-life of a radioisotope.

Number of Half-lives	Parent Isotope Remaining (%)
1	100
2	X
3	25
4	12.5
5	Y

7. Which replaces the letter X?

- A 40
- B 50
- C 62.5
- D 75

8. Which replaces the letter Y in the table above?

- A 0
- B 2.5
- C 3.13
- D 6.25

Part 2 Constructed Response

7.3.8

9. Why are fossils important? What information do they provide?

10. How could a fossil of an organism that lived in ocean water millions of years ago be found in the middle of North America?

11. Below is a graph showing the relationship between preservation potential and burial rate.

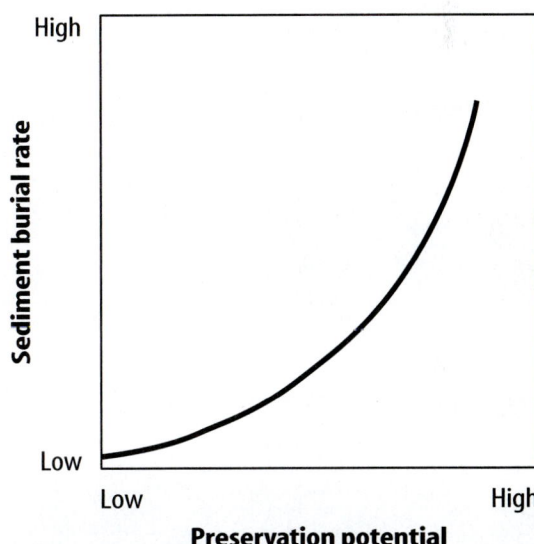

Relationship Between Sediment Burial Rate and Potential for Remains to Become Fossils

How does the potential for remains to be preserved change as the rate of burial by sediment increases? Why do you think this relationship exists?

7.3.8

12. What other factors affect the potential for the remains of organisms to become fossils?

STANDARDS REVIEW **681**

Student Resources

Student Resources

CONTENTS

Science Skill Handbook 684
Scientific Methods 684
   Identify a Question 684
   Gather and Organize
     Information 684
   Form a Hypothesis 687
   Test the Hypothesis 688
   Collect Data 688
   Analyze the Data 691
   Draw Conclusions 692
   Communicate 692
Safety Symbols 693
Safety in the Science Laboratory 694
   General Safety Rules 694
   Prevent Accidents 694
   Laboratory Work 694
   Laboratory Cleanup 695
   Emergencies 695

Extra Try at Home Labs 696
   Your Daily Drink 696
   Cell Sizes 696
   Expanding Eggs 697
   Putting Down Roots 697
   Vitamin Search 698
   Acid Defense 698
   Feeding Frenzy 699
   UV Watch 699
   Comparing Atom Sizes 700
   A Good Mix? 700
   Measuring Momentum 701
   Friction in Traffic 701
   The Heat is On 702
   Disappearing Dots 702
   Pattern Counting 703
   Big Stars 703
   Panning Minerals 704
   Changing Rocks 704
   Continental Movement 705
   Earth's Layers 705
   Getting Warmer 706
   Making Burrows 706

Technology Skill Handbook ...707
Computer Skills 707
   Use a Word Processing Program ...707
   Use a Database 708
   Use the Internet 708
   Use a Spreadsheet 709
   Use Graphics Software 709
Presentation Skills 710
   Develop Multimedia
     Presentations 710
   Computer Presentations 710

Math Skill Handbook 711
Math Review 711
   Use Fractions 711
   Use Ratios 714
   Use Decimals 714
   Use Proportions 715
   Use Percentages 716
   Solve One-Step Equations 716
   Use Statistics 717
   Use Geometry 718
Science Applications 721
   Measure in SI 721
   Dimensional Analysis 721
   Precision and Significant Digits ...723
   Scientific Notation 723
   Make and Use Graphs 724

Reference Handbooks 726
Use and Care of a Microscope 726
Rocks 727
Minerals 728
Physical Science Reference Tables ...730
Periodic Table of the Elements 732

English/Spanish Glossary 734

Index 755

Credits 774

Scientific Methods

Scientists use an orderly approach called the scientific method to solve problems. This includes organizing and recording data so others can understand them. Scientists use many variations in this method when they solve problems.

Identify a Question

The first step in a scientific investigation or experiment is to identify a question to be answered or a problem to be solved. For example, you might ask which gasoline is the most efficient.

Gather and Organize Information

After you have identified your question, begin gathering and organizing information. There are many ways to gather information, such as researching in a library, interviewing those knowledgeable about the subject, testing and working in the laboratory and field. Fieldwork is investigations and observations done outside of a laboratory.

Researching Information Before moving in a new direction, it is important to gather the information that already is known about the subject. Start by asking yourself questions to determine exactly what you need to know. Then you will look for the information in various reference sources, like the student is doing in **Figure 1.** Some sources may include textbooks, encyclopedias, government documents, professional journals, science magazines, and the Internet. Always list the sources of your information.

Figure 1 The Internet can be a valuable research tool.

Evaluate Sources of Information Not all sources of information are reliable. You should evaluate all of your sources of information, and use only those you know to be dependable. For example, if you are researching ways to make homes more energy efficient, a site written by the U.S. Department of Energy would be more reliable than a site written by a company that is trying to sell a new type of weatherproofing material. Also, remember that research always is changing. Consult the most current resources available to you. For example, a 1985 resource about saving energy would not reflect the most recent findings.

Sometimes scientists use data that they did not collect themselves, or conclusions drawn by other researchers. This data must be evaluated carefully. Ask questions about how the data were obtained, if the investigation was carried out properly, and if it has been duplicated exactly with the same results. Would you reach the same conclusion from the data? Only when you have confidence in the data can you believe it is true and feel comfortable using it.

684 STUDENT RESOURCES

Science Skill Handbook

Interpret Scientific Illustrations As you research a topic in science, you will see drawings, diagrams, and photographs to help you understand what you read. Some illustrations are included to help you understand an idea that you can't see easily by yourself, like the tiny particles in an atom in **Figure 2**. A drawing helps many people to remember details more easily and provides examples that clarify difficult concepts or give additional information about the topic you are studying. Most illustrations have labels or a caption to identify or to provide more information.

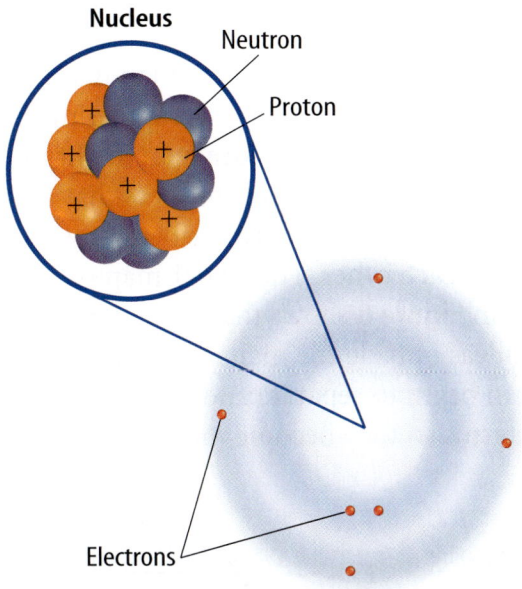

Figure 2 This drawing shows an atom of carbon with its six protons, six neutrons, and six electrons.

Concept Maps One way to organize data is to draw a diagram that shows relationships among ideas (or concepts). A concept map can help make the meanings of ideas and terms more clear, and help you understand and remember what you are studying. Concept maps are useful for breaking large concepts down into smaller parts, making learning easier.

Network Tree A type of concept map that not only shows a relationship, but how the concepts are related is a network tree, shown in **Figure 3**. In a network tree, the words are written in the ovals, while the description of the type of relationship is written across the connecting lines.

When constructing a network tree, write down the topic and all major topics on separate pieces of paper or notecards. Then arrange them in order from general to specific. Branch the related concepts from the major concept and describe the relationship on the connecting line. Continue to more specific concepts until finished.

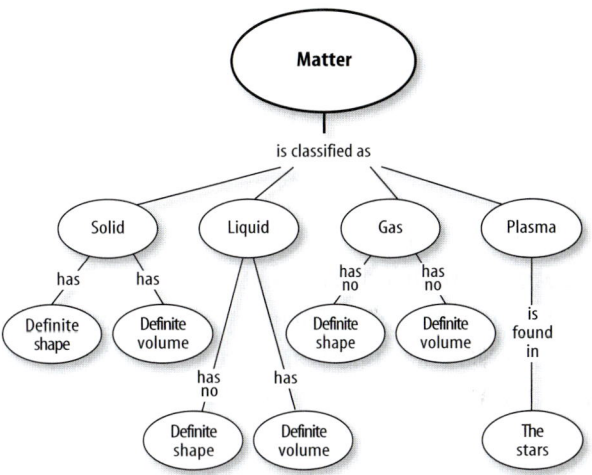

Figure 3 A network tree shows how concepts or objects are related.

Events Chain Another type of concept map is an events chain. Sometimes called a flow chart, it models the order or sequence of items. An events chain can be used to describe a sequence of events, the steps in a procedure, or the stages of a process.

When making an events chain, first find the one event that starts the chain. This event is called the initiating event. Then, find the next event and continue until the outcome is reached, as shown in **Figure 4**.

SCIENCE SKILL HANDBOOK 685

Science Skill Handbook

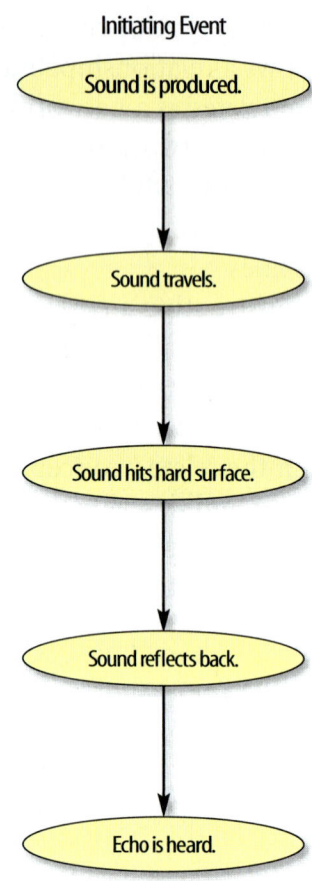

Figure 4 Events-chain concept maps show the order of steps in a process or event. This concept map shows how a sound makes an echo.

Cycle Map A specific type of events chain is a cycle map. It is used when the series of events do not produce a final outcome, but instead relate back to the beginning event, such as in **Figure 5**. Therefore, the cycle repeats itself.

To make a cycle map, first decide what event is the beginning event. This is also called the initiating event. Then list the next events in the order that they occur, with the last event relating back to the initiating event. Words can be written between the events that describe what happens from one event to the next. The number of events in a cycle map can vary, but usually contain three or more events.

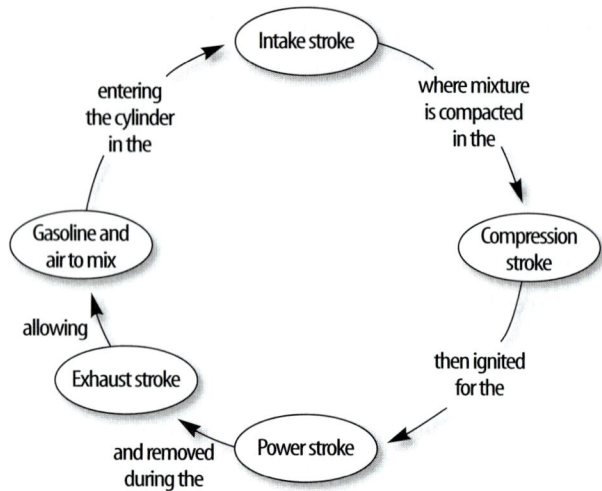

Figure 5 A cycle map shows events that occur in a cycle.

Spider Map A type of concept map that you can use for brainstorming is the spider map. When you have a central idea, you might find that you have a jumble of ideas that relate to it but are not necessarily clearly related to each other. The spider map on sound in **Figure 6** shows that if you write these ideas outside the main concept, then you can begin to separate and group unrelated terms so they become more useful.

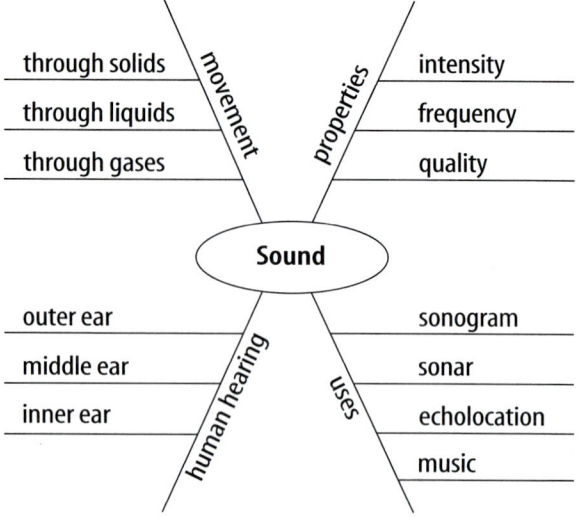

Figure 6 A spider map allows you to list ideas that relate to a central topic but not necessarily to one another.

686 STUDENT RESOURCES

Science Skill Handbook

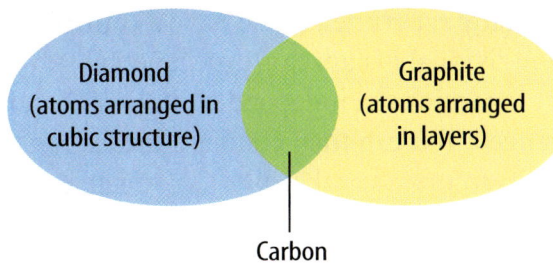

Figure 7 This Venn diagram compares and contrasts two substances made from carbon.

Venn Diagram To illustrate how two subjects compare and contrast you can use a Venn diagram. You can see the characteristics that the subjects have in common and those that they do not, shown in **Figure 7.**

To create a Venn diagram, draw two overlapping ovals that that are big enough to write in. List the characteristics unique to one subject in one oval, and the characteristics of the other subject in the other oval. The characteristics in common are listed in the overlapping section.

Make and Use Tables One way to organize information so it is easier to understand is to use a table. Tables can contain numbers, words, or both.

To make a table, list the items to be compared in the first column and the characteristics to be compared in the first row. The title should clearly indicate the content of the table, and the column or row heads should be clear. Notice that in **Table 1** the units are included.

Table 1 Recyclables Collected During Week			
Day of Week	Paper (kg)	Aluminum (kg)	Glass (kg)
Monday	5.0	4.0	12.0
Wednesday	4.0	1.0	10.0
Friday	2.5	2.0	10.0

Make a Model One way to help you better understand the parts of a structure, the way a process works, or to show things too large or small for viewing is to make a model. For example, an atomic model made of a plastic-ball nucleus and pipe-cleaner electron shells can help you visualize how the parts of an atom relate to each other. Other types of models can by devised on a computer or represented by equations.

Form a Hypothesis

A possible explanation based on previous knowledge and observations is called a hypothesis. After researching gasoline types and recalling previous experiences in your family's car you form a hypothesis—our car runs more efficiently because we use premium gasoline. To be valid, a hypothesis has to be something you can test by using an investigation.

Predict When you apply a hypothesis to a specific situation, you predict something about that situation. A prediction makes a statement in advance, based on prior observation, experience, or scientific reasoning. People use predictions to make everyday decisions. Scientists test predictions by performing investigations. Based on previous observations and experiences, you might form a prediction that cars are more efficient with premium gasoline. The prediction can be tested in an investigation.

Design an Experiment A scientist needs to make many decisions before beginning an investigation. Some of these include: how to carry out the investigation, what steps to follow, how to record the data, and how the investigation will answer the question. It also is important to address any safety concerns.

SCIENCE SKILL HANDBOOK 687

Science Skill Handbook

Test the Hypothesis

Now that you have formed your hypothesis, you need to test it. Using an investigation, you will make observations and collect data, or information. This data might either support or not support your hypothesis. Scientists collect and organize data as numbers and descriptions.

Follow a Procedure In order to know what materials to use, as well as how and in what order to use them, you must follow a procedure. **Figure 8** shows a procedure you might follow to test your hypothesis.

> **Procedure**
> 1. Use regular gasoline for two weeks.
> 2. Record the number of kilometers between fill-ups and the amount of gasoline used.
> 3. Switch to premium gasoline for two weeks.
> 4. Record the number of kilometers between fill-ups and the amount of gasoline used.

Figure 8 A procedure tells you what to do step by step.

Identify and Manipulate Variables and Controls In any experiment, it is important to keep everything the same except for the item you are testing. The one factor you change is called the independent variable. The change that results is the dependent variable. Make sure you have only one independent variable, to assure yourself of the cause of the changes you observe in the dependent variable. For example, in your gasoline experiment the type of fuel is the independent variable. The dependent variable is the efficiency.

Many experiments also have a control—an individual instance or experimental subject for which the independent variable is not changed. You can then compare the test results to the control results. To design a control you can have two cars of the same type. The control car uses regular gasoline for four weeks. After you are done with the test, you can compare the experimental results to the control results.

Collect Data

Whether you are carrying out an investigation or a short observational experiment, you will collect data, as shown in **Figure 9.** Scientists collect data as numbers and descriptions and organize it in specific ways.

Observe Scientists observe items and events, then record what they see. When they use only words to describe an observation, it is called qualitative data. Scientists' observations also can describe how much there is of something. These observations use numbers, as well as words, in the description and are called quantitative data. For example, if a sample of the element gold is described as being "shiny and very dense" the data are qualitative. Quantitative data on this sample of gold might include "a mass of 30 g and a density of 19.3 g/cm^3."

Figure 9 Collecting data is one way to gather information directly.

688 STUDENT RESOURCES

Science Skill Handbook

Figure 10 Record data neatly and clearly so it is easy to understand.

When you make observations you should examine the entire object or situation first, and then look carefully for details. It is important to record observations accurately and completely. Always record your notes immediately as you make them, so you do not miss details or make a mistake when recording results from memory. Never put unidentified observations on scraps of paper. Instead they should be recorded in a notebook, like the one in **Figure 10.** Write your data neatly so you can easily read it later. At each point in the experiment, record your observations and label them. That way, you will not have to determine what the figures mean when you look at your notes later. Set up any tables that you will need to use ahead of time, so you can record any observations right away. Remember to avoid bias when collecting data by not including personal thoughts when you record observations. Record only what you observe.

Estimate Scientific work also involves estimating. To estimate is to make a judgment about the size or the number of something without measuring or counting. This is important when the number or size of an object or population is too large or too difficult to accurately count or measure.

Sample Scientists may use a sample or a portion of the total number as a type of estimation. To sample is to take a small, representative portion of the objects or organisms of a population for research. By making careful observations or manipulating variables within that portion of the group, information is discovered and conclusions are drawn that might apply to the whole population. A poorly chosen sample can be unrepresentative of the whole. If you were trying to determine the rainfall in an area, it would not be best to take a rainfall sample from under a tree.

Measure You use measurements everyday. Scientists also take measurements when collecting data. When taking measurements, it is important to know how to use measuring tools properly. Accuracy also is important.

Length To measure length, the distance between two points, scientists use meters. Smaller measurements might be measured in centimeters or millimeters.

Length is measured using a metric ruler or meter stick. When using a metric ruler, line up the 0-cm mark with the end of the object being measured and read the number of the unit where the object ends. Look at the metric ruler shown in **Figure 11.** The centimeter lines are the long, numbered lines, and the shorter lines are millimeter lines. In this instance, the length would be 4.50 cm.

Figure 11 This metric ruler has centimeter and millimeter divisions.

SCIENCE SKILL HANDBOOK 689

Science Skill Handbook

Mass The SI unit for mass is the kilogram (kg). Scientists can measure mass using units formed by adding metric prefixes to the unit gram (g), such as milligram (mg). To measure mass, you might use a triple-beam balance similar to the one shown in **Figure 12.** The balance has a pan on one side and a set of beams on the other side. Each beam has a rider that slides on the beam.

When using a triple-beam balance, place an object on the pan. Slide the largest rider along its beam until the pointer drops below zero. Then move it back one notch. Repeat the process for each rider proceeding from the larger to smaller until the pointer swings an equal distance above and below the zero point. Sum the masses on each beam to find the mass of the object. Move all riders back to zero when finished.

Instead of putting materials directly on the balance, scientists often take a tare of a container. A tare is the mass of a container into which objects or substances are placed for measuring their masses. To mass objects or substances, find the mass of a clean container. Remove the container from the pan, and place the object or substances in the container. Find the mass of the container with the materials in it. Subtract the mass of the empty container from the mass of the filled container to find the mass of the materials you are using.

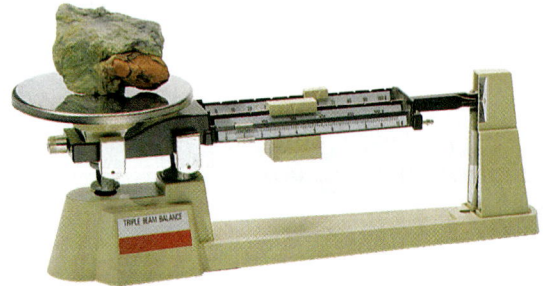

Figure 12 A triple-beam balance is used to determine the mass of an object.

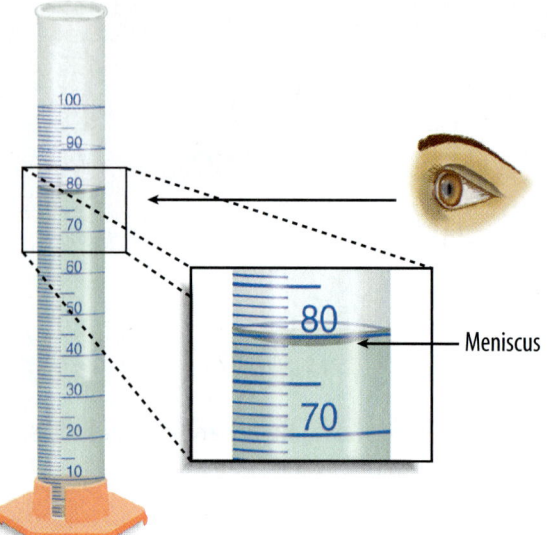

Figure 13 Graduated cylinders measure liquid volume.

Liquid Volume To measure liquids, the unit used is the liter. When a smaller unit is needed, scientists might use a milliliter. Because a milliliter takes up the volume of a cube measuring 1 cm on each side it also can be called a cubic centimeter ($cm^3 = cm \times cm \times cm$).

You can use beakers and graduated cylinders to measure liquid volume. A graduated cylinder, shown in **Figure 13,** is marked from bottom to top in milliliters. In lab, you might use a 10-mL graduated cylinder or a 100-mL graduated cylinder. When measuring liquids, notice that the liquid has a curved surface. Look at the surface at eye level, and measure the bottom of the curve. This is called the meniscus. The graduated cylinder in **Figure 13** contains 79.0 mL, or 79.0 cm^3, of a liquid.

Temperature Scientists often measure temperature using the Celsius scale. Pure water has a freezing point of 0°C and boiling point of 100°C. The unit of measurement is degrees Celsius. Two other scales often used are the Fahrenheit and Kelvin scales.

Science Skill Handbook

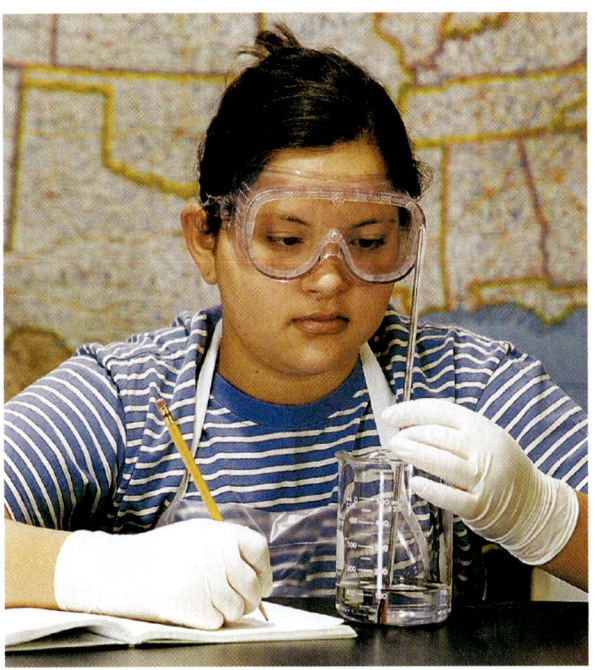

Figure 14 A thermometer measures the temperature of an object.

Scientists use a thermometer to measure temperature. Most thermometers in a laboratory are glass tubes with a bulb at the bottom end containing a liquid such as colored alcohol. The liquid rises or falls with a change in temperature. To read a glass thermometer like the thermometer in **Figure 14,** rotate it slowly until a red line appears. Read the temperature where the red line ends.

Form Operational Definitions An operational definition defines an object by how it functions, works, or behaves. For example, when you are playing hide and seek and a tree is home base, you have created an operational definition for a tree.

Objects can have more than one operational definition. For example, a ruler can be defined as a tool that measures the length of an object (how it is used). It can also be a tool with a series of marks used as a standard when measuring (how it works).

Analyze the Data

To determine the meaning of your observations and investigation results, you will need to look for patterns in the data. Then you must think critically to determine what the data mean. Scientists use several approaches when they analyze the data they have collected and recorded. Each approach is useful for identifying specific patterns.

Interpret Data The word *interpret* means "to explain the meaning of something." When analyzing data from an experiement, try to find out what the data show. Identify the control group and the test group to see whether or not changes in the independent variable have had an effect. Look for differences in the dependent variable between the control and test groups.

Classify Sorting objects or events into groups based on common features is called classifying. When classifying, first observe the objects or events to be classified. Then select one feature that is shared by some members in the group, but not by all. Place those members that share that feature in a subgroup. You can classify members into smaller and smaller subgroups based on characteristics. Remember that when you classify, you are grouping objects or events for a purpose. Keep your purpose in mind as you select the features to form groups and subgroups.

Compare and Contrast Observations can be analyzed by noting the similarities and differences between two more objects or events that you observe. When you look at objects or events to see how they are similar, you are comparing them. Contrasting is looking for differences in objects or events.

SCIENCE SKILL HANDBOOK 691

Science Skill Handbook

Recognize Cause and Effect A cause is a reason for an action or condition. The effect is that action or condition. When two events happen together, it is not necessarily true that one event caused the other. Scientists must design a controlled investigation to recognize the exact cause and effect.

Draw Conclusions

When scientists have analyzed the data they collected, they proceed to draw conclusions about the data. These conclusions are sometimes stated in words similar to the hypothesis that you formed earlier. They may confirm a hypothesis, or lead you to a new hypothesis.

Infer Scientists often make inferences based on their observations. An inference is an attempt to explain observations or to indicate a cause. An inference is not a fact, but a logical conclusion that needs further investigation. For example, you may infer that a fire has caused smoke. Until you investigate, however, you do not know for sure.

Apply When you draw a conclusion, you must apply those conclusions to determine whether the data supports the hypothesis. If your data do not support your hypothesis, it does not mean that the hypothesis is wrong. It means only that the result of the investigation did not support the hypothesis. Maybe the experiment needs to be redesigned, or some of the initial observations on which the hypothesis was based were incomplete or biased. Perhaps more observation or research is needed to refine your hypothesis. A successful investigation does not always come out the way you originally predicted.

Avoid Bias Sometimes a scientific investigation involves making judgments. When you make a judgment, you form an opinion. It is important to be honest and not to allow any expectations of results to bias your judgments. This is important throughout the entire investigation, from researching to collecting data to drawing conclusions.

Communicate

The communication of ideas is an important part of the work of scientists. A discovery that is not reported will not advance the scientific community's understanding or knowledge. Communication among scientists also is important as a way of improving their investigations.

Scientists communicate in many ways, from writing articles in journals and magazines that explain their investigations and experiments, to announcing important discoveries on television and radio. Scientists also share ideas with colleagues on the Internet or present them as lectures, like the student is doing in **Figure 15.**

Figure 15 A student communicates to his peers about his investigation.

Science Skill Handbook

SAFETY SYMBOLS	HAZARD	EXAMPLES	PRECAUTION	REMEDY
DISPOSAL	Special disposal procedures need to be followed.	certain chemicals, living organisms	Do not dispose of these materials in the sink or trash can.	Dispose of wastes as directed by your teacher.
BIOLOGICAL	Organisms or other biological materials that might be harmful to humans	bacteria, fungi, blood, unpreserved tissues, plant materials	Avoid skin contact with these materials. Wear mask or gloves.	Notify your teacher if you suspect contact with material. Wash hands thoroughly.
EXTREME TEMPERATURE	Objects that can burn skin by being too cold or too hot	boiling liquids, hot plates, dry ice, liquid nitrogen	Use proper protection when handling.	Go to your teacher for first aid.
SHARP OBJECT	Use of tools or glassware that can easily puncture or slice skin	razor blades, pins, scalpels, pointed tools, dissecting probes, broken glass	Practice common-sense behavior and follow guidelines for use of the tool.	Go to your teacher for first aid.
FUME	Possible danger to respiratory tract from fumes	ammonia, acetone, nail polish remover, heated sulfur, moth balls	Make sure there is good ventilation. Never smell fumes directly. Wear a mask.	Leave foul area and notify your teacher immediately.
ELECTRICAL	Possible danger from electrical shock or burn	improper grounding, liquid spills, short circuits, exposed wires	Double-check setup with teacher. Check condition of wires and apparatus.	Do not attempt to fix electrical problems. Notify your teacher immediately.
IRRITANT	Substances that can irritate the skin or mucous membranes of the respiratory tract	pollen, moth balls, steel wool, fiberglass, potassium permanganate	Wear dust mask and gloves. Practice extra care when handling these materials.	Go to your teacher for first aid.
CHEMICAL	Chemicals can react with and destroy tissue and other materials	bleaches such as hydrogen peroxide; acids such as sulfuric acid, hydrochloric acid; bases such as ammonia, sodium hydroxide	Wear goggles, gloves, and an apron.	Immediately flush the affected area with water and notify your teacher.
TOXIC	Substance may be poisonous if touched, inhaled, or swallowed.	mercury, many metal compounds, iodine, poinsettia plant parts	Follow your teacher's instructions.	Always wash hands thoroughly after use. Go to your teacher for first aid.
FLAMMABLE	Flammable chemicals may be ignited by open flame, spark, or exposed heat.	alcohol, kerosene, potassium permanganate	Avoid open flames and heat when using flammable chemicals.	Notify your teacher immediately. Use fire safety equipment if applicable.
OPEN FLAME	Open flame in use, may cause fire.	hair, clothing, paper, synthetic materials	Tie back hair and loose clothing. Follow teacher's instruction on lighting and extinguishing flames.	Notify your teacher immediately. Use fire safety equipment if applicable.

 Eye Safety Proper eye protection should be worn at all times by anyone performing or observing science activities.

 Clothing Protection This symbol appears when substances could stain or burn clothing.

 Animal Safety This symbol appears when safety of animals and students must be ensured.

 Handwashing After the lab, wash hands with soap and water before removing goggles.

Science Skill Handbook

Safety in the Science Laboratory

The science laboratory is a safe place to work if you follow standard safety procedures. Being responsible for your own safety helps to make the entire laboratory a safer place for everyone. When performing any lab, read and apply the caution statements and safety symbol listed at the beginning of the lab.

General Safety Rules

1. Obtain your teacher's permission to begin all investigations and use laboratory equipment.

2. Study the procedure. Ask your teacher any questions. Be sure you understand safety symbols shown on the page.

3. Notify your teacher about allergies or other health conditions which can affect your participation in a lab.

4. Learn and follow use and safety procedures for your equipment. If unsure, ask your teacher.

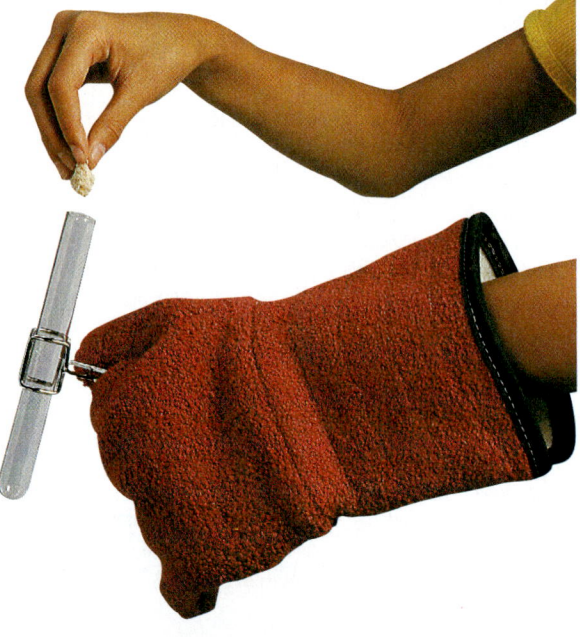

5. Never eat, drink, chew gum, apply cosmetics, or do any personal grooming in the lab. Never use lab glassware as food or drink containers. Keep your hands away from your face and mouth.

6. Know the location and proper use of the safety shower, eye wash, fire blanket, and fire alarm.

Prevent Accidents

1. Use the safety equipment provided to you. Goggles and a safety apron should be worn during investigations.

2. Do NOT use hair spray, mousse, or other flammable hair products. Tie back long hair and tie down loose clothing.

3. Do NOT wear sandals or other open-toed shoes in the lab.

4. Remove jewelry on hands and wrists. Loose jewelry, such as chains and long necklaces, should be removed to prevent them from getting caught in equipment.

5. Do not taste any substances or draw any material into a tube with your mouth.

6. Proper behavior is expected in the lab. Practical jokes and fooling around can lead to accidents and injury.

7. Keep your work area uncluttered.

Laboratory Work

1. Collect and carry all equipment and materials to your work area before beginning a lab.

2. Remain in your own work area unless given permission by your teacher to leave it.

Science Skill Handbook

3. Always slant test tubes away from yourself and others when heating them, adding substances to them, or rinsing them.

4. If instructed to smell a substance in a container, hold the container a short distance away and fan vapors towards your nose.

5. Do NOT substitute other chemicals/substances for those in the materials list unless instructed to do so by your teacher.

6. Do NOT take any materials or chemicals outside of the laboratory.

7. Stay out of storage areas unless instructed to be there and supervised by your teacher.

Laboratory Cleanup

1. Turn off all burners, water, and gas, and disconnect all electrical devices.

2. Clean all pieces of equipment and return all materials to their proper places.

3. Dispose of chemicals and other materials as directed by your teacher. Place broken glass and solid substances in the proper containers. Never discard materials in the sink.

4. Clean your work area.

5. Wash your hands with soap and water thoroughly BEFORE removing your goggles.

Emergencies

1. Report any fire, electrical shock, glassware breakage, spill, or injury, no matter how small, to your teacher immediately. Follow his or her instructions.

2. If your clothing should catch fire, STOP, DROP, and ROLL. If possible, smother it with the fire blanket or get under a safety shower. NEVER RUN.

3. If a fire should occur, turn off all gas and leave the room according to established procedures.

4. In most instances, your teacher will clean up spills. Do NOT attempt to clean up spills unless you are given permission and instructions to do so.

5. If chemicals come into contact with your eyes or skin, notify your teacher immediately. Use the eyewash or flush your skin or eyes with large quantities of water.

6. The fire extinguisher and first-aid kit should only be used by your teacher unless it is an extreme emergency and you have been given permission.

7. If someone is injured or becomes ill, only a professional medical provider or someone certified in first aid should perform first-aid procedures.

Extra Try at Home Labs

EXTRA Try at Home Labs

From Your Kitchen, Junk Drawer, or Yard

1 Your Daily Drink

Real-World Question
How much liquid do you consume in a day?

Possible Materials
- 500-mL measuring cup
- calculator

Procedure
1. When you drink a bottle or can of juice, soda, water, or other beverage, look on the label of the container to find the volume in milliliters.

2. Record the volumes of all the canned and bottled drinks you consume in one day in your Science Journal.
3. Use a measuring cup to measure the liquids that you pour from larger containers. Record these volumes in your Science Journal.
4. Add up the volumes of all the drinks you consumed during the day.

Conclude and Apply
1. How much liquid did you drink during the day?
2. Infer how you would measure the mass of the foods you ate in one day.

2 Cell Sizes

Real-World Question
How do different cells compare in size?

Possible Materials
- meterstick
- metric ruler
- white paper
- pencil
- pen
- masking tape

Procedure
1. Make a dot on a white sheet of paper with a pencil.
2. Use a metric ruler to make a second dot 1 mm away from the first dot. This distance represents the average length of a bacteria cell.
3. Measure a distance 8 mm away from the first dot and make a third dot. This distance represents the average length of a red blood cell.
4. Mark a spot on the floor with a piece of tape and use the meterstick to measure a distance of 7 m. Mark this distance with a second piece of tape. This distance represents the average length of an amoeba cell.

Conclude and Apply
1. The distance between the first and second dot is 1,000 times longer than the actual size of a bacterium cell. Calculate the length of an actual bacterium cell.
2. A large chicken egg is just one cell, and it is 100 times longer than an amoeba cell. Using your measurement from step 4, calculate the distance you would have to measure to represent the average length of a hen's egg.

Adult supervision required for all labs.

Extra Try at Home Labs

3 Expanding Eggs

Real-World Question
How can you observe liquids passing through a cell membrane?

Possible Materials
- glass jar with lid
- white vinegar
- medium chicken egg
- tape measure or string and ruler
- tongs
- measuring cup

Procedure
1. Obtain a glass jar with a lid and a medium egg.
2. Make certain your egg easily fits into your jar.
3. Measure the circumference of your egg.
4. Pour 250 mL of white vinegar into the jar.
5. Carefully place your egg in the jar so that it is submerged in the vinegar. Be careful not to crack or break the egg.
6. Observe your egg each day for three days. Measure the circumference of the egg after three days.

Conclude and Apply
1. Describe the changes that happened to your egg.
2. Infer why the egg's circumference changed. *HINT: A hen's egg is a single cell.*

4 Putting Down Roots

Real-World Question
Can cells from a plant's stem produce root cells for a new plant?

Possible Materials
- houseplant
- scissors
- metric ruler
- glasses or jars (3)
- water
- magnifying lens

Procedure
1. Examine the stems of a houseplant, such as *Pothos,* and locate a node on three different stems. A node looks like a small bump.
2. Cut 3 stems off the plant at a 45° angle about 3–4 mm below the node.
3. Place the end of each stem into a separate glass of water and observe them for a week.

Conclude and Apply
1. Describe what happened to the ends of the stems.
2. Infer how plant stem cells can produce root cells.

Adult supervision required for all labs.

Extra Try at Home Labs

5 Vitamin Search

Real-World Question
How many vitamins and minerals are in the foods you eat?

Possible Materials
- labels from packaged foods and drinks
- nutrition guidebook or cookbook

Procedure
1. Create a data table to record the "% Daily Value" of important vitamins and minerals for a variety of foods.
2. Collect packages from a variety of packaged foods and check the Nutrition Facts chart for the "% Daily Value" of all the vitamins and minerals it contains. These values are listed at the bottom of the chart.
3. Use cookbooks or nutrition guidebooks to research the "% Daily Value" of vitamins and minerals found in several fresh fruits and vegetables such as strawberries, spinach, oranges, and lentils.

Conclude and Apply
1. Infer why a healthy diet includes fresh fruits and vegetables.
2. Infer why a healthy diet includes a wide variety of nutritious foods.

6 Acid Defense

Real-World Question
How is stomach acid your internal first line of defense?

Possible Materials
- drinking glasses (2)
- milk
- cola or lemon juice
- masking tape
- marker
- measuring cup

Procedure
1. Pour 100 mL of milk into each glass.
2. Pour 20 mL of cola into the second glass.
3. Using the masking tape and marker, label the first glass *No Acid* and the second glass *Acid*.
4. Place the glasses in direct sunlight and observe the mixture each day for several days.

Conclude and Apply
1. Compare the odor of the mixture in both glasses after one or two days.
2. Infer how this experiment modeled one of your internal defenses against disease.

Extra Try at Home Labs

7 Feeding Frenzy

Real-World Question
How can you observe predation?

Possible Materials
- large jar with metal lid
- hammer and nail
- plant-eating insect
- insect net
- magnifying lens
- leaves, grass, flowers
- water

Procedure
1. Poke tiny holes in the metal lid of a jar with a nail so the insect has fresh air.
2. Observe a plant-eating insect in the wild. Collect one for indoor observation as well.
3. Put leaves, grass, and flowers in the bottom of the jar. Add a few drops of water.
4. Add the insect. Watch how it behaves.
5. When the experiment is finished, release the insect back into the wild.

Conclude and Apply
1. Describe the predation behaviors of the insect.
2. Compare the insect's behavior in the wild and in captivity. Did its diet change?

8 UV Watch

Real-World Question
How can you find out about the risks of ultraviolet radiation each day?

Possible Materials
- daily newspaper with weekly weather forecasts
- graph paper

Procedure
1. Use the local newspaper or another resource to get the weather forecast for the day.
2. Check the UV (ultraviolet light) index for the day. If it provides an hourly UV index level, record the level for 1:00 P.M.
3. Find a legend or do research to discover what the numbers of the UV index mean.
4. Record the UV index everyday for ten days and graph your results on graph paper.

Conclude and Apply
1. Explain how the UV index system works.
2. Research several ways you can protect yourself from too much ultraviolet light exposure.

Adult supervision required for all labs.

Extra Try at Home Labs

9 Comparing Atom Sizes

Real-World Question
How do the sizes of different types of atoms compare?

Possible Materials
- metric ruler or meterstick
- 1-m length of white paper
- transparent or masking tape
- colored pencils

Procedure
1. Tape a 1-m sheet of paper on the floor.
2. Use a scale of 1 mm: 1 picometer for measuring and drawing the relative diameters of all the atoms.
3. Study the chart of atomic sizes.
4. Use your scale to measure the relative size of a hydrogen atom on the sheet of paper. Use a red pencil to draw the relative diameter of a hydrogen atom on your paper.
5. Use your scale to measure the relative sizes of an oxygen atom, iron atom, gold atom, and francium atom. Use four other colored pencils to draw the relative diameters of these atoms on the paper.
6. Compare the relative sizes of these different atoms.

Atomic Sizes (picometers)	
Element	Diameter
Hydrogen	50
Oxygen	146
Iron	248
Gold	288
Francium	540

Conclude and Apply
1. Research the length of a picometer.
2. Using your scale, list the diameters of the atoms that you drew on your paper.

10 A Good Mix?

Real-World Question
Which liquids will dissolve in water?

Possible Materials
- cooking oil
- water
- apple or grape juice
- rubbing alcohol
- spoon
- glass
- measuring cup

Procedure
1. Pour 100 mL of water into a large glass.
2. Pour 100 mL of apple juice into the glass and stir the water and juice together. Observe your mixture to determine whether juice is soluble in water.
3. Empty and rinse out your glass.
4. Pour 100 mL of water and 100 mL of cooking oil into the glass and stir them together. Observe your mixture to determine whether oil is soluble in water.
5. Empty and rinse out your glass.
6. Pour 100 mL of water and 100 mL of rubbing alcohol into the glass and stir them together. Observe your mixture to determine whether alcohol is soluble in water.

Conclude and Apply
1. List the liquid(s) that are soluble in water.
2. List the liquid(s) that are not soluble in water.
3. Infer why some liquids are soluble in water and others are not.

Extra Try at Home Labs

11 Measuring Momentum

Real-World Question
How much momentum do rolling balls have?

Possible Materials
- meterstick
- orange cones or tape
- scale
- stopwatch
- bucket
- bowling ball
- plastic baseball
- golf ball
- tennis ball
- calculator

Procedure
1. Use a balance to measure the masses of the tennis ball, golf ball, and plastic baseball. Convert their masses from grams to kilograms.
2. Find the weight of the bowling ball in pounds. The weight should be written on the ball. Divide the ball's weight by 2.2 to calculate its mass in kilograms.
3. Go outside and measure a 10-m distance on a blacktop or concrete surface. Mark the distance with orange cones or tape.
4. Have a partner roll each ball the 10-m distance. Measure the time it takes each ball to roll 10 m.
5. Use the formula: velocity = $\frac{\text{distance}}{\text{time}}$ to calculate each ball's velocity.

Conclude and Apply
1. Calculate the momentum of each ball.
2. Infer why the momentums of the balls differed so greatly.

12 Friction in Traffic

Real-World Question
How do the various kinds of friction affect the operation of vehicles?

Possible Materials
- erasers taken from the ends of pencils (4)
- needles (2)
- small match box
- toy car

Procedure
1. Build a match box car with the materials listed, or use a toy car.
2. Invent ways to demonstrate the effects of static friction, sliding friction, and rolling friction on the car. Think of hills, ice or rain conditions, graveled roads and paved roads, etc.
3. Make drawings of how friction is acting on the car, or how the car uses friction to work.

Conclude and Apply
1. In what ways are static, sliding, and rolling friction helpful to drivers?
2. In what ways are static, sliding, and rolling friction unfavorable to car safety and operation?
3. Explain what your experiment taught you about driving in icy conditions.

Adult supervision required for all labs.

Extra Try at Home Labs

13 The Heat is On

Real-World Question
How can different types of energy be transformed into thermal energy?

Possible Materials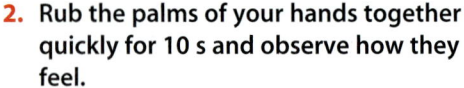
- lamp
- incandescent light bulb
- black construction paper or cloth

Procedure
1. Feel the temperature of a black sheet of paper. Lay the paper in direct sunlight, wait 10 min, and observe how it feels.
2. Rub the palms of your hands together quickly for 10 s and observe how they feel.
3. Switch on a lamp that has a bare light bulb. *Without touching the lightbulb,* cup your hand 2 cm above the bulb for 30 s and observe what you feel.

Conclude and Apply
1. Infer the type of energy transformation that happened on the paper.
2. Infer the type of energy transformation that happened between the palms of your hands.
3. Infer the type of energy transformation that happened to the lightbulb.

14 Disappearing Dots

Real-World Question
Do your eyes have a blind spot?

Possible Materials
- white paper
- metric ruler
- colored pencils

Procedure
1. Hold a sheet of white paper horizontally. Near the left edge of the paper, draw a black dot about 0.5 cm in diameter.
2. Draw a red dot 5 cm to the right of the black dot.
3. Hold the paper out in front of you, close your left eye, and look at the black dot with your right eye. Slowly move the paper toward you and observe what happens to the red dot.
4. Draw a blue dot 10 cm to the right of the black dot and a green dot 15 cm from the black dot.
5. Hold the paper out at arm's length, close your left eye, and look at the black dot with your right eye. Slowly move the paper toward you and observe what happens to the dots.

Conclude and Apply
1. Describe what happened to the red, blue, and green dots as you moved the paper toward you.
2. The optic nerve carries visual images to the brain, and it is attached to the retina in your eye. Infer why the dots disappeared.

Adult supervision required for all labs.

Extra Try at Home Labs

15 Pattern Counting

Real-World Question
What pattern is used to count in binary?

Procedure
1. Study the pattern used for counting in 4-bit binary.
2. Describe the pattern in your own words.
3. To test your understanding of the pattern, close the book and write the counting pattern from 0–15 by using your notes.

Conclude and Apply
1. Can this pattern continue past 15? Explain.
2. Develop a pattern to count to 32.

Decimal Number	Binary Number	Decimal Number	Binary Number
0	0000	8	1000
1	0001	9	1001
2	0010	10	1010
3	0011	11	1011
4	0100	12	1100
5	0101	13	1101
6	0110	14	1110
7	0111	15	1111

16 Big Stars

Real-World Question
How does the size of Earth compare to the size of stars?

Possible Materials
- metric ruler
- meterstick
- tape measure
- masking tape
- white paper
- black marker

Procedure
1. Tape a sheet of white paper to the floor.
2. Draw a dot in the center to the paper. Measure a 1-mm distance from the dot and draw a second dot. This distance represents the diameter of Earth.
3. Measure a distance of 10.9 cm from the first dot and draw a third dot. This distance represents the diameter of the Sun.
4. Measure a distance of 5 m from the first dot and mark the location on the floor with a piece of masking tape. This distance represents the average diameter of a red giant star.
5. Measure a distance of 30 m from the first dot and mark the location on the floor with a piece of masking tape. This distance represents the diameter of the supergiant star Antares.

Conclude and Apply
1. The diameter of Earth is 12,756 km. What is the diameter of the Sun?
2. What is the diameter of an average red giant?

Adult supervision required for all labs.

Extra Try at Home Labs

17 Panning Minerals

Real-World Question
How can minerals be separated from sand?

Possible Materials
- large, aluminum pie pan
- gallon jug filled with water
- empty gallon jug
- clean sand
- funnel
- coffee filter
- squirt bottle of water
- magnifying lens
- white paper
- hand magnet

Procedure
1. Conduct this lab outdoors.
2. Line the funnel with a coffee filter. Insert the funnel stem into an empty gallon jug.
3. Add a small amount of sand to the pie pan. Add some water and swirl the pan.
4. Continue to shake and swirl the pan until only black sand is left in the pan.
5. Use the squirt bottle to wash the black sand into the coffee filter. Repeat steps 3–5 until you have a good sample of black sand.
6. Let the black sand dry. Then observe it with a magnifying lens. Test the sand with a magnet.

Conclude and Apply
1. Why was black sand left in the gold pan after swirling it?
2. Describe how the sand looked under the lens. Did you see any well-shaped crystals?
3. What happened when you tested the sand with a magnet? Explain.

18 Changing Rocks

Real-World Question
How can the change of metamorphic rock be modeled?

Possible Materials
- soil
- water
- measuring cup
- bowl
- spoon
- shale sample
- slate sample
- schist sample
- gneiss sample

Procedure
1. Mix equal parts of soil and water in a measuring cup or bowl. Stir the mixture until you make mud.

2. Place the bowl of mud on the table near the top edge.
3. Lay a sample of shale below the mud, a sample of slate below the shale, a sample of schist below the slate, a sample of gneiss below the schist.
4. Observe the different stages of sedimentary and metamorphic rocks that are formed by heat and pressure over long periods of time.

Conclude and Apply
1. Identify which rock sample(s) are sedimentary rock and which sample(s) are metamorphic rock.
2. Infer which type of rock is found at the greatest depth beneath the surface of Earth.

Extra Try at Home Labs

19 Continental Movement

Real-World Question
How far will the continents move in the future?

Possible Materials
- meterstick or metric tape measure
- masking tape or sidewalk chalk
- tennis balls

Procedure
1. Go outside and measure a 1-cm distance. Mark this distance with two pieces of tape. This is the distance traveled by the slowest plate in one year.
2. Measure a 2.5-cm distance and mark this distance with two pieces of tape. This is the distance traveled by the North American plate in one year.
3. Measure a 15-cm distance and mark this distance with two pieces of tape. This is the distance traveled by the fastest plate in one year.
4. Measure the distances the slowest plate, North American plate, and fastest plate will travel in the next 50 years. Use tennis balls to mark your distances.
5. Measure the distances these three plates will move in the next 300 years. Use tennis balls to mark your distances.

Conclude and Apply
1. How many centimeters will these three plates travel in the next 50 years?
2. How many meters will these three plates travel in the next 300 years?

20 Earth's Layers

Real-World Question
What is the relative thickness of Earth's different layers?

Possible Materials
- meterstick
- masking tape

Procedure
1. Use a piece of masking tape to mark a spot on the floor. This spot represents the center of Earth.
2. Measure a distance of 1.22 m from the first tape mark and place a second piece of tape.
3. From the second piece of tape, measure a distance of 2.27 m and place a third piece of tape.
4. From the third piece of tape, measure a distance of 2.89 m and place a fourth piece of tape.
5. From the fourth piece of tape, make two measurements. Measure a distance of 0.005 m and a distance of 0.06 m. Place two more pieces of tape to mark these two distances.

Conclude and Apply
1. Identify the name of each of the levels you drew.
2. Calculate the scale you used for the thickness of your earth layers.

Adult supervision required for all labs.

Extra Try at Home Labs

21 Getting Warmer

Real-World Question
How do different surfaces affect temperature?

Possible Materials
- thermometer
- moist leaf litter
- large self-sealing bag
- stopwatch or watch

Procedure
1. Collect moist leaf litter in a large self-sealing bag.
2. Pile the leaf litter on a patch of grass that is exposed to direct sunlight.
3. Set the thermometer in the center of the leaf litter, wait 3 min, and measure the temperature.
4. Place the thermometer on the grass in direct sunlight, wait 3 min, and measure the temperature.
5. Place the thermometer on a cement surface in direct sunlight, wait 3 min, and measure the temperature.
6. Place the thermometer on an asphalt surface in direct sunlight, wait 3 min, and measure the temperature.

Conclude and Apply
1. Compare the temperatures of the different surfaces.
2. Explain how you measured the heat-island effect.

22 Making Burrows

Real-World Question
How does burrowing affect sediment layers?

Possible Materials
- clear-glass bowl
- white flour
- colored gelatin powder (3 packages)
- paintbrush
- pencil

Procedure
1. Add 3 cm of white flour to the bowl. Flatten the top of the flour layer.
2. Carefully sprinkle gelatin powder over the flour to form a colored layer about 0.25 cm thick.
3. The two layers represent two different layers of sediment.
4. Use a paintbrush or pencil to make "burrows" in the "sediment."
5. Make sure to make some of the burrows at the edge of the bowl so that you can see how it affects the sediment.
6. Continue to make more burrows and observe the effect on the two layers.

Conclude and Apply
1. How did the two layers of powder change as you continued to make burrows?
2. Were the "trace fossils" easy to recognize at first? How about after a lot of burrowing?
3. How do you think burrowing animals affect layers of sediment on the ocean floor? How could this burrowing be recognized in rock?

Technology Skill Handbook

Computer Skills

People who study science rely on computers, like the one in **Figure 16**, to record and store data and to analyze results from investigations. Whether you work in a laboratory or just need to write a lab report with tables, good computer skills are a necessity.

Using the computer comes with responsibility. Issues of ownership, security, and privacy can arise. Remember, if you did not author the information you are using, you must provide a source for your information. Also, anything on a computer can be accessed by others. Do not put anything on the computer that you would not want everyone to know. To add more security to your work, use a password.

Use a Word Processing Program

A computer program that allows you to type your information, change it as many times as you need to, and then print it out is called a word processing program. Word processing programs also can be used to make tables.

Learn the Skill To start your word processing program, a blank document, sometimes called "Document 1," appears on the screen. To begin, start typing. To create a new document, click the *New* button on the standard tool bar. These tips will help you format the document.

- The program will automatically move to the next line; press *Enter* if you wish to start a new paragraph.
- Symbols, called non-printing characters, can be hidden by clicking the *Show/Hide* button on your toolbar.
- To insert text, move the cursor to the point where you want the insertion to go, click on the mouse once, and type the text.
- To move several lines of text, select the text and click the *Cut* button on your toolbar. Then position your cursor in the location that you want to move the cut text and click *Paste*. If you move to the wrong place, click *Undo*.
- The spell check feature does not catch words that are misspelled to look like other words, like "cold" instead of "gold." Always reread your document to catch all spelling mistakes.
- To learn about other word processing methods, read the user's manual or click on the *Help* button.
- You can integrate databases, graphics, and spreadsheets into documents by copying from another program and pasting it into your document, or by using desktop publishing (DTP). DTP software allows you to put text and graphics together to finish your document with a professional look. This software varies in how it is used and its capabilities.

Figure 16 A computer will make reports neater and more professional looking.

Technology Skill Handbook

Use a Database

A collection of facts stored in a computer and sorted into different fields is called a database. A database can be reorganized in any way that suits your needs.

Learn the Skill A computer program that allows you to create your own database is a database management system (DBMS). It allows you to add, delete, or change information. Take time to get to know the features of your database software.

- Determine what facts you would like to include and research to collect your information.
- Determine how you want to organize the information.
- Follow the instructions for your particular DBMS to set up fields. Then enter each item of data in the appropriate field.
- Follow the instructions to sort the information in order of importance.
- Evaluate the information in your database, and add, delete, or change as necessary.

Use the Internet

The Internet is a global network of computers where information is stored and shared. To use the Internet, like the students in **Figure 17,** you need a modem to connect your computer to a phone line and an Internet Service Provider account.

Learn the Skill To access internet sites and information, use a "Web browser," which lets you view and explore pages on the World Wide Web. Each page is its own site, and each site has its own address, called a URL. Once you have found a Web browser, follow these steps for a search (this also is how you search a database).

Figure 17 The Internet allows you to search a global network for a variety of information.

- Be as specific as possible. If you know you want to research "gold," don't type in "elements." Keep narrowing your search until you find what you want.
- Web sites that end in *.com* are commercial Web sites; *.org, .edu,* and *.gov* are nonprofit, educational, or government Web sites.
- Electronic encyclopedias, almanacs, indexes, and catalogs will help locate and select relevant information.
- Develop a "home page" with relative ease. When developing a Web site, NEVER post pictures or disclose personal information such as location, names, or phone numbers. Your school or community usually can host your Web site. A basic understanding of HTML (hypertext mark-up language), the language of Web sites, is necessary. Software that creates HTML code is called authoring software, and can be downloaded free from many Web sites. This software allows text and pictures to be arranged as the software is writing the HTML code.

Technology Skill Handbook

Use a Spreadsheet

A spreadsheet, shown in **Figure 18**, can perform mathematical functions with any data arranged in columns and rows. By entering a simple equation into a cell, the program can perform operations in specific cells, rows, or columns.

Learn the Skill Each column (vertical) is assigned a letter, and each row (horizontal) is assigned a number. Each point where a row and column intersect is called a cell, and is labeled according to where it is located—Column A, Row 1 (A1).

- Decide how to organize the data, and enter it in the correct row or column.
- Spreadsheets can use standard formulas or formulas can be customized to calculate cells.
- To make a change, click on a cell to make it activate, and enter the edited data or formula.
- Spreadsheets also can display your results in graphs. Choose the style of graph that best represents the data.

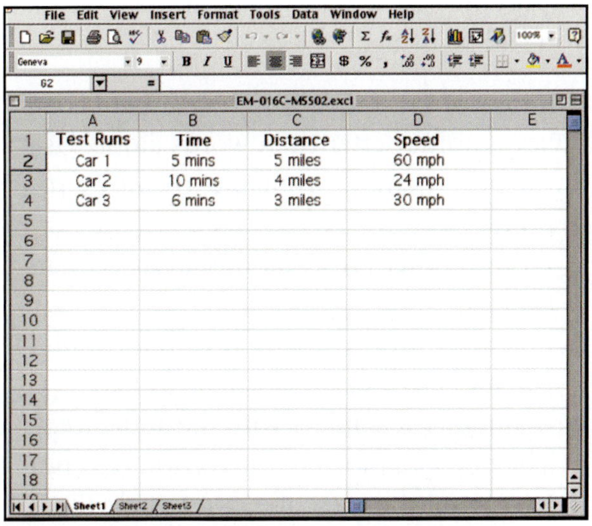

Figure 18 A spreadsheet allows you to perform mathematical operations on your data.

Use Graphics Software

Adding pictures, called graphics, to your documents is one way to make your documents more meaningful and exciting. This software adds, edits, and even constructs graphics. There is a variety of graphics software programs. The tools used for drawing can be a mouse, keyboard, or other specialized devices. Some graphics programs are simple. Others are complicated, called computer-aided design (CAD) software.

Learn the Skill It is important to have an understanding of the graphics software being used before starting. The better the software is understood, the better the results. The graphics can be placed in a word-processing document.

- Clip art can be found on a variety of internet sites, and on CDs. These images can be copied and pasted into your document.
- When beginning, try editing existing drawings, then work up to creating drawings.
- The images are made of tiny rectangles of color called pixels. Each pixel can be altered.
- Digital photography is another way to add images. The photographs in the memory of a digital camera can be downloaded into a computer, then edited and added to the document.
- Graphics software also can allow animation. The software allows drawings to have the appearance of movement by connecting basic drawings automatically. This is called in-betweening, or tweening.
- Remember to save often.

Presentation Skills

Develop Multimedia Presentations

Most presentations are more dynamic if they include diagrams, photographs, videos, or sound recordings, like the one shown in **Figure 19**. A multimedia presentation involves using stereos, overhead projectors, televisions, computers, and more.

Learn the Skill Decide the main points of your presentation, and what types of media would best illustrate those points.

- Make sure you know how to use the equipment you are working with.
- Practice the presentation using the equipment several times.
- Enlist the help of a classmate to push play or turn lights out for you. Be sure to practice your presentation with him or her.
- If possible, set up all of the equipment ahead of time, and make sure everything is working properly.

Figure 19 These students are engaging the audience using a variety of tools.

Computer Presentations

There are many different interactive computer programs that you can use to enhance your presentation. Most computers have a compact disc (CD) drive that can play both CDs and digital video discs (DVDs). Also, there is hardware to connect a regular CD, DVD, or VCR. These tools will enhance your presentation.

Another method of using the computer to aid in your presentation is to develop a slide show using a computer program. This can allow movement of visuals at the presenter's pace, and can allow for visuals to build on one another.

Learn the Skill In order to create multimedia presentations on a computer, you need to have certain tools. These may include traditional graphic tools and drawing programs, animation programs, and authoring systems that tie everything together. Your computer will tell you which tools it supports. The most important step is to learn about the tools that you will be using.

- Often, color and strong images will convey a point better than words alone. Use the best methods available to convey your point.
- As with other presentations, practice many times.
- Practice your presentation with the tools you and any assistants will be using.
- Maintain eye contact with the audience. The purpose of using the computer is not to prompt the presenter, but to help the audience understand the points of the presentation.

Math Review

Use Fractions

A fraction compares a part to a whole. In the fraction $\frac{2}{3}$, the 2 represents the part and is the numerator. The 3 represents the whole and is the denominator.

Reduce Fractions To reduce a fraction, you must find the largest factor that is common to both the numerator and the denominator, the greatest common factor (GCF). Divide both numbers by the GCF. The fraction has then been reduced, or it is in its simplest form.

Example Twelve of the 20 chemicals in the science lab are in powder form. What fraction of the chemicals used in the lab are in powder form?

Step 1 Write the fraction.
$\frac{\text{part}}{\text{whole}} = \frac{12}{20}$

Step 2 To find the GCF of the numerator and denominator, list all of the factors of each number.
Factors of 12: 1, 2, 3, 4, 6, 12 (the numbers that divide evenly into 12)
Factors of 20: 1, 2, 4, 5, 10, 20 (the numbers that divide evenly into 20)

Step 3 List the common factors.
1, 2, 4.

Step 4 Choose the greatest factor in the list.
The GCF of 12 and 20 is 4.

Step 5 Divide the numerator and denominator by the GCF.
$\frac{12 \div 4}{20 \div 4} = \frac{3}{5}$

In the lab, $\frac{3}{5}$ of the chemicals are in powder form.

Practice Problem At an amusement park, 66 of 90 rides have a height restriction. What fraction of the rides, in its simplest form, has a height restriction?

Add and Subtract Fractions To add or subtract fractions with the same denominator, add or subtract the numerators and write the sum or difference over the denominator. After finding the sum or difference, find the simplest form for your fraction.

Example 1 In the forest outside your house, $\frac{1}{8}$ of the animals are rabbits, $\frac{3}{8}$ are squirrels, and the remainder are birds and insects. How many are mammals?

Step 1 Add the numerators.
$\frac{1}{8} + \frac{3}{8} = \frac{(1+3)}{8} = \frac{4}{8}$

Step 2 Find the GCF.
$\frac{4}{8}$ (GCF, 4)

Step 3 Divide the numerator and denominator by the GCF.
$\frac{4}{4} = 1, \frac{8}{4} = 2$

$\frac{1}{2}$ of the animals are mammals.

Example 2 If $\frac{7}{16}$ of the Earth is covered by freshwater, and $\frac{1}{16}$ of that is in glaciers, how much freshwater is not frozen?

Step 1 Subtract the numerators.
$\frac{7}{16} - \frac{1}{16} = \frac{(7-1)}{16} = \frac{6}{16}$

Step 2 Find the GCF.
$\frac{6}{16}$ (GCF, 2)

Step 3 Divide the numerator and denominator by the GCF.
$\frac{6}{2} = 3, \frac{16}{2} = 8$

$\frac{3}{8}$ of the freshwater is not frozen.

Practice Problem A bicycle rider is going 15 km/h for $\frac{4}{9}$ of his ride, 10 km/h for $\frac{2}{9}$ of his ride, and 8 km/h for the remainder of the ride. How much of his ride is he going over 8 km/h?

Math Skill Handbook

Unlike Denominators To add or subtract fractions with unlike denominators, first find the least common denominator (LCD). This is the smallest number that is a common multiple of both denominators. Rename each fraction with the LCD, and then add or subtract. Find the simplest form if necessary.

Example 1 A chemist makes a paste that is $\frac{1}{2}$ table salt (NaCl), $\frac{1}{3}$ sugar ($C_6H_{12}O_6$), and the rest water (H_2O). How much of the paste is a solid?

Step 1 Find the LCD of the fractions.
$\frac{1}{2} + \frac{1}{3}$ (LCD, 6)

Step 2 Rename each numerator and each denominator with the LCD.
$1 \times 3 = 3,\ 2 \times 3 = 6$
$1 \times 2 = 2,\ 3 \times 2 = 6$

Step 3 Add the numerators.
$\frac{3}{6} + \frac{2}{6} = \frac{(3+2)}{6} = \frac{5}{6}$

$\frac{5}{6}$ of the paste is a solid.

Example 2 The average precipitation in Grand Junction, CO, is $\frac{7}{10}$ inch in November, and $\frac{3}{5}$ inch in December. What is the total average precipitation?

Step 1 Find the LCD of the fractions.
$\frac{7}{10} + \frac{3}{5}$ (LCD, 10)

Step 2 Rename each numerator and each denominator with the LCD.
$7 \times 1 = 7,\ 10 \times 1 = 10$
$3 \times 2 = 6,\ 5 \times 2 = 10$

Step 3 Add the numerators.
$\frac{7}{10} + \frac{6}{10} = \frac{(7+6)}{10} = \frac{13}{10}$

$\frac{13}{10}$ inches total precipitation, or $1\frac{3}{10}$ inches.

Practice Problem On an electric bill, about $\frac{1}{8}$ of the energy is from solar energy and about $\frac{1}{10}$ is from wind power. How much of the total bill is from solar energy and wind power combined?

Example 3 In your body, $\frac{7}{10}$ of your muscle contractions are involuntary (cardiac and smooth muscle tissue). Smooth muscle makes $\frac{3}{15}$ of your muscle contractions. How many of your muscle contractions are made by cardiac muscle?

Step 1 Find the LCD of the fractions.
$\frac{7}{10} - \frac{3}{15}$ (LCD, 30)

Step 2 Rename each numerator and each denominator with the LCD.
$7 \times 3 = 21,\ 10 \times 3 = 30$
$3 \times 2 = 6,\ 15 \times 2 = 30$

Step 3 Subtract the numerators.
$\frac{21}{30} - \frac{6}{30} = \frac{(21-6)}{30} = \frac{15}{30}$

Step 4 Find the GCF.
$\frac{15}{30}$ (GCF, 15)
$\frac{1}{2}$

$\frac{1}{2}$ of all muscle contractions are cardiac muscle.

Example 4 Tony wants to make cookies that call for $\frac{3}{4}$ of a cup of flour, but he only has $\frac{1}{3}$ of a cup. How much more flour does he need?

Step 1 Find the LCD of the fractions.
$\frac{3}{4} - \frac{1}{3}$ (LCD, 12)

Step 2 Rename each numerator and each denominator with the LCD.
$3 \times 3 = 9,\ 4 \times 3 = 12$
$1 \times 4 = 4,\ 3 \times 4 = 12$

Step 3 Subtract the numerators.
$\frac{9}{12} - \frac{4}{12} = \frac{(9-4)}{12} = \frac{5}{12}$

$\frac{5}{12}$ of a cup of flour.

Practice Problem Using the information provided to you in Example 3 above, determine how many muscle contractions are voluntary (skeletal muscle).

Math Skill Handbook

Multiply Fractions To multiply with fractions, multiply the numerators and multiply the denominators. Find the simplest form if necessary.

Example Multiply $\frac{3}{5}$ by $\frac{1}{3}$.

Step 1 Multiply the numerators and denominators.
$$\frac{3}{5} \times \frac{1}{3} = \frac{(3 \times 1)}{(5 \times 3)} = \frac{3}{15}$$

Step 2 Find the GCF.
$$\frac{3}{15} \text{ (GCF, 3)}$$

Step 3 Divide the numerator and denominator by the GCF.
$$\frac{3}{3} = 1, \frac{15}{3} = 5$$
$$\frac{1}{5}$$

$\frac{3}{5}$ multiplied by $\frac{1}{3}$ is $\frac{1}{5}$.

Practice Problem Multiply $\frac{3}{14}$ by $\frac{5}{16}$.

Find a Reciprocal Two numbers whose product is 1 are called multiplicative inverses, or reciprocals.

Example Find the reciprocal of $\frac{3}{8}$.

Step 1 Inverse the fraction by putting the denominator on top and the numerator on the bottom.
$$\frac{8}{3}$$

The reciprocal of $\frac{3}{8}$ is $\frac{8}{3}$.

Practice Problem Find the reciprocal of $\frac{4}{9}$.

Divide Fractions To divide one fraction by another fraction, multiply the dividend by the reciprocal of the divisor. Find the simplest form if necessary.

Example 1 Divide $\frac{1}{9}$ by $\frac{1}{3}$.

Step 1 Find the reciprocal of the divisor.
The reciprocal of $\frac{1}{3}$ is $\frac{3}{1}$.

Step 2 Multiply the dividend by the reciprocal of the divisor.
$$\frac{\frac{1}{9}}{\frac{1}{3}} = \frac{1}{9} \times \frac{3}{1} = \frac{(1 \times 3)}{(9 \times 1)} = \frac{3}{9}$$

Step 3 Find the GCF.
$$\frac{3}{9} \text{ (GCF, 3)}$$

Step 4 Divide the numerator and denominator by the GCF.
$$\frac{3}{3} = 1, \frac{9}{3} = 3$$
$$\frac{1}{3}$$

$\frac{1}{9}$ divided by $\frac{1}{3}$ is $\frac{1}{3}$.

Example 2 Divide $\frac{3}{5}$ by $\frac{1}{4}$.

Step 1 Find the reciprocal of the divisor.
The reciprocal of $\frac{1}{4}$ is $\frac{4}{1}$.

Step 2 Multiply the dividend by the reciprocal of the divisor.
$$\frac{\frac{3}{5}}{\frac{1}{4}} = \frac{3}{5} \times \frac{4}{1} = \frac{(3 \times 4)}{(5 \times 1)} = \frac{12}{5}$$

$\frac{3}{5}$ divided by $\frac{1}{4}$ is $\frac{12}{5}$ or $2\frac{2}{5}$.

Practice Problem Divide $\frac{3}{11}$ by $\frac{7}{10}$.

Math Skill Handbook

Use Ratios

When you compare two numbers by division, you are using a ratio. Ratios can be written 3 to 5, 3:5, or $\frac{3}{5}$. Ratios, like fractions, also can be written in simplest form.

Ratios can represent probabilities, also called odds. This is a ratio that compares the number of ways a certain outcome occurs to the number of outcomes. For example, if you flip a coin 100 times, what are the odds that it will come up heads? There are two possible outcomes, heads or tails, so the odds of coming up heads are 50:100. Another way to say this is that 50 out of 100 times the coin will come up heads. In its simplest form, the ratio is 1:2.

Example 1 A chemical solution contains 40 g of salt and 64 g of baking soda. What is the ratio of salt to baking soda as a fraction in simplest form?

Step 1 Write the ratio as a fraction.
$$\frac{\text{salt}}{\text{baking soda}} = \frac{40}{64}$$

Step 2 Express the fraction in simplest form.
The GCF of 40 and 64 is 8.
$$\frac{40}{64} = \frac{40 \div 8}{64 \div 8} = \frac{5}{8}$$

The ratio of salt to baking soda in the sample is 5:8.

Example 2 Sean rolls a 6-sided die 6 times. What are the odds that the side with a 3 will show?

Step 1 Write the ratio as a fraction.
$$\frac{\text{number of sides with a 3}}{\text{number of sides}} = \frac{1}{6}$$

Step 2 Multiply by the number of attempts.
$$\frac{1}{6} \times 6 \text{ attempts} = \frac{6}{6} \text{ attempts} = 1 \text{ attempt}$$

1 attempt out of 6 will show a 3.

Practice Problem Two metal rods measure 100 cm and 144 cm in length. What is the ratio of their lengths in simplest form?

Use Decimals

A fraction with a denominator that is a power of ten can be written as a decimal. For example, 0.27 means $\frac{27}{100}$. The decimal point separates the ones place from the tenths place.

Any fraction can be written as a decimal using division. For example, the fraction $\frac{5}{8}$ can be written as a decimal by dividing 5 by 8. Written as a decimal, it is 0.625.

Add or Subtract Decimals When adding and subtracting decimals, line up the decimal points before carrying out the operation.

Example 1 Find the sum of 47.68 and 7.80.

Step 1 Line up the decimal places when you write the numbers.
```
  47.68
+  7.80
```

Step 2 Add the decimals.
```
  47.68
+  7.80
  -----
  55.48
```

The sum of 47.68 and 7.80 is 55.48.

Example 2 Find the difference of 42.17 and 15.85.

Step 1 Line up the decimal places when you write the number.
```
  42.17
− 15.85
```

Step 2 Subtract the decimals.
```
  42.17
− 15.85
  -----
  26.32
```

The difference of 42.17 and 15.85 is 26.32.

Practice Problem Find the sum of 1.245 and 3.842.

Multiply Decimals To multiply decimals, multiply the numbers like any other number, ignoring the decimal point. Count the decimal places in each factor. The product will have the same number of decimal places as the sum of the decimal places in the factors.

Example Multiply 2.4 by 5.9.

Step 1 Multiply the factors like two whole numbers.
$24 \times 59 = 1416$

Step 2 Find the sum of the number of decimal places in the factors. Each factor has one decimal place, for a sum of two decimal places.

Step 3 The product will have two decimal places.
14.16

The product of 2.4 and 5.9 is 14.16.

Practice Problem Multiply 4.6 by 2.2.

Divide Decimals When dividing decimals, change the divisor to a whole number. To do this, multiply both the divisor and the dividend by the same power of ten. Then place the decimal point in the quotient directly above the decimal point in the dividend. Then divide as you do with whole numbers.

Example Divide 8.84 by 3.4.

Step 1 Multiply both factors by 10.
$3.4 \times 10 = 34$, $8.84 \times 10 = 88.4$

Step 2 Divide 88.4 by 34.

$$\begin{array}{r} 2.6 \\ 34\overline{)88.4} \\ -68 \\ \hline 204 \\ -204 \\ \hline 0 \end{array}$$

8.84 divided by 3.4 is 2.6.

Practice Problem Divide 75.6 by 3.6.

Use Proportions

An equation that shows that two ratios are equivalent is a proportion. The ratios $\frac{2}{4}$ and $\frac{5}{10}$ are equivalent, so they can be written as $\frac{2}{4} = \frac{5}{10}$. This equation is a proportion.

When two ratios form a proportion, the cross products are equal. To find the cross products in the proportion $\frac{2}{4} = \frac{5}{10}$, multiply the 2 and the 10, and the 4 and the 5. Therefore $2 \times 10 = 4 \times 5$, or $20 = 20$.

Because you know that both proportions are equal, you can use cross products to find a missing term in a proportion. This is known as solving the proportion.

Example The heights of a tree and a pole are proportional to the lengths of their shadows. The tree casts a shadow of 24 m when a 6-m pole casts a shadow of 4 m. What is the height of the tree?

Step 1 Write a proportion.
$$\frac{\text{height of tree}}{\text{height of pole}} = \frac{\text{length of tree's shadow}}{\text{length of pole's shadow}}$$

Step 2 Substitute the known values into the proportion. Let h represent the unknown value, the height of the tree.
$$\frac{h}{6} = \frac{24}{4}$$

Step 3 Find the cross products.
$h \times 4 = 6 \times 24$

Step 4 Simplify the equation.
$4h = 144$

Step 5 Divide each side by 4.
$$\frac{4h}{4} = \frac{144}{4}$$
$h = 36$

The height of the tree is 36 m.

Practice Problem The ratios of the weights of two objects on the Moon and on Earth are in proportion. A rock weighing 3 N on the Moon weighs 18 N on Earth. How much would a rock that weighs 5 N on the Moon weigh on Earth?

Math Skill Handbook

Use Percentages

The word *percent* means "out of one hundred." It is a ratio that compares a number to 100. Suppose you read that 77 percent of the Earth's surface is covered by water. That is the same as reading that the fraction of the Earth's surface covered by water is $\frac{77}{100}$. To express a fraction as a percent, first find the equivalent decimal for the fraction. Then, multiply the decimal by 100 and add the percent symbol.

Example Express $\frac{13}{20}$ as a percent.

Step 1 Find the equivalent decimal for the fraction.

$$\begin{array}{r} 0.65 \\ 20\overline{)13.00} \\ \underline{12\ 0} \\ 1\ 00 \\ \underline{1\ 00} \\ 0 \end{array}$$

Step 2 Rewrite the fraction $\frac{13}{20}$ as 0.65.

Step 3 Multiply 0.65 by 100 and add the % sign.
$0.65 \times 100 = 65 = 65\%$

So, $\frac{13}{20} = 65\%$.

This also can be solved as a proportion.

Example Express $\frac{13}{20}$ as a percent.

Step 1 Write a proportion.
$\frac{13}{20} = \frac{x}{100}$

Step 2 Find the cross products.
$1300 = 20x$

Step 3 Divide each side by 20.
$\frac{1300}{20} = \frac{20x}{20}$
$65\% = x$

Practice Problem In one year, 73 of 365 days were rainy in one city. What percent of the days in that city were rainy?

Solve One-Step Equations

A statement that two things are equal is an equation. For example, $A = B$ is an equation that states that A is equal to B.

An equation is solved when a variable is replaced with a value that makes both sides of the equation equal. To make both sides equal the inverse operation is used. Addition and subtraction are inverses, and multiplication and division are inverses.

Example 1 Solve the equation $x - 10 = 35$.

Step 1 Find the solution by adding 10 to each side of the equation.
$x - 10 = 35$
$x - 10 + 10 = 35 + 10$
$x = 45$

Step 2 Check the solution.
$x - 10 = 35$
$45 - 10 = 35$
$35 = 35$

Both sides of the equation are equal, so $x = 45$.

Example 2 In the formula $a = bc$, find the value of c if $a = 20$ and $b = 2$.

Step 1 Rearrange the formula so the unknown value is by itself on one side of the equation by dividing both sides by b.

$a = bc$
$\frac{a}{b} = \frac{bc}{b}$
$\frac{a}{b} = c$

Step 2 Replace the variables a and b with the values that are given.

$\frac{a}{b} = c$
$\frac{20}{2} = c$
$10 = c$

Step 3 Check the solution.
$a = bc$
$20 = 2 \times 10$
$20 = 20$

Both sides of the equation are equal, so $c = 10$ is the solution when $a = 20$ and $b = 2$.

Practice Problem In the formula $h = gd$, find the value of d if $g = 12.3$ and $h = 17.4$.

Math Skill Handbook

Use Statistics

The branch of mathematics that deals with collecting, analyzing, and presenting data is statistics. In statistics, there are three common ways to summarize data with a single number—the mean, the median, and the mode.

The **mean** of a set of data is the arithmetic average. It is found by adding the numbers in the data set and dividing by the number of items in the set.

The **median** is the middle number in a set of data when the data are arranged in numerical order. If there were an even number of data points, the median would be the mean of the two middle numbers.

The **mode** of a set of data is the number or item that appears most often.

Another number that often is used to describe a set of data is the range. The **range** is the difference between the largest number and the smallest number in a set of data.

A **frequency table** shows how many times each piece of data occurs, usually in a survey. **Table 2** below shows the results of a student survey on favorite color.

Table 2 Student Color Choice		
Color	Tally	Frequency
red	||||	4
blue	|||||	5
black	||	2
green	|||	3
purple	||||| ||	7
yellow	|||||		6

Based on the frequency table data, which color is the favorite?

Example The speeds (in m/s) for a race car during five different time trials are 39, 37, 44, 36, and 44.

To find the mean:

Step 1 Find the sum of the numbers.
$39 + 37 + 44 + 36 + 44 = 200$

Step 2 Divide the sum by the number of items, which is 5.
$200 \div 5 = 40$

The mean is 40 m/s.

To find the median:

Step 1 Arrange the measures from least to greatest.
36, 37, 39, 44, 44

Step 2 Determine the middle measure.
36, 37, <u>39</u>, 44, 44

The median is 39 m/s.

To find the mode:

Step 1 Group the numbers that are the same together.
44, 44, 36, 37, 39

Step 2 Determine the number that occurs most in the set.
<u>44, 44</u>, 36, 37, 39

The mode is 44 m/s.

To find the range:

Step 1 Arrange the measures from largest to smallest.
44, 44, 39, 37, 36

Step 2 Determine the largest and smallest measures in the set.
<u>44</u>, 44, 39, 37, <u>36</u>

Step 3 Find the difference between the largest and smallest measures.
$44 - 36 = 8$

The range is 8 m/s.

Practice Problem Find the mean, median, mode, and range for the data set 8, 4, 12, 8, 11, 14, 16.

Use Geometry

The branch of mathematics that deals with the measurement, properties, and relationships of points, lines, angles, surfaces, and solids is called geometry.

Perimeter The **perimeter** (*P*) is the distance around a geometric figure. To find the perimeter of a rectangle, add the length and width and multiply that sum by two, or $2(l + w)$. To find perimeters of irregular figures, add the length of the sides.

Example 1 Find the perimeter of a rectangle that is 3 m long and 5 m wide.

Step 1 You know that the perimeter is 2 times the sum of the width and length.
$P = 2(3\text{ m} + 5\text{ m})$

Step 2 Find the sum of the width and length.
$P = 2(8\text{ m})$

Step 3 Multiply by 2.
$P = 16\text{ m}$

The perimeter is 16 m.

Example 2 Find the perimeter of a shape with sides measuring 2 cm, 5 cm, 6 cm, 3 cm.

Step 1 You know that the perimeter is the sum of all the sides.
$P = 2 + 5 + 6 + 3$

Step 2 Find the sum of the sides.
$P = 2 + 5 + 6 + 3$
$P = 16$

The perimeter is 16 cm.

Practice Problem Find the perimeter of a rectangle with a length of 18 m and a width of 7 m.

Practice Problem Find the perimeter of a triangle measuring 1.6 cm by 2.4 cm by 2.4 cm.

Area of a Rectangle The **area** (*A*) is the number of square units needed to cover a surface. To find the area of a rectangle, multiply the length times the width, or $l \times w$. When finding area, the units also are multiplied. Area is given in square units.

Example Find the area of a rectangle with a length of 1 cm and a width of 10 cm.

Step 1 You know that the area is the length multiplied by the width.
$A = (1\text{ cm} \times 10\text{ cm})$

Step 2 Multiply the length by the width. Also multiply the units.
$A = 10\text{ cm}^2$

The area is 10 cm².

Practice Problem Find the area of a square whose sides measure 4 m.

Area of a Triangle To find the area of a triangle, use the formula:

$$A = \frac{1}{2}(\text{base} \times \text{height})$$

The base of a triangle can be any of its sides. The height is the perpendicular distance from a base to the opposite endpoint, or vertex.

Example Find the area of a triangle with a base of 18 m and a height of 7 m.

Step 1 You know that the area is $\frac{1}{2}$ the base times the height.
$A = \frac{1}{2}(18\text{ m} \times 7\text{ m})$

Step 2 Multiply $\frac{1}{2}$ by the product of 18×7. Multiply the units.
$A = \frac{1}{2}(126\text{ m}^2)$
$A = 63\text{ m}^2$

The area is 63 m².

Practice Problem Find the area of a triangle with a base of 27 cm and a height of 17 cm.

Math Skill Handbook

Circumference of a Circle The **diameter** (*d*) of a circle is the distance across the circle through its center, and the **radius** (*r*) is the distance from the center to any point on the circle. The radius is half of the diameter. The distance around the circle is called the **circumference** (C). The formula for finding the circumference is:

C = 2πr or C = πd

The circumference divided by the diameter is always equal to 3.1415926... This nonterminating and nonrepeating number is represented by the Greek letter π (pi). An approximation often used for π is 3.14.

Example 1 Find the circumference of a circle with a radius of 3 m.

Step 1 You know the formula for the circumference is 2 times the radius times π.
C = 2π(3)

Step 2 Multiply 2 times the radius.
C = 6π

Step 3 Multiply by π.
C = 19 m

The circumference is 19 m.

Example 2 Find the circumference of a circle with a diameter of 24.0 cm.

Step 1 You know the formula for the circumference is the diameter times π.
C = π(24.0)

Step 2 Multiply the diameter by π.
C = 75.4 cm

The circumference is 75.4 cm.

Practice Problem Find the circumference of a circle with a radius of 19 cm.

Area of a Circle The formula for the area of a circle is:
$A = \pi r^2$

Example 1 Find the area of a circle with a radius of 4.0 cm.

Step 1 $A = \pi(4.0)^2$

Step 2 Find the square of the radius.
$A = 16\pi$

Step 3 Multiply the square of the radius by π.
$A = 50$ cm^2

The area of the circle is 50 cm^2.

Example 2 Find the area of a circle with a radius of 225 m.

Step 1 $A = \pi(225)^2$

Step 2 Find the square of the radius.
$A = 50625\pi$

Step 3 Multiply the square of the radius by π.
$A = 158962.5$

The area of the circle is 158,962 m^2.

Example 3 Find the area of a circle whose diameter is 20.0 mm.

Step 1 You know the formula for the area of a circle is the square of the radius times π, and that the radius is half of the diameter.
$A = \pi\left(\frac{20.0}{2}\right)^2$

Step 2 Find the radius.
$A = \pi(10.0)^2$

Step 3 Find the square of the radius.
$A = 100\pi$

Step 4 Multiply the square of the radius by π.
$A = 314$ mm^2

The area is 314 mm^2.

Practice Problem Find the area of a circle with a radius of 16 m.

Math Skill Handbook

Volume The measure of space occupied by a solid is the **volume** (V). To find the volume of a rectangular solid multiply the length times width times height, or $V = l \times w \times h$. It is measured in cubic units, such as cubic centimeters (cm^3).

Example Find the volume of a rectangular solid with a length of 2.0 m, a width of 4.0 m, and a height of 3.0 m.

Step 1 You know the formula for volume is the length times the width times the height.
$V = 2.0 \text{ m} \times 4.0 \text{ m} \times 3.0 \text{ m}$

Step 2 Multiply the length times the width times the height.
$V = 24 \text{ m}^3$

The volume is 24 m^3.

Practice Problem Find the volume of a rectangular solid that is 8 m long, 4 m wide, and 4 m high.

To find the volume of other solids, multiply the area of the base times the height.

Example 1 Find the volume of a solid that has a triangular base with a length of 8.0 m and a height of 7.0 m. The height of the entire solid is 15.0 m.

Step 1 You know that the base is a triangle, and the area of a triangle is $\frac{1}{2}$ the base times the height, and the volume is the area of the base times the height.
$V = \left[\frac{1}{2}(b \times h)\right] \times 15$

Step 2 Find the area of the base.
$V = \left[\frac{1}{2}(8 \times 7)\right] \times 15$
$V = \left(\frac{1}{2} \times 56\right) \times 15$

Step 3 Multiply the area of the base by the height of the solid.
$V = 28 \times 15$
$V = 420 \text{ m}^3$

The volume is 420 m^3.

Example 2 Find the volume of a cylinder that has a base with a radius of 12.0 cm, and a height of 21.0 cm.

Step 1 You know that the base is a circle, and the area of a circle is the square of the radius times π, and the volume is the area of the base times the height.
$V = (\pi r^2) \times 21$
$V = (\pi 12^2) \times 21$

Step 2 Find the area of the base.
$V = 144\pi \times 21$
$V = 452 \times 21$

Step 3 Multiply the area of the base by the height of the solid.
$V = 9490 \text{ cm}^3$

The volume is 9490 cm^3.

Example 3 Find the volume of a cylinder that has a diameter of 15 mm and a height of 4.8 mm.

Step 1 You know that the base is a circle with an area equal to the square of the radius times π. The radius is one-half the diameter. The volume is the area of the base times the height.
$V = (\pi r^2) \times 4.8$
$V = \left[\pi\left(\frac{1}{2} \times 15\right)^2\right] \times 4.8$
$V = (\pi 7.5^2) \times 4.8$

Step 2 Find the area of the base.
$V = 56.25\pi \times 4.8$
$V = 176.63 \times 4.8$

Step 3 Multiply the area of the base by the height of the solid.
$V = 847.8$

The volume is 847.8 mm^3.

Practice Problem Find the volume of a cylinder with a diameter of 7 cm in the base and a height of 16 cm.

720 STUDENT RESOURCES

Math Skill Handbook

Science Applications

Measure in SI

The metric system of measurement was developed in 1795. A modern form of the metric system, called the International System (SI), was adopted in 1960 and provides the standard measurements that all scientists around the world can understand.

The SI system is convenient because unit sizes vary by powers of 10. Prefixes are used to name units. Look at **Table 3** for some common SI prefixes and their meanings.

Table 3 Common SI Prefixes			
Prefix	Symbol	Meaning	
kilo-	k	1,000	thousand
hecto-	h	100	hundred
deka-	da	10	ten
deci-	d	0.1	tenth
centi-	c	0.01	hundredth
milli-	m	0.001	thousandth

Example How many grams equal one kilogram?

Step 1 Find the prefix *kilo* in **Table 3**.

Step 2 Using **Table 3**, determine the meaning of *kilo*. According to the table, it means 1,000. When the prefix *kilo* is added to a unit, it means that there are 1,000 of the units in a "*kilo*unit."

Step 3 Apply the prefix to the units in the question. The units in the question are grams. There are 1,000 grams in a kilogram.

Practice Problem Is a milligram larger or smaller than a gram? How many of the smaller units equal one larger unit? What fraction of the larger unit does one smaller unit represent?

Dimensional Analysis

Convert SI Units In science, quantities such as length, mass, and time sometimes are measured using different units. A process called dimensional analysis can be used to change one unit of measure to another. This process involves multiplying your starting quantity and units by one or more conversion factors. A conversion factor is a ratio equal to one and can be made from any two equal quantities with different units. If 1,000 mL equal 1 L then two ratios can be made.

$$\frac{1,000 \text{ mL}}{1 \text{ L}} = \frac{1 \text{ L}}{1,000 \text{ mL}} = 1$$

One can covert between units in the SI system by using the equivalents in **Table 3** to make conversion factors.

Example 1 How many cm are in 4 m?

Step 1 Write conversion factors for the units given. From **Table 3**, you know that 100 cm = 1 m. The conversion factors are

$$\frac{100 \text{ cm}}{1 \text{ m}} \quad \text{and} \quad \frac{1 \text{ m}}{100 \text{ cm}}$$

Step 2 Decide which conversion factor to use. Select the factor that has the units you are converting from (m) in the denominator and the units you are converting to (cm) in the numerator.

$$\frac{100 \text{ cm}}{1 \text{ m}}$$

Step 3 Multiply the starting quantity and units by the conversion factor. Cancel the starting units with the units in the denominator. There are 400 cm in 4 m.

$$4 \text{ m} \times \frac{100 \text{ cm}}{1 \text{ m}} = 400 \text{ cm}$$

Practice Problem How many milligrams are in one kilogram? (Hint: You will need to use two conversion factors from **Table 3**.)

MATH SKILL HANDBOOK

Math Skill Handbook

Table 4 Unit System Equivalents	
Type of Measurement	**Equivalent**
Length	1 in = 2.54 cm
	1 yd = 0.91 m
	1 mi = 1.61 km
Mass and Weight*	1 oz = 28.35 g
	1 lb = 0.45 kg
	1 ton (short) = 0.91 tonnes (metric tons)
	1 lb = 4.45 N
Volume	1 in^3 = 16.39 cm^3
	1 qt = 0.95 L
	1 gal = 3.78 L
Area	1 in^2 = 6.45 cm^2
	1 yd^2 = 0.83 m^2
	1 mi^2 = 2.59 km^2
	1 acre = 0.40 hectares
Temperature	°C = $\frac{(°F - 32)}{1.8}$
	K = °C + 273

*Weight is measured in standard Earth gravity.

Convert Between Unit Systems Table 4 gives a list of equivalents that can be used to convert between English and SI units.

Example If a meterstick has a length of 100 cm, how long is the meterstick in inches?

Step 1 Write the conversion factors for the units given. From **Table 4,** 1 in = 2.54 cm.

$$\frac{1 \text{ in}}{2.54 \text{ cm}} \text{ and } \frac{2.54 \text{ cm}}{1 \text{ in}}$$

Step 2 Determine which conversion factor to use. You are converting from cm to in. Use the conversion factor with cm on the bottom.

$$\frac{1 \text{ in}}{2.54 \text{ cm}}$$

Step 3 Multiply the starting quantity and units by the conversion factor. Cancel the starting units with the units in the denominator. Round your answer based on the number of significant figures in the conversion factor.

$$100 \text{ cm} \times \frac{1 \text{ in}}{2.54 \text{ cm}} = 39.37 \text{ in}$$

The meterstick is 39.4 in long.

Practice Problem A book has a mass of 5 lbs. What is the mass of the book in kg?

Practice Problem Use the equivalent for in and cm (1 in = 2.54 cm) to show how 1 in^3 = 16.39 cm^3.

Math Skill Handbook

Precision and Significant Digits

When you make a measurement, the value you record depends on the precision of the measuring instrument. This precision is represented by the number of significant digits recorded in the measurement. When counting the number of significant digits, all digits are counted except zeros at the end of a number with no decimal point such as 2,050, and zeros at the beginning of a decimal such as 0.03020. When adding or subtracting numbers with different precision, round the answer to the smallest number of decimal places of any number in the sum or difference. When multiplying or dividing, the answer is rounded to the smallest number of significant digits of any number being multiplied or divided. Because a calculator may give you more digits than are significant, this method also is used to round the results of calculator operations.

Example The lengths 5.28 and 5.2 are measured in meters. Find the sum of these lengths and record your answer using the correct number of significant digits.

Step 1 Find the sum.

   5.28 m   2 digits after the decimal
 + 5.2 m   1 digit after the decimal
 ─────────
  10.48 m

Step 2 Round to one digit after the decimal because the least number of digits after the decimal of the numbers being added is 1.

The sum is 10.5 m.

Practice Problem How many significant digits are in the measurement 7,071,301 m? How many significant digits are in the measurement 0.003010 g?

Practice Problem Multiply 5.28 and 5.2 using the rule for multiplying and dividing. Record the answer using the correct number of significant digits.

Scientific Notation

Many times numbers used in science are very small or very large. Because these numbers are difficult to work with scientists use scientific notation. To write numbers in scientific notation, move the decimal point until only one non-zero digit remains on the left. Then count the number of places you moved the decimal point and use that number as a power of ten. For example, the average distance from the Sun to Mars is 227,800,000,000 m. In scientific notation, this distance is 2.278×10^{11} m. Because you moved the decimal point to the left, the number is a positive power of ten.

The mass of an electron is about 0.000 000 000 000 000 000 000 000 000 000 911 kg. Expressed in scientific notation, this mass is 9.11×10^{-31} kg. Because the decimal point was moved to the right, the number is a negative power of ten.

Example Earth is 149,600,000 km from the Sun. Express this in scientific notation.

Step 1 Move the decimal point until one non-zero digit remains on the left.
1.496 000 00

Step 2 Count the number of decimal places you have moved. In this case, eight.

Step 3 Show that number as a power of ten, 10^8.

The Earth is 1.496×10^8 km from the Sun.

Practice Problem How many significant digits are in 149,600,000 km? How many significant digits are in 1.496×10^8 km?

Practice Problem Parts used in a high performance car must be measured to 7×10^{-6} m. Express this number as a decimal.

Practice Problem A CD is spinning at 539 revolutions per minute. Express this number in scientific notation.

Math Skill Handbook

Make and Use Graphs

Data in tables can be displayed in a graph—a visual representation of data. Common graph types include line graphs, bar graphs, and circle graphs.

Line Graph A line graph shows a relationship between two variables that change continuously. The independent variable is changed and is plotted on the *x*-axis. The dependent variable is observed, and is plotted on the *y*-axis.

Example Draw a line graph of the data below from a cyclist in a long-distance race.

Table 5 Bicycle Race Data	
Time (h)	Distance (km)
0	0
1	8
2	16
3	24
4	32
5	40

Step 1 Determine the *x*-axis and *y*-axis variables. Time varies independently of distance and is plotted on the *x*-axis. Distance is dependent on time and is plotted on the *y*-axis.

Step 2 Determine the scale of each axis. The *x*-axis data ranges from 0 to 5. The *y*-axis data ranges from 0 to 40.

Step 3 Using graph paper, draw and label the axes. Include units in the labels.

Step 4 Draw a point at the intersection of the time value on the *x*-axis and corresponding distance value on the *y*-axis. Connect the points and label the graph with a title, as shown in **Figure 20**.

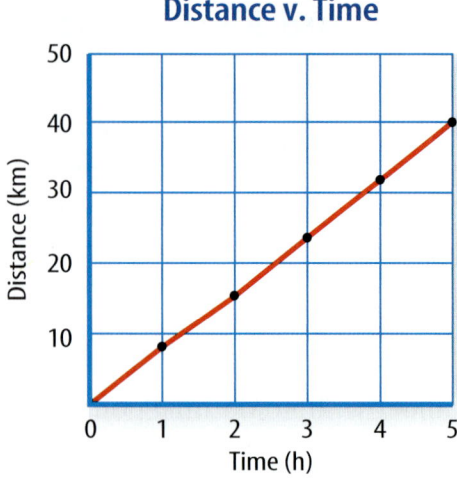

Figure 20 This line graph shows the relationship between distance and time during a bicycle ride.

Practice Problem A puppy's shoulder height is measured during the first year of her life. The following measurements were collected: (3 mo, 52 cm), (6 mo, 72 cm), (9 mo, 83 cm), (12 mo, 86 cm). Graph this data.

Find a Slope The slope of a straight line is the ratio of the vertical change, rise, to the horizontal change, run.

$$\text{Slope} = \frac{\text{vertical change (rise)}}{\text{horizontal change (run)}} = \frac{\text{change in } y}{\text{change in } x}$$

Example Find the slope of the graph in **Figure 20**.

Step 1 You know that the slope is the change in *y* divided by the change in *x*.
$$\text{Slope} = \frac{\text{change in } y}{\text{change in } x}$$

Step 2 Determine the data points you will be using. For a straight line, choose the two sets of points that are the farthest apart.
$$\text{Slope} = \frac{(40-0) \text{ km}}{(5-0) \text{ hr}}$$

Step 3 Find the change in *y* and *x*.
$$\text{Slope} = \frac{40 \text{ km}}{5 \text{ h}}$$

Step 4 Divide the change in *y* by the change in *x*.
$$\text{Slope} = \frac{8 \text{ km}}{\text{h}}$$

The slope of the graph is 8 km/h.

Math Skill Handbook

Bar Graph To compare data that does not change continuously you might choose a bar graph. A bar graph uses bars to show the relationships between variables. The *x*-axis variable is divided into parts. The parts can be numbers such as years, or a category such as a type of animal. The *y*-axis is a number and increases continuously along the axis.

Example A recycling center collects 4.0 kg of aluminum on Monday, 1.0 kg on Wednesday, and 2.0 kg on Friday. Create a bar graph of this data.

Step 1 Select the *x*-axis and *y*-axis variables. The measured numbers (the masses of aluminum) should be placed on the *y*-axis. The variable divided into parts (collection days) is placed on the *x*-axis.

Step 2 Create a graph grid like you would for a line graph. Include labels and units.

Step 3 For each measured number, draw a vertical bar above the *x*-axis value up to the *y*-axis value. For the first data point, draw a vertical bar above Monday up to 4.0 kg.

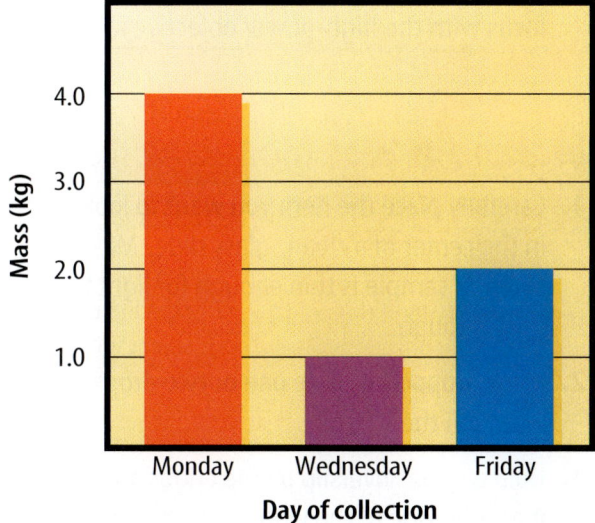

Practice Problem Draw a bar graph of the gases in air: 78% nitrogen, 21% oxygen, 1% other gases.

Circle Graph To display data as parts of a whole, you might use a circle graph. A circle graph is a circle divided into sections that represent the relative size of each piece of data. The entire circle represents 100%, half represents 50%, and so on.

Example Air is made up of 78% nitrogen, 21% oxygen, and 1% other gases. Display the composition of air in a circle graph.

Step 1 Multiply each percent by 360° and divide by 100 to find the angle of each section in the circle.

$$78\% \times \frac{360°}{100} = 280.8°$$

$$21\% \times \frac{360°}{100} = 75.6°$$

$$1\% \times \frac{360°}{100} = 3.6°$$

Step 2 Use a compass to draw a circle and to mark the center of the circle. Draw a straight line from the center to the edge of the circle.

Step 3 Use a protractor and the angles you calculated to divide the circle into parts. Place the center of the protractor over the center of the circle and line the base of the protractor over the straight line.

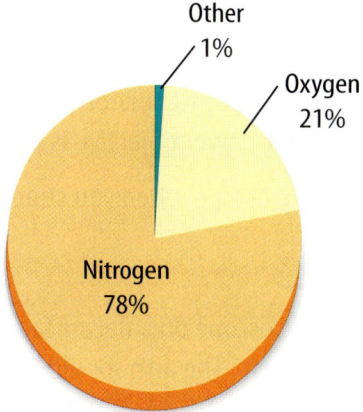

Practice Problem Draw a circle graph to represent the amount of aluminum collected during the week shown in the bar graph to the left.

Reference Handbooks

Use and Care of a Microscope

Eyepiece Contains magnifying lenses you look through.

Arm Supports the body tube.

Low-power objective Contains the lens with the lowest power magnification.

Stage clips Hold the microscope slide in place.

Coarse adjustment Focuses the image under low power.

Fine adjustment Sharpens the image under high magnification.

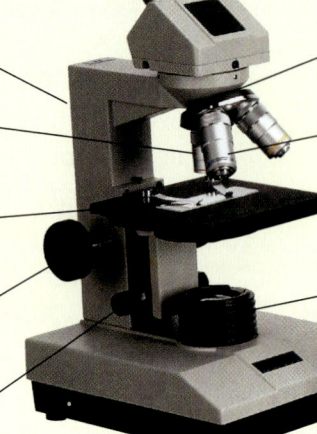

Body tube Connects the eyepiece to the revolving nosepiece.

Revolving nosepiece Holds and turns the objectives into viewing position.

High-power objective Contains the lens with the highest magnification.

Stage Supports the microscope slide.

Light source Provides light that passes upward through the diaphragm, the specimen, and the lenses.

Base Provides support for the microscope.

Caring for a Microscope

1. Always carry the microscope holding the arm with one hand and supporting the base with the other hand.
2. Don't touch the lenses with your fingers.
3. The coarse adjustment knob is used only when looking through the lowest-power objective lens. The fine adjustment knob is used when the high-power objective is in place.
4. Cover the microscope when you store it.

Using a Microscope

1. Place the microscope on a flat surface that is clear of objects. The arm should be toward you.
2. Look through the eyepiece. Adjust the diaphragm so light comes through the opening in the stage.
3. Place a slide on the stage so the specimen is in the field of view. Hold it firmly in place by using the stage clips.
4. Always focus with the coarse adjustment and the low-power objective lens first. After the object is in focus on low power, turn the nosepiece until the high-power objective is in place. Use ONLY the fine adjustment to focus with the high-power objective lens.

Making a Wet-Mount Slide

1. Carefully place the item you want to look at in the center of a clean, glass slide. Make sure the sample is thin enough for light to pass through.
2. Use a dropper to place one or two drops of water on the sample.
3. Hold a clean coverslip by the edges and place it at one edge of the water. Slowly lower the coverslip onto the water until it lies flat.
4. If you have too much water or a lot of air bubbles, touch the edge of a paper towel to the edge of the coverslip to draw off extra water and draw out unwanted air.

Rocks

Rocks		
Rock Type	**Rock Name**	**Characteristics**
Igneous (intrusive)	Granite	Large mineral grains of quartz, feldspar, hornblende, and mica. Usually light in color.
	Diorite	Large mineral grains of feldspar, hornblende, and mica. Less quartz than granite. Intermediate in color.
	Gabbro	Large mineral grains of feldspar, augite, and olivine. No quartz. Dark in color.
Igneous (extrusive)	Rhyolite	Small mineral grains of quartz, feldspar, hornblende, and mica, or no visible grains. Light in color.
	Andesite	Small mineral grains of feldspar, hornblende, and mica or no visible grains. Intermediate in color.
	Basalt	Small mineral grains of feldspar, augite, and possibly olivine or no visible grains. No quartz. Dark in color.
	Obsidian	Glassy texture. No visible grains. Volcanic glass. Fracture looks like broken glass.
	Pumice	Frothy texture. Floats in water. Usually light in color.
Sedimentary (detrital)	Conglomerate	Coarse grained. Gravel or pebble-size grains.
	Sandstone	Sand-sized grains 1/16 to 2 mm.
	Siltstone	Grains are smaller than sand but larger than clay.
	Shale	Smallest grains. Often dark in color. Usually platy.
Sedimentary (chemical or organic)	Limestone	Major mineral is calcite. Usually forms in oceans and lakes. Often contains fossils.
	Coal	Forms in swampy areas. Compacted layers of organic material, mainly plant remains.
Sedimentary (chemical)	Rock Salt	Commonly forms by the evaporation of seawater.
Metamorphic (foliated)	Gneiss	Banding due to alternate layers of different minerals, of different colors. Parent rock often is granite.
	Schist	Parallel arrangement of sheetlike minerals, mainly micas. Forms from different parent rocks.
	Phyllite	Shiny or silky appearance. May look wrinkled. Common parent rocks are shale and slate.
	Slate	Harder, denser, and shinier than shale. Common parent rock is shale.
Metamorphic (nonfoliated)	Marble	Calcite or dolomite. Common parent rock is limestone.
	Soapstone	Mainly of talc. Soft with greasy feel.
	Quartzite	Hard with interlocking quartz crystals. Common parent rock is sandstone.

Minerals

Minerals

Mineral (formula)	Color	Streak	Hardness	Breakage Pattern	Uses and Other Properties
Graphite (C)	black to gray	black to gray	1–1.5	basal cleavage (scales)	pencil lead, lubricants for locks, rods to control some small nuclear reactions, battery poles
Galena (PbS)	gray	gray to black	2.5	cubic cleavage perfect	source of lead, used for pipes, shields for X rays, fishing equipment sinkers
Hematite (Fe_2O_3)	black or reddish-brown	reddish-brown	5.5–6.5	irregular fracture	source of iron; converted to pig iron, made into steel
Magnetite (Fe_3O_4)	black	black	6	conchoidal fracture	source of iron, attracts a magnet
Pyrite (FeS_2)	light, brassy, yellow	greenish-black	6–6.5	uneven fracture	fool's gold
Talc ($Mg_3Si_4O_{10}(OH)_2$)	white, greenish	white	1	cleavage in one direction	used for talcum powder, sculptures, paper, and tabletops
Gypsum ($CaSO_4 \cdot 2H_2O$)	colorless, gray, white, brown	white	2	basal cleavage	used in plaster of paris and dry wall for building construction
Sphalerite (ZnS)	brown, reddish-brown, greenish	light to dark brown	3.5–4	cleavage in six directions	main ore of zinc; used in paints, dyes, and medicine
Muscovite ($KAl_3Si_3O_{10}(OH)_2$)	white, light gray, yellow, rose, green	colorless	2–2.5	basal cleavage	occurs in large, flexible plates; used as an insulator in electrical equipment, lubricant
Biotite ($K(Mg,Fe)_3(AlSi_3O_{10})(OH)_2$)	black to dark brown	colorless	2.5–3	basal cleavage	occurs in large, flexible plates
Halite (NaCl)	colorless, red, white, blue	colorless	2.5	cubic cleavage	salt; soluble in water; a preservative

Minerals

Minerals

Mineral (formula)	Color	Streak	Hardness	Breakage Pattern	Uses and Other Properties
Calcite ($CaCO_3$)	colorless, white, pale blue	colorless, white	3	cleavage in three directions	fizzes when HCl is added; used in cements and other building materials
Dolomite ($CaMg(CO_3)_2$)	colorless, white, pink, green, gray, black	white	3.5–4	cleavage in three directions	concrete and cement; used as an ornamental building stone
Fluorite (CaF_2)	colorless, white, blue, green, red, yellow, purple	colorless	4	cleavage in four directions	used in the manufacture of optical equipment; glows under ultraviolet light
Hornblende $(CaNa)_{2-3}(Mg,Al,Fe)_5-(Al,Si)_2Si_6O_{22}(OH)_2$	green to black	gray to white	5–6	cleavage in two directions	will transmit light on thin edges; 6-sided cross section
Feldspar ($KAlSi_3O_8$) ($NaAlSi_3O_8$), ($CaAl_2Si_2O_8$)	colorless, white to gray, green	colorless	6	two cleavage planes meet at 90° angle	used in the manufacture of ceramics
Augite $((Ca,Na)(Mg,Fe,Al)(Al,Si)_2O_6)$	black	colorless	6	cleavage in two directions	square or 8-sided cross section
Olivine $((Mg,Fe)_2SiO_4)$	olive, green	none	6.5–7	conchoidal fracture	gemstones, refractory sand
Quartz (SiO_2)	colorless, various colors	none	7	conchoidal fracture	used in glass manufacture, electronic equipment, radios, computers, watches, gemstones

Physical Science Reference Tables

Standard Units

Symbol	Name	Quantity
m	meter	length
kg	kilogram	mass
Pa	pascal	pressure
K	kelvin	temperature
mol	mole	amount of a substance
J	joule	energy, work, quantity of heat
s	second	time
C	coulomb	electric charge
V	volt	electric potential
A	ampere	electric current
Ω	ohm	resistance

Physical Constants and Conversion Factors

Acceleration due to gravity	g	9.8 m/s/s or m/s^2
Avogadro's Number	N_A	6.02×10^{23} particles per mole
Electron charge	e	1.6×10^{-19} C
Electron rest mass	m_e	9.11×10^{-31} kg
Gravitation constant	G	6.67×10^{-11} N $\times$ m^2/kg^2
Mass-energy relationship		1 u (amu) = 9.3×10^2 MeV
Speed of light in a vacuum	c	3.00×10^8 m/s
Speed of sound at STP		331 m/s
Standard Pressure		1 atmosphere
		101.3 kPa
		760 Torr or mmHg
		14.7 lb/in.^{2}

Wavelengths of Light in a Vacuum

Violet	$4.0 - 4.2 \times 10^{-7}$ m
Blue	$4.2 - 4.9 \times 10^{-7}$ m
Green	$4.9 - 5.7 \times 10^{-7}$ m
Yellow	$5.7 - 5.9 \times 10^{-7}$ m
Orange	$5.9 - 6.5 \times 10^{-7}$ m
Red	$6.5 - 7.0 \times 10^{-7}$ m

The Index of Refraction for Common Substances
($\lambda = 5.9 \times 10^{-7}$ m)

Air	1.00
Alcohol	1.36
Canada Balsam	1.53
Corn Oil	1.47
Diamond	2.42
Glass, Crown	1.52
Glass, Flint	1.61
Glycerol	1.47
Lucite	1.50
Quartz, Fused	1.46
Water	1.33

Heat Constants

	Specific Heat (average) (kJ/kg $\times$ °C) (J/g $\times$ °C)	Melting Point (°C)	Boiling Point (°C)	Heat of Fusion (kJ/kg) (J/g)	Heat of Vaporization (kJ/kg) (J/g)
Alcohol (ethyl)	2.43 (liq.)	−117	79	109	855
Aluminum	0.90 (sol.)	660	2467	396	10500
Ammonia	4.71 (liq.)	−78	−33	332	1370
Copper	0.39 (sol.)	1083	2567	205	4790
Iron	0.45 (sol.)	1535	2750	267	6290
Lead	0.13 (sol.)	328	1740	25	866
Mercury	0.14 (liq.)	−39	357	11	295
Platinum	0.13 (sol.)	1772	3827	101	229
Silver	0.24 (sol.)	962	2212	105	2370
Tungsten	0.13 (sol.)	3410	5660	192	4350
Water (solid)	2.05 (sol.)	0	–	334	–
Water (liquid)	4.18 (liq.)	–	100	–	–
Water (vapor)	2.01 (gas)	–	–	–	2260
Zinc	0.39 (sol.)	420	907	113	1770

Reference Handbooks

Standard Units

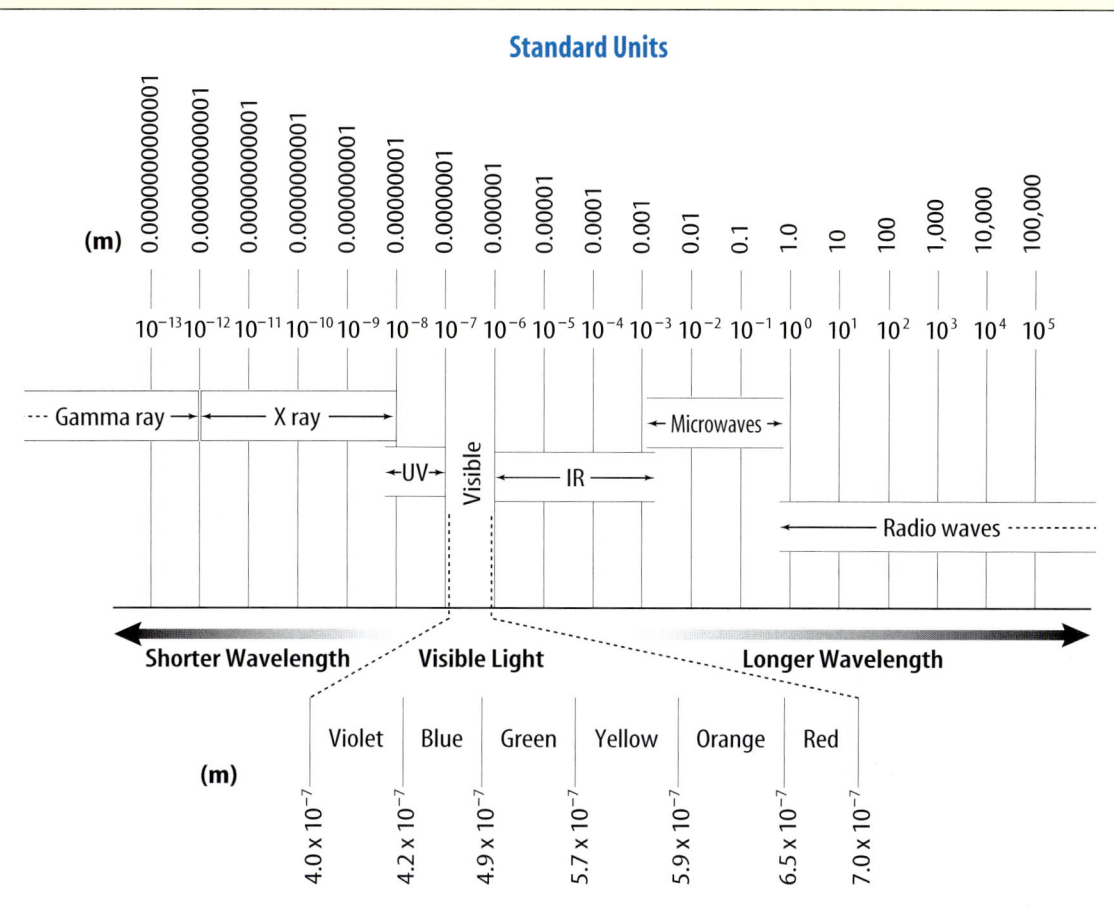

Heat Constants

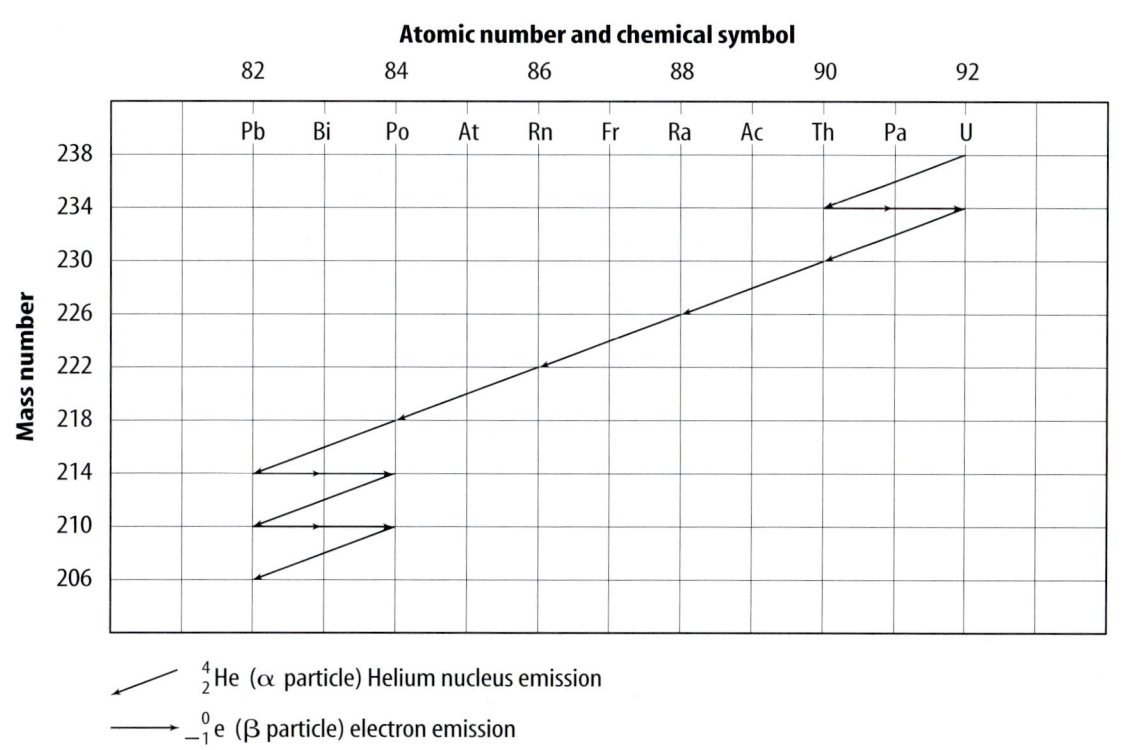

REFERENCE HANDBOOKS 731

Reference Handbooks

PERIODIC TABLE OF THE ELEMENTS

Columns of elements are called groups. Elements in the same group have similar chemical properties.

Element — Hydrogen
Atomic number — 1
Symbol — H
Atomic mass — 1.008
State of matter

- Gas
- Liquid
- Solid
- Synthetic

The first three symbols tell you the state of matter of the element at room temperature. The fourth symbol identifies elements that are not present in significant amounts on Earth. Useful amounts are made synthetically.

Period	1	2	3	4	5	6	7	8	9
1	Hydrogen 1 H 1.008								
2	Lithium 3 Li 6.941	Beryllium 4 Be 9.012							
3	Sodium 11 Na 22.990	Magnesium 12 Mg 24.305							
4	Potassium 19 K 39.098	Calcium 20 Ca 40.078	Scandium 21 Sc 44.956	Titanium 22 Ti 47.867	Vanadium 23 V 50.942	Chromium 24 Cr 51.996	Manganese 25 Mn 54.938	Iron 26 Fe 55.845	Cobalt 27 Co 58.933
5	Rubidium 37 Rb 85.468	Strontium 38 Sr 87.62	Yttrium 39 Y 88.906	Zirconium 40 Zr 91.224	Niobium 41 Nb 92.906	Molybdenum 42 Mo 95.94	Technetium 43 Tc (98)	Ruthenium 44 Ru 101.07	Rhodium 45 Rh 102.906
6	Cesium 55 Cs 132.905	Barium 56 Ba 137.327	Lanthanum 57 La 138.906	Hafnium 72 Hf 178.49	Tantalum 73 Ta 180.948	Tungsten 74 W 183.84	Rhenium 75 Re 186.207	Osmium 76 Os 190.23	Iridium 77 Ir 192.217
7	Francium 87 Fr (223)	Radium 88 Ra (226)	Actinium 89 Ac (227)	Rutherfordium 104 Rf (261)	Dubnium 105 Db (262)	Seaborgium 106 Sg (266)	Bohrium 107 Bh (264)	Hassium 108 Hs (277)	Meitnerium 109 Mt (268)

The number in parentheses is the mass number of the longest-lived isotope for that element.

Rows of elements are called periods. Atomic number increases across a period.

The arrow shows where these elements would fit into the periodic table. They are moved to the bottom of the table to save space.

Lanthanide series

Cerium 58 Ce 140.116	Praseodymium 59 Pr 140.908	Neodymium 60 Nd 144.24	Promethium 61 Pm (145)	Samarium 62 Sm 150.36

Actinide series

Thorium 90 Th 232.038	Protactinium 91 Pa 231.036	Uranium 92 U 238.029	Neptunium 93 Np (237)	Plutonium 94 Pu (244)

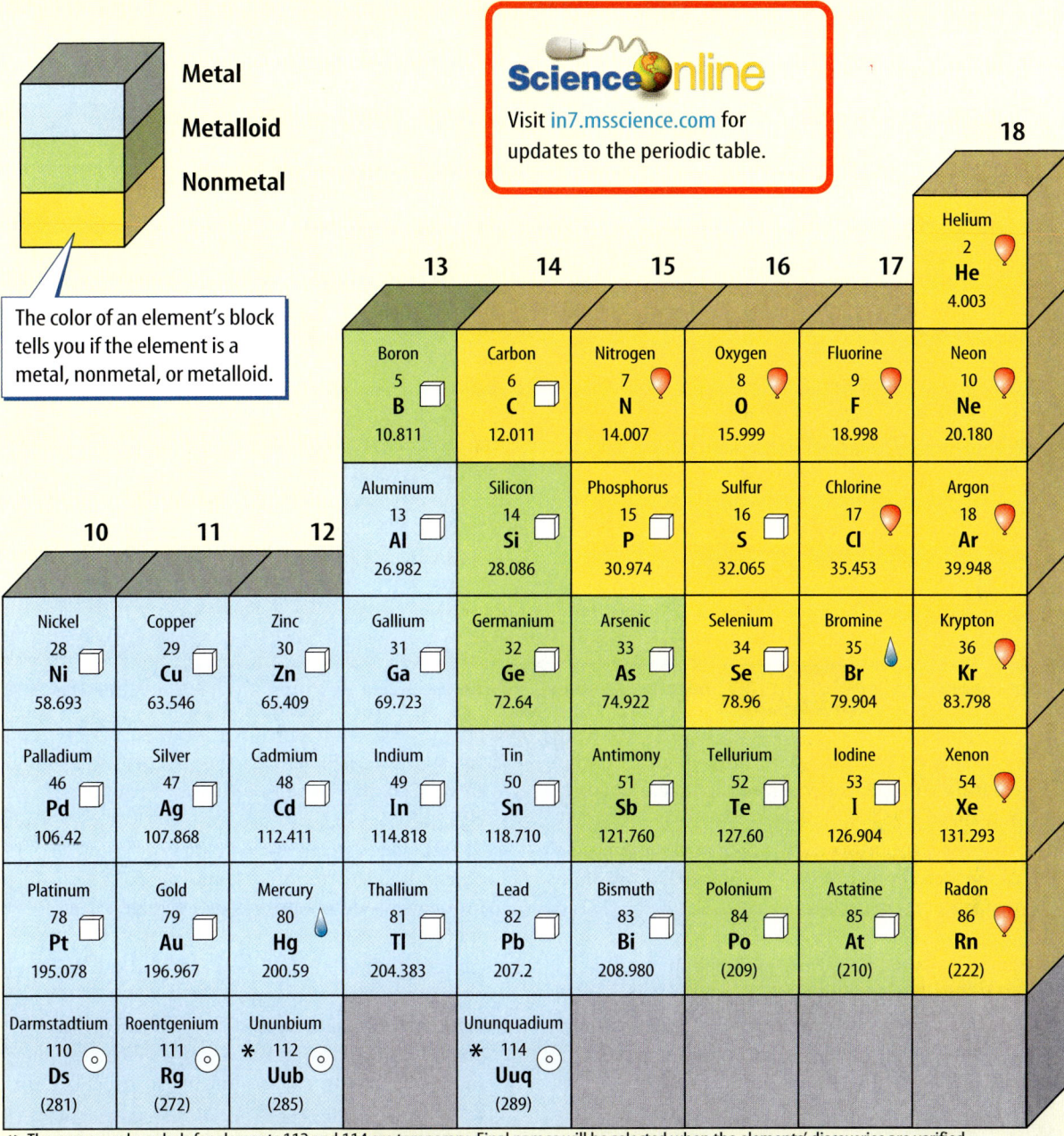

Glossary/Glosario

Cómo usar el glosario en español:
1. Busca el término en inglés que desees encontrar.
2. El término en español, junto con la definición, se encuentran en la columna de la derecha.

Pronunciation Key

Use the following key to help you sound out words in the glossary.

a............	back (BAK)	ew............	food (FEWD)
ay............	day (DAY)	yoo............	pure (PYOOR)
ah............	father (FAH thur)	yew............	few (FYEW)
ow............	flower (FLOW ur)	uh............	comma (CAH muh)
ar............	car (CAR)	u (+ con)......	rub (RUB)
e............	less (LES)	sh............	shelf (SHELF)
ee............	leaf (LEEF)	ch............	nature (NAY chur)
ih............	trip (TRIHP)	g............	gift (GIHFT)
i (i + con + e)..	idea (i DEE uh)	j............	gem (JEM)
oh............	go (GOH)	ing............	sing (SING)
aw............	soft (SAWFT)	zh............	vision (VIH zhun)
or............	orbit (OR buht)	k............	cake (KAYK)
oy............	coin (COYN)	s............	seed, cent (SEED, SENT)
oo............	foot (FOOT)	z............	zone, raise (ZOHN, RAYZ)

English — A — Español

abiotic (ay bi AH tihk) factor: any nonliving part of the environment, such as water, sunlight, temperature, and air. (p. 196)

absolute age: age, in years, of a rock or other object; can be determined by using properties of the atoms that make up materials. (p. 669)

absolute magnitude: measure of the amount of light a star actually gives off. (p. 474)

acceleration: equals the change in velocity divided by the time for the change to take place; occurs when an object speeds up, slows down, or turns. (p. 328)

acid: substance that releases H⁺ ions and produces hydronium ions when dissolved in water. (p. 302)

acid precipitation: precipitation with a pH below 5.6—which occurs when air pollutants from the burning of fossil fuels react with water in the atmosphere to form strong acids—that can pollute water, kill fish and plants, and damage soils. (p. 233)

active immunity: long-lasting immunity that results when the body makes its own antibodies in response to a specific antigen. (p. 176)

factor abiótico: cualquier parte no viva del medio ambiente, tal como el agua, la luz solar, la temperatura y el aire. (p. 196)

edad absoluta: edad, en años, de una roca u otro objeto; puede determinarse utilizando las propiedades de los átomos de los materiales. (p. 669)

magnitud absoluta: medida de la cantidad real de luz que genera una estrella. (p. 474)

aceleración: es igual al cambio de velocidad dividido por el tiempo que toma en realizarse dicho cambio; sucede cuando un objeto aumenta su velocidad, la disminuye o gira. (p. 328)

ácido: sustancia que libera iones H⁺ y produce iones de hidronio al ser disuelta en agua. (p. 302)

lluvia ácida: precipitación con un pH menor de 5.6—lo cual ocurre cuando los contaminantes del aire provenientes de la quema de combustibles fósiles reaccionan con el agua en la atmósfera para formar ácidos fuertes—que puede contaminar el agua, matar peces y plantas, y dañar los suelos. (p. 233)

inmunidad activa: inmunidad duradera que se presenta cuando el cuerpo crea sus propios anticuerpos como respuesta a un antígeno específico. (p. 176)

734 STUDENT RESOURCES

Glossary/Glosario

active transport: energy-requiring process in which transport proteins bind with particles and move them through a cell membrane. (p. 77)

adaptation: any structural or behavioral change that helps an organism survive in its particular environment. (p. 628)

allergen: substance that causes an allergic reaction. (p. 183)

alternative resource: new renewable or inexhaustible energy source; includes solar energy, wind, and geothermal energy. (p. 397)

alveoli (al VEE uh li): tiny, thin-walled, grapelike clusters at the end of each bronchiole that are surrounded by capillaries; carbon dioxide and oxygen exchange takes place. (p. 142)

amino acid: building block of protein. (p. 133)

amplitude: for a transverse wave, one half the distance between a crest and a trough. (p. 415)

analog signal: a electronic signal that carries information and varies smoothly with time. (p. 442)

antibody: a protein made in response to a specific antigen that can attach to the antigen and cause it to be useless. (p. 175)

antigen (AN tih jun): complex molecule that is foreign to your body. (p. 175)

apparent magnitude: measure of the amount of light from a star that is received on Earth. (p. 474)

aqueous (A kwee us): solution in which water is the solvent. (p. 294)

artery: blood vessel that carries blood away from the heart. (p. 170)

asexual reproduction: a type of reproduction—fission, budding, and regeneration—in which a new organism is produced from one organism and has DNA identical to the parent organism. (p. 101)

atom: a very small particle that makes up most kinds of matter and consists of smaller parts called protons, neutrons, and electrons. (p. 259)

atomic mass: average mass of an atom of an element; its unit of measure is the atomic mass unit (u), which is 1/12 the mass of a carbon-12 atom. (p. 270)

atomic number: number of protons in the nucleus of each atom of a given element; is the top number in the periodic table. (p. 269)

average speed: equals the total distance traveled divided by the total time taken to travel the distance. (p. 325)

transporte activo: proceso que requiere energía y en el cual las proteínas de transporte se unen con partículas y las trasladan a través de la membrana celular. (p. 77)

adaptación: cualquier cambio de estructura o comportamiento que ayude a un organismo a sobrevivir en su medio ambiente particular. (p. 628)

alergeno: sustancia que produce una reacción alérgica. (p. 183)

recurso alternativo: nueva fuente de energía renovable o inagotable; incluye energía solar, eólica y geotérmica. (p. 397)

alvéolos: racimos parecidos a las uvas, pequeños y de paredes finas encontrados en el extremo de cada bronquiolo, los cuales están rodeados de capilares y en donde se realiza el intercambio de dióxido de carbono y oxígeno. (p. 142)

aminoácido: bloque formador de las proteínas. (p. 133)

amplitud: para una onda transversal, es la mitad de la distancia entre la cresta y la depresión. (p. 415)

señal analógica: señal electrónica que conduce información y varía de manera uniforme con el tiempo. (p. 442)

anticuerpo: proteína creada como respuesta a un antígeno específico y que se puede adherir al antígeno inutilizándolo. (p. 175)

antígeno: molécula compleja extraña al cuerpo. (p. 175)

magnitud aparente: medida de la cantidad de luz recibida en la Tierra desde una estrella. (p. 474)

acuoso: solución en la cual el agua es el solvente. (p. 294)

arteria: vaso sanguíneo que transporta la sangre desde el corazón. (p. 170)

reproducción asexual: tipo de reproducción—fisión, gemación y regeneración—en el que un organismo da origen a uno nuevo de ADN idéntico al organismo progenitor. (p. 101)

átomo: partícula muy pequeña que constituye la mayoría de los tipos de materia y que está formada por partes más pequeñas llamadas protones, neutrones y electrones. (p. 259)

masa atómica: masa promedio de un átomo de un elemento; su unidad de medida es la unidad de masa atómica (u), la cual es 1/12 de la masa de un átomo de carbono-12. (p. 270)

número atómico: número de protones en el núcleo de un átomo de determinado elemento; es el número superior en la tabla periódica. (p. 269)

velocidad promedio: es igual al total de la distancia recorrida dividida por el tiempo total necesario para recorrer dicha distancia. (p. 325)

Glossary/Glosario

balanced forces/carbon film   **fuerzas balanceadas/película de carbono**

B

balanced forces: two or more forces whose effects cancel each other out and do not change the motion of an object. (p. 351)

basaltic: describes dense, dark-colored igneous rock formed from magma rich in magnesium and iron and poor in silica. (p. 539)

base: substance that accepts H^+ ions and produces hydroxide ions when dissolved in water. (p. 305)

Big Bang theory: states that about 13.7 billion years ago, the universe began with a huge, fiery explosion. (p. 493)

binary system: number system consisting of two digits, 0 and 1, that can be used by devices such as computers to store or use information. (p. 450)

binomial nomenclature (bi NOH mee ul • NOH mun klay chur): two-word naming system that gives all organisms their scientific name. (p. 24)

biogenesis (bi oh JEH nuh sus): theory that living things come only from other living things. (p. 19)

biosphere (BI uh sfihr): part of Earth that supports life—the top part of Earth's crust, all the waters covering Earth's surface, and the surrounding atmosphere; includes all biomes, ecosystems, communities, and populations. (p. 201)

biotic (bi AHT ihk) factor: any living or once-living organism in the environment. (p. 196)

black hole: final stage in the evolution of a very massive star, where the core's mass collapses to a point that it's gravity is so strong that not even light can escape. (p. 486)

bladder: elastic, muscular organ that holds urine until it leaves the body through the urethra. (p. 149)

bronchi (BRAHN ki): two short tubes that branch off the lower end of the trachea and carry air into the lungs. (p. 142)

fuerzas balanceadas: dos o más fuerzas cuyos efectos se cancelan mutuamente sin cambiar el movimiento de un objeto. (p. 351)

basáltica: roca ígnea densa de color oscuro que se forma a partir de magma rico en magnesio y hierro pero pobre en sílice. (p. 539)

base: sustancia que acepta los iones H^+ y produce iones de hidróxido al ser disuelta en agua. (p. 305)

teoría de la Gran Explosión: establece que hace aproximadamente 13.7 billones de años el universo se originó con una enorme explosión. (p. 493)

sistema binario: sistema numérico que consiste en dos dígitos, 0 y 1, que se puede usar con dispositivos como las computadoras para almacenar o usar información. (p. 450)

nomenclatura binomial: sistema de denominación de dos palabras que da a todos los organismos su nombre científico. (p. 24)

biogénesis: teoría que sostiene que los seres vivos sólo provienen de otros seres vivos. (p. 19)

biosfera: parte de la Tierra que alberga la vida, es decir, la parte superior de la corteza terrestre, toda el agua que cubre la superficie terrestre y la atmósfera circundante; incluye todas las biomasas, ecosistemas, comunidades y poblaciones. (p. 201)

factor biótico: cualquier organismo vivo, o que estuvo vivo, del medio ambiente. (p. 196)

agujero negro: etapa final en la evolución de una estrella masiva, en donde la masa del núcleo se colapsa hasta el punto de que su gravedad es tan fuerte que ni siquiera la luz puede escapar. (p. 486)

vejiga: órgano muscular elástico que retiene la orina hasta que ésta sale del cuerpo a través de la uretra. (p. 149)

bronquios: dos tubos cortos que salen del extremo inferior de la tráquea y llevan el aire a los pulmones. (p. 142)

C

capillary (KA puh ler ee): blood vessel that connects arteries and veins. (p. 170)

carbohydrate (kar boh HI drayt): nutrient that usually is the body's main source of energy. (p. 134)

carbon film: thin film of carbon residue preserved as a fossil. (p. 656)

capilar: vaso sanguíneo que conecta las arterias y las venas. (p. 170)

carbohidrato: nutriente que por lo general es la principal fuente de energía del cuerpo. (p. 134)

película de carbono: capa delgada de residuos de carbono preservada como un fósil. (p. 656)

736   **STUDENT RESOURCES**

Glossary/Glosario

cast/compaction

cast: a type of body fossil that forms when crystals fill a mold or sediments wash into a mold and harden into rock. (p. 657)

cell: smallest unit of an organism that can carry on life functions. (p. 14)

cell membrane: protective outer covering of all cells that regulates the interaction between the cell and the environment. (p. 38)

cell theory: states that all organisms are made up of one or more cells, the cell is the basic unit of life, and all cells come from other cells. (p. 51)

cell wall: rigid structure that encloses, supports, and protects the cells of plants, algae, fungi, and most bacteria. (p. 39)

cementation: sedimentary rock-forming process in which sediment grains are held together by natural cements that are produced when water moves through rock and soil. (p. 547)

center of mass: point in a object that moves as if all of the object's mass were concentrated at that point. (p. 362)

chemical energy: energy stored in chemical bonds. (p. 383)

chloroplast: green, chlorophyll-containing, plant-cell organelle that uses light energy to produce sugar from carbon dioxide and water. (p. 42)

chromosome: structure in a cell's nucleus that contains hereditary material. (p. 98)

chromosphere: layer of the Sun's atmosphere above the photosphere. (p. 477)

chyme (KIME): liquid product of digestion. (p. 131)

cinder cone volcano: relatively small volcano formed by moderate to explosive eruptions of tephra. (p. 604)

cleavage: physical property of some minerals that causes them to break along smooth, flat surfaces. (p. 513)

climate: average weather pattern in an area over a long period of time; can be classified by temperature, humidity, precipitation, and vegetation. (p. 624)

community: all of the populations of different species in a given area that interact in some way and depend on one another for food, shelter, and other needs. (p. 200)

compaction: process that forms sedimentary rocks when layers of sediments are compressed by the weight of the layers above them. (p. 546)

vaciado/compactación

vaciado: tipo de cuerpo fósil que se forma cuando los cristales llenan un molde o los sedimentos son lavados hacia un molde y se endurecen convirtiéndose en roca. (p. 657)

célula: la unidad más pequeña de un organismo que puede continuar con sus funciones vitales. (p. 14)

membrana celular: capa externa protectora de todas las células y reguladora de la interacción entre la célula y su entorno. (p. 38)

teoría celular: establece que todos los organismos están formados por una o más células, que la célula es la unidad básica de la vida y que las células provienen de otras células. (p. 51)

pared celular: estructura rígida que envuelve, sostiene y protege a las células de las plantas, algas, hongos y de la mayoría de las bacterias. (p. 39)

cementación: proceso de formación de la roca sedimentaria en el que las partículas de sedimento están unidas por cementos naturales producidos cuando el agua se mueve a través de la roca y el suelo. (p. 547)

centro de masa: punto en un objeto que se mueve como si toda la masa del objeto estuviera concentrada en ese punto. (p. 362)

energía química: energía almacenada en enlaces químicos. (p. 383)

cloroplasto: organelo de las células vegetales, de color verde, que contiene clorofila y que usa la luz solar para convertir el dióxido de carbono y el agua en azúcar. (p. 42)

cromosoma: estructura en el núcleo celular que contiene el material hereditario. (p. 98)

cromosfera: capa de la atmósfera del sol que se encuentra sobre la fotosfera. (p. 477)

quimo: líquido producido durante la digestión. (p. 131)

volcán de cono de cenizas: volcán relativamente pequeño formado por erupciones moderadas o explosivas de tefra. (p. 604)

exfoliación: propiedad física de algunos minerales que causa que se rompan junto a superficies planas y lisas. (p. 513)

clima: modelo meteorológico en un área durante un periodo de tiempo largo; puede clasificarse por temperatura, humedad, precipitación y vegetación. (p. 624)

comunidad: todas las poblaciones de diferentes especies en una determinada área, que interactúan de alguna forma y que dependen unas de otras en cuanto a alimento, refugio y otras necesidades. (p. 200)

compactación: proceso que forma rocas sedimentarias cuando las capas de sedimento son comprimidas por el peso de las capas superiores. (p. 546)

GLOSSARY/GLOSARIO 737

Glossary/Glosario

composite volcano/diffusion — **volcán compuesto/difusión**

composite volcano: steep-sided volcano formed from alternating layers of violent eruptions of tephra and quieter eruptions of lava. (p. 605)

compound: a substance produced when elements combine and whose properties are different from each of the elements in it. (p. 273)

compressional wave: mechanical wave that causes particles in matter to move back and forth along the direction the wave travels. (p. 413)

computer software: any list of instructions for a computer to follow that is stored in the computer's memory. (p. 453)

concentration: describes how much solute is present in a solution compared to the amount of solvent. (p. 299)

constellation: group of stars that forms a pattern in the sky that looks like a familiar object (Libra), animal (Pegasus), or character (Orion). (p. 472)

control: standard to which the outcome of a test is compared. (p. 9)

corona: outermost, largest layer of the Sun's atmosphere; extends millions of kilometers into space and has temperatures up to 2 million K. (p. 477)

crust: Earth's outermost layer that is thinnest under the oceans and thickest through the mountains and contains all features of Earth's surface. (p. 566)

crystal: solid in which the atoms are arranged in an orderly, repeating pattern. (p. 505)

cytoplasm: constantly moving gel-like mixture inside the cell membrane that contains heredity material and is the location of most of a cell's life processes. (p. 38)

volcán compuesto: volcán de costados inclinados formado por capas alternas producto de erupciones violentas de tefra y erupciones silenciosas de lava. (p. 605)

compuesto: sustancia resultante de la combinación de elementos cuyas propiedades son diferentes de los elementos que la componen. (p. 273)

onda de compresión: onda mecánica que hace que las partículas de materia se muevan hacia adelante y hacia atrás en la dirección en que viaja la onda. (p. 413)

software para computadoras: cualquier lista de instrucciones que debe realizar una computadora y que se almacena en la memoria de ésta. (p. 453)

concentración: describe la cantidad de soluto presente en una solución, comparada con la cantidad de solvente. (p. 299)

constelación: grupo de estrellas que forma un patrón en el cielo y que semeja un objeto (Libra), un animal (Pegaso) o un personaje familiar (Orión). (p. 472)

control: estándar contra el que se compara el resultado de una prueba. (p. 9)

corona: capa más externa y más grande de la atmósfera solar; se extiende millones de kilómetros dentro del espacio y tiene una temperatura hasta de 2 millones de grados Kelvin. (p. 477)

corteza: capa más externa de la Tierra, la cual es más delgada debajo de los océanos y más gruesa en las montañas y contiene todas las características de la superficie terrestre. (p. 566)

cristal: sólido en el que los átomos están alineados en forma ordenada y repetitiva. (p. 505)

citoplasma: mezcla parecida al gel y que está en constante movimiento dentro de la membrana celular, contiene material hereditario y es en donde tiene lugar la mayor parte de los procesos vitales de la célula. (p. 38)

D

deforestation: destruction and cutting down of forests—often to clear land for mining, roads, and grazing of cattle—resulting in increased atmospheric CO_2 levels. (p. 641)

diffraction: bending of waves around an object. (p. 418)

diffusion: a type of passive transport in cells in which molecules move from areas where there are more of them to areas where there are fewer of them. (p. 75)

deforestación: destrucción y tala de los bosques—a menudo el despeje de la tierra para minería, carreteras y ganadería—resultando en el aumento de los niveles atmosféricos de dióxido de carbono. (p. 641)

difracción: curvatura de las ondas alrededor de un objeto. (p. 418)

difusión: tipo de transporte pasivo en las células en el que las moléculas se mueven de áreas de mayor concentración de éstas hacia áreas de menor concentración. (p. 75)

digital signal: electronic signal that varies information that does not vary smoothly with time, but changes in steps between certain values, and can be represented by a series of numbers. (p. 443)

diode: a solid-state component made from two layers of semiconductor material that allows electric current to flow in only one direction and is commonly used to change alternating current to direct current. (p. 446)

diploid (DIHP loyd): cell whose similar chromosomes occur in pairs. (p. 104)

DNA: deoxyribonucleic acid; the genetic material of all organisms; made up of two twisted strands of sugar-phosphate molecules and nitrogen bases. (p. 110)

señal digital: señal electrónica que varía aquella información que no varía de manera uniforme con el tiempo, pero que cambia por grados entre ciertos valores y que puede ser representada por una serie de números. (p. 443)

diodo: componente de estado sólido conformado por dos capas de material semiconductor que permite el flujo de corriente eléctrica en una sola dirección y que comúnmente se utiliza para cambiar la corriente alterna a corriente directa. (p. 446)

diploide: célula cuyos cromosomas similares están en pares. (p. 104)

ADN: Ácido desoxirribonucleico; material genético de todos los organismos constituido por dos cadenas trenzadas de moléculas de azúcar-fosfato y bases de nitrógeno (p. 110)

earthquake: movement of the ground that occurs when rocks inside Earth pass their elastic limit, break suddenly, and experience elastic rebound. (p. 592)

ecology: study of all the interactions among organisms and their environment. (p. 196)

ecosystem: all of the communities in a given area and the abiotic factors that affect them. (p. 200)

egg: haploid sex cell formed in the female reproductive organs. (p. 104)

El Niño (el NEEN yoh): climatic event that begins in the tropical Pacific Ocean; may occur when trade winds weaken or reverse, and can disrupt normal temperature and precipitation patterns around the world. (p. 633)

electrical energy: energy carried by electric current. (p. 384)

electromagnetic spectrum: complete range of electromagnetic wave frequencies and wavelengths. (p. 426)

electromagnetic waves: waves that can travel through matter or empty space, include radio waves, infrared waves, visible light waves, ultraviolet waves, X rays and gamma rays. (p. 425)

electron: invisible, negatively charged particle located in a cloudlike formation that surrounds the nucleus of an atom. (p. 262)

electronic signal: a changing electric current that is used to carry information; can be analog or digital. (p. 442)

terremoto: movimiento del suelo que ocurre cuando las rocas del interior de la Tierra sobrepasan su límite de elasticidad, se rompen súbitamente y experimentan rebotes elásticos. (p. 592)

ecología: estudio de todas las interacciones entre los organismos y su medio ambiente. (p. 196)

ecosistema: todas las comunidades en un área determinada y los factores abióticos que las afectan. (p. 200)

óvulo: célula sexual haploide que se forma en los órganos reproductivos femeninos. (p. 104)

El Niño: evento climático que comienza en el Océano Pacífico tropical; puede ocurrir cuando los vientos alisios se debilitan o se invierten; puede desestabilizar los patrones normales de precipitación y temperatura del mundo. (p. 633)

energía eléctrica: energía transportada por corriente eléctrica. (p. 384)

espectro electromagnético: rango total de las frecuencias y longitudes de onda de las ondas electromagnéticas. (p. 426)

ondas electromagnéticas: ondas que pueden viajar a través de la materia o del espacio vacío; incluyen las ondas de radio, las infrarrojas, las de luz visible, las ultravioleta y los rayos X y gama. (p. 425)

electrón: partícula invisible con carga negativa, localizada en una formación parecida a una nube que rodea el núcleo de un átomo. (p. 262)

señal electrónica: corriente eléctrica dinámica que se usa para conducir información; puede ser analógica o digital. (p. 442)

element/fertilization **elemento/fertilización**

element: natural or synthetic material that cannot be broken down into simpler materials by ordinary means; has unique properties and is generally classified as a metal, metalloid, or nonmetal. (p. 266)

endocytosis (en duh si TOH sus): process by which a cell takes in a substance by surrounding it with the cell membrane. (p. 78)

endoplasmic reticulum (ER): cytoplasmic organelle that moves materials around in a cell and is made up of a complex series of folded membranes; can be rough (with attached ribosomes) or smooth (without attached ribosomes). (p. 43)

energy: the ability to cause change. (p. 380)

enzyme: a type of protein that speeds up chemical reactions in the body without being changed or used up itself. (pp. 71, 128)

epicenter: point on Earth's surface directly above an earthquake's focus. (p. 594)

equilibrium: occurs when molecules of one substance are spread evenly throughout another substance. (p. 75)

erosion: movement of soil from one place to another. (p. 239)

exocytosis (ek soh si TOH sus): process by which vesicles release their contents outside the cell. (p. 78)

extrusive: describes fine-grained igneous rock that forms when magma cools quickly at or near Earth's surface. (p. 537)

elemento: material natural o sintético que no puede ser descompuesto fácilmente en materiales más simples por medios ordinarios; tiene propiedades únicas y generalmente es clasificado como metal, metaloide o no metal. (p. 266)

endocitosis: proceso mediante el cual una célula capta una sustancia rodeándola con su membrana celular. (p. 78)

retículo endoplásmático (RE): organelo citoplasmático que transporta materiales dentro de una célula y está formado por una serie compleja de membranas plegadas; puede ser rugoso (con ribosomas adosados) o liso (sin ribosomas adosados). (p. 43)

energía: capacidad de producir cambios. (p. 380)

enzima: tipo de proteína que acelera las reacciones químicas en el cuerpo sin que ésta sufra modificaciones o se agote. (pp. 71, 128)

epicentro: punto de la superficie terrestre directamente encima del foco del terremoto. (p. 594)

equilibrio: ocurre cuando las moléculas de una sustancia están diseminadas completa y uniformemente a lo largo de otra sustancia. (p. 75)

erosión: movimiento del suelo de un lugar a otro. (p. 239)

exocitosis: proceso mediante el cual las vesículas liberan su contenido fuera de la célula. (p. 78)

extrusivo: describe rocas ígneas de grano fino que se forman cuando el magma se enfría rápidamente en o cerca de la superficie terrestre. (p. 537)

fault: fracture that occurs when rocks break and that results in relative movement of opposing sides; can form as a result of compression (reverse fault), being pulled apart (normal fault), or shear (strike-slip fault). (pp. 569, 593)

fault-block mountains: sharp, jagged mountains made of huge, tilted blocks of rock that are separated from surrounding rock by faults and form because of pulling forces. (p. 576)

fermentation: process by which oxygen-lacking cells and some one-celled organisms release small amounts of energy from glucose molecules and produce wastes such as alcohol, carbon dioxide, and lactic acid. (p. 84)

fertilization: in sexual reproduction, the joining of a sperm and egg. (p. 104)

falla: fractura que ocurre cuando al romperse una roca se presentan relativos movimientos de los lados opuestos; se pueden formar como resultado de una compresión (falla reversa), al separarse (falla normal) o al deslizarse (falla por desplazamiento). (pp. 569, 593)

montañas con bloques de fallas: montañas afiladas y dentadas formadas por enormes bloques de roca inclinados, separados de las rocas adyacentes por fallas y que se forman debido a fuerzas atrayentes. (p. 576)

fermentación: proceso mediante el cual las células carentes de oxígeno y algunos organismos unicelulares liberan pequeñas cantidades de energía a partir de moléculas de glucosa y producen desechos como alcohol, dióxido de carbono y ácido láctico. (p. 84)

fertilización: en la reproducción sexual, la unión de un óvulo y un espermatozoide. (p. 104)

Glossary/Glosario

focus/geothermal energy   **foco/energía geotérmica**

focus: point deep inside Earth where energy is released, causing an earthquake. (p. 594)

folded mountain: mountain that forms by the folding of rock layers caused by compressive forces. (p. 577)

foliated: describes metamorphic rock, such as slate and gneiss, whose mineral grains line up in parallel layers. (p. 543)

food chain: model that describes how energy passes from one organism to another. (p. 208)

food web: model that describes how energy from food moves through a community; a series of overlapping food chains. (p. 210)

force: a push or a pull. (p. 350)

fossil fuels: nonrenewable energy resources—coal, oil, and natural gas—that formed in Earth's crust over hundreds of millions of years. (p. 226)

fossils: remains, imprints, or traces of prehistoric organisms that can tell when and where organisms once lived and how they lived. (p. 655)

fracture: physical property of some minerals that causes them to break with uneven, rough, or jagged surfaces. (p. 513)

frequency: number of wavelengths that pass a given point in one second, measured in hertz (Hz). (p. 414)

friction: force that acts to oppose sliding between two surfaces that are touching. (p. 352)

foco: punto profundo de la Tierra donde se genera energía causando un terremoto. (p. 594)

montañas plegadas: montañas que se forman por el plegamiento de capas de rocas causado por fuerzas de tracción. (p. 577)

foliado: describe rocas metamórficas, como pizarra y gneis, cuyas vetas minerales se alinean en capas paralelas. (p. 543)

cadena alimenticia: modelo que describe la forma como pasa la energía de un organismo a otro. (p. 208)

red alimenticia: modelo que describe cómo la energía proveniente de los alimentos pasa a una comunidad; es una serie de cadenas alimenticias entrelazadas. (p. 210)

fuerza: presión o tracción. (p. 350)

combustibles fósiles: recursos energéticos no renovables—carbón, petróleo y gas natural—que se formaron en la corteza terrestre durante cientos de millones de años. (p. 226)

fósiles: restos, huellas o trazas de organismos prehistóricos que pueden informar cuándo, dónde y cómo vivieron tales organismos. (p. 655)

fractura: propiedad física de algunos minerales que causa que se rompan formando superficies irregulares, ásperas o dentadas. (p. 513)

frecuencia: número de longitudes de onda que pasan un punto determinado en un segundo; se mide en hertz (Hz). (p. 414)

fricción: fuerza que actúa para oponerse al deslizamiento entre dos superficies que se tocan. (p. 352)

G

galaxy: large group of stars, dust, and gas held together by gravity; can be elliptical, spiral, or irregular. (p. 488)

gem: beautiful, rare, highly prized mineral that can be worn in jewelry. (p. 515)

gene: section of DNA on a chromosome that contains instructions for making specific proteins. (p. 112)

generator: device that transforms kinetic energy into electrical energy. (p. 390)

genus: first word of the two-word scientific name used to identify a group of similar species. (p. 24)

geothermal energy: heat energy within Earth's crust, available only where natural geysers or volcanoes are located. (p. 229)

galaxia: grupo grande de estrellas, polvo y gas en donde todo está unido por gravedad; puede ser elíptica, espiral o irregular. (p. 488)

gema: mineral hermoso, raro y altamente valorado que puede usarse como joya. (p. 515)

gen: sección de ADN en un cromosoma, el cual contiene instrucciones para la formación de proteínas específicas. (p. 112)

generador: dispositivo que transforma la energía cinética en energía eléctrica. (p. 390)

género: primera palabra, de las dos palabras del nombre científico, que se usa para identificar a un grupo de especies similares. (p. 24)

energía geotérmica: energía calórica en el interior de la corteza terrestre disponible sólo donde existen géiseres o volcanes. (p. 229)

Glossary/Glosario

giant/host cell   **gigante/célula huésped**

giant: late stage in the life of comparatively low-mass main sequence star in which hydrogen in the core is deleted, the core contracts and temperatures inside the star increase, causing its outer layers to expand and cool. (p. 485)

global warming: increase in the average global temperature of Earth. (p. 640)

Golgi bodies: organelles that package cellular materials and transport them within the cell or out of the cell. (p. 43)

granitic: describes generally light-colored, silica-rich igneous rock that is less dense than basaltic rock. (p. 539)

greenhouse effect: natural heating that occurs when certain gases in Earth's atmosphere, such as methane, CO_2, and water vapor, trap heat. (pp. 234, 639)

gigante: etapa tardía en la vida de una estrella de secuencia principal, de relativamente poca masa, en la que el hidrógeno en el núcleo está agotado, el núcleo se contrae y la temperatura en el interior de la estrella aumenta, causando que las capas externas se expandan y enfríen. (p. 485)

calentamiento global: incremento del promedio de la temperatura global. (p. 640)

aparato de Golgi: organelo que concentra los materiales celulares y los transporta hacia adentro o afuera de la célula. (p. 43)

granítica: roca ígnea rica en sílice, generalmente de color claro y menos densa que la rocas basáltica. (p. 539)

efecto invernadero: calentamiento natural que ocurre cuando ciertos gases en la atmósfera terrestre, como el metano, el dióxido de carbono y el vapor de agua atrapan el calor. (pp. 234, 639)

H

habitat: place where an organism lives. (p. 207)

half-life: time it takes for half the atoms of an isotope to decay. (p. 670)

haploid (HAP loyd): cell that has half the number of chromosomes as body cells. (p. 105)

hardness: measure of how easily a mineral can be scratched. (p. 511)

hazardous wastes: waste materials, such as pesticides and leftover paints, that are harmful to human health or poisonous to living organisms. (p. 240)

hemoglobin (HEE muh gloh bun): a molecule in red blood cells that carries oxygen and carbon dioxide. (p. 163)

heterogeneous mixture: type of mixture where the substances are not evenly mixed. (p. 289)

hibernation: behavioral adaptation for winter survival in which an animal's activity is greatly reduced, its body temperature drops, and body processes slow down. (p. 630)

homeostasis: regulation of an organism's internal, life-maintaining conditions. (p. 15)

homogeneous mixture: type of mixture where two or more substances are evenly mixed on a molecular level but are not bonded together. (p. 290)

host cell: living cell in which a virus can actively multiply or in which a virus can hide until activated by environmental stimuli. (p. 52)

hábitat: lugar donde viven los organismos. (p. 207)

vida media: tiempo que le toma a la mitad de los átomos de un isótopo para desintegrarse. (p. 670)

haploide: célula que posee la mitad del número de cromosomas que tienen las células somáticas. (p. 105)

dureza: medida de la facilidad con que un mineral puede ser rayado. (p. 511)

desperdicios peligrosos: materiales de desecho como los pesticidas y residuos de pintura nocivos para la salud humana o dañinos para los organismos vivos. (p. 240)

hemoglobina: molécula presente en los glóbulos rojos que transporta oxígeno y dióxido de carbono. (p. 163)

mezcla heterogénea: tipo de mezcla en la cual las sustancias no están mezcladas de manera uniforme. (p. 289)

hibernación: adaptación del comportamiento para sobrevivir durante el invierno en la cual la actividad del animal se ve fuertemente reducida, su temperatura corporal se reduce y los procesos corporales disminuyen su ritmo. (p. 630)

homeostasis: control de las condiciones internas que mantienen la vida de un organismo. (p. 15)

mezcla homogénea: tipo de mezcla en la cual dos o más sustancias están mezcladas en de manera uniforme a nivel molecular pero no están enlazadas. (p. 290)

célula huésped: célula viva en la que un virus puede reproducirse activamente o en la que un virus puede ocultarse hasta que es activado por estímulos del medio ambiente. (p. 52)

STUDENT RESOURCES

Glossary/Glosario

hot spot: hot, molten rock material that has been forced upward from deep inside Earth, which may cause magma to break through Earth's mantle and crust and may form volcanoes. (p. 610)

hydroelectric power: electricity produced when the energy of falling water turns the blades of a generator turbine. (p. 227)

hydronium ion: hydrogen ion combines with a water molecule to form a hydronium ion, H_3O^+. (p. 302)

hypothesis: prediction that can be tested. (p. 8)

punto caliente: material de roca fundida, caliente, que ha sido lanzado hacia arriba desde lo más profundo de la Tierra y que puede producir que el magma se rompa a través del manto y la corteza pudiendo formar volcanes. (p. 610)

energía hidroeléctrica: electricidad producida cuando la energía generada por la caída del agua hace girar las aspas de una turbina generadora. (p. 227)

ion de hidronio: ion de hidrógeno combinado con una molécula de agua para formar un ion de hidronio, H_3O^+. (p. 302)

hipótesis: predicción que puede probarse. (p. 8)

I

igneous rock: rock formed when magma or lava cools and hardens. (p. 536)

index fossils: remains of species that existed on Earth for a relatively short period of time, were abundant and widespread geographically, and can be used by geologists to assign the ages of rock layers. (p. 659)

indicator: compound that changes color at different pH values when it reacts with acidic or basic solutions. (p. 308)

inertia: tendency of an object to resist a change in its motion. (p. 333)

inexhaustible resource: energy source that can't be used up by humans. (p. 397)

infectious disease: disease caused by a virus, bacterium, fungus, or protest that is spread from one person to another. (p. 179)

infrared waves: electromagnetic waves with wavelengths between about one thousandth of a meter and 700 billionths of a meter (p. 427)

inner core: solid, innermost layer of Earth's interior that is the hottest part of Earth and experiences the greatest amount of pressure. (p. 565)

inorganic compound: compound, such as H_2O, that is made from elements other than carbon and whose atoms usually can be arranged in only one structure. (p. 71)

instantaneous speed: the speed of an object at one instant of time. (p. 325)

integrated circuit: circuit that can contain millions of interconnected transistors and diodes imprinted on a single small chip of semiconductor material. (p. 447)

roca ígnea: roca formada cuando se enfría y endurece el magma o la lava. (p. 536)

fósiles índice: restos de especies que existieron sobre la Tierra durante un periodo de tiempo relativamente corto y que fueron abundantes y ampliamente diseminadas geográficamente; los geólogos pueden usarlos para inferir las edades de las capas rocosas. (p. 659)

indicador: compuesto que cambia de color con diferentes valores de pH al reaccionar con soluciones ácidas o básicas. (p. 308)

inercia: tendencia de un objeto a resistirse a un cambio de movimiento. (p. 333)

recurso inagotable: fuente de energía que no puede ser agotada por los seres humanos. (p. 397)

enfermedad infecciosa: enfermedad causada por un virus, bacteria, hongo o protista y que se propaga de una persona a otra. (p. 179)

ondas infrarrojas: ondas electromagnéticas con longitudes de onda entre aproximadamente una milésima y 700 billonésimas de metro. (p. 427)

núcleo interior: la capa sólida más interna del centro de la Tierra, la cual constituye la parte más caliente de ésta y en donde se ejerce la mayor cantidad de presión. (p. 565)

compuesto inorgánico: compuesto, como H_2O, formado por elementos distintos al carbono y cuyos átomos generalmente pueden estar organizados en sólo una estructura. (p. 71)

velocidad instantánea: la velocidad de un objeto en un instante de tiempo. (p. 325)

circuito integrado: circuito que puede contener millones de transistores y diodos interconectados y fijados en un solo chip de tamaño reducido y hecho de material semiconductor. (p. 447)

Glossary/Glosario

intensity/light-year — **intensidad/año luz**

intensity: amount of energy a wave carries past a certain area each second. (p. 420)

intrusive: describes a type of igneous rock that generally contains large crystals and forms when magma cools slowly beneath Earth's surface. (p. 537)

isostasy: principle stating that Earth's lithosphere floats on a plasticlike upper part of the mantle called the athenosphere. (p. 580)

isotopes (I suh tohps): two or more atoms of the same element that have different numbers of neutrons in their nuclei. (p. 269)

intensidad: cantidad de energía que transporta una onda al pasar por un área determinada en un segundo. (p. 420)

intrusivo: describe un tipo de roca ígnea que generalmente contiene cristales grandes y se forma cuando el magma se enfría lentamente por debajo de la superficie terrestre. (p. 537)

isostasía: principio que establece que la litosfera de la Tierra flota en la parte superior del manto, semejante a un plástico, llamada astenosfera. (p. 580)

isótopos: dos o más átomos del mismo elemento que tienen diferente número de neutrones en su núcleo. (p. 269)

K

kinetic energy: energy an object has due to its motion. (p. 381)

kingdom: first and largest category used to classify organisms. (p. 23)

energía cinética: energía que posee un objeto debido a su movimiento. (p. 381)

reino: la primera y más grande categoría utilizada para clasificar a los organismos. (p. 23)

L

larynx: airway to which the vocal cords are attached. (p. 142)

lava: molten rock flowing onto Earth's surface. (pp. 536, 601)

law: statement about how things work in nature that seems to be true consistently. (p. 10)

law of conservation of energy: states that energy can change its form but is never created or destroyed. (p. 386)

law of conservation of matter: states that matter is not created or destroyed but only changes its form. (p. 260)

law of conservation of momentum: states that the total momentum of objects that collide with each other is the same before and after the collision. (p. 335)

law of reflection: states that the angle the incoming wave makes with the normal to the reflecting surface equals the angle the reflected wave makes with the surface. (p. 417)

light-year: unit representing the distance light travels in one year—about 9.5 trillion km—used to record distances between stars and galaxies. (p. 475)

laringe: pasaje aéreo al cual están adheridas las cuerdas vocales. (p. 142)

lava: roca fundida que fluye en la superficie terrestre. (pp. 536, 601)

ley: enunciado acerca de cómo funciona todo en la naturaleza y que constantemente parece ser verdadero. (p. 10)

ley de la conservación de la energía: establece que la energía puede cambiar de forma pero nunca puede ser creada ni destruida. (p. 386)

ley de la conservación de la materia: establece que la materia no se crea ni se destruye, solamente cambia de forma. (p. 260)

ley de conservación de momento: establece que el momento total de los objetos que chocan entre sí es el mismo antes y después de la colisión. (p. 335)

ley de reflexión: establece que el ángulo que forman la onda que llega y la normal hacia la superficie reflejante es igual al ángulo que la onda reflejada forma con la superficie. (p. 417)

año luz: unidad que representa la distancia que la luz viaja en un año—cerca de 9.5 trillones de kilómetros—usada para registrar las distancias entre las estrellas y las galaxias. (p. 475)

Glossary/Glosario

limiting factor: any biotic or abiotic factor that limits the number of individuals in a population. (p. 205)

lithosphere (LIH thuh sfihr): rigid layer of Earth about 100 km thick, made of the crust and a part of the upper mantle. (p. 568)

luster: describes the way a mineral reflects light from its surface; can be metallic or nonmetallic. (p. 512)

lymph: fluid that has diffused into the lymphatic capillaries. (p. 173)

factor limitante: cualquier factor biótico o abiótico que limite el número de individuos en una población. (p. 205)

litosfera: capa rígida de la Tierra de aproximadamente 100 kilómetros de grosor, formada por la corteza y una parte del manto superior. (p. 568)

brillo: describe la forma en que un mineral refleja la luz desde su superficie; puede ser metálicos o no metálicos. (p. 512)

linfa: fluido que se encuentra difundido en los capilares linfáticos. (p. 173)

magma: hot, melted rock material beneath Earth's surface. (p. 507)

magnitude: a measure of the energy released by an earthquake. (p. 595)

mantle: largest layer of Earth's interior that lies above the outer core and is solid yet flows slowly. (p. 566)

mass: amount of matter in an object. (p. 333)

mass number: sum of the number of protons and neutrons in the nucleus of an atom. (p. 269)

matter: anything that has mass and takes up space and is made up of different kinds of atoms; includes all things that can be seen, tasted, smelled, or touched but does not include heat, sound, or light. (p. 258)

meiosis (mi OH sus): reproductive process that produces four haploid sex cells from one diploid cell and ensures offspring will have the same number of chromosomes as the parent organisms. (p. 105)

metabolism: the total of all chemical reactions in an organism. (p. 81)

metal: element that is malleable, ductile, a good conductor of electricity, and generally has a shiny or metallic luster. (p. 270)

metalloid: element that has characteristics of both metals and nonmetals and is a solid at room temperature. (p. 271)

metamorphic rock: forms when heat, pressure, or fluids act on igneous, sedimentary, or other metamorphic rock to change its form or composition, or both. (p. 541)

microprocessor: integrated circuit that controls the flow of information between different parts of the computer; also called the central processing unit or CPU. (p. 455)

magma: material rocoso fundido y caliente que se encuentra por debajo de la superficie terrestre. (p. 507)

magnitud: medida de la energía generada por un terremoto. (p. 595)

manto: la capa más grande del interior de la Tierra que yace sobre el núcleo exterior y que es sólida aunque fluye lentamente. (p. 566)

masa: cantidad de materia en un objeto. (p. 333)

número de masa: suma del número de protones y neutrones en el núcleo de un átomo. (p. 269)

materia: todo lo que tenga masa, ocupe espacio y esté hecho de diferentes tipos de átomos; incluye todo lo que se puede ver, saborear, oler o tocar, pero no incluye el calor, el sonido o la luz. (p. 258)

meiosis: proceso reproductivo que produce cuatro células sexuales haploides a partir de una célula diploide y asegura que la descendencia tendrá el mismo número de cromosomas que los organismos progenitores. (p. 105)

metabolismo: el conjunto de todas las reacciones químicas en un organismo. (p. 81)

metal: elemento maleable, dúctil y buen conductor de electricidad que generalmente tiene un lustre brillante o metálico. (p. 270)

metaloide: elemento que comparte características de los metales y de los no metales y es sólido a temperatura ambiente. (p. 271)

roca metamórfica: se forma cuando el calor, la presión o los fluidos actúan sobre una roca ígnea, sedimentaria u otra roca metamórfica para cambiar su forma, composición o ambas. (p. 541)

microprocesador: circuito integrado que controla el flujo de información entre diferentes partes de una computadora; también se lo denomina la unidad central de procesamiento o CPU. (p. 455)

Glossary/Glosario

mineral: naturally occurring inorganic solid that has a definite chemical composition and an orderly internal atomic structure. (pp. 136, 504)

mitochondrion: cell organelle that breaks down food and releases energy. (p. 42)

mitosis (mi TOH sus): cell process in which the nucleus divides to form two nuclei identical to each other, and identical to the original nucleus, in a series of steps (prophase, metaphase, anaphase, and telophase). (p. 98)

mixture: a combination of substances in which the individual substances do not change or combine chemically but instead retain their own individual properties; can be gases, solids, liquids, or any combination of them. (pp. 69, 275)

mold: a type of body fossil that forms in rock when an organism with hard parts is buried, decays or dissolves, and leaves a cavity in the rock. (p. 657)

momentum: a measure of how difficult it is to stop a moving object; equals the product of mass and velocity. (p. 334)

mutation: any permanent change in a gene or chromosome of a cell; may be beneficial, harmful, or have little effect on an organism. (p. 114)

mineral: sólido inorgánico que se encuentra en la naturaleza, tiene una composición química definida y una estructura atómica ordenada. (pp. 136, 504)

mitocondria: organelo celular que degrada nutrientes y libera energía. (p. 42)

mitosis: proceso celular en el que el núcleo se divide para formar dos núcleos idénticos entre sí e idénticos al núcleo original, a través de varias etapas (profase, metafase, anafase y telofase). (p. 98)

mezcla: una combinación de sustancias en la que las sustancias individuales no cambian ni se combinan químicamente pero mantienen sus propiedades individuales; pueden ser gases, sólidos, líquidos o una combinación de ellos. (pp. 69, 275)

moldura: tipo de cuerpo fósil que se formó en la roca cuando un organismo con partes duras fue enterrado, descompuesto o disuelto, dejando una cavidad en la roca. (p. 657)

momento: medida de la dificultad para detener un objeto en movimiento; es igual al producto de la masa por la velocidad. (p. 334)

mutación: cualquier cambio permanente en un gen o cromosoma de una célula; puede ser benéfica, perjudicial o tener un pequeño efecto sobre un organismo. (p. 114)

N

natural resources: parts of Earth's environment that supply materials useful or necessary for the survival of living organisms. (p. 224)

nebula: large cloud of gas and dust that contracts under gravitational force and breaks apart into smaller pieces, each of which might collapse to form a star. (p. 484)

nephron (NEF rahn): tiny filtering unit of the kidney. (p. 149)

net force: combination of all forces acting on an object. (p. 351)

neutralization (new truh luh ZAY shun): reaction in which an acid reacts with a base and forms water and a salt. (p. 308)

neutron: an uncharged particle located in the nucleus of an atom. (p. 264)

neutron star: collapsed core of a supernova that can shrink to about 20 km in diameter and contains only neutrons in the dense core. (p. 486)

recursos naturales: partes del medio ambiente terrestre que proporcionan materiales útiles o necesarios para la supervivencia de los organismos vivos. (p. 224)

nebulosa: nube grande de polvo y gas que se contrae bajo la fuerza gravitacional y se descompone en pedazos más pequeños, cada uno de los cuales se puede colapsar para formar una estrella. (p. 484)

nefrona: pequeña unidad de filtración en el riñón. (p. 149)

fuerza neta: la combinación de todas las fuerzas que actúan sobre un objeto. (p. 351)

neutralización: reacción en la cual un ácido reacciona con una base para formar agua y una sal. (p. 308)

neutrón: partícula sin carga localizada en el núcleo de un átomo (p. 264)

estrella de neutrones: núcleo colapsado de una supernova que puede contraerse hasta tener un diámetro de 20 kilómetros y contiene sólo neutrones en su denso núcleo. (p. 486)

Newton's first law of motion: states that if the net force acting on an object is zero, the object will remain at rest or move in a straight line with a constant speed. (p. 352)

Newton's second law of motion: states that an object acted upon by a net force will accelerate in the direction of the force, and that the acceleration equals the net force divided by the object's mass. (p. 356)

Newton's third law of motion: states that forces always act in equal but opposite pairs. (p. 363)

niche (NICH): role of an organism in the ecosystem, including what it eats, how it interacts with other organisms, and how it gets its food. (p. 207)

nonfoliated: describes metamorphic rock, such as quartzite or marble, whose mineral grains grow and rearrange but generally do not form layers. (p. 544)

noninfectious disease: disease that is not caused by a pathogen. (p. 183)

nonmetals: elements that are usually gases or brittle solids and poor conductors of electricity and heat; are the basis of the chemicals of life. (p. 271)

nonrenewable resources: natural resources, such as petroleum, minerals, and metals, that are used more quickly than they can be replaced by natural processes. (pp. 225, 394)

nuclear energy: energy contained in atomic nuclei. (pp. 228, 384)

nucleus (NEW klee us): organelle that controls all the activities of a cell and contains hereditary material made of proteins and DNA; positively charged, central part of an atom. (pp. 40, 263)

nutrients (NEW tree unts): substances in foods—proteins, carbohydrates, fats, vitamins, minerals, and water—that provide energy and materials for cell development, growth, and repair. (p. 128)

primera ley de movimiento de Newton: establece que si la fuerza neta que actúa sobre un objeto es igual a cero, el objeto se mantendrá en reposo o se moverá en línea recta a una velocidad constante. (p. 352)

segunda ley de movimiento de Newton: establece que si una fuerza neta se ejerce sobre un objeto, éste se acelerará en la dirección de la fuerza y la aceleración es igual a la fuerza neta dividida por la masa del objeto. (p. 356)

tercera ley de movimiento de Newton: establece que las fuerzas siempre actúan en pares iguales pero opuestos. (p. 363)

nicho: papel que juega un organismo en un ecosistema, incluyendo lo que come, cómo interactúa con los otros organismos y cómo consigue su alimento. (p. 207)

no foliado: describe rocas metamórficas, como la cuarcita o el mármol, cuyas vetas minerales se acumulan y reestructuran pero rara vez forman capas. (p. 544)

enfermedad no infecciosa: enfermedad que no es causada por un patógeno. (p. 183)

no metales: elementos que por lo general son gases o sólidos frágiles y malos conductores de electricidad y calor; son la base de los compuestos químicos biológicos. (p. 271)

recursos no renovables: recursos naturales, como el petróleo, los minerales y los metales, que son utilizados más rápidamente de lo que pueden ser reemplazados mediante procesos naturales. (pp. 225, 394)

energía nuclear: energía contenida en los núcleos de los átomos. (pp. 228, 384)

núcleo: organelo que controla todas las actividades de una célula y que contiene el material hereditario formado por proteínas y ADN; parte central con carga positiva del átomo. (pp. 40, 263)

nutrientes: sustancias en los alimentos (proteínas, carbohidratos, grasas, vitaminas, minerales y agua) que suministran energía y materiales para el desarrollo, crecimiento y reparación de las células. (p. 128)

O

ore: deposit in which a mineral exists in large enough amounts to be mined at a profit. (p. 519)

organ: structure, such as the heart, made up of different types of tissues that all work together. (p. 45)

mena: depósito en el que existe un mineral en cantidades suficientes para la explotación minera. (p. 519)

órgano: estructura, como el corazón, que consiste en diferentes tipos de tejidos que trabajan conjuntamente. (p. 45)

Glossary/Glosario

organelle: structure in the cytoplasm of a eukaryotic cell that can act as a storage site, process energy, move materials, or manufacture substances. (p. 40)

organic compounds: compounds that always contain hydrogen and carbon; carbohydrates, lipids, proteins, and nucleic acids are organic compounds found in living things. (p. 70)

organism: any living thing. (p. 14)

osmosis: a type of passive transport that occurs when water diffuses through a cell membrane. (p. 76)

outer core: layer of Earth that lies above the inner core and is thought to be composed mostly of molten metal. (p. 566)

ozone depletion: thinning of Earth's ozone layer caused by chlorofluorocarbons (CFCs) leaking into the air and reacting chemically with ozone, breaking the ozone molecules apart. (p. 235)

organelo: estructura del citoplasma de una célula eucariota que puede actuar como sitio de almacenamiento, procesamiento de energía, movimiento de materiales o elaboración de sustancias. (p. 40)

compuestos orgánicos: compuestos que siempre contienen hidrógeno y carbono; los carbohidratos, lípidos, proteínas y ácidos nucleicos son compuestos orgánicos que se encuentran en los seres vivos. (p. 70)

organismo: cualquier ser vivo. (p. 14)

ósmosis: tipo de transporte pasivo que ocurre cuando el agua se difunde a través de una membrana celular. (p. 76)

núcleo exterior: capa de la Tierra que yace sobre el núcleo interior y que se piensa que está compuesta principalmente de metal fundido. (p. 566)

agotamiento del ozono: adelgazamiento de la capa de ozono de la Tierra causado por los clorofluorocarbonos (CFC) que escapan al aire y reaccionan químicamente con el ozono rompiendo sus moléculas. (p. 235)

P

passive immunity: immunity that results when antibodies produced in one animal are introduced into another's body; does not last as long as active immunity. (p. 176)

passive transport: movement of substances through a cell membrane without the use of cellular energy; includes diffusion, osmosis, and facilitated diffusion. (p. 74)

pasteurization (pas chuh ruh ZAY shun): process in which a liquid is heated to a temperature that kills most bacteria. (p. 178)

peristalsis (per uh STAHL sus): waves of muscular contractions that move food through the digestive tract. (p. 130)

permineralized remains: fossils in which the spaces inside are filled with minerals from groundwater. (p. 656)

petroleum: nonrenewable resource formed over hundreds of millions of years mostly from the remains of microscopic marine organisms buried in Earth's crust. (p. 225)

pH: measure of how acidic or basic a solution is, ranging in a scale from 0 to 14. (p. 306)

photosphere: lowest layer of the Sun's atmosphere; gives off light and has temperatures of about 6,000K. (p. 477)

inmunidad pasiva: inmunidad que se presenta cuando los anticuerpos producidos en un animal son introducidos en el cuerpo de otro animal, la cual no es tan duradera como la inmunidad activa. (p. 176)

transporte pasivo: movimiento de sustancias a través de la membrana celular sin usar energía celular; incluye difusión, ósmosis y difusión facilitada. (p. 74)

pasteurización: proceso mediante el cual un líquido es calentado a una temperatura que mata a la mayoría de las bacterias. (p. 178)

peristalsis: ondas de contracciones musculares que mueven al alimento a través del sistema digestivo. (p. 130)

restos permineralizados: fósiles en los que los espacios interiores son llenados con minerales de aguas subterráneas. (p. 656)

petróleo: recurso no renovable formado durante cientos de millones de años, en su mayoría a partir de los restos de organismos marinos microscópicos sepultados en la corteza terrestre. (p. 225)

pH: medida para saber qué tan básica o ácida es una solución, en una escala de 0 a 14. (p. 306)

fotosfera: capa más interna de la atmósfera del sol; emite luz y tiene temperaturas de cerca de 6,000 grados Kelvin. (p. 477)

photosynthesis/radiant energy

photosynthesis: process by which plants and many other producers use light energy to produce a simple sugar from carbon dioxide and water and give off oxygen. (p. 82)

photovoltaic: device that transforms radiant energy directly into electrical energy. (p. 398)

phylogeny (fi LAH juh nee): evolutionary history of an organism; used today to group organisms into six kingdoms. (p. 23)

pitch: human perception of the frequency of sound. (p. 421)

plasma: the liquid part of blood, which is made mostly of water. (p. 162)

plate: section of Earth's crust and rigid, upper mantle that moves slowly around on the asthenosphere. (p. 568)

platelet: irregularly shaped cell fragments that help clot blood. (p. 163)

polar zones: climate zones that receive solar radiation at a low angle, extend from 66°N and S latitude to the poles, and are never warm. (p. 624)

pollutant: substance that contaminates any part of the environment. (p. 232)

population: all of the individuals of one species that live in the same space at the same time. (p. 200)

population density: number of individuals in a population that occupies an area of limited size. (p. 204)

potential energy: energy stored in an object due to its position. (p. 382)

precipitate: solid that comes back out of its solution because of a chemical reaction or physical change. (p. 290)

principle of superposition: states that in undisturbed rock layers, the oldest rocks are on the bottom and the rocks become progressively younger toward the top. (p. 662)

proton: positively charged particle located in the nucleus of an atom and that is counted to identify the atomic number. (p. 263)

fotosíntesis/energía radiante

fotosíntesis: proceso mediante el cual las plantas y muchos otros organismos productores usan la energía solar para producir azúcares simples a partir de dióxido de carbono y agua y desprender oxígeno. (p. 82)

fotovoltaico: dispositivo que transforma la energía radiante directamente en energía eléctrica. (p. 398)

filogenia: historia evolutiva de un organismo; usada hoy para agrupar a los organismos en seis reinos. (p. 23)

tono: percepción humana de la frecuencia del sonido. (p. 421)

plasma: parte líquida de la sangre compuesto principalmente por agua. (p. 162)

placa: sección de la corteza terrestre y del manto superior rígido que se mueve lentamente sobre la astenosfera. (p. 568)

plaqueta: fragmentos de célula de forma irregular que ayudan a coagular la sangre. (p. 163)

zonas polares: zonas climáticas que reciben radiación solar a un ángulo reducido, se extienden desde los 66° de latitud norte y sur hasta los polos y nunca son cálidas. (p. 624)

contaminante: sustancia que contamina cualquier parte del medio ambiente. (p. 232)

población: todos los individuos de una especie que viven en el mismo espacio al mismo tiempo. (p. 200)

densidad de población: número de individuos en una población que ocupa un área de tamaño limitado. (p. 204)

energía potencial: energía almacenada en un objeto debido a su posición. (p. 382)

precipitado: sólido que se aísla de su solución mediante una reacción química o un cambio físico. (p. 290)

principio de superposición: establece que en las capas rocosas no perturbadas, las rocas más antiguas están en la parte inferior y las rocas son más jóvenes conforme están más cerca de la superficie. (p. 662)

protón: partícula cargada positivamente, localizada en el núcleo de un átomo y que se cuenta para identificar el número atómico. (p. 263)

R

radiant energy: energy carried by light. (p. 383)

energía radiante: energía transportada por la luz. (p. 383)

Glossary/Glosario

radioactive decay/saturated

radioactive decay: process in which some isotopes break down into other isotopes and particles. (p. 669)

radiometric dating: process used to calculate the absolute age of rock by measuring the ratio of parent isotope to daughter product in a mineral and knowing the half-life of the parent. (p. 671)

random-access memory (RAM): temporary electronic memory within a computer. (p. 452)

read-only memory (ROM): electronic memory that is permanently stored within a computer. (p. 452)

recycling: conservation method that is a form of reuse and requires changing or reprocessing an item or natural resource. (p. 243)

refraction: change in direction of a wave when it changes speed as it travels from one material into another. (p. 417)

relative age: the age of something compared with other things. (p. 663)

renewable resources: natural resources, such as water, sunlight, and crops, that are constantly being recycled or replaced by nature. (pp. 225, 396)

respiration: process by which producers and consumers release stored energy from food molecules. (p. 83)

reverberation: repeated echoes of sound waves. (p. 423)

ribosome: small cytoplasmic structure on which cells make their own proteins. (p. 42)

rift: long crack, fissure, or trough that forms between tectonic plates moving apart at plate boundaries. (p. 609)

RNA: ribonucleic acid; a type of nucleic acid that carries codes for making proteins from the nucleus to the ribosomes. (p. 112)

rock: mixture of one or more minerals, rock fragments, volcanic glass, organic matter, or other natural materials; can be igneous, metamorphic, or sedimentary. (p. 532)

rock cycle: model that describes how rocks slowly change from one form to another through time. (p. 533)

desintegración radiactiva/saturado

desintegración radiactiva: proceso en el que algunos isótopos se desintegran en otros isótopos y partículas. (p. 669)

fechado radiométrico: proceso utilizado para calcular la edad absoluta de las rocas midiendo la relación isótopo parental a producto derivado en un mineral y conociendo la vida media del parental. (p. 671)

memoria de acceso aleatorio (RAM): memoria electrónica temporal dentro de una computadora. (p. 452)

memoria de sólo lectura (ROM): memoria electrónica almacenada permanentemente dentro de una computadora. (p. 452)

reciclaje: método de conservación como una forma de reutilización y que requiere del cambio o reprocesamiento del producto o recurso natural. (p. 243)

refracción: cambio de dirección de una onda al cambiar su velocidad cuando pasa de un material a otro. (p. 417)

edad relativa: la edad de algo comparado con otras cosas. (p. 663)

recursos renovables: recursos naturales, como el agua, la luz solar y los cultivos, que son reciclados o reemplazados constantemente por la naturaleza. (pp. 225, 396)

respiración: proceso mediante el cual los organismos productores y consumidores liberan la energía almacenada en las moléculas de los alimentos. (p. 83)

reverberación: ecos repetidos de ondas sonoras. (p. 423)

ribosoma: estructura citoplasmática pequeña en la que las células producen sus propias proteínas. (p. 42)

ruptura: grieta larga, fisura o hueco que se forma entre placas tectónicas que se separan en los límites de las placas. (p. 609)

ARN: ácido ribonucleico; tipo de ácido nucleico que transporta los códigos para la formación de proteínas del núcleo a los ribosomas. (p. 112)

roca: mezcla de uno o más minerales, fragmentos de roca, obsidiana, materia orgánica u otros materiales naturales; puede ser ígnea, metamórfica o sedimentaria. (p. 532)

ciclo de la roca: modelo que describe cómo cambian lentamente las rocas de una forma a otra a través del tiempo. (p. 533)

S

saturated: describes a solution that holds the total amount of solute that it can hold under given conditions. (p. 298)

saturado: describe a una solución que retiene toda la cantidad de soluto que puede retener bajo determinadas condiciones. (p. 298)

Glossary/Glosario

scientific methods: procedures used to solve problems and answer questions that can include stating the problem, gathering information, forming a hypothesis, testing the hypothesis with an experiment, analyzing data, and drawing conclusions. (p. 7)

season: short period of climate change in an area caused by the tilt of Earth's axis as Earth revolves around the Sun. (p. 632)

sedimentary rock: forms when sediments are compacted and cemented together or when minerals form from solutions. (p. 545)

sediments: loose materials, such as rock fragments, mineral grains, and the remains of once-living plants and animals, that have been moved by wind, water, ice, or gravity. (p. 545)

seismic safe: describes the ability of structures to stand up against the vibrations caused by an earthquake. (p. 599)

seismic waves: earthquake waves, including primary waves, secondary waves, and surface waves. (p. 594)

seismograph: instrument used to record seismic waves. (p. 595)

semiconductor: element, such as silicon, that is a poorer electrical conductor that a metal, but a better conductor than a nonmetal, and whose electrical conductivity can be changed by adding impurities. (p. 445)

sexual reproduction: a type of reproduction in which two sex cells, usually an egg and a sperm, join to form a zygote, which will develop into a new organism with a unique identity. (p. 104)

shield volcano: large, broad volcano with gently sloping sides that is formed by the buildup of basaltic layers. (p. 604)

silicate: mineral that contains silicon and oxygen and usually one or more other elements. (p. 508)

solubility (sahl yuh BIH luh tee): measure of how much solute can be dissolved in a certain amount of solvent. (p. 297)

solute: substance that dissolves and seems to disappear into another substance. (p. 290)

solution: homogeneous mixture whose elements and/or compounds are evenly mixed at the molecular level but are not bonded together. (p. 290)

solvent: substance that dissolves the solute. (p. 290)

specific gravity: ratio of a mineral's weight compared with the weight of an equal volume of water. (p. 512)

métodos científicos: procedimientos utilizados para solucionar problemas y responder a preguntas; puede incluir el establecimiento de un problema, recopilación de información, formulación de una hipótesis, comprobación de la hipótesis con un experimento, análisis de la información y presentación de conclusiones. (p. 7)

estación: periodo corto de cambio climático en un área, causado por la inclinación del eje de la Tierra conforme gira alrededor del sol. (p. 632)

roca sedimentaria: se forma cuando los sedimentos son compactados y cementados o cuando se forman minerales a partir de soluciones. (p. 545)

sedimentos: materiales sueltos, como fragmentos de roca, granos minerales y restos de animales y plantas, que han sido arrastrados por el viento, el agua, el hielo o la gravedad. (p. 545)

seguridad antisísmica: describe la capacidad de las estructuras de resistir las vibraciones producidas por los terremotos. (p. 599)

ondas sísmicas: ondas producidas durante los terremotos, las cuales pu ser primarias, secundarias y superficiales. (p. 594)

sismógrafo: instrumento usado para registrar las ondas sísmicas. (p. 595)

semiconductor: elemento, como el silicio, que no es tan buen conductor de electricidad como un metal, pero que es mejor conductor que un no metal y cuya conductividad eléctrica puede ser modificada al añadirle impurezas. (p. 445)

reproducción sexual: tipo de reproducción en la que dos células sexuales, generalmente un óvulo y un espermatozoide, se unen para formar un zigoto, el cual se desarrollará para formar un nuevo organismo con identidad única. (p. 104)

volcán escudo: volcán grande y ancho con lados ligeramente inclinados que se forma por la aparición de capas basálticas. (p. 604)

silicato: mineral que contiene sílice y oxígeno y generalmente uno o varios elementos distintos. (p. 508)

solubilidad: medida de la cantidad de soluto que puede disolverse en cierta cantidad de solvente. (p. 297)

soluto: sustancia que se disuelve y parece desaparecer en otra sustancia. (p. 290)

solución: mezcla homogénea cuyos elementos o compuestos están mezclados de manera uniforme a nivel molecular pero no se enlazan. (p. 290)

solvente: sustancia que disuelve al soluto. (p. 290)

gravedad específica: cociente del peso de un mineral comparado con el peso de un volumen igual de agua. (p. 512)

Glossary/Glosario

speed/transverse wave
rapidez/onda transversal

speed: equals the distance traveled divided by the time it takes to travel that distance. (p. 324)

sperm: haploid sex cell formed in the male reproductive organs. (p. 104)

spontaneous generation: idea that living things come from nonliving things. (p. 19)

streak: color of a mineral when it is in powdered form. (p. 513)

subduction: a type of plate movement that occurs when one plate sinks beneath another plate. (p. 571)

substance: matter that has the same composition and properties throughout. (pp. 273, 288)

sunspots: areas on the Sun's surface that are cooler and less bright than surrounding areas, are caused by the Sun's magnetic field, and occur in cycles. (p. 478)

supergiant: late stage in the life cycle of a massive star in which the core heats up, heavy elements form by fusion, and the star expands; can eventually explode to form a supernova. (p. 487)

symbiosis (sihm bee OH sus): any close interaction among two or more different species, including mutualism, commensalism, and parasitism. (p. 206)

rapidez: equivale a dividir la distancia recorrida por el tiempo que toma recorrer dicha distancia. (p. 324)

espermatozoides: células sexuales haploides que se forman en los órganos reproductores masculinos. (p. 104)

generación espontánea: idea que sostiene que los seres vivos proceden de seres inertes. (p. 19)

veta: color de un mineral en forma de polvo. (p. 513)

subducción: tipo de movimiento de placas que ocurre cuando una placa se ubica debajo de otra. (p. 571)

sustancia: materia que siempre tiene la misma composición y las mismas propiedades. (pp. 273, 288)

manchas solares: áreas en la superficie solar que son más frías y menos brillantes que las áreas circundantes, son causadas por el campo magnético solar y ocurren en ciclos. (p. 478)

supergigante: etapa tardía en el ciclo de vida de una estrella masiva en la que el núcleo se calienta, se forman elementos pesados por fusión y la estrella se expande; eventualmente puede explotar para formar una supernova. (p. 487)

simbiosis: cualquier interacción cercana entre dos o más especies diferentes, incluyendo mutualismo, asociaciones y parasitismo. (p. 206)

temperate zones: climate zones with moderate temperatures that are located between the tropics and the polar zones. (p. 624)

theory: explanation of things or events based on scientific knowledge resulting from many observations and experiments. (p. 10)

thermal energy: energy that all objects have that increases as the object's temperature increases. (p. 382)

tissue: group of similar cells that work together to do one job. (p. 45)

trachea (TRAY kee uh): air-conducting tube that connects the larynx with the bronchi, is lined with mucous membranes and cilia, and contains strong cartilage rings. (p. 142)

transistor: a solid-state component made from three layers of semiconductor material that can amplify the strength of an electric signal or act as an electronic switch. (p. 447)

transverse wave: mechanical wave that causes particles in matter to move at right angles to the direction the wave travels. (p. 413)

zonas templadas: zonas climáticas con temperaturas moderadas que están localizadas entre los trópicos y las zonas polares. (p. 624)

teoría: explicación de cosas o eventos basándose en el conocimiento científico resultante de muchas observaciones y experimentos. (p. 10)

energía térmica: energía que poseen todos los objetos y que aumenta al aumentar la temperatura de éstos. (p. 382)

tejido: grupo de células similares que trabajan conjuntamente para hacer una tarea. (p. 45)

tráquea: tubo conductor de aire que conecta a la laringe con los bronquios, está forrada con membranas mucosas y cilios y contiene fuertes anillos de cartílagos. (p. 142)

transistor: componente de estado sólido formado por tres capas de material semiconductor que puede amplificar la fuerza de una señal eléctrica o actuar a manera de interruptor electrónico. (p. 447)

onda transversal: onda mecánica que hace que las partículas de materia se muevan en ángulos rectos respecto a la dirección en que viaja la onda. (p. 413)

tropics: climate zone that receives the most solar radiation, is located between latitudes 23°N and 23°S, and is always hot, except at high elevations. (p. 624)

tsunami: powerful seismic sea wave that begins over an ocean-floor earthquake, can reach 30 m in height when approaching land, and can cause destruction in coastal areas. (p. 597)

turbine: set of steam-powered fan blades that spins a generator at a power plant. (p. 390)

trópicos: zonas climáticas que reciben la mayor parte de la radiación solar, están localizadas entre los 23° de latitud norte y 23° de latitud sur y siempre son cálidas excepto a grandes alturas. (p. 624)

tsunami: poderosa onda sísmica marina que comienza en un terremoto en el lecho oceánico, pudiendo alcanzar 30 metros de altura al acercarse a la tierra y causar gran destrucción en las áreas costeras. (p. 597)

turbina: conjunto de aspas de ventilador impulsadas por vapor que hacen girar a un generador en una planta de energía eléctrica. (p. 390)

ultraviolet waves: electromagnetic waves with wavelengths between about 400 billionths and 10 billionths of a meter. (p. 428)

unbalanced forces: two or more forces acting on an object that do not cancel, and cause the object to accelerate. (p. 351)

unconformity (un kun FOR mih tee): gap in the rock layer that is due to erosion or periods without any deposition. (p. 664)

uniformitarianism: principle stating that Earth processes occurring today are similar to those that occurred in the past. (p. 673)

upwarped mountain: mountain that forms when forces inside Earth push up the crust. (p. 577)

ureter: tube that carries urine from each kidney to the bladder. (p. 149)

ondas ultravioleta: ondas electromagnéticas con longitudes de onda entre aproximadamente 10 y 400 billonésimas de metro. (p. 428)

fuerzas no balanceadas: dos o más fuerzas que actúan sobre un objeto sin anularse y que hacen que el objeto se acelere. (p. 351)

discordancia: brecha en la capa rocosa que es debida a la erosión o a periodos sin deposición. (p. 664)

uniformitarianismo: principio que establece que los procesos de la Tierra que ocurren actualmente son similares a los que ocurrieron en el pasado. (p. 673)

montaña encorvada: montaña que se forma cuando las fuerzas internas de la Tierra levantan la corteza. (p. 577)

uréter: tubo que transporta la orina desde cada uno de los riñones hasta la vejiga. (p. 149)

variable: something in an experiment that can change. (p. 9)

vein: blood vessel that carries blood to the heart. (p. 170)

velocity: speed and direction of a moving object. (p. 327)

villi (VIH li): fingerlike projections covering the wall of the small intestine that increase the surface area for food absorption. (p. 131)

virus: a strand of hereditary material surrounded by a protein coating. (p. 52)

variable: condición que puede cambiar en un experimento. (p. 9)

vena: vasos sanguíneos que transportan la sangre al corazón. (p. 170)

velocidad: rapidez y dirección de un objeto en movimiento. (p. 327)

vellosidades: proyecciones en forma de dedo que cubren las paredes del intestino delgado y aumentan el área de superficie para la absorción de los alimentos. (p. 131)

virus: cadena de material hereditario rodeada por una membrana proteica. (p. 52)

Glossary/Glosario

vitamin/zygote vitamina/zigoto

vitamin: water-soluble or fat-soluble organic nutrient needed in small quantities for growth, for preventing some diseases, and for regulating body functions. (p. 135)

volcanic mountain: mountain that forms when magma is forced upward and flows onto Earth's surface. (p. 578)

volcano: cone-shaped hill or mountain formed when hot magma, solids, and gas erupt onto Earth's surface through a vent. (p. 601)

vitamina: nutriente orgánico soluble en agua o en grasa, necesario en pequeñas cantidades para el crecimiento, para prevenir algunas enfermedades y para regular las funciones biológicas. (p. 135)

montaña volcánica: montaña que se forma cuando el magma es empujado hacia arriba y fluye sobre la superficie terrestre. (p. 578)

volcán: colina o montaña cónica que se forma cuando el magma caliente, sólidos y gases, hacen erupción en la superficie terrestre a través de una abertura. (p. 601)

W

water cycle: continuous cycle of water molecules on Earth as they rise into the atmosphere, fall back to Earth as rain or other precipitation, and flow into rivers and oceans through the processes of evaporation, condensation, and precipitation. (p. 212)

wave: disturbance that moves through matter and space and carries energy. (p. 412)

wavelength: distance between one point on a wave and the nearest point moving with the same speed and direction. (p. 414)

weight: gravitational force between an object and Earth. (p. 357)

white dwarf: late stage in the life cycle of a comparatively low-mass main sequence star; formed when its core depletes its helium and its outer layers escape into space, leaving behind a hot, dense core. (p. 486)

ciclo del agua: ciclo continuo de las moléculas de agua en la Tierra en su proceso de subir a la atmósfera, regresar a la Tierra en forma de lluvia u otra forma de precipitación y fluir hacia los ríos y océanos a través de la evaporación, condensación y precipitación. (p. 212)

onda: perturbación que se mueve a través de la materia y el espacio y que transporta energía. (p. 412)

longitud de onda: distancia entre un punto en una onda y el punto más cercano, moviéndose con la misma rapidez y dirección. (p. 414)

peso: fuerza gravitacional entre un objeto y la Tierra. (p. 357)

enana blanca: etapa tardía en el ciclo de vida de una estrella de secuencia principal, de relativamente poca masa, formada cuando el núcleo agota su helio y sus capas externas escapan al espacio, dejando atrás un núcleo denso y caliente. (p. 486)

Z

zygote: new diploid cell formed when a sperm fertilizes an egg; will divide by mitosis and develop into a new organism. (p. 104)

zigoto: célula diploide nueva formada cuando un espermatozoide fertiliza a un óvulo; se dividirá por mitosis y se desarrollará para formar un nuevo organismo. (p. 104)

Index

Abdominal thrusts   **Anaphase**

Italic numbers = illustration/photo   **Bold numbers = vocabulary term**
lab = indicates a page on which the entry is used in a lab
act = indicates a page on which the entry is used in an activity

A

Abdominal thrusts, 143, *144*
Abiotic factors, 196–198; air, 198, *198;* light, 197, *197;* soil, 198, *198;* temperature, 197; water, 197, *197*
Absolute ages, 669–673
Absolute magnitude, 474
Acceleration, 328–332; calculating, 329–330, 330 *act,* 359, 359 *act;* equation for, 330; and force, 356, 356–357, 360; graph of, 332, *332;* modeling, 331 *lab;* and motion, 328–329; negative, 331, *331;* positive, 331; and speed, 328, 328–329; unit of measurement with, 357; and velocity, 328, 328–329, *329*
Accessory organs, 129
Accuracy, in record keeping, 689
Acetic acid, 292, *292,* 307, *307*
Acid(s), 302–304; in environment, 303, *304;* measuring strength of, 306, 306–308, *307,* 310–311 *lab;* neutralizing, 308–309, *309;* properties of, 302; reaction with bases, 308–309, *309;* uses of, 303, *303*
Acidophils, 306
Acid precipitation, 233, *233,* 233 *lab,* 304
Acid rain, *304*
Acquired Immune Deficiency Syndrome (AIDS), 182
Action, and reaction, 363–366, *364, 366*
Active immunity, 176
Active transport, 77, *77,* 79
Active viruses, 53, *53*
Activities, Applying Math, 44, 51, 85, 91, 102, 151, 185, 207, 230, 240, 271, 309, 324, 327, 330, 332, 334, 338, 359, 362, 368, 401 *act,* 416, 418, 423, 447, 487, 521, 539, 550, 551, 606, 612, 627, 673; Applying Science, 11, 107, 150, 181, 210, 244, 275, 299, 396, 451, 474, 512, 580, 626, 672; Chapter Review, 32–33, 60–61, 90–91, 120–121, 155–156, 190–191, 218–219, 250–251, 282–283, 314–315, 344–345, 374–375, 404–405, 436–437, 464–465, 498–499, 526–527, 556–557, 586–587, 618–619, 648–649, 678–679; Integrate Astronomy, 21, 357; Integrate Career, 50, 83, 198, 264, 299; Integrate Chemistry, 83, 110, 211, 233, 485, 519, 539, 548, 566, 603, 610, 657; Integrate Earth Science, 21, 178, 277, 394, 414; Integrate Environment, 44, 291, 295, 454; Integrate Health, 17, 77, 97, 132, 145, 236, 259, 421, 637; Integrate History, 165, 389; Integrate Language Arts, 580, 611; Integrate Life Science, 276, 306, 324, 351, 364, 387, 629, 660; Integrate Physics, 42, 50, 171, 486, 507, 535, 626; Integrate Social Studies, 17, 136, 227, 334; Science Online, 9, 15, 23, 53, 54, 70, 84, 97, 113, 115, 134, 145, 163, 172, 200, 204, 234, 244, 262, 267, 276, 289, 305, 308, 322, 326, 353, 364, 386, 396, 426, 445, 452, 456, 458, 477, 484, 518, 538, 542, 569, 578, 598, 603, 639, 641, 663, 666; Standards Review, 34–35, 62–63, 92–93, 122–123, 158–159, 192–193, 220–221, 252–253, 284–285, 316–317, 346–347, 376–377, 408–409, 438–439, 466–467, 500–501, 528–529, 558–559, 588–589, 620–621, 650–651, 680–681
Adaptations, 628–631; behavioral, *630,* 630–631, *631;* structural, 628, 629, *630*

Adenine, 111
Adenovirus, *52*
Age, absolute, **669**–673; relative, **663**–668, 668 *lab*
Agriculture, and soil loss, 239, *239*
AIDS (Acquired Immune Deficiency Syndrome), 182
Air pollution, 232–236; acid precipitation, 233, *233,* 233 *lab,* 304; and environment, 198, *198;* greenhouse effect, 234, *234,* 241 *lab;* indoor, 236, *236;* and ozone depletion, 235, *235;* smog, 232, *232*
Air quality, 70 *act,* 236. See also Air pollution
Air resistance, 361
Air temperature, 234, *234*
Alaska, volcanoes in, 646
Alcohol, 84, *84*
Algae, green, 197; and water pollution, 237
Allergen(s), 183
Allergies, 183
Alloys, 293, *293*
Alluvial fan, *534*
Almandine, 517, *517*
Alpha Centauri, 480
Alpha decay, 670, *670*
Alternative resources, 397 *lab,* **397**–399, *398, 399*
Altitude, and atmospheric pressure, 198
Aluminum, 519, *519;* recycling, 244
Alveoli, 142, *142,* 145
Amethyst, 515, 517, *517*
Amino acids, 133–134; in protein synthesis, 113, *113*
Amoeba, *96*
Amplitude, 415; of compressional wave, 415, *415;* and energy, 415; of transverse wave, 415, *415*
Analog devices, 442–443, *443*
Analog signal, 442, *444*
Anaphase, 98, *99,* 106, *106, 107,* 109

INDEX   **755**

Index

Andesite, 538
Andesitic rock, 538, 539
Anemia, 166
Angular unconformities, 664, 664, 665
Animal(s), behavioral adaptations of, 630, 630–631, 631; competition among, 205, 205; effect of momentum on motion of, 334; habitats of, 207; hibernation of, 630, 630; reproduction of, 96, 96, 97, 98, 99, 100, 100; speed of, 324
Animal cell, 41
Antacid, 308
Antarctica, food webs in, 210, 210
Antares, 483, 483
Antibiotics, 179, 183
Antibodies, 175; in blood, 165
Antigens, 165, **175**
Antihistamines, 183
Anus, 132
Anvil (of ear), 422, 422
Aorta, 169
Apatite, 511
Appalachian Mountains, 577, 577, 584, 584
Apparent magnitude, 474
Applying Math, Acceleration of a Bus, 330; Acceleration of a Car, 359; Calculate the Importance of Water, 72; Cell Ratio, 44; Chapter Review, 33, 61, 91, 121, 157, 191, 219, 251, 283, 315, 345, 375, 407, 437, 587; Coal Formation, 550; Momentum of a Bicycle, 334; P-wave Travel Time, 612; Section Review, 51, 85, 102, 151, 185, 207, 230, 240, 271, 309, 327, 332, 338, 362, 368, 401, 418, 423, 447, 487, 521, 539, 551, 606, 627, 673; Speed of Sound, 416; Speed of a Swimmer, 324
Applying Science, Are distance and brightness related?, 474; Deaths from Diseases, 181; Does temperature affect the rate of bacterial reproduction?, 11; How can chromosome numbers be predicted?, 107; How can glaciers cause land to rise?, 580; How can you compare concentrations?, 299; How do changes in Antarctic food webs affect populations?, 210; How do cities influence temperature?, 626; How does your body gain and lose water?, 150; How much information can be stored?, 451; Is energy consumption outpacing production?, 396; mineral identification, 512; What items are you recycling at home?, 244; What's the best way to desalt ocean water?, 275; When did the Iceman die?, 672
Applying Skills, 45, 55, 73, 109, 115, 132, 138, 146, 166, 173, 177, 201, 213, 245, 265, 277, 293, 300, 355, 384, 391, 431, 459, 476, 480, 493, 508, 514, 535, 544, 573, 581, 600, 631, 642, 661, 667
Aquatic ecosystems, freshwater, 197, 197
Aqueous solutions, 294–296, 295, 296
Area(s), of circles, 719; rectangles 718; triangles, 718
Aristotle, 22, 259
Arsenic, 446, 446
Arteries, 170, 170; coronary, 171
Ascorbic acid, 303
Aseptic techniques, 181
Asexual reproduction, 101, **101**–102, 102
Asthma, 145, 146
Atherosclerosis, 171
Atmosphere, ozone layer in, 198; particles in, 637, 637; pollution of, 639, 639, 641, 641, 642. See also Air pollution; of Sun, 477, 477
Atmospheric pressure, 198
Atom(s), 66, 68, 68, **259,** 669; electron cloud model of, 264–265, 265; mass number of, 269; model of, 66; models of, 260–265, 263, 264, 265; size of, 261, 261
Atomic mass, 270, 270
Atomic number, 269
Atomic theory of matter, 261
Atrium, 168
Aurora borealis, 479, 479
Automobiles, air bags in, 372, 372; hybrid, 387, 387, 404, 404; safety in, 340–341 lab, 372, 372
Average speed, 325, 325, 325 lab
Axis, 638
Ayers rock (Australia), 554, 554
Azurite, 510

B

Bacteria, and chemosynthesis, 211; in digestive system, 132; and diseases, 178, 181; and immune system, 174, 174; infectious, 178, 180 lab; reproduction of, 11; shapes of, 38; sizes of cells, 38, 38; use of energy by, 15
Bacteriophage, 54
Balanced forces, 351, 351
Balloon races, 369 lab
Barite, 506
Barium sulfate, 297
Basalt, 538, 539, 540 lab
Basaltic lava, 604, 604
Basaltic rock, 538, **539**
Base(s), 305; measuring strength of, 306, 306–308, 307, 310–311 lab; neutralizing, 308–309, 309; properties of, 305; reaction with acids, 308–309, 309; uses of, 305, 305
Bats, 630
Bauxite, 519, 519
B cells, 175, 176
Behavioral adaptations, 630, 630–631, 631
Beryl, 516, 516
Beta decay, 670, 670
Betelgeuse, 472, 472, 496, 496
Bicarbonate ions, 131
Big bang theory, 490, 492, **493**
Big Dipper, 473, 473
Bile, 131
Binary stars, 480
Binary system, 450, 450 lab, 451
Binomial nomenclature, 24
Biogenesis, 19
Biomechanics, 351
Biomes, 199, 200, 200, 200 act, 201
Biosphere, 199, **201**
Biotic factors, 196, 198–201, 199, 200

Index

Biotic potential, 206
Birds, how birds fly, 364 *act*
Bit, 450
Black hole, 357, **486**, *486*
Bladder, 149
Blood, 162–166; amount in body, 162; clotting of, 163, 164, *164;* diseases of, 166, *166;* filtering of, 173; functions of, 162; as mixture, 69, *69,* 275, *275,* 276; parts of, 162, *162;* purification of, 149; transfusion of, 165
Blood cells, red, 162, *162,* 163, *163,* 166; white, 162, *162,* 163, *163,* 163 *act,* 166, 175
Blood pressure, 171, *171;* high, 172, *172*
Blood types, 165, 186–187 *lab*
Blood vessels, 170, *170;* aorta, 169; arteries, 170, *170,* 171; capillaries, 142, *142,* 149, 170, *170;* as delivery system, 168, *168;* pressure in, 171, *171;* veins, 170, *170*
Blue shift, 491, *491*
Body, elements in, 67, *67;* oxygen use in, 75, *75;* regulating fluid levels in, 148; water in, 137, 150
Body systems, circulatory system, 162–187, *170, 171, 172;* immune system, 174, *174;* lymphatic system, 172–173, *173*
Body temperature, 389
Boiling point, of solvent, 300
Bond(s), covalent, 294, *294;* ionic, 295
Boomerangs, 342, *342*
Botanist, 6
Brass, *293*
Breastbone, 168
Breathing, 143, *143;* exhaling, 140, 142, 143, *143;* inhaling, 143, *143;* rate of, 127 *lab;* v. respiration, 140
Breccia, 547, 548
Brightfield microscope, 48
Bronchi, 142
Bronchioles, 142
Bronchitis, 145
Bryce Canyon National Park, 666, *667*
Budding, 102, *102*
Burning, 260, *260*
Byte, 451

Cactus, *630*
Calcite, 508, 511, 512, 514, 532, 544, 547, 548, 549
Calcium, 136
Calcium carbonate, 549, 657
Calcium hydroxide, 305, 305 *act*
Calcium phosphate, 71, 657
Calculators, 441 *lab*
Calorie, requirement, 133
Cancer, 58, *58,* 184–185; causes of, 184; early warning signs of, 185; prevention of, 185; and smoking, 145, 146, *146*
Cancer cells, division of, 97
Canis Major, 472
Canyonlands National Park, 666, *667*
Capillaries, 142, *142,* 149, **170,** *170*
Carbohydrates, 133, **134,** *134;* breaking down, 83; in living things, 70; and photosynthesis, 82, *82;* producing, 82
Carbonated beverages, 292, 298, 303 *lab*
Carbon cycle, 213, *213,* 642, *642*
Carbon dioxide, 274, in atmosphere, 639, *639,* 641, *641,* 642; and deforestation, 641, *641;* and greenhouse effect, 234, 241 *lab,* 639; and plants, 641, *641,* 642; in respiration, 140, 142, *142,* 143; in solution, 292, 298; as waste, 83, *83,* 84, *84,* 169
Carbon films, 655, *656*
Carbon-14 dating, 670, *670,* 670 *lab,* 671, *671,* 672 *act*
Carbonic acid, 303, 307
Carbon monoxide, 236, 274
Carcinogens, 146, 184
Cardiovascular disease, 171, 172, 172 *act*
Carrying capacity, 205
Car safety testing, 340–341 *lab*
Cassiopeia, 473
Cast, 657, *657*
Cathode rays, 262, *262*
Cave(s), formation of, 548; stalactites and stalagmites, 291, *291,* 303
Cell(s), 14, *15,* 36–55; active transport in, 77, *77, 79;* animal, *41;* B cells, 175, 176; comparing, 38, *38,* 46 *lab;* diploid, **104,** 105, 108, *109;* eukaryotic, 39, *39;* function, 38; haploid, **105,** 108; host, **52,** *53,* 54, *54,* 179; magnifying, 37 *lab,* 47, 47–50, 48–49; muscle, 14; nerve, 14; nucleus of, 40, *41;* organization of, 39–44, *40, 41;* osmosis in, 76, *76,* 80 *lab;* passive transport in, 74–77, *75, 76, 79;* plant, *41;* prokaryotic, 39, *39;* ratios in, 44 *act;* sex, 105, *105,* 108, 109; shapes of, 38, *38;* sizes of, 38, *38;* solar, 230, *230;* structure of, 38–45; T cells, 175, 182; trapping and using energy in, 81–85
Cell cycle, 96–97, *97*
Cell division, 96, *96,* 97, 99, 100, 104
Cell membrane, 38, 40, *40,* 70, 74, *74,* 76, 77, 78, 79
Cell nucleus, 99, 100, *100,* 101
Cell plate, 98, *98*
Cell reproduction. See Reproduction
Cell theory, 51
Cellular respiration, 140, *140,* 147
Cellulose, 39, 134
Cell wall, 39, *39,* 134
Cementation, 547, *547*
Central processing unit (CPU), 455, *455*
Centrifuge, 275
Centrioles, 98, *99,* 106
Centromere, 98, *98,* 106
Chadwick, James, 264
Chalk, 305, *534,* 549
Chemical digestion, 128, 130, 131
Chemical energy, 383, *383,* 387, *388*
Chemical formulas, 83, 274
Chemical processes, 288
Chemical sedimentary rocks, 548–549, *549*
Chemosynthesis, 211
Chicken pox, 176
Chlamydia, 181
Chlorine, isotopes of, 270, *270*

Index

Chlorofluorocarbons (CFCs), 235
Chlorophyll, 42, 82
Chloroplasts, 42, *42,* 82
Choking, 143, *144*
Cholesterol, 135
Chromatids, 98, *98, 99,* 106
Chromosome(s), 40, **98;** genes on, 112, *112;* in mitosis, 98, *98,* 99, 100, *100,* 101, 103 *lab;* predicting numbers of, 107 *act;* separating, 123, *123;* in sexual reproduction, 105, 106, *106,* 109, *109*
Chromosphere, 477, *477*
Chronic bronchitis, 145
Chronic diseases, 183–185
Chyme, 131, *132*
Cilia, 141, 174
Cinder cone volcano, 604, *604*
Circle chart, 725
Circuit, integrated, 447, *447,* 449, 452, *452*
Circular motion, 360–361, *361*
Circulation, 168, 168–173; coronary, 169; pulmonary, 169, *169;* systemic, 169
Circulatory system, 161 *lab,* 162–187; and blood pressure, 171, *171,* 172, *172;* blood vessels in, 169, 170, *170,* 171, *171*
Circumference, formula for, 718
Circumpolar constellations, 473
Cities, and climate, 626 *act,* 627, 644–645 *lab*
Citric acid, 303
Classification, 22–27; of climates, 628, *628,* 629; dichotomous key for, 26; of elements, 267, *267, 268;* field guides for, 25; history of, 22–23; of igneous rock, 538, 538–539; of metamorphic rocks, *543,* 543–544, *544;* modern, 23, *23;* of organisms, 5 *lab;* scientific names in, 24–25; of sedimentary rocks, 546–553, *547,* 552–553 *lab;* of sediments, 546 *lab;* of seeds, 27 *lab;* of stars, 482–483
Clay, *547*
Cleanliness, 181
Cleavage, 513, *513*
Climate, 622–646, **624;** adaptations to, 628–631, *630, 631;* around the world, 623 *lab,* 628; and atmospheric particles, 637, *637;* and burning fossil fuels, 641; change of, *636,* 636–642, *637, 638, 640,* 660, *660;* and cities, 626 *act,* 627, 644–645 *lab;* classification of, 628, *628,* 629; and crustal plate movement, 638; and deforestation, 641, *641,* 641 *act;* and El Niño, 633, 633 *lab,* 634–635; fossils as indicators of, 660, *660,* 661, *661;* and global warming, 639, 640, *640;* and greenhouse effect, 234, *234,* 241 *lab,* 639, *639,* 639 *act,* 643 *lab;* and La Niña, 633, *634–635;* and large bodies of water, 625, *625;* and latitude, 624, *624;* and meteorites, 637; microclimates, 644–645 *lab;* and mountains, 626–627, *627;* and ocean currents, 626; and plants, 628, *628,* 630, 641, *641,* 642; and seasons, 622, *632,* 632–633; and solar radiation, 235, *235,* 624, *624,* 625 *lab,* 637, 638, *638;* in tropics, 624, *624;* and volcanoes, 637, *637*
Clock, analog, 443
Clotting, 163, 164, *164*
Clouds of Magellan, 489, *489*
CMEs (coronal mass ejections), 479, *479*
Coal, 226, *226,* 394, *394,* 550, 550 *act,* 551, 657
Cobb, Jewel Plummer, 58, *58*
Coelacanth, 676, *676*
Collisions, 321 *lab,* 335, 335–338, *336, 337, 338,* 339 *lab,* 340–341 *lab*
Color, of minerals, 512; seeing, 431, *431*
Columbia River Plateau, 605, *605*
Combustion, 260, *260*
Commensalism, 206
Communicating Your Data, 27, 29, 46, 57, 80, 87, 103, 117, 153, 167, 187, 202, 215, 241, 247, 272, 279, 301, 311, 339, 341, 369, 371, 392, 403, 424, 433, 448, 461, 481, 495, 509, 523, 540, 553, 574, 583, 607, 615, 643, 645, 668, 675
Communities, 199, **200;** symbiosis in, 206, *206,* 206 *lab*
Compaction, 546, *546*
Complex carbohydrates, 134
Composite volcano, 605, *605*
Composting, 245, *245*
Compound(s), 68, *68,* 273, *273*–274, *274,* 288; comparing, 274 *lab;* inorganic, **71;** molecular, 294, 296, *296;* organic, **70**–71
Compound light microscopes, 56–57 *lab*
Compression, *570,* 571, 571 *lab,* 593, *593*
Compressional waves, 413, *413,* 414, *414;* amplitude of, 415, *415;* sound waves as, 419, *419*
Computer(s), 449–461; binary system in, 450, 450 *lab,* 451; and digital signals, 443–444, *444;* disposing of, 454; early, 449, *449;* and floppy disks, 458; hard disk of, 456, *456,* 456 *act,* 457; hardware of, 454–455, *454–455;* memory in, 451–452, *452,* 453 *lab,* 456; microprocessors in, 455, *455;* networks of, 459; software (programs) for, 452 *act,* **453,** *453;* storing information on, 451 *act,* 452, 456, 456–458, *457, 458;* viruses affecting, 460–461 *lab*
Computer information, 450–451, 451 *act*
Computer programming, 453
Concentration, 299 *act,* **299**–300; comparing, 299 *act;* measuring, 299–300, *300*
Concept Mapping, 115, 527
Conclusions, 9
Concrete, 548, *548*
Conductivity, of metalloids, 445–446, *446*
Cone(s), of eye, 431, *431*
Conglomerate, *547,* 547, 548, *548*
Conservation, 242–245; of energy, **386,** 393, 401; of fossil fuels, 226; of matter, **260;** of momentum, *335,* 335–338, *336, 337;* recycling, 243, 243–245, 244 *act, 245;* reducing, 242; reusing, 242, *242*
Constant speed, 325, *325*

Constellation, *472*, **472**–473, *473*
Consumers, 82, *83*, 208
Continent(s), *571*
Continental plates, 571, *571*
Control, 9
Convection, 572, *573*
Convergent plate boundaries, 571, 610
Convex lens, 50
Copper, 136, 512 *act*
Coquina, 549
Core(s), inner, **565**, *566*–*567*; outer, **566**, *566*–*567*
Cornea, 429, *429*
Corona, **477**, *477*
Coronary arteries, 171
Coronary circulation, 169
Corundum, 511, 517, *517*
Cotton, 224
Covalent bond, 294, *294*
CPU (central processing unit), 455, *455*
Crater(s), 578
Crick, Francis, 111
Crinoid, 661, *661*
Critical thinking, 7
Crust, of Earth, 508, *508*, **566**, *566*–*567*, 575–583, 582–583 *lab*; oceanic, 571; uplift of, 575–583, 582–583 *lab*
Crystal, *505*, **505**–507, *506*, *507*, 509 *lab*; ice, 73; from solution, 301 *lab*
Crystalline, 504
Crystallization, 290
Crystal systems, 505 *lab*, *506*
Current(s), and climate, 626
Cycles, carbon, 213, *213*, 642, *642*; nitrogen, 213; rock, *533*, **533**–535, *534*, 551; water, **212**, *212*, 212 *lab*
Cytoplasm, **38**, 40, 40 *lab*, 78, 84, 98, *99*
Cytosine, 111
Cytoskeleton, 40, *40*

D

Dalton, John, 261, 268
Dam, 227
Dark energy, 493
Darkfield microscope, 48
Data analysis, 9, 9 *lab*, 29 *lab*
Data Source, 116, 246, 402, 460, 582, 674
Dating, carbon-14, 666, 670, *670*, 671, *671*, 672 *act*; radiometric, *671*, **671**–672, *672*; relative, 663 *act*; of rocks, 659, *659*, 661, 671–672, *672*
Death rate, 181 *act*
Decibel scale, 421, *421*
Decomposers, 208, *208*
Decompression melting, 610
Deforestation, **641**, *641*, 641 *act*
Deformation, 593 *lab*
Democritus, 259, 280
Deoxyribonucleic acid (DNA), 40, 71, *110*–*111*, **110**–112, 111 *lab*
Desalination, 275 *act*, 289 *act*
Design Your Own, Blood Type Reactions, 186–187; Car Safety Testing, 340–341; Identifying a Limiting Factor, 214–215; Measuring Parallax, 494–495; Mineral Identification, 522–523; Modeling Motion in Two Directions, 370–371; Using Scientific Methods, 28–29
Detrital sedimentary rocks, 546–548, *547*
Development, 16, *16*, 17
Diabetes, 184, 524
Diagram(s), 685. *See also* Scientific illustration(s)
Dialysis, 151, *151*
Diamond, 502, 508, 511, *511*, 518, *518*
Dichotomous key, 26
Diffraction, **418**; of waves, 418, *418*
Diffusion, **75**, *75*; facilitated, 77, 79; of water, 75 *lab*, 76, *76*
Digestion, chemical, 128, 130, 131; enzymes in, *128*, 128–129, 131; mechanical, 128, 130, 152–153 *lab*; of plant structures, 134
Digestive system, 128–132, *129*; bacteria in, 132; functions of, 128–129; immune defenses of, 174; organs of, 129–132; peristalsis in, 130, 131
Digestive tract, 129, *129*
Digital information, 450–451, 451 *act*

Digital signal, **443**–444, *444*
Digitization, 444, *444*
Dinosaur(s), fossils of, 654, *654*, 655, *656*; tracks of, 658, *658*
Diodes, **446**, *446*, 448 *lab*
Diorite, *538*
Diploid cells, **104**, 105, 108, *109*
Diptheria, 176
Disconformity, 664, *665*
Disease(s), 178–185; of blood, 166, *166*; cardiovascular, 171, 172, 172 *act*; chronic, 183–185; and cleanliness, 181; fighting, 182–183; in history, 178–179; and human carriers, 181; infectious, 167 *lab*, **179**–181; noninfectious, 183–185; organisms causing, 178–179; percentage of deaths due to, 181 *act*; respiratory, 145–146; sexually transmitted (STDs), 181; sickle-cell, 166, *166*; urinary, 150–151, *151*
Disk(s), floppy, 458; hard, 456, *456*, 456 *act*, *457*; magnetic, 456, *456*, 456 *act*, *457*; optical, 458, *458*, 458 *act*
Displacement, and distance, 323, *323*
Dissolving, 290, 295, *295*
Dissolving rates, 287 *lab*, 297. *See also* Solubility; Solution(s)
Distance, and displacement, 323, *323*; in space, 474 *act*, 475, 490 *lab*
Distance-time graph, 326, *326*
Divergent plate boundaries, 609
DNA (deoxyribonucleic acid), 40, 71, *110*–*111*, **110**–112, 111 *lab*
Dolomite, 508
Dolphins, 23
Domain, 23, 23 *act*
Doping, 446, *446*
Doppler shift, 472–491, *491*
Drought, 633, *633*, 635
Ductility, 270
Duodenum, 131
Dust mites, *183*

E

Ear, 422, *422*
Earth, axis of, 638; crustal plate

Index

Earth history

movement on, 638; crust of, 566, *566–567*, 575–583, *582–583 lab*; inner core of, 565, *566–567*; interior of, *563 lab*, 564–566, *565*, *566–567*; layers of, *565*, 565–566, *566–567*; lithosphere of, 608, *609*; mantle of, 566, *566–567*; minerals in crust of, 508, *508*; moving plates of, 568–574, *569*, *571*, *572*, *573*, *574 lab*, 601, *601*, 608, *608*, *609*, *613*; orbit of, 638; outer core of, 566, *566–567*; structure of, *565*, 565–567, *566–567*; tilt of, *632*, 632–633, 638

Earth history, 652–675, *674–675 lab*; and absolute age, 669–673; and fossils, 654–661; and relative age, 663–668, *668 lab*

Earthquakes, 415, **592**–600; building for, *591 lab*, 616; causes of, *592*, 592–593; damage caused by, 598, 616, *616*; and Earth's plates, 569, *569*, 572, *572*, 611–613, *613*; epicenter of, 594, 596, *596*; and faults, 569, 572, *572*, 593, *593*, 594, *594*, 600; focus of, 594, *594*; locations of, 611, *611*; magnitude of, 595, 596, 598, *598 act*; measuring, 595, *595*, 596, 598; predicting, 600, *600*; preparation for, *591 lab*, 599, 599–600, 616; and seismic waves, 564, *564*, 565, *594*, 594–595, *596*, 612, *612*, *612 act*, 614–615 *lab*

Eating. *See also* Nutrition; eating well, 154; importance of, 133

E-books, 462, *462*

Echolocation, 423

Ecological pyramids, 211

Ecologist, 196, *196*

Ecology, **196,** 660

Ecosystems, *199*, **200,** *200;* balance of, *202 lab*; energy flow through, 208, 208–211, *209*, *210*, *211;* habitats in, 207; limiting factors in, 205, *205*, *214–215 lab*; populations in, *199*, 200, *200*

Egg(s), 94, **104,** *104*, *105;* fertilized, 104

Ehrlich, Gretel, 216

Einstein, Albert, 483
Elastic limit, 592, *592*
Elastic rebound, 592
Electrical energy, **384,** 389, *389*, *390*, 390–391, *391*
Electricity, consumption of, 396, 396 *act*, *402–403 lab*; generating, 227, 227–230, *228*, *390*, 390–391, *391*, 396 *act*, 397; power failure, 404; and water, 227; from wind power, 228
Electromagnetic spectrum, **426**–427, *427*
Electromagnetic waves, 414, 425, 426, *426*, 428, *428*
Electron(s), **262,** 669
Electron cloud model of atom, 264–265, *265*
Electronic(s), **442,** 442–448; analog devices, 442–443, *443*; calculator competition, *441 lab*; diodes in, 446, *446*, *448 lab*; integrated circuits in, 447, *447*, 449, 452, *452*; microprocessors, 455, *455*; semiconductors, 445 *act*, 445–446, *446*, 447; transistors in, 447, *447*
Electronic books, 462, *462*
Electronic devices, *441 lab*, 442–443, *443*, 445, *445*
Electronic signal, **442;** analog, 442, *444*; digital, **443**–444, *444*
Electron microscopes, 49, 50, 58
Element(s), 67, *67*, 68, *68*, **266**–272, 288; atomic mass of, 270, *270*; atomic number of, 269; classification of, 267, *267*, *268*; identifying characteristics of, 269–270; isotopes of, 269, *269*, 270, *270*, 669; metalloids, 271, 445–446, *446*; metals, 270, *270*; nonmetals, 271, *271*; periodic table of, 67, 267, *268*, 269, *272 lab*; synthetic, 266, *266*, 267 *act*
Elliptical galaxy, 489, *489*
El Niño, 633, *633 lab*, 634–635
Emerald, 516, *516*
Emphysema, 145
Endocytosis, 78, *78*, 79
Endoplasmic reticulum (ER), 42, *43*, 43

ENIAC

Energy, 378–404, *379 lab*, **380,** *380*, 386 *act*; alternative sources of, *397 lab*, 397–399, *398*, *399*; and amplitude, 415; chemical, **383,** *383*, 387, *388*; conservation of, **386,** 393, 401; consumption of, 396, *402–403 lab*; dark, 493; electrical, **384,** 389, *389*, *390*, 390–391, *391*; environmental consequences of obtaining, transforming, and distributing, 224–226, 394–396; and fermentation, 84, *84*, 85; flow through ecosystems, 208, 208–211, *209*, *210*, *211*; in food chain, 208, *209*; forms of, *382*, 382–384, *383*, *384*; from fossil fuels, 394, *394*; from fusion, 483–484, *484*; geothermal, **229,** *229*, 398–399, *399*; kinetic, 227, **381,** *381*, 386, *386*, 387, *388*; for life, 81–85, *86–87 lab*; and mass, 483; and matter, 208–213; of motion, 381, *381*; nuclear, **228,** *228*, **384,** *384*, 395, *395*; and photosynthesis, 82, *82*, 85, *85*, 208; potential, 227, **382,** *382*, 386, *386*; radiant, **383,** *383*; and respiration, 83, *83*, 85, *85*, *86–87 lab*; solar, 224, **229,** *229*–230, *230*, *231*, *246–247 lab*, 397–398, *398*, *399*, 404, *404*; sources of, *391*, 393–401, *402–403 lab*; storing, 390, *390*; thermal, **382,** *382*, 389–391, *390*; tidal, 400, *400*; transfer of, 380; transfer of between organisms, 208–211; transformation, 385–391; use by living things, 15; using, 393; and waves, 412, *412*; wind, 399, *399*

Energy-processing organelles, 42, *42*
Energy pyramids, 211, *211*
Energy transformations, *385*, 385–391, *392 lab*; analyzing, *387 lab*; chemical energy, 387, *388*; efficiency of, 387; electrical energy, 389, *389*; between kinetic and potential energy, 386, *386*; thermal energy, 389–390, *390*; tracking, 385
ENIAC, 449

Index

Environment, 196–202; abiotic factors in, 196–198, *197, 198;* acid in, 303, *304;* biotic factors in, 196, 198–201, *199, 200;* biotic potential of, 206; carrying capacity of, 205; and fossils, *660,* 660–661, *661;* and population, *199,* 200, *200*
Enzyme(s), 71, *71 lab, 112, 128,* **128**–129, 131; and metabolism, 81, *81;* and pathogens, 174; and photosynthesis, 82; and respiration, 83
Epicenter, 594, *596, 596*
Epiglottis, 130, 141
Equation(s), acceleration, 330; simple, *359 act, 416 act;* for wave speed, 416
Equilibrium, 75, *76*
Erosion, *223 lab,* **239,** *239;* of rocks, 546
Eruptions, 602, *602, 602 lab, 607 lab;* fissure, 605, *605;* largest, 606; quiet, 603, 605; violent, 603, 605; volcanic, *646, 646*
Esophagus, 130
Essential amino acids, 134
Etna, Mount (Italy), 378
Eukaryotic cell, 39, *39*
Evaporites, *507, 507*
Event horizon, 485
Evolution, of stars, *484 act,* 484–487
Excretory system, 147–151; functions of, 147; urinary system, *147,* 147–151, *148*
Exercise, 140
Exhaling, 140, 142, 143, *143*
Exocytosis, 78, *79*
Experiments, 8–9
Exponential notation, 723. See also Scientific notation
Extrusive rock, 537, *537,* 538
Eye, 429, 429–431, *430, 431*

Facilitated diffusion, 77, *79*
Fat(s), 70; body, 134, 135, *135;* dietary, 133, 134–135, *135 lab*
Fat-soluble vitamins, 135
Fault(s), 569, *572, 572,* **593,** *594;* measuring movement along, *600, 600;* types of, *593, 593*

Fault-block mountains, 576, *576*
Feldspar, 508, 511, 532, *532,* 543, 548
Fermentation, 84, *84,* 85
Fertilization, 104, *105,* 106
Fiber, 134, *134 act*
Fibrin, 164
Field guides, 25
Filovirus, *52, 54 act*
Fish, adaptations of, 631, *631;* early, *676, 676*
Fission, in reproduction, 101
Fissure eruptions, 605, *605*
Flight, *364 act*
Flood basalts, 605, *605*
Floppy disk, 458
Fluid levels, regulating, 148
Fluorescence microscope, *48*
Fluorite, *506,* 511, *512*
Focus, 594, *594*
Foldables, 5, 37, 65, 95, 127, 161, 195, 223, 257, 287, 321, 349, 379, 411, 441, 471, 503, 531, 563, 591, 623, 653
Folded mountains, 576, **577,** *577*
Foliated rocks, 543, *543*
Food, daily servings of, 138; fat content of, *135 lab;* lab*el*ing of, *12,* 138, *138;* particle size and absorption of, *152*–*153 lab;* spoilage of, 177, 298
Food chains, 208, *209*
Food groups, *137,* 137–138
Food web, 210, *210, 210 act;* global, 211, *211;* land, *209, 209;* ocean, 210, *210*
Fool's gold (pyrite), 510, *510,* 513
Force(s), *350,* **350**–351; and acceleration, *356,* 356–357, 360; action and reaction, 363–366, *364, 366;* balanced, **351,** *351;* combining, 351; compression, 570, 571, *571 lab;* effects of, *349 lab;* net, **351,** 360; shear, 593; tension, 569, *569, 570, 571 lab, 576;* unbalanced, **351;** unit of measurement with, 357
Force pairs, measuring, *367 lab*
Forest(s), and deforestation, *641, 641, 641 act;* as renewable resource, *224, 224*
Formaldehyde, 236

Formulas, chemical, 83, 274
Fossil(s), *654,* 654–661, *655;* and ancient environments, *660,* 660–661, *661;* and climate, *660, 660, 661, 661;* formation of, 655, *655;* index, **659,** *659, 666 act;* making model of, *653 lab;* minerals in, 656, *656;* organic remains, *658, 658;* preservation of, *655 lab,* 655–659, *656, 657, 658;* trace, *658, 658, 674*–*675 lab*
Fossil fuels, 226, *226;* alternatives to, 227–231; burning, 641; conservation of, 226; and greenhouse effect, 234; as source of energy, *394, 394*
Fossil-rich limestone, 549
Fracture, 513
Franklin, Rosalind, 111
Free fall, *367, 367,* 368
Freezing point, of solvent, 300
Frequency, 414; of light, 425; of sound waves, 421; unit of, 416
Freshwater ecosystems, *197, 197*
Friction, *352,* **352**–355, *354 lab,* 611; rolling, 355, *355;* sliding, 353, 354, *354, 355,* 359, 362; static, 354
Fruit flies, genes of, *115 act;* mutations in, 115; reproduction of, *100, 100*
Fungi, and diseases, 178, 179; infectious, 178
Fusion, 483–484, *484*

Gabbro, *538, 540 lab*
Galaxies, 470, **488**–489; clusters of, *471 lab,* 488; elliptical, *489, 489;* irregular, *489, 489;* spiral, *488,* 488–489
Galilei, Galileo, 352, *353 act,* 478
Galina, *512 act*
Gallium, 446
Galvanization, *520*
Gamma rays, 428
Garnet, 517, *517*
Gas(es), in digestive system, 132; natural, 226; solubility of, 298, *298 lab*

Index

Gaseous solutions

Gaseous solutions, 291, 298 *lab*
Gas-gas solution, 292
Gasoline, 393, 394
Gasoline engines, 387, *387*
Gems, 515, **515**–518, *516*, *517*, *518*, 518 *act*
Gene(s), 112, **112**–114; controlling, 114, *114*; of fruit fly, 115 *act*; in protein synthesis, 112–113, *113*
Generator, 390, *390*
Gene therapy, 55
Genetic information, 110–112
Genital herpes, 181
Genus, 24, *25*
Geothermal energy, 229, *229*, 398–399, *399*
Germ theory, 177
Germanium, 445
German measles (rubella), 176
Giants, 483, *483*, **485**, *485*, 486, *496*, *496*
Glaciers, 580 *act*, 636, *640*
Glass, recycling, 244
Global warming, 234, *234*, 234 *act*, 639, **640**, *640*
Glucose, 83, 84
Gneiss, *534*, *541*, 542, 543, 548
Gold, 512 *act*; identifying, 510, *510*, 513
Golgi bodies, 43, *43*
Gonorrhea, 181
Grand Canyon National Park, 666
Granite, 532, *532*, *538*, *539*, 540 *lab*, 543, 548
Granitic rock, *538*, **539**
Graph(s), of accelerated motion, 332, *332*; bar, 725; distance-time, 326, line, 724; of motion, 326, *326*; pie, 725; scale of, 724; speed-time, 332, *332*
Graphite, 504, *512*, 513
Graptolites, 656, *656*
Gravel, 547
Gravity, 357–358; and air resistance, 361; and motion, 357, 360, *360*, 361, *361*
Great Salt Lake, 312, *312*
Green algae, 197
Greenhouse effect, 234, *234*, 241 *lab*, 639, *639*, 639 *act*, 643 *lab*
Groundwater, pollution of, 238, *238*

Growth, 16, *16*; of seeds, 95 *lab*
Guanine, 111
Gypsum, *506*, 507, 511, 548

Habitat(s), **207**
Half-life, **670**, 671
Halite, 504, 507, *507*, *513*, 549, *549*. *See also* Salt(s)
Hammer (of ear), 422, *422*
Haploid cells, **105**, 108
Hard disk, 456, *456*, 456 *act*, *457*
Hardness, 511
Hardware, computer, 454–455, *454–455*
Harvey, William, 188
Hawaiian Islands, volcanoes in, 579, *579*, 604, *604*, 606, 610, *610*
Hazardous wastes, 240, *240*
Hearing, 421, *422*
Heart, *168*; blood circulation in, 169; chambers of, 168; open-heart surgery, 188
Heart attack, 169, 171
Heat island effect, 626 *act*, 627
Heat pumps, 399
Helper T cells, 175, 182
Hematite, 512 *act*, *513*, 519, 544, 547
Hemoglobin, 142, **163**
Hemophilia, 164
Heredity, laws of, 10
Herpes, 181
Hertz (Hz), 416
Hertzsprung, Ejnar, 482
Hertzsprung-Russell (H-R) diagram, 482, *482*, 483, 484
Heterogeneous mixture, 277, **289**
Hibernation, 630, *630*
High blood pressure, 172, *172*
Himalaya, 571, 575, *575*
Histamines, 183
HIV (human immunodeficiency virus), 182, *182*
Hodgkin, Dorothy Crowfoot, 524, *524*
Homeostasis, 15, 18, 132, 137
Homogeneous mixture, 277, **290**, *290*
Hooke, Robert, 51

Inexhaustible resources

Hornblende, 532, 544
Host cell, **52**, *53*, 54, *54*, 179
Hot spots, **610**, *610*, 613
Hubble, Edwin, 491
Hubble Space Telescope, 486, 493
Human Genome Project, 113 *act*
Human immunodeficiency virus (HIV), 182, *182*
Hutton, James, 535, 673
Hybrid cars, 387, *387*, 404, *404*
Hydra, 102, *102*
Hydrochloric acid, 71, 303, 307, *307*, 308; in digestive system, 131, 174
Hydroelectric power, 227, 396, 397
Hydrogen, isotopes of, 269, *269*, 669
Hydrogen peroxide, 274, *274*
Hydronium ions, **302**, *302*, 306, 307, 309, *309*
Hydroxide ions, 306, 307, 309, *309*
Hypertension (high blood pressure), 172, *172*
Hypothalamus, 148
Hypothesis, 8

Icebergs, 581, *581*
Ice cores, 636, *636*
Iceland, geothermal energy in, 229, *229*
Iceman, 672
Ideas, communicating, 25
Igneous rocks, 533, *533*, 534, **536**–540; classifying, *538*, 538–539; formation of, *536*, 536–538, *537*, 540 *lab*
Iguana, 25, *25*
Ilmenite, 520, *520*
Immune system, first-line defenses in, 174, *174*
Immunity, 174–177; active, **176**; passive, **176**, 177, *177*; specific, 175
Index fossils, **659**, *659*, 666 *act*
Indicators, **308**, 308 *act*, 310–311 *lab*
Indonesia, volcanoes in, 646
Indoor air pollution, 236, *236*
Inertia, 333, *333*
Inexhaustible resources, 397

Index

Infection, respiratory, 145
Infectious diseases, 179–181; and microorganisms, 167 *lab*
Inflammation, 175
Information, digital, 450–451, 451 *act;* storing on computers, 451 *act,* 452, *456,* 456–458, *457, 458*
Information gathering, 8
Infrared waves, 427
Ingestion, 130
Inhaling, 143, *143*
Inner core, 565, *566*–*567*
Inorganic compounds, 71
Instantaneous speed, 325, *325*
Insulin, 131, 184, 524
Integrate Astronomy, life's origins, 21
Integrate Career, Air Pollution Engineer, 198; Air Quality Control/Monitor, 641; Cell Biologist, 50; Computer Programmers, 454; Microbiologist, 83; Oncologist, 97; Pharmacist, 299; Physicists and Chemists, 264; Sedimentary Petrology, 548
Integrate Chemistry, acid precipitation, 233; adding impurities, 446; aluminum, 519; cave formation, 548; chemical formulas, 83; Chemosynthesis, 211; collisions, 298; Diploid Zygote, 105; discovering DNA, 110; Iron Core, 566; Melting Points, 610; Melting Rock, 539; volcano eruptions, 603; water cycle, 212; White Dwarf Matter, 485
Integrated circuits, 447, *447,* 449, 452, *452*
Integrate Earth Science, Energy Source Origins, 394; Oceans, 21; Rocks and Minerals, 277; seismic waves, 414
Integrate Environment, Recycling, 44; Recycling Computers, 456; Solutions, 295; stalactites and stalagmites, 291
Integrate Health, Air Quality, 236; development, 17; diseases and disorders of the respiratory system, 145; Hearing Damage, 421; Large Intestine Bacteria, 132; particulates, 637; Transport Proteins, 77
Integrate History, Atomism, 259; Blood Transfusions, 165; The Industrial Revolution, 389; Newton and Gravity, 357; 386 Supernova, 486
Integrate Language Arts, Friction, 611; The Isostasy Story, 580
Integrate Life Science, acidophils, 306; Ancient Ecology, 660; animals and ranchers, 216; Animal Speeds, 324; birds and Newton's laws, 364; Biomechanics, 351; blood, 276; flight, 364; pH Levels, 306; pollution, 248; separating mixtures, 276; structural adaptations, 629; transforming chemical energy, 387; water in plants, 88
Integrate Physics, blood pressure, 170; characteristics of water, 73; Crystal Formation, 507; energy processing, 42; evolution of stars, 484; matter and the rock cycle, 535; Mountain Air, 626; quasars, 486; radioactive decay, 669; waves, 564
Integrate Social Studies, Coal Mining, 657; Energy, 227; Forensics and Momentum, 334; Historical Mineralogy, 519; Salt Mines, 136; Social Development, 17
Intensity, 420; of sound, 420, *420,* 421
Interactions, among living things, 203–207; and space, 195 *lab,* 204, *204*
Interferons, 55
Interior, of Earth, 563 *lab,* 564–566, *565, 566–567*
International System of Units (SI), 12
Internet, 459, *459,* 460–461 *lab*
Interphase, 97, *97,* 98, 99
Intestine(s), large, 132; small, 131, *131*
Intrusive rock, 537, *537,* 538
Investigation(s), 684–695. *See also* Scientific method(s)
Iodine (dietary), 136
Ion(s), 68–69, *69,* 295
Ionic bond, 295
Iron, 515; as nonrenewable resource, 225, *225;* in ore, 519
Iron (dietary), 136
Irregular galaxy, 489, *489*
Isostasy, 580, *581,* 582–583 *lab*
Isotopes, 269, *269,* 270, *270,* 669

Jellyfish, *24*
Jenner, Edward, 54
Journal, 4, 36, 65, 94, 126, 160, 194, 222, 256, 286, 320, 348, 378, 410, 440, 470, 502, 530, 562, 590, 622, 652

Köppen, Wladimir, 628
Kashyapa, 259, 280
Kidney(s), *148,* 148–149, *149,* 150, 151
Killer T cells, 175
Kilogram (kg), 357
Kinetic energy, 227, **381;** and mass, 381, *381;* and speed, 381, *381;* transforming chemical energy to, 387, *388;* transforming to and from potential energy, 386, *386*
Kingdom, 23
Koch, Robert, 179, 180
Koch's Rules, 179, *180*

Lab(s), Balloon Races, 369; Bending Light, 428, 432–433; Classifying Seeds, 27; Collisions, 339; Comparing Cells, 46; Comparing Light Microscopes, 56–57; Crystal Formation, 509; Delicately Balanced Ecosystems, 202; Design Your Own, 28–29, 186–187, 214–215, 340–341, 370–371, 494–495, 522–523; Disruptive Eruptions, 607;

Index

Labeling

Earth's Moving Plates, 574; Elements and the PeriodicTable, 272; Greenhouse Effect, 241, 643; Growing Crystals, 301; Hearing With Your Jaw, 392; Identifying Vitamin C Content, 139; Igneous Rock Clues, 540; Investigating Diodes, 448; Launch Labs, 5, 37, 65, 95, 127, 161, 195, 223, 257, 287, 321, 349, 379, 411, 441, 471, 503, 531, 563, 591, 623, 653; Microclimates, 644–645; Microorganisms and Disease, 167; Mini Labs, 9, 40, 71, 101, 135, 164, 206, 233, 260, 298, 331, 367, 397, 428, 453, 490, 514, 546, 577, 593, 625, 670; Mitosis in Plant Cells, 103; Model and Invent, 246–247, 582–583, 674–675; Mystery Mixture, 278–279; Observing Osmosis, 80; Particle Size and Absorption, 152–153; Photosynthesis and Respiration, 86–87; Relative Ages, 668; Sedimentary Rocks, 552–553; Seismic Waves, 614–615; Sound Waves in Matter, 424; Sunspots, 481; Testing pH Using Natural Indicators, 310–311; Try at Home Mini Labs, 25, 50, 75, 111, 143, 176, 212, 226, 274, 303, 325, 354, 387, 417, 450, 473, 505, 533, 571, 602, 633, 655; Use the Internet, 116–117, 402–403, 460–461; Using Scientific Methods, 28–29

Labeling, of food, *12*, 138, *138*
Labradorite, *507*
Lactic acid, 84, *84*
Landfills, sanitary, 240, *240*
Landslide, *635*
Land speed, 326 *act*
La Niña, 633, *634–635*
Large intestine, 132
Large Magellanic Cloud, 489, *489*
Larynx, 142
Lasers, 426 *act*
Latent viruses, 53
Latitude, and climate, 624, *624*
Launch Labs, Breathing Rate, 127; Classify Organisms, 5; Clues to Life's Past, 653; Construct with Strength, 591; Distinguishing Rocks from Minerals, 503; Electronic and Human Calculators, 441; Energetic Marbles, 379; How do forces affect a ball?, 349; Magnifying Cells, 37; Measure Space, 195; Model Earth's Interior, 563; Motion After a Collision, 321; Observe and Describe Rocks, 531; Observe Matter, 257; Particle Size and Dissolving Rates, 287; Tracking World Climates, 623; Transportation by Road and Vessel, 161; What are some properties of waves?, 411; What happens when topsoil is left unprotected?, 223; Which cells of a seed become a plant?, 95; Why do clusters of galaxies move apart?, 471; Why does water enter and leave plant cells, 65

Lava, **536**–537, *537*, 538 *act*, 578, *578*, **601**, 603, 604, *604*, 605
Lava plateaus, 605, *605*
Lavoisier, Antoine, 260, *268*
Law(s), 10; of conservation of energy, **386**, 393; of conservation of matter, **260;** of conservation of momentum, *335*, **335**–338, *336*, *337;* Newton's first law of motion, **352**–355, *355;* Newton's second law of motion, **356**–362, *365;* Newton's third law of motion, **363**–368, *365*, 369 *lab;* of reflection, **417**, *417*
Leeuwenhoek, Antonie van, 47
Leeuwenhoek microscope, *48*
Length, measuring, 12
Lenses, convex, 50; of eye, 429, *429*
Leukemia, 166
Life. *See also* Living things; origins of, 19–21, *20*
Life scientist, 6
Light, 425–433; bending, 428, 432–433 *lab;* energy of, 383, *383;* and environment, 197, *197;* frequency of, 425; human eye's response to, 427, 429–431; seeing, 429; speed of, 425; visible, 427, *427;* wavelength of, 425
Light waves, in empty space, 425, *425;* perception of, 427, 429–431; properties of, 426, *426*
Light-year, 475
Lignin, 39
Lime, 305
Limestone, 544, 548, 549, 666, *666*
Limiting factors, 205, *205*, 214–215 *lab*
Linnaeus, Carolus, 23, 24
Lipids, 70, 134. *See also* Fat(s)
Liquid-gas solutions, 292, *292*
Liquid-liquid solutions, 292
Lister, Joseph, 181
Lithosphere, 566, *566*, **568**, 569, 608, *609*
Liver, 131
Living things, 14–18; characteristics of, 14–17; interactions among, 203–207; levels of organization of, *199*, 199–201; needs of, 17–18
Lizards, 25, *25*
Local Group, 488, 491
Lodestone, 514, *514*
Loudness, *420*, 420–421, *421*
Lung(s), 142, 143, *143;* pulmonary circulation in, 169, *169*
Lung cancer, 145, 146, *146*
Lungfish, 631, *631*
Luster, 270, **512,** *512*
Lye, 305
Lymph, 173
Lymphatic system, 172–173, *173*
Lymphocytes, 173, 175–176

Magma, 507, *507*, 533, 536, 536–537, *537*, 538, 578, *578*, 579, 603, 605; silica-rich, 603
Magma chamber, *578*
Magnesium hydroxide, 308
Magnetic disks, 456, *456*, 456 *act*, *457*
Magnetic properties, 514, *514*
Magnetite, 512 *act*, 514, *514*, 519
Magnification, 50, 50 *lab*

Index

Magnifying glass, 37 *lab*, 50
Magnitude, 595, 596, 598, 598 *act*; absolute, **474;** apparent, **474**
Main sequence, *482*, 482–483, 484–485
Malleability, 270, *270*
Mammoth, 658
Mantle, of Earth, **566,** *566–567*
Map(s), 327, *327*
Marble, 544, *544*
Marble launch, analyzing, 379 *lab*
Marmosets, 30, *30*
Mass, 333, *333*; and energy, 483; and kinetic energy, 381, *381*; measuring, 12; unit of measurement with, 357; and weight, 358
Mass number, 269
Materials, alloys, 293, *293*
Matter, 257 *lab*, **258;** atomic theory of, 261; atoms, 66, *66*, 68, *68*; compounds, 68, *68*, 70–71, *273*, 273–274, *274*; cycles of, *212*, 212 *lab*, 212–213, *213*; early beliefs about, 259, 280; elements, 67, *67*, 68, *68*; elements in, 266–272, *268*, 272 *lab*; and energy, 208–213; inorganic compounds, 71; ions, 68–69, *69*; law of conservation of, **260;** mixtures, 69, *69*; molecules, 68, *68*, 73; and motion, 322; organic compounds, 70–71; recycling, 487; and rock cycle, 535; structure of, 258–265
Mauna Loa, Hawaii, 604, *604*
Measles, 176
Measurement, of acid rain, 233 *lab*; of average speed, 325 *lab*; of concentration, 299–300, *300*; of earthquakes, 595, *595*, 596, 598; of force pairs, 367 *lab*; of movement along faults, 600, *600*; of parallax, 494–495 *lab*; of small object, 37 *lab*; in space, 475, 490 *lab*; of space, 195 *lab*; of strength of acids and bases, *306*, 306–308, *307*, 310–311 *lab*; units of, 12, 330, 357; of weight, 367, *367*
Mechanical digestion, 128, 130, 152–153 *lab*
Medicine, insulin, 524

Meiosis, *105*, **105**–109, *106–107*, 108
Melting point, 610
Memory, computer, 451–452, *452*, 453 *lab*, 456
Memory B cells, 176
Mendeleev, Dmitri, 268
Messenger RNA (mRNA), 113
Metabolism, 81, *81*
Metal(s), 270, *270*; as nonrenewable resource, 225, *225*; recycling, 244
Metal alloys, 293, *293*
Metalloids, 271, 445; conductivity of, 445–446, *446*
Metamorphic rocks, 533, *533*, 534, **541**–544; classifying, *543*, 543–544, *544*; formation of, *541*, 541–542, *542*
Metaphase, 98, *99*, 106, *106*, *107*, 109
Meteorite, 637, 672, *672*
Methane, 639
Metric units, 12
Mica, *513*, 532, *532*, 543
Mice, 26, *26*, 207, *207*
Microclimates, 644–645 *lab*
Microorganisms, beneficial, 84 *act*; and infectious diseases, 167 *lab*; in mouth, 182
Microprocessor, 455, *455*
Microscopes, *47*, 47–50, *48–49*, 56–57 *lab*; and discovering disease organisms, 178
Microwaves, 427
Mid-ocean ridge, 569, 573, *573*, 584
Milky Way Galaxy, 470, 488, *488*, 489
Miller, Stanley L., 20, 21
Mineral(s), 502–523, **504;** appearance of, 510, *510*; characteristics of, 504; cleavage of, 513, *513*; color of, 512; dietary, 133, **136;** distinguishing rocks from, 503 *lab*; in Earth's crust, 508, *508*; effects of mining, 226 *lab*; in fossils, 656, *656*; fracture of, 513; gems, 515, 515–518, *516*, *517*, *518*, 518 *act*; hardness of, 511; identifying, 510, 510–514, 512 *act*, 514,

522–523 *lab*; luster of, 512, *512*; magnetic properties of, 514, *514*; as nonrenewable resource, 225; physical properties of, *510*, 510–514, *512*, *513*, *514*, 522–523 *lab*; as pure substances, 277; rock-forming, 508; streak test of, 513, *513*; structure of, *505*, 505–507, *506*, *507*, 509 *lab*; unique properties of, 514; useful elements in, *519*, 519–521, *520*, *521*; uses of, 504, *504*, 515–521; vein, 520, *520*
Mineral grains, 537, 540 *lab*, *541*
Mini Labs, Analyzing Data, 9; Bending Light, 428; Building a Solar Collector, 397; Classifying Sediments, 546; Comparing the Fat Content of Foods, 135; Investigating the Unseen, 260; Measuring Acid Rain, 233; Measuring Distance in Space, 490; Measuring Force Pairs, 367; Modeling Acceleration, 331; Modeling Carbon-14 Dating, 670; Modeling Cytoplasm, 40; Modeling Mitosis, 101; Modeling Mountains, 577; Modeling Scab Formation, 164; Observe Enzymes Work, 71; Observing Deformation, 593; Observing Gas Solubility, 298; Observing Memory, 453; Observing Mineral Properties, 514; Observing Solar Radiation, 625; Observing Symbiosis, 206
Mining, 226 *lab*; of coal, 394
Mitochondria, 42, *42*, 84
Mitosis, 98, **98**–100, *99*, *100*, *101*, 101 *lab*, 103 *lab*
Mixture, 69, *69*
Mixtures, 274, *275*, **275**–279, 276 *act*, 289–290; heterogeneous, **289;** heterogenous, 277; homogeneous, **290,** *290*; homogenous, 277; identifying, 278–279 *lab*; separating, 275, 276, 289, *289*
Model and Invent, Isostasy, 582–583; Solar Cooking, 246–247; Trace Fossils, 674–675
Mohs, Friedrich, 511
Mohs scale of hardness, 511

INDEX 765

Index

Mold(s), of organic remains, 657, *657*
Molecular compounds, 294, 296, *296*
Molecule(s), 68, *68,* 73; nonpolar, 294, *294;* polar, 294, *294,* 296
Momentum, 334–338; calculating, 334 *act;* and collisions, 321 *lab,* *335,* 335–338, *336, 337, 338,* 339 *lab,* 340–341 *lab;* conservation of, 335, 335–338, *336, 337*
Monkey(s), 30, *30*
Montserrat volcano, 601, *601,* 602, *602,* 603, 603 *act,* 606, 609
Motion, 320, 322 *act,* 322–327, 348–371; and acceleration, 328–329, *356,* 356–357, 360; after a collision, 321 *lab;* and air resistance, 361; and changing position, 322, 322–323; circular, 360–361, *361;* energy of, 381, *381;* and friction, 352, 352–355; graphing, 326, *326,* 332, *332;* and gravity, 357, 360, *360,* 361, *361;* and matter, 322; modeling in two directions, 370–371 *lab;* and momentum, 334–338; Newton's first law of, **352**–355, *365;* Newton's second law of, **356**–362, *365;* Newton's third law of, **363**–368, *365,* 369 *lab;* on a ramp, 349 *lab;* relative, 323, *323;* and speed, 324–325, *325*
Mountains, 562, *562,* 584, *584;* and climate, 626–627, *627;* fault-block, **576,** *576;* folded, 576, **577,** *577;* formation of, 569, *569,* 571, *575,* 575–579, *576, 577, 578, 579,* 581; modeling, 577 *lab;* upwarped, **577;** volcanic, *578,* 578 *act,* **578**–579, *579*
Mount St. Helens eruption (Washington state), 605, 606, 646
Mount St. Helens (Washington state), 578
Mouth, 130, *130;* microorganisms in, 182
Mucus, 141, 174
Mumps, 176

Muriatic acid, 303
Muscle(s), transforming chemical energy to kinetic energy in, 387, 388
Muscle cell, 14, 38
Mutations, 114–115, *115,* 116–117
Mutualism, 206, *206*

N

Names, scientific, 24–25
Nanometer, 425
National Geographic Unit Openers, How are Canals and the Paleozoic Era Connected?, 468–469; How are Cargo Ships and Cancer Cells Connected?, 2–3; How are Chickens and Rice Connected?, 124–125; How are Radar and Popcorn Connected?, 318–319; How are Refrigerators and Frying Pans Connected?, 254–255; How are Rivers and Writing Connected?, 560–561
National Geographic Visualizing, Abdominal Thrusts, 144, *144;* Acid Precipitation, 304, *304;* The Big Bang Theory, 492, *492;* Cell Membrane Transport, 79, *79;* The Conservation of Momentum, 337, *337;* Crystal Systems, 506, *506;* El Niño and La Niña, 634, 634–635, *635;* Energy Transformations, 388, *388;* The Food Chain, 209, *209;* A Hard Disk, 457, *457;* Koch's Rules, 180, *180;* Microscopes, *48,* 48–49, *49;* Newton's Laws in Sports, 365, *365;* The Origins of Life, 20, *20;* The Periodic Table, 268, *268;* Polyploidy in Plants, 108, *108;* Rift Valleys, 570, *570;* The Rock Cycle, 534, *534;* Solar Energy, 231, *231;* Tsunamis, 597, *597;* Unconformities, 665, *665;* Vision Defects, 430, *430*
National Oceanic and Atmospheric Administration (NOAA), 646
Natural gas, 226

Natural resources, 224–230. *See also* Resources
Nebula, 484–485, 487, *487*
Needham, John, 20
Negative acceleration, 331, *331*
Nephrons, 149, *149*
Nerve cell(s), *14,* 38, *38,* 97 *act*
Net force, 351, 360
Network, computer, 459
Neutralization, 308, 308–309, *309*
Neutron(s), 264, *264,* 669
Neutron star, 486
Newton (unit of force), 357
Newton, Isaac, 352, 353 *act*
Newton's first law of motion, 352–355, *365*
Newton's second law of motion, 356–362, *365;* and air resistance, 361; and gravity, 357–358; using, *358,* 358–360, *360*
Newton's third law of motion, 363–368, *365,* 369 *lab*
Niche, 207
Nicotine, 173
Nitric acid, 303, 307
Nitrogen, 291, 292
Nitrogen cycle, 213
Nonconformity, 664, *665*
Nonfoliated rocks, 544, *544*
Noninfectious diseases, 183–184
Nonmetals, 271, *271*
Nonpolar molecules, 294, *294*
Nonrenewable resources, 225, *225,* 394, *394*
Normal fault, 593, *593*
Northern lights, 479, *479*
North Pole, 632, *633*
North Star (Polaris), 473, *473*
n-type semiconductors, 446, 447
Nuclear energy, 228, *228,* 384, *384,* 395, *395*
Nuclear fusion, 483–484, *484*
Nuclear waste, 228, 240
Nucleic acid, 70, 71
Nucleus, 40, *41,* 263, *263,* 669
Nutrient(s), 128; carbohydrates, 133, 134, *134;* daily servings of, 138; fats, 133, 134–135, 135 *lab;* minerals, 133, 136; proteins, 131, 133–134; vitamins, 132, 133, 135, 139 *lab;* water, 133, 136–137

766 STUDENT RESOURCES

Nutrition, 133–138; eating well, 154; and food groups, *137,* 137–138

Observation(s), 688–689; biased, 692
Obsidian, *538,* 540 *lab*
Ocean(s), energy from, 400, *400;* and environment, 197, *197*
Ocean currents, and climate, 626
Oceanic crust, 571
Oceanic plates, 571, *571*
Ocean water, 312, *312;* desalination of, 275 *act;* pollution of, 238, *238;* as solution, 295
Octopus, 96
Oil (petroleum), 394; as nonrenewable resource, 225, *225;* and pollution, 238, *238*
Olivine, 517, *517*
Oops! Accidents in Science, A Tangled Tale, 118, Jansky's Merry-Go-Round, 434, What Goes Around Comes Around, 342; The World's Oldest Fish Story, 676
Opal, 504
Oparin, Alexander I., 20, 21
Optical disks, 458, *458,* 458 *act*
Orbit, of Earth, 638; of satellite, 361; weightlessness in, 368, *368*
Order, 23
Ore, 519, *519*
Organ(s), 45, *45;* accessory, 129; of digestive system, 129–132; of respiratory system, *141,* 141–142; of urinary system, *148,* 148–149, *149*
Organelle(s), 40, 42–44; energy-processing, 42, *42;* manufacturing, 42–43; recycling, 44; storing, 43; transporting, 43
Organic compounds, 70–71
Organic sedimentary rocks, 549–550, *551*
Organism(s), 14, *199;* classification of, 5 *lab;* development of, 16, *16;* similarity among, 14–18
Orion, 472, *472,* 473
Oscillating model of universe, 490

Osmosis, 76, *76,* 80 *lab*
Ouachita Mountains (Arkansas), 575, *575*
Outcome, 714
Outer core, 566, *566*–567
Owl, 207, *207,* 209
Oxygen, 67, *68,* 288, 508; and respiration, 83; in respiration, 142, *142;* use in body, 75, *75*
Ozone depletion, 235, *235*
Ozone layer, 198

Pacific Ring of Fire, 610, 611
Pancreas, 131
Paper, recycling, 245
Parallax, 475, *475,* 494–495 *lab*
Parasite, 206
Particulates, 637
Passive immunity, 176, *177,* 177
Passive transport, 74–77, *75, 76,* 79
Pasteur, Louis, 19, 20, 22, 178
Pasteurization, 178
Pathogens, and immune system, 174, 175, 176
Pectin, 39
Pepsin, 131
Percentage(s), 716
Peridot, 517, *517*
Periodic table, 67, 267; metalloids on, 445
Periodic table of elements, 268, 269, 272 *lab*
Peristalsis, 130, 131
Permeable membrane, 74
Permineralized remains, 656, *656*
Perspiration, 174
Pertussis (whooping cough), 176
Petroleum, 225. *See also* Oil (petroleum)
pH, 233, **306**–308, 310–311 *lab*
Pharynx, 141
Phase-contrast microscope, 49
Phosphorus, 136, 213
Photosphere, 477, *477*
Photosynthesis, 82, *82,* 85, *85,* 86–87 *lab,* 208
Photovoltaic collector, 398, *398*
pH scale, *233,* 306, *306*
Phyllite, 542
Phylogeny, 23

Physical processes, 288, 289
Physical properties, appearance, 510, *510;* cleavage, 513, *513;* color, 512; fracture, 513; hardness, 511; luster, 512, *512;* of minerals, *510,* 510–514, *512, 513, 514,* 522–523 *lab;* streak, 512, 513, *513*
Physicist, 6
Pickling, 303
Pinatubo volcano (Philippines), 637
Pipe, *578*
Pitch, 421
Plant(s), and carbon dioxide, 641, *641,* 642; cell walls in, 39, *39,* 134; and climate, 628, *628,* 630, 631, 641, 642; photosynthesis in, 82, *82,* 85, *85,* 86–87 *lab,* 208; polyploidy in, *108;* reproduction of, 95 *lab,* 97, 98, *98,* 101, *101,* 103 *lab;* stone, *6;* transport in, 76, *76,* 77, *77;* use of energy by, 15; use of raw materials by, 18; water in, 65 *lab,* 72, 76, *76*
Plant cell, 41
Plasma, in blood, **162,** *162,* 163, 164
Plastics, recycling, 243, *243*
Plate(s), 568, *578;* collisions of, 571, *571;* continental, 571, *571;* and earthquakes, 569, *569,* 572, *572,* 611–613, *613;* movement of, 568–574, *569, 571, 572, 573,* 574 *lab,* 608, *608, 609, 613;* oceanic, 571, *571;* and volcanoes, 601, *601,* 608, 608–610, *609*
Plate boundaries, 569 *act,* 569–572, *571;* convergent, 571, 610; divergent, 609; transform, 572, *572*
Platelets, 162, *162,* **163,** *163*
Polar bears, 630
Polaris (North Star), 473, *473*
Polar molecules, 294, *294,* 296
Polar zones, 624, *624*
Poles, of Earth, *632,* 633
Pollutants, 232
Pollution, 232–240; of air, 198, *198,* 232, *232*–236, *233, 234, 235,* 241 *lab, 304;* of atmosphere, 639, *639,* 641, *641,* 642; and fossil fuels, 394; and nuclear power, 228; of soil, 239–240, *240;* of water, 237, 237–238, *238*

Index

Polyploidy, in plants, *108. See* Haploid cells. *See also* Diploid cells
Population(s), 200; characteristics of, 203–206; and competition, 205, *205;* and environment, *199,* 200, *200;* and food webs, 210, *210,* 210 *act;* limits on growth, 205, 206; size of, 203, *203;* spacing of, 195 *lab,* 204, *204*
Population density, 204, *204,* 204 *act*
Position, changing, *322,* 322–323
Positive acceleration, 331
Potassium, 136
Potassium chromate, 297
Potato leafroll virus, *52,* 54
Potential energy, 227, **382,** *382,* 386, *386*
Power, 402–403 *lab;* geothermal, 399, *399;* hydroelectric, **227,** 396, *397;* nuclear, 228, *228;* wind, 228
Power failure, 404
Power plants, *390,* 390–391
Precipitate, 290, *290,* 291, 301 *lab*
Precipitation, acid, **233,** *233,* 233 *lab,* 304
Precision, degree of, 723
Predators, 207, *207*
Pressure, atmospheric, 198; and metamorphic rocks, 542; and solubility, 298
Prey, 207, *207*
Principle of superposition, 662, *662*
Principle of uniformitarianism, 673, *673*
Probability, estimation of, 714; of outcome, 714
Problem solving, *7,* 7–10, 11 *act*
Producers, 82, *83,* 208
Program(s), computer, 452 *act,* 453, *453*
Programming, computer, 453
Prokaryotic cell, 39, *39*
Prominences, 478, *479*
Properties, of acids, 302; of bases, 305; of gems, 515; of light waves, 426, *426;* magnetic, 514, *514;* physical. *See* Physical properties; of waves, 411 *lab,* 414, 414–416, *415*
Prophase, 98, *99,* 106, *106, 107*
Proteins, 70, 71, 133–134; complete, 134; digestion of, 131; incomplete, 134; sources of, *133;* transport, 77
Proteins, making, 112–113, *113*
Protist(s), and diseases, 178, *179*
Proton(s), 263, *263,* 669
Proxima Centauri, 475, 480
p-type semiconductors, 446, *447*
Pulmonary circulation, 169, *169*
Pumice, *538,* 540 *lab*
Pyrite (fool's gold), 510, *510,* 513
Pyroclastic flows, 602, *602,* 603

Quarantine, 55
Quarks, 265
Quartz, 505, *505,* 508, 511, 512, 513, 517, *517,* 518, 532, *532,* 543, 544, 547, 548
Quartzite, 544
Quasars, 486

R

Rabies vaccinations, 55, *55*
Radiant energy, 383, *383*
Radiation, from Sun, 185, 235, *235,* 624, *624,* 625 *lab,* 637, 638, *638;* ultraviolet, 235
Radio, 389, *389,* 392 *lab*
Radioactive decay, 669–670, *670*
Radioactive waste, 228, 240, 395
Radiocarbon dating, 670, *670,* 670 *lab,* 671, *671,* 672 *act*
Radiometric dating, 671, **671**–672, *672*
Radio waves, 427
Radon, 236, *236*
Rain, acid, 233, *233,* 233 *lab,* 304; and water pollution, 237, *237*
Rainbow, 258
Rain forests, destruction of, 641, *641*
Rainier, Mount, *534*
Rainier, Mount (Washington state), 605
Rain shadow, 627, *627*
Rajalakshmi, R., 154
RAM (random-access memory), 452, 453 *lab,* 456

Random-access memory (RAM), 452, 453 *lab,* 456
Ratios, 44 *act*
Reaction, and action, 363–366, *364, 366*
Reading Check, 9, 10, 15, 17, 19, 23, 25, 39, 40, 43, 44, 45, 51, 54, 67, 69, 75, 76, 83, 84, 98, 101, 105, 106, 111, 114, 129, 131, 135, 136, 140, 143, 148, 151, 164, 165, 170, 173, 174, 176, 179, 184, 196, 198, 205, 206, 211, 225, 235, 240, 243, 245, 258, 262, 269, 271, 274, 275, 288, 290, 292, 295, 296, 297, 298, 300, 306, 307, 308, 323, 325, 332, 353, 354, 356, 381, 383, 386, 390, 397, 398, 413, 415, 420, 421, 426, 427, 443, 450, 452, 474, 478, 483, 485, 486, 489, 505, 511, 513, 519, 520, 533, 535, 537, 538, 542, 543, 546, 548, 566, 568, 577, 579, 592, 594, 604, 605, 609, 610, 624, 626, 629, 630, 632, 641, 657, 659, 664, 666, 669, 672
Read-only memory (ROM), 452, 453 *lab,* 456
Read/write head, 457
Real-World Questions, 27, 28, 46, 56, 86, 103, 116, 139, 152, 167, 186, 202, 214, 241, 246, 272, 278, 301, 310, 339, 340, 369, 370, 392, 402, 424, 432, 448, 460, 481, 494, 509, 522, 540, 552, 574, 582, 607, 614, 643, 644, 668, 674
Rectum, 132
Recycling, 44 *act,* **243,** 243–245, 244 *act, 245,* 487; of computers, 454; organelles, 44
Red blood cell(s), 38, *38,* 162, *162, 163, 163,* 166
Red giants, 483, *483,* **485,** *485,* 486, 496, *496*
Redi, Francesco, 20
Red shift, 491, *491*
Reducing, 242
Reflection, law of, **417,** *417;* of sound, 423; of waves, 417, *417,* 417 *lab*
Refraction, 417; of waves, 417, *417*
Regeneration, 97 *act,* 102, *102*
Relative ages, 663–668, 668 *lab*
Relative dating, 663 *act*

Relative motion, 323, *323*
Renewable resources, *224,* **224**–225, *225,* **396,** *397*
Reporting results, 10
Reproduction, 17, *17,* 94–117; of animals, 96, *96,* 97, 98, 99, 100, *100;* asexual, *101,* **101**–102, *102;* of bacteria, 11; fission, 101; meiosis, *105,* 105–109, *106–107, 108;* mitosis, *98,* 98–100, *99, 100, 101,* 101 *lab,* 103 *lab;* and mutations, 114–115, *115,* 116–117; of plants, 95 *lab,* 97, 98, *98,* 101, *101,* 103 *lab;* sexual, *104,* **104**–109, *105, 106–107, 109;* of viruses, 52
Reproduction rates, determining, 176 *lab*
Resources, alternative, 397 *lab,* 397–399, *398, 399;* conservation of, 242–245; importance of, 222; inexhaustible, **397;** natural, **224**–230; nonrenewable, **225,** *225,* **394,** *394;* renewable, *224,* **224**–225, *225,* **396,** *397*
Respiration, 83, *83,* 85, *85,* 86–87 *lab,* 126; v. breathing, 140; breathing rate, 127 *lab;* cellular, 140, *140,* 147
Respiratory infections, 145
Respiratory system, 140–146; diseases and disorders of, 145–146; functions of, 140; organs of, *141,* 141–142
Retina, *429,* 429, 431, *431*
Reusing, 242, *242*
Reverberation, 423
Reverse fault, 593, *593*
Rh factor, 165
Rhodonite, *506*
Rhyolite, *538,* 540 *lab*
Ribonucleic acid (RNA), 71, **112**–113, *113,* **114**
Ribosome, 42, *43*
Richter scale, 596, 598
Ridge, mid-ocean, 569, 573, *573,* 584
Ridge-push, 573, *573*
Rift, 609
Rift valleys, 569, *570*
Rift zones, 610
Rigel, 474
Ring of Fire, 610, 611

RNA (ribonucleic acid), 71, **112**–114, *113,* 114
Rock(s), 530–554, *532;* absolute ages of, 669–673; andesitic, *538,* 539; basaltic, *538,* **539;** cementation of, 547, *547;* common, 532, *532;* compaction of, 546, *546;* dating, 659, *659,* 661, 671–672, *672;* distinguishing minerals from, 503 *lab;* erosion of, 546; extrusive, **537,** *537, 538;* foliated, **543,** *543;* fossils in, 659, *659,* 660, 661, *661;* granitic, *538,* **539;** igneous, 533, *533, 534,* 536, 536–540, *537, 538,* 540 *lab;* intrusive, **537,** *537, 538;* melting, 539; metamorphic, 533, *533, 534, 541,* **541**–544, *542, 543, 544;* as mixtures, 277; modeling, 533 *lab;* nonfoliated, **544,** *544;* observing and describing, 531 *lab;* and principle of superposition, 662, *662;* relative ages of, 663–668, 668 *lab;* sedimentary, 533, *533,* **535**–553, 552–553 *lab;* stacked, 545, *545;* structure of, 507, *507;* weathering of, 546
Rock cycle, *533,* **533**–535, *534,* 551
Rocket(s), balloon, 369 *lab;* launching, 366, *366*
Rock-forming minerals, 508
Rock gypsum, 548
Rock layers, matching up, *666,* 666–667, *667;* unconformities in, 664, *664,* 665
Rock salt, 549, *549*
Rods, of eye, 431, *431*
Rolling friction, 355, *355*
ROM (read-only memory), 452, 453 *lab,* 456
Rubella (German measles), 176
Rubies, 516, *516,* 518
Rushmore, Mount, *532*
Russell, Henry, 482
Rutherford, Ernest, 263, 264
Rutile, 520, *520*

Safety, 13; and air bags, 372, *372;* in automobiles, 340–341 *lab,* 372, *372;* in earthquakes, 591 *lab,* 599, 599–600, 616
Saliva, 130, *130,* 174, 312
Salt(s), 69, *69,* 71; crystal structure of, 505, 505 *lab;* dissolving in water, 295, *295;* rock, 549, *549;* uses of, 504
Saltwater, 289, 289 *act,* 292, 312, *312*
Sample, choice, 687
San Andreas Fault, 572, *572,* 616
Sand, *547*
Sandstone, 544, *547,* 548
San Francisco earthquake (1906), 616, *616*
Sanitary landfills, 240, *240*
Sapphire, 517, *517*
SARS (severe acute respiratory syndrome), 178
Satellite(s), 361
Saturated fats, 135
Saturated solution, 298, *298*
Scab, 164, *164,* 164 *lab*
Scanning electron microscope (SEM), *49,* 50, *58*
Scanning tunneling microscope (STM), 50
Schist, 542
Schleiden, Matthias, 51
Science, 6 13; critical thinking in, 7; laws in, 10; problem solving in, 7, 7–10, 11 *act;* safety in, 13; theories in, 10; types of, 6; work of, 6
Science and History, Ancient Views of Matter, 280; Cobb Against Cancer, 58; Dr. Dorothy Crowfoot Hodgkin, 524, *524;* Have a Heart, 188; Overcoming the odds, 154; Quake, 616; The Year There Was No Summer, 646
Science and Language Arts, Beauty Plagiarized, 248, "The Solace of Open Spaces," 216; "Tulip," 88
Science and Society, Air Bag Safety, 372; Australia's Controversial Rock Star, 554, *554;* E-Lectrifying E-Books, 462; Monkey, 30
Science Online, Air Quality, 70; Beneficial Microorganisms, 84; Calcium Hydroxide, 305; Cardiovascular Disease, 172; Collisions, 336; Computer

Software, 452; Controlled Experiments, 8; Correlating with Index Fossils, 666; Deforestation, 641; Desalination, 289; Disease Theory, 178; Domains, 23; Earthquake Magnitude, 597; Earth's Biomes, 200; Energy and Energy Resources, 396; Energy Transformations, 386; Evolution of Stars, 484; Fiber, 134; Filoviruses, 54; Fruit Fly Genes, 115; Galileo and Newton, 353; Gemstone Data, 518; Global Warming, 234; Greenhouse Effect, 639; Hodgkin's Disease, 172; Homeostasis, 15; How Birds Fly, 364; The Human Genome Project, 113; Human Population, 204; Human White Blood Cells, 163; Hydroelectricity, 396; Indicators, 308; Isotopes in Ice Cores, 672; Land Speed Record, 326; Lasers, 426; Magnetic Disks, 456; Mixtures, 276; Montserrat Volcano, 603; Nerve Cell Regeneration, 97; New Elements, 267; Optical Disks, 458; Plate Boundaries, 569; Recycling, 244; Relative Dating, 663; Rock Formation, 538; Secondhand Smoke, 145; Semiconductor Devices, 445; Shale Metamorphism, 542; Space Weather, 479; Studying Motion, 322; Sub-Atomic Particles, 262; Virus Reactivation, 53; Volcanic Mountains, 578

Science Stats, Energy to Burn, 404; Mountains, 584; Salty Solutions, 312; Stars and Galaxies, 496,

Scientific contribution(s). *See* Dalton, Lavoisier, Thomson, Rutherford, Democritus

Scientific illustration(s), 685

Scientific laws, 10

Scientific Methods, 7, *7*–10, 27, 28–29 *lab*, 46, 56–57, 80, 86–87, 103, 116–117, 139, 152–153, 167, 186–187, 202, 214–215, 241, 246–247, 272, 278–279, 301, 310–311, 339, 340–341, 369, 370–371, 392, *402*, 402–403, 424, 432–433, 448, 460–461, 481, 494–495, 509, 522–523, 540, 552–553, 574, 582–583, 607, 614–615, 643, 644–645, 668, 674–675, 684–695; Analyze Your Data, 9, 9 *lab*, 29, 57, 117, 187, 215, 247, 279, 341, 369, 371, 403, 433, 461, 495, 523, 675; Answering Questions through, 11; Conclude and Apply, 8, 27, 29, 46, 57, 80, 87, 103, 117, 139, 153, 168, 187, 202, 215, 241, 247, 272, 279, 301, 311, 339, 341, 369, 371, 392, 403, 424, 433, 448, 461, 481, 495, 509, 523, 540, 553, 574, 583, 607, 615, 643, 645, 668; Follow Your Plan, 187, 371, 461; Form a Hypothesis, 8, 10, 28, 56, 116, 186, 214, 340, 370, 402, 494, 522; Information Gathering, 8; Make a Plan, 187, 371, 460; Make the Model, 247, 583; Making the Model, 675; Planning the Model, 675; Plan the Model, 583; Test the Model, 247; Test Your Hypothesis, 8–9, 29, 57, 187, 215, 341, 370, 403, 494–495

Scientific names, 24–25

Scientific notation, 723

Scientific units, 12

Scoria, *538*

Sea anemone, *5*

Sea lions, *24*

Seasons, 622, *632*, 632–633

Sea star, 102, *102*

Secondhand smoke, 145, 145 *act*

Sediment(s), 545; classifying, 546 *lab*; size and shape of, 547, *547*

Sedimentary rocks, 533, *533*, **535**–553; chemical, 548–549, *549*; classifying, 546–553, *547*, 552–553 *lab*; detrital, 546–548, *547*; formation of, 545, *545*; materials found in, 548, *548*; organic, 549–550, *551*

Seeds, classification of, 27 *lab*; growth of, 95 *lab*

Seismic-safe structures, 591 *lab*, *599*, 599–600, 616

Seismic waves, 414, 415, 564, *564*, *565*, *594*, **594**–595, 596, 612, *612*, 612 *act*, 614–615 *lab*

Seismograph, 595, *595*, 596, *596*

Semiconductors, 445 *act*, **445**–446, *446*, 447

Sense(s), hearing, 421, 422; vision, 429–431, *430*

Serpentine, 544

Server, 459

Serveto, Miguel, 188

Severe acute respiratory syndrome (SARS), 178

Sex cells, 105, *105*, 108, *109*

Sexually transmitted diseases (STDs), 181

Sexual reproduction, 104, **104**–109, *105*, *106*–*107*, *109*

Shale, *534*, 542 *act*, *547*, 548

Shark, *655*

Shear forces, 593

Shearing, 572

Shield volcano, 604, *604*

Siccar Point, Scotland, 535, *535*

Sickle-cell disease, 166, *166*

Sight. *See* Vision

Signals. *See* Electronic signal

Significant figures, 723

Silicates, 508

Silicon, 445, 446, *446*, 508

Silt, *547*

Siltstone, *547*, 548

Silver, 512 *act*

Simple carbohydrates, 134

Sirius, 472, 474

Skin, functions of, 174

Slab-pull, 573, *573*

Slate, 542, 543, *543*

Sliding friction, 353, 354, *354*, *355*, 359, 362

Small intestine, 131, *131*

Smallpox, 54

Smelting, 519

Smog, 232, *232*

Smoking, and cancer, 145, 146, *146*, 184; and high blood pressure, 172, *172*; and indoor air pollution, 236; and secondhand smoke, 145, 145 *act*

Soap scum, 290, *290*

Sodium, 136

Sodium bicarbonate, 71

Sodium chloride, 295, *295*, 504. *See also* Salt(s)

Index

Sodium hydroxide, 305
Software, computer, 452 *act,* **453,** *453*
Soil, as abiotic factor in environment, 198, *198;* loss of, 223, 239, *239;* pollution of, 239–240, *240;* topsoil, 223 *lab,* 239, *239*
Solar cells, 230, *230*
Solar collector, 397 *lab,* 398, *398*
Solar cooking, 246–247 *lab*
Solar energy, 224, *229,* 229–230, *230, 231,* 246–247 *lab,* 397–398, *398, 399,* 404, *404*
Solar flares, 478, *479*
Solar radiation, 184, 235, *235*
Solid solutions, 293, *293*
Solid waste, 239
Solubility, 297–298; factors affecting, *297,* 297–298; of gas, 298, 298 *lab;* and pressure, 298; of similar and dissimilar substances, 296, *296;* and temperature, 297, *297*
Solute, 290, 292, 300
Solution(s), 69, **290**–300; aqueous, **294**–296, *295, 296;* concentration of, 299 *act,* 299–300, *300;* crystals from, 301 *lab,* 507, *507;* formation of, *290,* 290–291, *291;* saturated, **298,** *298;* supersaturated, 298, 301 *lab;* types of, 291–293, *292, 293;* unsaturated, 298
Solvent, 290, 292; boiling point of, 300; freezing point of, 300; water as, **294**–296, *295, 296*
Soufrière Hills volcano (Montserrat), 601, *601,* 602, *602,* 603, 603 *act,* 606, 609
Sound, intensity of, 420, *420,* 421; loudness of, *420,* 420–421, *421;* pitch of, 421; reflection of, 423; speed of, 416 *act,* 420
Sound waves, 410, 416 *act,* 419–424; as compressional waves, 419, *419;* frequency of, 421; making, 419, *419;* in matter, 424 *lab;* perception of, 421–422
South Pole, 632, 633
Space, distance in, 474 *act,* 475, 490 *lab;* light waves in, 425, *425;* measurement in, 475, 490 *lab;* measuring, 195 *lab;* and populations, 195 *lab,* 204, *204;* weather in, 477 *act*
Space shuttle, 368, *368*
Spallanzani, Lazzaro, 20
Species, 23
Specific immunity, 175
Spectroscope, 476
Spectrum, electromagnetic, **426**–427, *427;* of star, 476, *476,* 491, *491*
Speed, 324–325; and acceleration, *328,* 328–329; of animals, 324; average, **325,** *325,* 325 *lab;* calculating, 324 *act;* constant, 325, *325;* and distance-time graphs, 326, *326;* instantaneous, **325,** *325;* and kinetic energy, 381, *381;* land, 326 *act;* of light, 425; and motion, 324–325, *325;* of sound, 416 *act,* 420; and velocity, 327; of waves, 416
Speed-time graph, 332, *332*
Sperm, 104, *104,* 105
Sphalerite, 520, *520*
Spindle fibers, 98, *99,* 106, *106*
Spinel, 516, *516*
Spiral galaxy, 488, *488, 489*
Spoilage, food, 177, 298
Spontaneous generation, 19, *19*
Sports, Newton's laws in, 365
Stacked rock, 545, *545*
Stalactites, 291, *291,* 303
Stalagmites, 291, *291,* 303
Standards Review, 34–35, 92–93, 122–123, 158–159, 192–193, 220–221, 252–253, 284–285, 316–317, 346–347, 438–439, 500–501, 528–529, 558–559, 620–621, 650–651, 680–681
Star(s), 472–476, absolute magnitude of, 474; apparent magnitude of, 474; binary, 480; classifying, 482–483; constellations of, *472,* 472–473, *473;* evolution of, 484 *act,* 484–487, *485;* fusion reaction in, 483–484, *484;* life cycle of, 484–487, *485;* main sequence, *482,* 482–483, 484, 485; neutron, **486;** patterns of, 473 *lab;* properties of, 476, *476;* spectrum of, 476, *476,* 491, *491;* Sun as, 477, 480; triple, 480
Starch, 134
Star cluster, 480, *480*
Static friction, 354
Steady state theory, 490
Steel, 293, *293;* recycling, 244
Stereomicroscopes, 56–57 *lab*
Sternum, 168
Stirrup (of ear), 422, *422*
Stomach, 130–131
Stone plants, 6
Streak, 512, 513, *513*
Strike-slip fault, 593, *593*
Structural adaptations, 628, 629, *630*
Study Guide, 31, 59, 89, 119, 155, 189, 217, 249, 281, 313, 343, 373, 405, 435, 463, 497, 525, 555, 585, 617, 647, 677
Sub-atomic particles, 262 *act*
Subduction, 571
Subduction zones, 610
Substance, 273, 277, **288**
Sugar, 134
Sulfur, 213, 233
Sulfur dioxide, 233
Sulfuric acid, 303, 304
Sun, 477–481, 487; atmosphere of, 477, *477;* corona of, 477, *477;* electromagnetic waves from, 428, *428;* layers of, 477, *477;* radiation from, 185, 235, *235,* 624, *624,* 625 *lab,* 637, 638, *638;* as star, 477, 480; surface features of, *478,* 478–479, *479;* temperature of, 477
Sunlight, ultraviolet waves in, 428
Sunset Crater, Arizona, 604, *604*
Sunspots, 478, *478,* 481 *lab,* 637
Supergiants, 483, *483,* **486**
Supernova, 486
Superposition, principle of, **662,** *662*
Supersaturated solution, 298, 301 *lab*
Surface area, comparing, 143 *lab*
Surface water, 237, *237*
Suspension, 69
Sweat, 174
Switch, 451

Index

Symbiosis, 206, *206,* 206 *lab*
Symbols, for safety, 13
Synthetic elements, 266, *266,* 267 *act*
Syphilis, 181
Systemic circulation, 169

Talc, 511
Tanzanite, 516, *516*
T cells, 175, 182
Technology, alloys, 293, *293;* analog devices, 442–443, *443;* centrifuge, 275; computers. *See* Computer(s); dialysis machine, 151, *151;* diodes, 446, *446,* 448 *lab;* electronics, *442,* 442–448, *445,* 448 *lab;* floppy disks, 458; gasoline engines, 387, *387;* generator, 390, *390;* gene therapy, 55; hard disks, 456, *456, 456 act,* 457; heat pumps, 399; *Hubble Space Telescope,* 486, 493; integrated circuits, 447, *447,* 449, 452, *452;* lasers, 426 *act;* microprocessors, 455, *455;* microscopes, *47,* 47–50, *48–49,* 56–57 *lab,* 178; nuclear power generation, 228, *228;* optical disks, 458, *458,* 458 *act;* photovoltaic collector, 398, *398;* power plants, *390,* 390–391; for predicting earthquakes, 600, *600;* radio, 389, *389,* 392 *lab;* rockets, 366, *366,* 369 *lab;* satellites, 361; seismograph, 595, *595,* 596, *596;* semiconductors, 445 *act,* 445–446, *446,* 447; solar collector, 397 *lab,* 398, *398;* space shuttle, 368, *368;* spectroscope, 476; transistors, 447, *447;* Tsunami Warning System, *597;* turbine, 227, *227,* 228, 390, *390;* vacuum tubes, 445, *445,* 449; wheelchairs, 521, *521;* windmill, 399, *399;* World Wide Web, 459, *459;* X-ray crystallography, 524, *524*
Tectonic plates. *See* Plate(s)
Telescopes, *Hubble,* 486, 493
Television, vacuum tubes in, 445, *445*

Telophase, 98, *99,* 106, *106, 107*
Temperate zones, 624, *624*
Temperature, of air, 234, *234;* and bacterial reproduction, 11; of body, 389; and environment, 197; influence of cities on, 626 *act;* and metamorphic rocks, 542, *542;* and solubility, 297, *297;* of Sun, 477
Tension, 569, *569, 570,* 571 *lab, 576*
Tephra, 601, 605
Tetanus, 176
Teton Range (Wyoming), 576, *576*
Theory, 10
Thermal collector, 398, *398*
Thermal energy, 382, *382,* 389–390, *390*
Thickness, calculating, 550 *act*
Thirst, 137
Thomson, J. J., 262, *262,* 263, *263*
Thymine, 111
Tidal energy, 400, *400*
TIME, Science and History, 58, 188, 280, 524, *524,* 616, 646; Science and Society, 30, 154, 372, 462, 554
Tissue, 45, *45*
Titanium, 520, 520–521, *521*
Topaz, 511, 516, *516*
Topsoil, loss of, 223 *lab,* 239, *239*
Trace fossils, 658, *658,* 674–675 *lab*
Trachea, 142
Tracks, of dinosaurs, 658, *658*
Traits, and mutations, 116–117 *lab*
Transfer RNA (tRNA), 113
Transform boundary, 572, *572*
Transistors, 447, *447*
Transmission electron microscope (TEM), *49,* 50
Transport, active, **77,** *77, 79;* passive, **74**–77, *75, 76, 79;* in plants, 76, *76, 77, 77*
Transverse waves, 413, *413,* 414, 415, *415*
Treatment(s), differences in historical and modern, 177, 181
Triceratops, 654
Triple stars, 480
Tropics, 624, *624*
Try at Home Mini Labs, Analyzing Energy Transformations, 387; Communicating Ideas, 25;

Comparing Compounds, 274; Comparing Surface Area, 143; Determining Reproduction Rates, 176; Diffusion, 75; Inferring Salt's Crystal System, 505; Measure Average Speed, 325; Modeling an Eruption, 602; Modeling DNA Replication, 111; Modeling El Niño, 633; Modeling Rock, 533; Modeling Tension and compression, 571; Modeling the Water Cycle, 212; Observing a Nail in a Carbonated Drink, 303; Observing Friction, 354; Observing Magnified Objects, 50; Observing Mineral Mining Effects, 226; Observing Star Patterns, 473; Predicting Fossil Preservation, 655; Reflecting Waves, 417; Using Binary Numbers, 450
Tsou Yen, 280
Tsunami, *597,* **598**
Turbine, 227, *227,* 228, **390,** *390*
Tyrannosaurus rex, 655

Ultraviolet radiation, 235
Ultraviolet waves, 428
Uluru (Australia), 554, *554*
Unbalanced forces, 351
Unconformities, 664, *664,* 665
Uniformitarianism, 673, *673*
Universe, expansion of, 471 *lab,* 490–491, *490–491,* 493; origin of, 490, *492,* 493
Unsaturated fats, 135
Unsaturated solution, 298
Upwarped mountains, 577
Uranium, 228, 395
Ureter, 149, 151
Urethra, 149, 151
Urey, Harold, 20, 21
Urinary system, *147,* 147–151, *148;* diseases and disorders of, 150–151, *151;* organs of, *148,* 148–149, *149*
Urine, 149
Ursa Major, 473, *473*

Index

Use the Internet, Does your computer have a virus?, 460–461; Energy To Power Your Life, 402–403; Mutations, 116–117

Vaccination, 176–177, *177*
Vaccines, 54, 55, *55*, 176–177, *177*
Vacuoles, 43
Vacuum tubes, 445, *445*, 449
Variable, 9
Vein mineral deposits, 520, *520*
Veins, 170, *170*
Velocity, 327; and acceleration, *328*, 328–329, *329*; and speed, 327
Vent, *578*
Ventricles, 168
Vesicles, 43, 78
Villi, 131, *131*
Vinegar, 292
Virchow, Rudolf, 51
Virus(es), 52–55; active, 53, *53*; computer, 460–461 *lab*; and diseases, 178, 179; effects of, 54; fighting, 54–55; latent, 53; reactivation of, 53 *act*; reproduction of, 52; shapes of, 52, *52*
Visible light, 427, *427*
Vision, 429–431, *430*
Vision defects, *430*
Vitamin(s), 132, 133, **135;** fat-soluble, 135; identifying, 139 *lab*; water-soluble, 135
Vitamin B, 132
Vitamin C, 139 *lab*
Vitamin D, 135
Vitamin K, 132, 135
Volcanic glass, 538
Volcanic mountains, *578*, 578 *act*, 578–579, *579*
Volcano(es), 601–607; and climatic changes, 637, *637*; and Earth's plates, 569, *571*, 579, *579*, 601, *601*, 608, 608–610, *609*; energy from, 378, *378*; eruptions of, 602, *602*, 602 *lab*, 603, 605, 606, 607 *lab*, 646, *646*; formation of, *601*, 601–603, 609–610, *610*; and formation of igneous rock, 536, 536–537, *537*; forms of, 603–605, *604*, 605; risks of, 603, *603*
Volume(s), 690, 720; measuring, 12, 690; of rectangular solids, 720

Waste(s), cellular, 169; excretion from body, 147–151; and exhaling, 142; hazardous, **240,** *240*; radioactive, 228, 240, 395; solid, 239
Water, 71–73; balancing gain and loss in body, 150; characteristics of, 73; and climate, 625, *625*; as compound, 68, *68*, 288; diffusion of, 75 *lab*, 76, *76*; and environment, 197, *197*; freezing, 73; in generation of electricity, 227; groundwater, 238, *238*; importance of, 72; in living things, 71; molecules of, 68, *68*, 73, *73*; as nutrient, 133, 136–137; in oceans, 238, *238*; in plant cells, 65 *lab*, 72, 76, *76*; as solvent, 294–296, *295*, *296*; surface, 237, *237*; use by living things, 18
Water cycle, 212, *212*, 212 *lab*
Water pollution, 237, 237–238, *238*
Water-soluble vitamins, 135
Water waves, 410
Watson, James, 111
Wave(s), 412–418; amplitude of, 415, *415*; changing direction of, 417, 417–418, *418*; compressional, **413,** *413*, 414, *414*, 415, *415*, 419, *419*; diffraction of, 418, *418*; electromagnetic, 414, 425, 426, *426*, 428, *428*; and energy, 412, *412*; frequency of, 414; infrared, 427; microwaves, 427; properties of, 411 *lab*, 414, 414–416, *415*; radio, 427; reflection of, 417, *417*, 417 *lab*; refraction of, 417, *417*; seismic, 414, 415, 564, *564*, 565, *594*, **594**–595, *596*, *612*, 612 *act*, 613, 614–615 *lab*; sound. *See* Sound waves; speed, 416–417, 420, 425; transverse, **413,** *413*, 414, 415, *415*; tsunami, *597*, **598;** types of, 412–414, *413*; ultraviolet, **428;** visible light, 427, *427*; water, 410
Wavelength, 414, *414;* of light, 425
Weathering, of rocks, 546
Weather, in space, 477 *act*
Web site, 459, *459*
Weight, 357–358; and mass, 358; measuring, 367, *367*
Weightlessness, *367*, **367**–368, *368*
Wheelchairs, 521, *521*
White blood cells, 162, *162*, 163, *163*, 163 *act*, 166, 175
White dwarf, 483, **485,** *485*
Whooping cough (pertussis), 176
Williams, Daniel Hale, 188
Wind energy, 399, *399*
Windmill, 399, *399*
Wind power, 228
World Wide Web, 459, *459*

X-ray crystallography, 524, *524*
X rays, 428

Yeast, 84, *84*

Zinc, 520
Zircon, 506
Zoisite, 516, *516*
Zoologist, 6
Zygote, 104, *105*, 109

INDEX **773**

Credits

Magnification Key: Magnifications listed are the magnifications at which images were originally photographed.
LM–Light Microscope
SEM–Scanning Electron Microscope
TEM–Transmission Electron Microscope

Acknowledgments: Glencoe would like to acknowledge the artists and agencies who participated in illustrating this program: Absolute Science Illustration; Andrew Evansen; Argosy; Articulate Graphics; Craig Attebery, represented by Frank & Jeff Lavaty; CHK America; John Edwards and Associates; Gagliano Graphics; Pedro Julio Gonzalez, represented by Melissa Turk & The Artist Network; Robert Hynes, represented by Mendola Ltd.; Morgan Cain & Associates; JTH Illustration; Laurie O'Keefe; Matthew Pippin, represented by Beranbaum Artist's Representative; Precision Graphics; Publisher's Art; Rolin Graphics, Inc.; Wendy Smith, represented by Melissa Turk & The Artist Network; Kevin Torline, represented by Berendsen and Associates, Inc.; WILDlife ART; Phil Wilson, represented by Cliff Knecht Artist Representative; Zoo Botanica.

Photo Credits

Cover i ii (bkgd)Sharon Gerig/Tom Stack & Assoc., (bl)Steve Raymer/CORBIS, (r)Zephyr/Photo Researchers; **vii** Aaron Haupt; **viii** John Evans; **ix** (t)PhotoDisc, (b)John Evans; **x** (l)John Evans, (r)Geoff Butler; **xi** (l)John Evans, (r)PhotoDisc; **xii** PhotoDisc; **xiii** Michael Fogden/Earth Scenes; **xiv** (t)Roland Seitre-Bios/Peter Arnold, Inc., (b)KS Studios; **xv** AFP/CORBIS; **xvi** Ray Massey/Getty Images; **xvii** (t)Breck P. Kent/Earth Scenes, (c)Charles D. Winters/Photo Researchers, (b)Matt Meadows; **xviii** (t)PhotoTake NYC/PictureQuest, (b)David Hosking/CORBIS; **xix** Tim Courlas; **xx** (t)Dennis Johnson/Papilio/CORBIS, (b)Joe McDonald/CORBIS; **xxi** Alexis Duclos/Getty News Images; **xxiii** (l)Archivo Iconografico, S.A./CORBIS, (r)John Reader/Science Photo Library/Photo Researchers; **xxiv** Aaron Haupt; **xxvi** George Bernard/Earth Scenes; **1** David W. Hamilton/Getty Images; **2** Microworks/PhotoTake NYC; **2–3** Doug Wilson/CORBIS; **4–5** A. Witte/C. Mahaney/Getty Images; **6** Kjell B. Sandved/Visuals Unlimited; **8 9** Mark Burnett; **11** Tek Image/Science Photo Library/Photo Researchers; **12 13** Mark Burnett; **14** (t)Michael Abbey/Science Source/Photo Researchers, (bl)Aaron Haupt, (br)Michael Delannoy/Visuals Unlimited; **15** Mark Burnett; **16** (tcr)A. Glauberman/Photo Researchers, (tr)Mark Burnett, (bl bcl br)Runk/Schoenberger from Grant Heilman, (others)Dwight Kuhn; **17** (t)Bill Beaty/Animals Animals, (bl)Tom & Therisa Stack/Tom Stack & Assoc., (br)Michael Fogden/Earth Scenes; **18** Aaron Haupt; **19** Geoff Butler; **22** (t)Arthur C. Smith III From Grant Heilman, (bl)Hal Beral/Visuals Unlimited, (br)Larry L. Miller/Photo Researchers; **23** Doug Perrine/Innerspace Visions; **24** (l)Brandon D. Cole, (r)Gregory Ochocki/Photo Researchers; **25** (l)Zig Leszczynski/Animals Animals, (r)R. Andrew Odum/Peter Arnold, Inc.; **26** Alvin E. Staffan; **27** Geoff Butler; **28** (t)Jan Hinsch/Science Photo Library/Photo Researchers, (b)Mark Burnett; **29** Mark Burnett; **30** Marc Von Roosmalen/AP; **31** (l)Mark Burnett, (r)Will & Deni McIntyre/Photo Researchers; **32** KS Studios/Mullenix; **33** Jeff Greenberg/Rainbow; **34** Dwight Kuhn; **35** Dave Spier/Visuals Unlimited; **36–37** Nancy Kedersha/Science Photo Library/Photo Researchers; **39** David M. Phillips/Visuals Unlimited; **40** (t)Don Fawcett/Photo Researchers, (b)M. Schliwa/Visuals Unlimited; **42** (t)George B. Chapman/Visuals Unlimited, (b)P. Motta & T. Naguro/Science Photo Library/Photo Researchers; **43** (t)Don Fawcett/Photo Researchers, (b)Biophoto Associates/Photo Researchers; **47** (l)Biophoto Associates/Photo Researchers, (r)Matt Meadows; **48–49** David M. Phillips/Visuals Unlimited; **48** (cw from top)Kathy Talaro/Visuals Unlimited, Michael Abbey/Visuals Unlimited, Michael Gabridge/Visuals Unlimited, David M. Phillips/Visuals Unlimited, David M. Phillips/Visuals Unlimited, courtesy Nikon Instruments Inc.; **49** (tl)Michael Abbey/Visuals Unlimited, (tr)Bob Krist/CORBIS, (cl)courtesy Olympus Corporation, (cr)James W. Evarts, (bl)Karl Aufderheide/Visuals Unlimited, (br)Lawrence Migdale/Stock Boston/PictureQuest; **52** (l)Richard J. Green/Photo Researchers, (c)Dr. J.F.J.M. van der Heuvel, (r)Gelderblom/Eye of Science/Photo Researchers; **55** Pam Wilson/Texas Dept. of Health; **56 57** Matt Meadows; **58** (t)Quest/Science Photo Library/Photo Researchers, (b)courtesy California University; **59** (l)Keith Porter/Photo Researchers, (r)NIBSC/Science Photo Library/Photo Researchers; **61** Biophoto Associates/Science Source/Photo Researchers; **62** P. Motta & T. Naguro/Science Photo Library/Photo Researchers; **64–65** Jane Grushow/Grant Heilman Photography; **67** Bob Daemmrich; **69** (t)Runk/Schoenberger from Grant Heilman, (b)Klaus Guldbrandsen/Science Photo Library/Photo Researchers; **74** (l)John Fowler, (r)Richard Hamilton Smith/CORBIS; **75** KS Studios; **76** Aaron Haupt; **77** Visuals Unlimited; **78** Biophoto Associates/Science Source/Photo Researchers; **80** Matt Meadows; **82** Craig Lovell/CORBIS; **83** John Fowler; **84** David M. Phillips/Visuals Unlimited; **85** (l)Grant Heilman Photography, (r)Bios (Klein/Hubert)/Peter Arnold; **86** (t)Runk/Schoenberger from Grant Heilman, (b)Matt Meadows; **87** Matt Meadows; **88** Lappa/Marquart; **89** CNRI/Science Photo Library/Photo Researchers; **90** Biophoto Associates/Science Source/Photo Researchers; **94–95** Zig Leszcynski/Animals Animals; **96** (l)Dave B. Fleetham/Tom Stack & Assoc., (r)Cabisco/Visuals Unlimited; **98** Cabisco/Visuals Unlimited; **99** (tl)Michael Abbey/Visuals Unlimited, (others)John D. Cunningham/Visuals Unlimited; **100** (l)Matt Meadows, (r)Nigel Cattlin/Photo Researchers; **101** (l)Barry L. Runk from Grant Heilman, (r)Runk/Schoenberger from Grant Heilman; **102** (l)Walker England/Photo Researchers, (r)Tom Stack & Assoc.; **103** Runk/Schoenberger from Grant Heilman; **104** Dr. Dennis Kunkel/PhotoTake NYC; **105** (tl)Gerald & Buff Corsi/Visuals Unlimited, (r)Fred Bruenner/Peter Arnold, Inc., (bl)Susan McCartney/Photo Researchers; **107** (l)John D. Cunningham/Visuals Unlimited, (c)Jen & Des Bartlett/Bruce Coleman, Inc., (r)Breck P. Kent; **108** (tl)Artville, (tr)Tim Fehr, (c)Bob Daemmrich/Stock Boston/PictureQuest, (bl)Troy Mary Parlee/Index Stock/PictureQuest, (br)Jeffery Myers/Southern Stock/PictureQuest; **114** Stewart Cohen/Stone/Getty Images; **116** (t)Tom McHugh/Photo Researchers, (b)file photo; **117** Monica Dalmasso/Stone/Getty Images; **118** (t)Philip Lee Harvey/Stone, (b)Lester V. Bergman/CORBIS; **120** Walker England/Photo Researchers; **122** Barry L. Runk from Grant Heilman; **123** Cabisco/Visuals Unlimited; **125** Don Mason/The Stock Market/CORBIS; **124–125** Birgid Allig/Stone/Getty Images; **126–127** Chris Trotman/NewSport/Corbis; **129** Geoff Butler; **133 134** KS Studios; **135** Visuals Unlimited; **137 138** KS Studios; **140** Dominic Oldershaw; **141** Bob Daemmrich; **144** Richard T. Nowitz; **146** Renee Lynn/Photo

Credits

Researchers; **151** Richard Hutchings/Photo Researchers; **152** KS Studios; **153** Matt Meadows; **154** (t)Lane Medical Library, (b)Custom Medical Stock Photo; **155** (l)Ed Beck/The Stock Market/CORBIS, (r)Tom & DeeAnn McCarthy/The Stock Market/CORBIS; **160–161** Julian Calder/CORBIS; **163** National Cancer Institute/Science Photo Library/Photo Researchers; **166** Meckes/Ottawa/Photo Researchers; **167** Aaron Haupt; **170** Matt Meadows, (inset)StudiOhio; **171** Aaron Haupt; **173** Runk/Schoenberger from Grant Heilman; **175** CC Studio/Science Photo Library/Photo Researchers; **178** Holt Studios International (Nigel Cattlin)/Photo Researchers; **179** (tc br)Visuals Unlimited, (tr bl)Jack Bostrack/Visuals Unlimited, (cl)Cytographics Inc./Visuals Unlimited, (cr)Cabisco/Visuals Unlimited; **181** Oliver Meckes/E.O.S/Gelderblom/Photo Researchers; **182** Andrew Syred/Science Photo Library/Photo Researchers; **186** Matt Meadows/Peter Arnold, Inc.; **187** Matt Meadows; **188** (bkgd)Science Photo Library/Photo Researchers, TIME; **189** (tl)Manfred Kage/Peter Arnold, Inc., (tr)K.G. Murti/Visuals Unlimited, (bl)Don W. Fawcett/Visuals Unlimited; **192** Aaron Haupt; **194–195** Clem Haagner/A.B.P.L./Photo Researchers; **196** WM. J. Jahoda/Photo Researchers; **197** (t)Stuart Westmorland/Photo Researchers, (c)Michael P. Gadomski/Earth Scenes, (b)George Bernard/Earth Scenes; **198** Francis Lepine/Earth Scenes; **200** (t)Roland Seitre-Bios/Peter Arnold, Inc., (bl)Robert C. Gildart/Peter Arnold, Inc., (br)Carr Clifton/Minden Pictures; **202** Bob Daemmrich; **204** Dan Suzio/Photo Researchers; **205** (t)Tim Davis/Photo Researchers, (b)Arthur Gloor/Animals Animals; **206** Gilbert Grant/Photo Researchers; **207** John Gerlach/Animals Animals; **208** Michael P. Gadomski/Photo Researchers; **209** (bkgd bl)Michael Boys/CORBIS, (t)Joe McDonald/CORBIS, (c)David A. Northcott/CORBIS, (bc)Dennis Johnson/Papilio/CORBIS, (br)Kevin Jackson/Animals Animals; **211** (from top)Ray Richardson/Animals Animals, Suzanne L. Collins/Photo Researchers, William E. Grenfell Jr./Visuals Unlimited, Zig Leszczynski/Earth Scenes; **214** (t)Geoff Butler, (b)KS Studios; **215** Matt Meadows; **216** Allen Russell/Index Stock; **217** (l)Richard Reid/Earth Scenes, (r)Helga Lade/Peter Arnold, Inc.; **218** Helga Lade/Peter Arnold, Inc.; **220** (l)George Bernard/Earth Scenes, (r)Tim Davis/Photo Researchers; **221** Arthur Gloor/Animals Animals; **222–223** Grant Heilman Photography; **224** (l)Keith Lanpher/Liaison Agency/Getty Images, (r)Richard Thatcher/David R. Frazier Photolibrary; **225** (t)Solar Cookers International, (bl)Brian F. Peterson/The Stock Market/CORBIS, (br)Ron Kimball Photography; **226** Larry Mayer/Liaison Agency/Getty Images; **229** (tr)Torleif Svenson/The Stock Market/CORBIS, (bl)Rob Williamson, (br)Les Gibbon/Cordaiy Photo Library Ltd./CORBIS; **230** Sean Justice; **231** (t)Lowell Georgia/Science Source/Photo Researchers, (cl)NASA, (c)CORBIS, (cr)Sean Sprague/Impact Visuals/PictureQuest, (bl)Lee Foster/Bruce Coleman, Inc., (br)Robert Perron; **232** Philippe Renault/Liaison Agency/Getty Images; **233** (l)NYC Parks Photo Archive/Fundamental Photographs, (r)Kristen Brochmann/Fundamental Photographs; **237** (l)Jeremy Walker/Science Photo Library/Photo Researchers, (c)John Colwell from Grant Heilman, (r)Telegraph Colour Library/FPG/Getty Images; **238** Wilford Haven/Liaison Agency/Getty Images; **239** (tl)Larry Mayer/Liaison Agency/Getty Images, (tr)ChromoSohm/The Stock Market/CORBIS, (cr)David R. Frazier Photolibrary, (br)Inga Spence/Visuals Unlimited; **240** (r)Andrew Holbrooke/The Stock Market/CORBIS, (Paint Cans)Amanita Pictures, (Turpantine, Paint thinner, epoxy)Icon Images, (Batteries)Aaron Haupt; **242** Paul A. Souders/CORBIS; **243** Icon Images; **245** Larry Lefever from Grant Heilman; **246** (t)Howard Buffett from Grant Heilman, (b)Solar Cookers International; **247** John D. Cunningham/Visuals Unlimited; **248** Frank Cezus/FPG/Getty Images; **250** Robert Cameron/Stone/Getty Images; **251** (l)Steve McCutcheon/Visuals Unlimited, (r)James N. Westwater; **252** David R. Frazier Photolibrary; **254** CORBIS/PictureQuest; **254–255** Stephen Frisch/Stock Boston/PictureQuest; **256–257** Russell Dohrman/Index Stock; **257** Morrison Photography; **258** (l)Gary C. Will/Visuals Unlimited, (c)Mark Burnett/Stock Boston, (r)CORBIS; **260** Mark Burnett; **261** (l)Mark Burnett, (r)NASA; **262** Van Bucher/Photo Researchers; **266** Fermi National Accelerator Laboratory/Science Photo Library/Photo Researchers; **267** Tom Stewart/The Stock Market/CORBIS; **268** (br)New York Public Library, General Research Division, Astor, Lenox, and Tilden Foundations, (others)Bettmann/CORBIS; **270** Emmanuel Scorcelletti/Liaison Agency/Getty Images; **272** Doug Martin; **273** NASA; **274** Mark Burnett; **275** Klaus Guldbrandsen/Science Photo Library/Photo Researchers; **276–277** KS Studios; **276** (tl)Mark Thayer, (tr)CORBIS, (bl)Kenneth Mengay/Liaison Agency/Getty Images, (bc)Arthur Hill/Visuals Unlimited, (br)RMIP/Richard Haynes; **278** (t)Mark Burnett, (b)Michael Newman/PhotoEdit, Inc.; **280** (tl)Robert Essel/The Stock Market/CORBIS,(tr)John Eastcott & Yva Momatiuk/DRK Photo, (cl)Ame Hodalic/CORBIS, (cr)Diaphor Agency/Index Stock, (br)TIME; **286–287** Joseph Sohm/ChromoSohm, Inc./CORBIS; **289** (l)Stephen W. Frisch/Stock Boston, (r)Doug Martin; **290** (t)HIRB/Index Stock, (b)Doug Martin; **291** Richard Hamilton/CORBIS; **292** John Evans; **293** (l)SuperStock, (r)Annie Griffiths/CORBIS; **296** John Evans; **298** Richard Nowitz/Phototake/PictureQuest; **300** Aaron Haupt; **301** KS Studios/Mullenix; **303** John Evans; **304** (l)Joe Sohm, Chromosohm/Stock Connection/PictureQuest, (c)Andrew Popper/Phototake/PictureQuest, (r)A. Wolf/Explorer, Photo Researchers; **305** John Evans; **306** (tl tr)Elaine Shay, (tcl)Brent Turner/BLT Productions, (tcr)Matt Meadows, (bl bcl)CORBIS, (bcr)Icon Images, (br)StudiOhio; **310 311** KS Studios; **312** CORBIS; **314** Royalty-Free/CORBIS; **317** Stephen W. Frisch/Stock Boston; **318–319** Matthew Borkoski/Stock Boston/PictureQuest; **319** L. Fritz/H. Armstrong Roberts; **320–321** Brian Snyder/Reuters Newmedia Inc./CORBIS; **322** Telegraph Colour Library/FPG/Getty Images; **323** Geoff Butler; **326** Richard Hutchings; **329** Runk/Schoenberger from Grant Heilman; **331** Mark Doolittle/Outside Images/Picturequest; **333** (l)Ed Bock/The Stock Market/CORBIS, (r)Will Hart/PhotoEdit, Inc.; **335** (t)Tom & DeeAnn McCarthy/The Stock Market/CORBIS, (bl)Jodi Jacobson/Peter Arnold, Inc., (br)Jules Frazier/PhotoDisc; **336** Mark Burnett; **338** Robert Brenner/PhotoEdit, Inc.; **339** Laura Sifferlin; **340 341** Icon Images; **342** Alexis Duclos/Liaison/Getty Images; **343** (l r)Rudi Von Briel/PhotoEdit, Inc., (c)PhotoDisc; **348–349** Wendell Metzen/Index Stock; **349** Richard Hutchings; **350** (l)Globus Brothers Studios, NYC, (r)Stock Boston; **351** Bob Daemmrich; **352** (t)Beth Wald/ImageState, (b)David Madison; **353** Rhoda Sidney/Stock Boston/PictureQuest; **355** (l)Myrleen Cate/PhotoEdit, Inc., (r)David Young-Wolff/PhotoEdit, Inc.; **356** Bob Daemmrich; **358** (t)Stone/Getty Images, (b)Myrleen Cate/PhotoEdit, Inc.; **360** David Madison; **362** Richard Megna/Fundamental Photographs; **363** Mary M. Steinbacher/

Credits

PhotoEdit, Inc.; **364** (t)Betty Sederquist/Visuals Unlimited, (b)Jim Cummins/FPG/Getty Images; **365** (tl)Denis Boulanger/Allsport, (tr)Donald Miralle/Allsport, (b)Tony Freeman/PhotoEdit/PictureQuest; **366** (t)David Madison, (b)NASA; **368** NASA; **369** Richard Hutchings; **370 371** Mark Burnett; **372** (t)Tom Wright/CORBIS, (b)Didier Charre/Image Bank; **373** (tl)Philip Bailey/The Stock Market/CORBIS, (tr)Romilly Lockyer/Image Bank/Getty Images, (bl)Tony Freeman/PhotoEdit, Inc.; **377** Betty Sederquist/Visuals Unlimited; **378–379** Chris Knapton/Science Photo Library/Photo Researchers; **379** Matt Meadows; **380** (l c)file photo, (r)Mark Burnett; **381** (t b)Bob Daemmrich, (c)Al Tielemans/Duomo; **382** KS Studios; **383** (l r)Bob Daemmrich, (b)Andrew McClenaghan/Science Photo Library/Photo Researchers; **384** Mark Burnett/Photo Researchers; **385** Lori Adamski Peek/Stone/Getty Images; **386** Richard Hutchings; **387** Ron Kimball/Ron Kimball Photography; **388** (t)Judy Lutz, (b)Lennart Nilsson; **390 392** KS Studios; **398** (t)Dr. Jeremy Burgess/Science Photo Library/Photo Researchers, (b)John Keating/Photo Researchers; **399** Geothermal Education Office; **400** Carsand-Mosher; **401** Billy Hustace/Stone/Getty Images; **402** SuperStock; **403** Roger Ressmeyer/CORBIS; **404** (tl)Reuters NewMedia, Inc./CORBIS, (tr)PhotoDisc, (br)Dominic Oldershaw; **405** (l)Lowell Georgia/CORBIS, (r)Mark Richards/PhotoEdit, Inc.; **410–411** Mark A. Johnson/CORBIS; **412** (l)David W. Hamilton/Getty Images, (r)Ray Massey/Getty Images; **417 418** Richard Megna/Fundamental Photographs; **420** David Young-Wolff/Photo Edit, Inc.; **421** (tl)Ian O'Leary/Stone/Getty Images, (tr)David Young-Wolff/PhotoEdit, Inc., (bl)Mark A. Schneider/Visuals Unlimited, (bc)Rafael Macia/Photo Researchers, (br)SuperStock; **423** AFP Photo/Hector Mata/CORBIS; **424** Matt Meadows; **425** James Blank/Getty Images; **430** (t)Nation Wong/CORBIS, (b)Jon Feingersh/CORBIS; **431** Ralph C. Eagle Jr./Photo Researchers; **432 433** Matt Meadows; **434** (t)Bettmann/CORBIS, (bl br)image courtesy of NRAO/AUI; **439** (l)Edward Burchard/Index Stock, (r)David Young-Wolff/Photo Edit, Inc.; **440–441** Andrew Syred/Science Photo Library/Photo Researchers; **442** Willie L. Hill, Jr./Stock Boston; **443** (l)Icon Images, (c)Russ Lappa, (r)Doug Martin; **445** CMCD/PhotoDisc; **446** Amanita Pictures; **447** (t)Amanita Pictures, (b)Charles Falco/Photo Researchers; **448** Charles Falco/Photo Researchers; **449** (l)Bettmann/CORBIS, (r)Icon Images; **452** (t)courtesy IBM/Florida State University, (b)Andrew Syred/Science Photo Library/Photo Researchers; **455** file photo; **456** Thomas Brummett/PhotoDisc; **458** (l)Dr. Dennis Kunkel/PhotoTake, NYC, (r)Aaron Haupt; **459** Timothy Fuller; **460** David Young-Wolff/PhotoEdit, Inc.; **461** Frank Cezus; **462** Tek Images/Science Photo Library/Photo Researchers; **463** (tr)Amanita Pictures, (l)Aaron Haupt, (br)Keith Brofsky/PhotoDisc; **467** Thomas Brummett/PhotoDisc; **469** Mary Evans Picture Library; **468–469** Coco McCoy from Rainbow/PictureQuest; **470–471** TSADO/ESO/Tom Stack & Assoc.; **475** Bob Daemmrich; **478** (t)Carnegie Institution of Washington, (b)NSO/SEL/Roger Ressmeyer/CORBIS; **479** (l)NASA, (r)Picture Press/CORBIS, (b)Bryan & Cherry Alexander/Photo Researchers; **480** Celestial Image Co./Science Photo Library/Photo Researchers; **481** Tim Courlas; **483** Luke Dodd/Science Photo Library/Photo Researchers; **486** AFP/CORBIS; **487** NASA; **489** (t)Kitt Peak National Observatory, (b)CORBIS; **493** R. Williams (ST ScI)/NASA; **494** Matt Meadows; **496** Dennis Di Cicco/Peter Arnold, Inc.; **497** (l)file photo, (r)AFP/CORBIS; **502–503** SuperStock; **504** Matt Meadows; **505** (l)Mark A. Schneider/ Visuals Unlimited, (inset)John R. Foster/Photo Researchers; **506** (tr br)Mark A. Schneider/Visuals Unlimited, (cl)A.J. Copley/Visuals Unlimited, (cr bl)Harry Taylor/DK Images, (bc)Mark A. Schneider/Photo Researchers; **507** (inset) Patricia K. Armstrong/Visuals Unlimited, (r)Dennis Flaherty Photography/Photo Researchers; **509** KS Studios; **510** (l)Mark Burnett/Photo Researchers, (c)Dan Suzio/Photo Researchers, (r)Breck P. Kent/Earth Scenes; **511** (t)Bud Roberts/Visuals Unlimited, (b)Charles D. Winters/Photo Researchers, (inset) Icon Images; **512** (l)Andrew McClenaghan/Science Photo Library/Photo Researchers, (r)Charles D. Winters/Photo Researchers; **513** (t)Goeff Butler, (bl)Doug Martin, (br)Photo Researchers; **514** Matt Meadows; **515** Reuters NewMedia, Inc./CORBIS; **516** (Beryl, Spinel)Biophoto Associates/Photo Researchers, (Emerald, Topaz)H. Stern/Photo Researchers, (Ruby Spinel, Tanzanite)A.J. Copley/Visuals Unlimited, (Zoisite)Visuals Unlimited, (Uncut Topaz)Mark A. Schneider/Visuals Unlimited; **517** (Olivine)University of Houston, (Peridot) Charles D. Winters/Photo Researchers, (Garnet) Arthur R. Hill/Visuals Unlimited, (Almandine)David Lees/CORBIS, (Quartz, Corundum)Doug Martin, (Amethyst) A.J. Copley/ Visuals Unlimited, (Blue Sapphire)Vaughan Fleming/Science Photo Library/Photo Researchers; **518** (l) Francis G. Mayer/ CORBIS, (r) National Museum of Natural History/© Smithsonian Institution; **519** (l)Fred Whitehead/Earth Scenes, (inset)Doug Martin; **520** (t)Matt Meadows, (bl)Paul Silverman/Fundamental Photographs, (br)Biophoto Associates/Photo Researchers; **521** Jim Cummins/Getty Images; **522** Matt Meadows; **523** (t)Doug Martin, (bl)Andrew J. Martinez/Photo Researchers, (br)Charles D. Winter/Photo Researchers, (inset)José Manuel Sanchis Calvete/CORBIS; **524** (bkgd)Science Photo Library/Custom Medical Stock Photo, (bl)Bettmann/CORBIS; **525** José Manuel Sanchis Calvete/ CORBIS; **526** R. Weller/Cochise College; **528** José Manuel Sanchis Calvete/CORBIS; **529** Breck P. Kent/Earth Scenes; **530–531** Michael T. Sedam/CORBIS; **532** (l)CORBIS, (r)Doug Martin; **533** (tl)Steve Hoffman, (cl)Brent Turner/BLT Productions, (r)Breck P. Kent/Earth Scenes; **534** (bkgd) CORBIS/PictureQuest, (t)CORBIS, (bl)Martin Miller, (bc)Jeff Gnass, (br)Doug Sokell/Tom Stack & Assoc.; **535** Russ Clark; **536** USGS/HVO; **537** (t)Breck P. Kent/Earth Scenes, (b)Doug Martin; **538** (basalt)Mark Steinmetz, (scoria, obsidian)Doug Martin, (pumice)Tim Courlas, (others)Breck P. Kent/Earth Scenes; **540** (t)Breck P. Kent/Earth Scenes, (r)Doug Martin/Photo Researchers; **541** (t)Breck P. Kent/Earth Scenes,(l)Breck P. Kent/Earth Scenes, (bl)Courtesy Kent Ratajeski & Dr. Allen Glazner, University of North Carolina, (br)Alfred Pasieka/Photo Researchers; **543** (l)Aaron Haupt, (r)Robert Estall/CORBIS; **544** Paul Rocheleau/Index Stock; **545** (l)Timothy Fuller, (r)Steve McCutcheon/Visuals Unlimited; **547** (l)Icon Images, (cl)Doug Martin, (cr)Andrew Martinez/Photo Researchers, (r)John R. Foster/Photo Researchers; **548** (l)Breck P. Kent/Earth Scenes, (r)Aaron Haupt; **549** (bkgd) Georg Gerster/Photo Researchers, Icon Images; **551** Beth Davidow/Visuals Unlimited; **552** (l)Icon Images, (r)Breck P. Kent/Earth Scenes; **553** (l)Jack Sekowski, (r)Tim Courlas; **554** (bkgd)Y. Kawasaki/Photonica,(inset)Matt Turner/Liaison Agency; **556** Breck P. Kent/Earth Scenes; **557** Jeremy Wood-house/DRK Photo; **561** Robert Caputo/ Aurora/ Picture-Quest; **560–561** Thierry Borredon/Stone/Getty Images; **562–563** Steve Razzetti/Getty Images; **564** Aaron Horowitz /CORBIS; **565** (t)Barry Sweet/AP/Wide World Photos, (b)Mark Burnett;**566** Dewitt Jones/CORBIS;

Credits

570 National Geographic Maps; **574** Amanita Pictures; **575** (l)Chris Noble/Getty Images, (r)Buddy Mays/CORBIS; **576** David Muench; **577** Mark Burnett/Stock Boston; **578** AFP/CORBIS; **579** Michael T. Sedam/CORBIS; **580** Mark E. Gibson/Visuals Unlimited; **582** (t)Ralph A. Clevenger/CORBIS, (b)Paul Chesley/Getty Images; **583** KS Studios; **584** (tl)Sharon Gerig/Tom Stack & Assoc., (l)Dale Wilson/Masterfile, (r)SuperStock; **585** (tr)David Muench/CORBIS, (bl)Robert Lubeck/Earth Scenes, (br)I & V/TLC/Masterfile; **587** Pat Hermansen/Getty Images; **589** Mark Burnett/Stock Boston; **590–591** Reuters NewMedia Inc./CORBIS; **592** KS Studios; **595** (t)Krafft/Explorer/Photo Researchers, (b)Jean Miele/The Stock Market/CORBIS; **598** (bkgd)Galen Rowell/CORBIS, (others)NOAA; **599** (t)KS Studios, (b)Pacific Seismic Products, Inc.; **600** Roger Ressmeyer/CORBIS; **602** AP/Wide World Photos; **604** (t)Breck P. Kent/Earth Scenes, (b)Dewitt Jones/CORBIS; **605** (t)Lynn Gerig/Tom Stack & Assoc., (b)Milton Rand/Tom Stack & Assoc.; **607** Otto Hahn/Peter Arnold, Inc.; **608** Spencer Grant/PhotoEdit, Inc.; **610** Image courtesy NASA/GSFC/JPL, MISR Team; **614 615** Aaron Haupt; **616** (t)Ted Streshinky/CORBIS, (b)Underwood & Underwood/CORBIS; **617** (t)James L. Amos/CORBIS, (c)Michael Collier, (b)Phillip Wallick/The Stock Market/CORBIS; **622–623** Andrew Wenzel/Masterfile; **627** (l)William Leonard/DRK Photo, (r)Bob Rowan, Progressive Image/CORBIS; **628** John Shaw/Tom Stack & Assoc.; **629** (tl)David Hosking/CORBIS, (tr)Yva Momatiuk & John Eastcott/Photo Researchers, (b)Michael Melford/Getty Images; **630** (t)S.R. Maglione/Photo Researchers, (c)Jack Grove/Tom Stack & Assoc., (b)Fritz Pölking/Visuals Unlimited; **631** Zig Leszczynski/Animals Animals; **633** (l)Jonathan Head/AP/Wide World Photos, (r)Jim Corwin/Index Stock; **635** (t)A. Ramey/PhotoEdit, (b)Peter Beck/Pictor; **636** Galen Rowell/Mountain Light; **640** John Bolzan; **641** Chip & Jill Isenhart/Tom Stack & Assoc.; **643** Matt Meadows; **645** Doug Martin; **646** Alberto Garcia/Saba; **647** Steve Kaufman/DRK Photo; **652–653** Hugh Sitton/Getty Images; **654** (t)Mark E. Gibson/Visuals Unlimited, (b)D.E. Hurlbert & James DiLoreto/Smithsonian Institution; **655** Jeffrey Rotman/CORBIS; **656** (t)Dr. John A. Long, (b)A.J. Copley/Visuals Unlimited; **658** (t)PhotoTake, NYC/PictureQuest, (bl br)Louis Psihoyos/Matrix; **660** David M. Dennis; **661** (l)Gary Retherford/Photo Researchers, (r)Lawson Wood/CORBIS; **662** Aaron Haupt; **665** (bkgd)Lyle Rosbotham, (l)IPR/12-18 T. Bain, British Geological Survey/NERC. All rights reserved, (r)Tom Bean/CORBIS; **666** Jim Hughes/PhotoVenture/Visuals Unlimited; **667** (l)Michael T. Sedam/CORBIS, (r)Pat O'Hara/CORBIS; **669** Aaron Haupt; **670** James King-Holmes/Science Photo Library/Photo Researchers; **672** Kenneth Garrett; **673** WildCountry/CORBIS; **674** (t)A.J. Copley/Visuals Unlimited, (b)Lawson Wood/CORBIS; **675** Matt Meadows; **676** Jacques Bredy; **677** (tl)François Gohier/Photo Researchers, (tr)Sinclair Stammers/Photo Researchers, (b)Mark E. Gibson/DRK Photo; **680** Tom Bean/CORBIS; **684** Tom Pantages; **688** Michell D. Bridwell/PhotoEdit; **689** (t)Mark Burnett, (b)Dominic Oldershaw; **690** StudiOhio; **691** Timothy Fuller; **692** Aaron Haupt; **694** KS Studios; **695** Matt Meadows; **696 697** Aaron Haupt; **698** KS Studios; **699** Donald Specker/Animals Animals; **700** John Evans; **701** First Image; **702** John Evans; **704** (t)Matt Meadows, (b)Doug Martin; **706** Doug Martin; **707** Amanita Pictures; **708** Bob Daemmrich; **710** Davis Barber/PhotoEdit.

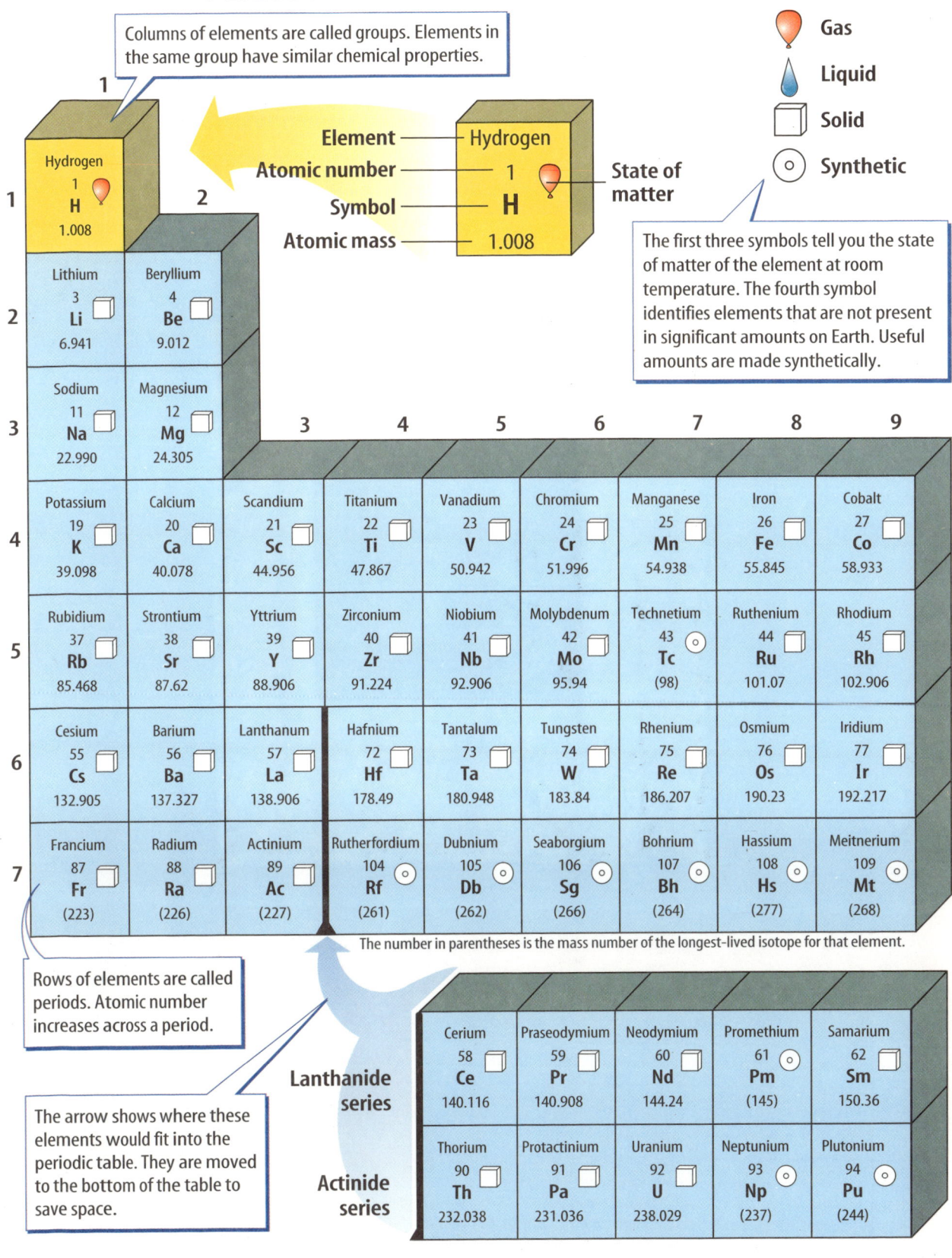

ST. FRANCIS COLLEGE LIBRARY

3 9318 01045625 0

The Library
University of Saint Francis
2701 Spring Street
Fort Wayne, Indiana 46808